HANDBOOK OF PARAPSYCHOLOGY

HANDBOOK OF PARAPSYCHOLOGY

Benjamin B. Wolman
Editor

Laura A. Dale
Gertrude R. Schmeidler
Montague Ullman

Associate Editors

VAN NOSTRAND REINHOLD COMPANY
NEW YORK   CINCINNATI   ATLANTA   DALLAS   SAN FRANCISCO
LONDON   TORONTO   MELBOURNE

Van Nostrand Reinhold Company Regional Offices:
New York Cincinnati Atlanta Dallas San Francisco

Van Nostrand Reinhold Company International Offices:
London Toronto Melbourne

Published by Van Nostrand Reinhold Company
135 West 50th Street, New York, N.Y. 10020

Published simultaneously in Canada by Van Nostrand Reinhold Ltd.

15 14 13 12 11 10 9 8 7 6 5 4 3

Library of Congress Cataloging in Publication Data
Main entry under title:

Handbook of parapsychology.

    Includes bibliographies and index.
    1. Psychical research—Addresses, essays, lectures.
I. Wolman, Benjamin B. [DNLM: 1. Parapsychology—
Handbooks. BF1031 H236]
BF1031.H254   133   77-8336
ISBN 0-442-29576-6

To

GARDNER MURPHY

with affection and appreciation

Authors' Biographies

Joseph M. Backus, Ph.D., Professor of English, University of Hawaii, Manoa Campus, Honolulu.

John Beloff, Ph.D., Senior Lecturer, Department of Psychology, University of Edinburgh, Scotland; Vice-President, former President, The Society for Psychical Research Inc.; Council member, former President, Parapsychological Association.

Donald Smiley Burdick, Ph.D., Department of Mathematics, Duke University, Durham, North Carolina.

James Clinton Carpenter, Ph.D., Assistant Professor of Psychology, University of North Carolina, Chapel Hill.

C. T. K. Chari, Ph.D., Chairman, Department of Philosophy and Psychology, Professor and Chairman, Department for Research and Teaching, Honorary Professor for Research, Madras Christian College, India.

Walter Houston Clark, Ph.D., Former Professor of Psychology of Religion, Andover Newton Theological School; Founder and Past President, Society for the Scientific Study of Religion; President, Academy of Religion and Psychical Research.

Laura A. Dale, Research Associate, American Society for Psychical Research (1943-1959); Editor, *Journal and Proceedings* of the American Society for Psychical Research (1943-   ).

Jan Ehrenwald, M.D., Fellow, American Psychiatric Association, New York Academy of Medicine; Consulting Psychiatrist, Roosevelt Hospital, New York, New York.

Jule Eisenbud, M.D., Med. Sci. Dr., Associate Clinical Professor of Psychiatry, University of Colorado Medical School.

Alan Ogilvie Gauld, Ph.D., Lecturer in Psychology, University of Nottingham, England.

Charles Honorton, Director of Research, Division of Parapsychology and Psychophysics, Department of Psychiatry, Maimonides Medical Center, Brooklyn, New York; Member, Board of Trustees, American Society for Psychical Research; Member, Parapsychological Association.

Edward Francis Kelly, Ph.D., Postdoctoral Research Fellow, Department of Electrical Engineering, Duke University, Durham, North Carolina; Member, Gardner Murphy Research Institute.

Arthur Koestler, LL.D., Fellow, Royal Society of Literature, England.

Robert Lyle Morris, Ph.D., Lecturer, Tutorial Program, University of California, Santa Barbara.

Gardner Murphy, Ph.D., Past Chairman, Department of Psychology, City College of the City University of New York; Past Director of Research, Menninger Foundation, Topeka, Kansas; Past President, American Society for Psychical Research.

J. Fraser Nicol, Corresponding Member, former Member of Council, former Chairman of Research Committee, Society for Psychical Research, London; Member, American Statistical Association.

John Albert Palmer, Jr., Ph.D., Associate Professor, Department of Psychology, University of California, Davis; Member, Gardner Murphy Research Institute.

Joseph Gaither Pratt, Ph.D., Professor of Psychiatry (Psychology), Research Staff, Division of Parapsychology, University of Virginia, Charlottesville.

Joseph Banks Rhine, Ph.D., Professor Emeritus of Psychology, Past Director, Parapsychology Laboratory, Duke University, Durham, North Carolina; Executive Director, Foundation for Research on the Nature of Man.

Louisa Ella Rhine, Ph.D., Former Research Associate, Parapsychology Laboratory, Duke University, Durham, North Carolina; Member, Board of Directors, Foundation for Research on the Nature of Man; Coeditor, *Journal of Parapsychology*.

William George Roll, B. Litt. (Oxon), Former Research Associate, Parapsychology Laboratory, Duke University, Durham, North Carolina; Project Director, Psychical Research Foundation, Durham, North Carolina.

Gertrude R. Schmeidler, Ph.D., Professor of Psychology, City College of the City University of New York; Vice-President, American Society for Psychical Research; Past President, Parapsychological Association.

Rex G. Stanford, Ph.D., Director of the Center for Parapsychological Research, Austin, Texas.

Ian Stevenson, M.D., Carlson Professor of Psychiatry; Director, Division of Parapsychology, Department of Psychiatry, University of Virginia Medical Center, Charlottesville.

Charles T. Tart, Ph.D., Professor of Psychology, University of California, Davis; Fellow, International Institute of Integral Human Sciences, Montreal.

Montague Ullman, M.D., Director, Division of Parapsychology and Psychophysics, Maimonides Medical Center, Brooklyn, New York; President, American Society for Psychical Research; Faculty, Westchester Center for the Study of Psychoanalysis and Psychotherapy; President, Gardner Murphy Research Institute.

Robert L. Van de Castle, Ph.D., Professor of Clinical Psychology (Psychiatry), Director of the Sleep and Dream Laboratory, University of Virginia Medical Center, Charlottesville; Member, Gardner Murphy Research Institute.

Rhea A. White, M.A. (Library Science), Reference Librarian, East Meadow Public Library, New York; Director of Information, American Society for Psychical Research; Managing Editor, *Advances in Parapsychological Research: A Biennial Review.*

J. H. M. Whiteman, Ph.D., Professor of Mathematics, University of Cape Town, South Africa.

Benjamin B. Wolman, Ph.D., Professor of Psychology, Doctoral Program in Clinical Psychology, Long Island University, Brooklyn, New York; President, International Organization for the Study of Group Tensions; Editor-in-Chief, *International Encyclopedia of Psychiatry, Psychology, Psychoanalysis, & Neurology.*

Howard M. Zimmerman, B.A., Staff member, Office of the Assistant Secretary for Health, U.S. Department of Health, Education, and Welfare; Executive Secretary, Parapsychological Association.

Introduction

Howard M. Zimmerman

The "Great Books of the Western World," published by Encyclopaedia Britannica, begins with a volume entitled *The Great Conversation*—a review of the continuing dialogue among societal spokesmen, from Homer and Plato to Freud and James, whose views and thoughts have contributed so importantly to the evolution of Western culture.

> It is the task of every generation to readdress the tradition in which it lives, to discard what it cannot use and to bring into context with the distant and immediate past the most recent contributions to the Great Conversation (Hutchins, 1952, Vol. 1, p. xi).

By making available in permanent form much of the most important work and thought achieved in the field of parapsychology, the editors of the *Handbook of Parapsychology* have made a valuable offering to "The Great Conversation." The contributors to this volume have brought to this dialogue the history, achievements, scope, and problems as well as the implications and issues of an emerging science. Taken together, they represent the major lines of inquiry in the pursuit of knowledge and understanding of extrasensory expression and perception among people, and between people and their environment. While some of their observations and conclusions provide *prima facie* evidence that has withstood the test of time and reason, other observations suggest that the road to understanding and the resolution of basic issues is a long and arduous one. What are the issues that parapsychology brings to the "Great Conversation"?

From the vantage point of historical hindsight, two basic issues are clearly implicit in parapsychology and can be viewed as having guided the scientific explorations of several generations of investigators.

1. Does humankind have paranormal abilities and potentials for awareness, communication, and action that are not fully realized?
2. Do these capacities continue to function even when muscles and nerves cease to function, i.e., is there some sense in which humankind survives the experience of physical death?

Nearly a century of research had addressed and attempted to clarify these issues—with more apparent success in clarifying the former than the latter. The systematic study of spontaneous cases and experimental laboratory investigations of selected subjects (or similar studies of unselected subjects on the assumption that these abilities are universal in nature) has refined fundamental methodologies for detection and measurement. In the process, a series of subsidiary questions bearing on these issues was uncovered—questions, as reflected in this volume, that are receiving increased attention by contemporary researchers and thoughtful observers of the field.

1. What factors facilitate (or inhibit) the functioning of these paranormal abilities?
2. Can we develop them well enough so that they can be easily observed, measured, and evaluated?
3. Can we learn to use them more effectively so that they can be usefully and beneficially applied, thereby increasing or improving our well-being and the well-being of others?
4. When, and how, do we knowingly (or unknowingly) misuse them?

The basic issues are not particularly unique ones. They have been woven into the "Great Conversation" since the dawn of recorded history. In one sense, they are historically derived from prescientific classical inquiries, particularly those of philosophy and religion, which have raised similar questions from other than scientific perspectives in attempting, as Teilhard de Chardin (1965) notes, "to discover the universal hidden behind the exceptional" (p. 56). Perhaps they are also implicitly asked by most of us in the quiet embassy of personal reflection when we ponder the ultimate life questions—Who am I? Why am I here? Where am I going?

What is new about these issues is that they have become integrated into a scientific matrix of systematic inquiry that emphasizes the dimension of empirical observations and critical evaluation—distinct from, although often complementary to, transcendental insight and intuition—in arriving at an understanding of human nature and the world in which we live. Some of the seminal and personally significant, yet anomalous, experiences of everyday life that transcend our ability for rational interpretation and explanation have slowly become amenable to the scientific method. Thus aided by empirical reference points, the subject matter of this volume is an ally to some of the deepest traditions of our culture and not only ignites scientific curiosity and inquiry, but also rekindles philosophical issues, arouses many of our long-standing questions, and stimulates our thinking on issues of both personal and societal significance.

In the Foreword to *Dream Telepathy* (Ullman and Krippner, with Vaughan, 1973) Gardner Murphy hints at the challenge of this generic significance:

> Can we adapt to the experimental and quantitative requirements of the laboratory, the vast floating psychological energies of the living human mind, so complex, so challenging, so full of both inspiration and terror—as we see its conscious and unconscious expressions in civilizations and in the forces which tear civilizations apart? Can parapsychology move from the realm of the bizarre, absurd and occasionally demonic to the realm of verifiable and intelligible expressions of latent human nature? What are these hidden forces at work within us? Our seventeenth-century ancestors knew that blankets gave off sparks in cold weather. But what was electricity good for? Today, electricity drives our machines, lights our halls, monitors our studies of man, (p. xiii).

Are there seeds of extrasensory expression and perception latent in human nature that have not yet fully germinated and sprouted? If so, then a portion of our human ability is lying fallow, and the human landscape of tomorrow, given adequate nourishment, will exhibit a ripening of a more varied fruit of human abilities.

Documented by indicators from both "life and lab," a gradual social evolution appears to be moving toward a consensual view that such abilities are more than a mere possibility. Many of the milestones leading to this view are reflected in the contributions to this volume that bring into focus paranormal or extrasensory interactions between living organisms and their environment—interactions that are not limited by time and space. Other observations have suggested that the functioning of these capacities is associated with physiological and psychological variables of some complexity, including facilitating factors of belief and a friendly relaxed interest, and inhibiting factors such as disbelief, reserve, distrust, and inhibition. More recent studies suggest that the variables which create favorable conditions for the observation and measurement of psi abilities are gradually becoming amenable to the kind of orchestration that will permit their functioning to be more easily observed, recorded, and evaluated. While little systematic effort has been devoted to studying the misuse of these latent abilities, there is universal concern among thoughtful persons about the ethical and moral milieu that will accompany any future development of these abilities. The misapplication of new discoveries in recent history has stimulated more than one observer to comment that "perhaps they should remain largely latent until the issue as to how they will be used is no longer in doubt."

The second basic issue is equally important. Do these potentials continue to function even when muscles and nerves cease to function? Do they function as facets of something that we may view as a "surviving personality"? This question has always been a part of the "Great Conversation." The biblical query "If a man die, shall he live again?" is inherent in virtually every religious and philosophical belief system. By demonstrating that sense experience alone is not always required to discover factual information that tests the truth of general statements about the nature of things, parapsychology has provided an important interface between science, religion, and philosophy, and the beginnings of a framework within which these fields can cooperate for the mutual benefit and understanding of humankind. While a consensus on the survival question is importantly circumscribed by the researchability of the issue itself, many individuals, groups, and organizations are currently evaluating the information being obtained through parapsychological research and attempting to integrate it, from their own perspectives, with the body of knowledge attendant on a scientific, religious, or philosophical understanding of human nature. In addition, they are exploring its relationship and application to the delivery of services intended to aid the health and well-being of people.

Society has seldom spoken with one voice in considering these issues. The larger population has consistently maintained a high level of interest and belief that such experiences do occur, a belief measured in more recent times by public opinion polls and the sale of publications related to ESP. Historically, however, the scientific community has not always accorded its colleagues working in parapsychology the reception that would be conducive to nurturing the balance, dignity, and charity that these workers in parapsychology have nonetheless maintained in transforming a field of uncritical speculation into a field of vigorous scientific inquiry. Opinion surveys directed to this segment of the population have only recently begun to suggest some kind of consensus that ESP phenomena are either an established fact or a likely possibility.

This gradually narrowing gap between the general public and the scientific community has been accompanied by an increasingly widespread public and professional interest in experiences and explorations related to parapsychology. Books, articles, and media coverage of ESP and related topics have proliferated significantly in the last few years. Parapsychology is being introduced into the curriculum of a growing number of schools and colleges. In addition, several Federal agencies have participated in supporting parapsychological research, and the Smithsonian Institution is sponsoring a nation-wide showing of the first scientific exhibit of the activities and accomplishments of workers in parapsychology. These developments appear to reflect the beginnings of a gradual socialization of parapsychology and suggest, hopefully, that the distribution of public funds for support of research should more fully mirror the needs and interests of the society providing that support. A prospective speculation might expect that parapsychology will evolve to enjoy the same status and access to public support as other branches of science in the national research portfolio—a status characterized, in part, by an appreciation of the importance of the research findings and the issues involved.

A gradually broadening consensus of viewpoint and interest is perhaps influenced to some extent by the important implications of parapsychological research.

—it implies interactions between mental activity and physical processes that transcend present understanding.

—it implies modes of interaction among individuals that is stimulating revision in our thinking about the potential possibilities for human development and communication.

—it shows that the kinds of communication channels assumed by religious belief systems are at least available.

—it suggests the researchability of the question of continued existence of human personality after physical death.

During the century-long history of parapsychology and psychical research, these issues and their implications, as indicated elsewhere in this volume, have occasionally provided an arena where the dynamics of critical discussion generated more heat than light. This dynamic may be helpfully viewed from within the perspective expressed by Thomas Kuhn, a philosopher of science. In the *Structure of Scientific Revolutions* (1962) Kuhn advances the idea that scientific progress ebbs and flows within a theoretical framework or "paradigm" that identifies the limits and boundaries for acceptable scientific inquiry. The question and answer dialogue between scientist and nature is importantly circumscribed by the limits of this paradigm. The pre-Copernican model of the sun revolving around the earth was consistent with the existing paradigm, while the observations supporting the Copernican model of the earth revolving around the sun exceeded accepted limits. While observations that conflict with established paradigms are seldom made or reported, when such anomalies do occur and are reported, they are first ignored, then disputed, and are eventually articulated as a shared group of assumptions by a minority of adherents. The result is a "paradigm clash." As an outcome of the "clash," the old will suppress the new into extinction or to an underground existence, or will somehow accommodate the new and make it fit. Or, alternatively as a basis for future progress, a search is made for new models which will fit all, not just some of the data.

While the outcome of the paradigm clash created by the findings of parapsychology is yet to be determined, the dynamic nature of the confrontation was described 50 years ago by William McDougall. In *A Plea For Psychical Research* (in Van Over and Oteri, 1967), he identified the dichotomy of opposing viewpoints between the leaders of scientific orthodoxy and "practically all the rest of mankind" who believed that the issues inherent in parapsychology (then called psychical research) were still an open question and that further investigation was needed to resolve the issues. As a solution he suggested that psychical research should be adequately supported financially by organized science for 50 years in a concentrated and sustained effort to settle the issues involved:

> If [organized science] would support psychical research freely and unreservedly then every type of the alleged supernormal phenomena could be investigated adequately and evaluated critically. And if after fifty years of psychical research thus supported and cultivated, no such evidence should be found to have withstood the application of scientific method, then at last, science will be able to maintain with justice the attitude which at present it assumes dogmatically and uncritically (p. 41).

Although this injunction for unreserved support and cultivation was unfortunately not fulfilled, much additional evidence has been found, and the issues involved remain as an integral part of the "Great Conversation." They have again been joined in a contemporary segment of that dialogue in both a prominent scientific journal and in the news media.

An editorial opinion in *Nature* (1974) accompanied publication of an experimental report by two Stanford Research Institute scientists "where the claim is made that information can be transferred by some channel whose characteristics apparently fall 'outside the range of known perceptual modalities.' Or, more bluntly, some people can read thoughts and see things remotely." Perhaps recognizing that important issues are not resolved in the dark crypts of social concealment, the editors cited both positive and negative factors leading to the decision to publish the report, hoping to "stimulate and advance the controversy rather than keep it out of circulation for a further period." Believing that publication would create a "stir" in the scientific community, the editorial noted that publication was not intended as an indication of endorsement by the "establishment" but "rather, it is a serving of notice on the [scientific] community that there is something worthy of their attention and scrutiny" (pp. 559–560).

A "stir" was also created in the world of scientific journalism. A subsequent *New York Times* editorial (November 4, 1974), citing the publication in *Nature,* added the observation that scientific orthodoxy is becoming "increasingly remote from the interest and beliefs of a generation of Americans as well as long neglected thinkers from early in the century."

This volume is intended to help reduce that "remoteness" and to provide a systematic framework within which "attention and scrutiny" can be pursued. We are often reminded that there is virtually no area of contemporary life where our knowledge is adequate to the challenges we face. While parapsychology is not a scientific panacea for any of the world's challenges and problems, it does show promise for providing some illumination for our collective obscurity. If, as I believe, present trends harbor long-term values, the findings of parapsychology, in the future, will be more broadly examined in relation to their importance to fundamental issues—both basic and applied—rather than as patterns of anomaly, statistical artifact, ·delusion, or accident. We will then bring out of the shadows of neglect potentials to which humankind may well be prone. And we will be constrained to look at processes of learning, coping, and adaptation rather than avoidance and indifference.

The "Great Conversation" is a continuing dialogue where

> Everybody is to speak his mind. No proposition is to be left unexamined. The exchange of ideas is held to be the path to the realization of the potentialities of the race (Hutchins, 1952, Vol. 1, p. 1).

Perhaps one of the greatest contributions of the *Handbook of Parapsychology* is to direct attention to some of those "potentialities of the race." As such, it is also a handbook for change, for it provides visions of possibility for a new frontier of learning and understanding. It is a frontier of social and individual change whose precise dimensions are blurred but where a rough outline may be dimly discerned. It is a frontier where individual and mutual effort can begin to explore another aspect of "latent human possibility" and its beneficial application to the learning and helping professions. But while challenges in the past were often concerned with mastery of the external environment, the challenge of the new frontier is an internal one, the challenge of awakening, with wisdom, slumbering abilities within the self.

REFERENCES

Hutchins, R. *The Great Conversation.* (Vol. 1, *Great Books of the Western World.*) Chicago: Encyclopaedia Britannica, Inc., 1952.

Kuhn, T. S. *The Structure of Scientific Revolutions.* Chicago: University of Chicago Press, 1962.

Nature. Editorial: Investigating the paranormal. October 18, 1974, **251**, 559–560.

Teilhard de Chardin, P. *The Phenomenon of Man.* New York: Harper & Row, 1965.

Ullman, M., and Krippner, S., with Vaughan, A. *Dream Telepathy.* New York: Macmillan, 1973.

Van Over, R., and Oteri, L. (Eds.). *William McDougall, Explorer of the Mind.* New York: Garrett/Helix, 1967.

Contents

HANDBOOK OF
PARAPSYCHOLOGY

Part I
HISTORY OF PARAPSYCHOLOGY

1

Historical Overview

John Beloff

INTRODUCTION

The existence of a concept of paranormality presupposes a relatively sophisticated level of scientific development. Early science was so riddled with occult and magical notions that the question of drawing a firm line between what is and is not possible in nature could scarcely have arisen. With the advent of Newtonian science, on the other hand, there emerged for the first time a picture of the physical world that was both clear enough and comprehensive enough to leave no room for mystery. What nowadays we refer to as psychic phenomena (or, more technically, "psi phenomena") were, of course, known under one name or another to every society of which there is record; what was lacking until comparatively recently was the critical attitude which dared to question their authenticity. In the late seventeenth and early eighteenth centuries, all kinds of traditional beliefs were subjected to a fresh scrutiny as a result of which they rapidly began to lose their credibility. Among the first to go, mercifully, was the belief in witchcraft, a belief that had wrought such terrible havoc and slaughter during the preceding century when it prevailed not only among the credulous masses but also among men of learning and intelligence. Against this somber background of superstition the skepticism and scorn of a Hume and a Voltaire can be heard as a resounding blast of the liberated human intellect.

THE ORIGINS OF PARAPSYCHOLOGY

Mesmerism

The age of reason eventually gave way to the romantic era with its new-found appetite for marvels and mysteries. It was then that a development occurred that was to have profound consequences for the emergence of a parapsychology. This was the rise and spread of the mesmeric movement. The idea of a super-subtle fluid pervading the universe and regulating, according to its distribution, the harmony of nature and the health of man was one that found an immediate echo in an age much given to speculative metaphysics and nature-mysticism. Indeed, so potent was its appeal that the idea survived repeated demonstration that the mesmeric phenomena were due to nothing more recondite than sugges-tion or imagination. Mesmer, who settled in Paris in 1776 where he enjoyed a flourishing practice, thought of himself as a man of the Enlightenment and a medical innovator whose new technique could be used as a panacea for every kind of infirmity. To his followers, however, he soon came to be regarded as the prophet of a new revelation, and before the turn of the century the movement had become a worldwide cult (Ellenberger, 1970, Chaps. 2 and 3).

Following the discovery of the hypnotic trance, first observed in 1784 by Puységur, Mesmer's foremost French disciple, interest began to focus as much on the remarkable phenomena associated with this special state as on the healing potentialities of the practice as such. It was believed that a person who attained a certain stage of trance, the so-called state of lucidity, could freely manifest a variety of clairvoyant powers, in particular the power of viewing distant places with the mind's eye that was known as "traveling clairvoyance." Based on the analogy of sleep-walking, Puységur thought that he had discovered a method of artificially inducing somnambulism, hence the expression "somnambules" for those who succumbed to this treatment. Certain of these psychic somnambules became widely known in their day, and there were even public demonstrations in which they participated. The Didier brothers, who flourished in Paris in the 1840s, were probably the most famous exponents of this tradition (Dingwall, 1968).

The direction taken by the mesmerists in pursuit of the paranormal had the unfortunate effect of diminishing the chances of hypnotism gaining official recognition as an adjunct of medicine and surgery, especially as the movement inevitably attracted charlatans in large numbers. It took, in fact, a hundred years, after the adverse report on mesmerism by the French Royal Commission of 1784, before the French Academy of Sciences acknowledged the validity of hypnosis in deference to Charcot, then at the height of his fame, who had intro-duced it at the Salpêtrière in connection with his studies of hysteria (Owen, 1971). By then a close link had been forged between mesmerism or hypnotism and psychical research so that it is not altogether surprising to find Janet, in 1886, reporting on the case of "Leonie," a somnambule of Le Havre, who appeared susceptible to hypnosis at a distance (Dingwall, 1968; Ellenberger, 1970, Chap. 6).

In summary, one can say that the mesmeric movement provided the earliest examples of what we now call extrasensory perception (ESP) being demonstrated under controlled conditions, even if the reports are seldom detailed enough for us to be able to evaluate their authenticity with much assurance. It was, moreover, the study of hypnosis which laid the foundations of a depth psychology which was to have such a profound influence on parapsychological thinking, commencing with Myers' theory (1903, Introduction) of the "subliminal self." Perhaps the current enthusiasm for altered states of consciousness among parapsychologists may best be viewed as one of the long-term legacies of the mesmeric movement.

Spiritualism

The other principal precursor of parapsychology in the nineteenth century was the movement usually referred to as "Spiritualism," although the more accurate designation would be spiritism. The movement, which erupted quite suddenly at the mid-point of the century in the United States, ensured a steady flow of mysterious phenomena that cried out for investigation. The story of the hauntings at Hydesville, involving the Fox family, usually taken as having precipitated the movement, is too well known to require retelling (Podmore, 1902) but, at all events, within a few years it had spread from its home ground in upper New York State across the length and breadth of Europe. No doubt its passage had been eased by the earlier conquests of the mesmerists. The role of trance medium fitted neatly the niche previously occupied by the somnambules, and not a few of those who began as mesmerists made the transition to Spiritualism. Its spread may also have been facilitated by the existence of the Swedenborgian sect whose beliefs about a spirit world derived from the arcane writings of Emanuel Swedenborg, a Swedish contemporary of Hume and Voltaire, who combined the career of a practical scientist with that of a visionary.

In some respects Spiritualism represented a regression to a cruder and more outlandish conception of the paranormal. Its key idea, that of communicating with the spirits of the deceased, stems from a venerable occult tradition—shamans and witch-doctors were forerunners of the medium. What was new about Spiritualism was its prosaic matter-of-factness and its cosy conception of the relationship between the two worlds. In this it faithfully reflected the outlook of the times when the romantic era had been superseded by a new faith in technology and progress. If survival were a fact, it ought to be possible to demonstrate this like any other fact of science. There is nothing, it seems to me, in basic spiritualist doctrine that could not be expressed quite adequately in purely secular terms. Death itself, after all, is to be conceived as a natural metamorphosis, not as the prelude to any kind of supernatural resurrection.

It is, however, one of the paradoxes of the Victorian age that it was not only an age of unprecedented material progress; it was also an age of intense religious activity, of church-building and church-going, coupled with a strong dose of sentimental religiosity. Inevitably, the spiritualist movement soon acquired the trappings of a religion with its own churches and its own priesthood of trained mediums. Its devotees, after all, were drawn mainly from the ranks of pious Christians who, in the face of bereavement, sought a more substantial consolation than could be obtained through conventional worship. Thus, from the outset, the movement exhibited this twofold character: at the one level it was a new religious revelation, one of the many to come out of nineteenth-century America, while on another level it was an incipient science of interest to scholars and researchers. In the end there is no doubt that it had far more influence on the emergence of parapsychology than did mesmerism.

One clear advantage that Spiritualism possessed over mesmerism was its claim to produce paranormal physical phenomena. The idea was that the spirits could communicate not just by inspiring the medium to convey messages, but also through direct physical manifestations. These included raps which, used in conjunction with an agreed code, could spell out messages, direct voice utterances, and, more tangibly, table-tilting or table-levitation. But the most spectacular way whereby the discarnate entity could signalize its presence was by means of a so-called materialization consisting of a partial or total reproduction, in quasiphysical form, of the deceased individual during the course of a séance. The accepted theory of materialization that came to prevail in spiritualist circles was that the spirit-form was composed of a peculiar substance drawn from the medium's own body to which Richet gave the name "ectoplasm" (Fodor, 1966, *Ectoplasm*).

Before the advent of Spiritualism the only source of paraphysical phenomena, practically speaking, was that represented by haunts and poltergeists (Owen, 1964). The significance of the spiritualist approach was that it sought to tame these wild sporadic phenomena by using the medium as a channel through which they could manifest in an orderly and meaningful way. The gravest drawback of this approach was the irresistible opportunity it afforded for every manner of trickery or fraudulent simulation, especially when the séance was conducted in the customary way in semi-darkness or even pitch darkness. It is hardly surprising, therefore, that, from the very beginning, starting with the Fox sisters, the first professional mediums, the movement was hag-ridden with fraud and with the suspicions, accusations, exposures, and confessions that went with it

(Podmore, 1902, Vol. 1). The debasement of the movement was indeed more rapid and shameless than the similar debasement of the earlier mesmeric movement, for there was more money to be gained by successful imposture in the case of Spiritualism. Moreover, like so much else in the nineteenth century, the age-old craft of conjuring was making headway and there must have been a standing temptation for the unscrupulous practitioner of the craft to make a lucrative living from the deception of those who appeared to desire so passionately to be deceived! The fact is that nearly all psychic phenomena, mental and physical, can be simulated given sufficient ingenuity and provided the simulator is allowed to retain the initiative. At all events, from the time of Houdini to the present day, members of the magicians' fraternity have always been the most vociferous skeptics whenever paranormal claims have been mooted.

What made the situation peculiarly exasperating for the would-be investigator was that there seemed to be no way of segregating the honest mediums from the dishonest ones. With one notable exception, to which we shall return, nearly all the outstanding physical mediums on record must be considered in some degree at least as contaminated. The question at issue was not whether they ever cheated—it was taken for granted that cheating was second nature to them—but whether any of their phenomena could be accepted as genuine. This is illustrated most strikingly in the case of Eusapia Palladino who was more thoroughly investigated by more independent investigators than any other physical medium before or since. They all knew that she would take advantage of any relaxation in the test conditions to perpetrate a deception; nevertheless some of the most experienced among them were convinced that she was able at times to produce phenomena that could only be called paranormal (Carrington, 1913, Pt. 2; Feilding, Baggally, and Carrington, 1909).

The Special Case of D. D. Home

The one notable exception was, of course, D. D. Home. He, at any rate, was never discredited whatever his enemies may have said or thought about him and whatever reservations may have been voiced by later critics (Hall, 1965; Podmore, 1902; Solovovo, 1930). Were it not for Home, there would be a strong argument for dismissing the entire physical phenomena of Spiritualism as, at best, unproven, and, at worst, a monstrous testament to human credulity. His case, however, is so important, not only for its great intrinsic interest but for its repercussions on the history of parapsychology, that I make no apologies for dwelling on it at some length. For it may well be doubted whether, but for his prodigious reputation, Spiritualism would ever have acquired the influence which brought it to the attention of the learned world.

The principal facts of Home's career have been recounted many times, first by himself (Home, 1863), then posthumously by his second wife (Mme. Home, 1888), and subsequently by various authors including Podmore (1902), Dingwall (1962, Chap. 5), and Burton (1948). He was born near Edinburgh in 1833 but from the age of 9 was brought up in Connecticut at a time when Spiritualism was just beginning to impinge on the American social scene. Already as an adolescent he was attracting attention on account of his physical phenomena and was taken up by leading American Spiritualists. Then, in 1855, he moved to London and thereafter spent the rest of his life in Europe until his death in 1886. With no visible means of support he always contrived to mix in the highest social and literary circles and was a welcome guest at the courts of Europe where he gained the special patronage of the Empress Eugénie of France, Queen Sophie of Holland, and Tzar Alexander II of Russia. The last two decades of his life were spent mainly in England where he came to the attention first of Lord Adare (later Earl of Dunraven), who wrote a long account of his experiences with Home (Dunraven, 1926); and, later, of Sir William Crookes, one of the most eminent scientists of the time. In 1871 Crookes published a report in the *Quarterly Journal of Science*, of which he was editor, on experiments which he and his associates had carried out with Home at his laboratory and in his home (see Crookes, 1874, 1889). Although Crookes encountered bitter opposition from his colleagues for his stance (he failed to persuade Faraday to be a witness to the phenomena), there can be no doubt that Crookes, more than anyone, was responsible for establishing Home as a scientific wonder, and this in itself was of some importance in the events that led to the founding of the Society for Psychical Research (S.P.R.) in 1882.

What was it, we must now ask, that Home could do that so astounded our Victorian forebears? For it would be a mistake to suppose that the Victorians, or, at any rate, the educated ones, were any more credulous than we are. If anything, the contrary was true, for they were less inhibited about expressing a contemptuous disbelief in anything "spooky" or supernatural. The scientific ethos, after all, had not yet lost any of its luster. The answer must be sought in the plain facts of Home's performances. To begin with, Home normally operated in good illumination, that is, with ample candlelight or gaslight. Indeed, he himself poured scorn on those mediums who had to have recourse to darkness. This is a point we must bear in mind when considering the possibility of sheer malobservation at his séances. A typical Home séance (there were, of course, innumerable variations) would proceed somewhat as follows. First, there would come a tremendous shaking of the room and all its contents (the earthquake effect). By and by—and usually the sitters were apprised of what to expect next—the table would start to tilt and eventually would rise into the air, sometimes even above the heads of the sitters, remain suspended in mid-air for a short while, and then gently descend. If the table tilted, the objects on it were never observed to slide off. After a time, the sitters would feel themselves touched as if by invisible hands, and objects would be deposited in their laps or snatched away from them. Finally, towards the close of the séance, the spirits, who often announced their identities through Home, might be requested to play a favorite tune on an accordion specially provided for the purpose (this was sometimes held by Home in one hand on the side opposite the keyboard; at other times it might be left under the table or even appear to float in the air!). Home did not usually go into a trance but sat quietly in a chair, occasionally conversing with the sitters. His more fantastic displays involving the visible materialization of hands, arms, etc., were usually reserved for the company of true believers. For these phenomena low illumination was the rule, as it was for his self-levitations, which likewise were kept for special occasions.

Various hypotheses were put forward, already during Home's lifetime, to avoid having to accept the observations at their face value. The most widely canvassed, then and subsequently, was the idea that Home was really some sort of a supermesmerist who could simply bewitch his sitters into seeing or hearing anything that he wanted them to see or hear. Alternatively, it was suggested that Home was a superconjurer who made good use of his feet or of concealed appliances; thus a stuffed glove at the end of a rod could deputize nicely for a spirit hand! An idea favored by Podmore (1902) was that Home's amateur status allowed him the privilege of deciding who should receive an invitation to a séance and that he took care to invite only the most gullible and impressionable. Appeal was also made to the notorious fallibility of human testimony (Besterman, 1932; Davey, 1887), and it was pointed out that at the time of Home it was not yet the practice to take notes at the sittings and many of the extant accounts were written months or years later.

Recent historical research (Zorab, 1975), however, has made all of these hypotheses difficult to sustain. We can discount straight away the use of machinery, at least where the table levitations were concerned, for the tables in question were not flimsy little card-tables of the sort that one could hoist on the end of one's toes but massive mahogany dining-room tables of the sort that could seat a dozen or more at dinner! Next, the idea that Home exercised a veto on those who were to be admitted to the séance does not square with the facts. Podmore (1902) grossly underestimated the total number of different individuals who witnessed the phenomena during Home's lifetime, and while no doubt many of them were his friends and supporters, they included also some of his bitterest enemies and critics. Likewise, if many sitters were already convinced beforehand of the truths of Spiritualism, others were professed skeptics, like the Dutch rationalists who invited Home to Amsterdam hoping to expose him but then had to acknowledge that there was no explanation for what they had observed with their own eyes (Zorab, 1970). The "defective-memory" hypothesis is also quite inadequate to account for more than minor discrepancies.

Some of the reports were penned on the same day, and a comparison between contemporaneous and delayed reports shows none of the progressive embroidery of the incidents that one would expect on this hypothesis. Thus, the hypnotic hypothesis remains the only serious contender that stops short of a paranormal explanation; after all, there were as yet no recording instruments to prove that the events described actually took place.

Nevertheless, the theory that the events were purely hallucinatory runs into grave difficulties. In the first place, the annals of hypnotism and mesmerism provide no independent evidence of any powers of comparable magnitude. But even if, *faute-de-mieux*, we attribute to Home this unique power over his sitters we would have to suppose that he could wield it with 100 per cent efficacy. If even one witness for even part of the time had failed to succumb to it, the game would have been up. Yet there is no record of even one such witness failing to see, say, a table-levitation, which every one else present claimed to observe, and this is the more telling inasmuch as investigators were well aware of the danger of falling a victim to Home's charisma and took strenuous precautions against it (Dingwall, 1953; Zorab, 1970). There is also some evidence of tables being broken by a too precipitate descent which is hard to reconcile with an hallucinatory explanation.

In summary, we must, it seems, resign ourselves to the fact that Home remains as much an enigma to us as he was to his contemporaries. The most we can say by way of reducing dissonance is that Home's career ran its course somewhat before psychical research had become properly organized. The trouble is that we have to view him from across a gulf in time where there is nothing truly comparable. Of course, there were a great many physical mediums after Home. Some of these are of considerable interest, like the amazing Kluski, a Polish medium of the post–World War I period, who not only allegedly materialized hands and arms but obtained casts of these in paraffin-wax that are still extant (Geley, 1927). Perhaps the last in the succession to Home to arouse widespread interest was the young Austrian medium, Rudi Schneider, who between the Wars was tested independently and with positive results in Munich, Paris, and London (Besterman, 1968, Chaps. 21–22; Gregory, 1968; Hope, 1933). But, for the most part, the latter-day physical phenomena were no more than a pale reflection of those reported in such abundance with Home, and they seldom excited much concern outside the narrow circle of psychical researchers. To find a parallel to Home we may have to turn to the ambiguous figure of Uri Geller who, at the present time, has created something of the same stir both among the general public and among the scientific community. He, of course, does not belong to the spiritualist tradition and his repertoire is entirely different, but, like Home, he has already begotten a host of lesser imitators, and it is not inappropriate to think of him as a Home for the age of the mass-media.

THE HEROIC AGE 1882-1930

The Society for Psychical Research (S.P.R.)

In the next period to which we must now turn there was a decisive shift of interest away from physical phenomena, which by this time had acquired a thoroughly bad odor. The accent was now on telepathy (a term coined by F. W. H. Myers) and on survival of bodily death as evidenced by the verbal communications of mediums. These two topics are not unrelated since it can be argued that if telepathy between the living could be established, this would render more plausible communication between the living and the dead. This shift is well illustrated by the career of Mrs. Leonore Piper, a brilliant medium from Boston, who was discovered by no less a person than the great William James and then retained by the S.P.R., who put Richard Hodgson in charge of her investigation. She was steered away from any involvement in physical phenomena, but, as a mental medium, she has remained unsurpassed.

The founding of the S.P.R. in London in 1882 is one of the few unmistakable turning points which an historian of parapsychology can seize upon. For it set the pattern which the field was to assume for the next five decades—the pattern of earnest, high-minded amateurs who were fearless in the face of public ridicule and dedicated to the objective study of phenomena which none of the existing sciences were yet ready to tackle. The S.P.R. became the model for numerous similar societies in other countries, especially those of France, Germany, and Poland where there was most of the activity. America, for all that it was the homeland of Spiritualism, was slow to take to psychical research. An American S.P.R. was founded as early as 1885, with the blessing of William James, but it soon ran into financial difficulties and in 1887 was amalgamated with the London Society and managed by its representative, Richard Hodgson, until his death in 1905, when it regained its independence. It was not until our next period that America was to establish its unquestioned leadership in this field, a leadership which it still retains.

It is worth pausing at this juncture to look at the composition of the S.P.R. in its early days (Gauld, 1968; Nicol, 1972). There was first what might be called the Cambridge group: Henry Sidgwick, the philosopher, a Fellow of Trinity College, who served as its first president, and two younger men who had known Sidgwick when they were students at Trinity, Frederic Myers and Edmund Gurney. All three could be described as products of the conflict between science and religion which came to a head in Victorian England with the advent of Darwin. They were men who had lost their faith in revealed religion but who were temperamentally averse to the prevailing scientific materialism. Myers, poet and classicist, was the great enthusiast of this group who combined a passionate concern with the problem of survival with a deep interest in the new depth psychology (he was probably the first person in England to show an interest in what Freud was doing). His thought is enshrined in his *Human Personality and its Survival of Bodily Death*, a two-volume work that was published posthumously in 1903 and at once became a classic in the literature of psychical research. Gurney, a man of wide-ranging interests, began his career as a musicologist and then studied both medicine and law, without practicing either, until he eventually found his vocation in becoming the first honorary secretary of the Society to which he thereafter devoted his prodigious energies until his premature death in 1888. He was the senior author (with Myers and Podmore) of the two-volume *Phantasms of the Living*, published in 1886, a collection of spontaneous case material centering upon the so-called crisis apparition, the experience of seeing an hallucination of someone who, it later transpires, was then at the point of death.

A second group is represented by the Balfour family, which comprised Arthur, First Earl of Balfour, philosopher, classicist, and statesman, who was Prime Minister from 1902 to 1905 and later Foreign Secretary under Lloyd George when he gave his name to the Balfour Declaration; his brother Gerald, who was much more active as a psychical researcher; and, most important of all, their sister Eleanor (Nora) Mildred, who married Henry Sidgwick. She was not merely one of the leading lights of the Society for many years but, by all accounts, one of the most remarkable women of her generation. Before her marriage she had studied physics and worked under Lord Rayleigh, and, as Mrs. Sidgwick, she became one of the champions of higher education for women and Principal of Newnham College, Cambridge.

The third group consisted of the scientists. Besides Crookes, whom we have already mentioned, there were Sir William Barrett, professor of physics at the Royal College of Science in Dublin, and a number of other physicists of varying degrees of eminence including Lord Rayleigh, J. J. Thomson, and Sir Oliver Lodge. By 1887 the Society numbered no less than eight Fellows of the Royal Society among its Council and Honorary Members. On the Continent, too, scientists were starting to take an interest in the phenomena. The most eminent of these was Charles Richet, professor of physiology at the Sorbonne and later Nobel Laureate. He made intensive studies of Eusapia Palladino, whom he took to be genuine, and it is noteworthy that even the Curies found time to attend some sittings which Palladino held in Paris. Mention should also be made of the Swiss psychologist, Théodore Flournoy, who held a chair of experimental psychology at the University of Geneva.

Perhaps the culmination of the "heroic age" of psychical research, as we have dubbed it, was the appearance upon the scene of what became known as the "cross correspondences" (Balfour, 1960; Murphy, 1961, Chap. 7; Salter, 1963; Saltmarsh, 1938; see also Gauld's chapter in this volume). These consisted, essentially, of an enormous number of automatic scripts, produced by a dozen or so different mediums or automatists operating independently in different parts of the world, which when pieced together conveyed intelligible, if cryptic, messages.   The ostensible communicators were mainly the Society's own founders, Myers, Gurney, and Sidgwick, all of whom had by 1901 quit this life. The cross correspondences began around 1902 and lasted until 1930 or even later, and their geographical ramifications took in America, Britain, Egypt, and India. Mrs. Piper was the only professional medium of this group; the rest were upper-class women, some of them well-known figures in public life who used pseudonyms and kept their mediumship a closely-guarded secret even from their friends.

The most salient feature of the scripts is their profusion of literary puzzles with learned allusions to Greek and Latin texts. In this respect they reflect well the erudition of their purported discarnate authors but were quite beyond the attainments of their mediums with the notable exception of Mrs. A. W. Verrall, who was herself a classicist. But, if this was an experiment intitiated from the beyond to demonstrate survival, it must be admitted that it was sadly misconceived. For it demanded almost a lifetime of study combined with exceptional scholarly gifts in order to interpret and evaluate this huge body of material. And, even then, it allowed too much latitude to the ingenuity of the interpreter.   Clearly, it was not by such recherché strategies as this that the bastions of skepticism would be stormed.

Some Traditional Psychic Skills

The fortunes of the Spiritualist movement in Europe revived with the advent of the First World War when the legion of the bereaved which the holocaust created put a premium on the services of the medium. The best known of English mediums, Mrs. Gladys Osborne Leonard, flourished at this time, and it was through her that Sir Oliver Lodge claimed to have made contact with his son Raymond, killed in action in 1915, as described in his book *Raymond* (1916). Yet Spiritualism and the survival problem was never more than one of the many strands that went to make up the fabric of parapsychology. The original mesmeric belief in latent powers of mind that could be released by special means persisted and continued to show itself in a variety of ways both at the level of folk belief and at the level of research. Even the mediumistic evidence did not necessarily imply a spiritistic explanation. Crookes (1889), for example, also believed that, in D. D. Home, he had discovered a new force in nature, the "psychic force." As for the verbal communications, there was always the possibility that the information came not from a discarnate communicator but from the medium's own powers of telepathy or clairvoyance which her unconscious had dramatized in the form of direct speech. Indeed, where the communicator was clearly fictitious, or was someone who was later ascertained to be alive, there was little option but to interpret the evidence in this way—assuming, that is, that the information was veridical and could not have been known to the medium by normal means. To this day parapsychologists are still divided as between survivalists and nonsurvivalists (Ducasse, 1961; Roll, 1974a; see also Gauld's chapter in this volume).

Most mediums, in any case, claimed to possess psychic skills of one kind or another which owed nothing to spirit intervention. These included psychic diagnosis, psychic healing, and, of special importance in this context, psychometry (the term dates from 1842) where the medium tries to gain impressions from a "token object" of its owner or its provenance. In due course these or similar feats were appropriated by individuals who were not Spiritualist mediums but were variously known as psychics, sensitives, clairvoyants, seers, paragnosts, etc. A striking example from our own day is the celebrated Dutch clairvoyant Gerard Croiset, who has been extensively studied by W. H. C. Tennhaeff of Utrecht (Pollack, 1964). Croiset, working largely through psychometry, has acquired something of a reputation as a "psychic detective."

An earlier exponent of psychometry was Pascal Forthuny, who flourished in Paris during the 1920s and whose exploits have been described at length by his investigator, Eugène Osty (1923). Forthuny was not a professional psychic but a writer and artist who discovered his mediumistic gifts only in middle life following the death of his son in an air crash. At first this took the form of automatic writing, but soon he switched to psychometry. He was the first to attempt a "chair test" which later Croiset was to make a prominent feature of his repertoire. For this the clairvoyant has to concentrate on a particular chair in an auditorium before the audience arrives and to try and gain impressions of the person who will shortly occupy that chair, the seats being assigned at random.

Another psychometrist of this period was the woman known in the literature as Señora Maria Reyes de Z. She was the patient of a German physician, Gustav Pagenstecher, who practiced in Mexico, and it was while she was undergoing hypnosis that she first accidentally revealed her clairvoyant powers. Her most remarkable feat was to produce information concerning the background and history of some token object such as a stone when this was handed to her while in the hypnotic trance. A committee of the medical society of Mexico City, to whom Pagenstecher reported his observations in 1919, upheld his claims that they were of a paranormal nature (Pagenstecher, 1922; Prince, 1921; Roll, 1967).

At about the same time, in Munich, another medical man, Rudolf Tischner (1925), was studying a group of clairvoyant subjects who could perform an even more exacting psychic task which he called "cryptoscopy"; this consisted of apprehending the contents of a sealed opaque envelope which usually contained as a target an inscription or a drawing. One of the first such cases to arouse scientific interest had occurred in Russia in the 1890s where the subject was a woman patient of the Russian psychiatrist A. N. Khovrin. He had brought her to the attention of his medical colleagues who had conducted a number of tests on her, and in 1898 he published a monograph on the case; this began to attract attention in the West after it appeared in a German translation in 1919, shortly before Tischner published his own findings in German in 1921. An interesting sidelight of cultural history is provided by the fact that Khovrin's patient could distinguish colors by touch and in certain tests he used colored liquids in test-tubes (Zielinski, 1968, Vol. 3). In our own day, Roza Kuleshova, who has been vouched for by no less an authority than A. R. Luria, became for a short while a world celebrity as an exponent of just such a skill. As so often happens, many others then came forward with similar claims, but whether this ability was a species of clairvoyance or a new "dermo-optical" sense-mechanism remained a matter of dispute.

A much more flamboyant example of "reading" sealed target material which baffled a number of scientists early in the century, including the great Thomas Edison, was the case of a Polish immigrant to the United States who called himself Bert Reese. Being a professional psychic and billet-reader, he was a natural object of suspicion and, in a letter to Conan Doyle, Houdini claimed that he had detected the trick. Certainly, Reese's billet-readings were so fluent and accurate that it is very hard to suppose that they could have been genuine unless his powers exceeded anything that has ever been known in this line; and yet Edison, for one, never wavered in his conviction, based on his own tests with Reese, that the phenomenon was paranormal (See Fodor, 1966, *Reese*; also Ebon, 1971, Chap. 11).

More evidential is the case of Stefan Ossowiecki, who flourished in Warsaw during the Inter-War years, since he was tested by some of the best known researchers from France, England, and Germany, as well as those of his native Poland (Besterman, 1968). He displayed clairvoyant powers of a high order that included both cryptoscopy and psychometry. Unlike Reese, he was not a professional psychic; he was an engineer and an educated man, and he used his rare gifts exclusively in the interests of science or for the benefit of friends who sought his help in personal matters. He perished in the Warsaw uprising of 1944.

One other outstanding sensitive of this period who played an important part in the history of parapsychology was Mary Craig Sinclair, the wife of the popular novelist, Upton Sinclair. In his book *Mental Radio* (1962), first published in 1930, Sinclair describes with illustrations the series of experiments which he carried out on the telepathic transmission of simple line drawings with his wife as subject and himself as sender. This type of experiment had a long history; indeed, it figures in the very earliest volumes of *S.P.R. Proceedings* in connection with the Guthrie experiments in Liverpool which had attracted the attention of Oliver Lodge; and, in Paris, at much the same time as the Sinclairs, René Warcollier (1938) was conducting successful experiments along these lines. What gave special importance to the case of Mrs. Sinclair, however, was that she became known to William McDougall, a pioneer of experimental psychology in England, who at that time held the chair of psychology at Duke University. He conducted his own tests with her, and although the results were less striking than those she had achieved with her husband or with her brother-in-law, R. L. Irwin, they were sufficiently impressive to encourage McDougall to persevere with his own plans to establish a parapsychological research center in his department at Duke (Sinclair, 1962).

McDougall, who was a formidable polemicist, had long been engaged in a running battle against the mechanistic outlook in psychology as represented especially by the school of behaviorism which was then coming into prominence. While teaching at Harvard in 1926—he first met a young biologist by the name of J. B. Rhine, who was to play the key role in the next stage of our story. It was also during McDougall's stay at Harvard that there occurred a scandal destined to have far-reaching consequences for the direction which parapsychology in America was thereafter to take. "Margery" (Mrs. Mina Crandon), the attractive wife of a prominent Boston surgeon, had begun to manifest physical phenomena of the most bizarre and spectacular sort, ostensibly under the guidance of her deceased brother Walter. Soon she was the center of a stormy controversy into which many well-known scientists and parapsychologists were drawn. By all accounts she must have been a formidable woman since she even managed to outwit Houdini. Whether there was ever a core of genuine phenomena in the Margery mediumship is still a matter of speculation, but, at all events, in due course she was exposed as guilty of gross fraud, and her husband too was implicated as her accomplice. This traumatic denouement very nearly shattered the American S.P.R. which, by then, was already heavily committed in her favor. Fortunately, both McDougall and Rhine had expressed skepticism in their reports of the séances, and the lesson was not lost on Rhine, who was determined to rebuild parapsychology on a cooler, less frenetic basis (Dingwall, 1926; McDougall, 1967, Pt. 1, Chap. 8; Roll, 1974b; Tietze, 1973).

THE RHINE ERA 1930–1960

This brings us to the second critical turning point of our story, the founding of the Duke University Parapsychology Laboratory. McDougall moved to Duke in 1927 and was joined there the same year by J. B. Rhine and his wife and coworker, Louisa. Soon they were in charge of the newly formed parapsychology laboratory. There were two interrelated aspects of the "Rhine

Revolution" which we must now examine. First, it represented a bid on behalf of parapsychology for university status and for recognition as an accredited academic discipline (McDougall, 1927). Secondly, it represented the substitution of a quantitative, statistical approach in place of the search for qualitative evidence of a self-evidently paranormal character. This latter move, it was hoped, would not only overcome the bottleneck created by the scarcity of phenomena and thereby enhance the general credibility of the evidence, but would also demonstrate that psychic ability was part of the universal birthright of mankind, not just the freakish gift of certain rare sensitives.

Let us now consider each of these two major programmatic objectives. In pursuance of the first, the attempt was made to standardize both the nomenclature and the techniques of the new discipline. Thus, in introducing the term *parapsychology* McDougall was trying to carve out from the broader, looser field of psychical research an area that would become the preserve of the academic researcher. The latter would include the careful documentation of spontaneous cases but could be entrusted to the devoted amateur. Here, however, in keeping with the best current usage we have been using the terms *parapsychology* and *psychical research* interchangeably (already in the nineteenth century the Germans were using "parapsychologie" as the equivalent for what the British called "psychical research" and the French "la métapsychique"). Some textbooks and encyclopedias still use "parapsychology" in its original McDougallian sense as denoting the strictly experimental and quantitative subdivision of psychical research, but more and more it has come to replace the older expression as embracing the critical study of the paranormal in all its aspects.

The expression *extrasensory perception*, soon to be replaced for most purposes by its acronym *ESP*, was introduced to designate, indifferently and under one single rubric, telepathy, clairvoyance, and precognition in all their many guises. The use of the word *perception* was unfortunate, for all that is implied by ESP is an acquiring of information about the external world by means other than through the known sensory channels. Operationally speaking, the subcategories of ESP could now be related to the particular procedure used in the standard card-guessing test for ESP: whether the target card was or was not known to another person, whether it was selected before or only after the subject had recorded his guess, and so on. The term *psychokinesis* (PK) to cover the paraphysical phenomena was introduced somewhat later in connection with the dice-throwing tests, which soon became a stock part of the laboratory repertoire, although the evidence these provided was markedly inferior to that yielded by the ESP tests. The contrast between PK in this narrow operational sense, as a kind of gambler's lucky streak, and the phenomena traditionally associated with poltergeist cases and physical mediumship is particularly glaring. Finally the term *psi*, as the generic expression covering both ESP and PK, became part of the new vocabulary carrying with it a tacit implication of a single fundamental "psi process" which could take either a cognitive or a motor form.

The idea of using probability theory to test for psi ability was by no means a novel one. Charles Richet, as early as 1884, had carried out tests of telepathy using playing cards and had explained in the *Revue Philosophique* how probability theory could be exploited for this purpose. At much the same time William Barrett was conducting card tests to demonstrate telepathy, and since then accounts of similar efforts can be found scattered throughout the literature. Of special importance in this connection is the work with playing cards of Ina Jephson (1928) of the S.P.R. in London. She was able to apply to her data formulas specially devised by R. A. Fisher, the great statistician (McVaugh and Mauskopf, 1976). A simplification of the necessary calculations followed when Rhine replaced the playing-card pack with a specially designed ESP pack consisting of the five "Zener symbols" repeated five times.

The new dispensation soon began to assert itself. Rhine published his first report on the work of the Laboratory entitled *Extrasensory Perception* in 1934, and it soon attracted widespread attention among the general public as well as in academic circles. In 1937, a year before McDougall died, the *Journal of Parapsychology* was launched as a forum for the new movement, and when, in 1940, Pratt and his associates published *Extrasensory Perception after Sixty Years*, it really did begin to look as if parapsychology had at least arrived on the academic scene. The "sixty years" of the title of their volume was an allusion to the founding of the S.P.R., but the book was essentially a comprehensive survey and evaluation of the work of the Laboratory since its inception. More and more in the public estimation scientific parapsychology was becoming identified with the products of the Rhine school.

And yet these early successes were deceptive. Enthusiasts soon learned to their cost that the vast majority of ESP tests end, as they begin, by reaffirming the laws of chance. In retrospect we can now see that the early years at Duke were blessed with an almost unbelievable share of good fortune. For there appeared, out of the blue, a whole cluster of first-rate subjects who could not only score consistently above chance but who, on occasion, could produce phenomenal scores on a given run. *Extrasensory Perception* deals with no less than eight such subjects starting with A. J. Linzmayer and culminating in Hubert Pearce. Never again were we to witness such an auspicious concentration of psychic talent. Cynics have attributed this to the relatively lax conditions that prevailed during this exploratory phase, suggesting that it was bound to vanish once conditions had been tightened up in deference to external criticism (Hansel, 1966). However, Rhine (1934) himself makes a persuasive case when he points out that there was, in those early days, a unique atmosphere of fun and excitement which could never be recaptured either there or anywhere else. Certainly, one can never ignore such psychological imponderables.

At all events, it soon became apparent that a good guessing subject is just as rare a commodity as a good medium or a good clairvoyant. This was clearly shown in the work of S. G. Soal, a mathematician at London University and the chief exponent of the Rhine approach in England. Soal labored doggedly for years, testing hundreds of volunteer subjects without the glimmer of a significant result, and became more and more skeptical in the process, until at last he discovered his two star performers, Basil Shackleton and Gloria Stewart (Soal and Bateman, 1954). Yet even this modest harvest made Soal a focus of suspicion when no other good scorers could subsequently be found in Britain.

The most notable subject of recent years is Pavel Stepanek of Prague, who was discovered in 1962 by the Czech parapsychologist Milan Ryzl. The investigation of Stepanek, initially sponsored by Rhine and spanning the next 10 years, was mainly the work of J. G. Pratt (1973, 1974), for long Rhine's second-in-command, in collaboration with various other visiting parapsychologists. Stepanek, whose stereotyped repertoire was confined to a specific binary guessing task, could boast a longer record of significant scoring than any previous subject, yet the very fact that no better subjects were available nearer home tells its own story.

With the virtual disappearance of the consistent scorer, the work of the Duke Laboratory might have ground to a halt had it not been for the discovery of the differential scoring effect. One new fact that came to light, and could only have done so with a quantitative measure of ESP, was the existence of negative scoring. Some subjects under certain conditions would score consistently *below* chance expectation. This would suggest some kind of unconscious censoring of the psi information, as if the subject knew the correct answers but dare not admit it! Following the lead of Gertrude Schmeidler of the City College, New York, this anomaly became linked at first with differences of attitude. Her idea was that subjects could be divided into sheep and goats according to whether they accepted or rejected the possibility of ESP. Sheep could be expected to score positively, goats negatively. Later, other personality correlates became associated with this bidirectionality in the scoring pattern (Schmeidler and McConnell, 1958). Much of the work of the Duke Laboratory and of other centers from then on was given up to the search for personality correlates of psi ability and to the study of differential scoring effects between two specially selected groups.

It cannot yet be said that any clear personality profile has emerged that would identify the good scorer or even that the sheep/goat hypothesis has been consistently upheld. Nevertheless, this trend did do something toward broadening the scope of the field beyond a mere preoccupation with proving the existence of psi and toward bringing it closer to the work of psychologists and personality theorists. It also helped to revive the idea that psi is a regular feature of our mental life, not a rare attainment, an idea that is still strongly cherished by one school of thought among parapsychologists.

In 1965, when Rhine was due to retire, Duke University, the first in the world to open its doors to parapsychology, severed all further connections with it. The Laboratory, which was well funded, continued to function as before, but as a private research organization outside the campus walls. At the present time, parapsychology is being taught in an ever-increasing number of colleges in the United States, but whether this represents a tribute to its achievements or a concession to the greater intellectual permissiveness of our age (the initiative usually comes from the student body for whom its unorthodoxy constitutes its principal recommendation!) is a debatable point. There are, however, encouraging signs that parapsychology is being accorded a greater measure of recognition by the scientific community; thus, in 1969 the Parapsychological Association was admitted to affiliation with the American Association for the Advancement of Science. But as an academic discipline it remains precarious and peripheral so that McDougall's hopes for its future remain to be realized.

THE CONTEMPORARY SCENE

I will deal only cursorily with the later developments in the field as they will be adequately covered elsewhere in this volume. The decline of behaviorism in the 1960s produced a certain rapprochement between psychology and parapsychology. The newfound interest in inner experience and altered states of consciousness alerted parapsychologists to the possibility that psi might be less a function of personality traits than of mood and state of mind. One of the most significant developments of the decade was the work of the Dream Laboratory of the Maimonides Hospital, New York. Using the instrumentation of a sleep research laboratory, the attempt was made to demonstrate a telepathic influence on dream content and imagery, the idea being that the REM stage of sleep might be specially conducive to psi receptivity. In the end, however, it transpired that even in sleep success largely depends on having the right subject (Ullman and Krippner, with Vaughan, 1973). However, these important studies inspired further work at the Maimonides and elsewhere on psi and altered states of consciousness, including hypnosis, sensory deprivation, sensory bombardment, deep relaxation, meditation, and so forth (see Honorton's chapter in this volume).

With the passing of the Rhine era parapsychology became bolder with respect to the kinds of phenomena that it sought to encompass. Thus psychic photography, for so long shunned for its associations with fraudulent mediums, made a startling reappearance during the 1960s with the unlikely figure of Ted Serios. Although his authenticity remains a matter of dispute, it can at least be said that few subjects have ever been studied more intensively or kept under closer surveillance than Serios was by his chief investigator, the psychiatrist Jule

Eisenbud (1967, and in this volume), and by other investigators (Stevenson and Pratt, 1968, 1969).

Another development which made parapsychological history during the 1960s was the work of Ian Stevenson, a psychiatrist of the University of Virginia, whose monumental case studies culled from all over the world of children who appeared to recollect a previous existence on earth carved out a niche for the study of reincarnation as a reputable field of parapsychological scholarship (Stevenson, 1974, and in this volume).

Perhaps the chief lesson that can be learned from this brief overview of the field is that if a science is to prosper it must have a source of stable phenomena that can be systematically manipulated and forced to yield specific answers to specific questions.

Meanwhile, such progress as has been achieved lies mainly in the area of methodology and experimental design. Thus, at the present time, automated testing has largely superseded the classic card-guessing or dice-throwing techniques as the standard method of testing for ESP or PK (Schmidt, 1974). This, combined with the computer analysis of scoring data, can virtually eliminate human error and bias from the test procedure. It also makes possible a much more rapid screening of subjects.   But, alas, it cannot guarantee results. Methodological rigor and sophistication can never be a substitute for concrete discoveries in science or for theoretical understanding.   When it comes to the basic nature of psi, we are still almost as much in the dark as were our pioneers. Theories and models in plenty have been put forward, but they are little more than speculative exercises which so far lack empirical support (see Chari's chapter in this volume).

There are at the present time two guiding philosophies within parapsychology. According to one, the concept of the paranormal has no permanent validity but is simply an expression of our ignorance. In the fullness of time, parapsychology will be integrated into a unified conceptual framework embracing all the sciences. Such a framework may have to be extended in various unexpected ways, but there is no danger of its being stretched to bursting point. According to the other school of thought, which has been the dominant one in parapsychological history, the significance of the paranormal is precisely that it signals the boundary of the scientific world-view. Beyond that boundary lies the domain of mind liberated from its dependence on the brain. On this view, parapsychology, using the methods of science, becomes a vindication of the essentially spiritual nature of man which must forever defy strict scientific analysis. Which of these two antithetical philosophies will prevail remains a question for the future. In the meanwhile, there is no reason whatever why both parties should not cooperate in furthering our knowledge in this, the most perplexing field of inquiry ever to engage the curiosity of our species.

REFERENCES

Balfour, J. The "Palm Sunday" case: New light on an old love story. *Proceedings of the Society for Psychical Research*, 1960, **52**, 79–267.

Besterman, T. The psychology of testimony in relation to paraphysical phenomena: Report of an experiment. *Proceedings of the Society for Psychical Research*, 1932, **40**, 365–387.

Besterman, T. *Collected Papers on the Paranormal*. New York: Garrett/Helix, 1968.

Burton, J. *Hey-Day of a Wizard*. London: Harrap, 1948.

Carrington, H. *Personal Experiences in Spiritualism*. London: Laurie, n.d. [1913].

Crookes, W. *Researches in the Phenomena of Spiritualism*. London: James Burns, 1874.

Crookes, W. Notes of séances with D. D. Home. *Proceedings of the Society for Psychical Research*, 1889, **6**, 98–127.

Davey, S. J. The possibilities of mal-observation and lapse of memory from a practical point of view. (With an introduction by R. Hodgson.) *Proceedings of the Society for Psychical Research*, 1887, **4**, 381–495.

Dingwall, E. J. Report on a series of sittings with the medium Margery. *Proceedings of the Society for Psychical Research*, 1926, **36**, 79–158.

Dingwall, E. J. Psychological problems arising from a report of telekinesis. *British Journal of Psychology*, 1953, **44**, 61–66.

Dingwall, E. J. *Some Human Oddities*. Secaucus, N.J.: University Books, 1962.

Dingwall, E. J. Hypnotism in France 1800–1900. In E. J. Dingwall (Ed.), *Abnormal Hypnotic Phenomena*, Vol. I. New York: Barnes and Noble, 1968.

Ducasse, C. J. *A Critical Examination of the Belief in a Life After Death*. Springfield, Ill.: Charles C Thomas, 1961.

Dunraven (Earl of). Experiences in spiritualism with D. D. Home. *Proceedings of the Society for Psychical Research*, 1926, **35**, 1–285. (This account first appeared in 1870 in a book printed for private circulation.)

Ebon, M. *They Knew the Unknown*. New York: World, 1971.

Eisenbud, J. *The World of Ted Serios*. New York: Morrow, 1967.

Ellenberger, H. F. *The Discovery of the Unconscious*. New York: Basic Books, 1970.

Feilding, E., Baggally, W. W., and Carrington, H. Report on a series of sittings with Eusapia Palladino. *Proceedings of the Society for Psychical Research*, 1909, **23**, 209–569.

Fodor, N. *Encyclopedia of Psychic Science*. Secaucus, N.J.: University Books, 1966.

Gauld, A. *The Founders of Psychical Research*. New York: Schocken, 1968.

Geley, G. *Clairvoyance and Materialization*. London: T. F. Unwin, 1927.

Gregory, A. K. *The Medium Rudi Schneider and His Investigators*. Unpublished manuscript, 1968. (Available in Library of the S.P.R.)

Gurney, E., Myers, F. W. H., and Podmore, F. *Phantasms of the Living*. London: Trübner, 1886. 2 vols.

Hall, T. *New Light on Old Ghosts*. London: Duckworth, 1965.

Hansel, C. E. M. *ESP: A Scientific Evaluation*. New York: Scribner's, 1966.

Home, D. D. *Incidents in My Life*. London: Longmans, Green, 1863.

Home, Mme. D. D. *D. D. Home: His Life and Mission*. London: Trübner, 1888.

Hope, C. Report of a series of sittings with Rudi Schneider. *Proceedings of the Society for Psychical Research*, 1933, **41**, 255–330.

Jephson, I. Evidence for clairvoyance in card-guessing. *Proceedings of the Society for Psychical Research*, 1928, **38**, 223–271.

Lodge, O. *Raymond, or Life and Death*. London: Methuen, 1916.

McDougall, W. Psychical research as a university study. In C. A. Murchison (Ed.), *The Case For and Against Psychical Belief*, pp. 149–162. Worcester, Mass.: Clark University Press, 1927.

McDougall, W. *William McDougall: Explorer of the Mind.* Comp. and ed. by R. van Over and L. Oteri. New York: Garrett/Helix, 1967.

McVaugh, M., and Mauskopf, S. H. J. B. Rhine's *Extra-Sensory Perception* and its background in psychical research. *Isis,* 1976, **67**, 161-189.

Murphy, G. *The Challenge of Psychical Research.* New York: Harper & Row, 1961.

Myers, F. W. H. *Human Personality and its Survival of Bodily Death.* London: Longmans, Green, 1903. 2 vols.

Nicol, J. F. The founders of the S.P.R. *Proceedings of the Society for Psychical Research,* 1972, **55**, 341-369.

Osty, E. *Supernormal Faculties in Man.* London: Methuen, 1923.

Owen, A. R. G. *Can We Explain the Poltergeist?* New York: Garrett Publications, 1964.

Owen, A. R. G. *Hysteria, Hypnosis, and Healing.* New York: Garrett Publications, 1971.

Pagenstecher, G. Past events seership: A study in psychometry. *Proceedings of the American Society for Psychical Research,* 1922, **16**, 1-136.

Podmore, F. *Modern Spiritualism: A History and a Criticism.* London: Methuen, 1902. 2 vols.

Pollack, J. H. *Croiset the Clairvoyant.* New York: Doubleday, 1964.

Pratt, J. G. A decade of research with a selected ESP subject: An overview and reappraisal of the work with Pavel Stepanek. *Proceedings of the American Society for Psychical Research,* 1973, **30**, 1-78.

Pratt, J. G. In search of the consistent scorer. In J. Beloff (Ed.), *New Directions in Parapsychology,* pp. 95-121. London: Elek, 1974. (Reprinted by Scarecrow Press in 1975.)

Pratt, J. G., Rhine, J. B., Smith, B. M., Stuart, C. E., and Greenwood, J. A. *Extrasensory Perception after Sixty Years.* New York: Holt, 1940. (Reprinted by Branden in 1966.)

Prince, W. F. Psychometric experiments with Señora Maria Reyes de Z. *Proceedings of the American Society for Psychical Research,* 1921, **15**, 189-314.

Rhine, J. B. *Extrasensory Perception.* Boston: Boston Society for Psychic Research, 1934. (Reprinted, with a new introduction, by Branden in 1964.)

Roll, W. G. Pagenstecher's contribution to parapsychology. *Journal of the American Society for Psychical Research,* 1967, **61**, 219-240.

Roll, W. G. Survival research: Problems and possibilities. In E. D. Mitchell et al., *Psychic Exploration,* pp. 397-424. New York: Putnam's, 1974. (a)

Roll, W. G. Review of *Margery,* by T. R. Tietze. *Journal of the American Society for Psychical Research,* 1974, **68**, 417-424. (b)

Salter, W. H. The rose of Sharon. *Proceedings of the Society for Psychical Research,* 1963, **54**, 1-22.

Saltmarsh, H. F. *Evidence of Personal Survival from Cross Correspondences.* London: Bell, 1938.

Schmeidler, G. R., and McConnell, R. A. *ESP and Personality Patterns.* New Haven: Yale University Press, 1958. (Reprinted by Greenwood Press in 1973.)

Schmidt, H. Instrumentation in the parapsychological laboratory. In J. Beloff (Ed.), *New Directions in Parapsychology,* pp. 13-37. London: Elek, 1974. (Reprinted by Scarecrow Press in 1975.)

Sinclair, U. *Mental Radio.* Springfield, Ill.: Charles C Thomas, 1962. (Originally published in 1930.)

Soal, S. G., and Bateman, F. *Modern Experiments in Telepathy.* New Haven: Yale University Press, 1954.

Solovovo, P. P. Some thoughts on D. D. Home. *Proceedings of the Society for Psychical Research,* 1930, **39**, 247-265.

Stevenson, I. *Twenty Cases Suggestive of Reincarnation.* (2nd ed., rev.) Charlottesville: University Press of Virginia, 1974.

Stevenson, I., and Pratt, J. G.   Exploratory investigations of the psychic photography of Ted Serios. *Journal of the American Society for Psychical Research*, 1968, **62**, 103–129.

Stevenson, I., and Pratt, J. G.   Further investigations of the psychic photography of Ted Serios. *Journal of the American Society for Psychical Research*, 1969, **63**, 352–365.

Tietze, T. R. *Margery.* New York: Harper & Row, 1973.

Tischner, R. *Telepathy and Clairvoyance.* (2nd ed.) New York: Harcourt, Brace, 1925.

Ullman, M., and Krippner, S., with Vaughan, A. *Dream Telepathy.* New York: Macmillan, 1973.

Warcollier, R. *Experimental Telepathy.*   Boston: Boston Society for Psychic Research, 1938.

Zielinski, L.   Dr. A. N. Khovrin and the Tambov experiments.   In E. J. Dingwall (Ed.), *Abnormal Hypnotic Phenomena*, Vol. III.   New York: Barnes and Noble, 1968.

Zorab, G.   Test sittings with D. D. Home at Amsterdam. *Journal of Parapsychology*, 1970, **34**, 47–66.

Zorab, G. *D. D. Home the Medium: A Biography and a Vindication.*   Unpublished manuscript, 1975 (Published in Italian as *D. D. Home, il Medium*. Milano: Armenia Editore 1976).

2

History of Experimental Studies

J. B. Rhine

INTRODUCTION

Parapsychology is largely an experimental science today; therefore a full account of this aspect of the field would be much too extensive for a single chapter. This will therefore have to be only an outline of the development of psi experiments. Fortunately little needs to be said about all the many experimental efforts attempted over the last century which have not yielded anything of scientific value; and even the many problems that have not yet been solved can be by-passed except to note briefly that they are perhaps being shelved for a later and more advanced stage of methodology. It is not that these decisions about what problems to investigate in parapsychology are unimportant; they are extremely important. In fact, problem selection is an essential part of experimental method, and questions of whether a given problem can be solved experimentally will confront us in this chapter more than once. But there will not be space to pursue either the methods that have proved inadequate or the problems that do not lend themselves to known procedures. I shall simply outline the progress made in experimental parapsychology up to 1975 and the methods that made it possible. For convenience, I shall divide the last century of research into four periods of 25 years each.

THE FIRST PERIOD: 1876-1900

It seems proper to begin the first period with 1876, the year in which the physicist William Barrett gave his report on thought-transference experiments with hypnotized subjects as part of the program of the British Association at its convention in Glasgow. In the experiments he reported, he was the experimenter; the subject and the hypnotist were in adjoining rooms, with the door between them left open and Barrett standing in the doorway. The two participants were out of each other's line of vision. The subject was instructed to try to identify the sensation (e.g., a specific taste) which the hypnotist was experiencing (Barrett, 1882, pp. 47-48). The successful results led to further experiments in thought-transference. Oliver Lodge (1884), another physicist, conducted tests with pairs of young women reputed to have telepathic ability. The two participants, both unhypnotized, were seated back to back in a large room and were provided with paper and pencil with which they were to make drawings. The one acting as the subject succeeded remarkably well in drawing what the other, acting as agent, had drawn.

In 1889 the French physiologist Charles Richet published an account of tests of clairvoyance which he conducted with a hypnotized subject who had shown spontaneous manifestations of that ability. Richet enclosed playing cards in opaque envelopes and asked the subjects to identify the concealed cards. Richet (1884) had earlier introduced the mathematics of probability to calculate the chance expectancy in the tests—first the average percentage to be expected from chance and second the odds against a chance explanation of his results. This great step forward in method became the most important instrument in psychical research, as the new study was then called in Britain.

Richet (1889) also learned that his subject's ability (which he called "lucidity") was a very unstable one in spite of the highly successful results he obtained. When he arranged a demonstration before a group of fellow scientists in Cambridge, she produced only chance results; but she recovered her ability on her return to Paris. It was also important that Richet discovered that others showed the ability without being hypnotized and could achieve some success in his tests even though at a relatively low rate. He discovered, too, that long runs of many trials led to a decline in scoring rate within the run, and accordingly he recommended the use of short runs.

This small selection of only three notable investigators of what today we call ESP will serve to illustrate the experimental beginnings. They introduced methods that were followed by others, and the methods had enough in common to offer a sound basis for further study. It is noteworthy that two of the men were physicists and one a physiologist and that all were experimentalists whose work in other fields gave them unusual eminence. The fact that the two Englishmen investigated what later came to be called "telepathy" and that the Frenchman investigated what came to be called "clairvoyance" reflects national differences in culture. The English were more interested in post-mortem survival and favored telepathy because it fitted better with their interest in the question of spirit communication through mediums. Richet did not share that interest.

THE SECOND PERIOD: 1901–1925

Most of the attention of those active in psychical research during both the first and second periods was given to the study of mediums, but on a somewhat declining scale over the years. The second period, however, showed some progress in the amount of experimentation with telepathy. For one thing, psychical research penetrated a few universities and even their psychology departments. This was a notable advance in itself. The field was no longer left to the leadership of physical scientists, although at the very beginning that leadership had been a great advantage indeed.

To represent this period, I shall pass on to its last decade and select only four experiments, all conducted by psychologists in their own departments and located neither in France nor England but in the U.S.A. and Holland. This group represents the main line of advance in psi experiments. It is noteworthy, too, that all four of these experiments were aimed at telepathy (as thought-transference was now called), which indicated that the British influence was stronger than the French at that time.

The first of these telepathy experiments was reported in 1917 by John E. Coover of Stanford University. Coover, like Richet, used playing cards, but only a 40-card deck. Instead of enclosing the cards to screen them, as Richet had done, Coover used two adjoining rooms, with the sender and the experimenter in one and the subject in the other. The cards were shuffled between trials. Coover also introduced a control; by throwing a die before each trial he decided whether the sender would look at the card or would not. (Actually what he intended as a control was simply the test condition for clairvoyance.) Using 105 students as percipients and 97 as senders, he amassed a total of 10,000 trials and obtained a significant positive deviation. However, Coover, who was under a great deal of stress because of the critical attitude of psychology in his day, concealed the significance of his findings so that it was not until many years later that it was discovered. Actually, his experiment was well conducted for the stage at which it was done, and his findings gained something from the author's reluctance to acknowledge them publicly.

About the same time, Leonard T. Troland (n.d., *ca.* 1917) of Harvard's Department of Psychology carried out a small series of "telepathy" tests, also quite advanced in method. He introduced the first ESP test machine, one that automatically selected the target, recorded it, and also recorded the subject's response. He used the same statistics as Richet, but in his 605 trials the odds against chance were only 14 to 1. The most interesting feature about these results is that his subjects scored *below* chance expectation, and Troland recognized that the direction of the deviation made no difference in its significance. In fact, this target avoidance and the method of measuring it came out in the next period as a most important advance.

The third experiment in this selection of reports was done about 10 years later, also at Harvard. It was the work of George H. Estabrooks (1927), then a graduate student, who carried out his experiment under the sponsorship of William McDougall; he obtained significant results, this time in the form of a positive deviation from the chance mean. Estabrooks used a pair of adjoining rooms to separate his subject from himself as the sender, with a device which operated to signal each trial to the subject. He used volunteer Harvard students as subjects, endeavoring to select those who were more positively interested. Each subject was given a series of 20 trials with playing cards as targets. The results were highly significant, giving odds for success (on suits) of millions to 1 in his three main series. In his fourth series, in which the subjects were sent to a more distant room with better isolation, the scoring rate dropped, not to a chance level, but well below it. Also, Estabrooks, like Richet, found a decline of scoring within the run, even though his runs were short compared to Richet's. Later investigators made a point of the significance of this decline, in which the scoring in the first half of the run was significantly above that of the second half; but Estabrooks was not ready then to appreciate this statistical differentiation nor the equally important fact that his fourth series was an independently significant one.

The fourth telepathy experiment representing this quarter century was carried out at the University of Groningen, and except for one weak point, it was the most definite advance in method for this period. It was reported by H.I.F.W. Brugmans (1922), and the tests were all made with a single subject, a man who had been an entertainer and claimed an ability to locate hidden objects. In the Psychology Laboratory of the University of Groningen, the experimenter and agent sat in a room above that in which the subject was seated. The agent looked through a window in the floor of the upper room, attempting to influence the subject to locate one of 48 squares on the table in front of him. The target squares in a 6 × 8 arrangement were concealed from the subject by a heavy curtain through which his hand extended. With a pointer moving over the squares, he would indicate his guess on each trial. The results were strikingly successful, although it was found later that the selection of the targets was not random and tended to favor the more centrally located squares, which would render a conclusion unreliable.

The advance in method by Brugmans consisted mainly of the introduction of physiological variations and measurements accompanying the tests. For example, when the subject was given alcohol, it appeared to elevate his rate of success. Also the galvanic skin response of the subject was measured in connection with his successful and unsuccessful trials, and there were suggestive indications of a relationship.

The second period left some excellent new methods and some suggestions of great importance as well as many unsettled questions. The subject of telepathy had received some attention in major universities on two continents even though, as will be seen, telepathy as a major subject of investigation ended with this period. This did not invalidate the findings, for they still belong to the wider category of extrasensory perception. The shift of experimental study in psychical research to American universities has had significance for succeeding periods, but there is an important explanatory factor that should not be overlooked: both of the American universities that harbored telepathy experiments during this period were supported in this bold step by financial aid from philanthropy. This, of course, associates lay interest with these university initiatives, a circumstance that must itself be given considerable importance.

THE THIRD PERIOD: 1926–1950

It is essential in tracing the experimental progress of parapsychology to continue to be guided by the same thread of success that has been followed through the two preceding periods. Actually, the dominant interest in psychical research circles during the half century already reviewed had been in mediumship and post-mortem survival; and yet, in 1925, no scientific conclusion was even in sight to back them up. There was no successful method to follow (just as there is none today, another half century later). Telepathy, the principal experimental problem of psychical research in the preceding periods, was being challenged early in the third period as not yet being an acceptable experimental problem (i.e., in terms of its stated meaning of mind-to-mind exchange). During the second period, increasing attention was given to clairvoyance, even in Britain. Now, in the third period, beginning in 1927, telepathy was challenged for the first time, after it was discovered that clairvoyance as a counterhypothesis had never yet been excluded in telepathy tests. Since I shall have to record that, by the end of this period, still no method had been found to provide an adequate test of telepathy, I think it is excusable to omit the complicated efforts made to produce a conclusive test of this form of psi. It will then be left not only for the fourth period but, as now seems fairly certain, for some still more distant one.

This strict pursuit of only the main trail of psi experimentation is more than a matter of economizing space. It is also a necessary path for the research to follow in order to raise the quality of our methods of inquiry. The kind of loose design that kept telepathy as a prime experimental problem in psychical research for more than 50 years (that is, with the clairvoyance hypothesis equally applicable in every experiment) is sharp enough warning of the need to reexamine our entire methodology. It does not matter which problem is concerned, how important the issue seems, how much money is available for research support, or any other essentially irrelevant consideration. Therefore I have no compunction in deleting from current consideration, in the interest not only of brevity but of scientific clarity and objectivity, problems for which no adequate methods are known.

Development of Methods at Duke

Even at the end of the second period the conditions of the Richet tests of clairvoyance seemed to offer the best starting point for a renewal of the search for conclusive proof of psychic ability. Of all the claims made in parapsychology at the time, clairvoyance was the most easily testable. Only one subject was necessary. The target object had only to be selected at random and to be completely concealed. The record-taking was the simplest, since only one record was needed during the test—that of the subject's responses. Richet himself had found that unselected subjects showed some evidence of clairvoyant ability, but he had also found gifted individuals—at least one. History showed that hypnosis was not essential. Much had been learned by others in the tests of so-called telepathy which was in general agreement with Richet's findings regarding clairvoyance.

However, as we began at Duke in 1927 with this considerable inheritance from the past, it still remained to be seen whether or not the earlier experiments could in some way and degree be replicated, and if they could, to see if the test methods could be improved.

Most of the new steps taken at first consisted of relatively minor additions, either for convenience or for added assurance regarding reliability. One of the first was to design a more suitable deck of test cards than the standard playing cards. Five geometric symbols, star, circle, cross, waves, and square, were selected from the wide range considered and, after some improvements in early usage, were identified as ESP cards, 25 to the pack.

The emphasis was placed on the testing of clairvoyance with a view to arriving if possible at an adequately decisive test of its occurrence. This selection of topic was considered only an advantageous starting point; that is, it seemed by far the best point of entry into parapsychology. Once adequate evidence of it was obtained, the long-view aim called for adding on another type of psychical claim, if possible, and then of course another, as long as unverified claims remained and adequate methods could be devised. Some had to be bypassed for the time; I have explained the difficulty concerning telepathy as an example.

This testing of the reality of psychic claims and their elementary types was the main-line research, as it more or less had to be. But it was only a slightly more distant objective to ask whether these various claims represented distinctive powers, faculties, or abilities, or whether they were basically unitary in principle and only different as phenomena.

A second larger relationship would have to be cleared up if and as the search for these abilities was successful. This would be to find where the abilities fitted into the rest of psychology and biology and how they related to the physical world.

New Evidence for Clairvoyance

It was a very good question in our minds, as my colleagues and I began testing for clairvoyance at Duke in the early 1930s, whether we could obtain any reliable evidence of any of these psychic claims. Great difficulty and uncertainty had been indicated in the past work. Richet (1889) himself was not always successful, even with his special hypnotic subject. The clairvoyance aspect of Coover's test was not significant by itself. Ina Jephson (1929) had success in her first clairvoyance experiment and failure in the next. Estabrooks' "telepathy" experiment succeeded for him but was said to have failed the next year when repeated by an assistant. So there was much more uncertainty to it than just the design of the test itself or even the question of whether the subjects actually possessed the ability.

The program at Duke therefore had to begin in a broadly exploratory way. Along with testing for clairvoyance, an attempt was made to see if the telepathy hypothesis could be verified in tests when clairvoyance was excluded; that is, without the sender having any objective target in relation to which clairvoyance could play a part. It was a new experiment. What would it produce? Again, tests were carried out both with subjects in the normal waking state and when they were hypnotized; it was an open question as to which would be better. A wide variety of ways of presenting the target objects was tried, and quite a range of classes of subjects was explored. The subjects were tested in many types of situations—in groups as in the classroom, and individually in the laboratory, at home, or at a distance. In all of these exploratory approaches the first aim was to find the most favorable setting, the best test device, and the most conducive subject-experimenter relation.

On the side of precautions, in experiments that were intended to be conclusive, it was required in the experimental design that the target cards should be completely out of the subject's sensory range and the order unknown to all concerned. Opaque envelopes or boxes were adequate but less convenient than opaque screens. The latter were acceptable when additional assurance against sensory cues was provided. This led to the use of different rooms and even different buildings, with still further precautions; for example, an assistant to provide independent observation. The type of experiment that led to a conclusion about clairvoyant ESP was represented by the Pearce-Pratt Series carried out in 1933. The first subseries of this experiment was published in my monograph, *Extrasensory Perception*, in 1934. J. G. Pratt, then a graduate student in psychology, was put in charge of this experiment in which the most successful subject (H.P.) found among the Duke students was asked to identify cards 100 yards away in another building. The cards were handled by Pratt. The two men worked with synchronized watches, and each provided me (in advance of his own checkup) with a sealed independent record of his end of the test. This "distance" experiment was so successful (H. P.'s results were as good as those he had obtained when in close proximity to the target cards) that further series were carried out with certain variations in procedure. The distance was increased and another building was the site of the target cards. In still another subseries I stayed with Pratt to see that the conditions were carried through properly and received the records before the two men commenced their own checkup.

First Experiments in Precognition

At that point the case for the clairvoyance type of ESP seemed strong enough to warrant the next advance, and the first precognition experiment was designed (J. B. Rhine, 1938). It was made with as little innovation in the technique as possible. The same subject, H. P., who had already succeeded with ESP at a distance, was now asked to guess what the card order would be after the deck was shuffled. If space was no barrier to ESP, time should not be expected to be either. A definite type of shuffle was agreed upon and the control was to be a card-guessing type of clairvoyance in which the subject called "down through" another deck as it lay in its box at the time. Both methods gave significant results, and the time discrepancy seemed not to matter. It looked as though precognition were taking place.

At this point a member of the research staff, Charles E. Stuart, thought it was possible that clairvoyance might enter into the shuffling of the cards to make them match the subject's calls, and he attempted to demonstrate that such a "psychic shuffle" was possible. He was successful, as were some others, and the "psychic shuffle" itself then became a technique for the testing of psi ability.

Of course, we had to change the method of randomizing the target order for a test of precognition. This led to the introduction of mechanical methods of shuffling the target cards, and for a time this seemed to fill the need. The success of the precognition project continued in general (as it went on doing, or I would not now be reviewing the progress in its methodology).

Experiments in Psychokinesis

In January 1934, our confidence in the method of precognition testing was given another jolt. While these tests had been going on with considerable success, circumstances had precipitated interest in another psychic claim, this one dealing with the effect popularly known as "mind over matter," which came to be called psychokinesis, or PK. A young gambler who had visited the laboratory because of an interest in ESP strongly asserted his belief in the mind-over-matter principle as represented in a gambler's successful control (under certain conditions) over the fall of dice. He himself had made some preliminary tests which supported that view, and when I invited him, he was willing to attempt to demonstrate the effect. He and H. P. were soon engaged in dice-throwing tests in my office. PK research had begun, although it was not to be reported until 1943.

The same statistical methods that had been applied to the evaluation of the card-guessing results applied to the dice-throwing results as well. It was necessary, however, to make sure that skilled throwing of the dice was not involved in trying to influence them to fall with a designated face or combination of faces upward. Over a period of more than 9 years before the first publication was released, a variety of methods of dice-throwing was used, beginning with simple hand-throwing and extending through many changes and devices to a completely mechanical method eventually. However, the ability of subjects to influence the dice psychokinetically persisted through these many variations and techniques. In fact, the subjects seemed generally to do as well when the dice were thrown mechanically as when other methods, such as shaking them in a dice cup, were involved.

The problem of avoiding the effect of imperfections in the cubes was not difficult to solve since, even if the dice were imperfect (as was assumed to be the case), the imperfections would be neutralized if an equal number of throws were made for each face as the target. If one face were physically disfavored, other faces would be correspondingly favored. The problem of avoiding recording errors in the PK experiments was a little more difficult than in ESP testing. For the highest level of precautions it was found desirable to have independent records taken by two observers. Eventually automatic photographic recording was introduced (by McConnell, Snowdon, and Powell, 1955; see also Dr. Stanford's chapter on psychokinesis in this *Handbook*; and L. E. Rhine, 1970).

Precognition and PK Methods in Conflict

Not all of the problems had been fully solved, however, when it was realized that the establishment of PK would make a difference in the methods of testing for precognition. It was recognized that the mechanical shuffling apparatus used in precognition tests could itself possibly be influenced by means of PK. Perhaps the subject could influence falling cards just as he evidently could influence falling dice. Another staff member, Burke M. Smith, then found that he was able to influence the cards in the shuffler sufficiently to make them significantly match a designated target series. This PK shuffle effect thus brought an end to the use of the mechanical shuffler in the precognition research.

But the precognition enthusiasts among us went on immediately to design a way of generating the future target order by using a system that began with the temperature readings in a designated newspaper report on a certain date fixed in advance, going on from there to get the figures for cutting the deck of cards. Years later, however, another procedure was adopted after the "weather cut" method was criticized. The next device interposed an intricate mathematical calculation, carried out electrically, that was considered far beyond human powers to achieve mentally. This too has had a challenger, Robert L. Morris (1968), also at the time associated with the Duke Laboratory. This difficulty of distinguishing precognition from PK, although primarily belonging to this period, runs over into the next. (For a more detailed account of the precognition study, see L. E. Rhine, 1967.)

It is necessary now to go back to where we left the PK work, in the mid-40s. At that time a reverse reaction occurred in this methodological conflict between the two subtypes, PK and precognition. It was argued that in a PK experiment the subject's precognition of the way the dice were likely to fall could enable him to choose the most favorable target face of the dice for a given test run. If so, precognition would account for the PK test results. Fortunately, this counterhypothesis was relatively easy to control; it was only necessary not to allow the subject to have such a choice of targets. Instead, a routine order of the six target faces was imposed in advance and followed consistently throughout the experiment.

By the end of the third period the question had at least been well raised as to whether PK and precognition could be adequately distinguished experimentally; the answers were not definitely final either way, although they were suggestive. At the same time, however, the impression was fast growing that enough similarity was being found between these subtypes that their unitary character now seemed more important than the fine points of their differences.

Some Problems that Had to be Shelved

The three subtypes of parapsychic ability (or psi, as it is now called)—clairvoyance, precognition, and PK—gave rather conclusive experimental results, as we have seen, even though we may need to carry over beyond the end of this period the debatable points of difference between PK and precognition. However, not all the claims of special psychic abilities succeeded so well. I have mentioned that it was found that telepathy could not be tested in a way that clearly excluded clairvoyance (J. B. Rhine, 1974b). Similarly, no way had been found to test the claim of post-mortem survival so as to exclude the medium's psi exchange with the living and the terrestrial environment as the sources of the information in the "messages" (J. B. Rhine, 1960).

Other claims, too, were considered during this period, but they had to be shelved because of the inadequacy of the methods available to apply to them. Retrocognition, or the ESP of past events, was one of these. Some of the precognition enthusiasts thought retrocognition logically followed from precognition, but this was only an untestable speculation. No one could think of a way to test it conclusively enough to justify the pursuit of the problem at that stage (i.e., to distinguish it from simple clairvoyance). (Retroactive PK, which is closely associated, did not get much attention until the next period.) Early exploration of the idea of mental projection in some extrasomatic (out-of-body) form did receive attention, especially in the period when hypnosis was being explored. However, no clear method was known that distinguished it from normal psi ability (plus the subject's highly adaptable imagination). One of the leading exponents of projection, John Björkhem of Sweden, was invited to Duke to demonstrate his method and to discuss his own extensive results, but no conclusions were possible on the point of "extrasomatic projection." This too was rated as a "bad-risk" problem.

The research reviewed in this section leaves the reminder that such success as was attained owed much to the discipline of adhering to problems that were logically possible to solve with the methods available. Only through this discipline can we make parapsychology a firm science.

Progress Toward Reliability

Good evidence of psi ability is not only more difficult to obtain than that of the whole range of sensorimotor exchange; it is also harder to accept. Therefore, it requires more security in the way of test conditions, perhaps the most of any field. The history of parapsychology bears this out. At the beginning of the third period the main emphasis was on *subject* reliability: the subjects in psi tests were not to be trusted as far as they were in other psychological experiments. In fact, it had to be made impossible for subjects to cheat. The ways in which subject cheating has been avoided, taken together, are quite convincing. The greatest degree of dependability is in the testing of precognition in which the subject simply has no opportunity at all to cheat since the future target order does not exist. Even in PK experiments, if the subject is not allowed to handle the dice or keep his own records, he has no chance for trickery in a normally well-observed test situation.

The question of dishonesty in the experimenter was also in the focus of attention at that time if only as secondary to that of cheating by the subject. At the suggestion of Professor McDougall, I arranged that I myself would oversee one section of the Pearch–Pratt series. If anyone still wanted more support on the honesty of such a team of investigators, he had then to look for independent confirmations by other teams of experimenters. Fortunately, even in the third period a few other centers were being started, centers in which some (although not all) of those who attempted to replicate the Duke experiments were successful.

A survey of the contents of the *Journal of Parapsychology* during those years (1937–1950) will indicate the progress that was made in getting supporting confirmations. It offers some satisfaction on this point even though the independent replication aspect in the third period was slow compared to that in the fourth. Because of the peculiar nature of the unconscious psi functions, it was difficult to know just how the experimenter could best bring out the elusive ability. Many would-be experimenters naturally were not prepared for such a new undertaking and failed to get any evidence in their first efforts at ESP testing. In any case, it is easier and very much safer to suspend judgment about a claim in which there has not been sufficient confirmation than it is to put undue weight on individual reports.

It is now possible, however, to point to certain kinds of effects in these accumulated psi test records that provide evidence against which no reasonable suspicion can arise; for example, consider the Estabrooks results. It is not the best example, but it has already been described. The best evidence in his data consists of findings that he did not at that time recognize as significant. It will be recalled that in his fourth series he put the subjects in a room remote from the agent and that their rate of success as a group fell below mean chance expectation. At the time this was for Estabrooks only a puzzling result for which he attempted to offer a speculative explanation; but it was found later to be a statistically significant result showing a definite avoidance of the target through a negative deviation (J. B. Rhine, 1969a). He knew, too, that in all his four series there was a falling-off in his subjects' scoring in the test runs, but he did not realize that this decline had an important meaning for ESP (J. B. Rhine, 1969b). It created a top–bottom difference between the halves of the run that was later analyzed by others and found to be very significant. Obviously this was not something he had wanted or even could have understood then; but it was a finding that, along with later findings by others, helped to show how the psi function works in such a test situation. It revealed one of the peculiar "signs of psi" (J. B. Rhine, 1974a) that was to be discovered years after his experiment was over.

This kind of evidence is particularly important because it is well beyond the question of the honesty either of the experimenter or the subjects (or even of the reviewer, since anyone can recheck these figures). It puts the findings onto a basis in which honesty is no longer a counterhypothesis. The third period produced a great deal of this kind of evidence, although it was not until the next period that the realization of its extent and its bearing on the question of reliability began to be recognized (J. B. Rhine, 1975).

The Search for Psi Properties

The next major question of this third period was: What is psi ability like? Even during the 1930s, as it began to look as if there must indeed be one or more types of psi ability, this question of its general characteristics started inquiries in a number of directions. It was logical, of course, that one of them should concern a possible physical explanation. This was a question that had come up in earlier periods. Was there some known energetic principle that might explain the results? Did this type of communication between a person and his environment resemble the known methods of sensorimotor communication in having some discoverable physical mode of energy transfer? The Pearce–Pratt Series tested the effect of distance and found no suggestion that the inverse square law applied. In fact, during this period, many physical comparisons were made, but there were no results that gave a clue to a hidden physical principle applicable to these mental interactions.

Then came the precognition experiments, which gave what seemed to be a more distinctive ruling-out of any known physical explanations. This evidence of nonphysicality has been reviewed many times, and this general characteristic of psi was a widely accepted one by the end of this period. At least it was conceded that no known physical principle could be applied.

At this point, then, another aspect of the relationship between psi and the physical world became even more important: If the psi process and the physical order of nature are so *different*, how are they able to interact? Here we need to remember that we do not yet know even how sensory experience bridges its somewhat comparable gap. But this identification of a nonphysical quality in psi reminds us that it is not only on the physical side of such interaction that we have acceptable methods, but on the mental side as well; in short, with the very elementary methods of physics itself, we had ruled out physicality as a property of the psi function. But this will come up later on in the following period with the use of new methods and a broader basis for judgment. Here it may be mentioned that wholly independent experimental confirmation of the nonphysical nature of ESP was carried out by L. L. Vasiliev (1963) of Leningrad early in this period (although it was not published until later). Vasiliev tested the possible effect on ESP ("telepathy") not only of long distance but also of an electromagnetic screening of the subject during the test. Neither one interfered with the subject's ESP.

Here for the time being the question may be left. By the criteria of physics itself, psi had been shown to be nonphysical; yet it had evidenced the earmarks of a reliable principle in nature—human nature, of course. It exerted influence. It exhibited the "capacity to do work," the general definition of energy. What kind of energy could this be? Psi energy? That could only be a small starting point on the real question of interaction, but it is a start that I think has already been made.

Biological Questions about Psi

Beyond question, psi is a biological function too. To bring forward a biological function that was also nonphysical was plainly to introduce into biology something unknown and most unwelcome; but it is interesting to note that the discoveries about psi in the living organism fitted well with the fact that psi is not physical. No localizations of psi functions (analogous to those of the sense organs or muscles in the sensorimotor order) have as yet even been seriously suggested. No definitive evidence of localization of function within the nervous system has come forth, although a few speculative suggestions have been made.

Yet, even without direct experimental evidence, we do have to infer that psi capacity has to be a part of the genetic system of the organism. Certainly it is not something learned. No reliable linkage has been found thus far as to sex or age differences; nor has any other biological (e.g., ethnic) grouping been discovered with which it can be said to be associated. The working hypothesis that emerged in the third period is that probably everyone in the human species has potential psi ability to some extent and that the great differences among individuals are the result of psychological (and perhaps other unknown) factors that may affect its limitation and use.

As this period ended parapsychologists were prepared to go beyond the human species in search of the possibly wider biological distribution of psi ability. It should be noted that biologists themselves, as a "subspecies," showed almost no interest in parapsychology during this or even earlier periods; but the next period marked at least a break in this indifference.

Psychology of Psi

As we have seen, the relation of psi research to general psychology was very different from what it had been back through the second period. It was an important circumstance that the research laboratory at Duke, in which most of the leading developments of the third period occurred, was connected with the Department of Psychology, which was headed (1927-1938) by William Mc-Dougall. (Only in 1950 did the Parapsychology Laboratory become independent of the Department.) McDougall's (1911) interest in psi was preeminently in what it indicated about the nature of man in relation to his physical world. This is the mind-body problem which psychology has had on the shelf for 50 years. The very fact that psi occurred showed that human nature could not be completely physical—that a qualitatively distinctive mental ability existed, one that could even be experimentally demonstrated as nonphysical. Psychology now had a validly objective claim to being more than just an obscure branch of the less illuminated side of physics. In a word, the mind after all was experimentally real.

More immediately important, if anything could be, was the discovery (or rediscovery) of the fact that psi is an unconscious function. Parapsychology was thus adding to the psychological sciences an objectively experimental entré to the area of unconscious mental processes. During this third period psychology had not had from its other branches such quantitative techniques for probing into this unconscious level.

The growing recognition that psi is unconscious opened up to further study some of its obscure but distinctive lawful relations. I have mentioned the early discovery by Troland, and incidentally by Estabrooks, that the subject under certain ESP test conditions unconsciously avoids the target. Later in the third period, Gertrude Schmeidler's tests of sheep-goat attitudes brought out this point more consistently (Schmeidler and McConnell, 1958). She found that negative attitudes toward ESP favored negative deviations from chance. Such findings illustrated the importance of discovering distinctively psychological characteristics for the psi function, which, as I have said above, consistently fails to show any physical characteristics.

Perhaps the main burden of psychological studies of psi in the third period was borne by three leading searchers for psychological correlates at the time: C. E. Stuart (Stuart, Humphrey, Smith, and McMahan, 1947), Gertrude R. Schmeidler (1948, 1960), and Betty M. Humphrey (1945, 1950, 1951-52). Using psychological methods for the study of individual differences and correlating such measures with performance in ESP tests, these three and a few others amassed a large collection of results that brought the psychology of psi into prominence in the field and contributed some interesting new insights.

First was the generalization that a group of subjects (e.g., a psychology class) tested for ESP and then divided into two sections on the basis of psychological tests usually diverge from the chance line (e.g., with one group scoring above chance and one below). In Schmeidler's case the sheep went above and the goats below, with a difference that was generally significant. The pooled group results as a whole might, and often did, show no total significance because the two deviations completely cancelled each other. Does this separation show that the trait measured (let us say, extraversion, a belief in ESP, a state of anxiety, or an expansive type of personality) is correlated with the *amount* of ESP ability? No, that cannot be said. What can be said is that the trait is correlated with the *direction* taken by the performance of the subject in the ESP tests. The subject is led, by whatever lies back of the psychological measure, to score positively in the ESP test, or, by the opposite type of trait, to score on the negative side. These psychological tests and ratings divide subjects in terms of how they are able to *use* their psi ability, positively or negatively (J. B. Rhine, 1969a).

It is safe to say that we do not know of anything that does affect the actual *amount* of psi except the subject's general motivation. If subjects are indifferent, uninterested, and yet still take part in a test for some reason or other, they are likely to score only at chance levels. If they are interested, then their characteristics as measured by these more-or-less standard and familiar psychological tests simply divide them into the two groups showing plus or minus scoring tendencies. They are at the time and in these particular tests either psi-hitters or psi-missers.

As it gradually emerged in our minds over a couple of decades, this turned out to be no minor discovery. It helped to explain much of what was baffling about psi testing and indicated that the job of finding out about the psi process was going, first of all, to be more typically psychological than parapsychological. It would consist of the disentangling of the elusive psi ability from the more familiar functions of mental life, and the methods of dealing with this psi-differential tendency were going to be distinctly psychological. This emphasis on distinctly psychological (nonphysical) methods belongs to the fourth period, it is true, but the first and perhaps the best basis for it in test data was already available in the psychological studies of psi at this earlier time.

The Search for Methods of Psi Control

It was recognized at an early stage that anyone who wants to experiment with psi ability must of course be able to find evidence of it and that this was the number one hurdle for any experimenter to overcome. No one will ever know how many people have tried to experiment with psi and, having met with no success, simply (and wisely) turned to something they could do successfully. By the beginning of the third period it was fairly well known that the experimenter himself had something to do with the success or failure of the experiment. Estabrooks had worked with that idea in mind in preparing and selecting his subjects.

Hypnosis had been associated with psi ability, even before the first period began. However, no clear-cut demonstration had ever been made to show that it was necessary or even helpful. The point that was overlooked was the need of a comparison of the hypnosis and nonhypnosis experimental conditions. When experimenting began at Duke, this kind of comparison became a part of the exploratory phase; and in the course of time it seemed that we could get about the same order of results without hypnosis that we could with it if we gave the subjects comparable encouragement and personal attention. Hypnosis, which took a lot of time, was then abandoned except for special experiments in which it was only an incidental feature, used perhaps to prepare the subject for a particular attitude not easy to induce without it. In any research using hypnosis during the third period, I think, the question of its usefulness was properly left out.

During this period some exploratory tests on the use of drugs were also conducted. None of them was more than preliminary, made to see whether good ground for a more thorough study could be found. As I look back over these efforts today, I can see that they provided guidance on the question of the timeliness of that type of experiment at that stage. Our tests of alcohol, sodium amytal, caffeine, and dexedrine gave us two guiding decisions: (a) We could definitely influence the subject to some extent, especially the good performer with whom we had worked previously. We could reduce his high rate of scoring by administering narcotic drugs in large dosages and could counteract that with caffeine. (b) Under exploratory conditions, however, we could not know whether we were keeping the psychological relationship otherwise normal and neutral. We might, for instance, be making the subject less motivated since, with sodium amytal, he probably wanted only to be let alone so that he could go to sleep. In a word, we had a bigger order of research on our hands than we were able to manage at that stage in our laboratory and with our limited staff.

The other point which I think was indicated was that mainly we were attacking the physical system of the individual in the physiological tests, and it was through this system that the subject's psi function was needing to express itself. A clearly adequate design for such an experiment would have required better facilities than we had for so ambitious an undertaking as that of properly investigating the psi function with subjects under the influence of drugs, for example. As it was, many more immediate and simpler problems were inviting attention.

Probably the most important development of this third period with respect to control of the psi-testing operation was the discovery that the most important condition of the psi test is the experimenter—or rather, the subject-experimenter relation—and that probably the greatest limitation in the research field then (and still today) was the lack of adequately selected and sufficiently trained research staff, for on such a staff almost everything in the field depends. It has been distressing to see that some of the most able subjects could not perform well with certain experimenters, and even worse to find that certain experimenters could do well only with subjects who, with the help of other experimenters, had already acquired confidence in their ability. Since there was no method of selecting entrants to the field, the experimenter had to find out the hard way and often with no adequate instruction as to how to play his part. We were fortunate in discovering at an early stage how this situation could in some instances be handled. Unsuccessful experimenters could play a highly important role in conjunction with those who were more successful in eliciting good psi performance from their subjects. For the most part these differences would seem to be matters of personality, but they might, with a fair opportunity, yield to adjustment under training. By the end of this period we were at least aware of the need to find or make good psi-testers, much as we had learned earlier of the need to select and develop good subjects.

THE FOURTH PERIOD: 1951-1975

The turn of the mid-century left parapsychology in a somewhat more advanced status than hitherto. Other research centers besides the Duke laboratory were beginning to appear. The parapsychical work at Duke itself had become increasingly diversified. Interaction of parapsychologists with other related fields was gradually growing more free and extended, and a few more research workers from these fields turned to parapsychology as a possible career field, some of them after having been well established in professions of their own. All of this was gradual; nothing radical was taking place. Rather, the stormy winds of controversy that had been active up until about 1940 had little effect inside the field as we entered the decade of the 1950s.

One of the more innovative steps taken at the Duke laboratory at this stage was the decision to reexamine the spontaneous case material of parapsychology. (For a fuller account, see the chapter in this volume by Louisa E. Rhine.) The method involved in this reevaluative study was intended to be different from that used in the case material of the past. This time it was to be part of a two-pronged approach to the larger problems of parapsychology—a combination of nature's own offering as to the way psi exhibits itself spontaneously and the results yielded in the laboratory by controlled studies. Those studies show the two as generally confirming each other. It is interesting to see emerging within the same period a new combination of the spontaneous or intuitive psi-functioning and the experimental method in the work of Rex Stanford (1974a, 1974b). There are indications that the careful use of the spontaneous psi happenings will play a bigger part in the future than in the past, especially in the efforts to understand psi ability.

Even more venturesome, perhaps, was the launching of the search for psi in animals. This also began as a roundup of case material to get the information necessary for guidance in developing a test method in making the best selection of species for test subjects. By coincidence certain government interests in such studies developed at the same time and these, along with the Laboratory, provided financial support. Experiments with cats conducted by Karlis Osis (1952) and Esther Foster (Osis and Foster, 1953) were carried out at about the same time that studies of possible ESP factors in pigeon homing were made by J. G. Pratt (1953). My own tests (1971) with a man-dog team were carried out to discover whether dogs had the ability to locate underground objects by ESP. Perhaps the best by-product of these exploratory animal studies was Esther Foster's (Osis and Foster, 1953) idea of what has been called the "random behavior" (RB) analysis. It was put to its best use first in the later work of Duval and Montredon (1968) in tests for precognition in mice. The principle in the RB analysis was to select for the actual test results (before checking the data for success) only those trials in which psi was logically possible (as when a response habit was broken and the way was left open for a true choice). In principle, this was a great step forward. In practice, at least, the indications have been favorable, but more research is needed for testing the extent of the applicability and the actual merit of the new methodological device.

On the whole, the work with animal subjects since the Duval and Montredon experiments, which initiated the tests of precognition in rodents, has aroused wider interest than anything else in this period (discounting completely all of the work of Walter J. Levy, Jr., as too uncertain for acceptance [J. B. Rhine, 1974c]). Not all of this interest is likely to cease even though careful reexamination of much of the research already reported is necessary. New results are still coming in, and the animal psi program seems reasonably likely to be a major one in the period to follow the present one.

Another vigorous drive in the fourth period was made on ESP testing in the schools. It was begun in Holland by J. G. Van Busschbach (1953) of Amsterdam and was picked up for repetition at the Duke laboratory by Anderson and White (1958), then with less success by others, leaving it currently in a somewhat doubtful status. It may have depended at the beginning on the kind of enthusiastic leadership that is likely to be shown by those who initiate new developments. Psi testing at best is not an easy matter and is definitely not for everyone, but with a classroom situation there are factors such as combinations of experimenters, preparatory training, experience, and still other circumstances that add to the uncertainty of what to expect and how to explain success or failure.

One of the interesting developments back in the second period was the introduction of the study of physiological correlates of ESP in the work of Brugmans at Groningen. Very little of this type of research was attempted in the third period, but at least a few beginnings were made in the fourth. There were a number of attempts to find a correlation between ESP and measurements of the EEG alpha rhythm during or in connection with ESP tests. For the most part these can be considered as exploratory successes which have no conclusive confirmation as yet. Among some of the other physiological measures introduced experimentally in psi testing are the plethysmograph, the galvanic skin response, and the rapid eye movement (REM) measured when the subject is asleep to identify dreaming. Correlations with ESP have been sought also for a number of physiological states of more general character, such as physical relaxation, deep-breathing exercises, the menstrual cycle, and various special conditions of sensory awareness. On this last condition, the matter of sensory stimuli or deprivation, the correlation is more psychological than physiological, having to do with degrees or special types of sensory awareness.

In turning to the more or less parallel effort to correlate psychological variables and psi scoring rate, we come onto somewhat more familiar ground. I have already referred to the very considerable amount of work in the third period in which parapsychical and other mental measurements were examined for significant correlations. The main orientation of the psychological studies of psi has been the search for the mental states most conducive to psi functioning. Hypnosis, the first great hope in the past, seemed not to justify such expectations as time passed.   Early in the third period I dropped it as an important factor in psi testing.   In general the claims for it have not been confirmed, and the main benefit in any case might possibly come not from the hypnosis *per se* but from the special encouragement given to the subject incidentally.

One of the major new methodologies in the fourth period was the use of the dream state and the REM technique to determine when to awaken the subject for a dream report.   This work at Maimonides Medical Center in Brooklyn, initiated by Montague Ullman (Ullman and Krippner, with Vaughan, 1973) and assisted by Stanley Krippner and Charles Honorton, among others, has rightly claimed a great deal of interest in and out of parapsychology.   Still in the stage of proving itself in terms of easy repetition, special or unique contributions, and the like, the inquiry will extend into the fifth period before it can be seen how much of a role it should have and what in the way of special interest and contribution it can make.   Methodological improvements will doubtless make clear whether the results are due to the subject, the experimenter, or the judges.   The complex method involves a setting which in itself has awakened widespread interest, especially in medical circles.

One of the shifts of some interest in this most recent period has been the concentration (again as in the early Duke work) on long series of investigations with individual subjects.   The work of H. Kanthamani and E. F. Kelly (1974) at the Foundation for Research on the Nature of Man (FRNM) with the subject B.D. is illustrative, and another example is the long series of studies (by a number of investigators) with Sean Harribance at the Psychical Research Foundation and the FRNM.   Among other advantages, the use of a special subject considerably reduces the uncertainty and loss of time required by the search for and selection of subjects from the general population.   Obviously, certain types of experiment call for one or the other of these ways of obtaining and using subjects.   Perhaps the main thing to be learned from keeping this comparison in mind is how best to obtain and prepare subjects from the general population, and, on the other hand, how best to find the good subjects and keep them good. These lessons, which need to be learned better than they have been thus far, are of very great and basic importance to the whole field.

Much of the popular and even the scientific interest in parapsychology in recent years has been aroused by the sensational demonstration of PK by special subjects.   It will be recalled that the occurrence of PK was established with moving targets, mostly with dice.   By the time of the fourth period, the interest in psychic healing led to the initiation of experimental testing of PK on animals and even plants.   Among the first investigators was Bernard Grad of McGill University.   Grad (1965) tested the psi influence of a healer, first on the rate of wound-healing in mice and later on the growth of seedlings.   Tests were introduced at the FRNM to see if people who believed they could influence plant growth could register electrically recorded changes in the plant.   Later still, tests were introduced to see if healers could more quickly resuscitate etherized mice than control mice. These tests all offer a certain success in the way of methods and a clear justification for continuing research. In other words, the limiting factors are not the lack of design or the reliability of method. These too are experiments in which special subjects are needed.

The PK type of psi has come into prominence in a number of other types of manifestation; for example, the PK of static targets has become a line of experimental work in this period. The first outstanding subject was Ted Serios, who was investigated mainly by Jule Eisenbud (1967). More recently the claims of Uri Geller have been in the foreground, and probably the greatest popular interest during the past hundred years has been directed toward his claims and demonstrations, along with those of others who are imitating him. A sharper experimental focus must be made before it can be determined whether some of the phenomena are clearly and safely acceptable as genuine psi occurrences. Nonexperimental demonstrations alone are not sufficient for scientific conclusions.

Just as this fourth period is about to end, I must, anticlimactically, raise a question that concerns the whole basic methodology of this field. It is in fact a crisis in the methodology of parapsychology. Thus far most of our methods, like those in the other sciences, have depended on physical principles. Now, however, I recognize that all the reliance on physical conditions for the containment of psi have been futile, based as they have been on a now discredited assumption—discredited by the psi research itself. All the relevant research of the past has shown that psi cannot be screened out by physical barriers, whether space, or time, or any other known physical condition.

This realization was forced upon me when the need arose to decide whether a PK result was due to the subject or to the experimenter. It had to be recognized that no physical separation of the two could be considered adequate. This fact came to a head especially in the animal research of the last few years when it was necessary to consider carefully before attempting to draw a conclusion that the animal was in fact the real subject. To draw such a conclusion, the possible direct influence of the experimenter himself had to be ruled out, and that could not be done by physical methods.

As I have recently written elsewhere (J. B. Rhine, 1975), when I came to recognize the sweeping consequences of the fact that physical methods were inadequate for a psi-test methodology, I realized that I had long been aware of the beginnings already made on the use of nonphysical methods in psi research without generalizing on the extent of the important difference involved. I was now led further to the view, as stated in the article mentioned, that while physical methods are of great convenience in excluding sensorimotor influences in psi testing (i.e., barring all physical sources of information), they are inapplicable beyond that point for parapsychology—a very real distinction indeed.

These nonphysical methods already in use may be conveniently illustrated by one of the most familiar experiments, Schmeidler's use of sheep–goat attitudes as a basis for dividing the subjects in her classroom tests of clairvoyance. The physical conditions in her experiments were the same for all subjects, but it was the mental attitudes which made the essential difference in the tests. They constituted a simple but effective nonphysical psychological test device. By building on this psychological type of method, it seems possible that parapsychological research can take more advantage in the future of this uniquely nonphysical methodology. In the article mentioned I suggested some of the more distinctive types of parapsychical methods already available. While I think the distinction is still too new to justify settled convictions about just where the lines are to be drawn, it may be a challenge to parapsychologists to explore the identifying features of the phenomena and principles of their own field.

REFERENCES

Anderson, M. L., and White, R. A. A survey of work on ESP and teacher–pupil attitudes. *Journal of Parapsychology*, 1958, **22**, 246–268.

Barrett, W. F. Appendix to the report on thought-reading. *Proceedings of the Society for Psychical Research*, 1882, **1**, 47–64.

Brugmans, H. I. F. M. A report on telepathic experiments done in the psychology laboratory at Groningen. *Le Compte Rendu Officiel du Premier Congrès International des Recherches Psychiques*. Copenhagen, 1922.

Coover, J. E. *Experiments in Psychical Research*. Palo Alto: Stanford University Press, 1917.

Duval, P., and Montredon, E. ESP experiments with mice. *Journal of Parapsychology*, 1968, **32**, 39–55.

Eisenbud, J. *The World of Ted Serios*. New York: Morrow, 1967.

Estabrooks, G. H. A contribution to experimental telepathy. *Bulletin of the Boston Society for Psychic Research*, 1927, **5**, 1–30. (Reprinted in the *Journal of Parapsychology*, 1961, **25**, 190–213.)

Grad, B. Some biological effects of the "laying on of hands": A review of experiments with animals and plants. *Journal of the American Society for Psychical Research*, 1965, **59**, 95–127.

Humphrey, B. M. An exploratory correlation study of personality measures. *Journal of Parapsychology*, 1945, **9**, 116–123.

Humphrey, B. M. Score level prediction by a combination of measures of personality. *Journal of Parapsychology*, 1950, **14**, 193–206.

Humphrey, B. M. The relation of some personality ratings to ESP scores. A review of recent research. *Journal of the Society for Psychical Research*, 1951–52, **36**, 453–566.

Jephson, I. Evidence for clairvoyance in card-guessing. *Proceedings of the Society for Psychical Research*, 1929, **38**, 223–268.

Kanthamani, H., and Kelly, E. F. Awareness of success in an exceptional subject. *Journal of Parapsychology*, 1974, **38**, 355–382.

Lodge, O. J. An account of some experiments in thought-transference. *Proceedings of the Society for Psychical Research*, 1884, **2**, 189–200.

McConnell, R. A., Snowdon, R. J., and Powell, K. F. Wishing with dice. *Journal of Experimental Psychology*, 1955, **50**, 269–275.

McDougall, W. *Body and Mind*. London: Methuen, 1911.

Morris, R. L. Obtaining non-random entry points: A complex psi task. In J. B. Rhine and R. Brier (eds.), *Parapsychology Today*, pp. 75–86. New York: Citadel Press, 1968.

Osis, K. A test of the occurrence of a psi effect between man and the cat. *Journal of Parapsychology*, 1952, **16**, 233–256.

Osis, K., and Foster, E. B.   A test of ESP in cats.   *Journal of Parapsychology*, 1953, **20**, 158–186.

Pratt, J. G.   The homing problem in pigeons.   *Journal of Parapsychology*, 1953, **17**, 34–60.

Rhine, J. B.   *Extrasensory Perception.*   Boston: Boston Society for Psychic Research, 1934. (Reprinted by Branden Press in 1964.)

Rhine, J. B.   Experiments bearing on the precognition hypothesis.   *Journal of Parapsychology*, 1938, **2**, 38–54.

Rhine, J. B.   Incorporeal personal agency: The prospect of a scientific solution.   *Journal of Parapsychology*, 1960, **24**, 279–309.

Rhine, J. B.   Psi-missing re-examined.   *Journal of Parapsychology*, 1969, **33**, 1–38. (a)

Rhine, J. B.   Position effects in psi test results.   *Journal of Parapsychology*, 1969, **33**, 136–157. (b)

Rhine, J. B.   Location of hidden objects by a man–dog team.   *Journal of Parapsychology*, 1971, **35**, 18–33.

Rhine, J. B.   Security versus deception in parapsychology.   *Journal of Parapsychology*, 1974, **38**, 99–121. (a)

Rhine, J. B.   Telepathy and other untestable hypotheses.   *Journal of Parapsychology*, 1974, **38**, 137–153. (b)

Rhine, J. B.   A new case of experimenter unreliability.   *Journal of Parapsychology*, 1974, **38**, 218–225. (c)

Rhine, J. B.   Psi methods re-examined.   *Journal of Parapsychology*, 1975, **39**, 38–58.

Rhine, L. E.   *ESP in Life and Lab.*   New York: Macmillan, 1967.

Rhine, L. E.   *Mind Over Matter: Psychokinesis.*   New York: Macmillan, 1970.

Richet, C.   La suggestion mentale et le calcul des probabilités.   *Revue Philosophique*, 1884, **18**, 608–674.

Richet, C.   Further experiments in hypnotic lucidity or clairvoyance.   *Proceedings of the Society for Psychical Research*, 1889, **6**, 66–83.

Schmeidler, G. R.   The 1948 symposium: Personality correlates of ESP as shown by Rorschach studies.   *Journal of Parapsychology*, 1948, **12**, 23–30.

Schmeidler, G. R.   ESP in relation to Rorschach test evaluation.   *Parapsychological Monographs No. 2.*   New York: Parapsychology Foundation, 1960.

Schmeidler, G. R., and McConnell, R. A.   *ESP and Personality Patterns.*   New Haven: Yale University Press, 1958.

Stanford, R. G.   An experimentally testable model for spontaneous psi events. I. Extrasensory events.   *Journal of the American Society for Psychical Research*, 1974, **68**, 34–57. (a)

Stanford, R. G.   An experimentally testable model for spontaneous psi events. II. Psychokinetic events.   *Journal of the American Society for Psychical Research*, 1974, **68**, 231–356. (b)

Stuart, C. E., Humphrey, B. M., Smith, B. M., and McMahan, E.   Personality measurements and ESP tests with cards and drawings.   *Journal of Parapsychology*, 1947, **11**, 117–146.

Troland, L. T.   *A Technique for the Experimental Study of Telepathy and Other Alleged Clairvoyant Processes.*   Albany, n.d. (*ca.* 1917). (Reprinted in the *Journal of Parapsychology*, 1976, **40**, 194–216.)

Ullman, M., and Krippner, S., with Vaughan, A.   *Dream Telepathy.*   New York: Macmillan, 1973.

Van Busschbach, J. G.   An investigation of extrasensory perception in school children.   *Journal of Parapsychology*, 1953, **17**, 210–214.

Vasiliev, L. L.   *Experiments in Mental Suggestion.*   Hampshire, England: Institute for the Study of Mental Images, 1963.

3

William James and Psychical Research*

Gardner Murphy

Everything conspired to make William James a pioneer in psychical research. One could almost see it coming 100 years ahead. One might look first at his ancestry and early rearing; then at his more formal education; then at his career in medicine and in philosophy, and his integration of these studies with psychology; his determination to investigate the margins and edges of all that is known; and consequently his discovery, in psychical research, of a kind of inquiry that fulfilled the cravings accumulated from all these many areas of experience.

The family history usually begins with "William of Albany," his grandfather, who made a fortune and enabled his many children to start off in life with some degree of freedom from the current struggle to exist. Among his sons, Henry James, Sr., the father of William James and of Henry James the novelist, early chose for himself a life of study, contemplation, speculation. He was a "seeker," who in the nineteenth-century effort to find a new, solid ground to stand on, explored one philosophy or religious movement after another. Having suffered a series of amputations upon a leg as a child, he had been deprived to some degree of normal social intercourse, yet managed to preserve a vivid, earnest, hearty enthusiasm, and a real gift for friendship with all sorts of fellow-seekers. His warm response to the teachings of Swedenborg—who, against the background of an amazing scientific achievement had nevertheless seen fit to identify

*Reprinted from the *Journal of the American Society for Psychical Research*, Vol. 43, July, 1949, by permission of the author and the Society.

himself with his great vision of the beyond—was characteristic of his deep sympathies, though he never joined the Swedenborgian fold. He created in the home atmosphere an exhilarating sense of the worthwhileness of pursuing problems of cosmic dimensions, of asking forever one more question as to the place of man in this world and as to the real basis for ethics and religion; everybody in the family was apparently always ready for a debate which wound up with humor and with agreement to live and let live.

William (born in 1842) and Henry (born in 1843) shared this atmosphere. As their letters show, there was a rugged intensity of fellowship despite their profound temperamental differences. The contrast appears in the fact that while Henry James had sought the meanings of life in introspection and in the subtleties of self-observation, it was William James' determination to look for answers in the new scientific world of the evolutionary period, and to attempt to support his personal faith with the knowledge and wisdom of empirical inquiry. Both were empiricists, but in a very different sense, Henry James looking for the shadings and overtones of daily experience, William trying always to accumulate more facts from every quarter.

The freedom of the family to roam about reached its richest values for William James during the journeys to England, France, Switzerland, and Germany. A special importance should perhaps be attached to a year in Geneva in which, as he entered upon adolescence, William James found his enthusiasm fired by a mixture of science and art. He loved, for example, to draw the skeletons in the Geneva museum. Soon he was thinking of becoming a painter.

Returning to the United States, he entered upon his studies at Harvard (1861). Ill health dogged him all during these years. He was obviously unfit for military service, and his chemistry professor noted the long hours in which he had to lie still and rest, being unable to stand at his table and his test tubes as most students did. His interest in science, especially biology, led ultimately into medicine. Medicine meant, however, much more for him than the continuation of scientific studies. Indeed, his one attempt to be a pure scientist, his journey with Agassiz to the Amazon to collect and barrel fishes, resulted in a tremendous breakdown and a long illness. Medicine, however, he could ultimately master, with hopes, as he said, that he could not only "support W. J., but Mrs. W. J. as well."

During these medical years, moreover, he was carrying forward the kinds of thinking which another journey to Europe had set going within him. He had exposed himself to the physiological psychology of Helmholtz, and the other giants of the period, and wrote to his brother that he hoped that these beginnings of a new experimental science of psychology had something to offer, and he wanted to see what he could do in this area too.

After finishing medical school, and going on into further studies in physiology, he attracted the attention of President Eliot of Harvard, who asked him to teach comparative anatomy and physiology to Harvard undergraduates. This led rapidly to more and more work in experimental physiology, and later, psychology, where both subjects were carried forward by James as he rapidly rose to fame through a series of brilliant publications which began in 1876.

As a matter of fact, during these early years he had made a contract with Henry Holt for his *Principles of Psychology*, and over a 12-year period, from 1878 to 1890, he turned out chapter after chapter of this monumental work. As he began his Harvard career, he had been married to Alice Gibbens, and a quiet and happy home life in Cambridge made possible a period of relative freedom from the strain and illness which had frequently been his lot. The question has often been debated as to what factors, other than his marriage and his steady work at Harvard, had turned the semi-invalid into such a productive and effective teacher and writer. The answer which he himself apparently emphasized most was that the restitution of his health came from the study of that branch of evolutionary philosophy represented by the French philosopher Renouvier, who taught that *spontaneity, genuine freedom*, is available to the individual who strikes out on a new path for himself, and creatively remakes his personal life, including his health as well as his intellectual and spiritual goals. Evidently James' long sufferings, his backaches, his eye-aches, his periods of semi-invalidism, his pathetic and futile journeys to the mud-baths of Bohemia, all of which left him still an invalid, were things of the past when once he realized, in the language of Renouvier, that he could spontaneously, arbitrarily recreate his own life. Though he never became really rugged, his physical and intellectual vitality were in some measure a response to this new conviction.

But this philosophy of spontaneity was an aspect of a still larger movement of thought within him. He was more and more convinced that the threadbare abstractions which characterized German idealistic philosophy and British idealistic philosophy almost to the same degree could make no real contact with the tough, vital, throbbing, everyday realities with which our immediate life is concerned. Always give us realities, give us facts, give us concreteness. In later years, for example, when asked to tell what "pragmatism" was really about, he stressed the fact that it dealt with the practical *and the concrete*, and that if one must choose between the two, to be concrete was even more important than to be practical. He was moving toward "radical empiricism," the habit of thrusting oneself forward into the world of experience to make the richest possible contact with the concrete, the immediate, the real.

The extraordinary series of lectures that he gave at Edinburgh in 1901, which appeared in the volume *The Varieties of Religious Experience*, is a consummation of this faith in the importance of the concrete and the personal. Religion is to be judged not in terms of the abstract representation of an invisible world, but in terms of the living fiber of its substance as we feel it moving through us; and even the mystic is to be understood in terms of the kinds of reality with which he makes contact, the "window" into an unseen world, said James, upon which one's own personal vision depends. As R. B. Perry (1935,

Vol. II, p. 704) put it in his final evaluation of James, James always "knew there was more." No summary, no scheme can ever contain the creative totality of the real. Indeed, those last extraordinary 10 years of his life from 1900 to 1910, in which he turned out such a series of epoch-making philosophical contributions, represent the constantly changing, many-faceted expression of his determination to make contact everywhere with the concrete and the vital. Just as he never constructed a *system* of psychology, so he never constructed a *system* of philosophy. He wrote many psychologies and many philosophies; it was evidently his wish to let posterity decide what it could use.

The interest in psychical research came, then, as a perfectly normal and "predictable" response to this kind of attitude toward life. In the home environment one did not laugh at the claims of Swedenborg. One studied them, played with them, tossed them about, rejected some aspects of them, took other aspects more seriously, just as one did with regard to Christian Science, or any of the other new winds of doctrine that swept through the intellectual atmosphere. Questions about telepathy or survival were just as reasonable as any other kind of question. Such questions were not to be decided *a priori*, or in deferential regard for authority, but by recourse to rigorous investigation. When, therefore, the Society for Psychical Research was founded in London in 1882 under the able leadership of scholars of the stature of Henry Sidgwick, Sir William Barrett, and Frederic Myers, he shared warmly in the whole enterprise. Shortly thereafter he played a leading part in forming an American Society for Psychical Research, which after a few years became the American Branch of the London Society. (The present American Society for Psychical Research later replaced this American Branch.)

During these years William James was eagerly and actively concerned with the investigations by these societies into alleged hauntings, apparitions, and communications with the deceased. He himself was drawn as early as 1885 to investigate the extraordinary phenomena of Mrs. L. E. Piper, who was purported while in deep trance to give information to sitters regarding which she could have had no normal knowledge. In the first sittings which he held, sometimes in the company of his wife, highly personal material was given which he and his wife were morally certain could never have been known normally to Mrs. Piper— indeed some of which was apparently known to no living person but themselves. Other sitters had similar success. In James' (1886) own words:

> To turn to the . . . case of Mrs. P. This lady can at will pass into a trance condition, in which she is "controlled" by a power purporting to be the spirit of a French doctor, who serves as intermediary between the sitter and deceased friends. This is the ordinary type of trance-mediumship at the present day. I have myself witnessed a dozen of her trances, and have testimony at first hand from twenty-five sitters, all but one of whom were virtually introduced to Mrs. P. by myself.

Of five of the sittings we have *verbatim* stenographic reports. Twelve of the sitters, who in most cases sat singly, got nothing from the medium but unknown names or trivial talk. Four of these were members of the society, and of their sittings *verbatim* reports were taken.

Fifteen of the sitters were surprised at the communications they received, names and facts being mentioned at the first interview which it seemed improbable should have been known to the medium in a normal way. The probability that she possessed no clew as to the sitter's identity, was, I believe, in each and all of these fifteen cases, sufficient. But of only one of them is there a stenographic report; so that, unfortunately for the medium, the evidence in her favor is, although more abundant, less exact in quality than some of that which will be counted against her.

Of these fifteen sitters, five, all ladies, were blood relatives, and two (I myself being one) were men connected by marriage with the family to which they belonged. Two other connections of this family are included in the twelve who got nothing. The medium showed a most startling intimacy with this family's affairs, talking of many matters known to no one outside, and which *gossip* could not possibly have conveyed to her ears. The details would prove nothing to the reader, unless printed *in extenso*, with full notes by the sitters. It reverts, after all, to personal conviction. My own conviction is not evidence, but it seems fitting to record it. I am persuaded of the medium's honesty, and of the genuineness of her trance; and although at first disposed to think that the "hits" she made were either lucky coincidences, or the result of knowledge on her part of who the sitter was and of his or her family affairs, I now believe her to be in possession of a power as yet unexplained (pp. 103–104).

This did not establish for William James, of course, any *prima facie* case for survival as such, but it indicated, as he said over and over again (James, 1897), a "lightning stroke" of conviction that there were received by Mrs. Piper's mind many items which she had never normally acquired. He continued to have sittings through his life. He did not hesitate to go out to Concord to see the curious physical phenomena produced by Mr. Foss, in whose home the table charged about in the darkness like a wild beast, and he made it his business to keep informed regarding Mrs. Piper, through the extensive reports offered by Richard Hodgson. He was in the meantime closely following the studies of phantasms of the living and of the dead, and the whole realm of phenomena to which his friend Frederic Myers was applying the conception of the "subliminal self." In his review of Myers' posthumous treatise, *Human Personality and its Survival of Bodily Death*, he wrote: "Any one with a healthy sense for evidence, a sense not methodically blunted by the sectarianism of 'Science,' ought now, it seems to me, to feel that exalted sensibilities and memories, veridical phantasms, haunted houses, trances with supernormal faculty, and even experimental thought-transference, are natural kinds of [phenomena] which ought, just like other natural events, to be followed up with scientific curiosity" (1903, p. 23).

When in 1905 Richard Hodgson suddenly died, it was James' task to edit and report upon that long series of communications purporting to come from the deceased Hodgson through the trance communications of Mrs. Piper (James, 1909). Here he poured himself into a systematic and critical task of editing and evaluation, in which both the strength and the weakness of the evidence for the surviving personality of Hodgson were carefully appraised. An example is the following incident from his report:

> The American Branch had never fully paid its expenses; and although the Secretary's salary had always been very small, Hodgson had, after the first years, been reluctant to have any part of it charged to the mother-country. The result had occasionally been pecuniary embarrassment on his part. During his last visit to England, shortly after Myers' death, this embarrassment had been extreme; but an American friend, divining it in the nick of time, rescued him by an impulsive and wholly unexpected remittance. To this remittance he replied by a letter which contained some banter and, among other things, cited the story of a starving couple who were overheard by an atheist who was passing the house, to pray aloud to God for food. The atheist climbed the roof and dropped some bread down the chimney, and heard them thank God for the miracle. He then went to the door and revealed himself as its author. The old woman replied to him: "Well, the Lord sent it, even if the devil brought it."
>
> At this friend's sitting of Jan. 30th, R. H. suddenly says:
>
> "Do you remember a story I told you and how you laughed, about the man and woman praying?"
>
> Sitter: "Oh, and the devil was in it. Of course I do."
>
> "Yes, the devil, they told him it was the Lord who sent it if the devil brought it.... About the food that was given them.... I want you to know who is speaking."
>
> The sitter feels quite certain that no one but himself knew of the correspondence, and regards the incident as a good test of R. H.'s continued presence. Others will either favor this interpretation of it, or explain it by reading of the sitter's mind, or treat it as a chance coincidence, according to their several prepossessions. I myself feel morally certain that the waking Mrs. Piper was ignorant of the incident and of the correspondence. Hodgson was as likely to have informed *me*, as any one, of the affair. He had given me at the time a vivid account of the trouble he had been in, but no hint of the quarter from which relief had come (pp. 26–27).

The final verdict was that the representation of his deceased friend, and the evidence given of his personal identity, was of such a sort as to suggest that Richard Hodgson himself, or a "spirit counterfeit" of him was there. But James' (1909) whole concluding statement should be noted; it reads as follows:

> Fechner in his *Zend-Avesta* and elsewhere assumes that mental and physical life run parallel, all memory-processes being, according to him, co-ordinated

with material processes. If an act of yours is to be consciously remembered hereafter, it must leave traces on the material universe such that when the *traced parts of the said universe systematically enter into activity together* the act is consciously recalled. During your life the traces are mainly in your brain; but after your death, since your brain is gone, they exist in the shape of all the records of your actions which the outer world stores up as the effects, immediate or remote, thereof, the cosmos being in some degree, however slight, made structurally different by every act of ours that takes place in it. Now, just as the air of the same room can be simultaneously used by many different voices for communicating with different pairs of ears, or as the ether of space can carry many simultaneous messages to and from mutually attuned Marconi-stations, so the great continuum of material nature can have certain tracts within it thrown into emphasized activity whenever activity begins in any part or parts of a tract in which the potentiality of such systematic activity inheres. The bodies (including of course the brains) of Hodgson's friends who come as sitters, are naturally parts of the material universe which carry some of the traces of his ancient acts. They function as receiving stations, and Hodgson (at one time of his life at any rate) was inclined to suspect that the sitter himself acts "psychometrically," or by his body being what, in the trance-jargon, is called an "influence," in attracting the right spirits and eliciting the right communications from the other side. If, now, the *rest of the system of physical traces* left behind by Hodgson's acts were by some sort of mutual induction throughout its extent, thrown into gear and made to vibrate all at once, by the presence of such human bodies to the medium, we should have a Hodgson-system active in the cosmos again, and the "conscious aspect" of this vibrating system might be Hodgson's spirit redivivus, and recollecting and willing in a certain momentary way. There seems fair evidence of the reality of psychometry; so that this scheme covers the main phenomena in a vague general way. In particular, it would account for the "confusion" and "weakness" that are such prevalent features: the system of physical traces corresponding to the given spirit would then be only imperfectly aroused. It tallies vaguely with the analogy of energy finding its way from higher to lower levels. The sitter, with his desire to receive, forms, so to speak, a drainage-opening or sink; the medium, with her desire to personate, yields the nearest lying material to be drained off; while the spirit desiring to communicate is shown the way by the current set up, and swells the latter by its own contributions.

It is enough to indicate these various possibilities, which a serious student of this part of nature has to weigh together, and between which his decision must fall. His vote will always be cast (if ever it be cast) by the sense of the dramatic probabilities of nature which the sum total of his experience has begotten in him. *I myself feel as if an external will to communicate were probably there*, that is, I find myself doubting, in consequence of my whole acquaintance with that sphere of phenomena, that Mrs. Piper's dream-life, even equipped with "telepathic" powers, accounts for all the results found. But if asked whether the will to communicate be Hodgson's, or be some mere spirit-counterfeit of Hodgson, I remain uncertain and await more facts, facts which may not point clearly to a conclusion for fifty or a hundred years (pp. 119–121).

Thus, while he had early and repeatedly expressed his conviction regarding the reality of telepathy, he apparently never reached conviction on the question of the evidence for survival. One finds, nevertheless, a constant insistence on the legitimacy and importance of the inquiry. Indeed, he had published a little book on *Human Immortality* in 1898 in which he had suggested that perhaps the brain acts as a transmitter rather than as an originator of mental processes, so that the deceased may perfectly well be able to carry on a transphysical existence. He believed, however, that Frederic Myers' studies of the "subliminal consciousness" showed such a vast array of paranormal powers possessed by the deeper strata of the living personality that it is difficult to tell which, if any, phenomena of trance mediumship, or of psychical research in general, may require an interpretation transcending the action of these deeper subliminal powers.

But it was not simply the research that James carried on, nor the views he expressed, which gave him the permanent place which he holds in psychical research. It was in large measure the courage and energy with which he stressed the importance of these inquiries; his eager insistence upon the definitive nature of the evidence that at least telepathy exists; his demand that the instruments of such research, such as spiritualist mediums, be respected, honored, and studied with an open mind; his emphatic recognition and *insistence* that an organized type of research enterprise must be set up, with continuity over the years; his deep conviction that a long-range empirical investigation, rather than anybody's religious or philosophical opinion, was the only guide which a thoughtful and literate public could accept. He believed that regardless of the question whether the demonstration of continued existence beyond death is ever possible, psychical research has epoch-making implications for the extension of our understanding about the deeper levels of personality, and of the relation of personality to the universe in which it is placed.

REFERENCES

James, W. Report of the Committee on Mediumistic Phenomena. *Proceedings of the American Society for Psychical Research*, 1886, **1**, 102–106.

James, W. *The Will to Believe, and other Essays in Popular Philosophy*. New York: Longmans, Green, 1897.

James, W. *Human Immortality: Two Supposed Objections to the Doctrine*. Boston: Houghton Mifflin, 1898.

James, W. Review of *Human Personality and its Survival of Bodily Death*, by F. W. H. Myers. *Proceedings of the Society for Psychical Research*, 1903, **18**, 22–33.

James, W. Report on Mrs. Piper's Hodgson control. *Proceedings of the Society for Psychical Research*, 1909, **13**, 2–121.

Perry, R. B. *The Thought and Character of William James*. Boston: Little, Brown, 1935. 2 vols.

Part II
RESEARCH METHODS IN PARAPSYCHOLOGY

1

Research Methods with Spontaneous Cases

Louisa E. Rhine

INTRODUCTION

Spontaneous cases in parapsychology are personal experiences in which an individual gets information about, or causes effects on, the external world without the use of the senses or muscles. For convenience in methods of study, such occurrences are divided into the recurrent kind—mainly poltergeists and haunting effects (see W. G. Roll's chapter in this volume)—and the nonrecurrent kind, which are the more isolated experiences of individuals such as veridical dreams, premonitions, etc. The nonrecurrent type of case forms the subject matter of this chapter.

Although nonrecurrent psi experiences have been reported in practically all cultures, they have not figured directly in modern parapsychological research, which has been devoted to experimental methods almost exclusively. Case material, however, has been used in occasional research projects, and the methods of study used in them will be examined here.

Almost by necessity it would seem that the methods employed in any research must depend on the objectives of the individual project. Of course, they must also be based on the background of knowledge in the field as well as on the general standards of science that prevail at the time. However, for several reasons many of the case study projects in parapsychology have not fulfilled these expectations. Since the earliest ones predated the recognition of psi as a human ability, they were not undertaken in order to gain greater insight into the cases themselves, but rather for the light the investigators hoped they might shed on other problems. Even the later studies were often approached from this point of view. This meant that only a specific kind of case was picked out and that it was studied in isolation rather than in the context of psi experiences in general.

Then, too, the studies have been scattered and generally peripheral to the main advance of parapsychology. Moreover, they were sometimes carried out by persons not informed of or not in sympathy with the experimental kind of inquiry. Consequently, the methods used tended to become fixed by tradition rather than to be adapted to advances in the knowledge of psi. Still, minor changes in method were introduced as the needs of individual projects dictated. The following account, covering the majority of the case studies on record, will show this. Only studies involving human subjects are included, although animals too are involved in spontaneous cases.

ORIGINAL CASE STUDY MODEL

A convenient starting point in the survey of methods of case studies is the project carried out by Gurney, Myers, and Podmore of the Society for Psychical Research in London in the 1880s and reported in *Phantasms of the Living* (Gurney, Myers, and Podmore, 1886). The research method developed for this project overshadowed any earlier one and became the classic model for those succeeding it to such an extent that its influence is still felt today. On that account and because it is an excellent example of the fitting of the method to the objective of a particular research project, it must be described in some detail although it is a remnant of a day long before any type of extrasensory perception had been established and when even the concept of telepathy was not accepted in orthodox scientific circles.

The objective of this research was implicit in the reason for which the Society was established. As stated in the first paragraph of the first number of the *Proceedings* of the S.P.R. in 1882, the objective was to investigate "that large group of debatable phenomena designated by such terms as mesmeric, psychical, and Spiritualistic." In the background was the fact that the materialistic trend of science was crowding out the recognition of the psychical aspect of man on which the religions depended. The psychical researchers felt that possible evidence for this aspect might lie in such obscure and overlooked phenomena as telepathic experiences.

Myers, in his introduction to *Phantasms* argued that if telepathy be admitted, "an element is thus introduced which constitutes a serious obstacle to the materialistic synthesis of human experience" (p. 1). The case project, he said, was designed to "deal with all classes of cases where there is reason to suppose that the mind of one human being has affected the mind of another . . . by other means than through the recognised channels of sense" (p. xxxv). A few lines later he stated further that they proposed to deal also with "a vast class of cases which seem at first sight to involve something widely different from a mere transference of thought." "I refer to apparitions . . . " he said. Later it became clear that apparitions were included because they seemed to involve telepathy.

Thus, to prove that telepathy occurs would be only preliminary to the great question of survival. For proof on so great a thesis, the best possible method must be used. Consequently, the one that was developed—the analysis of spontaneous cases that appear to involve telepathy—was in accordance with the general scientific criteria of the day which, in the 1880s, still permitted emphasis on the use of anecdotal material with only secondary attention to the results of experiments. (Some experiments suggesting telepathic exchange had already been made.) Also, although the use of statistics in the evaluation of test results was beginning, methods for its general application were not yet in wide use. These early workers felt the need of statistical method, as is frequently evident in their reports.

The material which seemed the most directly applicable as proof of telepathy— even more pertinent than the experimental evidence then available—was certain spontaneous experiences that seemed to involve telepathy. These experiences depend, of course, on human testimony. But such testimony is notably unreliable, and it would be necessary, first of all, to find a way by which it could be so strengthened that it would constitute proof of the thesis. Then, as a second step, would come the analysis of these cases according to the kinds of impressions the percipients had had. This would show the ways in which information coming from the agents could impress the percipients. It could thus prove that telepathy is a reality and that it can explain various kinds of experiences, including apparitions.

The method of screening that was developed was logical in view of the objective. It had to exclude errors of testimony, and cases in which this could not be done with a high degree of reliability would not be accepted. The completeness with which the investigators were aware of and guarded against possible errors is shown in Chapter 4 of *Phantasms* under the title "General Criticism of the Evidence for Spontaneous Telepathy," which covers 58 pages. It shows that the authors were alert to the danger of errors—of observation, inference, narration, memory (including the percipient's memory of his own impression of the agent's crisis), and pertinent dates. All of this pointed to the necessity for even the best of witnesses to have made a report or record of his experience before he learned of the related event and could have been influenced by it. Only by such a record could this testimony be corroborated by a second party and thus strengthened sufficiently that it could be considered reliable.

Also, the timing of each element would have had to be exact. It was assumed that in telepathy the impression of the percipient and the crisis of the agent would be simultaneous. But in apparitions at the time of a death (the kind of case that was of the greatest interest) it might be impossible to know exactly when death occurred. It was therefore decided that it would be reasonable to accept cases in which a time discrepancy of up to 12 hours occurred, but to reject those in which it was longer.

The first step in the method that was developed was to collect a large number of cases of the type that seemed to involve telepathy. The individual cases were then processed according to the standards that had been set, including witnesses' statements covering all aspects of the occurrence. Since the criteria were so high, the task was a formidable one. It entailed, wherever possible, firsthand contact between collector and percipient, written statements from witnesses, the validation of testimony to ensure truthfulness and eliminate unconscious error, the following-up of details from all possible sources, travels to significant locations, the tracing-down of evidence from old letters, diaries, newspapers, and archives of every sort. But the criteria were followed meticulously, and cases were rejected if any hint remained that an extraneous factor might have entered in or if sufficient corroboration could not be produced. All of this did not mean, of course, that rejected cases might not involve telepathy but that the testimony could not be corroborated and that those that were accepted were as reliable as such material could be.

Eventually 702 cases were found that withstood the rigors of validation, but that was only the first step. The most important part of the method came second. It was the analysis of the impressions of the percipients in the accepted cases. This step was carried out just as carefully and exhaustively as the validation had been.

The analysis yielded a breakdown of the material which showed the importance in which hallucinatory experiences were held in the proof of telepathy. There was a major division of the cases into two great families (p. 186): (a) cases in which the impression was sensory and externalized and (b) cases in which it was not.[1]   The strongest evidence, the authors implied, came from the first group, a judgment supported by the fact that these (apparitions) occurred in the waking state, as had all the experiments made earlier that suggested telepathy.

This analysis of the entire collection of cases, including many more points than can even be suggested here, enabled the researchers to feel that they had accomplished their mission and had shown beyond reasonable doubt that telepathy was a reality and that apparitional experiences belonged in that category. The study thus went as far as possible to establish its point.

---

[1]Dreams, of course, were included here, but tentatively and almost with apology, for in the 1880s their status was very low. A discussion of their value as evidence of telepathy (pp. 303–310) included an attempt at a statistical evaluation of the probability that some dreams of the death of an agent were the result of something other than chance.

However, no widespread acceptance of telepathy followed, then or later. Perhaps no proof of any kind could have been generally accepted at that time. But the times were changing, and the scholarly demand for experimental results that could be evaluated statistically was increasing; it was being recognized more and more that case material of any kind, no matter how well the *bona fides* of the testimony might be established, still could be explained in terms of chance or other possible causes which the method could not screen out.

In spite of this inherent weakness of case material, the aspect of this historical case study that impressed many of the succeeding workers most strongly seems to have been the stringent validation of the cases rather than the second step in the process, the analysis of the impressions of the percipients, although it was the results of this analysis that permitted the authors to feel that they had been successful.

THE "CENSUS OF HALLUCINATIONS": AN ADVANCE TOWARD STATISTICAL ANALYSIS

The desirability of having statistical evaluations when seeking proof of a point was recognized in effect in 1889 by members of the S.P.R. Under the leadership of Henry Sidgwick, they undertook to introduce such an element into the next S.P.R. study. The case collection that had been used earlier had included only telepathy cases. This new one was still more select. It included only the hallucinatory form of the telepathic experiences.

The project was reported as the "Census of Hallucinations" (H. Sidgwick and Committee, 1894). Its aim was to see if a reason could be found to "refer to a supernatural cause" those experiences in which a dying or a deceased person had been seen or otherwise manifested to a percipient in such a way that it seemed as if he were actually there. In *Phantasms*, the authors had tried to prove that telepathy occurs; the "Census" attempted to show statistically that in the hallucinatory form of telepathic experience a relationship exists between the dying person and the percipient's experience. The counterargument which would have to be ruled out was the same one, of course, that had been leveled at telepathy cases in general: that the correspondence between the thoughts of the percipient and agent was just the result of chance. The same counterargument applied to apparitions too. But in the earlier collection, the investigators had been impressed in particular by the frequency of hallucinations of the dying. Now, for this new project, cases of this kind seemed to provide an opportunity to find a statistical basis for ruling out this counterargument because it might be possible to show that apparitions of the dying occurred too often to be the result of chance. The method used to accomplish this began with the issuing of a questionnaire to determine what percentage of the population had had hallucinatory experiences. From this the investigators could estimate the proportion of the experiences that involved dying agents. Then, since the actual death rate was a known figure (19.15 per thousand over the preceding 10 years in England), a comparison would show whether the rate of death-coincident apparitional experiences was greater than that to be expected by chance. The investigators hoped to get replies to the questionnaire from a large enough number of people to make an adequate sample.

With 410 helpers working over a 3-year period, the inquiry was closed when 17,000 replies had been received. Of these, 2,272 were affirmative. This meant only that these persons testified to having had experiences of a hallucinatory nature; but the experiences were of many different kinds. Then, by careful winnowing from this number those coincident with death and by an ingenious rationale too detailed to describe here, they arrived at an estimate which showed the hallucinations involving dying agents to have occurred many times too frequently to have been the result of chance.[2]

The point made by this "Census" that has withstood the changes of the last 70 years is that hallucinatory experiences at the time of death very well may involve something more than chance—may at least involve the operation of one form of ESP. The method, that of seeking a numerical evaluation of spontaneous cases in such a study, is enlightening today mainly in showing the dawning realization of these investigators that the old case method needed the support of statistics.

STUDIES OF PRECOGNITIVE AND APPARITIONAL CASES

Over the next decades, less ambitious projects which involved two special kinds of cases, the hallucinatory and the precognitive, were made. For example, in 1889, Eleanor Mildred Sidgwick (1888–89) of the S.P.R. reported a study of cases suggesting precognition. These cases had been excluded from *Phantasms* because they lacked the time coincidence which had been one of the criteria imposed in that study. Mrs. Sidgwick's method was simply to take the individual case reports which had already been validated and analyze the likelihood that something more than chance was involved. She found a few which she could not easily dismiss and which strongly suggested precognition.

While Mrs. Sidgwick's study pointed up the unsolved question of precognition by the analysis of cases suggesting it, a somewhat different method was publicized in 1927 by J. W. Dunne. He had noted certain of his own dreams which came true, and therefore he began recording them. His book, *An Experiment*

---

[2] The reasoning behind the method they used covers three pages in the Sidgwick report (1894) and has been conveniently summarized by several later writers (Salter, 1960; Tyrrell, 1942). The method has had a long influence in psychical research circles but today is of historical interest only. In its day it was, and still is, testimony to the ingenuity and dedication of the authors to the theme of their research.

with Time (1927), was the account of his diary method and the theory of time he was able to build upon it. Dunne supposed also that many persons, like himself, might dream precognitively and that the diary method might show it.

One result of the interest in the possibility of precognition that was aroused by Dunne's book was an attempt by Theodore Besterman (1932–33) to confirm the idea that some of the ordinary dreams of many people may be precognitive. Besterman's method, accordingly, was to ask subjects to record their dreams regularly and systematically over a 3-week period and note events that later seemed to be connected with them. He secured 43 subjects and 430 dream records. Of these, he thought 18 showed sufficient similarity between the dream and the later event to which it was associated that they might have been precognitive, but only two of them seemed to him to be "good cases." He added, however, that he had secured no "conclusive instances of precognition" and that his figures were only a "personal estimate" since with "free" material, which gives no basis for statistical evaluation, "there must always be room for difference of opinion" (p. 204).

Although Besterman drew his conclusion from a much larger number of dreams than Dunne had at his command, his result was hardly a confirmation of Dunne's idea. But Dunne was evaluating his own experiences, Besterman those of others. This may have been a factor in the difference in their conclusions. Or Dunne may have been an especially good subject for precognition. In any event, the methods of these men in trying to get conclusive evidence of precognition from dreams alone can now be seen as unrealistic.

In 1928, Walter Franklin Prince reported a collection of cases from what he called "noted witnesses." The witnesses from whom he collected experiences were scientists, clergymen, literary personages, lawyers, and statesmen; but curiously, he found no names of well-known psychic researchers. This fact struck Prince as testimony against the common charge that the "will to believe" accounts for those persons who have convictions regarding parapsychological topics. He noted that as many scientists as clergymen had entries in his list.

At this point Prince showed his awareness of the rising desirability to have statistical evaluations of results, but he steered clear of the trap of attempting such evaluations when data of the kind necessary for them were lacking, remarking that "no true statistical result can be obtained unless the proper basis for it can be established."

Experiences that seemed to be precognitive had continued to be reported, authenticated, and published from time to time in the *Journal* of the S.P.R. They stimulated another S.P.R. member, H. F. Saltmarsh (1934), to undertake a study of them. His method went further in one way than Dunne's because he was not restricted to only one person's experiences and because, by using already authenticated cases, he did not get deeply enmeshed in that aspect. Instead, he gave his main attention to the analysis of the material. He found 349 cases, which he divided into groups in several ways, including criteria of form and content. With respect to form, he found they occurred as dreams, borderline waking experiences, waking cases (which he called impressions), and hallucinations, as well as mediumistic and crystal-gazing cases. The content or themes involved ranged from illness or death to quite trivial incidents.

These analyses gave Saltmarsh an insight into the particular state of mind of the percipient that produced the different forms. They led also to the observation that while 100 of the 349 cases, or fewer than a third, involved death, 35 of the 63 cases of hallucinations, or over half, were death coincidences. This preponderance of death coincidences in the hallucinatory form was large enough to be impressive just by inspection. But on the advice of Whately Carington, he worked out a mathematical formula and by its use was able to show that the proportion was statistically significant (see p. 100 of his report for the formula).

Death, of course, is an emotionally charged topic; and in the "Census of Hallucinations," for instance, it had been shown that emotionally charged situations predominated in hallucinatory experiences involving present situations. Now Saltmarsh's study showed that the same was true in these precognitive situations too often to be explained by chance. It appeared therefore that the future emotional situation was having an effect in the present.

In 1942, G. N. M. Tyrrell, in his Myers Memorial Lecture to the S.P.R., returned to the old question of apparitions and their meaning. He reported on a study of 61 such cases, most of which had been collected, checked, and validated at the S.P.R. With this reasonably large collection of "ready-made" material at his command, Tyrrell, as part of his method, made an *interpretation* of the phenomenon by analyzing the individual cases with regard to the principal *characteristics* of the apparitions described. He found the same characteristics being reported again and again, not all of them in every case, but all of them appearing repeatedly in different cases. They were so consistent that he constructed a hypothetical "perfect" apparition from them, and it turned out to be one that was quite different from the popular "ghost" of fiction. This fact seemed to speak for a reality not produced by imagination, and it meant that "this kind of experience can be originated by psychological factors in the personality" of the percipient.

Tyrrell knew of course that telepathy was a possibility. In the years since the S.P.R.'s attempt to prove it by case studies, it had come to be rather generally considered as experimentally established, and so he could draw upon it now. He suggested that the mental content of the agent could be transferred telepathically to the percipient, who could then himself project the appropriate sense data into the hallucinatory form. The apparitional experience would then be an effect *created* by the percipient in response to the telepathic information drawn from the agent, a concept that did not call for recourse to a spiritistic theory.

Later, in a survey of investigations of spontaneous cases, D. J. West (1946–49) concluded that "formidable obstacles" stood in the way of using cases as proof of psi. J. B. Rhine (1948) of the Duke Parapsychology Laboratory gave a similar opinion. West had urged the collecting of "more good modern cases that incorporated all the necessary criteria." Rhine, however, urged that case material was miscast if used as proof of a thesis (i.e., proof of psi) because it was essentially too weak for that and could not be sufficiently strengthened. But cases, he said, did have great suggestive value; suggestions raised by them had led to experiments in parapsychology in the first place and could do so again. He pointed out that suggestions so raised could be tested experimentally and their validity decided; and if so established, the results could prove the thesis whereas the untested suggestions alone could not. Rhine therefore called for a return to the use of cases in psi research.

A study of "ESP projection" was reported a few years later by Hornell Hart (1954), the chairman of a committee appointed for the purpose at an international congress in Europe. Hart defined a "full-fledged" projection ideally as a situation in which a "projected" individual carries within himself "full memories and purposes" during his projection out of his body and afterwards.[3] Hart's major interest was to prove survival, and projection as it was envisaged by his definition would show that the mind of an individual may actually be separable from the body (as it would have to be in survival).

The question was whether the separation in such projection is actual. Hart recognized that it had never been proven and that therefore, as he said, more rigorous methods than had been used on the question would be necessary. The method that he thought could produce such proof was based on the assumption that if full-fledged projection could be produced experimentally, survival could be proved in principle, even though the projected individual's body was not dead.

Hart was able to collect 99 cases after eliminating all that did not conform to the S.P.R. standards of authenticity. Since the objective was to find a way to produce full-fledged projections experimentally, the 99 cases were divided into groups according to the manner by which the projection had been obtained—by hypnosis, concentration, or self-projection by methods more complex than mere concentration.

Each of the cases in these groups was then subjected to an "evidentiality rating" which, he explained in a later paper (Hart, 1956, p. 157), was not for the exclusion of nonevidential cases but was "merely for the purpose of giving as accurate a measure as feasible" of the relative success which various case reporters and investigators demonstrated in presenting proofs that the alleged

---

[3] "ESP projection," "astral projection," and "out-of-body experiences" are nearly, if not entirely, synonymous terms.

evidentiality is dependable (p. 157). The mean scores of each of the groups was then found, and the variance was calculated. Whether the variance figures show anything beyond another item added to their authentication is not clear; but if, as would seem necessary, they provide an estimate of the degree to which any of the groups produced full-fledged cases, none did so. On a scale of 0–1, the mean scores varied between .177 and .431.

The rest of the method could be called a resort to argument against the possibility that explanations of the case material could be anything other than projection. These counterarguments he listed as (a) faulty memory, etc., on the part of witnesses, (b) coincidence, (c) fraud, and (d) ESP. The first three were ruled out by argument, and the fourth, ESP, by definition. He defined ESP as not involving the projection of the viewpoint of the percipient and thus attempted to distinguish it from "projection." The general conclusion in spite of lack of support by the facts was that the most promising avenue for producing full-fledged projection was hypnosis. The mean score for the hypnosis cases was only .424 while that for concentration was .431. Nevertheless, Hart concluded that by hypnosis a full-fledged projection could be produced and could thus provide evidence that the spirit is separable from the body.

In his second paper, already mentioned, Hart (1956) used essentially the same method as in the first insofar as he attempted by rigorous validation to arrive at numerical values. In this study, however, the objective was to compare the characteristics of apparitions of the dying and the dead with those of full-fledged projections (apparitions) of the living and thereby show that by their similarity, apparitions of the dead are evidence for survival.

Again he divided the cases into groups, this time according to the situation of the agents: those dead 12 hours or longer; those dead less than 12 hours; death-coincident apparitions; living persons who remembered being projected; and those who did not remember. Then, using Tyrrell's idea but not his interpretation, Hart made up a list of the traits of the apparitions in the five groups. The percentage of cases in each group showing each characteristic was computed. Then, by using a criterion "for chance occurrences" (the critical ratio), he concluded that the difference in characteristics of the several groups was no greater than would be expected by chance. On his results he based the hypothesis that apparitions are "semi-substantial."

BREAKING THE OLD MODEL

In response to Rhine's call for case studies in 1948, I undertook such a study at the Duke Parapsychology Laboratory. Initially the general objective of the project was to explore the possible suggestive value of case material in order to provide an adjunct to the planning of experiments. Later the purpose was extended to include any objectives that the material itself suggested. Eventually it grew into an extensive study of psi as a human ability as it seems to be indicated in spontaneous experiences.

Until 1948, only experimental, not case material, had been used in the Laboratory. But, with psi experimentally established, emphasis was shifting to a study of its nature. For this it was logical to think that spontaneous experiences might give clues.

Hundreds of reports of occurrences that individuals thought might involve psi had accumulated at the Laboratory, and I undertook to study them with the idea of finding suggestions as to the processes that produced them. For that, it was necessary to make a survey of all the ways in which psi occurs naturally, i.e., when not restricted by laboratory conditions.

In the choice of a method by which to accomplish this, two difficulties presented themselves. One concerned the old practice of validating the material to guard against all the possible weaknesses of human testimony, much as if preparing evidence for a court case. Even with full awareness of those weaknesses, the labor of attempting to process by the old criteria all the reports already on hand and continuing to come in was beyond the time and effort I could give, except, of course, to the extent that I could eliminate accounts with obvious weaknesses upon first reading. (Over half of those received were rejected at this initial stage.)

The second difficulty was even worse. Even if a few acceptable cases could be salvaged by the old methods, this would certainly narrow the range of material for the collection because some kinds of experience are obviously less open to corroboration than others. For instance, many dreams might not be reported before the occurrence of the related events as required, because the dreamers would not then know they were significant. A hallucinatory experience, on the other hand, was likely to be mentioned whether or not significant just because it was striking and unusual. The effect of setting up restrictions prematurely was well illustrated by the fact that precognitive experiences had been eliminated in the early S.P.R. model because of the timing criterion that had been imposed.

The solution to both problems was achieved by a method that fitted the new situation. It was based on the idea that human testimony is at least partly reliable and that most people, when going to the trouble of reporting a puzzling personal event, will try to do so correctly. The likelihood that their reports will be relatively correct, while not strong enough for strict scientific certainty, is good enough to raise suggestions about the experiences that can then be tested— especially if the experience is of a kind that is repeated by persons entirely unconnected. A method was developed, accordingly, in which the necessary level of reliability of the material was achieved by numbers of individual cases featuring a given point, rather than by the attempted validation of individual reports.

In order to avoid selection of experiences at this preliminary stage, and to include all possible varieties of them, it was decided to accept tentatively for study all reports that were intelligently written and in apparent good faith, *if they fulfilled the definition*, that is, if, as reported, they seemed to be instances in which information was received without the senses or effects were produced without the muscles.

This method could not have been used 50 years earlier, before psi was established experimentally; now, however, it was necessary to conclude that psi must also occur spontaneously. The question was, When? The ever-present alternative was that a seeming psi experience might only be a coincidence between the experience and the event. But in this study, in order not to exclude cases that might tell something about the psi process, the benefit of the doubt would have to be given if the case fulfilled the definition. This method made certain that no premature exclusion of significant kinds of cases would occur.

It was planned that the cases would be classified and filed but would not be considered ready for study until a large number of instances showing a given feature had been collected. This, as mentioned, was done on the theory that any valid kind or form of experience would tend to be reported again and again and that even rare kinds of experiences would eventually recur if they did involve psi.

After the method of treating cases had been decided upon, the first step was to draw up an outline of the general topics that were of most pressing concern to the experimenters in the Laboratory at the time so that cases could be filed for later use accordingly. This outline fell into two main sections which have remained the same over the years, with subdivisions being added as new needs have arisen. The two main sections were:

Section I. Problems bearing on the nature of the different types of psi. A. Precognition; B. Telepathy; C. Clairvoyance; D. Psychokinesis.
Section II. Problems connected with the way psi is experienced. A. Manner (or psychological form of consciousness); B. Extent of knowledge conveyed.

As they came in, the cases were classified and filed under these various headings. Of course, every case could have found an appropriate place in both sections, but since there was no scarcity of material, it seemed best to use each one only once, so that numbers would be independent. Accordingly, each case was put in the category to which it seemed it would contribute the most.

From the cases collected and classified according to these criteria, a number of separate studies (18 in all) were made and published between 1951 and 1967. The method included no attempt to introduce statistical evaluations since case material is unmeasurable in precise terms. Even kinds of cases and their frequency in a collection depend on external variables. On that account, the basic method used was analytical but modified in each study according to the specific objective. In some studies the purpose was best suited by the use of all the cases on hand at the time; in others, only pertinent sections of them.

The overall objective of these studies was to see what the basic psi process seemed to be. Toward this end, several of the studies, as it turned out, were especially suggestive, although all of them contributed to the general objective, at least in a minor way, by leading (me, especially) on to a glimpse of the possible underlying meaning. Among the more definitive ones, the most important of all (L. E. Rhine, 1953), I think, identified the main forms (intuitions, hallucinations, unrealistic dreams, and realistic dreams) in which psi is expressed in consciousness, a survey which had never been made in entirety before and which perhaps could be done only in a case study.[4]   In fact, here was the payoff for not using the discriminatory criteria of the early S.P.R. model, for in the present collection of cases, it could well be assumed that no form of psi experience had been excluded.[5]

The method used in this instance was simply to analyze each case in order to find its basic form beneath the superficialities. This might seem easy to do, at least when a gross difference like that of sleep versus wakefulness was involved. But even on that point the question soon arose about classifying cases on the borderline between the two psychological states. In the borderline area, the person's own testimony as to whether he was awake or not could not be considered reliable. A distinction that did prove reliable, however, was found to be the kind of imagery displayed. For instance, the majority of the dreams appeared as if modeled on reality. They could therefore be called realistic. In others, a bit of imagination, fantasy, and even symbolism was introduced, making them by contrast unrealistic. More than that, a few of both the realistic and unrealistic forms occurred when the person was not sleeping, and this was the reason why the state of consciousness did not discriminate exactly.

Then, in the hallucinatory kind of experience, often the person was in bed, and his state of wakefulness could be questioned. However, here too the kind of imagery discriminated reliably because it was different from that of dreams. The person *thought* he was awake, and the imagery accordingly was modeled on sense experience, although actually it was only pseudosensory. The majority of experiences that occurred when the person was really awake (not in bed or reclining), however, had no imagery but were indistinguishable in form from ordinary intuitions.

The method here, based on an analysis of the kind of imagery or lack of it, did succeed in making possible a distinction in the forms of psi in consciousness. This, in turn, led on to later studies, by somewhat modified methods, in which the genesis of psi experience at unconscious mental levels could be traced (L. E. Rhine, 1962a, 1962b). The difference in the method used in these studies was

[4]In a later study (L. E. Rhine, 1963) PK experiences were analyzed, and their apparent function as a form of psi was noted.

[5]In 1953 the collection included about 1,000 ESP cases, but at the last count (1973) the total number was 12,659; of PK cases there were 178. To date, no form not in the 1953 survey has been reported.

that cases that seemed to involve meaningful errors or omissions of information were studied for suggestions as to the reason for their imperfections, reasons which, in turn, seemed to be related causally to the form the experience took in consciousness.

One block of three separate studies was on apparitions and was a diversion from the main objective of my other case studies. With the analysis of the cases according to their form in consciousness just mentioned, apparitions had fallen into place as one subdivision of hallucinatory experiences in general, usually those that involved the human figure, or voice, or both. It seemed of interest now to see what this classification of them as only a selected part of a larger group would mean in regard to the early S.P.R. tentatively held hypothesis that they had a bearing on the survival question.

In the first (L. E. Rhine, 1956b) of these three studies the purpose was to see what differences might exist between the old collections and the new by comparing their outstanding characteristics in regard to the sense modality (whether visual, auditory, or other) and type (telepathy, clairvoyance, or precognition). In old collections, the outstanding sense modality had been visual; in the new, the visual hallucinatory experiences made up only about a fourth of all. In the old, the type had been telepathic; in the new, besides the telepathic, some of the experiences were of the clairvoyant, the precognitive, and the GESP types. In the second study (L. E. Rhine, 1957a) the nature of the imagery when the agents were living, dying, and dead was contrasted to see if the action appeared to originate with the agent or, as it had seemed to do in my study of telepathy (L. E. Rhine, 1956a), with the percipient. The third study (L. E. Rhine, 1957b) was a contrast between the degree of complexity of imagery in cases in which the agent was living and those in which he was dead. The result of all three studies was to show that if apparitions have any bearing on the survival question, it cannot be because of the hallucinatory *form* of the experience. That, it was shown, is one of the basic ways in which psi is expressed in consciousness.

The rest of the projects cannot be specified here; but each one called for a modification of the general method and contributed suggestions about psi as a process. Together they bear witness, just as the experimental methods of the present are doing, to the large psychological factor in the genesis of a psi experience. These case studies thus have yielded tentative insights into the psi process, many of which will be established when proper experimental research can be completed.

A method similar to mine was followed in a case study undertaken in Germany by Sannwald (1963). The study involved a collection of 1,000 cases resulting from newspaper publicity. The method separated the cases into their types, forms, state of consciousness, and degree of meaningfulness. An attempt was also made to find the underlying motivation that may have been relevant to the experiences. Also, the cases were analyzed for their content, from which the effects of anxiety and concern for others and for the self were noted.

Sannwald found that over 47 percent of the cases were realistic, with the symbolic form making up about 15 percent, intuitive cases about 25 percent, and hallucinations, 10 percent. His precognitive and contemporary experiences were about equal in number. None of the differences in relative numbers between Sannwald's percentages and my own were greater than might be expected from the differences in kind of publicity that elicited the cases of the two collections. I had found such response to vary, depending not only on the magazine or newspaper from which it was drawn, but also on the topic that was featured in the article: if dreams, then in the responses dreams preponderated; if precognitive effects, then that type of experience was the most frequent. Case collecting of this kind is to some extent an instance of reaping what has been sown, and this fact always makes overall numbers tentative and not a basis for strict statistical reliability.

RETURN TO EARLY MODEL WITH SOME ADAPTATIONS

In 1955, an international congress held in Cambridge, England, was devoted specifically to the discussion of spontaneous cases and the methods of research to be used in studying them. The result was that the old traditional methods were advocated, and at a later conference in Paris the objectives of further case studies were given as those of obtaining material on cultural anthropology, the role of psi in normal psychological activity, etc. (Salter, 1960, p. 93). A questionnaire was compiled and distributed to S.P.R. members and the press. "The intention was that all cases reported should first be screened. Those that seemed of interest should then be followed up with a view to verification along the lines *traditionally followed by the Society's investigators* . . . [my italics] " (Salter, 1960, p. 93).

The result was that about 300 cases were collected. As reported by Rosalind Heywood (1960), they were eventually turned over to Celia Green (1960), who introduced a new element by not rejecting all those that did not pass the "verification" test perfectly. Instead, she graded them A, B, or C according to the level they reached, thereby, no doubt, reducing somewhat the selection of kinds that can result from the authentication process. She then tabulated the cases according to relevant previous classifications (pp. 99–117) plus some new ones. These were coded as required for computer analysis, and the data were compiled on a wide range of topics, the more obvious being age, sex, marital status, as well as type, telepathic, clairvoyant, or precognitive, degree of conviction, etc. Green was aware of the difficulty of judging some of the more important aspects of case material such as motivation and the emotional element. Her work contributed a method and suggestions which she hoped would provide hints for improved experiments. It also provided a backlog of material which presumably future researchers might find adaptable to whatever objectives they might have. Thus far, however, no reports on them have appeared.

Another result of the renewed interest in case studies following the 1955 convention was a project reported in 1962 by Dale, White, and Murphy, who made an appeal for cases via a newspaper (*This Week*, a Sunday Supplement). About 12,000 replies were received, nearly all of which were "chaff"; only a few hundred of the replies contained possible grains of wheat. Even these, when properly authenticated, produced only 17 that were considered acceptable. These experiences, when presented with the detailed questions of corroboration that were asked of each percipient along with the replies to them, fill about 40 pages of the report. The criteria for corroboration were that the experience be veridical; that there should be independent witnessing; and that a record of the experience should be made within the ensuing 5 years. However, the old restriction followed in *Phantasms* regarding timing was not imposed.

The cases were presented in the report according to the psychological state of the percipient—asleep, borderline, or waking—and a distinction was made between contemporaneous and future events. The number of cases of course was much too small to permit meaningful generalizations. But it was hoped that with larger numbers further studies of psychological attributes could be carried out "similar to those that [were] carried out by Louisa E. Rhine on cases *unselected* from the standpoint of authentication" (p. 46). (If this were done, however, it should be expected that the selection imposed by the need for independent witnessing, etc., would considerably limit the results.)

After the Aberfan disaster in England (Barker, 1967) an attempt was made to use spontaneous cases of precognition in a practical way. It had developed (as is often true of public disasters) that this calamity in which many lives were lost had been the topic of a number of apparently premonitory experiences. The resulting action was the formation of two registries—first, one in England, and later, one in the United States[6]—to which persons with premonitions of impending disasters were invited to report beforehand. The idea, according to Ian Stevenson (1970a), was the possible formation of a "distant early warning system, alerting persons or communities threatened with some disaster so that they [might] take precautionary measures to avert it" (p. 207).

In 1970, Ian Stevenson returned to the old method of case collecting in his book *Telepathic Impressions* (1970b), the subject matter of which, the author explained, was cases that lack imagery and involve only simple impressions[7] or

---

[6]The addresses are: British Premonitions Bureau, Grove House, 14 W. Grove, London, S.E., England; and Central Premonitions Registry, Box 482, Times Square Station, New York, N.Y. 10036.

[7]"Impressions" are the kind of experience that I characterized as intuitive and as comprising practically all waking experiences except hallucinations (L. E. Rhine, 1953, 1962a). Cases involving telepathic impressions necessarily make a group that is limited both as to type (telepathy) and form (impression), for telepathic experiences do not occur only in the form of impressions. They often occur with imagery, as in hallucinations and dreams. Neither is the impression form limited to the telepathic type of experience; both clairvoyant and pre-

intuitions about a distant person. Since they lack detail it is difficult to establish the fact that these cases, standing alone as they do here, involve ESP, because the chance hypothesis is difficult to rule out. Stevenson's objective in the study was to show that even these imageless experiences might be the result of ESP, and that if they were, they might contribute to an understanding of the process of extrasensory perception.

The method of procedure, reverting to the S.P.R. model, involved first the collecting of cases of this kind from the older literature. Stevenson found 160 which, already authenticated as they were, he reviewed and analyzed. He then summarized their common features and characteristics: the relation of agent and percipient, and the variation in amount of information transmitted. With this as a background, he presented as the main burden of the book, 35 new cases that he had collected. For the treatment of these, four criteria were set up by Stevenson (1970b):

1. The percipient believed that the distant agent "needed" him or was in some "significant and unusual situation."
2. The percipient's statement about the need was also unusual.
3. The correspondence in time between impression and related event was close.
4. The report had to satisfy standards of authenticity. It had to include independent corroboration to show that the percipient had his experience before he learned normally of the related events, for which independent verification was also required (summarized from pp. 10–11).

The first three criteria limited the cases to the specified type. In No. 1, by including only cases with agents (telepathic), any that might be clairvoyant were excluded. The restriction as to timing in No. 3 excluded all but very short-term precognitive cases. No. 4, of course, involved the S.P.R. kind of authentication, and the manner of presentation of the material was also similar to that of the S.P.R. in that corroborative statements of the witnesses were all presented in full. They cover many more pages of the text than the cases themselves or their discussion.

When the 35 new cases were subjected to the four criteria, some of them ap-

---

cognitive cases may occur as impressions. The group as delineated (as telepathic impressions) was only a selected part of each category.

In my classification, cases of this kind, when they contributed a complete item of information, could have been placed under Section IIA, the form being intuitive; if the information was incomplete, they would have been classified as emotional or compulsory only and put under IIB.

The varying amounts of information received in different cases suggest an effect resulting from difficulties in the transfer of unconscious items into consciousness. The range in relative amount varies all the way from complete items like "John is dead" down to those that are so incomplete that only an appropriate emotion or compulsion to action indicates that a psi event may have occurred. This narrowing of the amount of information in many instances seems similar to the imperfections sometimes produced in another psychological process, that of recall.

peared to be precognitive or "variant" in other ways, so that only 23 fitted the model precisely. The "variants," however, seemed to involve ESP just as convincingly as the others. (They thus showed that the designation "telepathic impressions" was narrow and arbitrary.)

Once the matters of definitions and criteria were settled, the method Stevenson followed was essentially that of comparison. His group of new cases was shown to have characteristics similar to the old ones. And so the author was able to conclude that while no individual case provided *proof* of extrasensory perception, this seemed "the best available present interpretation" of such cases. The generalization followed that if this is so, ESP experiences probably occur more frequently than has been recognized and that people may be linked to each other in hidden ways, even though this may be noticeable mostly between persons emotionally close. It was also concluded that further study of these interactions could not "fail to increase our still very small understanding of the nature of human personality" (p. 187).

Another psychiatrist, Berthold Eric Schwarz, published a book in 1971 based on a unique method of case collecting. It was essentially a diary method, which began at the birth of his first child, Lisa, and recorded each episode that seemed telepathic between the child and her parents until she reached the age of 9. The same kind of record was kept from the birth of the second child, Eric, until he was 7 years and 9 months of age. When the book was written, 504 episodes had been recorded.

As a second part of his method, Schwarz analyzed the episodes in various ways, both psychological and psychiatric. General observations included the fact that in most instances the episodes took place when children and parents were in a state of rapport; that no conscious control was evidenced; and that the episodes seemed to occur most often at the "intersection of the parents' and child's emotional needs" (p. 222). Schwarz felt that a parent can learn to recognize and develop telepathic ability between himself and others. While the criteria for telepathy that he used were broad and in some instances conjectural, at least the method he used with his children appeared to give strong anecdotal evidence of ESP.

A still more recent study of spontaneous cases was reported by John Palmer and Michael Dennis (1975). In this study the method used was adapted to the objective, which was an attempt to get a representative sample of psychic experiences in the general population and their frequency of occurrence. For practical reasons the attempt was limited to a single community, that of Charlottesville, Virginia, and suburbs.

The first step in the method was to procure the names of a thousand persons randomly selected, 700 from the City Directory, 300 from the University of Virginia Student Directory. The names from the City Directory were obtained by door-to-door canvassing of all numbered street addresses, and names of any students among them were excluded from the 300 taken from the Student Directory.

Next, a complicated questionnaire, covering too many points to be listed in detail here, was mailed to those on this list of 1,000 names. Something of the range of items covered, however, is indicated by the five categories of questions asked. They were (a) demographic, ranging from sex and marital status to education and income levels; (b) experiences and practices of possible relevance to psi, such as dream recall, drug usage, etc.; (c) psychic experiences ranging from *déjà vu* to out-of-body experiences and hauntings; (d) attitudes toward the occult, survival, parapsychology, etc.; (e) sociological questions concerning the effects and possible values of psychic experiences. Usable questionnaires were returned by 89 percent of the students and 51 percent of the town sample. The numbers in the various categories obviously could be used for computer analysis of the various topics. A few generalizations were reported, e.g., that *déjà vu* experiences were more frequent among younger than older persons and that more women than men reported experiences occurring when awake. The percentage of persons reporting apparitional (visual) experiences were equally balanced with tactile and auditory ones. Students reported more out-of-body experiences than did the townspeople and also a greater use of drugs. Significantly related to drugs were the numbers reporting out-of-body experiences and seeing the aura. These were also greatest among the student group. Some tendency was shown for the same people to have more than one kind of psychic experience and for psychic experiences to be most prevalent among those who reported good dream recall and mystical experiences.

SUMMING UP

As was remarked at the beginning of the chapter, case studies have been peripheral to the main advances in parapsychology regardless of the methods used. This has been so, first of all, because of the inherent weakness of case material, which is impossible to authenticate perfectly and difficult to interpret exactly. The early attempt to strengthen the experiences by careful authentication went as far as the method permitted to establish its thesis. That thesis was that telepathy does occur. But the evidence from the cases was largely ignored by the scholarly world, as was also the possible significance of experiences that "came true," until experimental evidence for both telepathy and precognition was produced. Even with that evidence, acceptance has come only gradually.

The situation regarding psi apparitions and their interpretation is different. Even yet, no direct experimental study of them has been made. But after the establishment of psi experimentally, they fell in line as belonging to one of the forms psi takes in consciousness—that of hallucinatory effects.

The reason why later studies have remained peripheral is, first of all, because *science in general* has now advanced from the anecdotal stage to the experimental, so that material of this kind can no longer be used to prove a point, although it still may have suggestive value in showing the way nature *seems* to be going about her business. But naturally, perhaps, the age-old reverence for authentication has lingered on and methods, to a large extent, have been directed mainly to collecting and authenticating cases for only vague reasons like "an inquiry into possible psychological motives" (Salter, 1960, p. 93). Stevenson and Palmer were among the few who had more specific objectives. Green (1960) and Dale, White, and Murphy (1962) recognized the need for wider analysis of significant characteristics in spontaneous material, and my own attempt was to get a broader viewpoint at the expense of the old fixation on authentication of individual cases; but so far that fixation has been too strong for all but one investigator, Sannwald (1963).

However, in a general way not easy to pin down, the atmosphere surrounding spontaneous cases may be changing a bit. At least one experimental parapsychologist (Stanford, 1974a, 1974b) has even attempted to reverse the process and go from experiments to cases and to apply certain insights derived from experimental findings to more obscure spontaneous experiences which earlier, and certainly by the older criteria, would not have been considered among the possible instances of spontaneous psi. They are those tantalizing occurrences in which an apparent coincidence could mean that psi had operated "under cover," as it were. But such a conjecture could not have been made until the old blinders regarding the criteria for cases worthy of study were lifted. Even so, of course, connections such as Stanford suggests—like points made in other case studies—must remain in the realm of conjecture until some way is found to check experimentally just how much in such cases is only a nonsignificant coincidence and how much is actual psi.

And this thought brings up the reason why case studies must always be peripheral. They never *prove* anything, by themselves. They only suggest. Originally, cases suggested that psi occurs. They still suggest a great deal about the process of psi, even in ways, areas, and degrees not as yet very clearly recognized. (As one of the simpler instances, outstanding "sensitives" suggest greater degrees of both ESP and PK than have yet been established by reliable methods.)

Case studies, then, if pursued by insightful methods, can still have a useful function, even if peripheral. They can give tentative hints on which the slower methods of experimentation can capitalize. Besides that, the results of their study can afford a measure of relief and satisfaction to persons baffled by psi experiences of their own. Such persons need not await the time of absolutely definitive scientific answers or be deterred entirely because the material is anecdotal.

REFERENCES

Barker, J. C. Premonitions of the Aberfan disaster. *Journal of the Society for Psychical Research*, 1967, **44**, 169–181.

Besterman, T. Report of an inquiry into precognitive dreams. *Proceedings of the Society for Psychical Research*, 1932–33, **41**, 186–204.

Dale, L. A., White, R., and Murphy, G. A selection of cases from a recent survey of spontaneous ESP phenomena. *Journal of the American Society for Psychical Research*, 1962, **56**, 3–47.

Dunne, J. W. *An Experiment with Time*. New York: Macmillan, 1927.

Green, C. Analysis of spontaneous cases. *Proceedings of the Society for Psychical Research*, 1960, **53**, 97–161.

Gurney, E., Myers, F. W. H., and Podmore, F. *Phantasms of the Living*. London: Trübner, 1886. 2 vols.

Hart, H. ESP projection: Spontaneous cases and the experimental method. *Journal of the American Society for Psychical Research*, 1954, **48**, 121–146.

Hart, H. Six theories about apparitions. *Proceedings of the Society for Psychical Research*, 1956, **50**, 153–239.

Heywood, R. Immediate background to Celia Green's analysis of spontaneous cases. *Proceedings of the Society for Psychical Research*, 1960, **53**, 94–96.

Palmer, J., and Dennis, M. A community mail survey of psychic experiences. In J. D. Morris, W. G. Roll, and R. L. Morris (Eds.), *Research in Parapsychology 1974*, pp. 130–133. Metuchen, N.J.: Scarecrow Press, 1975.

Prince, W. F. *Noted Witnesses for Psychic Occurrences*. Boston: Boston Society for Psychic Research, 1928.

Rhine, J. B. The value of reports of spontaneous psi experiences. *Journal of Parapsychology*, 1948, **12**, 231–235.

Rhine, L. E. Subjective forms of spontaneous psi experiences. *Journal of Parapsychology*, 1953, **17**, 77–114.

Rhine, L. E. The relationship of agent and percipient in spontaneous telepathy. *Journal of Parapsychology*, 1956, **20**, 1–32. (a)

Rhine, L. E. Hallucinatory psi experiences. I. An introductory survey. *Journal of Parapsychology*, 1956, **20**, 233–256. (b)

Rhine, L. E. Hallucinatory psi experiences. II. The initiative of the percipient in hallucinations of the living, the dying, and the dead. *Journal of Parapsychology*, 1957, **21**, 13–46. (a)

Rhine, L. E. Hallucinatory psi experiences. III. The intention of the agent and the dramatizing tendency of the percipient. *Journal of Parapsychology*, 1957, **21**, 186–226. (b)

Rhine, L. E. Psychological processes in ESP experiences. Part I. Waking experiences. *Journal of Parapsychology*, 1962, **26**, 88–111. (a)

Rhine, L. E. Psychological processes in ESP experiences. Part II. Dreams. *Journal of Parapsychology*, 1962, **26**, 172–199. (b)

Rhine, L. E. Spontaneous physical effects and the psi process. *Journal of Parapsychology*, 1963, **27**, 84–122.

Salter, W. H. Historical background to 1959 report on enquiry into spontaneous cases. *Proceedings of the Society for Psychical Research*, 1960, **53**, 83–93.

Saltmarsh, H. F. Report on cases of apparent precognition. *Proceedings of the Society for Psychical Research*, 1934, **42**, 49–103.

Sannwald, G. On the psychology of spontaneous paranormal phenomena. *International Journal of Parapsychology*, 1963, 5, 274–292.

Schwarz, B. E. *Parent-Child Telepathy*. New York: Garrett Publications, 1971.

Sidgwick, E. M. (Mrs. H.) On the evidence for premonitions. *Proceedings of the Society for Psychical Research*, 1888–89, 5, 288–354.

Sidgwick, H., and Committee. Report on the census of hallucinations. *Proceedings of the Society for Psychical Research*, 1894, 10, 25–422.

Stanford, R. G. An experimentally testable model for spontaneous psi events. I. Extrasensory events. *Journal of the American Society for Psychical Research*, 1974, 68, 34–57. (a)

Stanford, R. G. An experimentally testable model for spontaneous psi events. II. Psychokinetic events. *Journal of the American Society for Psychical Research*, 1974, 68, 321–356. (b)

Stevenson, I. Precognition of disasters. *Journal of the American Society for Psychical Research*, 1970, 64, 187–210. (a)

Stevenson, I. *Telepathic Impressions*. Charlottesville: University of Virginia Press, 1970. (b)

Tyrrell, G. N. M. *Apparitions*. London: The Society for Psychical Research, 1942. (Republished by Macmillan in 1962.)

West, D. J. The investigation of spontaneous cases. *Proceedings of the Society for Psychical Research*, 1946–49, 48, 264–300.

2

Statistical Methods in Parapsychological Research

Donald S. Burdick and Edward F. Kelly

INTRODUCTION

Quantitative methods entered parapsychology at a very early date. The recognition that many aspects of psychical phenomena could be investigated by statistical study of simple card-guessing and dice-throwing experiments goes back at least to Francis Bacon (Bell, 1964), and the first systematic attempts to apply statistical theory to such experiments occurred within just a few years of the founding of the Society for Psychical Research in London in 1882 (Edgeworth, 1885, 1886; Richet, 1884).

Although qualitative studies of spontaneous psi occurrences and the phenomena of mediumship continued to dominate the literature for the next half century, the quantitative tradition steadily gained force, ultimately crystallizing in the work of J. B. Rhine and his associates at Duke University in the 1930s. The Rhine school, building on earlier quantitative efforts, institutionalized a family of simple experimental and analytical methods based upon a "standard" ESP card deck, containing five each of five geometric symbols.

The first systematic report of the Duke work (Rhine, 1934) quickly generated a very active controversy, as critics attacked numerous aspects of Rhine's experimental and analytical methodology. Much of this criticism was ill-founded, but some was not, and the ensuing period was a very healthy one for parapsychology, in which all aspects of the methodology were vigorously tested and, where necessary, improved.   In addition, the controversy led directly to a number of technical developments in statistical theory itself.

More detailed treatments of the early history of quantitative parapsychology can be found in Rhine, Pratt, Stuart, Smith, and Greenwood (1940) and in McVaugh and Mauskopf (1976).   For present purposes it will suffice to point out that as early as 1937 the statistical aspects of the controversy were largely settled.   The incumbent president of the Institute of Mathematical Statistics declared in a public statement:

> . . . assuming that the experiments have been properly performed, the statistical analysis is essentially valid.   If the Rhine investigation is to be fairly attacked it must be on other than mathematical grounds (Camp, 1937).

Despite Camp's statement, statistical criticism persisted, and even today long-discredited objections to the basic Rhine methodology are occasionally resurrected.   Nevertheless, by 1940 the volume of criticism had diminished to the point where the parapsychologists felt that the period of controversy was behind them and they could go on about their experimental business without further interruption.   This sentiment is clearly expressed by the authors of *Extrasensory Perception After Sixty Years* (Rhine et al., 1940):

> In the main, the mathematical requirements of the ESP research have been taken care of by the mathematical procedures that were generally available, together with the special adaptations that have already been reviewed in Chapter II. *At present then, the need for further statistical advances is not an acute one so far as the main problems of the ESP investigations are concerned* (p. 349; italics ours).

We stress the final sentence, because it seems to us to anticipate an unfortunate characteristic of the ensuing period of research.   Doubtless there were other contributing factors (for example, the dislocations produced by World War II and the loss of some key personnel), but most importantly many parapsychologists seemed to construe the endorsements of the statisticians in an excessively absolutist fashion.   Although new statistical techniques appeared in the parapsychology literature from time to time, the period of active dialogue and development largely ceased, and the experimental work went forward for many years on an essentially fixed body of methods, isolated from the rapidly developing methodological specialties.

In our view this kind of professional isolation was both unnecessary and unhealthy.   On the one hand the modern researcher confronting the parapsychological literature for the first time encounters even in much recent work outdated statistical procedures and terminologies which may obscure the fundamental soundness of given pieces of research. Much more importantly, parapsychologists have so far barely begun to make effective use of the greatly expanded resources of contemporary research methodology.

Accordingly, one of the main themes of this chapter is to stress the importance of reestablishing the kind of active dialogue between experimenter and statistician that existed in the 30s and early 40s. Indeed, we hope this chapter will exemplify the potential benefits of such dialogue. Fortunately, this theme is by no means original with us, and there are abundant signs of methodological renaissance in the field. We hope in this chapter to provide a benchmark for these developments by taking stock of the present statistical resources of the field in a way that will contribute maximally to their effective deployment in future research.

The core of our presentation is therefore an updated and integrated catalog of statistical procedures particularly useful in the analysis of "typical" psi experiments. We will draw from various sources such as previous catalogs (Greenwood and Stuart, 1937; Rhine et al., 1940; Rhine and Pratt, 1957), scattered reports in the parapsychological literature, and other methodological developments which we feel have relevance to psi research. Our principal objectives in developing this material are:

1. To provide a reasonably complete though not exhaustive inventory of generally useful procedures, in sufficient detail for the chapter to be largely self-contained and useful as a reference. We do not present mathematical derivations in detail. References to sources of such detail are provided where appropriate;
2. to provide a coherent overall organization of available procedures, so that each particular technique is located appropriately in the more general scheme;
3. to present material in greater generality than has been typical of the parapsychology literature, in order to encourage diversification of experimental materials and methods;
4. to emphasize connections among topics and in particular to emphasize the essential continuity of forced-choice and free-response methods;
5. to introduce at least at the level of suggested directions for further investigation a number of new topics and analysis procedures;
6. to indicate how the relatively specialized procedures we will describe for analysis of parapsychological data fit into a broader perspective of modern concepts of experimental design and analysis. Here we can only provide general suggestions and pointers, since we cannot possibly incorporate the content of a sound basic course in the space available to us.

Thus, we will necessarily presume some familiarity with the central concepts and techniques of statistics, at a level that might typically be encountered in a college-level elementary introduction, plus willingness to work through difficult sections. To complete the preliminaries, we must also remind the reader that we are not generally concerned here with matters of experimental procedure or conditions. As always, statistical results can provide useful guides for decision-making, but the interpretation of an observed result will depend ultimately on the conditions of the experiment, and such matters lie largely outside the scope of this chapter. To put it another way, we will assume that the data we are analyzing have been collected under sound experimental conditions, so that the failure of null hypotheses to adequately explain the data can be attributed to psi rather than to sensory leakage or other experimental artifacts.

Our first step toward providing an organizational framework is to classify experiments as forced choice or free response. A forced-choice experiment consists of a sequence of trials. On each trial the subject produces a response consisting of one of a fixed set of possible targets. If the subject's response agrees with the actual target for that trial, a hit is scored. Otherwise, the result is a miss. Card-guessing ESP experiments and dice-tossing PK experiments both fall into this category. In its restriction of the subject's responses to a fixed number of specified alternatives, the forced-choice experiment resembles a multiple choice examination.

A free-response experiment does not limit the subject to a fixed list of specified responses. It does usually have a fixed set of targets such as target persons or pictures, but the subject may draw a picture, describe the target verbally, or respond in some other way that is not tantamount to a selection from a specified set of alternatives. To continue our analogy with examinations, a free-response experiment resembles an essay examination. The fact that a judge is needed to assess agreement between protocols and targets corresponds to the fact that essay examinations are difficult to grade.

Although a clear distinction can be drawn between forced-choice and free-response experiments, the statistical methods for analyzing them are remarkably similar. Our discussion of these methods will be given first in the setting of forced-choice experiments because of the greater simplicity of that setting.

FORCED-CHOICE EXPERIMENTS

To begin, consider the following gross model of the entire performance of a single respondent ("subject"):

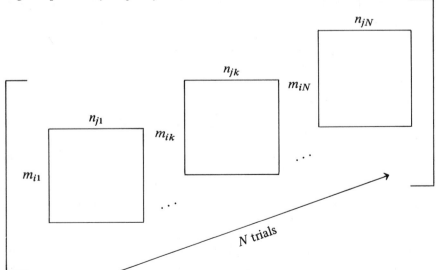

Here n_{jk} stands for the target on trial k, and m_{ik} for the corresponding response. The target might be a specified die face in a PK task or a specified symbol in an ESP task. Correspondingly, the response might be the die face actually obtained or the symbol which the respondent actually chose. Both targets and responses are drawn from a fixed stock of s possibilities. The experimenter generally has control over the target order, and the process by which a target-order is generated can provide the basis for statistical tests. In the model each successive matrix or "frame" represents a single trial; for the usual case in which each trial consists of a single response, each matrix can be imagined as containing all zeroes except for a "1" in the cell corresponding to the pairing of target and response observed on that trial. The entire experiment consists of a sequence of N such trials. The trials might further be organized into natural blocks or *runs*, typically of equal length, representing units of testing (passes through randomized decks of ESP cards, for example). In more general cases there could also be multiple entries in the appropriate column of each trial matrix (for example, if multiple respondents are guessing at a single target order), and for cases of this type it will later prove convenient to conceive of the experiment as consisting of two separate but parallel orders, a response-by-trial order and a target-by-trial order.

Much detail is deliberately left out of this model—for example, details concerning the type of experiment, processes generating the target order, and so on. At this level of abstraction, it serves a useful heuristic function in quickly directing our attention to the basic dimensions of the experimental performance and thus to the corresponding kinds of analytical procedure we will want to develop. In particular it emphasizes aspects of the data structure that in our view have not so far received sufficient attention in parapsychological research.

Synchronic Analyses (Analyses Ignoring Sequential Structure)

Overall Test of Association Between Targets and Responses. Under the null hypothesis of no psi, there should be no evidence of any kind of systematic association between responses and targets. The most appropriate test of this hypothesis can be carried out in two stages: First, accumulate the performance over all trials to form a single overall response-target matrix, often called a "confusion matrix." (We strongly recommend reporting forced-choice data in this form, particularly in extended studies with exceptional performers.) Second, test for independence of the rows and columns of the confusion matrix. The general procedure is Pearson's chi-square test of association for contingency tables.[1] Good introductions to the theory and practice of such tests can be found in many standard texts, for example, Hays (1963, Chap. 17). Here we shall simply outline the computational scheme.

[1]This test is also recommended as the most appropriate overall test by Greenwood and Stuart (1937), but it has rarely been used this way in parapsychology. For the initiate, we remark that the open-deck and closed-deck situations are asymptotically equivalent (Roy and Mitra, 1956).

Suppose we have a confusion matrix C with entries c_{ij} representing the frequency of pairing of response i with target j. The expected frequency e_{ij} for the ij cell is determined by the relation

$$e_{ij} = \frac{M_i N_j}{N} \tag{1}$$

where M_i is the total (marginal) frequency of response i, N_j is the marginal frequency of target j, and N is the total number of trials.

Now the χ^2 statistic can be computed from

$$\chi^2 = \sum_{i=1}^{s} \sum_{j=1}^{s} \frac{(c_{ij} - e_{ij})^2}{e_{ij}} \tag{2}$$

Under appropriate conditions χ^2 follows the chi-square distribution with $(s - 1)(s - 1)$ degrees of freedom, and an observed result can be evaluated simply by entering the ordinary chi-square tables for an upper-tail test. Although more complex rules are sometimes given, a simple and conservative rule for applicability of the test would be to require that all cells have expected values over 5.

In the special case of a 2-by-2 table, the deviations $(c_{ij} - e_{ij})$ are all equal except for sign and should be reduced in absolute value by .5 (Yates' correction for continuity) before squaring. If in addition any e_{ij} is close to zero, it may be desirable and feasible to compute the exact probability of obtaining by chance a table as extreme as that observed, or more so (Fisher's exact test). These matters, plus a variety of tests of strength of association, are discussed in detail in Hays (1963, Chap. 17).

A significant overall association between targets and responses is evidence for psi and reflects in general the presence of either or both of two main kinds of effects: systematic excess or deficiency of observations on the main diagonal (direct hitting); and systematic structure in the off-diagonal cells, indicating consistent but erroneous association of targets and responses (consistent missing). We now present ways of investigating these possibilities.

Quantity of Direct Hits. This topic has been by a wide margin the dominant focus of traditional research, and in fact most discussions of the methodology in the parapsychology literature are specialized to a few cases corresponding to "standard" experimental procedures.

In this section, however, we will systematically develop a unified general framework for analysis of forced-choice hitting, which will include the "standard" situations as special cases. We hope thereby to encourage experimentation with more diverse sorts of target materials and to expose clearly the underlying connections between the general theory of forced-choice analysis and the various methods for analysis of free-response data which will be discussed subsequently.

The True Binomial or "Open-Deck" Situation with Equal-Probability Targets.
To begin with the simplest case, suppose we have s equiprobable targets sampled repeatedly and at random. For example, target orders for an ESP task might be generated (a) using a random number table; (b) by selection from a very large pool containing equal frequencies of the targets, with or without replacement after each trial; or (c) by sampling from a small pool, but replacing the target and rerandomizing the pool after each trial.

Under these or like conditions, successive trials may be regarded as independent, and the outcome of each can be classified as either a hit or a miss. Furthermore, the probability p of a hit is constant over trials, and $p = 1/s$. If we define X as the number of hits in N trials, then X is a random variable which follows the binomial distribution. Specifically,

$$p(X = x) = \binom{N}{x} p^x (1 - p)^{N-x} \tag{3}$$

where $\binom{N}{x}$ is the number of ways of obtaining x hits in N trials and equals $N!/(x!)\,(N-x)!$; and the rest of expression (3) is the probability of any single arrangement of N trials containing exactly x hits.

If in a given N-trial experiment we observe x hits, we actually need to evaluate the probability of observing x or more; hence, letting $q = 1 - p$

$$p(X \geqslant x) = \sum_{r=x}^{N} \binom{N}{r} p^r q^{N-r} \tag{4}$$

For small N, or extreme x, or with the aid of a computer, exact computation of binomial probabilities may be feasible. In most circumstances, however, it is appropriate and convenient to utilize a different approach which leads to results closely approximating the exact probabilities. If we let $E[X]$ be the mean, or expected value, or mean chance expectation (MCE) of X, and σ_X^2 be the variance of X, then as is shown in most introductory texts (for example, Hays, 1963, pp. 169, 183, 227),

$$E[X] = Np \tag{5}$$

$$\sigma_X^2 = Npq \tag{6}$$

and

$$p(X \geqslant x) \cong p(Z \geqslant z) \tag{7}$$

where

$$z = \frac{x - Np \pm .5}{\sqrt{Npq}} \quad \text{and } Z \text{ is the standard normal deviate.}$$

The value of z is thus a total deviation (reduced by .5 in absolute value to adjust for a continuous approximation to a discrete distribution) divided by a standard deviation, and it is evaluated simply by entering the usual table of the cumulative normal probability at $Z = z$, giving the upper-tail probability.[2]

It can be shown that as N becomes large the binomial distribution converges upon the normal for any p. However, for fixed N the approximations deteriorate as p decreases from .5, leading to increased skewness (asymmetry) of the binomial. In general, the normal approximation will be quite good if Np is greater than 10, and p is not extremely small. For very small p, say .05 or less, and moderate values of N (such that Np is less than 10), calculations may be simplified using the Poisson approximation to the binomial (Mood and Graybill, 1963, p. 70). For very large N the normal approximation again takes over.

In the next section we give more detailed results on quality of approximation for the special case $\ell = N = 25$ and $p = 1/5$, which figured heavily in the early debates.[3]

The Basic "Closed-Deck" Situation with Equal-Probability Targets. In practice, especially beginning with the work of Rhine's group at Duke, the target order for each run was typically generated not by independent random selection of successive targets but through randomization (by thorough shuffling or other means) of a standard "closed" deck containing five each of five different target cards. Nevertheless, the hit results were evaluated by the binomial methods given above. Critics correctly pointed out that the stated conditions do not precisely meet the assumptions of the binomial model, because of the correlations introduced among successive targets in the fixed pack. This led to deeper mathematical and empirical study of the closed-deck situation and eventually to slight revisions of method for the closed-deck case. We briefly review these developments here.

The fundamental difference between the models lies in the source of randomness involved. In the "open-deck" situation each successive target (or response)

---

[2]Equivalently, we could analyze the mean run score, assuming runs of equal length. Suppose there are m runs of length ℓ, so that $N = \ell m$. Then by the above method

$$z = \frac{x - \ell mp \pm .5}{\sqrt{\ell mpq}}.$$

By the run-score method

$$z = \frac{x/m - \ell p \pm .5}{\sqrt{\ell pq/m}} = \frac{x - \ell mp \pm .5}{\sqrt{\ell mpq}},$$

so the results are identical. However, the run-score form is more likely to raise a question about the use of the theoretical standard deviation vs. the observed (cf. Kellogg and other early critics). We state flatly that the use of the theoretical SD is perfectly appropriate here, and in fact, the observed variance is itself a random variable which can be tested for departure from theoretical expectation (see section below entitled "Central Tendency").

[3]Another topic, which we shall not discuss here, is the use of Charlier's series to provide more exact approximations in cases where direct calculation is ruled out, but the normal approximation is thought inadequate. See Rhine et al. (1940, p. 364).

must be chosen at random, independently of all others. In the "closed-deck" case, however, the composition of the target series for each run is taken as fixed, and we randomize only its order; the question then arises as to precisely what theoretical distribution of hit scores arises under these conditions.

It was quickly demonstrated that under the standard test conditions with absence of trial-by-trial feedback, $p = 1/s$ on every trial irrespective of aspects of target and response orders (Greenwood and Stuart, 1937; Herr, 1938; Stuart and Greenwood, 1937.) Thus the binomial expectation continues to hold for equal-probability targets under the closed-deck model.

However, as shown by Greenwood (1938a) for the "standard" 5×5 deck and (1938c) for the general $r \times s$ deck containing r each of s symbols, the interdependence among successive targets *does* alter the variance, in a manner dependent on the observed frequencies of the possible responses. Specifically, the variance ranges from zero when the same response occurs on every trial, to a maximum when all responses occur equally often. The first part of this statement is self-evident, and the second part may be seen in the following way: As shown by Greenwood (1938c) and Greville (1941), for the general $r \times s$ case in which the unit of randomization is a deck of ℓ cards, and $N = \ell = rs$,

$$\sigma^2 = \frac{r}{\ell(\ell - 1)} \left(\ell^2 - \sum_{i=1}^{s} M_i^2 \right) \tag{8}$$

where M_i is the number of responses with symbol i. This variance will be maximized when $\Sigma_{i=1}^{s}, M_i^2$ is minimized, and this occurs in the event all M_i are equal. Then

$$\sigma_{max}^2 = \frac{r}{\ell(\ell - 1)} (\ell^2 - sr^2) \tag{9}$$

This situation, the "worst-case," was called the matching hypothesis, because it corresponds to the situation in which one $r \times s$ deck is shuffled against another. The next question naturally concerns the relative magnitude of the matching variance and the binomial variance. A little further algebra reveals that in the general $r \times s$ case the maximum closed-deck variance is always $\ell/(\ell - 1)$ times the corresponding binomial. Thus as the deck size becomes larger the matching variance converges toward the binomial.

In analyzing direct hits in a series comprised of multiple closed-deck runs, one is therefore faced with three options in selecting a denominator for the z-score: (a) assume the approximately correct binomial variance, Npq; (b) assume the maximum possible (matching) variance, $\ell Npq/(\ell - 1)$; or (c) compute the exact variance for each run, based on the observed call frequencies, and sum over successive runs.

Clearly, strategy (b) will always lead to a conservative test, and the matching variance is in any event generally only slightly larger than the binomial, so that the penalty for conservatism is in this respect minor. Even for a deck as small as the "standard" 5×5, for example, $\sigma_{max}^2 = 4.16$ vs. 4.00 for the binomial, and the conservative rule thus multiplies the binomial SD by $\sqrt{4.16/4.00} = 1.02$.

The potential advantage of strategy (c), which might offset the associated increase in (manual) computational difficulty, is that it would capitalize on the reduced variance that would be associated with extreme calling patterns to yield a more powerful test. More generally, unlike either of the other methods, it would lead in any given case to an exact value for the variance. (We should also remark here that formula (8) itself is a special case of more general formulas to be presented subsequently.)

We have thus established that the binomial and matching hypothesis models will lead to direct-hit analyses that are only trivially different for typical closed target-decks. We still have an open question, however, about the characteristics of the "true" chance run-score distributions that would arise empirically from the closed-deck model, under conditions representative of actual experiments, and the detailed relationships holding among these empirical distributions and our three mathematical models—binomial, matching, and normal.

These questions were studied most intensely in the context of the $\ell = 25$, $p = 1/5$ case, which was naturally of central importance in the early controversy. The details of that situation were very carefully scrutinized, both mathematically and empirically. Greville (1938, for the 5×5 deck; 1941, for decks of arbitrary composition) carried the analysis of the matching model a step further by working out the exact frequency distribution of run-scores under the matching hypothesis and found that the matching p-values are nearly identical to their binomial counterparts. (This was perhaps to be expected since the means are identical and the variances nearly so, but note that these can be obtained from the frequency distribution, but not vice-versa.)

The normal distribution is of course symmetric, but with $p = 1/5$ and ℓ only 25, the binomial is still slightly skewed to the right, and the matching distribution slightly more so. What about the empirical distribution of run-scores under conditions which seem to exclude psi effects?[4]

Greenwood (1938b) attempted to answer this question (and several others) by carefully constructing a control series of 500,000 trials (20,000 runs). His procedure involved matching 100 prerecorded call runs (the first 20 runs of each of 5 high-scoring subjects) repeatedly against target orders generated by a multiperson shuffling scheme. The results in brief indicated that there was nothing

---

[4]In light of subsequent experimental work typified by Morris (1968), it no longer seems so clear that Greenwood's investigation can safely be regarded as free of psi effects, but the results are sufficiently in line with those of the surrounding theoretical studies to give moderate assurance that the psi effects, if any, must be rather slight.

inherently hit-producing in the call-sequences of the special subjects (as some critics had argued) and that the "true" chance run-score distribution under standard conditions of ESP guessing lies between the binomial and matching models. In fact, the chance distribution could not be statistically distinguished from either of these models in 20,000 runs, although it appeared to lie closer to the binomial.

The (symmetrical) normal approximation, however, slightly underestimates the probability of large run-scores, and the underestimation is clearly large enough to lead to highly significant departures of a chance empirical distribution from normal expectation in even moderate numbers of runs. The net implications are these:

1. For testing the distribution of run-scores (see section below entitled "Overall Test"), either in the 5 × 5 case or more generally for any (open or closed) deck such that ℓp is less than 10, it is clearly better to use either the matching or binomial probabilities as the basis of the test rather than the normal. The binomial probabilities can be obtained from equation (3) or from tables (Harvard Computation Laboratory, 1955) and the slightly conservative matching probabilities, at cost of greater labor, from Greville (1941).

2. The matching model is essentially identical with its simpler rival, the binomial. Both fit the empirical closed deck situation very closely, and both are adequately approximated for most purposes by the normal. In particular, the basic method for evaluating direct hits is still safe, because it essentially treats a set of short runs as one long run, and the approximation improves rapidly with increasing N.

The Generalized "Closed-Deck" Situation–Matching 2 Decks of Arbitrary Composition. The next level of generality is reached if we consider the matching of two closed decks of completely arbitrary composition. One corresponds to a target order, and the other to a set of responses made to that order.

A general treatment of this situation is provided by Greville (1941), who obtained the exact frequency distribution and from it the mean and variance. This approach is relatively difficult, however, and provides more information than will generally be useful. We will base our discussion rather on the paper by Stevens (1939a), which derives the mean and variance by a much simpler and more direct argument. In our (modified) notation, with $N = \ell$,

$$E[X] = \frac{1}{N} \sum_{i=1}^{s} M_i N_i \qquad (10)$$

$$\sigma_X^2 = \frac{1}{N^2(N-1)} \left[\left(\sum_{i=1}^{s} M_i N_i \right)^2 - N \sum_{i=1}^{s} M_i N_i (M_i + N_i) + N^2 \sum_{i=1}^{s} M_i N_i \right] \qquad (11)$$

where symbol i appears as a target N_i times and as a response M_i times. Several things should be pointed out about these results:

1. Various specialized closed-deck results given above can be obtained directly from the Stevens formulas. For example, it is readily seen that in the $r \times s$ closed deck where $N_1 = N_2 = \ldots = N_s = r$, $E[X] = r$. Somewhat less readily, it can be seen that (8) is a special case of (11).

2. The Stevens formulas provide a precise basis for evaluating direct hits in any single-response performance utilizing closed target decks, whatever the structure of the target decks and whatever the response pattern. As noted earlier for the special case of the $r \times s$ deck, the formulas must be applied run-by-run to obtain the correct overall variance, but the extra labor could pay off in the presence of extreme calling patterns, which reduce the theoretical variance considerably.

3. The Stevens results also open up extended possibilities for experimental work. In particular, we are free to construct target decks containing arbitrary proportions of the symbols. Thus the structure of the target decks can be freely manipulated and the effects of such manipulations on ESP performance studied. For some reasons why this might be useful see Scott (1961), and for an exploratory investigation along these lines see Child and Kelly (1973).

Matching Open or Closed Decks of Arbitrary Composition—"Multiple-Response" Case. The highest level of generality is reached if we consider the problem of matching multiple decks of arbitrary composition, *all but one of which have fixed orders.* This problem was solved by Greville (1944), in response to the so-called stacking effect problem which arises when multiple respondents guess a single target order, as in the Zenith radio experiments. The problem, of course, is that respondents may tend to possess shared guessing habits which happen to coincide with the structure of the single target order so as to produce a spurious apparent excess or deficiency of hits, if the guesses are treated as independent. That is, the independent-guess treatment spuriously increases the number of trials.

Greville's multiple-deck problem is clearly an appropriate model of the stacking situation. However, it is essential to realize that it is also an appropriate model for a wide variety of other situations which have arisen (or might profitably arise) in parapsychological research. These applications, many previously unrecognized, include a variety of situations in free-response work and some novel procedures for forced-choice experimentation. Thus Greville's procedure is the cornerstone of our treatment of the analysis of direct hits, and we will describe it in some generality and detail.

We will first attempt to convey a sense of the statistical rationale of the procedure. Imagine that we have completed a forced-choice experiment with multiple respondents guessing at a single target order. We now have before us a response X trial matrix. That is, each column represents a trial, and the entry in each row within that column is the total number of responses with the corresponding symbol. In addition, we have the target order itself, that is, a target X trial array, or, more compactly, the sequential list of targets. The response array is taken as fixed (in fact, it is immaterial where it came from, and this underlies the great generality of the method). The statistical problem is to evaluate the probability of obtaining a number of hits as large or larger than that observed, *given the response array.*

As usual, there are two cases to consider, depending on the source of randomness in the target order. In the open-deck case, a mean and variance for number of hits can be obtained separately for each trial and summed over consecutive trials to obtain the total mean and variance for the experiment. The more difficult closed-deck cases require a different approach, in which we investigate the probability of the observed score relative to the total distribution of scores that would be obtained under all possible permutations of the target order. The closed-deck model leads to somewhat different expressions for the mean and variance of the total score and hence to a different assessment of the probability for a given observed score. Thus the model one chooses is important and especially so when N is small; we will return to this question later, especially in discussing free-response methods.

To expedite both understanding and computation, we have modified Greville's formulas to more directly parallel forms. The notation, computational scheme, and illustrations of the application of the methods to data from a wide variety of experiments appear later in the chapter (Appendix A) by which point the full generality of the techniques will best be appreciated. It will still be helpful to refer to that section in working through the remainder of this one, as we discuss some general properties of the Greville methods.

First, we emphasize that the Greville results include all our previous results as special cases. In the closed-deck case with one response per trial, some algebra shows that Greville's equations reduce to the Stevens formulas and hence cover all cases covered by Stevens' method. (Be sure to note also that Greville's closed-deck equations apply to the unit of randomization, i.e., the run.) In the open-deck case, with equal-probability targets and one response per trial, Greville's formulas reduce all the way down to the standard binomial expressions for mean and variance.

In short, these single-response cases can be handled (and probably would be if computations are done manually) by simplified versions of Greville's formulas. Nevertheless, it is useful to recognize that all the cases can be treated within the unified framework. Appendix A gives both the general calculations and the simplified expressions for a wide variety of cases. It is also worth noting that since the Greville calculations can become rather cumbrous with increasing N and s, a computer program implementing Greville's method would be very handy, and for such a program the differences among the various cases would be computationally inconsequential.

Meanwhile, the cases of maximum difficulty and interest are the multiple-response cases, and we will now attempt to convey some feeling for the properties of the methods in these cases. To simplify matters we will discuss the equal-p open-deck case (once the equal-p case is clear, the extension to unequal-p is reasonably clear but very hard to describe compactly; and the generalizations we will offer for the open-deck case hold at least approximately for the closed-deck case as well, although some qualifications will be made subsequently).

First note that the expectation depends only on the total of the entries in the response array, since the p_i's are by design all equal to p, and p comes outside the summation. The variance on the other hand, is greatly affected by the distribution of responses. It can be seen from formula (30) that the variance will be maximized when on each trial all responses are attached to one target only (in the closed-deck case there is a further condition, that each target must be so favored equally often). This is because the sum of sums-of-squares is maximized and all cross-product terms go to zero. Correspondingly, the variance reduces to zero when on each trial every target receives the same number of responses.

The response matrix can be pictured as containing bets about the targets, trial by trial. The bet for each trial (column) is represented in the distribution of numbers within that column. No matter where those numbers came from, the interpretation is the same: A uniform distribution across the rows is effectively a pass, or no bet at all, and allocating everything to a single target is the strongest possible bet. Intermediate cases represent bets of strength corresponding to their associated variances. The successive bets are used by Greville's method essentially to *weight* the trials (cf. Burdick and Roll, 1971). Thus a strong bet on the right target scores a lot of points; the risk is higher (inflates the variance), but if target-related information really underlies the bet, the payoff will more than compensate for the increased variance.

The best result obtainable by Greville's method occurs when the strongest bet in every trial is also correct. This corresponds to what would be achieved by a single perfect guesser or judge operating under the same experimental conditions. For the open-deck model the minimum p-value is thus p^N, and for the closed-deck it is

$$\frac{\prod_{i=1}^{s} N_i!}{N!}$$

The open-deck model for the same data will carry a lower minimum p-value (but that is of course no guarantee that this additional range will be utilized).

An alternative to the Greville technique, which would apply in all of the multiple-response cases, is the majority-vote technique suggested by Thouless and Brier (1970).[5] Taking the equal-p case again to simplify discussion, the majority-vote procedure simply replaces each column of the original response x trial matrix with a single response representing the collective best-bet determined by the entries in that column. In the cases we are discussing, that would be the response with the largest m_{ik}.[6] The reduced string of majority-vote responses can then be evauated by the appropriate single-response method.

This method is clearly very much simpler than the Greville technique and has somewhat similar properties, so it is worth discussing their relationships in more detail. First, note that the majority-vote procedure has the same "best-result," namely simulation of a perfect guesser or judge, and that this result occurs under the same conditions for both procedures. The important difference between the methods becomes apparent, however, as soon as misses enter the picture. Under the majority-vote procedure, every trial is like every other and is either a miss or a hit. Each additional miss therefore leads to a sharp decrement in the obtained result. By contrast, Greville's method takes account of the *degree* of hitting and missing and thus more sensitively reflects the structure of the response system. The cost of a miss, in particular, will depend on the strength of the associated bet and may therefore be very slight.

In short, the majority-vote procedure purchases computational simplicity at potentially considerable cost of sensitivity. We should point out, however, that the actual cost might depend somewhat on the source of the data. For example, in a forced-choice environment with multiple respondents, it is plausible to suppose that the tendency to select the correct target would be weakly but fairly consistently present across trials, and the structure of the response system correspondingly consistent. In that event the majority-vote results might fairly approximate those by Greville's method. If the data represent judgings of free-response material, however, we might expect a different situation to hold: Specifically, if some free-response protocols are strongly and obviously related to their corresponding targets, whereas others are not, then these differences will show up in the rankings/ratings/etc. of the judges. The "strong" trials will tend to be associated with strong bets, and so on. On current evidence this sort of thing does appear to be characteristic of free-response data, and to the extent this is true the advantage conferred by the extra sensitivity of Greville's method would become correspondingly great.

---

[5]Earlier suggestions about fixed "correction rules" (for example, to compute an independent-guess z-score and reduce it by 10% to allow for the nonindependence of the guesses) can be rejected as inappropriate.

[6]Ignoring the possible problem of ties. We will not go further into the general theory of majority-vote techniques in this chapter, nor into other topics related to possible techniques for psi-amplification. We hope to do so subsequently in another report.

We also wish briefly to indicate some further applications of Greville's method to forced-choice experimentation. As mentioned, the source of the "multiple-response" matrix is immaterial. Thus it could in fact represent the judgments of one or more respondents who on each trial allocate scores of some sort to targets, reflecting degree of confidence in each. A good system might be to allot to each respondent a total number of points, say twice the number of targets; then on each trial each respondent must allot all of his points, but in whatever way he chooses. Data of this sort could then be analyzed by Greville's multiple-response method for the corresponding case (open or closed deck, equal or unequal p).

Another large class of applications of the methods will be outlined in the next section, and they will also figure prominently throughout our discussion of free-response methods. To conclude the general discussion here, however, we need to issue a word of caution concerning the adequacy of the approximation underlying the Greville methods (see also Scott, 1972). The approximation will be good if the score distributions within trials have similar spread. Suppose now that we start with such a situation and then change one trial so that it has a markedly different distribution, for example containing a very extreme score. Thus on top of the essentially normal distribution based on the remaining trials, we superimpose a secondary peak corresponding to occasions when the extreme score represents a correct bet. In general, then, extreme fluctuations of score distribution across trials will distort the normal approximation, especially when N is very small. The approximation will improve rapidly with increasing N, particularly if the score distributions can be kept within reasonably consistent bounds. A rule of thumb that presently seems useful is to trust the approximation if the number of trials is several times the ratio of the largest to the smallest within-trial range of scores. Near-marginal results obtained under other conditions should be regarded at present with some skepticism, pending further study of the empirical properties of the method. In some cases exact enumeration of cases is readily possible (cf. Roll and Burdick, 1969; Scott, 1972), and we see possibilities for the future development of a more general enumeration algorithm. Monte-Carlo techniques can also be applied to obtain estimates of the exact probabilities. We hope to prepare a report on these matters subsequently.

Target-Sets With Given Internal Structure. The discussions so far have assumed what amount to categorical target sets with no internal structure. Each target is indivisible, and there is no a priori or assumed structure of relationships among the targets in the set. This has been the dominant tradition by far, but there has also been some investigation of target-sets that come with an assumed metric of some sort, allowing for notions of "distance" and differential credit for responses according to their distance from the designated target. The small amount of work that has been carried out with such target-sets suggests that the extra sensitivity of the generalized measures may actually capture evidence of psi that would otherwise go undetected. This kind of result is important in itself and may provide further clues to the nature of the psi process, inasmuch as it suggests that in various situations, responses may enter the "neighborhood" of the target even when they are not exactly correct. Thus the extra labor involved in analysis of this kind of data should be amply justified. The approaches of this section should be regarded as parallel to those of the next: Here we assume a metric and observe whether psi responses follow it, whereas the methods of the next section are intended to use the data to tell us what, if any, metric exists in the target set as filtered through whatever mechanisms underlie the psi processes at work in a given task.

We will first briefly outline the approaches that have so far appeared in the literature and then sketch a generalized application of Greville's method that will encompass these and numerous others. Although methods could in principle also be developed for continuous target structures (for example, a point moving with uniform random distribution within a geometric figure), we will confine ourselves here to discrete structures.

There is a class of transitional cases in which the targets have multiple attributes which can be scored independently, and no attempt is made to impose a distance metric. For example, playing cards can be treated as composed of a number attribute and a suit attribute. The target system is thus implicitly an array with 13 rows corresponding to the numbers and 4 columns corresponding to the suits. Related types of target systems would include any kind of explicit array of two or more dimensions (the more conventional target-sets amount to one-dimensional arrays). In such cases the attributes can clearly be analyzed separately by the standard methods. They can also be analyzed jointly by the same methods (for example, exact hits on playing cards with $p = \frac{1}{52}$), but the joint test and the attribute tests are not independent. An interesting question, in fact, is whether success in guessing one attribute is independent of success on the other, and this is answered by constructing the 2 X 2 table of success and failure for each attribute and testing for association (see section above entitled "Overall Test of Association Between Targets and Responses"; Foster, 1952).

An integrated system for scoring all attributes simultaneously and weighting hits according to their improbability was devised by R. A. Fisher (Saltmarsh and Soal, 1930). Assuming N *open-deck* trials on each of which k *independent* attributes are guessed, then the total score for the performance is obtained by

$$x = \sum_{i=1}^{k} (Np_i - x_i) \log p_i \qquad (12)$$

where x_i is the number of correct guesses of attribute i, with probability p_i. By the structure of the scoring system, MCE is zero, and

$$\sigma_x^2 = N \sum_{i=1}^{k} p_i q_i (\log p_i)^2 \qquad (13)$$

For a worked example, see Rhine et al. (1940, p. 385).

We know of only three attempts in the literature to develop some kind of distance measure. All three assume open-deck testing methods. The first is another method developed by R. A. Fisher, for scoring playing card targets (Fisher, 1924; Jephson, 1928). Briefly, Fisher constructed a system of weights which reflects the degree of proximity between target and response, as measured by the *improbability* of the nine classes of correspondence he considered (a 3 × 3 array consisting of no correspondence/color/suit vs. no correspondence/rank [face card or pip]/number).

A second method was developed by Cadoret (1955) using a 5 × 5 array as the target system. On each trial, the geometric distance between target square and response square is measured, taking the side of a square as unit length and measuring between centers. Note that the distribution of possible distances depends in this case on the response location, and thus the overall test must take account of respondents' call patterns. There are exactly six types of calls for the 5 × 5, and each is associated with a distribution of possible distances which is readily determined. The overall test is constructed on this basis.

The third method was developed by Fisk and Mitchell (1953). They used a circular array containing 12 target positions (hence the name "clock-cards"). In this scheme the distribution of possible distances from the target (in ordinal position) is always the same for any call location. There is one way to obtain 0 distance (exact hit), one way to obtain a 6 (exact opposite), two ways to obtain all others. Assuming an open-deck test procedure and k possible distances, the distribution of the sum of the distances in N trials is developed on the model of a k-sided die rolled N times, where faces 1 and k of the die have probability $1/k$ and the remaining faces, $2/k$. We refer you to Fisk and Mitchell (1953) for details but mention here that there is a close kinship between this method and the exact method for evaluating preferentially-ranked free-response data (see section below entitled "Preferential Ranking and Rating Methods").

Finally, we briefly sketch a general approach to distance-measure problems. (We will find it convenient to speak of proximity rather than distance, actually, to make everything positive; this simply inverts the scoring system.) With any target-set, we can associate an arbitrary matrix of scores which we will denote S, whose rows are possible targets, columns possible responses, and cell entries the proximity scores to be assigned given that combination of target and response. In the "standard" hit-or-miss case, this matrix is an "identity matrix";

all entries on the main diagonal are "1," and all others "0." For the cases of interest, however, we assume that we have somehow been able to work up a reasonable set of scores, in some sense reflecting proximity to the true target. Next, suppose we run an experiment and obtain a response x trial matrix M (which may be either single-response or multiple-response). Now the essential idea is to transform the given response matrix into a new *weighted* response matrix T, utilizing the scores. In matrix notation, $\underset{s \times N}{T} = \underset{s \times s}{S} \underset{s \times N}{M}$, and the analysis by Greville's method then proceeds as usual. A simple example will clarify the procedure: Imagine that we are using simplified clock cards with four positions, 3, 6, 9, and 12. Then our score matrix and a possible five-trial single response matrix might be as follows:

target \ response	12	3	6	9		response \ trial	1	2	3	4	5
12	2	1	0	1		12	1	0	0	0	0
3	1	2	1	0		3	0	0	0	1	1
6	0	1	2	1		6	0	1	0	0	0
9	1	0	1	2		9	0	0	1	0	0

$\underset{4 \times 4}{S} = $ (left matrix) $\underset{4 \times 5}{M} = $ (right matrix)

Then the transformed response matrix T is:

weighted response \ trial	1	2	3	4	5
12	2	0	1	1	1
3	1	1	0	2	2
6	0	2	1	1	1
9	1	1	2	0	0

$\underset{4 \times 5}{T} = $

We stress that the score matrix is quite arbitrary. It can be constructed on any principle that seems appropriate, such as probability, geometric distance, or whatever, but essentially constitutes a guess about the definition of "neighborhood" relative to whatever psi processes are at work in the given task. We turn now to more direct methods of attacking this question.

Consistent Missing. Our elaborate discussion of the direct-hits problem will serve us well when we turn to free-response methods. Meanwhile we turn to other topics in the analysis of forced-choice data.

The other primary source of overall association between responses and targets is systematic erroneous association, or consistent missing. As indicated, this kind of information can be extremely valuable in revealing aspects of the mechanisms underlying successful performance in psi tasks, and this fact fully justifies the considerably greater labor associated with the analysis procedures.

The first question is naturally whether the overall confusion matrix contains evidence of consistent missing, independent of any evidence of direct hitting. Cadoret and Pratt (1950) present a method for detecting the presence of overall nonrandomness in the off-diagonal cells alone; that is, discounting the effects of the direct hitting represented on the main diagonal. The method uses an iterative procedure to obtain a "neutral" main diagonal which permits appropriate revision of the off-diagonal expectations. The overall χ^2 test of association is then carried out as usual, except for reduction of the degrees of freedom by the number of diagonal cells (i.e., targets). Since only the off-diagonal cells contribute to the revised χ^2, it constitutes an appropriate measure of systematic erroneous association. The procedure is manually laborious but can readily be implemented in a computer program for any number of targets.[7]

A significant overall χ^2 tells us only that there *is* consistent missing and nothing about its character. For small matrices (say, $s < 10$), the characteristics of the confusion structure may be directly discoverable through inspection of the pattern of contributions to χ^2. Apart from random fluctuation, the *strength* of association between responses and targets corresponds to the size of the χ^2 in the corresponding cells, and the *direction* (selection or avoidance) is indicated by excess or deficiency of observations relative to expectation.

For larger matrices, particularly with large N so that the evidence of a confusion structure becomes stable, direct inspection can be supplemented by the powerful technique of multidimensional scaling. The essential aim of this technique is to extract relationships implicit in the complex mass of data contained in the confusion matrix and to represent them compactly in a geometric structure of low dimensionality. Specifically, a structure is found which represents the targets as points in a space, such that targets which are highly confusable are represented by points which lie close together and targets which are rarely confused are represented by points which are far apart. Thus, the confusions data themselves are used to fracture the target system into a set of underlying dimensions reflecting its metric relative to whatever mechanisms underlie the psi performance. By examining the distribution of the targets in the scaled space it may be possible to infer directly something of the properties of those mechanisms.

---

[7] As in the overall test, the open-deck and closed-deck results will be asymptotically equivalent with increasing N (Roy and Mitra, 1956). We should also mention that apparent consistent missing can under some circumstances arise from sources other than target confusion, for example, if the respondent shows systematic scoring on the *next* target (+1 displacement) coupled with strong sequential call patterns. Displacement should therefore be checked before more extensive analysis.

We cannot go further into this complex subject here. A good introduction to multidimensional scaling is provided by Shepard, Romney, and Nerlove (1972, Vol. 1), and an excellent and widely-available general purpose scaling program is reported by Young (1973). Examples of application of the basic techniques to some unusually strong ESP data are contained in Kelly, Kanthamani, Child, and Young (1974), along with extensions of the procedures to problems involving comparison of confusions structures between bodies of data. The confusions methodology opens up a rich set of possibilities for investigating the mechanisms of psi, and we hope it will be vigorously applied in future work.

Diachronic Analyses (Analyses Taking Account of Sequential Structure)

There are numerous ways in which the sequential distribution of hits within runs, or run-scores within a series, can depart from expectation under the basic model. Here we catalog the major possibilities and ways of approaching them. (Throughout this section we are dealing with standard simple target-sets; although some of the tests could be extended to multiattribute targets, we make no general effort to do so here. Likewise, we will confine ourselves to the equal-p case, which is much simpler, and we will assume that the runs are all of equal length, corresponding to standard units of testing.)

Run-Score Distribution. Here we preserve the identity of individual runs, but ignore their order. From an appropriate model (binomial or matching) we can predict the structure of the observed distribution and test various kinds of departure from our predictions.

Overall Test. An overall test of conformity to expectation is easily constructed in the following way: Given the exact probability distribution of run-scores under the null hypothesis (binomial or matching), we obtain the corresponding distribution of expectations for a set of m runs simply by multiplying each probability by m. For the test we are about to describe, the minimum expected value should not be less than 5, and this will require some grouping of extreme run-scores depending on the size of m. Then for each of the resulting k categories, we will have an expected number of runs e_i and an observed number o_i. Form

$$\chi^2 = \sum_{i=1}^{k} \frac{(o_i - e_i)^2}{e_i} \tag{14}$$

and refer to the chi-square tables with $k - 1$ degrees of freedom for an upper-tail test. An alternative which we will not describe here for reasons of space is the Kolmogorov-Smirnov 1-sample goodness-of-fit test (Siegel, 1956, pp. 47-

52). This test can be applied to small samples, does not require combining of categories, and is generally more powerful than the chi-square test, and on these grounds should probably be the method of choice.

The overall tests are intended to detect any kind of departure from the theoretical model. As always, a more specific alternative hypothesis lends itself to a more specific and hence powerful test. There are two main cases to consider.

Central Tendency. First, the mean run-score could be displaced in either direction from its expectation ℓ/s where ℓ is the number of trials per run and s is the number of targets in the set. As indicated above (footnote 2), the test of the mean is equivalent to the test of the total score using the appropriate standard method.

Variability. The second major possibility is that the *variance* of the observed run-score distribution could be larger or smaller than expected, whatever its *location.* For example, respondents might display strong fluctuations in scoring which would show up in the variance, even when the mean run-score is close to chance.

To construct the test, we begin by computing the variance of our sample of m run-scores. Let x_i be the score in run i.

$$\hat{s}^2 = \frac{m \sum_{i=1}^{m} x_i^2 - \left(\sum_{i=1}^{m} x_i \right)^2}{m(m-1)} \tag{15}$$

The test then follows from a theorem proved in most introductory texts, for example, Hays (1963, p. 343):

$$\chi^2 = \frac{(m-1)\hat{s}^2}{\sigma^2} \sim \chi^2 \text{ with } m-1 \text{ df} \tag{16}$$

To complete the test, we have to choose an appropriate denominator. If the length of the individual runs is ℓ, this would be the binomial variance (ℓpq) for an open-deck test, and for a closed-deck test it could be either the (approximately correct) binomial variance, the conservative matching variance $[(\ell/\ell - 1) (\ell pq)]$, or an exact theoretical variance computed by Stevens' formula (formula 11 above).

As is typical for procedures based on chi-square, the result is exact only if the underlying population of run-scores is normally distributed, but it should be approximately valid for psi data, even when ℓp is less than 10 for moderate values of p.

An extended use of the variance lies in comparing variability of scoring between segments of the performance. For example, suppose we suspect that variance declines over the course of a long series of runs. Specifically, let us hypothesize that runs in the first half of the series will show greater run-score variance than those of the second. To test this hypothesis, compute the variance for each batch of runs separately. To be general suppose that the numbers of runs in the two batches are m_1 and m_2, which need not be equal (the run *lengths* however must be identical, so that ℓpq is constant). Then if $\hat{s}_1^2$ and $\hat{s}_2^2$ are the two sample variances,

$$F = \frac{\chi_1^2/m_1 - 1}{\chi_2^2/m_2 - 1} = \frac{\hat{s}_1^2}{\hat{s}_2^2} \sim F \text{ with } m_1 - 1 \text{ and } m_2 - 1 \text{ df} \qquad (17)$$

Clearly, sets of runs chosen on the basis of any appropriate experimental hypothesis can be compared in this way. It is of course *not* appropriate, except as an exploratory device, to frame the hypothesis following examination of the data.

The tests we have described are properly single-respondent tests. One way of extending them to multiple respondents is to pool runs across subjects (essentially creating a super-subject) and then to carry out the same tests on the pooled data (Rogers and Carpenter, 1966). An alternative which we feel is preferable, because it preserves the individual respondent's performance as the unit of analysis, is to compute the relevant statistic for each respondent and then test the distribution of *those* scores against an appropriate MCE, using the t-test. For example, on the null hypothesis the χ^2 scores computed using formula (16) should follow the chi-square distribution with $m - 1$ degrees of freedom. That distribution has mean $(m - 1)$, and if m is large (say over 30) the distribution is nearly normal. (The logarithm of a χ^2 score is even more nearly normal.) Furthermore, since the t-test is robust against moderate departures from normality, considerably smaller values of m would in practice yield a valid test. If in doubt, one could also apply a nonparametric alternative to the t-test (Siegel, 1956). Similar remarks hold for the F-test comparing variances; see, for example, Hays (1963, p. 348). In both cases, the nonparametric approach may be safer, if less powerful.

Finally, it should be noted that the interpretation of variance effects is not quite straightforward. To say that psi is operating to change the distribution of exact hits is to say that p is changing, and as p changes the theoretical variance must also change. Consequently, "variance" effects detected by the above tests are partly confounded with direct-hitting effects. Although we cannot develop this topic here, one possible approach to separating the effects cleanly might lie in the use of the arc-sine transformation (Greenwood, 1943b), under which the theoretical variance becomes asymptotically independent of p. We also point out that in all the above tests we are implicitly assuming that fluctuations in p are roughly stable over stretches of trials approximately coincident with the runs. A collection of more general techniques for studying episodic occurrences is presented in the section below entitled "Unsystematic Occurrences."

Nonrandom Distribution of Scoring.   We will now consider various categories of nonrandom distribution of scoring in forced-choice data.

Systematic Trends.   One class of nonrandom occurrences in the distribution of scoring involves various possibilities of systematic correlation of the scoring with *location* of one or another type, for example, location in the run, in the series, or in the structure of the recording sheet. A substantial amount of work has been done in this area, as surveyed by Rhine (1969), and effects of this sort are widely regarded as one of the more dependable manifestations of psi processes.

The main kinds of effects that have been analyzed can be called linear and quadratic trends.   Examples of linear trends are the steady decline of scoring across segments of the run and the "diagonal decline" from the upper left- to lower right-hand quarter of the recording sheet.   Quadratic trends include the tendency for scoring to be more extreme at the ends of runs than in the middle ("terminal salience"), leading to U-shaped or inverted-U distributions of scoring by position within the run (Rhine, 1969).

The main statistic used for analysis of linear trends has been the so-called CR_d, or critical ratio of the difference, which can be used to test whether two groups of trials arise from the same (known) binomial population.   Consistent with our earlier usage, we will call this statistic Z_d. If the two groups contain n_1 and n_2 trials, with x_1 and x_2 hits, respectively, then

$$Z_d = \frac{(x_1/n_1) - (x_2/n_2)}{[pq(1/n_1 + 1/n_2)]^{1/2}} \tag{18}$$

In the analysis of linear trends, this statistic has been applied simply by constructing sets of trials representing the extremes of the trend, for example, in the upper left vs. lower right quarter analysis.   Trials were also typically pooled across subjects.

An extension of the basic method was devised to handle the quadratic trends. In the case of quadratic trends within the run, for example, the standard run was first divided into five 5-trial segments, and a standard CR (z) computed for each segment, pooling trials over runs and subjects.   Then each z was squared, yielding a chi-square with 1 df.   Finally, the sum of the two terminal chi-squares was divided by the sum of the three interior ones to obtain an F-ratio with 2 and 3 df.

While these techniques have served a useful purpose in developing much evidence of systematic trends, we feel they can now be greatly extended, particularly through application of procedures associated with the analysis of variance. The basic idea, which we can only sketch here, would be to construct a two-way design in which the rows represent run segments and the columns, series segments. Sizes of segments would be determined by considerations of sample size but would be equalized in each direction.   Each respondent would contribute a score to every cell, but these scores can plausibly be treated as independent, particularly if obtained under an open-deck testing regime. The scores could be raw scores, or deviations, or absolute values of deviations if the difference between hitting and missing is to be ignored. The total size of the performance would be fixed in advance and identical for all respondents.

This approach has several important virtues relative to the earlier methods. First, it makes the respondent the unit of analysis, rather than the trial. Second, the analysis of each effect can be based on a more detailed breakdown of the corresponding data. And finally, we can analyze simultaneously for run effects, series effects, and interactions, including breakdowns of each into linear, quadratic, and possibly even higher-order components (Hays, 1963, Chaps. 14 and 16).

Another kind of systematic trend which may merit attention is the cyclic or periodic trend. This is also a very large subject which we cannot develop here, but we would suggest that under the right circumstances techniques of autocorrelation and spectral analysis could sensibly be applied to psi data to extract any evidence of periodicity in the scoring. A detailed introduction can be found in Bendat and Piersol (1971).

Unsystematic Occurrences. The other main category of nonrandom occurrences in the distribution of scoring involves transient and aperiodic fluctuations in hit rate, revealed by clustering or "bursts" of hits. In this section we present some basic techniques for studying these kinds of events.

A concept fundamental to our discussion is that of the *window*, a sequence of trials of fixed length L. By introducing the techniques in terms of a window of arbitrary size, we immediately obtain their specializations to the two cases of maximum practical importance, $L = 1$ (the individual trial) and $L = \ell$ (the run), as well as any others that might prove of interest. We shall assume that an entire series of N trials has been partitioned into N_W consecutive nonoverlapping windows of length L.

1. *Dichotomous situations:* Here we first assume that a criterion of some sort has been established together with the choice of L. Each window can be categorized as either satisfying the criterion, in which case we will call it a success locus (s), or failing to satisfy it, in which case we call it a failure locus (f). For example, we may classify single-trial windows as s or f according to whether they are hits· or misses, respectively; and we might choose to classify a run-length window as s if it satisfies some score criterion, such as 10 or better. For some purposes we will also want to associate a probability with satisfaction of the criterion; we will denote this p_s.

a. *Clustering of success and failure loci:* An overall test of clustering effects for the case where p_s is a known constant was developed by Wishart and Hirshfeld

(1936). Defining a "join" as any point at which the sequence of success and failure loci alternates (i.e., switches from s to f or vice versa), they find the mean and variance of the number of joins J in a series of N_W windows to be:

$$E[J] = 2 (N_W - 1) p_s q_s \qquad (19)$$

$$\sigma_J^2 = 4 N_W p_s q_s (1 - 3 p_s q_s) - 2 p_s q_s (3 - 10 p_s q_s) \qquad (20)$$

As N_W becomes large, the distribution of J becomes normal, and if it is very large, the second term may effectively be disregarded (Rhine et al., 1940, p. 381).   To test an observed number of joins, compute a z-score in the usual manner (including the continuity correction), and refer to the normal table. Note that clustering will be reflected in a reduced number of joins and hence in a negative z-score.

This procedure can be applied to trial-length windows with $p_s = p$, but note that it assumes independence between successive windows, implying an open-deck test regime.   Also, if the boundaries between runs cannot be ignored, the total mean and variance for the series of runs should be obtained by computing the mean and (exact) variance for a single run and multiplying by the number of runs.   The procedure can also be applied to run-length windows, including runs of closed-deck data.   The criterion might be, say, x or more hits in the run. Then p_s can be computed from the binomial formula (3) for an open-deck procedure, or from Greville's (1941) results for the closed-deck procedure.

A special case occurs if $p_s = q_s = 1/2$; then, the exact distribution is binomial with $N_W - 1$ "trials" and $p = 1/2$.

It should be pointed out that the Wishart-Hirshfeld technique uses known theoretical probabilities and will confound true clustering effects with the secondary effects of alterations of hit rate.   If the question to be asked is not simply whether clustering occurs, but whether it occurs *given the observed hit rate*, a technique developed by Wald and Wolfowitz (Siegel, 1956, pp. 136–145) is the method of choice.[8]   The sample statistic to be tested is the total number of *runs* of successes and failures in the sequence of windows: For example, if the sequence is /sssfsffs/, we will have five runs total, three of s's and two of f's. We also need the total number of occurrences of s and f loci which we will denote m and n, respectively.   (In the example, $m = 5$, $n = 3$.)   Given the observed values of m and n, the number of runs (r) follows a known exact distribution, and critical values have been tabulated for m and n less than 20 (Siegel, 1956, p. 252; Swed and Eisenhart, 1943).   For cases outside these tables, r is approx-

---

[8] A nearly identical procedure was developed by Stevens (1939b), and applied to the analysis of psi data by Pratt (1947). Our selection of the Wald-Wolfowitz technique is based solely on the fact that it is now more widely known in the general research community.

imately normally distributed with

$$E[r] = \frac{2mn}{m+n} + 1 \tag{21}$$

and

$$\sigma_r^2 = \frac{2mn\,(2mn - n - m)}{(m+n)^2\,(m+n-1)} \tag{22}$$

To test an observed r, form the z-score as usual, including the continuity correction, and enter the normal tables. As in the case of the joins method, clustering will be reflected in a reduced number of runs and hence in a negative z-score.

The Wald-Wolfowitz method makes no assumptions about the probability of a correct response (except that it is constant), resting entirely on the possible ways of arranging the observed numbers of successes and failures. It can therefore be applied either to open-deck or closed-deck data, even at the trial level. In the trial-level case it would again be appropriate to observe run boundaries, accumulating totals across runs.

b. *Distribution of lengths for runs of successes:* The tests just reviewed are concerned only with the overall amount of clustering. We now present methods which can reveal more of the detailed structure of clustering effects. These methods enable us to construct theoretical expectations for the frequencies of success-groups of different lengths, which we can at least informally compare with the observed distribution of lengths. (Note that the techniques of the section above entitled "Overall Test" should not be applied, because of the correlations among run lengths in the observed data.) As in the overall clustering test, there are two cases.

First, we may want to construct a distribution based on the theoretical probability of success in each window, p_s. Although we will not carry out the demonstration here, it can readily be shown that if n_k is the number of runs of exactly length k in a sequence of N_W windows,

$$E[n_k] = N_W\,p_s^k q_s^2 - (k+1)p_s^k q_s + 2p_s^k q_s \tag{23}$$

Here again use of the theoretical probability p_s will lead to a confounding of clustering effects with secondary effects of altered hit rate. Soal and Bateman (1954, p. 380) circumvented the problem by substituting the observed hit rate for p_s and applying formula (23). For their very large body of data the results of that strategy should be nearly exact. However, a better approach would be based, like the Wald-Wolfowitz test, on the observed numbers of s's and f's. The same sort of methods that lead to formula (23) lead to the result we need; if m

and n are again the total numbers of success and failures, respectively, and n_k is the number of success runs of length k,

$$E[n_k] = \frac{m^{(k)}}{N_W^{(k+1)}} [n (n + 1)] \tag{24}$$

Here $m^{(k)}$ is the kth factorial power of m, defined as $m(m - 1)(m - 2) \cdots (m - k + 1)$.

c. *Longest-run problems:* Uspensky (1937, pp. 77–84) presents a method for determining the probability of a run of successes of length k or longer in a sequence of N_W independent windows with constant probability of success p_s. The method is too complex to present here but could be useful if unusually large clusters are observed. Note that it would require open-deck data for trial-level applications and that it would again confound clustering effects with secondary effects of altered hit rate. We assume that a version could be developed based on *observed* successes and failures but have not attempted it. Meanwhile, a provisional solution would be to substitute the observed proportion of successes into Uspensky's method. This should be adequate if N is large relative to k.

2. *Ordinal/interval situations:* If our windows are larger than trial-length, or even in the trial-length case if we have an appropriate distance metric, dichotomous classification of windows as s or f loci can waste valuable information. Although the complexity of the subject precludes detailed development here, we want at least to mention the kinds of procedures that might be appropriate in such situations, plus sources of more detailed information.

Rhine et al. (1940, p. 392) present a method developed by Greenwood and illustrate its application to ESP run-score data. The test statistic ρ is formed by summing the first pair of adjacent scores, squaring the sum, continuing to the next (overlapping) pair, and so on, finally dividing the grand sum of squared sums by N_W. The distribution of ρ is strongly nonnormal even for rather large N_W, however, which limits its usefulness.

A statistic with better distributional properties would be obtained by using successive differences rather than sums, and this problem has been investigated by von Neumann (1941).

In general, the kind of problem involved here falls under the heading of serial correlation techniques. A detailed exposition at an advanced level is contained in Kendall and Stuart (1966, Vol. 3, Chap. 48). Finally, we would suggest that autocorrelation procedures might also be useful devices for extracting information about the presence and duration of clustering tendencies. The autocorrelation function can be pictured as a plot of serial correlations at increasing displacement from the reference window. At zero displacement the correlation is one, and in the absence of clustering or periodic trends all correlations at larger displacements will approximate zero.   Clustering will be reflected in a slower decline to zero, with the size of clusters reflected in the slope of the decline; and periodic trends would appear as secondary peaks in the function.   For details see Bendat and Piersol (1971) and Kendall and Stuart (1966, Vol. 3).

FREE-RESPONSE EXPERIMENTS

The forced-choice methodology of the Rhine school was the first and major response to the need for quantitative methods of evaluating evidence of psi. Together with its subsequent extensions it has allowed—and will certainly continue to allow—investigation of a wide variety of questions about the nature and conditions of occurrence of psi phenomena.   Nevertheless, many investigators have felt that something vital was lost in the transposition of psi from its natural settings into the forced-choice paradigm and have sought ways of extending quantitative techniques back into situations which more nearly resemble the conditions of spontaneous psi occurrences.

At the present time in particular, a strong revival of interest in such situations appears to be in progress, as reflected in a number of chapters in this *Handbook*. However, there is also still a good deal of uncertainty on the quantitative side, as reflected in the welter of techniques which have appeared in the literature, often specialized to particular experimental methods or materials.   Although the uncertainty has partly to do with empirical properties of the methods, and will thus be resolved only by further empirical study, we hope in this section to clarify the theoretical aspects of the situation by providing the first comprehensive and unified survey of available techniques.

We begin by grossly characterizing the kinds of situations typically encountered.   A medium or sensitive, for example, may give verbal descriptions of various deceased persons or of the owners of concealed "psychometric" objects. More commonly at present, respondents may be asked to give their impressions of a series of remote target situations in whatever form seems appropriate, including verbal descriptions, dream or imagery reports, or drawings, possibly in any combination.   The basic data-structure of such an experiment will therefore consist of a set of targets or target-representations on the one hand, and on the other a set of response protocols hopefully containing information related to the corresponding targets.   The essential difference from the forced-choice situation is that the resemblance of successive target-response pairs cannot be determined simply, or on an absolute basis, but only relative to the overall structure of pairwise resemblances between the sets.   Furthermore, the role of the *judge*, reduced to a minimum in the forced-choice case, becomes conspicuously important.   Thus the evaluation procedure is not so intimately joined to the test procedure, and this leads to the curious situation that the final quantitative assessment of a fixed experimental result may depend strongly on properties of the judging scheme by which it is evaluated.   Nevertheless, we emphasize that there is also underlying continuity between the general theory of forced-choice hitting and the various kinds of free-response analysis we will now describe.[9]

Two main classes of analytical procedure have appeared in the literature, one aimed at the evaluation of overall or global resemblance of targets and protocols, and the other analyzing targets and protocols into simpler elements and evaluating piecewise correspondence.   We will call these the *holistic* and *atomistic* approaches, respectively.   Historically, the two classes have tended to evolve somewhat independently, in conjunction with differing kinds of experimental material.   For example, the atomistic techniques grew up primarily in response to the problem of evaluating verbal material such as mediumistic utterances, whereas holistic procedures arose principally in conjunction with the results of drawing tests, which are naturally more resistant to atomization.   Nevertheless, these differences are incidental, and we present the methods here in a unified manner.

Holistic Approaches

The central idea of these approaches is to capitalize on the sophisticated pattern-recognition capabilities of the human judge to evaluate overall resemblances between sets of objects.   There are two main subclasses.

Forced-Matching Techniques.   Suppose we run a free-response experiment consisting of N trials, on each of which we collect a single response protocol corresponding to a single target.   The standard experimental procedure would follow a closed-deck format in which the number of targets, s, equals the number of trials, N, with order of target presentation randomized.   Following the experiment, judging begins.   Judges might be persons involved in the experiment (respondent, or "agent") or independent persons; and there might be just one judge or several.   Each judge is confronted with the entire collection of targets and protocols, with the target order randomized as appropriate.   His task is to match the two sets pairwise, eliminating each pair successively from the pool.   Thus, he first finds the pair that seems to correspond maximally, then the next best, and so on.   The score he obtains is the number of correct matches. The exact probability distribution of x matches in N tries was first worked out by Chapman (1934) and is also given by Feller (1968, Vol. 1, pp. 107–108), and a very convenient table can be found in the appendix to Scott (1972).   Scott's table also encompasses the case of k independent judgings, each involving N

[9]Parallels to other aspects of forced-choice analysis could in principle be developed as well, but this would be a much more difficult undertaking than we are presently prepared to attempt.

pairs. (Note carefully that the *pools themselves* must be independent; multiple judging of single pools is a different case altogether. Chapman's [1934] paper unfortunately failed to distinguish these cases, and the error regrettably but understandably slipped into the parapsychology literature in J. G. Pratt's [1937] application of the method to results of some drawing experiments.)

Scott's table will probably cover most of the cases of practical significance, but there are also limiting results which may be useful as approximations. For example, as s becomes large, the matching distribution approaches the Poisson with parameter 1. In fact even for values of s as small as 6 the approximation is fairly good (see table in Feller, 1968, Vol. 1, p. 108). Also for k independent matchings, the sum of the correct matchings is approximately Poisson with parameter k. Then for large k, the sum of the correct matchings will be approximately normal with mean and variance both equal to k. (Note incidentally that these mean and variance results are exact and can be derived directly from Stevens' formulas, which reveal that the mean and variance for a single matching are both 1, independent of N.) If the normal approximation is used, the continuity correction should be incorporated in calculating the z-score.

In practice, the multiple-judgings case of greater practical interest is the one in which each pool is force-matched by several different judges. The two main approaches to handling the resulting dependency among judges will by now be familiar. Greenwood (1940), suggested treatment of each set of matchings as a single matching, using the average number of correct matches obtained by the various judges as their collective score for the match and using 1 as the variance (the variance of a single-judge forced matching). Then these scores could be summed over independent sets of data as usual.

It should be recognized that Greenwood's suggestion of 1 for the variance is a very conservative one. The true variance is at most equal to 1 and can be calculated by applying Greville's method for the closed-deck situation. It would probably be desirable, though not necessary, for successive judges to encounter the targets in different random orders, to minimize order effects in the matching. The final response array will in any event consist of a response x trial (target) matrix in which the order assigned to the targets is arbitrary, but each column will contain the numbers of times each possible protocol was matched with that target. Then the analysis proceeds as usual.

Preferential Ranking and Rating Methods. It was recognized as a defect of the forced-matching method by Carington (1940) and Stuart (1942) that unless the correspondences between responses and their targets were very striking (which they often were not), all-or-none judgements would tend to become insensitive. For example, suppose a judging pool contains two rather similar responses, each made to one of two rather similar targets. A judge might clearly recognize the resemblance of the two pairs but fail to match them correctly. More generally, judges may often have some partial sense of what goes with what, even when they cannot determine correspondences exactly.

To circumvent this problem, Stuart (1942), with the aid of Greenwood (1943a), developed a technique of preferential ranking, which in essence is simply a device for allowing partial credit. In making each successive comparison of a response protocol with a possible target, a judge is no longer required to make an all-or-nothing decision but rather to *rank* or *rate* the resemblance of the given pair.

Unlike the forced-match, which inherently involves a closed-deck analysis, preferential ranking and rating methods can be applied in either a closed-deck or open-deck setting. Stuart's initial application clung to the pattern of earlier forced-matching procedures, whereas recent investigations have tended to favor the open-deck approach; however, the distinctions and their analytical consequences have not previously been clearly noted.

Open-Deck Cases. The essential feature here is, as usual, that targets are sampled with replacement. (A variation which has appeared commonly in recent work is one in which both the targets and the associated judging pools for successive trials are constructed by sampling with replacement from a much larger set; this is done to maintain novelty and unfamiliarity in the target materials over successive trials and leads to no essential complications in the analysis.) On each of N trials, a judge is required to rank the members of the associated judging pool according to their correspondence to the response protocol, by assigning integers from 1 through s, where s is the number of possible ranks (= number of items in the pool, including the actual target).

Under open-deck conditions and with only one judge per target, the sum of the ranks assigned to the true targets follows an exact probability distribution of known form. Morris (1972) presented a general formula, plus a table applicable to various cases in which the number of trials is equal to the number of ranks. Solfvin, Kelly, and Burdick (in press) have recently extended Morris' work in two ways: first, by providing complete tables of exact probabilities for all cases in the range $4 \leqslant N \leqslant 20$ and $4 \leqslant s \leqslant 10$; and second, by developing a more generalized approach which allows a normal approximation to the probability distribution of an arbitrarily weighted sum of the ranks. Solfvin et al. also give tables of estimated percent-points of the distributions for several potentially useful weighting schemes and representative cases and illustrate how the weighted-sum statistics could give greater power against specific alternative hypotheses.

It remains possible that the ranking procedure is still too restrictive and that by relaxing it we can get more sensitive tests. One possibility, utilized earlier in a forced-choice context, would be to allot the judge a quota of points (equal, say, to the sum of the possible ranks $s(s + 1)/2$) and request him to allocate those points however he wishes on any given trial. This might be regarded as a conservative species of rating scheme. In the general rating situation, the judge is allowed to assign any ratings he chooses within some specified range, such as 0–30 (Stanford and Mayer, 1974), with no restrictions on their sum. (It should be pointed out that ranks can always be recovered from ratings, provided tied ratings are not allowed; this is a strong argument for using a rating procedure, particularly at the present exploratory stage in development of the methods.)

With either of these extended scoring procedures, both of which use the entire score distribution on each trial rather than just the score assigned to the true target, Greville's (open-deck) method can be applied as usual (but note that in the variant design mentioned above, the targets have to be represented by a convention such as ordinal position in the judging pool rather than by their literal identities, to accommodate the changing membership of the pools).

Moreover, Greville's method extends automatically to cover cases in which the same free-response data are ranked, extended-ranked, or rated by each of a number of judges. This feature should be a decisive advantage of the method in the likely event that multiple judges collectively can do a better job of detecting the "true" correspondence existing in a set of data than could any one of them singly.

If a single-judge evaluation scheme is acceptable, an alternative procedure suggested by Stanford and Mayer (1974) might be useful. It uses the rating method, and on each trial it converts the rating assigned to the target to a z-score, by subtracting the mean rating and dividing the result by the standard deviation of all the ratings. These z-scores can then be used as dependent measures, for example, in a t-test of the null hypothesis that their own mean μ_z is zero. Of course the fact that these scores are called z-scores does not imply that they are even approximately normally distributed, and available information suggests they may actually be excessively nonnormal in practice. Possibly the normality could be improved by adjustments in the range of ratings, number of objects rated, and instructions to judges (Stanford and Mayer, 1974), and in seriously nonnormal cases nonparametric tests could be applied (Siegel, 1956). Furthermore, the z-scores could themselves be used as the basis of a Greville analysis, obviating the need to make distributional assumptions; this transformation would also tend to stabilize the distribution of possible scores, while still taking into account on each trial the overall distribution of the ratings.

Closed-Deck Cases. Here the composition of the target sequence is fixed, only its order being subject to randomization. An example appears in the work of Stuart (1942), who had respondents produce four drawings, one each in response to four target pictures, and then had the same respondents preferentially-rank each of the drawings against all of the targets. (Stuart also complicated the situation further by having the respondent then rank each target against all of the drawings, and by repeating the whole process with other judges.)

It should be clearly recognized that neither Morris' exact procedure nor any other open-deck analysis strictly applies here. Stuart was aware of the problem and supplemented his (approximate) open-deck method with a second method based on a constrained open-deck model under which the judge acts independently from trial to trial except for avoiding the giving of maximum rank to any target more than once. The statistical basis of this method was worked out by Greenwood (1943a). We will not present it here in further detail because we feel that parapsychologists will generally want to avoid routine use of methods which require potentially controversial assumptions about respondents' behavior.

Having said that, we can quickly dispose of the closed-deck cases: Greville's closed-deck method makes no assumptions about the respondents and can be applied as earlier to ranks, extended-ranks, or ratings contributed by one or multiple judges. The z-score method should be avoided here because of the dependency among trials, except possibly as an intermediate stage in the Greville analysis. We close by remarking that the open-deck methods appear to us to be both experimentally and statistically preferable.

Atomistic Approaches

The general aim of these more laborious procedures is to capitalize on the detailed relationships of targets and responses in order to obtain a more sensitive scoring procedure. Before turning to the general case, we mention one specialized technique which has recently appeared.

Specially Constructed Target Sets. Honorton (1975) has constructed an elaborate pool of free-response targets with the special property that each member represents exactly one of the 2^{10} possible combinations of 10 independent binary attributes. Thus each free-response trial using a target randomly sampled from this pool can be treated as a set of 10 binary forced-choice trials, as well as in the usual manner. In the extreme case where only the forced-choice aspect is considered, the complications of judging analysis are eliminated altogether. Although the scheme of binary attributes only grossly characterizes the content of any given target, it is sufficiently detailed to permit 1-trial significance down to the 1/1024 level and is very easily evaluated. Work currently being conducted with this target system should help to clarify its functional properties.

More Detailed Atomization Procedures. Historically, the atomization methods originated in analysis of verbal material, such as mediums' verbal descriptions of living or deceased persons. We will introduce the methods in that context and then extend to the general case.

Excellent reviews of the history of methods for analyzing verbal material are available in Pratt (1960, 1969). Briefly, the early methods all attempted to use the Saltmarsh-Soal (1930) method to obtain the total probability of the observed number of correct statements, taking into account the estimated a priori probability that each given statement would be true. Despite steady improvements in the experimental controls and methods for estimating the individual probabilities, the basic approach remained flawed because it required independence among the items or statements derived from the medium's protocol. The problem was finally solved when J. G. Pratt (Pratt and Birge, 1948) recognized the applicability of Greville's method.

The basic procedure is essentially as follows: the medium produces a protocol or series of protocols containing statements intended for each of a set of target persons. These target persons can be "sampled" in either a closed-deck or open-deck manner. (The traditional method has been closed-deck, but an open-deck analysis may be justified procedurally or by argument, as discussed in Roll and Burdick, 1969). Subsequently the protocol is reduced to a set of individual statements, often by merely inserting parentheses between successive statements in the original order, but preferably (Scott, 1972) randomizing the order of the statements as well. Then the statement-protocol is given independently to the several target-persons, each of whom now functions as a judge by checking (or otherwise scoring) all statements for their applicability to his own situation. This leads to a matrix of scores suitable for analysis by the appropriate version of Greville's method.

For greater detail in the mediumistic situation, the above references should be consulted. Here we want to point out that this situation has special peculiarities which are not inherent in the method. Specifically, the number of trials (N) is generally equal to the number of target-persons (s), and the target-persons are necessarily also judges. In a more general setting we can think of analyzing protocols containing verbal and other responses to remote targets of any sort. Thus, any of the general cases could in principle apply, for example, open or closed deck and equal or unequal p. The only fixed feature is a result of the atomization process itself, which leads necessarily to dependence among items and therefore to the multiple-calling analysis, whether single or multiple judges are in fact involved.

There is obviously a great deal of work involved in these procedures, and it is fair to ask whether it is worth it. Unfortunately, we can give no general answer based solidly on either theoretical or empirical considerations. Our feeling is that it would be, the more so to the degree that protocols contain detailed and nonredundant information selectively relevant to their intended targets. In particular, the more detailed study provides entry to a set of interesting questions about precisely what aspects of targets are correctly obtained and what kinds of systematic distortion occur (Roll, Morris, Damgaard, Klein, and Roll

1973). It is also worth observing that the costs of the method would be greatly reduced by a relatively simple package of computer programs to handle the manual chores involved in setting up the statements and constructing the judging protocols. This would be particularly true of an interactive system. See Scott (1972) for related discussion.

Finally—and these remarks pertain to all the many applications of Greville's methods throughout this section—the ability of the methods to reflect detailed correspondences is partly dependent on statistical considerations. Clearly our object should be to develop for any situation a scoring system which will be maximally sensitive, consistent with the requirement that we can safely analyze the results. Since the origin of the response matrix is arbitrary, we can in principle extend the scoring in arbitrary ways to increase the weighting of strong-bet trials. Thus, for example, Schmeidler (1958) carried out analyses in which correct items received scores of 1–10 to reflect their antecedent improbability and in further analyses even multiplied the scores obtained on adjacent correct items. While proper in principle, these kinds of extensions may in practice severely undermine the quality of Greville's approximations, as stressed particularly by Scott (1972). The problem is especially serious in view of the small N typically involved in free-response work. A principle which can always be applied is to make N as large as possible in the given situation. Beyond that we can only offer provisional advice—follow the ratio-of-ranges rule and regard marginal results with considerable skepticism. Better guidelines will surely be developed as experience with the methods accumulates.

CONCLUDING OBSERVATIONS: EXPERIMENTAL DESIGNS IN PARAPSYCHOLOGICAL RESEARCH

Throughout this chapter we have artificially isolated the performance of the single respondent in order to effectively display aspects of that performance that seem worthy of study. However, in many if not most investigations, that performance would be just one of many that go to make up a larger experimental design. The question therefore arises as to the role the individual scores play in the overall analysis. At various points we have made specific suggestions, but here we wish to discuss the subject briefly in a more general way.

Certainly one of the most conspicuous trends in recent psi research is an accelerating shift of emphasis from the "demonstration" orientation of the early days to "process-oriented" research.[10] In its early stages this shift was marked by awkward, limited, and sometimes erroneous extensions of trial-based bi-

---

[10]Correspondingly, there is increasing recognition of the importance of Type II errors, in contrast to the early preoccupation with Type I errors (Stanford, 1974; Zenhausern, 1974), and concern for *strength* as well as *statistical significance* of observed relationships (Stanford, 1974).

nomial methods to situations in which the respondent is the appropriate unit of analysis. The most common case involves the use of the CR_d to investigate differences in exact-hitting performance of two groups representing some experimental variable. As clearly demonstrated by Stanford and Palmer (1972), this procedure is unsound even in the sole case where it applies, and it cannot be extended even to one-way designs involving more than two groups.

More generally, many of the measures we have discussed could function as dependent variables in an experiment designed to study relationships between aspects of psi performance and possible predictor variables. This could be a one-way design with any number of treatments, or any kind of higher-order design, and could use selected measures either singly (univariate designs) or in concert (multivariate). Correct application of these more complex designs could greatly increase the yield of information from psi experiments and consequently accelerate progress toward understanding and control. It is also important to stress that increased complexity of a design does not necessarily or in general require any disturbance of the delicate interface with the respondent. We also point out that evidence of significant group differences in an ANOVA design (or evidence of significant regression) is prima facie evidence of the occurrence of psi (assuming the experiment is properly controlled). This is true even in the absence of analyses localizing its presence in the performance of any single group. The precise sources of the effects in the experiment can always be investigated by appropriate secondary analyses (Palmer, 1975).

Statisticians have developed a wide variety of specialized tools for experimental inquiry. The modern parapsychologist, like any other modern researcher, needs to have good command of these extremely valuable resources. Many parapsychologists already do, and the level of sophistication is steadily rising. Clearly, quantitative parapsychology is moving into a new phase in which it will make extensive and effective use of all relevant aspects of modern technology, choosing techniques on the basis of appropriateness to problems rather than on artificial considerations of simplicity of analysis or ease of understanding. We hope in this chapter to have encouraged these developments, and we close by urging that no potentially interesting problem be abandoned merely because it appears inaccessible to any existing quantitative procedure. We venture the suggestion that virtually any qualitatively rich-looking phenomenon will prove amenable to some appropriate form of statistical modeling and analysis. Let us take phenomena as we find them and develop our methods accordingly.

APPENDIX A

In this appendix we illustrate the wide applicability of the Greville formulas by applying them to hypothetical data in a variety of situations. The situations covered are single or multiple responses, open or closed decks, and equal or unequal probabilities for targets. We begin by presenting the notation and formulas in general.

NOTATIONS AND GENERAL FORMULAS

s = number of targets (symbols, persons, pictures, etc.).

N = number of trials (cards, protocols).

N_i = number of trials containing i^{th} target. $i = 1, \ldots, s$ (appears in closed-deck formulas).

p_i = probability that a trial will contain i^{th} target. $i = 1, \ldots, s$ (appears in open-deck formulas).

m_{ik} = number of responses of ith target on k^{th} trial. $i = 1, \ldots, s; k = 1, \ldots, N$.

M_i = total number of response of ith target = $\Sigma_{k=1}^{N} m_{ik}$.

Response matrix:

$$M_{s \times N} = (m_{ik}) \, i = 1, \ldots, s; k = 1, \ldots, N \tag{25}$$

Lambda matrix:

$$\lambda = MM' = (\lambda_{ij}) = \left(\sum_{k=1}^{N} m_{ik} m_{jk} \right) i = 1, \ldots, s; j = 1, \ldots, s \tag{26}$$

Adjustment matrix:

$$A = (a_{ij}) = \left(\frac{M_i M_j}{N} \right) i = 1, \ldots, s; j = 1, \ldots, s \tag{27}$$

Gamma matrix:

$$\Gamma = \lambda - A = (\gamma_{ij}) = (\lambda_{ij} - a_{ij}) \tag{28}$$

Open-Deck Formulas:

$$\text{Expectation} = \sum_{i=1}^{s} p_i M_i \tag{29}$$

$$\text{Variance} = \sum_{i=1}^{s} p_i \lambda_{ii} - \sum_{i=1}^{s} \sum_{j=1}^{s} p_i p_j \lambda_{ij} \tag{30}$$

Closed-Deck Formulas:

$$\text{Expectation} = \left(\sum_{i=1}^{s} N_i M_i \right) / N \tag{31}$$

$$\text{Variance} = \left(\sum_{i=1}^{s} N_i \gamma_{ii} \right) / (N - 1) - \left(\sum_{i=1}^{s} \sum_{j=1}^{s} N_i N_j \gamma_{ij} \right) / N(N - 1) \tag{32}$$

GENERAL DESCRIPTION

Each of our hypothetical experiments consists of a run containing 18 trials and 3 targets. Thus, we shall always have $N = 18$ and $s = 3$. The variable aspects will be single (SR) or multiple (MR) responses, open (OD) or closed (CD) deck targets, and equal (E) or unequal (U) target probabilities. Furthermore, in each of the cases to be described below the data can be considered to have arisen from either a forced-choice or a free-response experiment.

The basic procedure involves matching a response sequence to a target sequence to obtain a hit score. The hit score is combined with the appropriate mean and variance to obtain a CR. There are two response sequences (SR, MR), each of which will be compared to each of the four target sequences (E-OD, E-CD, U-OD, U-CD) to obtain eight hypothetical data sets for analysis. The response data will be described first.

RESPONSE DATA

Single-Response Data

The response matrix M^{SR} for the single response case is presented below.

	Target	1	2	3	4	5	6	7	8	9	10	11	12	13	14	15	16	17	18	Total
M^{SR}:	a	0	0	0	1	0	1	1	0	0	0	1	0	1	0	0	0	1	0	6
	b	1	0	1	0	0	0	0	0	0	1	1	0	0	0	1	0	0	0	0	5
	c	0	1	0	0	1	0	0	1	0	0	0	0	1	0	0	1	1	0	1	7

The response matrix M^{SR} could have arisen from a forced-choice card-guessing experiment involving a single subject guessing one of three target symbols for each card of an 18-card deck. It could also have arisen in a free-response experiment as the result of single judge matching each of 18 verbal descriptions (protocols) produced by a subject to one of three target pictures.

The essential feature of an SR response matrix which distinguishes it from the more general MR response matrix is the property that each column has exactly one "1" with the other entries in the column being "0." The "1" for a column (trial) is entered in the row corresponding to the target which was chosen as the response for that trial. This particular SR matrix indicates that target b was called on the first trial, c was called on the second, b on the third, etc.

For the data in M^{SR} we have:

$$M_1^{SR} = 6 \qquad M_2^{SR} = 5 \qquad M_3^{SR} = 7 \qquad (33)$$

$$\lambda^{SR} = \begin{pmatrix} 6 & 0 & 0 \\ 0 & 5 & 0 \\ 0 & 0 & 7 \end{pmatrix} \qquad (34)$$

$$A^{SR} = \tfrac{1}{18}\begin{pmatrix} 36 & 30 & 42 \\ 30 & 25 & 35 \\ 42 & 35 & 49 \end{pmatrix} = \begin{pmatrix} 2.000 & 1.667 & 2.333 \\ 1.667 & 1.389 & 1.944 \\ 2.333 & 1.944 & 2.722 \end{pmatrix} \qquad (35)$$

$$\Gamma^{SR} = \tfrac{1}{18}\begin{pmatrix} 72 & -30 & -42 \\ -30 & 65 & -35 \\ -42 & -35 & 77 \end{pmatrix} = \begin{pmatrix} 4.000 & -1.667 & -2.333 \\ -1.667 & 3.611 & -1.944 \\ -2.333 & -1.944 & 4.278 \end{pmatrix} \qquad (36)$$

Notice that M_i^{SR} is just the number of trials on which the ith target was called. Notice also that λ is a diagonal matrix with M_i^{SR} in the ith position on the diagonal. Both of these features are characteristic of single response data for which each column of the response matrix M has exactly one "1" and the other entries "0."

Multiple-Response Data

The response matrix M^{MR} for the multiple-response case is presented below.

	Target	1	2	3	4	5	6	7	8	9	10	11	12	13	14	15	16	17	18	Total
M^{MR}:	a	1	0	1	4	0	2	4	1	1	3	1	3	1	6	4	0	5	3	40
	b	8	4	1	1	2	0	1	2	5	1	3	0	5	2	1	3	0	2	41
	c	4	2	6	2	1	1	0	4	3	2	2	1	3	4	2	1	3	4	45

A multiple-response matrix such as M^{MR} can arise in a number of ways. For example, it could be the result of several subjects responding to the same target sequence. This example was mentioned by Greville (1944) in his article dealing with the stacking effect. Alternatively, M^{MR} could be the result of a single subject who is permitted to cast multiple "votes" on each trial with heavy, decisive votes coming on trials for which the subject is confident of his response (e.g., trials 1, 3, 7) and more scattered voting patterns occurring on trials for which the subject is unsure of his response (e.g., trials 5, 6, 10, 11, 18). Multiple-response data can also arise from preference ranking procedures. For example, the response for trial #10 could be the result of a single subject who rated a as the most likely target, c as the second most likely, and b as the least likely target for that trial.

Multiple-response data can and frequently does arise in a free-response setting. The free-response analog of the stacking effect occurs when several judges each match the same set of N protocols to the s targets. With this interpretation the numbers in column 4 of M^{MR} indicate that four judges felt that protocol #4 matched target a best, one judge felt that it matched target b, and two judges felt that it matched target c. This situation has sometimes been called the "cookie problem."

For another possible interpretation suppose that the protocols are verbal descriptions of target persons which have been broken down into items. Each target person is asked to check the items which pertain to him. Using this interpretation we see that target person a checked four items on the fourth protocol, target person b checked one item on the fourth protocol, and target person c checked two items on that same protocol.

Preference rankings are another source of MR data which can arise in a free-response setting just as easily as in a forced-choice experiment. The interpretation is strictly analogous.

When several subjects (judges) each make a single call (match) for every trial, then the column totals will be the same for every column in the multiple-response matrix. The column totals would also be equal if one or more subjects gave preference rankings for every trial. However, in the item-checking example there is no reason to expect the column totals to be equal. Equality of column totals is a property that is often present, but it is not necessary for the validity of the Greville method. Consequently, there is no need to require every subject to respond on every trial of a matching or preference ranking experiment. Unequal column totals resulting from missing responses (or any other reason) can be readily handled by the Greville method. For that reason we have chosen a multiple-response matrix with unequal column totals for our illustrative example.

There is one note of caution that must be sounded as a counterpoint to the theme of freely changing columns. The Greville method employs a critical ratio whose distribution is approximately normal. Very wild fluctuations between columns will cause the approximation to be poor. The key feature here is within-column variability rather than totals. As a rough and ready procedure for assessing this feature we suggest that you calculate the ratio of the maximum within-column range to the minimum. If the number of trials is several times larger than this ratio, the normal approximation is probably adequate.

In our example the largest within-column range is 7 which occurs on trial #1. The smallest is 2 which occurs on trials #5, 6, 10, 11, and 18. The ratio is $3\frac{1}{2}$, and the number of trials is more than five times this ratio.

It should be emphasized that this recommended procedure is based purely on guesswork. Unfortunately, that is the best we can do as of this writing. As experience with the Greville method accumulates, we can expect more soundly based recommendations to appear.

The purpose of the preceding remarks has been to emphasize the generality of the multiple-response matrix and the broad applicability of the Greville method. The examples were chosen to illustrate the variety of experimental situations which can be fit into this framework and not to provide a complete listing of all possible applications of the Greville method.

For the data in M^{MR} we have:

$$M_1^{MR} = 40 \qquad M_2^{MR} = 41 \qquad M_3^{MR} = 45 \qquad (37)$$

$$\lambda^{MR} = \begin{pmatrix} 146 & 57 & 100 \\ 57 & 169 & 117 \\ 100 & 117 & 151 \end{pmatrix} \qquad (38)$$

$$A^{MR} = \tfrac{1}{18}\begin{pmatrix} 1600 & 1640 & 1800 \\ 1640 & 1681 & 1845 \\ 1800 & 1845 & 2025 \end{pmatrix} = \begin{pmatrix} 88.889 & 91.111 & 100 \\ 91.111 & 93.389 & 102.5 \\ 100 & 102.5 & 112.5 \end{pmatrix} \qquad (39)$$

$$\Gamma^{MR} = \tfrac{1}{18}\begin{pmatrix} 1028 & -614 & 0 \\ -614 & 1361 & 261 \\ 0 & 261 & 693 \end{pmatrix} = \begin{pmatrix} 57.111 & -34.111 & 0 \\ -34.111 & 75.611 & 14.5 \\ 0 & 14.5 & 38.5 \end{pmatrix} \qquad (40)$$

DATA ANALYSIS FOR EXAMPLE CASES

The Equal Probability Open-Deck Case

The target sequence for this case was generated by rolling a die 18 times. The target was a if the die roll was "1" or "6," b if "2" or "5," and c if "3" or "4." The results are presented in the table below. Hits for the single-response data are indicated with an asterisk.

Trial	1	2	3	4	5	6	7	8	9	10	11	12	13	14	15	16	17	18	Total Hits
Target	a	b	a	c	a	a^*	a^*	c^*	c	c	a^*	b	c	c	b	a	b	b	4
MR Score	1	4	1	2	0	2	4	4	3	2	1	0	3	4	1	0	0	2	34

Single Response. For single-response data the open deck equal probability model is identical to the binomial model, and the Greville formulas for expectation and variance reduce to (5) and (6) respectively. We have

$$\text{Expectation} = \sum_{i=1}^{3} p_i M_i = Np = 6 \qquad (41)$$

$$\text{Variance} = \sum_{i=1}^{3} p_i \lambda_{ii} - \sum_{i=1}^{3}\sum_{j=1}^{3} p_i p_j \lambda_{ij} = Np(1-p) = 4 \qquad (42)$$

Observed Hit Total = 4

(i) Continuity-corrected deviation (psi-hitting) = -2.5

$$CR = -2.5/\sqrt{4} = -1.25, P = .8944$$

(ii) Continuity-corrected deviation (psi-missing) = -1.5

$$CR = -1.5/\sqrt{4} = -.75, P = .2266$$

Multiple Response. There is no special simplifying feature here other than the fact that the target probabilities are equal. We have

$$\text{Expectation} = \sum_{i=1}^{3} p_i M_i = p \sum_{i=1}^{3} M_i = \tfrac{1}{3}(40 + 41 + 45) = 42 \qquad (43)$$

$$\text{Variance} = \sum_{i=1}^{3} p_i \lambda_{ii} - \sum_{i=1}^{3}\sum_{j=1}^{3} p_i p_j \lambda_{ij} = p \sum_{i=1}^{3} \lambda_{ii} - p^2 \sum_{i=1}^{3}\sum_{j=1}^{3} \lambda_{ij}$$

$$= \tfrac{1}{3}(146 + 169 + 151) - \tfrac{1}{9}[146 + 169 + 151 + (2 \times 57)$$

$$+ (2 \times 100) + (2 \times 117)] = 155\tfrac{1}{3} - 112\tfrac{2}{3} = \tfrac{128}{3} = 42.667 \quad (44)$$

Observed Hit Total = 34

(i) Continuity-corrected deviation (psi-hitting) = -8.5

$$CR = -8.5/\sqrt{128/3} = -1.30 \; P = .9032$$

(ii) Continuity-corrected deviation (psi-missing) = -7.5

$$CR = -7.5/\sqrt{128/3} = -1.15 \; P = .1251$$

The Equal Probability Closed-Deck Case

The target sequence for this case was generated from an 18-card deck consisting of six hearts (a), six clubs (b), and six spades (c). Thus, $N_1 = N_2 = N_3 = 6$. The results are presented in the table below. Hits for the single-response data are indicated with an asterisk.

Trial	1	2	3	4	5	6	7	8	9	10	11	12	13	14	15	16	17	18	Total Hits
Target	c	b	b*	a*	b	a*	b	a	b*	a	b	c*	a*	c	c*	c*	c	a	8
MR Score	4	4	1	4	2	2	1	1	5	3	3	1	1	4	2	1	3	3	45

Single Response. For single-response data in the equal probability closed-deck case the second term in the variance formula is identically zero. This is a consequence of the fact that the column totals are equal for M^{SR}. Thus, we have

$$\text{Expectation} = \tfrac{1}{18} \sum_{i=1}^{3} N_i M_i = \tfrac{6}{18}(6 + 5 + 7) = 6 \quad (45)$$

$$\text{Variance} = \frac{1}{N-1} \sum_{i=1}^{3} N_i \gamma_{ii} - 0 = \frac{6}{17}(4.000 + 3.611 + 4.278) = 4.196 \quad (46)$$

Observed Hit Total = 8

Continuity-corrected deviation = 1.5

$$CR = 1.5\sqrt{4.196} = .73, P = .2327$$

This case is very common in parapsychology. Besides card guessing it often occurs in a free-response setting as a forced-matching experiment. In forced matching the number of trials (protocols) is equal to the number of targets ($N = s$). A judge makes a one-to-one matching of protocols to targets yielding a response pattern such as occurs on trials #7, 8, 9 of the single response data or alternatively on trials #10, 11, 12 or on trials #13, 14, 15. The characteristic feature of a forced-matching experiment is that it is closed deck, single response with each $N_i = 1$ and each $M_i = 1$. These conditions also imply the equal target probability property and the fact that $N = s$.

Multiple Response.   Using the closed-deck formulas we have

$$\text{Expectation} = \frac{1}{18} \sum_{i=1}^{3} N_i M_i = \frac{6}{18} (40 + 41 + 45) = 42 \tag{47}$$

$$\text{Variance} = \frac{1}{17} \sum_{i=1}^{3} N_i \gamma_{ii} - \frac{1}{18 \times 17} \sum_{i=1}^{3} \sum_{j=1}^{3} N_i N_j \gamma_{ij}$$

$$= \frac{6}{17} (57.111 + 75.611 + 38.5) - \frac{36}{18 \times 17 \times 18} [1028 - (2 \times 614)$$

$$+ 1361 + (2 \times 261) + 693] = \frac{2290}{51} = 44.902 \tag{48}$$

Observed Hit Total = 45

Continuity-corrected deviation = 2.5

$$CR = 2.5/\sqrt{44.9} = .37, P = .3557$$

The multiple response, equal probability, closed-deck case often occurs in a free-response setting where the protocols are verbal descriptions of target persons produced by a medium and each number that appears in the MR matrix is the number of items on the protocol that the target person has checked as applicable to him. In this context we also have $N = s$, and the Greville method is identical to the one suggested by Pratt and Birge (1948).

The Unequal Probability Open-Deck Case

As an example of unequal target probabilities we chose to have $p_1 = \frac{1}{6}$, $p_2 = \frac{1}{3}$, $p_3 = \frac{1}{2}$. A target sequence with these probabilities was obtained from die rolls where the target was a if the die roll was "1," b if "2" or "5," and c if "3," "4," or "6." The results, based on the same set of die rolls which generated the equal probability open-deck target sequence, are presented in the table below. Hits for the single response data are indicated with an asterisk.

Trial	1	2	3	4	5	6	7	8	9	10	11	12	13	14	15	16	17	18	Total Hits
Target	c	b	a	c	c*	c	a*	c*	c	c	a*	b	c	c	b	a	b	b	4
MR Score	4	4	1	2	1	1	4	4	3	2	1	0	3	4	1	0	0	2	37

Single Response. Since the target probabilities are unequal, the Greville formulas do not simplify to the binomial as they did in the SR-E-OD case. However, the simple structure of the λ matrix for SR data does lead to a simplification of the open-deck variance formula.

$$\text{Expectation} = \sum_{i=1}^{3} p_i M_i = (\tfrac{1}{6} \times 6) + (\tfrac{1}{3} \times 5) + (\tfrac{1}{2} \times 7) = \tfrac{37}{6} = 6.167 \qquad (49)$$

$$\text{Variance} = \sum_{i=1}^{3} M_i p_i (1 - p_i) = (6 \times \tfrac{1}{6} \times \tfrac{5}{6}) + (5 \times \tfrac{1}{3} \times \tfrac{2}{3}) + (7 \times \tfrac{1}{2} \times \tfrac{1}{2})$$

$$= \tfrac{133}{36} = 3.694 \qquad (50)$$

Observed Hit Total = 4

(i) Continuity-corrected deviation (psi-hitting) $= -\tfrac{8}{3} = -2.667$

$$CR = -2.667/\sqrt{3.694} = -1.39, P = .9172$$

(ii) Continuity-corrected deviation (psi-missing) $= -\tfrac{5}{3} = -1.667$

$$CR = -1.667/\sqrt{3.694} = -.867, P = .193$$

Multiple Response

$$\text{Expectation} = \sum_{i=1}^{3} p_i M_i = (\tfrac{1}{6} \times 40) + (\tfrac{1}{3} \times 41) + (\tfrac{1}{2} \times 45) = \tfrac{257}{6} = 42.833 \quad (51)$$

$$\text{Variance} = \sum_{i=1}^{3} p_i \lambda_{ii} - \sum_{i=1}^{3} \sum_{j=1}^{3} p_i p_j \lambda_{ij} = (\tfrac{1}{6} \times 146) + (\tfrac{1}{3} \times 169) + (\tfrac{1}{2} \times 45)$$

$$- [(\tfrac{1}{6} \times \tfrac{1}{6} \times 146) + (\tfrac{1}{3} \times \tfrac{1}{3} \times 169) + (\tfrac{1}{2} \times \tfrac{1}{2} \times 151)$$

$$+ 2(\tfrac{1}{6} \times \tfrac{1}{3} \times 57) + 2(\tfrac{1}{6} \times \tfrac{1}{2} \times 100) + 2(\tfrac{1}{3} \times \tfrac{1}{2} \times 117)] = \tfrac{1209}{36}$$

$$= 33.583 \qquad (52)$$

Observed Hit Total = 37

(i) Continuity-corrected deviation (psi-hitting) $= -\tfrac{19}{3} = -6.33$

$$CR = -6.33/\sqrt{33.538} = -1.09, P = .8621$$

(ii) Continuity-corrected deviation (psi-missing) $= -\tfrac{16}{3} = -5.33$

$$CR = -5.33/\sqrt{33.583} = -.92, P = .1788$$

The Unequal Probability Closed-Deck Case

The target sequence for this case was generated from an 18-card deck consisting of three hearts (*a*), six clubs (*b*), and nine spades (*c*). Thus, $N_1 = 3, N_2 = 6,$

$N_3 = 9$. The results are presented in the table below. Hits for the single-response data are indicated with an asterisk.

Trial	1	2	3	4	5	6	7	8	9	10	11	12	13	14	15	16	17	18	Total Hits
Target	b*	c*	c	b	c*	b	c	b	c	c	b	a	b	a	c*	a	c	c*	5
MR Score	8	2	6	1	1	0	0	2	3	2	3	3	5	6	2	0	3	4	51

Single Response. It is worth noting that for SR data the closed-deck case is equivalent to matching two decks of arbitrary composition. Stevens formulas (10) and (11) are equivalent to the Greville formulas for this case. Since the Stevens formulas are not appreciably simpler, we will use the Greville formulas (31) and (32). Note also that in contrast to formula (46) the second term in the variance formula (54) is not identically zero when the target probabilities are not equal.

$$\text{Expectation} = \left(\sum_{i=1}^{3} N_i M_i \right) / N = \tfrac{1}{18} [(3 \times 6) + (6 \times 5) + (9 \times 7)] = \tfrac{37}{6} = 6.167$$

$$(53)$$

$$\text{Variance} = \left(\sum_{i=1}^{3} N_i \gamma_{ii} \right) / (N - 1) - \left(\sum_{i=1}^{3} \sum_{j=1}^{3} N_i N_j \gamma_{ij} \right) / N(N - 1)$$

$$= [(3 \times 4) + (6 \times 3.611) + (9 \times 4.278)]/17 - [(9 \times 4)$$
$$+ (36 \times 3.611) + (81 \times 4.278) - 2(18 \times 1.667) - 2(27 \times 2.333)$$
$$- 2(54 \times 1.944)]/(18 \times 17) = 4.245 - .381 = 3.864 \qquad (54)$$

Observed Hit Total = 5

(i) Continuity-corrected deviation (psi-hitting) $= -\tfrac{5}{3} = -1.667$

$$CR = -1.667/\sqrt{3.864} = -.85, P = .8023$$

(ii) Continuity-corrected deviation (psi-missing) $= -\tfrac{2}{3} = -.667$

$$CR = -.667/\sqrt{3.864} = -.34, P = .3669$$

Multiple Response

$$\text{Expectation} = \left(\sum_{i=1}^{3} N_i M_i \right) / N = \tfrac{1}{18} [(3 \times 40) + (6 \times 41) + (9 \times 45)] = \tfrac{257}{6}$$

$$= 42.833 \qquad (55)$$

$$\text{Variance} = \left(\sum_{i=1}^{3} N_i \gamma_{ii} \right) / N - \left(\sum_{i=1}^{3} \sum_{j=1}^{3} N_i N_j \gamma_{ij} \right) / N(N-1) = [(3 \times 57.111)$$

$$+ (6 \times 75.611) + (9 \times 38.5)]/17 - [(9 \times 57.111)$$

$$+ (36 \times 75.611) + (81 \times 38.5) - 2(18 \times 34.111)$$

$$- 2(54 \times 14.5)]/(18 \times 17) = 57.147 - 21.871 = 35.276 \qquad (56)$$

Observed Hit Total = 51

Continuity-corrected deviation = $\frac{23}{3}$ = 7.667

$$CR = 7.667/\sqrt{35.276} = 1.29, P = .0985$$

REFERENCES

Bell, M. Francis Bacon: Pioneer in parapsychology. *International Journal of Parapsychology*, 1964, **6**, 199–208.

Bendat, J. S., and Piersol, A. G. *Random Data: Analysis and Measurement Procedures.* New York: Wiley-Interscience, 1971.

Burdick, D. S., and Roll, W. G. Differential weighting of ESP responses. *Journal of the American Society for Psychical Research*, 1971, **65**, 173–184.

Cadoret, R. The reliable application of ESP. *Journal of Parapsychology*, 1955, **19**, 203–227.

Cadoret, R., and Pratt, J. G. The consistent missing effect in ESP. *Journal of Parapsychology*, 1950, **14**, 244–256.

Camp, B. H. (Statement in Notes section.) *Journal of Parapsychology*, 1937, **1**, 305.

Carington, W. W. Experiments on the paranormal cognition of drawings. *Journal of Parapsychology*, 1940, **4**, 1–134.

Chapman, D. The statistics of the method of correct matchings. *American Journal of Psychology*, 1934, **46**, 287–298.

Child, I. L., and Kelly, E. F. ESP with unbalanced decks: A study of the process in an exceptional subject. *Journal of Parapsychology*, 1973, **37**, 278–297.

Edgeworth, F. Y. The calculus of probabilities applied to psychical research. *Proceedings of the Society for Psychical Research*, 1885, **3**, 190–199.

Edgeworth, F. Y. The calculus of probabilities applied to psychical research, II. *Proceedings of the Society for Psychical Research*, 1886, **4**, 189–208.

Feller, W. *An Introduction to Probability Theory and Its Applications.* (3rd ed.) New York: Wiley, 1968. 2 vols.

Fisher, R. A. A method of scoring coincidences in tests with playing cards. *Proceedings of the Society for Psychical Research*, 1924, **34**, 181–185. (See also appendix to Jephson, ·1928.)

Fisk, G. W., and Mitchell, A. M. J. ESP experiments with clock cards: A new technique with differential scoring. *Journal of the Society for Psychical Research*, 1953, **37**, 1–14.

Foster, E. B. Multiple-aspect targets in tests of ESP. *Journal of Parapsychology*, 1952, **16**, 11–22.

Greenwood, J. A. Variance of the ESP call series. *Journal of Parapsychology*, 1938, **2**, 60–64. (a)

Greenwood, J. A. Analysis of a large chance control series of ESP data. *Journal of Parapsychology*, 1938, **2**, 138–146. (b)

Greenwood, J. A. Variance of a general matching problem. *Annals of Mathematical Statistics*, 1938, **9**, 56–59. (c)

Greenwood, J. A. A caution on the use of the method of correct matchings. *American Journal of Psychology*, 1940, **53**, 614–615.

Greenwood, J. A. A preferential matching problem. *Psychometrika*, 1943, **8**, 185–191. (a)

Greenwood, J. A. On the evaluation of differences of success ratios from binomial populations. *Journal of Parapsychology*, 1943, **7**, 277–280. (b)

Greenwood, J. A., and Stuart, C. E. Mathematical techniques used in ESP research. *Journal of Parapsychology*, 1937, **1**, 206–225.

Greville, T. N. E. Exact probabilities for the matching hypothesis. *Journal of Parapsychology*, 1938, **2**, 55–59.

Greville, T. N. E. The frequency distribution of a general matching problem. *Annals of Mathematical Statistics*, 1941, **12**, 350–354.

Greville, T. N. E. On multiple matching with one variable deck. *Annals of Mathematical Statistics*, 1944, **15**, 432–434.

Harvard Computation Laboratory. *Tables of the Cumulative Binomial Probability Distribution.* Cambridge, Mass.: Harvard University Press, 1955. (Volume 35 of the Annals of the Computation Laboratory of Harvard University.)

Hays, W. L. *Statistics for Psychologists.* New York: Holt, Rinehart, and Winston, 1963.

Herr, D. L. A mathematical analysis of the experiments in extrasensory perception. *Journal of Experimental Psychology*, 1938, **22**, 491–496.

Honorton, C. Objective determination of information rate in psi tasks with pictorial stimuli. *Journal of the American Society for Psychical Research*, 1975, **69**, 353–359.

Jephson, I. Evidence for clairvoyance in card-guessing. *Proceedings of the Society for Psychical Research*, 1928, **38**, 223–271.

Kelly, E. F., Kanthamani, H., Child, I. L., and Young, F. W. On the relation between visual and ESP confusion structures in an exceptional ESP subject. *Journal of the American Society for Psychical Research,* 1975, **69**, 1–31.

Kendall, M. G., and Stuart, A. *The Advanced Theory of Statistics.* London: Griffin, 1966. 3 vols.

McVaugh, M., and Mauskopf, S. H. J. B. Rhine's *Extrasensory Perception* and its background in psychical research. *Isis*, 1976, **67**, 161–189.

Mood, A. M., and Graybill, F. A. *Introduction to the Theory of Statistics.* New York: McGraw-Hill, 1963.

Morris, R. L. Obtaining non-random entry points: A complex psi task. In J. B. Rhine and R. Brier (Eds.), *Parapsychology Today*, pp. 75–86. New York: Citadel, 1968.

Morris, R. L. An exact method for evaluating preferentially matched free-response material. *Journal of the American Society for Psychical Research*, 1972, **66**, 401–407.

Palmer, J. Three models of psi test performance. *Journal of the American Society for Psychical Research*, 1975, **69**, 333–339.

Pratt, J. G. The work of Dr. C. Hilton Rice in extrasensory perception. *Journal of Parapsychology*, 1937, **1**, 239–259.

Pratt, J. G. Trial-by-trial grouping of success and failure in psi tests. *Journal of Parapsychology*, 1947, **11**, 254–268.

Pratt, J. G. Methods of evaluating verbal material. *Journal of Parapsychology*, 1960, **24**, 94–109.

Pratt, J. G. On the evaluation of verbal material in parapsychology. *Parapsychological Monographs No. 10.* New York: Parapsychology Foundation, 1969.

Pratt, J. G., and Birge, W. R. Appraising verbal test material in parapsychology. *Journal of Parapsychology*, 1948, 12, 236-256.

Rhine, J. B. *Extrasensory Perception*. Boston: Boston Society for Psychic Research, 1934.

Rhine, J. B. Position effects in psi test results. *Journal of Parapsychology*, 1969, 33, 136-157.

Rhine, J. B., and Pratt, J. G. *Parapsychology: Frontier Science of the Mind*. Springfield, Ill.: Charles C Thomas, 1957.

Rhine, J. B., Pratt, J. G., Stuart, C. E., Smith, B. M., and Greenwood, J. A. *Extrasensory Perception after Sixty Years*. New York: Henry Holt, 1940.

Richet, C. La suggestion mentale et le calcul des probabilités. *Revue Philosophique*, 1884, 18, 609-674.

Rogers, D. P., and Carpenter, J. C. The decline of variance of ESP scores within a testing session. *Journal of Parapsychology*, 1966, 30, 141-150.

Roll, W. G., and Burdick, D. S. Statistical models for the assessment of verbal and other ESP responses. *Journal of the American Society for Psychical Research*, 1969, 63, 287-302.

Roll, W. G., Morris, R. L., Damgaard, J. A., Klein, J., and Roll, M. Free verbal response experiments with Lalsingh Harribance. *Journal of the American Society for Psychical Research*, 1973, 67, 197-207.

Roy, S. N., and Mitra, S. K. An introduction to some nonparametric generalisations of analysis of variance and multivariate analysis. *Biometrika*, 1956, 43, 361.

Saltmarsh, H. F., and Soal, S. G. A method of estimating the supernormal content of mediumistic communications. *Proceedings of the Society for Psychical Research*, 1930, 39, 266-271.

Schmeidler, G. R. Analysis and evaluation of proxy sessions with Mrs. Caroline Chapman. *Journal of Parapsychology*, 1958, 22, 137-155.

Scott, C. Models for psi. *Proceedings of the Society for Psychical Research*, 1961, 53, 195-225.

Scott, C. On the evaluation of verbal material in parapsychology. A discussion of Dr. Pratt's monograph. *Journal of the Society for Psychical Research*, 1972, 46, 79-90.

Shepard R. N., Romney, A. K., and Nerlove, S. B. (Eds.). *Multidimensional Scaling: Theory and Applications for the Behavioral Sciences*. New York: Seminar Press, 1972. 2 vols.

Siegel, S. *Non-parametric Statistics for the Behavioral Sciences*. New York: McGraw-Hill, 1956.

Soal, S. G., and Bateman, F. *Modern Experiments in Telepathy*. New Haven: Yale University Press, 1954.

Solfvin, G. L., Kelly, E. F., and Burdick, D. S. Some methods of analysis for preferential-ranking data. *Journal of the American Society for Psychical Research*, in press.

Stanford, R. G. Concept and psi. In W. G. Roll, R. L. Morris, and J. D. Morris (Eds.), *Research in Parapsychology 1973*, pp. 137-162. Metuchen, N. J.: Scarecrow Press, 1974.

Stanford, R. G., and Mayer, B. Relaxation as a psi-conducive state. A replication and exploration of parameters. *Journal of the American Society for Psychical Research*, 1974, 68, 182-191.

Stanford, R. G., and Palmer, J. Some statistical considerations concerning process-oriented research in parapsychology. *Journal of the American Society for Psychical Research*, 1972, 66, 166-179.

Stevens, W. L. Tests of significance for extrasensory perception data. *Psychological Review*, 1939, 46, 142-150. (a)

Stevens, W. L. Distribution of groups in a sequence of alternatives. *Annals of Eugenics*, 1939, 9, 10-17. (b)

Stuart, C. E. An ESP test with drawings. *Journal of Parapsychology*, 1942, 6, 20–43.

Stuart, C. E., and Greenwood, J. A. A review of criticisms of the mathematical evaluation of ESP data. *Journal of Parapsychology*, 1937, 1, 295–304.

Swed, F., and Eisenhart, C. Tables for testing randomness of grouping in a sequence of alternatives. *Annals of Mathematical Statistics*, 1943, 14, 66–87.

Thouless, R. H., and Brier, R. M. The stacking effect and methods of correcting for it. *Journal of Parapsychology*, 1970, 34, 124–128.

Uspensky, J. V. *Introduction to Mathematical Probability.* New York: McGraw-Hill, 1937.

von Neumann, J. Distribution of the ratio of the mean square successive difference to the variance. *Annals of Mathematical Statistics*, 1941, 12, 367–395.

Wishart, J., and Hirshfeld, H. O. A theorem concerning the distribution of joins between line segments. *Journal of the London Mathematical Society*, 1936, 11, 227.

Young, F. W. POLYCON: A program for multidimensionally scaling one-, two-, or three-way data in additive, difference, or multiplicative spaces. *Behavioral Science*, 1973, 18, 152–155.

Zenhausern, R. Damn lies or statistics? *Journal of the American Society for Psychical Research*, 1974, 68, 281–296.

3

Methods for Controlled Research on ESP and PK

Gertrude R. Schmeidler

INTRODUCTION

From a broad perspective, all scientific methods are alike. They demand, by definition, accurate observations with a full statement of the relevant conditions. But (as students who have had laboratory courses in diverse fields know too well) when we focus upon a particular area like geology or psychology, we find that it has special techniques, and the various scientific techniques seem to have little overlap.

From this narrower point of view, parapsychology's methods are essentially those of good psychological research: specification of the stimulus, subject, and response variables; double-blind controls; statistical evaluation of the data; checks for contaminants such as response bias and experimenter effects; a search for physiological concomitants; and so on.

When next we turn our viewer to high magnification, we find that parapsychology, like other specialized fields, has developed a variety of distinctive techniques. It uses built-in controls, methods of eliciting an appropriate instructional set, and ways of examining the data which are unfamiliar even to most psychologists. It is these special methods, as they apply to ESP and PK research, that the following discussion will emphasize.

EXTRASENSORY PERCEPTION (ESP)

ESP refers to information which is not obtained through the senses or by inference. Obviously, then, ESP research must include controls for sensory input and for inference, and a measure of the information. The simplest experimental techniques delimit the target (stimulus) population to a few prespecified items and ask the subject to call (respond to) those targets by stating their order. With this simple method, responses are forced choice. Sensory input is controlled by eliminating it: the targets are concealed. Inference is similarly controlled by eliminating all possibility of it: the targets are arranged in random order. A measure of the ESP information comes from comparison of the accuracy of the calls with the likelihood of chance success. Where it seems desirable, the estimate of chance success can be corrected for response bias by "diagonal scoring": data are recorded in a square with targets designating the columns and responses designating the rows. Each call is tallied in the appropriate box, and hits (accurate calls) appear in the diagonal. Success is evaluated by analysis of variance, assigning one degree of freedom to the diagonal.

The simple forced-choice method was used early. In 1889, for example, Sidgwick, Sidgwick, and Smith reported research where the targets were the two-digit numbers from 10 to 90, selected in random order, and where they found the spectacular success rate of 117 accurate calls in 664 trials, i.e., more than 17 per cent. Coover (1917) used playing cards with the face cards removed as his targets and found success that was significantly above chance expectation under both clairvoyant and telepathic conditions. It was only in the 1930s, however, through the efforts of J. B. Rhine, that the forced-choice method came into wide use.

Rhine established what is now the classical target population for such research: five cards (a circle, cross, square, star, and set of three wavy lines) arranged in decks of 25. These are usually called ESP cards and are a variant of the symbols proposed to Rhine by Zener, which were called Zener cards. With these simple targets there is usually relatively little response bias; and more than a dozen more or less satisfactory methods of working with ESP cards have been developed (Rhine and Pratt, 1962).

But even with ESP cards, there are pitfalls for the unwary. Consider, for example, a well-meaning but naive experimenter who used a deck of 25 ESP cards, with five symbols of each type, in the following way. He sits across a table from his subject, shuffles the cards a few times, looks at the top one, asks his subject to guess what it is, records card and guess, tells the subject what the card is, and continues thus through the deck; then shuffles again and repeats. Let us say that the subject had five right on the first run and eight right on the second, and our experimenter decides he will forget the first run because it was just a warm-up. He concludes that the second high score gave evidence of ESP and therefore terminates his session. A quick rundown of everything that was wrong here can suggest the controls necessary for ESP research.

In the first place, sensory input was not properly controlled. It is well known that if light strikes the back of an ESP card at the right angle, it is possible to read the symbol through the back of the card. Further, the subject may have glimpsed top or bottom cards during the shuffling, or seen any card as the experimenter lifted it. He might have seen a reflection of the target, perhaps in the experimenter's eyeglasses. The backs of some cards could have been defaced, so that they would be recognized on the second run. Also, the experimenter might have unconsciously given sensory cues by responding to what he was looking at, perhaps by smiling at his favorite symbol or by stiffening at an angular one and relaxing at a curved one.

In the second place, cards were not adequately randomized. Some might stick together in shuffling, so that sequences reappear; the first or last cards might have stayed in position.

In the third place, inference was not eliminated. As soon as the subject learned what the first card was, he knew there were only four chances that the same symbol would follow, but there were five chances for each of the other symbols—and on his 25th call he had not a guess, but a certainty.

In the fourth place, the experimenter was not blind when he recorded the calls and targets. He may have made the "autistic" error of writing what he wished the subject had said, or what he wished the target was.

In the fifth place, it invalidates research to change the rules after the data are known, or to stop as soon as one likes the pattern of results. Eliminating some of the data (in this case, the score of the first run) for reasons that are thought up after seeing those data is a method which, if run into the ground, can give spurious confirmation of any hypothesis.

In the sixth place, a single score of eight correct calls in a deck of ESP cards could occur so often by chance that, in isolation, it proves nothing.

What methods have been worked out for coping with these difficulties? How can we set up an adequately controlled procedure? Some examples follow.

Concealing the Targets

If targets are near the subject, they must be in an opaque container, unopened until the subject's responses have been recorded. With ESP cards, for example, a deck may be in a box which is not opened until all calls at the deck are on record; or each card may be in its own opaque, closed envelope. A method I like with ESP symbols is to record the order of symbols on a target sheet, by-passing the cumbersome cards altogether. This not only saves a lot of preparation time, but by simplifying the method, it makes errors in target preparation less likely.

The next step is to wrap the target sheet on both sides with aluminum foil or put cardboard on both sides of it. The next is to put it into a manila envelope with a response sheet aligned on top, so that the spaces on the response sheet are over the written targets. The final step is to staple the assembly so that it stays in place. The subject is asked to write, in each empty box of the response sheet, a response that corresponds to the target directly beneath it. The one further precaution necessary with this method is that the person who put the targets into their envelopes, and who thus might be able to identify any target order, should either not be in contact with the subject or else should not see which envelope the subject is using.

The difficulty which necessitates this final precaution is that an experimenter who knows the target order may inadvertently give cues about the first target or others. A necessary part of target concealment, therefore, is that the experimenter and everyone else in normal contact with the subject be blind about target order. Since small differences between containers might identify target order, either an assistant should do the whole job of target arrangement, or (if requiring so much labor from an assistant is impractical) the experimenter should prepare the targets, then have an assistant (a) put all targets into their containers and (b) randomize the order of the containers.

Different types of targets require different precautions. A later section lists many kinds of targets which are currently being used, and obviously some need quite another kind of control for sensory input. With machine selection of targets, for example, the machine must not show by clicks or other external changes which target it chooses.

When the research design permits telepathy, it is necessary that the *agent* (sender) as well as the *targets* be out of the sensory range of the percipient (subject). Visual cues can be prevented by having agent and percipient in different rooms with closed doors. To guard against auditory cues, the rooms should be insulated, or separated by an air space, not merely by a single wall. Timing presents an added difficulty here. If the agent signals when he is ready to send the target, he may signal somewhat differently for different targets. Timing must therefore be set by the percipient, or by some automatic signal, or by a blind experimenter.

When the research deals with precognition, target concealment is no problem because targets have not yet been determined.

Randomizing the Targets

If targets are cards to be shuffled, it is necessary to have a well-trained shuffler, clean cards that are not dog-eared, many shuffles, and then two cuts with a knife edge (the first to ensure that both top and bottom cards are changed; the second to permit the first card to return to the top.) The method is clumsy and is little used.

Machines may be constructed to mix targets and feed them out serially; but such machines must of course be carefully pretested to check that their mixing is adequate. A computer may be programmed to supply random lists. In the modern, sophisticated variant of machine mixing, target order is determined by radioactive emission.

If targets are not to be reused, each target (or set of targets, treated as a unit) may be put into an opaque container, e. g., a heavy envelope, and the order of the containers randomized. It is essential that this be done by a person not otherwise connected with the experiment, so that small differences in the appearance of the containers do not identify them and their contents. The subject or experimenter may then choose one container as the target. This simple method is the one that is commonly used when pictures are the targets, as in experiments where the subject is asked to dream about a target or to produce a series of images or free associations relevant to it.

If targets are to be reused, the whole population must be concealed, perhaps in an opaque box where a shielded opening permits the experimenter to put his hand in and select one. After its use, that target must be returned to the container, and all targets thoroughly mixed before the next is selected. This has the obvious problem of inadequate mixing, perhaps because some targets change shape after use and then are more or less readily accessible. A check on whether such systematic errors occurred can come at the end of the experiment, by finding if the targets were appropriately balanced and if target sequences fell within chance limits.

The usual method of target randomization depends on random number tables. Each target is assigned a digit or a set of digits. With ESP symbols, for example, 0 and 1 might be assigned to the circle, 2 and 3 to the cross, and so on; or with the 12 positions on the face of a clock, 01 might designate 1, 02 designate 2, and so on to 12 (and the paired digits 13, 14 . . . 99, 00, would not designate targets). Entry into the random number table should be random, for example, by throwing ten-sided dice to determine page, column, and row for initial entry. The random digits then determine target order. The experimenter or his assistant reads down the designated column or columns, then down the next, and treats the table as circular. Successive series of targets are allocated to successive subjects, so that only one point of entry is needed. An advantage of this method is that a written record of the targets is made before the experiment. The wise experimenter prepares more lists than he expects to need, so that there will be an emergency supply in case some procedural error or difficulty arises.

Since each target list is called only once, response bias should not affect the overall data. When all subjects call the same lists, it is necessary to use Greville's (1944) correction for a possible response bias or "stacking" effect.

Open and Closed Series

If target order is randomized and the series of targets is "open" (i.e., any item used as a target is then replaced and usable again), there is no possibility of inference.   Conventional statistics may be used.   But the mathematics are different with a "closed" set of targets (a predesignated number of each target, e.g., five of each of the ESP symbols in a deck of 25).   Further, a subject who is calling a closed series and is given feedback after each response (told if each call is right or wrong) needs to have fresh odds calculated for each response. This would be so cumbersome that experimenters avoid it; feedback experiments use open series.   Subjects ordinarily expect target choice to be orderly rather than truly random and thus often try to "balance" their calls (i.e., to give equal frequencies of response for the various targets).   This gives them no advantage with the usual open series, and there is evidence (Stanford, 1967) that such a cognitive attitude is unfavorable for ESP success.   I therefore like to make the situation clear to my subjects by a concrete example and typically include in the instructions some such paragraph as this:

> The way we decided on the order wasn't exactly like this, but it was as if we had a big box with 500 of these cards in it—a hundred circles, a hundred crosses, a hundred squares, a hundred stars, a hundred waves.   I'd put my hand in, mix them up, take one out, and that would be the first on your list. Then I'd *put that one back*, mix them up again, take one out, and that would be your second one.   And keep on that way, putting them back each time. You see with that way of doing it, a particular one could repeat itself any number of times, and some other one might be left out.   There's no way of figuring it.   You shouldn't try to make them come out even.

Double-Blind Methods

Without machine scoring, it is essential that the target record be made by some-one who is ignorant of the subject's responses and also that the response record be made by the subject or by someone else who is ignorant of the target.   It is desirable to have someone blind to the hypothesis score the records.   And be-cause we all make mistakes, it is essential that records be rescored by someone ignorant of the initial scoring.

An alternative is to use a machine which records the targets and responses and which scores the responses automatically.

Scoring ESP Responses

Forced Choice Responses.   The usual ESP score is number of hits (calls which match the targets), but there are many other appropriate scores.   A list of six is given below.

Certain calls may be predesignated as the only ones to be used. Fisk and West (1955), for example, found a subject who made more hits on circles than on the other targets and who reported that he thought of circles as erotic, female symbols. In a follow-up experiment with the same subject, they designated circle targets as the items of particular interest. Fahler and Osis (1966) asked their subjects to say which calls they felt most confident about and then scored only those calls to test their hypothesis.

Displacements may be presented as scorable responses. After pretests, for example, Soal found two subjects who typically responded with the target which preceded or followed the "correct" one. He then scored later tests to find if this pattern continued (Soal and Bateman, 1954). The conventional notation for a response scored against the target immediately *after* the correct one is to write it as (+1) displacement; for a response scored against the target two places ahead, to write (+2); for a response scored against the target immediately *preceding* the correct one, to write (-1), and so on. Many experimenters routinely score for (-1), 0, and (+1) displacement, then of course correct mean chance expectation to correspond. Occasionally a subject will be found on pretest to have some other displacement pattern, such as calling a wave for a circle, and so long as the pattern is designated before the experiment begins, it is legitimate to score for it.

When targets can be arranged in a meaningful sequence, "difference scores" are a more sensitive measure than direct hits. If the 12 standard positions on a clock face are targets, they may be arranged to form a circle, as may various other targets, such as the colors from red to orange, green, purple, and back to red again. Here a direct hit is scored 0, an adjacent target is scored 1, a target two away is scored 2, and so on. Lower scores show greater success; standard statistics can be used (Fisk and Mitchell, 1953).

When forced-choice targets cannot be arranged into a meaningful sequence, ranked-target scoring yields more information than the simple score of hit (right) or miss (wrong). For each call, targets are put into a random rank order. If the call matches the first ranked target it obtains the maximum score; if it matches the second ranked target its score is one lower; and so on (Friedman, Schmeidler, and Dean, 1976). This method is practicable with computer scoring and target determination but would be intolerably time-consuming if done by hand.

Variance of scores is sometimes used as the measure of ESP. With an open series of 25 ESP symbols, for example, the mean variance expected by chance is 4. If the subject's run scores are unusually flat or unusually variable, standard statistics show whether the run variance departs significantly from either the theoretical run variance or the empirical variance derived from the subject's scores. Score variance seems a sensitive indicator of mood: eager excitement tends to be associated with high variance (Rogers and Carpenter, 1966) and apathy or withdrawal with flat scores and low variance (Rogers, 1967; Stanford, 1966).

When there is a very large number of targets, such as all the drawable words in a dictionary, data are best evaluated by a special formula developed by R. A. Fisher (Carington, 1944). The baseline for chance expectation is determined by the number of responses for a word (or other item) when it was *not* the target. The method thus requires many test administrations with diverse targets, to provide a large response pool. (Having a large response pool is especially important because Carington, after years of working with the technique, found that it is advisable to use narrow categories for scoring a hit. For example, he reports a substantially higher hit ratio when "elm" was scored correct only for the target "elm" than when elm, along with oak, maple, poplar, etc., were all classed together as hits for any kind of tree.) A problem here is that any particular catalogue of response frequencies, such as the one Carington prepared, may be inappropriate for subjects drawn from a different population or tested at a different time.

Open-ended Responses. When the target is complex, no response is likely to be completely right or wrong. The standard way of scoring such data is to use blind judges who score each response against each of the targets. For example, a subject may try on ten nights to dream about whatever target picture an agent happened, that night, to select from a target pool. Then each of three blind judges (whose scores will be averaged) is presented with a 10 × 10 array. Along the top are listed the ten pictures, in random order; down the side are the dream reports. The judge rates (for example, on a scale of 0 to 100) how well the dream reports for the first night correspond to each of the ten pictures. He then continues with ratings for each of the subsequent nights. Analysis of variance of the array shows whether the ten correct target-response pairings are significantly different from the 90 incorrect pairings.

An alternative with the same general approach is to have the blind judge *rank* each response for how well it matches the various targets. With ten possibilities, he would enter into the array 1, 2, 3 . . . 10 for each response. Some experimenters choose to class all high ranks together, and all low ranks together, but such pooling of scores discards so much information that it seems inadvisable.

Similar ratings or rankings can be used to judge the accuracy of "readings" (life histories). Good research must be double blind. The person for whom the reading is held is absent. The proxy sitter (a blind notetaker) asks for the reading and records it. The best judge of the accuracy of a reading is ordinarily the absent sitter for whom the sitting was held. Each absent sitter is then presented with the entire set of readings, coded so that he does not know which was intended for him, and is asked to rate or to rank them. The experimenter puts these ratings or rankings into an array for analysis of variance: readings are the columns, and sitters' scores are the rows.

In scoring, an alternative to such global ranking or rating requires that a blind experimenter put a pair of parentheses after each scorable item in the responses.

Parentheses would, for example, litter the protocol thus: "I think this is a man ( ) of about 50 or 55 ( ) who is going to have a lot of happiness in his future. He has had some troubles in his past, but things will go better for him soon. He is very close to someone named Anna ( ). He wears a green ( ) jacket ( ) with brass ( ) buttons ( )." The subject is asked to respond to each item singly, so far as possible, so that a woman of 55 who wore a red sweater with a brass clasp should respond affirmatively to the age and the brass, but not to the man, green, jacket, or buttons. Responses typically consist of entering each pair of parentheses with a check if the item is clearly right, a cross if it is wrong, and a question mark if it is ambiguous. (Subjects find this easier than entering only checks and crosses.) Checks are then summed, and the frequency of checks for each reading is entered into the protocol X subject array.

The items on any of these protocols may be subdivided, and a different array set up for each division. Dream protocols, for example, may have items evaluated separately for responses that were or were not associated with color. Readings for absent sitters may have items subdivided for personality descriptions of the sitters, references to living individuals, references to dead individuals, etc.

Open-ended Responses Scored as Forced Choice. A method for retaining both freedom in the subject's response and also the simplicity of forced-choice scoring is to use complex material for the target but take only prespecified categories as the scorable responses. Schmeidler and Lewis (1969) prepared a set of 81 pictures which showed all combinations of three levels for four variables: sex (two males, two females or one male and one female); age (young, adult but not old, old); activity (passive, normal, active); and emotion (unhappy, neutral, happy). Subjects were told that each picture showed two people; they were asked to describe the picture; and responses were scored for accuracy on the four variables. Honorton (1975) has recently prepared an assembly of 1,024 pictures which permits binary scoring (present or absent) for all combinations of ten variables.

Physiological Measures. When targets are preselected as emotionally neutral or emotionally charged, the subject's physiological changes can appropriately be used as the response measure. Tart (1963) applied painful electric shock to the agent on some trials of a GESP experiment and measured subjects' responses by GSR, EEG, plethysmograph, and key taps (conscious report). Each of the physiological measures showed a significant difference between shock and nonshock trials, but the key taps did not. Another example is research reported by Dean (1966), who made use of only a single physiological measure. In his procedure, the subject lay quietly in a darkened room. A plethysmograph record showed changes in his finger's fluid volume (a measure of autonomic activity). The agent in another room looked at names, randomly ordered, of three types: persons important to the subject but not to the experimenter; persons important to the experimenter but not to the subject; and persons known to neither. Timing was recorded on the plethysmograph record. Scoring of plethysmograph changes was blind. Dean's data, and those of several similar experiments, showed increase in autonomic activity when the agent contemplated a name personally relevant to the subject. Typically, as found by Tart, the subject reported no awareness of the target.

Other possibilities are obvious but have not as yet been adequately explored. No controlled research has been published on the wave form of the cortical evoked potential, e.g., for auditory vs. visual ESP targets. Only preliminary investigation reports similarity in the timing of alpha waves as the ESP response in paired subjects.

Selection of Appropriate ESP Targets

The experimenter, obviously, need not restrict himself to using ESP cards as targets. There is an infinite number of possibilities, and for some subjects or some hypotheses, other target possibilities are preferable to a set of five symbols. The range of choice might be suggested by the following list, culled from 5 years of reports in a single journal. The *Journal of the American Society for Psychical Research*, in 1970-1974, published ESP research with these targets: cards that were green on one side and white on the other; the inner containers that concealed these cards; ESP cards; multiple-choice questions, each consisting of four items relevant to a story that the subject had heard; elaborate pictures (usually art prints or magazine illustrations); slides of patterns and faces (including the subject's own face); names (including the subject's own name); the sex of a person in a concealed photograph; a particular square within a 5 X 5 matrix; red vs. black papers; Identi-Kit components to match the face of a target person; a multisensory environment which the subject would soon experience; erotic pictures affixed to some ESP cards; the timing of radioactive emissions from a Schmidt machine; several sets of five nature cards; the 12 positions of a clock face; audio-visual programs of slides and music; geometric symbols; the five vowels; a pool of 100 simple line drawings of objects, with their names; characteristics of the persons who would sit in specified auditorium chairs; word associates; relevant statements about individuals in concealed photographs; series of thematically related stereoscopic slides.

Selection of Appropriate Subjects

Species. Humans are not necessarily the subjects of choice. Though no systematic work has been done in comparative parapsychology, extrachance data have been reported for such diverse animals as cockroaches, lizards, rodents, cats, dogs, horses, and humans. Probably the two best directives for the research worker are: (a) to study psi in the species where he is himself most expert as an experimentalist; and (b) to set up the laboratory conditions and reinforcement schedules which most sensitively elicit meaningful data in other types of research.

Demographic Variables. Since psi has been demonstrated in young children, adolescents, and adults, in males and females, and in many races, the same directives apply as in the preceding paragraph. In general, the experimenter should work with the subjects with whom he feels most comfortable and whom he is most competent to test.

Preselection of Subjects. If the experimenter wants to study the relation of psi to some other variable, such as imagery, creativity, extroversion, or psychosis, he may choose to use preselected criterion groups. It may be even more necessary in psi than in other research, however, to do careful pretesting to ensure that such special conditions as the choice of targets, the setting, or the connotations of the wording of the instructions do not in themselves have a differential effect upon the groups.

In the more common case of preselection, the experimenter may choose to use gifted subjects. Here he can fall into a trap. The natural way to find gifted subjects is to look for those who have shown marked psi success outside of the laboratory, but this is often counterproductive. A subject who considers himself gifted while working under his own conditions will often feel either a sullen or a fierce resentment of laboratory restrictions, and this attitude may defeat the experimenter's purpose in selecting him.

A method recently used successfully (Tart, 1976), and which may serve as a model, used two preselection steps. The first consisted of group testing by an experimenter who told his subjects that he was looking for good subjects for later work and who used rather dull targets. Subjects with promising scores were invited to come to the laboratory, where the same experimenter had them work on two types of interesting ESP machines. Those with the better scores were invited for a third session with the same experimenter, in which they worked with the machine that they preferred. Their scores on the third session were remarkably high.

The three conspicuous virtues of this approach are: (a) the subject's goal during the selection trials is to do well enough for later laboratory work, and thus the later work comes as no surprise to him; (b) the experimenter effect is controlled, since it is the experimenter for whom the subject produced earlier high scores who works with him later; and (c) test conditions become increasingly pleasant.

Selection of Targets with Appropriate Probability Levels

Comparison of the "psi quotient" for targets with different probability levels has not given unequivocal evidence that scoring is better with high probability of chance success, with low, or with some middle level. Many factors can guide the experimenter's choice of targets, and a few are listed below.

Psi-Missing. If there is reason to expect target avoidance, perhaps because of unpleasant testing conditions, or because of a negativistic group of subjects, or merely because the experimenter wants to leave all possibilities open, the research design should permit equal opportunity for extrachance low scores and extrachance high ones. Binary targets are therefore desirable.

Feedback to the Subject. If an experimenter reports after each call whether it was right or wrong, to find if this will help his subject learn to increase ESP success, he is faced with a dilemma. Targets with a low probability of chance success will probably yield a long string of failures; and this is likely to discourage the subject and induce a set which is unfavorable for learning. On the other hand, targets with a high probability of chance success, like $1/4$ or $1/5$, are inappropriate. This is because the subject is told he is right both for ESP hits and for chance hits; and there will be so many false positives that the subject is likely to develop "superstitious" behavior.

The method of choice is to avoid both horns of the dilemma by using targets which permit differential scoring or else by using targets which are qualitatively complex. With either, (a) the subject receives more information from feedback than a simple "Right" or "Wrong"; and (b) a response which is not completely correct may still be near enough to the target to provide some encouragement.

Attention Span of the Subject. Subjects who are unfamiliar with a set of targets are likely to be confused by a large set and to omit some targets from their calls. (It is especially important to keep this in mind when working with young children.) It is possible to compensate for this difficulty to some extent by organizing the targets into an ordered display. Examples are the circular arrangement of a color wheel or a clock face, or a 5 × 5 matrix which shows five colors for each of the five ESP symbols.

Efficiency of Research. With a gifted subject who has many ESP hits, targets with long odds will achieve meaningful results more quickly than targets with short odds. Lower odds demand longer series of calls.

Selection of Appropriate Motivating Conditions

When the target is distant, and especially if an experiment is conducted by mail, many subjects feel that the set-up is so discouragingly impersonal as to preclude

ESP. Carington (1972) and other experimenters who worked under these conditions reported higher scores when the subjects were provided with a "K-object": a concrete link to the target or the experimenter. Examples of such K-objects are a photograph of the room in which the target will be displayed, or a personal belonging of the experimenter's. This seems comparable to the "token object" (something which belongs to an absent sitter) which is often used in "psychometry" experiments. K-objects have been interpreted as carrying associative bonds to the target, and token objects have been interpreted as carrying a psi field, imparted by prior events, which is informative. A more conservative interpretation is that each encourages the subject to feel intimacy and closeness; that they make the whole project more motivating to him; and that they demonstrate the personalized interest, or even the solicitude of the experimenter. From this point of view, the equivalent in a face-to-face situation might be the experimenter's effort to make the subject feel at ease or showing concern and interest in the outcome of the session.

In general, appropriate motivating conditions vary with the experimenter-subject relationship. In classroom experiments, for example, a colleague told me he found higher scores when he offered a prize, such as money or theater tickets, for the subject with the highest ESP scores. For me, offering an extrinsic reward for competitive success would be embarrassing, and I would therefore expect my classes to react unfavorably to it. My own finding has been that scores tend to be higher if my class has developed an intrinsic interest in the topic of ESP. In general, perhaps, each experimenter should choose the motivating condition which he has found most effective in his prior work on other topics.

The subject's mood seems, from well-replicated research, to be a key factor in his ESP scoring. Many experimenters report unusually high ESP scores if they induce a dreamy, relaxed state of consciousness, for example, by a ganzfeld, partial perceptual deprivation, or by instructions for progressive relaxation. The most desirable mood, however, probably depends both on the individual subject's needs and the experimental situation. Social affection, for example, has been found to relate negatively to ESP scores in an impersonally administered precognition task; but it relates positively to ESP scores in a GESP task conducted in a warm, friendly atmosphere.

Appropriate Research Design

There are several well-replicated findings within parapsychology. It is often wise to build them into a research design, either to control for them, or to find if they interact with the other variables one is examining, or to vary them in the effort to sharpen scoring differences. Four such findings are listed below.

The Differential Effect. When subjects use two procedures or two sets of targets and their scores are compared for the preferred vs. the nonpreferred (each subject's preference being taken singly), there is usually a significant difference between scores on the preferred and the nonpreferred condition (Rao, 1965).

When overall scores are above mean chance expectation, the scores on the preferred condition are usually higher, and vice versa. The experimenter may therefore be better able to evaluate the factors which interest him if he has subjects go through two procedures and uses for hypothesis-testing only the scores on the procedure which each subject preferred.

The Sheep-Goat Effect. Subjects who think there is *no* possibility of ESP success with a certain procedure (goats) will usually have lower average scores than subjects (sheep) who admit at least some possibility of ESP success with that method (Palmer, 1971; Schmeidler and McConnell, 1973). There is also some evidence that subjects who report unqualified certainty that their own scores will be high because of their ESP ability (supersheep) will have unpredictable, highly variable scores (Beloff and Bate, 1970).

The experimenter may find his data cleaner if he administers a multiple choice question to test attitude toward success on the ESP task. (He may also choose to include other questions to check general negativism, withdrawal, or excessive ego-involvement.) His prestated research design can then properly be to discard (or examine separately) the scores of goats, supersheep, or other unsuitable subjects; he will examine his hypothesis only by using the scores of appropriately cooperative subjects.

Decline Effects. Both ESP hits and run-score variance tend to decline with many repetitive trials, though there is sometimes an upswing when the subject knows he is near the end of the task. Most experimenters therefore plan to have relatively few ESP calls in a session. Depending on the subjects and the targets, "relatively few" may mean perhaps two to five responses to pictures or other complex targets, or 50–100 calls for ESP symbols, or 500–1,000 quick button presses on one of Schmidt's machines. Pretests are desirable to find the appropriate number.

Response Bias. Kreitler and Kreitler (1973) in GESP experiments and Stanford (1967) in clairvoyance-type research using signal detection report that ESP seems most effective for targets where baseline data show a response bias *against* calling them. The experimenter may therefore state different hypotheses for the targets where the subject has shown a positive or a negative response bias.

Telepathy

To investigate telepathy as a distinctive form of ESP, it is necessary to set up conditions which preclude clairvoyance or clairvoyant precognition. This is difficult. Targets cannot be written or even spoken, because the record or the sound waves would constitute a target for clairvoyance. Targets must be identified only by the agent's thought. (Even the most rigorous controls cannot, of course, exclude brain or other body changes associated with the thoughts as possible clairvoyant targets.)

Special techniques for such experiments have been described by McMahan (1946), Birge (1948), and others. The basic design asks the subject to respond to the agent's thoughts in a particular set of forced choices. Let us say the choices are the usual ESP symbols. The agent makes a private code which translates digits into ESP symbols, for example, by saying to himself that three will translate as a circle because last night he and two friends sat around a circular table; and five will translate as a cross because there are five houses between his home and the nearest cross street. He then enters a random number table at random and follows its digit order: he tries to send telepathically a circle whenever 3 comes in the column, a cross whenever 5 comes, and so on. The subject, so far away that he cannot hear or see the agent, writes the ESP symbols which he feels the agent is thinking of. The agent scores the responses against the digit series. Independent checking of hits can be done by a friend of the agent, to whom the code is transmitted by allusion without specific statement. A significant excess of hits above chance expectation with this method is taken as evidence of "pure telepathy," since only the agent's thoughts specified the target.

Most research on telepathy is impure, since it permits interpretation as clairvoyance. The punctilious therefore call it "GESP" or "general ESP." Internal comparisons within such experiments may, however, suggest strongly that telepathy rather than clairvoyance was operative. For example, the difference in scores when (unknown to the subject) different agents try to send the recorded targets, or the difference in scores when the agents' attitudes are different, or the difference when there is an agent as opposed to when there is none would seem to imply that the agent was effective (Schmeidler, 1961; Soal and Bateman, 1954).

An interesting technique reported to yield high GESP scores (Guarino, 1971) consisted of having each percipient select his own two target words: any two words which he considered distinctively different. The words were used as targets for a large number of trials, and their order was determined from a random number table. The percipient made his calls slowly. During the entire period that the percipient was trying to call a word, the agent wrote the target word again and again. A special advantage of this method might be that it permits telepathic transmission from either the agent's initial focal awareness of the target or from a later fuguelike state where the agent is writing automatically while his conscious thoughts drift elsewhere.

Clairvoyance

To investigate clairvoyance as a distinctive form of ESP, it is necessary to preclude telepathy or precognitive telepathy. Targets must therefore be determined and scored without anyone's ever knowing them, either at the time of the experiment or in the future. The use of machines which select random targets and score responses and then register only the total score of a long series is the method of choice. With a long series, it is unlikely that the subject will be correct on all targets (or with binary targets, that the subject will be incorrect on all); and without these extreme scores, no one can know what any particular target was.

The careful experimenter who uses this method may be troubled about machine accuracy. Some check can be provided by comparison with series which permit hand scoring. Another looser check comes from convergent validity. If prior or concurrent GESP research shows that certain conditions are associated with a higher hit rate (perhaps, for example, higher scores for more relaxed subjects, or for runs when the subject reports more confidence) and if the same pattern of differential success appears in the clairvoyance procedure, it adds some modicum of confidence to the assumption of machine accuracy (Schmeidler, 1964).

Precognition

In most precognition research, targets are either randomly selected, or else are observed according to some prestated scheme, *after* the subject has tried to call them. In either case, it may be argued that extrachance correspondence between calls and targets shows PK rather than precognition. The subject (or experimenter) may have influenced by PK the apparently random selection of targets, or he may by PK have determined the target's occurrence. If, for example, the experimenter throws dice to determine the point of entry into a random number table, his PK may have determined the outcome of the throw. Or if emissions of a radioactive element determine the target (Schmidt, 1969), PK may have slowed down or speeded up the radioactivity.

No method has been proposed for making a clean choice between these alternatives. However, a number of methods have been used which make the precognition interpretation attractive because it is simple and the PK interpretation so absurdly elaborate that most of us would choose not to hold it. I give two examples of such methods.

The first method is to use a complicated way of selecting targets. One that has been fairly frequently used is the following. Targets are given by a random number table. The point of entry into the table is determined by temperatures of the principal cities of the United States as printed in a given newspaper on 12 specified future dates. On each date, the right-hand digits in the temperature column are added, and the right-hand digit of the sum is used in the following computations (Mangan, 1955).   The digits, in order, give four three-place numbers. The four numbers are multiplied by each other, and their product is multiplied by its own digits in reverse order. This product is divided by a four-digit number composed of the middle digits of the original numbers. The sum of the digits in the quotient gives the directive for page, column, and row for entering the random number table. One point of entry determines the successive sets of targets for the (prenumbered) subjects. For PK to be effective here, it would have to change the temperature (or the printed statement of temperature) so as to make the computations designate that entry point in a random number table which will produce extrachance results.

A second approach, usable either with this method of entering the random number table or with a simpler one, involves making a number of different hypotheses about the subjects' scores. The hypotheses may be based on such familiar parapsychological findings as the decline effect or the preferential effect, or may relate to individual differences among the subjects; preferably they would be of both types. Where several such hypotheses are significantly confirmed by the data, determination by PK of the entry point which resulted in all these findings seems unlikely. The precognition thesis can thus be supported by convergent validity.

Other investigations examine precognition of events outside the laboratory. One ingenious example comes from Cox (1956), who put forth the hypothesis that accidents tend to be precognized and therefore that railroad trains about to have accidents will carry fewer passengers than usual. He used, as baseline for what was usual, the number of passengers carried on the same train run for each of its preceding 7 days and also for the same weekday, 2, 3, and 4 weeks earlier.

Retrocognition

When a subject tries to get ESP information about past events, we can check his accuracy only if there are records of those events. But with such records, clairvoyance is not precluded (even if the records are now buried and not yet known to us).   Perhaps because of this difficulty, no laboratory research on retrocognition has been published; reports of it come only from spontaneous cases.

One laboratory method seems usable, though it has not been tried as yet: the cipher method.   Some records of ancient civilizations have not yet been deciphered by the experts who have tried to do so. If a subject tried by retrocognition to find the meaning of those records and succeeded in giving the key to them, this would provide a strong argument for retrocognition. The point would be that the translation which shows his accuracy would not have existed in the absence of his retrocognitive success.

Special Problems in ESP Research

Nonrandomness in Random Number Tables. Most modern ESP experiments compare different conditions to test the hypothesis that they will show significantly different ESP scores. In older research, however, many experiments merely compared ESP scores with theoretical chance expectation. Spencer-Brown (1957), attacking these older experiments, argued that if ESP targets were arranged according to random number tables, and if the numbers in those tables were not truly random, evidence for ESP would go down the drain.

He attempted to show that random number tables were nonrandom by the naive method of selecting a short sample of digits from the table, then entering the table at arbitrarily selected points and matching his initial sequence with these new ones. He found significant correspondences, followed by declining correspondences. They supported his argument but alternatively could be interpreted as showing his successful use of ESP (or PK) in his first choices of the "right" places to enter the table.

The appropriate method of examining his argument is obvious, though expensive. It is to program a computer to match all possible entry points in a random number table against an appropriate set of initial selections.

Distance Experiments. A question of major theoretical interest is whether ESP becomes weaker as distance from the target increases. Two methodological problems arise in attempts to find an answer.

One is the subject's motivation. Some subjects may be challenged by knowing their targets are unusually far away and may score higher as a result. Other subjects may be discouraged and score lower. Both patterns have been found. It is necessary that the subject be blind and also, because of the possibility of unconscious cuing, that everyone in normal contact with the subject be blind. (In theory, it would also be desirable to shield against the subject's using ESP to learn about distance, but we do not know how to do such shielding.)

The second methodological problem comes from precognition. Suppose that a subject comes to the experimenter's laboratory and there calls targets which are thousands of miles away. The targets are later mailed to the experimenter for scoring. If the subject's calls were guided by precognition, distance between call and target has been reduced. Initially it was thousands of miles; now it is a few feet or inches. The solution to this difficulty is to have targets prepared at a distant location, to send the responses there for scoring, and to have only total scores, but not the targets, returned to the experimenter. ESP research which used these precautions has shown no consistently significant effects of distances on the earth.

Dowsing. For dowsing, two factors need to be controlled. One is familiarity with the topography and microclimate of a region. Someone who has lived for a long time in the hills of Vermont may, for example, be able to infer the location of underground water from the plant growth and the dips of the ground. He may thus be better qualified than even an expert geologist to make accurate inferences about a familiar area. The second factor extends to the cutting edge of research on sensory sensitivity: it now seems possible that humans may share with other animals some faint sensitivity to electromagnetic changes of the kind that could be produced by running water. The success of a dowser who is at the site is thus attributable to sensory information or to inference. A method which controls for these factors and which seems to have yielded successful results for some of those few dowsers willing to try it consists of presenting the subject with a flat map of a region where he has never been and asking him to identify underground features from the map alone. This method, however, obviates the distinction between dowsing and other forms of ESP.

Auras. It is often claimed that a psychic aura surrounds a person and that observing this aura can show the person's physical well-being and mental state. Tart (1972) has proposed several more or less tightly controlled methods for testing such claims, such as having the target person stand behind a screen which covers him but not the space around him. Auditory and olfactory cues would need to be controlled, and blind scoring of the responses is requisite. No adequately controlled research has tested the claims of an aura.

Ad-Hoc Investigations. Occasionally a unique problem presents itself for investigation, usually an individual's claim that he shows ESP ability only under certain special conditions. An ingenious research worker is sometimes able, with the appropriate combination of rigor and flexibility, to arrange for a meaningful investigation. For example, a sensitive may claim to be able to give a proper reading only if the sitter is nearby but may accept having an unknown sitter unseen in a nearby room. Or the sensitive may insist on touching a token object which the sitter has often used but may accept objects which give no clues for any sitter, like uniform ballpoint pens which the experimenter supplied to all sitters a few weeks earlier. One further example follows.

Bleksley (1963) received a letter from a man living 900 miles away, who was sure he could waken at a time which he had preset, without looking, on a broken alarm clock. Bleksley arranged that the subject send him this clock, learned the subject's normal sleep hours (between midnight and 7:59) and arranged the 480 minutes of sleep time according to a random number table. Bleksley then set the broken clock to the times given by the random number sequence for each of 135 nights; and the subject wrote him, for each night, the time at which he woke. Bleksley thus retained the special conditions congenial to his subject and still performed an experiment that could be properly evaluated. In a second longer experiment, control conditions included keeping the clock set at an inappropriately late time and (a) recording the times specified by the random number table or (b) recording the random number but not computing the time it specified until after the subject's report. Significantly higher scores when the clock was appropriately set attested to this subject's need for the arrangement to which he was accustomed rather than one which the experimenter might think equivalent.

Different subjects make different demands, and some require conditions which no careful experimenter would accept. We infer, perhaps improperly, that such subjects are either fraudulent or else desperately clinging to a means of self-deception. Ordinarily, however, as in Bleksley's research, adequate controls which meet the subject's needs can be set up.

PSYCHOKINESIS (PK)

PK refers to the direct effect of mental processes upon external objects or events. Tests for it must therefore control for the effect of the subject's muscular, glandular, or other physiological changes and also, of course, for normal non-random changes in the target. With inanimate objects the appropriate controls present little difficulty. However, with living organisms, as in psychic healing, determination of the normal range of changes becomes harder. And for some research with living beings, it seems impossible to differentiate between direct changes due to PK and indirect changes produced by telepathy.

PK with Inanimate Objects

Dice, Coins, etc. Most published PK experiments have dealt with throwing or releasing dice so that they come to rest with the desired face uppermost; and methods which apply to them are appropriate for similar research with coins, discs, etc. Major factors that need to be controlled are the subject's muscular skill, imperfections in the objects, and of course recording errors. None presents a theoretical difficulty.

A skilled subject, we are told, can largely determine the way a die falls if it does not bounce, if it bounces once, and perhaps even if it bounces twice. A safe procedure therefore requires many bounces. This can be produced by having the die or dice fall down a chute with many corrugations, or into a chamber with many baffles, or come to rest after being rotated in a cage. Further precautions consist of arranging the dice in the same position before all trials, of having a release mechanism which the subject activates only by pushing a button, of enclosing the apparatus in glass, etc. Though these may be only gilding the lily, careful experimenters like to use them to make the procedure especially sure. (The usual statement of this, a quotation from an unknown sage, is: "You don't have to be paranoid to be a good experimenter, but it helps.")

But suppose that the dice or the coins are imbalanced. Usually they are. (Dice which are supposed to be perfect when they come from the factory need to be specially ordered and are expensive; and even they will develop imperfections with use.) Control for imbalance is easily established by requiring each subject to try an equal number of times for each die face. When all trials are summed, imperfections balance out and can safely be disregarded.

Two methods have been used for blind recording: photographing the dice after they come to rest (McConnell, Snowdon, and Powell, 1955) and having a subject make the record while ignorant of the correct target, i.e., having the subject, alone, try to make the dice come out "right" without knowing what face had been assigned in any trial (Fisk and West, 1958). Both are difficult to arrange. Photography is expensive, and many subjects will object to being ignorant of the target. It is therefore unfortunately common to have records made nonblind. Standard procedure is to have subject and experimenter (or two experimenters) make independent records, in the expectation that where there are no discrepancies, errors are unlikely. The method is not impeccable and has been subject to legitimate criticism (Girden, 1962).

Most subjects grow bored quickly when they make repeated throws or releases for the same target. A method often selected for scoring PK with dice is a comparison of first and later throws at the same target. Standard technique is to have 24 throws without target change and to predict higher scores for the first six throws than for the others.

The optimal number of dice for a single throw varies with the subject. Usually scores are lower with one die or only a few and are also lower with very many. The interpretation is that with a single die, the subject is insufficiently stimulated; with many, there is a feeling of overload.

Placement Tests. A method used with spectacular success by Forwald (McConnell and Forwald, 1967) is to release objects over the middle line of a table and try to use PK to make them fall to one of the sides. As with dice, a mechanical release is used, and the objects are put into the release box in a uniform way. An equal number of tries for the left and right side will control for imbalance. Recording must, of course, be blind.

In theory, an advantage of this method is that the trajectory of the moving object can be recorded. This has not yet been done but could be informative. Anomalies in the trajectories could provide a clue as to how or when PK operated.

Other Moving Objects. Various other methods for studying PK with moving objects have been devised, notably by Cox (1974). In one, for example, ball bearings fall down a medial chute into columns and in the absence of PK demonstrate the familiar Gaussian curve. The subject is asked to produce imbalances.

Scores are the number of balls in each column. With a variety of such devices available, the experimenter can prevent boredom or study the differential effect.

Radioactive Emissions. Schmidt (1974) has constructed sophisticated devices using radioactive emissions which, in the absence of PK, determine target change. The machines are carefully pretested for randomness, then human subjects are asked to influence them or animal subjects are used under such conditions that influencing them provides reinforcement. These are excellent but expensive techniques, with automatic recording of scores; they are now being widely used. Among their special advantages is that minor changes make them adaptable for many purposes. One, for example, registers with a hand on a dial face: rapid emissions make the hand move in one direction and slow emissions in the other. An entire lecture audience may simultaneously try to make the hand move in a given direction and obtain immediate feedback by watching it. Another use to which Schmidt has put his devices is to have the feedback display attached by a concealed switch to one or another machine. He can throw the switch without the subject's being aware of it, and thus change the physical mechanism for feedback. His data, showing similar extrachance scores before and after such changes, provide a method for demonstrating that the subject's effectiveness in PK or ESP does not depend on information about the physical nature of the process.

Temperature. In the PK methods discussed above, measurements are discontinuous. A recent method for observing continuous PK change used polygraph recordings of temperature in an insulated object (Schmeidler, 1973). A device sensitive to small temperature changes, such as a thermistor or a thermocouple, was connected to a recording machine and insulated in a thermos jug or Dewarr flask. To control for changes in the system, the subject was required to try an equal number of times to make the target hotter and colder. Trials were, of course, counterbalanced. Two advantages of this method are that it permits a detailed study of the time course of any significant changes, and that it readily permits a record of what is occurring nearby, in nontarget thermistors or in the subject's body. The method thus allows us to study field effects produced by PK, and the data so far suggest that the target's PK change in one temperature direction is compensated by opposite temperature changes in the nearby field.

Magnetometer, Laser, etc. A variety of sophisticated ways of studying PK are reported by Targ and Puthoff (1977). They describe change in direction of a laser beam, changes in the decay curve of a well-shielded magnetometer, etc. It is clear that such methods, which are perhaps appropriate only when used with selected subjects, can produce strong evidence for PK. If the claims are replicated, they will offer the same advantages as studying temperature change: they permit continuous records and examination of field effects. Chemical changes, e.g., in enzymes, are also appropriate PK targets (Smith, 1972).

Motion of Stationary Objects. Gifted subjects have on occasion produced movement in a stationary object. The first scientific report was from Crookes (1874), who shielded a lever from vibration and air change, recorded its position on smoked paper, and published curves which were initially flat but showed perturbations when his subject tried to produce movement. Green (1971) attached a knitting needle to a pivot and shielded his subject's face with a mask. His subject "at the word of command" made the knitting needle move. Targ and Puthoff (1977) report a change in a scale on which a weight was resting, presumably produced by PK. Other subjects, notably Kulagina, a Russian woman, have been reported to produce movement of nonmagnetic objects under nonlaboratory conditions; but even the movie records of this activity are as yet in the gray area between controlled observations and naturalistic ones (Keil, Ullman, Herbert, and Pratt, 1976).

Table-tipping was a standby of the nineteenth-century séance; and a series of remarkable recent reports describes massive movements of a table and other objects (Brookes-Smith, 1973). The precondition seems to be a lively, loose social atmosphere, most unusual in controlled research, with shouting, cheering, and a priming of the pump by normally produced movements of the table. Brookes-Smith's ingenious technique for this priming of the pump consists of wiring the lower surface of the table so that pressure on it will be recorded and having one subject (selected by his drawing a joker from a set of cards) move the table upward by finger pressure. Records permit differentiating such built-in "cheating" from table movements without normal pressure. Recording of table movements is automatic.

Photography. Conditions for research on "psychic photography" include full control of the exposure field; the use of film still sealed as it came from the manufacturer; a pretested, standard camera; and blind, careful developing, e.g., with polaroid film. Fraudulent manipulations have been so common that the method fell into disrepute, but careful research by Eisenbud (1967) and his colleagues suggests that it is possible for a gifted subject to produce photographic changes by willing. The special advantage of this method is that it can give simultaneous data about both PK and ESP, if the subject produces a picture which conforms to concealed instructions. Since this is a free-response rather than a forced-choice technique, it is potentially an especially rich source of qualitative information about the dynamics of ESP information interacting with PK output.

PK with Living Organisms

Microcellular Organisms. Richmond (1952) reported influencing the direction of movement of paramecia by willing. Research here must include, as Richmond's did not, a blind recording of movement. It must also include equal numbers of trials, ordered or counterbalanced, for the various movement directions.

Recommendations so far are parallel to PK with inanimate objects. With volatile organisms, however, time factors become more important. Microconditions within the medium where the organism swims may change rapidly; movement in one direction may nonrandomly be followed by movement in another; and so on. It therefore seems essential that there be a baseline of control periods and that movement patterns during the baseline be the point of departure for determining appropriate balancing of PK trials.

Plant Activity. Electrical change in plants can be monitored and taken as a response in a PK experiment. It is of course necessary to control a large number of factors known to affect plant activity, such as humidity. It is also necessary to have a baseline for comparison. Most claims about "plant telepathy" are notorious for the absence of such controls and also for the possibility of contamination because electrical changes associated with the "telepathy" stimulus may directly affect the recording device. A good research design has been described by Brier (1969), where two shielded plants were simultaneously monitored. One or the other, in random order, was the target for PK. Records of electrical change were scored blind.

Plant Growth. Long-term research, as on seed germination or plant growth, is especially liable to experimental error. It seems essential to have plants tended only by a blind assistant or experimenter and to have random assignment or carefully matched assignments to experimental and control conditions. Grad (1964) has described what seems an appropriately careful experiment, with affirmative results, where apparently the only difference between control and experimental plants, all watered from flasks of distilled water, was that sealed flasks of the water for the experimental plants were held by a "healer" before use. Measurement of growth was from photographs taken against a scaled background.

Grad reported that pilot research had given null results until all plants were injured by watering with a mild saline solution. Replication may show whether this precondition is generally necessary for positive findings or whether it was only a special requirement for Grad's subject. (Since the subject thought of himself as a healer, he might have needed to know that there was an injury to heal, before he could work effectively.)

Animal Recovery from Injury. Attempts to find if psychic healing can aid the recovery of animals after injury, or facilitate their normal growth, demand controls parallel to those described for plants. Animals should be of pure stock, and the minor differences in size, vitality, and other potentially relevant factors that occur even in pure strains should be matched or otherwise controlled. Rearing, tending, handling, and measurement should be blind. Injuries should be comparable. Either the healer should be allowed no physical contact with the animals or a strong attempt should be made to have controls receive comparable stimulation, perhaps by nonhealers, or by mechanical means, or by subjects who wish them ill. An example of what seems to be well-controlled research with positive findings is given by Grad, Cadoret, and Paul (1961), who made tracings of the outlines of surgical wounds inflicted on mice and of changes in the wounds during recovery. The healer held the outside of the animals' cage; some of the controls' cages were held by others for comparable lengths of time.

Psychic Surgery. To investigate the fairly frequent claims that surgical operations can be performed psychically, it is necessary to have careful medical diagnosis before and after the operation, to observe the purported surgery under good conditions, and to have standard pathological examination of the tissues or blood which the "surgeon" claims came from the patient's body. These conditions have not yet been met. When movies of the operation are permitted, they have been found inadequate because key areas are shielded from the camera. As of now, however, one technique has been sufficient to disprove the claims which it tested: examination of tissue or stones purportedly removed from human patients have shown the tissue or blood to be nonhuman, and the stones inorganic.

Nonsurgical Psychic Healing. The conditions for good research on psychic healing are easy to set forth on paper but as of now seem to have been met only in one experiment with null results (Joyce and Welldon, 1965). For humans, they begin with full diagnosis of patients, then division into matched pairs or matched groups, and then random assignment within the matches to experimental and control conditions. They demand double blind methods. Psychic healers must work at a distance, so that neither patients nor those who have to do with the patient know the assignment. Scores should be derived from competent physicians' blind description of the medical condition and the patient's self-report. Such projects have been difficult to arrange.

Special Problems in PK Research

Distance Experiments. Research on the relation of PK effects to the distance of the subject from the target requires the same double blind conditions as does an

ESP experiment on distance. Since it has long been recognized that the experimenter's PK may interact with the subject's, further necessary precautions are that no one connected with the experiment be nearer the target than the subject is. Automatic recording is essential, especially since timing may be critical. No well-controlled experiment on this problem has yet been performed; but nonblind experiments up to distances of 100 feet indicate no lessening of the PK effect as distance increases.

Ad-Hoc Investigations. As with ESP, special instances sometimes occur where there seems evidence of PK under unusual or unique conditions. This is most frequent in poltergeist cases. The two examples that follow describe controls introduced ad hoc to permit checking such observations.

Bender (1969) investigated a poltergeist case where small objects seemed to move in inexplicable ways. To monitor these small objects he constructed a box which he put in the "poltergeist house," then placed some of the family's knickknacks in the box. The box was open on one side, and its opening was monitored by a photoelectric "light curtain" so that anything which crossed the box's opening would trigger at least one of three cameras, which among them covered the whole open side. On one occasion when all the house's occupants were outside the house with the investigators, a figurine fell within the box. Photoelectric signals and cameras showed that the opening had not been penetrated.

Roll and Pratt (1971) investigated a poltergeist case in a warehouse where shelves were filled with small objects. They had observed that certain objects were particularly likely to move and designated these objects as targets. They placed target objects on the rear of a shelf, arranged other objects in front of them, then carefully monitored the area. On two occasions when no one was or had been near the targets, the target objects fell to the floor although the objects in front of them were still in place.

Experimenter Effects. Humphrey (1947) found subjects' PK scores were significantly higher when an observer tried to help them along than when he or she tried to hinder them. This demonstration of an observer's possible effect upon the data raises difficult methodological problems, especially since we cannot be sure that distance diminishes PK effectiveness. Removing an experimenter from the experimental room will not necessarily remove the experimenter's influence. An experimenter who tries to keep a neutral attitude about success in the conditions which he hypothesizes will be effective and those he hypothesizes will be ineffective may not succeed in neutralizing himself—and if he does, he may be acting to hinder the subject's PK. Perhaps the best safeguard against experimenter effects here is to pretest experimenters on PK under conditions where they are motivated to succeed, then examine separately the data from experimenters whose own PK is weak or is strong.

Ambiguity between PK and ESP. Several experimental methods have studied responses which might be interpreted as PK or as ESP. Vasiliev (1963) describes hypnosis at a distance. The subject was in a Faraday cage; the hypnotist was in a distant room; and Vasiliev reports that the time at which subjects entered a hypnotic trance showed that they were responding to the hypnotic suggestions. Goodrich (1976) describes subjective feelings when psychic healers tried to do distant healing. Patients and healers were notified when to hold each session but were not informed that some sessions were set at different times for the healer and the patient. Blind judges evaluated synchronous and nonsynchronous sessions on the basis of protocols and mood checklists from both healer and patient and showed a significant difference in favor of the synchronous sessions. A third technique, for which only pilot work has so far been done, is to monitor a patient's spontaneous motor behavior (e.g., while he is reading) and find the baseline for such spontaneous movements as crossing the knees or touching the face. An agent can then send randomly ordered PK messages to make one or another type of movement, and differences between experimental and control conditions can be evaluated for PK (or telepathic) effects.

In research of this type, it seems impossible to distinguish between direct PK effects upon the subject's activity and telepathic messages which the subject acts upon. Perhaps the best solution to this difficulty is to bypass it and class the responses under the neutral label of "psi."

REFERENCES

Beloff, J., and Bate, D. Research report for the year 1968-1969. *Journal of the Society for Psychical Research*, 1970, 45, 297-301.

Bender, H. New developments in poltergeist research. *Proceedings of the Parapsychological Association*, 1969, 6, 81-102.

Birge, W. R. A new method and an experiment in pure telepathy. *Journal of Parapsychology*, 1958, 12, 273-288.

Bleksley, A. E. H. An experiment on long-distance ESP during sleep. *Journal of Parapsychology*, 1963, 27, 1-15.

Brier, R. M. PK on a bio-electrical system. *Journal of Parapsychology*, 1969, 33, 187-205.

Brookes-Smith, C. Data-tape recorded experimental PK phenomena. *Journal of the Society for Psychical Research*, 1973, 47, 69-89.

Carington, W. Experiments on the paranormal cognition of drawings. *Proceedings of the American Society for Psychical Research*, 1944, 24, 3-107.

Carington, W. *Telepathy: An Outline of Its Facts, Theory, and Implications*. New York: Gordon Press, 1972. (First published in 1945.)

Coover, J. E. *Experiments in Psychical Research*. Palo Alto, Calif.: Stanford University Press, 1917.

Cox, W. E. Precognition: An analysis, II. *Journal of the American Society for Psychical Research*, 1956, 50, 99-109.

Cox, W. E. PK tests with a thirty-two channel balls machine. *Journal of Parapsychology*, 1974, 38, 56-68.

Crookes, W. *Researches in the Phenomena of Spiritualism*. London: J. Burns, 1874.

Dean, E. D. Plethysmograph recordings as ESP responses. *International Journal of Neuropsychiatry*, 1966, **2**, 439–446.

Eisenbud, J. *The World of Ted Serios*. New York: Morrow, 1967.

Fahler, J., and Osis, K. Checking for awareness of hits in a precognition experiment with hypnotized subjects. *Journal of the American Society for Psychical Research*, 1966, **60**, 340–346.

Fisk, G. W., and Mitchell, A. M. J. ESP experiments with clock cards. *Journal of the Society for Psychical Research*, 1953, **37**, 1–14.

Fisk, G. W., and West, D. J. ESP tests with erotic symbols. *Journal of the Society for Psychical Research*, 1955, **38**, 1–7.

Fisk, G. W., and West, D. J. Dice-casting experiments with a single subject. *Journal of the Society for Psychical Research*, 1958, **39**, 277–287.

Friedman, R. M., Schmeidler, G. R., and Dean, E. D. Ranked-target scoring for mood and intragroup effects in precognitive ESP. *Journal of the American Society for Psychical Research*, 1976, **70**, 195–206.

Girden, E. A review of psychokinesis (PK). *Psychological Bulletin*, 1962, **59**, 353–388.

Goodrich, J. Studies of paranormal healing. *New Horizons*, 1976, **2**, 21–24.

Grad, B. A telekinetic effect on plant growth. II. Experiments involving treatment of saline in stoppered bottles. *International Journal of Parapsychology*, 1964, **6**, 472–498.

Grad, B., Cadoret, R. J., and Paul, G. I. The influence of an unorthodox method of treatment on wound healing in mice. *International Journal of Parapsychology*, 1961, **3**, 5–24.

Green, E. *Report to the Third Interdisciplinary Conference on the Voluntary Control of Internal States*. Council Grove, Kansas, 1971.

Greville, T. N. E. On multiple matching with one variable deck. *Annals of Mathematical Statistics*, 1944, **15**, 432–434.

Guarino, S. Un nuovo metodo per esperimenti quantitativi di suggestione mentale (telepatico): a "selezione nella memoria." *Rendiconti ed Atti del' Academia di Scienze Mediche a Chirurgiche della Societa' Nazionale di Scienze Lettere ed Arti in Napoli*, 1971, **125**, 40–46.

Honorton, C. Objective determination of information rate in psi tasks with pictorial stimuli. *Journal of the American Society for Psychical Research*, 1975, **69**, 353–359.

Humphrey, B. M. Help-hinder comparison in PK tests. *Journal of Parapsychology*, 1947, **11**, 4–13.

Joyce, C. R. B., and Welldon, R. M. C. The objective efficacy of prayer. *Journal of Chronic Diseases*, 1965, **18**, 367–377.

Keil, H. H. J., Ullman, M., Herbert, B., and Pratt, J. G. Directly observable voluntary PK effects. *Proceedings of the Society for Psychical Research*, 1976, **56**, 197–235.

Kreitler, H., and Kreitler, S. Subliminal perception and extrasensory perception. *Journal of Parapsychology*, 1973, **37**, 163–168.

Mangan, G. L. Evidence of displacement in a precognition test. *Journal of Parapsychology*, 1955, **19**, 35–44.

McConnell, R. A., and Forwald, H. Psychokinetic placement: II. A factorial study of successful and unsuccessful series. *Journal of Parapsychology*, 1967, **31**, 198–213.

McConnell, R. A., Snowdon, R. J., and Powell, K. F. Wishing with dice. *Journal of Experimental Psychology*, 1955, **50**, 269–275.

McMahan, E. A. An experiment in pure telepathy. *Journal of Parapsychology*, 1946, **10**, 224–242.

Palmer, J. Scoring in ESP tests as a function of belief in ESP. Part I. The sheep-goat effect. *Journal of the American Society for Psychical Research*, 1971, **65**, 373–408.

Rao, K. R. The bidirectionality of psi. *Journal of Parapsychology*, 1965, **29**, 230–250.

Rhine, J. B., and Pratt, J. G. *Parapsychology: Frontier Science of the Mind*. (Rev. ed.) Springfield, Ill.: Charles C Thomas, 1962.

Richmond, N. Two series of PK tests on paramecia. *Journal of the Society for Psychical Research*, 1952, **36**, 577–588.

Rogers, D. P. Negative and positive affect and ESP run-score variance—Study II. *Journal of Parapsychology*, 1967, **31**, 290–296.

Rogers, D. P., and Carpenter, J. C. The decline of variance of ESP scores within a testing session. *Journal of Parapsychology*, 1966, **30**, 141–150.

Roll, W. G., and Pratt, J. G. The Miami disturbances. *Journal of the American Society for Psychical Research*, 1971, **65**, 409–454.

Schmeidler, G. R. Evidence for two kinds of telepathy. *International Journal of Parapsychology*, 1961, **3**, 5–48.

Schmeidler, G. R. An experiment in precognitive clairvoyance. *Journal of Parapsychology*, 1964, **28**, 1–27, 93–125.

Schmeidler, G. R. PK effects upon continuously recorded temperature. *Journal of the American Society for Psychical Research*, 1973, **67**, 325–340.

Schmeidler, G. R., and Lewis, L. A search for feedback in ESP: Part III. The preferential effect and the impatience effect. *Journal of the American Society for Psychical Research*, 1969, **63**, 60–68.

Schmeidler, G. R., and McConnell, R. A. *ESP and Personality Patterns*. Westport, Conn.: Greenwood Press, 1973. (First published 1958.)

Schmidt, H. Precognition of a quantum process. *Journal of Parapsychology*, 1969, **33**, 99–108.

Schmidt, H. Comparison of PK action on two different random number generators. *Journal of Parapsychology*, 1974, **38**, 47–55.

Sidgwick, H., Sidgwick, E. M., and Smith, G. A. Experiments in thought-transference. *Proceedings of the Society for Psychical Research*, 1889, **6**, 128–170.

Smith, M. J. Paranormal effects on enzyme activity. *Human Dimensions*, 1972, **1**, 15–19.

Soal, S. G., and Bateman, F. *Modern Experiments in Telepathy*. New Haven, Conn.: Yale University Press, 1954.

Spencer-Brown, G. *Probability and Scientific Inference*. London: Longmans, Green, 1957.

Stanford, R. G. A study of the cause of low run-score variability. *Journal of Parapsychology*, 1966, **30**, 236–242.

Stanford, R. G. Response bias and the correctness of ESP test responses. *Journal of Parapsychology*, 1967, **31**, 280–289.

Targ, R., and Puthoff, H. *Mind-Reach*. New York: Delacorte Press, 1977.

Tart, C. T. Physiological correlates of psi cognition. *International Journal of Parapsychology*, 1963, **5**, 375–386.

Tart, C. T. Concerning the scientific study of the human aura. *Journal of the Society for Psychical Research*, 1972, **46**, 1–21.

Tart, C. T. *Learning to Use Extrasensory Perception*. Chicago: University of Chicago Press, 1976.

Vasiliev, L. L. *Experiments in Mental Suggestion*. Church Crookham, Hampshire, England: Institute for the Study of Mental Images, 1963.

Part III

PERCEPTION, COMMUNICATION, AND PARAPSYCHOLOGY

1

Extrasensory Perception

J. B. Rhine

INTRODUCTION

The term *extrasensory perception* (ESP) was introduced in 1934 in my book bearing that title (Rhine, 1934). This term was chosen after considerable thought and some discussion with colleagues; but had I realized what a wide usage the expression would receive in the course of years, I would certainly have given it further thought in the hope of arriving at a more convenient and adaptable term. *Supersensory perception* was an expression used in some circles, but I thought the prefix *super* might not really apply as well as the neutral one, *extra*. *Extrasensory cognition* was not specific enough, and the various descriptive terms involving the word *normal* begged the question too much for so exploratory a stage in parapsychology. I had noted the difficulties psychology had had with its various "normals."

DEFINITION

At an early stage I was challenged on the question of whether or not we could say with confidence that what we were studying in our experiments in clairvoyance and telepathy was actually beyond *all* sensory range. For a few years I compromised by using the definition "perception beyond the known senses." But eventually the experiments themselves settled this issue; they showed that in the test results there was no evidence of any need of stimuli; this was well confirmed by the absence of any indication of physical intermediation. I think we can say, therefore, that the experimental results have determined the definition. At the same time, both the abbreviation and the wording have been a challenge to inventive minds, and I have little doubt that eventually there will be a new and better terminology for the entire field.

However, at the time of the 1930s there was need of a general descriptive expression, particularly since there were disagreements over the importance of the various abilities now embraced under the term *extrasensory perception*. The British parapsychologists were particularly interested in telepathy, and the French in clairvoyance. In America we were interested in both if they were verifiable, and in Germany Hans Driesch had taken the position that both were important and should be distinguished as basically different. For me, ESP was meant as a descriptive expression useful for purposes of exchange. It simply designated a territory marked off for investigation, bounded by one of the most formidable distinctions science was capable of making—a distinction between the sensory and the extrasensory orders of experience.

ESP AND PK

ESP is only a part of the subject matter of parapsychology (or psychical research). Before the question of terminology arose, there had been studies of unexplainable (or parapsychical) physical happenings along with the cognitive type of ESP experiences. In fact, by the time the 1934 book appeared, I had been working for some months on a new technique for testing the direct mental influence on moving objects (dice), and I welcomed the term *psychokinesis* (PK) when I found it already in the dictionary and defined as "the direct action of mind on matter." In the present volume the article on PK is a chapter in itself, but it will be necessary here to make frequent references to the relationships between the two types of parapsychological phenomena. Most parapsychologists have come to prefer the use of the Greek letter *psi* as representing the inclusive parapsychical subject matter of parapsychology. This was proposed by Robert H. Thouless and B. P. Wiesner (1948) to include the two divisions of ESP and PK which they designated as psi-gamma and psi-kappa.

CLAIMS WHICH HAVE PROVED TESTABLE

The trend toward unified thinking about psi and its various types of phenomena is constructive and useful, but it was not easy during the 1930s and 1940s to distinguish and evaluate the various psychic phenomena for which strong claims were being made. As I have indicated in my chapter in Part I, we began at the Duke Laboratory with concurrent investigations of telepathy and clairvoyance, and the monograph *Extrasensory Perception* was a report of the first main period of these studies, which was largely concerned with clairvoyance. On the other hand, telepathy, defined as mind-to-mind thought transference, was difficult to test with a conclusive design—one that adequately excluded other types of psi ability. In due course, precognition (ESP of the future) lent itself well to conclusive experimental testing, while retrocognition (the ESP of past events) did not. As a matter of fact, it was decided eventually that no conclusion on the latter could be considered valid. Psychokinesis also yielded to dependably clear conclusions, although there were certain other claims of "psychic ability" that failed to do so. For instance, the claims that involved an alleged separation of mind and body were based on untested assumptions that weakened the test design beyond acceptability. The simplest case, the claim that the mind could "project" or leave the body and provide evidence of its existence elsewhere, was found to be logically untestable; and likewise, the widespread belief that mediums could produce messages from still existing discarnate spirits was found after years of critical consideration to be experimentally unprovable.

These judgments did not deny the importance of the problems, and the rationale behind them was not a philosophical one. The decisions were scientifically empirical and were based on whether or not there were experimental methods by which the questions could be objectively determined. Naturally we chose the questions we could answer, as far as could be determined at the time, and in these decisions there was a high level of concurrence among the researchers who were involved. Accordingly, it was with clairvoyance, precognition, and psychokinesis that most of the research was done, and it is still much the same today.

The efforts to determine whether the subtypes of psi ability were experimentally distinguishable, one from the other, have been discussed in Part I. I will say here only that the degree of unity among these types which allows us to consider psi as one general system of ability, reversible in its direction from ESP to PK, is one of the most useful generalizations in the field today. It need not be considered as an absolutely settled judgment; rather, unanswered questions about the methodology of psi research make it wise to keep an open mind as to whether we are still asking the right questions about how far these distinctions between types really extend.

THE NEED TO KEEP FLEXIBLE

It seems probable that before long we will be talking about the psi process with sufficient understanding that these special testing designations, ESP and PK, so useful in the past, will be rephrased in an even more apt and insightful manner. We cannot even now think of how PK could function apart from ESP, although we have been laboring to distinguish it experimentally and still need to do so for the present. Again, it is hard to get along without the concept of telepathy, and yet it is simply a violation of all that we hold reliable in science to go on thinking about it according to the untestable definition which came down to us from the past. Still further, it is impossible to think of precognition as anything more than clairvoyance of the future. (We have no acceptable evidence of telepathy of the future.) At the same time it is difficult enough to think of precognition in any rationally theoretical way at all. Rather, it is for the present simply a scientific fact, unless or until some way of extending the PK hypothesis is found that can reasonably well explain the evidence for this form of psi. But while we keep our minds open on the question of just which subtypes of psi ability can be experimentally investigated and how distinctive one from the other the special phenomena really are, there still remains one question about ESP (and psi ability as a whole) on which we cannot justify any compromise; and to that I will turn next.

HOW SATISFACTORY IS THE EVIDENCE?

The century-long study of the development of methods to deal with psi ability, as I have outlined it in my earlier chapter, ought to be sufficient on certain points of evidentiality. That the psi-testing methods have been sufficiently thorough in excluding sensory cues in ESP (and various motor influences in PK) ought not to need any great amount of further amplification. Likewise, the experimental design has adequately covered the possibility of recording errors, particularly in much of the ESP research. None of these remains a serious enough question to disturb the reader of the literature in parapsychology. Rather, I come again to the somewhat inflamed but still entirely proper question of whether the ESP research (as well as parapsychology as a whole) can stand the most vigorous scrutiny of honestly critical minds on the question of whether its experimenters have been trustworthy. I touched on this general question of experimenter honesty more fully in the chapter on the history of experimental development. Here I will present it from another point of view, supplementary perhaps, and certainly not in conflict with the other.

I have written elsewhere (Rhine, 1974a) about the importance of building into the design of an experiment the essential safeguards against overdependence on any one person. The requirement that there be a two-experimenter design, double-blind conditions, and maximum security regarding the records and evaluations will greatly reduce any likelihood or even possibility of one person's falsifying data or manipulating results to influence their interpretations. I have emphasized also the commonly accepted reliance on independent confirmations by other workers and even other laboratories, and the suspension of judgment until ample confirmation has been reached. No one doubts the wisdom of these provisions if judiciously and constructively managed and quietly enforced. Laboratories are becoming increasingly well equipped to make all these features more widely feasible.

We have at our disposal, however, a further source of psi evidence of unquestionable quality. I refer to something that has appeared over and over again in a wide variety of experiments when the data were reexamined in search of identifying signs of psi. One of these signs is the tendency of subjects to decline in their scoring rate as testing proceeds. Other characteristic indications of psi have also been discovered incidentally by a number of researchers, too many for review here. When these special signs are discovered in test data long after the experiment has been completed, when they have been discovered even by a different worker, the new finding is safe against suspicion of dishonesty on the part of the original experimenter (or his subjects, assistants, or other participants).

I introduced this kind of evidence in my paper in Part I by reference to the work of Estabrooks at Harvard. Years after he conducted his telepathy experiment, I reexamined his results, looking for possible evidence he might have overlooked or some on which his own conclusions had not depended—in other words, for evidence not dependent on his honesty. I found that, among other points, the CR of the total score difference between the top and bottom halves of his subjects' runs was quite significant in itself. This was a measure of significance of which he was unaware, and it therefore constituted independent proof. I had already found many similar declines in the run in other data, also with significant top–bottom differences. To me this additional evidence was confirmatory, but it was news to Estabrooks that such a test of significance could be applied. Many "position effects" of this type have been found in the reanalysis of results at some later stage, too late for the suspicion to arise that the experimenter himself could have planted the data in such a way as to produce the effect. Much of this type of evidence has been summed up in my article on position effects in psi-test results (Rhine, 1969b) and in my psi-missing paper (Rhine, 1969a). Such analyses can be repeated as often as is desired, and new searches can be made for more new findings of the same type. No one knows how much more remains to be discovered.

By far the most outstanding body of evidence of this kind was found in connection with the PK research when, after long years of collecting records and delaying publication, it was decided that the time had come to hold off no longer and that a comparative study of declines should be made in the total available data. As a result, one of the most extensive analyses of internal hit distributions ever published was reported in 1944-1945. The patterning of hits on the record sheet from series to series was found to show a significant drop between the scores of the upper left quarter of the record page and those of the lower right, thus resulting in a diagonal decline in the distribution of the scores of the four quarters of the page (Rhine and Humphrey, 1944a). There was no possibility that either the subjects or the experimenters could have manipulated the data in that large collection of test records. The analysis was then entirely rechecked by an independent but experienced parapsychologist (Pratt, 1944);

moreover, at the time of these reports further rechecking by qualified persons was publicly invited (Editorial, 1944). In addition, an independent breakdown of the data (Rhine and Humphrey, 1944b) resulted in a highly significant confirmation. I can conceive of no stronger evidence of psi, even today after 30 years have passed. Finally, I could go on to many other types of hidden evidence, but this example will at least introduce the kind of proof that allows no question of experimenter honesty to arise; it is a type of proof that has been produced in both the ESP and the PK branches of psi research.

The problem of experimenter reliability sums up to this: we can tolerate the unavoidable uncertainties of psi research that still remain, even while we labor to remove them in the future research program of the field; and we look forward to the time when it will be possible to carry out the major part of the test program in such a way that there will be little or no need to trust the tester. Technology in this, as in almost every field, is moving to the stage where no mistakes, intentional or innocent, can endanger the results. Some of the test methods are already close to that stage. But to me, in looking over experimental results for nearly 50 years, it seems that scores of times the more incontestable answers have come when I have discovered new hidden evidence which was unknown to the individual experimenter but which fitted into the pattern that many workers have come to recognize as the peculiar way in which psi operates. These signs of psi have, for many of us, contributed more to our confidence than anything else.

WHAT IS ESP LIKE?

When it is fairly certain that psi does occur, it is justifiable and even necessary to look for its properties and its characteristics. What is it like? It is so distinctive as to be, for many critical minds, almost incredible. This is one reason for considering the reliability of evidence so cautiously before opening up this further question of the nature of ESP.

The very first characteristic of ESP (and psi in general) I shall mention is a most amazing one, even though the concept certainly did not originate with anybody now living. In fact, in one form or another it was recognized down through the ages wherever psi phenomena were familiar. I refer to the fact that psi is not in any known shape or form a recognizable physical process. Physicists have attempted to offer explanations, usually in terms of current physical theories. One finds field theories of psi, electromagnetic wave theories, and before these were current in physics still other notions were suggested on such lines as unknown cosmic forces. Earlier still, in the various theologies, the types of psi we investigate today were attributed to divine agency. Even among the physicists who dominated the nineteenth-century period of psychical research, there were some who frankly favored a nonphysical interpretation of thought transference.

Tests of Physicality

At the Duke Laboratory, the first main inquiry into the question of the nature of ESP was to make a comparison of different distances from the targets on the success of the subject. An even more stringent test of possible physical influences on ESP was the inquiry into time as a barrier. On the question of distance effects, enough comparisons have taken place over the last half century of parapsychology to discourage any thought of applying the inverse square law to the results; and neither have the tests involving increasing time periods shown any effect on the scoring rate. In a word, no differences in ESP results have been found to compare lawfully with any of the physical conditions tested (Rhine and Pratt, 1962, Chap. 4; Rhine, Pratt, Smith, Stuart, and Greenwood, 1940, Chap. 13).

The Biology of ESP

We can begin with the biology of ESP by saying that biology is logically the field that is most basic to psi; but biologists have been very cautious about parapsychology, perhaps because of their deeply ingrained fear of vitalism and their extraordinary loyalty to the doctrine of mechanism. But the facts are there: only living creatures manifest psi capacity. Certain further general observations can be made, at least as working hypotheses. It appears definite now that psi is part of the genetic heritage of the organism, and so far no indication has been found either of an organic localization of the ability or of an equivalent of the sensorimotor organs. Should we logically expect physical localization for a function that is not in itself physical? I do not know the anwer, but I like the question.

It begins to look as though the human species has no monopoly on psi, in spite of the disavowal of the Levy work on precognition in rodents (Rhine, 1974b; 1975b). There are still enough findings from ESP tests on cats, dogs, and rodents to keep the question of psi in animals an open one (Morris, 1970). Psi tests with animals as subjects do offer a special difficulty, one that has been taken more seriously in recent years, namely the role of the experimenter in the production of the results. It has been difficult to design an experiment in which it can be established with reasonable certainty that the experimenter himself may not be the source of the psi effects. This is the main reason I put my summary statement about the possibility of psi in animals with some reserve. However, as I have explained elsewhere, I feel confident of a way out of this seeming impasse (Rhine, 1975a, pp. 44–46). I also think it probable that animals can exert PK on their environment. There is sufficient evidence to support the suggestion and to stimulate new investigation on the topic.

Little as is known about the biology of psi, it still can be said that psi should be expected to be a factor in the living system. Since it has given evidence of exerting an intelligent, forceful influence in tests with human beings in the laboratory, it may confidently be assumed to have played a part in the evolution of life and species. John Randall (1976), a biologist himself, touches on the topic more positively in his recent book *Parapsychology and the Nature of Life*. He points out that if psi can be traced to an involvement in the origin of species (even if, for the present, only inferentially), it would seem proper to inquire about the possibility that it might persist right on through the termination of life, leaving a postmortem trace that science can eventually capture. This might be a new starting point on the old question of the finality of death. After all, science has made a rather successful start on the question of man's origin and has done so of necessity by way of the biological approach. The feasibility of research on the continuity of psi through the terminal phase of organic life in animals and men is at least indicated as a research problem.

Psi and Psychology

It is the psychology of psi, however, that should claim our major attention. Parapsychology, of course, belongs to the broadly conceived field of psychology, but the fact that psi seems to be completely extrasensorimotor sets this branch apart—at least on the surface—from most of the rest of the field. A further fact is that psi phenomena are not only unconscious but are among the most unconscious of the range of functions within that classification of experiences.

However, once these two main lines of distinction are firmly drawn, the interrelation between psi and general psychology becomes rather striking. Even the unconscious extrasensorimotor functions show intelligent behavior, subject of course to the limitations of consciousness. In fact, most manifestations of psi effects typically convert to familiar psychological functions (e.g., dreams, intuitions, and hallucinations) for purposes of communication. We might even say that only in PK phenomena is there an overt kind of psi expression. That is, the physical psi effect (PK) *is* the subject's expression of the message. On the other hand, the other forms of psi manifestation are "covert" in that they become known in such disguises as intuitions, dreams, and hallucinations. Ordinarily, of course, such vehicles are not laden with psi messages. Finally, there is room for another form of psi response, neither wholly overt nor wholly covert. The following example will illustrate: There is on file the case of a woman who parapsychologically experienced her daughter's parturition taking place at a great distance; and without advance notice as to the day of the birth, she suffered severe pains, although her daughter did not. Other paraphysiological experiences which have been reported raise the question about the variety and range of PK.

Or again, consider the findings of the studies of personality correlates with psi, which I have reviewed briefly in Part I. The occurrence of psi in a test response seems to be completely at the mercy of the psychological state of the individual. Schmeidler found that if a subject rejected the possibility of ESP under the test conditions, he tended to avoid the target and thus to help produce negative deviations for the group; on the other hand, if he accepted the possibility, he scored above chance (Schmeidler and McConnell, 1958). And so it is with other psychological ratings; the unconscious psi process is influenced by the favoring or hindering mental state of the subject at the time.

It seems clear now after many confirmations that the amount of psi ability possessed by a test subject can well be regarded as approximately the same whether it registers on the positive side of the chance average or on the negative. ESP has no free port of entry of its own. Instead, the dominant mood or attitude of the subject seems to direct it except when it takes the form of a PK effect. But PK, too, can be shown to be subject to this same plus or minus direction of deviation. The main point is that the amount of psi a subject shows may be expected to register the same on either side of the chance mean; but which of the two it takes depends upon the mental attitude of the subject at the moment.

This does not mean that the unconsciousness of psi must block all efforts at volitional control over the ability. This problem has already been dealt with. Psi tests could not be made if the subject were unable to make a choice as to whether or not to identify a certain designated target card or to try to influence a certain pair of rolling dice. The unconsciousness of an ability can be recognized in many sensorimotor functions; but here in the extrasensory area there are differences. First, *all* psi functions are unconscious, whereas the unconscious sensorimotor processes are only a limited part of the entire range of sensory capability. On the other hand, the psi abilities, even though totally unconscious, are subject to a large degree of voluntary, even intelligent, control. The limits of the state of unconsciousness are, of course, to some extent relative, and one may conjecture that research may discover a way to alter this limitation.

It is here, in the common unconscious functions of both sensorimotor and extrasensorimotor (or psi) character, that parapsychology comes closest to psychology. The current researches on both sides of the gap between the two may narrow it further, perhaps bridge it over or even close it. On the other hand, there may be a greater chasm between the psi and nonpsi functions that we can at present anticipate. It will be advisable to keep our attention on all the psychological research on unconscious mental activities, watching for similarities and differences. Does anything like the signs of psi occur in nonpsi experiments?

Perhaps the greatest challenges to those interested in the psychology of psi now lie in the need of parapsychologists for practical psychological help. First of all, it is greatly needed in the training of subjects. It is surprising to realize that even after a century of study of psi no systematic schooling or preparation of the people who are going to perform in the tests has been developed. It is true that there have been classes and schools to train mediums, and in the earlier stages of parapsychology efforts were made to prepare subjects with the aid of hypnosis. To my knowledge, however, little has come down to us from those efforts that could help with today's needs on the matter. But a great deal of useful, relevant knowledge has accumulated that could, if well compiled and made available to experimenters, bring about more efficient selection and training of test subjects.

However, it is not only the subjects who need selection and training. It is even more important to give these advantages to experimenters, rather than to allow and even encourage them to get into the laboratory without the training that normally would be given to professional people in any branch of study. I understand of course how difficult it is to manage these larger needs when it is difficult enough to find opportunity and willing investigators to do the research without the added burdens of preparation. Obviously, we need a school for this; but a school does not just happen. Even an instruction staff for such a school, a staff experienced in research and fully aware of the needs that trainees must be prepared to meet, has had to wait. Parapsychology has slowly been advancing toward this stage, however.

THE MEANING OF ESP

This topic actually covers the whole territory of psi. It has become my own habit of thought to conceive of psi as a unitary system and, even more than that, as a very integral part of the total personality. But I cannot even stop there, because one is never really separable from his universal setting. From the beginning, then, when ESP was found to occur regardless of distance, not only man but even his universe took on a larger meaning. Was this not a different kind of world than had been generally conceived of if it allowed the subject, and perhaps all of us, to transcend distance so objectively? It showed human beings as in some degree having more potential than had been supposed. On the other hand, the world was more subject to human thought than I had realized. I have been carried along during these years with this optimism which was started by the psi researches. To me they were pointing the way to the discovery of a more meaningful concept of the relation of a person to his world than any I had found in studying the other sciences. As I have continued over the years, I have come to feel the need the founders of religions must have felt in exploring the meaning and use of these powers and expanding the concept of them in a universal way. I myself want most to know, as far as possible, what the presence of these abilities connotes about the universe of which they are a part, if perhaps only a fragment. They add something distinctive to the universe which otherwise has been conceived of only in physical terms. Man himself is very different—how much we cannot yet say—because of the gradual discovery of psi. Can we think of the universe as any less expanded when we contemplate so distinctive an addition to its constitution?

While I refuse to go into lines of thought that would represent more wishful thinking or an act of faith whose validity is beyond my ability to check, I can better understand how the thinkers of the past developed the systems of thought which helped them to guide their conduct and to make sense of life. They could not have done so had there been in their time no such concept of psychic powers to stimulate their awareness of capacities beyond the physical bounds. I am conceding now only that they were correct in principle in their supernaturalism—superphysicalism to us—and that we have more to account for in the origins of man than science has hitherto recognized. Certainly in the universe somewhere there is something which has made it possible for psi capacity to emerge, a capacity that was first interpreted theologically, as perhaps was more suitable to times past than to ours. But to find these psi phenomena, emerging eventually in a careful scientific laboratory approach today, has led me to think that, hand in hand with psychology, and with help, too, from some of the other branches, we are approaching a point at which a perspective at least as broad as that which the ancients had in their time may be possible. We might find out enough about man's nature to increase his control over the unconscious psi functions, to strengthen his self-control and self-understanding, and to lay the basis for a sense of values in which mankind could place the confidence that tested knowledge alone can yield (Rhine, 1972).

In a word, if ancient man could in his time deify these mysterious powers we are investigating and the magicians of the ages could build systems of practice around them, perhaps the psychologists of tomorrow, with the increasing contribution of parapsychology, may design an authentic psychology of conduct that will meet the demands of life and the challenges of the future.

REFERENCES

Editorial: The PK research at the point of decision. *Journal of Parapsychology*, 1944, 8, 1–2.

Morris, R. L. Psi and animal behavior: A survey. *Journal of the American Society for Psychical Research*, 1970, 64, 242–260.

Pratt, J. G. A reinvestigation of the quarter distribution of the (PK) page. *Journal of Parapsychology*, 1944, 8, 61–63.

Randall, J. L. *Parapsychology and the Nature of Life*. New York: Harper & Row, 1976.

Rhine, J. B. *Extrasensory Perception*. Boston: Bruce Humphries, 1934. (Reprinted by Branden Press in 1973.)

Rhine, J. B. Psi-missing re-examined. *Journal of Parapsychology*, 1969, 33, 1–38. (a)

Rhine, J. B. Position effects in psi test results. *Journal of Parapsychology*, 1969, 33, 136–157. (b)

Rhine, J. B. Parapsychology and man. *Journal of Parapsychology*, 1972, 36, 101–121.

Rhine, J. B. Comments: Security versus deception in parapsychology. *Journal of Parapsychology*, 1974, 38, 99–121. (a)

Rhine, J. B. A new case of experimenter unreliability. *Journal of Parapsychology*, 1974, 38, 218–225. (b)

Rhine, J. B. Comments: Psi methods reexamined. *Journal of Parapsychology*, 1975, 39, 38–58. (a)

Rhine, J. B. Second report on a case of experimenter fraud. *Journal of Parapsychology*, 1975, 39, 306–325. (b)

Rhine, J. B., and Humphrey, B. M. The PK effect: Special evidence from hit patterns. I. Quarter distributions of the page. *Journal of Parapsychology*, 1944, 8, 18–60. (a)

Rhine, J. B., and Humphrey, B. M. The PK effect: Special evidence from hit patterns. II. Quarter distributions of the set. *Journal of Parapsychology*, 1944, 8, 254–271 (b)

Rhine, J. B., and Pratt, J. G. *Parapsychology: Frontier Science of the Mind* (Rev. ed.) Springfield, Ill.: Charles C Thomas, 1962.

Rhine, J. B., Pratt, J. G., Smith, B. M., Stuart, C. E., and Greenwood, J. A. *Extrasensory Perception After Sixty Years*. New York: Henry Holt, 1940. (Reprinted by Branden Press in 1966.)

Schmeidler, G. R., and McConnell, R. A. *ESP and Personality Patterns*. New Haven: Yale University Press, 1958. (Reprinted by Greenwood Press in 1973.)

Thouless, R. H., and Wiesner, B. P. On the nature of psi phenomena. *Journal of Parapsychology*, 1948, 12, 192–212.

2

Attitudes and Personality Traits in Experimental ESP Research

John Palmer

INTRODUCTION

This chapter will survey published experimental research on the relationships between certain attitudes and personality traits and performance on tests of extrasensory perception (ESP). A comprehensive review of early research on these topics has been written by Mangan (1958). The nonexperimental literature on personality and psi, including psi within the framework of personality theories such as psychoanalysis, will be covered in other chapters.

For purposes of this chapter, personality variables or "traits" refer to behavioral dispositions or tendencies that are relatively stable over time for a particular individual and are so structured that each individual can be placed on a continuum for which that trait is an appropriate label. For example, introversion might be defined as a tendency to behave in an aloof manner toward other individuals. This tendency is sufficiently stable that we find it meaningful to call some people introverts and others extraverts, and we can place individuals on a continuum going from extreme introversion to extreme extraversion.

Certain types of variables often considered as personality variables will not be so considered in this chapter. These include so-called cognitive variables, i.e., variables that measure cognitive abilities or dominant modes of cognitive functioning rather than behavioral dispositions as such. Examples are intelligence, creativity, imagery ability, and field dependence.

175

The only attitude variable to be considered will be belief in psi or belief in one's ability to demonstrate psi in an experiment, the so-called sheep-goat variable (Schmeidler and McConnell, 1973).

THE RELIABILITY PROBLEM

Eysenck (1967) has stressed the importance of the reliability of ESP scores in determining their evidential value. As he points out, few experimenters have bothered to compute, or at least report, the reliability of the ESP scores obtained in their experiments. Based on the few cases where such reliabilities have been reported (e.g., Brodbeck, 1969; Honorton, Ramsey and Cabibbo, 1975; Schmeidler, 1964), as well as my own experience, I would estimate the average reliability to be in the low-positive range, in the neighborhood of +.30. More importantly, reliabilities are apt to vary widely from experiment to experiment, some approaching normally acceptable levels and others being negative!

The low and variable reliability of ESP scores implies that correlations between such scores and personality variables are likely to be very small and unstable. For this reason, I consider it hazardous to draw any conclusions—positive or negative—from most individual experiments of this type. Fortunately, personality-ESP experiments are very easy to conduct, and a large number of them have been reported in the literature. Several personality and attitude variables are represented in a large enough number of such experiments that patterns of relationships have emerged. Such patterns are more likely to provide information about what genuine relationships (if any) exist between ESP and personality variables than are the results of single experiments.

We might begin our evaluation of such conglomerates by asking what pattern one would expect if there is no relationship between ESP and variable X; i.e., what is the null hypothesis. Two findings we clearly should expect are the following:

1. An approximately equal number of experiments should show positive and negative relationships between ESP and variable X, regardless of significance level.
2. An approximately equal number of the *statistically significant* relationships between ESP and variable X should be in each direction. (Unless otherwise specified, "statistically significant" in this chapter means $P < .05$, two-tailed.)

Substantial departures from either of these patterns would suggest that there is a genuine and generalizable relationship between ESP and variable X, *even though only a small proportion of the sample relationships were statistically significant*, a likely possibility considering the unreliability of ESP scores.

Of course, this method of analysis assumes that one begins with a sample of experiments that is unbiased on relevant parameters. A frequent criticism of both parapsychology and psychology is that experiments with significant results are much more likely to be published than experiments with nonsignificant results (e.g., Greenwald, 1975). Despite the fact that one of the leading parapsychological journals indeed has the general policy (apparently shared by many psychological journals) of publishing only significant experiments (see Rhine, 1975), the reader will see as this chapter progresses that the personality-ESP literature nevertheless includes many nonsignificant outcomes. In any event, however, a mere bias toward reporting only significant results would not affect either of the two analyses proposed above, because both involve a comparison of experiments with respect to the direction of the findings rather than to their significance. Because of the otherwise unfortunate tendency over the years for parapsychologists to worship statistical significance rather than meaningfulness, it is especially unlikely that a significant finding would be suppressed because it contradicted a theoretical hypothesis (although even here there is no way to be sure).

Therefore, my approach in this chapter will be to analyze *patterns* of results between ESP and personality variables in the manner outlined above. In so doing, I naturally will be concentrating on those variables that have been studied most extensively in relation to ESP. The other side of this coin is that some experiments involving less popular variables will be omitted. I am quite aware of the imperfections of the pattern analysis approach, especially the fact that experiments included in such samples are never entirely comparable and classification of studies in terms of direction or significance of the relationship sometimes depends partly on arbitrary decisions. Although I have tried to include all experiments published in the English-language journals and proceedings that used relevant predictor variables, this does not allow me to say that my sample is exhaustive. Therefore, I cannot guarantee that my conclusions in this paper would be the same if the sample were exhaustive. Despite these difficulties, I am firmly convinced that the pattern approach is the most valid method of analysis that can be applied to the data at hand and that the conclusions derived therefrom deserve at least tentative acceptance.

One final digression. Some of the earlier ESP experiments to be discussed in this chapter employed statistical analyses where the single trial rather than the subject's (S's) total ESP score was the unit of analysis, the most common example being the critical ratio or CR (see chapter on statistical methods). Studies using such methods will be identified where appropriate. Without attempting to defend the use of illegitimate statistics, I nevertheless would note that when the number of trials per S is less than 100, I have found that the CR and the t test (using S as the unit of analysis) give almost identical results. For a less charitable discussion of this statistical indiscretion, see Stanford and Palmer (1972).

Unless otherwise noted, all experiments to be reviewed in this chapter used more or less standard forced-choice testing techniques. The particular type of test employed generally will not be mentioned unless it is unorthodox or germane to the results.

PERSONALITY VARIABLES

Neuroticism

I will use the term *neuroticism* to refer broadly to tendencies toward maladaptive behavior caused either by anxiety or defense mechanisms against anxiety. Although decisions as to which experiments to include in this section were somewhat arbitrary, I have tried to include only studies involving variables which rather unequivocally reflect level of emotional adjustment. The section will be organized in terms of particular personality scales, as experiments using the same predictors are obviously the most comparable.

Cattell 16PF and HSPQ. Cattell's personality scales were developed by factor analytic techniques. The 16PF yields 16 primary factors or "source traits," which in turn can be combined in various ways to produce eight secondary factors, one of which is labeled "adjustment vs. anxiety" (Cattell, Eber, and Tatsuoka, 1970). The High School Personality Questionnaire (HSPQ) contains 14 of these 16 primary source traits derived from testing adolescents. One of its secondary factors is also anxiety, which contributes to another second-order factor labeled "neuroticism" (Cattell and Beloff, 1962).

Nicol and Humphrey (1953) used the 16PF in an ESP experiment with 36 adults. Each was tested individually and given 400 trials. Significant correlations with ESP scores were found for three of the nine source traits evaluated (C, O, and Q4). Each of these contributes to the anxiety factor, and in each case the direction of the relationship indicated higher ESP scores among less anxious Ss. Guilford's STDRC (G1) and GAM1N (G2) scales were also administered. According to Guilford (1959), scales C, D, I, and N reflect neurotic tendency. Correlations between ESP scores and each of these scales supported the relationship found with the 16PF, significantly so for D, I, and N.

In an attempted replication with 32 new Ss, Nicol and Humphrey (1955) succeeded primarily in demonstrating statistical regression to the mean. None of the correlations between ESP and personality scales were significant, nor were there any clear directional trends. When results of the two studies were combined, however, all relevant scales supported a negative relationship between anxiety and ESP, the correlations with factor C (emotional stability) of the 16PF and Guilford's I and N retaining significance.

Kanthamani and Rao (1973a) used the HSPQ in four separate series, samples consisting of from 22 to 50 Indian high school students. Ss were tested individually with a card-matching technique, completing 100 trials in each of two sessions. In each of these four experiments, Ss scoring below the theoretical mean on neuroticism scored significantly higher on the ESP test than Ss scoring above the mean, as evaluated by t tests. Results on the component anxiety factor were somewhat less consistent. Low-anxious Ss nevertheless scored better than high-anxious Ss in three of the four series, significantly so in one.

In general, results on Cattell's scales reflect higher ESP scores among less "neurotic" Ss.

Eysenck (Maudsley) Personality Inventory. The Maudsley Personality Inventory (H. J. Eysenck, 1959), later revised as the Eysenck Personality Inventory (Eysenck and Eysenck, 1965), was also derived from factor analysis. These inventories consist of two essentially orthogonal factors, extraversion (E) and neuroticism (N).

Nielsen (1970a, 1970b) gave the EPI and 75 ESP trials to classes of 33 college students and 19 high school students respectively. Two sets of targets were used in each study: a single target sequence for the whole group and separate target sequences for individual Ss. Ss were divided into high and low groups on the N factor based on published norms. In both studies there was a significant interaction between neuroticism and type of target: high-N Ss scored better on the group targets and low-N Ss on the individual targets. However, these findings apparently were not significantly confirmed in three subsequent experiments.

Randall (1974) used the Junior EPI (S. B. G. Eysenck, 1965) in six classroom ESP tests with grammar school boys. Sample sizes ranged from 18 to 31. The ESP test consisted of 100 trials, and Ss were divided at the grand mean of the N factor for all series combined. No significant differences between high- and low-N Ss on ESP scores were found in any of these series, although low-N Ss scored best in four of the six. However, across all series, high-N Ss had significantly high "subject variance," i.e., the deviations of their scores from chance in either direction were greater than expected if the null hypothesis were true.

Green (1966b) gave the MPI and 100 ESP trials to 40 college students tested individually. On the basis of a post-hoc analysis including only 14 of these Ss with the most extreme ESP scores, she found that the positive scorers were significantly higher on N than the negative scorers.

The EPI was used in three other experiments (Brodbeck, 1969; Freeman, 1970; Osis, Turner, and Carlson, 1971), but the results involving the EPI were not reported in such a way that the basic relationship between neuroticism and conventional ESP scores could be determined.

In summary, no clear trends relating neuroticism and ESP have emerged from research with the EPI or MPI.

Manifest Anxiety Scale. The MAS is a personality inventory consisting of 50 MMPI items selected by clinical psychologists as characterizing "the presence of persistently heightened skeletal and visceral tensions, which disturb a person's habitual rhythms of living and predispose him generally to give exaggerated and inappropriate responses on relatively slight provocation" (Taylor, 1953).

In two papers, Freeman and Nielsen (1964) and Nielsen and Freeman (1965) reported the results of 17 series using various forced-choice ESP tests. All but one involved group testing in a classroom setting. Ss were divided into high, medium, and low anxiety groups on the basis of their MAS scores. High anxious Ss scored highest on the ESP test in 13 of the 17 series, although this trend was significant in only one series. The fact that some "series" consisted of trials from the same session and that only certain trials were selected for analysis in three others render these trends somewhat ambiguous, however.

In contrast, Rao (1965) found a correlation of −.36 between ESP and MAS scores among 49 high school Ss previously tested by Freeman. He used multilingual ESP targets, leading him to speculate, based on Hull's (1943) learning theory, that the reason for the reversal of findings was that his test was more "complex" than Freeman's. A nonsignificant trend interpreted as providing additional support for this hypothesis was reported by Honorton (1965), some of whose data were included in the analyses of Nielsen and Freeman (1965). Honorton merely told his Ss that one testing procedure was complex and the other was simple.

Finally, Carpenter (1971) tested 19 junior high school students individually with a 150-trial blind-matching procedure. Two sets of key cards in opaque envelopes were used as targets. Unbeknownst to the Ss, one set contained erotic pictures attached to the key cards. Ss were divided into three groups on the MAS according to the method of Freeman and Nielsen (1964). In support of the prediction, analysis of variance revealed a significant interaction, with high anxious Ss scoring best on the neutral targets and low anxious Ss scoring best on the theoretically more anxiety-arousing erotic targets.

With neutral targets, however, the general trend seems to be for high scorers on the MAS to score better on ESP tests than low scorers, a reversal of the trend found with Cattell's scales.

Defense Mechanism Test. The DMT is a projective test designed to measure Freudian defense mechanisms (Kragh, 1960, 1962). TAT-like pictures are presented tachistoscopically at progressively longer intervals, and S is asked after each exposure to state what is happening in the picture. The DMT has a standard scoring for defensiveness on a nine-point scale (high scores reflecting a lack of defensiveness), as well as scoring procedures for particular defense mechanisms.

Carpenter (1965) reported a series with ten high school students who were given 40 ESP trials. He found a significant rank-order correlation of +.79 between ESP scores and the DMT scored in the standard manner. He briefly mentioned two other studies with the DMT, one of which produced a significant confirmation of the previous finding.

Johnson and Kanthamani (1967) reported an experiment by Nordbeck, who gave 50 ESP trials to each of 60 Swedish college students. Selecting the ten highest and ten lowest scorers, he found a significant negative relationship between these scores and a DMT measure of "isolation." Johnson and Kanthamani

(1967) then reported an experiment in the U.S. where pairs of Ss who were friends were tested together to induce a competitive spirit. A significant correlation (+.67) between ESP and standard DMT scores was obtained in the first series ($N = 16$). In the second series ($N = 11$), the correlation was of similar magnitude (+.59) but was not significant.

Thus, there is a quite consistent tendency for Ss showing superior adjustment on the DMT to produce the highest ESP scores.

Other Scales. Humphrey (1945) reported correlations between ESP and scores from the Bernreuter Personality Inventory (Super, 1942) in three series where Ss were tested individually and given from 500 to 2,500 trials, 250 to 500 per session. Sample sizes ranged from 14 to 22. Correlations with the BPI subscale labeled "neurotic tendency" were negative in all three series (-.14, -.21, -.38). The general pattern of correlations indicated higher ESP scoring among the better adjusted Ss, although there was no evidence of statistical significance not attributable to sampling bias.

Smith and Humphrey (1946) gave each of three classes of students 100 ESP trials in a classroom setting. Ss had already been given the first 25 items of the Maslow Security-Insecurity Questionnaire (Maslow, Hirsh, Stein, and Honigmann, 1945) and were divided at the overall mean on this scale for all Ss in the experiment. In the first two series, "secure" Ss scored highest on the ESP test, while in the third series this trend was reversed. The effect in the first series was significant. Some of these Ss were later tested individually by McMahan (1946) in a 100-trial "pure telepathy" experiment, but the "secure" and "insecure" groups were selected so as to differ simultaneously on other variables relevant to ESP success.   Thus, although the "insecure" Ss scored significantly better than "secure" Ss by CR analysis, these results are really uninterpretable as far as the MSIQ is concerned.   Stuart, Humphrey, Smith, and McMahan (1947) reported the results of two other series in which Ss were given the MSIQ. One series involved individual testing ($N = 33$), and the other involved group testing ($N = 63$). The ESP test consisted of a four-trial free response drawing test plus 50–100 card-guessing trials. Ss were divided at the mean of the MSIQ, based on normative data. In the individual series, "secure" Ss scored better than "insecure" Ss on both types of tests. This trend was reversed in the group series. All results were nonsignificant.

Rivers (1950) correlated scores from 400 ESP trials with scores on the Mental Health Analysis-Secondary Series (no reference cited) in each of two series, one with high school students ($N = 36$) and one with college students ($N = 36$). All Ss were tested individually. Using a post-hoc cutoff at the 60th percentile based on published norms, she was able to demonstrate a significant negative relationship between ESP and an MHA subscale labeled "freedom from nervous mannerisms" for the high school group. No data were reported for the college group, although it was mentioned that the results were not significant.

Kahn (1952) found a significant positive relationship between ESP scores and adjustment as measured by the Heston Personal Adjustment Inventory, or HPAI (Heston, 1949), among a group of 47 college student volunteers.

Nash (1966) reported a matrix of correlations between ESP scores and the Minnesota Multiphasic Personality Inventory (Dahlstrom, Welsh, and Dahlstrom, 1972) across eight experiments with sample sizes ranging from 18 to 38. Although the number of significant correlations was no greater than expected by chance, the correlations for all 165 Ss combined were negative for all the clinical scales except masculinity-femininity. They were significant for the hypochondriasis and psychasthenia scales, the latter being the most relevant of the subscales to the concept of anxiety. The overall pattern of Nash's results support a slight but consistent tendency for higher ESP scores to be associated with an absence of psychopathology as measured by the MMPI.

On the other hand, Nash and Nash (1967) found no consistent relationships across 11 experiments between ESP scores and the "emotional stability" scale of the Guilford-Zimmerman Temperament Survey, or GZTS (Guilford and Zimmerman, 1949). Three of these 11 experiments were included in Nash's survey of results with the MMPI.

Discussion. It is evident that attempts to correlate measures of ESP and "neuroticism" have yielded conflicting results. Some of this inconsistency seems to be related to the specific personality test used. Particularly noteworthy in this connection is the generally positive relationship between ESP and the MAS, as relationships between ESP and the other tests tended to be negative or nonexistent. Such a discrepancy is especially frustrating because the MAS tends to be highly and positively intercorrelated with the other objective measures of neuroticism considered in this chapter (e.g., Brockbill and Little, 1954; H. J. Eysenck, 1959; Hundleby and Connor, 1968). Nevertheless, none of these scales can be considered equivalent. On the other hand, the very high correlation (+.91) found between the MAS and Byrne's Repression-Sensitization Scale (Joy, 1963) suggests that low scores on the MAS may reflect not so much superior emotional adjustment as the use of repression-based defense mechanisms to cope with anxiety (see Lazarus and Alfert, 1964). Following this logic, the MAS-ESP results, particularly in light of the strong and consistent negative relation found between ESP and use of defense mechanisms as measured by the DMT, could be interpreted to mean that coping with anxiety by "sensitization" is associated with high ESP scoring while coping with anxiety by "repression" is associated with low scoring. Inconsistent with such an argument, however, is the fact that in the MAS studies summarized by Nielsen and Freeman (1965) it was Ss who scored in the midrange rather than the low end of the MAS who scored most poorly on the ESP tests. Also difficult to explain by such a theory would be Carpenter's (1971) finding that low MAS Ss (repressors) scored better on "erotic" ESP targets than did high MAS Ss (sensitizers).

A more promising means of extracting order from the apparent chaos is suggested by the fact that most instances where the relationship between neuroticism and ESP was positive involved classroom testing of students. If the general tendency of neurotic Ss to score poorly on ESP tests reflects their inability to be comfortable in the test situation, one would expect this effect to be mitigated in group testing situations where such a person could "lose himself in the crowd." This would be particularly true in a classroom setting, where both the environment and the other group members would be familiar and nonthreatening.

When experiments involving group testing are eliminated, the remaining studies reveal a highly consistent pattern in support of a negative relationship between ESP and neuroticism. Table 1 includes all published experimental series covered so far in this chapter where it is clear from the report that Ss were not tested in groups and the direction of the relationship between ESP and neuroticism could be determined. In cases where more than one inventory was used, the classificatory decision was based on the average correlation between ESP and the scales of these inventories supposedly reflecting neuroticism. If the trends were inconsistent for the two inventories, the outcome was considered indeterminate and not included in the table. Thus in the Nicol and Humphrey (1953, 1955) studies the decision was based on the average correlation with the 16PF scales contributing to the anxiety factor and Guilford's D, C, I, and N scales. A similar procedure was followed with the Nashs' (Nash, 1966; Nash and Nash, 1967) experiments, two of which involved both the MMPI (where "psychasthenia" was used as the criterion scale) and the GZTS (where "emotional stability" was used). In cases where significant conflicting trends emerged for different types of targets, classification was based on results with the most conventional type. Thus the classification of Carpenter's (1971) experiment was based on results with the neutral (not erotic) targets. Statistical significance was not listed for experiments where claims for such significance were based on unorthodox or questionable analyses. Thus the experiments by Green (1966b) and Nordbeck (Johnson and Kanthamani, 1967) were not considered significant because only extreme ESP scores were analyzed. Rivers' (1950) results were not considered significant because classification of Ss on neuroticism was made on the basis of the ESP scores. These decisions were somewhat arbitrary, and all I can say is that I tried to be reasonable and objective.

Among the 24 series in Table 1 classified according to the above standards, 18 were in the predicted direction. This trend is associated with a chi-square value of 6.00, $df = 1$, $P < .02$. Even more impressive is the fact that all seven of the statistically significant relationships were in the predicted direction. In conclusion, by the criteria of analysis set forth at the beginning of this chapter, there is evidence for a consistent negative relationship between neuroticism and scoring on ESP tests when Ss are not tested in groups.

TABLE 1. SUMMARY OF PUBLISHED EXPERIMENTS RELATING ESP TO NEUROTICISM WITH GROUP EXPERIMENTS ELIMINATED.

Negative Relationships

Author	Pred.	Exps.	Sign.
Humphrey (1945)	BPI	3	0
Stuart et al. (1947)	MSIQ	1	0
Nicol and Humphrey (1953, 1955)	16PF; G1, 2	2	1
Carpenter (1965)	DMT	1	1
Nash (1966)–Exps. 1 and 4	MMPI; GZTS	2	0
Nash (1966)–Exp. 6	MMPI	1	0
Nash and Nash (1967)–Exp. 6	GZTS	1	0
Johnson and Kanthamani (1967)	DMT	3	1
Kanthamani and Rao (1973a)	HSPQ	4	4
Total		18	7

Positive Relationships

Author	Pred.	Exps.	Sign.
Rivers (1950)	MHA	1	0
Nielsen and Freeman (1965)	MAS	1	0
Green (1966b)	MPI	1	0
Nash and Nash (1967)–Exps. 10 and 11	GZTS	2	0
Carpenter (1971)	MAS	1	0
Total		6	0

Extraversion

Another personality variable that has received considerable attention in parapsychological research is extraversion. It is also a prominent variable in personality research, defined as a major factor in the conceptual systems of both Cattell (1965) and H. J. Eysenck (1960).

Many of the experiments cited in the previous section utilized personality inventories that included measures of extraversion. The combined results of Nicol and Humphrey (1953, 1955) reflected low positive correlations between ESP and extraversion measures on Cattell's 16PF and Guilford's STDRC. (According to Guilford [1959], the S, T, and R scales reflect introversion-extraversion.) The correlation with Guilford's T scale (thinking extraversion) and R scale (Rhathymia) were significant. With Ss divided at the theoretical mean on the extraversion factor of Cattell's HSPQ, Kanthamani and Rao (1972b) found extraverts scoring higher than introverts in all four of their experimental series, the difference reaching statistical significance in three of these.

Results with the Eysenck scales, however, have been less encouraging. Using the Junior EPI with classroom testing of grade school students, Randall (1974) obtained nonsignificant positive relationships between ESP and extraversion in only two of six classroom experiments, although extraverts had significantly high subject variance in their ESP scores in the six series combined. Brodbeck (1969), Freeman (1970), Green (1966a, 1966b), Nielsen (1970a, 1970b), and Osis, Turner, and Carlson (1971) found no significant simple relationships between conventional ESP scores and extraversion as measured by the MPI or EPI, but the directions of such relationships could not be determined from the reports. The only significant finding with one of Eysenck's scales was in an experiment by Aström (1965). He gave the MPI and 125 ESP trials to 48 college students tested in groups and found significantly higher scoring among the extraverts.

Humphrey (1945) found nonsignificant negative correlations between ESP and the Bernreuter (BPI) introversion scale in each of her three series discussed in the previous section. In a later paper (Humphrey, 1951a), she reanalyzed the results of two of these series and one additional series. Ss were divided at the theoretical mean of the introversion scale. Extraverts scored higher than introverts in each series, significantly so in the first two. Unfortunately, the statistical significance she claimed for individual series was based on CR analysis. The fact that each S in these experiments completed at least 500 trials renders her claims of significance highly questionable. Casper (1952) used the BPI introversion scale in an experiment where pairs of Ss matched for mutual like and dislike served reciprocally as subject and agent in a GESP paradigm. Each S completed 100 trials. When Ss were divided at the theoretical median on the introversion scale, extraverts scored significantly higher on the ESP test than introverts. In this case the CR analysis was supplemented by a more appropriate consistency test. Based on her most complete analysis, Nielsen (1970c) found slightly more positive scoring among BPI extraverts than introverts in a precognition experiment with 14 Ss, but the difference was not significant.

Nash (1966) found negative correlations between ESP scores and the social introversion scale of the MMPI in five of eight experiments, the correlation being significant in one of these five.

There was no consistent relationship between ESP and the extraversion scales (S, T, R) of the Guilford-Zimmerman Temperament Survey in the 11 experiments reported by Nash and Nash (1967).

Finally, Shields (1962) reported the results of two exploratory experiments ($N = 21, 98$) with emotionally disturbed children. On the basis of various tests and reports of those making referrals, the children were classified as "withdrawn" or "not withdrawn." The experimental procedures were designed to produce a gamelike atmosphere. In both experiments, highly significant differences in favor of the "not withdrawn" Ss were reported. Statistical analysis was by the CR method, but the large magnitude of the effects combined with the fact that most Ss only completed 40-50 trials suggests that the differences still would have been significant had more appropriate statistics been applied.

Discussion. As Table 2 reveals, there is evidence for a positive relationship between extraversion and ESP scoring even when studies involving group testing are included. Of the 33 experimental series where the direction of the relationship between extraversion and conventional ESP scores could be determined, the relationship was positive in 23. This trend is associated with a chi-square value of 5.12, $df = 1$, $P < .05$. Furthermore, all eight of the legitimately significant relationships were in the positive direction.

However, the lack of independence between neuroticism and extraversion on most of the inventories used in these studies renders interpretation ambiguous. Kanthamani (1968) reported a correlation of $-.63$ among her Ss between the neuroticism and extraversion factors of Cattell's HSPQ. When neuroticism was partialled out of the relationship between extraversion and ESP, this relationship became nonsignificant. On the other hand, partialling out extraversion had little effect on the neuroticism-ESP relationship. The correlation between the "neurotic tendency" and "introversion" scales of the BPI is greater than $+.90$ (Guilford, 1959). There also is considerable common variance among the clinical scales of the MMPI, the psychasthenia (Pt) and social introversion (Si) scales each having loadings greater than .75 on the same factor in one sample of 334 college students (Jackson and Messick, 1962). The Heston Inventory used by Kahn (1952) included two introversion scales, but the scales comprising the Heston are so highly intercorrelated that Kahn did not even bother to analyze them separately. Only in Eysenck's scales and the GZTS are extraversion and

TABLE 2. SUMMARY OF PUBLISHED EXPERIMENTS RELATING ESP TO EXTRAVERSION.

Positive Relationships

Author	Pred.	Type[a]	Exps.	Sign.
Humphrey (1945, 1951a)	BPI	I	4	0
Casper (1952)	BPI	I	1	1
Nicol and Humphrey (1953, 1955)	16PF; G1, 2	I	2	0
Åström (1965)	EPI	G	1	1
Shields (1965)	Misc.	I	2	2
Nash (1966)— Exps. 6, 7	MMPI	I, ?	2	1
Nash (1966)— Exps. 1, 4, 5	MMPI	I, ?	3	0
Nash and Nash (1967)— Exp. 11	GZTS	I	1	0
Nielsen (1970c)	BPI	I	1	0
Kanthamani and Rao (1972b)	HSPQ	I	4	3
Randall (1974)	EPI	G	2	0
Total			23	8

Negative Relationships

Author	Pred.	Type	Exps.	Sign.
Nash (1966)—Exp. 8	MMPI	?	1	0
Nash (1966)—Exp. 2	MMPI	?	1	0
Nash and Nash (1967)— Exps. 2, 3, 6, 7	GZTS	I, G	4	0
Randall (1974)	EPI	G	4	0
Total			10	0

[a] I—Individual testing or testing in pairs
G—Group or classroom testing
?—Indeterminant

neuroticism reasonably orthogonal, but these scales have not been consistent predictors of ESP performance.

Given this state of affairs, it would appear most reasonable and parsimonious to interpret the findings in this section as reconfirming the more general conclusion that ESP scoring tends to be highest among Ss with superior emotional adjustment, particularly as this affects their ability to adapt to social situations such as psychological experimentation. A different interpretation of the extraversion-ESP relationship is presented by H. J. Eysenck (1967), who suggests that extraverts score better on ESP tests because of lower cortical arousal.

Graphic Expansiveness

A number of studies have been reported comparing ESP scores to ratings of the formal characteristics of freehand drawings. The particular measure used was a rating of "expansiveness-compressiveness" (E-C) proposed by Elkisch (1945) and validated as a measure of maladjustment in children. However, results with this measure in the context of ESP testing suggest that it lacks sufficient stability over time to be clearly interpretable as measuring a personality trait (e.g., Humphrey, 1946b; Stuart et al., 1947), and it seems more reasonable to interpret it as a reflection of mood and reaction to the test situation, at least for generally well-adjusted Ss (West, 1950). Nevertheless, it has been treated as a between-Ss variable in most ESP research and so will be included in this chapter.

During the 1940s, a type of ESP test was frequently used where Ss were asked to reproduce hidden drawings or pictures, usually in sets of four. Two blind and independent judges then would attempt to match the responses and targets. From these matchings ESP scores could be derived.

Humphrey (1946a) informally analyzed data from several Ss who had previously participated in ESP drawing experiments, comparing their ESP scores to scores derived from applying four of Elkisch's rating scales to the ESP drawings. She found the E-C scale to be a good predictor of ESP scoring and commenced formal reanalyses of all available data. Each drawing was rated separately as expansive (1), compressive (0), or indeterminant (.5), the rater being blind to the S's ESP score. Ss rated two or above on the sum of all four drawings were labeled "expansive," the rest "compressive." Humphrey found that expansive Ss obtained higher ESP scores than compressive Ss in each of four series using clairvoyance testing procedures. The difference was significant for the four series combined and for the first series separately. On the other hand, in six series where an agent was concentrating on the target pictures during the trial (GESP), this trend was reversed in all six series (Humphrey, 1946b). Statistical significance was again demonstrated for all six series and for one series individually. Despite slight bias due to pooling of trials, the overall results indicate a consistent interaction between E-C and type of ESP test.

These trends were somewhat confirmed in two experiments by Bevan (1947a, 1947b), who gave his Ss in alternating sequence two drawing trials under clairvoyance conditions and two under GESP conditions. There was only one expansive S in his first experiment, but the 11 compressive Ss scored significantly higher on the clairvoyance trials than on the GESP trials. In his second experiment, where he had about equal numbers of expansive and compressive Ss, the interaction between E-C and type of test was in the predicted direction but not significant. The reports suggest that Ss from the first experiment may have been included in this experiment. Stuart et al. (1947) were able to demonstrate higher scoring among expansive than compressive Ss in each of their two clairvoyance series, but the trend was only significant for the group series. On the other hand, nonsignificant reversals of the predicted trend were found among four expansive and 44 compressive college students in a clairvoyance series (Nash and Richards, 1947) and for both clairvoyance and GESP among 50 Ss tested by West (1950) in England.

The E-C measure has also been used to predict the results of card tests given in the same session as drawings, the latter in some cases not being used as ESP tests themselves. Stuart et al. (1947) found the predicted relationship between E-C and ESP card-guessing scores only in their individual series. Smith and Humphrey (1946), on the other hand, found the predicted trend (E > C) in all three of their classroom clairvoyance series, as did Kahn (1952) among 73 Ss tested in groups. Bevan (1947a) found the predicted trend in his first experiment but did not report these results for his second (Bevan, 1947b). None of the trends in the above series were significant, although the trends were generally consistent. Kanthamani and Rao (1973b), using a more objective criterion for classifying subjects on the E-C dimension than used by earlier experimenters, found significantly higher scoring among expansive Ss in their four combined clairvoyance series. (Results for separate series were not reported.)

As for GESP, McMahan (1946) found, as predicted, that her 15 compressive Ss scored higher than her nine expansive Ss on a 100-trial card test, the difference reported as significant by CR analysis. She also used the drawings as an ESP test, but these results were not reported. West (1950), however, found nonsignificant reversals of the predicted trends for both clairvoyance and GESP, his Ss completing 50 trials of each. Casper (1951) found no significant relationship between E-C drawings and either clairvoyance or GESP card guessing trials, although the direction of the trends could not be determined from his report.

Humphrey (1951b) reported a summary of results from all E-C experiments conducted up to that time, including some results otherwise unpublished. Among experiments where ESP scores were derived from drawings, 10 of 12 clairvoyance series and 8 of 9 GESP series yielded trends in the predicted direction. Among 29 experiments where ESP scores were derived from card guessing, there were 17 confirmations of the predicted trends, 9 reversals, and 3 showing no difference. She notes that the trends were strongest in the four experiments involving individual testing. Although a more detailed summary of these experiments would have been desirable, there appears to be a fairly consistent tendency for expansive Ss to score better on clairvoyance tests and compressive Ss to score better on GESP tests, especially when ESP scores are derived from the drawings themselves. As Table 3 reveals, this interaction is also demonstrated among separately published experiments where the direction of the relationship could be determined.

The interpretation of this interaction, however, is anything but clear. Humphrey (1946b) suggested that compressiveness in a GESP paradigm may reflect greater attentiveness to the agent on the part of S, thus accounting for his better ESP scoring in relation to the expansive S, who presumably is more wrapped up in his own fantasy. Kanthamani and Rao (1973b) suggested an interpretation based on combining expansiveness and extraversion, but their reasoning is too complicated to discuss here.

Discussion. Although E-C is a less than ideal personality variable, the ESP results with this scale still appear to have some relevance to the relationships discussed earlier between ESP and neuroticism and extraversion. Referring to Elkisch, West (1950, p. 298) described the prototypical compressive as a "neurotically developed introvert." Treating E-C as measuring a transient state, West offered the observation that his own compressive Ss seemed especially uncomfortable in the test situation, and it was suggested earlier in this review that such discomfort may be why neurotic and introverted Ss score poorly in certain testing situations.

If one thus takes the latitude of equating compressiveness with neuroticism and introversion, the results with the E-C variable support the trend found with the other predictors only for clairvoyance experiments. It is noteworthy that almost all the experiments discussed in the sections on neuroticism or extraversion used clairvoyance (or precognition) procedures. With reference to Table 1, for example, only one of the three series by Humphrey (1945) and the experiment by Rivers (1950) employed GESP procedures as defined for the E-C experiments, and the latter employed clairvoyance trials as well. Thus the results with the E-C variable suggest caution in generalizing conclusions reached in the previous sections to test situations involving GESP or telepathy.

Aggression

A series of studies by Schmeidler explored the relationship between ESP and the Rosenzweig Picture Frustration Test, a projective test measuring how people cope with their aggressive impulses (Rosenzweig, 1945). Encouraged by the results of a preliminary experiment (Eilbert and Schmeidler, 1950), Schmeidler (1950) found in a reanalysis of data from 446 college students tested in a class-

TABLE 3. SUMMARY OF PUBLISHED EXPERIMENTS RELATING ESP TO GRAPHIC EXPANSIVENESS.

Section A. Drawing Tests

Confirming Cases (Clairv.: E > C and/or GESP: C > E)				Disconfirming Cases (Clairv.: C > E and/or GESP: E > C)			
Author	Type[a]	Exps.	Sign.	Author	Type	Exps.	Sign.
Humphrey (1946a)	C	4	1[b]	Nash and Richards (1947)	C	1	0
Humphrey (1946b)	G	6	1[b]	West (1950)	C, G	1	0
Bevan (1947a, 1947b)	C, G	2	1[b]				
Stuart et al. (1947)	C	2	1	Total		2	0
Total		14	4				

Section B. Card Tests

Confirming Cases				Disconfirming Cases			
Author	Type	Exps.	Sign.	Author	Type	Exps.	Sign.
McMahan (1946)	G	1	1[b]	Stuart et al. (1947)	C	1	0
Smith and Humphrey (1946)	C	3	0	West (1950)	C, G	1	0
Bevan (1947a)	C, G	1	0				
Stuart et al. (1947)	C	1	0	Total		2	0
Kahn (1952)	C	1	0				
Kanthamani and Rao (1973b)[c]	C	1	1				
Total		8	2				

[a]C = clairvoyance; G = GESP.
[b]Significance based on *CR* analysis.
[c]Four series of necessity treated as one.

room setting that ESP scores were significantly negatively correlated with the RPFT measure of "extrapunitiveness" (directing of aggression outward) and positively with "impunitiveness" (evasion or avoidance of aggression). Thus the least aggressive Ss scored best on the ESP test. This finding was confirmed in another sample of 266 Ss, but only on a post-hoc basis for those who rated themselves as moderately annoyed during the ESP test (Schmeidler, 1954). Further support for this general type of relationship comes from Nicol and Humphrey (1953, 1955), who found in their combined experiments a significant negative correlation between ESP and Cason's Test of Annoyance (Cason, 1931). Van de Castle (1958) found a nonsignificant reversal of the trend obtained by Schmeidler with the RPFT, but this was a psychokinesis experiment where the psychological quality of the task (i.e., intrusive rather than receptive) may be more compatible with an extrapunitive response style. More research is needed before sufficient data will be available to draw generalized conclusions about the relationship between ESP and manner of handling aggressive impulses.

Stuart Interest Inventory

A different approach to the prediction of ESP scoring is represented by the Stuart Interest Inventory (Stuart, 1946). The scale consists of 60 items, each one an event, topic, or object thought to be of interest to students at that time. S rates each item on a five-point scale, ranging from "dislike very much" (-2) to "like very much" (+2). S's score is the sum of these 60 ratings.

Based on earlier research suggesting a relationship between ESP and "affectability" (Stuart, 1941), Stuart chose to compare Ss who scored at the extreme ends of the scale with those who scored in the midrange. However, such divisions were based on the empirical distribution of scores, which was positively biased. As Humphrey (1949b) later pointed out, such a strategy caused persons with mean scores near zero to be included in the "extreme" category, thus making Stuart's classification questionable as a measure of affectability. A more appropriate measure would have been the mean absolute value of the ratings.

Whatever the scale as scored by Stuart was measuring, it did seem to have some success in predicting performance on ESP card tests. Humphrey (1949b) applied Stuart's analysis to the results of 16 card-guessing experiments involving 517 Ss for whom SII scores were available. A highly significant difference in favor of midrange scorers on the SII was demonstrated in the combined series by both the CR test and a chi-square test using S as the unit analysis. Continued success was reported when the sample was extended to 32 series totaling 900 Ss (Humphrey, 1951b). On the other hand, Casper (1951) was unable to significantly replicate these findings with a sample of 146 college students.

In a more directly empiricist approach to predicting ESP scoring from the SII, Humphrey (1950a) took the highest and lowest ESP scorers from the first three series reported earlier (Humphrey, 1949b) and selected the 14 SII items which most clearly discriminated these two groups. This separation was cross-validated to a statistically significant degree in the 13 remaining series by both *CR* and chi-square analyses. Unfortunately, it did not hold up in the still later series reported by Humphrey (1951b), although it was confirmed in a precognition experiment by Carpenter (1969). Honorton (1964, 1966) successfully utilized this version of the SII to predict the direction of scoring of *S*s undergoing a hypnotic induction procedure, but it was not successful with these same *S*s in the "waking" control condition.

Correlations between the 14-item scale and the original 60-item scale scored by Stuart's method have never been reported.

ATTITUDES

Belief in ESP

Perhaps the most extensively studied predictor of ESP test performance has been *S*'s attitude toward the existence of ESP or its likelihood of occurrence in the testing situation. In a classic series of experiments, Schmeidler asked *S*s whether they accepted the possibility of paranormal success under the conditions of the experiment (Schmeidler and McConnell, 1973). Those who admitted this possibility were labeled "sheep" while those who denied it were called "goats." In seven series of individual testing involving a total of 111 sheep and 40 goats, she found that the sheep scored significantly above chance and the goats significantly below chance. Analysis of variance yielded a highly significant difference between the two groups ($P < 8 \times 10^{-6}$). This relationship was confirmed in 14 series of classroom testing of 692 sheep and 465 goats. Although the effect was weaker in magnitude than in the individual series, sheep and goats again scored significantly above and below chance respectively, and analysis of variance again revealed a highly significant difference ($P < 3 \times 10^{-5}$). With the exception of the first three individual series where uniform testing procedures were not employed, each *S* received from 200–225 trials using standard forced-choice procedures.

A large number of subsequent experiments employing the sheep-goat dichotomy have since been published. These experiments used varying methodologies, varying definitions of the sheep-goat variable, and varying means of classifying undecided *S*s. In a review of sheep-goat experiments published in full in the major parapsychological journals from 1947 to 1970, Palmer (1971) found that among 17 experiments using standard forced-choice procedures, 13 were in the predicted direction (i.e., sheep scoring higher than goats). Six of these yielded significant results by a uniform two-tailed statistical test, all in the predicted direction. Among seven other experiments using less orthodox testing procedures, four yielded differences in the predicted direction, one in the reverse direction, and two were indeterminant. One of the positive experiments was statistically significant. Thus all significant sheep-goat differences covered in the review were in the predicted direction. With reference to the 17 experiments in his review that used orthodox testing procedures, Palmer was able to show that the 13 to 4 ratio of positive to negative directional trends follows closely the predicted ratio assuming a "real" sheep-goat difference in the population of the same magnitude found by Schmeidler in her group series, the most stable sample estimate available.

Experiments published since 1970 continue to confirm this same basic pattern. Lowy significantly confirmed the sheep-goat effect in an experiment with 20 college students in which clock faces were used as targets (Schmeidler, 1971). In a precognition experiment conducted 10 years earlier, Nielsen (1970c) reports significantly more positive scoring among a group of believers than among neutral ("open-minded") Ss (there were no skeptics in the sample), the effect being attributable to runs completed when Ss were in an "extreme" rather than a "moderate" mood. In a follow-up to his experiment with erotic and neutral targets, Carpenter (1971) found a significant sheep-goat difference (one-tailed) when the erotic and neutral trials were pooled. Ss were 31 male college students. Honorton (1972) found a positive but nonsignificant sheep-goat difference among 28 adults each given 125 ESP trials. Barrington (1973) also found a positive sheep-goat difference among a group of 47 members of the (British) Society for Psychical Research given a complicated free-response ESP test camouflaged as a memory task. She gamely demonstrated statistical significance by showing that her four subgroups of Ss classified on the sheep-goat continuum scored in perfect predicted order on the ESP test, although the two goat subgroups contained only two and three Ss respectively. Palmer (1973) analyzed data from two college classes tested by Schmeidler. Thirty-nine sheep and 18 goats produced a significant sheep-goat difference in the predicted direction using a modified version of Schmeidler's definition of the sheep-goat variable, but nonsignificant reversals were found using three other definitions.

A significant reversal of the sheep-goat effect was found by Moss, Paulson, Chang, and Levitt (1970) in a telepathy experiment where each of 23 agents attempted to transmit the contents of emotionally arousing slides to paired percipients located in a separate room. However, this experiment is not comparable to the other sheep-goat experiments reviewed in this chapter for at least two reasons. First, the Ss in the Moss experiment were selected because they either had previous psi experiences or had scored well on a previous ESP test of the same type. Thus, it is especially unlikely that the sample of "goats" in this experiment were representative of nonbelievers in general or comparable to "goats" in most other ESP experiments. Second, some of the Ss were hypnotized and given suggestions of success on the ESP test, a procedure which was significantly related to ESP scores in this experiment as in many previous experiments (Van de Castle, 1969). However, assignment to the hypnosis condition was not random but based on subject preferences. Unfortunately, the report does not allow a determination of the degree of confounding between hypnosis and belief.

Beloff and Bate (1970) reported a tendency for Ss who expressed belief that they themselves had ESP ability to score differently than other Ss to a statistically significant degree on a forced-choice ESP task. However, the direction of the effect differed from sample to sample and was independently significant in only two of the seven. This classification has been one of the least successful of the sheep-goat criteria in previous research (see Palmer, 1971).

Nonsignificant sheep-goat differences were reported in two other studies (McCollam and Honorton, 1973; Schmeidler and Craig, 1972), but the results were not reported in sufficient detail to allow determination of the direction of the effect.

For a theoretical discussion of the sheep-goat effect and review of other data related to this general issue, see Palmer (1972).

MULTIVARIATE APPROACHES

Up to this point the discussion has been restricted primarily to univariate relationships between ESP and personality or attitudinal variables. In his 1973 Presidential Address to the Parapsychological Association, Stanford (1974) echoed the feeling of many parapsychologists that such an approach is overly simplistic. Indeed, it is obvious that personality variables interact not only with other personality variables but also with the experimental situation and S's mood in determining level of scoring on ESP tests. Stanford also stressed the need for more, and more sophisticated, conceptualization in the personality-ESP area.

Unfortunately, most personality-ESP research has not been very sophisticated conceptually, and few studies have explored interactions among variables. A notable exception is Schmeidler's (1960) sheep-goat research. In addition to questions concerning S's beliefs about ESP occurring in the test situation, Schmeidler included various personality tests, including the Rorschach. Post-hoc examination of the data indicated that the sheep-goat effect appeared only for Ss rated as "socially adjusted" on a Rorschach scale developed by Munroe (1945). This interaction was confirmed to a significant degree among the 1,004 remaining Ss in her sample by analysis of variance.

Schmeidler then reexamined data from the first 250 Ss of this latter group and found seven Rorschach "signs," the presence of which in Ss' protocols seemed to counterindicate the sheep-goat effect in a manner similar to high scores on the Munroe checklist. (Unfortunately, correlations between these two

Rorschach measures were not reported.) This interaction was then confirmed at a significant level on the 754 remaining Ss in the series. The results seemed interpretable as the sheep-goat effect being eliminated for either overly constrained or overly impulsive Ss. As an oversimplified but generally valid conclusion from this body of research, it may be stated that the sheep-goat effect was attenuated for persons relatively low on social or emotional adjustment as measured by the Rorschach.

In one analysis of variance, Schmeidler (1960) also found the sheep-goat effect to be significantly stronger for females than males. Finally, analysis of 114 of her Ss indicated a stronger sheep-goat difference among those with a strong theoretical orientation on the Allport-Vernon Study of Values (Schmeidler and McConnell, 1973). However, the effect was very weak and not replicated in subsequent research (see Palmer, 1971).

Palmer and Miller (1970) reported a significant interaction reflecting elimination of the sheep-goat effect among Ss offered a monetary reward of ten dollars for the highest score. Ss were 47 college students tested in groups. Carpenter's (1971) research with the Manifest Anxiety Scale and erotic vs. neutral targets is another example of a more sophisticated and conceptually oriented approach to the study of personality and psi.

Finally, several experimenters have demonstrated increased discriminability of high and low ESP scorers by combining predictors. Examples are the Stuart Interest Inventory and graphic expansiveness (Humphrey, 1949a, 1950b) and subscales of Cattell's HSPQ (Kanthamani and Rao, 1972a). Such an approach is of little theoretical interest, although it may have some value as a screening device for selecting Ss most likely to benefit from attempts at training psi. Unfortunately, however, we know even less about the test-retest reliability of ESP scores than we do about their internal consistency. Thus, there is no guarantee that personality variables can predict potential or actual psi ability conceptualized as a *trait*.

A more complicated multivariate approach to ESP research using multiple regression techniques is illustrated by Osis et al. (1971).

SUMMARY

Because of the low reliability of ESP scores, it was a premise of this review that conclusions could only be drawn by examining trends in a large number of studies employing conceptually related predictors, including experiments where the results did not reach statistical significance. This approach was not introduced as ideal, but as the best among a group of less-than-ideal alternatives.

Keeping these reservations in mind, the data seem to suggest that two kinds of people are most likely to perform best on laboratory tests of ESP, at least the first time they are tested individually with a clairvoyance procedure: (a) people who are relatively well adjusted, and (b) people who believe in ESP. There is also evidence from Schmeidler's research that under certain circumstances, at least, these two factors can interact; i.e., believers only score better than nonbelievers if the *S*s are well adjusted or (if you prefer) well-adjusted *S*s only score better than their more poorly adjusted counterparts if the *S*s believe in psi. It also seems to be the general consensus of opinion that the reason believers and/or well-adjusted *S*s score best is that they are more comfortable in the test situation, thereby better able to exercise the relaxed spontaneity thought to be necessary for high scoring.

In order to transcend this probably oversimplified conclusion, more sophisticated research, more sophisticated theory, and (alas!) more reliable ESP scores will be needed. The first two requirements can be fulfilled by personality-ESP researchers themselves; the third, however, will almost certainly have to come from other approaches. However, if theoretical principles uncovered through personality-ESP research can provide insights for those working with these other approaches, this research will have been well worth the effort.

REFERENCES

Aström, J. GESP and MPI measures. *Journal of Parapsychology*, 1965, **29**, 292–293.

Barrington, M. R. A free response sheep/goat experiment using an irrelevant task. *Journal of the Society for Psychical Research*, 1973, 47, 222–245.

Beloff, J., and Bate, D. Research report for the year 1968–69. University of Edinburgh Parapsychology Unit. *Journal of the Society for Psychical Research*, 1970, **45**, 297–301.

Bevan, J. M. ESP tests in light and darkness. *Journal of Parapsychology*, 1947, **11**, 76–89. (a)

Bevan, J. M. The relation of attitude to success in ESP scoring. *Journal of Parapsychology*, 1947, **11**, 296–309. (b)

Brockbill, G., and Little, K. B. MMPI correlates of the Taylor-Scale of Manifest Anxiety. *Journal of Consulting Psychology*, 1954, **18**, 433–436.

Brodbeck, T. J. ESP and personality. *Journal of the Society for Psychical Research*, 1969, **45**, 31–32.

Carpenter, J. C. An exploratory test of ESP in relation to anxiety proneness. In J. B. Rhine (Ed.), *Parapsychology: From Duke to FRNM*, pp. 68–73. Durham, N.C.: Parapsychology Press, 1965.

Carpenter, J. C. Further study on a mood adjective check list and ESP run-score variance. *Journal of Parapsychology*, 1969, **33**, 48–56.

Carpenter, J. C. The differential effect and hidden target differences consisting of erotic and neutral stimuli. *Journal of the American Society for Psychical Research*, 1971, **65**, 204–214.

Cason, H. An annoyance test and some research problems. *Journal of Abnormal and Social Psychology*, 1931, **25**, 224–238.

Casper, G. W. A further study of the relation of attitude to success in ESP scoring. *Journal of Parapsychology*, 1951, **15**, 139–145.

Casper, G. W. Effect of receiver's attitude toward sender in ESP tests. *Journal of Parapsychology*, 1952, **16**, 212–218.

Cattell, R. B. *The Scientific Analysis of Personality*. Baltimore: Penguin Books, 1965.

Cattell, R. B., and Beloff, H. *Handbook for the Jr.-Sr. High School Personality Question-naire*. (2nd ed.) Champaign, Ill.: Institute for Personality and Ability Testing, 1962.

Cattell, R. B., Eber, H. W., and Tatsuoka, M. M. *Handbook for the Sixteen Personality Factor Questionnaire (16PF)*. Champaign, Ill.: Institute for Personality and Ability Testing, 1970.

Dahlstrom, W. G., Welsh, G. S., and Dahlstrom, L. E. *An MMPI Handbook*. (Rev. ed.) Minneapolis: University of Minnesota Press, 1972.

Eilbert, L., and Schmeidler, G. R. A study of certain psychological factors in relation to ESP performance, *Journal of Parapsychology*, 1950, **14**, 53–74.

Elkisch, P. Children's drawings in a projective technique. *Psychological Monographs*, 1945, **58**, 1–31.

Eysenck, H. J. *The Maudsley Personality Inventory*. San Diego: Educational and Industrial Testing Service, 1959.

Eysenck, H. J. *The Structure of Human Personality*. London: Methuen, 1960.

Eysenck, H. J. Personality and extrasensory perception. *Journal of the Society for Psychical Research*, 1967, **44**, 55–71.

Eysenck, H. J., and Eysenck, S. B. G. *The Eysenck Personality Inventory*. San Diego: Educational and Industrial Testing Service, 1965.

Eysenck, S. B. G. *The Junior Eysenck Personality Inventory*. London: University of London Press, 1965.

Freeman, J. A. Mood, personality, and attitude in precognition tests. *Proceedings of the Parapsychological Association*, 1970, **7**, 53–54.

Freeman, J. A., and Nielsen, W. Precognition score deviations as related to anxiety levels. *Journal of Parapsychology*, 1964, **28**, 239–249.

Green, C. E. Extrasensory perception and the extraversion scale of the Maudsley Personality Inventory. *Journal of the Society for Psychical Research*, 1966, **43**, 337. (a)

Green, C. E. Extrasensory perception and the Maudsley Personality Inventory. *Journal of the Society for Psychical Research*, 1966, **43**, 285–286. (b)

Greenwald, A. G. Consequences of prejudice against the null hypothesis. *Psychological Bulletin*, 1975, **82**, 1–20.

Guilford, J. P. *Personality*. New York: McGraw-Hill, 1959.

Guilford, J. P., and Zimmerman, W. S. *Guilford-Zimmerman Temperament Survey*. Beverly Hills, Calif.: Sheridan Supply Co., 1949.

Heston, J. C. *Heston Manual and Personal Adjustment Inventory*. Yonkers-on-Hudson, N.Y.: World Book Co., 1949.

Honorton, C. Separation of high- and low-scoring ESP subjects through hypnotic preparation. *Journal of Parapsychology*, 1964, **28**, 251–257.

Honorton, C. The relationship between ESP and manifest anxiety level. *Journal of Parapsychology*, 1965, **29**, 291–292.

Honorton, C. A further separation of high- and low-scoring ESP subjects through hypnotic preparation. *Journal of Parapsychology*, 1966, **30**, 172–183.

Honorton, C. Reported frequency of dream recall and ESP. *Journal of the American Society for Psychical Research*, 1972, **66**, 369–374.

Honorton, C., Ramsey, M., and Cabibbo, C. Experimenter effects in extrasensory perception. *Journal of the American Society for Psychical Research*, 1975, **69**, 135–139.

Hull, C. L. *Principles of Behavior*. New York: Appleton, 1943.

Humphrey, B. M. An exploratory correlation study of personality measures and ESP scores. *Journal of Parapsychology*, 1945, **9**, 116–123.

Humphrey, B. M. Success in ESP as related to form of response drawings: I. Clairvoyance experiments. *Journal of Parapsychology*, 1946, **10**, 78–106. (a)

Humphrey, B. M. Success in ESP as related to form of response drawings: II. GESP experiments. *Journal of Parapsychology*, 1946, **10**, 181–196. (b)

Humphrey, B. M. ESP subjects rated by two measures of personality. *Journal of Parapsychology*, 1949, **13**, 274–291. (a)

Humphrey, B. M. Further work of Dr. Stuart on interest test ratings and ESP. *Journal of Parapsychology*, 1949, **13**, 151–165. (b)

Humphrey, B. M. A new scale for separating high- and low-scoring subjects in ESP tests. *Journal of Parapsychology*, 1950, **14**, 9–23. (a)

Humphrey, B. M. ESP score level predicted by a combination of measures of personality. *Journal of Parapsychology*, 1950, **14**, 193–206. (b)

Humphrey, B. M. Introversion-extraversion ratings in relation to scores in ESP tests. *Journal of Parapsychology*, 1951, **15**, 252–262. (a)

Humphrey, B. M. The relation of some personality ratings to ESP scores. *Journal of the Society for Psychical Research*, 1951, **36**, 453–466. (b)

Hundleby, J. D., and Connor, W. H. Interrelationships between personality inventories: The 16PF, the MMPI, and the MPI. *Journal of Consulting and Clinical Psychology*, 1968, **32**, 152–157.

Jackson, D. N., and Messick, S. Response styles on the MMPI: Comparison of clinical and normal samples. *Journal of Abnormal and Social Psychology*, 1962, **65**, 285–299.

Johnson, M., and Kanthamani, B. K. The Defense Mechanism Test as a predictor of ESP scoring direction. *Journal of Parapsychology*, 1967, **31**, 99–110.

Joy, V. L. Repression-sensitization and interpersonal behavior. Paper presented at the Seventy-first Annual Meeting of the American Psychological Association, Philadelphia, Pa., 1963.

Kahn, S. D. Studies in extrasensory perception: Experiments utilizing an electronic scoring device. *Proceedings of the American Society for Psychical Research*, 1952, **25**, 1–48.

Kanthamani, B. K. The ESP subject: An inquiry into the personality patterns of psi-hitters and missers. Unpublished doctoral dissertation, Andhra University, Waltair, India, 1968.

Kanthamani, B. K., and Rao, K. R. Personality characteristics of ESP subjects. II. The Combined Personality Measure (CPM) and ESP. *Journal of Parapsychology*, 1972, **36**, 56–70. (a)

Kanthamani, B. K., and Rao, K. R. Personality characteristics of ESP subjects. III. Extraversion and ESP. *Journal of Parapsychology*, 1972, **36**, 190–212. (b)

Kanthamani, B. K., and Rao, K. R. Personality characteristics of ESP subjects: IV. Neuroticism and ESP. *Journal of Parapsychology*, 1973, **37**, 37–50. (a)

Kanthamani, B. K., and Rao, K. R. Personality characteristics of ESP subjects: V. Graphic expansiveness and ESP. *Journal of Parapsychology*, 1973, **37**, 119–129. (b)

Kragh, U. The Defense Mechanism Test: A new method for diagnosis and personnel selection. *Journal of Applied Psychology*, 1960, **44**, 4.

Kragh, U. Prediction of success of Danish attack divers by the Defense Mechanism Test (DMT). *Perceptual and Motor Skills*, 1962, **7**, 103–106.

Lazarus, R. S., and Alfert, E. The short circuiting of threat by experimentally altering cognitive appraisal. *Journal of Abnormal and Social Psychology*, 1964, **69**, 195–205.

Mangan, G. L. A review of published research on the relationship of some personality variables to ESP scoring level. *Parapsychological Monographs No. 1*. New York: Parapsychology Foundation, 1958.

Maslow, A. H., Hirsh, E., Stein, M., and Honigmann, I. A. A clinically derived test for measuring psychological security-insecurity. *Journal of General Psychology*, 1945, **33**, 21–41.

McCollam, E., and Honorton, C. Effects of feedback on discrimination between correct and incorrect ESP responses: A further replication and extension. *Journal of the American Society for Psychical Research*, 1973, **67**, 77–85.

McMahan, E. A. An experiment in pure telepathy. *Journal of Parapsychology*, 1946, **10**, 224–242.

Moss, T., Paulson, M. J., Chang, A. F. and Levitt, M. Hypnosis and ESP: A controlled experiment. *American Journal of Clinical Hypnosis*, 1970, **13**, 46–56.

Munroe, R. L. Prediction of the adjustment and academic performance of college students by a modification of the Rorschach method. *Applied Psychological Monographs*, No. 7, 1945.

Nash, C. B. Relation between ESP scoring and the Minnesota Multiphasic Personality Inventory. *Journal of the American Society for Psychical Research*, 1966, **60**, 56–62.

Nash, C. B., and Nash, C. S. Relations between ESP scoring level and the personality traits of the Guilford-Zimmerman Temperament Survey. *Journal of the American Society for Psychical Research*, 1967, **61**, 64–71.

Nash, C. B., and Richards, A. Comparison of two distances in PK tests. *Journal of Parapsychology*, 1947, **11**, 269–282.

Nicol, J. F., and Humphrey, B. M. The exploration of ESP and human personality. *Journal of the American Society for Psychical Research*, 1953, **47**, 133–178.

Nicol, J. F., and Humphrey, B. M. The repeatability problem in ESP-personality research. *Journal of the American Society for Psychical Research*, 1955, **49**, 125–156.

Nielsen, W. Studies in group targets: A social psychology class. *Proceedings of the Parapsychological Association*, 1970, **7**, 55–57. (a)

Nielsen, W. Studies in group targets: An unusual high school group. *Proceedings of the Parapsychological Association*, 1970, **7**, 57–58. (b)

Nielsen, W. Relationships between precognition scoring level and mood. *Journal of Parapsychology*, 1970, **34**, 93–116 (c).

Nielsen, W., and Freeman, J. A. Consistency of relationship between ESP and emotional variables. *Journal of Parapsychology*, 1965, **29**, 75–88.

Osis, K., Turner, M. E., Jr., and Carlson, M. L. ESP over distance: Research on the ESP channel. *Journal of the American Society for Psychical Research*, 1971, **65**, 245–288.

Palmer, J. Scoring in ESP tests as a function of belief in ESP. Part I. The sheep-goat effect. *Journal of the American Society for Psychical Research*, 1971, **65**, 373–408.

Palmer, J. Scoring in ESP tests as a function of belief in ESP. Part II. Beyond the sheep-goat effect. *Journal of the American Society for Psychical Research*, 1972, **66**, 1–26.

Palmer, J. ESP scoring as predicted from four definitions of the sheep-goat variable. In W. G. Roll, R. L. Morris, and J. D. Morris (Eds.), *Research in Parapsychology 1972*, pp. 37–39. Metuchen, N.J.: Scarecrow Press, 1973.

Palmer, J., and Miller, A. Monetary incentive and the sheep-goat effect. *Proceedings of the Parapsychological Association*, 1970, **7**, 11–12.

Randall, J. L. Card-guessing experiments with school boys. *Journal of the Society for Psychical Research*, 1974, **47**, 421–432.

Rao, K. R. ESP and the Manifest Anxiety Scale. *Journal of Parapsychology*, 1965, **29**, 12–18.

Rhine, J. B. Comments: "Publication policy regarding nonsignificant results." *Journal of Parapsychology*, 1975, **39**, 135–142.

Rivers, O. B. An exploratory study of the mental health and intelligence of ESP subjects. *Journal of Parapsychology*, 1950, **14**, 267–277.

Rosenzweig, S. The picture-association method and its application in a study of reactions to frustration. *Journal of Personality*, 1945, **14**, 3–23.

Schmeidler, G. R. Some relations between picture-frustration ratings and ESP scores. *Journal of Personality*, 1950, **18**, 331–344.

Schmeidler, G. R. Picture-frustration ratings and ESP scores for subjects who showed moderate annoyance at the ESP task. *Journal of Parapsychology*, 1954, **18**, 137–152.

Schmeidler, G. R. ESP in relation to Rorschach test evaluation. *Parapsychological Monographs No. 2*. New York: Parapsychology Foundation, 1960.

Schmeidler, G. R. An experiment on precognitive clairvoyance: Part IV. Precognition scores related to creativity. *Journal of Parapsychology*, 1964, **28**, 102–108.

Schmeidler, G. R. Mood and attitude on a pretest as predictors of retest ESP performance. *Journal of the American Society for Psychical Research*, 1971, **65**, 324–335.

Schmeidler, G. R., and Craig, J. G. Moods and ESP scores in group testing. *Journal of the American Society for Psychical Research*, 1972, **66**, 280–287.

Schmeidler, G. R., and McConnell, R. A. *ESP and Personality Patterns*. Westport, Conn.: Greenwood Press, 1973. (Originally published, 1958.)

Shields, E. Comparison of children's guessing ability (ESP) with personality characteristics. *Journal of Parapsychology*, 1962, **26**, 200–210.

Smith, B. M., and Humphrey, B. M. Some personality characteristics related to ESP performance. *Journal of Parapsychology*, 1946, **10**, 269–289.

Stanford, R. G. Concept and psi. In W. G. Roll, R. L. Morris, and J. D. Morris (Eds.), *Research in Parapsychology 1973*, pp. 137–162. Metuchen, N.J.: Scarecrow Press, 1974.

Stanford, R. G., and Palmer, J. Some statistical considerations concerning process-oriented research in parapsychology. *Journal of the American Society for Psychical Research*, 1972, **66**, 166–179.

Stuart, C. E. An analysis to determine a test predictive of extra-chance scoring in card-calling tests. *Journal of Parapsychology*, 1941, **5**, 99–137.

Stuart, C. E. An interest inventory relation to ESP scores. *Journal of Parapsychology*, 1946, **10**, 154–161.

Stuart, C. E., Humphrey, B. M., Smith, B. M., and McMahan, E. Personality measurements and ESP tests with cards and drawings. *Journal of Parapsychology*, 1947, **11**, 118–146.

Super, D. E. The Bernreuter Personality Inventory: A review of research. *Psychological Bulletin*, 1942, **39**, 94–125.

Taylor, J. A. A personality scale of manifest anxiety. *Journal of Abnormal and Social Psychology*, 1953, **48**, 285–290.

Van de Castle, R. L. An exploratory study of some personality correlates associated with PK performance. *Journal of the American Society for Psychical Research*, 1953, **52**, 134–150.

Van de Castle, R. L. The facilitation of ESP through hypnosis. *American Journal of Clinical Hypnosis*, 1969, **12**, 37–56.

West, D. J. ESP performance and the expansion-compression rating. *Journal of the Society for Psychical Research*, 1950, **35**, 295–308.

3

Intrasubject and Subject-Agent Effects in ESP Experiments

James C. Carpenter

INTRASUBJECT EFFECTS

The Variable Subject

If the world had been constructed with the parapsychologist's convenience in mind it would be peopled by two distinct types: those who possessed the faculty for acquiring knowledge nonsensorially and those without it. These types would be simply distinguishable, as by the Dvorine patterns used to select the color-blind from the color-seeing. The psychic person would correctly identify all of the targets in an ESP deck each time he tried, the nonpsychic would always identify only a coincidental few. Possession of the faculty would be linked to a physiological receptor system in the brain, the occurrence of which obeyed clear genetic laws. The physical properties of the stimuli to which psychics respond would be understood, and extreme ranges of those stimuli, to which psychics would be insensate, would be established.

This fantasy bears little resemblance to the array of observations one encounters in attempting to assess a body of parapsychological research. If it did, there would be no "para" describing the research, and long ago it would have occupied a secure if curious niche in general psychology, alongside the responsiveness of bees to polarized light and the olfactory powers of bloodhounds. In fact, the constructs advanced by parapsychologists refer to hypothetical processes whose very existence seems contrary both to everyday experience and to the world-view erected by the physical sciences. This is what makes them at once so audacious, so intriguing, and so dismissable. It would be a mistake to forget that the person designing an ESP experiment, for all his sober method and pedestrian statistics, is setting the stage for a miracle. It may transpire or it may not. If it does, it may have to be fished out with a statistical net to be evident. Consider the predicament of the ESP subject. You, the experimenter, have elicited his cooperation. Next you refer to some information which you assure him is not accessible to him, for example a sealed deck of cards in another city. Then in the same breath you ask him to tell you the order of the cards in that deck. "If people could do that," I remember a former psychology professor of mine saying, "don't you think someone would have noticed by now?" Is it any wonder then that performance in such a situation is nothing if not variable? The important question becomes: Is the variability observed "mere coincidence"?

"Mere coincidence" is a concept with a kind of negative substance for science. We may speak loosely of something being "due to chance," but really that is incorrect since by chance, or coincidence, we mean to assert an absence of any causal connection between two series of events. On each of two billiard tables one ball may strike another at the same moment. Both impacts would impart force in a predictable, lawful way; yet their concurrence in time would be "mere coincidence," each causal series being insulated from the other. I am persuaded to think of science as a human effort to wrest meaning from the flux of ongoing events, to construe recurrent elements in experience, test the expectations to which they give rise, revise the constructs in the light of experience, and test again. The scientist, particularly in primitively developed sciences like psychology, is not so different from Everyman in this respect, motivated as we all are to make predictive sense of our lives. "Mere coincidence" is the scientist's conceptual no man's land where nothing is, no theories need be constructed, no hypotheses tested. We would not be too far wrong, I think, to view the development of experimental parapsychology as a continuing assault against some areas of "mere coincidence," an effort to make sense where no sense has been generally supposed to be.

Sir Francis Bacon (cited by Thouless, 1972) in a work published in 1627, advocated a methodical approach to the examination of alleged phenomena now construed as "paranormal." In assessing telepathy, or the "binding of thought," Bacon suggested guessing tests using cards or names and advised: "You are to note whether it hit for the most part though not alway." As Thouless remarks in his reference to the advice, "for the most part though not always," was a good anticipation of how matters have generally gone.

The performance of subjects in ESP tests is variable. Success is virtually always partial and undependable. This has been an almost ubiquitous observation and at times a very vexing one. William James (cited in Murphy and Ballou, 1960), in relating his "final impressions of a psychical researcher," exclaimed that the many hours he had spent in studying mediumistic material had left him "tempted to believe that the Creator has eternally intended this department of nature to remain *baffling*, to prompt our curiosities and hopes and suspicions all in equal measure" (p. 310).

J. B. Rhine (1934), in his historic first monograph, noted that even his best subjects experienced dips of scoring to a chance or below-chance level and turned to "psychological conditions" as offering hope for explanations. Perhaps psychology was seen as itself sufficiently riddled with uncertainty and unpredictability as to promise a good match with these psychic vagaries. Soal and Bateman (1954) seem to have thought so, as they said: "Physical phenomena are characterized by their uniformity and psychological phenomena in general by their greater variability. As we pass from physics to biology, thence to classical psychology, through psychotherapy to psychical research, we find an ever increasing degree of variability in the results of experiment. In parapsychology, each subject's performance represents the reaction of his own personality to the experimental situation, and this reaction is modified by the extra-personal relations of the group in which he is working" (p. 318). Psychical research, we are to judge, is somewhat more intrinsically unruly than dealing with madness. In summarizing a lengthy and careful series of studies on conditions supposed to favor success, Woodruff and George (1937) can almost be glimpsed throwing up their hands as they come to conclude: "The ability to perform under different conditions varies widely and in different directions among individuals" (p. 30). Or perhaps one might put it: "Anything may happen, unless it doesn't."

There has been a quality of hard-headed persistence and determination to modern parapsychology, perhaps best typified by the long labors of J. B. and L. E. Rhine, which has doggedly refused to take refuge in an "instrinsic lawlessness" kind of solution (which would only be a reassertion of mere coincidence) and has instead forged new constructs in an effort to anticipate variations in performance and render them intelligible. This has occurred both on the side of the dependent variables (the psychic abilities) and of the independent variables. In the next few paragraphs I will sketch some of the elaborations of the dependent variable side which have transpired. The various intrasubject and interpersonal dimensions which have been employed as independent variables will then provide a structure for the review of research to follow.

Telepathy vs. Coincidence. That part of the no-man's land of coincidence which first attracted the attention of the psychical researchers of the nineteenth century (Gauld, 1968) was the relationship between the concurrent thoughts and experiences of two people who were not in sensory communication. Framing their notions in the form of bipolar constructs, one might say they asserted a "telepathy vs. coincidence" construct. In mediumistic séances intimate and obscure information pertinent to a sitter was sometimes given by the medium when no way for her to have learned the information could be imagined. From the medium's point of view the knowledge was given by an intangible spirit of someone deceased; another hypothesis had her acquiring it from the sitter. Either way, if the knowledge was truly neither coincidence nor fraud, the boundaries of private experience seemed more permeable than had been assumed. With the development late in the century of probability theory, the parameters of mere coincidence had been described, and the relative unlikelihood of some set of observations having no causal interrelation could be determined. Armed with the statistics of probability, a few researchers turned their efforts to forced-choice guessing tasks, the results of which could be statistically assessed. Richet (1884) carried out almost 3,000 trials with ordinary subjects guessing the suits of playing cards being looked at by another person. The results were not unlike those reported many times since. Overall, the number of correct guesses exceeded chance expectation to a degree conventionally considered significant ($P = .015$), but the variable subject was evident. Even in these significantly correct data 2,138 of the guesses were wrong, and only 789 were right. Another element of subject-variability was also noticed by Richet, which also portended later findings. When subjects worked at long series of guesses (100 or more trials), their pooled data were at flat chance; when they worked in shorter bouts, their performance was quite significant ($P = .005$).

The "telepathy vs. coincidence" construct was fairly soon expanded experimentally to include apprehension of information not known to another person, or clairvoyance (Jephson, 1928). Later, J. B. Rhine and his co-workers (1938) added precognition and called the three together extrasensory perception.

Since late in the last century, experimental parapsychologists have found and carried out repeated testing on several unusually consistent and gifted subjects, all of whom have sooner or later shown the waning of ability which Thouless (1972) has called "long term decline." This within-subject pattern of variation found with the special subjects will be described below.

Psi-hitting vs. Psi-missing. Naturalistically inclined researchers have criticized the laboratory procedures developed by J. B. Rhine (1934) and Soal and Bateman (1954) as being dull and not liable to produce the dramatic and vivid results reported in "spontaneous cases." One point in favor of the laboratory method is its fruitfulness in producing new constructs which would never have been invented in the "field." The subatomic entities of modern physics are examples of laboratory-bred concepts. The construct of psi-hitting vs. psi-missing (referred to subsequently as ψH and ψM) is also such an invention. The idea that ESP correspondences can be consistently and meaningfully *wrong* could scarcely have occurred to a collector of spontaneous cases since an error would presumably be experienced as a nonrelation and never reported to anyone, except as a refutation of the ESP hypothesis (i.e., as representing coincidence). The elaboration of ESP vs. coincidence into ψH *or* ψM vs. coincidence was perhaps at first a matter of making do with an apparently bad situation. Except for a handful of "low-aim" tests (described below), data yielding negative deviations during the early years of ESP testing were as desirable as a cockroach in a coffee-cup: it is *something* but not what one really wants. Since then, however, ψH vs. ψM has become the primary dependent-variable construct for parapsychologists and the relation between the two poles, and conditions making for each, have been areas of intense theoretical and empirical interest (Rao, 1965b; J. B. Rhine, 1952, 1969a, 1969b; L. E. Rhine, 1965).

Patterns in which ψH, ψM, and apparently chance scoring trends replace one another in a subject's ESP performance have received considerable attention under the label of position effects (J. B. Rhine, 1969b). Perhaps the most often reported position effect has been the "episodic decline" (Thouless, 1972). Declines have been found within the run (usually 25 calls), within a "segment" of the run (usually five calls), within a "page" of runs (usually ten), and within a series of runs (usually some number greater than ten). Jephson (1928), in her pioneering study of clairvoyant card-guessing, observed a U-curve pattern of success across the set of five guesses each of her subjects carried out per day. This combination of decline and recovery has since been found often enough to warrant a name: "terminal salience" (J. B. Rhine, 1941).

Scoring effects, including psi-hitting, declines to chance, declines to psi-missing, salience, etc., have tended to follow a common pattern of evolution in parapsychology. First a scoring effect is noticed, tested for statistical significance, and then reported as an instance of the "psi-faculty" in operation; i.e., as a refutation of mere coincidence. Then its replicability is seen as partial, and it is described more vaguely as an "earmark" of psi, or something "commonly found." Finally, it becomes seen as a dependent variable, a dimension along which performance may shift, whose occurrence is contingent upon factors potentially specifiable and experimentally controllable.

Another position effect to receive attention has been the apparent ψH or ψM contingencies between the guess and the targets just before or after the one intended for it. Carington (1940), in a series of telepathy experiments in which subjects tried to make drawings which would match target drawings several hundred miles distant, noted that subjects often produced drawings which matched the target just before or after the one drawn on the day of the trial. Carington urged S. G. Soal to look for the effect. Soal and Bateman (1954) did reexamine data which had been collected on 76 subjects in an unsuccessful effort to find a high-scoring card guesser and to their surprise found that two subjects had large ψH deviations on the targets next-in-the-future from the direct target. This displacement effect, as it was called, seemed not to be an accident, since one of the subjects (Basil Shackleton) upon retesting produced it again with significant consistency. Analyses for displacement effects are not commonly reported so it is difficult to judge how pervasive they may be or on what factors their occurrence depends. They have been especially important in extended research with two special subjects, Shackleton and Pavel Stepanek.

Another scoring effect, which incorporates the ψH-ψM construct, is the differential effect. This has been construed rather loosely and in fact has been used to refer to at least three kinds of experimental results in a repeated-measures design. The three cases can be illustrated by three relatively older studies. First, the phrase has been used to describe studies in which the same subjects are tested in two different circumstances, and the different circumstances tend to elicit performances which are modally opposite for each subject. Stuart, Humphrey, Smith, and McMahan (1947) tested 63 subjects using two modes of response: calling ESP cards and producing free-response drawings. Forty-two of the 63 subjects had opposite-mode scoring rates on their two tasks; that is, those who scored ψH on drawings tended to score ψM on card-calling, and vice versa. The proportion of subjects reversing mode was significant, with a Z (sign test) = 2.52. There was no significant consistency *across* subjects in their "preference," only an apparent power of the two response-conditions to pull both above and below chance performance from the same individuals.

The second major type of result which has been called a differential effect is that in which a group of subjects (or a single subject on repeated occasions) is tested with each of two different tasks or conditions, and the results as a whole show an accumulated ψH effect for one condition and an accumulated ψM effect for the other. Thouless (1949) carried out 144 sessions of repeated self-testing making three DT runs per session, one run (A) being a clairvoyance-type (preshuffled and precut); another (B) being a "simple" precognition-type (preshuffled, randomly cut after guessing); and the last (C) a "complex" pre-cognition-type (both shuffled and randomly cut after the guessing was completed). He varied their order within the session in a balanced manner. The results showed, overall, a ψH effect for condition C ($Z = 2.33, P < .02$), a ψM effect for condition A ($Z = -2.54, P < .01$), and a nonsignificant deviation on condition B. The contrasting performance in the A and C conditions represents a differential effect of this type. That this effect is *not* the same as the one just cited from Stuart et al. is indicated both by the absence of overall significant scoring trends in either experimental condition in the Stuart study and by the absence of a negative correlation within each testing session between Thouless' type A and C runs. If a cross-mode differential effect within the session was present, a negative correlation of the two sets of run-scores should be found. In fact, there was an insignificant positive (+ .06) correlation value reported.

The third case that has been called a differential effect is akin to the second in all respects except that neither of the cumulative ψH and ψM trends are statistically significant; instead, the two trends are found to be significantly different *from each other*. A study by Skibinsky (1950) is often cited as illustrating a differential effect. In that research the experimenter reasoned that personally salient bits of information might intrude more successfully into the subject's consciousness when used as ESP targets than the more neutral geometric symbols commonly used. Three series of guesses were carried out with six subjects. Each day each subject (in New York City) made one run of 25 guesses using names followed by one run using symbols trying to match target orders prepared that day by the experimenter in North Carolina. When the results for all series were pooled, the scoring rates on the two target-types were significantly different (Z of the difference = 2.7). The modality of the results was opposite to the original expectation: significant ψM on the names and a nonsignificant ψH trend on the symbols (Z's = -2.4 and 1.4, respectively, my calculations).

Apparently by convention the term *differential effect* has not been used to describe the case in which a repeated-measures design yields a significant overall difference between two scoring rates when one of them is at or very close to chance.

Palmer (1974) has urged that only the first case just reviewed should be termed differential effect, since the latter two only represent cases in which some conditions have been found which will tend to elicit ψH and ψM trends. The broader usage implies that the contiguity of the two tasks or conditions is responsible for the separation of modal trends. Actually, Palmer reasons, the same difference in trends could well be obtained by testing independent groups in the two conditions; that is, in a design not employing repeated measures on the same subjects. If so, the repeated-measure aspect would be falsely credited with having a differentiating power it did not have.

It seems to be an empirical question (largely unaddressed) whether or not the presentation to a single subject of two contrasting conditions (Rao, 1965a, 1965b) is responsible in part for our second and third kinds of differential effects. If the Skibinsky study were replicated using two groups of subjects, one guessing family names as targets, and the other symbols, would the modal differentiation be replicated? It would certainly seem advisable for researchers to heed Palmer's warning at least to the extent of replicating repeated-measures differential effects using *both* repeated-measures and independent-group designs. The actual power of the within-subject contrast effect could then be ascertained. For purposes of this review, to avoid confusion only the first case (within-session modal differentiation) will be termed a differential effect. The other two types of result will be referred to as "preferential effects" (Rao, 1962), with no answer being assumed to the above question. Unfortunately, in many cases a study might embody both kinds of result, but analyses pertinent only to one being reported, we are prevented from examining the interesting question of how the two effects might tend to covary.

The final set of intrasubject scoring effects to be covered here pertains to the fluctuation of performance in both ψH and ψM directions: the variance of scoring. Assessing the size of the variance of a set of scores blurs across ψH and ψM trends and focuses on the size of deviations *per se*, rather than their mode. Results have not typically been reported in these terms, perhaps mostly because of the curiously anachronistic fashion in parapsychology of analyzing data using the critical ratio (Z score) or χ^2 rather than statistics such as t or F which rely on empirically observed scoring variations in their calculation (Stanford and Palmer, 1972). Even so, variance effects seem particularly descriptive in examining within-subject differences and have been reported to some extent. The units whose variation have been examined have included the segment (five calls, or 1/5 of a standard run), the half-run, the run, the session, and the "subject" (i.e., all the data contributed by each subject).

To summarize, experimental results will be presented in terms of the kinds of intrasubject variation reported. Perhaps the reasonable place to begin is with the unusual subject whose performance proved to be relatively *in*variant in terms of modal shift: the "stars" of ESP research.

The Stars. Consistent, dependable extrachance ESP performance has always been a matter of degree. Extremely rare have been those subjects whose performance has been steady enough to constitute anything close to an extrachance baseline against which could be studied experimentally manipulated changes.

Still, they have been found. J. B. Rhine in his early monograph (1934) ventured the opinion based upon his experiences with Duke students that an experimenter might expect one subject in every five to show consistent extrachance performance. He seems to have been far too optimistic. His own best subject, Hubert Pearce, tended to show drops in performance when conditions of testing were first changed, but he typically rebounded quickly and produced for about 2 years an extraordinary ψH performance. The end seemed to come one day when he reported to his major experimenter, J. G. Pratt, that he had just received very distressing news from home and added that he did not expect to do well. With that single flash of prescience, his starhood ended.

The anonymous young female subject of B. F. Riess (1937) produced the highest sustained ψH performance ever recorded. In 74 25-call runs with ESP cards conducted with a quarter-mile separating the subject and the targets, she achieved an average run-score of 18.24 hits. This phenomenal performance was interrupted by a "general breakdown" for which the subject was hospitalized and treated for a thyroid condition. After the illness, resumed testing showed a nonsignificant scoring rate.

Basil Shackleton continued his extrachance precognitive (forward displacement) card guessing for about 3 years, accumulating almost 4,000 trials with a hitting rate of 27 percent (chance expectation = 20 percent). The odds against such a record being attributable to chance are very great (Soal cites $P = 10^{-35}$).

Soal's other major subject, Gloria Stewart, showed even greater longevity, performing at a high rate for 4 years. As with many long-term declines, her own loss of ability seemed linked with growing disinterest in the task. As Soal and Bateman (1954) said: "We have no explanation to account for this ultimate collapse of her powers. Even under the most favorable conditions, guessing at the names of five animals year in and year out must conduce to a soul-deadening monotony that can only end early or late as a 'sad mechanic exercise,' bereft of all spontaneity" (p. 310). By then, totaling all her work in the basic GESP condition, she amassed 37,100 trials and an overall scoring rate of 25.4 percent. The odds against chance are even greater than with Shackleton. Soal estimates them at 10^{-70} to 1.

The only subject to surpass Mrs. Stewart in long-term productivity is the Czech Pavel Stepanek. Trained with a hypnotic procedure, Stepanek was tested by Milan Ryzl in a clairvoyance task in which Stepanek would try to identify the uppermost color (green or white) of a card in a sealed, opaque cover. Stepanek managed to sustain ψH performance on this task for a 4-year period, accumulating (Ryzl and Beloff, 1965) 42,598 trials with a 59.7 percent scoring rate (chance = 50 percent). This includes only published results, although the authors assure us the rate would be even higher if all work done were reported. At this point, his performance became less stable, sometimes falling to chance, sometimes rebounding, sometimes shifting to the missing mode. He remained an active subject for several years thereafter, because Ryzl, J. G. Pratt, and others noticed that his performance was showing other target-guess contingencies than the one consciously aimed for. This will be discussed further below.

At least two other subjects have more recently appeared whose stabilized ψH abilities may not yet have suffered long-term decline: Lalsingh Harribance (Roll and Klein, 1972) and Bill Delmore (Kanthamani and Kelly, 1974).

It is difficult to venture any but the most tentative generalizations about the more stable subjects. Most investigators did not describe their subjects' personalities and life-circumstances in any depth, and what items they mentioned seem as much an idiosyncratic interest of the investigator as a truly salient characteristic of the subject. Rao (1966) reviews some descriptions of several major subjects and concludes that most of them had three characteristics in common: most were artistic (some by profession), most felt themselves (and often close family members) to be generally intuitive in their daily lives, and most were extraverted and sociable. Another feature shared by the majority was serious religiosity, usually not of a conventional sort. Perhaps another hint can be gleaned from the handful of 8- and 9-year-old children who produced extraordinarily high bursts of performance (sometimes at a 100 percent rate) then declined rapidly (Banham, 1966; Freeman, 1966a; Reeves and Rhine, 1942; J. B. Rhine, 1964). The gamelike potential of a guessing task, combined with an intense interest and pleasure in succeeding, all in a warmly appreciative interpersonal context, seemed to combine for those preadolescent children in heights of success not reached by the more stable adult "stars."

The even greater instability of the ψH and ψM trends in unselected subjects has been indicated by the low and nonsignificant test-retest reliability coefficients usually reported in ESP experiments (Schmeidler, 1964a) and in the failure of most mass-testing strategies for discovering high-scoring subjects. Retesting of subjects found to score positively on "screening tests" have generally not yielded consistent scorers (Fisk, 1951; C. B. Nash, 1963; J. B. Rhine, 1962).

Tracking the Variable Subject

Low-aim Tests. One of the attempts made by the early Duke workers to live with the unpleasant reality of ψM deviations was the effort to cause them deliberately by asking the subject who was succeeding at ψH to switch his aim and try to miss. Pearce (J. B. Rhine, 1934), during a period when he was said to be averaging about 40 percent (twice the chance rate), carried out 225 trials with a low-aim set and got only 17 hits, or 8 percent. Another subject, Stuart, was performing at a less dramatic (but quite significant) rate of 26 percent for 1,300 trials in the ψH set, and in the 1,300 trials with the ψM set got only 182 hits, or 14 percent. Schmidt (1969) reported a series of work done by six subjects who were selected on the basis of strong interest in ESP and a prior showing of some success in the experimental task, which was clairvoyant guessing of one of four lights on a mechanical device, the selection of targets being controlled by random digits punched on a paper tape. The subjects were allowed to choose a high- or low-aim set before their guessing and to change it if they wished. This flexibility in procedure was seen as an effort to add an element of spontaneity to the task. A total of 15,000 trials was carried out. In the high-aim condition, 7,091 targets were guessed with a hit rate of 27 percent (chance = 25 percent); and in the low-aim condition the 7,909 trials yielded a scoring rate of 23 percent. Both are independently significant, and the difference between them is highly significant ($P < .6 \times 10^{-6}$). Another study employing a high-aim vs. low-aim contrast was reported by Ratte (1961). She used an ESP game procedure in which each of two players (subjects) made a series of high- or low-aim guesses the success of which moved counters across a game board toward a goal. By the exchange of ψH and ψM sets, Ratte hoped like Schmidt to impart an element of spontaneity to the task. Three series of 5,000 trials each were carried out. In all three a significant difference in scoring rates in the attempted directions was found. While Ratte's scoring rates are not dramatic, they were produced by unselected subjects. It seems rather surprising that high- vs. low-aim procedures have not been more fully explored and also surprising that this game-device has apparently received no further use. Particularly in the testing of children something like it would seem to have promise.

Whatever the combinations of conditions which may someday be found to elicit sustained ψH performance, clearly for the time being it is the mixed and unstable performances which are most regularly observed, and it is to these that parapsychologists have increasingly turned in an effort to construct those twin features which Gardner Murphy (1971) has said are so necessary yet painfully absent in this area: rationality and repeatability.

Position Effects: Episodic Declines. Thouless (1972) has termed "episodic declines" those patterns of results in which the subject displays a falling-off of success over a period of effort, followed by a rebounding in a new period. Intra-run declines have attracted considerable attention. The Jephson (1928) U-curve across her runs of five guesses, already cited, is one early example of a decline and rebound pattern within the set, suggesting a "terminal salience." Another early report of an intrarun decline (without terminal rebound) was in the work of Estabrooks (1927). His overall results from three series of well-controlled GESP experiments using playing cards as targets were significantly in the ψH direction. When he broke the 20-trial runs into top and bottom halves of ten trials each, he found a strong concentration of ψH in the top halves and a nonsignificant deviation in the bottom. A top-bottom decline similar to Estabrooks' was reported by Woodruff and Rhine (1942) who found significant ψH in the first run-halves (12 trials) of the 25-trial precognition runs and near-chance scores in the second halves. Humphrey (1943) reported a similar top-to-bottom ψH to chance decline. Anderson (1959), in a precognition experiment comparing target-selection delays of a few days and one year, found that her subject showed a linear decline across the segments, with the fifth dropping into ψM. The first and fifth segments were found to differ significantly $(P = .01)$.

Cadoret (1952) carried out a self-testing study comparing DT performance using three general kinds of procedures. In his "new system" runs he used any novel device he could imagine to inspire freshness and spontaneity in his calling. Examples he gives include: "Reciting poetry, both aloud and to myself . . . reading and reciting prose; singing aloud; studying; whistling . . . In short, I tried to use any system that kept my mind off the task and the goal of scoring high, with all its attendant anxieties" (p. 194). Some systems were used only once, others were repeated. Upon repetition, they constituted his second condition: "old system" runs. The third condition he called "control runs" in which he simply wrote his calls without employing any system. Sometimes his runs were quite short (as few as one trial), others as long as the standard 25 trials. Among his interesting findings, both the old system and the control runs produced significant top-half vs. bottom-half scoring differences $(P = .03$ and $.04$, respectively) with ψH trends in the top halves and ψM (P = .01 and .02, respectively) in the bottom. The "new system" runs showed no decline but rather strong ψH in both halves.

Pratt (1953a, 1953b), in examining the accumulated data of Soal's subject Gloria Stewart, found significant within-run position effects which differed for the two runs (A and B) on each record sheet. For the A runs, a significant decline across the five segments was found, although all five remain above chance. In column B a general incline was found, giving the entire 50 trials a U-curve. Since only a slight pause separated the two runs, Pratt assumed that they were experienced as a single block of effort. In column B, another and much more idiosyncratic effect was noticed as well: a strong tendency for differential scoring rates between the odd-numbered and even-numbered trials, the latter giving much the stronger ψH.

U, or salience curves like Jephson's across the five segments of the run have been reported frequently as well as declines. This pattern tended to be the rule for the major subjects in the early Duke work (J. B. Rhine, 1934). Considering only DT clairvoyance work, the U-pattern was followed by the four male subjects Pearce, Cooper, Stuart, and Linzmayer. Only Miss Ownbey was an inadvertent nonconformist, producing instead an inverted U. Significant U-curves were also reported by Pegram (1937) and Gibson (1937) in DT testing. Humphrey and J. B. Rhine (1942) found them in a precognition study, and Pratt (1961) found them strongly in an earlier clairvoyance study using the screened-touch matching technique. Unfortunately, analyses pertinent to within-run decline and salience effects have not been regularly reported by experimenters, particularly in more recent years. Because of this, it is difficult to assess how general they really are, and what conditions favor each. They seem generally to have been found post hoc. Only two studies, one by Stanford (1964) and one by Carpenter (1966), seem to have been carried out with an eye to the manipulation of the decline effect as a dependent variable. The Carpenter study is discussed below under variance effects. Stanford selected the high-scoring subjects (N = 160) from a previous experiment. Some were "sheep" (believers in ESP) and some were "goats" (disbelievers). Stanford hypothesized that the sheep should score with a decline pattern across the run-halves, and goats show an incline. His reasoning was based on cognitive dissonance theory. The task was an arduous and time-consuming one, in that the subject was required to make three calls at each target: a best guess, second-best guess, and third-best guess. Without feedback as to success, Stanford reasoned that the task would be an unpleasant one for most subjects. Disbelievers going through such a task might be expected to begin their performance with a chance-level scoring rate matching their disbelief, but to shift to ψH as cognitive dissonance built up over the continuing compliance (implying belief) in the test. The sheep might experience the test at first as interesting and ψH accordingly but then shift downward as the boredom and implied doubt of making three ranked guesses built up dissonance for them. The pattern found was as predicted: the sheep declined across the halves and the goats inclined.

A second sort of episodic decline is that observed across the runs in a session or across the sessions in the series performed by each subject. Soal's subject Basil Shackleton (Soal and Bateman, 1954), although his hits were distributed equally within each run, showed decline across the four runs (two target sheets) of each session. Examining data done at a normal rate of calling with the major agents Elliott and Aldred, Shackleton's average run-score on first-page runs is 7.77, and his average on last-page runs is 6.60, the difference being significant ($P < .005$).

Another intrasession episodic decline was found by Kahn (1952), who carried out five well-controlled series using standard IBM scoring sheets and an automated scoring device. Both sides (150 trials per side, or six standard runs) were filled out by the subject. Overall, Kahn found a significant deviation ($Z = 3.26$), all of which was contributed by the side-1 guesses. The side-2 guesses were at chance. He also carried out further repeated testing of 19 subjects, each still filling out the entire page at each of six sittings. These subjects showed a significant decline from side-1 to side-2 and also a significant intersession decline from ψH on the first three weeks to ψM on the last three ($Z = 3.64$).

Rose and Rose (1951), in a study of GESP in a group of six Australian aborigines, found a highly significant overall scoring rate of 23 percent in 296 runs. The largest number of runs and the highest scoring rate (29 percent) were contributed by the 75-year-old Lizzie Williams. When her 68 runs are divided chronologically into four 17-run quarters, the scoring rates are 34 percent, 26 percent, 29 percent, and 25 percent. The trend is quite significant. Freeman (1962) carried out a study with seven Duke students comparing the success rate on precognition and clairvoyance tasks when instructions led the subjects to believe the precognitive one was the easier and more conducive to good results. His major result will be discussed below; but in a secondary analysis Freeman compared the scoring rates at the first and second two-run sittings performed by each subject. A significant decline across sittings was found ($Z = 2.46$), between a scoring rate of 27 percent and one of 19 percent (chance = 20 percent).

Novelty in Task. A number of writers (Jephson, 1928; J. B. Rhine, 1952; Thouless, 1949) have supposed that the episodic decline effects represent the action of a fatiguing or inhibiting force which somehow builds up as the subject repetitively works at a task. Considering this, some studies on the rejuvenating effect of task-novelty bear mentioning. Pratt and Woodruff (1939) set out to study, with 66 subjects, the relative effects of the physical size of the target symbols used in a clairvoyance procedure. Two series were carried out, the symbol sizes varying from $1/16''$ to $2\ 1/4''$ in size. In some cases the subjects were made aware when a new target-type was introduced, and in others they were led to believe that the targets were remaining unchanged. When the results were tallied there were no differential results due to target-size; but there was a strong difference between performance on new targets and that on targets which had been previously used. In 1,238 trials with "old" targets there was an average run-score of 5.09 (chance expectation = 5) and with "new" targets an average run score of 5.33. This difference was contributed almost entirely by those cases in which the subjects knew of the change (average run scores for "new" and "old" = 5.34 and 5.04, respectively), while in those cases in which the change was not known, a slight and nonsignificant difference was observed.

A self-testing study by Thouless (1949) mentioned above as an example of one kind of differential effect, produced results which were interpreted (post hoc) as representing the effect of "inhibition" due to previous amounts of work with the testing procedures. Thouless carried out 144 sessions in which three types of DT tests were carried out in balanced order. The first (condition A) was the standard clairvoyance procedure which Thouless had used for "a good many years" with some success; the second (B) was a precognitive task which he had been using for about a year; and the third (C) was a more complex precognitive task which he had just devised and with which he thought success was very unlikely. To his surprise condition A produced ψM $(P < .01)$; B produced a chance rate; and C yielded ψH $(P < .02)$.

An attempt at experimentally manipulating a novelty effect was reported by Hallett (1952). He first conducted a pilot study, with 13 fellow research staff members as subjects, which he hoped would shed light on some questions having to do with dual-aspect ESP tests. This is a procedure in which each target is composed of two aspects, such as the number and suit of playing cards, both of which are guessed. Hallett used ESP symbols, each of which was placed in one of five spaces for the trial. The subject guessed both the position of the target and its content. A hit could be scored in terms of either aspect, or both. Each subject carried out 50 trials with this task. The results were not in accord with Hallett's original hunch. What he did find was an overall ψH rate of 25 percent on the position aspect $(P = .002)$ and a ψM rate of 16 percent $(P = .01)$ for the symbol aspect. Since all of the subjects had been well-practiced with the symbol-guessing task, but new to the position-aspect, Hallett saw a suggestion of a novelty effect. He then set up another study to test these impressions. He tested 40 new subjects, all of whom had no prior experience with any kind of ESP test. Half the subjects were first tested with ten runs using symbols as targets. Each subject then carried out 50 dual-aspect trials as in the pilot study. No significant effect emerged from the latter test. It is possible that the ten-run exposure is insufficient to be comparable to the years-long acquaintance Thouless' and Hallett's colleagues had with their familiar procedures.

Cadoret (1952), in the self-testing study mentioned above, found significant ψH in his "new system" runs (P = .005), significant ψM in his "old system" and "control" runs (P = .03 and .02, respectively), and a significant difference between the "new systems" and the other two combined. Cadoret ventured an analogy to peripheral vision in discussing his results and suggested that the novel activities served to focus his attention elsewhere than the ESP task, permitting ψH, much as one looks most effectively at an object in poor light by focusing just away from it, permitting the rods in the retinal periphery to be used.

It should be added here that changed conditions have sometimes been found to have debilitating consequences. For at least two of the "star" subjects, changes apparently caused scoring to drop. J. B. Rhine's (1934) subject Pearce was reported to respond to the introduction of visitors in the testing situation with a temporary drop in scoring, which was followed by a later recovery as he apparently acclimated. The same kind of temporary drop was caused by a change in experimental conditions; as, for example, a shift from GESP (agent looking) to clairvoyance procedures which caused a drop to a chance level. Six other changes of task led to similar drops followed by recovery. Gertrude Johnson, the apparently gifted subject of Tyrrell (1936) had been scoring well with a simple mechanical device containing 5 boxes one of which was lit by the experimenter for each trial. When a more complex device was introduced her scores fell for a time to chance, then recovered to a high ψH rate of 39 percent. Her scoring dropped still again to chance when Tyrrell added a commutator to the device in order to remove his own knowledge of the target from the situation. Even when Tyrrell mixed up trials employing the commutator with others not using it, the subject still showed ψH without it and chance scores with it. Finally, after returning from a vacation, Tyrrell's patience was rewarded when Miss Johnson scored at a high rate for over 4,000 trials with the commutator in circuit for a highly significant result.

Perhaps a suggestion which might help resolve this contradiction is to be found in another study on Pearce, this one done after the subject had stopped performing at a reliably high rate. Zirkle (J. B. Rhine, Pratt, Smith, Stuart, and Greenwood 1940) tested Pearce for 272 runs under 21 different experimental conditions such as "staring at a fixed point, looking into a crystal ball, following a rhythmic tapping, or walking about the room during the tests" (p. 282). As soon as Pearce tired of one condition he was switched to another. When the runs done under each condition were divided chronologically into halves, a significant difference was noted between an average run-score of 5.44 from the first-half runs and one of 4.90 for the second-half. The findings suggest a kind of Hawthorne effect (Roethlisberger and Dickson, 1939) for parapsychology, such that novel conditions are facilitative of ψH, at least for the great majority of subjects who are not able to produce stable ψH performance;

while for those special subjects who are able to score well, changes might be expected to reduce the efficiency of the performance. The latter is offered with less confidence since some special subjects (e.g., Kanthamani, 1974) seem unaffected by changed conditions.

Displacement Effects. This class of intrasubject scoring effects is made up of some oddities of performance which have been collected by parapsychologists at their most empirical, following the data wherever they might lead. The term *displacement* refers to hitting or missing contingencies between a response and certain targets other than the one for which it was intended, generally targets in the immediate vicinity of the intended one.

A relatively simple and impressively consistent form of displacement is that found with Soal's subject Basil Shackleton (Soal and Bateman, 1954). Shackleton had been selected for retesting, as mentioned above, because of his success at hitting not the target contemporaneous with his guess but the one which would next be selected (randomly) by the agent. These hits on the +1 targets (as they were called) persisted throughout the long confirmatory series, accumulating odds against chance which were astronomical. Soal construed this success as precognitive: a knowing of the future by the subject. The first experiments used lists of random numbers, coded to five animal pictures, to provide targets. A counterhypothesis to precognition could be that Shackleton was "sensing" the number next on the list, and unconsciously decoding it, thus making the process a complex clairvoyance one. Since parapsychologists must deal in preposterous possibilities anyway, Soal thought this one not unworthy of testing. In order to do this some series were run in which targets were selected by the agent pulling a colored counter from a bowl at random. The +1 success was as high as before, 28 percent correct out of 1,578 trials. A fascinating discovery was then made. The testing routine which had been first established had Shackleton make his guess in response to a signal that a target was ready, then call for a new target which was then selected (out of his sight, of course). His work at this quickly became routinized and brisk, and his call to the agent was dropped since his response always followed immediately after the signal to guess (the trial number) was called by an experimenter. The latency of his response was timed, and scarcely ever exceeded 2/5 of a second. The period of time between successive calls was thus very regular, averaging about 2.8 seconds. A new series was instituted in which the rate of calling and target selection was doubled. The ψH effect then shifted to the target two trials ahead, keeping constant the little gulf of time across which Shackleton was "seeing."

Several analyses have appeared over the years on displacement effects in Mrs. Stewart's data. Although she had been selected for her +1 hits, when retesting commenced her ψH appeared and stayed on the contemporaneous (direct hit) targets. Upon summing all of her work, scored for forward and backward displacements as well as direct hits, Soal found that her +1 and −1 hits were fewer than chance expectation to a significant degree ($Z = -4.6$ and -3.5, respectively). These effects are far weaker than her ψH results on direct targets, but they appeared quite real. Some of this displacement was apparently due to an odder effect found later (Soal and Pratt, 1951) that had to do with a nonrandom feature of Mrs. Stewart's response pattern: a strong tendency to avoid repeating target calls sequentially. When targets were divided sequentially into pairs, it was found that Mrs. Stewart tended to ψH on targets which were followed by a different target and to ψM on targets which were followed by a repeat of the same target. In a later analysis (Pratt, 1967) it was reported that in those parts of her overall high-scoring data in which ψM scores were obtained, +1 and −1 hits rose to a significant ψH level. All of these findings have been taken to indicate that Mrs. Stewart's responses were complexly determined by a total array or *gestalt* of targets in the neighborhood of the direct one and not solely by the direct target. A similar conclusion about some of Shackleton's work had been suggested by analyses carried out by Pratt (1951).

Displacement effects were also found in the data of the two very high scoring subjects whose work had been reported by Martin and Stribic (1940). Pratt and Foster (1950) found a previously unnoticed ψM rate of correspondence with +1 targets. Thus, like Stewart, these subjects seemed to be responding to a *gestalt* of targets (at least the direct and the +1) so as to differentially hit one and avoid the other.

Fisk (1951) found displacement effects (ψM on both +1 and −1) in a series of tests of 177 subjects who scored at chance on the direct targets.

The Focusing Effect. Perhaps the most peculiar and intriguing version of a displacement effect has been that found in the work of Pavel Stepanek, Ryzl's star subject, particularly after his long-continued ψH performance had begun to falter. This reviewer collected over 20 publications on this matter, the most generally informative being the monograph by Pratt (1973). Because of varying publication delays the dates cited do not follow a strict chronology. After a number of publications reporting stable ψH (e.g., Blom and Pratt, 1968; Ryzl and Pratt, 1963a), it was noticed (Ryzl, Barendregt, Barkema, and Kappers, 1965) that in some series of overall high success, Stepanek's scoring rate was consistently higher on some cards than others (in the Ryzl procedure the same target cards, covered in opaque envelopes, are periodically reversed in their envelopes, mixed in order, and given to the subject for another round of guessing). This selective success on certain targets was the first hint of a "focusing effect." A bit later Ryzl and Pratt (1963b) reported a series in which the card-envelope packages were further enclosed in an outer cover. In addition to overall ψH, strong call and target-side contingencies were found, sometimes right and sometimes wrong. That is, the call "green" would be found to have been called very preponderantly for a certain target-side whenever it appeared in its double-cover. A later study (Ryzl and Pratt, 1963c) reported that these contingencies persisted even when the cards were enclosed in new envelopes and a new series run. From this point on the results are more complex, and they cannot be covered here in any detail. Papers by Pratt (1968a, 1968b) and Pratt and Roll (1968) attempt to follow (as the titles suggest) "the trail of the focusing effect"; and a winding, odd trail it is. In the broadest terms, it seemed that Stepanek tended to shift from the targets to the envelopes containing the targets and/or to the covers around the envelopes and to form consistent calling contingencies with those aspects of the target-complex. At times the contingencies seemed extrasensory (to some hidden aspect of the target-pack) and at times possibly sensory, connected to the outer cover. In further studies the target-envelope-cover sets were themselves enclosed in jackets (Keil and Pratt, 1969), and the call-cover contingencies which had formed to the covers when they had previously been sensorially available were found to persist when they were out of sight. Further research (Pratt and Keil, 1969) provided evidence that guessing habits formed on the basis of some sensorially available feature would persist for this subject when that feature was itself covered. By now the target-cover-jackets sets were enclosed in jiffy bags (actually the original target cards had been dropped out, the effect having shifted to the outer covers). At this point this reviewer confesses to having the fantasy of tractor-trailers pulling slowly in front of Stepanek for his call of green or white which would by then have become focused to the sides of huge crates carried within. Still further papers (Pratt, Keil, and Stevenson, 1970; Pratt and Ransom, 1972; Stanford and Pratt, 1970) have reported clearer experimental control over this process of apparent sensory habits turning to extrasensory ones for this subject, and a complex correlational analysis has shown that the response-cover contingencies are pervasive throughout the entire set of targets, including consistent mixed-calling for some targets along with predominant green or white calling for others. The doggedness and ingenuity with which all this work was developed (Pratt, 1973) sets a high-water mark for parapsychologists in pursuing the phenomena relentlessly and without regard for its changes nor discouragement at what might most easily have been construed as a loss of ability.

The Self-reflectivity of ESP "Awareness."   A question posed early by the experimental parapsychologists was: Are correct guesses experientially distinguishable from incorrect ones? Do they *feel* different? The answer to this question at first generally appeared to be No. Guessing tended to feel like guessing, even for the better subjects when the guesses were right. Drops in scoring performance fell upon subjects unawares, and in spite of their conscious efforts. For example, Soal and Bateman (1954) argued: "ESP is not in the true sense a form of cognition, because the subject has no inkling of how he arrives at his impressions; it is more akin to guessing" (p. 182). Their subject Shackleton sometimes ventured the opinion that he was doing well or poorly, but his notions did not correspond to the facts. During a period when he marked trials of whose success he was particularly confident, his marked guesses were actually a bit less successful (25 percent) than his unmarked (28 percent). J. B. Rhine (1958) concluded that ESP, unlike sensory cognition, has no experientially distinguishable modality but makes itself known to the subject in an entirely unconscious manner from whence it rises to expression only in "borrowed" ways (e.g., a visual hallucination) or in some dissociated, automatism-like manner. In that paper and in others, J. B. Rhine (1952, 1969a, 1969b) argued that it is this nonreflectivity, or unconsciousness of ESP, that gives rise to the problem of ψM, the shifting of performance without volitional control into the negative mode.

Although a lack of self-reflective awareness seems to be true as a rule, some investigators have continued to inquire into the matter of the subjects's own experience of his success and failure. Scherer (1948) compared guesses which felt like a strong, spontaneous "hunch" to the subject with those collected in more routine calling. Strong ψH was found in the "hunch" calls, a chance hit-rate in the remainder. Humphrey and Nicol (1955) studied the "feeling of success" by asking subjects to mark with confidence-checks those trials in which they felt especially confident. Subjects were urged to make about 5-10 such checks in each run. Each subject carried out eight runs with trial-by-trial feedback and eight runs with no feedback until the end of the run. They found that in the no-feedback condition those subjects who complied with the instructions to check 5-10 calls per run got significant ψH on their checked trials, at a rate significantly higher than their nonchecked trials. The feedback runs showed a nonsignificant trend in the same direction. Scores from the Guilford-Martin Personality Inventory were also available on the subjects and it was found that the first factor, "self-confidence," was an important moderating variable: subjects low in self-confidence scored very well on the confidence calls, more confident subjects did not show a significant difference. Subjects who had checked too many or too few trials per run were scored separately, and it was seen that they tended to check a higher proportion of misses than of hits.

Nash and Nash (1958) also asked their subjects to make 5-10 confidence-checks per run. All subjects were pooled (although some checked fewer than five), and they found that hits were checked at a higher rate (26 percent than misses (23 percent). However, in a later study Nash (1960), without specifying the number to check, found that misses were checked at a higher rate than hits (14 percent vs. 12 percent). Since the number of checks reported is low, it seems that much of Nash's data would have been excluded had he used the five-check criterion. He also collected success estimates for each run as a body. Interestingly, he found that the ψM trend on the confidence-checks was concentrated in those runs which were estimated to show poor success. As Nash said, "predictions of below-average success was followed by below-average success in *checking* hits" (p. 30).

Eilbert and Schmeidler (1950) asked subjects who had just performed five ESP runs without scoring which of the five they felt had the highest score. They were successful in making this judgment to a significant degree.

Schmeidler carried out two studies in which she gave subjects the "low-pressure" suggestion that they check any calls on which they felt confident. In the first study (1961) (a telepathy experiment) the subjects' data were analyzed according to the number of checks per run: less than one, one to four, five to ten, and more than ten. In general, a higher proportion of hits were checked in the lower-frequency groups.

In the second study (1964b) (precognition) she asked for an indefinite number of confidence checks and also asked subjects after their guessing how well they thought they had done. The confidence checks proved to be associated with ψH scoring for the low frequency (one to six-check) group as before, but only if the targets were those which had been earmarked to be shown the subject. Two other target-conditions were also used in which the results were not to be so shown. She also found that those subjects who gave differentiated judgments as to their success (some runs high and some low) discriminated accurately ($P = .004$), while those giving a single, global judgment did not. Schmeidler also confirmed Nash's finding of ψM on confidence checks in runs judged as poor by the subject.

In passing, it may be worth noting that the number of calls checked in response to Schmeidler's unstructured suggestion might be expected to relate positively to the Bernreuter "self-confidence" scale; i.e., those checking relatively few calls might be somewhat equivalent to the "low confidence" subjects of Humphrey and Nicol (1955). If so, Schmeidler's findings could be said to be confirmatory of this aspect of the earlier work. In a precognition study, Fahler and Osis (1966) studied confidence checks of two subjects who had been hypnotized and given the suggestion that "on some trials they might have impressions of correctness or feelings that certain calls were 'different' from the others" (p. 341). They found a very strong tendency for the confidence calls to be associated with hits ($P = .00000002$).

In three experiments attempting to enhance confidence-checking ability, Honorton (1970, 1971) and McCollam and Honorton (1973) examined the effects of feedback on the ability to discriminate between correct and incorrect calls. The design was similar for all three experiments, involving pretesting of three runs with "about five" confidence calls requested per run, followed by runs with feedback (three in the first two studies), then followed by three more runs with confidence checks and no feedback. In each study, half the subjects were assigned to an "experimental group" which was given correct feedback, and half to a control group given false feedback. In the first two studies, a significant increase in the success rate of confidence checks followed correct but not incorrect feedback. In the third study, there was no false-feedback control group, but instead four experimental groups with zero, three, six, and nine runs of feedback were run. Contrary to expectation, the groups with six and nine runs of feedback did not gain in confidence-call success. The group with three runs did gain significantly in confidence-call success ($P = .01$) and in overall hitting rate as well ($P < .01$). The subjects were also asked to describe what cues they relied upon in making confidence calls. Those subjects who reported multiple cues (e.g., visual and somatic) showed more gain ($P = .03$) than those reporting no cues. The no cue group actually lost from pre- to post-test. Other subjects, who reported using only visual cues or only "intuitive feelings" had intermediate gains.

That awareness of hits can occur in a least one "special subject" was indicated by Kanthamani and Kelly (1974) who worked with Bill Delmore in tasks involving the guessing of playing cards. In two series using a modified "psychic shuffle" procedure with $p = 1/52$, Delmore accumulated 67 direct hits in 468 trials, an excess over chance expectation of 58. More important for our concern here, he also made 50 confidence calls, before check-up, all 50 of which were correct. The authors cite no P-figure for this result, which is quite understandable. This reviewer calculated a $Z = 51$ for the result for whatever that is worth. The reader might appreciate the result better by knowing that a result of only three right out of the 50 would reach conventional levels of significance. In a third series, under quite rigidly controlled conditions, 20 confidence calls yielded 14 direct hits, and the other six were partial hits (on number or suit only). The odds against chance are again phenomenal.

All this work taken together certainly belies the assumption that ESP knowledge is never self-reflective. An absence of over-confidence, a tendency to judge discriminatingly and with attention to multiple internal cues, hypnotic suggestions for internal scanning, and a moderate amount of feedback as to guessing success and failure all seem to hold out some promise for success in aiding self-reflectivity; and the Delmore phenomenon suggests that it is at least humanly possible to have flashes of ESP cognizance which are as reliable as vision in broad daylight.

Preferential Effects

Preferential Effects for Different Modes of Response. The single most studied mode-of-response difference is that of preferred vs. nonpreferred rates of responding. Stuart (1938) studied 41 subjects in matching tests. After a preferred rate of responding was established by a metronome, subjects were asked to make some of their responses at that rate, and others at a different rate. A significant difference in scoring levels favoring the preferred rate was found. A replication attempt (Stuart and Smith, 1942) failed to produce any difference in scoring rates. Shackleton, besides the rapid rate tests mentioned above, also carried out some "slow rate" guessing, waiting about twice as long as usual to make his guesses. He complained to Soal that this procedure "was enough to drive him mad," and his scoring dropped to a chance level. Van de Castle (1953) had his subject make clairvoyance guesses at each of five time intervals: 0–2 seconds, 3–10 seconds, 11–30 seconds, 31–60 seconds, and 61 or more. The subject preferred the longer intervals since she liked to let her decisions "gestate in her unconscious" as she distracted herself with other things such as conversation or smoking. She produced significant ψH on the 31–60 and 61+ intervals and chance scoring on the remainder. Osis and Pienaar (1956), in a long-distance GESP test between the United States and Northern Rhodesia, tested two subjects at two rates of calling: a slow rate (look at target for 10 seconds, pause 10 seconds, look at next target) and a rapid rate (look at target for 5 seconds, no pause, look at next target for 5 seconds). Watches were synchronized between the agents and percipients. The subjects strongly favored the slower rate as they thought of the task as a telepathic one and feared that in the rapid rate condition errors in timing would be greater than the period allowed to call. ψH was produced on the favored rate, and ψM on the disfavored.

Three other studies have been reported on other kinds of favored and disfavored response modes. Sanders (1962) had 20 female subjects do two series of precognition runs, using both verbal and written modes of response. In the first series (three runs of each) a significant differential effect was found (in the sense of Palmer's criterion, mentioned above) in that subjects tended to produce individually significant differences in scoring rates between the two response modes. Before the second series, each subject was asked her preference of the two modes, and four more runs of each kind were done. Again a differential effect was found ($P < .005$), and an overall preferential effect was found as well, with the preferred modes showing a ψH trend, the nonpreferred significant ψM, and a significant difference between them. No preferential effect for the two modes *per se* was found. The fact that subjects knew their first series results before a preference was stated makes it impossible to attribute the scoring difference with certainty to the factor of preference. The subjects might have tended to prefer the mode with which they scored well and then been simply self-consistent in scoring pattern in series 2. Information which might help examine this point was not provided in the report. Schmeidler and Lewis (1969) reported a study employing four-aspect targets in which subjects guessed all four aspects in half their trials and were given information on two of the aspects in the other half. Forty-five of the 50 subjects reported a strong preference for one condition or the other, and their scoring was in line with their preference. Another study examining different rates of success for different modes of response was carried out with the special subject Lalsingh Harribance (Roll,

Morris, Damgaard, Klein, and Roll, 1973). This was a free verbal response study, in which "readings" were given to 20 concealed, undeveloped target photographs of persons (ten male, ten female). The ten protocols for males were then ranked for personal appropriateness by the ten male target persons, and likewise for the females. Overall a significantly correct set of rankings ($P < .02$) was obtained. The protocol items were then sorted by a content analysis into 11 content categories (physical description, health, vocation, family, love life, future, wants, interests, needs, personal character, and other). Target persons then rated all the individual statements. For the female target persons it was found that Harribance had strong ψH in the areas of physical description and love life; and for the males on physical description and family. The effects were stronger for the female than the male target persons. No information is given as to whether or not the subject in any sense "favored" the content categories he did so well on; but it is known that he was a young bachelor in a strange country at the time of the experiment, and his ψH for the women was focused in areas which might certainly be imagined to have been especially salient for him.

The general matter of a preferential response being elicited predictably by preferred vs. nonpreferred response modes has been studied far too little and too unsystematically to permit conclusions. It seems suggestive, however, that all of the preferential effects due to response modes that could be found were a product of the subject's conscious preference (as opposed to the results with preferential effects related to target differences, where the relation to conscious preference will be seen to be much less secure). The suggestion is certainly raised that juxtaposition of two response conditions which are differentially favored by the subject will tend to produce scoring differences in favor of the better-liked mode of response. On the other hand, lest an undue sense of Murphy's "rationality and repeatability" be given at this point, attention should be shifted to another set of studies having to do with another form of response "preference" with quite the opposite trend of findings.

Response Bias. Stanford (1967) formulated what he called the response-bias hypothesis which, simply stated, holds that a bias toward infrequency of response content favors ψH on that response content. He first marshalled a collection of observations culled from earlier work which he construed as pointing to this possibility. Martin and Stribic (1940) in reporting the results of their two clairvoyance experiments had noted a significant inverse relationship between call frequency for a symbol and success-rate with the symbol. Pavel Stepanek (Ryzl and Pratt, 1963a), during the period of his strong direct-hitting, had a strong tendency to call "green" more often than "white," and had ψH rates on them of 55 percent and 59 percent respectively. One of Pratt's (1967) findings from his post-hoc analyses of Mrs. Stewart's data showed a strong response bias against calling a given symbol twice in succession. When she *did* repeat a symbol, her guesses showed an unusually high rate of correctness ($P = 10^{-11}$). In an unpublished study by Freeman, subjects had made ESP guesses by checking one of five columns across the page. Some columns received a higher rate of checking than others. Columns less frequently checked showed ψH ($P < .04$) and those more frequently checked showed ψM ($P < .02$). Stanford (1967) also reported a study of his own carried out to test this hypothesis. He devised a "radar" record sheet for use with high school students. The sheet showed a circular "radar screen" divided into 36 sectors. Twenty-eight subjects were asked to use ESP "like radar" to locate the 12–18 sectors per sheet which contained an ESP target and indicate their choices by checking the sectors. Each subject did two sheets of guesses. Sheets were divided at the median in terms of frequency of checking. Significant ψH was found on those with fewer checks ($P < .0005$), and ψM on those with more ($P < .06$). That this was not simply tapping an individual-differences dimension pertinent to ψH and ψM was indicated by the data of 12 subjects who contributed both kinds of sheet and whose data followed the general trend. Stanford also checked for an inadvertent correlation between the number of responses checked on a page and the number of targets which had been randomly assigned to it. Had such been present, it would have contributed spuriously to the effect reported; but there was no relationship ($r = -.08$).

Stanford has reported two more studies pertinent to this hypothesis and has tried to construct an account of how ESP information might intrude upon everyday cognitions. In the first, a study on "memory," Stanford (1970) read subjects a passage and then gave them a "memory quiz" on it. The memory quiz was made up of three kinds of five-choice items: determinate (the correct response had explicitly occurred in the passage); partially determinate (the correct response had been implied by the story); and indeterminate (neither given nor implied). ESP targets had also been determined for the "memory quiz," one of each multiple-choice set picked at random. Some responses were pro-story (on the correct item), and some were counter-story. Stanford expected a frequency response bias in favor of the correctly remembered items, particularly those explicitly read, and the frequency of responses showed that to be true. He hypothesized that counter-story responses would contain the highest ψH rate and particularly those rarer counter-story responses which were given on determinate items. Pro-story items which were determinate were not scored, and those partially determined were expected to yield ψM. The results generally conformed to expectations. The determinate counter-story responses were significantly positive ($P < .004$); the partially determinate pro-story responses scored negatively ($P < .025$); and the partially determinate counter-story responses had an insignificant ψH trend. Another bit of confirmation for the response-bias hypothesis came from the fact that the preferential effect just mentioned was contributed primarily by those subjects with the better memories (i.e., those who gave fewer counter-story responses).

In his next study, Stanford (1973) turned his attention to the associative processes elicited by word association tests. Most of the work focused on a word association task of 36 items, all of which had strong norms established for "primary" (most frequently given) and "secondary" (next most frequently given) associates. ESP targets were assigned to either the primary or secondary response for each word, and a response was scored for ESP only if it was one of the two. Thus the author ingeniously captured some of the better features of both forced-choice and free-response kinds of testing. The results were mixed in terms of the major hypothesis. Overall, there was ψH on the primary responses and ψM on the secondary responses. This would seem counter to the hypothesis (the author construes it as supportive of Roll's (1966) memory-trace hypothesis). At the same time, an interaction effect was observed between subject's actual response frequencies and the relative success on response-type (their conformity to the prior norms was unexpectedly weak). Those subjects who had relatively more secondary responses in their runs showed a preferential effect favoring the primary responses; while those with relatively more primary responses got ψH scoring on their secondaries and ψM on their primaries. Another relationship favoring the response-bias hypothesis depended upon the fact that primary associations are most commonly found with short response-latencies, while longer latencies give higher proportions of nonprimaries. Stanford found an interaction between the subjects' average latency of response and their preferential effect: those subjects with longer average reaction times scored higher on primary than on secondary targets; those with shorter latencies did better on secondary than on primary targets. No attention was given to estimate the strength of these last two findings relating to actual response frequency and latency time independent of each other; so one assumes that they are to some extent dependent and overlapping.

Some confirmation for the response-bias hypothesis has come from three studies reported by Kreitler and Kreitler (1972), testing, like Stanford's, the possible intrusion of ESP targets into the response of subjects engaged in other tasks. In each of the studies an agent, unknown to the subjects, was trying to interject certain target content via ESP into the response of subjects engaged in the following tasks: (a) identification of subliminally presented letters, (b) perception of movement-direction while watching a stable light source (the autokinetic effect), and (c) telling stories to TAT cards. In all cases there was an overall ψH effect, most strongly in the first two. In both of these there was also a clear tendency for the ψH to be associated only with responses of a generally low probability of occurrence. A trend in the same direction was noted in the third study.

Additional confirmation has come from Glidden (1974) and Morris (1971). Glidden had his subjects trace paths through a circular maze, made of concentric circles and broken lines, starting from the center and attempting to exit at the edge. The maze structure was partially defined for the subject, but some of it was unknown (ESP targets). The subject could move outward, inward, and to either side provided no line blocked his way. His task was to avoid by ESP the unknown lines which also "blocked his way" in the various directions. His score was determined by the proportion of "invisible lines" he crossed in his moves out of the circle. A response-bias is set up naturally by this task in that, no visible barrier to the contrary, the subject will tend to respond in an outward direction, and will also, if moving to the right or left, either tend to continue that direction if unblocked or else tend to turn outward. Responses contrary to these tendencies (an unforced change of direction not in the quickest apparent route to the edge) were called "random behavior trials" by Glidden. Two series were run, one with trial-by-trial feedback (which was slow and irritating to the subjects) and one with no check-up until the end. In the first no preferential effect was observed; in the second the random-behavior trials showed ψH ($P < .05$). Morris (1971), in a comparison of high scoring (11 hits or more) and chance-scoring runs from a 1,000-run series with the special subject Harribance, found a negative correlation between the response frequency of a symbol in the run and the success rate on the symbol; that is, the less frequently it was called, the more likely it was a hit. Other observations congruent with the response bias hypothesis come from Freeman (1973) and Otani (1968a).

An instructive study on the response frequency issue comes from Kreitler and Kreitler (1973). These authors deduced from their previous findings the hypothesis that only GESP targets which are perceptually discrepant with the consciously perceived target situation would elicit ψH. They set out to test this and to examine the effect of agent-set also.

Subjects were given an ostensive perceptual discrimination task. They were shown pairs of identically sized circles and lines and asked to choose the larger. The subjects' perceptual response tendency was manipulated by very faint subliminal projections superimposed upon the visible lines or circles such that, were they supraliminally seen, they would act to make one of the targets seem larger than the other by optical illusion.

The subliminal elements of the illusions were projected at a level so faint that they did not elicit the perceptual illusions (established by pretest) and presumably would not unless augmented by the ESP "stimulus." A two-factor repeated-measures design was used. Factor A (agent set) had two levels: agent merely thinking of the ESP target and agent "actively trying" to interject the target content into the unseen subjects' perception. There were three levels of factor B (relation of ESP and subliminal stimuli): b1, no subliminal stimulus; b2, subliminal stimuli congruent with ESP stimulus; b3, subliminal stimulus incongruent with ESP stimulus. Strong interaction effects were observed between factors A and B from the data on two of the three illusions (the two which have been found to have the most perceptual strength) such that a strong ψH performance was observed in the active agent-discrepant content treatment condition. This was in particularly strong contrast with a ψM deviation in the active agent-congruent content condition. However, the significance of the latter is not reported (the authors apparently being less concerned with ψM-mode scoring). The Kreitlers reason that the results confirm the supposition that ESP information is of a different kind than sensory information and will not add to the probability of a response already boosted in probability by sensory information; but it will add to the probability of a response if it contradicts the sensory information and is of sufficient intensity (presumably the agent-set was a manipulation of intensity, turning up the extrasensory volume, so to speak).

Failures to confirm the response-bias hypothesis have been reported by Bottrill (1969) and Mischo (1968). Bottrill found that seven of his 56 subjects called one or more of the five ESP symbols significantly more accurately than the others but found no relationship between these preferential effects and the response frequencies. Mischo, in a distance GESP test, found that two subjects achieved significant ψH. The stated symbol preferences of these subjects were positively related to their frequency of usage; but neither were associated with success-rate.

It seems likely that the response-bias ψH-ψM relationship will evolve in the way noted above for other ESP scoring effects: From its original status as a nominated "feature" of extrasensory performance it will itself become a dependent variable, and its occurrence, reversals, and failures to occur will themselves become seen as dependent upon some causal or predictive features which parapsychologists will try to catch in their constructions and experiments.

Target-Type Preferential Effects: "Types" of ESP. Modern parapsychologists, inheriting the "faculty" constructs from workers in the nineteenth century, have used a cluster of notions defining "types" of ESP in terms of the nature of the presumed source of information, assuming barriers to sensory-inferential knowledge. Telepathy is the faculty of knowing another person's experience, clairvoyance that of knowing nonexperienced objective events, precognition knowing something which has not yet transpired. A few other faculties, such as retrocognition, and some exotic hybrids like precognitive telepathy have also been advanced (psychokinesis, of course is outside the scope of this review). Because of various assumptions, workers have sometimes felt that one or some of these proposed faculties are more preposterous than others and have conducted research contrasting different kinds of target-conditions to attempt to determine their relative possibility of occurrence. In the process, juxtaposed target-types have sometimes produced the kinds of scoring we are calling preferential effects. Several studies have been done, for example, contrasting scoring under telepathy (someone looking at the target contemporaneously with the guessing) versus clairvoyant (no one looking) target conditions. Discussion of these will be reserved for the section on interpersonal factors. A number of studies have also been carried out contrasting telepathic and/or clairvoyant scoring when the contemporaneous targets are at various distances from the subject. Since these studies have not tended to produce preferential effects (ψH-ψM group separations), they will not be reviewed. Analogous to the distance studies, some workers in precognition have compared scoring rates when subjects are guessing targets which will be determined after the lapse of different periods of time. Hutchinson (1940) asked her subjects to perform ten runs each, five to be matched against cards shuffled within 24 hours and five to be scored after 10 days. Feedback on results was to be given after the check-up. ψH performance was observed on the 24-hour runs, ψM on the 10-day, and a significant difference was reported. This might be construed as a target "preference" (next section) since she reported that the subjects expressed more interest in the 24-hour results. Bastin and Green (1953) reported high ψH performance (38 percent when 17 percent was chance) in a precognitive task which required the subject to make precognitive guesses by forming a visual image of a digit from 1 to 6. As soon as a vivid image appeared in her mind's eye, the subject announced her choice. The experimenter then shuffled and cut a deck of cards, took the top one, formed a vivid image of it in his own mind, and then announced the target. The experimenter felt that this procedure made the guess-to-target sequence an "aesthetic whole" for the subject and reasoned that breaking up that whole should lower success. Another series was taken up in which, in balanced orders, the above procedure was intermixed with guesses which were to be scored after a 15-minute delay, following the collection of all such guesses. Scoring on the original procedure fell to a still-significant ψH rate of 26 percent; in the delay-condition results were at chance.

Anderson (1959) conducted a long precognition experiment with one subject who had previously scored well in other testing. The subject carried out two five-run series per month while in France, sending her guesses to Anderson in North Carolina. Five runs of the ten were chosen at random for target-determination and checking at that time, and results were then sent back to the subject; the other five were set aside for checking the following year. The delayed scoring was generally done in the presence of the subject, by then back at Duke. The sets of scores on the delayed-check showed significant ψH (23.4 percent), and the immediate check did not differ from chance.

Osis (1955) compared the precognitive performance of a single subject who guessed various numbers of ESP runs per session in New York over a period of 8 months, sending the guesses to Osis in North Carolina for target selection and checking at some indefinite time in the future. She did not want to know her scores, and no feedback was sent. Osis scored the batches of guesses at convenient times, and at intervals varying from 1 to 33 days after the guesses had been performed. The 240 runs were divided into two sets in terms of delay (1–

7 days and 30–33 days) and compared: ψM was observed in both sets, both at the rate of 18 percent. Thus no difference was produced. All of these studies suggest that the factor of different amounts of time elapsing before checking is not liable to produce a preferential effect unless one interval is strongly preferred by the subject. ψH performance may tend to be associated with the scoring-condition which most interests and excites the subject, even if, as in the Anderson study, the excitement and interest are (appropriately enough, given the topic) "somewhere" in the future.

A couple of studies have examined the effect of the physical constitution of aspects of the target situation in clairvoyance testing. Chauvin and Darchen (1963) reported two series in which targets screened by glass received ψM scoring while targets screened by wood were called in the ψH mode. Roll and Pratt (1968) tested an hypothesis derived from Roll's theory to the effect that targets composed of organic material should elicit ψH scoring while inorganic material should not be extrasensorially "perceived" at all. The special subject Stepanek produced a significant ψH series ($P < .001$) with cardboard and aluminum targets, in which only the cardboard targets were called at an extrachance rate.

Target-Type Preferential Effects: Consciously Preferred vs. Not-Preferred Targets. Freeman (1962) reported a suggestive study in which he manipulated subjects' attitudes as to the relative likelihood of succeeding in clairvoyance and precognition. He told them that precognition was the more likely. ψH was observed for the precognitive runs; chance for the clairvoyant. All the ψH deviation came from the first session (out of a total of five) in which the subject had just been exposed to the instructions. Unfortunately, this study seems never to have been followed by one manipulating belief in a pro-clairvoyance way as well and testing the recency of instructions as an independent variable. Of course, similar regrets can be expressed all too often throughout these researches.

Freeman (1969c) did report another study conducted with a group of high school science teachers as subjects, the results of which are consistent with the idea that target preference accounts for the scoring pattern rather than an intrinsic difference between precognition and clairvoyance. In a lecture and discussion period he spent with the group, Freeman noted a great many questions and a sense of hostility regarding the possibility of precognition, which seemed particularly incredible to the group. Each of the 33 subjects carried out one standard run of clairvoyance, which was immediately scored, followed by one run of precognition trials to be scored at some indefinite time in the future. When final scoring was done, ψM scoring on the precognition runs was noticed ($P = .002$), and chance results on the clairvoyant.

Rao (1962) asked each of six female undergraduates to select five targets to which she had favorable emotional associations. These were put onto cards.

Working in a competitive gamelike clairvoyance procedure, four subjects took turns in guessing the personal targets and the standard ESP targets. Another subject worked alone in a DT procedure, guessing both kinds of targets, and the sixth guessed at a mixed pack of 50 cards using a BT procedure. For all six subjects performance was higher on personal than standard symbols. The overall difference between the target-types was significant $(P < .002)$. The difference diminished as the number of runs per subject increased. What seemed a simple relationship became quickly complicated when Rao (1963a) replicated his target-contrast procedure with five more subjects, with the procedural differences of a blind screen-touch-matching procedure in individual-testing routines. Two subjects contributed most of the 100 runs per target-type. Under these conditions a reversed difference from the previous one was found. Personal targets received a ψM trend (not significant) and standard symbols a significant ψH rate. Rao attributed the reversal to the changed condition of subject "blindness": the fact that with covered key cards and response cards face-down and handled by the experimenter, the subjects did not know which runs represented personal and which standard targets. No new series contrasting blind and nonblind procedures seems to have been done, however. In his next study, Rao (1963c) kept the subjects blind but changed from a run-by-run target-type distinction to a trial-by-trial distinction. He did this by putting two targets, one personal and one standard, into each key-envelope, and the two kinds of response cards into a 50-card deck of both kinds. Thus each blind-matching response (signaling the experimenter to place a face-down card next to a key envelope) represented either a personal target or a standard target guess, the subject not knowing which. Rao conducted a pilot and a confirmatory experiment with this procedure. The pilot was composed of two parts: the first made up of 21 two-run sessions with the experimenter and subject; and the second 22 two-run sessions in which an observer also was present. Rao tallied his results and found a complex and shifting pattern. In the first runs of each session the personal targets showed a ψH trend; the symbol targets a ψM trend; but all the second runs showed a reversed pattern $(P = .05)$. This was complicated by the fact that the first-part sessions (no observer) showed a standard-over-personal preference and the second part sessions (observer) showed the reverse. Rao attempted to clear this up by conducting another series of tests in which all two-run sessions would share the no-observer condition. When these were tallied a stronger run-1 vs. run-2 preference reversal was repeated (run 1 personal > standard; run 2 standard > personal, all $P < .01$). The strength of this pattern was still stronger when the first-run first-session scores were contrasted with the last-run last-session scores.

Nash and Nash (1968) reported a classroom test in which "choice" targets (the five "favorite things" of the group, determined by voting) were compared to digits as targets in both clairvoyance and precognition paradigms. The effect of order was controlled by balancing. The choice targets received ψH scoring in both clairvoyance and precognition tests, and the digit targets received ψM in both (P of difference $<$ .01). Schmeidler (1964a) had subjects carry out dual-aspect precognition runs in which each trial required both a number and a color guess. Some subjects reported liking some colors or numbers and disliking others. The scoring rates of the liked and disliked targets were compared, and a ψH trend found on the liked, ψM on the disliked, and a significant difference ($P <$ .02) between them. Chauvin (1961) and Buzby (1968b) found preferential effects for target-types in experiments in which the more successful targets might be supposed to have been consciously favored by the subjects, although they seem not to have been asked. Chauvin tested himself, his son and daughter, and two nieces. The children ranged in age from 10 to 14 years. The targets to be guessed were 36 cards, carrying the digits 1 or 2. On nine cards of each digit the numbers were 12 mm high. On the other targets there was glued a micro-filmed digit so small as to be unreadable without a magnifying lens. Two runs per session were carried out with immediate check-up after each run. Each subject guessed 648 trials with each target-type. The first runs-per-session were analyzed separately from the second runs-per-session, and results were presented as series A and B, respectively. Overall a ψH trend was found on the normal digits, ψM on the microfilmed, and a significant difference ($P =$ .02) was observed. All of the preferential effect was contributed by series A runs, and all by the four children. In series A the normal symbols were hit at a 52 percent rate, and the microfilmed at a 46 percent rate (Z of the difference = 3.65, $P =$ .00026). In series B the hit-rates did not depart significantly from chance. Buzby (1968b) reported an analysis of two sets of data in which subjects had done one sitting each made up of five DT clairvoyance runs and five precognition runs. Check-up and feedback followed the completion of each set. Unfortunately, order was confounded with target-type, the precognition always coming first. Subjects had also been tested with the Draw-a-Man Test which was scored by the criteria used by Witkin, Lewis, Hertzman, Machover, Meissner, and Wapner (1954) and by Witkin, Dyk, Faterson, Goodenough, and Karp (1962) to separate subjects into high and low groups in terms of degree of differentiation (accurate detail) of body image shown. In a post-hoc analysis of his first batch of data, Buzby found that his low body-sophistication subjects had exhibited a clairvoyance-over-precognition preferential effect. His second series confirmed that pattern for the same type of subject. Buzby speculates that a conscious target-preference might account for the pattern.

Target-Type Preferential Effects: Emotional Significance of Target Material.
The relative preference subjects feel for two kinds of targets is one way in which their emotional significance for the subject can be described. Other research has been addressed to other kinds of difference in emotional meaning. Skibinsky

(1950), in the study mentioned above, tested his three sisters and three friends in tests using both the names of members of his immediate family and standard ESP symbols. Presumably the names had much more emotional significance to the subjects than the standard targets, the difference being greatest for the family members. Overall, scoring was ψM on the names ($P < .001$), and ψH trend on the symbols. The difference was strongest for the family members. The data were collected in three series. For the family members the first shows the strongest difference and the only difference which is significant ($P < .01$). Rao (1964b) compared results on targets with a milder emotional disparity, using standard ESP cards and a set of cards drawn by an artist (M. Higbee), each of which used one of the standard symbols as a dominant motif but developed it into an arresting primitive-mask design. The blind-matching procedure with a mixed 50-card deck and double-loaded key envelopes was used again. A total of 100 runs for each target-type were performed by several subjects (varying numbers of runs contributed by different subjects). ψH was observed on mask targets, ψM on standard, with a significant difference between the two.

Fisk and West (1955a, 1955b) reported a series of tests in which certain targets had profound emotional significance for the subject. In analyzing the S.P.R.'s home-testing experiments they had found one subject who had greatly over-called two of the five ESP symbols. When the subject was asked about this he explained the difference by saying that the symbols (+ and 0) were especially salient for him at the time since they represented for him the male and female sex, respectively. This young man was apparently wrestling with an existential dilemma concerning his sexual orientation (homosexual or heterosexual), and the two poles of that dilemma were signified by the two symbols. In what appears to have become as much a sensitive counseling relationship as an experimental one, the subject and Fisk agreed to carry out a series of GESP runs using the five targets, with the + and 0 deliberately altered to the gender symbols ♀ and ♂. Ten runs were collected with significant overall ψH scoring, all of which was contributed by the high success rate on the gender-linked targets.

Three studies have been carried out to test the possible effect of target differences of which the subject is unaware. Johnson and Nordbeck (1972) tested a reputedly psychic young woman, who had also been given extensive clinical testing using standard projective devices and a "defense mechanism test" examining patterns of responsiveness in a subliminal-perception situation. Her protocols were scrutinized and six terms were picked, three of which were expected to have strong positive significance for the subject and three strong negative significance. She was tested in four 30-trial runs using a blind-matching procedure, without knowing the content of the response-cards or key envelopes, and obtained significant ψH on the positive words and significant ψM on the negative. The difference was contributed mostly by the first two runs ($Z = 4.15$) and only slightly by the last two ($Z = 1.71$) my calculations. After this series she learned of the targets and the means by which they had been determined and became annoyed at the experimenters for their intrusiveness. Testing conducted at this point yielded null results for both target types.

Carpenter (1971) tested subjects in a blind-matching procedure in which a deck of 75 standard ESP cards were matched against 10 key-envelopes (two for each symbol). Subjects were told only that each symbol was represented by two different target-envelopes. Unknown to them, erotic pictures of men and women engaged in explicit sexual activity were taped inside one set of target-envelopes, and blank cards of similar bulk and weight taped inside the other five. Two experiments using this procedure were reported. The first involved junior high school students who had also been tested on the Taylor Manifest Anxiety Scale. Two runs of 75 trials each were collected per subject in a single session. Effects of target-type and anxiety level (high, mid-range, low) were tested by analysis of variance. Neither main effect was significant, but an interaction ($P < .01$) was observed. The preferential pattern of high-anxious subjects was ψH on erotic targets and ψM on neutral. The mid-range and low-anxious subjects showed the opposite pattern. Males performed no differently than females. In the second experiment 31 college males also performed two 75-trial runs without awareness of the target difference. Subjects were also tested with the Mosher Guilt Scale (Mosher, 1960) and asked if they believed or disbelieved in the possibility of ESP in that situation. The effects of sex-guilt and target-type were tested by separate analyses of variance for sheep and goats. For the sheep, target-type had the only significant effect (erotic ψH, neutral ψM, $P < .05$). The goats' performance was affected by guilt level ($P < .05$) and by the interaction of guilt and target-type: high-guilt Ss ψH on erotic, ψM on neutral; low-guilt Ss vice versa, ($P < .05$). Ballard (1975) has used a similar testing procedure and found somewhat congruent results. The factor of anxiety was reported to interact with the erotic-neutral target-type for female subjects ($P < .01$), but the modal pattern of the interaction is not described. Judging from the Johnson and Nordbeck, Carpenter, and Ballard studies, subject awareness of the target-differential is apparently not necessary for the elicitation of a preferential response.

Freeman and Nielsen have reported several studies using a single ESP testing procedure and emotional target-differences—a welcome change from the diversity of procedures which characterizes most of the work reviewed. Freeman (1964) developed a "Word Reaction Test": a list of 25 words with five blank spaces by each. The subject was asked to react to each word by registering an L for like and a D for dislike and to make a precognitive ESP guess at the same time by placing the letter in one of the five spaces. Freeman's initial hunch (that people with relatively more L responses would score better than people with relatively fewer L's) was not supported in pilot testing. Instead, when subjects were classified into "likers" and "dislikers" by dividing their $\Sigma L/\Sigma L + \Sigma D$ proportions at the median, they were found to ψH on their "primary" responses (L for likers, D for dislikers) and to ψM on their "secondary" responses. Forty subjects in a high school science club were tested after a 20-minute talk on ESP by the experimenter, and the primary-ψH, secondary-ψM pattern was confirmed. Most of the effect was contributed by the dislikers.

Freeman and Nielsen (1964) retested the same high school group the following year, and reconfirmed the effect ($P = .03$). Some new wrinkles were added, in that subjects were asked to scale their responses in terms of extremity of rating and were also tested on the Taylor Manifest Anxiety Scale. Closer examination showed that the primary vs. secondary effect was contributed this time entirely by the dislikers and showed also that only high and midrange anxiety subjects generated the effect. No analysis of correlation between the MAS and the liker-disliker dichotomy is given nor a multivariate analysis which would permit one to assess the independent and interacting effects of the individual-difference variables.

Nielsen and Freeman (1965) next reported the findings of testing done with two criterion and seven follow-up groups of high-school and college students. Overall, the primary vs. secondary effect was not confirmed. A different preferential effect was observed consistently for high anxious dislikers: ψH on extremely rated words and ψM on moderately rated words. Freeman (1969b) reported finding the primary vs. secondary effect in another high-school group of 20 subjects. As before, the dislikers contributed most of the effect. In his last report on the matter, Freeman (1970c) reported another failure to confirm the original primary-secondary effect or any of the variations with moderating variables. A new, very complex relationship was reported between neuroticism, mood ratings, and the primary-secondary distinction. As no confirmation of this has been reported it will not be described in detail. These studies are difficult to generalize from. In two of them what may be called the most persistent effect was confirmed: that dislikers score ψH on disliked words and ψM on liked words. In another it was confirmed only for mid- and high-anxious subjects, and in another it was not found at all. As the latter involved several experimenters and diverse groups (many subjects older than the ones in the more replicative reports) the effects may somehow be tied to the major experimenter and his lecture-discussion-test procedure which has become idiosyncratic to him; or else it may be found with high-school age subjects only.

Target-Type Preferential Effects Moderated by Sex of Subject. Two relatively sustained lines of research on preferential effects mediated by subject-gender have been carried out, the first mostly by Rao, the other by Freeman. Rao (1963b) reported a study in which 56 subjects (33 boys and 23 girls) were challenged to use ESP to "cross the language barrier." Each subject made 50 precognition guesses using five English words as responses when those words were targets and 50 more with the same words when their translated equivalents in

Telugu (an Indian language) comprised the targets. The boys showed a preferential effect between strong ψH on Telugu targets ($Z = 4.2$) and a chance rate on English. Girls had a weaker preferential effect with marginal ψM on Telugu and a chance rate on English. A more complex blind screened touch matching study followed (Rao, 1964a) in which each subject matched a 50 card mixed deck of Telugu and English words against two sets of key cards, one in English and the other in Telugu. A second series was carried out with a blind matching procedure, in which five key-envelopes were used which were doubly loaded with one English and one (different) Telugu word. The preferential effect, mediated by sex, appeared in both series but only on the same-language matchings. Rao interpreted this as having bearing on the question of what is responded to in an ESP test: if to the meaning of a target then cross-language matchings should be as effective as within-language matchings. He took the results to suggest that the appearance (form) of the target is critical. Boys ψH on Telugu responses matched to Telugu targets, and ψM on English-English; girls did the opposite on their same-language matchings. The relationship failed to be confirmed in a group test with 57 high school students (Rao, 1965a). A variant of this procedure was used by Kanthamani (1965) in three series. She used five English words and their Hindi equivalents as responses and targets. Overall, in each of her series ψH was found on English targets and ψM on Hindi. No effect of subject gender was found.

Freeman (1965) developed a group testing procedure for preschool and primary school children in booklet form which contained six pages of targets in five rows of five pictures per page. Three pages were comprised of rows made of "same" objects (e.g., five identical teddy bears) and three of "different" objects (e.g., five different toys). The ESP task was to guess the one object out of the row of five that was the target. In two pilot studies, one of a class of mentally retarded children and one of a kindergarten group, an unexpected tendency was found for girls to ψH on same-object pages and ψM on different-object pages, and for boys to show the opposite pattern. Three confirmatory studies are reported. In two of them, in a California elementary school and a fifth grade class in Illinois, significant differences were observed when the pooled predicted ψH pages (girls same, boys different) were contrasted with the predicted ψM pages. A third group from a New Jersey nursery school showed a nonsignificant trend in the predicted direction. The girls showed the stronger pattern in all three. Another elementary school group was tested with a ten-page version of the booklet containing pages of symbols and words (Freeman, 1970b), and a confirmation of the effect was reported ($P < .02$). There was no word vs. symbol difference in the effect. Extension of the method to older subjects brought mixed and increasingly complex results. In the first study carried out on a high school group, Freeman (1966b) used a six-page booklet with pages of same-words, different-words, same-symbols, and different-symbols. From pilot-testing Freeman expected the responses to words to vary as those of the younger children had to pictures: boys ψH on different, ψM on same, and girls vice versa. On symbols the opposite pattern had been observed: boys ψM on different and ψH on same; girls vice versa. Four confirmatory series with high school students were carried out. Contrasting the pooled "predicted ψH" to the pooled "predicted ψM" trials yielded significant effects ($P < .05$) in the first two and trends in the predicted directions in the others. In other studies Freeman (1967, 1970a) tested two accelerated seventh grade and two normal eighth grade classes looking for the complex effect described above, also hypothesizing that the spatial ability scores of the Primary Mental Abilities Test would differentiate scores as well as the sex grouping. High spatial subjects (using median score for appropriate sex group) were expected to follow the preferential pattern expected of boys; low spatial subjects were expected to conform to the girls' pattern. Both of these predictions were borne out by data from the seventh graders and from one group of the eighth, but not from the other where results were near chance in all conditions. An attempt (Freeman, 1970d) to extend the spatial ability x target-type interaction to a group of college subjects failed. A final series with five seventh grade classes (Freeman, 1970e) showed a trend toward reversing the expected relationship in terms of spatial ability, and Freeman accounted for the inconsistency by hypothesizing a maturational period between the seventh and eighth grades when the development of spatial ability takes on special salience. A further report (Freeman, 1971) gave some partial confirmation to that possibility by demonstrating in two of four seventh grade groups the sex x target-type relationship but no effect due to Primary Mental Abilities dimensions. Aside from the fairly clear effects reported in the elementary school groups, this set of findings is difficult to assess. One wishes that the increasing complexity of design had been matched by multivariate methods of analysis and detailed reports of results. Contrasting the total scores in two complexly constituted, pooled groups makes precision in understanding difficult to achieve. In general it seems that one can say of sex-linked preferential effects that they have been reported sufficiently often that they seem to point to a potentially fruitful line of inquiry but that they also seem to depend upon other factors for their occurrence (sex of experimenter, kind of ESP task, age and maturational levels of subjects all seem possibilities) and that future work should aim at greater delineation and experimental control of these factors.

Regarding target-type preferential effects in general it seems clear that more sustained and systematic research must be done before reliable generalizations will be possible. Several potentially fruitful lines of pursuit seem to have been laid down. Results of those studies which have been characterized here as involving the conscious preference of the subject (including the time-delay precognition studies) or the emotional significance of the target for the subject may bear brief summarization.

Considering first the "conscious preference" studies there seems to be a clear tendency, shared by 11 studies, for ψH to be associated with preferred targets and ψM or chance to be associated with the nonpreferred. The only exception is a study by Rao (1963a) in which standard targets received ψH scoring and personal targets a ψM trend. That is the only study which was carried out with separate runs of each target-type and the subject blind as to which was which.

In the studies comparing target-differences in emotional meaningfulness for the subject, consider first those studies in which more and less interesting (or significant) targets are contrasted in which the subjects know of the contrast. For Rao (1964b) and Fisk and West (1955a, 1955b) the more interesting targets elicited ψH and the less interesting ψM and chance, respectively. Skibinsky's (1950) apparently contrary result might be accounted for by the possibility that the family names aroused not so much an interest as a fear of failure. The subjects (including the experimenter) might have shared an implicit theory that important relationships should "channel more ESP" than meaningless designs and felt that their feelings toward the family were being evaluated by the procedure. Such threat could have caused a "moving away" (ψM) from the "favored" target and a "moving toward" the more neutral one.

Another trend which may be suggested by the studies is a tendency for the preferential effect to be itself a transient thing, tending toward a kind of episodic decline either across the runs in a session or across the sessions in a series. Unfortunately, most studies were not analyzed in these terms or reported in such detail as would permit an assessment. Of the two studies reporting scoring patterns across the runs within each session (Chauvin, 1961; Freeman, 1962), both reported the effect declining. Of the six studies reporting scoring trends across the sessions of the experiment, four reported declines (Freeman, 1962; Johnson and Nordbeck, 1972; Rao, 1962; Skibinsky, 1950). One reported an incline (Anderson, 1959) and one a correlated drop in hitting for both target types and no change in strength of preference (Fisk and West, 1955a). Enough of a trend is suggested to warrant regular analysis and reporting of preferential effects in terms of within-session and between-session order effects.

Differential Effects (Palmer Criterion). The first differential effect (modal difference in scoring for each subject between two ESP tasks) seems to have been reported by Stuart et al. (1947) and was described above. The scoring differences were later found to have been mediated by a mood variable (Humphrey, 1949). Osis (1956) compared scoring rates in GESP tests in which the targets were at close and far distances (in the subject's room in Germany vs. in North Carolina). Three series were carried out. In each series there was a negative correlation between the scores for the two distance tasks. In none of the series was a preponderant preference found, but each showed a tendency toward a modal-separation within the session: r's for the three series = $-.70$, $-.44$, and $-.30$; with $-.54$ overall ($P < .01$).

Freeman (1961) asked 12 undergraduate subjects to provide five emotionally significant objects as targets and compared their success guessing them and guessing standard symbols. No overall preference was found but a differential effect was. Sanders (1962), in a study also mentioned, found differential effects between scoring using verbal and written response modes. The directions of the differences proved to be predictable by the response-mode preference of the subject. Schmeidler (1964a) carried out a precognition study in which subjects completed runs which would be treated in three different ways: some would be scored and sent to the subject (S sees), some would be scored and seen only by the experimenter (E sees), and some would be scored automatically by a computer, but no records of anything but total scores would be printed out. A differential effect was observed for the S-sees and E-sees runs ($r = -.41$, $P = .0005$), but not for the other target-type contrasts. Rao (1964b) reported a study, mentioned above, in which he had subjects carry out two testing procedures by which he had been studying the preferential effect: a mask-and-symbol test and a Telugu-English test. No preferential effects were observed within the two tests, but a differential effect was found between the total scores for each. The reversal of scoring between tasks was observed for all ten subjects and was independently significant for eight of the ten. I venture no generalizations from these six studies.

Effects of Mood

With ψH and ψM effects so intermixed in the performances of the single subject, it becomes of interest to examine the predictive powers of psychological variables which are themselves characterized by intrasubject shift. A fairly widely-studied variable of that sort has been the subject's mood at the time of testing. A large portion of work relevant to this topic, such as change-of-state, effects of hypnosis, or of meditation, etc. are being treated by Charles Honorton in this volume so they will not be mentioned here. Another set of mood studies has treated the variance of scoring, and they are discussed under variance effects.

Results Suggestive of Mood Effects. The first systematic experimentation to be done with a mood variable did not use repeated-measures designs, but it has been influential in later work, so it will be briefly surveyed. The graphic expansiveness of drawings has received usage as a clinical technique (Elkisch, 1945; Machover, 1949). Humphrey (1946a) used Elkisch's criteria for expansion and compression ratings and scored the drawings produced by subjects as free-responses in a clairvoyance test which had previously (Stuart, 1942) been thought to yield null results. She found that the expansive response drawings showed ψH and the compressive ψM, with a significant difference between them ($P = .003$). Stuart et al. (1947) replicated the finding in another clairvoyance drawing test. Drawings not scored as an ESP response but used as a mood indicator were also found to discriminate significantly different ψH-ψM trends in subjects performing clairvoyance card-guessing (Smith and Humphrey, 1946). Kanthamani and Rao (1973) used the House-Tree-Person test to distinguish expansive and compressive subjects and found that expansives did score more successfully than compressives in a clairvoyance task ($P < .05$), and when the variable was treated with the Eysenck Personality Inventory scale for extraversion as a moderator, its effect was strengthened. In predicting GESP performance (with an agent looking at the target) the device was found to be predictive in the opposite way: compressives scored ψH, expansives ψM (Humphrey, 1946b). McMahan (1946) confirmed the latter pattern in a "pure telepathy" test. Other studies have not found the predicted relationships (Casper, 1951; Kahn, 1952; West, 1950). It should be noted that the expansive-compressive criterion is rated by judges and that interrater reliabilities are typically not very high. Some of the failures of replication with it may have come from that fact.

There are any number of studies in which one might infer the moods of subjects in certain conditions. Some of those in which the reviewer feels greatest confidence are cited. Schmeidler and Lewis (1968) had subjects call triple-aspect targets and immediate feedback was given on aspects 1 and 2. On those trials in which both 1 and 2 were correct, the third also tended strongly to ψH. The authors interpret this as a momentary result of exhilaration or confidence. Hudesman and Schmeidler (1971) compared the ESP scores from tests done by patients in psychotherapy after sessions rated as good or bad by the therapist. The highest ratings were associated with ψH scoring ($P = .02$) while the others were at chance. A mood of well-being or personal satisfaction might be expected to have accompanied the highest ratings. Schmeidler (1970) reported high ESP scores after a talk by a swami on meditation and deep-breathing exercise, suggesting that a calm and alert mood was facilitative of ψH scoring. Pretalk scores had been at chance. Sailaja and Rao (1973) reported three studies comparing ESP scores before and after an interview for admission to a course or being accepted for employment. Subjects in the pretest were led to believe that their success in the test would influence the outcome of their request. Significantly higher scores were found after the interview. A mood of anxiety could be said to have been elicited by the preinterview circumstance, and that anxiety alleviated by the time of the later run.

An indirect assessment of mood was used by Schmeidler (1964b) in a study on confidence checks. Subjects were given a low-structure suggestion about checking some calls to indicate special feelings of success. Subjects were classified in terms of the number of checks they made: 0, 1-6, 7-29, and 30-60. The 0 group (which Schmeidler considered to be taking a withdrawn stance in the situation) had overall ψM across the three target-conditions in the experiment. The 1-6 group were assumed to be taking a participative but unpressured stance. They showed ψH in runs the results of which they would later see.

Studies of Subject-Rated Mood. Some investigators have constructed mood scales of their own. Osis (1968) reported a correlation between ψM tendencies (measured independently of ψH tendencies) and ratings on an elation-depression scale. Osis and Bokert (1971) reported a complex and complexly analyzed study on mood responses to meditation. Ratings on numerous mood items were factor-analyzed and yielded three major, stable factors which they named: self-transcendence and openness, mood brought to session, and meaning-dimension. Performance on two ESP tests, a forced-choice and a free-response, was related to the mood variables by a correlational analysis. Two separate groups conducted repeated-testing after each meditation session. The strongest effects were relations between self-transcendence with ψH trends for one group and mood brought to session related to ψH for the other. Neither effect was replicated across groups. Osis, Turner, and Carlson (1971) and Osis and Carlson (1972) used similar scales to rate the moods of experimenters who prepared clairvoyance targets and compared those mood ratings to the performance of subjects, using the technique of canonical correlation. The reader is referred to the papers for details, as the results are too complex to summarize here.

Nielsen (1956b) also reported the use of a mood scale which she devised measuring physical vitality, emotional well-being, and mental alertness. Eight subjects carried out 20 five-run sessions, checking off mood ratings at each session. She divided her scales at the midpoints and termed top and bottom ratings "positive" and "negative." In all her data pooled, ψH was observed. A breakdown of performance showed that ψH was contributed by the mood-profiles which were consistently high and consistently low across all three scales, and scores were at chance for the mixed ratings. In a later study (Nielsen, 1970) this pattern was found again for her ten sheep subjects but was reversed for her four "uncertain" subjects.

Still another scale was made up by Fisk and West (1956). A total of 162 subjects did at least three clock-calls (type of target) per day over a 56-week period. Subjects rated their moods daily. Ratings were: A, exaltation or pleasure; B, neutral; C, unpleasure or depression. A χ^2 analysis showed that A ratings were associated with ψH days, C associated with ψM days, and B had no predominant relationship. The authors also averaged the mood ratings for each subject to make an individual-differences dimension. Correlations were then calculated between subjects' total ESP score and their average mood ratings. The correlations were: for A, $r = +.25$ $(P = .001)$; for B, $r = -.15$ $(P = .038)$; for C, $r = -.11$ (n.s.). Thus the more consistently happy people tended on the whole to ψH scoring and the less consistently happy tended to ψM; while those who most often called themselves neutral tended to overall ψM, and those who used the neutral rating less tended to ψH. Thus the individual-differences dimension which is suggested for future work appears to be a construct of "consistently happy vs. consistently neutral or noncommittal" rather than one of "consistently happy vs. consistently unhappy."

A few studies have been reported using the mood-adjective check list (MACL) scales developed by Nowlis (1965). Schmeidler (1971) tested a group with both MACL and an ESP clairvoyance test. She predicted that hitting rate on the ESP test should correlate positively with a sum of the MACL scale scores for surgency, social affection, and concentration. The results were in the expected direction but not significant. Hitting was strongly predicted by surgency and concentration; but social affection had the reversed relationship. As the task was an asocial clairvoyance one, the reversal of the meaning of social affection seemed reasonable to the author. Schmeidler decided to establish idiosyncratic mood and attitude patterns for a given group on a pretest and then predict its replication on a posttest. The strategy was applied to a new group, and mood and run-score variance effects were predicted and successfully replicated. The strategy was used once more by Schmeidler and Craig (1972) with three groups. Only one showed a strong ψH-ψM pattern on pretest. A group of animated and achievement-oriented young men showed a pattern of hitting associated with a mood score made up of scores for egotism minus aggression and anxiety. On retests the predicted relationship was observed ($P = .05$). McGuire, Percy, and Carpenter (1974) reported an experiment in which predictive equations for ESP hitting, run score variance, and subject variance were derived empirically using a multiple regression procedure. The battery of tests included the MACL. On the equation predictive of hitting, the MACL scales which appeared were vigor and elation (loaded positively) and concentration, egotism, and skepticism (loaded negatively). No confirmatory work with the equation has been reported.

Carpenter (1975) reported the development of a scale of MACL items taken from a set with which Nowlis (1961) had distinguished pharmacologically elated and sedated states. Carpenter analyzed a body of precognition runs accompanied by MACL responses with a multiple regression procedure and generated a scale postdictive in those data of hitting rate. Application of the scale to a new group of subjects was carried out, and the scale did succeed in separating high- and low-scoring sets of data, particularly when the moderator variable of authoritarianism was also used. Low-authoritarian subjects produced data more predictable by the scale. It may be important that all of these ESP data were gathered in self-testing conditions, with the subjects alone. The scale might not be expected to predict scoring trends in other testing circumstances.

On the whole the work on mood seems to offer general support for the common-sense assumption that happier and more consistently (or firmly) expressed moods accompany more successful scoring, and unhappier and less consistently expressed moods go with ψM trends. At the same time, factorial studies of mood (Nowlis, 1965) make it clear that moods are discriminable into far more discrete types, and work taking account of these discriminations should be most instructive. Attitudinal and situational variables seem to interact with mood effects, so it would be wise for future research to take increasing account of them.

Variance Effects

The final way to be discussed in which parapsychologists have attempted to come to terms with intrasubject scoring variability has been by studying variance effects. The variance of a set of scores is a measure which represents their amount of scatter around their central tendency or mean. The expected variance (σ^2) can be as easily specified by probability theory as the expected mean, and departures from it can be tested for significance. In ESP research, workers have sometimes employed the "theoretical variance" (calculated in terms of deviations of scores from the theoretical mean determined by probability theory) and sometimes the "empirical variance" (dispersion around the empirically observed mean). When the observed mean for a set of data does not differ much from chance the two are roughly equivalent, but when a modal trend is strong throughout the data as a body, the two may differ greatly, and appropriate interpretations may be different. A large theoretical variance observed in data with a large overall ψH deviation may be telling the experimenter nothing new: only that too many subjects had strong ψH deviations to attribute the results to chance. When overall deviations are large, care must be taken in noting the kind of variance reported. The first report focusing on score variance as such seems to have been by West (1951). Reports of analyses in terms of the parameter have remained relatively sparse, although the past 10 years have seen some increase of interest. As noted above, reliance on Z and χ^2 statistics kept workers from having to compute empirical variances as a matter of course, and disinterest may also have come from the fact that effects in terms of variance have probably appeared to represent a loss of information relative to the modal-difference analyses. A large theoretical variance means that the scores in the set scatter more widely above *and* below chance expectation than one would expect by chance. The ψH-ψM distinction is blurred over. Even so, ESP test performances are most often not strongly consistent in mode, and variance as a construct for a pattern of ESP performance has been applied in the hope of making sense of data that might have seemed construable only as "chance" without it. We will discuss first work which has been done on run-score variance (referred to hereafter as RSV). Discussion of other variance effects and attempts to explain and predict them will follow.

Variance of Run Scores. Several studies have indicated that the subject's attitudes about ESP, or toward the test, may affect RSV. Whittlesey (1960) found significantly constricted RSV in a group of psychiatric outpatients who carried out one standard clairvoyance run before and one after taking LSD-25. Many of the subjects commented that they found the test "ridiculous, petty, mundane, etc." (p. 221). Van de Castle (1957) found relationships between RSV and the sheep-goat dimension. Van de Castle used a projective device—an incomplete sentences blank—to elicit subjects' attitudes about ESP. A rater judged the protocols and scored them in four categories: high-sheep, sheep, conflict, and goats. A total of 194 subjects was tested in a clairvoyance paradigm. The means of the groups did not differ significantly from each other nor from chance, but the conflict and goat groups both had large RSV, and the high-sheep and sheep had small RSV, the difference being significant. Using the same attitude device, Osis and Dean (1964) replicated the results for three of the subject categories: high-sheep and sheep had small RSV, and conflict had large; but the RSV of goats was found to be small. The effects do not appear to be general for the sheep-goat dimension (no difference in RSV between sheep and goats was found by Schmeidler [Schmeidler and McConnell, 1958] for her much larger sample), and it may be somehow specific to the Van de Castle measure. Unreported analyses I carried out on data contributed by almost 300 sheep and goats (Schmeidler's criterion) also showed no difference. Some other RSV effects in which the sheep-goat variable played an interacting part will be mentioned below under the topic of mood.

Relations between RSV and other individual-difference variables have been reported. Freeman (1969a), using the Word Reaction Test mentioned above, reported that a group of "likers" (who gave relatively more liked than disliked response-words) produced a significantly small RSV. No analyses for RSV were reported in his several other studies with this procedure, so one cannot ascertain the generality of this finding. Schmeidler and LeShan (1970) perused data previously collected in group ESP tests by subjects who had also taken the Rorschach test. Sheep subjects were selected for three groups on the basis of performance in their ESP tests (all of eight or nine runs in length): A, high means and large (theoretical) RSV; B, chance means and small RSV; C, chance means and chance RSV. Subjects in those groups whose Rorschach protocols were too short were excluded, and the remaining protocols were scored for Fisher and Cleveland's barrier and penetration dimensions. The subjects with ψH means and large RSV (group A) scored relatively high on penetration and low on barrier, the subjects with chance means and small RSV (group C) had a relatively large preponderance of barrier over penetration, and the ψH and chance RSV group (B) was in between. Within the nonpathological ranges found here, the authors concluded that the group A subjects were relatively open and responsive and not especially reliant on repressive defenses, while group C subjects were relatively closed, withdrawn, and repressive in their defensive style. Additional evidence for the group C interpretation was found in the fact that subjects in that group had proportionately many more Rorschach protocols with too few responses to score. In the Rorschach literature, a small number of responses is generally taken to indicate repressiveness. What might sheep, high sheep, likers, and high-barrier subjects have in common that might facilitate their producing small RSV? Only more research on these intriguing possibilities could determine an answer.

Declines of Variance. The matter of changes of run score variance within a subject's performance was brought up by Rogers and Carpenter (1966) and Carpenter and Carpenter (1967). These studies suggested that RSV may be expected to decline across a series of runs done at a single sitting. Previous unpublished pilot testing by Carpenter and Rogers of a single subject who had been dosed with a stimulating drug revealed an interesting phenomenon across his 30 runs (*N* trials per run = 20; $p = \frac{1}{2}$). The scatter of run scores above and below the expected mean of 10 was significantly large overall, although after the 20th run, when the subject reported that the stimulant effect had worn off, the scatter dropped to the point that a below-chance RSV was found in the last ten runs. The two RSV's (first 20 vs. last 10 runs) were significantly different ($P < .01$). Although this observation was post hoc, it serves to illustrate what is meant by large and small variance scoring.

The Carpenter and Carpenter (1967) data were comprised of 29 sets of self-testing and had been collected before the above observation was made. A re-analysis of RSV was done in order to see if a decline of RSV might be found in these other series in which no drugs had been used. The number of runs of the sessions varied (from 16 to 88), but when each was divided at its midpoint a significant proportion (76 percent) showed a decline from first half to second half. When the sittings were divided into longer and shorter sessions at the median, the effect was found confined to the shorter-session set. There the first-half RSV was significantly large ($P < .01$) and the second-half RSV significantly small ($P < .01$). For the longer series (40 runs or more) both RSV's were at chance. The Rogers and Carpenter (1966) study represented an attempt to apply the hypothesis to new subjects who carried out relatively short series. Their 20 subjects carried out 20 precognition runs (two pages) while in a room alone. Their RSV's declined with significant consistency ($P < .01$) from the first to the second page. Analyses for declines in RSV from the first to the last half of five-run series of runs have been reported by Carpenter (1968a, 1969). When data from three series were analyzed a decline was found in one, a significantly large first-half RSV (but no significant decline) in another, and null results in the third. These very spotty results might suggest that a five-run series is too short to evoke a consistent effect. No other analyses pertinent to RSV declines have been reported, so one can say very little about the generality of the effect.

Variance declines within the run have been reported. A decline of the variance of half-run scores was found by Carpenter (1966) in self-testing data and replicated across seven confirmatory series ($P < .01$). Another replication of the effect was reported (Carpenter and Carpenter, 1967) in runs which had been carried out in the same mode of response ($P < .05$) and reversed in runs which had been done in a "constricted" response mode (calls drawn in a very tiny, neat, way and timed) ($P < .05$). A decline in half-run score variances can probably be inferred from a report by Stump, Roll, and Roll (1970) on some work with Lalsingh Harribance. Seven series gave overall a high ψH rate of calling ($P < 10^{-10}$). A decline within the runs of the ψH effect was found, such that very strong and consistent positive deviations were found in the top, and near-chance scoring in the bottom. Construing this as a decline in theoretical variance seems very likely correct, although redundant to the ψH to chance decline noted. It might be, however, that variance declines are more general than hitting declines, as most of the latter have only been looked for in cases in which, like this one, an overall ψH deviation was first found. The more general case of intrarun decline might be the decline of variance (of hitting *and* missing) of which only the hitting cases have tended to be selected because of researchers' habits and editorial policies. Until many more studies are analyzed in terms of variance of part-run scores, this possibility cannot be evaluated.

The data from Carpenter's (1966) first seven confirmatory series were also scored by segments and the variance of segment scores analyzed. A significant decline was observed, and top segment variance was significantly large ($P < .01$). Freeman (1968) and Brier (1969) reported weak but significantly consistent sex differences in size of segment variances between the thousands of junior high school boys and girls who took part in a mail-in ESP test solicited by a national magazine. Boys tended to have larger segment variances than girls. Evaluations for decline effects were not reported.

West (1951) reported a decline of half-series score variance in a reanalysis of some unpublished GESP data collected by Nicol and Osborn, although he did not construe it as that. He had been alerted to do this by the results of a study which had purported to test the effects of a euphoria-producing drug (which was misdosed and produced no euphoria) in which he had noticed a significantly large dispersion (or, in later terms, subject variance) for the total scores of his five subjects. The Nicol and Osborn data provided an opportunity to look for the effect again, but West thought that since their testing series was longer than his, it would most likely occur only in the first part (16 runs) of the series. When scores for the 16-run blocks were checked for large dispersion, the effect was found ($P = .01$). The dispersion of the scores of the later-run blocks was near to chance expectation. In an analysis of another set of data from Fisk (1951), only a trend ($P = .10$) toward the effect was found. Rogers and Carpenter (1966) also reported a significant difference between the two page-scores (ten-run blocks) produced by their subjects ($P < .03$), with the first larger than σ^2, and the second smaller. Freeman (1969a) also found a significant decline of run-block variances. Using a 12-page booklet made of three four-page sections (each with a different class of targets) Freeman found a significantly large variance of first-section scores and a significantly small variance for second- and third-section scores. As with run scores and part-run scores, run-block scores have not typically been analyzed for variance position effects. The possibility that these too represent more general phenomena, of which the ψH declines are a subgroup, cannot be examined until more such analyses are reported.

Run Score Variance and Mood.   The suggestion was drawn by workers who reported variance declines that the declines had been accompanied by changes of mood in the subject, from fresh, spontaneous interest at first, to cramped monotony at the end.   Rogers (1966) set out to test the possibility that positive and negative moods could directly affect RSV.   He first carried out ten ten-run sessions of precognition self-testing when he found himself in states of "negative affect" toward the test (defined as feeling neither interested, enthusiastic, nor confident of success), followed by ten series in which he was in a "positive affect" state.   The variances tended to depart from chance as expected, with the negative affect RSV significantly smaller than chance expectation ($P < .01$), but only a largeness trend in the positive affect sessions.   The difference was significant ($P < .01$).   Rogers (1967b) then repeated the procedure with five other subjects.   The small variance for the negative state was replicated ($P < .01$), and a chance RSV was found for the positive, with the difference still significant ($P = .025$).

Carpenter (1968a, 1969) attempted to develop a more objective measure of mood which would capture the states Rogers had studied.   A mood-adjective check list (MACL) was made up of items which had been found to discriminate elated and sedated states, plus some "filler" items.   Three studies were reported in which subjects completed four or five precognition runs at a sitting, followed by an MACL.   In the first, a simple separation of the MACL scores into "positive" and "negative" groups by dividing at the median did not serve to significantly isolate low and high RSV scoring.   Both sets of scores were separated into more moderate and more extreme groups; and by this post-hoc division, an isolation of RSV effects seemed to have been achieved.   The moderate positive and negative scores predicted as had been expected, but the extreme scores did the reverse.   Carpenter followed with two more studies which replicated this more complex discrimination.   After this he shifted his tack in hopes of finding a more direct and powerful way of scoring the mood scale.   All data that had been collected were analyzed by a stepwise multiple-regression procedure, and a set of the most strongly postdictive items were selected.   Work to validate this scale has been carried out (Carpenter, 1973, 1975) on six different sets of subjects.   The scale has been significantly predictive in its consistent discrimination of large and small sets of RSV.   When the moderator variables of authoritarianism and sheep-goat attitude are taken into account, its power is enhanced.   Performance of sheep and of low-authoritarian (by California F-scale) subjects is more predictable.

Schmeidler and co-workers have reported several studies in which the Nowlis (1961) 23-item mood scale was used to predict RSV.   Schmeidler (1971), as she had with modal predictions, set upon the strategy of testing a group twice, finding the most powerful mood-RSV relationship in the first testing, and predicting its recurrence in the second. A group comprised of 11 supersheep (who expect personally to score well) and 40 sheep were administered MACL's and clairvoyance tests. On the pretest, summed scores for surgency, social affection, and concentration were found to correlate positively with RSV for supersheep, while the sheep showed an inverse relationship. Upon retesting the group the effect for supersheep was replicated, the one for sheep was not. This strategy was also applied to three other groups (Schmeidler and Craig, 1972), and an RSV prediction was made for one of them based on pretesting. Members of an adult YMCA class on the occult showed a positive pretest relation between RSV and the Nowlis scale combination of scores for vigor minus fatigue, egotism, and anxiety. Upon retest a positive correlation was found, but it was not significant.

Stanford reported two studies in which RSV was related to factors probably associated with mood. He hypothesized that an effortful, overrational response set should make for small RSV and a spontaneous set for large RSV. In one study (1966a) he manipulated the response sets of subjects doing two 25-trial clairvoyance runs. In his open-deck condition (targets drawn from random numbers, and symbol frequencies in the deck not usually equal), subjects were told that a spontaneous, nonrational approach would be best. In the closed-deck condition (five each of five symbols per run), he urged them to keep careful count of the number of times they called each symbol. The open-deck condition did elicit large RSV ($P < .0007$) and the closed-deck condition a small RSV trend ($P < .10$). He then thought of checking runs for their call frequencies, taking even-frequency runs as a likely indication of such a rational response style, and nonequal frequencies as representing a freer style. In a reanalysis of data borrowed from Rao and Morris the nonequal runs had large RSV ($P < .03$) and the equal had small RSV ($P < .02$). Stanford and Stanford (1969), examining runs during which EEG alpha wave dominance had undergone a marked shift from the top half of the run to the bottom half, reasoned that cognitive work should be represented by the alpha-decrease runs and absence of such work by the alpha-increase runs. The alpha-decrease runs did show a large RSV ($P < .01$), but the alpha-increase RSV, though smaller than chance, was not significant. Examination of the call-frequencies of these two sets of runs found a significant tendency for more balanced calling in the alpha-decrease runs. A similar suggestion came from a study by Stanford and Palmer (1973) in which a reputed psychic was tested in a free-response study of personality "readings." EEG activity was recorded during the session and during a prior period of meditation. Sessions were divided into two groups on the basis of mean alpha frequency during the meditation period. Marked deviations from chance in both ψH and ψM directions were almost entirely associated with sessions in the high frequency group.

The Problem of Small Variance.   Large variance scoring can be construed rather easily in terms of the ψH–ψM construct.   The ESP "force" is acting to make scores depart from chance; only the modality of the deviations is not consistent. Small variance scoring, on the other hand, seems to present something of a conceptual problem since the scores would not seem to represent either psi-hitting or psi-missing.   In fact, they are seen to hover *so closely to chance expectation that it is extra chance.*   "Chance" level scores, long the refuse of parapsychology, in the above studies had been construed for the first time as nonchance.   But how could sense be made of it?   One possibility which received some empirical test was that of an internal cancellation effect.   J. B. Rhine (1969b) reasoned that if runs with small deviations are scored by segments, and the segment scores tallied, and further if a "position effect" across the segments is observed with some deviations above and some below chance, then the small run-score deviation could be understood as a result of the cancelling-out effect of the within-run position effect.   Rogers (1967a), Stanford (1966b), and Bednarz and Verrier (1969) all reported segmental position effect analyses for sets of data which had yielded significantly small RSV.   In the Rogers array, a one-way analysis of variance was not significant, but a ψH trend was found in the first four segments and a ψM trend in the fifth.   A post-hoc test of the difference between the average scores on the first four versus the fifth was significant ($P <$ .02), and the majority of runs (53 of 77) were found to follow the pattern. Stanford (1966b) reported a post-hoc separation of segments 1 and 2, vs. segments 3, 4, and 5 in two groups of subjects ($P < .03 < .04$).   No analysis of variance or consistency tests were reported.   Bednarz and Verrier (1969) reported a pattern of segments 2, 3, and 4 being ψH, 1 and 5 ψM.   No statistical assessment was reported.   All of these studies would have presented stronger cases if a significant tendency for the individual runs to obey the ostensive pattern had been demonstrated.   The one-way analysis of variance would seem to be the logical choice for trying to isolate such a tendency, but its use has not been encouraging.

Another tack was taken by Crumbaugh (1968), who also postulated an internal cancellation of ψH and ψM tendencies to account for small RSV, but he did not use the idea of a position effect consistent across runs. He suggested the existence of a ψH–ψM stimulator-inhibitor mechanism. In an analogy to Hull's concept of reactive inhibition, he reasoned that ψH may cause a strain in the organism which brings on the protective response of ψM. The notion that ψH is maladaptive and must be defended against in favor of focused and manageable sensory channels of information goes back at least to Bergson (1920), but Crumbaugh gives the idea a more precise formulation. He postulates that differing strengths of these stimulating and inhibiting mechanisms could account for subjects with different patterns of scoring rate and RSV. The small RSV situation is accounted for by a rapid oscillation of stimulating and inhibiting forces cancelling out to a zero overall deviation. Crumbaugh's assumption that types of subjects exist whose performance would show certain characteristic scoring features seems unwarranted by the low levels of test-retest reliabilities subjects generally show. No empirical tests are reported for the model, but the tests proposed would depend upon acquiring self-consistent scorers, which would probably be difficult. Carpenter (1968b) also hypothesized the idea that ψH and ψM normally occur as oscillating functions whose rate of oscillation could be imagined to vary as a function of unspecified factors. A large deviation set of runs would be one in which a slow rate of oscillation is occurring, a rate no faster than the period taken for a single run to be done. A small RSV set of runs would be one in which the rate of oscillation is rapid enough that nearly equal pulls in the ψH and ψM directions will be expected for every run, keeping the scores close to mean chance expectation. These two models—position-effect cancellation and cancellation by rate of oscillation of serial ψH and ψM tendencies—could both be developed to the point that hypotheses could be derived and tested. Whatever the facts may eventually prove to be, it may not be unwarranted to think of small-variance runs as representing modally-balanced performance and of large-variance runs as representing modally-imbalanced performance.

Subject Variance as a Function of Individual Differences. A number of studies have given results which suggest that subjects for whom the ESP test is most salient or emotionally involving produce the largest deviation (or greatest modal imbalance) across all their guesses. This hypothesis was put forth by Palmer (1972) on the basis of a research review. The run-block variance declines mentioned above suggest such an effect, assuming that emotional involvement might decrease as the task proceeds. Sanders (1962) did not report a run-block variance analysis, but his report permitted me to compare the SV on two target-types: preferred and not preferred. The SV is significantly larger on the preferred targets than on the nonpreferred ($P < .05$). Another study reporting target differences that affected SV was one by Woodruff (1960) in which 100 subjects did ten runs each, guessing ostensibly black lists of targets (examples were shown). In the experimental series, 40 percent of the targets for each subject were, without their knowledge, stamped in red ink. Scores on black and the unexpected red targets were tallied separately, and the SV was significantly large for the red material, but at chance for the black.

Van de Castle (1957) reported that his high-sheep had very large SV's, the sheep and goats small, and the conflict intermediate. Osis and Dean (1964) replicated this pattern. Otani (1968b) tested subjects both under the condition in which they knew their response would be scored against ESP targets and under the condition in which they did not have that knowledge. In the knowledge condition the variance of 125-trial blocks of data was larger than in the no-knowledge condition. The knowledge condition could be assumed to be more salient or emotionally arousing. Jones and Feather (1969) asked subjects the frequency of their presumed psi experience in daily life and gave them ESP tests. Subjects reporting more such experiences had larger SV's in several groups tested. Buzby (1967a, 1967b) asked subjects to rate their amount of interest in obtaining positive results. He called "vital interest" those subjects who wanted success because of its personal implications for their own potentialities, and "casual interest" those subjects who checked a more impersonal degree of curiosity. In one study (Buzby, 1967a) his "vital interest" groups scored significantly large SV in the precognition condition in both of two experiments. Each subject was tested with five runs of precognition followed by five runs of clairvoyance. The superiority of the precognition SV may be attributable then to the task or to its position as first and thereby most salient. In another study (Buzby, 1967b) a subset of the same data was analyzed in terms of the "global vs. analytic" dimension on the imbedded figures test (EFT), and significantly large SV was found in the data of the "global" subjects. Further work by Buzby (1968b, 1969) and by Nash and Nash (1968) failed to replicate the "vital-casual" difference. Buzby (1968a) studied ratings of high-body sophistication taken from figure drawings. He found that the effect of the "global-analytic" distinction was moderated by the high or low body sophistication the subjects displayed. It was the subjects who were both global and high in body-sophistication who had the largest SV, as contrasted to small SV obtained by the other groups. Nash and Nash (1968) replicated the global-analytic SV effect.

Randall (1972) found and replicated in two groups of schoolboys relations between SV and the Eysenck Personality Inventory variables of extraversion and neuroticism. The more extraverted and more neurotic subjects had larger SV's. Price (1973) measured the degree of his subjects' control of imagery on the Gordon Imagery Scale. His less controlled imagers had larger SV than his controlled imagers. Price suggested that the dimension may be related to a general factor of cognitive control.

Perusing these SV findings, one feature stood out to this reviewer which all of these studies had in common: all of the multi-run guessing tasks which elicited the large SV and small SV effects were uninterrupted both by run-by-run scoring and by change of task. That is, all of the blocks of work carried out were not internally broken up and were presumably experienced by the subjects as continuous blocks of effort and not as a combination of disparate tasks. This suggests that it might be a necessary, although not sufficient, condition for work yielding SV effects to be continuous and uninterrupted. Besides that, the Palmer (1972) hypothesis of greater emotional involvement accompanying larger SV seems consistent with the results for high sheep and conflict vs. sheep and goats, knowledge of ESP test vs. no knowledge, more psi experiences vs. fewer, and vital interest vs. casual. In all of these the subject who is expressing more emotional involvement in the task, or who is in a situation likely to elicit more involvement, scored in a larger SV manner. In terms of the hypothesis mentioned above (of the importance of situationally continuous and unbroken testing circumstances), more bits of a pattern might be glimpsed. Long, sustained, continuous testing activity might be expected to yield high SV for subjects whose attention and motivation could be expected to be relatively consistent. Both the global subject and the uncontrolled imager, and possibly the extravert as well, might be expected to experience such a sustained condition as an unbroken whole, not eliciting changes in attention and motivation, while the controlled imager, the analytic, and the introvert might to expected to analyze, reflect upon, and break apart the experience as it proceeds. An unbroken experience might be expected to produce modal imbalance across the task, with one ψ-mode maintaining its relative predominance; while the broken-apart experience might be expected to yield modally balanced scoring, with both ψH and ψM tendencies called into play and cancelling each other out.

The importance of the unbroken conditions might be better ascertained by examining some sets of studies in which no large SV effects were obtained. Such a case seems represented by the differential effect studies mentioned above. A subject whose scoring is in one mode for one condition and in the other mode for another condition is not likely, on the whole effort, to obtain large SV.

In all of these studies (Freeman, 1961; Osis, 1956; Rao, 1964b; Sanders, 1962; Schmeidler, 1964a; Stuart et al., 1947) it can be seen that the tasks were experienced as interrupted in some way by the subject's performing them: either by change of response mode, scoring, knowledge of a change in targets, or by a new testing session. An overall hypothesis can be stated for future research: large SV scoring will be elicited by testing procedures which are internally uninterrupted (whether by scoring, change of task, interpolated task, or change of session) and by subjects who find the task emotionally involving and who have cognitive styles not prone to analysis and conscious control. Small SV scoring will be elicited in the opposite circumstances.

SUBJECT-AGENT EFFECTS

The Importance of an Agent

One of the first questions to preoccupy parapsychologists was whether or not it was necessary for an agent (or sender) to be thinking of the target material for success to be observed in ESP guessing. Results published in J. B. Rhine's monograph (1934) indicated clearly that it was not. Pearce and others performed as well when no one was looking at the cards as when they were. Although the question of *possibility* seemed settled (see also Musso and Granero, 1973), subject differences in this regard still appear to be important. Soal's subjects (Soal and Bateman, 1954) Stewart and Shackleton dropped abruptly to chance levels of scoring when clairvoyance conditions were substituted for GESP conditions, even when the subjects were not aware of the change (although it should be noted that Foster, 1956, has reported extrachance effects in the Shackleton clairvoyance work). European and American streams of research have differed somewhat in the assumptions shared by experimenters and subjects in the two continents. Some European workers have tended to find telepathy more "reasonable" than clairvoyance, while for some Americans that has not been the case. The different assumptive structures can be illustrated by two large-scale reviews of subject-agent factors in apparently telepathic spontaneous cases which appeared the same year in British and American journals. Dalton (1956), reviewing cases from *Phantasms of the Living* (Gurney, Myers, and Podmore, 1886) and other sources, concluded that the quality of experience in the agent at the moment of "transmission" was the critical factor determining the nature of the percipient's experience (death being apparently the most salient experience an agent is likely to have). L. E. Rhine (1956), reviewing spontaneous cases from the Duke collection, noted that the apparent motivation for the experience (its need-value, we might say) was generally greater for the percipient than for the agent. Because of this, she reasoned that the "experiencing person" (E-person, in her phrase) was most likely the active member, and the "target person" (T-person) functioned generally as an ESP target more or less like any other.

Soal may somehow have carried his "agent-necessary" phenomenon with him. At least this is suggested by a study of Langdon-Davies (Langdon-Davies, Langdon-Davies, Bateman, and Soal, 1955), who had found an apparently gifted subject who scored consistently above chance in both GESP and BT (clairvoyance) conditions. In a session supervised by Soal and Bateman, her performance continued to be good in GESP, but dropped to chance in BT. Bender (1970) is another researcher who has continued to stress the importance of the sender and has reported results in which unannounced changes from GESP to clairvoyance resulted in an abrupt drop of scores to chance. The special subject Harribance, who had been performing at a very high rate in clairvoyance tests, nevertheless fell to chance in clairvoyance trials in a study (Klein, 1971) in which they were contrasted with GESP trials, even though Harribance was kept blind as to the two conditions. Kreitler and Kreitler (1973) found different results when agents were trying to actively "send" the target material vs. when they were asked merely to think of it, without mention that the situation was an ESP test. The "active sending" condition, matched with one target-content condition, elicited significantly ψH scoring. There also seems to have been a trend, not evaluated by the authors, for the "passive thinking" matched with the same target content to have elicited ψM scoring. From these findings we may conclude that an active agent may not be necessary for ψH (or other scoring effects) to occur, but that contrasting an agent with some other condition may prove to be an effective independent variable.

A number of studies have been done on the question of the relative efficacy of different agents. That there are differences has been suggested by several studies which have found post-hoc differences of scoring rate when different agents were "sending" (Bednarz and Verrier, 1969; Bender, 1970; Louwerens, 1960; Michie and West, 1957; Nicol and Humphrey, 1953; Soal and Bateman, 1950; Thouless, 1947; West and Fisk, 1953).   Soal and Bateman (1954) reported that Mrs. Stewart was able to score well with only about half of the people who acted as agent, and with certain agents her success rates seemed unusually high. Soal's impression was that she tended to score well with agents whom she liked. Shackleton was able to score well with only three out of over a dozen agents who were tried. The unsuccessful agents were dropped quickly, so one cannot guess whether Shackleton's and Mrs. Stewart's hitting rates might have improved had they persisted. Zotti and Cohen (1970) used prior success as a receiver to predict success as an agent, much as Soal had done. In ten sessions of two runs each, subjects guessed first at targets looked at by a "gifted" agent (by his own previous ESP results) and then at targets looked at by a nongifted agent, and the very large difference in hitting rates (both ψH) of 27 percent was observed favoring the gifted agent.

Type of Agent-Percipient Relationship

Looking at two collections of reports on spontaneous cases, Green (1960) tallied the numbers of times different family members appeared to be playing the roles of agent and percipient. By far the two highest combinations were son as agent and mother as percipient, and son as agent and father as percipient. These cases were reported with twice the frequency of the next highest combinations. This seems congruent with anecdotal evidence discussed by Ehrenwald (1954) to the effect that the child-parent relationship, with its "biological symbiosis," is productive of ESP exchange, as is the intensive transference-phase of the psychoanalytic relationship. These leads do not appear to have been followed up experimentally, but several studies have been done comparing the degree of intimacy of the relationship existing between agent and percipient. Stuart (1946) reported that his intimately-related couples worked more successfully as agent-percipient teams than his unrelated couples. Rice and Townsend (1962) reported a strong difference in scoring when four engaged or married couples and four previously unacquainted couples alternated in the agent and percipient roles. Strong ψH was observed for the related couples and strong ψM for the unrelated. This was not a preferential effect, as members of each couple were only tested with each other. Haraldsson (1970) compared the success in close (married or related) and casual (friends) dyads in a study in which the percipient's plethysmograph recordings were checked for changes coincident with the agent's looking at a meaningful name. Overall mean differences were not found, but it was observed that the degree of emotional meaningfulness of the name for the percipient correlated highly with success for the intimate pairs but not for the casual. ψH effects were reported for close (husband-wife and mother-daughter) percipient-agent pairs (Rice, Williss, Lafferty, Little, and Mauldin, 1966), but no comparison or control conditions were used. In a study in which Rorschach protocols were used in an attempt to predict percipient-agent success, Schmeidler (1960, 1961) found that her predictions were strongly verified in one series in which percipient and agent had briefly met beforehand and received chance results in other series in which they were not allowed to meet, suggesting that the presence or absence of even so brief a relationship can be important. Congruent results as to importance of agent and percipient having met were reported by Bleksley (1963). Moss and Gengerelli (1968), on the other hand, found that the degree of intimacy in relationship had no effect on their GESP results, while Beloff (1969) failed to find any extrachance results at all when the agent-percipient pairs were couples in love.

The degree of liking or feeling of closeness between two friends has curiously been found to be negatively related to GESP success. Casper (1952) tested ten male and ten female college students all of whom were acquainted and each of whom had ranked all ten subjects of the opposite sex in terms of liking. Each subject then acted as percipient with two opposite sex agents: the one most liked and the one least liked. Two runs each of BT and GESP were done by each pair. In the GESP runs the subject scored ψM with the liked agent and ψH with the disliked one. Carpenter, in an unpublished study on the effects of subject-rated mood of closeness between married couples who carried out several sessions in both percipient and agent roles, found no relation of GESP scoring to that mood variable.

Two attempts to experimentally manipulate the effectiveness of agents by hypnosis have been reported. McBain, Fox, Kimura, Nakanishi, and Tirado (1970) hypnotized their agents and suggested that they would concentrate, feel rapport with the percipient, and reach emotionally to the targets. Overall ψH was observed ($P = .025$). That the manipulation had some effect was suggested by a significant positive correlation ($P < .01$) found between the agent's hypnotizability and the scoring rate. Casler (1969) divided subjects into same-sex dyads and in one condition suggested to agents that the percipients were their closest friends; in another condition he suggested to percipients that the agents were closest friends; and in another condition did no hypnosis. Results were at chance across the board. No analysis in terms of hypnotizability was reported. As mentioned above, Schmeidler (1960, 1961), using Rorschach protocols plus interviews assessing a person's willingness to permit deep emotional contact, made clinical predictions as to percipient-agent pairs which were expected to show ψH and ψM scoring, and when the two had met the predictions were significantly accurate.

The Teacher-Pupil Relationship

The most extensively tested kind of relationship between agent and percipient has been that of the teacher and pupil. Van Busschbach (1953) reported a high level of scoring success in 21 Dutch primary school classes tested with the teacher acting as agent. The children were mostly in the age range of 10–12. Van Busschbach thought that the good rapport generally established between teacher and students should facilitate such an effect, and this was verified. He attempted (1955, 1959) to extend the effect to secondary school classes and to first and second grade classes, and strong ψH scoring was found in the latter, but not the former. A successful cross-cultural replication was carried out (Van Busschbach, 1956) on fifth and sixth grade pupils in American schools. An attempt to extend it (Van Busschbach, 1961) to first and second grade American schools was only partially successful. Significant ψH scoring was found in the first half of the testing but not in the second. The author noted that the level of cooperation from the teacher and rapport with the class did not seem as high as he had found in Dutch schools. Louwerens (1960) found very high scoring in a GESP study with nursery school children in The Netherlands, but only under the condition in which the teacher, not the experimenter, was acting as agent. Randall (1972) also failed to find overall ψH in a similar teacher-student GESP task with students who were in secondary school. High success rates with both primary and secondary Dutch school children have been reported by Bierman and Camstra (1973). However, the trend of the findings published seems to favor the idea that the teacher-pupil relationship will most reliably favor GESP success in primary-school groups.

Other Problems

Soal and Bateman (1950) addressed the question as to whether or not two agents working simultaneously would reduce each other's effectiveness when in "competition" (looking at different targets) or augment the success level when looking at the same targets. In the competition series Mrs. Stewart "selected" one agent and continued her previous success rate on those targets, while scoring at chance on the other. When the competing agents were liked to different degrees, she tended to pick the better liked. In the series with joint "sending" of the same targets success was not augmented: it remained at the same ψH rate as with one agent alone. White and Angstadt (1963a, 1963b) attempted to study this preferential selection between competing agents by asking two classes of students each to elect an agent from their number. Guessing was done while both classes' agents were looking at different targets. In the first study the elected agent received significant ψH scoring, the other agent ψM; but the effect failed to replicate in the second study.

Some studies have indicated that even the experimenter in a clairvoyance situation can be an agent in the sense that the mood or set of the experimenter can have an effect on scoring. Carlson (1970) and Osis and Carlson (1972) have reported complex effects on subjects' scoring of the mood-scale ratings of the experimenter who prepared the targets. Price (1973) found that one period of unusual distress on the part of the experimenter preparing the targets was associated with the most pronounced ψH scoring in the study. An experimental manipulation of the wishes for success or failure on the part of an experimenter was carried out by Schmeidler (1958). Experimenters acted as active agents (GESP) in one condition, hoped for the subjects' success while handling the targets without looking at them in another, and hoped for failure in the third. No overall differences were found, but a significant negative correlation was found between GESP scores and scores in the wish-for-failure condition, suggesting that the experimenter's set or wish can have an effect in the clairvoyance situations. A follow-up study (Schmeidler, 1961) offered further support for this general contention.

An interesting bit of speculation on the importance of the agent and some relevant data have come from Langdon-Davies (1956), who considers the agent to function as a *point d'appui*. After many tedious series of DT self-testing taking account of variables such as the weather, health, drugs, fatigue, mood, etc., a very frustrating flat chance result was found, with none of the hypothesized variables showing consistent relations to scoring. He then decided to select an object of focus for dramatic exteriorization, someone (not there) to "appeal to," "blame for," etc., the phenomena. The medium Eileen Garrett (whom he had never met) was selected and her picture erected as an imaginary agent. He proceeded to scold her vigorously when results were bad, feel intense gratitude when they were good, etc. The tests took on a new liveliness and excitment, and over 200 runs of testing significant ψH ($Z = 4$) were observed. The author hypothesized that this "dramatic exteriorization" is the function of the target person for the successful medium or psychic and of the agent in successful GESP tests. The possibility is an interesting one, although the fact that a few *agent* (mood and set) effects, as noted just above, have been reported suggests that the agent's conscious experience may act as an orienting variable, if not as a literal transmitter of information.

SUBJECT-SUBJECT EFFECTS AND EXPERIMENTER EFFECTS

Subject-subject variables have been very sparely studied by parapsychologists. A few findings suggest that they might bear further looking into. J. B. Rhine (1964), reviewing some cases of exceptionally high ESP scoring, noted that an atmosphere of contagious enthusiasm and of intense "audience appreciation" for the successful scorer was an important feature. Steen (1957) and Ratte (1961) both found a gamelike ESP test to promote enthusiasm and ψH scoring. Kanthamani (1966) carried out a pilot and three experimental series in which pairs of same-sex junior high school students took turns picking and guessing ESP cards enclosed in envelopes in a pile on a table. The experimenter urged them to compete for the greatest number of hits and tried to promote a warm, excited, and appreciative interpersonal atmosphere. Using her impressions of each pair's initial interaction, and the first run-score with each pair as bases, Kanthamani made and recorded a prediction as to which of the pair would score higher. The first runs were excluded from the calculations. The predicted-higher scorers produced ψH scoring in all series, and the predicted-lower scorers produced ψM in all series, the total differences in all series being significant ($P < .01$). Testing the possibility that relative dominance was responsible for the difference, she administered the Allport Ascendance-Submission Scale and solicited teachers' ratings of dominance; but neither related to success. Kanthamani spelled out several factors which could have contributed to the effect and urged further research on them; but none has been reported.

The area of experimenter effects is outside the scope of this paper (see Rhea White's chapter in this volume), but is mentioned in passing since it clearly suggests, as do the agent-percipient and subject-subject studies, that the network of interpersonal relations containing the experiment cannot be avoided if a full account of effective factors is ever to be constructed. In a relatively large number of studies the experimenter himself or herself has been noticed to have exerted differential effects on scoring (e.g., Pratt and Price, 1938; Sharp and Clark, 1937, Woodruff and Dale, 1950). A relatively long series of studies (e.g., Anderson and Gregory, 1959; Anderson and White, 1958) has been reported on the mutual effect of students' evaluative attitudes toward the teachers and the teachers' toward the students, when students were tested by teachers in classroom clairvoyance tests. These relationships were retested about as widely as any have been in parapsychology, and although relatively replicative, enough failures occurred to indicate that they did not provide "the repeatable experiment" as the authors had apparently hoped.

One study by Honorton, Ramsey, and Cabibbo (1975) can be mentioned in more detail as an example of the potential importance this area seems to have. Precognitive guesses were elicited from subjects after they had first been involved in a 15-minute interaction with an experimenter who was deliberately either "friendly, casual, and supportive" or "abrupt, formal, and unfriendly." Both of two experimenters played each role half of the time. Manipulation checks showed the subjects experienced the interactions in the ways that had been intended. Those subjects who had been treated in a friendly way scored ψH and the others scored ψM.

A final study to be mentioned is that of Akolkar and Ghate (1969) because of the interesting similarity of its results to those found by Skibinsky (1950), comparing family names to symbols as targets, and by Casper (1952) comparing most-liked and least-liked opposite-sex agents. Akolkar and Ghate conducted BT tests in which the students acting as experimenters (handling the target cards) were those who had been rated as the "emotionally closest" and "emotionally most distant" by each student acting as subject. To their surprise, the researchers found ψH trends in the "distant" agent-subject pairs and ψM in the "close" (P of difference = .01). Pooling these results, I would like to phrase an hypothesis which could receive future test: whenever a subject is exposed to two contiguous and contrasting experimental conditions, he is likely to believe that the experiment is "about" the difference between those conditions; and if the difference he perceives fits in with his own implicit "theories of psi" and appears to subject something important to him to critical scrutiny, then a fear of failure will result which will show itself as an avoidance (ψM) of the favored and threatening material and as an acceptance (ψH) of the contrasting threat-relieving material.

SOME CONCLUDING REMARKS

If the above material represents, as I have conjectured, an "assault upon coincidence," what may be said to be the outcome of the engagement? Clearly it is still being waged, and no definite settlement can be glimpsed. There do, however, appear to be some trends in the more recent literature which seem to make an ultimate settlement more promising; and I would like to mention and endorse them and suggest some other directions of change which might be facilitative.

Harder Heads

A trend toward greater sophistication in experimental design, logic, method, and analysis can be observed. Fewer major independent variables are left confounded with order, fewer statistical assumptions are being grossly violated, and, in the better recent work, complex multivariate correlational or analysis of variance designs are being appropriately applied to multivariate problems, in place of the approach of roaming about a multivariate array and stumbling onto the "ESP in" some treatment-combination. The better reports are being presented in adequate detail to permit discerning appraisal. Another development, as this review attests, is that attention to the whole range of experimental results has tended to replace argument over the value of large positive deviations as evidence for ESP. The presidential address of Gertrude Schmeidler (1959) to the Parapsychological Association in which that change was urged may have been somewhat pivotal in this respect. The model of a stable "ESP faculty" is being decently laid to rest, and the facts of the profound variability of ESP results are being squarely faced and dealt with as the meat for experiments. A helpful next step, or at least it seems so to me, would be the development of some channels by which null results could be made as easily accessible as positive results. Publication costs and the logically less-instructive nature of nonsignificant results may make it unreasonable to give such results much journal space. But some other centralized mechanism for recording null results and making them available to working researchers seems important. A recent suggestion by J. B. Rhine (1975) is pertinent and helpful in this respect. By his plan, such reports would be presented in abstract form in the scientific journals and be available in more detail upon individual request. With the burgeoning number of quantitative effects that have been construed as "psi," some way of appraising null results is necessary if workers are to protect themselves and their colleagues from self-deception. And it would seem just as helpful if they are to build a nomothetic set of constructs for use in piecing together the flux and vagary of experimental observations.

Construction vs. Inexplicability

The not-very-distant roots of parapsychology lie in the tradition of trying to account for odd anecdotes and to substantiate their occurrence through multiple corroboration of witnesses, character references, etc. In making an account, the psychical researcher tried to eliminate "normal" explanation and sometimes succeeded in leaving afterward a hard lump of undeniable mystery.

Substantiating the occurrence of odd anecdotes and proving their inexplicability is not a final goal for a scientist. It does not always seem appreciated by parapsychologists that the use of experimental method and statistical analysis does not by itself raise one above the level of establishing anecdotes. Statistics and method may provide assurance that "something" really happened, but no more than that. Scientific work depends upon the erection and test of conceptual continuents which are relentlessly applied to the press of future events, discarded or modified, and tested again. Some concepts in use by parapsychologists are not of much use as continuents. For example, this reviewer found the concept "strength of ESP" used to refer to overall significant positive deviations, negative deviations, large subject variance, large (positive and negative) run-score variances, small variances, and to a change of position effect pattern linked to both chance variances and overall chance deviation. Language so fluid is misleading since it implies reference to some continuent in nature when none is really intended. Constructs which are specific enough to carry testable implications are being ventured in more studies in recent years (examples are Stanford's [1967] "response-bias" hypothesis and Kreitler and Kreitler's [1974] "content-congruent vs. content-discrepant" construct, among others), and more such work seems necessary if progress is to be made in constructing replicative, nomothetic accounts of experimental phenomena.

What Kind of World?

The trends just mentioned toward more methodological sophistication, a broadened attention to all observations including null, and an effort to construct testable nomothetic continuents, are all ways in which parapsychologists have been trying to catch up with the best work now being done in other areas of psychology. There is another respect in which the parapsychologist may make a kind of contribution which would likely come from no other area of work, but how it might be done this reviewer confesses to having little idea. The kinds of impermeable boundaries between person and world and between person and person which are implied by the behavioristic assumptions which undergird most psychological research seem to be contradicted in principle by the kinds of findings parapsychologists report. For one thing the boundary often assumed between the experimenter and the subject, and between the experimenter and his observed results, may be no more obdurate than cheesecloth to a wispy guess, a vaporous wish. The Honorton, Ramsey, and Cabibbo (1975) findings, that seem to translate the experimenter's attitudes directly into the language of his findings, are stunning. It seems that the experimenter will not remain able to keep himself out of his descriptions of the world of process if he is a major source of those forces. A few other psychologists have been coming to feel increasingly confined by the mechanistic language which we have inherited as a science, particularly when wanting to deal with the intimacies of human meaning and relationship with others and the world. According to Harold McCurdy (1968), we may need to develop a language that is both dynamic and bipolar (including both observer and observed):

> To put it succinctly in an example; "she is growing beautiful," must not be dissociated from "I *see* that she is growing beautiful," or even "*because* I look at her as I do, she is growing beautiful." "She is growing beautiful" can be as factual as "the rocket is accelerating," but the experiment is different. To be sure, the acceleration of a rocket also depends on some human pre-conditions. But in the case of "she is growing beautiful" the bipolarity of observer and observed is peculiarly essential. To report the fact accurately we must include ourselves in the description and admit that if our manner of looking has changed her, her manner of change affects in turn our manner of looking. We must describe, that is, a whole relational universe (p. 321).

It is toward such an understanding of the world that the parapsychologists with their constructions also seem to be struggling.

REFERENCES

Akolkar, V. V., and Ghate, A. K. Emotional distance and ESP test scores. *Journal of Parapsychology*, 1969, 33, 158.

Anderson, M. A precognition experiment comparing time intervals of a few days and one year. *Journal of Parapsychology*, 1959, 23, 81–89.

Anderson, M., and Gregory, E. A two-year program of tests for clairvoyance and precognition with a class of public school pupils. *Journal of Parapsychology*, 1959, **23**, 149–177.

Anderson, M., and White, R. The relationship between changes in student attitude and ESP scoring. *Journal of Parapsychology*, 1958, **22**, 167–174.

Ballard, J. A. A psi task with hidden erotic and neutral stimuli. *Journal of Parapsychology*, 1975, **39**, 34.

Banham, K. M. Temporary high scoring by a child subject. *Journal of Parapsychology*, 1966, **30**, 106–113.

Bastin, E. W., and Green, J. M. Some experiments in precognition. *Journal of Parapsychology*, 1953, **17**, 137–143.

Bednarz, K., and Verrier, M. Role of the experimenter in GESP tests. *Journal of Parapsychology*, 1969, **33**, 159.

Beloff, J. The "sweethearts" experiment. *Journal of the Society for Psychical Research*, 1969, **45**, 1–7.

Bender, H. Differential scoring of an outstanding subject on GESP and clairvoyance. *Journal of Parapsychology*, 1970, **34**, 272–273.

Bergson, H. *Mind Energy*. New York: Henry Holt, 1920.

Bierman, D. J., and Camstra, B. GESP in the classroom. In W. G. Roll, R. L. Morris, and J. D. Morris (Eds.), *Research in Parapsychology 1972*, pp. 168–170. Metuchen, N.J.: Scarecrow Press, 1973.

Bleksley, A. E. An experiment on long-distance ESP during sleep. *Journal of Parapsychology*, 1963, **27**, 1–15.

Blom, J. G., and Pratt, J. G. A second confirmatory ESP experiment with Pavel Stepanek as a "borrowed" subject. *Journal of the American Society for Psychical Research*, 1968, **62**, 28–45.

Bottrill, J. Frequency as related to accuracy of ESP card calls. *Journal of Parapsychology*, 1969, **33**, 70–71.

Brier, R. M. A mass school test of precognition. *Journal of Parapsychology*, 1969, **33**, 125–135.

Buzby, D. E. Subject attitude and score variance in ESP tests. *Journal of Parapsychology*, 1967, **31**, 43–50. (a)

Buzby, D. E. Precognition and a test of sensory perception. *Journal of Parapsychology*, 1967, **31**, 135–142. (b)

Buzby, D. E. Precognition and psychological variables. *Journal of Parapsychology*, 1968, **32**, 39–46. (a)

Buzby, D. E. Precognition and clairvoyance as related to the Draw-a-Man test. *Journal of Parapsychology*, 1968, **32**, 237–243. (b)

Buzby, D. E. Further search for evidence of a pattern in the functioning of psi. *Journal of Parapsychology*, 1969, **33**, 323.

Cadoret, R. J. Effect of novelty in test conditions on ESP performance. *Journal of Parapsychology*, 1952, **16**, 192–203.

Carington, W. W. Experiments on the paranormal cognition of drawings. *Journal of Parapsychology*, 1940, **4**, 1–129.

Carlson, M. L. Subject and "experimenter" moods and scoring on a correspondence ESP test. *Journal of Parapsychology*, 1970, **34**, 273–274.

Carpenter, J. C. Scoring effects within the run. *Journal of Parapsychology*, 1966, **30**, 73–83.

Carpenter, J. C. Two related studies on mood and precognition run-score variance. *Journal of Parapsychology*, 1968, **32**, 75–89. (a)

Carpenter, J. C. Psi prediction with the use of run-score variance and mood-sampling techniques. *Journal of Parapsychology*, 1968, **32**, 258–259. (b)

Carpenter, J. C. Further study on a mood-adjective check list and ESP run-score variance. *Journal of Parapsychology*, 1969, 33, 48–56.

Carpenter, J. C. The differential effect and hidden target differences consisting of erotic and neutral stimuli. *Journal of the American Society for Psychical Research*, 1971, 65, 204–214.

Carpenter, J. C. Validating research on a mood-adjective scale for predicting run-score variance. In W. G. Roll, R. L. Morris, and J. D. Morris (Eds.), *Research in Parapsychology 1972*, pp. 145–148. Metuchen, N.J.: Scarecrow Press, 1973.

Carpenter, J. C. Toward the effective utilization of enhanced weak-signal ESP effects. Paper presented at the annual meeting of American Association for the Advancement of Science, New York, N.Y., Jan. 27, 1975.

Carpenter, J. C., and Carpenter, J. C. Decline of variability of ESP scoring across a period of effort. *Journal of Parapsychology*, 1967, 31, 179–191.

Casler, L. Hypnotically induced interpersonal relationships and their influence on GESP. *Journal of Parapsychology*, 1969, 33, 337–338.

Casper, G. W. A further study of the relation of attitude to success in ESP scoring. *Journal of Parapsychology*, 1951, 15, 139–145.

Casper, G. W. Effect of the receiver's attitude toward the sender in ESP tests. *Journal of Parapsychology*, 1952, 16, 212–218.

Chauvin, R. ESP and size of target symbols. *Journal of Parapsychology*, 1961, 25, 185–189.

Chauvin, R., and Darchen, R. Can clairvoyance be influenced by screens? *Journal of Parapsychology*, 1963, 27, 33–43.

Crumbaugh, J. C. Variance declines as indicators of a stimulator-suppressor mechanism in ESP. *Journal of the American Society for Psychical Research*, 1968, 6?, 356–365.

Dalton, G. F. Operative factors in spontaneous telepathy. *Journal of the Society for Psychical Research*, 1956, 38, 287–319.

Ehrenwald, J. Telepathy and the child-parent relationship. *Journal of the American Society for Psychical Research*, 1954, 48, 43–55.

Eilbert, L., and Schmeidler, G. R. A study of certain psychological factors in relation to ESP performance. *Journal of Parapsychology*, 1950, 14, 53–74.

Elkisch, P. Children's drawings in a projective technique. *Psychological Monographs*, 1945, 58, 1–31.

Estabrooks, G. H. A contribution to experimental telepathy. *Bulletin of the Boston Society for Psychic Research*, 1927, 5, 1–30.

Fahler, J., and Osis, K. Checking for awareness of hits in a precognition experiment with hypnotized subjects. *Journal of the American Society for Psychical Research*, 1966, 60, 340–346.

Fisk, G. W. Home-testing ESP experiments: A preliminary report. *Journal of the Society for Psychical Research*, 1951, 36, 369–370.

Fisk, G. W., and West, D. J. ESP tests with erotic symbols. *Journal of the Society for Psychical Research*, 1955, 38, 1–7. (a)

Fisk, G. W., and West, D. J. ESP tests with erotic symbols: Corrections, and interpretation of results. *Journal of the Society for Psychical Research*, 1955, 38, 134–136. (b)

Fisk, G. W., and West, D. J. ESP and mood: Report of a "mass" experiment. *Journal of the Society for Psychical Research*, 1956, 38, 320–329.

Foster, E. B. A re-examination of Dr. Soal's "clairvoyance" data. *Journal of Parapsychology*, 1956, 20, 110–120.

Freeman, J. A. An ESP test involving emotionally toned objects. *Journal of Parapsychology*, 1961, 25, 260–265.

Freeman, J. A. An experiment in precognition. *Journal of Parapsychology*, 1962, 26, 123–130.

Freeman, J. A. A precognition test with a high-school science club. *Journal of Parapsychology*, 1964, **28**, 214–221.

Freeman, J. A. Differential response of the sexes to contrasting arrangements of ESP target material. *Journal of Parapsychology*, 1965, **29**, 251–258.

Freeman, J. A. A sequel report on a high-scoring child subject. *Journal of Parapsychology*, 1966, **30**, 39–47. (a)

Freeman, J. A. Sex differences and target arrangement: High-school booklet tests of precognition. *Journal of Parapsychology*, 1966, **30**, 227–235. (b)

Freeman, J. A. Sex differences, target arrangement, and primary mental abilities. *Journal of Parapsychology*, 1967, **31**, 271–279.

Freeman, J. A. Evidence of precognition in sex differences in the *Read* test. *Journal of Parapsychology*, 1968, **32**, 133.

Freeman, J. A. Decline of variance in school precognition tests. *Journal of Parapsychology*, 1969, **33**, 72–73. (a)

Freeman, J. A. The psi-differential effect in a precognition test. *Journal of Parapsychology*, 1969, **33**, 206–212. (b)

Freeman, J. A. A precognition experiment with science teachers. *Journal of Parapsychology*, 1969, **33**, 307–310. (c)

Freeman, J. A. Sex differences in ESP response as shown by the Freeman Picture-Figure Test. *Journal of Parapsychology*, 1970, **34**, 37–46. (a)

Freeman, J. A. Ten-page booklet tests with elementary-school children. *Journal of Parapsychology*, 1970, **34**, 192–196. (b)

Freeman, J. A. Mood, personality, and attitude in precognition tests. *Journal of Parapsychology*, 1970, **34**, 226–227. (c)

Freeman, J. A. Personality, PMA, and target differentiation in precognition tests. *Journal of Parapsychology*, 1970, **34**, 227–228. (d)

Freeman, J. A. Shift in scoring direction with junior-high-school students: A summary. *Journal of Parapsychology*, 1970, **34**, 275. (e)

Freeman, J. A. Sex differences in an ESP test. *Journal of Parapsychology*, 1971, **35**, 58–59.

Freeman, J. A. The psi quiz: A new ESP test. In W. G. Roll, R. L. Morris, and J. D. Morris (Eds.), *Research in Parapsychology 1972*, pp. 132–134. Metuchen, N.J.: Scarecrow Press, 1973.

Freeman, J. A., and Nielsen, W. Precognition score deviations as related to anxiety levels. *Journal of Parapsychology*, 1964, **28**, 239–249.

Gauld, A. *The Founders of Psychical Research*. New York: Schocken Books, 1968.

Gibson, E. P. A study of comparative performance in several ESP procedures. *Journal of Parapsychology*, 1937, **1**, 264–275.

Glidden, S. H. A random-behavior maze test for humans. *Journal of Parapsychology*, 1974, **38**, 324–331.

Green, C. E. Analysis of spontaneous cases. *Proceedings of the Society for Psychical Research*, 1960, **53**, 97–161.

Gurney, E., Myers, F. W. H., and Podmore, F. *Phantasms of the Living*. London: Trübner, 1886. 2 vols.

Hallett, S. J. A study of the effect of conditioning on multiple-aspect ESP scoring. *Journal of Parapsychology*, 1952, **16**, 204–211.

Haraldsson, E. Psychological variables in a GESP test using plethysmograph recordings. *Journal of Parapsychology*, 1970, **34**, 276.

Honorton, C. Effects of feedback on discrimination between correct and incorrect ESP responses. *Journal of the American Society for Psychical Research*, 1970, **64**, 404–410.

Honorton, C. Effects of feedback on discrimination between correct and incorrect ESP responses: A replication study. *Journal of the American Society for Psychical Research*, 1971, 65, 155–161.

Honorton, C. Ramsey, M., and Cabibbo, C. Experimenter effects in extrasensory perception. *Journal of the American Society for Psychical Research*, 1975, 69, 135–149.

Hudesman, J., and Schmeidler, G. R. ESP scores following therapeutic sessions. *Journal of the American Society for Psychical Research*, 1971, 65, 215–222.

Humphrey, B. M. Patterns of success in an ESP experiment. *Journal of Parapsychology*, 1943, 7, 5–19.

Humphrey, B. M. Success in ESP as related to form of response drawings. I. Clairvoyance experiments. *Journal of Parapsychology*, 1946, 10, 78–106. (a)

Humphrey, B. M. Success in ESP as related to form of response drawings. II. GESP experiments. *Journal of Parapsychology*, 1946, 10, 181–196. (b)

Humphrey, B. M. The relation of ESP to mode of drawing. *Journal of Parapsychology*, 1949, 13, 31–46.

Humphrey, B. M., and Nicol, J. F. The feeling of success in ESP. *Journal of the American Society for Psychical Research*, 1955, 49, 3–37.

Humphrey, B. M., and Rhine, J. B. A confirmatory study of salience in precognition tests. *Journal of Parapsychology*, 1942, 6, 190–219.

Hutchinson, L. Variations of time intervals in pre-shuffle card-calling tests. *Journal of Parapsychology*, 1940, 4, 249–270.

James, W. The final impressions of a psychical researcher. In G. Murphy and R. O. Ballou (Eds.), *William James on Psychical Research*, pp. 309–325. New York: Viking Press, 1960.

Jephson, I. Evidence for clairvoyance in card-guessing. *Proceedings of the Society for Psychical Research*, 1928, 38, 223–271.

Johnson, M., and Nordbeck, B. Variation in the scoring behavior of a "psychic" subject. *Journal of Parapsychology*, 1972, 36, 122–132.

Jones, J. N., and Feather, S. R. Relationship between reports of psi experiences and subject variance. *Journal of Parapsychology*, 1969, 33, 311–319.

Kahn, S. D. Studies in extrasensory perception: Experiments utilizing an electronic scoring device. *Proceedings of the American Society for Psychical Research*, 1952, 25, 1–48.

Kanthamani, B. K. A study of the differential response in language ESP tests. *Journal of Parapsychology*, 1965, 29, 27–34.

Kanthamani, B. K. ESP and social stimulus. *Journal of Parapsychology*, 1966, 30, 31–38.

Kanthamani, B. K., and Rao, K. R. Personality characteristics of ESP subjects: V. Graphic expansiveness and ESP. *Journal of Parapsychology*, 1973, 37, 119–129.

Kanthamani, H. Psi in relation to task complexity. *Journal of Parapsychology*, 1974, 38, 154–162.

Kanthamani, H., and Kelly, E. F. Awareness of success in an exceptional subject. *Journal of Parapsychology*, 1974, 38, 355–382.

Keil, H. H. J., and Pratt, J. G. Further ESP tests with Pavel Stepanek in Charlottesville dealing with the focusing effect. *Journal of the American Society for Psychical Research*, 1969, 63, 253–272.

Klein, J. A comparison of clairvoyance and telepathy. *Journal of Parapsychology*, 1971, 35, 335.

Kreitler, H., and Kreitler, S. Does extrasensory perception affect psychological experiments? *Journal of Parapsychology*, 1972, 36, 1–45.

Kreitler, H., and Kreitler, S. Subliminal perception and extrasensory perception. *Journal of Parapsychology*, 1973, 37, 163–188.

Kreitler, H., and Kreitler, S. Optimization of experimental ESP results. *Journal of Parapsychology*, 1974, 38, 383–392.

Langdon-Davies, J. What is the agent's role in ESP? *Journal of the Society for Psychical Research*, 1956, **38**, 329–337.

Langdon-Davies, J., Langdon-Davies, P., Bateman, F., and Soal, S. G. ESP tests with a Spanish girl. *Journal of Parapsychology*, 1955, **19**, 155–163.

Louwerens, N. G. ESP experiments with nursery school children in the Netherlands. *Journal of Parapsychology*, 1960, **24**, 75–93.

Machover, K. *Personality Projection in the Drawing of the Human Figure*. Springfield, Ill.: Charles C Thomas, 1949.

Martin, D. R., and Stribic, F. P. Studies in extrasensory perception: III. A review of all University of Colorado experiments. *Journal of Parapsychology*, 1940, 4, 159–248.

McBain, W. N., Fox, W., Kimura, S., Nakanishi, M., and Tirado, J. Quasi-sensory communication: An investigation using semantic matching and accentuated affect. *Journal of Parapsychology*, 1970, **34**, 66–67.

McCollam, E., and Honorton, C. Effects of feedback on discrimination between correct and incorrect ESP responses: A further replication and extension. *Journal of the American Society for Psychical Research*, 1973, **67**, 77–85.

McCurdy, H. G. Personal knowing and making. In T. A. Langford and W. H. Poteat (Eds.), *Intellect and Hope: Essays in the Thought of Michael Polanyi*, pp. 315–340. Durham, N.C.: Duke University Press, 1968.

McGuire, K., Percy, E., and Carpenter, J. C. A multivariate approach to the prediction of ESP test performance. In W. G. Roll, R. L. Morris, and J. D. Morris (Eds.), *Research in Parapsychology 1973*, pp. 34–35. Metuchen, N.J.: Scarecrow Press, 1974.

McMahan, E. A. An experiment in pure telepathy. *Journal of Parapsychology*, 1946, **10**, 224–242.

Michie, D., and West, D. J. A mass ESP test using television. *Journal of the Society for Psychical Research*, 1957, **39**, 113–133.

Mischo, J. The Achtert-Zutz GESP experiments over a distance. *Journal of Parapsychology*, 1968, **32**, 283–284.

Morris, R. L. Guessing habits and ESP. *Journal of Parapsychology*, 1971, **35**, 335–336.

Mosher, D. J. The development and multi-trait-method matrix analysis of three measures of three aspects of guilt. *Journal of Consulting Psychology*, 1960, **30**, 25–29.

Moss, T., and Gengerelli, J. A. ESP effects generated by affective states. *Journal of Parapsychology*, 1968, **32**, 90–100.

Murphy, G. The problem of repeatability in psychical research. *Journal of the American Society for Psychical Research*, 1971, **65**, 3–16.

Murphy, G., and Ballou, R. O. (Eds.). *William James on Psychical Research*. New York: Viking, 1960.

Musso, J. R., and Granero, M. An ESP drawing experiment with a high-scoring subject. *Journal of Parapsychology*, 1973, **37**, 13–36.

Nash, C. B. Can precognition occur diametrically? *Journal of Parapsychology*, 1960, **24**, 26–32.

Nash, C. B. Retest of high-scoring subjects in the Chesebrough-Pond's ESP television contest. *Journal of the American Society for Psychical Research*, 1963, **57**, 106–110.

Nash, C. B., and Nash, C. S. Checking success and the relationship of personality traits to ESP. *Journal of the American Society for Psychical Research*, 1958, **52**, 98–107.

Nash, C. S., and Nash, C. B. Effect of target selection, field dependence, and body concept on ESP performance. *Journal of Parapsychology*, 1968, **32**, 249–257.

Nicol, J. F., and Humphrey, B. M. The exploration of ESP and human personality. *Journal of the American Society for Psychical Research*, 1953, **47**, 133–178.

Nielsen, W. An exploratory precognition experiment. *Journal of Parapsychology*, 1956, **20**, 33–39. (a)

Nielsen, W. Mental states associated with success in precognition. *Journal of Parapsychology*, 1956, **20**, 96–109. (b)

Nielsen, W. Relationships between precognition scoring level and mood. *Journal of Parapsychology*, 1970, **34**, 93–116.

Nielsen, W., and Freeman, J. A. Consistency of relationship between ESP and emotional variables. *Journal of Parapsychology*, 1965, **29**, 75–88.

Nowlis, V. Methods for studying mood changes produced by drugs. *Revue de Psychologie Applique*, 1961, **11**, 373–386.

Nowlis, V. Research with the mood-adjective check list. In S. S. Tomkins and C. E. Izard (Eds.), *Affect, Cognition and Personality*, pp. 352–389. New York: Springer, 1965.

Osis, K. Precognition over time intervals of one to thirty-three days. *Journal of Parapsychology*, 1955, **19**, 82–91.

Osis, K. ESP tests at long and short distances. *Journal of Parapsychology*, 1956, **20**, 81–95.

Osis, K. Transient states and ESP. *Journal of Parapsychology*, 1968, **32**, 292–293.

Osis, K., and Bokert, E. ESP and changed states of consciousness induced by meditation. *Journal of the American Society for Psychical Research*, 1971, **65**, 17–65.

Osis, K., and Carlson, M. L. The ESP channel—open or closed? *Journal of the American Society for Psychical Research*, 1972, **66**, 310–320.

Osis, K., and Dean, D. The effect of experimenter differences and subjects' belief level upon ESP scores. *Journal of the American Society for Psychical Research*, 1964, **58**, 158–185.

Osis, K., and Pienaar, D. C. ESP over a distance of seventy-five hundred miles. *Journal of Parapsychology*, 1956, **20**, 229–232.

Osis, K., Turner, M. E. Jr., and Carlson, M. L. ESP over distance: Research on the ESP channel. *Journal of the American Society for Psychical Research*, 1971, **65**, 245–288.

Otani, S. Call patterns related to scoring on a clairvoyance test. *Journal of Parapsychology*, 1968, **32**, 57–58 (a)

Otani, S. ESP testing with and without knowledge of participation. *Journal of Parapsychology*, 1968, **32**, 134. (b)

Palmer, J. Scoring on ESP tests as a function of belief in ESP. Part II. Beyond the sheep-goat effect. *Journal of the American Society for Psychical Research*, 1972, **66**, 1–26.

Palmer, J. Review of "Experimental studies of the differential effect in life setting," by P. Sailaja and K. R. Rao. *Journal of the American Society for Psychical Research*, 1974, **68**, 104–109.

Pegram, M. H. Some psychological relations of extrasensory perception. *Journal of Parapsychology*, 1937, **1**, 191–205.

Pratt, J. G. The reinforcement effect in ESP displacement. *Journal of Parapsychology*, 1951, **15**, 103–117.

Pratt, J. G. ESP success and trial position. *Journal of the American Society for Psychical Research*, 1953, **47**, 33–37. (a)

Pratt, J. G. Position effects in the Stewart ESP data. *Journal of Parapsychology*, 1953, **17**, 130–136. (b)

Pratt, J. G. Run salience in the Pratt-Woodruff series. *Journal of Parapsychology*, 1961, **25**, 130–135.

Pratt, J. G. Computer studies of the ESP process in card-guessing: I. Displacement effects in Mrs. Gloria Stewart's data. *Journal of the American Society for Psychical Research*, 1967, **61**, 25–46.

Pratt, J. G. Seeking the trail of the focusing effect: Part I. An exploratory investigation of Pavel Stepanek in Prague. *Journal of the American Society for Psychical Research*, 1968, **62**, 158–170. (a)

Pratt, J. G. Seeking the trail of the focusing effect: Part II. The first stage of ESP research with Pavel Stepanek in Charlottesville. *Journal of the American Society for Psychical Research*, 1968, **62**, 171–189. (b)

Pratt, J. G. A decade of research with a selected ESP subject: An overview and reappraisal of the work with Pavel Stepanek. *Proceedings of the American Society for Psychical Research*, 1973, **30**, 1–78.

Pratt, J. G., and Foster, E. B. Displacement in ESP card tests in relation to hits and misses. *Journal of Parapsychology*, 1950, **14**, 37–52.

Pratt, J. G., and Keil, H. J. The focusing effect as patterned behavior based on habitual object-word associations: A working hypothesis with supporting evidence. *Journal of the American Society for Psychical Research*, 1969, **63**, 314–337.

Pratt, J. G., Keil, H. J., and Stevenson, I. Three-experimenter ESP tests of Pavel Stepanek during his 1968 visit to Charlottesville. *Journal of the American Society for Psychical Research*, 1970, **64**, 18–39.

Pratt, J. G., and Price, M. M. The experimenter-subject relationship in tests for ESP. *Journal of Parapsychology*, 1938, **2**, 84–94.

Pratt, J. G., and Ransom, C. Extrasensory perception or extraordinary sensory perception? A recent series of experiments with Pavel Stepanek. *Journal of the American Society for Psychical Research*, 1972, **66**, 63–85.

Pratt, J. G., and Roll, W. G. Confirmation of the focusing effect in further ESP research with Pavel Stepanek in Charlottesville. *Journal of the American Society for Psychical Research*, 1968, **62**, 226–245.

Pratt, J. G., and Woodruff, J. L. Size of stimulus symbols in extrasensory perception. *Journal of Parapsychology*, 1939, **3**, 121–158.

Price, A. D. Subjects' control of imagery, "agent's" mood, and position effects in a dual-target ESP experiment. *Journal of Parapsychology*, 1973, **37**, 298–322.

Randall, J. Group ESP experiments with schoolboys. *Journal of Parapsychology*, 1972, **36**, 133–143.

Rao, K. R. The preferential effect in ESP. *Journal of Parapsychology*, 1962, **26**, 252–259.

Rao, K. R. Studies in the preferential effect. I. Target preference with types of target unknown. *Journal of Parapsychology*, 1963, **27**, 23–32. (a)

Rao, K. R. Studies in the preferential effect. II. A language ESP test involving precognition and "intervention." *Journal of Parapsychology*, 1963, **27**, 147–160. (b)

Rao, K. R. Studies in the preferential effect. III. The reversal effect in psi preference. *Journal of Parapsychology*, 1963, **27**, 242–251. (c)

Rao, K. R. Studies in the preferential effect. IV. The role of key cards in preferential response situations. *Journal of Parapsychology*, 1964, **28**, 28–41. (a)

Rao, K. R. The differential response in three new situations. *Journal of Parapsychology*, 1964, **28**, 81–92. (b)

Rao, K. R. ESP and the manifest anxiety scale. *Journal of Parapsychology*, 1965, **29**, 12–18. (a)

Rao, K. R. The bidirectionality of psi. *Journal of Parapsychology*, 1965, **29**, 230–250. (b)

Rao, K. R. *Experimental Parapsychology*. Springfield, Ill.: Charles C Thomas, 1966.

Ratte, R. Three exploratory studies of ESP in a game situation. *Journal of Parapsychology*, 1961, **25**, 175–184.

Reeves, M. P., and Rhine, J. B. Exceptional scores in ESP tests and the conditions. I. The case of Lillian. *Journal of Parapsychology*, 1942, **6**, 164–173.

Rhine, J. B. *Extrasensory Perception*. Boston: Boston Society for Psychic Research, 1934.

Rhine, J. B. Experiments bearing on the precognition hypothesis: I. Preshuffling card-calling. *Journal of Parapsychology*, 1938, **2**, 38–54.

Rhine, J. B. Terminal salience in ESP performance. *Journal of Parapsychology*, 1941, **5**, 183–244.

Rhine, J. B. The problem of psi-missing. *Journal of Parapsychology*, 1952, **16**, 90–129.

Rhine, J. B. On the nature and consequences of the unconsciousness of psi. *Journal of Parapsychology*, 1958, **22**, 175–186.

Rhine, J. B. The precognition of computer numbers in a public test. *Journal of Parapsychology*, 1962, **26**, 244–251.

Rhine, J. B. Special motivation in some exceptional ESP performances. *Journal of Parapsychology*, 1964, **28**, 42–50.

Rhine, J. B. Psi-missing re-examined. *Journal of Parapsychology*, 1969, 33, 1–38. (a)

Rhine, J. B. Position effects in psi test results. *Journal of Parapsychology*, 1969, 33, 136–157. (b)

Rhine, J. B. Comments: "Publication policy regarding nonsignificant results." *Journal of Parapsychology*, 1975, **39**, 135–142.

Rhine, J. B., Pratt, J. G., Smith, B. M., Stuart, C. E., and Greenwood, J. A. *Extrasensory Perception after Sixty years*. New York: Holt, 1940.

Rhine, L. E. The relationship of agent and percipient in spontaneous telepathy. *Journal of Parapsychology*, 1956, **20**, 1–32.

Rhine, L. E. Toward understanding psi-missing. *Journal of Parapsychology*, 1965, **29**, 259–274.

Rice, G. E., Williss, D., Lafferty, C., Little, J., and Mauldin, C. H. Emotional closeness, communication of affect, and ESP. *Journal of Parapsychology*, 1966, **30**, 282–283.

Rice, G. E., and Townsend, J. Agent-percipient relationship and GESP performance. *Journal of Parapsychology*, 1962, **26**, 211–217.

Richet, C. La suggestion mentale et le calcul des probabilités. *Revue Philosophique*, 1884, **18**, 609–674.

Riess, B. F. A case of high scores in card-guessing at a distance. *Journal of Parapsychology*, 1937, **1**, 260–263.

Roethlisberger, F. G., and Dickson, W. J. *Management and the Worker*. Cambridge, Mass.: Harvard University Press, 1939.

Rogers, D. P. Negative and positive affect and ESP run-score variance. *Journal of Parapsychology*, 1966, **30**, 151–159.

Rogers, D. P. An analysis for internal cancellation effects on some low-variance ESP runs. *Journal of Parapsychology*, 1967, **31**, 192–197. (a)

Rogers, D. P. Negative and positive affect and ESP run-score variance—Study II. *Journal of Parapsychology*, 1967, **31**, 290–296. (b)

Rogers, D. P., and Carpenter, J. C. The decline of variance within a testing session. *Journal of Parapsychology*, 1966, **30**, 141–150.

Roll, W. G. ESP and memory. *International Journal of Neuropsychiatry*, 1966, **2**, 505–521.

Roll, W. G., and Klein, J. Further forced-choice ESP experiments with Lalsingh Harribance. *Journal of the American Society for Psychical Research*, 1972, **66**, 103–112.

Roll, W. G., Morris, R. L., Damgaard, J. A., Klein, J., and Roll, M. Free verbal response experiments with Lalsingh Harribance. *Journal of the American Society for Psychical Research*, 1973, **67**, 197–207.

Roll, W. G., and Pratt, J. G. An ESP test with aluminum targets. *Journal of the American Society for Psychical Research*, 1968, **62**, 381–386.

Rose, L., and Rose, R. Psi experiments with Australian Aborigines. *Journal of Parapsychology*, 1951, **15**, 122–131.

Ryzl, M., Barendregt, J. T., Barkema, P. R., and Kappers, J. An ESP experiment in Prague. *Journal of Parapsychology*, 1965, **29**, 176–184.

Ryzl, M., and Beloff, J. Loss of stability of ESP performance in a high-scoring subject. *Journal of Parapsychology*, 1965, **29**, 1–11.

Ryzl, M., and Pratt, J. G. A further confirmation of stabilized ESP performance in a selected subject. *Journal of Parapsychology*, 1963, 27, 73–83. (a)

Ryzl, M., and Pratt, J. G. A repeated-calling ESP test with sealed cards. *Journal of Parapsychology*, 1963, 27, 161–174. (b)

Ryzl, M., and Pratt, J. G. The focusing of ESP upon particular targets. *Journal of Parapsychology*, 1963, 27, 227–241. (c)

Sailaja, P., and Rao, K. R. Experimental studies of the differential effect in life setting. *Parapsychological Monographs No. 13.* New York: Parapsychology Foundation, 1973.

Sanders, M. S. A comparison of verbal and written responses in a precognition experiment. *Journal of Parapsychology*, 1962, 26, 23–34.

Scherer, W. B. Spontaneity as a factor in ESP. *Journal of Parapsychology*, 1948, 12, 126–147.

Schmeidler, G. R. Agent-percipient relationships. *Journal of the American Society for Psychical Research*, 1958, 52, 47–69.

Schmeidler, G. R. Exploring the parameters of research variables. *Journal of Parapsychology*, 1959, 23, 238–250.

Schmeidler, G. R. Changing field relations of an ESP experiment. In J. G. Peatman and E. L. Hartley (Eds.), *Festschrift for Gardner Murphy*, pp. 94–105. New York: Harper & Row, 1960.

Schmeidler, G. R. Evidence for two kinds of telepathy. *International Journal of Parapsychology*, 1961, 3, 5–48.

Schmeidler, G. R. An experiment in precognitive clairvoyance. Part II. The reliability of the scores. *Journal of Parapsychology*, 1964, 28, 15–27. (a)

Schmeidler, G. R. An experiment on precognitive clairvoyance. Part V. Precognition scores related to feelings of success. *Journal of Parapsychology*, 1964, 28, 109–125. (b)

Schmeidler, G. R. A search for feedback in ESP: Part I. Session salience and stimulus preference. *Journal of the American Society for Psychical Research*, 1968, 62, 130–142.

Schmeidler, G. R. High ESP scores after a swami's brief instruction in meditation and breathing. *Journal of the American Society for Psychical Research*, 1970, 64, 100–103.

Schmeidler, G. R. Mood and attitude on a pretest as predictors of retest ESP performance. *Journal of the American Society for Psychical Research*, 1971, 65, 324–335.

Schmeidler, G. R., and Craig, J. G. Moods and ESP scores in group testing. *Journal of the American Society for Psychical Research*, 1972, 66, 280–287.

Schmeidler, G. R., and LeShan, L. An aspect of body image related to ESP scores. *Journal of the American Society for Psychical Research*, 1970, 64, 211–218.

Schmeidler, G. R., and Lewis, L. A search for feedback in ESP: Part II. High ESP scores after two successes on triple-aspect targets. *Journal of the American Society for Psychical Research*, 1968, 62, 255–262.

Schmeidler, G. R., and Lewis, L. A search for feedback in ESP: Part III. The preferential effect and the impatience effect. *Journal of the American Society for Psychical Research*, 1969, 63, 60–68.

Schmeidler, G. R., and McConnell, R. A. *ESP and Personality Patterns.* New Haven: Yale University Press, 1958.

Schmidt, H. Clairvoyance tests with a machine. *Journal of Parapsychology*, 1969, 33, 300–306.

Sharp, V., and Clark, C. C. Group tests for extrasensory perception. *Journal of Parapsychology*, 1937, 1, 123–142.

Skibinsky, M. A comparison of names and symbols in a distance ESP test. *Journal of Parapsychology*, 1950, 14, 140–156.

Smith, B. M., and Humphrey, B. M. Some personality characteristics related to ESP performance. *Journal of Parapsychology*, 1946, 10, 269–289.

Soal, S. G., and Bateman, F. Agents in opposition and conjunction. *Journal of Parapsychology*, 1950, **14**, 168–192.

Soal, S. G., and Bateman, F. *Modern Experiments in Telepathy*. New Haven: Yale University Press, 1954.

Soal, S. G., and Pratt, J. G. ESP performance and target sequence. *Journal of Parapsychology*, 1951, **15**, 192–215.

Stanford, R. G. Differential position effects for above-chance scoring sheep and goats. *Journal of Parapsychology*, 1964, **28**, 155–165.

Stanford, R. G. The effect of restriction of calling upon run-score variance. *Journal of Parapsychology*, 1966, **30**, 160–171. (a)

Stanford, R. G. A study of the cause of low run-score variance. *Journal of Parapsychology*, 1966, **30**, 236–242. (b)

Stanford, R. G. Response bias and the correctness of ESP test responses. *Journal of Parapsychology*, 1967, **31**, 280–289.

Stanford, R. G. Extrasensory effects upon "memory." *Journal of the American Society for Psychical Research*, 1970, **64**, 161–186.

Stanford, R. G. Extrasensory effects upon associative processes in a directed free-response task. *Journal of the American Society for Psychical Research*, 1973, **67**, 147–190.

Stanford, R. G., and Palmer, J. Some statistical considerations concerning process-oriented research in parapsychology. *Journal of the American Society for Psychical Research*, 1972, **66**, 166–179.

Stanford, R. G., and Palmer, J. Meditation prior to the ESP task: An EEG study with an outstanding ESP subject. In W. G. Roll, R. L. Morris, and J. D. Morris (Eds.), *Research in Parapsychology 1972*, pp. 34–36. Metuchen, N.J.: Scarecrow Press, 1973.

Stanford, R. G., and Pratt, J. G. Extrasensory elicitation of sensorially acquired response patterns? *Journal of the American Society for Psychical Research*, 1970, **64**, 296–302.

Stanford, R. G., and Stanford B. E. Shifts in ESG alpha rhythm as related to calling patterns and ESP run-score variance. *Journal of Parapsychology*, 1969, **33**, 39–47.

Steen, D. Success with complex targets in a PK baseball game. *Journal of Parapsychology*, 1957, **21**, 133–146.

Stuart, C. E. The effect of rate of movement in card matching tests of extrasensory perception. *Journal of Parapsychology*, 1938, **2**, 171–183.

Stuart, C. E. An ESP test with drawings. *Journal of Parapsychology*, 1942, **6**, 20–43.

Stuart, C. E. GESP experiments with the free response method. *Journal of Parapsychology*, 1946, **10**, 21–35.

Stuart, C. E., Humphrey, B. M., Smith, B. M., and McMahan, E. Personality measurements and ESP tests with cards and drawings. *Journal of Parapsychology*, 1947, **11**, 118–146.

Stuart, C. E., and Smith, B. M. A second study of the effect of tempo rates of matching. *Journal of Parapsychology*, 1942, **6**, 220–231.

Stump, J. P., Roll, W. G., and Roll, M. Some exploratory forced-choice ESP experiments with Lalsingh Harribance. *Journal of the American Society for Psychical Research*, 1970, **64**, 421–431.

Thouless, R. H. Experimental investigation by the Cambridge Psychical Research Group. *Journal of the Society for Psychical Research*, 1947, **34**, 112–115.

Thouless, R. H. A comparative study of performance in three psi tasks. *Journal of Parapsychology*, 1949, **13**, 263–273.

Thouless, R. H. *From Anecdote to Experiment in Psychical Research*. London: Routledge and Kegan Paul, 1972.

Tyrrell, G. N. M. Further research in extrasensory perception. *Proceedings of the Society for Psychical Research*, 1936, **44**, 99–168.

Van Busschbach, J. G. An investigation of extrasensory perception in school children. *Journal of Parapsychology*, 1953, **17**, 210–214.

Van Busschbach, J. G. A further report on an investigation of ESP in school children. *Journal of Parapsychology*, 1955, **19**, 73–81.

Van Busschbach, J. G. An investigation of ESP between teacher and pupils in American schools. *Journal of Parapsychology*, 1956, **20**, 71–80.

Van Busschbach, J. G. An investigation of ESP in the first and second grades of Dutch schools. *Journal of Parapsychology*, 1959, **23**, 227–237.

Van Busschbach, J. G. An investigation of ESP in first and second graders in American schools. *Journal of Parapsychology*, 1961, **25**, 161–174.

Van de Castle, R. L. An exploratory study of some variables relating to individual ESP performance. *Journal of Parapsychology*, 1953, **17**, 61–72.

Van de Castle, R. L. Differential patterns of ESP scoring as a function of differential attitudes toward ESP. *Journal of the American Society for Psychical Research*, 1957, **51**, 43–61.

West, D. J. ESP performance and the expansion-compression rating. *Journal of the Society for Psychical Research*, 1950, **35**, 295–308.

West, D. J. Dispersion of scores in ESP experiments. *Journal of the Society for Psychical Research*, 1951, **36**, 361–366.

West, D. J., and Fisk, G. W. A dual ESP experiment with clock cards. *Journal of the Society for Psychical Research*, 1953, **37**, 185–197.

White, R. A., and Angstadt, J. Student preferences in a two classroom GESP experiment with two student-agents acting simultaneously. *Journal of the American Society for Psychical Research*, 1963, **57**, 32–42. (a)

White, R. A., and Angstadt, J. A second classroom GESP experiment with student-agents acting simultaneously. *Journal of the American Society for Psychical Research*, 1963, **57**, 227–232. (b)

Whittlesey, J. R. B. Some curious ESP results in terms of variance. *Journal of Parapsychology*, 1960, **24**, 220–222.

Witkin, H. A., Dyk, R. B., Faterson, H. F., Goodenough, D. R., and Karp, S. A. *Psychological Differentiation: Studies of Development*. New York: Wiley, 1962.

Witkin, H. A., Lewis, H. B., Hertzman, M. Machover, K., Meissner, P. B., and Wapner, S. *Personality Through Perception*. New York: Harper & Row, 1954.

Woodruff, J. L. Effect on ESP scoring of an unexpected qualitative change in ESP material. In J. G. Peatman and E. L. Hartley (Eds.), *Festschrift for Gardner Murphy*, pp. 106–116. New York: Harper & Row, 1960.

Woodruff, J. L., and Dale, L. A. Subject and experimenter attitudes in relation to ESP scoring. *Journal of the American Society for Psychical Research*, 1950, **44**, 87–112.

Woodruff, J. L., and George, R. W. Experiments in extrasensory perception. *Journal of Parapsychology*, 1937, **1**, 18–30.

Woodruff, J. L., and Rhine, J. B. An experiment in precognition using dice. *Journal of Parapsychology*, 1942, **6**, 243–262.

Zotti, E., and Cohen, D. B. Effect of an ESP transmitter vs. a non-ESP transmitter in telepathy. *Journal of Parapsychology*, 1970, **34**, 232–233.

4

The Influence of Experimenter Motivation, Attitudes, and Methods of Handling Subjects on Psi Test Results

Rhea A. White

INTRODUCTION

The experimenter has been a neglected variable in parapsychological research. Yet it is the hypothesis of this article that there could hardly be a more significant area of investigation than the role of the experimenter, because not only may the achievement of extrachance results depend on the experimenter, but the experimenter may also affect the nature of the results obtained. Since only a few experiments bearing directly on the role of the experimenter have been reported (Crumbaugh, 1958; Honorton, Ramsey, and Cabibbo, 1975; Moss, 1966; Nash, 1960, 1968; Parker, 1975; Pratt and Price, 1938; and West and Fisk, 1953), this survey of the literature will necessarily contain many post-hoc analyses, observations, and clinical impressions about the role of the experimenter in parapsychological investigations. Its purpose, then, is not only to review what is known about the experimenter's role but to survey conjectures about it as well in the hope of suggesting as many leads as possible for future research.

This chapter will review the literature bearing on the role of the experimenter in eliciting psi test results, variations in results due to his attitude toward the experiment, and/or his methods of handling the subjects. Relevant material on data collectors, who serve in lieu of experimenters, will also be discussed. However, material on psi-mediated experimenter effects, effects associated with individual experimenters, and the relation of the experimenter to decline effects, the reversal effect, as well as the effect of other personnel taking part in experiments such as agents, observers, randomizers, and checkers to psi test results have deliberately been omitted from this chapter due to lack of space.

SUGGESTIONS REGARDING THE ROLE OF THE EXPERIMENTER IN ELICITING PSI TEST RESULTS

In any ESP or PK situation the experimenter-subject relationship may not only be an important determinant of whether the scores will be positive or negative, but it could also be *the* determining factor in whether any results of significance will be obtained at all. This led J. B. Rhine (1961) to define a psi experimenter not simply, as would commonly be supposed, as one who rules out all normal cues to the target and administers a randomized set of targets to the subject, but rather as one who can succeed in "liberating the psi function" (p. 2) under adequate testing conditions. Rhine and Pratt (1957) point out that the experimenter must be able to provide "the psychological conditions under which psi can operate" (p. 131). They stress that even though we cannot now describe the necessary psychological prerequisites for psi testing, we must nevertheless recognize that they exist and that any budding experimenter, before committing himself to an ambitious research project, had better find out by preliminary tests whether or not he can administer ESP or PK tests and get significant results, even if he cannot specify exactly how he does it.

Try hard as they may, not everyone can do this. For example, James Crumbaugh, although actively interested in parapsychology from his student days, has rarely been able to obtain significant results in an ESP test in spite of several attempts, one an elaborate study of experimenter attitudes and ESP test results (Crumbaugh, 1958). Donald West (West and Fisk, 1953) numbers himself along with Denys Parsons among those who get null results. John Beloff (1973) has eloquently remarked on the widespread inability of anyone on the eastern side of the Atlantic to obtain significant results in ESP experiments:

> There have been occasions this year when, getting together with my friends at the Society for Psychical Research in London, we have asked one another, in mournful tones, whether perhaps ESP is not just something that happens in America! . . . I must beg my American friends to believe me when I say that we have not been entirely idle over here. I do not wish to cite my own paltry efforts in this context (I may just be an incompetent investigator), but I cannot help recalling my indomitable friend Dr. George Medhurst who unhappily died about a year ago . . . . In addition to a distinguished career as an electrical engineer, Dr. Medhurst devoted practically all his leisure hours to parapsychology. Over the years he tested literally thousands of individuals, always hoping that another Shackleton might turn up or, at the very least, that he would obtain some firm evidence for the reality

of ESP. He died, alas, a disappointed man. Yet his experience was so common by British standards that it never evoked any comment; no one suggested, for example, that he had a negative effect on the phenomena (p. 197).

And yet, with all due respect to Drs. Beloff and Medhurst, it would appear that the latter did exercise a negative effect; yet this liability is not confined to British experimenters. In all justice I would have to add myself to the list of those who are unable to elicit psi in their subjects, a fact made most apparent when I was testing school children in Burlington, North Carolina, with my colleague, Dr. Margaret Anderson, who, on the contrary, is a highly gifted psi experimenter. While testing different classes at the same grade level and in the same schools and at the same time, she obtained significantly positive results ($CR = 3.1$, $P = .002$) while my subjects scored at chance (Van Busschbach, 1956). The CR of the difference between our scores was suggestive ($P = .03$).

Adrian Parker (1974), when a graduate student working under Beloff at the University of Edinburgh, tried to account for the dearth of significant ESP and PK test results in the British Isles by suggesting that it may be due to "some kind of experimenter factor, masking as a cultural difference" (p. 21).

Thus, although adequate controls in psi tests can be provided for according to the canons of science, getting subjects to demonstrate psi on such tests is an art. In fact, as long ago as 1949, Gardner Murphy (1949) suggested that there is no such thing as a gifted ESP subject *per se*. Rather, he proposed that whether or not a subject scores well in a psi test depends on the person who does the testing and the nature of the experimental conditions.

The Experimenter's Motivation

What is it about a successful psi experimenter that enables him to obtain significant results in a psi test? In the same article Gardner Murphy (1949) provided the following insightful suggestions:

> One of the outstanding things about the Duke University research, I think, has been the inculcation of certain attributes in certain experimenters which make it possible for them to set free something with certain individual subjects. This does not mean that they can always set it free, nor that what they obtain from one subject is the same as what they obtain from another. But my mind goes back to the year 1934, in which I first visited Rhine at Duke University, and saw the rugged force of the demands which he made upon his co-workers and subjects. In the light of his glowing intensity, it became possible to begin to understand the accounts given in his book of the way in which he had driven some of his subjects in the demand to get extrasensory phenomena. It may well have been this intensity which produced the results—including some of the best-authenticated long distance results which

we have in all this field. In the case of Schmeidler's studies in clairvoyance I believe the results may well have arisen from a very different kind of intensity, namely her sheer unwillingness to let people fail. And it was, I am convinced, the intensity of Mrs. Dale's devotion to her first independent PK experiment, of which she was so proud, and in which so much ego was invested, from which her brilliant positive results emerged. Whately Carington's methods were successful time and again with groups that he organized, and which caught his spirit; but no such comparable results have been easily obtainable away from the white heat of his own brilliant personality . . . . I doubt whether we can go on with the tradition that an experimenter—any experimenter—undertakes to test a subject—any subject—with a standard method—any standard method—for ESP or PK. If an experimenter in the abstract tests a subject in the abstract with a method in the abstract, experience shows that we can be pretty certain that we shall have nothing to show for our pains (pp. 13–14).

An example of a productively motivated experimenter not associated with Rhine was David Kahn. J. G. Pratt (1953) reviewed Kahn's (1952) experiment, which was the first experiment to record and check responses by machine, and asked why it succeeded when there were so many factors involved that one would expect to have inhibited results. First, marking IBM cards was not particularly likely, from a psychological point of view, to lead to significant results; and second, it was conducted in the Harvard Psychology Department, which had, if anything, a negative attitude toward parapsychology. Pratt suggests that the fact that Kahn succeeded against these odds in obtaining significant results over an extended period of testing might

lie in the personality and motivation of the chief experimenter himself. Kahn has a family background of long and deep interest in parapsychological phenomena. Furthermore, in his Sophomore year at Harvard, he took the lead in forming the Harvard Society for Parapsychology, an organization of undergraduate students whose aim was scientific study and research in parapsychology. Where others probably would have had no hope of success, Kahn was able to interest some members of the Psychology Department and of other departments in the University in his research and to get their cooperation at different stages of the investigation.

When the report is considered as the product of an undergraduate student working in such a difficult area of research under these circumstances, it is clear how strongly motivated he must have been and how unusual were the social gifts employed. The procedure, one in which machine scoring was used for the first time, assumed great importance for him and provided a worthy objective. This all creates a picture of a young experimenter, full of a deep sense of the importance of his work and driven to even greater heights of enthusiasm by the feeling that this was the research to end all criticism of ESP.

Kahn believed that one of the advantages of the machine-scoring test procedure was that it enabled the experimenter to keep in the background. A more likely interpretation is that the experimenter was a central factor, and a very large one indeed, in the success of the investigation (p. 221).

Others have also emphasized the social gifts of the effective experimenter, as well as the necessity for strong motivation. Rhine and Pratt (1957) say that "the fine art of interpersonal relations has probably never been better put to test than it has been in the development of a finely poised sense of the challenge of a psi experiment" (p. 134). Stanford, Zenhausern, Taylor, and Dwyer (1975) suggest that an extraverted experimenter is more effective than an introverted one. Schmeidler (1969) says of Margaret Anderson, who is well known for her ability to elicit psi in test subjects, that "she has a quality of controlled and organized enthusiasm which is infectious and can create in others the same kind of eagerness" (p. 89). Schmeidler and McConnell (1958) have suggested that "it may be that the subject-experimenter relationship . . . is largely a matter of the kind of mood which the experimenter tends to engender in his subjects. The successful experimenter might be one whose personality (or presentation of the task) evokes relatively uniform moods, which then allow the emergence of consistent ESP-personality effects" (p. 106).

J. B. Rhine has said many valuable things about the art of psi testing. Perhaps the most complete presentation of his ideas on this subject is contained in his article, "Conditions favoring success in psi tests" (1948). It is both a description of the role of the experimenter and a valuable personal statement of what he experienced when he was actively experimenting—and surely he was one of the most gifted experimenters this field has known. One quote will serve to provide the flavor of the entire article:

> Anyone who has taken part in a successful psi experiment knows that the pitch of interest developed is something out of the ordinary. Nobody could maintain it indefinitely, and it is not to be put on and taken off with a laboratory coat. Once the experimenter's high level of motivation runs its course, once he satisfies his intellectual curiosity and is thoroughly convinced of the occurrence of the psi phenomenon in question, he comes down to a more relaxed plane of living. As one looks back to his own days of most productive work with psi tests, he recalls a sense of adventure, of suspense, of concentration on the problem that one can acquire only through a very genuine and quite profound personal interest in knowing what the experiment will reveal. But once he is well satisfied, he cannot hope to recover the same spirit again over the same problem, not genuinely (p. 74).

And so an experimenter may have to ask a question of "profound and personal interest" that can be incorporated in or at least symbolized by the psi test situation, or results are not likely to be forthcoming. Rex Stanford appears to be deeply motivated in demonstrating nonintentional ESP and PK in the laboratory, and he is succeeding in doing so (Stanford, 1970, 1973;

Stanford et al., 1975). Charles Honorton is highly interested in demonstrating a relationship between psi and altered states of consciousness and has done so in several experiments (for example, Honorton, 1972a, 1972b; Honorton, Drucker, and Hermon, 1973; and Honorton and Harper, 1974). I have yet to be creative enough to devise a psi test that would concern my deep personal interests in parapsychology. Is that why I have failed as an experimenter?

Adrian Parker (1974) has pointed out that the demonstration of ESP is often associated with changes in consciousness and suggests that "it may be that some experimenters are good at inducing this state or change in state in the subject while others are not" (p. 21). The description of psi testing quoted from Rhine gives the impression that he himself may have been in an altered state when he was experimenting. I have personally observed Margaret Anderson to be in what appeared to be an exalted or at least elevated—if not an altered—state before, during, and after conducting an experiment. This state appears to be highly infectious, and it is easy to see how it could be a factor in eliciting psi test results. As it happens, Rhine and Pratt (1957) mention something similar in their textbook where they describe the most potent factor in an ESP experiment as "the quality of infectious enthusiasm that accompanies the initial discoveries of the research worker" (p. 132). It was the "discovery" of ESP and PK that fired Rhine's imagination and the flame was passed to his subjects and students. A different fuel stoked Anderson's fire, and doubtless something else fans the flame of a Stanford or an Honorton, but whatever it is, it looks as if it exalts the experimenter, is transmitted to the subject, and results in significant evidence of psi.

Need for Research on the Role of the Experimenter

Gardner Murphy (1948), in a clarion call for research on the personality of the experimenter in parapsychological research, wrote:

> Everyone who knew J. B. Rhine during the early days of the Duke work knew that a great deal depended upon the combination of flexibility and terrific determination which characterized him—attributes often thought to be mutually exclusive. An iron will and an irresistible determination to get a real performance out of his good subjects were combined with great gentleness and charm in dealing with each person as a person. Partly through modesty, but partly because he was blind to the fact himself, he never brought out clearly the role of the experimenter. The result was that the little paper by Pratt and Price which featured the differences in scoring level which were related to different experimenters came as something of an oddity or something of a shock. From all I have seen of these elusive phenomena over thirty years, I'm convinced that they come to certain people and not to others largely because of deep-seated personality factors in those investigating them and that the searchlight should be turned for a while di-

rectly upon the investigator. I know of no one anywhere who is doing this, and I regard it perhaps as the most striking example of blind spots among parapsychologists. Why not put the experimenters themselves through the works? (pp. 17–18).

Ten years later James Crumbaugh (1958) set out to do just that. Convinced by his own inability to get results that the most important factor in psi testing was the personality of the experimenter, he decided to investigate personality and attitudinal variables in both experimenters and subjects thought to be important ingredients of successful psi experiments. He conferred with the Duke Parapsychology Laboratory staff in designing the experiment and used a factorial design to manipulate the variables of self-confidence, insecurity, belief in ESP, and disbelief in ESP in 16 subjects and 16 experimenters working in long and short sessions. The results in the long sessions were marginally significant and mostly in the predicted direction. He therefore conferred once more with the Duke staff, further refined his experiment and repeated it using only the long sessions, and got chance results, which when added to the results from the long sessions in the first experiment, produced a total right at chance. Could it be that Crumbaugh, one of parapsychology's confirmed skeptics, somehow inhibited his own results? Whatever the answer, there is no question but that we are here in the presence of a great mystery. In the face of such a rebuff one must turn elsewhere to search for the key to the perplexities involved in psi testing. Some have suggested the answer may lie in the experimenter's attitude toward the subjects and his method of handling them. One thing is fairly certain—different experimenters obtain different results in psi tests.

DIFFERENTIAL RESULTS RELATED TO THE EXPERIMENTER IN PSI EXPERIMENTS

Differences Between Experimenters

Whatever it is that a successful experimenter does, it has often been observed that differential results are obtained by different experimenters when testing the same or similar subjects.

MacFarland (1938) tested five subjects who made 15,300 calls at two different target decks simultaneously handled by an experimenter who had previously obtained consistently positive results and an experimenter who had only obtained chance results. Again significant positive scoring ($CR = 11$) occurred on the targets handled by the first experimenter while only chance results were obtained on the second experimenter's targets. The CR of the difference was highly significant: 7.7. Neither experimenter was in the same room as the subjects during the testing. (Kennedy [1939] found recording errors in MacFarland's data, but Stuart [1940] reexamined the data following Kennedy's criticism and found that the results were still highly significant even when the recording errors were taken into account.)

Nicol and Humphrey (1953) found striking differences in the results of the same subjects when each served as an experimenter using the same test and under similar conditions. Bednarz and Verrier (1969) each administered individual GESP tests to 50 of their college classmates. For the 100 subjects tested, half the time one experimenter administered the test while the other acted as an observer and recorded the results. The total results were significantly negative $(P = <.01)$. The bulk of the negative deviation, however, was contributed by the subjects tested by only one of the experimenters (K. B.). The report does not say whether the difference in scoring between the subjects tested by the two experimenters was significant. Presumably it was not.

Unfortunately the preceding experimental reports do not provide sufficient information to allow for any inferences to be made as to what factors associated with the experimenters led to the differential results. Several experiments, however, have provided such clues. An important difference that has been singled out is the experimenter's method of handling his subjects. The first experiment to test experimenter differences was carried out by Pratt and Price (1938). Both experimenters had previously conducted independent research with the same subjects and under similar conditions but only one of them, Price, obtained significant results, Pratt's subjects having scored at chance. In order to see if the differences in scoring were due to the experimenter's handling of the subjects, a second experiment was done using subjects from the same population but with Price only handling the subjects while Pratt attended to precautions against sensory cues and accurate recording of the scores. Throughout the testing Price did not know the targets. The experiment was in two parts. In the first part, Price compared two methods of handling the subjects, one thought to be "favorable" and one thought to be "unfavorable." The authors report that

> the favorable condition . . . consisted of introducing a subject to the situation by one-half hour of general conversation before starting the tests and then continuing the conversation during the test. The "unfavorable" one was characterized by starting to test a subject without delay and in deliberately keeping him out of the conversation as much as possible. Two subjects, one in each of the two conditions, were usually tested together in Section I. M.M.P. used these two objectively-defined conditions against her expressed better judgment for the next four experimental days. She insisted all the while that she did not feel capable of "slighting" subjects and claimed that she was not able, under the conditions imposed, to establish with any of the subjects the experimenter-subject relationship which she considered most favorable (p. 91).

The upshot was that only chance results were obtained in both conditions, the "favored" subjects scoring only slightly higher than the controls.

It was then decided to run Section II of the experiment, in which Price was allowed to work with the subjects without any restrictions with the aim of obtaining the best scores possible. The results of Section II were significantly positive and at the same level of scoring as was obtained in the initial experiment in which Price worked alone.

In analyzing the results of the two preliminary experiments in which Price and Pratt worked independently, some interesting suggestions are offered concerning favorable working atmospheres for ESP testing. Since so little has been recorded about favorable testing conditions, these remarks will be quoted in full.

> Objectively, the clearest difference between the two experimenters detectable from their records is that of the number of trials. M.M.P. generally obtains about two-thirds as many scores as does J.G.P. in an equal time. It might appear superficially that this indicates a difference in the rate of guessing. Actually, however, the subjects worked for each experimenter at their own natural rates, and the difference in the total number of trials was due to a difference in the amount of time taken between runs. M.M.P. avoids hurrying her subjects and encourages a free social atmosphere in which general conversation flourishes. She has a way of directing the subject's attention to the task at hand and of explaining what is to be done with a few simple, well-directed remarks. After she has once got the subject started at the test, she usually manages to get his attention on something other than the testing process. As long as the responses are made without hesitation or evidence of too serious effort, she permits, and even encourages, the subject to talk about something besides the test. When she sees any evidence of a misunderstanding of the test, she corrects the subject as briefly as possible, sometimes in a scolding tone, and then returns at once to the interrupted conversation. In this way her subjects are first consciously oriented with respect to their task and are then diverted as much as possible to permit them to still keep that orientation. They "play" at the tests without getting any strong feeling of needing to win or of having a duty to perform.
>
> J.G.P.'s approach, on the other hand, has always been to direct the subject's attention as much as possible to the task and to keep it there. He felt that full explanations were due the subject, even when the information given was not necessary for taking the tests. All in all, his subjects were given a more serious view of the tests, looked upon them as a pleasant duty, and were encouraged to concentrate upon the task at hand to the exclusion of other things, e.g., conversation while working (pp. 92–93).

It is relevant to point out that the runs which Price ran in Section I were the only trials conducted by this experimenter in which she did not obtain significant results. She has been cited in the literature as an outstanding psi experimenter (Bates and Newton, 1951), and the results of the Pratt-Price experiment here described indicate that the favorable experimenter-subject relationship may be (and in the case of Price, apparently was) a spontaneous one which is disturbed when the investigator is placed under conditions which are psychologically restricting.   In line with these remarks about Price's outstanding ability as a psi experimenter is the outcome of another experiment conducted by Price but which was reported by Bates and Newton (1951), in which she worked with mental patients as subjects trying to get them to score high on some occasions and negatively on others.   She was able to get them to do both to a significant degree.

Sharp and Clark (1937), in group tests carried out to locate high-scoring subjects, used several experimenters (or observers, as Sharp and Clark call them) who administered the ESP tests, and variations in scoring associated with different experimenters were noted.   These scoring variations appeared to be related to the experimenter's attitude toward ESP.   The attitudes of the experimenters and the corresponding scoring averages of the subjects they tested were as follows: Sharp, who was very positive in his attitude toward ESP, had an average run score of 5.36; Davidson, who was also positive, had an average score of 5.88; Berger, who was uncommitted, had an average run score of 4.86; while Myers, who was decidedly skeptical, obtained an average run score of 4.30, which was significantly negative.

It is likely that Myers had a depressing effect on the results not only because of his attitude toward ESP but due to his mannerisms.   Sharp and Clark report that "one of our subjects, who has done a great deal of work, stated privately that Myers distracted her to such a point that she was unable to think of what she was doing.   While conducting the tests Myers kept swinging his watch chain and talked about extracurricular activities.   He manifested little interest in the work at hand.   At that time, he had little or no interest in the experiments" (p. 136).

In a series of ESP and PK tests with children, McMahan and S. L. Rhine (1952) found a decided difference in the results depending on which of them had been the experimenter, one being positive and the other significantly negative.   They suggest that the experimenter who obtained the negative results did so because she was new to the experiment, and her anxiety and concern to conduct the test properly may have created tension in the children.

Sailaja and Rao (1973) report that in studying differences in ESP test results obtained before and after an interview conducted in connection with being admitted to graduate school, an unanticipated finding was that "the differential scoring between the pre- and post-interview tests was more pronounced with one experimenter (BK) than with the other (PS). Also the decline of the effect from the first to the second runs is greater with PS than with BK" (p. 66). The authors suggest that the scoring difference between the two experimenters was due to the fact that "BK's handling of the subjects caused little change in their mental set or mood whereas the way PS handled her subjects caused loosening of the set with which they came, as they proceeded with the ESP test" (p. 70). Unfortunately no further information on how the two experimenters handled the subjects is given.

In an attempted replication of the sheep-goat work of Schmeidler (Schmeidler and McConnell, 1958) and Van de Castle (1957), Osis and Dean (1964) conducted psi test sessions with lecture audiences. Although both experimenters used the same lecture outline, test directions, and slides, there was a significant difference between the scores of each group with the results of Osis' subjects being positive ($P = .03$), Dean's insignificantly negative, and the difference between the positive and negative ESP scores for the two experimenters as measured by chi square yielding $P = .02$. There were also differences in the results of both experimenters in regard to repeating the findings of Schmeidler and Van de Castle. In an attempt to describe the differences in the testing approaches of the two experimenters, they report:

> The assistant (S.V.S.) who helped in the experiments and heard both lecturers remarked that whereas K.O.'s speech was presented in a relaxed, humorous, and confident manner, D.D. was rather tense, less secure about the subject matter, and very seriously intent on getting the audience to accept his point of view. In self-observations by both experimenters it was discovered that K.O. loves to give talks and thoroughly enjoys such occasions; D.D., on the other hand, did not enjoy giving talks at that time and became nervous when confronting an audience. Both experimenters are definitely convinced of the existence of ESP. If there is any difference in level of belief between the two, D.D.'s belief would be more intensely positive than K.O.'s. Is it possible that the experimenter who enjoys the lecture session for the fun of it gets good scores, while the one for whom it is a difficult task fails to get positive scores? (pp. 179–180).

Two experiments in which two experimenters independently tested the same subjects in the all-male sophomore biology class at St. Joseph's College was reported by C. B. Nash and C. S. Nash (1962). There was positive scoring when C.S.N. was the experimenter (16 subjects scored positively to eight negatively scoring subjects), and only seven scored positively while 14 scored negatively when C.B.N. was the experimenter. The total deviation for C.B.N.'s subjects was −112 while it was +42 for C.S.N.'s subjects. Moreover, when each subject's score with one experimenter was correlated with his score with the other experimenter, the $r = -.69$ ($P < .001$), indicating that the degree to which "the subject expressed ESP to produce a positive deviation in one experiment varied directly with the degree to which he expressed ESP to produce a negative deviation in the other" (p. 83). The authors suggest that the differences that may have led to positive scoring with one experimenter and negative scoring with the other could have been as follows: (a) C.S.N. tested subjects individually whereas C.B.N. used a group test; (b) C.S.N. was a female experimenter testing 11 male subjects whereas C.B.N. was a male testing all male subjects; (c) C.S.N.

offered a reward to the highest scoring individual whereas C.B.N. offered a reward to members of the highest scoring section; (d) C.S.N. told each subject of his results at once whereas C.B.N. posted the scores; (e) C.S.N. provided immediate feedback whereas C.B.N.'s subjects had to wait until the next meeting of their section; and (f) C.S.N. recorded the subject's calls whereas the subjects recorded their own calls in C.B.N.'s experiment. With so many variables involved, it is impossible to say what factors accounted for the differential results obtained by the two experimenters, but it seems likely that the differences were associated in some way with the individual experimenter.

Honorton (Honorton and Barksdale, 1972) tested six subjects who tried to exert a group PK effect on a random number generator under conditions of muscle tension versus muscle relaxation. Honorton personally favored the muscle tension hypothesis, and the results confirmed it. Next Barksdale attempted a replication with ten subjects working individually but obtained insignificant results. In a third study, Honorton himself served as the subject, and he not only scored highly significantly above chance on the muscle tension runs $(P < .00005)$, but the relaxation runs were significantly negative to the same extent $(P < .00005)$. This raises the question of whether, in Honorton's words, "the first experiment may not have involved *seven* Ss rather than six—or perhaps just *one*" (p. 213). He goes on to point out, "If the PK hypothesis is to be taken seriously, it would appear that traditional boundaries between Ss and experimenters cannot easily be maintained" (p. 213). This is an experiment in which one experimenter obtained highly significant results while another got only chance results, but in addition, it indicates that the senior experimenter's motivation may have been directly responsible for the significant results.

Although two experimenters were not involved, an experiment reported by Nash and Richards (1947) obtained results which also suggest that the experimenter's motivation may have affected the results of a PK experiment. The experimenter, Richards, compared PK results at two distances from the target. An incline in scoring in the experiment as a whole as well as in various subsections of it was noted, instead of the more customary decline effects. As an explanation for this and other results, they suggest that the experimenter was responsible for the results:

> In the first place, the significant chronological incline is undoubtedly independent of the individual subject. While it is possible that the subjects of the first half were naturally low-scoring subjects and those of the second half were naturally high-scoring, it is most plausible to suppose that the subjects were not essentially different and that the experimenter herself underwent a progressive change, acquiring greater familiarity and deeper interest as the experiment advanced. If this is so, the other inclines would be likely to be associated with, and to some extent patterned after, the chronological incline—as they seem to be.

There is no way of reliably ascertaining which of the two persons present in the test is actually responsible for the PK that was exerted. It is logically plausible, however, to suppose that, of the two, the experimenter was the more strongly motivated toward discovering whether PK was equally possible at 30 feet and at three. If so, she would naturally exert stronger volitional action at the longer distance than at the shorter; whereas, generally speaking, the neutral and disinterested attitude of the subject would not lead him to favor either distance. We therefore submit the purely speculative suggestion that the results and the distribution are due to A.R.'s own PK effect (pp. 281–282).

Honorton, Ramsey, and Cabibbo (1975) reported on an experiment in which two experimenters interacted with the subjects in a positively toned manner as contrasted with interacting with them in a negatively toned manner. The positive orientation consisted of informal conversation with the subject which could be characterized as "friendly," "casual," "supportive," while in the negative condition subjects were given the ESP task immediately and treated in a formal, abrupt, unfriendly manner. The positive subject treatments were associated with significantly higher scores than the negative interactions.

In a number of experiments aimed at training subjects to use ESP, Tart (1975) found that of ten subjects, five obtained independently positive scores, and these were tested by the same experimenter (out of 11 experimenters employed in the entire range of experiments). Tart characterizes this experimenter as "a very patient experimenter, as his subjects often worked very slowly" (p. 79).

Differences Related to Experimenter-Subject Attitudes Toward One Another

In addition to the experimenter's method of handling the subjects affecting the results of ESP and PK tests, it has often been suggested that the attitudes and feelings the experimenter and subject entertain for each other may also have a bearing on the results.

Woodruff and Dale (1950) were the first to formally test the role of mutual subject-experimenter attitudes on ESP scoring level. Questionnaires were devised to independently assess the attitudes of subject and experimenter toward each other, and these were completed immediately following the ESP test which consisted of 20 DT runs with one experimenter on one day and 20 with the second experimenter on another day. Neither the overall results nor the experimenter comparison in terms of total scores was significant. However, to a significant extent for Woodruff ($P = .01$) and to a lesser extent for Dale ($P = .12$) subjects who gave low experimenter ratings obtained positive ESP scores and vice versa. When the results for both experimenters were combined, the resulting CR of the difference was 2.61 ($P = .0045$).

In regard to the experimenter's ratings of the subjects, the average ESP score for those subjects Dale rated highly was 5.15, while those subjects she gave a low rating to had an average ESP score of 4.88. The *CR* of the difference between the two groups is 2.14 (*P* = .016). However, the ESP results in relation to Woodruff's rating of the subjects was in the opposite direction although not significantly so: The subjects he rated highly had an average ESP score of 4.99, and those he gave a low rating to had an average score of 5.05.

Finally, when both experimenter and subject gave each other mutually low or high ratings, the average run score for Dale's subjects was 5.06 when the ratings were high and 4.99 when they were low. This is not significant. However, for Woodruff's subjects, mutually high ratings were associated with an average run score of 4.83 and mutually low attitudes with a mean ESP score of 5.20. The *CR* of the difference is 2.94 (*P* = .0016). The authors point out that "in most cases the members of the so-called 'low-rating' group did not express strong antipathy toward the experimenters or the experimental situation. As a matter of fact, ratings of plus 1 were often placed in the low-rating category because of the frequency of plus 2 ratings. The results seem to indicate not that *antipathy* is positively related to high ESP scoring, but that a more or less *neutral attitude* may be" (p. 108).

Another experiment dealing with experimenter-subject attitudes was reported by Waldron (1959). He tested the hypothesis that the sheep-goat differential effect was largely dependent on the subject's reaction to the experimenter and his conception of the experimenter's attitude to ESP rather than to a direct effect of belief on scoring (thus we have the first attempt in parapsychology to manipulate and assess experimenter bias). He tested five groups of college students for clairvoyance. The first and fifth groups were told nothing about the experimenter's own belief in ESP; one group was assured that the experimenter believed in ESP and another the opposite; the remaining group, the control, was told it was being tested for subliminal perception. Of four interactions, two were significant and bore out the hypothesis that the subject's reaction to the experimenter was an important factor in determining whether "sheep" would obtain higher ESP scores than "goats."

Nash (1968) also investigated the effect of the experimenter's attitudes on the subject's scores in three experiments. The subjects of all three experiments were divided into two groups according to whether they were liked or disliked by the experimenter. He reports that "the correlation coefficient between the 79 pairs of run score averages of the liked and disliked subjects has a value of -.27 which is at the .02 level of probability" (p. 410). He also tested the effect of the subject's attitude toward the experimenter on the ESP score level by correlating 74 pairs of run-score averages of subjects who liked and disliked the experimenter and obtained an *r* of -.35 (*P* = .01).

Differential Results Obtained by the Same Experimenter

The preceding experiments in this section have dealt with differential ESP or PK test results associated with different experimenters. A number of reports have included incidental observations concerning differential scoring associated with the *same* experimenter's differential treatment of or attitude toward the subjects. These studies are summarized next.

Hutchinson (1940) carried out two series of experiments comparing pre-shuffle card calling in which scores were checked after 1- and 10-day intervals. No difference between conditions was noted in Series I, but a striking one occurred in Series II. In Series I the subjects were not informed of their scores in either condition until the experiment was over, whereas in Series II the subjects were informed of their scores on the 1-day runs the day they were checked. Hutchinson offers several hypotheses to account for the contrasting results of the two series, stressing the fact that the experimenter had little contact with the subjects in the first session except for providing the initial instructions, whereas in the second session she felt there was more freedom and that she had greater contact with the subjects through discussing the daily scores. Moreover, from the beginning she had wanted to inform the subjects of their scores the day they were checked and felt constrained by not doing so. (This situation is similar to Price's experience in Series I of the Pratt-Price [1938] experiment.) Hutchinson felt the subjects had a more favorable attitude toward the experiment in Series II because of the experimenter-subject relationship.

Another experiment which indicated that sufficient preparation of the participants in an ESP test is important was noted by Van Busschbach (1956) when he came to the United States to attempt to repeat his successful work in Holland in obtaining positive GESP scores in the school classroom with the teacher as agent. In the first block of American tests two members of the laboratory staff, Margaret Anderson and myself, and Rosa Tillett, supervisor of elementary grades, conducted the tests. At the end of 6,714 trials, a negative deviation of -45.8 had accrued. Although school administrators had been contacted before we entered the schools to do the testing, it was hypothesized that the preparation of the teachers for the experiment had been inadequate. As Van Busschbach reports it:

> From that point on ... each teacher was visited by the experimental assistants a couple of days before the tests took place, and the program was explained. The appointment for the test was cleared, and every effort was made to see that the tests were properly anticipated. Thereafter, in the 14,818 trials that followed, a deviation of +78.4 was obtained ... the difference between the two stages ... gives a CR of 2.06, which is not far short of being acceptably significant (p. 77).

In Schmeidler's (1943) first sheep-goat experiment in which subjects believing in the possibility of ESP under the conditions of the experiment (sheep) obtained positive scores on a clairvoyance test while skeptical subjects (goats) obtained negative scores, it is likely that the differential scoring patterns were attributable not only to the different attitudes about ESP but to the demand characteristics provided by the experimenter who artfully used the testing situation to reinforce the positive or negative sets of the subjects to a rather extreme degree. She writes:

> Both my rooms were generally considered quite suitable for research; so I put the skeptics in the "dark room" and their cards in my office, reversing this for the open-minded group. There was a battered laboratory table in the "dark room"; I left it there for the skeptics to work on—and as often as not, supplied them with the stub of a pencil, not overly sharp. For the other group I used a table with a fairly nice surface and set it under a window so that they could look out at Harvard Yard. Pencils were always freshly sharpened. There were cigarettes and an ashtray available; sometimes I offered them candy. Probably none of these differences mattered very much to the subjects (with the exception of the candy!) and yet they may have served to establish something of the atmosphere of dullness and drudgery on the one hand, and friendly cooperation on the other.
>
> When a skeptic finished a run, he pressed a telegraph key which flashed a small light in the room where I was waiting. I then took away the deck he had been guessing; put the next one on the table; and pressed the corresponding telegraph key, to signal that he could begin another run. The signal in his room was a rather raucous buzzer.
>
> With the more docile group, there was a longer interruption after each run. As soon as a subject signalled that he was done, I would go into [his room] with a list of the cards he had been guessing. We would go over the scores together, discuss the methods the subject used, his impressions of success or failure, or anything else he wanted to talk about. This took up so much time that there was never more than ten runs in an hour; whereas in the same period there were fifty runs with the other procedure (pp. 106–107).

(This is reminiscent of the Pratt-Price experiment.)

In later experiments Schmeidler (Schmeidler and McConnell, 1958) tested both sheep and goats under similar conditions, and the difference between attitude and positive or negative ESP scoring held up, although the scores for the sheep were not as high, while the goats, paradoxically, scored more negatively when tested under the more favorable conditions!

Sharp and Clark (1937), in group tests aimed at discovering high scoring subjects, incidentally noted that significant changes in individual scoring were obtained with different experimenters. Specifically, they offer the post-hoc observation that the senior experimenter, Sharp, obtained significant positive results for the first 4 weeks of testing, at which point his wife became critically ill and it was doubtful whether she would live. While she was hospitalized, testing continued. After 3 weeks she recovered sufficiently to go home. During the weeks of her hospitalization Sharp had been very upset and distracted, and his subjects scored below chance. Testing continued for an eighth and final week after his wife returned home, and his subjects once more scored positively. The *CR* of the difference between the tests Sharp conducted during the 5 weeks his wife was not hospitalized as opposed to the 3 when she was is 2.87.

Rivers (1950) individually tested 36 high school boys and 36 college men for clairvoyance and GESP. Although the total results were significant, it was due entirely to the scores of the high school students. She suggests that one possible cause of the difference in scoring between the two groups was that

> the writer feels that she did not exert herself with the college group to the extent that she did with the high school group in trying to get high scores from the individual subject for fear that undue enthusiasm on her part might make her appear unscientific in her approach. Perhaps this greater pitch of tension and enthusiasm, which she did employ with Series I, is necessary for favorable response from the subject (pp. 276–277).

In an experiment designed primarily to test Schmeidler's sheep-goat hypothesis, Casper (1951) ran two series of tests in which 146 subjects did two clairvoyance and two GESP runs apiece. The most significant finding of the experiment was a decline between the first and second halves of Session B (*CR* 3.4). In trying to account for the decline, the only difference between the two halves of the series which he could think of was a change in his own attitude. In the beginning of the series he had been unhurried and had been "free and easy with each subject and allowed them to take as long as they wished to do the test." But, he continues,

> . . . as time passed, it became apparent to me that the experiment was not proceeding rapidly enough for me to get back to my classes at Duke at the beginning of the semester there. I therefore made the schedule sheet more readily available to get more subjects, and I speeded up the testing process as much as possible. This meant that I was tired at the end of a day and was not as friendly and sociable with the subjects as I had been previously. And it also meant that the subjects were hurried through the testing procedure one after another because I was anxious to finish the experiment and return to Duke. In the light of the facts, this experiment would seem to indicate again what ESP workers have emphasized so much, that the attitude of the experimenter is a prime factor in getting good results (p. 144).

In testing subjects with ESP targets consisting of words in English and Hindi, Kanthamani (1965a) found in three series that subjects obtained more hits on the familiar language targets (those in English), which was the opposite of what

Rao (1963, 1964) had found in earlier work along similar lines comparing targets in English and Telugu. To test the possibility that the difference was due to the method of presenting the experiment to the subjects, Kanthamani (1965b) ran three more series with different subjects, this time using a method of presentation as much like Rao's as possible. In these experiments she obtained results in line with Rao's, i.e., positive scores on the unfamiliar language (Hindi) and negative scores on the familiar language (English). Unfortunately her report does not describe the way in which her initial treatment differed from Rao's nor what she did specifically to make the directions employed in the later tests similar to the manner in which he had presented his tests.

Birge (1949) designed five ingenious game variations of clairvoyance tests and conducted several experiments with college undergraduates as subjects. But in spite of having provided what seemed to be optimum test conditions favoring spontaneity and interest, the only evidence of ESP was a suggestive difference between forward and backward displacement. In accounting for his disappointing results, Birge suggests that

> his own excessive eagerness may have inhibited the ESP of his subjects. For example, in Series II he keenly anticipated finding the same run position effects which he found in Series I. In Series III he had great hopes that the games Scoop and New Metapoker would continue to elicit positive scoring. Neither of these expectations was fulfilled, and it is at least plausible to assume that the tensions aroused by these anticipations may have created a psychological situation which insured their failure (p. 206).

Martin Johnson (1971) attempted to manipulate the experimenter-subject relationship so that the subjects would score as predicted, either above or below chance, depending on how he treated them. He tried to obtain positive scores in the first of two sessions with 13 students in his clinical interviewing course and negative scores in a later test with the same subjects. On the last day of the semester he presented the subjects with envelopes containing either a blank paper or a paper with one of the questions to be given in the final exam written on it. The ESP task was to select the envelopes containing the test information. The subjects were allowed to open the envelopes they selected and thus to read the exam questions they had correctly chosen. They succeeded to a significant extent in opening the envelopes concealing the questions ($P = .013$).

In the second half of the experiment, about which the subjects had been given no preparation, they were unexpectedly and preemptorily called to the experimenter's office a few days after the final exam. They were treated in a rude and inconsiderate manner and were made to take a second test similar to the first while standing in the hall. They scored right at chance, not negatively, as predicted. The difference between the two experimental halves was significant, however ($P = .025$, two-tailed). Although Johnson does not suggest it, the second test may have failed because guessing the envelopes containing test questions was no longer a matter of real-life concern since the exam had already been taken.

Johnson and Johannesson (1972) attempted to treat one group of subjects so that they would score above chance and another group so they would score below. Johannesson was the experimenter and there were six subjects in each group who were tested by means of a blind matching clairvoyance test. The predicted positive group consisted of sheep to begin with, and they were paid for participating; they were promised rewards for high scoring; they were tested in a friendly, warm, comfortable atmosphere in the experimenter's home; they were given relaxing suggestions; refreshments were served; music was played; breaks were allowed; and they responded at their own speed. The predicted negative group, however, was tested in an unpleasant room; they were not rewarded or paid for participating; they were made to wait; they were not served refreshments; no music was played; no relaxing suggestions were given; no breaks were allowed; and the responses had to be made within a specific time period. The experimenter behaved in an authoritarian, abrupt manner. He reported that "the treatment of the 'negatives' was so unfriendly, so stereotyped and boring that most of the subjects were very close to the 'breaking-point' at the end of the experiment" (p. 5).

In spite of all the encouragement, the positive group obtained an insignificant negative score while the negative group managed to score very nicely below chance as anticipated ($P = .0002$, two-tailed). Five of the six subjects in the negative group scored below chance and one at chance.

This experiment had been viewed as an extension of Johnson's (1971) experiment, but whereas Johnson had obtained significant positive scores when he wanted to, yet was unable to obtain significant negative scores, Johannesson got the reverse. The authors suggest that this difference may have been an experimenter effect.

Differential Results Obtained by Different Data Collectors

In most parapsychological experiments the person who conceives the idea of the experiment and designs the method of testing it is also the person who actually conducts the experiment. This is not always the case, however, and as parapsychology enlarges its foothold in the university and the number of students doing research increases, to a greater extent than at present the number of persons other than the senior investigator who are running experiments, or data collectors, will be bound to increase. It is of considerable relevance here to examine experiments indicating differences in results in ESP and PK tests associated with different data collectors. These results are comparable to those already reviewed in the foregoing sections in that the data collectors, as the experimenters, were the ones who handled the subjects and administered the test(s). However, motivationally speaking, data collectors are likely to be one step removed from the experimenter, since presumably it is not their own ideas that they are testing but those of someone else. It is not known if this makes a difference, but since it is likely that it may, this material on variations in psi tests results with different data collectors is presented separately.

In much of his later research Van Busschbach (1956, 1959) depended on the use of data collectors, or "test leaders," as he called them, to gather data in his classroom GESP tests with school children using the teacher as the agent. Unfortunately, as a rule his reports do not provide a breakdown of results according to individual data collectors, but that there were differences involved was certainly the case when he came to the Duke Parapsychology Laboratory in 1956 to repeat in the United States the results he had obtained in Holland (Van Busschbach, 1956). The overall *CR* he obtained in this country was very like those he obtained at home: in Amsterdam the *CR* was 2.79; in Utrecht it was 2.73; and in North Carolina it was 2.70. However, the significance obtained in North Carolina was entirely due to the scores of the pupils in classes where Margaret Anderson served as test leader. The *CR* for the results of her subjects was over 3, but when these scores were added to those of the other test leaders (of which there were four, none of whom obtained even suggestive *CR*s), the *CR* for the entire experiment dropped to 2.7.

On his return to Holland, Van Busschbach (1959) tested 40 first- and second-grade classes in Amsterdam and Dordrecht. Only the latter tests yielded significant positive results, but these were quite high and when added to those from Amsterdam a *CR* of 5.16 resulted, and there was a chi-square test of the difference between the two cities yielding a *P* of < .000001. In trying to account for the difference in the results obtained in the two cities, Van Busschbach pointed out that a simpler test was used in Dordrecht and "there may also be other factors that influenced the results, such as the unavoidable personal difference between the manner in which the tests were presented by the different test leaders in the two cities, the difference between large and small cities, and the difference between classes" (p. 236). Of the possibilities he mentions, the likeliest to have affected the results is the difference in data collectors used, as was the case with the work in North Carolina.

The Anderson-White (1956, 1957, 1958b) experiments investigating teacher-pupil attitudes toward each other as measured by questionnaires and clairvoyance test results necessarily employed data collectors in the form of classroom teachers. As was pointed out in a review of all the Anderson-White experiments and attempted replications of their work (White and Angstadt, 1965):

> It is the teacher who introduces the experiment to the students, supervises the test, and collects the data. As far as the student-subjects are concerned, the teacher *is* the experimenter. They have no contact with the "real" experi-

menter—the distant person who had conceived the experiment, designed it, who will check it and be identified with the results. The only knowledge the subjects have of the experimenter is a dim awareness of a person in Durham, New York, or Istanbul who has sent the materials to the teacher. In this sense, the experimenter is as remote from the students as the person or persons responsible for designing the achievement tests which the teacher also administers (p. 77).

Unfortunately no breakdown is available for each teacher in all of the replications of the Anderson-White work that have been carried out, but for those studies where this information is available (the work conducted by Anderson [1957], Anderson and White [1956, 1957, 1958b], and White and Angstadt [1965]), almost all of the significant scoring was done in the classes of those teachers who knew Anderson and White, but particularly Anderson personally (White and Angstadt, 1965). And Anderson was the senior investigator whose imagination had certainly been captured by the idea being tested. Was some of this enthusiasm transmitted to the teachers she contacted? Certainly it was not shared extensively by the other investigators, including Angstadt and myself, whose emphasis was primarily on the importance of the experimental design as a means of providing a repeatable ESP test situation.

Rilling, Adams, and Pettijohn (1962) attempted a replication of the Anderson-White studies of teacher-pupil attitudes and clairvoyance test results at the college level. They used four professors who collected data from their classes. Although the attitude of the student toward the professor was not related to the ESP scores, it appeared that a form of sheep-goat effect was evident in the overall results obtained by each professor. They point out that Professor A could best be characterized as having a belief in ESP, and the average score for his class was 5.23. Professor B had a neutral attitude, and his students scored an average of 4.96, almost at chance. Professors C and D were skeptical about ESP, and the average scores for their classes were 4.86 and 4.64, respectively. These results are reminiscent of those of Sharp and Clark (1937) who observed marked variations in scoring possibly associated with the attitudes of the experimenters toward ESP. It will be remembered, however, that Crumbaugh (1958) used data collectors who were selected in part for their attitudes toward ESP, but these attitudes did not prove to be related to the ESP score level of the subjects they tested.

In an experiment comparing intentional as opposed to nonintentional PK results reported by Stanford et al. (1975), Stanford and Zenhausern were the organizing experimenters while Taylor and Dwyer served as data collectors. The scores of the subjects tested by Experimenter 1 (that is, Data Collector 1) were not significant for either condition, but the subjects tested by Experimenter 2 (that is, Data Collector 2) were significant for both the conscious and unconscious PK tests. This is particularly interesting in that the overall results of the intentional PK test are reported as being insignificant, due to the scores of the subjects of Data Collector 1 which vitiated the significant results obtained by Data Collector 2. If the results had not been reported separately by the data collector, as one suspects is often the case, the results would appear in an entirely different (and inaccurate) light. The authors propose that personality differences of the experimenters (that is, data collectors) be examined as a means of predicting how their subjects will do on psi tests. They add, "personality differences which relate to the quality of social interaction provided by the experimenter can logically be expected to have importance here. This suggestion is underscored by the fact that the experimenter in this study who was judged to be the [more] extraverted of the two obtained the best results with her subjects" (p. 132).

Nash (1960) studied subject-experimenter attitudes by using nine college students who served alternately as subject and experimenter. This experiment is being reviewed in this section on data collectors because the students were not genuine experimenters, in the sense that their ideas were not being tested in the experiment nor did they have a hand in designing it. And, in a certain sense, they could even by viewed as subjects, whether they were administering the ESP test or being tested; for, as Lester (1969) pointed out in an article on subject bias in psychology experiments, in experiments where an experimenter has students run subjects (i.e., serve as data collectors), there is some justice in saying that the only experimenter is the senior investigator and that the student experimenters are in fact his subjects. Lester's example was drawn from experiments on experimenter bias, but it could apply just as well to other types of psychology experiments and to parapsychology investigations as well.

Nash's student experimenters took turns administering a clairvoyance test to their classmates. Each student conducted two sessions as data collector while the remaining eight students served as subjects. At each session both the data collector and each subject listed the four classmates he preferred of the eight participating in addition to himself. The rater was judged as having a "positive" attitude toward the four students he listed and a "negative" attitude toward the remainder. The results are reported as follows:

> . . . positive scoring was associated with positive attitudes and negative scoring with negative attitudes, the subject's attitude exerting a greater effect than the experimenter's. There was a statistically significant difference between the positive scores obtained by the subjects who were "positive" toward the experimenter and the negative scores by those who were "negative." [P = .01.] The difference between the scores when the subject and experimenter were mutually positive toward each other and when they were mutually negative, combining both general factors, was statistically even more significant [P = .003] in spite of the reduced amount of data. The results were consistent when analyzed in terms of individual subjects within each session and throughout the series (p. 189).

The data from sessions in which the attitude of subject or data collector differed in the second session from that in the first were of interest. (The two sessions administered by each data collector were separated by an average of 50 days.) The subject's attitude changed in 18 instances, the data collector's in 12, and in one case the attitude change was mutual. Nash reports that the average run score was higher or lower, respectively, according to whether the attitude had changed from negative to positive or from positive to negative. However, there were too few cases to reach statistical significance. Unfortunately, data on the number of subjects scoring above or below chance in the changed attitude categories are not given. The results of this experiment suggest the advisability of having actual experimenters and subjects routinely register their attitudes toward one another by means of a standardized set of questions, regardless of what other variables are being studied.

Another experiment dealing with attitude changes between a data collector and his subjects was reported by Anderson and White (1958a). In this experiment a teacher who had taken part in the successful repetition (Anderson and White, 1957) of the first Anderson and White experiment (Anderson and White, 1956) served as the data collector on this second occasion. He administered a clairvoyance test to one of his classes on the fourth day of school in the fall semester and repeated the test again near the close of that semester. The purpose of the experiment was to see if any changes in the attitude of teacher and students toward one another over the course of the semester would be associated with changes in ESP scoring level. The attitudes of teacher and pupils were measured by questionnaire at the same time the two clairvoyance tests were given. At the end of the semester 14 students became more positive in their attitude toward the teacher. The average run score for these subjects was 4.57 in the first clairvoyance test and 5.66 in the second. The *CR* of the difference is 3.21 ($P = .001$). Seven students became more negative in their attitude toward the teacher, and their average score dropped to 5.20 in the second experiment as opposed to 5.57 in the first. The remaining eight students did not change their attitude toward the teacher over the course of the semester, and their average run scores also remained about the same: 4.95 on the second test as compared to 4.80 on the first. A chi square test of the number of students scoring above or below chance divided according to whether their attitudes became more positive or more negative yielded a *P* of .017 (exact method). The relationship between ESP score and attitude change on the part of the teacher as well as the mutually combined attitudes of teacher and students was not significant.

This experiment and other experiments in which the teacher served as the data collector (Anderson and White, 1956, 1957, 1958b), and Nash's experiment (1960) in which students who knew each other not only in class but outside of it suggest that if an experimenter cannot run his own subjects, it might be worthwhile to use as data collectors persons who already have a relationship with the persons who will serve as subjects. Although exploiting an already existing relationship between data collector and subjects is likely to raise the probability that a psi test in such a situation will yield significant results, there is still much room for failure, as evidenced by the unsuccessful repetitions of the Anderson-White work (White and Angstadt, 1965). However, perhaps the probability of error would be lowered if Schmeidler's (1969) suggestion were considered: she proposed the introduction of a method of evaluating the teacher's attitude toward the experimental task, suggesting that some of the repetitions of the Anderson and White work failed because "the teachers' attitudes toward the experiment were an uncontrolled variable" (p. 91).

Although the foregoing experiments indicate that data collectors can influence ESP or PK test results, unlike the next two to be described, they were not deliberately designed to study such an influence. Johnson, Cronquist, Danielsson, and Mondejar (1972) investigated the experimenter-subject relationship in 52 children between the ages of 3 and 7. The children were distributed randomly in two groups of 26 each and were individually tested for clairvoyance by means of a test specifically designed to be suitable for that age group. In one group a parent (usually the mother) served as the experimenter, whereas in the other group the experimenter was an outsider. The first group scored significantly above chance ($P = .02$, two-tailed) while the other group obtained an insignificant positive deviation. The difference between the scores of the two groups was not significant.

Recently Adrian Parker (1975) reported on an experiment which was specifically designed to test the role of experimenter bias or expectancy in parapsychological research. As in the other experiments described in this section, the experimenter did not collect the data himself but used others for that purpose. Eighteen undergraduate psychology students were employed: six as experimenters, six as subjects, and six as agents. The six experimenters were further separated into two groups of three each, Group A consisting of "those with a strong prior bias toward belief in ESP" (p. 43) and Group B consisting of "those with a strong bias toward disbelief" (p. 43). The two groups of data collectors, or experimenters, were then separately given two differing lectures on ESP and ESP testing. Parker says that the experimenters in

> Group A were told that ESP had been "proven" by scientific research using methods such as they were going to experiment with. They were then given instructions as to how to perform a GESP test and told to expect between seven and ten hits per run.
>
> The experimenters from group B were given instructions aimed at promoting the opposite expectancy. They were told that ESP research is riddled with flaws and errors, and that there is no reliable evidence for the existence of ESP. After they were given instructions for carrying out the GESP test, they were told that if the experiments were conducted in a strict controlled manner they should obtain scores close to the chance expectation of five hits per run (p. 43).

Each experimenter ran two 25-trial runs with each subject-agent pair and then exchanged pairs with the other experimenter and completed two more runs. The overall results were insignificant but as predicted, the scores of the subject-pairs tested by Group A experimenters were significantly higher than those of the B experimenters (CR diff. = 1.64; P = .05, one-tailed). The bulk of the positive scoring was made by the subjects tested by two of the three A experimenters whose subjects obtained independently significant results (P = .02 and .05, respectively). One of these experimenters whose subjects scored significantly above chance had a strong previous bias in favor of ESP.

These results are particularly interesting because of the level of significance achieved with such a small sample. At this stage, however, it is not possible to determine whether this experiment shows that subjects' ESP scoring level can be influenced by the expectancies of the person who administers the ESP test or that data collectors (surrogate experimenters) will obtain results in line with the expectations of the original experimenter (in this case Parker), as suggested by Lester (1969). Either way, Parker's experiment demonstrates that experimenter expectancies can influence ESP scoring level.

Because of our ignorance as to what factors are responsible for significant psi test results, it is important that we routinely gather data on every likely variable. Certainly the differing results associated with individual data collectors reviewed here indicates that whenever more than one data collector is employed in an experiment, the ESP or PK test results collected by each one should be reported separately regardless of whatever other variables are under study.

Moreover, since in essence a data collector is a person who is carrying out another person's experiment, and since whether or not extrachance results will be forthcoming in any given experiment may depend heavily not only on the experimenter but on the quality of his interest and enthusiasm, it stands to reason that his surrogate, the data collector, must share that enthusiasm and motivation if the experiment is to succeed.

Finally, since whether due to motivation, personality factors, or whatever, it is clear that some people are able to succeed as psi experimenters and others are not. Rhine and Pratt (1957) suggested long ago that before undertaking to investigate any experimental question, the experimenter should do a pilot test under conditions similar to those that would prevail in the formal experiment in order to see if he can elicit significant results under those conditions. This is sound advice and should be applied in the case of data collectors as well.

SUMMARY AND CONCLUSIONS

Although not enough attention has been paid to the experimenter's role in parapsychological research, it is probably one of the most important variables of all. Some experimenters have reported not being able to obtain significant results on

ESP or PK tests while others often seem able to get significant results. Others are successful only with certain subjects or under certain testing conditions. It appears that whether or not a subject provides evidence of psi depends on how he is handled by the experimenter. A favorable subject-experimenter relationship favors psi test results. In addition, the motivation of the experimenter in carrying out his experiment appears to be an important factor in whether he will succeed or fail, although this supposition has not been tested. The experimenter's attitude toward and his method of handling the subject not only determine whether or not there will be extrachance results but appear also to be related to whether psi-hitting or psi-missing or perhaps both will occur. It is hypothesized that successful experimenters are able to pose questions in their research which are of great personal importance and that the possibility that that question might be answered in a particular experiment may induce an altered state in the experimenter which in turn affects the subject(s). In other words, experimenter expectancies may be necessary in order to induce psi results, and the more unconscious they are the more effective they may be. In a sense data collectors other than the organizing experimenter are just as important as the latter, for they contact the subjects, and the way they handle the subjects will have a major influence on whether and how the subjects perform. If the experimenter's motivation in conducting an experiment has something to do with whether and what results are obtained, it may be essential that data collectors share this interest and enthusiasm. In future experiments it might be wise to routinely record in advance of the actual ESP or PK testing the motivation in the particular experiment of the experimenter, data collectors, if any, or other persons playing an important role in any aspect of the investigation.

In any case, it is time that the experimenter himself be the subject of parapsychological investigations. If psi is a reality, it would be impossible to rule out the experimenter in the results of any investigation. Therefore we must do the next best thing: delineate in as much detail as possible exactly what the experimenter's influence is and how far it can be expressed. Just as survival research has foundered because parapsychologists do not know the limits of psi on the part of the living in producing "survival" evidence, so we cannot obtain reliable information about the subjects in psi experiments, whether animal or human, until we learn how much of the subject's response is attributable to the experimenter.

REFERENCES

Anderson, M. Clairvoyance and teacher-pupil attitudes in fifth and sixth grades. *Journal of Parapsychology*, 1957, **21**, 1–12.

Anderson, M., and White, R. Teacher-pupil attitudes and clairvoyance test results. *Journal of Parapsychology*, 1956, **20**, 141–157.

Anderson, M., and White, R. A further investigation of teacher-pupil attitudes and clairvoyance test results. *Journal of Parapsychology*, 1957, **21**, 81–97.

Anderson, M., and White, R. The relationship between changes in student attitude and ESP scoring. *Journal of Parapsychology*, 1958, **22**, 167–174. (a)

Anderson, M., and White, R. A survey of work on ESP and teacher-pupil attitudes. *Journal of Parapsychology*, 1958, **22**, 246–268. (b)

Bates, K. E., and Newton, M. An experimental study of ESP capacity in mental patients. *Journal of Parapsychology*, 1951, **15**, 271–277.

Bednarz, K., and Verrier, M. Role of experimenter in GESP tests. *Journal of Parapsychology*, 1969, **33**, 159.

Beloff, J. Belief and doubt. In W. G. Roll, R. L. Morris, and J. D. Morris (Eds.), *Research in Parapsychology 1972*, pp. 189–200. Metuchen, N.J.: Scarecrow Press, 1973.

Birge, W. R. A clairvoyance game experiment. *Journal of Parapsychology*, 1949, **13**, 197–207.

Casper, G. W. A further study of the relation of attitude to success in ESP scoring. *Journal of Parapsychology*, 1951, **15**, 139–145.

Crumbaugh, J. C. Are negative ESP results attributable to traits and attitudes of subjects and experimenters? *Journal of Parapsychology*, 1958, **22**, 294–295.

Honorton, C. Significant factors in hypnotically-induced clairvoyant dreams. *Journal of the American Society for Psychical Research*, 1972, **66**, 86–102. (a)

Honorton, C. Reported frequency of dream recall and ESP. *Journal of the American Society for Psychical Research*, 1972, **66**, 369–374. (b)

Honorton, C., and Barksdale, W. PK performance with waking suggestions for muscle tension versus relaxation. *Journal of the American Society for Psychical Research*, 1972, **66**, 208–214.

Honorton, C., Drucker, S. A., and Hermon, H. C. Shifts in subjective state and ESP under conditions of partial sensory deprivation: A preliminary study. *Journal of the American Society for Psychical Research*, 1973, **67**, 191–196.

Honorton, C., and Harper, S. Psi-mediated imagery and ideation in an experimental procedure for regulating perceptual input. *Journal of the American Society for Psychical Research*, 1974, **68**, 156–168.

Honorton, C., Ramsey, M., and Cabibbo, C. Experimenter effects in extrasensory perception. *Journal of the American Society for Psychical Research*, 1975, **69**, 135–149.

Hutchinson, L. Variations of time intervals in pre-shuffle card-calling tests. *Journal of Parapsychology*, 1940, **4**, 249–270.

Johnson, M. An attempt to manipulate the scoring direction of subjects by means of control of motivation of the subjects. *Research Letter of the Parapsychological Division of the Psychological Laboratory of the University of Utrecht*, 1971 (Dec.), 1–8.

Johnson, M., Cronquist, A., Danielsson, B. I., and Mondejar, A. A. A test of clairvoyance especially designed for children: A study on the effect of the experimenter-subject relationship on ESP-performance. *Research Letter of the Parapsychological Division of the Psychological Laboratory of the University of Utrecht*, 1972 (Mar.), 9–15.

Johnson, M., and Johannesson, G. An attempt to control scoring direction by means of treatment of the subjects. *Research Letter of the Parapsychological Division of the Psychological Laboratory of the University of Utrecht*, 1972 (Mar.), 1–8.

Kahn, S. D. Studies in extrasensory perception; Experiments utilizing an electronic scoring device. *Proceedings of the American Society for Psychical Research*, 1952, **25**, 1–48.

Kanthamani, B. K. A study of the differential response in language ESP tests. *Journal of Parapsychology*, 1965, **29**, 27–34. (a)

Kanthamani, B. K. The experimenter's role in language ESP tests. *Proceedings of the Parapsychological Association*, 1965, **2**, 34. (b)

Kennedy, J. L. A critical review of "Discrimination shown between experimenters by subjects." *Journal of Parapsychology*, 1939, **3**, 213–225.

Lester, D. The subject as a source of bias in psychological research. *Journal of General Psychology*, 1969, **81**, 237–248.

MacFarland, J. D. Discrimination shown between experimenters by subjects. *Journal of Parapsychology*, 1938, **2**, 160–170.

McMahan, E., and Rhine, S. L. ESP and PK tests as related to intelligence ratings. Unpublished manuscript. Described in J. B. Rhine, The problem of psi-missing. *Journal of Parapsychology*, 1952, **16**, 90–129.

Moss, T. S. A study of experimenter bias through subliminal perception. Unpublished doctoral dissertation, University of California, Los Angeles, 1966.

Murphy, G. What needs to be done in parapsychology. *Journal of Parapsychology*, 1948, **12**, 15–19.

Murphy, G. Psychical research and human personality. *Proceedings of the Society for Psychical Research*, 1949, **48**, 1–15.

Nash, C. B. The effect of subject-experimenter attitudes on clairvoyance scores. *Journal of Parapsychology*, 1960, **24**, 189–198.

Nash, C. B. Comparison of ESP run-score averages of groups liked and disliked by the experimenter. *Journal of the American Society for Psychical Research*, 1968, **62**, 411–414.

Nash, C. B., and Nash, C. S. Negative correlations between the scores of subjects in two contemporaneous ESP experiments. *Journal of the American Society for Psychical Research*, 1962, **56**, 80–83.

Nash, C. B., and Richards, A. Comparison of two distances in PK tests. *Journal of Parapsychology*, 1947, **11**, 269–282.

Nicol, J. F., and Humphrey, B. M. The exploration of ESP and human personality. *Journal of the American Society for Psychical Research*, 1953, **47**, 133–178.

Osis, K., and Dean, D. The effect of experimenter differences and subjects' belief level upon ESP scores. *Journal of the American Society for Psychical Research*, 1964, **58**, 158–185.

Parker, A. The experimenter effect. *Parapsychology Review*, 1974, **5**(2), 21.

Parker, A. A pilot study of the influence of experimenter expectancy on ESP scores. In J. D. Morris, W. G. Roll, and R. L. Morris (Eds.), *Research in Parapsychology 1974*, pp. 42–44. Metuchen, N.J.: Scarecrow Press, 1975.

Pratt, J. G. A review of Kahn's "Studies in extrasensory perception." *Journal of Parapsychology*, 1953, **17**, 215–222.

Pratt, J. G., and Price, M. M. The experimenter-subject relationship in tests for ESP. *Journal of Parapsychology*, 1938, **2**, 84–94.

Rao, K. R. Studies in the preferential effect. II. A language ESP test involving precognition and "intervention." *Journal of Parapsychology*, 1963, **27**, 147–160.

Rao, K. R. Studies in the preferential effect. IV. The role of key cards in preferential response situations. *Journal of Parapsychology*, 1964, **28**, 28–41.

Rhine, J. B. Conditions favoring success in psi tests. *Journal of Parapsychology*, 1948, **12**, 58–75.

[Rhine, J. B.] New experimenters in parapsychology. *Parapsychology Bulletin*, 1961, No. 58, 1–4.

Rhine, J. B., and Pratt, J. G. *Parapsychology: Frontier Science of the Mind*. Springfield, Ill.: Charles C Thomas, 1957.

Rilling, M. E., Adams, J. Q., and Pettijohn, C. A summary of some clairvoyance experiments conducted in classroom situations. *Journal of the American Society for Psychical Research*, 1962, **56**, 125–130.

Rivers, O. B. An exploratory study of the mental health and intelligence of ESP subjects. *Journal of Parapsychology*, 1950, **14**, 267–277.

Sailaja, P., and Rao, K. R. Experimental studies of the differential effect in life setting. *Parapsychological Monographs No. 13*. New York: Parapsychology Foundation, 1973.

Schmeidler, G. R. Predicting good and bad scores in a clairvoyance experiment: A preliminary report. *Journal of the American Society for Psychical Research*, 1943, 37, 103–110.

Schmeidler, G. R. (Ed.). *Extrasensory Perception*. New York: Atherton Press, 1969.

Schmeidler, G. R., and McConnell, R. A. *ESP and Personality Patterns*. New Haven: Yale University Press, 1958.

Sharp, V., and Clark, C. C. Group tests for extrasensory perception. *Journal of Parapsychology*, 1937, 1, 123–142.

Stanford, R. G. Extrasensory effects upon "memory." *Journal of the American Society for Psychical Research*, 1970, 64, 161–186.

Stanford, R. G. Extrasensory effects upon associative processes in a directed free-response task. *Journal of the American Society for Psychical Research*, 1973, 67, 147–190.

Stanford, R. G., Zenhausern, R., Taylor, A., and Dwyer, M. A. Psychokinesis as psi-mediated instrumental response. *Journal of the American Society for Psychical Research*, 1975, 69, 127–133.

Stuart, C. E. An examination of Kennedy's study of the MacFarland data. *Journal of Parapsychology*, 1940, 4, 135–141.

Tart, C. T. The application of learning theory in ESP performance. *Parapsychological Monographs No. 15*. New York: Parapsychology Foundation, 1975.

Van Busschbach, J. G. An investigation of ESP between teacher and pupils in American schools. *Journal of Parapsychology*, 1956, 20, 71–80.

Van Busschbach, J. G. An investigation of ESP in the first and second grades of Dutch schools. *Journal of Parapsychology*, 1959, 23, 227–237.

Van de Castle, R. L. Differential patterns of ESP scoring as a function of differential attitudes toward ESP. *Journal of the American Society for Psychical Research*, 1957, 51, 43–61.

Waldron, S. Clairvoyance scores of sheep versus goats when subjects' attitude toward the experimenter and the purpose of the experiment are manipulated. *Journal of Parapsychology*, 1959, 23, 289.

West, D. J., and Fisk, G. W. A dual ESP experiment with clock cards. *Journal of the Society for Psychical Research*, 1953, 37, 185–196.

White, R. A., and Angstadt, J. A review of results and new experiments bearing on teacher-selection methods in the Anderson-White high school experiments. *Journal of the American Society for Psychical Research*, 1965, 59, 56–84.

Woodruff, J. L., and Dale, L. A. Subject and experimenter attitudes in relation to ESP scoring. *Journal of the American Society for Psychical Research*, 1950, 44, 87–112.

Part IV

PARAPSYCHOLOGY AND PHYSICAL SYSTEMS

1

Historical Background

J. Fraser Nicol

INTRODUCTION

Though paranormal physical phenomena were reported in very early times, the quality of the accounts was dubious, to put it mildly. Thus Moses (ca. 1200 B.C.) was supposed, with divine help, to have parted the waters of the Red Sea, allowing the Israelites to cross unharmed; and then by reversing the process he caught the pursuing Egyptians and drowned them all (Exodus, Chap. 14).

The sardonic Edward Gibbon (1910) recalled the tale from the days of Mohammed of how the moon "stooped from her station in the sky, . . . saluted Mohammed in the Arabian tongue, and suddenly contracting her dimensions, entered at the collar, and issued forth through the sleeve of his shirt" (Vol. 4, p. 242).

Fortunately, in the next thousand years there was some improvement in standards of evidence, as witness that avid collector of strange experiences, John Aubrey (1890), who narrated: "There was in Scotland one (an obsessus) carried in the air several times in the view of several persons, his fellow-sòldiers. Major Henton hath seen him carried away from the guard in Scotland, sometimes a mile or two. Sundry persons are living now (1671) that can attest this story. I had it from Sir Robert Harley . . . who married Major Henton's widow; as also from E.T.D.D." (p. 153). The initials may possibly stand for Aubrey's reverend friend Ezreel Tongue, D.D. The significant feature of the account is not of course the incredible story but the fact that John Aubrey realized the importance of corroborative evidence, though in this instance he was only able to obtain it at second-hand.

Joseph Glanvil, a contemporary of Aubrey, wrote a substantial book (1700) of psychical cases, some of which he had personally investigated, including the famous Drummer of Tedworth poltergeist.

In the next century another ardent psychical researcher, Daniel Defoe (1840), during his many investigations, exposed a fraudulent poltergeist case near Dorking in Surrey.

In the course of several centuries the quality of investgations was slowly improving, while at the same time the variety of phenomena was greatly extended. Hitherto most of the reported occurrences were of the spontaneous or poltergeist types, but by the middle of the nineteenth century experimental methods began to emerge. Credit for this development is attributable solely to the rise of modern Spiritualism. This fact need cause us little surprise and no embarrassment for, after all, nearly all the established sciences have been the creatures of strange parents: pure mathematics born from Pythagorean numerology, astronomy from astrology, chemistry from alchemy, medicine from Galenic delusions, and so on. Considered historically, therefore, it may be that the origins of psychical research are slightly more respectable than those of the traditional sciences.

The controversial nature of the modern physical phenomena will be readily imagined by merely listing some of the claims. Raps and other percussive sounds were the earliest form of physical phenomena and together with telekinesis (or psychokinesis) are perhaps the best evidenced, though under loose experimental conditions they are easy to imitate by trickery. Less plausible to critically-minded investigators were: personal levitation in the séance room; direct writing on paper or slates without apparent human aid; direct speech ostensibly originating at some point in the air distant from a medium; ectoplasm (effusion of a semisolid substance from a medium); materializations ("ghosts" in solid form); apports (passage of solid objects through matter); and teleportation (transit of a person or object over considerable distances).

The modern investigation of physical phenomena began in 1848 when in the month of March at a cottage in Hydesville, New York, two young daughters of Mr. and Mrs. J. D. Fox, Catherine (age 11) and Margaretta (age 14), heard rapping sounds in their bedroom. After a time, Kate, wondering if the knocks had an intelligent source, cried, "Do as I do, Mr. Splitfoot!" and clapped her hands. The sounds were echoed in raps. Mrs. Fox asked, "Are you a spirit? If you are rap twice." Two knocks, and modern Spiritualism was born (Capron, 1855; Pond, 1947). The Fox girls, and also their married sister Leah, gave demonstrations for many years, separately or together. Kate was the most notable performer. Emigrating to Britain, she was investigated by the scientist (Sir) William Crookes, who wrote:

> . . . it seems only necessary for her to place her hand on any substance for

loud thuds to be heard in it, like a triple pulsation, sometimes loud enough to be heard several rooms off. In this manner I have heard them in a living tree—on a sheet of glass—on a stretched iron wire—on stretched membrane . . . Moreover, actual contact is not always necessary; I have had these sounds proceeding from the floor, walls, &c., when the medium's hands and feet were held. . . (cited in Medhurst, Goldney, and Barrington, 1972, p. 113).

Mrs. E. M. Sidgwick (1886b) had several séances with Kate (then Mrs. Jencken) in 1874 and 1885, and though she discovered no fraud, she remained unconvinced. Lord Rayleigh (1919), the future Nobel physicist, had sittings with Mrs. Jencken at his country house which left him unable to form a definite opinion one way or the other. One thing he could not explain on normal grounds was floating lights as much as 6 and 8 feet distant from the medium.

After her husband's death Kate Jencken returned to the United States where she and Margaretta (also a widow) were soon reported sunk in poverty and alcoholism. In 1888 they publicly "confessed" to a history of fraud, but a month later Margaretta recanted, and in a few years all three sisters were dead. The importance of the Foxes rests solely in the fact that they initiated the modern movement for the investigation of physical phenomena. How much, if any, of their experiences were genuine is impossible to assess, the séance conditions being usually insufficient to exclude normal causes.

Though within a few years mediums cropped up all over the United States and in Europe, scientists were slow to investigate. An exception was Robert Hare (1781–1858), emeritus professor of chemistry at the University of Pennsylvania and famous for his inventions including the oxy-hydrogen blowpipe. For his mediumistic investigations he constructed and used an ingenious mechanism for the measurement of the hypothetical psychic force. Nevertheless, he got a skeptical reception at the annual meeting in 1854 of the American Association for the Advancement of Science when he described "an experiment made with the greatest care and precision, which proved the existence of a power independent of any possible or conceivable mortal agency" (Hare, 1856, p. 431). When in the following year he submitted a preliminary letter to the President of the Association, the standing committee resolved that the subject did not fall within the objects of the Association.

In 1857 a committee of Harvard professors and others, including Louis Agassiz and Benjamin Peirce, investigated a number of physical mediums. A promised report never saw the light, but in a brief pronouncement at the close of the séances the committee deemed it their "solemn duty to warn the community against this contaminating influence [psychic séances], which surely tends to lessen the truth of man and the purity of woman" (Sargent, 1869, p. 10).

The Victorian tone of moral disapproval was not entirely out of place, for fraud and deception by bogus mediums were commonplace occurrences of mediumistic performances in darkened rooms. Nevertheless, many séance-room shams were exposed—usually by Spiritualists themselves but occasionally by non-Spiritualists, as witness the long and negative investigations of the Seybert Commission on Spiritualism appointed by the University of Pennsylvania under the will of Henry Seybert. The Commission investigated numerous physical mediums almost all of whom they discovered to be fraudulent or guilty of dubious practices at best (Preliminary Report, 1887).

Although many séance reports read like adventures in the absurd, they are historically important because it was by learning such hard lessons by bitter experience that serious psychical researchers were enabled to toughen their methods and thereby defeat imposture. For instance, on the side of credulity there was the Londoner Gambier Bolton, author of zoological works, who claimed that at a séance held by the materialization medium Frederick Craddock he had caressed the materialized form of his lately deceased pet monkey; and that at the same sitting in the dark a pet seal, a few days dead, had flopped out of the medium's cabinet (Bolton, 1900). In agreeable contrast to the bemused zoologist we have the young psychologist William McDougall attending another dark sitting with Craddock when the latter's "spirit control" appeared from the cabinet, his face made visible by means of a luminous plaque. "This awe-inspiring vision," McDougall (1906) reported, "began to make the tour of our semi-circle, showing to each in turn the face dimly lit by the phosphorescent pasteboard. When my turn came I rose and seized the head in my arms and dragged it, together with the violently resisting body of the 'medium,' into the gaslight of the next room. There was a scene of some confusion while the 'medium' and his agent received corporal chastisement" (p. 276).

Not all mediumistic frauds were done for financial gain. Henry Sidgwick (1894) knew of "half-a-dozen instances [of] deception in cases where no motive of pecuniary interest could come in." One deceiver was a learned gentleman who could cause a small table to rise—by the simple trick of using two rods concealed under his sleeves and outstretched hands.

The list of questionable claims to physical phenomena could be extended indefinitely. Fully formed materialized spirits (as the sitters believed them to be) appeared in many séance rooms, as many as a dozen such phantoms in an evening, walking about the room in dim light, talking, kissing their surviving friends. Mrs. Mary M. Hardy of Boston produced paraffin wax molds of spirit hands and feet. Under cover of darkness a spirit supposedly plunged a limb into a pail of melted paraffin, then into a pail of cold water. The wax hardening, the spirit dematerialized the hand, leaving the mold behind from which a plaster cast could be made. But as Walter Franklin Prince (1933) afterwards recalled from history, on one occasion "when Mrs. Hardy was going to a sitting with a Spiritualist friend, a paraffin hand fell out of her bag, in which it was not supposed to be, in advance of the 'demonstration.'" In London a great stir was created when it was claimed by numerous witnesses that an amateur medium, Mrs. Agnes Guppy, had been teleported from her home in north London to a closed room in a house 3 miles away where a séance happened to be in progress (Holms, 1925).

But incidents like the above and many others resembling them seem rather minor affairs when compared with the extraordinary marvels associated with Mme. H. P. Blavatsky, member of an upper-class Russian family and a founder of the Theosophical Society. In particular there were many reports of letters supposedly apported from alleged "Mahatmas" in Tibet to Mme. Blavatsky's friends, who were usually in her neighborhood or in the vicinity of one of her junior associates. A Committee of the newly founded Society for Psychical Research in London, after conducting considerable inquiries among leading Theosophists (First Report, 1884) sent one of their number, Dr. Richard Hodgson, to India where he made investigations on the spot at the Theosophical Headquarters at Adyar. As a result of Hodgson's devastating 200-page report and other information, the Committee concluded: "For our own part, we regard her [Mme. Blavatsky] neither as the mouthpiece of hidden seers, nor as a mere vulgar adventuress; we think that she has achieved a title to permanent remembrance as one of the most accomplished, ingenious, and interesting impostors in history" (Report, 1885, p. 207).

Not all physical phenomena could be dismissed as merely bogus. Table-tilting (typtology) has a long history dating from Roman times. In modern activities it is customary for a medium to sit at a small table with her hands near the edge. One tilt of the table stands for the letter A, two for B, and so on. By this means Spiritualists believed they obtained messages from the dead. Michael Faraday, however, devised an ingenious experiment which showed that the usual type of tilting could be explained by the conscious or unconscious pressure of the operator's fingers on the table edge. Though Faraday's demonstration was impressive, it shed no light on the content of the messages which in some cases were at least telepathic from distant sources. Nor could Faraday explain how in other cases, as with the medium D. D. Home, a table would tilt or even move across a room in good light without being touched at all.

Of great historic importance were the manifestations (real or supposed) called direct-writing or psychography. Their significance rests in the fact, as will be seen below, that a close study of them led to a revolution in the methods and attitudes of psychical researchers with respect to all kinds of physical phenomena.

In psychographic experiments writing mysteriously appeared on paper or slates without (it was claimed) human aid or mechanism. The earliest exponent was the erudite Baron Louis de Guldenstubbé (ca. 1820–1873) who published an extraordinary book (1873) describing many of his 2,000 experiments. For his first attempt, on 1 August 1856, he put paper and pencil in a small box which he locked. Twelve days later he found that the paper had been written on. Many of his subsequent experiments took place in churches and graveyards. In the cloisters of Westminster Abbey he invited Oriana T. Greenfield to place two pieces of paper and a pencil upon a stone, which she did and covered them with a handkerchief. The baron walked to the other side of the cloisters while the lady and two friends protected the objects. When on the baron's return the lady removed the handkerchief she found inscribed on the papers a faint cross and the word *Life* (Greenfield, 1892). Unfortunately for the many Guldenstubbé reports by himself or others, essential details are so lacking that it is impossible to draw favorable conclusions.

Slate-writing was witnessed by Charles Dickens in 1853 at Boulogne. The performance, however, was by a conjuror who did not pretend that the display was any more than a trick. Charles Dickens was completely baffled (Blyton, 1892).

In the 1860s the American medium Henry Slade rose to fame, claiming that his slate-writing was the work of spirits. The highlight of his checkered career was an investigation by the astrophysicist Professor J. C. F. Zöllner and other German scientists who were deeply impressed, particularly by a different type of phenomenon, namely the apparent production of a knot in an endless cord. Out of this manifestation Zöllner (1882) conceived a theory of the fourth dimension. Some years later Slade submitted himself to the Seybert Commission, which repeatedly detected him cheating and concluded that his demonstrations were "fraudulent throughout" (Preliminary Report, 1887).

It was the British medium William Eglinton (1857-1933) who unwittingly— and paradoxically—paved the way for a drastic new outlook and a transformation of methods in the investigation of physical phenomena. Beginning his mediumship as a teenager, Eglinton obtained wide publicity for his materialized ghosts (Aksakof, 1895). But, turning his talents to slate-writing he soon showed himself an abler performer than Henry Slade. Several conjurors wrote testimonials to his genuineness. But trouble was on the way—at the hands of a talented woman, Mrs. E. M. Sidgwick. Having attended three slate-writing sittings with Eglinton at which nothing happened, she published (1886a) and discussed reports of other investigators. Those reports were on the whole favorable to Eglinton or noncommittal, and no sitter detected fraud. Nevertheless Mrs. Sidgwick had her doubts: "Certainly some of the phenomena *as described* seem to be inexplicable by the known laws of nature; but this proves nothing by itself, since the question still remains, Are they correctly described?" (pp. 331-332). Those four words epitomize almost the whole problem of physical phenomena research. Mrs. Sidgwick further pointed to the human difficulty of exercising *continuous* observation, unbroken over a period of time. In this connection it has to be noted that at Eglinton's séances the sitters' attention was frequently diverted by such incidents as the medium dropping a slate or passing into a convulsive, gasping state, well contrived to interrupt the sitters' "continuous observation." Mrs. Sidgwick's final judgment on Eglinton was: "For

myself I have now no hesitation in attributing his performances to clever conjuring" (p. 332). Eglinton was later discovered in an act of trickery.

Meanwhile there was an astonishing development, which lives in history. A
young S.P.R. member, S. John Davey (ca. 1863-1890), having at first been
deeply impressed by Eglinton sittings he had attended, began to have doubts.
These he followed up by conceiving and privately practicing trick methods of
producing slate writing effects in the style of Eglinton. Using a fictitious name
he offered his services as a "medium," with Richard Hodgson present as an observer. The numerous sitters were requested to write reports of their experiences. When those accounts were compared with the true séance facts the
contrast was devastating. Sitters misreported commonplace incidents. They
reported things that never happened. And all the time they failed to observe
and remember the most crucial happenings to the slates, even though the latter
were only 3 feet from their eyes. On a few occasions sitters were informed before a séance that trickery would be used. They detected nothing (Hodgson,
1892; Hodgson and Davey, 1886-87).

The Davey and Hodgson reports on malobservation have long been numbered
among the several great classics of psychical research. Almost half a century
later Theodore Besterman (1931-32) conducted comparable research in which
members of the S.P.R. were candidly invited to have their powers of observation tested in a situation resembling a séance, except that there was no trickery.
Six séances were attended by an average of seven sitters—42 in all. Each séance
lasted only 25 minutes, and the incidents at all sittings were identical. At the
end of each sitting the participants were invited to answer a questionnaire about
their observations. The replies were scored not in simple terms of right-or-
wrong, but according to the difficulty of the questions and precision of detail;
and as Besterman reported, "the scoring was all done with a definite bias in
favour of the sitter" (p. 369). Nevertheless, the best score was only 61 percent
correct, the worst 5.9 percent, and the average for all sitters 33.9 percent.
Roughly speaking, twice out of three times the testimony could not be trusted.
Thirteen sitters experienced illusions.

In summary, the overwhelming number of reports on mediumistic physical
phenomena offer no valid evidence. Fortunately, there are a few cases which
the majority of critically minded students find it unreasonable to dismiss.

The most impressive history is that of the Scotsman Daniel Dunglas Home
(1833-1886). When as an adolescent he was living with an aunt in Connecticut,
raps were heard and pieces of furniture were seen to move about the room. The
aunt, becoming alarmed, turned Daniel out of the house. These poltergeist
phenomena continued elsewhere, and formal séances began to be held in various parts of New England. Impressive features of Home's demonstrations were
that they almost always took place in good light, and Home sat among the
observers, never using a medium's cabinet. He moved to London where he

was investigated and approved by Lord Brougham (a famous judge), Bulwer Lytton (novelist and occultist), and numerous other notable persons. Most of his phenomena were telekinetic in various forms, but occasionally a supernumerary hand would be seen coming from under some Victorian dining-table. At various times he demonstrated before the Emperor Napoleon III, the Tsar of Russia, and other royalties, and numerous scientists, scholars, and statesmen. No malpractice was ever discovered in hundreds of sittings over 25 years.

Scientifically, the most striking experiments were conducted by William Crookes (Medhurst et al., 1972) who, improving on Robert Hare's method (1856) for measuring psychic force, constructed an apparatus consisting of a board 36 inches long and about 9 inches wide; the board was suspended at one end from a spring balance which was furnished with an automatic recording device, and, near the other end, it rested upon a fulcrum on a table. On the board above the fulcrum was a large cylindrical bowl filled with water, and in the upper part of the water was a perforated copper vessel independently supported. When Home dipped the fingers of his right hand in the copper vessel, while his left hand and feet were held by experimenters, the board moved, registering a force of 5,000 grains (about 11 ounces). Using simpler apparatus Crookes and his colleagues found the force registering up to 6 pounds.

A curious Home phenomenon was the apparent paranormal playing of an accordion. Crookes tightened the customary conditions by building a small cage open at the top and obtaining a new accordion which Home had never seen. Home as usual held the instrument inverted at its base, the keys therefore being at the bottom and out of his reach, protected by the cage. His free hand and feet were controlled by the investigators. The accordion played a well-known melody. On some occasions it played when untouched by anyone (Medhurst et al., 1972).

On numerous occasions in his career Home was personally levitated from the floor. Crookes once recalled to the well-known psychical researcher, Sir Ernest Bennett (1927): "On that very hearthrug where you are standing I saw Home raised eighteen inches from the ground in broad daylight and verified the phenomenon *visu et tactu.*"

The Italian medium Eusapia Palladino (1854–1918) was an illiterate peasant whose psychic gifts emerged at puberty when she was asked to join a Spiritualist circle in southern Italy. In 1888 she was brought to the attention of the scientific world when Professor Chiaia of Naples challenged the skeptic Professor Lombroso to investigate the medium himself. Lombroso did so (1909) and was completely convinced that her telekinetic and other powers were genuine.

Though Palladino used a cabinet, she customarily sat outside it at a small table. Frequently not only did the table rise into the air—and was there photographed —but the cabinet curtains bulged out as if blown by some strong wind in the cabinet. When Palladino was tied prostrate to a bed the phenomena continued.

To add to the Palladino mystery, in spite of the genuineness of some of the phenomena (which exhausted her physically and mentally) she was on some occasions caught cheating—by slipping one of her hands from a researcher's control. However, according to the neurologist Professor Enrico Morselli (who in 1908 published a 1000-page book about her) her trance was genuine. In that condition she could not be held morally blameworthy. Palladino was an extraordinary person in many ways. She never denied accusations of fraud. She usually knew—from internal sensations, no doubt—when a phenomenon was about to happen; and there is at least one memorable occasion when she cried out in her Neapolitan dialect, "Hold me tight or I'll cheat!" or words to that effect.

The Institut Général Psychologique in Paris seems to have imposed fairly strict controls on Palladino during 43 sittings through the years 1905–1908 and appears to have been satisfied. The investigators, who included Pierre and Marie Curie, d'Arsonval, Bergson, and others, made good use of instrumental methods. Palladino discharged an electroscope without touching it, and she caused a lever balance to register up to 7 kilograms without contact (Courtier, 1908). An even more impressive investigation was conducted at Naples in 1908 by three research experts, the Hon. Everard Feilding, W. W. Baggally, and Hereward Carrington, all of whom as the fruit of many years' investigation of physical mediums had found nothing but fraud and delusion. Their 260-page report (1909) is probably the most thorough and reliable account of physical phenomena that has ever been published. Minute by minute a shorthand writer recorded the spoken pronouncements of the investigators—what they saw, heard, and felt through 11 séances. Once during a dimly lit period in the third séance, Carrington detected the medium escaping his hand control, but the phenomena were feeble. On many other occasions in good light, and the medium's hands and feet controlled, the table repeatedly ascended into the air, and in the cabinet—behind Palladino—a guitar was strummed, a bell rung, and a table in the cabinet "walked" into the séance room. The three investigators beginning as suspicious skeptics were forced to the conviction that Palladino did produce evidence of a force not known to official science.

Among many mediums who have appeared since Palladino's time, Franek Kluski of Poland, sitting in the dark, produced paraffin wax moulds of "spirit" hands some of which had the appearance of adult's hands but were the size of a small child's. The ectoplasm that issued from the mouth of the Frenchwoman Marthe Béraud ("Eva C.") was the subject of much controversy. In Boston Mina ("Margery") Crandon, a surgeon's wife, was several times photographed in the dark showing an object shaped like a hand seemingly coming out of her mouth or, on other occasions, apparently from her vagina. Anatomy experts, however, said the hand was "undoubtedly cut out of lung tissue of some animal" (Prince, 1934, p. 79). At some Crandon dark séances thumb prints on wax were obtained that were said to be those of the medium's deceased brother. In fact they were the prints of the medium's dentist who had originally given her some dental wax (Tietze, 1973).

An impressive case for genuineness of physical phenomena can be made for the Austrian Rudi Schneider who, in addition to causing objects to move without contact, was able, when firmly controlled by French investigators, to produce paranormal interference in a beam of infra-red rays (Osty and Osty, 1931). Similar Schneider phenomena, though more subdued, were obtained by Lord Charles Hope and other researchers in London (Hope, 1933).

Aside from mediumistic séances, various instruments were constructed over the years which it was claimed showed the existence of a human paranormal force. They have all passed into the discard. The best known was Dr. Paul Joire's sthenometer, which consisted of a straw pointer resting on a needle point and protected by a glass shade. When a hand was held above and at right angles to the pointer the latter revolved toward alignment with the hand. F. J. M. Stratton and P. Phillips (1906) showed that the effect was due to the heat of the hand.

One of the most controversial phenomena is the "direct voice": that is, a voice ostensibly originating not in the medium's vocal organs but from a point in space a short distance away. An internationally famous practitioner was Mrs. Etta Wriedt (1859–1942) of Detroit. Like most "psychophonic" mediums, she employed a trumpet which in the darkness of the séance room was apparently levitated into the air and in the next hour or so trumpet voices conversed with the sitters. It was said that sometimes voices of the dead spoke in foreign languages. Incidents were reported of two voices being heard simultaneously, and there were instances when, it was claimed, Mrs. Wriedt (always in a conscious state) could be heard speaking to a sitter while simultaneously a trumpet voice was speaking to another sitter (Holms, 1925).

Among notable persons who attended her London séances were W. B. Yeats, W. L. Mackenzie King, and W. T. Stead. Everard Feilding had two sittings with Mrs. Wriedt in 1911. He privately reported that the phenomena might have been due to trickery. In the following year, when the medium gave further sittings in London, Feilding and his friend Baggally were "specifically excluded" (Carrington, 1957). This was a pity because if her claims were genuine there were no two men in London better qualified to confirm them.

Physiologically, a most peculiar case of purported direct voice concerns Mrs. Elizabeth Blake. Her phenomena came to involve a theory that her voices were produced—apparently unconsciously, though she was never entranced—by subvocal articulation. This curious form of speech production has been known for centuries. In 1727 Daniel Defoe (1840) reported the case of a servant girl in Hertfordshire, England, being "possessed of the Devil" who spoke through her "by the organ of her voice, though without any apparent motion of her tongue or lips, or any part of her mouth."

Mrs. Blake spent almost the whole of her long life in the village of Bradrick on the north side of the Ohio River. She became the wife of "a humble farmer" in the neighborhood and the mother of a family. In childhood she had "heard voices in her ears," but it was not until much later that she began practice as a medium. At first her sittings were unpaid, but later she charged ten cents and eventually a dollar.

At her voice sittings, usually held in daylight or in good artificial light, she used a trumpet about 2 feet long, 2 inches wide at the center, and tapering to about $\frac{1}{2}$ inch at each end. Seated on a chair, she held one end of the trumpet to her ear while the sitter held the other end to his ear. Though she kept her mouth closed, a voice or voices would presently be heard in the trumpet. The sounds were usually whispered, but occasionally they could be heard clearly by independent observers even at a distance.

Mrs. Blake was almost unknown to the psychical world until David Abbott, a conjuring expert and psychical researcher, heard of her and informed Dr. J. H. Hyslop, leader of the American Society for Psychical Research. They and one or two others journeyed to Bradrick where they conducted a considerable investigation, their reports filling more than 200 pages of print (Hyslop, Guthrie Abbott, Clawson, and Clawson, 1913). Mrs. Blake was found to be an "elderly and frail lady." All the experimenters were greatly impressed by what they observed through two series of voice sittings. Hyslop concluded that she was "consciously honest." It was soon noticed that when voices were heard in the trumpet Mrs. Blake's mouth was tightly closed. But Hyslop and Abbott when acting as observers saw that her throat muscles twitched simultaneously with the voice sounds in the trumpet. Mrs. Blake's physician, Dr. L. V. Guthrie, suggested the theory that the voices were produced in the medium's throat from which they passed (her lips being closed) through the Eustachian tube to the tympanum of the ear.

The investigators found that "ventriloquism" was not a plausible explanation of their experiences. Moreover, all the sitters received what purported to be communications from their departed relatives and friends. Some were highly evidential. When a sitter, Mr. G. W. Clawson, asked a communicator (ostensibly his deceased daughter) for her former fiancé's name, she correctly replied, "Archimedes" and spelled the name.

When Mrs. Blake died in April, 1920, it was recorded "that four hours after she was first pronounced dead by a physician she revived and that she continued to live for several days" (Prince, 1920a).

Purported phenomena not of the direct voice but apparently related to it and involving telekinesis have occasionally been reported in the last 60 years. In 1915 David Wilson, a Londoner and a qualified solicitor, believed he had obtained paranormal messages by "wireless telegraphy." His apparatus included a galvanometer. One day the galvanometer needle suddenly jerked for no discoverable reason. Some days later when the needle made short and long movements Wilson wondered whether they might represent the Morse code. So it seemingly proved, according to Wilson (1915), who thereafter received brief messages which indicated that the sender (if such there were) had a knowledge of Wilson, his family, and certain psychical experiments he had supervised.

Wilson persuaded a friend to learn the Morse alphabet, and the two men made separate records as they watched the galvanometer. Their interpretations of the needle's movements tended to vary. On one occasion Wilson believed that the meaning in the two records was: "Try eliminate vibrations. ARTK."

The galvanometer was subsequently replaced by an instrument that provided dots and dashes by sound. A duplicate instrument was set up in Paris, the experimenter being Wilson's friend "J. F." On March 19 at 11.1 P.M. Wilson recorded the following from his receiver: "Message received in Russian: 'Nyet leezdyes Kogoneebood Kto govoreet poroossky.' Translation: 'Is there anyone who speaks Russian here?' Six minutes later, 1.7 P.M. J. F. in Paris received this: 'Nyet . . . lee . . . [incoherent] . . . Kto . . . poroosski.'" Wilson did not think the messages came from spirits of the dead but rather that they were mundanely telepathic from unknown sources. His reports were criticized in the pages of *Light*. Perhaps it was all delusion and wishful thinking. On the other hand it might be argued that Wilson possessed some telepathic gift and that what he thereby received he unconsciously transferred to a sensitive electronic instrument by means of some small telekinetic influence. We shall never know unless someone tries to repeat Wilson's research with technological improvements and safeguards.

In 1918 an anonymously written book was published in Boston, in which the author (Geldert, 1918) claimed to have received paranormal radio communications from her dead son. The writer's name was revealed 9 years later as Mrs. Louis Napoleon Geldert. Her son Bob had been a radio buff, an interest which his passionately devoted mother tried to share. When the United States entered the first World War, Bob was officially ordered to dismantle his wireless installation. He soon became an Army officer specializing in wireless and was sent to the Western Front. One day, while Mrs. Geldert was reading one of Bob's letters, suddenly "the wireless signaled 'attention,'" It was a message in Morse from Bob saying he had been killed in battle "near Lens." The mother recorded further quite long Morse messages from Bob in the receipt of which (according to her) she never once erred in the interpretation of thousands of Morse signals (alphabetical letters).

Dr. J. H. Hyslop despatched to the publisher a list of questions to be forwarded to the anonymous author. She refused to answer. Hyslop (1919) in a review said the book read like "a piece of imagination dressed up to make it miraculous." Dr. Walter F. Prince (1920b) judged the work "an imposture . . . a book made to sell, and I have no doubt it has fulfilled its purpose." In fact, when the book was reprinted during the Second World War, the publisher revealed that the first edition sold 31,407 copies. The Geldert affair is of historical interest because it typifies a vast range of stories that impress the unthinking section of the public and therefore require critically-minded investigators like Hyslop and Prince to defend the subject from such errors.

In the last two decades an allegedly new type of voice phenomenon has been reported—"voices on the tapes," i.e., voices faintly heard (it is claimed) when unused magnetic tapes are played and listened to by means of earphones. They were first apparently heard by Raymond Bayless and a colleague in Los Angeles in 1956 (Bayless, 1959). Further reports have been published by F. Jurgenson (Sweden) and the late Dr. K. Raudive (Latvian living in Germany) (Raudive, 1971). Raudive's claims have been subjected to much criticism, rising at times to total disbelief (Cutten, 1971). A frequently expressed view is that the voices are illusory, being false interpretations of static and other meaningless sounds.

In telekinesis research during half a dozen decades there had been some development in laboratory techniques. The purported telekinetic abilities of Kathleen Goligher (later Mrs. S. G. Donaldson) were brought to public notice by Dr. W. J. Crawford (1916, 1919), college lecturer in engineering at Belfast, who in 1914 began his 6-year investigation of the medium. Miss Goligher was born in 1898, one of numerous children of a poor family. Her mediumship seems to have begun about the age of puberty. According to Crawford six other members of the family were also mediums "in a greater or less degree," but Kathleen, the youngest daughter, was the "medium of outstanding merit." Raps were a minor phenomenon at her séances, and to confirm their reality Crawford made phonographic records of them as they occurred.

Miss Goligher was usually quite conscious during her séances. The family customarily sat in a circle of about 5 feet diameter with a table or stool—the objects of psychic activity—in the center. The room was illuminated with a dim red light shining from a 4-foot high mantlepiece. Crawford was thus able (if his senses were not otherwise engaged) to see every one of the six or more persons in the room. Kathleen's feet, however, were not usually visible, being concealed by the shadow of the table; and judging from a plan of the room any one of the six members of the Goligher family sitting opposite the mantlepiece would also have his/her legs hidden by the table or its shadow.

The phenomena were chiefly telekinetic, the usual experimental object being the table weighing 10½ pounds, occasionally the stool. The table was often levitated into the air where it hovered for as long as 5 minutes on end. The medium's chair stood on a platform scale. Crawford found that the registered weight increased simply by the weight of the table. There were other experiments which seemed to show that the weight was partly borne by some of the sitters. Crawford devised the theory that the table was raised by a cantilever of ectoplasm extruded from the lower part of the medium's body. There were occasions when a strong man trying to force the table down to the floor completely failed. Various other phenomena were tested with scientific instruments, to Crawford's complete satisfaction.

Sir William Barrett (1920) in 1915 and Whately Smith (later Carington) (1920) in 1916 had brief experiences of.the mediumship and were convinced of its genuineness; but 4 years later Carington, making a return visit, found a "conspicuous and startling deterioration" and (as he long afterwards informed me) concluded that the initially honest mediumship had sunk into fraud.

Crawford committed suicide in July, 1920. He left a message saying that the reason for his death was not Miss Goligher's mediumship, of which his high opinion was unchanged.

Three months after Crawford's death, F. M. Stevenson (1920) held a sitting at which he was accompanied by some of his friends, including two women doctors who searched Miss Goligher before the séance. Miss Goligher's attendant relatives were also searched. "Plasma," described as "a clammy gripping substance," seemingly produced from the medium's body, was photographed by five cameras. Stevenson believed the phenomena were genuine.

In 1922 the physicist and psychical researcher Dr. E. E. Fournier d'Albe (1922) had 20 sittings with Miss Goligher and her family and reported that he observed no paranormal phenomena but did see fraud. After publication of Fournier's report Miss Goligher refused all further investigation. It might charitably be argued (as indeed has been argued for other mediums of comparable history) that Miss Goligher did in her early days produce genuine telekinetic effects but that when later her "power" declined, she consciously provided a fake substitute. Whatever the verdict, Dr. Crawford deserves to be remembered for the variety of technological equipment and methods (too numerous to be described here) which he introduced to the study of physical phenomena.

A more impressive investigation of telekinetic mediumship concerned a Danish woman, Mrs. Anna Rasmussen (b. 1898), whose apparent gifts began to manifest at the age of 12 when she caused tables to move. Later, raps were heard in her presence. She also produced automatic writing and mirror-writing. More importantly for scientific investigation, she was able to deflect the scales of a balance.

Professor Christian Winther (1928) of the Polytechnic Academy, Copenhagen, held 116 séances with her—usually in normal light—in his laboratory and elsewhere. His research colleagues usually included one or more scientists and physicians. The experiments were designed to test Mrs. Rasmussen's ability to move a balance paranormally. The medium was accommodated on cushions in a basket chair facing a table on which stood two balances. The latter was soon activated. Winther was convinced that the movements here and in all other experiments could not be explained on normal grounds. Then, one day, without forewarning the medium he produced a pendulum apparatus he had carefully constructed in private. The pendulum bobs were on different occasions made of steel, wood, rubber, glass, sugar, and other substances, and they were suspended by either wire, sewing thread, or wool inside a stout glass case placed on a table. Two pendulums were used simultaneously in order that the medium could be requested to move one but not the other. This she did frequently. She could also cause them to move at different amplitudes. All the movements were automatically recorded on instruments.

At one session when a glass of water was placed on the table, the surface of the water "remained calm while the pendulums went into strong action." Working on his own, Winther tried to produce the effects by normal means. By applying "rhythmic pressure upon the floor" he was able by "extreme physical effort" to produce a swing of "one centimeter or so," whereas with Mrs. Rasmussen swings were often recorded of 8 to 10.5 centimeters. By pressing against the tabletop or legs he obtained swings but not without affecting the water in the glass; and apparently he was unable to produce differential effects on two pendulums.

In the hope of ruling out all possibility of trickery by vibration or otherwise, Winther had a concrete pillar built into the concrete floor of a cellar. The glass case and its pendulums were fixed on top of the pillar. Two series of experiments were held with Mrs. Rasmussen. The pendulums never moved. The medium's purported spirit control "Dr. Lasaruz" attributed the failure to the dampness of the cellar.

Dr. Nandor Fodor (1964) was disappointed by the results of an investigation of Mrs. Rasmussen he and colleagues carried out in London 15 years later, in 1938. He found that the pendulums moved only when the medium was "allowed to place her hands on the table leaf and make rhythmic pulls at the wood." To sum up, perhaps the safest—and most charitable—conclusion to draw from the Rasmussen history is that she might originally have possessed some gift which over the years forsook her. Then unwilling to abandon her international fame she indulged in trivial fakery. At any rate, Winther's massive reports displaying not only his ingenious instrumental methods but also giving accounts of the medium's peculiar temperament seem well deserving of study by psychologists and psychiatrists as well as by physicists.

The telekinetic powers of Stella C. (Stella Cranshaw, later Mrs. Leslie Deacon) were investigated in the late Harry Price's National Laboratory of Psychical Research in London, beginning in 1923 when Stella was about 23 years old. She was a hospital nurse and dispenser. The sittings were held in good red light. The usual séance table contained a built-in meshwork cage which accommodated musical instruments and a "telekinetoscope." This instrument consisted of a contact-maker in a brass cup covered by a strong soap bubble (soap, glycerine, water) and over all a glass bowl. The contact-maker was connected by cable to a battery and red pea lamp on the table top. The purpose was to test whether the telekinetic force could operate the lamp by penetrating the soap bubble without breaking it. The experiment was tried several times and succeeded once.

The musical instruments emitted sounds on many occasions. One of several tables was violently broken. Seemingly paranormal lights were occasionally seen. Numerous researchers of critical minds and long experience took part in the investigations and were evidently impressed. But Stella's interest in psychical phenomena (which she had experienced spontaneously since childhood) was slight; her powers in the course of several years declined, and she gracefully retired from the scene (Price, 1973).

To the Polish psychologist and philosopher Professor Julian Ochorowicz belongs the credit of discovering a rare type of telekinesis. The young medium was Stanislawa Tomczyk (later Mrs. Everard Feilding). Usually, in good light, Miss Tomczyk would place her hands on a table a few inches on either side of some small object such as a matchbox. Raising her hands a foot or so, the box rose along with them. Among the many things levitated in this way were a tumbler, a compass, a handbell, a pencil, and a lighted cigarette. During experiments she experienced a cold breeze in her vicinity and her hands sweated profusely. On one occasion Ochorowicz felt a thread but could not see it. At another time he did see a thread; it was black. A committee of physiologists, physicians and others confirmed Ochorowicz's findings (Janikowski et al., 1910). In numerous photographs taken by Ochorowicz and later investigators a thread was sometimes visible, sometimes not. Ochorowicz (1909) believed it was a paranormal physical extrusion from her fingers, and he called it "ideoplasm."

A photograph by the German neurologist Baron Albert von Schrenck-Notzing showed the experimental object, a ball, apparently *balanced* on a thread or filament of uneven thickness. Schrenck was convinced of Miss Tomczyk's genuineness; so were the Nobel physiologist Charles Richet and the Swiss psychologist Theodore Flournoy. The young lady, however, was not above extending her activities illegitimately. Flournoy (1911) recalled how at one investigation the medium tried to perform certain other more complicated experiments "which were manifestly purely fraudulent." And one winter day in Poland she professed to apport a snowball into a closed room.

Phenomena very similar to Miss Tomczyk's were reported of Miss Melita P., of Zurich, who was investigated by Dr. Kharis (1921) and another physician. With her hands a short distance from a small box, Melita's raising her hands caused the box to rise in the air. As with Miss Tomczyk, the experimenters observed a fine filament extending from each hand to object. When Kharis passed his hand between the box and the medium's hand he felt nothing, but the box dropped to the table. A photograph confirmed the existence of the filament.

To sum up, it will be gathered from these glimpses of background history that physical phenomena are the most uncertain part of the paranormal field. Many students convinced of telepathy and other forms of paranormal cognition have had doubts about the existence of physical phenomena. The reason is that physical phenomena are more difficult to investigate satisfactorily, and for a hundred years the subject has been infected with frauds beyond counting. In addition, there have been doubts about the quality of human testimony—"malobservation and lapse of memory" as experimentally proved by Davey and Hodgson and later by Besterman. Skepticism has been particularly strong—and even scornful—about asserted evidence for supposed materialized phantoms, apports, spirit photographs, and some other spectacular claims. Nevertheless, when all allowance is made for the possibilities of human error, it does appear from the histories of Home, Palladino (at her best), Rudi Schneider, Stella C., and perhaps a few others that on the question of telekinesis, percussive sounds, and possibly other reported occurrences, a surprisingly impressive case can be made out for their genuineness and therefore for the reality of the phenomena.

REFERENCES

Aksakof, A. *Animisme et spiritisme*. Paris: Librairie des Sciences Psychiques, 1895.

Aubrey, J. *Miscellanies Upon Various Subjects*. (5th ed.) London: Reeves and Turner, 1890.

Barrett, W. F. Report of physical phenomena taking place at Belfast with Dr. Crawford's medium. *Proceedings of the Society for Psychical Research*, 1920, **30**, 334-337.

Bayless, R. Correspondence. *Journal of the American Society for Psychical Research*, 1959, **53**, 35-38.

Bennett, E. N. *Apollonius or the Present and Future of Psychical Research*. New York: Dutton, 1927.

Besterman, T. The psychology of testimony in relation to paraphysical phenomena: Report of an experiment. *Proceedings of the Society for Psychical Research*, 1931-32, **40**, 363-387.

Blyton, T. Charles Dickens's association with mesmerism and spiritualism. *Light*, 1892, **12**, 136-137.

Bolton, G. Some personal experiences. *Light*, 1900, **20**, 199.

Capron, E. W. *Modern Spiritualism*. Boston: Bela Marsh, 1855.

Carrington, H. (Ed.) *Letters to Hereward Carrington*. Mokelumne Hill, Cal.: Health Research, 1957.

Courtier, J. *Rapport sur les séances d'Eusapia Palladino à l'Institut Général Psychologique en 1905, 1906, 1907 et 1908*. Paris: Institut Général Psychologique, 1908.

Crawford, W. J. *The Reality of Psychic Phenomena*. London: Watkins, 1916.

Crawford, W. J. *Experiments in Psychical Science*. London: Watkins, 1919.

Cutten, J. H. Review of K. Raudive, *Breakthrough*. *Journal of the Society for Psychical Research*, 1971, **46**, 187-191.

Defoe, D. *The Secrets of the Invisible World Disclos'd: Or an Universal History of Apparitions*. (New ed.) London: Thomas Tegg, 1840.

Feilding, E., Baggally, W. W., and Carrington, H. Report on a series of sittings with Eusapia Palladino. *Proceedings of the Society for Psychical Research*, 1909, **23**, 309-569.

First Report of the Committee of the Society for Psychical Research Appointed to Investigate the Evidence for Marvellous Phenomena Offered by Certain Members of the Theosophical Society. Private and confidential. London: Society for Psychical Research, n.d. [1884].

Flournoy, T. *Spiritism and Psychology*. New York: Harper, 1911.

Fodor, N. *Between Two Worlds*. West Nyack, N.Y.: Parker, 1964.

Fournier d'Albe, E. E. *The Goligher Circle*. London: Watkins, 1922.

[Geldert, Mrs. L. N.] *Thy Son Liveth*. Boston: Little, Brown, 1918.

Gibbon, E. *The Decline and Fall of the Roman Empire*. London: Dent, 1910.

Glanvil, J. *Saducismus Triumphatus*. (3rd ed.) London: Tuckyr, 1700.

Greenfield, O. T. Letter to the editor. *Light*, 1892, **12**, 630-631.

Guldenstubbé, Baron L. de. *Pneumatologie positive: la realité des esprits et le phénomène merveilleux de leur ecriture directe*. Paris: Published by the author, 1873.

Hare, R. *Experimental Investigation of the Spirit Manifestations*. (4th ed.) New York: Partridge and Brittan, 1856.

Hodgson, R. Mr. Davey's imitations by conjuring of phenomena sometimes attributed to spirit agency. *Proceedings of the Society for Psychical Research*, 1892, 8, 253–310.

Hodgson, R., and Davey, S. J. The possibilities of mal-observation and lapse of memory from a practical point of view. *Proceedings of the Society for Psychical Research*, 1886–87, 4, 381–495.

Holms, A. C. *The Facts of Psychic Science and Philosophy*. London: Kegan Paul, Trench, Trübner, 1925.

Hope, C. Report of a series of sittings with Rudi Schneider. *Proceedings of the Society for Psychical Research*, 1933, 41, 255–330.

Hyslop, J. H. Survey and comment. *Journal of the American Society for Psychical Research*, 1919, 13, 3–9.

Hyslop, J. H., Guthrie, L. V., Abbott, D. P., Clawson, G. W., and Clawson, Mrs. G. W. The case of Mrs. Blake. *Proceedings of the American Society for Psychical Research*, 1913, 7, 570–788.

Janikowski, L., Kalinowski, S., Lebiedzinski, P., Leski, J., Sosnowski, J., and Zatorski, B. Rapport d'une commission de naturalistes. *Annales des Sciences Psychiques*, 1910, 20, 33–39.

Kharis, Dr. Les "fils" télékinésiques. *Revue Métapsychique*, 1921, 1, 215–216.

Lombroso, C. *After Death–What?* Boston: Small, Maynard, 1909.

McDougall, W. Exposures of Mr. Craddock. *Journal of the Society for Psychical Research*, 1906, 12, 275–276.

Medhurst, R. G., Goldney, K. M., and Barrington, M. R. *Crookes and the Spirit World*. New York: Taplinger, 1972.

Morselli, E. *Psicologia e "spiritismo."* Turin: Fratelli Bocca, 1908.

Ochorowicz, J. Un nouveau phénomène mediumique. *Annales des Sciences Psychiques*, 1909, 19, 1–10, 45–51, 65–77, 97–106, 129–133.

Osty, E., and Osty, M. Les pouvoirs inconnus de l'esprit sur la matière. *Revue Métapsychique*, 1931, 11, 393–427; 12, 1–59, 81–122.

Pond, M. B. *The Unwilling Martyrs*. London: Spiritualist Press, 1947.

Preliminary report of the Commission Appointed by the University of Pennsylvania to Investigate Modern Spiritualism in Accordance with the Request of the Late Henry Seybert. Philadelphia: Lippincott, 1887.

Price, H. *Stella C.* (New ed.) London: Souvenir Press, 1973.

Prince, W. F. Death of Mrs. Elizabeth Blake. *Journal of the American Society for Psychical Research*, 1920, 14, 319.(a)

Prince, W. F. Additional notes on two books. *Journal of the American Society for Psychical Research*, 1920, 14, 615–626. (b)

Prince, W. F. "Impossible" and "supernormal." *Bulletin of the Boston Society for Psychic Research*, 1933, 19, 4–39.

Prince, W. F. Some high lights. *Bulletin of the Boston Society for Psychic Research*, 1934, 22, 74–85.

Raudive, K. *Break-through*. New York: Lancer Books, 1971.

Rayleigh, Lord. Presidential address. *Proceedings of the Society for Psychical Research*, 1919, 30, 275–290.

Report of the committee appointed to investigate phenomena connected with the Theosophical Society. *Proceedings of the Society for Psychical Research*, 1885, 3, 201–400.

[Sargent, E.] *Planchette: Or, the Despair of Science*. Boston: Roberts Brothers, 1869.

Sidgwick, E. M. (Mrs. H. Sidgwick). Mr. Eglinton. *Journal of the Society for Psychical Research*, 1886, **2**, 282-334. (a)

Sidgwick, E. M. (Mrs. H. Sidgwick). Results of a personal investigation into the physical phenomena of spiritualism. *Proceedings of the Society for Psychical Research*, 1886, **4**, 45-74. (b)

Sidgwick, H. Disinterested deception. *Journal of the Society for Psychical Research*, 1894, **6**, 274-277.

Smith, W. W. (Carington). The reality of psychic phenomena. (Review and discussion of W. J. Crawford's book of the same title.) *Proceedings of the Society for Psychical Research*, 1920, **30**, 306-333.

Stevenson, F. M. A test séance with the Goligher circle. *The Psychic Research Quarterly*, 1920, **1**, 113-117.

Stratton, F. J. M., and Phillips, P. Some experiments with the sthenometer. *Journal of the Society for Psychical Research*, 1906, **12**, 335-339.

Tietze, T. R. *Margery*. New York: Harper & Row, 1973.

Wilson, D. The ethereal transmission of thought. *Light*, 1915, **35**, 123-124. See also *Light*, **35**, Index, s.v. Radiograms.

Winther, C. Experimental inquiries into telekinesis. *Journal of the American Society for Psychical Research*, 1928, **22**, 25-33, 82-99, 164-180, 230-239, 278-290.

Zöllner, J. C. F. *Transcendental Physics*. London: W. H. Harrison, 1882.

2

Experimental Psychokinesis: A Review from Diverse Perspectives

Rex G. Stanford

HISTORICAL PERSPECTIVE

Studies of the physical phenomena of mediumship dominated the early decades of psychical research. Diverse and interesting happenings were observed and studied, but constant allegations, suspicions, and evidence of fraud eventually soured most investigators on the usefulness of pursuing research into such claims. These circumstances had the salutary effect of encouraging researchers to study physical psi phenomena under the more desirable degree of control afforded by the laboratory. This review focuses primarily upon statistically-evaluated studies of psychokinesis (PK) by humans upon nonliving systems.

The Early Quantitative-Experimental Period (1934–1950)

During this period the emphasis was on providing statistical evidence of PK, and the predominant method was that of releasing dice and "willing" or "wishing" a particular face to turn up. J. B. Rhine, inspired by the claims of a gambler, was the first to use this method in formal research. This work was begun in 1934 but was not reported until 1943 (Rhine and Rhine, 1943). Carroll B. Nash independently used this method in 1940 and published his work in 1944. With the die-face method 24 die-falls are said to constitute a "run," and because the intrinsic nonpsi "hit" (success) probability for a given fall is $1/6$, mean chance expectation per run is four hits. The subjects tested were not mediums or psychics, typically, but volunteers who were in some studies preselected on the basis of ability to succeed.

The PK work from 1934 to 1943 was not uniformly successful, and often the methods employed were less than rigorous. Their weaknesses frequently included hand-thrown dice, the improved but still suspect use of cup-thrown dice, the problem of die-bias uncorrected by adequate balancing of trials across the die faces, and an overemphasis on or the exclusive use of the highly suspect six-face as target. (Pitted dice usually have a tendency for the higher faces to turn up because they are lighter.) Given these facts plus the undesirability of rapidly introducing one incredible claim (PK) on top of another (ESP), it is little wonder that J. B. Rhine waited 9 years to publish the early PK evidence.

The event that triggered publication of the early PK results was the retrospective discovery that PK success was unequally distributed over the time of testing, that success over time followed a typical pattern. The pattern was a general decline in success throughout a test session such that when the results for the session—usually recorded on a single record page—were divided into first, second, third, and fourth quarters of testing, the performance for the first quarter typically was better than for the last quarter. Eighteen studies could be thus analyzed (Rhine and Humphrey, 1944b), and when their results for the first versus fourth quarters were pooled, the outcome was very improbable on a chance basis ($P < 10^{-8}$). The vast majority of the studies had shown better performance in the first than in the last quarter.

Subsequent studies with comparable methodology have sometimes confirmed and sometimes failed to confirm the quarter-decline (QD) effect. One study which confirmed the effect involved a large mass of data gathered under very careful conditions including photographic recording of die falls resulting from machine throwing of dice (McConnell, Snowdon, and Powell, 1955).

The success with the QD for the session (usually the page) analysis led to further, more minute, analyses to examine possible temporal trends in performance (Pratt, 1946, 1947a, 1947b; Rhine and Humphrey, 1944c; Rhine, Humphrey, and Pratt, 1945). These analyses included the quarter distribution of results for the "set" (a "set" usually consisting of three runs grouped on the basis of pauses for scoring or changes in the target) and the "half-set." Success was most likely on the first column of the set and often on the first trial of that column. In some data, performance turned upward at the bottom of the column.

The interest in such internal effects was partly because of their relevance to the psychology of PK success, but it was perhaps primarily derived from a feeling that these effects were particularly immune to nonpsi interpretations such as die-bias. Die-bias should not become less as the session progresses. Nevertheless, die bias can cause such internal effects if, for example, target face is suitably co-varied with the unit of the internal analysis. Controls against such a possibility were often lacking because analyses of this kind were not anticipated in planning the studies. Spurious internal effects might, in fact, occur in a number of ways having nothing to do with psi. These matters have been discussed by authors such as Parsons (1945), Thouless (1951), and Girden (1962a). Girden's review is a highly critical examination of the PK evidence. (With respect to Girden's review, see also Murphy, 1962, and Girden, 1962b).

Although the internal-effects data looked psychologically lawful, such retrospective analyses were not followed up with systematic experimentation designed to test hypotheses about the nature and causes of such effects as the QD.

Two studies during this period deserve special mention because they involved large amounts of data, produced clear-cut results favoring the PK hypothesis, and were methodologically superior to most contemporary work (Dale, 1946; Gibson, Gibson, and Rhine, 1944). The Dale study also provided evidence of internal reliability in subjects' performance. However, a later attempted replication was unsuccessful (Dale and Woodruff, 1947).

Some studies during this period directly contributed to our knowledge of PK function as well as added to the evidence for PK. They will be discussed later. New testing methods were explored. McMahan (1945, 1946, 1947) and Thouless (1945) studied PK by observing the fall of disks and coins, respectively. Certain die-face studies falling just outside this period (Fisk and West, 1958; Mitchell and Fisk, 1953; Thouless, 1951) included work which carefully eliminated specific methodological problems discussed earlier. Thouless' work (1951) was, in part, a serious attempt to come to grips with the psychological nature of internal effects.

The Middle Period (1951-1969)

During this period the die-face method largely gave way to the placement method. In placement work the subject tries to influence one or more objects (e.g., dice or balls) to move in one direction rather than the other such that at the end of their fall, roll, or whatever, they will come to rest in one position or place rather than another. Since the object(s) are subjected to randomizing influences upon their movement, and since target-side alternation is used to rule out place bias, the results can be evaluated on the basis of probability theory.

Two workers stand out during this period: W. E. Cox, associated with J. B. Rhine's laboratory, and Haakon Forwald, a Swedish engineer. Cox initiated placement work in the U.S.A., but it is unclear whether Forwald adopted the method following Cox or whether he developed it independently. Both researchers tested specific hypotheses about PK function, usually with the placement method, but occasionally with the die-face approach. The placement method was used by others besides Cox and Forwald, for example, Cormack (Pratt, 1951), Wilbur and Mangan (1956, 1957), and Fahler (1959).

The placement method provided an opportunity to increase the level of measurement of the PK effect. When dice or cubes are used one can measure the distance of displacement of each die from some standard position on the apparatus. Thus one can learn not only how many objects stop their movement in the proper position but also the actual extent of the movement involved. This, Forwald (1954) asserted, should allow a computation of the energy involved in the PK interaction. In his "scaled displacement method" he simplified the procedure by releasing cubes onto a surface already marked off into squares of a standard size.

A similar refinement was developed for the die-face method (Mitchell and Fisk, 1953; Fisk and West, 1958). This "die-orientation method" involved scoring die-face results according to whether the target face turned up, one of the four faces on an adjacent side (to the target face), or the face on the opposite side. This method seemed to have some advantages over the traditional hit-or-miss classification.

Forwald studied the influence of physical conditions such as surface texture of cubes (1955), weight of cubes (varied in terms of material), the material coating of cubes, and their thickness (1957, 1959). Guided by such studies, he made several rather unsuccessful attempts to conceptualize the nature of the PK force. The concepts he developed were never consistently borne out in his work or in that of others. His most recent effort attempted to relate his findings to gravity (1969). This hypothesis-oriented work was burdened by Forwald's almost exclusive use of himself as subject.

During a visit to Duke University (Pratt and Forwald, 1958) and back in his own laboratory under improved conditions suggested by Robert A. McConnell (McConnell and Forwald, 1968), Forwald reinforced the impression of himself as a good PK subject. As his own subject he independently confirmed an important internal-effect finding, that of outstanding success on the first trial (for a given target side) of the set. This was precisely analogous to an earlier finding in the die-face work. He made several other important contributions.

Cox used the placement method in many applications and in devices of his own design and construction. He had his subjects work with dice, marbles, metal balls, water drops, electrical current through a saline solution, and electrical relays. He focused on questions such as whether some dice in placement tests tend regularly to respond contrary to the subject's intention and others, positively; whether the simultaneous use of larger numbers of target objects would provide a way to increase the magnitude of the total result of a study; and whether through the use of multiple target objects a cumulative measure of the effect (such as using the "majority vote" principle on each multiple-target trial) in placement tests would yield overall better results than simply counting the results of the totality of the individual target objects in the study.

Other workers were active during the period, and new lines of research developed to examine possible PK upon living organisms, upon radioactive decay, and with targets unknown to the subject. There was little work on specifically psychological variables despite the fact that results from many studies seemed to be influenced by such variables.

The 1960s evinced a clear decrease in the number of PK studies done and reported. Some investigators seemed to feel that PK results were difficult to get and were weaker and less reliable than in the case of ESP. Could Girden's (1962a) negative review have taken a toll? At the very least the climate among experimenters was not a good one for undertaking PK research.

The Contemporary Scene

Recently several factors have combined to rekindle interest in PK research, and these factors have exerted a powerful influence upon the directions of the research.

1. Electronic technology has changed the entire complexion of research by making possible compact random event generators (REG's, sometimes called "random number generators" or just "random generators"). These devices allow variable rates of automatic target generation; variable chance hit probabilities; new, instantaneous, and exciting modes of feeding back success information to subjects; and automatic recording of experimental outcomes. Helmut Schmidt, a physicist now working with the Mind Science Foundation in San Antonio, Texas, did much to encourage the development of this technology. He did this by building such devices himself—including one with β emission from a strontium-90 source as the basis of its randomicity (1970a, 1970c)—and by using them with great success and ingenuity in his own research.

2. The success of Schmidt and others using the radioactivity-based REG in both ESP and PK work has captured the interest not only of parapsychologists but of other scientists, particularly physicists, because it has provided evidence that an "intrinsically unpredictable" quantum process can be both predicted and controlled through psi means. No doubt these results produced excitement for some physicists and bad nights for others, but, if valid, Schmidt's conclusions surely have immense theoretical significance. By a mere change in the PK target system, the potential excitement of PK research for scientists outside parapsychology was amplified many times.

3. Although the large bulk of PK research is still done using subjects who do not think of themselves as being "psychic," around 1970 parapsychologists began to become interested once more in persons who claimed to be PK superstars, and the latter have subsequently shared at least some of the limelight with "nonpsychic" subjects. The interest of nonparapsychologists, too, was attracted by the claims of persons such as Nina Kulagina of the Soviet Union and Uri

Geller of Israel, now living in the U.S. Somehow it is easier to ignore a mere "significant statistic" than a moving cigar holder or a bending spoon even if one's only response is to label the latter "fraudulent." Some parapsychologists in the U.S. have been able to undertake at least a small amount of PK work with supposed superstars such as Geller (Cox, 1974b; Puthoff and Targ, 1974) and Ingo Swann (Puthoff and Targ, 1974; Schmeidler, 1973). Kulagina has been observed several times by workers from the U.S. and from other non-Soviet countries (Pratt and Keil, 1973; Pratt and Ransom, 1971; Ullman, 1971, 1974). Work has also been reported with Felicia Parise, another possible PK superstar, from the U.S. (Honorton, 1974; Watkins and Watkins, 1974). Such observations, some formal, most informal, have so far taught us little if anything about PK function, and the supposed PK superstars have generally been difficult to get into the laboratory or to keep there for systematic work. Such work must be regarded as preliminary and still in need of tightening up to eliminate possible subject fraud and nonpsi artifact. Nonetheless, it would seem that this work had led not only to an increased interest in PK, but also to a revitalized interest in statistically analyzed PK studies.

4. The importance of PK research has become more evident with a growing interest in conceptualization and theory building. Recent psi research, which has been aimed at understanding rather than simply "proof," has given some workers the feeling that the pieces of the psi puzzle may be falling into some meaningful patterns. This has given impetus to theory building (e.g., Schmidt, 1975b; Stanford, 1974b). These efforts at theory building have made it evident that significant conceptual advances will require incisive investigation into the PK problem, something of which there has been all too little. Already it has become evident that the problems of ESP and PK are closely, if not inextricably, intertwined. It is quite conceivable that PK research will recast our understanding of what we have termed ESP. These and related issues will be developed in a later part of this chapter.

The new wave of PK investigation has brought with it further diversification of target systems and new concern with continuous, scaled measurement of PK effects (e.g., Schmeidler, 1973; Stanford and Fox, 1975). There have been further studies of PK on biological systems. Work has been initiated on the possibility of PK by nonhuman organisms. Much research now involves direct experimental manipulation of independent variables, including psychological ones. Work is being reported on nonintentional but need-relevant PK, studies in which subjects never know they are involved in psi research and thus never deliberately attempt to use psi. Such studies are beginning to provide experimental support for the hypothesis that intentionality is not necessary for the occurrence of PK, something which has long been suggested by spontaneous case reports. There is a growing interest in the possibility of facilitating or training PK performance through biofeedback and/or immediate feedback regarding trial-by-trial success. The excitement about PK is also causing renewed interest in the problem of active-agent telepathy. Such telepathy is sometimes considered as a possible form of PK (Stanford, 1974b).

It is fair to say that within a 5-year span (1970–1975) PK research has developed from a minor concern within parapsychology to a position at least on a par with ESP research.

PSYCHOLOGICAL PERSPECTIVE

Belief and Attitude: A Sheep-Goat Effect?

In none of three studies involving the die-face PK-test paradigm was there significant evidence that belief regarding PK influenced performance either positively or negatively (Dale, 1946; Nash, 1946; Van de Castle, 1958). The studies used somewhat different questions about belief, but since none produced a significant effect related to belief, there is little point in examining the specific questions involved. Similarly, Mischo and Weis (1973) examined PK performance on an electronic REG under two psychological conditions, but in neither did they find evidence that answers to a PK attitude questionnaire related reliably to performance.

Curiously, in some less conventional PK-test paradigms, subjects' answers to questions about their belief in ESP (not PK!) related positively to PK success. Rubin and Honorton (1971) reported that ESP-sheep as contrasted with ESP-goats were better at using the toss of pennies to derive a meaningful or accurate hexagram from the *I Ching* (an ancient Chinese text used with tossed coins or sticks for augury). Watkins, Watkins, and Wells (1973) tested unselected subjects on their ability to differentially influence the arousal rate of two centrally anesthetized mice. They found that subjects' belief in ESP was positively and significantly related to performance, whereas their attitude toward success in the experiment was negatively and significantly related to performance.

Three studies have examined the possibility that self-perceptions of one's "luckiness" may relate to PK performance (Greene, 1960; Ratte, 1960; Ratte and Greene, 1960). The first study cited involved a methodology which would have allowed precognition as well as PK to occur; it produced no evidence that persons perceiving themselves as lucky did better than those perceiving themselves otherwise. The second and third studies both produced results which the authors construed as evidence that self-perceived lucky individuals may perform better at PK than their unlucky counterparts. However, the statistical analyses in both studies are inappropriate for supporting any such conclusions. It can only be said that such work certainly leaves open the possibility that in some probably weak and possibly complex way self-perceived luckiness may be related to PK performance.

Anecdotal and quasi-experimental material suggests that observers' beliefs and cognitions may be important in manifestations of "macro-PK." Many psychics and mediums have professed that skeptics present at a demonstration can inhibit or block the phenomena, whereas the presence of friendly, enthusiastic observers can aid in their production. Investigators of quasi-experimental, possible macro-PK phenomena (Batcheldor, 1966; Brookes-Smith, 1973; Brookes-Smith and Hunt, 1970) have noted that to start things happening it is often useful to produce, through normal means, bogus physical phenomena, after which presumably genuine effects often immediately begin.

Perhaps if a person believes that psi events are beginning to happen, he will develop the feeling that some force external to himself is already at work, and his own capacities to produce such phenomena may be turned loose, perhaps due to cessation of egocentric efforts to make something happen, or perhaps due to the cessation of willing, wishing, watching, and waiting for something to happen. These may be inhibitory factors. Cognitions which place outside oneself (i.e., externalize) the responsibility for potential PK events appear to facilitate such events provided those events are seen as being actuated by an efficacious outside agency. The most dramatic of possible-PK events seem almost invariably associated with beliefs that some efficacious agency outside oneself is responsible for their occurrence, albeit usually with one's consent, request, supplication, etc., as in the case of appeal for such events to God, supernatural beings or forces, spirits, etc. (Even in the exception to this rule, that of poltergeist cases, the poltergeist agent or focus is normally not aware of causing the events himself, though he may recognize that they are in some way associated with himself. Poltergeist events are thus an example of the general case into which the externalization-of-responsibility phenomenon fits—PK as basically ego-alien [Stanford, 1974b]. Furthermore, in many poltergeist cases, historically speaking, there has been the belief in the household of some external agency causing the events.)

Apropos of the externalization-of-responsibility hypothesis, Owen and Sparrow (1974) recently claimed that their group had evoked apparently genuine PK phenomena through the expedient of role-playing communication with an imaginary, totally fictional spirit. Similarly, recent reports on possible PK events following TV appearances by the metal-bending "psychic" Uri Geller noted that persons in the homes or places of work where objects bent or broke most often believed that Geller himself was directly responsible for the events (Bender, Vandrey, and Wendlandt, 1976; Keil and Hill, 1975). Such TV appearances may be vast, unplanned, and poorly controlled experiments on the hypothesis that PK is facilitated through externalization of responsibility through belief in an efficacious external agency. Curiously, Geller himself is reported to believe that extraterrestrial beings make possible his displays of what he claims are PK and ESP (Puharich, 1974).

Motivation and Incentive-Value of Goal Events

Gatling and Rhine (1946), in a die-face study, pitted four divinity students interested in PK as a possible basis for the efficacy of prayer, against four reputedly good crap shooters. The outcome was that both groups turned in an exceptionally good and highly significant PK performance. Perhaps the unique set of circumstances created an unusual level of motivation which aided performance. Another study for which an ad-hoc motivational interpretation might be appropriate is one in which McMahan (1947) tested children for PK at parties. She had previously (1946) tested the same children under conditions of light, but now she gave them trials in both light and darkness. The trials in the darkness were certainly more novel, and they may have been perceived as more challenging and exciting. Results in neither condition were statistically significant, but there was about equally strong positive performance in the dark condition as there was below-chance performance in the light. The difference was significant. Part of this difference may have been contributed by task juxtaposition rather than by the intrinsic influence of each condition. We will later consider such effects in their own right.

Of possible relevance to motivation are studies which apparently aimed at obtaining good PK results by embedding the PK task in a game. Steen (1957), Ratte and Greene (1960), and Ratte (1960) all tried this approach and reported some success with it. The latter study was perhaps the most ambitious, methodologically speaking, of the three. It compared game and nongame circumstances in competitive and noncompetitive settings. Results were generally quite promising with the game and competitive situations and less promising with the nongame and noncompetitive ones. There was statistically significant evidence for better results with games than nongames. This series of three studies at least suggests that there may be some virtue in presenting the PK task in a way which is challenging, fun, and motivating but which does not produce a deadly serious attitude toward what is being undertaken.

Nash and Richards (1947) tried to directly manipulate motivation by contrasting conditions in which they did or did not give two movie tickets for good PK performance. Performance under these two conditions was not reliably different, and it was slightly better in the nonreward condition. Could it have been that the college students tested were affronted by the idea that they would have to be induced to perform in an exciting study of a new scientific area by an offer of movie tickets? The paradigm would have seemed more suitable for junior-high students, perhaps, in that era.

In both pilot and confirmatory series Pantas (1971) contrasted results when subjects attempted PK on an electronic REG generating targets at two rates (60 or 240 per minute). Subjects were first allowed to establish which of the two rates they preferred by actually working under each rate. Then they were tested under both rates, and the order of the two was counterbalanced across subjects.

In both series subjects did better at the preferred rate, significantly so in the pilot series, but not quite significantly in the confirmatory one. In both series results in the preferred condition were positive, and they were significantly so in the confirmatory series. Rate of target generation *per se* did not relate to performance. The outcomes of this study may or may not be related to motivation, though they can be interpreted in that light.

A recent study by Schmidt (1976) suggests that, in psychological terms (not Schmidt's), the *incentive value* (potential total reward value) of REG outcomes may be positively related to level of success. Earlier Schmidt (1975a) had reported results suggesting that PK can operate with time displacement; that is, even if the PK "test results" are generated by an REG before a subject participates in the experiment and are then played to him during the experiment, good results are possible. In the more recent study (1976) Schmidt found that, in accord with his theory (1975b), in time displacement PK a good level of performance can be had by playing the "test results" back (with visual and auditory displays) to the subject four times (when he does not realize the trials are prerecorded). Prerecorded trials were alternately mixed in with present-time generated trials, the latter involving four times the number of actual trials as in the prerecorded condition since the latter were played back four times. Results were significantly better for the time-displaced outcomes than for the contemporaneous-generation outcomes, though both were significant and positive. The results of this study support an incentive theory of PK outcomes, a concept which is perhaps even more clearly enunciated in the PMIR theory (Stanford, 1974b) than in Schmidt's own conceptualization (Schmidt, 1975b). However, the study in question confounds incentive (or amount of feedback as Schmidt might prefer to term it) with time and rate of generation of targets.

The results of two recent studies (Schmidt, 1975a; Stanford, Zenhausern, Taylor, and Dwyer, 1975) of nonintentional PK are very compatible with the view that subjects will act upon an REG if the outcomes have potential incentive value for them. These studies did not involve actual manipulations of motivation or incentive, and they will be described in a later section.

Thouless (1951) tested himself as PK subject and provided some introspective insights about how motivation related to his own success. He felt that when motivation was too high this resulted in an anxiety about success which was self-defeating. An interest involving a detached, gamelike view of the proceeding was likely to be successful, an observation which accords with experimental results discussed earlier. A real effort to succeed, Thouless felt, led directly to failure. He described the proper attitude as "effortless intention to succeed," one in which "I want to succeed but I don't really care whether I do or not" (p. 123). Stanford (1974b) has expressed the similar view that while motivation is important for PK success, it can have self-defeating consequences when for any reason (e.g., fear of failure) it leads to a direct effort to "make things happen." No one knows how things really work in PK or how to actually make them happen, so such efforts may really be "wrong effort" that can waste energy by misdirection of intention. Such efforts, as we shall see, are largely devoid of fruitful outcomes. Perhaps conscious effort can be effective if it is expended on a ritual believed to aid or cause things to happen. Such a ritual, because it usually involves an appeal to powerful being(s) or force(s) outside oneself, can be effective in actually reducing egocentric efforts to try to make things happen.

Conscious Effort versus Mere Intention

The common belief of mediums and psychics that their physical phenomena originate from outside their individuality may not be a mere "superstition" even if the particular beliefs concerning this are not literally true. Such beliefs are probably based upon an important introspective observation, that the psychic does not feel personally responsible for the events. This doctrinal acknowledgment of that feeling may play an important role in allowing physical events to happen, for it obviates egocentric efforts to make things happen. A number of experiments point to the conclusion that egocentric efforts to make things happen are usually ineffective.

Camstra (1973) found that subjects asked *not* to concentrate on their task were significantly successful in PK, while those asked to concentrate on the task were not successful. Similarly, subjects who did not know the nature of the task did significantly better than those who knew they were involved in a PK task.

Honorton and Barksdale (1972) reported that during a rather ritualistic exercise in which subjects tested as a group pointed at a Schmidt REG with arm muscles tensed, positive and significant results occurred only when they were asked not to try to exert any effort to affect the outcome. When they made such an effort, results were close to chance. The muscle-tensing ritual was, in short, effective only when it was used in a way analogous to a true religious-magic ritual. In such a ritual one does not think one has, personally, to make something happen, and therefore one does not concentrate on trying to make something happen. One simply involves oneself with the ritual.

Steilberg (1975) had each subject use two approaches to influence die-face. One of these involved the subject's visualizing the target face while looking away from the test apparatus. This might, from our perspective, be regarded as only moderately egocentric in its approach to the task. The other method had the subject attentively watch the falling dice while tensing his body and consciously focusing his willpower to force them to stop with the target-face upward. This approach could be considered highly egocentric. The less egocentric approach yielded a moderately strong positive deviation which, however, fell short of significance. The highly egocentric approach resulted in self-defeat (i.e., significant psi-missing).

Steilberg's less egocentric condition was probably relatively egocentric as contrasted with the ritualistic noneffort condition employed in the Honorton-Barksdale study described above. Visualizing the desired target face probably produces a certain amount of ego-involvement with the task even if the subject is not looking at the falling dice. Furthermore, it may be that if subjects have trouble visualizing the target face, this produces further egocentric involvement. In the Honorton-Barksdale study the ritualistic muscle-tensing combined with no effort to influence the REG was something anyone could easily do. Also, the ritual muscle-tensing provided a strong internal stimulus onto which the subject could focus attention and not worry about the REG and its outcomes.

Thouless (1951) in testing himself as subject reported that he was able, at least temporarily, to dramatically and significantly recover from a period of poor performance by the simple expedient of reading poetry to himself during the course of the experiment. At least some of the effectiveness of this method might have derived from the distraction provided by the poetry from a task about which he had probably become rather tense. This interpretation is bolstered by Thouless' observation that results with the poetry reading declined after this reading had lost some of the qualities it would have needed to keep his attention from focusing upon the PK task. One is reminded of Batcheldor's report (1966) that presumed macro-PK effects would not occur while his group was tensely awaiting their occurrence but would break out after they diverted themselves with joking, singing, etc.

Release of Effort

Folk tradition concerning effective prayer often urges the supplicant to pray but then to "let go and leave it in the hands of God." Uri Geller, the Israeli "psychic" who claims to be a PK superstar, has told me that frequently when his effort to psychically bend some object has failed, it will begin to bend just after he has "given up" and is apologizing for a failure. In a different vein we experience something similar when confronted with a problem for which we cannot find a solution but have certainly been trying. Often, dismissing the problem from the mind, we later suddenly find ourselves with a creative insight into its solution. The tip-of-the-tongue phenomenon is similar in character. Later we shall see that these diverse phenomena may not be as unrelated as they at first seem. What does the experimental PK literature indicate about a possible release-of-effort effect?

Pratt (Pratt and Woodruff, 1946), in an analysis of data from himself as subject, noted significant, positive scoring for the just-abandoned die-face on the trials following a switch to a new target face even though his overall results, scored in the usual way, were unimpressive. Other workers have informally noted the same thing.

In each of two studies of PK influence upon the arousal of centrally anesthetized mice (Watkins, Watkins, and Wells, 1973), a statistically significant "lag effect" was demonstrated. Effects of subjects' efforts over a period of trials to psychically produce early arousal of the animal on a randomly chosen side of the test apparatus were shown to "carry over" to animals on that side in subsequent trials. Curiously, the "lag effect" in both studies was actually greater in magnitude than the effect when subjects were concentrating on the target, albeit not significantly greater. As Roger Wells and Graham Watkins themselves later noted (1975) in commenting on these results, the posteffort effect "may be a more reliable finding than the main effect" (p. 145). These studies were made with selected or "talented" subjects.

Stanford and Fox (1975) studied three different experimental conditions in order to directly test the hypothesis that there is a release-of-effort effect in PK. All three conditions had in common that 12 unselected subjects tried to influence the output of a light-stimulated photocell housed in a light-tight container. Periods of effort to influence the photocell were alternated with periods in which the subject read aloud from a magazine under instructions not to try to influence the photocell. In all three conditions of the study the magnitude of change in the photocell output was significantly greater during the posteffort distraction period than during the period of effort.

Millar (1976) reported work in which subjects attempted to influence the resistance of a thermistor. There was no evidence of an overall PK effect either during the effort or during the release-of-effort period. Of 20 subjects studied, only one showed a significant effect, and this was during the release-of-effort period. Statistical artifact is the likely explanation. It would appear that the periods of effort and release-of-effort involved in the Millar study were not comparable to those in the Stanford and Fox (1975) study.

Conceivably related to the release-of-effort issue is a study by McConnell (1955) in which he and eight other persons attempted to program themselves prior to sleep to exert PK influence while asleep on the fall of machine-thrown dice. A single target face was used during a given night. The overall results were not significant, but the experimenter's own sleep results, constituting nearly one-third of the total trials, were statistically significant. His data consisted of more than 5,500 trials.

Secondary Objective Studies

What happens when a subject simultaneously has two nonconflicting objectives in a PK task but makes one the focus of his effort and does not think about the other?

Cox (1951) had subjects throw 24 dice at a time onto a surface marked off into squares. Each square had a number (1, 2, 3, 4, 5, or 6), and there were equal numbers of squares with each number. Thus two objectives were possible using the dice; placement of the dice to fall into squares having a designated target number; and die-face. On each trial the die-face target was the same number as was used for the placement target. For each trial one of the objectives was regarded as primary and the other as secondary. Which was primary and which, secondary was alternated, so each objective was primary and secondary half the time. Subjects on each trial concentrated upon the primary objective. Cox in this paper reported three separate series which examined this problem. In each series a highly significant difference (measured by CR_d) favored the primary objective. Ironically, the PK effect was contributed almost entirely by the secondary objective. Pooling the results of the three series, there was a positive but nowhere near significant deviation for the primary objective and a negative and significant deviation for the secondary objective ($P < .0000002$). The pooled difference for the two objectives was also significant. There was no difference in performance level for placement versus die-face, and scoring level for neither showed significance. Such results, consistent across three series, once more suggest the inhibitory effect upon PK performance of an effort to "make it happen." Although the results with the secondary objective showed a negative deviation, this objective was the source of the PK effect. The negative deviation can probably be accounted for by the fact that subjects were not trying for this objective and may have implicitly devalued it as contrasted with the primary objective.

Later Cox (1954) replicated this effect, but this time his subjects worked with a lateral placement task. On each throw 24 cubes and 24 spheres were released. Which type of object constituted the primary focus of attention was alternated in blocks of eight releases of the objects. The subjects produced a small, non-significant negative deviation on the primary objective and, most importantly, a sizeable, significant ($P = .03$) negative deviation on the secondary objective, confirming the earlier work. The difference of the two objectives failed to reach significance in this study.

Cox's work thus produced remarkably consistent confirmation that a secondary objective, one not concentrated upon in a PK task, produces good evidence of PK and generally better evidence than a primary objective. The results generalized across two rather different PK tasks.

The studies by Cox involved unselected subjects, or at least persons not known to be outstanding PK subjects. Given the findings discussed in earlier sections, perhaps such subjects are persons who may take a maladaptive, egocentric approach toward whatever is their conscious PK objective. They may show their strong PK effect upon the secondary objective because their attitude toward that objective, which is not one of "make it happen," is less egocentric and therefore more suitable for the occurrence of PK. But what of someone known to be relatively proficient at PK, someone who presumably approaches his primary objective in a more suitable fashion? Will such a person show more evidence of PK on a secondary objective?

Only one study bears on this question. Forwald (1952b), an outstanding experimenter-subject in the PK area, did placement work in which he simultaneously released cubes of two different materials and attempted to influence only one type of cube. The type of cube, with each combination, that he tried to influence was the type which seemed to him to be the more difficult of the two to control. The cubes he attempted to influence showed a significant positive deviation, whereas those he did not attempt to influence showed a miniscule negative deviation. The divergence of this study from the results reported by Cox might derive from Forwald being an outstanding PK subject, from his special interest in the cubes which constituted his primary focus, from a combination of these factors, or from some other source of variation. In any event, it is difficult to make generalizations on the basis of work with a single subject.

Randall (1974) studied three schoolboys preselected on the basis of ESP performance. He compared their PK performance on a Schmidt-type REG when they were engaged in the PK task alone and when the PK task was more or less a secondary objective. In the latter case they were focused on an ESP task. He found no evidence of PK ability in these subjects and no evidence that the results differed under the two conditions. This study differs in several respects from the work described earlier concerning secondary objective.

Hidden-Target Studies

If *not* trying to "make it happen" in PK work removes some factors associated with failure, what, then, would happen if someone attempted to make the die-face accord with a hidden, unknown target? It is not possible to try to make "it" happen if one does not know what "it" is. Such a study would have not only the interest just mentioned but could also provide some basic information about psi processes, as will be shown below.

There have been five published studies concerned exclusively or in major part with the hidden target paradigm (Fisk and West, 1958; Forwald, 1963; Mitchell and Fisk, 1953; Osis, 1953; Thouless, 1951). Each of these studies was at least moderately successful, and most were very strikingly so. It certainly does not appear that being unaware of the target at all inhibits success. Forwald discovered that in his hidden-target work he did not show his characteristic, rapid decline in performance. Dr. J. Blundun, the major subject in the Mitchell-Fisk study and the sole subject in the Fisk-West report, continued to produce significant, positive die-face deviations during the course of approximately 24,000 trials using the hidden-target method. Nonetheless, one should not conclude that position or decline effects do not occur with the hidden-target paradigm, for Thouless (1951) reported evidence of a decline within each occasion of testing. It does appear that the method may have some advantages over known targets, at least for some subjects. In any event, it does not seem to depress results.

Thouless (1951, p. 116) reports that he found this form of experiment successful with others as well as with himself, and he states that Betty Humphrey (at that time of the Duke laboratory) had informed him that she had had good success with it. Thouless felt the success of the method probably derived from the subject being less tempted to use conscious volition. He further observed, "We seem to be asking the subject to perform an impossible task, and the attitude he is inclined to adopt to an impossible task is a good attitude for psi performance" (p. 117).

In a more recent study Cox (1974a) has reported confirmatory but perhaps less satisfactory evidence for hidden-target PK. He tested one subject who was unaware of the targets in a placement study but who obtained a highly significant result with respect to one of the analyses done on the data (p. 60). This subject was not even aware that he was being studied for PK performance.

In the five major studies cited earlier the task was presented to the subject as a PK task, one with hidden targets. Two studies have appeared which used a physically similar paradigm but which were presented to subjects as studies of augury, divination through "chance" events (Rubin and Honorton, 1971; Stanford, 1972). These studies did not show overall significant results, but, instead, showed that individual differences in subjects determine the effectiveness with which they can use the augury method. The outcome of the Rubin-Honorton study, which involved the *I Ching*, was described above ("Belief and Attitude" section). The Stanford study involved using die-faces to call standard ESP symbols and examined differences in suggestibility as related to success. Seventy subjects were tested, and low-suggestible subjects were more successful with augury than were high-suggestible subjects. Whether these findings would generalize to the situation in which unselected subjects are asked to do "PK with hidden targets" rather than "augury, an ancient system of divination through random events," remains to be seen. Certainly the psychological settings are quite different. Whatever the answer to this query, the Rubin-Honorton and the Stanford studies clearly provide further evidence for the reality of PK with hidden targets.

Although there is not space to discuss the matter here, methodological, empirical, and logical considerations make it quite unlikely that the results of hidden-target PK studies can be explained away by the concept of experimenter precognition used in providing random arrangements of hidden PK targets.

As will be shown below, the PK literature is replete with examples of success at PK tasks in which subjects are lacking many sorts of information which would "reasonably" seem to be required for success. We have already seen an instance in which subjects definitely performed better, given less rather than more information about the PK task (Camstra, 1973). Others have found similar trends which, however, fell short of significance (Cox, 1965a; Stanford et al., 1975). Let us examine further evidence that PK function (and probably psi function in general) is not at all dependent upon subjects' being given information about the kind of system with which they are working or even about the fact that they are in a PK test.

Unknown Target Systems

Stanford et al. (1975) found evidence that subjects could bias the outputs of an electronic REG in a way that would help them to escape an unpleasant task and enjoy a more pleasant one. Most importantly, they were able to do this when they did not know that an REG was running and knew nothing about their fate being contingent upon its outputs. Similarly, Schmidt (1975a) found that subjects, without knowing they were in a PK study, biased the outputs of an REG in accord with a psychological disposition—one might say, a need—induced by the experimental setting. Schmidt found that it made no difference whether the running of the REG (relative to the time of the subject being in the laboratory) was contemporaneous or time-displaced, for results were comparable. Subjects knew nothing of the time element involved.

Schmidt (1974a) has obtained other evidence that major shifts related to the target system do not prevent PK, at least when the subject is unaware of these shifts. He tested subjects on randomly alternating trials with different (simple and complex) REGs. The simple REG generated events slowly, and the complex REG, more rapidly (1 binary event versus 100 binary events per 3-second period, respectively). Both subjects and experimenter were unaware of which generator was the target generator on a given trial. Going beyond the analyses which Schmidt reported, I have pooled the trials of both his pilot and confirmatory series. Significant, positive PK was obtained with each of the generators when it was the target ($P < .01$, for each). Subjects were somehow able to determine which generator was the target at a given time and were able to selectively influence it. This is obvious because the simple generator was left running even when it was not the target generator, and results on it at that time were well within the range of chance operation. Thus subjects implicitly discriminated which generator was the target on a given trial and were able to selectively influence it. The simple generator had as its basis of randomness the time of arrival at a Geiger counter of decay particles from a strontium-90 (radioactive) source, whereas the complex generator's randomicity was based upon the time at which the noise from an electronic noise generator exceeded a certain threshold amplitude.

In a similar vein, Schmidt and Pantas (1972) found that under psychologically identical conditions, including instructions, subjects did essentially equally well and significantly above chance under two very different internal conditions of the REG. The two different internal conditions were precognition- and PK-oriented modes of REG function. In another phase of the same study, Pantas himself was the sole subject, and even though he knew about the difference of the two types of test, his performance with the two REG modes was statistically indiscriminable and significantly above chance for each.

The independence of PK from sources of sensory information has long been noted by parapsychologists. J. B. Rhine has often pointed out (e.g., Rhine and Pratt, 1957, p. 71) that sensory guidance is not necessary for PK operation since even the early dice work seemed to rule out sensory perception as the guiding principle behind PK.   As we have seen, modern PK research is achieving remarkable success with some rather complicated REGs based upon quantum and/or electronic processes. In such studies subjects are typically *not* given a description of the technical aspects of the PK device, its circuit, function, etc. Instead, they are usually told only that some kind of display which they will witness is controlled by a REG and that they are to cause some specific thing to occur in the display controlled by the outputs of the REG. For example, the subject is to observe a circle of nine lamps of which one is lighted at a time and is to cause the light, which can only move one step at a time, to move consistently in a specified direction (Schmidt, 1970a); or the subject is to cause clicks presented through headphones to occur in one ear rather than in the other (Schmidt, 1973). Sometimes they are not told even this much and are unaware of participating in a PK study. In this case something in the subject's experience—perhaps the possibility of something enjoyable occurring—is, unknown to him, controlled by an REG. In the face of all such ignorance PK still occurs in these studies, and the magnitude of the effect observed does not appear to depend upon giving the subject knowledge of the technicalities of what is required for a favorable outcome.

In short, PK success does not depend upon knowing the PK target, upon knowing the nature or existence of the REG, upon knowing one is in a PK study, upon the complexity or the design of the REG, or upon subjects knowing anything about the mechanics of the REG. These findings are highly consistent and appear in different forms throughout the PK literature. They suggest that PK somehow occurs such that the favorable outcome (or goal event) is directly accomplished without mediation through sensory guidance *and probably without any form of computation or information processing by the organism.* This formulation suggests that even extrasensory guidance is inadequate to explain what happens in PK. Extrasensory guidance as it is normally conceptualized would still depend upon the processing of ESP information inside the organism; it would still depend upon the information-processing capacities of the organism made possible by the complex neuronal networks of the nervous system and brain.   Later we shall see that evidence of PK associated with relatively simple organisms further adds to the impression that the function of PK in no way depends upon information processing.

In any event, we cannot explain PK function in terms of extrasensory guidance for the very simple reason that we cannot explain anything merely by labeling it. "ESP" is simply a label we have placed upon a body of findings which we do not understand.   As will be shown later, so-called PK events can help us to reconceptualize "ESP events" and tentatively to subsume both under a single construct.

These radical implications of the PK findings can in a sense be summarized by saying that PK is *goal oriented*. As Schmidt (1974c) has explained, experiments such as those outlined above suggest that ". . . PK may not be properly understood in terms of some mechanism by which the mind interferes with the machine in some cleverly calculated way but that it may be more appropriate to see PK as a goal-oriented principle, one that aims successfully at a final event, no matter how intricate the intermediate steps" (p. 190).   It in fact seems that all psi is goal-oriented in this sense.

Altered States of Consciousness

Certainly we know that so-called altered states of consciousness are not necessary for PK to occur. Almost all the laboratory work has been done with subjects in the normal, waking state.   Even the dramatic forms of supposed PK events often occur without the medium or psychic being in a trance. A good example is the case of D. D. Home, one of the greatest physical mediums of all time.   Nevertheless, many mediums, including some who may well have produced genuine physical phenomena (such as Eusapia Palladino), often produced such phenomena while ostensibly in trance—whatever being in "trance" may mean.   Possibly, trance aided some mediums in producing such effects. If so, going into trance and letting supposed spirits "take over" could be another way of externalizing responsibility for such events and thereby reducing the ego-involvement which can block their occurrence.

The state of the direct experimental evidence on "altered states" and PK is much less than satisfactory. We earlier discussed McConnell's effort (1955) to have subjects do PK while asleep. J. B. Rhine's (1946) attempt to influence PK performance through hypnotic suggestion (including suggestions of eagerness, ability to concentrate on the task, and strong confidence) produced no systematic results.   Two laboratories, Stanford Research Institute (Puthoff and Targ, 1974) and City College (Schmeidler, 1973) report somewhat anecdotal evidence that when Ingo Swann attempted to mentally inspect or "probe" a piece of laboratory equipment attached to a chart recorder or polygraph, the apparatus exhibited marked changes in its output. Swann claims to "externalize" his awareness during such "probing," so these effects might, by certain criteria, be regarded as having occurred during an altered state of consciousness.

The most promising area of investigation so far is that of meditation. Many traditional schools of meditation involve the meditator in learning to focus attention steadily and, ultimately, noneffortfully upon some object of concentration. Matas and Pantas (1971) reasoned that such practice at steadily focusing attention might be related to success at PK. They recruited 25 persons who had practiced some form of meditation or similar self-culture for at least 6 months and compared their PK performance on a Schmidt REG to that of 25 control subjects, visitors to their laboratory, or students, who were interested in being tested but who had never practiced meditation. Subjects were tested individually, and the meditators were allowed 15 minutes for meditation prior to testing. (Of the 25 meditators, 21 meditated at that time.) The meditators produced significant positive results; the nonmeditators, nonsignificant below-chance results. The difference was significant, but weaknesses in the experimental design prevent conclusions about the cause of the observed difference.

In the Schmidt-Pantas (1972) study discussed above, Pantas served very successfully as the sole subject in one phase of the work. Prior to each session Pantas practiced Zen meditation for about 20 minutes in front of the test machine. Then he attempted to remain in the meditation-induced relaxed but alert state while he made 25 trials on the machine at the rate of one trial per minute. These trials constituted a session, and he usually did only one session per day. His striking results cannot, however, unambiguously be attributed to the meditation, for there was no control group or series conducted at this exceptionally slow-paced rate (both within-session and in terms of only one session with 25 trials per day).

Another tantalizing but inconclusive linkage of the practice of meditation and successful PK performance occurred in a study by Honorton and May (1976). Ten subjects tried to influence outcomes of an electronic REG, and each engaged in equal numbers of high- and low-aim runs. Aside from the overall analysis of results, the investigators reported that five of the ten subjects achieved individually significant differences of performance on high- and low-aim runs. Four of the five persons producing a significant difference were meditators. Six of the ten subjects were meditators, and thus two-thirds of the meditators produced significant results. Also, each of the four meditators showing significance had also had biofeedback experience. By contrast, only one-fourth of the nonmeditators achieved significant results. Any decision as to whether these differences are meaningful, and, if so, what interpretation should be put on them, must await further work. Personality factors related to self-selection for meditation and biofeedback training might well be involved. (Some of the data discussed above are not included in the work cited; they were personally communicated to me by Charles Honorton.)

In a study by Schmeidler (1973) something similar was noted. Of two graduate students tested, only one showed significant PK results. This was the one who had practiced meditation. In the same study the psychic Ingo Swann was involved, and he was successful at the PK task. He had previously been involved in an unconventional form of mind training, and he felt he was able at will to dissociate ("externalize") his consciousness from his body.

Observations such as these from the Honorton-May and the Schmeidler studies can at this time only be regarded as showing the need of further investigations in these areas.

Workers at the University of Houston (Texas) have recently studied the influence upon PK performance of "nonanalytic" versus "analytic" modes of thinking (Andrew, 1975; Braud, Smith, Andrew, and Willis, 1976). These studies have compared PK performance of subjects engaged in listening to music and nonlinguistic sounds, solving spatial tasks, appreciating depth, and imaging in visual, kinesthetic, and other modalities with PK performance of subjects engaged in analytical, verbal, mathematical, and logical tasks. There have been three such studies, and the analytic and nonanalytic tasks differed somewhat in them, as did various other details. In two of the three studies subjects in the nonanalytic condition performed significantly better than those in the analytic condition, and when results from all three studies were pooled, performance of subjects in the nonanalytic condition was significantly better than that of subjects in the analytic condition. Subjects tested in the nonanalytic condition (with results pooled across the three studies) produced significant positive scoring ($P = .0014$), but not those in the analytic condition, who scored about at chance level. Such results are certainly not self-explanatory, and they surely do not prove (and the workers at Houston did not contend that they proved) that the right hemisphere of the brain is responsible for PK and that the left acts counter to its expression. These results fit in well with the weak evidence we already have that the practice of meditation, which is usually a "nonanalytic" activity, might aid PK performance. The findings on nonanalytic versus analytic mode may also be related to a distinction discussed earlier, that an active, egocentric, "I've got to make it happen" approach blocks PK performance, whereas the passive volition approach is more favorable. Many of the analytic tasks used were strongly directed toward some particular solution which could be arrived at through effort. Many of the nonanalytic tasks had no definite solution but resulted in passively appreciating some source of stimulation. It is also possible that the attempts to manipulate analytic and nonanalytic modes of thinking also manipulated mood and, in particular, the pleasantness or unpleasantness of the experimental setting.

Personality Factors

Some studies have simply correlated personality measures with PK performance under a single test condition. Nash and Richards (1947) studied 48 subjects and found no significant relationship of PK scores with intelligence or with expansion-compression ratings. Van de Castle (1958), working with 31 PK subjects, tried a number of personality measurements, including a measure of intelligence (Raven Progressive Matrices), a test of expansion-compression, the Rosenzweig Picture Frustration Test, and Rorschach measures of spontaneity. Neither intelligence nor measures based upon the Rosenzweig Picture Frustration Test related significantly to PK performance. But expansive subjects as contrasted with compressives tended to do well on the PK task (rank order correlation of +.38, $P = .05$), and two Rorschach-based measures of spontaneity (one based on average reaction time, the other on response protocols), especially when combined, tended quite strongly to differentiate PK performance. Seven out of eight subjects who were high spontaneous by *both* criteria scored above chance, and seven out of eight who were highly inhibited by *both* criteria scored below chance. Watkins, Watkins, and Wells (1973), in their study of PK arousal of centrally anesthetized mice, administered a battery of psychological tests to their subjects, including the Eysenck Personality Inventory and the Lüscher Color Test. They reported no significant relationships with PK performance of the variables derived from these tests, but in their report there is no mention of the number of subjects studied. In recent work Schmeidler, Mitchell, and Sondow (1975) studied subjects' ability to influence thermistor temperature registrations, and in a post-hoc analysis found some weak evidence that certain measures derived from a projective test, the Hand test, were related to PK performance, at least on the day (the first PK session) the Hand test was given. Still more recently Schmeidler, Gambale, and Mitchell (1976) reported no significant differences for successful and nonsuccessful PK (thermistor) subjects on the Hand test, on whether subjects saw an illusory staircase as going up or down, or on Rotter's I-E scale. The number of successful subjects (i.e., those producing significant results) was, however, very small ($N = 4$).

Some recent studies have employed two kinds of PK tasks (or two task orientations) and have related success with these to one or more individual difference variables. Such studies can have considerable value in elucidating the relationship of an individual difference variable to PK performance, and they indicate the importance of recognizing and exploring possible boundary conditions for personality-psi correlations. They suggest the importance of considering possible interactions of task and individual differences.

Stanford (1969) found that subjects who normally tended to organize their thinking around sensory imagery obtained better die-face PK results when visualizing the desired target face than when using another strategy ("associative activation of the unconscious"), but that subjects whose thinking was not normally dominated by sensory imagery did better with the "associative activation" method than with the visualization strategy. This study involved 20 subjects. Steilberg (1975) tried a similar approach. Each of his ten subjects did PK die-face trials using a visualization strategy similar to but not identical with that used by Stanford (1969) and also using the intense concentration method described earlier in this review. He attempted to relate success with these methods to the measure of sensory imagery in thought used by Stanford, to expansion-compression ratings, and to sex of subject. He, however, found no significant relationships. Part of the difficulty might have been in the very small sample size used in his study. Unfortunately, the directions of the nonsignificant outcomes in his study are not specified; nor is the specific nature of his statistical analyses stated. Mischo and Weis (1973) had each of 50 subjects do two series of PK trials, the first under conditions of nonfrustration and the second following a deliberately induced frustration. The PK trials were with an electronic REG. PK scores following frustration were significantly and positively related to calmness and sociability and significantly and negatively related to depressivity, neuroticism, and inhibition. There were no significant correlations of personality variables and PK scores contributed during the nonfrustration condition. Subjects were always tested under frustration after being tested under nonfrustration, so conclusions which might be drawn from the study are hampered by the confounding of the frustration variable (nonfrustration versus frustration) with order of testing. Such a study should ideally use an independent-groups design.

The attempt to relate seemingly stable personality traits to PK performance would appear to presuppose some stability over time of PK performance. This matter has not been approached in the direct way of retesting subjects and computing a correlation coefficient for test-retest reliability. However, in a number of studies investigators have pretested PK subjects and have used them in later, formal work if they showed initial indications of being successful. The fact that this has been a useful method at least suggests that subjects showing promise in PK at one time tend to do well at a later time (e.g., Schmidt, 1970a, 1973, 1974a). An interesting example of prediction of PK scoring level from past PK performance is a study by Fahler (1959). On the basis of preliminary PK testing he selected two small groups of subjects, one predicted to psi miss ($N = 4$) on the placement PK task, the other predicted to hit ($N = 5$). Both groups did as expected to a significant degree. The difference in the performance of the two was also significant. Since, however, the analysis had the "set" as its basis rather than subject scores, some reservation is in order.

There are several indications of this form of consistency spread throughout the literature (e.g., in the early die-face work), and there are even some indications that subjects who showed marked ESP ability are often also able to demonstrate PK ability (e.g., Schmidt and Pantas, 1972). Indeed, the history of parapsychology is replete with examples of persons who seemed to be both outstanding PK and ESP subjects and who could demonstrate results rather repeatedly over a period of time, sometimes with rather different PK and ESP tasks. A recent example has been reported by Kelly and Kanthamani (1972).

As far as consistency within a test session is concerned, Dale (1946) reported a +.46 Spearman-Brown correlation (based on odd-even sheets for 54 subjects), a highly significant result. However, in a second study (Dale and Woodruff, 1947) which attempted to replicate the one just cited, the obtained correlation for odd-even sheets (N = 54 subjects) was insignificantly negative. In reference to the problem broached above, that of whether PK and ESP performance may be correlated, the Dale-Woodruff study yielded only a +.12 nonsignificant correlation of ESP and PK scores. Because subjects took an ESP test prior to the PK test and were offered a monetary reward for high scores on the latter but not on the former, there may have been a reduction in the correlation.

Stanford et al. (1975) found a positive (+.18) but nonsignificant correlation between PK scores (on an electromechanical REG) when subjects deliberately tried to influence the REG and when it functioned in a nonintentional PK setting (N = 40 subjects). The latter setting produced significant, positive performance, but the former, only chance results.

There is a need for formal studies of PK test-retest reliability utilizing the same PK task on test and retest.

Mood

André (1972) gave tiny samples of subjects (three in one study and six in another) a paper-and-pencil mood questionnaire and found no relationship between mood and PK performance. She did note that in both series trials contributed during morning sessions were significantly above chance and were somewhat better than those contributed at other times. Interestingly, Wadhams and Farrelly (1968) reported that in testing themselves for PK the only glimmer of success was on trials which one of them had contributed during the early morning. These were significantly above chance. Similarly, Thouless (1951) noted that his own PK results were best during the morning. He felt this was not an artifact of a simple decline in performance from morning to afternoon, for he noted the same effect comparing morning and afternoon trials from different days (with both groups of trials being beginning trials). No conclusion should, however, be drawn from such convergence of unanticipated findings. Systematic study of the time-of-day factor is needed for any conclusion. It is possible that morning superiority, if it is a real phenomenon, might hold for some subjects but not for others. If real, it might be a function of circadian changes in the body, or perhaps simply of being rested, feeling fresher, etc. Further work is needed on the time-of-day factor.

Mood and/or motivational factors may have played a role in studies noting differences of PK performance under conditions of darkness versus light (in the test room) (Gibson and Rhine, 1943; McMahan, 1947). In a study involving only two subjects (Feather and Rhine, 1969), the mood of one of the subjects may have influenced the effect of a "help-hinder" manipulation. (See "Number of Subjects" topic within the "Physical Perspective" section.)

Drugs

No methodologically adequate studies of the effects of drugs on PK have appeared. What we have are two highly exploratory studies. One (Averill and Rhine, 1945) involved alcohol. A pre- to post-drug decline was observed in both subjects tested. Both had imbibed 100 cubic centimeters of gin mixed with an equal quantity of ginger ale; both became sick as a result. The decline was slight in the subject who got sick and vomited, possibly losing much of his alcohol. The one who had become sick but retained his alcohol showed a significant decline in performance from strong above-chance scoring to slight psi-missing. The other study concerned caffeine (Rhine, Humphrey, and Averill, 1945), or, more accurately, Coca-Cola. It involved three subjects and provided evidence of a pre- to post-Coca-Cola increase in PK performance. Both drug studies had many limitations, and they were frankly acknowledged as highly exploratory. The many limitations include no blind element being involved, lack of a proper control group, and the presence of the drug being confounded with the presence of other substances such as sugar.

Social Factors

The evidence bearing on social influences in PK work is essentially indirect or unsystematic. Here we shall be concerned with the studies, such as they are, which have a reasonably direct relevance to the topic of social influence. We shall ignore studies in which a purely ad-hoc interpretation of results has been made in terms of social factors or experimenter influence.

Margaret M. Price and J. B. Rhine (1944) reported a study on subject-experimenter relationships. Price challenged an outstanding PK subject, J. S. Woodruff, with the claim that she could so distract him during PK testing that his performance would suffer. To establish comparison data Woodruff worked alone in a pretest series of 60 runs and obtained a mean run score of 4.97, quite exceptional performance. On the following day when Price attempted to distract him during 60 runs, his mean run score was 3.83, a significant decrement. But since experimental treatment had been confounded with order of testing, it was possible that the poor performance on the second day of the study was the result of whatever factors typically cause declines of success with time rather than the effect of Price's efforts. To help eliminate such a possibility, 16 days later another single session consisting of 20 runs was undertaken in which Price again attempted her negative influence. Despite the shorter session and 'the time lapse, results here were again poor (mean run score = 3.85).

Another early study provides at least a weak suggestion that personality factors may interact with social conditions to influence PK performance. Edmond and Lottie Gibson, a husband-wife team, compared the performance of each other as subjects when working alone or in the presence of the other. Mr. Gibson's performance seemed to suffer when he was alone as compared to when he was in the company of his wife, but Mrs. Gibson showed an opposite trend (Gibson, Gibson, and Rhine, 1943). No general conclusions can be drawn from this work involving only two subjects, but such outcomes suggest the possible value of studying the interaction of socially-related personality variables (e.g., extraversion-introversion) with the social conditions of experimentation. No such work has been reported.

A possible psi-mediated social or experimenter effect was observed in a blind-target PK study by Fisk and West (1958) of the outstanding PK subject, Dr. J. Blundun. This study was inspired by earlier work on ESP in which subjects had performed poorly on targets prepared by West and had done well with those prepared by Fisk even though they did not know that both men were preparing targets and of course had no idea as to which targets were prepared by whom (West and Fisk, 1953). In one phase of their work reported in 1958, PK targets were, on alternate days, displayed in Fisk's home and in West's home, unknown to Dr. Blundun. The idea was to see if something comparable to their 1953 results would happen in this blind-target PK study. In accord with expectation, results were significant on Fisk's targets but not on West's. Such results do not prove the effect was a psi-mediated social or experimenter one, for alternative interpretations are possible.

Certain casual observations made in and outside of the laboratory have suggested to some of us specific avenues for the exploration of social facilitation of PK performance. One such observation is of how easy it often appears for "ordinary persons" to accomplish some rather striking psi feats after observing a "psychic," in person, do the same. The psi events seem to happen, at least with the psychic, quickly and rather easily, and the psychic may often assure the observer that they are possible for others as well. Thus social facilitation of psi events may occur through making subjects aware, concretely, of the effects as being real and even probable and expected. Next, there are the instances, as noted earlier, in which persons watch Uri Geller on TV or hear him on the radio and report dramatic possible-PK events happening in their own homes. In this case contact with a psychic via such media may allow an externalization of responsibility for PK events, for, as was mentioned earlier, most persons reporting such events believed Geller was personally responsible for those events. Another observation is that of a person who thinks of himself or herself as psychic "coming on like a light" and accomplishing possible psi-mediated feats of unaccustomed strength or of previously unattained character after witnessing another psychic (perhaps on film) do something outside the observer-psychic's current repertory. This seems especially likely when other observers appear impressed by the feats of the psychic being observed. Here motivation may be augmented through a little social facilitation of professional envy. Finally, each of us may be a showman, potentially, and the presence of TV or movie cameras during an effort at PK may prove facilitating much as it would seem to have been for free-response ESP work at the Maimonides Medical Center's parapsychology laboratory (personal communication to me from Charles Honorton of that center). Each of these observations could lead to some interesting research.

Span of Psi "Attention"

Much of the early die-face work involved as target, not a single die face, but either a "high" or "low" combination of faces (with two dice). If a high combination was the target, the objective was that the two dice would stop with their upward faces adding to eight or more. A large part of the early work involved the high-combination target. This was unfortunate because if the dice were pitted dice, as they often were, any bias would likely favor a "high" combination. The lighter "high" faces would be more likely to turn up. Occasionally, too, work was done with the target as "sevens" (the two faces adding up to seven) or as "low" combinations (e.g., J. B. Rhine, 1945). It is difficult to evaluate the extent to which such early work, frankly recognized by the investigators as exploratory, was successful because of PK, die bias, perhaps both, or other sources of possible error.

If PK were the cause of any of the success, it looks as though subjects could through psi mediation somehow select particular combinations of faces to be favored. This psi versatility intrigued workers then as it does now. Humphrey (1947b) reported a remarkable study which explored the limits of what might be termed the span of psi "attention." As her own subject, she threw 12 dice simultaneously, six red and six white. The one-face was target on all of the trials, and the intention was to cause one of the colors to produce an excess of ones, the other color, a deficit. Which color was to be "high" aim and which "low" (in the sense just specified) was alternated. The basic problem posed by the study was whether simultaneous high- and low-aim could be successfully realized. Taking the data as a whole, the deviation of the number of ones in the anticipated direction was significant ($P = .014$). Although this result does not of itself prove that the two objectives were being realized simultaneously, further analyses of the data suggested that simultaneous realization of the two objectives had occurred to a statistically significant degree.

Other early studies added to the evidence that PK can function in complex tasks. Examples are studies by Steen (1957), Ratte (1960), and Ratte and Greene (1960). Steen's study was a PK analogue of baseball, whereas those of Ratte were an analogue of basketball. These studies were considered above in the section on motivation. As an example of the complexity involved, in Steen's study there was evidence of extrachance success by his two subjects even though success appeared to require the coordinated manipulation of three dice on a given play. In the work of Ratte, subjects were successful in producing the selected doubles which were of maximal value in certain aspects of the game.

Early work has suggested the possibility of success with doubles involving the six-face (Reeves and Rhine, 1945), but this work must be viewed with caution because of methodological deficiencies including possible die bias. Forwald (1962) demonstrated that he could either encourage or discourage the appearance of doubles in general (i.e., denomination of the doubles was unimportant). His work aimed, in one part, at producing a specified number of doubles in as few throws as possible, and in the other part it aimed at going as many trials as possible without producing the specified number of doubles. The success of the work indicated that he could systematically encourage or discourage the occurrence of doubles in general. This Forwald work had the drawback of the dice having been shaken and released from cupped hands.

Rate of Target Generation

The recent development of electronic REGs with their capacity to generate targets at varied speeds raises the question of whether PK success is in any way functionally related to generation speed. Conclusions about this matter are complicated by a number of issues, sometimes interrelated. These include the following: (a) If a subject works at two generation rates for an equal period of time, the total work at the fast rate required to attain the same rate of success as with the slow rate increases directly with the speed of generation involved in the faster rate. For example, if the fast rate is ten times the slow rate, equal success rates, granted equal periods of time at the two rates, will require ten times the net effort (work accomplished) at the fast rate as at the slow rate. (b) Given the fact summarized in (a), how does one equate, psychologically, the task for subjects? Would cutting down the working time at the fast rate, in proportion to the rate, be an adequate solution? (c) REGs which run at different speeds sometimes function on different principles and thus may not be equally easy to influence by PK. As only one example, generation rate may be confounded with complexity of the device. (d) How "hits" or "success" are assigned may be an important factor.   Sometimes 100 trials with a fast rate are automatically evaluated on a majority-vote basis (e.g., 51 out of 100 of the events going in the desired direction equals a hit), and the outcome of this process is fed back to the subject as a hit or a miss (e.g., Schmidt, 1974a). (e) Psychological factors may be important, such as whether the mode of feedback to the subject betrays the generation rate. As one of many possibilities in this connection, if the subject knows there are two such rates, and especially if he has a preference for one of them and knows when that rate is occurring, this may make a difference (Pantas, 1971). Also, the meaningfulness of the individual trial and the incentive value of success on it may be influenced by generation rate. (f) The experimenter's purpose, interest, or hypothesis in the study may make a difference (e.g., whether he is interested in actual trial-by-trial hit rate, efficiency with respect to time, or whatever).

Several studies have allowed a direct comparison of generation rates (Millar and Broughton, 1976; Pantas, 1971; Schmidt, 1973, 1974a, 1976).

Pantas (1971) found no direct effect of target generation rate (60 versus 240 trials per minute), but he was working with subjects who had specified a preferred rate on the basis of experience with the REG and who knew which rate was being generated.   He found some tendency for the preferred rate to have more success than the nonpreferred one, but this difference was contributed largely by slow-generation trials.   Under the psychological conditions of this study, more effective PK at the slower rate might produce just such an effect, but the possible interaction of preference with generation rate was not statistically evaluated, it would seem.

Schmidt (1973) found that on a binary-trial basis there was significantly better performance at a slow- than at a fast-generation rate (rates of 30 and 300 events/second, respectively).   In this study subjects knew two speeds were being compared and often knew which rate was being used at a given time.   Whether the feedback mode itself betrayed the generation rate seemed not to affect the scoring difference for the two rates.   Both rates showed positive, significant scoring.

Schmidt (1974a) compared performance on "fast" (complex) and "slow" (simple) generators under conditions such that subjects could not distinguish the generation rate of the generators (1 binary trial during 3 seconds versus 100 binary trials during 3 seconds).   For the fast generator the 100 trials (per 3-second period) were not individually recorded but were used to make a single binary decision, hit or miss, on the basis of a majority-vote principle, and this information was immediately fed back to the subject as the outcome for that "trial."   Such "trials" alternated with actual binary trials on a random basis. Subjects received feedback on the latter, slow-generator trials, too. Pooling the results of Schmidt's pilot and confirmatory series (something he did not do), we find that the hit-rate for the slow generator (producing true binary trials) is significantly greater than that for the fast generator (producing artificial binary "trials") even though results for both generators are significantly positive.

This confirms the impression developed from the earlier Schmidt study (1973) and the Pantas study (1971) that performance is, for some reason, better on slow generators or at slower generation rates. Note, however, that in the study discussed in the paragraph above, generation rate was confounded with type of generator used. Generators were not confounded with generation rate in the Schmidt (1973) study, nor in the Pantas (1971) work. It is tempting, therefore, to conclude that increases in generation rate can impair performance level, especially when generation rate is quite high, perhaps 30 events per second or more. But why should this be the case?

Apparently, any such effect is not solely a function of generator complexity since generation rate and generator type were not confounded in two of the three studies considered. Perhaps complexity of the generation mode of a given generator is involved, but the work discussed so far cannot clarify this question. One is tempted to think that neither complexity of generator nor of generation mode would be a factor, given the findings reviewed earlier concerning the apparent independence of the PK effect from changes in task complexity (e.g., the ease of success with hidden targets).

A recent study by Schmidt (1976) may help in deciding this issue. An REG generated targets at the rate of 300 per second, the rate which gave such poor results (50.4 percent) in Schmidt's 1973 study; and these were stored in an electronic memory for later playback to subjects (in a time-displaced PK study) at the rate of ten per second, a rate which had earlier given reasonably good (51.6 percent) results. The prerecorded sequence was played back to the subject four times such that the psychological "value" (incentive value) of each hit would presumably have been increased. These prerecorded targets, which had been generated at 300 trials per second, yielded an average scoring rate (across subjects) of 52.92 percent as contrasted with 50.18 percent for "momentarily-generated" trials produced at the rate of ten per second. The difference of these rates is statistically significant, and each rate is independently significant (as contrasted with mean chance expectation).

The results of this ingenious study clearly indicate that there is no intrinsic limiting factor in a generation rate of 300 targets per second. The results suggest that the poor results often shown at such high rates may be caused by the decreased distinctiveness and/or the decreased psychological value (incentive value) of the individual trial at a higher generation rate. Psychologically speaking, at such fast rates the trial may no longer be especially meaningful as a unit, and success on the individual trial may be less rewarding. But when fast-generated targets are played back to subjects at a slow rate, each trial is more distinctive and the value of a hit on it may be increased, especially given that it is played back several times. There are two possible factors at work here, the *slow* playback (ten per second of targets generated at 300 per second) and the *multiple* feedback (four-fold) for each target. Unfortunately, the Schmidt (1976) study confounds these factors. There was no condition, for instance, in which the fast-generated trials were played back at ten per second but were heard only once. Nor was there a condition in which prerecorded feedback occurred without the events being slowed down during feedback but with multiple feedback. It is possible that both factors may work in some interactive fashion, and only further studies which disconfound these factors can clarify this issue.

It is doubtful that the Millar-Broughton (1976) study, which showed no significant results under any of the target-generation rates (1000, 100, 10, and 1 binary trial(s) per second), casts light on the problem at hand. Methodologically it differed considerably from Schmidt's work, and in any event there is no evidence that subjects were induced to produce PK in the study.

In summary, there are some consistent indications that very high-target-generation rates can impair PK success. Both direct and indirect evidence suggest that this finding may be related more to how the subject experiences and responds to the individual trial (psychological factors) than to any intrinsic limitations of PK in acting on complex generators or generators operating at fast rates. More research is certainly needed on this very important and fundamental problem.

"Strings" of PK Success and Failure?

Conceivably related to the topic of attentional processes and PK performance, which we have been considering, is the question of whether hits and misses in PK testing are randomly distributed throughout the unit of analysis (e.g., the column, set, or page) or whether they tend to cluster or "string" more (or less) than one would expect by chance. Pratt (1947c) failed to find evidence of such patterning in data collected by other researchers. Schmidt and Pantas (1972) failed to find such patterning whether the REG was in a PK- or in a precognition-oriented mode. Both the papers just cited considered data which showed evidence of extrachance performance. The psychological interpretation of the failure to find "strings" in the several kinds of data analyzed in the reports cited would vary from experiment to experiment. What is striking is that none of the data showed such effects.

The Use of Same-Subjects Designs

It is very common practice for each subject in a PK study to be tested under two conditions, with two REGs, with two generation rates, etc., during a single experimental session. Sometimes more than two such factors are studied with the same subject during a given session, through the two-condition study is the rule. Experimental psychologists have long been aware of the peculiar vicissitudes often associated with such same-subjects designs, but these problems somehow seem not to have bothered parapsychologists.

The problems of same-subjects designs can be summarized as follows: (a) The presence of sequence relevant variables (order and carry-over effects) necessitates counterbalancing to prevent their effects being confounded with the effects of the experimental manipulation. However, counterbalancing, to be effective, requires symmetry of transfer, i.e., that the carry-over effects operating from one condition to the next be of the same magnitude and kind when the order is reversed. This assumption is often hard to justify (Poulton and Freeman, 1966). (b) The presence in same-subjects designs of range effects (Poulton, 1973, 1974)—the influence upon performance in a given condition of the range of other conditions to which the subject has been exposed—can result in unanticipated and undersirable influences upon outcomes. (c) Task-juxtaposition effects—e.g., the development of a preference for one condition over the other; or other effects comparable to perceptual contrast phenomena—can spuriously increase or decrease the observed difference of means. (d) The exposure of subjects to more than one condition can often either give them clues as to the nature of the hypothesis and thereby possibly lead to spurious confirmation; or such exposure can cause subjects to make wild guesses about the hypothesis, which can inflate error variance. Problems such as these should give an investigator considerable pause in selecting a same-subjects design in spite of the economic and statistical advantages which are often associated with such designs. D'Amato (1970) has discussed some of these problems in greater detail, and Poulton (1973, 1974) has discussed range effects at some length. Poulton (1973) feels that "The day should come . . . when no reputable psychologist will use a within-subject design, except for a special purpose, without combining it with a separate-groups design" (p. 119). It is well known that within-subject designs (same-subjects designs) often lead to different conclusions than those based upon separate groups even when lower animals (perhaps not so subject to task-juxtaposition influences) are involved (e.g., D'Amato, 1955; Schrier, 1958).

Same-subjects designs have been the rule in PK studies and in ESP work as well. Although parapsychologists have very rarely acknowledged their troublesome character, they have recognized that such designs produce some peculiar effects. Specifically, when subjects are given two tasks or function under two conditions in a study, it often appears that their performance under the two conditions is directionally polarized. Rao (1965) discussed such effects at length in his Presidential Address to the Parapsychological Association, and he termed them "preferential" or "differential" effects. Same-subjects designs have, in some instances, apparently been preferred by parapsychologists precisely because they tend to produce polarized differences of means. However, this expediency in the interest of obtaining statistical significance is very short-sighted. Usually when a study compares two conditions, target classes, tasks, etc., the purpose is to compare performance levels occasioned by the two compared conditions. We are interested in the performance level in each condition in its own right. Usually we are not interested in the problem of how subjects react specifi-cally to the juxtaposition of the two conditions in question. Nor do we wish our two means or their difference to be influenced by sequence relevant variables which go uncontrolled whenever there is asymmetry of transfer.

In short, when parapsychological studies are planned, we must avoid being hypnotized by the relative ease of finding significant differences of means when using same-subjects designs. We should show more concern for what can or cannot actually be learned from the conditions we study. To do this we must generally avoid same-subjects (within-subject) designs or couple them with separate-groups designs. Otherwise, we may have no idea what a given difference of means, however significant, really signifies.

The review by Rao (1965) cited earlier mentions a number of instances of probable "differential" effects in PK work. These effects of task-juxtaposition (and/or confounding by sequence relevant variables) often, though not always, show up in parapsychological studies as psi-hitting in one condition and psi-missing in the other. Some very striking and more recent examples of probable such effects can be found in work by Cox (1971), Honorton and Barksdale (1972), and Stanford (1969, 1972). The later two studies are perhaps the most informative about the origin of such effects for they considered the interaction of psychological individual differences with the two kinds of tasks presented to each subject.

Intention

The entire history of laboratory PK research bespeaks the ability of subjects to deliberately bias outcomes of random events in a particular direction. Much of that search has also shown the ability of subjects to deliberately and effectively shift that biasing influence as the target changes throughout an experiment. Sometimes this ability to shift the direction of the PK influence has become the focus of a particular study. We have already discussed Humphrey's (1947b) study of simultaneous "high-" and "low-aim" on different colors of dice. Cer-tain workers undertook to see whether with "high" or "low" die faces as targets subjects could succeed. Studies by Knowles (1949) and Mangan (1954) yielded success, but not that of Parsons (1945). Honorton and May (1976) tested sub-jects with an electronic REG and showed that they could intentionally bias the REG either to favor or disfavor a certain feedback outcome. (To prevent any artifact of possible REG bias, the event inside the REG which would produce the intended form of feedback was alternated on each trial; generation rate was ten per second. Despite this rapid switching of the event which objectively had to be influenced, subjects were still successful. This is further evidence of the goal-directed character of psi function.)

Possibly related to the topic of intention are two placement PK studies by Cox with dice falling down a three-tier apparatus (1959) and with metal balls falling down a five-tier apparatus (1962a). He studied results in each of the tiers, but only the bottom tier in each device was associated with a significant, positive deviation. It is quite likely that these results were caused by the seemingly greater interest in and attention paid to the bottom tier(s) by subjects. In the five-tier work Cox at times covered the lower tier so that it could not be seen, and the rate of scoring there was then reduced.

In summary, the evidence reviewed immediately above plus much if not all of the other PK evidence reviewed herein indicate that the subject's intention is a directive factor in intentional PK tasks. Keeping in mind a matter discussed above, this intention factor should not be confused with egocentric concentration upon a task.

The Majority-Vote Technique

Several PK studies have, at least in part, addressed themselves to the problem of whether through the use of multiple trials as the unit of statistical analysis—such as using the "majority vote" of numerous dice released at the same time to designate the outcome and thus a single hit or miss for that unit—it is possible to obtain better overall results than by simply counting the results of the totality of the individual trials in the study. Several studies have provided data yielding a higher percentage of "hits" when treating a multiple-trial unit as a single trial (using majority vote) than when considering the single trials pooled (Cox, 1962a, 1965b, 1966, 1974a, the latter summarizing such results; Morris, 1965; Schmidt, 1973). However, as Schmidt (1973) noted, the simple assumption that subjects uniformly exert some PK effect upon individual trials automatically leads to a higher percentage of success if we pool groups of trials for a majority vote than if we simply consider the individual trials as the unit of analysis. He provides the example (p. 111) in which if the hit rate for individual trials is 51.4 percent, consideration of 100 trials at a time (using the majority vote) leads to an expected hit rate of about 61 percent.

Nonetheless, Schmidt's explanation for increased hit-rate using the majority-vote procedure may not be the entire story. Cox (1974a) points out that in his own work or that of persons working under him (cited above), in six out of seven units of experimental work the critical ratio (CR or z score) produced by the majority-vote procedure was greater than that based upon single trials. He says that this effect, if a genuine one, would not be expected on a purely statistical basis since the CR computed from the majority-vote procedure is based upon fewer "trials."

Schmidt, on the other hand, found that in only one out of eight blocks of data from his own studies was the CR computed from the majority-vote procedure greater than that computed on the basis of trials. The results for the two experimenters, Cox and Schmidt, are thus strikingly dissimilar. Perhaps differential interests of the two experimenters in the majority-vote method and different concepts about the significance of hit-rates with the method influenced the outcomes of their studies with respect to it, either indirectly by some form of influence upon their subjects or directly by experimenter psi influences upon the PK target system. Interestingly, the only study in which Cox did not find a higher CR for the majority-vote method was the earliest study (1962a) when his attention was not so crucially focused on the "cumulation hypothesis" as he later (1965b) termed it. In that study (1962a) there was improvement in hit rate with the majority-vote method, albeit not improvement which suggests anything other than statistical principles in operation.

Cox (1974a) states without giving details that several studies (Cox, 1965b, 1966, 1974a; Morris, 1965) have provided some evidence that a "relatively large percentage of majority-vote hits were produced by a differential of only one or two balls" (p. 67). (Cox was working with machines which used balls.) Cox's reasoning (1974a) seems to suggest the possibility that a principle of economy may have been operating in his work such that through psi just enough was done to win the majority vote, but little or nothing more. However, the paper by Cox (1974a) does not establish any such claim, for detailed analyses would be required which are not reported therein. It would seem that to demonstrate majority-vote efficiency not explainable on a purely statistical basis one would have to show that hits on the original, binary trials are more uniformly distributed across the various blocks (upon which the majority-vote is based) than would be expected by chance.

It appears certain that if there is ever any increased efficiency in the majority-vote method that cannot be attributed to statistical artifact, it is not a universal phenomenon. Schmidt found no support for this idea. It is clear, too, that Cox's original "cumulation hypothesis" (1965a)—that "the more separate events available per trial for PK to operate upon, the greater the chance of success for that particular trial" (p. 166)—has found no definitive support beyond what one would expect from an artifact of how the data are treated when PK acts quite uniformly across the trials of an experiment. Nor has Cox reported any measure of statistical significance for the increase in CRs which he finds with the majority-vote method.

Some Curious Performance Effects

Cox, Feather, and Carpenter (1966) followed up earlier work (Cox, 1965a) involving PK on an electromechanical system which controlled the distance traveled by the hand of a target clock as it moved first in a clockwise and then in a counterclockwise direction. The difference in the length of the two sweeps was compared with the difference for a control clock. In an analysis based upon data gathered in earlier work (Cox, 1965a), but not reported there, Cox et al. (1966) divided trials into two kinds with respect to the observed difference of the two final clock-hand positions: those with large differences (greater than .01 second) and those with small (.01 second or less). They found a significant, positive PK effect for the large-difference (L-D) trials, but not for the small-difference (S-D) trials, though performance on the latter was positive. In the 1966 paper Cox et al. reported new work in which the same effect was evident. They also noted, both in the earlier and in the later data, a tendency for the percent of trials producing hits to be rather directly related to the size of the clock differential, though no statistical analysis of that effect was reported. They also mention that earlier data of Cox's (1962b) involving possible PK on water drops had shown an opposite effect, namely S-D trials yielding a larger percentage of hits than L-D trials. The work, when examined on the basis of subseries (exclusive of the water-drop study) yielded fairly consistent results favoring L-D trials, in addition to the overall significant effect. The interpretation of such findings is still very uncertain.

In a more recent study Cox (1974a) noted an interesting effect. In this work 1,200 small steel balls were released down an incline and rolled into 16 pairs of chutes alternately colored red and green. In each pair scoring was by majority vote according to whether the majority of balls was in the target-color chute. Several series consistently showed higher scoring rates in chute-pairs where the balls in either chute did not exceed a fixed number approximating the median than in chute-pairs where the balls in either or both chutes did exceed the median. While the difference was not significant in all the series, the trend was constant across series, and the difference pooled for the series was significant. Only an ad-hoc psychological interpretation can be given for such an outcome, and Cox does not attempt any at all. If the effect stands up with attempted replication, it is conceivable that here may be a parapsychological manifestation of Weber's Law from psychophysics. Only new studies could test that possibility.

Is There Evidence That PK Can Be Trained?

In PK research the possibility that immediate feedback regarding success might facilitate performance through a learning effect has received little *explicit* attention. This is probably because almost every PK study done has employed immediate feedback to the subject, and in many cases decline effects, not functions resembling learning curves, have been observed! Even a steady rate of performance seems very much the exception rather than the rule. With electronic REGs, which perhaps allow optimal feedback regarding success (e.g., the appropriate light immediately comes on), reports of significant inclines of performance with experience are not evident in the literature. Recently, Honorton and May (1976) reported a significant decline in work involving an electronic REG and immediate feedback. This occurred even though the test session was very short and the overall results were statistically significant. In most studies with electronic REGs and immediate feedback, results have been quite good, but, nonetheless, there has emerged no significant incline with performance. This set of circumstances does not favor the learning hypothesis.

On the other hand, such work may be associated with fewer significant declines than in the die-face work. If one takes this impression seriously and feels that feedback is more adequate in the recent work, this could be construed as at least some weak support for the learning hypothesis. But it is very weak evidence. Both the early and the recent work involved reasonably good feedback, and the relative lack of significant declines in the current work may, perhaps, be most parsimoniously attributable to the ease and swiftness with which trials can be done on the electronic REGs and the shortened length of typical sessions.

In the only study in the literature which was specifically aimed at training PK through immediate feedback, Thouless (1945) used a coin-spinning task with himself as subject and obtained a nonsignificant, positive deviation along with a statistically significant decline across sessions.

In summary, most of the work to date on PK has involved essentially immediate feedback regarding success. Incline effects, even nonsignificant ones, are quite rare. Declines seem, rather, the rule. This state of the evidence should not, however, discourage further exploration of the possibility that, given the interesting feedback possibilities inherent in modern electronic devices, training of PK performance may be possible. More direct efforts are needed to study these possibilities, efforts fully informed by and built around the principles of operant conditioning.

PHYSICAL PERSPECTIVE

Questions concerning physical variables as related to PK performance are of the greatest importance, but they have not received the systematic study they would seem to deserve. The studies of such factors, which we do have, generally have not controlled for contaminating or confounding by psychological factors.

Subject-to-Target Distance

Three studies (Dale and Woodruff, 1947; Nash, 1946; Nash and Richards, 1947) directly compared two distances of the subject from the target dice. None of the studies provided evidence of a decline of effect with distance. In the Nash (1946) study the experimenter was always near the target dice, and only the distance of the subject from the dice was varied; this may not have been an adequate test of a possible distance effect since the "experimenter" might have been the "subject." The studies by Nash involved distances of 3 and 30 feet. In the Dale-Woodruff study the distances were 100 feet and essentially zero distance from the test appratus. Nash found significant, positive performance at 30 feet in both studies but significant performance at 3 feet only in the earlier study. Dale and Woodruff found nonsignificant results at both distances. None of these studies controlled for the possible psychological effect of knowledge of distance (e.g., greater motivation due to a sense of challenge).

A placement study by Fahler (1959) showed that success could be had when both subject and experimenter were at a distance of approximately 27 yards from the test appratus. The study also involved an essentially zero-distance condition, and, although performance in the two conditions was not compared, it was somewhat better in the long-distance condition.

McConnell's study (1955) of PK during sleep involved a minimum distance between the subject and the dice of about 1 mile, but there was no effort to study the effect of distance *per se*. The overall results were not significant, but McConnell's own results, a large proportion of the total trials, were significant. If one takes seriously this ad-hoc finding, the possibilities for PK at a distance are considerably extended.

In some of the work in which subjects were blind as to PK targets the dice were with the subjects but the targets were at a distance. This distance ranged from 3 to 300 miles in the Mitchell and Fisk work (1953) and was 200 miles during part of the Fisk and West study (1958). This cannot be termed "PK at a distance," but, rather, it is "PK with distant targets." The distance of the targets made no obvious difference.

Temporal "Distance"

Earlier, Schmidt's studies (1975a, 1976) of possible time-displaced PK were mentioned. An REG was set into operation prior to the time the subject received any feedback about its outputs. The time span varied from a matter of days (1975a) to, apparently, a matter of minutes (1976). Subjects never knew that a sequence of events was being prepared for them, and some attempts were made to reduce the possibility of experimenter effects (contemporaneous) upon the REG. Nevertheless, positive, significant results were forthcoming. Although, as Schmidt notes, these studies cannot completely rule out an experimenter-psi interpretation, they at least open up the question of whether PK, like, possibly, ESP (as precognition), can have a time-displaced form. They broach the question of whether PK is time-independent or time-dependent. These studies simply asked whether time-displaced PK is possible. If such PK does occur, other work is needed to determine whether the magnitude of the effect is independent of the *length* of time involved.

Die-Size Comparisons (Uncontrolled for Weight)

Several studies have failed to show any significant or consistent effect of die-size on results (Hilton, Baer, and Rhine, 1943; Hilton and Rhine, 1943; Humphrey and Rhine, 1945; Rhine and Humphrey, 1944a). A number of these studies have some potentially serious methodological flaws which might mean that they measured something else than or in addition to PK.

A more sophisticated study of die-size was conducted by Forwald (1961). He studied 5- and 13-mm dice thrown for die face onto two types of surfaces, soft cardboard or a hard tabletop. This 2 X 2 design allows for some interesting possibilities, for instance, that which type of die is most effective may depend upon the type of surface onto which it is thrown (i.e., an interactive effect). Two separate sections of the study (conducted at different times) each produced significant, positive overall deviations. Of the four combinations of die size and surface, the smaller dice thrown onto the harder surface produced by far the greatest proportion of the total deviation in both sections of the study. This combination also produced the most bouncing of the dice. Could that fact have been related to the greater success for that circumstance? It is not possible to say, but this work certainly deserves being followed up. It may provide vital clues as to the application of the PK influence.

Material (With Size Constant)

The study of mass with size held constant is equivalent to studying different materials, at least in the PK research to date. Thus mass *per se* was usually confounded with type of material and also, usually, with surface material and thus, possibly, differences in friction.

Let us first consider the placement work. Cormack did work which was reported by Pratt (1951), and some of this involved holding size constant and using different weights of cubes (i.e., different materials). Results across series were inconsistent as concerns weight, and it certainly did not look as though the heavier cubes were any more difficult to influence. In an early study of placement Forwald (1952a) worked with cubes made of wood, paper (hollow), aluminum, Bakelite, and steel. Total results and results in individual series were nonsignificant. Results with each of the various materials were close to chance. Although in some of his work Forwald found suggestions that heavier cubes moved less far (e.g., 1952b, 1957), his most interesting finding in relation to this problem complicates matters a bit. When in later work he employed the scaled displacement method and computed the dynes presumably involved in the effect observed with a given material, it was obvious that while more massive cubes sometimes moved less, the computed energy involved in the interaction with such cubes was considerably greater than that for the less massive cubes

(1957, 1959). In his work he observed a number of effects along these lines. For instance, he found that as the thickness of the metal coating increased (and, thus, its mass, I might add), so did the computed energy involved in the PK effect. He felt the function was an exponential one. The kinds of metal used were varied and included aluminum, cadmium, copper, lead, and silver. From this kind of outcome, it certainly does not look as though a fixed amount of energy is available in PK work for application to each cube of a given size, and such results immensely complicate any attempt at a simplistic physical explanation of this work. Certainly such results would be much more interesting were the subject blind as to the existence of more than one type of cube in the study (or at the very least, as to which is which type). Such problems are compounded by Forwald's tendency to work as his own subject. In summary, with regard to Forwald's work on mass, although he sometimes found that more massive cubes moved less, their distance of movement was not inversely proportional to their mass; and when he computed the amounts of energy theoretically involved in such interactions, the amounts of energy expended on more massive objects were greater than for less massive ones and were out of proportion to the increase in mass. The increase in energy was greater than the increase in mass. As for the placement work in general, there is no convincing evidence that the mass of the object to be placed influences the outcome, and, if anything, PK seems more than able to rise to the occasion. However, the work done to date has involved very poor methodology for studying such questions, and later work with adequate methodology might produce different results. Studies involving double-blind methodology are sorely needed.

Turning now to die-face work, Cox (1971) has reported the use of two densities of dice under conditions such that subjects were seemingly blind as to the fact that two densities were involved. Furthermore, experimenters did not know about this fact except for a small segment of the work in which Cox himself unavoidably was required to be experimenter, and in that segment Cox was unaware of the target face. The dice used in the test apparatus were three lead dice (12.5 grams each) and three celluloid dice (1.7 grams each), all 7/16 inches on a side. In both pilot and confirmatory phases performance was significantly higher on the celluloid than on the lead dice; however, both types of dice had approximately equal deviations, the celluloid, positive and the lead, negative. Apparently, PK was active to an essentially equal degree on both types of dice, but some factor caused subjects to consistently differentiate their performance on the two densities involved.

If density of target object makes essentially no difference in die-face work, why not? Do subjects expend more energy on heavy dice than with less heavy ones even though they are blind as to the existence of the two types of dice? Or does PK for die-face targets really require no more energy for heavier dice? Nash (1955) has suggested that the PK force in such studies may act at a point of unstable equilibrium of the die and thus, he concludes, more energy might not be required for heavier dice. Whether Nash's argument is a cogent one from the physicist's standpoint, I, as a psychologist, am not prepared to say. Even if cogent, the question of its validity would still remain unanswered.

Studies such as those reviewed immediately above really raise more questions than they have answered, and the questions they raise are extremely important ones. Although very little work is currently being undertaken using dice, essentially similar questions are being raised with the newer, more efficient modes of PK testing: For example, why is there an essentially comparable success level whether subjects are attempting to influence an atomic-disintegration-based REG or one based upon the thermal emission of electrons?

Number of Dice

Several studies bearing on this problem have shown either slightly better performance with an increased number of dice or at least no decrease in rate of success (Hilton, Baer, and Rhine, 1943; Nash, 1944; Rhine, 1944; Rhine and Humphrey, 1944a, 1945). Some of these studies are quite poor methodologically—e.g., excessive use of the high faces or the six face (studies reported by Rhine and Humphrey) or hand-throwing of dice (Rhine, 1944).

Some studies have shown the possibility of PK with even very large numbers of dice at a time (96 dice, e.g., Rhine, Humphrey, and Averill, 1945). However, the level of performance in such studies does not allow the conclusion that it is possible to influence *many* dice at the same time. There is no compelling basis so far to conclude that more than one die is influenced on a single throw, although "no compelling basis" does not mean it does not or cannot happen.

In attempting to draw conclusions in this area we should also bear in mind that in the studies at hand many potentially relevant psychological variables covaried with changes in the number of dice used. One very obvious one is the intertrial interval, since tallying results for many dice thrown at a time takes longer than for a few dice thrown simultaneously.

Selected Physical Features of Apparatus

Some investigators have varied such features as the roughness of the cubes used in PK placement (Forwald, 1955), the size of the sphere rolling down a roughened incline (and thus the "relative roughness"), the roughness of the surface of the incline (with size of sphere held constant but slope of the incline confounded with roughness), and roughness of incline held constant but slope varied (Wilbur and Mangan, 1956, 1957). The Wilbur-Mangan work showed no effect of physical conditions. The Forwald study provided no evidence of a difference when 16-mm Bakelite cubes with their natural surface were compared with similar cubes with fine indentations on their surface, though there was a significant difference when the naturally surfaced ("smooth") Bakelite cubes were compared with the same type of cube covered with fine sand held in place with glue. The difference favored the rougher-surfaced cubes, which showed an independently significant, positive deflection (using the scaled displacement method). The smooth cubes showed a nonsignificant deflection in the direction opposite to the subject's effort. Here we may have a task-juxtaposition effect.

Number of Subjects

There are few studies which could even cast light upon the seemingly fundamental problem of the number of subjects.

Humphrey (1947a) made a systematic attempt to see if two subjects trying for the same target face (using six dice at a time) would perform better than if the two were trying for a different face. The person who threw the dice at a given time was ignorant of whether the "observer" was going to try for the same or for another face; however, the "observer" was not ignorant of whether his effort was contrary to or concordant with that of the thrower. The role of thrower and observer alternated. The outcome for the "help" trials was positive and significant ($P = .0001$), and the outcome for the "hinder" section of the data was not significant. The difference between the two conditions was significant.

Sara Feather and Louisa Rhine (1969) reported "help-hinder" work in which both PK agents were ignorant of whether at a given time their targets were the same or different. Overall performance was slightly but not significantly better under the different-target ("hinder") condition than under the same-target ("help") condition. Run-score variance (about the theoretical or "chance" mean) for the same-target condition was considerably, but not significantly, greater than the theoretical variance. Same-target run-score variance was significantly greater than different-target run-score variance. There was some evidence that the effect of different- or same-target conditions depended upon the mood of one of the subjects whose mood varied considerably from one day of testing to another. The authors were the only subjects involved in the study.

It simply is not possible at this time to make any form of definitive statement about the effect of increasing the number of subjects in PK studies. The importance of this problem justifies much more work being directed toward it. A recently published theory of psi (Schmidt, 1975b) includes an addition theorem for combining the effects of independent psi sources. The availability of closed-circuit TV should aid in doing studies of this problem in which the various subjects are blind as to the total number of subjects "working on" an REG at a given time. In any event, such work must give very careful consideration to controlling psychological factors which could confound the experiment.

Observations with Possible Relevance to Field Theory

Roll (1975) summarized evidence based on poltergeist cases which suggests that the physical events occur less frequently with increasing distance of potentially affectable objects from the poltergeist agent. He also adduced evidence that an object previously influenced in such a case is more likely to be subsequently influenced than is an object not previously influenced. It is difficult to know whether such generalizations are valid until experimental work is brought to bear upon them. This is particularly true because both generalizations are highly compatible with the theory of fraud being involved in poltergeist causes.

Consideration was given earlier to the "lag effect" found by Graham Watkins and his colleagues in studies of PK awakening of anesthetized mice (Watkins, Watkins, and Wells, 1973). These authors appear to interpret their finding as involving a physical influence, such as a field, which decays with time (Wells and Watkins, 1975), but this interpretation is problematic. As noted in an earlier section, the "lag effect" in these studies was larger than the initial effect itself. This seems incompatible with the proposed physical explanation in terms of an effect which decays with time, unless one makes some very specific ad-hoc assumptions. Earlier we examined an alternative interpretation of such observations, the concept of a psychologically based release-of-effort effect. The proper interpretation of such findings as those just discussed can only be ascertained through further experimentation.

Graham and Anita Watkins (Watkins and Watkins, 1974) and Roger Wells with Graham Watkins (Wells and Watkins, 1975) have reported some other data which they construe as supporting the reality of a physically based (and probably field-based) "linger effect," as they now term what they formerly termed a "lag effect" (Watkins, Watkins, and Wells, 1973). These data include the observation, while testing an outstanding subject, of an influence upon a compass needle which had a long time-course and which gradually dissipated with time and the presence of differential "exposure" of photographic film at different distances from the compass in question. The report on this effect (Watkins and Watkins, 1974) states that the amount of "exposure" decreased in proportion to the distance between the film and the compass. However, such a claim cannot be taken seriously in the absence of quantitative measures made upon each developed film and in the absence of such measures being demonstrated by actual computation to be directly proportional to the distance of each film from the compass. No such measures were reported in the published form of this paper, and none were reported in the oral delivery of the paper at the convention where it was presented. Unfortunately, prints of these films have never been published, but from my recollection of the convention presentation the fogging on some of the films was sufficiently nonuniform that one should question its having its origin in anything like radiation or a uniform physical field. Odd effects on such film can occur with irregularities in development or by means of other normal factors. The long-term effect upon the compass needle had never been previously observed with this (or any other) subject. It has not been observed since this occasion.

Whatever the nature of the effects reported in this study, it is doubtful that any such energy as was posited to explain the effects observed could conceivably be the energy typically involved in PK effects. The kind of energy supposedly involved in this study would have to readily and nondiscriminately interact with sundry objects in its path from photoplates to compass needles to metal detectors. (One of the latter was also involved in this case.) It would seem that such an energy would quickly lose power and would be capable of effective action only over short distances. Could any such energy conceivably produce the highly specific, goal-oriented and long-distance effects which we know do occur with PK? If what these studies have detected is genuine, perhaps what is involved is not the basic energy of the PK interaction but an indirect, spatially localized, influence which is a kind of residue from the occurrence of an initial PK interaction. There are many possibilities. In any event, such effects are well worth following up, and they surely need following up before any conclusions can be drawn. Such observations could provide important clues about the PK interaction or its aftereffects.

Reports of physical phenomena associated with spirit mediumship often involved reports of temperature drops in the room about the time a supposedly paranormal physical event was occurring. Price (1925) claimed that in work with Stella C. he had physically measured such drops in temperature. If such reports have physical validity, they may be of great theoretical importance. Some persons have wondered whether at the time of such observations energy was being "drained off" from the air in the room and was being used in producing the phenomena. This particular explanation will not appear reasonable to physicists. Nevertheless, if the observations in question are reliable, they may be of considerable importance. Perhaps relevant to these older observations is a recent one by Schmeidler (1973). She found evidence that when Ingo Swann, a well-known psychic, produced presumably psychokinetic changes in a target thermistor, there were sometimes changes in the opposite direction in a thermistor at another location, particularly when the second thermistor was a considerable distance from the target thermistor. Often a thermistor close to the target one showed similar changes to the target thermistor. Because of the intriguing patterns observed, this study has attracted considerable interest. However, Millar (1976) has criticized the design of the study with Swann, and his criticisms might in principal explain the odd correlations of thermistor readings. His criticisms would not so easily explain why when two other subjects than Swann were involved in the study they did not get comparably good results as did the famous psychic. More recent thermistor work by Schmeidler and associates

(Schmeidler, Gambale, and Mitchell, 1976; Schmeidler, Mitchell, and Sondow, 1975) employed essentially the same design but was generally less successful and apparently did not replicate the pattern of interthermistor results found with Ingo Swann. Millar (1976) himself modified the design to one he felt was more satisfactory, and he obtained nonsignificant results. The Millar study involved, in addition to a different design, a different experimenter and unselected subjects rather than Ingo Swann. Other workers have also failed to obtain significant results for PK with thermistors (Placer, Breese, Corcoran, Crane, and Morris, 1976). The latter study, like that of Millar, and like the later two studies by Schmeidler, employed unselected subjects.

In summary, the literature to date does not adequately support any form of "field" interpretation of PK, but it does offer some intriguing observations which should be further and more systematically explored.

Variety of Target Systems

Earlier discussion has covered a considerable variety of target systems with which PK success has been reported.

Cox has reported promising results with falling water drops (1962b), with a combination of saline solution and low-voltage relays, and with relays alone (Cox, 1965a; Cox et al., 1966). Binski's (1957) work with an outstanding subject, Kastor Seibel, illustrates the ease with which subjects often seem able to change from one PK target system to another and to maintain comparable degrees of success, in this case with coins and with a roulette wheel. Studies with spheres (metal balls or marbles) have sometimes been successful (Cox, 1962a, 1965b, 1966, 1974a; Morris, 1965) and sometimes not (Cox, 1951, 1954; L. E. Rhine, 1951; Wilbur and Mangan, 1956, 1957). Although it is difficult to generalize about why some studies with spheres were successful and some were not, examination of the sources cited at once suggests that the use of multiple spheres with the majority-vote method applied may be important. Also, consideration of the physical circumstances suggests that the successful studies may have provided more opportunities for PK influence on the movement of balls. That is, successful studies often have provided for more definite and/or numerous interruptions in the path of rolling or falling spheres. The suggestion seems to emerge that spheres rolling very fast and/or without interruptions or with minimal interruptions are unlikely to be influenced. Further work on these possibilities might reveal important relationships, and the results of the studies just reviewed seem to converge with Forwald's observation (1961) that small dice thrown on a hard surface produced the best results in a study in which both large and small dice were thrown onto hard and soft surfaces. The latter study involved die-face work, and the smaller dice thrown onto the hard surface bounced more than did dice in the other three combinations. In this general connection, it is of interest that Cox et al. (1966) found decreased PK performance in work involving an electromechanical system when, unknown to both subjects and experimenters (who worked with them), only two electrical relays were used rather than the usual four. (However, earlier work [Cox, 1965a] had failed to show an increment in success when the number of pulses per relay had been increased.)

One of the most important suggestions of a physical kind which emerges from the PK literature is that changes in the state of a physical system (including its movement) may in some sense be opportunities for PK influence to occur and that the number as well as the existence of such opportunities may be important. But these are only suggestions, and they call for systematic follow-ups. Work on the time and circumstance of PK influence is one of the most important avenues for future investigation. Worthy of investigation is the closely related proposal (Stanford, 1974a, 1974b) that in a complex system in which PK might operate in several possible ways to produce a desired end result, it will operate in the specific circumstance(s) which provide the most ready opportunity for the easy accomplishment of the desired end results.

The suggestion that PK can readily influence systems in a transitional or indeterminate phase between states may have a parallel in PK work on quantum-indeterminate events such as the time of emission of radioactive decay particles or the time-course of outputs from an electronic source of noise. Both these events have recently been used as the basis for constructing REGs.

The study of possible PK influence upon radioactive decay was first undertaken by Beloff and Evans (1961) who asked subjects alternately to increase or decrease the count-rate of a Geiger counter subjected to a source of alpha particles (uranyl nitrate). This study was unsuccessful. Chauvin and Genthon (1965) found that two out of seven children (8–17 years of age) who were relatives or friends of the experimenters produced outstanding, highly significant results in trying to influence the count-rate of a Geiger counter subjected to a uranium source. Wadhams and Farrelly (1968) tested themselves and found no overall evidence that they could influence the count-rate of a Geiger counter subjected to strontium-90, a source of beta particles.

Schmidt (1970a) developed a PK test apparatus which in effect interfaced a source of beta particles (strontium-90) with a 1,000,000 Hz electronic switch. The electronic switch is "caught" in one of two positions any time a pulse is received from a Geiger tube, and this pulse is produced whenever a beta particle enters the Geiger tube. Since any radioactive source should theoretically emit decay particles at random times, the probability of catching the electronic switch in the two positions is theoretically equal and REG outputs should be random across time. The objective of the subject in PK work with this device is, technically stated (ignoring whatever means may be chosen to display the outcomes to the subject), to bias the results such that one switch position is favored over the other. This device has the advantage that it cannot be biased by changes in the voltage supplied to the Geiger tube or by the introduction (intentionally or nonintentionally) of an additional source of radioactivity. Work by several experimenters has confirmed that subjects can influence the output of such a "Schmidt machine" (André, 1972; Honorton and Barksdale, 1972; Kelly and Kanthamani, 1972; Schmidt, 1970b, 1970c, 1974a).

Interest in purely electronic REGs as PK target generators has recently developed because of a need for REGs which can generate targets at faster rates than can realistically be had with a radioactivity-based REG. Fast generation rates with the latter type of REG would require the use of more potent radioactive sources which could pose health hazards. Several successful studies with fast electronic REGs have recently been reported (Honorton and May, 1976; Kelly and Kanthamani, 1972; May and Honorton, 1976; Schmidt, 1973, 1974a, 1974b, 1975a, 1976).

Other PK target systems new to parapsychology have recently received study. Puthoff and Targ (1974) reported successful work with Uri Geller and Ingo Swann using magnetometers, and workers at the University of California, Santa Barbara, have reported encouraging but inconclusive results with a cryogenic magnetometer (Jarrard, Corcoran, Mayfield, and Morris, 1976). Puthoff and Targ (1974) also found evidence for PK effects by Geller on a precision laboratory balance with an electrical readout; effects mimicking both "more" and "less" weight were obtained.

In summary, there are good indications that PK can influence a vast variety of target systems, systems which vary in both type and complexity. This is a fact with which any physical theory of PK must eventually cope. So far there appear to be no limits as to the kinds of systems which can be influenced by PK even though, as noted above, the likelihood of its influencing specific systems may depend upon specific opportunities for it to do so. Cases of possible spontaneous PK (in both recurrent and nonrecurrent forms) converge with the laboratory evidence on the conclusion that PK interaction can occur with respect to a multitude of different target systems. If this conclusion is granted and is combined with the evidence discussed earlier that PK is goal oriented, any attempt to explain PK on the basis of known energies seems, at least for the present, futile and simplistic. The possibility should at least be entertained that we are here concerned with an entirely new class of interaction.

SOME CONCLUDING THOUGHTS

As discussed above, it now appears that the favorable outcome in PK tasks is accomplished without sensory guidance and probably without any form of computation or information processing by the organism. In short, many of the outcomes summarized above seem to suggest a noncybernetic view of PK function.

In a cybernetic view of PK the organism must, by some means (perhaps ESP), receive information about the system it wishes to control and, while acting on that system (via PK), it must monitor and guide its PK influence in light of the information (feedback) received. This monitoring and guidance would require active, efficient information processing by the organism. Considerable masses of data suggest that the efficiency of PK function is not reduced by increases in the complexity of the target system, by speed of target generation, or by even radical (and sensorially unknown) changes in the nature of that target system. These are all outcomes which would not be expected were the cybernetic view of PK function a viable one.

One implication of abandonment of the cybernetic view of PK function is that it is inappropriate to think of the organism involved in that interaction as being the "source" of the effect. That kind of language makes sense only with the cybernetic view according to which an organism is actively "PKing" an REG in a manner analogous to a person hitting a ball or steering an automobile. If the noncybernetic view of PK is correct, the possibility of nonhuman and even very simple organisms being involved in PK interactions no longer seems puzzling or preposterous. The organism's nervous system is no longer thought to be responsible for monitoring and guiding the application of PK force to a perhaps rather complex and rapidly functioning target system. The evidence of possible PK by nonhuman organisms (reviewed by Robert L. Morris in this volume) is at once less an offense to reason. Such evidence in fact adds something to the case for a noncybernetic view of PK.

If PK is interpreted as noncybernetic in character, how, then, is it to be interpreted? One possibility which seems to do no violence to the facts is to view it as an entirely new class of interaction which occurs under a specifiable set of circumstances.

In order to approach PK within this new framework and to free ourselves from prior conceptions which might block understanding, let us put a new name on the events heretofore called "PK." Let us term them examples of "conformance behavior," a new class of interaction, and let us examine the circumstances under which this interaction may be observed.

Several elements are involved whenever conformance behavior is observed. One such element is a *disposed system*, a system which, on its own and over time tends to change in a particular direction. Studies of conformance behavior have, to date, considered as disposed systems only living organisms and usually rather complex ones at that. There is, however, nothing in this proposal which would rule out conformance behavior with respect to a disposed system of a nonliving kind. Whether any dispositions in nonliving systems can play the kind of role (described here) in conformance behavior remains to be seen and should be actively explored. Living systems can readily be seen as disposed in that their needs dispose them to act consistently in particular ways which will satisfy those needs. Another element present whenever conformance behavior is observed is the *possibility of* what could be termed *a favorable event*. Such an event is one which, if it is encountered by the disposed system, will result in changes in the direction favored by the disposition. For instance, the consumption of food by a hungry (disposed) organism is a favorable event in that it will eventuate in changes (physiological ones) favored by the disposition in question. Another element present whenever conformance behavior is observed is a *source of incompletely determinate alternative states (or events)*. An example of this is an REG as used in modern PK studies. It will be convenient to abbreviate "source of incompletely determinate alternative states (or events)" as "REG." This convenient notation should not, however, be misunderstood. The concept thus labeled is much broader than the class of such devices specifically produced for and used in PK experiments. It might, for instance, include the brain, in which circumstances at synapses may often exist in a quantum-indeterminate state (Eccles, 1953). A final key element in conformance behavior is a *contingent relationship such that the probability of a favorable event is linked to the REG outputs*. This means that among the REG outputs is one or more which, if selected, will eventuate in or increase the probability of a favorable event. For instance, in Schmidt's studies whether or not a signal is given to the subject indicating a "hit" (success) depends upon the event generated by the REG on that trial.

When these four key elements—a disposed system, the possibility of a favorable event, an REG, and a contingent relationship (of the type described)—all eventuate in the REG outputs actually controlling the probability of a favorable event, *conformance behavior* is observed. This means that REG outputs will be biased so as to increase the probability of a favorable event.

The term *favorable event* should not, incidentally, be construed in a narrow, common-sense fashion. If an organism, for instance, is disposed toward hurting itself, an REG outcome which leads to its being hurt would be a "favorable event," albeit not by our common-sense definition of that term.

The reader should bear in mind that this noncybernetic (or nonpsychobiological) interpretation of PK posits a new class of interaction, conformance behavior, an interaction in which a disposed system is intimately involved but of which that disposed system cannot properly be said to be the cause. By analogy, when two like charges repel, which can be said to be the cause? It is the relationship between the two which is important. In the case of conformance behavior it is likewise the contingent relationship (of the circumstances in question) which is important.

This interpretation of PK as conformance behavior is clearly built around and attempts to interpret the finding that PK is goal-oriented. Because of this and because of the way this theory is structured, it can subsume both "PK events" and "ESP events." In the case of a typical ESP test the REG which exhibits conformance behavior is the brain or nervous system of the organism tested, and it becomes biased such that outputs are selected which will produce a match with the ESP target. This is precisely analogous to the studies of PK with hidden targets, but in those studies the REG was the fall of dice. To the extent that there are incompletely determinate circumstances in the brain associated with alternative states which could increase the probability of a favorable outcome, conformance behavior is possible. This view is fully compatible with the growing mass of evidence that constraints upon mental processes (e.g., logical constraints or psychological inhibition) or preoccupations (e.g., "noise," internal or external) reduce the possibility for effective ESP; and it is compatible with the developing evidence that preestablished associations are the mediational basis of extrasensory response (see Stanford, 1975). The former (constraints and preoccupations) may reduce the indeterminacy present during neural activity, whereas the latter (preestablished associations somehow relevant to the ESP target), when activated, are brain states (or neural events) which can increase the probability of a favorable outcome (e.g., an ESP "hit").

When "ESP events" are seen as conformance behavior occurring with neural processes, it is no longer surprising that no one has turned up evidence of an "ESP organ" or "receptor." There is no receptor since conformance behavior does not involve the transfer of energy or information across space. Rather, the brain is a wonderfully complex and sophisticated REG which has available, usually, a number of alternative states (or neural events) which, if selected through conformance behavior, will increase the probability of a favorable outcome.

The conformance behavior interpretation of psi interaction makes a clean break with both cybernetic views and with information-transfer views. It is true that for many kinds of "ESP events" the neural events selected through conformance behavior may be said in a sense to encode information about the "ESP target." But this fact is incidental to the basic conception of what is occurring here. According to the conformance behavior view, in all ESP experiences the specific neural events involved are selected not because they in some sense correspond to the target material, but because those specific neural events increase the probability of a favorable outcome. In perceptual-cognitive tests of ESP— the traditional kinds of tests—subjects are disposed toward coming up with images, etc., which correspond to the target, so neural events are selected which will make this possible. In many other cases which would certainly be called ESP, this is not the case. One example is recent work in which subjects have exhibited "unconscious ESP" by showing a selectively decreased reaction time when, unknown to them, their doing this increased their probability of experiencing a favorable event (Stanford and Stio, 1976).

Conformance behavior theory also provides an understanding of so-called active-agent telepathy, or, as it has been termed elsewhere (Stanford, 1974b), "mental or behavioral influence of an agent" (MOBIA). The conformance behavior view makes it appear likely that such a phenomenon exists even though there is need of much more research into this question. MOBIA is conceptualized as conformance behavior occurring in the nervous system of one person in accord with a disposition existing in another.

The concept of conformance behavior at once raises the possibility that in parapsychology we have so far been studying only "the cat's whisker." Could conformance behavior be involved in other aspects of mental activity than those we traditionally call psi mediated? Might it play a role in processes such as creative insight or memory retrieval? Certainly we have no evidence for this but the theory of conformance behavior requires that we look more broadly for evidence of psi interaction. We know that there are some curious parallels between psi-conducive mental states and those which are associated with creative insight (preparation, incubation, and illumination stages), with memory retrieval (as in the need for releasing effort in the tip-of-the-tongue phenomenon), and with biofeedback success (passive volition). (For discussion of some of these parallels, see Stanford, 1974b; and see Kreitler and Kreitler, 1974, for discussion of the possibility that psi may be involved in cognitive processes.) Should future research show that conformance behavior occurs with respect to dispositions in nonliving systems this would open up the possibility that psi influence might be involved in the development of life itself. Certainly the theory of conformance behavior demands that we study the possibility of this proposed interaction occurring with respect to both simple biological systems and nonliving ones. The theory does not require that the interaction occur with respect to nonliving systems, but it is open-ended with regard to this possibility. It encourages exploration of the range of possible disposed systems with respect to which conformance behavior can be observed.

The above discussion should not be regarded as a full exposition of the conformance behavior interpretation of psi events, but as an outline of its essentials. Elsewhere I hope to develop the theory and its ramifications in more detail. The reader may wish to compare and contrast this theory with another which has recently been put forward by Schmidt (1975b).

Only a considerable amount of research can determine the correctness of the conformance behavior view of psi interaction. Whatever the outcomes of such research, the speculative framework just developed will have salutary effects if it causes those interested in this area to carefully examine the too often implicit and unexamined premises which have traditionally guided—or perhaps confined—our research.

REFERENCES

André, E. Confirmation of PK action on electronic equipment. *Journal of Parapsychology*, 1972, **36**, 283–293.

Andrew, K. Psychokinetic influences on an electromechanical random number generator during evocation of "left-hemispheric" vs. "right-hemispheric" functioning. In J. D.

Morris, W. G. Roll, and R. L. Morris (Eds.), *Research in Parapsychology 1974*, pp. 58–61. Metuchen, N.J.: Scarecrow Press, 1975.

Averill, R. L., and Rhine, J. B. The effect of alcohol upon performance in PK tests. *Journal of Parapsychology*, 1945, **9**, 32–41.

Batcheldor, K. J. Report on a case of table levitation and associated phenomena. *Journal of the Society for Psychical Research*, 1966, **43**, 339–356.

Beloff, J., and Evans, L. A radioactivity test of psychokinesis. *Journal of the Society for Psychical Research*, 1961, **41**, 41–46.

Bender, H., Vandrey, R., and Wendlandt, S. The "Geller Effect" in Western Germany and Switzerland: A preliminary report on a social and experimental study. In J. D. Morris, W. G. Roll, and R. L. Morris (Eds.), *Research in Parapsychology 1975*, pp. 141–144. Metuchen, N.J.: Scarecrow Press, 1976.

Binski, S. R. Report on two exploratory PK series. *Journal of Parapsychology*, 1957, **21**, 284–295.

Braud, W., Smith. G., Andrew, K., and Willis, S. Psychokinetic influences on random number generators during evocation of "analytic" vs. "nonanalytic" modes of information processing. In J. D. Morris, W. G. Roll, and R. L. Morris (Eds.), *Research in Parapsychology 1975*, pp. 85–88. Metuchen, N.J.: Scarecrow Press, 1976.

Brookes-Smith, C. Data-tape recorded experimental PK phenomena. *Journal of the Society for Psychical Research*, 1973, **47**, 69–89.

Brookes-Smith, C., and Hunt, D. W. Some experiments in psychokinesis. *Journal of the Society for Psychical Research*, 1970, **45**, 265–281.

Camstra, B. PK conditioning. In W. G. Roll, R. L. Morris, and J. D. Morris (Eds.), *Research in Parapsychology 1972*, pp. 25–27, Metuchen, N.J.: Scarecrow Press, 1973.

Chauvin, R., and Genthon, J.-P. Eine Untersuchung über die Moglichkeit psychokinetscher Experimente mit Uranium und Geigerzähler. *Zeitschrift für Parapsychologie und Grenzgebiete der Psychologie*, 1965, **8**, 140–147.

Cox, W. E. The effect of PK on the placement of falling objects. *Journal of Parapsychology*, 1951, **15**, 40–48.

Cox, W. E. A comparison of spheres and cubes in placement PK tests. *Journal of Parapsychology*, 1954, **18**, 234–239.

Cox, W. E. Three-tier placement PK. *Journal of Parapsychology*, 1959, **23**, 19–29.

Cox, W. E. Five-tier placement PK. *Journal of Parapsychology*, 1962, **26**, 35–46. (a)

Cox, W. E. The placement of falling water. *Journal of Parapsychology*, 1962, **26**, 266. (b)

Cox, W. E. The effect of PK on electromechanical systems. I. The first electrical clock experiments. *Journal of Parapsychology*, 1965, **29**, 165–175. (a)

Cox, W. E. A cumulative assessment of PK on multiple targets. *Journal of Parapsychology*, 1965, **29**, 299–300. (b)

Cox, W. E. Multiple PK placement using 135 balls per throw. *Journal of Parapsychology*, 1966, **30**, 299.

Cox, W. E. A comparison of different densities of dice in a PK task. *Journal of Parapsychology*, 1971, **35**, 108–119.

Cox, W. E. PK tests with a thirty-two channel balls machine. *Journal of Parapsychology*, 1974, **38**, 56–68. (a)

Cox, W. E. Note on some experiments with Uri Geller. *Journal of Parapsychology*, 1974, **38**, 408–411. (b)

Cox, W. E., Feather, S. R., and Carpenter, J. C. The effect of PK on electromechanical systems. II. Further experiments and analysis with PK clocks machine. *Journal of Parapsychology*, 1966, **30**, 184–194.

Dale, L. A. The psychokinetic effect: The first A.S.P.R. experiment. *Journal of the American Society for Psychical Research*, 1946, **40**, 123–151.

Dale, L. A., and Woodruff, J. L. The psychokinetic effect: Further A.S.P.R. experiments. *Journal of the American Society for Psychical Research*, 1947, **41**, 65–82.

D'Amato, M. R. Secondary reinforcement and magnitude of primary reinforcement. *Journal of Comparative and Physiological Psychology*, 1955, 48, 378–380.

D'Amato, M. R. *Experimental Psychology: Methodology, Psychophysics, and Learning.* New York: McGraw-Hill, 1970.

Eccles, J. C. *The Neurophysiological Basis of Mind.* Oxford, England: The Clarendon Press, 1953.

Fahler, J. Exploratory "scaled" PK placement tests with nine college students with and without distance. *Journal of the American Society for Psychical Research*, 1959, 53, 106–113.

Feather, S. R., and Rhine, L. E. PK experiments with same and different targets. *Journal of Parapsychology*, 1969, 33, 213–227.

Fisk, G. W., and West, D. J. Dice-casting experiments with a single subject. *Journal of the Society for Psychical Research*, 1958, 39, 277–287.

Forwald, H. A further study of the PK placement effect. *Journal of Parapsychology*, 1952, 16, 59–67. (a)

Forwald, H. A continuation of the experiments in placement PK. *Journal of Parapsychology*, 1952, 16, 273–283. (b)

Forwald, H. An approach to instrumental investigation of psychokinesis. *Journal of Parapsychology*, 1954, 18, 219–233.

Forwald, H. A study of psychokinesis in its relation to physical conditions. *Journal of Parapsychology*, 1955, 19, 133–154.

Forwald, H. A continuation of the study of psychokinesis and physical conditions. *Journal of Parapsychology*, 1957, 21, 98–121.

Forwald, H. An experimental study suggesting a relationship between psychokinesis and nuclear conditions of matter. *Journal of Parapsychology*, 1959, 23, 97–125.

Forwald, H. A PK experiment with die faces as targets. *Journal of Parapsychology*, 1961, 25, 1–12.

Forwald, H. A PK dice experiment with doubles as targets. *Journal of Parapsychology*, 1962, 26, 112–122.

Forwald, H. An experiment in guessing ESP cards by throwing a die. *Journal of Parapsychology*, 1963, 27, 16–22.

Forwald, H. Mind, matter, and gravitation. *Parapsychological Monographs No. 11.* New York: Parapsychology Foundation, 1969.

Gatling, W., and Rhine, J. B. Two groups of PK subjects compared. *Journal of Parapsychology*, 1946, 10, 120–125.

Gibson, E. P., Gibson, L. H., and Rhine, J. B. A large series of PK tests. *Journal of Parapsychology*, 1943, 7, 228–237.

Gibson, E. P., Gibson, L. H., and Rhine, J. B. The PK effect: Mechanical throwing of three dice. *Journal of Parapsychology*, 1944, 8, 95–109.

Gibson, E. P., and Rhine, J. B. The PK effect: III. Some introductory series. *Journal of Parapsychology*, 1943, 7, 118–134.

Girden, E. A review of psychokinesis (PK). *Psychological Bulletin*, 1962, 59, 353–388. (a)

Girden, E. A postscript to "A review of psychokinesis (PK)." *Psychological Bulletin*, 1962, 59, 529–531. (b)

Greene, F. M. The feeling of luck and its effect on PK. *Journal of Parapsychology*, 1960, 24, 129–141.

Hilton, H., Jr., Baer, G., and Rhine, J. B. A comparison of three sizes of dice in PK tests. *Journal of Parapsychology*, 1943, 7, 172–190.

Hilton, H., Jr., and Rhine, J. B. A second comparison of three sizes of dice in PK tests. *Journal of Parapsychology*, 1943, 7, 191–206.

Honorton, C. Apparent psychokinesis on static objects by a "gifted" subject. In W. G. Roll, R. L. Morris, and J. D. Morris (Eds.), *Research in Parapsychology 1973*, pp. 128–131. Metuchen, N.J.: Scarecrow Press, 1974.

Honorton, C., and Barksdale, W. PK performance with waking suggestions for muscle tension versus relaxation. *Journal of the American Society for Psychical Research*, 1972, 66, 208–214.

Honorton, C., and May, E. C. Volitional control in a psychokinetic task with auditory and visual feedback. In J. D. Morris, W. G. Roll, and R. L. Morris (Eds.), *Research in Parapsychology 1975*, pp. 90–91. Metuchen, N.J.: Scarecrow Press, 1976.

Humphrey, B. M. Help-hinder comparison in PK tests. *Journal of Parapsychology*, 1947, 11, 4–13. (a)

Humphrey, B. M. Simultaneous high and low aim in PK tests. *Journal of Parapsychology*, 1947, 11, 160–174. (b)

Humphrey, B. M., and Rhine, J. B. PK tests with two sizes of dice mechanically thrown. *Journal of Parapsychology*, 1945, 9, 124–132.

Jarrard, R., Corcoran, K., Mayfield, R., and Morris, R. Psychokinesis experiments with a cryogenic magnetometer. In J. D. Morris, W. G. Roll, and R. L. Morris (Eds.), *Research in Parapsychology 1975*, pp. 64–66. Metuchen, N.J.: Scarecrow Press, 1976.

Keil, H. H. J., and Hill, S. "Mini-Geller" PK cases. In J. D. Morris, W. G. Roll, and R. L. Morris (Eds.), *Research in Parapsychology 1974*, pp. 69–71. Metuchen, N.J.: Scarecrow Press, 1975.

Kelly, E. F., and Kanthamani, B. K. A subject's efforts toward voluntary control. *Journal of Parapsychology*, 1972, 36, 185–197.

Knowles, E. A. G. Report on an experiment concerning the influence of mind over matter. *Journal of Parapsychology*, 1949, 13, 186–196.

Kreitler, H., and Kreitler, S. ESP and cognition. *Journal of Parapsychology*, 1974, 38, 267–285.

Mangan, G. L. A PK experiment with thirty dice released for high- and low-face targets. *Journal of Parapsychology*, 1954, 18, 209–218.

Matas, F., and Pantas, L. A PK experiment comparing meditating versus nonmeditating subjects. *Proceedings of the Parapsychological Association*, 1971, 8, 12–13.

May, E. C., and Honorton, C. A dynamic PK experiment with Ingo Swann. In J. D. Morris, W. G. Roll, and R. L. Morris (Eds.), *Research in Parapsychology 1975*, pp. 88–89. Metuchen, N.J.: Scarecrow Press, 1976.

McConnell, R. A. Remote night tests for PK. *Journal of the American Society for Psychical Research*, 1955, 49, 99–108.

McConnell, R. A., and Forwald, H. Psychokinetic placement. III. Cube-releasing devices. *Journal of Parapsychology*, 1968, 32, 9–38.

McConnell, R. A., Snowdon, R. J., and Powell, K. F. Wishing with dice. *Journal of Experimental Psychology*, 1955, 50, 269–275.

McMahan, E. PK experiments with two-sided objects. *Journal of Parapsychology*, 1945, 9, 249–263.

McMahan, E. A PK experiment with discs. *Journal of Parapsychology*, 1946, 10, 169–180.

McMahan, E. A PK experiment under light and dark conditions. *Journal of Parapsychology*, 1947, 11, 46–54.

Millar, B. Thermistor PK. In J. D. Morris, W. G. Roll, and R. L. Morris (Eds.), *Research in Parapsychology 1975*, pp. 71–73. Metuchen, N.J.: Scarecrow Press, 1976.

Millar, B., and Broughton, R. A preliminary PK experiment with a novel computer-linked high speed random number generator. In J. D. Morris, W. G. Roll, and R. L. Morris (Eds.), *Research in Parapsychology 1975*, pp. 83–84. Metuchen, N.J.: Scarecrow Press, 1976.

Mischo, J., and Weis, R. A pilot study on the relations between PK scores and personality variables. In W. G. Roll, R. L. Morris, and J. D. Morris (Eds.), *Research in Parapsychology 1972*, pp. 21-23. Metuchen, N.J.: Scarecrow Press, 1973.

Mitchell, A. M. J., and Fisk, G. W. The application of differential scoring methods to PK tests. *Journal of the Society for Psychical Research*, 1953, 37, 45-61.

Morris, R. L. Further PK placement work with the Cox machine. *Journal of Parapsychology*, 1965, 29, 300.

Murphy, G. Report on a paper by Edward Girden on psychokinesis. *Psychological Bulletin*, 1962, 59, 520-528.

Nash, C. B. PK tests of a large population. *Journal of Parapsychology*, 1944, 8, 304-310.

Nash, C. B. Position effects in PK tests with twenty-four dice. *Journal of Parapsychology*, 1946, 10, 51-57.

Nash, C. B. The PK mechanism. *Journal of the Society for Psychical Research*, 1955, 38, 8-11.

Nash, C. B., and Richards, A. Comparison of two distances in PK tests. *Journal of Parapsychology*, 1947, 11, 269-282.

Osis, K. A test of the relationship between ESP and PK. *Journal of Parapsychology*, 1953, 17, 298-309.

Owen, I. M., and Sparrow, M. H. Generation of paranormal physical phenomena in connection with an imaginary "communicator." *New Horizons*, 1974, 1 (No. 3), 6-13.

Pantas, L. PK scoring under preferred and nonpreferred conditions. *Proceedings of the Parapsychological Association*, 1971, 8, 47-49.

Parsons, D. Experiments on PK with inclined plane and rotating cage. *Proceedings of the Society for Psychical Research*, 1945, 47, 296-300.

Placer, J., Breese, G., Corcoran, K., Crane, W., and Morris, R. L. Stable system psychokinesis studies using temperature differential between thermistors. In J. D. Morris, W. G. Roll, and R. L. Morris (Eds.), *Research in Parapsychology 1975*, pp. 69-71. Metuchen, N.J.: Scarecrow Press, 1976.

Poulton, E. C. Unwanted range effects from using within-subject experimental designs. *Psychological Bulletin*, 1973, 80, 113-121.

Poulton, E. C. Range effects are characteristic of a person serving in a within-subjects experimental design—a reply to Rothstein. *Psychological Bulletin*, 1974, 81, 201-202.

Poulton, E. C., and Freeman, P. R. Unwanted asymmetrical transfer effects with balanced experimental designs. *Psychological Bulletin*, 1966, 66, 1-8.

Pratt, J. G. Lawfulness of position effects in the Gibson cup series. *Journal of Parapsychology*, 1946, 10, 243-268.

Pratt, J. G. Restricted areas of success in PK tests. *Journal of Parapsychology*, 1947, 11, 191-207. (a)

Pratt, J. G. Rhythms of success in PK test data. *Journal of Parapsychology*, 1947, 11, 90-110. (b)

Pratt, J. G. Trial-by-trial grouping of success and failure in psi tests. *Journal of Parapsychology*, 1947, 11, 254-268. (c)

Pratt, J. G. The Cormack placement PK experiments. *Journal of Parapsychology*, 1951, 15, 57-73.

Pratt, J. G., and Forwald, H. Confirmation of the PK placement effect. *Journal of Parapsychology*, 1958, 22, 1-19.

Pratt, J. G., and Keil, H. H. J. Firsthand observations of Nina S. Kulagina suggestive of PK upon static objects. *Journal of the American Society for Psychical Research*, 1973, 67, 381-390.

Pratt, J. G., and Ransom, C. Exploratory observations of the movement of static objects without the apparent use of known physical energies by Nina S. Kulagina. *Proceedings of the Parapsychological Association*, 1971, **8**, 20–21.

Pratt, J. G., and Woodruff, J. L. An exploratory investigation of PK position effects. *Journal of Parapsychology*, 1946, **10**, 197–207.

Price, H. *Stella C.* London: Hurst & Blackett, 1925.

Price, M. M., and Rhine, J. B. The subject-experimenter relation in the PK test. *Journal of Parapsychology*, 1944, **8**, 177–186.

Puharich, A. *Uri: A Journal of the Mystery of Uri Geller.* New York: Anchor/Doubleday, 1974.

Puthoff, H., and Targ, R. PK experiments with Uri Geller and Ingo Swann. In W. G. Roll, R. L. Morris, and J. D. Morris (Eds.), *Research in Parapsychology 1973*, pp. 125–128. Metuchen, N.J.: Scarecrow Press, 1974.

Randall, J. L. An extended series of ESP and PK tests with three English schoolboys. *Journal of the Society for Psychical Research*, 1974, **47**, 485–494.

Rao, K. R. The bidirectionality of psi. *Journal of Parapsychology*, 1965, **29**, 230–250.

Ratte, R. J. A comparison of game and standard PK testing techniques under competitive and noncompetitive conditions. *Journal of Parapsychology*, 1960, **24**, 235–244.

Ratte, R. J., and Greene, F. M. An exploratory investigation of PK in a game situation. *Journal of Parapsychology*, 1960, **24**, 159–170.

Reeves, M. P., and Rhine, J. B. The PK effect: The first doubles experiment. *Journal of Parapsychology*, 1945, **9**, 42–51.

Rhine, J. B. The PK effect: Early singles tests. *Journal of Parapsychology*, 1944, **8**, 287–303.

Rhine, J. B. Early PK tests: Sevens and low-dice series. *Journal of Parapsychology*, 1945, **9**, 106–115.

Rhine, J. B. Hypnotic suggestion in PK tests. *Journal of Parapsychology*, 1946, **10**, 126–140.

Rhine, J. B., and Humphrey, B. M. PK tests with six, twelve, and twenty-four dice per throw. *Journal of Parapsychology*, 1944, **8**, 139–157. (a)

Rhine, J. B., and Humphrey, B. M. The PK effect: Special evidence from hit patterns. I. Quarter distribution of the page. *Journal of Parapsychology*, 1944, **8**, 18–60. (b)

Rhine, J. B., and Humphrey, B. M. The PK effect: Special evidence from hit patterns. II. Quarter distribution of the set. *Journal of Parapsychology*, 1944, **8**, 254–271. (c)

Rhine, J. B., and Humphrey, B. M. The PK effect with sixty dice per throw. *Journal of Parapsychology*, 1945, **9**, 203–218.

Rhine, J. B., Humphrey, B. M., and Averill, R. L. An exploratory experiment on the effect of caffeine upon performance in PK tests. *Journal of Parapsychology*, 1945, **9**, 80–91.

Rhine, J. B., Humphrey, B. M., and Pratt, J. G. The PK effect: Special evidence from hit patterns. III. Quarter distribution of the half-set. *Journal of Parapsychology*, 1945, **9**, 150–168.

Rhine, J. B., and Pratt, J. G. *Parapsychology: Frontier Science of the Mind.* Springfield, Ill.: Charles C Thomas, 1957.

Rhine, L. E. Placement PK tests with three types of objects. *Journal of Parapsychology*, 1951, **15**, 132–138.

Rhine, L. E., and Rhine, J. B. The psychokinetic effect: I. The first experiment. *Journal of Parapsychology*, 1943, **7**, 20–43.

Roll, W. G. Earlier RSPK cases. In J. D. Morris, W. G. Roll, and R. L. Morris (Eds.), *Research in Parapsychology 1974*, pp. 134–139. Metuchen, N.J.: Scarecrow Press, 1975.

Rubin, L., and Honorton, C. Separating the yins from the yangs: An experiment with the *I Ching*. *Proceedings of the Parapsychological Association*, 1971, **8**, 6–7.

Schmeidler, G. R. PK effects upon continuously recorded temperature. *Journal of the American Society for Psychical Research*, 1973, **67**, 325–340.

Schmeidler, G., Gambale, J., and Mitchell, J. PK effects on temperature recordings: An attempted replication and extension. In J. D. Morris, W. G. Roll, and R. L. Morris (Eds.), *Research in Parapsychology 1975*, pp. 67–69. Metuchen, N.J.: Scarecrow Press, 1976.

Schmeidler, G. R., Mitchell, J., and Sondow, N. Further investigation of PK with temperature records. In J. D. Morris, W. G. Roll, and R. L. Morris (Eds.), *Research in Parapsychology 1974*, pp. 71–73. Metuchen, N.J.: Scarecrow Press, 1975.

Schmidt, H. A PK test with electronic equipment. *Journal of Parapsychology*, 1970, **34**, 175–181 (a)

Schmidt, H. PK experiments with animals as subjects. *Journal of Parapsychology*, 1970, **34**, 255–261. (b)

Schmidt, H. A quantum mechanical random number generator for psi tests. *Journal of Parapsychology*, 1970, **34**, 219–224. (c)

Schmidt, H. PK tests with a high-speed random number generator. *Journal of Parapsychology*, 1973, **37**, 105–118.

Schmidt, H. Comparison of PK action on two different random number generators. *Journal of Parapsychology*, 1974, **38**, 47–55. (a)

Schmidt, H. PK effect on random time intervals. In W. G. Roll, R. L. Morris, and J. D. Morris (Eds.), *Research in Parapsychology 1973*, pp. 46–48. Metuchen, N.J.: Scarecrow Press, 1974. (b)

Schmidt, H. Psychokinesis. In E. D. Mitchell et al., *Psychic Exploration: A Challenge for Science*, pp. 179–193. New York: Putnam's, 1974. (c)

Schmidt, H. Observation of subconscious PK effects with and without time displacement. In J. D. Morris, W. G. Roll, and R. L. Morris (Eds.), *Research in Parapsychology 1974*, pp. 116–121. Metuchen, N.J.: Scarecrow Press, 1975. (a)

Schmidt, H. Toward a mathematical theory of psi. *Journal of the American Society for Psychical Research*, 1975, **69**, 301–319. (b)

Schmidt, H. PK experiment with repeated, time displaced feedback. In J. D. Morris, W. G. Roll, and R. L. Morris (Eds.), *Research in Parapsychology 1975*, pp. 107–109. Metuchen, N.J.: Scarecrow Press, 1976.

Schmidt, H., and Pantas, L. Psi tests with internally different machines. *Journal of Parapsychology*, 1972, **36**, 222–232.

Schrier, A. M. Comparison of two methods of investigating the effect of amount of reward on performance. *Journal of Comparative and Physiological Psychology*, 1958, **51**, 725–731.

Stanford, R. G. "Associative activation of the unconscious" and "visualization" as methods for influencing the PK target. *Journal of the American Society for Psychical Research*, 1969, **63**, 338–351.

Stanford, R. G. Suggestibility and success at augury–divination from chance outcomes. *Journal of the American Society for Psychical Research*, 1972, **66**, 42–62.

Stanford, R. G. An experimentally testable model for spontaneous psi events. I. Extrasensory events. *Journal of the American Society for Psychical Research*, 1974, **68**, 34–57. (a)

Stanford, R. G. An experimentally testable model for spontaneous psi events. II. Psychokinetic events. *Journal of the American Society for Psychical Research*, 1974, **68**, 321–356. (b)

Stanford, R. G. Response factors in extrasensory performance. *Journal of Communication*, 1975, **25**, 153–161.

Stanford, R. G., and Fox, C. An effect of release of effort in a psychokinetic task. In J. D.

Morris, W. G. Roll, and R. L. Morris (Eds.), *Research in Parapsychology 1974*, pp. 61–63. Metuchen, N.J.: Scarecrow Press, 1975.

Stanford, R. G., and Stio, A. A study of associative mediation in psi-mediated instrumental response. *Journal of the American Society for Psychical Research*, 1976, **70**, 55–64.

Stanford, R. G., Zenhausern, R., Taylor, A., and Dwyer, M. A. Psychokinesis as psi-mediated instrumental response. *Journal of the American Society for Psychical Research*, 1975, **69**, 127–133.

Steen, D. Success with complex targets in a PK baseball game. *Journal of Parapsychology*, 1957, **21**, 133–146.

Steilberg, B. J. "Conscious concentration" versus "visualization" in PK tests. *Journal of Parapsychology*, 1975, **39**, 12–20.

Thouless, R. H. Some experiments on PK effects in coin spinning. *Proceedings of the Society for Psychical Research*, 1945, **47**, 277–280.

Thouless, R. H. A report on an experiment in psychokinesis with dice, and a discussion on psychological factors favoring success. *Proceedings of the Society for Psychical Research*, 1951, **49**, 107–130.

Ullman, M. An informal session with Nina Kulagina. *Proceedings of the Parapsychological Association*, 1971, **8**, 21–22.

Ullman, M. PK in the Soviet Union. In W. G. Roll, R. L. Morris, and J. D. Morris (Eds.), *Research in Parapsychology 1973*, pp. 121–125. Metuchen, N.J.: Scarecrow Press, 1974.

Van de Castle, R. L. An exploratory study of some personality correlates associated with PK performance. *Journal of the American Society for Psychical Research*, 1958, **52**, 134–150.

Wadhams, P., and Farrelly, B. A. The investigation of psychokinesis using β-particles. *Journal of the Society for Psychical Research*, 1968, **44**, 281–289.

Watkins, G. K., and Watkins, A. M. Apparent psychokinesis on static objects by a "gifted" subject: A laboratory demonstration. In W. G. Roll, R. L. Morris, and J. D. Morris (Eds.), *Research in Parapsychology 1973*, pp. 132–134. Metuchen, N.J.: Scarecrow Press, 1974.

Watkins, G. K., Watkins, A. M., and Wells, R. A. Further studies on the resuscitation of anesthetized mice. In W. G. Roll, R. L. Morris, and J. D. Morris (Eds.), *Research in Parapsychology 1972*, pp. 157–159. Metuchen, N.J.: Scarecrow Press, 1973.

Wells, R., and Watkins, G. K. Linger effects in several PK experiments. In J. D. Morris, W. G. Roll, and R. L. Morris (Eds.), *Research in Parapsychology 1974*, pp. 143–147. Metuchen, N.J.: Scarecrow Press, 1975.

West, D. J., and Fisk, G. W. A dual ESP experiment with clock cards. *Journal of the Society for Psychical Research*, 1953, **37**, 185–197.

Wilbur, L. C., and Mangan, G. L. The relation of PK object and throwing surface in placement tests: I. Preliminary series. *Journal of Parapsychology*, 1956, **20**, 158–165.

Wilbur, L. C., and Mangan, G. L. The relation of PK object and throwing surface in placement tests: Further report. *Journal of Parapsychology*, 1957, **21**, 58–65.

3

Poltergeists

William G. Roll

INTRODUCTION

When you look up *Poltergeist* in the *New Cassell's German Dictionary* (Better-ridge, 1965) you will find it in the section under *Polterabend*. *Polterabend* is an eve-of-the-wedding-party when the couple gets together with friends for a bois-terous good-bye to chastity. Glasses and old crockery are broken for good luck, and there is a great deal of noise. Sometimes the bride-to-be is "abducted" by one of the friends of the groom and the groom has to find her. *Poltern* as a verb also means to make knocking or rumbling sounds or to bluster and scold.

This is very apropos of the poltergeist. Here, too, there is usually breakage of glasses and plates and a lot of noise, such as knocks and raps. Sometimes pieces of furniture topple over or move, the commotion lasting anywhere from a few days to several months.

Though the poltergeist usually does not confine itself to one *abend* or evening, it too mostly involves young people. These are often of premarital age, around puberty or adolescence. It is interesting that for both poltergeists and polter-abends the turbulence seems to be associated with sexual development or maturity. As we shall see later, the poltergeist is perhaps also scolding about something.

Who or what is a poltergeist? The word *geist* can refer to either an incorporeal spirit or the mind of somebody living. The phenomena are usually associated with a living person; in fact, it seems to have become part of the meaning of poltergeist that there be such a connection. This suggests that the events may be cases of psychokinesis (PK) produced by that person, or perhaps by an incorporeal entity which has attached itself to him or her (Stevenson, 1972). In any case, if the phenomena are as reported, we seem to be dealing with PK so we now often use the phrase *recurrent spontaneous psychokinesis* (RSPK) for poltergeist incidents.

During the past several years it has become clear that RSPK research may provide strong evidence for PK and, more importantly, clues to its nature. For an adequate evaluation of the evidence the original reports should be read. For cases after 1950 I suggest the Runcorn poltergeist (Dingwall and Hall, 1958, p. 68-85), the Seaford case (Pratt and Roll, 1958), the Sauchie case (Owen, 1964, pp. 129-169), the Newark case (Roll, 1969), the Indianapolis case (Roll, 1970) the Pratt-Palmer case (1976), and especially the Rosenheim (Bender, 1968; Karger and Zicha, 1968), Miami (Roll and Pratt, 1971), and Oliver Hill cases (Roll and Stump, 1969). The studies I have been involved with are also reported in my book (Roll, 1976).

Many of the older reports are as interesting as the newer ones. Some of them can be found in the books by Barrett (1918), Flammarion (1924), Carrington and Fodor (1951), Thurston, (1954), Sitwell (1959), and Owen (1964). There are also useful survey papers by Barrett (1911), Cox (1961), and Zorab (1964, 1973).

In a poltergeist study the investigator has left the security of his laboratory to become immersed in startling, sometimes violent events. In spite of the turmoil, the poltergeist is often amenable to observation under controlled conditions. In the first part of this survey I shall explore for patterns in the data, knowledge of which will aid in the design of research. I shall then examine these and other poltergeist characteristics for indications about the nature of RSPK. First some words about the cases to be examined.

ONE HUNDRED AND SIXTEEN POLTERGEISTS

Sources and Witnesses

The first scientist to take the poltergeist seriously may have been the British physicist and chemist Robert Boyle. While visiting Geneva, Boyle met a Protestant minister, Francis Perrault, who gave him a report of inexplicable noises and movements of objects which suddenly began at his home in Mascon, France, in September, 1612. Boyle's discussions with Perrault and the account itself had the effect "at length to overcome in me (as to this narrative) all my settled indisposedness to believe strange things" (Thurston, 1954, p. 40). Perrault's treatise on "the devil in Mascon" was published in English on Boyle's recommendation and is probably the first detailed description of a poltergeist outbreak; it is also the first of the 116 reports in the present survey. I have limited this to cases (a) which have appeared in print, and, for cases since 1850, in professional parapsychological publications; (b) in which the author was present during one or more of the occurrences or had interviewed witnesses who were; (c) in which the author is known and generally accepted as a truthful person; and (d) in which one or more physical incidents took place while the author or witnesses were present which they could not explain in familiar terms.

I have divided the cases into four groups: 1612–1849, 19 cases; 1850–99, 25 cases; 1900–49, 38 cases; and 1950–74, 34 cases.

The strength of the evidence for RSPK in these cases differs considerably. In some it is rather weak, as in the Pavarino case where Lombroso (1906) only spoke to the witnesses 10 years afterwards; but "my researches, incomplete as they were, had been sufficient to persuade me that the phenomena . . . must be genuine as a whole" (p. 367). There is another type of uncertainty in the Wem case (Podmore, 1896–97) where clearly fraudulent occurrences were mixed with incidents which could not be easily dismissed. F. S. Hughes, on behalf of the Society for Psychical Research, interviewed the witnesses and suggested that this case "might, with some degree of probability," be included among those in which "trickery and genuine preternatural phenomena" are combined (p. 65). At the other extreme are such cases as the Rosenheim (Bender, 1968; 1969, pp. 93–95) and Miami (Roll and Pratt, 1971) where two or more investigators testified to the phenomena.

Any material due to human testimony may be colored by erroneous perception and recall. This is especially true for events which seem mysterious to begin with. For instance, objects are often described as having been "thrown" though no ordinary hand was seen; from this it may be a short step to suppose and then see an apparitional one or to imagine peculiarities in the trajectories of the object. One hopes, however, that the sample is large and reliable enough so that spurious elements are overshadowed by real effects.

The professions of the witnesses to the events are relevant in evaluating the reports. In 25 of the 116 cases, some of the occurrences were witnessed by members of parapsychological research organizations. In 19 other cases police officers were the main outside witnesses. Three resulted in court trials, and the accounts largely consisted of court testimony. In three cases the witnesses included government officials; in seven, psychologists, physicians, scientists, or lawyers; in ten, members of the clergy; in six, teachers, an "official committee," a navy officer, or a fireman. In other words, in 73 of the cases the witnesses supposedly had experience in observing events and people and in evaluating and reporting what they saw (or in the court trials, were under oath to tell the truth and were questioned by people whose profession it was to ferret this out).

In 32 other cases there were also outside witnesses, but their professions are not stated or they were nonprofessional neighbors or visitors. In 11 cases all the

testimony came from members of the family or group involved in the RSPK outbreak. The fact that 105 of the cases included witnesses from outside the family,
73 with professional training, adds to the confidence of the material.

Though I think the reports must be taken seriously, they are not necessarily a
representative sample of RSPK. The criteria for inclusion may have caused a
bias in favor of cases which remained active with visitors or investigators on the
scene. The sample may also be weighted by long-lasting occurrences—the short
outbreaks may not be reported and are less likely to be observed by outsiders.
For similar reasons, there may be an overemphasis on cases with striking physical
effects, such as frequent movements of objects, as against those restricted to less
dramatic incidents, such as knocking or rapping sounds.

Geographic Distribution

The largest clusters of RSPK reports came from the United States with 31 cases;
the British Isles (England, Scotland, and Ireland) with 26 cases; and Germany,
Austria, and Switzerland with 21 cases. Other parts of Europe were also well
represented. There were nine Italian cases; seven French; five Dutch and Bel-
gian; four Scandinavian (from Finland, Iceland, and Sweden); two Russian; and
one Czechoslovakian. The rest of the world was represented by five cases from
Indonesia, four from India, and one from Mauritius.

Social, national, linguistic, and geographical factors undoubtedly affected the
sample. The collection is confined largely to Europe and the United States,
probably the result of easy mass communication and the presence of parapsychologists. There were only ten cases outside these regions. Though it would
be interesting to have had cases from Africa, Asia, and the Far East, many of
those from Europe and the United States occurred in isolated areas and among
people who seemed to have no prior knowledge or expectancy about such
events; this is painfully clear from the way most of the people reacted to the disturbances. Nevertheless, the cases show striking similarities. However, the explanation of the events, say in terms of demonic visitations, and the way people
tried to deal with the situation, as by exorcism, seem related to cultural and
social conditions.

CONNECTION WITH A PERSON

In November, 1960, the minister of Sauchie, Scotland, Rev. T. W. Lund, visited
the home of Virginia Campbell, an 11-year-old girl, in whose room unexplained
knockings and other events had taken place for two days. He found "Virginia
awake . . . in the double bed. About eight people (family and neighbors) were
already present in the room. The loud knocking noise continued and appeared
to emanate from the bed-head. Mr. Lund moved Virgina down in the bed so

she could not strike or push the bed-head with her head, and he also verified that her feet were well tucked in under the bed-clothes, and held in by them. The knocking continued. During the knocking, Mr. Lund held the bed-head. He felt it vibrating in unison with the noises. The bed-head was at no time in contact with the wall." A linen chest weighing about 50 pounds stood about 1½ feet from the bed. Mr. Lund saw this chest "go through a lateral rocking motion together with a spasmatic and uneven rising from the floor." It then moved sidewise "with a jerky kind of motion through a distance of about 18 inches and back again." The phenomena ceased when Virginia fell asleep (Owen, 1964, pp. 148-149). Two physicians and Virginia's teacher witnessed other events at the home and also at school.

Among the 116 cases, 92 seemed to be associated with a particular person, or occasionally two persons. For the 19 cases prior to 1849, in 14 there seemed to have been focal persons; the 25 cases, 1850-99, showed focal persons in 19; in the 1900-49 collection of 38 cases, there was such a connection in 30; and in the recent 34 cases, 1950-74, 29 showed this relation. This slight increase over the four periods of cases with focal persons is not statistically significant.

In some cases, the events followed the focal person out-of-doors, during visits to relatives, and so on. This was true for 39 of the 92 cases. The distribution over the four periods is six, seven, 13, and 13. In two other cases no focal person was identified, but the phenomena followed the family when they moved. A common factor runs through these cases which further points to the link with a person: There were generally no disturbances when the focal person was asleep.

Sex and Age

In the 92 cases with focal persons, 56 involved females and 36 males. (When more than one person was involved, I counted the person who seemed to be most closely associated with the phenomena; I did the same in calculating ages.) The difference may be of borderline significance (at the .05 level) depending on the proportions of males and females in the general population in the times and places involved. This favoring of women, however, was due to the two early periods. During 1612-1849 there were ten females versus four males, and during 1850-99, 16 versus three. The proportions then evened out for 1900-1949 to 16 versus 14, and for 1950-1974 to 14 versus 15. Apparently sex was generally not important in determining agency.

The ages of the poltergeist centers were reported for 74 cases and ranged from 8 to 78 (actually a man said to be in his late 70s; similarly a woman in her 70s is entered as 75 years old). The average for the 43 females was 15 years and for the 31 males 17 years, but the medians were only 13 in both cases. This difference was the result of two people in their 70s in the fourth period. For the four time periods, the average ages for females were 12, 15, 12, and 19; and for males 15, 13, 14, and 21. The medians for females were 12, 13.5, 15, and 13; and for males 14, 12, 15, and 14.

Of the 13 women whose ages were not stated, nine apparently were above 13 years old. The same was true for three of the five males. If account is taken of these people, the medians for both sexes would probably increase to 14 years.

THE MAIN OCCURRENCES

Movements, Sounds, Light, and Water

Several objects had moved when Roger, a 12-year-old boy was near, but it had happened out of my sight. This was in his home in Kentucky, December, 1968. I therefore stayed as close to Roger as I could. One time he went out to the kitchen while I followed a few feet behind. When he came to the area between the sink and the kitchen table he turned around facing me. At that moment the table jumped into the air, rotated about 45 degrees, and came down on the backs of the four chairs that stood around it, its four legs off the floor. No one else was in the area, and I was unable to discover any ordinary explanation for the event (Roll, 1976, p. 134).

Of the 116 cases, 105 involved recurrent movements of objects. There were 63 cases which had percussive sounds, usually knocks or raps, but sometimes explosive sounds (when I speak about sounds in the following, I refer to such effects). In 55 there were both movements and sounds. In 50 there were movements but no sounds, and in eight sounds but no movements. In ten cases there were lights, but only one, the Clayton case (Roll, 1976, pp. 59-69), consisted entirely of light flashes. Two cases involved only the appearance of water (Bender, 1974, pp. 138-141; Cox, 1961, pp. 68-69).

If we look at the distribution of incidents over the four time periods, we see that the proportions of movements and percussive sounds remained about the same. The number of cases with movements were 16, 24, 36, and 29 of the totals, and with sound 11, 15, 20, and 17.

Sometimes objects that moved were said to be warm to the touch. Of the 105 cases with moving objects, in six some of them felt hot or warm. In the total of 116 cases, seven had accounts of cold areas or feelings of cold and one of a room that felt hot.

Palmer has raised the question, based on two of his studies (Palmer, 1974; Pratt and Palmer, 1976), whether RSPK cases might tend to begin with sounds and develop to movements. In the 31 cases where we know which came first, 17 began with sounds and 14 with movements. The slight difference is due to the fourth period where the proportion was seven to two. Though the overall difference is insignificant, it should be kept in mind that there may be a tendency to ignore or not report sound phenomena and that this tendency may have been reduced in the recent, more thorough investigations. In other words, if we had more details, we might learn that a greater number of cases with movements were preceded by sound.

Duration

The duration of the RSPK disturbances varied from 1 day to 6 years. The average for the 98 cases where this was recorded was 5.1 months. The median, however, was only 2 months. Looking at the four collections separately, the average durations were 9.6 months, 4.15 months, 2.5 months, and 5.5 months. The medians were 3 months, 2 months, 1.3 months, and 1.95 months. The fluctuations are due mainly to long-lasting cases in the first and last periods.

Attenuation Effects

In February, 1921, Mrs. Ernest Sauerbrey of Hopfgarten, Germany, was gravely ill and in addition was plagued by inexplicable knocks and movements of objects. In the presence of Commissioner of Police Pheil from Weimar, some objects moved while no one was near. Pheil stated, "A police officer set a jug of water two metres away from Frau Sauerbrey. At the very moment that he turned away, the jug was already in motion. The same thing happened with a water basin." The case resulted in a court trial and the Magistrate, Justizrat Thierbach, observed that "generally speaking the movements were more marked in proportion to their nearness to Frau Sauerbrey" (Schrenck-Notzing, 1922, p. 204; I take "more marked" to mean more numerous).

The proximity effect, or put differently, the attenuation of the number of incidents with increased distance from the focal person reinforces the impression that he or she is the agent for the phenomena. This effect can only be clearly demonstrated if the distances have been measured and if the attenuation of incidents is statistically significant. Such attenuations, first reported in 1968 (Artley and Roll, 1968; Roll, 1968), have now been found in ten of the 34 cases in the 1950-1974 period (Eisler, 1975; Palmer, 1974; Roll, 1968, 1969, 1970; Roll, Burdick and Joines, 1973; Roll and Stump, 1969; Solfvin, Harary, and Batey, 1976).

I know of only one case where an analysis was made for attenuation, but none was found. In the Scherfede water case (Bender, 1974, pp. 138-141) there was no decrease in the number of times water appeared in relation to the position of the 13-year-old girl who seemed to be the agent. However, the distances measured were those between the girl and the place where the water appeared, its origin being unknown, while in the other studies the distances were those between the person and the starting place of the moving object.

Unusual Trajectories

In 1818 a teacher of mathematical physics in Austria, H.J. Aschauer, was told by his son-in-law that strange things were happening in the latter's home in Münchoff.   Shortly after Aschauer arrived and while he, his daughter, and a neighbor, Mr. Koppbauer, were in the kitchen "a big iron spoon suddenly left the shelf on which it was lying and came straight at Koppbauer's head. Weighing about a pound and travelling with great velocity it might have been expected to inflict a serious bruise, but the stricken man declared he felt only a light touch and the spoon dropped perpendicularly at his feet." The next day when a maid who "had been rasping some loaves laid the loaves and the bread rasp upon a wooden tray, the tray proceeded to float gently across the room, grazing the surface of the big stove, after which it suddenly dropped on to the floor so that the tray rebounded and the bread was scattered about." Aschauer "as a student of physics, was keenly interested" (Thurston, 1954, pp. 30-31).

Taking a look at the 105 cases with moving objects, "floating," "wavering," "zigzag," "sinuous," "hovering," or "fluttering" movements are often reported. There are also changing speeds in flight, levitations of objects, and objects coming around corners or rotating in the same spot.   Forty-three of the 105 cases show one or more of these features. The proportions do not differ greatly in the four groups: 5, 14, 11, and 13.

Such events, if reliably reported, increase the difficulty of ordinary explanations of the events. More importantly, they may help throw light on the nature of the RSPK process. As I pointed out in a previous section, there is some uncertainty about eye-witness accounts of moving objects, especially if the event seems strange to begin with. However, the reports are sufficiently numerous to suggest that slow, changing, and curved movements are characteristic of a large proportion of RSPK cases.

Teleportation

Mr. Adam, whose law office in Rosenheim, Germany, had earlier been the scene of RSPK disturbances, became interested in such occurrences and visited a family in Nicklheim where RSPK occurrences were taking place in 1968. "They had told him that objects which disappeared were later seen falling outside the house. He put bottles containing perfume and tablets on the kitchen table, asked the inhabitants of the house to go outside, closed all the windows and doors, and then left himself. After a short time, the perfume bottle appeared in the air outside the house, and a bit later on, the bottle of tablets appeared in the air at the height of the roof and fell to the ground in a zigzag manner" (Bender, 1969, p. 96).

Cases with apparent instances of teleportation are scattered throughout the collection, with 18 in the total of 105 showing recurrent movement of objects. The teleportation cases are distributed over the four groups as follows: 1, 2, 10, and 5. Teleportation presents a special challenge and opportunity for the RSPK investigator. It is fairly easy to provide for sealed rooms or containers. If an object appears in or disappears from such an area, the investigator is likely to be able conclusively to discount familiar causes, human as well as physical.

Focusing

In a village near Siena, Italy, in 1928, "showers of stones" were seen near a funeral monument when Silvia Giardi, a 15-year-old girl, passed by. "With several witnesses present, stones flew up from the ground for some height and dropped once more. They appeared to be the stones lying on the ground in the vicinity of the monument. The police lieutenant, Callaioli, a number of his men, a farmer living nearby, some journalists and others, and Silvia and her friend Ida Sali (age 15) went to the monument after the phenomena had attracted the attention of the authorities. A police cordon was put around the monument, but at the moment Silvia walked past the monument everyone present saw the stones nearby rise as described above" (Zorab, 1964, p. 121).

The term focusing is used for RSPK effects which repeatedly involve the same or similar objects or which recur in the same place. There are three types of focusing: on particular objects, on types of objects, and on areas, such as a room or a shelf. The example given before is a case of area focusing. Though Sylvia probably often walked by similar stones at other places, these near the monument were for some reason singled out by the RSPK energy.

The case also illustrates a rather common form of object focusing, namely on rocks and stones. In the Giardi case and several others only rocks or stones were involved and in others they were among the objects most commonly affected.

If the focal person in an RSPK outbreak spends a large part of his time in a certain place, such as his home, or near certain objects, such as the contents of his room, we would expect these areas and objects to be frequently involved because of the person's prolonged proximity to them.

I have tried to determine whether focusing might arise as an artifact from the proximity effect and whether one kind of focusing could be reduced to another (Roll, 1968, 1975). In the three cases for which we had sufficient data for analyses, there was evidence for focusing on types of objects, individual objects, and areas which could not be easily dismissed in other terms.

It is rarely possible to isolate the focusing effect from the proximity effect in the present RSPK cases. But in 107 of the total of 116 cases there is prima facie focusing of one or more kinds. In 89 there is focusing on objects, either individual or types of objects (in 12 of these there is also area focusing), and in 18 on areas.   The evidence for focusing runs about equally strongly through the four collections: 17, 21, 38, and 31.

RSPK is not only spontaneous and recurrent, but the recurrence often involves the same objects and places.   This feature is a powerful aid in research.   When the investigator has discovered that certain objects or areas in the locality are more prone than others to become targets for RSPK, he can concentrate on them, rather than attempt to survey all the contents of the home.   Focusing offers a means for experimental studies of RSPK.

EXPERIMENTING WITH POLTERGEISTS

The poltergeist has been a "subject" in RSPK tests from the first accounts in our survey to the last.   In September, 1612, soon after "the devil of Mascon" first visited the parsonage of Francis Perrault, Perrault reported the incidents to Francois Tornus, royal notary and procurator of Mascon.   "Mr. Tornus, coming to my house about noon, would know whether the devil was there still, and whistled in several tones, and each time the devil whistled to him in the same tone.   Then the devil threw a stone at him, which being fallen at his feet without any harm to him, he took it up and marked it with a coal, and flung it into the backyard of the house, which is near the town wall and the river Saone, but the devil threw it up to him again; and that it was the same stone, he knew by the mark of the coal.   Tornus taking up that stone found it very hot, and said he believed it had been in hell since he had handled it first" (Thurston, 1954, pp. 45-46).

In October, 1974, J. G. Pratt made a study of RSPK knocking associated with a boy and a girl aged 9 and 10 who were living with their grandmother (Pratt and Palmer, 1976).   "On Saturday evening around 6:00 p.m. . . . the grandmother's sister came for a short visit.   When I asked if she would like to hear some of the noises, she thought I was offering to play some tapes for her and she said that she did not have time.   I explained that I meant that we would arrange to have the noises occur just for her benefit . . . I direct(ed) the children regarding their movements . . . during which the unexplained noises occurred two times, once in the basement beyond the range of our direct observation and the second time on the glass of the back door when we were expecting the sounds to come there and were looking directly at it" (Pratt, personal communication, 1975).

Tests involving movements or sounds were reported in 48 of the 116 cases.   Of these 46 were successful.   They were distributed as follows over the four periods: 10, 8, 17, and 11.   Through few of the tests would qualify even as "exploratory experiments" by parapsychologists, it is interesting that RSPK phenomena often occurred in situations involving this type of challenge.

It is curious that the lowest proportion of RSPK tests appeared in the most recent period.   On the other hand, standard ESP or PK trials, usually with cards or dice, were sometimes used. In six studies such tests were reported. Four also involved RSPK tests of the types discussed before. Three of the four ESP tests gave significant results and so did three of the six PK tests.

In Bender's (1974) experience "in all cases where laboratory experimentation with the subject was possible, we found highly significant ESP scores but could not elicit experimental PK" (p. 130). With regard to PK research in poltergeist studies, the most fruitful approach is to use the objects and places on which the activity already centers. I shall mention other examples in later sections.

Fraud Incidents

Objects and pieces of furniture had been toppling over in an apartment in the Bronx, New York City, in February, 1974. Victoria, the 8-year-old adopted daughter of an elderly couple, was usually near when something happened. An insurance agent, Mr. Barclay, the 24-year-old son of another family in the building, visited in the hope of observing and filming the incidents. While he was with the girl in the master bedroom, a lamp fell over twice in another part of the room. The last time he saw it as it fell. He told me there was no way the girl could have caused this event since she was behind him, several feet from the lamp, and since the cord of the lamp was on its other side. No one else was in the room. He then replaced a night table which had fallen earlier, preparing to film it if it should fall again. When Victoria thought that Mr. Barclay was not looking, she quickly touched the table, turning it over. He commented, "she thought this was fun, so she helped" (Eisler, 1975; Roll, unpublished notes, 1974).

In 19 of the 116 cases one or more incidents were discovered where the focal person, or in one case a relative, produced one or more events by trickery (I found no instances of fraud in cases without focal persons). In four of these the person experienced dissociated states, and it seemed likely that the events were done in such a state, but in the others the trickery was probably done consciously.

Cox (1961) draws a distinction between "imitative" and "total" fraud. In imitative fraud the person copies the genuine RSPK phenomena by trickery while cases of total fraud are entirely made up of deception. Cases of total fraud have presumably been sifted from the present collection, but some instructive examples are presented by Owen (1964, pp. 27–87).

If we look at fraud incidents over the four periods, the distribution is 2, 3, 3, and 11. There is a significant increase in the detection of fraud in the last period ($P < .05$, two-tailed). I believe this is a function of the increased scrutiny of RSPK cases in recent years, especially of the focal person (also reflected, as we saw before, in the slight increase of cases over the four periods where such persons were identified). In early times, if events took place which clearly were not caused by anyone living, they were usually presumed to be due to devils or spirits, and the observers might ignore as irrelevant instances where the maid or child who was usually present caused some of them normally.

The increase in reports of fraud may not be entirely due to better observation and reporting. As in the Bronx case, it sometimes seems that the visitor or investigator who wants "something to happen" may help to bring this about. Young children may be more susceptible to this kind of influence than older people. The average age for the focal persons who were discovered in trickery is 12.9, and the median age is 12. These are lower than the average (16 years) and and median (14 years) for the total sample.

As we shall see in the next section, the observer sometimes seemed to enhance the genuine RSPK occurrences as well.

If there are instances of fraud in a case where other events have been witnessed under good conditions, this should not cause the researcher to dismiss the case. As we shall later see, RSPK occurrences seem to be due to psychological or physiological tensions and not to any desire to provide scientific proof of psychical phenomena. When the events are simulated, they should be studied together with the apparently genuine events for any light they may shed on the psychological features of the case.

Fraud incidents emphasize that RSPK occurrences are person-oriented. They also emphasize that the most plausible normal explanation for ostensible RSPK events is deception by the person around whom they occur. The main effort of poltergeist researchers in determining whether a case includes genuine RSPK effect consists in setting up controlled conditions which will exclude normal interference by the focal person or anyone else in the group among whom the disturbances occur.

Controlled Research

Area focusing and control of the agent was the basis of RSPK experiments with moving objects which Pratt and I (Roll and Pratt, 1971) did in 1967 in a warehouse in Miami, Florida. Before we came, police officers and others had noticed that glasses, beermugs, and ashtrays, as well as cartons of merchandise, were more likely to move if placed on certain shelves in the stockroom than on others. This room contained three free-standing wooden tiers of shelves and one along the wall, as well as desks and shipping tables. Some of the shelves of the tiers were particulary prone to be the scene of disturbances, in other words, there was area focusing.

We chose the most active places on the shelves as target areas and placed on them some of the kinds of objects which had moved, such as beermugs and glasses, taking advantage also of object focusing. We carefully examined the shelves for stability and faulty construction and for magical devices which might have been installed to simulate parapsychological occurrences. The target objects that we placed in these areas were similarly examined. After the areas had been prepared, we kept them under surveillance. Ten objects moved when we had the area under observation both prior to and during the event; none of the employees had been near since we examined it last, nor was anyone near when the events took place.

The focal person for these events was Julio, a 19-year-old shipping clerk. For seven of the movements of target objects, Pratt or I had him in direct view; the description of one of these illustrates the detailed observation which is possible under such circumstances:

> At 11:27 a.m., a Zombie glass from the target area b on Tier 2 broke in the middle of Aisle 2. This glass had . . . been 12 inches from the edge of the shelf and there was a spoondrip tray, a water globe, and some notebooks in front of it. During this event there were three people in the warehouse aside from myself: Miss Roldan who was at her desk, Mr. Hagmeyer who was in the southwest corner of the room, and Julio. At the time of the event, Julio was sitting on his haunches at the north end of Aisle 3, placing a plastic alligator on the bottom shelf of Tier 3. I [W.G.R.] was between five and six feet from him and facing him when this event happend. He had no visible contact with Tier 2. The position of the glass was four feet from his back. It moved away from him. None of the objects in front of the glass were disturbed. It therefore must have risen at least two inches to clear these (Roll and Pratt, 1971, pp. 446–447).

In addition to enabling the investigator to control the situation, the experimental approach to RSPK enables him to obtain more detailed information than otherwise is possible. Since Pratt and I not only knew the place the objects landed but also their starting position, as well as Julio's location in the room, we could plot the exact distances and directions the objects moved on our charts. As we shall later see, this provided important information about the RSPK process.

Instrumental Explorations

In December, 1968, Hans Bender (1969, pp. 93–95) brought in two physicists to determine the nature of the energy which caused the electrical equipment in a lawyer's office in Rosenheim, Germany, to malfunction in strange ways. Lamps "exploded," fuses blew though the current was stable, and the phone company registered calls no one had made. The occurrences were connected with a 19-year-old secretary and included conventional poltergeist movements of objects and furniture. The physicists F. Karger and G. Zicha (1968) reported that "on December 8, 1967, the line recorder of the power station was fitted with a voltage magnifier and set up in the passageway of the lawyer's office to record the main voltage. Between 4:30 p.m. and 5:48 p.m. the recorder registered about 15 strong deflections at irregular intervals. At about the same time we heard loud bangs similar to those produced by discharging spark gaps, but not for every deflection. The noises were tape-recorded." The physicists ruled out deception as well as known physical forces and attributed the incidents to "mechanical influence without apparent cause" (pp. 33–34). The investigators also succeeded in filming swinging ceiling lamps and wall pictures.

Bender and his associates have used electronic devices for controlled studies of teleportation. At Neusatz (Bender, 1969, pp. 88–89) the poltergeist seemed to retreat in face of the electronic gear. But in Nicklheim, Bender (1969, pp. 95–99) had at least partial success: An object, which had been involved in previous incidents, fell again after it had been placed in a box protected by an electric curtain.

American investigators have been dreaming about mobile electronic laboratories (Artley and Joines, 1969; Joines, Owen, Osis, Roll, and Bender, 1970; Tart, 1965), but so far the realities are modest. Tape recorders and cameras are common. RSPK sounds have been recorded (Pratt and Palmer, 1976) and a swinging lamp filmed (Rosenberg, 1974). More sophisiticated equipment is usually beyond the financial resources of the researcher.

One aspect of many poltergeist cases which cries out for instrumental research are the unusual trajectories of objects. Video or film recording of moving objects would help to verify or falsify the reports of such trajectories and provide insight into the RSPK process. The equipment of course should be brought in without upsetting the psychological situation on which the phenomena may depend.

Influence of Observer

My arrival at the Miami warehouse in January, 1967, seemed to check the pace of the poltergeist (Roll and Pratt, 1971). Things generally only happened when I was not on the premises. The poltergeist was not nearly so shy with police officers and others who had come to investigate; I suspected that it was the notion of the poltergeist specialist which changed the psychological situation for Julio, the center for the events. When Pratt joined the investigation, I was careful to introduce him as a casual visitor and then to absent myself. There were several occurrences when Pratt had Julio under observation and when I was away. But then things began to happen when I too was present. Finally, a number of events took place when I was not only present but looking at or speaking to Julio; I described one of them in the previous section. It seemed that I was actually enhancing the phenomena.

I have studied the 116 RSPK accounts for observer effects, distinguishing between cases where the presence of outside witnesses apparently inhibited, enhanced, or had no effect on the phenomena. In some cases, one observer seemed to have no effect while another inhibited or enhanced the phenomena. Sometimes recent arrivals suppressed the events at first but later had no effect or enhanced the events. Large crowds usually inhibited RSPK. Disregarding these, I have listed the cases according to whether the observer tended to suppress or enhance the events. In the majority, 67 of the total, the observers did not seem either to add or detract from the incidents, in 16 they seemed to inhibit the events, and in 23 to enhance them. For the other cases, the reports did not indicate what effect if any the observer had. In other words, for 90 of the cases, the witnesses either had no effect on the events or actually enhanced them. The proportion of cases where this held true is large in each period, though somewhat lower in the last: 15, 20, 31, and 24. In general, RSPK should provide good opportunities for investigation.

Other Observer Effects

In September, 1903, falls of stones were reported by an Associate of the Society for Psychical Research living in Sumatra. The stones came through the roof of the bedroom, landing near the bed. He tried to catch them, "but I could never catch them; *it seemed to me that they changed their direction in the air as soon as I tried to get hold of them.* I could not catch any of them before they fell on the floor. Then I climbed up . . . and examined [the roof just above it from which] the stones were flying. They came right through the 'Kadjang,' but there were no holes in the kadjang. When I tried to catch them there at the very spot of coming out, I also failed. . . . This kadjang is of such a kind that it cannot be penetrated (not even with a needle) without making a hole. Each 'kadjang' is one single flat leaf of about 2 by 3 feet in size. It is a speciality of the neighborhood of Palembang. It is very tough and offers a strong resistance to penetration" (Grottendieck, 1906, pp. 262-263).

Many RSPK cases show a related effect: Objects are often flung about with great violence, but people are rarely hurt. The missiles may seem to be aimed at someone, and to move with great speed, but they usually hit lightly or veer off.

In some poltergeist cases, observation had a special inhibitory effect. Whether or not the witnesses to the events seemed to suppress these, a direct gaze on objects appeared to inhibit or retard movement. John Bristow, the main witness of disturbances in a carpenter's workshop in Swanland, Yorkshire in 1849 told F. W. H. Myers (1891-92) that "sometimes one of us would look fixedly for many minutes at a bit of wood on the floor. It never moved while we looked at it. But once let our attention be relaxed and that very bit of wood would come flying at us from some distant point. Mr. Crowther . . . used sometimes to sit in the shed for two or three hours at a time, watching to see a piece of wood start on its course. He never saw one start; though, like the rest of us, he saw many which seemed to have just started" (pp. 390-391).

Among the 105 cases involving movements of objects, visual fixation seemed to have had an inhibiting effect in 47 and to have had no effect in 43. (I am not here distinguishing between outside witnesses and the people primarily involved.) In 15 cases the influence, if any, of direct observation could not be determined. These proportions are closely reflected in the four periods. If we restrict ourselves to cases where the beginning of the movements were seen, the figures are 6, 10, 14, and 13. The cases where direct observation seemed to inhibit are roughly the same.

A parapsychologist who plans to investigate an RSPK case should be prepared for the possibility that direct observation may retard movements and also for the more remote possibility that his presence may inhibit the events. It is fairly easy, especially if there is focusing, to provide for controlled observation of an area without having the objects located in this area in direct view. In the Miami case (Roll and Pratt, 1971) we often had the target areas under complete surveillance when objects moved—though we never saw them take off.

The situation is more difficult if the visitor suppresses the events by his mere presence. In that case he might obtain the help of a colleague who does not have this effect or rely on other witnesses, such as police officers, whose presence does not affect the phenomena. Video recordings or other means of electronic surveillance might also be tried.

APPARITIONS, VOICES, AND OTHER EFFECTS

At the age of 13 an epileptic girl in the Midlands, England, began to have hallucinations of people. "At first she saw an old man, who was taken to be her long-deceased grandfather. Then, in 1971, she repeatedly saw a young girl who claimed to have been strangled in 1808 and who wished to be buried in consecrated ground. . . . Involvement of the rest of the family and of friends began when they witnessed ostensible poltergeist phenomena such as doors and curtains opening and shutting, objects moving. . . . Apparitions . . . then began to be seen by others, both singly and collectively. These were not only of dead persons, but also of persons known to be alive. Dogs, bears, birds and devilish 'horny things' were also seen—a coldness was usually experienced in the part of the body nearest to the apparition. Shared apparitions sometimes appeared, to different observers, to be differently dressed" (McHarg, 1973, pp. 17-18).

In 46 of the 116 cases one or more of the following effects were reported. In 27, apparitions were seen, representing human figures, animals, demons, hands, fingers, or amorphous shapes. In 13, intelligible voices were heard, including whispering and singing. Seven of these also had apparitions. In eight others there were special sound phenomena variously referred to as sounds of wind, whistling, groans, laughter, screams, and so on. In five cases one or more persons were wounded or slapped by some unknown agency or stigmata appeared on their bodies. In five cases people were pulled or lifted. In four cases feces appeared, usually smeared on people's faces. The victims of the woundings and other unpleasantries were usually the poltergeist agents. In four cases unexplained fires occurred, in three writing, and in two the manes or tails of livestock were braided. Several other cases showed peculiarities of their own.

Aside from the movements and sounds, most of the effects were not common enough to be regarded as typical for RSPK. If we arbitrarily set 10 per cent as the cut-off place, the apparitions and voices remain. The 27 cases with apparitions are distributed as follows over the four periods: seven, seven, six, and seven; and the 13 cases with intelligible voices: six, two, two, and three. There is a decrease in both over the four periods. The figures, however, cannot be assumed to be independent since hearing voices and seeing visions may be related and since both were reported in seven of the accounts. In any case only the decrease in the proportion of cases with voices from the first period to the last three is significant ($P < .05$, chi-square test).

The decrease may be associated with a reduced tendency in more recent times to personify RSPK phenomena. In the early cases, the observers may have been more likely to suppose that they were dealing with a personal entity which, if it could make knocks and throw things, should also be able to speak and make itself visible. This is not to say that the experiences were necessarily hallucinatory: Several of them were shared by the observers present, including visitors and investigators. Though collective hallucinations may be produced by suggestion—no doubt heightened by the (other) RSPK disturbances—an objective basis for some of the experiences remains a possibility.

There was a total of 33 cases with apparitions (20 cases), voices (six cases), or both (seven cases). In eight the RSPK agents were the only ones to see or hear anything; in 17 the apparitions or voices were experienced by relatives or other members of the household either by themselves or in addition to the RSPK agent; and in eight people outside the immediate group witnessed the phenomena. The two former categories may consist predominantly of subjective experiences or the effects of suggestion. The eight collective experiences, sometimes involving police officers and other professional witnesses, raise the possibility that there was an objective or physical basis to some of the experiences.

Next let us consider the information provided by the experiences. In addition to the visions and voices, intelligible information was occasionally provided by writing which would mysteriously appear on walls and other places; by Ouija board spellings; and by mediumistic-type communications received by the agent. The knocks and raps which were common in many of these cases provided information through the use of conventional codes, such as indicating the letters of the alphabet by the number of raps. These methods often supplemented the information produced by the apparitions or voices. In addition there was one case where the information only came by writing and another only by mediumistic communications (I am disregarding the few cases where professional mediums were called in to identify the entities; the material in any case was either indefinite or contradictory). There were 11 cases where the information came only by raps.

Altogether there were 47 cases of the 116 where meaningful information appeared by one of these means. In about half, 24, some kind of entity was identified, and in 23 there was no personal entity or its origin or nature could not be determined. In the former group, three main types of entities were manifested. In eight cases of the 47, deceased persons appeared; in three, deceased persons, living people, and demons were manifested at different times; ten cases only featured demons or imaginary characters; and in three cases living people only were represented.

In a case reported by Pierce (1973) where a deceased person was suspected of being responsible for the events, no living RSPK agent was identified. In our sample of 116 cases, there were 24 cases with no agents. As we saw before, there were 11 cases with apparitions or other effects suggestive of discarnate agency; four of these had no known living RSPK agents. This is a higher proportion than for the total, though not statistically significant.

Some of the 11 cases provided correct information about the deceased, in others it was false or implausible, or the information could not be verified.

Haunting RSPK

Three of the cases suggestive of discarnate agency and lacking a living agent were haunting-type cases (Cornell and Gauld, 1960; Pierce, 1973; Stevenson, 1972, p. 243–246).

As a rule, haunting phenomena are distinguished from poltergeist occurrences. Hauntings are thought to be "place oriented"; that is, to be associated with a special location, usually a "haunted house" (haunting comes from the same root as home and literally means homing, presumably by a discarnate entity to his or her earthly habitat). Poltergeists, on the other hand, are "person oriented." As a rule things only happen when a particular individual is present. At the same time, there usually is a tendency for the disturbances to be concentrated on certain objects or on certain areas, so-called object or area focusing; to that extent RSPK is also "place oriented." Occasionally the (primary) agent is not at home during an incident (Roll, 1970; 1976, p. 151). Perhaps the RSPK "charge" on a focused object is then triggered by someone else.

Haunting phenomena are sometimes said to go on for years with different families in the haunted house or place reporting the incidents. Such cases are difficult to investigate because the physical incidents, if any, are generally few and far between. Typically, haunting occurrences are hallucinatory, that is, only certain individuals hear or see anything while others who are present experience nothing. This personal association may be true also for the physical aspects of haunting: Sometimes these seem to subside when another family moves in, only to resume when that family has left and a third family has taken over. To an extent hauntings, too, may be person oriented.

There are other similarities, such as hallucinatory or apparitional experiences which are typical in hauntings and as we saw, not uncommon in poltergeist cases. Also, as we shall later observe, RSPK outbreaks sometimes take place in haunted houses.

This survey is limited to cases with recurrent physical effects. As a result there are few ostensible hauntings. Since the investigator of hauntings cannot expect to be present when physical occurrences take place, and thus may be unable to satisfy himself whether these are parapsychological, he is likely to emphasize the ESP possibilities of the case rather than its PK possibilities. An important methodological advance in judging this aspect of hauntings has been made by Schmeidler (1966) and Moss and Schmeidler (1968).

THE NATURE OF RSPK

There are two main areas to examine for clues about the RSPK process, the agent and the occurrences themselves.

The RSPK Agent

Physical and Mental Health. In May, 1904, knocking sounds erupted around Karin Nauckhoff, a young housewife living in southern Sweden. Six years before, she had contracted a "nervous disease" when she would collapse, cry, and have tremors. This happened about twice a day. Later the fainting fits were replaced by anxiety attacks. Bjerre (1947), who investigated the knocks, found that they were preceded by an anxiety attack which receded when the knocks came. Her eyes then assumed a staring expression, and she seemed absent-minded. During his study, she had a fainting fit with convulsions.

Of the 92 RSPK agents, 49 appeared to have more or less severe medical or psychological problems. In the accounts, 22 agents were described as having seizures or dissociative states, or as being prone to such states. Sixteen of the 22 were observed one or more times as having muscular contractions, comas, convulsions, fainting fits, trances, seizures, or other dissociative episodes. Four others had been diagnosed as epileptics. Of these, three were treated for the disease at the time of the RSPK outbreak and one had previously shown epileptic spikes in the EEG. A fifth, whose EEG was taken some months after the incidents, produced a short burst of such spikes. This RSPK agent and one other were prone to dissociative episodes according to their psychological tests.

If we examine the distribution over the four periods, 1612-1849, 1850-1899, 1900-1949, and 1950-1974, the 22 RSPK agents prone to seizures or dissociative states are distributed as follows: three, five, five, and nine. The slightly higher figure in the last period is probably due to increased interest in the behavior of the RSPK agent and improved methods of observation, such as the EEG. It seems likely that the other figures would have been larger if similar diagnostic tools had been available then. In this context it is relevant that there were no diagnosed epileptics in the two first periods; the first appeared in the third period, with three in the fourth period, not counting the borderline case, who was also in the fourth. We will discuss the question of a possible association of RSPK eruptions with epilepsy in a section below.

Among the remaining RSPK agents 27 had other problems. One was dwarfed and lame, another terminally ill, and a third had a kidney disease. The latter and three others were also said to suffer from hysteria. In two cases, however, this may have been brought on by the RSPK disturbances. One of the hysterics also had a consumptive tendency and another was a victim of nightmares and somnambulism. Two were said to be neurasthenic; one of them had rickets and was sickly, and the other had tried suicide and showed somnambulism. Disturbed sleep was common to several, including one who sweated and trembled during sleep. One of the RSPK agents was a schizophrenic, another in a state of nervous collapse, and a third a violent alcoholic. Two children were hyperactive; one of these also had a low IQ and behavior problems. Three others were mentally retarded, one of these being tubercular; and three children had behavior problems.

In the fourth period, as a result of parapsychological investigations or because the family had sought professional help on their own, several of the RSPK agents received psychological or psychiatric examinations. The 13 RSPK agents who participated in such studies were found to have repressed aggression or low tolerance of frustration. Four of them were also among the agents with dissociative episodes, and four were in the group with miscellaneous problems (the two hyperactive children, the schizophrenic, and the violent alcoholic). Repressed aggression was probably also part of the problem for many of the RSPK agents in the previous periods, particularly the hysterics and neurotics. Aggression and irritability are also common among epileptics. Five of the agents in the fourth period seemed normal except for the aggression shown on the psychological tests. The 27 persons suffering from miscellaneous organic or functional disorders were distributed over the four time periods as follows: 1, 7, 5, and 14. The significant ($P < .05$, chi-square test) increase in the proportion of people with such problems in the last period is probably the result of improved methods of observation and increased interest in the RSPK agent. Of the total of 49 agents with more or less severe medical or psychological problems, 23 were in the fourth period, representing 79 percent of the RSPK agents in this period.

Some of the dissociative episodes and hysteric outbreaks seemed to result from the psychological stress associated with the RSPK disturbances. Those cases only suggest a predisposition to the symptoms shown rather than any preceding, overt symptomology.

The best estimate of the proportion of RSPK agents with organic or functional problems may come from the fourth period. If anything, 79 per cent may be an underestimation. It should be kept in mind that the attention of observers usually centers on the RSPK incidents themselves rather than on the agent and furthermore that the period of observation is generally confined to the duration of the RSPK occurrences. With more attention to the agent and more thorough medical and psychological studies, more psychological or medical problems may emerge.

Inherited Traits and Family Situation. If little is known about most of the RSPK agents, even less is known about their parents and families. In the search for inherited traits, I could only find six cases with relevant information. In two cases, one in the first and the other in the third period, one or both of the parents of the agent had reputations of witchcraft. It is uncertain whether they possessed psychical abilities or whether their reputation was due to unusual behavior patterns. In a case in the third period, RSPK phenomena had been associated with an older brother of the agent and their mother was insane. In a case in the first period the father of the agent had "spells"; in a case in the second period the mother was an imbecile, and in another a hysteric-epileptic and other members of the family had supplementary fingers.

Palmer has observed (Pratt and Palmer, 1976) that in two RSPK cases he studied (Palmer, 1974; Pratt and Palmer, 1976) the children were not living with their natural parents at the time of the RSPK outbreaks. Palmer's observation made me look at this aspect of the data.

If we set 18 as the age when a person can normally be expected to leave home, there were 61 girls and boys at this age or lower for whom we know where they lived (I have included seven whose exact ages are not given, but who are referred to as boys, girls, or teenagers). Of these, 38 were living away from home and 23 were at home when the events began. Among the 23 who were living at home, in four cases there was only one parent in the home and in three, the child was a late-comer to elderly parents.

Of the 38 children who were living away from home, 18 were 13 years or less. Since we do not know how many children, in the populations and periods under consideration, did not live with their natural parents, a statistical assessment is not possible. It would appear, however, that many of the RSPK children may have been subjected to more psychological stress during childhood than others at their age.

Precipitating Events

Changes and Stress. In November, 1970, a 13-year-old girl and her sister were living with their grandmother in Pursruck, Germany, when a person in the house died. The day after, "Helga, who looked from her window directly over the cemetery and the mortuary where the corpse had been taken, was frightened and could not fall asleep. She was thinking of a ghost story which her teacher had told months ago. When she first heard the tappings, she thought that the dead man was announcing himself in this way.... The second poltergeist period at the end of May 1971 was preceeded by anxiety dreams which clearly showed puberty problems (a man standing in her bed is threatening her with vipers)" (Bender, 1974, p. 137).

In 38 of the 92 cases with focal persons, the RSPK events began at a time when there were changes or problems in the family which may have affected the agent. In 15 the RSPK incidents started up after the agent or the family had moved, when a parent was away, or when the agent, usually a child, had to share his bed with somebody else; in 12 cases the focal person was ill or subject to unusual psychological stress; in eight, the incidents erupted after a move to a reportedly haunted house or followed mediumistic or spiritistic communications, or RSPK occurrences reportedly took place in the previous home of the focal person or had centered around a relative. In two cases the incidents followed shortly after the death of relatives or friends, and in one case RSPK knocking came after the person had been startled by normal knocks on the door. In the latter case, the agent had also just moved into a house believed to be haunted.

The cases where precipitating events were identified are distributed as follows over the four periods, 4, 7, 13, and 14. Again, the slight increase over the four periods is probably the result of increased attention to the agent and to the possibility that he or she, and therefore the events, may be affected by external circumstances. Some of the precipitating events were clearly stressful. With respect to the moves or other changes in the family situation, we do not know how these affected the focal person, but changes of this type require adaptations to a new social and physical environment and may be stressful, especially for children.

Termination Attempts

Exorcism. Captain Jandachenko was commanding a calvary post in Liptsy, Russia, in January, 1853, when cups and wooden platters began moving about in the kitchen of the small house where he was lodged with his wife. The parish priest sprinkled the house with holy water but the events continued. The next day three priests came bringing the icons from the church and "... a solemn service was read. Hardly had they begun, when a stone was thrown in the kitchen, which was empty, and smashed a window in the sight of all. Then a piece of wood, followed by a pail of water, flew out of the kitchen into the midst of the assembly, the latter upsetting in the midst. The culminating horror was the fall of a stove into the basin of holy water itself.... as the phenomena still continued, the captain begged two of the priests to return and read the formal prayers for the exorcism of evil spirits. . . . The phenomena continued in the presence of several fresh witnesses" (Leaf, 1897, p. 320).

Since poltergeist occurrences were first described, the most common way of trying to make them go away was by exorcism and other religious or spiritistic interventions. Among the 116 cases, exorcism and related activities were tried in 30. These attempts were distributed as follows over the four periods: 4, 4, 13, and 9. It is interesting that such attempts were about as common in the twentieth century as in earlier ages.

Of the 30 attempts, the RSPK phenomena ceased after four, there was a temporary relief after four and the exorcism had no effect in 21 cases, except in five cases where the occurrences seemed to intensify during the rites.

In one case it could not be determined whether the religious rites temporarily enhanced the phenomena or caused them to quiet down: Movements of objects and knocking sounds had been going on in Sauchie, Scotland, for 8 days in November, 1960; on the ninth day it was quiet, and on the tenth a service of intercession was conducted by four ministers (Owen, 1964, p. 134). The knocks resumed during the service and continued for three quarters of an hour afterwards but then the phenomena died down—though there were sporadic occurrences at least until January 23, 1961.

It is uncertain if the four cases which ceased after the rites did so as a result of these. For two of the four cases the duration of the RSPK eruption was not known. In two others they were 2 and 3 months. Since the median duration of an RSPK outbreak was 2 months, these two cases had perhaps run their course when the religious rites were tried. In general exorcism seems to be ineffective as a means for dealing with RSPK.

Moves and Reduction of Stress. Once it had been noticed that the phenomena followed a servant or other employee, this person was sometimes dismissed, or if a member of the family, he or she was sent to another relative. Occasionally the family as a whole or some member would move. The phenomena at times followed the family or the focal person to the new location, but sometimes they ceased. (In two of the cases the house was burnt or severely damaged by fires supposedly set by the poltergeist thereby bringing an end to the events).

Of the 116 cases, in 35 the incidents terminated after the focal person or someone with whom he or she had frequent interaction moved away. The distribution over the four periods is 1, 13, 10, and 11. The proportion of the total for the first period is significantly lower than for the others ($P < .02$, chi-square test). This was probably the result of few families taking this recourse—understandable in view of the common belief that devils rather than people were responsible for the turmoil.

To determine whether such moves actually tended to shorten the course of the events we need to examine the durations of the cases. In 31 where duration is recorded the median is 1.13 months versus 2 months for all the cases. To evaluate the difference statistically, the averages have to be used: 52.4 versus 155.6 days. This difference is significant ($P < .05$, one-tailed) and suggests that the moves tended to shorten the duration of the incidents.

In 11 cases the occurrence seemed to terminate for other reasons, but usually this happened so late in the course of the events that the causal connection seems doubtful. For instance, one case ceased after a year with the inception of the girl's menses, in another after 2 years of psychoanalysis. Only three such cases ceased before 2 months. In one it was after payment of a debt incurred by a deceased person believed to haunt the area, in another by hypnotic suggestion, and in the third when the 10-year-old agent returned to school after having to stay home with a back injury.

A PSYCHOPHYSICAL MODEL FOR RSPK

The present survey suggests that the RSPK agent at the time of the incidents is often in a poor state of health, either mentally or physically. The existence of precipitating factors reinforces the impression of pathological conditions which are triggered into overt expression when the situation becomes overly stressful.

Most RSPK researchers concur that the incidents are related to psychological tensions (Bender, 1969; Mischo, 1968; Owen, 1964; Palmer, 1975; Rogo, 1974; Roll, 1976, pp. 153–161; Zorab, 1964). Let us now examine the possibility that there may be a physiological basis to RSPK occurrences.

Central Nervous System Eruptions and RSPK

The first RSPK agent to have an EEG examination was a 13-year-old boy who was the center in 1961 of the Newark disturbances (Roll, 1969). The record showed a slight indication of epileptic discharges of the type sometimes found in adolescents who have behavioral problems and experience dissociated episodes (a burst of 14 per second positive spikes during a short period when the boy was resting). This fitted evidence from psychiatric and other studies that he sometimes carried out activities without knowing what he was doing. Julio, the center for the Miami disturbances, was also prone to dissociative behavior according to the psychological tests, but showed a normal EEG (Roll, 1976, p. 159). Then in 1975, Gerald Solfvin and I (Solfvin and Roll, 1976) studied a case where the 21-year-old focal person suffered from grand mal. This fact and the apparent relation between the RSPK incidents and the progress of the disease made us speculate that RSPK events are sometimes related to unusual neural discharges. The impression was reinforced by the present survey. As we saw above, the RSPK agents include a small number of known epileptics and several others with convulsions and other symptoms suggestive of disorders of the central nervous system (CNS). This raises the possibility of a causal relation between RSPK and CNS disturbances.

The Swedish psychiatrist Bjerre (1947), who investigated the RSPK knockings around Karin, suggested in 1905 that electric current in brain cells was converted to another energy form which was then radiated into the environment and produced the RSPK knocks. Bjerre diagnosed Karin's fainting fits, convulsions, and anxiety attacks as "organic hysteria."

The exploration of the possible relation between brain events and psychic occurrences was greatly stimulated by the advent of the electroencephalograph (EEG). Hans Berger (1940), the discoverer of the EEG, had a theory for telepathy rather similar to Bjerre's. He thought that the electrical energy produced by nerve cells may be transformed to psychical energy and that this is the vehicle for telepathic transmission. He pictured this energy as similar to but not identical with electromagnetic waves.

So far brain wave studies in parapsychology have focused on the reception of information (ESP) or energy rather than on its transmission. In PK we seem to deal with transmission and in RSPK with sudden and recurrent transmission. If these are the results of CNS eruptions, poltergeist incidents may be regarded as a special class of epileptic-like symptoms.

It is interesting that the term epilepsy implies spirit intervention, as does poltergeist. Epilepsy comes from the Greek verb to seize or to be possessed (by a spirit or a god). The word long ago lost its occult connotation and is now defined as the "sudden and recurrent disturbances in mental function, state of consciousness, sensory activity or movements of the body, caused by paroxysmal malfunctions of the cerebral nerve cells" (*Encyclopaedia Britannica*, 1974).

In addition to the fact that RSPK incidents have been reported around epileptics and people with symptoms suggestive of epilepsy, several other factors make the CNS theory deserve the attention of RSPK researchers. Many epileptics show "irritability . . . with sudden and unpredictable variations of mood: they are suspicious, quarrelsome, egocentric, circumstantial, religious, and [show] a slowness and stickiness of thought that borders onto mental subnormality" (Pond, 1974, pp. 580–581).

The theme of aggression recurs in both the personalities of RSPK agents and in the nature of the events themselves. The "stickiness of thought" or perseveration in patients with brain dysfunctions refers to their tendency to have the same thought or carry out the same activity repeatedly. This trait does not come out strongly in the personality tests of RSPK agents, but it does seem to be expressed in the incidents themselves. The focusing effects and the repetitive incidents involving an object or area are characteristic of RSPK.

Epilepsy can be brought on by a variety of developmental and congenital defects. Some of the 27 RSPK agents described above as having miscellaneous complaints had problems which are sometimes associated with epilepsy. The disease may be found in children who are hyperactive, who have behavior distur- bances, and in mentally retarded people. It can be caused by birth injuries, tuberculosis, and alcoholism.

Epilepsy is reported to be more common in men than in women (Robb, 1974). In a recent study of petit mal in 100 patients, however, there was an equal distri- bution (Robb, 1974). RSPK was more common among women than men in the early periods, but since 1900 the sexes are equally divided.

Epilepsy is concentrated in the lower age brackets: "Over half of known cases appear before age 15" (Goldenson, 1970, p. 407). Petit mal usually ceases before adulthood. The median age for RSPK outbreaks is 14, that is, about half of the cases in the survey erupted before the age of 15.

In patients with epilepsy "seizures may be brought on by particular odors, cer- tain types of music, by reading, by a loud voice or other startling stimuli" (Robb and McNaughton, 1974, p. 272). Emotional and psychological disturbances (Robb and McNaughton, 1974) may also bring on an epileptic attack. Similarly, RSPK occurrences may be triggered by startling or stressful events in the life of the agent. Epileptic attacks can sometimes be controlled by adjustments in the social situation of the patient. The same seems to be true for RSPK.

Epileptics sometimes have visual and auditory hallucinations. A number of the RSPK cases in our group were associated with the seeing of apparitions and hear- ing of voices. Of the 33 such cases, 12 involved agents who reportedly experi- enced dissociated episodes or were prone to them. In other words, more than half of the 22 agents in this group saw apparitions or heard voices, or relatives or visitors had such experiences. This relationship is significant ($P < .05$, chi-square test). If the usual RSPK movements and knocks result from CNS eruptions, it appears as if the more complex brain states of the RSPK agent can be exter- nalized as well.

RSPK Energy and CNS Transmission

Some aspects of RSPK suggest familiar energy patterns. For instance, lighter household objects usually move greater distances than heavy pieces of furniture. The strongest evidence that we are dealing with energy comes from the attenua- tion studies where the number of disturbed objects were found to decrease with distance from the focal person. In five of these, the attenuation was studied more closely: In four of the cases (Roll, 1968, 1969; Roll, Burdick, and Joines, 1973; Roll and Stump, 1969), the decrease followed the exponential decay func- tion better than the inverse function (the case where the inverse function gave the better fit may have been complicated by dual RSPK agency [Roll, 1970]). In other words, the pattern in which kinetic energy (i.e., movements of objects) appeared in the space surrounding the agent suggests that this energy resulted from the transformation of an unidentified energy.

The evidence that RSPK energy was concentrated near the agent seems to be inconsistent with another pattern: In all five studies it was found that distant objects tended to move greater distances than objects close to the agent. To throw light on this curiosity, we selected the Miami case for which we had the greatest number of reliable data and made a correlation analysis between the various aspects of motion (Roll et al., 1973). We found that objects close to the agent tended to be short, clockwise, and to point away from him, while distant objects moved further, were counterclockwise, and pointed slightly inwards. Such a pattern could result if energy waves were radiated from two positions on the agent's body and if they were nonsynchronous. The pattern of interaction between the waves might then become a beam which moved around the agent and varied from short and fat to long and thin. Some of the peculiarities of RSPK motion such as the floating or fast-slow speeds and the rotating and circular motions could result if the objects were picked up and carried along by the beam, then dropped, picked up by another sweep, and so on. An analysis of the Olive Hill disturbances (Roll et al., 1974) supported the rotating beam theory. The focusing effect could also be explained in terms of wave theory (Joines, 1975).

The theory that recurrent paroxysmal events in the central nervous system are related to RSPK helps to complete the picture. In epilepsy the neural discharge begins in a particular location (the epileptic focus) and then rapidly spreads to other parts of the brain. In a computer study Brazier (1973, pp. 153–177) was able to trace the timing and speed of discharges from the trigger zone to other parts of the brain. She found a regular progression along anatomical pathways lasting from a few to many milliseconds. The EEG transmissions resulting from different parts of the brain were out of phase and might provide several loci of CNS discharges in addition to the place of origin. The theory that recurrent CNS disturbances are related to RSPK seems to complement the rotating beam theory.

The most direct way of testing the CNS theory for RSPK is to take EEG recordings of the agent during the RSPK incidents. This has been attempted in two studies (Pratt and Palmer, 1976; Solfvin and Roll, 1976). The transmitting unit, which was designed by Fritz Klein of the Department of Anesthesiology, Duke University, is about the size of a package of cigarettes and is connected to scalp electrodes. It has an antenna which transmits to a nearby FM receiver and tape recorder. The unit can be kept in a pocket and allows the subject to move about normally. In neither case were there any incidents when the focal persons were wearing the EEG electrodes and carrying the telemetry units.

EEG measurements can also be made during conventional PK tests. Palmer (1975) has suggested that attempts be made to create the psychological conditions in the laboratory which seem to facilitate RSPK. During periods of high PK scoring, it could be determined if there are reflections in the EEG of the CNS storms which may be associated with RSPK. Other facets of RSPK could also be explored experimentally, such as the attenuation and focusing effects.

CONCLUDING REMARKS

In this survey I have examined the poltergeist from two points of view. I have looked for patterns in the occurrences which may help in the design of research, and I have looked for patterns which may point to the nature of RSPK.

The cases span four centuries and 17 countries in three continents; Europe, North America, and Asia as well as the islands of Iceland, Indonesia, and Mauritius. The cases have a basic similarity consisting of spontaneous and repetitive physical occurrences, usually movements of objects or percussive sounds. Over and above this similarity there is variability which seems to be due to the psychological, social, and other circumstances of the focal person.

Some of the messages we get from the poltergeist are garbled, but one comes over clearly: An active poltergeist is an excellent prospect for research, including controlled experimental research.

A small proportion of RSPK agents have been diagnosed as suffering from the sudden and recurrent disturbances of the central nervous system known as epilepsy; many others show mental and behavioral characteristics consistent with this or have problems which may bring on CNS disturbances. While only a few poltergeist agents are known to have suffered from epilepsy, it nevertheless seems possible that RSPK may be associated with CNS eruptions, whether or not these also result in epileptic symptoms. In any case, epilepsy provides some interesting parallels to poltergeist attacks and may offer insights into the nature of "seizures" outside the physical organism. The etiology of this form of CNS dysfunction and the conditions which tend to enhance or inhibit seizures have parallels in many poltergeist agents and in the development of RSPK disturbances.

A theory for RSPK, however, must be more than a simple extension of neurology. It requires a radical change in thinking. Usually advances in science are marked by new concepts: to understand the poltergeist, it may be fruitful to forfeit some old ones. One aged pair, now often excluded from polite discourse, but still turning up in one guise or another, is the mind-matter couple (sometimes with its relatives, the animate-inanimate, nonphysical-physical, and observer-object pairs). If we do not assume a sharp distinction between a mental or inner world and a physical or outer one, RSPK phenomena become less paradoxical. This approach does not result in a paucity of conceptual tools but in a great wealth: The laws and regularities which have been discovered by the physical sciences become hypotheses in the exploration of psychical processes, and the patterns which have been found in psychical processes become hypotheses in the exploration of physical events.

RSPK occurrences are psychophysical. They simultaneously express patterns which we generally call physical and patterns which we call mental. A simple RSPK occurrence, such as the glass in the Miami warehouse which lifted itself over the objects in front of it, suggests intelligent guidance. At the same time, the events conformed to the attenuation pattern and in other ways suggested an energetic process. Similarly, the focusing effects appear to be examples of perseveration at the same time as they can be understood in terms of wave theory (Joines, 1975). Fast-slow movements, the "floating," curved, and rotating trajectories make sense in terms of the rotating beam theory (Roll et al., 1974) —assuming a built-in guidance system.

Teleportations, if real, show in a particularly striking manner the psychological side of RSPK. Our thoughts are not limited by walls and closed space: We can easily and immediately call up ideas or images relating to distant objects. Mentation has another framework: It is a function, at least in part, of the associative cortex. Perhaps a neural discharge of sufficient strength which combines two images, such as mirror and bedroom, is reflected in the sudden appearance of an actual mirror in the room.

Here, physical and mental space become complementary or synonymous. The things in a poltergeist house are at the same time the thoughts of the people who live there. When an investigator enters the space surrounding an RSPK agent, in a literal sense he enters that person's mind, and he is liable to change that mind; in other words, to affect the course of RSPK events.

RSPK outbreaks are rare, but usually highly traumatic to the family or group they descend upon. The possibility that they are related to brain dysfunctions makes it possible to envisage a poltergeist therapy similar to treatments for epilepsy (Solfvin and Roll, 1976). The main interest of RSPK phenomena, however, may be what they suggest about ordinary people and the everyday world. As Bender (1974) says, "Poltergeist phenomena are . . . a *via regia* or royal road to an extended understanding of man, of his position in nature and of nature herself" (p. 142).

REFERENCES

Artley, J. L., and Joines, W. T. Research approaches to parapsychological phenomena in natural environments. *Proceedings of the Parapsychological Association*, 1969, 6, 55–57.

Artley, J. L., and Roll, W. G. Mathematical models and the attenuation effect in two RSPK (poltergeist) cases. *Proceedings of the Parapsychological Association*, 1968, 5, 29–31.

Barrett, W. F. Poltergeists, old and new. *Proceedings of the Society for Psychical Research*, 1911, 25, 377–412.

Barrett, W. F. *On The Threshold of the Unseen.* New York: Dutton, 1918.

Bender, H. An investigation of "poltergeist" occurrences. *Proceedings of the Parapsychological Association*, 1968, 5, 31–33.

Bender, H. New developments in poltergeist research: Presidential address. *Proceedings of the Parapsychological Association*, 1969, **6**, 81-102.

Bender, H. Modern poltergeist research. In J. Beloff (Ed.), *New Directions in Parapsychology,* London: Elek Science, 1974. pp. 122-143.

Berger, H. *Psyche.* Jena, Germany: Gustav Fischer, 1940.

Betteridge, H. T. (Ed.) *The New Cassell's German Dictionary.* New York: Funk and Wagnalls, 1965.

Bjerre, P. *Spökerier.* Stockholm, Sweden: Centrum, 1947.

Brazier, M. A. B. Electrical seizure discharges within the human brain: The problem of spread. In M. A. B. Brazier (Ed.), *Epilepsy: Its Phenomena in Man*, pp. 153-170. New York: Academic Press, 1973.

Carrington, H., and Fodor, N. *Haunted People.* New York: Dutton, 1951.

Cornell, A. D., and Gauld, A. A Fenland poltergeist. *Journal of the Society for Psychical Research*, 1960, **40**, 343-358.

Cox, W. E. Introductory comparative analysis of some poltergeist cases. *Journal of the American Society for Psychical Research*, 1961, **55**, 47-72.

Dingwall, E. J., and Hall, T. H. *Four Modern Ghosts.* London: Duckworth, 1958.

Eisler, W. The Bronx poltergeist. In J. D. Morris, W. G. Roll, and R. L. Morris (Eds.), *Research in Parapsychology 1974*, pp. 139-143. Metuchen, N.J.: Scarecrow Press, 1975.

Encyclopaedia Britannica. Chicago: Benton, 1974.

Flammarion, C. *Haunted Houses.* New York: Appleton, 1924.

Goldenson, R. M. *The Encyclopedia of Human Behavior: Psychology, Psychiatry, and Mental Health*, pp. 403-410. Garden City, N.Y.: Doubleday, 1970. 2 vols.

Grottendieck, W. G. A poltergeist case. *Journal of the Society for Psychical Research*, 1906, **12**, 260-266.

Joines, W. T. A wave theory of psi energy. In J. D. Morris, W. G. Roll, and R. L. Morris Eds.), *Research in Parapsychology 1974*, pp. 147-149. Metuchen, N. J.: Scarecrow Press, 1975.

Joines, W. T., Owen, A. R. G., Osis, K., Roll, W. G., and Bender, H. Symposium: The future of the poltergeist. *Proceedings of the Parapsychological Association.* 1970, **7**, 33-37.

Karger, F., and Zicha, G. Physical investigation of psychokinetic phenomena in Rosenheim, Germany, 1967. *Proceedings of the Parapsychological Association*, 1968, **5**, 33-35.

Leaf, W. Review of Predvestniki Spiritizma za polednie 250 lyet, by A. M. Aksakoff. *Proceedings of the Society for Psychical Research*, 1897, **12**, 319-330.

Lombroso, C. The "Haunted Houses" which I have studied. *The Annals of Psychical Science,* 1906, **3**, 361-372.

McHarg, J. F. Poltergeist and apparitional haunting phenomena affecting the family and associates of an adolescent girl with well-controlled epilepsy. In W. G. Roll, R. L. Morris, and J. D. Morris (Eds.), *Research in Parapsychology 1972*, pp. 17-19. Metuchen, N.J.: Scarecrow Press, 1973.

Mischo, J. Personality structure of psychokinetic mediums. *Proceedings of the Parapsychological Association*, 1968, **5**, 35-37.

Moss, T., and Schmeidler, G. R. Quantitative investigation of a "haunted house" with sensitives and a control group. *Journal of the American Society for Psychical Research*, 1968, **62**, 379-410.

Myers, F. W. H. On alleged movements of objects, without contact, occurring not in the presence of a paid medium. *Proceedings of the Society for Psychical Research*, 1891-92, **7**, 383-394.

Owen, A. R. G. *Can We Explain the Poltergeist?* New York: Garrett/Helix, 1964.

Palmer, J. A case of RSPK involving a ten-year-old boy: The Powhatan Poltergeist. *Journal of the American Society for Psychical Research*, 1974, **68**, 1-33.

Palmer, J. PK on the loose: Some clues from the poltergeist. Paper read at the convention of the American Psychological Association, Chicago, September, 1975.

Pierce, H. W. RSPK phenomena observed independently by two families. *Journal of the American Society for Psychical Research*, 1973. **67**, 86-101.

Podmore, F. Poltergeists. *Proceedings of the Society for Psychical Research*, 1896-97, **12**, 45-115.

Pond, D. A. Epilepsy and personality disorders. In P. J. Vinken and G. W. Bruyn (Eds.), *Handbook of Clinical Neurology*, Vol. 15, *The Epilepsies*, pp. 576-592. Amsterdam, Holland: North-Holland Publishing Co., 1974.

Pratt, J. G., and Palmer, J. An investigation of an unpublicized family poltergeist. In J. D. Morris, W. G. Roll, and R. L. Morris (Eds.), *Research in Parapsychology 1975*, pp. 109-115. Metuchen, N.J.: Scarecrow Press, 1976.

Pratt, J. G., and Roll, W. G. The Seaford disturbances. *Journal of Parapsychology*, 1958, **22**, 79-124.

Robb, P. Epidemiology of epilepsy. In P. J. Vinken and G. W. Bruyn (Eds.), *Handbook of Clinical Neurology*, Vol. 15, *The Epilepsies*, pp. 491-497. Amsterdam, Holland: North-Holland Publishing Company, 1974.

Robb, P., and McNaughton, F. Etiology of epilepsy. In P. J. Vinken and G. W. Bruyn (Eds.), *Handbook of Clinical Neurology*, Vol. 15, *The Epilepsies*, pp. 271-273. Amsterdam, Holland: North-Holland Publishing Company, 1974.

Rogo, D. S. Psychotherapy and the poltergeist. *Journal of the Society for Psychical Research*, 1974, **47**, 433-446.

Roll, W. G. Some physical and psychological aspects of a series of poltergeist phenomena. *Journal of the American Society for Psychical Research*, 1968, **62**, 263-308.

Roll, W. G. The Newark disturbances. *Journal of the American Society for Psychical Research*, 1969, **63**, 123-174.

Roll, W. G. Poltergeist phenomena and interpersonal relations. *Journal of the American Society for Psychical Research*, 1970, **64**, 66-99.

Roll, W. G. Earlier RSPK cases. In J. D. Morris, W. G. Roll, and R. L. Morris (Eds.), *Research in Parapsychology 1974*, pp. 134-139. Metuchen, N. J.: Scarecrow Press, 1975.

Roll, W. G. *The Poltergeist*. Metuchen, N.J.: Scarecrow Press, 1976.

Roll, W. G., Burdick, D. S. and Joines, W. T. Radial and tangential forces in the Miami poltergeist. *Journal of the American Society for Psychical Research*, 1973, **67**, 267-281.

Roll, W. G., Burdick, D. S., and Joines, W. T. The rotating beam theory and the Olive Hill poltergeist. In W. G. Roll, R. L. Morris, and J. D. Morris (Eds.), *Research in Parapsychology 1973*, pp. 64-67. Metuchen, N.J.: Scarecrow Press, 1974.

Roll, W. G., and Pratt, J. G. The Miami disturbances. *Journal of the American Society for Psychical Research*, 1971, **65**, 409-454.

Roll, W. G., and Stump, J. P. The Olive Hill poltergeist. *Proceedings of the Parapsychological Association*, 1969, **6**, 57-58.

Rosenberg, R. A haunting in New Jersey. *Theta*, 1974, **39-40**, 17-18.

Schmeidler, G. R. Quantitative investigation of a "haunted house." *Journal of the American Society for Psychical Research*, 1966, **60**, 137-149.

Schrenck-Notzing, A. von. The Hopgarten poltergeist case. *Journal of the Society for Psychical Research*, 1922, **20**, 199-207.

Sitwell, S. *Poltergeists.* New Hyde Park, N.Y.: University Books, 1959.

Solfvin, G., Harary, B., and Batey, B. A highly publicized case of RSPK. *Journal of Parapsychology*, 1976, **40**, 48-49.

Solfvin, G., and Roll, W. G. A case of RSPK with an epileptic agent. In J. D. Morris, W. G. Roll, and R. L. Morris (Eds.), *Research in Parapsychology 1975*, pp. 115-120. Metuchen, N.J.: Scarecrow Press, 1976.

Stevenson, I. Are poltergeists living or are they dead? *Journal of the American Society for Psychical Research*, 1972, **66**, 233-252.

Tart, C. T. Applications of instrumentation in the investigation of haunting and poltergeist cases. *Journal of the American Society for Psychical Research*, 1965, **59**, 190-201.

Thurston, H. *Ghosts and Poltergeists.* Chicago: Henry Regnery, 1954.

Zorab, G. A further comparative analysis of some poltergeist phenomena: Cases from Continental Europe. *Journal of the American Society for Psychical Research*, 1964, **58**, 105-127.

Zorab, G. The Sitoebondo Poltergeist (Java, 1893): A firsthand account written soon after the events. *Journal of the American Society for Psychical Research*, 1973, **67**, 391-406.

4

Paranormal Photography

Jule Eisenbud

INTRODUCTION

For almost as long as the history of photography, which began in 1849 with the daguerreotype, there have been claims that what looked like regular photographic images could be obtained on chemically sensitized surfaces through means that transcended known modes of energy transfer. Since the images that appeared in the early days were usually of persons no longer living, it was widely assumed that the agencies responsible for them were surviving aspects of those who had suffered physical death. In fact, the first known example of such an occurrence, reported in 1861 by a Boston jewelry engraver who obtained a so-called extra (a normally inexplicable image of someone appearing in addition to—and usually alongside of—a person sitting for a photographic portrait), was hailed by the Spiritualist press as conclusive proof of the continuation of life after death. Of course it was not, but the very suggestion of such a tie-in was enough to stimulate intense interest in what soon became known as "spirit photography."

William Mumler, the jewelry engraver who was the first to report the strange new phenomenon, soon capitalized on his discovery. Not long after obtaining his first "extra" he opened a studio specializing in "spirit photographs" where he did a brisk trade until it was discovered that one of his extras was alive and well. Since it was beyond the comprehension of many of those interested in the new phenomenon that extras could occur without the agency of discarnate entities, accusations of fraud followed, and Mumler was at length forced to leave Boston. In 1869 he moved his studio to New York City where he became so widely known that he was soon brought to trial on the charge of "having by means of what he termed spiritual photographs swindled many credulous persons." To the surprise of many, Mumler was acquitted, not only because the prosecution failed to sustain its case, but also on the strength of the many eminent witnesses who testified in his favor (Coates, 1911).[1]

Since Mumler's time more than two dozen persons in a number of countries have become known as spirit photographers or, latterly, psychic photographers. Some claimed the ability to impress images directly on nonexposed film without the mediation of a camera, called "scotography" (Fukurai, 1931; Henslow, 1919; Johnson, 1936; Sudre, 1960, p. 285; Warrick, 1939); others claimed to get film messages in the handwriting of deceased persons, called "psychography" (Doyle, 1923; Fukurai, 1931; Henslow, 1919; Johnson, 1936; Warrick, 1939). Edward Wyllie, an American psychic photographer, was allegedly able to obtain images of deceased persons if articles that had belonged to them were sent to him (Coates, 1911; Cook, 1916; Fodor, 1966). Sometimes many extras appeared on a single portrait, as shown in Figure 1, one of the photos of Alexander Martin, a Denver portrait photographer of the beginning of the twentieth century who, according to his chief investigator, was often embarrassed by the unbidden appearance of these images (Cook, 1916).

Unfortunately, trickery lay all too readily at hand as a means of satisfying the demands of both a credulous public and the incredulous critics (Edmunds, 1965; Price, 1922, 1925), and it appears hardly worth while at this date to attempt to disentangle the mass of claims and counterclaims on this point. "Mediumship," wrote Coates in his 1911 review volume, *Photographing the Invisible*, "implies neither manliness, honesty nor spiritual worth." It seems certain that fraud was practiced, though how widely will never be known. One man in France was actually sent to jail on his own confession, which he later claimed he was coerced into making (Coates, 1911). Often what was considered evidence of fraud, however, was entirely circumstantial, or simply that the allegedly paranormal photos *looked* fake. At the same time it was alleged that in certain instances the cases against psychic photographers accused of fraud were rigged (Doyle, 1923; Fukurai, 1931; McKenzie, 1923a, 1923b) and that impartial investigation was impossible or even refused by the accusers (McKenzie, 1923a). Indeed, according to James H. Hyslop in his 1915 review of Coates (and of the entire subject, including E. M. Sidgwick's much quoted 1891 indictment of spirit photogra-

---

[1] In his memoirs, published in 1875, Mumler tells of a woman who gave her name at a sitting as Mrs. Lindall, but whose true identity became known when an extra of her late husband, President Abraham Lincoln, appeared. During the 7 years she lived after the publication of Mumler's account, Mrs. Lincoln, to the embarrassment of at least one biographer (Ross, 1973), continued to express her belief in the spiritual origin of the extra.

phy), the evidence for fraud was in large part so dubious as to be virtually worthless. "I have found fraud requiring as much proof as spirits," Hyslop concluded, "and I think there is as much credulity shown by many believers in fraud as was ever shown by believers in spirits" (p. 175).

Today it seems plain that the essential question should be not whether fraud was ever committed, but solely whether the disputed effects were ever obtained under conditions which rendered fraud highly unlikely, if not impossible. While there can be no final answer to this, it would seem that claimed instances of extras recognized as deceased family members by sitters who allegedly turned up incognito and without prior arrangement (Cushman, 1922; Doyle, 1923), or of extras of persons who were never known to have been photographed during their lifetime (Henslow, 1919; Johnson, 1936; Morse, 1909; Wallace, 1874), or which were totally unlike any known photographs of such persons (Doyle, 1923) might make a presumption of trickery somewhat difficult to defend, whatever the circumstances of the sitting. But sittings were apparently rigorously controlled on occasion. One such was supervised by a well-known "ghost-breaker" who was also an expert photographer and conjurer. Despite every precaution (". . . the plates, camera, etc., were mine, and I did all the manipulations"), an inexplicable even if somewhat fake-looking hand appeared as an extra (Tubby, 1924; see also *Journal of the American Society for Psychical Research*, 1925). In another sitting, reported in 1893 by the editor of the *British Journal of Photography*, observers and cameras were trained upon him, the chief investigator, as well as upon the medium, who was not allowed anywhere near the camera or dark slide. Extras still appeared, but looked "as if cut oval out of a photograph with a can opener" (Taylor, 1893; see also Coates, 1911, p. 55; Sudre, 1960).

The term *thoughtography* was introduced by Tomokichi Fukurai of Japan, who in 1910 came upon this branch of what was by now being referred to as psychic photography, purely by accident. He was trying to see if a clairvoyant medium with whom he was experimenting could pick up the latent image of a calligraphic character impressed upon a film plate that had been allowed to remain undeveloped. It was discovered that another plate lying around had been somehow imprinted with this character, leading Fukurai to undertake further tests to see if his subject could deliberately imprint film plates with characters chosen by him. In one trial the medium was asked to put one half of a selected character on one plate and the complementary half on a second (Figure 2). In another trial the medium imprinted, on request, only the middle one of a stack of three film plates placed inside two boxes, one inside the other. The successful outcome of this experiment, concluded Fukurai (1931) in what must surely rate as one of the most notable throw-away lines in parapsychological literature, was "pregnant with a great meaning in the study of the psychic problem" (p. 181).

From the very beginning Fukurai's work came under severe attack. A pair of physicists, one the former president of the Imperial University of Tokyo where

Fukurai held a professorship, attempted maliciously (according to Fukurai) to rig one of his experiments so that the medium would appear to have cheated and then saw to it that she, Fukurai, and thoughtography were roundly attacked by the press. Despite a confession of "carelessness" and an apology by the former university president when the true facts came out, the accused medium vowed never to take part in another experiment and a few weeks later fell ill and died ("of influenza"), while another medium Fukurai was working with committed suicide when she learned of the first medium's supposed disgrace. The publication in Japan in 1913 of Fukurai's work with these and several other sensitives, moreover, led to his forced resignation from the university. Fukurai nonetheless went on with his experiments, and in 1931 his *Clairvoyance and Thoughtography,* which incorporated additional data, appeared in English.

Experiments along thoughtographic lines were carried out in America (Carrington, 1919, 1953; Hyslop, 1914), in France (Hyslop, 1911; Joire, 1916; Ochorowicz, 1912; Sudre, 1960), where a Comité d'Etude de Photographie Transcendental awarded a research prize in 1911, and in other countries. In England a Society for the Study of Supernormal Pictures, composed mainly of professional photographers, flourished between 1918 and 1923. In 1920 its members placed on record the fact that "after many tests and after the examination of thousands of pictures, they are unanimously of the opinion that results have been obtained supernormally on sensitive photographic plates under reliable test conditions . . . excluding the possibility of fraud" (Fodor, 1966, p. 352). Time was on the side of the opposition, however, as allegations of fraud (in which no one seems to have taken to heart Hyslop's strictures on the evaluation of the evidence) against several of the best known psychic photographers resulted in ever more acrimonious controversy (Barlow and Rampling-Rose, 1933; McKenzie, 1923a, 1923b; Price, 1922). The two photographers about whom controversy was most heated were William Hope and Mrs. Emma Deane, both of whom over a period of years gave what appears to have been evidence of paranormal photography (Carrington, 1925; Cushman, 1922; Doyle, 1923; Fukurai, 1931; Johnson, 1936; Sudre, 1960), but both of whom may well on occasion have slipped into fraudulent practices. F. W. Warrick, who described extensive work with Mrs. Deane in his much neglected *Experiments in Psychics* (1939), admitted as much in her case. At all events, after a damaging exposé of spirit photography by Barlow and Rampling-Rose in 1933, the entire subject of paranormal photography fell into disrepute. References to it in the literature all but disappeared for the next 30 years (Morris, 1967).

THE PARANORMAL PHOTOGRAPHY OF TED SERIOS

"For an essential part of [an] experiment," wrote Barlow in the above-mentioned exposé (Barlow and Rampling-Rose, 1933), "a dark room is necessary, so that if one is up against deception it is more difficult to detect. An additional disadvantage is that before arriving at the final results, the photographic plates registering those results have to go through many different processes—in and out of boxes, in and out of dark slides, in and out of the camera, in and out of solutions and so on; and at every single step there is a loophole for fraud" (p. 121). Although it should hardly have been as difficult to eliminate these loopholes as some critics made it out to be, the fact that they existed at all seemed to discourage investigation. With the advent of Ted Serios in the mid-50s, however, paranormal photography took a new turn. Ted was able to produce pictures repeatedly under close observation while the newly invented Polaroid camera, which became the sole laboratory for the development of its exposed film, provided him with just what was needed for the demonstration of his abilities.

Ted was in his middle 30s and working as an elevator operator in a Chicago hotel when his abilities first came to light. One day a fellow employee, who had found that Ted was an excellent hyponotic subject, conceived the idea of putting him into the role of so-called traveling clairvoyant and having him search for buried treasure in this way. To aid Ted in what seems to have been his "out-of-body" jaunts under hypnosis, his mentor, George Johannes, suggested as a spirit guide Jean Laffite, the notorious buccaneer (and probably as good as anyone when it came to buried treasure). After a fairly profitless initial period, it was suggested to Ted that he get hold of a camera and try to get pictures of the places to which, he claimed, Laffite would take him. At first an ordinary box camera was used. To everyone's astonishment (including Ted's, as he felt at the beginning that he was being tricked), pictures of unidentified places and scenes began to appear. This happened rather infrequently at the start, but soon the pictures began to come through often enough to cause considerable stir in certain Chicago circles, especially when Ted switched to a Polaroid camera and started getting pictures before everyone's eyes. Under the tutelage of a professional hypnotist who was later called into the picture to strengthen Ted's and Johannes' resolve about what they were doing, Ted's technique changed from simply pointing the camera at a blank wall when he shot to pointing at his own face and staring intently into the lens. In front of the lens he now began to hold a small open cylinder—usually a half-inch cut section of the 5/8 inch wide squeegee tube that came with each roll of film—which, it was suggested, would keep his fingers out of the way of the light (and, no doubt, of mischief). This cylinder later underwent several modifications, including having the open ends sealed with blackened tape. It ultimately became known as "the gismo."

For several years, with interruptions, Ted kicked around Chicago doing his psychic photography for various persons, groups, and institutions, including a 3-month stint at a Borg-Warner research laboratory near Chicago. But he failed to secure the type of sustained scientific investigation he and a few of his supporters were hoping would eventuate. It was rumored that it was during this discouraging period that Ted became a confirmed alcoholic, but Ted himself admits to having been a heavy drinker since the age of 16. Whatever the truth, drinking came to play a large part in Ted's story.

Early in 1964 Curtis Fuller, publisher of *Fate*, sent me a reprint of an article in that magazine by Pauline Oehler (1962), a member of the Illinois Society for Psychical Research, in which the story of these years was told and a number of examples of Ted's work given. At Fuller's urging, and with Mrs. Freda Morris, a graduate student in psychology, acting as go-between, a meeting with Ted was set up for me in Chicago in late April. At that meeting, to which I had gone with scant hope of anything really worth while, Ted impressed me and a co-observer I had invited to be present sufficiently to warrant my immediately arranging for him to come to Denver for further investigation.

Between May, 1964, when Ted began his work in Denver, and June, 1967, when the structured image phase of his "thoughtography" came to an abrupt end, Ted worked with more than three dozen scientifically trained observers— physicians, physicists, physiologists, engineers, and others—under a variety of conditions. During this period over 400 normally inexplicable images on over 100 different themes were obtained, as well as hundreds of "blackies," prints from which light seemed inexplicably to have been totally or almost totally excluded, and "whities," prints rendered totally or almost totally white, as if markedly overexposed in an equally inexplicable manner. (Many of the latter were produced with all visible light sources blocked from entering the camera.) During this period Ted also consumed, it is estimated, several thousand quarts of hard liquor and beer as heavy drinking turned out to be a regular part of the picture taking ritual.

Ted was most comfortable with Polaroid cameras of the older model 95 series (which did not have the "electric eye"), but he never objected to whatever other Polaroid models were brought by witnesses. (Other makes were not encouraged only because they did not permit immediate on-the-spot development.) He frequently alternated between several cameras during a session and these were usually set at infinity and the aperture fixed at the 3 opening, which provided the equivalent of 1/30th second at f 11. For the most part a winklight, which bounced light off Ted's face or torso when he was working close to the camera, was in use in addition to variable room lighting. (Ted had no particular specifications on this point.) Investigators were invited to bring their own cameras and film, which were appropriately marked. After the first few sessions, gismos were constructed on the spot from the black paper which came with the type 47, 3,000 speed black and white film rolls used in the model 95 cameras. They usually measured about an inch in width and about an inch or slightly more in length and, because the earlier gismos which were taped shut to prevent anything being inserted into them invariably became objects of suspicion, they were left open (which of course could not then fail to render them objects of constant suspicion).

From the start, efforts with Ted were aimed at identifying and eliminating whatever normal means of image production could conceivably come into play within his usual manner of working, which there seemed to be no pressing reason to interfere with. (An early attempt to bring about a change in Ted's style led only to a lengthy period of completely normal prints.) It was quickly determined that, with cameras and film completely out of Ted's control, the only normal (i.e., "trick") means of producing a film image other than what would ordinarily be obtained with the camera would be by having light pass into the camera lens through a transparency mounted onto a suitable auxiliary lens held in front of the camera lens. Figure 3 shows an image obtained with a 1/8 inch wide plano-convex lens made from the tip of a pocket flashlight bulb onto whose plane surface a tiny transparency had been mounted. Ted inducted me into the intricacies of this method of getting false paranormal images at the very start of our work in Denver, having learned the trick, he claimed, from the people at Borg-Warner. No secret to the cogniscenti, one or another variant of this method (e.g., a ¼ by ½ inch collimated system) was soon seized upon by critics as the most likely means whereby Ted produced his effects, while the ever-mysterious gismo was indicted as the prop in which such a lens-transparency gimmick could be conveniently concealed (Eisendrath, 1967; Reynolds, 1967). The fact that devices of width less than the 5/8 inch of the camera lens would require shielding to prevent the camera "seeing" around the gimmick was somehow ignored by the experts, as well as the problem of having an adequate light source handy. (It required a 200-watt bulb 3 feet away from the camera lens and shielded gimmick to produce the print shown in Figure 3.) Also ignored was that the gismo used by Ted at the start of our work (and earlier) was a cylinder taped at both ends, at least one opaquely, through which little light could pass. (Figure 4 shows one print obtained with such a gismo held on a string around one investigator's neck, to avoid sleight-of-hand substitution, and covered by this investigator's hand when the camera was triggered [Eisenbud, 1967b].) Further ignored was the fact that for several years after he began his extraordinary picture-taking, Ted didn't use a gismo at all.

Viewed in isolation, nevertheless, several features of Ted's images are consistent with a gimmick hypothesis. Some of the pictures, for instance, are demonstrably copies of pictures reproduced in books or magazines (Eisenbud and associates, 1967; Oehler, 1964). Successive images of the same scene, moreover, do not show relative motion where moving persons or vehicles are pictured. And rarely, in multiple versions of a given image, do we see changes in perspective or in the size of an image or in its basic detail (Eisenbud and associates, 1970b). Except for these features, however (features which in any case do not exclusively favor a gimmick hypothesis), nothing about Ted's images or his manner of producing them support a normal explanation.

It would be virtually impossible, to begin with, for any gimmick, whatever its size, to long escape detection under the conditions of observation in force in the Denver studies (Frey, Lehrburger, Marx, Merrill, Paley, and Wheeler, 1968). It wasn't as if Ted would come up with only one or two strange images in scores of trials where, as has been suggested (Reynolds, 1967), the witnesses' attention might be dulled or distracted. At his peak, Ted produced as many as 50 images or part images during sessions of perhaps 60 to 80 trials, with 10 to 20 not rare in sessions of fewer trials. The appearance of imagery was frequently preceded by a progressive darkening of the normal prints, up to complete blackouts, and invariably, when the images started coming, the attention of witnesses reached a high pitch of concentration. Characteristically, several types of image themes would emerge, often in rapid succession on one or more cameras (Eisenbud and associates, 1970a). For each of these a separate auxiliary lens-transparency gimmick would have been required, as would have been the case also in those infrequent but significant instances in which a given image did vary in size and important detail (Eisenbud, 1967b, pp. 115ff., 172 ff.)

During sessions Ted was constantly monitored. Except for two completely out-of-character instances where, unmanageably drunk, he took offense at and resisted the demand that he show his gismo for inspection (Eisenbud, 1967a; Reynolds, 1967), there was never any bar to inspection of Ted's gismo or his hands or of what he was doing between trials. When Ted handled the camera himself, moreover, no witness was ever denied the opportunity to look directly through his invariably empty gismo from any position deemed advantageous. Figure 5 shows what many witnesses saw and what any witness might have seen if he had taken the trouble to look over Ted's shoulder as he was shooting. Stevenson and Pratt (1968, 1969), who obtained a number of "abnormal" pictures in their work with Ted at the University of Virginia during interludes in the Denver studies, wrote in 1969: "We have ourselves observed Ted in approximately 800 trials, and we have never seen him act in a suspicious way in the handling of the gismo before or after a trial" (p. 359). And Pratt (1973), noting in his book *ESP Research Today* that no witness had ever reported any direct evidence pointing to Ted's use of trickery in several thousand trials, observed that "only a single clumsy action, one slip-up, would have been enough to expose him" (p. 114). The fact is that, despite claims on radio and television by some professional conjurers that it would be possible successfully to deploy a palmed gimmick under the conditions of observation obtaining during Ted's sessions, none have met a long-standing challenge (Eisenbud, 1967a) to attempt to do so—not hundreds of times, be it noted, but only often enough to demonstrate that it could be done at all. Several eminent conjurers have declined personal invitations to meet this challenge, while the ingenious efforts of one to avoid such a confrontation are now part of the record (Eisenbud, 1975a; Fuller, 1974).

Whether or not it might be possible to execute such sleight-of-hand under the conditions of observation employed with Ted is somewhat academic, however, as the relevance of such a possibility is drastically reduced when certain other features of Ted's work are taken into account. First, Ted on occasion has produced well-defined images in complete darkness and on unexposed, opaquely wrapped film pack (Eisenbud, 1970). (Unfortunately, his yield with film pack was too low to warrant spending much time on it.) Next were Ted's blackies and whities, which he produced by the hundreds under a variety of conditions—blackies at considerable distances from the camera (Eisenbud, 1972b) and whities with normal sources of light eliminated (Eisenbud, 1967b). He also produced an electronic equivalent of blackies with the film replaced by light sensors (Eisenbud, 1972b). Conjurers, not surprisingly, are unanimous in their avoidance of claims in these areas where the futility of plain or fancy gimickry is acknowledged. Finally, there was the separation of Ted from the camera, where the role of the gismo and anything it could possibly conceal was obviated entirely, and also the use of randomly selected target images. This last feature, despite the difficulties involved in the interpretation of some of the data, came to constitute, for some persons at least, as strong an argument against sleight-of-hand as any of the purely physically-based arguments.

Separation of Ted from the Camera

Ted undertook to wean himself from the camera and the gismo when he was at the peak of his productivity and increasingly confident of his powers. At first he would allow witnesses to trigger the camera, or to hold the gismo and trigger the camera while he held it, or to hold and trigger the camera while he held the gismo up to it. Finally, he allowed the cameras, sometimes two or three at a time, to be held at varying distances from him with gismos being held either by him, by the person holding and triggering the camera, or by a third person whom he would occasionally instruct in the art of its delicate manipulation. (The gismo was to be given a slight squeeze, for example, at the precise moment he signaled for the camera to be triggered.) At times Ted would operate an empty dummy camera while one or two of the loaded cameras were being triggered simultaneously by witnesses some feet from him (Eisenbud, 1974). Ted himself generally gave the signal to trigger, but now and then he would ask someone else to call the shot. Since it was early found that best results were achieved when Ted himself improvised the procedures used, it was left mostly up to him as to when the cameras would be given to others to operate.

Over a period of about a year beginning some 10 months after the start of the Denver studies, more than three dozen variegated images were produced with Ted separated from the camera at distances of 1 to 66 feet. These were observed on 12 occasions in nine separate locations by a dozen witnesses besides myself.

The chief significance of Ted's being separated from the camera was, as mentioned earlier, that such a maneuver completely eliminated the possibility of an unlooked-for image being produced normally (i.e., fraudulently) by anything on or about Ted or in his gismo. For this result to be achieved, it was not necessary for Ted to be separated from the camera by inches or feet; a fraction of an inch was sufficient. Figure 6 shows what resulted when the same auxiliary lens-transparency system that produced the picture shown in Figure 3 was held at a distance of ½ inch away from the camera lens and with the same 200-watt bulb used in the production of that picture at about the same distance from the camera. Nothing like an image can be discerned in the dark blob near center which represents the gimmick inside a gismo. One-quarter inch from the camera lens, which is actually less than the distance at which Ted frequently held his gismo when operating the camera himself (Figure 5), shows only a larger blob with the surrounding scene still coming through. More than ½ inch, even with gimmicks of larger diameter, would show decreasingly smaller blobs and more surrounding scene. The fact is that, given a separation of ¼ inch or more from the Polaroid camera, a conjurer can safely be allowed the use of any prop or gimmick of his choice—entirely in the open, and with no need to avoid detection—with complete assurance that no unexpected image will result. Just as certain is the important fact that the expected normal image cannot be made thus to disappear as it did in Ted's pictures (Eisenbud, 1974, p. 320, and Figure 6).

The pictures that were obtained with Ted at varying distances from the camera ranged from indistinct or embryonic forms of images gotten in clearer form under other circumstances to images about as clear as were ever obtained by him. So far as could be judged, the distinctness and the degree of "exposure" of the print had little to do with Ted's distance from the camera or, for that matter, with the amount of ambient light. Figure 7 shows an indistinct image obtained by Dr. Johann R. Marx holding a camera and gismo about 1 foot from Ted. It can be seen to be a partial representation of the unidentified scene (Figure 8) which emerged from Ted's camera some trials later during a triple shooting in which Dr. Henry Frey, standing about 3 feet away from Ted and manning a camera whose lens was covered by Dr. Marx's hand, obtained the impossible-to-duplicate montage shown in Figure 9. (All three shots were caught on 16-mm movies taken during this session.) Several days before this, Ted was operating a dummy camera while Dr. Laurence B. Hall, on Ted's instructions, stood behind a partition in a fairly dark room about 18 feet away and aimed his camera, to which Ted had had no access, at a typewriter a few inches away on a table. Figure 10 shows what he got—a partial whitie and some books on a shelf 90 degrees northward from the direction in which the camera was pointing. (This picture could not be duplicated in ordinary control shots.)

Two days later an unidentified image, shown in Figure 11, was obtained with a camera held by Dr. Aaron Paley and triggered at a signal given by Ted standing 66 feet away. This should normally have been a fairly dark print or a blackie as Dr. Paley, at Ted's improvised suggestion, was holding his camera and gismo "eyeball to eyeball" up to a camera and gismo (held up to the lens) by Dr. Frey. Ted hadn't been within 66 feet of either camera during several previous trials.

The more usual distance shot obtained with Ted is exemplified by one, shown in Figure 12, of two such gotten by Dr. F. Bruce Merrill when holding the camera and gismo about 2 feet away from Ted inside a radiology laboratory (Eisenbud and associates, 1968).

Several pictures (as well as blackies and whities) were obtained while Ted was separated from the camera by the wire screen door of a so-called Faraday cage, a room (with double steel walls in this case) lined with wire mesh to shield out radio waves. Two gismos were in use, one held inside the cage by Ted and one held outside by either James A. Hurry, a physicist who arranged and supervised the procedures, or myself. In a report of the experiment, Hurry (1967) wrote that "the cameras held either by Dr. Eisenbud or myself were at least one (1) foot or more from the subject [Ted] when [the picture shown in Figure 13] and others were obtained with Ted inside the shielded room and Dr. Eisenbud and myself outside . . ." In reference to this picture (Figure 13), Hurry wrote, "Dr. Eisenbud held the camera and I held the gismo on the outside of the shielded lab (door closed). I looked through the 'gismo' used by Ted in the inside of the room—there was nothing visible inside Ted's 'gismo'." Ted remained inside the Faraday cage from the time the experimentation began until it was concluded.

Target Responses

When the classical spirit photographers obtained extras of deceased members of sitters' families, they were, whether or not the objective of the sittings had been so defined, coming up with successful responses to implied target tasks. In cases where a correspondence was clear, and where the medium had no prior way of knowing who the sitter was to be (to say nothing of the sitter's relatives), the only way to circumvent a verdict of paranormality was to insinuate that the facts as given were incorrect or, as was frequently the case, to ignore the matter entirely. With Ted Serios this became more difficult to do.

It is obvious that if Ted were to produce a picture corresponding in an extra-chance matter to a target more or less randomly selected and about which he could have had no prior knowledge, the likelihood of this being accomplished through normal means (short of collusion) would be extremely small. Unfortunately, no figures can be given for the number of Ted's successful target responses for the reason that, except for a few that can be immediately perceived as correspondences close enough to warrant being rated as hits, most of the responses that can be considered relevant at all require some degree of interpretation. This simply does not lend itself to convenient techniques of quantification. Another difficulty is that in several instances (Eisenbud, 1972a; Eisenbud and associates, 1967) relevant connections between a given target and Ted's re-

Figure 1.

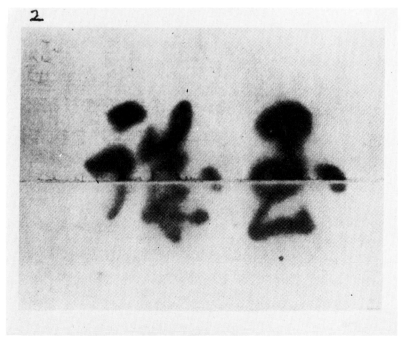

Figure 2.

Figure 3.

Figure 4.

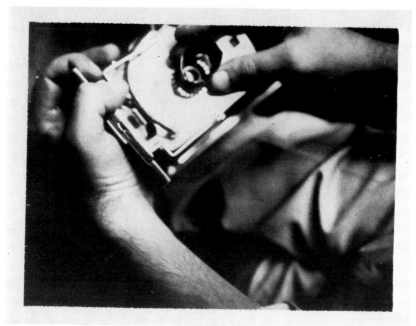

Figure 5.

Figure 6.

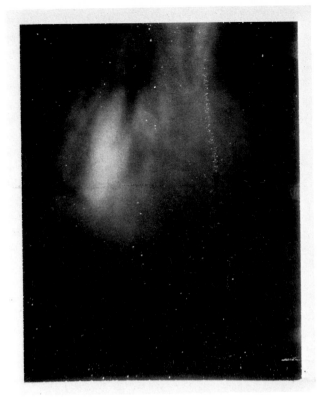

Figure 7.

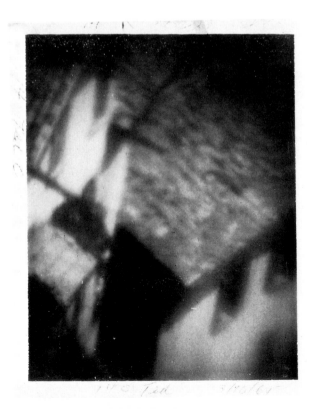

Figure 8.

Figure 9.

Figure 10.

Figure 11.

Figure 12.

Figure 13.

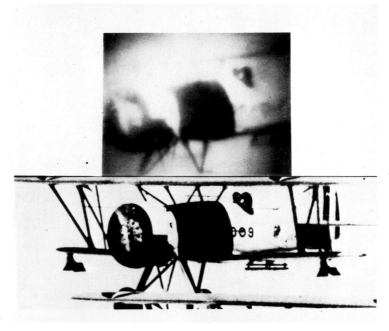

Figure 14.

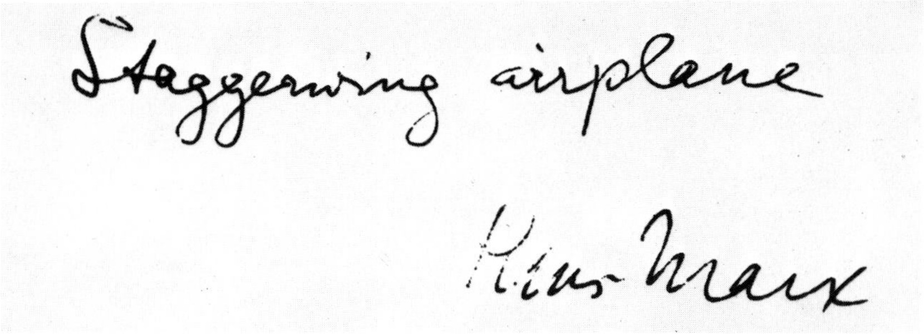

Staggerwing airplane

Klaus Marx

Figure 15.

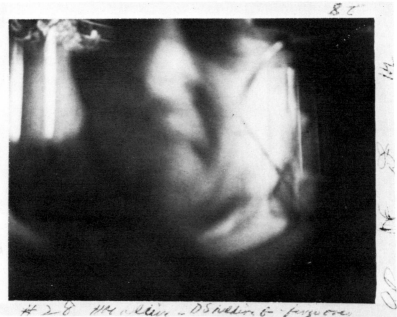

Figure 16.

Figure 17.

Figure 18.

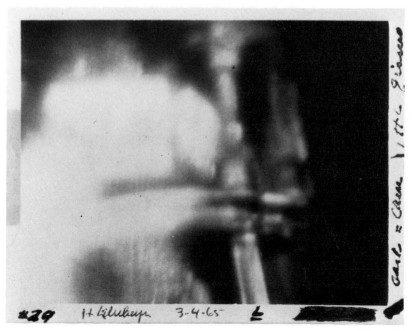

Figure 19.

Figure 20.

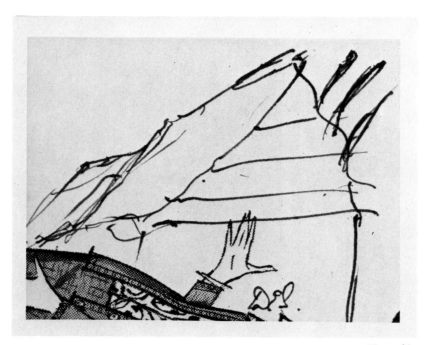

Figure 21.

Figure 22.

Figure 23.

Figure 24.

Figure 25.

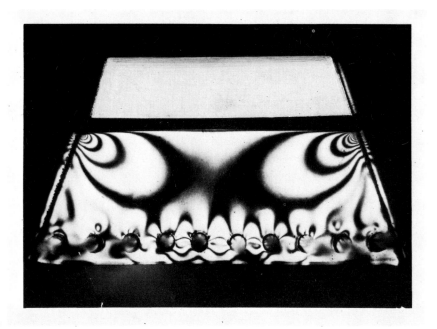

Figure 26.

Figure 27.

Figure 28.

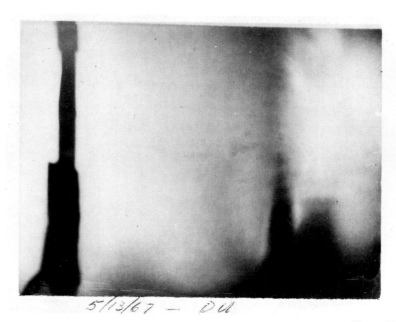

5/13/67 — DU

Figure 29

sponses were revealed only by chance a considerable time later, leading to the supposition that all returns may not yet be in. Ted was, nevertheless, able often enough to come through with responses of a striking nature—either intuitively striking or when relevant background material was known—to render normal hypotheses highly improbable.

Ted generally requested that targets be hidden from him, and he tended to do as well with hidden targets as with targets he was allowed to see. Striking responses to a hidden target occurred in a session in which target ideas ("The Statue of Liberty," "The Great Wall of China," and other suggestions) were written on slips of paper by each of six witnesses. Without having been shown to either Ted or me, the slips were handed to a notetaker for safekeeping (Eisenbud and associates, 1967). During the session Ted came up with five versions of an unidentifiable image that was referred to at one point in the notes as a "lobster" and at another as a "spider." Through a series of chance events, it was found almost 2 years later that the clearest of these images (Figure 14, upper) was a "copy" (though a poor one) of a picture of an airplane in one of Ted's own books (Figure 14, lower). Then it was recalled that one of the six hidden targets of that session had been a "staggerwing airplane." Luckily, the slip on which this was written was still among the notes of the session (Figure 15). The plane in Figure 14 was identified in Ted's book as a "Marine F-4 B staggerwing."[2] Another print that turned up during this session shows, approximately where Ted's right eye is hidden in the shadow, what appears to be a staggerwing plane seen head-on (Figure 16). This print, obtained on a camera held by one witness about 1 foot from Ted, should normally have been a blackie as a second witness, at Ted's suggestion, had his finger over the open end of the gismo he was holding in front of the camera lens (see Figure 40 in Eisenbud, 1967b). The other structures in the print (Figure 16) have not been identified.

Another instance of a striking correspondence occurred when Ted was asked to get a close-up of one of his own typically chiaroscuro pictures, itself a target hit of sorts (Eisenbud, 1967b, p. 187). This picture, shown in Figure 17, has since been identified as that of a portion of Munich's City Hall (Figure 18), but with the dancing figures apparently reversed and possibly somewhat altered. Ted didn't oblige with his close-up until several shots later, when the print

[2] Some persons (e.g., Randi, 1968) have felt that Ted's ownership of the book which was the apparent source of the pictures corresponding to one of the targets was suggestive of possible fraud (on Ted's part, presumably). The fact, however, that Ted himself—purely gratuitously, it would seem—drew attention to the ownership of the book does not support such an hypothesis. Indeed, if Ted did wish to perpetrate such a fraud (assuming that it would have been possible for him to do so, given the circumstances under which the pictures were obtained), he could easily have disposed of his book during the (almost) 2 years that elapsed before the discovery of its relevance and contrived to have the significant correspondences come to light, as if by chance, in some other manner. The fact that nothing of this sort actually did occur would therefore seem, if anything, to strengthen rather than weaken the case for paranormality in this instance.

shown in Figure 19 came through. This was obtained on a "lensless" camera[3] held about 3 feet away from him, up to which Dr. Henry Lehrburger held a gismo. Even though this doesn't show dancing figures (which were really what was wanted) and appears to have been "shot" from a different angle, it is plainly a version either of the structure shown in Figures 17 and 18 or of one very much like it.

Most of what might be adjudged successful responses by Ted showed varying degrees of distortion and transformation of the target image of the kind seen in experiments in tachistoscopic perception, eidetic imagery, and in fact in tele-pathic drawing experiments (see, e.g., Warcollier, 1938). The lines along which such distortions and transformations took place were, as in much normal and dream imagery, configurational and ideational, sometimes both. An instance of a pure configurational transformation occurred in response to a target picture, shown in Figure 20, chosen randomly from a book. Ted scarcely looked at this picture before the book was shut, whereupon he drew on a piece of newspaper his general impression of it (Figure 21). Then, after a few blackies and whities, he came up with four versions of the image shown in Figure 22. It can be seen to represent a sort of condensation of the target and Ted's sketched impressions of it. (The image shown in Figure 12 represents a similar condensation.)

In another instance in which it was not too difficult to perceive the configura-tional relevance of Ted's distorted response, the target, whose impromptu selec-tion was made shortly after the session had begun, was an etching of a medieval town (Figure 23). Ted indicated that he would not get exactly the buildings shown (the target was not hidden in this instance) but something *like* them. He then proceeded to get the prints shown in Figures 24 and 25. The first exhibits the general conformation and grouping of the buildings in the target picture, as well as the prominently displayed angle of the roof. Both prints show the Roman archway theme. The second print, which Ted indicated would be a de-parture from the actual target, also showed interesting departures from its known original source (Eisenbud, 1967b, p. 167).

An example of a response in which transformation of a target picture took place along ideational lines is seen in Figure 13, cited earlier in connection with shots where Ted was separated from the camera. The target which Ted selected out of a batch of several shown him was a picture of stress lines in a belt section (Figure 26). Ted saw this as "eyes looking at a line of people," which is what three pairs of eyes in Figure 13 can be said to be doing. (The idea of a parade

---

[3] Model 95 Polaroid cameras from which an optically essential part of the lens system had been removed were called "lensless." Their use in tests with Ted became largely pointless when it was discovered that fairly clear images could be obtained with them when certain auxiliary lens-transparency devices were held flat against the forward lenses that had been left in as dust shields.

or troop review may have been suggested by the fact that the session took place on Washington's Birthday.)

Many of Ted's responses were more cryptic than this, and some seemed to have been based upon unconscious equations that perhaps only the clinically trained depth psychologist would appreciate to best advantage (Eisenbud, 1967b, pp. 194ff). It was precisely responses of this sort, however, that brought the highest degree of conviction to some persons as to the paranormality of Ted's productions, as such responses are more consistent with the type of creative work of the mind seen in dreams and other types of unconscious elaborations than the more direct hits. (The remarkable thing, in fact, is that Ted was able to obtain any of the latter at all, as the problem would seem to be something like having to produce a dream on a consciously selected theme.)

REPORTS OF OTHER PRESENT-DAY PARANORMAL PHOTOGRAPHERS

Of the handful of persons other than Ted currently known to claim paranormal photographic ability, the only ones who have been investigated to any noteworthy extent are the Russian physical psychic known as Nina Kulagina and three members of the Veilleux family of Waterville, Maine. Kulagina has allegedly been able to fog film and to impress on it simple patterns like plus signs (Herbert, 1972; *Journal of Paraphysics*, 1971; Kulagin, 1971). The Veilleux family, father Joseph and grown sons Alfred and Richard, claim several hundred paranormal Polaroid prints since the beginning of this aspect of their variegated paranormal experience in 1967 (Eisenbud, 1975b; Smith, 1974). Many of their pictures are in the style of the classical extras, but a number are full-frame prints of persons and scenes (some still unidentified) much in the manner of Ted Serios. Although none of these pictures have been obtained under conditions which conclusively eliminate normal means of image production (Waterville is not located near major centers of research, for one thing), a sufficient number of foggings, bleachings, and other anomalies have been witnessed under restrictive enough conditions to warrant continued investigative efforts (Artley, 1969; Eisenbud, 1975b; Rindge, Cook, and Owen, 1972).

In addition to Kulagina, the Veilleux, and others who claim to get paranormal photos repeatedly, there are persons professing no particular paranormal ability who have nevertheless obtained a number of possibly paranormal photographs during some particular period of stress in their lives. One university professor claimed to have fogged all film she handled over a period of several years, after which this unwanted tendency ceased and she was again able to take ordinary snapshots. A considerable number of persons, moreover, have claimed single instances of seemingly inexplicable pictures or extras. These too, judging from some that have come to my attention, appear to have been associated with stress or high motivation: for example, a child obtaining, on an ordinary snapshot, an extra of her father long absent on military duty in Vietnam; a mother who had not been heard from for a long time appearing as an extra alongside a girl posing for a graduation snapshot. An officer of a large film manufacturing concern which receives hundreds of such reports annually is certain that every one of the pictures can be explained by intentional or unintentional double-exposure. But it would seem unwarranted to make any judgment at all where the circumstances involved are not thoroughly known. Several persons who sent me pictures that baffled them claimed that double-exposure was impossible on the cameras they used.

In any event, the factors that go into the ability to obtain paranormal photographs are still obscure. If the ability is related to anything that goes on in the brain, this has yet to be demonstrated. Nothing unusual showed up when Ted Serios obtained excellent images while being monitored electroencephalographically (Eisenbud, 1967b, pp. 254–255). Other areas remain equally dark. While many of the classical spirit photographers were known as gifted mediums, other strong psychics and mediums have reported little or nothing along paranormal photography lines. Even Uri Geller, who has been said to have produced simple geometric designs on Polaroid prints while experimenting with Kirlian photography (Skutch, 1973) and has allegedly been able to obtain images of his face through the barrier of a lens cap (Reynolds, 1974), has apparently not come up with anything like the intricately patterned extras that ordinary persons seem to have called out of thin air in moments of stress or longing. Whatever is involved in paranormal photographic ability, finally, does not appear to be related to any particular type of personality structure, if we can judge from the seeming lack of features common to the devoutly religious William Hope (Fodor, 1966), the "humble white mouse of a person" Mrs. Deane (Doyle, 1923), the ambitious and socially inclined John Myers (Barbanell, 1964), the impulsive and erratic Ted Serios (Eisenbud, 1967b), and the rather different from the others and from each other Veilleux (Eisenbud, 1975b, Smith, 1974).

THE ENERGY PROBLEM

As to what modes of information or energy transfer might be involved in paranormal photography, all that can be said at present is that not only is there no direct evidence pointing to any known process, but there are many data radically restricting the conceivable possibilities. If we accept Fukurai's account (1931), his subject would seem to have ruled out all known radiative possibilities with one stroke when she succeeded in imprinting only the middle photographic plate of a three-decker film sandwich. (This was subsequently done by other Fukurai subjects.) The Serios data not only do not contradict this result but add to it confirmation upon confirmation. To begin with, the type of film used is not sensitive to electrostatic or magnetic field forces or to infrared radiations; and although it is sensitive to beta and gamma radiations, not a trace of these was picked up when Ted obtained several target hits while being monitored in a whole body radiation counting chamber (Eisenbud, 1967b, p. 258). Ordinary shielding ruled out visible and ultraviolet light, as well as any unlikely effects from alpha radiation (Eisenbud, 1967b, 1970). Shielding with several thicknesses of leaded x-ray glass in and out of radiology laboratories effectively eliminated x-ray as a possibility (Eisenbud, 1967b; Eisenbud and associates, 1968), while the Faraday cage experiment (cited earlier) provided high enough attenuation to virtually eliminate all long-wave radio and radar waves. No plausible hypothesis, finally, has been advanced to account for blackies, their electronic equivalent with photo cells, and the fact that (in Ted's case, anyway) normal light rays have to be somehow blocked out each time a paranormal image is obtained.

The enigmatic nature of the physical aspects of paranormal photography goes beyond the mere absence of positive data on radiations or fields; major phenomenological inconsistencies and anomalies in what data we have add to the puzzle. This can be illustrated by a series of prints obtained in a 1973 session with Ted. Figure 27 shows a partial whitie which immediately followed an almost total blackie on a fresh roll of film. Ted's face, which was normally seen when (as in this instance) he held the camera pointing at himself, is completely bleached out. (My on-the-spot notation on this print was "Where Ted?") Cardboard bars used (in a series of experiments not yet reported) for mounting sensors immediately in front of the film are seen, as they normally were, as strong black shadows. In the next shot (Figure 28), however, these bars have all but disappeared; only the dim gray shadow of part of one of them shows on a print which is otherwise without a molecule remaining on its surface. (The grayish tone of the reproduction in Figure 28 doesn't quite do this justice.) The following shot was a control done by David Clint, a professional photographer on the staff of Denver University. It showed the bars again and, as expected, Clint's face. All of this took place within 3 or 4 minutes.

Now there is no conceivable normal way of bleaching out the bars as shown in Figure 28 with visible light entering the camera through the lens or otherwise. (If the shutter were kept open 60 seconds the black bars would still remain.) And, as in Fukurai's experiment, penetrating radiation would have been expected to have affected other film in the roll. The question then is: what acted upon the molecules of the film surface through or behind the bars, and how did it circumvent the bars to get to these molecules? (Figure 29, which shows a print of an earlier experiment in which "light" seems to be curling around a bar almost like a fluid, does not provide the answer.) Why, finally, did this happen on this occasion and not at other times?

It is tempting to imagine that there might be an as yet undiscovered realm of causation in which what takes place in paranormal photography would be found to be mediated by an identifiable process that would follow some sort of lawful pattern. But this would at best merely push the essential problem one step backward. This problem, as in all psi phenomena, is: What governs whatever physical or quasi-physical mode of causation that may yet turn out to be involved? Simply to say "mind" is not entirely satisfactory. Whether the problem will ever be formulated and dealt with in clearer form is anybody's guess.

REFERENCES

Artley, J. Report of a visit to the Veilleux family. Personal communication, 1969

Barbanell, M. *He Walks in Two Worlds: The Story of John Myers.* London: Jenkins, 1964.

Barlow, F., and Rampling-Rose, W. Report of an investigation into spirit-photography. *Proceedings of the Society for Psychical Research,* 1933, **41**, 121-138.

Carrington, H. *Modern Psychical Phenomena.* New York: Dodd, Mead, 1919.

Carrington, H. Experiences in psychic photography. *Journal of the American Society for Psychical Research,* 1925, **19**, 258-267.

Carrington, H. We photographed thoughts. *Fate,* June, 1953, 64-72.

Coates, J. *Photographing the Invisible.* London: Fowler, 1911.

Cook, C. H. Experiments in photography. *Journal of the American Society for Psychical Research,* 1916, **10**, 1-56, 57-63.

Cushman, A. S. An evidential case of spirit photography. *Journal of the American Society for Psychical Research,* 1922, **16**, 132-151.

Doyle, A. C. *The Case for Spirit Photography.* New York: Doran, 1923.

Edmunds, S. *"Spirit" Photography.* London: The Society for Psychical Research, 1965.

Eisenbud, J. The cruel, cruel world of Ted Serios. *Popular Photography,* November, 1967, 31ff. (a)

Eisenbud, J. *The World of Ted Serios.* New York: Morrow, 1967. (b)

Eisenbud, J. Correspondence: Light and the Serios images. *Journal of the Society for Psychical Research,* 1970, **45**, 424-427.

Eisenbud, J. Gedanken zur Psychofotographie und Verwandten. *Zeitschrift für Parapsychologie und Grenzgebiete der Psychologie,* 1972, **14**, 1-11. (a) (Reprinted in E. Bauer, Ed., *Psi und Psyche,* pp. 37-44. Stuttgart: Deutsche Verlags–Anstalt, 1974.)

Eisenbud, J. The Serios "blackies" and related phenomena. *Journal of the American Society for Psychical Research,* 1972, **66**, 180-192. (b)

Eisenbud, J. Psychic photography and thoughtography. In E. D. Mitchell and others (ed. by J. White), *Psychic Exploration: A Challenge for Science,* pp. 314-331. New York: Putnam's, 1974.

Eisenbud, J. Correspondence: On Ted Serios alleged "confession." *Journal of the American Society for Psychical Research,* 1975, **69**, 94-96. (a)

Eisenbud, J. The merveilleux Veilleux. *Fate,* Part I, November, 1975, 46-54; Part II, December, 1975, 72-81. (b)

Eisenbud, J., and associates. Some unusual data from a session with Ted Serios. *Journal of the American Society for Psychical Research,* 1967, **61**, 241-253.

Eisenbud, J., and associates. Two experiments with Ted Serios. *Journal of the American Society for Psychical Research,* 1968, **62**, 309-320.

Eisenbud, J., and associates. An archeological *tour de force* with Ted Serios. *Journal of the American Society for Psychical Research,* 1970, **64**, 40-52. (a)

Eisenbud, J., and associates. Two camera and television experiments with Ted Serios. *Journal of the American Society for Psychical Research,* 1970, **64**, 261-276. (b)

Eisendrath, D. B. An amazing weekend with the amazing Ted Serios. Part II. *Popular Photography,* October, 1967, 85ff.

Fodor, N. *Encyclopaedia of Psychic Science*. New Hyde Park, N.Y.: University Books, 1966.

Frey, H., Lehrburger, H., Marx, J. R., Merrill, F. B., Paley, A., and Wheeler, B. W. Correspondence. *Journal of the American Society for Psychical Research*, 1968, 62, 330-331.

Fukurai, T. *Clairvoyance and Thoughtography*. London: Rider, 1931.

Fuller, C. Dr. Jule Eisenbud vs. the Amazing Randi. *Fate*, August, 1974, 65-74.

Henslow, G. *The Proofs of the Truth of Spiritualism*. New York: Dodd, Mead, 1919.

Herbert, B. Report on Nina Kulagina. *Parapsychology Review*, 1972, 3, 8-10.

Hurry, J. A. Letter of June 4, 1967, to Dr. R. A. McConnell (copy sent to Dr. J. Eisenbud).

Hyslop, J. H. (Trans.). Experiments of Dr. Ochorowicz. Report of a commission of naturalists. *Journal of the American Society for Psychical Research*, 1911, 5, 678-730.

Hyslop, J. H. Some unusual phenomena in photography. *Proceedings of the American Society for Psychical Research*, 1914, 8, 395-465.

Hyslop, J. H. Review of *Photographing the Invisible*, by J. Coates. *Journal of the American Society for Psychical Research*, 1915, 9, 148-175.

Johnson, G. L. *Does Man Survive? The Great Problem of the Life Hereafter and the Evidence for its Solution*. New York: Harper, 1936.

Joire, P. *Psychical and Supernormal Phenomena*. Chicago: Marlowe Press, 1916.

Journal of the American Society for Psychical Research, 1925, 19, 417-419. (Unsigned statement, "Our foreign research officer.")

Journal of Paraphysics, 1971, 5, back cover.

Kulagin, V. V. Nina S. Kulagina. *Journal of Paraphysics*, 1971, 5, 54-62.

McKenzie, J. H. Fraud charges in psychic photography: The Price-Hope case. *Psychic Science*, 1923, 1, 378-394. (a)

McKenzie, J. H. The "Price-Hope" case: Conclusion. *Psychic Science*, 1923, 2, 58-62. (b)

Morris, F. A history of psychic photography. *Fate*, March, 1967, 69-85.

Morse, J. J. *A Brief History of Spirit Photography*. Manchester, England: Two Worlds Publishing Company, 1909.

Mumler, W. H. *Personal Experiences of William H. Mumler in Spirit Photography*. Boston: Colby and Rich, 1875.

Ochorowicz, J. Les mains fluidiques et la photographie de la pensée. *Annales des Sciences Psychiques*, 1912, 22, 97-104, 147-153, 164-170, 204-209.

Oehler, P. The psychic photography of Ted Serios. *Fate*, December, 1962, 68-82.

Oehler, P. Personal communication, 1964.

Pratt, J. G. *ESP Research Today: A Study of Developments in Parapsychology Since 1960*. Metuchen, N. J.: Scarecrow Press, 1973.

Price, H. A case of fraud with the Crewe circle. *Journal of the Society for Psychical Research*, 1922, 20, 271-283.

Price, H. Psychic photography: Some scientific aids to spurious phenomena. *Journal of the American Society for Psychical Research*, 1925, 19, 570-587, 617-636.

Randi, J. ("The Amazing Randi"). Correspondence. *Popular Photography*, January, 1968, 4.

Reynolds, C. An amazing weekend with the amazing Ted Serios. Part I. *Popular Photography*, October, 1967, 81ff.

Reynolds, C. The making of a psychic. *Popular Photography*, June, 1974, 74ff.

Rindge, J. P., Cook, W., and Owen, A. R. G. An investigation of psychic photography with the Veilleux family. *New Horizons*, 1972, 1, 28-32.

Ross, I. *The President's Wife, Mary Todd Lincoln*. New York: Putnam's, 1973.

Sidgwick, E. M. (Mrs. H.). On spirit photographs; A reply to Mr. A. R. Wallace. *Proceedings of the Society for Psychical Research*, 1891, 7, 268-289.

Skutch, J. Personal communication, 1973.

Smith, S. Psychic photography in Maine. *Psychic*, September/October, 1974, 13-18.

Stevenson, I., and Pratt, J. G. Exploratory investigations of the psychic photography of Ted Serios. *Journal of the American Society for Psychical Research*, 1968, **62**, 103–129.

Stevenson, I., and Pratt, J. G. Further investigations of the psychic photography of Ted Serios. *Journal of the American Society for Psychical Research*, 1969, **63**, 352–364.

Sudre, R. *Parapsychology*. New York: Citadel Press, 1960.

Taylor, J. T. "Spirit photography" with remarks on fluorescence. *British Journal of Photography*, March 17, 1893, 167–169.

Tubby, G. O. Notes and comment. *Journal of the American Society for Psychical Research*, 1924, **18**, 299–300.

Wallace, A. R. *On Miracles and Modern Spiritualism*. London: Burns, 1874.

Warcollier, R. *Experimental Telepathy*. Boston: Boston Society for Psychic Research, 1938.

Warrick, F. W. *Experiments in Psychics*. New York: Dutton, 1939.

Part V

PARAPSYCHOLOGY AND ALTERED STATES OF CONSCIOUSNESS

1

Psi and Internal
Attention States

Charles Honorton

INTRODUCTION

Psi interactions involve information flow between events or processes in the outer environment and sensorially-noncontingent internal processes or events within the organism. In this chapter, we will explore the role of *internal attention states* in the detection and recognition of psi interactions. I will use this term to designate any condition in which conscious awareness is maintained in the absence of patterned exteroceptive and proprioceptive information. These conditions include spontaneously generated states, such as hypnagogic reverie, as well as those which are deliberately induced, such as meditation and hypnosis.

In order to promote conceptual clarity and avoid controversies which are irrelevant to this discussion, I shall use traditional "state" terms, such as hypnosis and meditation as operational designations of specific techniques or procedures for inducing internal attention states, rather than as descriptors of hypothetical attributes of such states. Similarly, I shall use traditional parapsychological terms, such as telepathy, clairvoyance, and precognition as operational designations of specific experimental procedures for detecting and measuring psi interactions, rather than as phenomenal categories for discrete processes.

We will mainly be concerned with the following questions. Do internal attention states enhance the detection of psi interactions? If so, how is this accomplished, and what is the common denominator underlying such enhancement? These questions are of considerable interest, both in terms of practical applications and theoretical implications. On the level of practical application, we will be primarily interested in the utilization of internal attention states in the development of techniques for the reliable production of psi interactions. On the level of theory, we will be concerned with the extent to which internal attention states provide a framework for assimilating a wide array of parapsychological findings.

INTERNAL ATTENTION STATES AND PSI DETECTION CRITERIA

Let us begin by briefly examining the conditions which are necessary for the detection of a psi interaction. Suppose that the output of an information source serves as an influence on a sensorially-remote receiver. In order for the receiver influence to be detected and identified with its source, each of the following conditions is necessary and must be fulfilled:

1. The receiver influence must be detected. With human receivers, this means that the influence must take the form of a conscious experience which the receiver can and does attend to.
2. The experience must be sufficiently prominent, or carry sufficient impact, to allow the receiver to distinguish it from among the many other (nonpsi) inputs which are concurrently influencing him. In this context, normal perceptual, somatic, and cognitive influences on the receiver constitute sources of noise.
3. The experience must be retained and reported prior to receiver-source contact through normal channels; otherwise it is not evidential of psi interaction.
4. There must be subsequent confirmation of a meaningful correspondence between the source output and the receiver output. Such correspondence need not be literal or exact—there may be information loss—but it must be sufficiently accurate and consistent over repeated transmissions to eliminate chance coincidence as a reasonable explanation.

These detection criteria account for some of the most prominent features of spontaneous psi experiences. The high incidence of psi interactions between friends and relatives, and the low incidence between remote acquaintances and strangers (Stevenson, 1970), would be expected, since there is naturally a greater likelihood of confirmation in the former case. Unless receiver and source know each other and come into frequent contact, the probability of confirmation is very low. Furthermore, unless the relationship between them permits some degree of intimacy, it is unlikely that they would be sufficiently uninhibited to share unusual personal experiences.

Similarly, the high incidence of "crisis" cases, involving information pertaining to unexpected situations of emotional importance to the receiver, would be expected, since such experiences will more likely be recognized by the receiver as unusual, thereby increasing attention to them and increasing the likelihood that they will be retained and reported.

The high incidence of spontaneous psi experiences which are mediated through dreams and other internal attention states (Rhine, 1962) makes especially good sense when viewed in relation to these detection criteria. Since such states are associated with deafferentation (sensory-somatic noise reduction) and deployment of attention toward internal processes such as thoughts and images, which can mediate psi information into consciousness, internal attention states should increase the likelihood of initial detection of psi interactions.

It is obvious that these detection criteria are seldom all fulfilled in everyday life situations, and it now seems likely that those psi interactions which are detected and recognized are merely the tip of the proverbial iceberg. C. D. Broad (1953) went so far as to suggest that psi interactions may be occurring continuously on an unconscious level, affecting our moods and dispositions in subtle ways. Broad distinguished between psi *interactions* which may occur without conscious registration, and psi *experiences* which are detected and represented in consciousness.

Support for the hypothesis that psi interactions are much more common than psi experiences is available from both spontaneous case studies and experimental studies. It is suggested by case studies involving noncognitive "intuition" or "impression" cases (Rhine, 1962; Stevenson, 1970) and in cases of mundane psi "coincidences" (Heywood, 1964). Experimental support for this hypothesis has come in recent years from a series of studies involving nonintentional psi interactions (Kreitler and Kreitler, 1972; Stanford, 1974). The primary importance of this to the discussion of psi and internal states is that it shifts attention from the popular but unanswerable question of what conditions are necessary for the *occurrence* of psi interactions to what conditions are necessary for their *detection*.

MEDITATION

Psychophysical Noise Reduction

The association between psi and meditation can be traced back as far as the *Vedas* of ancient India. Claims of *siddhis* ("paranormal powers") manifest as by-products of meditation were common in all of the early writings on yoga. Patanjali, who is generally regarded as the founder of the Raja system of yoga, devoted one of the four chapters of his *Yoga Sutras* to the classification of *siddhis*. Patanjali's dates are unknown, but he is believed to have lived around 1500 B.C. His *Yoga Sutras* is the oldest surviving textbook of yoga and has been translated with commentaries by various Indian scholars (Mishra, 1967; Prabhavananda and Isherwood, 1953; Taimni, 1961; Vivekananda, 1955). The eight stages of Raja yoga may be described as a progressive system of psychophysical noise reduction.

Reducing External Distractions. The first five stages were designed to systematically reduce the external causes of mental distraction. The first two stages (*Yama* and *Niyama*) involve the reduction of distractions associated with emotion and desire. The second two (*Asana* and *Pranayama*) involve reduction of somatic distractions. The fifth stage (*Pratyahara*) involves detaching attention from the sensory organs in order to isolate consciousness from external perception.

Reducing Internal Distractions. Freed from external somatosensory noise, the last three stages of Patanjali's system involve the elimination of internal cognitive distractions. This is accomplished by maintaining attention on a single object or image. These three stages designate increasing durations of concentration. The object of concentration serves to focus and limit attention within a narrowly-defined area. Concentration (*Dharana*) is achieved when attention is confined within the boundaries of a single object or image for a specified period of time. In this stage, attention is free to fluctuate within the defined area but may not wander outside of it. Meditation (*Dhyana*) involves the maintenance of concentration for a longer period of time. It is characterized by less movement of attention within the boundaries of the object or image, which is experienced with greater continuity. In the final stage (*Samadhi*), concentration is maintained for a still longer period. This stage is characterized by total continuity of attention on the object or image. Attention is said to be "absorbed" in the object and there is a dissolution of subject-object differentiation which is associated with an experience of transcending space-time. Collectively, these last three stages constitute a process which Patanjali calls *Samyama*. According to Patanjali, paranormal phenomena may be produced by performing *Samyama*.

Psychophysiological Correlates. The claim that meditation can be used to effectively tune out environmental stimulation is supported by psychophysiological studies. During meditation, the organism is shut down to a slow idle, with significant decreases in oxygen consumption and heart rate. Decreases in responsiveness to external stimulation are associated with increases in skin resistance and EEG alpha rhythm activity (Wallace, 1970; Wallace, Benson, and Wilson, 1971). Advanced practitioners of yoga meditation show particularly strong increases in alpha abundance and amplitude, a progressive slowing of the dominant alpha frequency, and the absence of normal alpha blocking response to photic stimulation (Anand, Chhina, and Singh, 1961).

Experimental Studies of Psi and Meditation

The first systematic study of psi and meditation was by Gertrude Schmeidler (1970). The subjects were six graduate students in an experimental psychology course given by Schmeidler. With one exception, the students were described as having little knowledge or interest in either parapsychology or meditation. Each completed a psi guessing task before and after instructions in yoga meditation and a breathing exercise administered by an Indian swami. Psi performance prior to the meditation period was at chance, while postmeditation psi performance was significantly above chance ($P = .01$). Given the small number of trials per subject and the fact that psi guessing procedures usually yield very low information rates (Honorton, 1975), these results are quite impressive.

Three correlational studies of psi and meditation were performed by Osis and Bokert (1971). Weekly meditation sessions were held at the American Society for Psychical Research, and the participants were encouraged to use their own preferred techniques of meditation. Two psi tasks were employed. One was a closed-circuit TV version of the Brugmans test in which the psi receiver attempted to locate a target square on a checkerboard array, while a remote sender monitored the receiver's success on a TV screen. The second psi task was a pictorial slide retrieval test. Changes in state of consciousness associated with meditation were assessed by means of scaled-item questionnaires and transcripts of subjects' descriptions. Pre- and post-session questionnaires were administered. The psi tasks were performed after the meditation periods. Questionnaire material was factor-analyzed, and three stable factors emerged, one of which ("Self-transcendence and Openness") appeared to be related to psi performance. It is difficult, however, to assess the validity of these findings because of the large number of analyses which were performed on the data. Also, the post-session questionnaire relations to psi performance are of questionable validity inasmuch as the subjects' knowledge of their success on the psi tasks could have served as an influence on their subsequent questionnaire responses (Palmer and Lieberman, 1975). No analysis was presented of overall psi performance in relation to meditation.

Dukhan and Rao (1973) reported a series of experimental studies on psi and yoga meditation with students of an ashram in South India. These investigators used the term *meditation* to designate a combination of practices: Mandala gazing, pranayama (breath control), kundalini yoga, mantra yoga, and karma yoga. A blind-matching psi guessing task was employed. Each student was tested individually before and after meditation, over a series of sessions. In each experiment, the participants were divided into two groups, "juniors" who were just beginning to study meditation, and "seniors" who were more advanced practitioners.

The first experiment constituted a pilot study and involved 27 students, all Westerners attending a residential yoga teacher training course. The juniors obtained significant psi-missing results in the premeditation condition and significant psi-hitting in the postmeditation condition. The difference between conditions was significant. The seniors produced chance results in both conditions.

The second experiment involved 18 students, again, all Westerners. The

TABLE 1. PROBABILITIES ASSOCIATED WITH CARD-MATCHING
PERFORMANCE IN THE DUKHAN AND RAO EXPERIMENTS ON THE EFFECTS OF
MEDITATION ON PSI GUESSING PERFORMANCE

Study	Juniors			Seniors		
	Pre-	Post-	Diff.	Pre-	Post-	Diff.
Pilot	.005	.03	.01	n.s.	n.s.	n.s.
Expt. 1	.0001	.0001	6.5×10^{-5}	.03	.02	.004
Expt. 2	.006	n.s.	.05	.01	.00012	.006
Combined	10^{-6}	10^{-4}	10^{-5}	.012	10^{-4}	2×10^{-4}

Note: The combined analysis was not reported by Dukhan and Rao. It was computed by
the author using the formula $\chi^2 = -2 \log_e P$, with 2 *df* per entry (J. P. Guilford, *Fundamental Statistics in Psychology and Education*. New York: McGraw-Hill, 1956, p. 245). In this
and later evaluations involving combining probabilities from different series, where nonsignificant results are reported without specifying the *P*-value, I have assumed the worst case
(i.e., *P* = .99).

juniors obtained highly significant psi-missing in the premeditation condition,
equally significant psi-hitting in the postmeditation condition, and a significant
difference between conditions. The seniors also produced significant psi-missing
in the premeditation condition, significant psi-hitting in the postmeditation
condition, and a significant difference between conditions.

The third and final study involved 14 students, all Indians and practicing
Hindus. The juniors obtained significant psi-missing results in the premeditation
condition, nonsignificant results in the postmeditation condition, and a significant difference between conditions. The seniors obtained significant psi-missing
in the premeditation condition, highly significant psi-hitting in the postmeditation
condition, and a significant difference between conditions. The significance
levels obtained in these studies are given in Table 1.

The occurrence of highly significant psi-missing in the premeditation conditions
of these experiments raises a question as to whether these truly remarkable
results were due to the practice of meditation, *per se*, or to the practitioners'
expectations and motivation to produce higher scores following meditation. This
interpretation seems particularly appropriate in the first two studies where all of
the participants were Westerners who had traveled great distances to study yoga
meditation and who were probably very eager to demonstrate the benefits of
such practices in an experimental setting that was quite obviously designed to do
just that. For this reason, it appears that the same-subjects design is not appropriate for research of this type. It is to be hoped that the work of Dukhan and
Rao will be followed up and extended in such a way as to more specifically
pinpoint the contributions of meditation apart from the motivations and expectations of the meditator. This, of course, is a problem which plagues meditation
research in general and is not limited to parapsychological studies.

A number of exceptionally gifted psi practitioners (e.g., Lalsingh Harribance, Malcolm Bessent) routinely utilize meditation techniques in preparation for psi testing sessions. Unfortunately, only one study has thus far been reported involving the efficacy of such preparation with gifted subjects. Stanford and Palmer (1973) conducted a pilot study with Bessent in which he attempted to engage psi in order to provide descriptions of 20 remote target persons. Prior to each session, he meditated with eyes closed for 15-20 minutes while EEG activity was monitored from the right occipital cortex. Overall psi results were not statistically significant, though a post-hoc analysis of EEG frequency data showed a tendency for stronger psi deviations to be contributed by sessions in which Bessent produced a relatively high mean alpha frequency during the meditation period ($P < .005$).

Although not strictly comparable, conceptually dissimilar findings were reported by Stanford and Stevenson (1972). Occipital EEG data were taken from the receiver who used meditation techniques to prepare for retrieval of pictorial targets viewed by a remote sender. The EEG record was marked to distinguish "mind-clearing" and "image-development" periods. Slower EEG alpha frequencies during the mind-clearing phase were associated with higher psi performance ($P < .035$), and superior psi performance was associated with an acceleration of EEG alpha frequency from the mind-clearing phase to the image-formation period ($P < .03$). The overall psi results were not statistically significant. These findings replicated two earlier studies involving nonmeditators (Stanford, 1971; Stanford and Lovin, 1970).

Several studies have been reported involving meditation and psychokinetic performance. Matas and Pantas (1971) compared PK performance in two groups of subjects. One group consisted of 25 subjects who had pursued some form of meditation for at least 6 months prior to the experiment. The other group consisted of 25 visitors or students who had expressed interest in being tested but who had not practiced any form of meditation. The meditation group was given 15 minutes to meditate prior to the PK task, and the procedure was otherwise identical for the two groups. The subjects were tested individually for PK influence on an electronic random event generator. Their task was to concentrate on a globe lamp and keep it turned on. The meditation group was successful in keeping the feedback lamp on ($P = .014$), while the nonmeditation group was not. The PK performance of the meditators was significantly superior to that of the nonmeditators ($P = .003$).

Schmidt and Pantas (1971) reported three series of experiments with a single subject who practiced Zen meditation for 20 minutes prior to an electronic PK task. In the preliminary series, he completed 14 sessions with overall significant PK influence ($P = .012$). Twenty sessions were completed in the second experiment, with highly significant PK results ($P = 6.3 \times 10^{-5}$). The same number of sessions were completed in the third experiment which also yielded overall significant PK influence ($P = .0093$). The combined results for these three experiments are highly significant ($P = 2.2 \times 10^{-6}$).

Honorton and May (1976) performed a study designed to assess volitional control in an electronic PK task. Each of ten subjects completed an equal number of PK trials attempting to enforce high scores and low scores. The subjects received auditory feedback pertaining to the magnitude of deviation in either direction and visual feedback providing directional information. A significant directional (volitional) PK influence was obtained ($P = .035$), and five of the ten subjects obtained individually significant ($P < .05$) differences in the expected direction ($P = .00006$). Four of the five individually successful subjects were meditators. There were six meditators altogether, and the probability that four of the six would obtain independently significant results at the .05 level is itself highly significant ($P = .00009$).

Summary of Experimental Meditation Studies. The combined results for all of the studies involving psi tasks during or following meditation are highly significant ($P = 6 \times 10^{-12}$). Nine of the 16 experimental series are independently significant at the .05 level or lower, whereas .8 significant series would be expected on the basis of chance error. The exact binomial probability of nine significant series out of 16 is highly significant ($P = 1.62 \times 10^{-8}$). It appears that meditation is an effective means of producing controlled psi interactions.

HYPNOSIS

The "Higher Phenomena" of Hypnotism

Reports of ostensible psi interactions in hypnosis go back to the days of Mesmer who himself gave demonstrations of "mental suggestion at a distance" (Moser, 1968). In fact, ostensible psi interactions were so common in early studies of mesmerism that they were for a time considered to be "the higher phenomena of hypnotism." The phenomena reported may be grouped in four categories: (a) transposition of the senses, including claims of "eyeless vision" and finger reading; (b) community of sensation, in which hypnotized subjects were reported to have responded to sensory stimuli presented to a distantly-located hypnotist; (c) mental suggestion, in which the hypnotist is alleged to have exerted an influence on the subject's behavior, while in "trance," posthypnotically, or by hypnotic induction at a distance; and (d) traveling clairvoyance, billet reading, and claims of paranormal medical diagnosis.

The early "magnetizers," embracing as they did a physical (magnetic fluid) theory, viewed the subject or "somnambule" as an animated automaton, and phenomena such as those reported in the nineteenth-century literature were frequently interpreted as evidence of direct physical influence between magnetizer and somnambule. This view was promulgated by Mesmer's most influential follower, the Marquis de Puységur, who was one of the first experimenters to report cases of mental suggestion. In fact, Puységur believed mental suggestion to be "the principal characteristic of somnambulism in its most complete form" (Dingwall, 1968, Vol. 1, p. 13).

Even among the early mesmerists, however, there were those who rejected the physical theory of magnetic fluids in favor of a psychological interpretation involving imagination and compliance.

Most of the cases supporting claims of the "higher phenomena" are of little value when assessed by contemporary standards of experimental control. Rarely, for example, is it possible to feel confidence in the methods employed to eliminate sensory contact during demonstrations of "eyeless vision," in which the magne-tizers eagerly encouraged the use of elaborate albeit easily manipulated blind-folds, while rejecting simpler methods which would have more effectively screened the somnambule from his target. Experiments involving community of sensation, while often impressive, were seldom conducted with sufficient distance between hypnotist and subject to eliminate potential sources of sensory contamination, especially on trials involving the use of olfactory stimuli. Simi-larly, reports of hypnosis at a distance suffer from the same problem encountered in contemporary hypnosis research in general; namely, what criteria were em-ployed to assess the presence of the hypnotic state? Apparently most of the cases bearing on this claim were deemed successful if the subject "appeared" to be "asleep." The "hypnotic appearance," however, must be regarded as a dubious criterion of hypnosis in light of modern experimental studies (Orne, 1959) which have demonstrated that even highly experienced hypnotists are unable to discriminate between "real" and "simulating" subjects on a better than chance basis.

Some of the early cases are not, however, so easily dismissed. There are, for example, a number of cases of traveling clairvoyance in which the subject provided specific information about distant events, occasionally with details unknown at the time to those present, which seem particularly suggestive of psi.

Psi Guessing Studies with Hypnosis

Hypnosis versus "Waking" Comparisons.   Sixteen experimental studies have com-pared psi guessing performance in hypnosis and waking conditions. Some of these studies have also explored the effects of different types of hypnotic suggestions on psi performance. While some of these studies employed measures of hypnotic susceptibility, they all suffer from the same difficulty confronting hypnosis research in general; namely, the lack of clear-cut objective correlates of the hypnotic state. For this reason, hypnosis must be defined (and differenti-ated from "waking") primarily through the use of hypnotic induction procedures.

From the standpoint of this discussion, we are less concerned with the controversy over interpretation of hypnotic state constructs than with the efficacy of hypnotic induction procedures as a means of enhancing psi performance.

The first systematic study was reported by Grela (1945). Eleven subjects were assigned to a hypnosis group and ten to a waking suggestion group. Subjects in the hypnosis group completed ESP guessing tasks in three conditions. The first condition was a waking state "baseline," not involving hypnotic induction procedures or explicit suggestions. The second condition involved hypnotic induction. with positive suggestions aimed at instilling belief in ESP and confidence in the subject's ability to demonstrate ESP. The third condition involved negative hypnotic suggestions aimed at instilling disbelief in ESP and doubt in the subject's ability to demonstrate it. Subjects in the waking suggestion group were given suggestions similar to those in the second hypnosis condition. The hypnosis subjects obtained significant psi guessing accuracy in the condition with positive suggestions ($P = .007$). The lowest psi scoring rate was in the negative suggestion condition for the hypnosis group, though this was not independently significant. The difference between the positive and negative suggestion conditions was significant ($P < .05$). Subjects in the waking suggestion condition and those in the waking baseline hypnosis condition obtained chance results.

Fahler (1957) reported a study in which four subjects completed both clairvoyance and precognitive guessing tasks in hypnosis and waking conditions. Hypnotic psi performance was significant for both the clairvoyance procedure ($P = .001$) and the precognitive procedure ($P < .05$). Chance performance was obtained in the waking condition and was significantly lower than that obtained in hypnosis ($P < .01$).

Fahler's initial work was replicated and extended in three experiments by Fahler and Cadoret (1958). Series A was a preliminary pilot study and yielded significant psi scoring rates in both waking ($P = .00027$) and hypnosis ($P = 7.2 \times 10^{-12}$) conditions. The difference between conditions was significant ($P < .05$). Series B involved 11 subjects, each of whom completed clairvoyant psi guessing tasks in both hypnosis and waking conditions. The waking condition yielded chance results, while the hypnosis condition provided highly significant psi performance ($P = 8.4 \times 10^{-9}$). The difference between conditions was highly significant ($P = .00012$). Twelve subjects participated in series C. Again, chance results were obtained in the waking condition and highly significant psi performance was obtained in hypnosis ($P = 6.8 \times 10^{-13}$). The level of psi performance was significantly superior in the hypnosis condition ($P = 1.3 \times 10^{-9}$). Given the high levels of success achieved in these studies, it is highly unfortunate that while the investigators adequately describe conditions and controls associated with psi testing, they provide no description whatsoever of the hypnotic techniques used, types of suggestions (if any) that were given, or criteria for subject selection.

An important series of psi experiments with hypnosis has been reported by

Lawrence Casler. In his first report, Casler (1962) described two experiments. The first, preliminary, experiment involved 48 subjects divided into four groups. One group carried out clairvoyant psi guessing under two conditions in hypnosis. One condition involved positive hypnotic suggestions for high ESP performance and the other condition involved psi guessing in hypnosis but without explicit suggestions for high scoring. A second hypnosis group was identical but involved a telepathic psi guessing task. The two waking groups were similar but involved no prior hypnotic induction. Since the clairvoyance and telepathy data produced nearly identical performance rates, they were combined. Significant psi performance was obtained in the hypnosis condition with positive suggestions $(P = .0042)$, and chance results were obtained in hypnosis without explicit suggestions. The difference between these two hypnosis conditions was significant $(P = .006)$. Chance results were obtained in both waking conditions. The hypnotic condition with positive suggestions yielded significantly higher psi performance waking suggestion condition $(P = .031)$. The confirmatory experiment involved 15 subjects. Each subject completed clairvoyant psi guessing tasks in both hypnosis and waking conditions. Positive suggestions were given for high ESP scores, in both conditions. Psi guessing accuracy was significant for the hypnosis condition $(P = .0093)$ and at chance for the waking condition. The difference between conditions was significant $(P = .007)$.

Casler (1964) conducted a telepathic guessing study in which both sender and receivers were hypnotized during half of the psi runs and in the waking state for the remainder. Receivers were allowed to instruct the sender, prior to beginning the session, as to how they wanted her to concentrate on the target symbols. No explicit suggestions were given regarding psi performance, which was significant for the hypnosis condition $(P = .046)$ and at chance for the waking condition. Hypnotic psi performance was significantly superior to waking performance $(P = .01)$.

The effects of different types of hypnotic suggestions on psi performance were explored in another study (Casler, 1967). Casler hypothesized that "while . . . suggestions aimed at higher scoring had been successful, greater effectiveness may be expected from specific suggestions that are particularly meaningful to the individual subject." While in hypnosis, Casler instructed subjects to generate suggestions which they believed would enhance their psi performance. Twenty-one subjects completed psi guessing tasks in hypnotic and waking conditions. Hypnotic psi performance was not independently significant in this study, though it was significantly superior to waking performance $(P < .025)$.

In a later study, Casler (1969) tested the hypothesis that close emotional relationships between senders and receivers facilitate telepathic psi interactions. Initially unacquainted senders and receivers were (at different times) given hypnotic suggestions that such a relationship existed between them. Each of the 15 sender-receiver teams completed three conditions: both sender and receiver in a waking condition with explicit suggestions; sender hypnotized but not the receiver; and, receiver hypnotized but not the sender. Chance results were obtained in each of these conditions, and the differences among conditions were nonsignificant. It would seem that a more adequate test of the hypothesis that emotional bonds facilitate psi would involve hypnotic reinforcement of previously formed bonds, rather than attempting to artificially induce emotional bonds in total strangers. This could, in fact, have effects opposite those intended, e.g., instilling elements of anxiety, threat, and resentment.

Van de Castle and Davis (1962) reported a study with 56 subjects who were divided into three groups on the basis of hypnotic susceptibility. Each group carried out psi guessing tasks in five conditions: waking, task-motivated waking, hypnosis, hypnosis with positive suggestions, and posthypnotic. The mean psi scores for the three hypnosis conditions were higher than either of the two waking conditions, but the difference was not significant. Psi performance for the combined hypnosis conditions was significantly superior to the combined waking conditions ($P < .01$). Posthypnotic psi performance was superior to both waking performance ($P < .05$) and performance in the hypnosis condition with positive suggestions ($P < .02$).

Nash and Durkin (1959) obtained a nonsignificant difference favoring psi performance in the waking condition ($P = .07$) in a short experiment with two subjects. Rao (1964) reported significantly superior psi performance in hypnosis ($P < .02$) in another short experiment with a single subject.

Edmunds and Jolliffe (1965) obtained chance results in a study with four subjects, each of whom completed ten sessions involving psi guessing tasks before, during, and after hypnosis. Positive suggestions were given in hypnosis to instill belief in ESP and confidence in the subject's ability to demonstrate ESP.

Using the Stuart Interest Inventory (SII) which had previously been found to be a predictor of psi-hitting and psi-missing, Honorton reported two studies to test the hypothesis that hypnosis would increase the magnitude of deviation in the direction predicted by the SII. In the first study (Honorton, 1964), six subjects completed a clairvoyant psi guessing task in hypnosis and waking conditions, following administration of the SII. The experimenter was blind as to SII predictions until the end of the session. Positive hypnotic suggestions, patterned after those used by Casler (1962), were given prior to the psi task. Four of the six subjects were predicted by the SII to be high-scorers, and they scored at chance in both hypnosis and waking conditions. The two predicted low-scorers, however, showed highly significant psi-missing in hypnosis ($P = .00023$) and chance performance in the waking condition. The difference between hypnosis and waking performance was significant for these subjects ($P = .025$), and the difference between SII predicted high- versus low-scorers was significant for the hypnosis condition ($P = .002$).

Similar procedures were followed in a subsequent replication study involving

20 subjects (Honorton, 1966). As in the initial study, the predicted high-scorers performed at chance in both hypnosis and waking conditions. The predicted low-scorers showed significant psi-missing in hypnosis ($P = .015$) and chance results in the waking condition. Their scoring level was significantly lower in hypnosis than in the waking condition ($P = .017$) and was significantly lower than the predicted high-scoring subjects ($P = .0058$).

To summarize these studies comparing psi performance in waking and hypnosis conditions, it is clear that hypnotic induction procedures enhance psi guessing accuracy. Of the 19 hypnosis-waking comparisons made in these 16 studies, ten showed overall significant psi performance in hypnosis. Only one (Fahler and Cadoret's series A) showed overall significant psi performance under waking conditions. Hypnotic psi performance was significantly superior to waking performance in 12 of the 19 comparisons. Waking performance was not superior to hypnotic performance in any of the comparisons. The exact binomial probability of ten or more significant comparisons ($P < .05$) out of 19 total comparisons is less than one in a million.

Other Guessing Studies.   Ryzl (1962) developed what he claimed to be an hypnotic training procedure for ESP. Unlike most of the investigators whose work is reviewed above, Ryzl described his hypnotic techniques in great detail. Ryzl's procedure involved intensive hypnotic training, culminating in the subject's ability to experience very complex and vivid visual imagery. The psi "training" involved informal free response psi tasks with immediate feedback in hypnosis, evolving toward reduced dependence upon hypnosis and formal forced choice guessing tasks. Ryzl claimed to have developed several reliable ESP subjects in this manner. Extensive work with one such subject, Pavel Stepanek, carried out over a 10-year period by numerous investigators, has been reviewed elsewhere (Pratt, 1973). In the initial report on Stepanek, Ryzl and Ryzlova (1962) described two experiments involving binary targets. Stepanek's guessing performance in hypnosis was highly significant ($P = 10^{-9}$). The second series was completed with Stepanek in what was described as a self-induced hypnotic state. The results were again highly significant ($P = .00008$). Unfortunately, no comparisons were made with waking state performance, and Stepanek's later history as an outstanding ESP performer did not involve the use of hypnosis.

Several studies were subsequently reported involving attempts to replicate Ryzl's general approach (Beloff and Mandleberg, 1966; Haddox, 1966; Stephenson, 1965). These investigators were uniformly unsuccessful in validating Ryzl's training claims. In fairness to Ryzl, it was pointed out elsewhere (Honorton and Krippner, 1969) that none of these studies followed Ryzl's procedures at all closely. However, it must now be added that Ryzl has not, himself, reported further work along these lines.

Fahler and Osis (1966) reported a study with two subjects in which hypnotic suggestions were given to facilitate the subjects' ability to discriminate between correct and incorrect psi impressions. The hypnotized subjects were instructed to call "Mark" whenever they felt particularly confident that their responses were correct. Their confidence calls were accurate to a highly significant degree ($P = 2 \times 10^{-8}$).

ESP targets selected on the basis of similarity of concept ratings by senders and receivers were used in an hypnosis study by McBain, Fox, Kimura, Nakanishi, and Tirado (1970). After posthypnotic suggestions to accentuate affective reactions to specific concepts, close rapport with partners, and ability to concentrate, subjects both sent and received random lists of those concepts at three weekly sessions. Psi guessing performance was significant overall ($P = .025$), was higher for same-sexed teams ($P = .001$), and was related to the hypnotizability of the senders ($r = .64, P < .01$).

Psi Picture Retrieval Studies with Hypnosis

There has been a noteworthy shift in psi hypnosis research in the last 5 years, away from the use of forced-choice guessing psi tasks, toward free-response tasks in which hypnotized subjects produce spontaneous hypnotic imagery in response to remote target pictures. Statistical evaluation of these studies involves blind rating or ranking procedures in which target pictures are compared for similarity to receiver mentation reports.

Waking, dream, and hypnotic imagery was utilized as a vehicle for psi mediation in a study by Krippner (1968). Sixteen subjects were alternately assigned to hypnosis or waking groups. They attempted to retrieve remote target pictures viewed by a distant sender, under three conditions: positive suggestions to promote target-relevant imagery; a nap in the laboratory, following suggestions to dream about the target picture; and postsession dream diaries, maintained for one week following the laboratory session. For the hypnosis group, the posthypnotic nap condition was associated with significant target-mentation correspondences ($P = 6 \times 10^{-5}$). For the waking group, the postsession dream diary material corresponded significantly to the target material ($P < .01$). The combined hypnosis conditions were associated with significant psi retrieval ($P < .001$).

Moss, Paulson, Chang, and Levitt (1970) reported a study with eight hypnotized and nine nonhypnotized sender-receiver teams. All subjects had either participated successfully in prior psi studies or claimed personal psi experiences. The target material consisted of emotional slide episodes. The receivers free-associated during the sending periods and later were shown sample slides from two episodes for judging. The hypnotized teams showed overall significant psi retrieval ($P < .001$), while the nonhypnotized teams performed at chance.

Seven studies have involved psi retrieval through hypnotically induced dreams. Honorton and Stump (1969) selected six subjects who were in the upper quartile of the Barber Suggestibility Scale. Each subject was given suggestions in hypnosis to dream, while in hypnosis, about the contents of concealed target pictures. Following each hypnotic dream period, subjects were dehypnotized and asked to report their hypnotic dream imagery, after which they were rehypnotized and the procedure repeated until each subject completed four hypnotic dreams to four different targets. At the end of the session, the subject was shown the four target pictures and asked to blind rank them with respect to correspondences with each of their four hypnotic dreams. The subjects were able to match their hypnotic dream imagery to the appropriate target pictures with a significant level of accuracy ($P = .016$).

This study was replicated and extended by Honorton (1972). Sixty subjects were assigned to hypnosis or waking groups, matched in terms of hypnotic susceptibility. Four hypnotic dreams were elicited to four concealed targets for subjects in the hypnosis group. Subjects in the waking group were asked to have daydreams about the targets. Self-ratings of degree of inwardly-directed attention were elicited following each hypnotic dream or daydream. Vividness of imagery was also self-rated after each target trial. Hypnosis subjects in the upper quartile of the Barber Suggestibility Scale produced significant target-mentation correspondences ($P = .033$), replicating the initial findings of Honorton and Stump. Hypnosis subjects with high state reports indicating internally-directed attention were significantly more accurate in identifying target-dream material than were those with low state reports, indicating externally-directed attention ($P < .05$). Vivid hypnotic dreams were more accurately identified with their targets than hypnotic dreams with weak imagery ($P < .05$). Significantly higher vividness ratings were given to the last two hypnotic dreams than to the first two ($P = .002$), and this was associated with significantly superior psi performance in the last two hypnotic dreams ($P = .029$). Subjects in the waking group produced chance results in the psi task.

Keeling (1971) reported a study with three highly susceptible hypnosis subjects who each contributed four sessions. The first two sessions were devoted to training in hypnosis with stress on hypnotic dreaming. In the two psi sessions, one subject served as sender while the other two served as receivers. Sender and receivers were hypnotized (by different experimenters) and given suggestions to have hypnotic dreams. The hypnotic dream stimulus for the sender was a randomly selected one- or two-sentence description. This served also as the target for the receivers' hypnotic dreams, and the receivers were oriented toward having hypnotic dreams corresponding to that of the sender. The overall results were significant ($P < .03$), and like the Honorton (1972) study, the results were better for the second half, which was independently significant ($P < .002$).

Glick and Kogen (1971) reported a study with two hypnotized receivers, each of whom produced hypnotic imagery in response to five concealed target pictures. Significant target-mentation correspondences were obtained by all three judges for one subject ($P < .001$) and by one of the judges for the other subject ($P < .01$).

A pilot study involving psi and hypnotic dreams was reported by Rechtschaffen (1970). Both sender and receiver were hypnotized and given suggestions to dream about specific contents suggested to the sender. Overall significant correspondences were obtained between target and mentation data ($P < .01$). As with the other hypnotic dream psi studies, the qualitative correspondences between targets and subjects' mentation were sometimes very impressive.

Parker and Beloff (1970) reported two studies involving attempts to replicate the findings of Honorton and Stump. The first experiment involved eight subjects, each of whom contributed two sessions, following the instructions and procedures used by Honorton and Stump. Significant target-mentation correspondences were obtained in the first session ($P = .018$), and there was a significant decline in performance between the two sessions ($P = .011$). The second study involved ten subjects, each completing a single session. The overall results of this study were nonsignificant, though Parker (1975) later reported a significant association between psi performance and self-reports of internally-focused attention ($P = .046$), confirming the state report findings of Honorton (1972), whose study was then still in progress.

Psi and Hypnosis: Conclusions from Experimental Work

Hypnotic Enhancement of Psi. I believe the conclusion is now inescapable that hypnotic induction procedures enhance psi receptivity. Whereas chance error would predict 2.1 "significant" series (at the .05 level), of the 42 series, 22 were actually significant at or below the .05 level. That is, 52 percent of studies were significant, compared to a chance expectation of 5 percent.

Of the studies involving waking state comparisons, only one produced significant psi performance in the waking state. Waking group subjects in one additional study (Krippner, 1968) obtained significant psi performance, but only in a condition involving nocturnal dream recall. The fact that *none* of these studies provided significantly superior psi performance in waking conditions while 12 out of 22 studies produced significantly superior hypnotic psi performance is itself highly significant ($P = .00024$).

Both studies comparing positive versus negative hypnotic suggestions (Grela, 1945; Casler, 1962) obtained significant differences in psi performance favoring positive suggestions. This work provides the first successful functional manipulation of the sheep-goat variable (Schmeidler and McConnell, 1958), which has been one of the few consistent predictors of psi performance in waking state studies without internal state procedures (Palmer, 1971).

Guessing versus Imagery as Psi Mediators in Hypnosis. The hypnosis-psi literature provides the only area of internal states work in which a sufficiently large data base is available to permit comparisons of psi information rates in guessing

TABLE 2. PSI INFORMATION RATE IN FREE RESPONSE VERSUS GUESSING EXPERIMENTS WITH HYPNOSIS.

Free response studies (n = 12)	Mean $PQ\%$ = 7.70
Guessing studies (n = 30)	Mean $PQ\%$ = 0.76
Difference: t = 3.54, 40 df, $P < .001$	

Note: $PQ\%$ is a measure of information rate, more strictly of statistical efficiency, based on the ratio of the observed PQ to its maximal value, where $PQ = \chi^2 / N$ trials.

versus free-response tasks. Table 2 shows the information rates for each procedure. The information rate in free-response hypnosis studies is of an order of magnitude significantly greater than the information rate associated with psi guessing studies ($P < .001$). This finding directly supports spontaneous case findings that psi is most frequently mediated through imagery and other spontaneous mentation processes.

RELAXATION

In an article that ushered in the systematic exploration of psi and internal states, Rhea White (1964) analyzed introspective reports from a number of exceptionally successful psi percipients in early prequantitative free response studies. She concluded that relaxation was a common factor in their attempts to enter a psi receptive mode of functioning:

> The early reports place a great deal of emphasis on achieving a state of deep mental and physical relaxation. Deliberate attempts are made to still the body and mind, and these techniques are, in most cases, incorporated in a kind of ritual . . . . In most of the cases reviewed here, specific techniques are made an integral part of the method for achieving a relaxed state 1964, pp. 28-29).

White quotes Mary Craig Sinclair, an unusually articulate and successful psi percipient, who offered this advice, based on her own experience, to prospective psi percipients:

> By making the body insensitive I mean simply to relax completely your mental hold of, or awareness of, all bodily sensations . . . . Relax all mental interest in everything in the environment; inhibit all thoughts which try to wander into consciousness . . . . Drop your body, a dead weight, from your conscious mind . . . . To make the conscious mind a blank it is necessary to "let go" of consciousness of the body. If, after you have practiced "letting go" of the body, you find that your mind is not a blank, then you have not succeeded in getting your body rid of all tension (In U. Sinclair, 1930, pp. 181-182).

These practices bear more than a superficial similarity to the meditative and hypnotic techniques discussed above, which are also associated with mental and physical relaxation. The kind of mental relaxation described by Mary Craig Sinclair seems to involve effortless intention, or what some present-day biofeedback researchers call "passive volition" (Green and Green, 1973–74). This is a mind-set which is characterized by "allowing it to happen" with a minimum of ego involvement and conscious *striving*. At the same time, there is conscious *intent*, which serves to guide attention in a goal-directed fashion, whether it be to meditate on an object, control a physiology-contingent feedback signal, or retrieve a remote target picture.

Stilling the mind, or reducing the internal noise level, is the object of concentration in Patanjali's system of Raja yoga, and it is clear from the organization of his system as well as the experiential description of Craig Sinclair, 3,500 years later, that it must be approached in stages. Physical relaxation is a necessary prerequisite for this kind of mental relaxation and reorientation.

The first systematic experimental investigation of the role of relaxation in psi performance was initiated by Gertrude Schmeidler (1952). Using a clairvoyant psi guessing task, she reported significantly superior psi performance from hospitalized concussion patients than from patients suffering other disorders ($P = .002$). Based on interview data and analysis of Rorschach protocols, Schmeidler hypothesized that the superior performance of the concussion patients was due to their greater relaxation, receptivity to the experiment, and their "uncritical willingness to respond to the outside world." This hypothesis was put directly to the test in a subsequent study with maternity patients (Gerber and Schmeidler, 1957). Patients judged (by an evaluator who was blind to their ESP scores) relaxed and acceptant of the experimental situation produced significant psi-hitting performance ($P = 3 \times 10^{-5}$), while those judged not relaxed obtained significant psi-missing ($P = .006$). These results were highly consistent, with 13 of the 15 relaxed patients scoring positively on the psi task ($P = .0037$), while none of the patients who were not relaxed scored positively.

Progressive Muscular Relaxation

Based on these and similar findings Braud and Braud (1973) introduced a variation of Jacobson's (1929) progressive relaxation exercises to assess the effects of induced relaxation on psi retrieval of remote pictures. Their general procedure is as follows. The subject-receiver sits in a comfortable armchair with eyes closed and is given tape-recorded instructions to relax his entire musculature by alternately tensing and relaxing each muscle group from toes to forehead. This is continued until a state of deep muscle relaxation is achieved. The receiver is then given instructions to relax mentally, first by imaging pleasant scenes, and then by "blanking" the mind and becoming as passive as possible. At the outset of the experimental session, the receiver is told to "keep somewhere in the back of his mind" the fact that a target picture will be "transmitted" by a sender and that he is to receive impressions of this picture.

A 5-minute "impression" period, accompanied by white noise follows these instructions. While the receiver is relaxing, a sender located in a remote location, randomly selects a target picture and concentrates on its "raw sensory information." The sender in all of the Brauds' studies has been one of the experimenters.

Correspondences between targets and receiver-mentation reports are assessed by blind ranking each mentation report against a pool of five control pictures and the actual target.

In their first report (Braud and Braud, 1973), these investigators reported two major experiments. Experiment 1 involved repeated sessions with a single subject-receiver, described as a "twenty-seven year old male assistant (now associate) professor of psychology at the University of Houston." While he had no prior history of psi experiences, he was "firmly convinced of the reality of psi and enthusiastically felt that he would perform well under the conditions of the experiment." The receiver was able to match his mentation to the correct target with perfect accuracy in all six sessions of the experiment ($P = .0014$), and the target-mentation correspondences were quite striking. The target for one session was a Coca-Cola ad showing two frosted bottles of Coke, partially covered with ice. The receiver's mentation report included, " . . . a glass, a frosted glass filled with Coca-Cola."

Experiment 2 involved a single session with each of six different subject-receivers who were advanced undergraduate or graduate students from the University of Houston. All were classified as believers in ESP and were "convinced that they would perform well," although only two had reported prior psi experiences. As in the first study, the receivers were able to match targets with mentation reports with perfect accuracy ($P = .0014$). Again, the target-mentation correspondences were quite striking. In one session, the target picture showed a cow with horns, and the receiver reported " . . . two structures which looked like the claws of a crab . . . then they became horns with a cow's head attached . . . a cow's head with horns on it . . . "

Experiments 3–7 were group tests in which between 6 and 11 subjects all tried to gain impressions of a single target. Three of these experiments produced significant results, but because of statistical problems involved in multiple calling of the same target, the results of each group session were reduced, by majority vote, to a single response, and the overall results were not independently significant ($P = .188$).

In a subsequent report Braud and Braud (1974) described two additional studies which confirmed and extended their initial findings. In Experiment 1, 16 subject-receivers contributed one session each. They were all undergraduate psychology students enrolled in one of the experimenters' experimental psychology courses. None of them had participated in prior psi research, and none had any striking psi experiences, though they were all believers in ESP. The instructor-experimenter served as sender for each of the receivers. The same general procedure described above was employed. After completing their mentation reports at the end of the session, the receivers self-rated their degree of relaxation during the "impression" period. They then blind-judged their mentation reports in relation to each of the six potential targets in the judging pool. The subject-receivers were successful in matching their mentation reports with the correct target pictures ($P = .038$). Self-ratings of relaxation were significantly higher for receivers who accurately identified the correct target pictures than for those who were unsuccessful ($P < .04$).

Degree of relaxation was systematically manipulated and objectively measured in Experiment 2. Twenty volunteer students each contributed one session as psi receivers. They were randomly assigned to two groups. The relaxation group underwent the same procedures used in the Brauds' prior studies, with psi retrieval following tape-administered relaxation exercises. The tension group carried out the same psi retrieval task following tension-inducing instructions administered via another tape. Level of relaxation was assessed through self-ratings and evaluation of electromyograms (EMG) taken from the frontalis (forehead) muscles. Significant psi retrieval was obtained in the relaxation group ($P = .011$), while chance results were obtained by the tension group. Psi performance for the relaxation group was significantly superior to that of the tension group ($P < .025$). Subjects in the relaxation group showed significant decreases in EMG activity ($P < .005$), while tension subjects showed significant increases in EMG level ($P < .025$). During the psi impression period, EMG tension levels were significantly lower for the relaxation group than for the tension group ($P < .001$). Questionnaire data provided a converging measure of degree of relaxation, with self-rated tension levels differentiating the two experimental groups at about the same level as the EMG measure. EMG level, physical state rating, and mental state rating were intercorrelated positively and significantly, whether measured in terms of initial values, psi-impression period values, or degree of shift from beginning to end of session.

A successful independent replication of the University of Houston relaxation work was reported by Stanford and Mayer (1974). The subjects were 21 volunteer students from the University of Virginia, each of whom contributed one session. Unlike the Houston work, this study involved a clairvoyance psi procedure. Subjects were instructed that their mentation during a 5-minute impression period would "likely relate to the picture inside an opaque container on the other side of the room." The procedure, including relaxation instructions, was otherwise identical to the Houston studies. Overall significant psi retrieval results were obtained in this study ($P = .019$). Psi retrieval was examined in relation to a number of predictor variables involving self-ratings by subjects prior to target-mentation judging at the end of the session. Mental quietude correlated positively and significantly with psi retrieval ($r = 0.38, P < .05$). When dichotomized at the median with respect to this item, the high mental relaxation group showed significant psi retrieval ($P < .008$), whereas the low mental relaxation group produced chance results.

Miller and York (1976) examined psi retrieval following progressive relaxation exercises in relation to a tachistoscopic measure of perceptual defensiveness. They hypothesized that the group showing the least amount of perceptual filtering would score significantly higher on a free-response clairvoyance test than the group showing the greatest amount of perceptual filtering. Seventeen subjects each completed a single psi retrieval session following a session involving tachistoscopic perceptual defense measurement. The results were in the hypothesized direction, with better psi retrieval from the less perceptually defensive subjects, but not to a significant degree ($P < .10$).

Altom and Braud (1976) used musical selections as targets in a study with 30 psi receivers. Subjects were randomly assigned to a telepathic or clairvoyant group. Following a 15-minute tape-administered relaxation exercise, the receivers attempted to gain psi impressions of the musical target, while their auditory input was held constant with white noise. The difference between groups was that the musical target was audible to a remote agent in the telepathy group but was inaudible in the clairvoyance group. At the end of the session, the receiver blind ranked four different musical selections in relation to psi impressions during the session. Psi performance was approximately the same for the two groups and was significant overall ($P = .049$). Some subjects actually reported hearing music in the white noise. One reported bagpipe music while the sender listened to a bagpipe rendition of "Hieland Laddie."

The use of an incubation period to augment psi retrieval was explored by Braud and Thorsrud (1976). Sixteen subject-receivers attempted to gain psi impressions of target pictures viewed by remote senders following 25 minutes of muscular, autogenic, and mental relaxation exercises. After the subject blind-judged in-session mentation in relation to the target pool, a 15-minute "incubation" period began, involving an irrelevant task. At the end of the incubation period, the subject was asked for any additional details which might have come to mind about the target and was asked to make a second judgment of the four target pictures. Psi retrieval before and after the incubation period was identical. Subjects were successful in accurately relating their in-session mentation reports to the remote target pictures viewed by the sender ($P = .038$).

These procedures were extended to psychokinetic psi tasks in three studies reported by Braud, Smith, Andrew, and Willis (1976). Subjects in these studies were assigned to two groups. Both groups, prior to the PK task, listened to tape-recorded relaxation instructions. One group then listened to a tape including music, environmental sounds, and electronically synthesized sounds suggesting depth and imagery which was intended to stimulate right hemisphere brain functioning. The other group listened to a tape including linear prose, problem solving, counting etc., intended to stimulate left hemisphere functioning. The investigators hypothesized significantly superior PK performance for the group processing right hemisphere material. The PK task involved influencing the frequency of occurrence of two colored display lamps on an electronic random event generator. Experiment 1 involved ten subjects in each group. The group receiving right hemisphere material ("mode 1") obtained a significant positive PK influence ($P = .02$), while the left hemisphere group ("mode 2") obtained a significant negative PK influence ($P = .011$). The difference between groups was significant ($P = .002$). In Experiment 2, 20 subjects were assigned to each group. The "mode 1" group again displayed significant positive PK influence ($P = .025$) while the "mode 2" group produced chance results. The difference between groups was again significant ($P < .05$). Experiment 3 was essentially identical to Experiment 2. The results for both groups were nonsignificant. The combined results for the three experiments showed significant PK influence for subjects processing the "mode 1" material ($P = .0014$) and chance results for those processing "mode 2" material. The overall difference between the two groups was significant ($P < .01$).

A picture retrieval procedure, with sensory relaxation exercises, for group administration was developed by Barker, Messer, and Drucker (1976). The procedure involves showing each group a 20-minute film on the work of the Maimonides laboratory, in which two of the experimenters are seen participating successfully as psi receivers, themselves, in dream and psi ganzfeld procedures. The experimenters then discuss different ways psi influences may be mediated into conscious experience through images, memories, and associations. They present examples of ostensible psi interactions in everyday life, drawing from their own personal experiences in and out of the laboratory. The group is given a crash-course in what is believed to be necessary to detect and recover psi impressions, including the usefulness of sensory relaxation. Relaxation exercises are then given by the experimenter who will later serve as sender. These involve directing attention to the various muscle groups, releasing tension from each area, and allowing the body as a whole to relax and grow heavy. The experimenter-sender leaves for another room to send the target picture while the group continues relaxing with directions to simply observe their internal mental processes. After a 5–10-minute impression period, the group members are asked to briefly record their impressions and code them with respect to the presence or absence of content in ten binary categories which represent the population from which the target picture is randomly selected. The targets are contained in a special pool of 1,024 pictures which have been produced such that each picture represents a unique permutation of content in the ten categories. Each target picture can therefore be represented by a ten-digit binary number and matched against the ten-bit number representing the receiver's mentation code (Honorton, 1975). Targets for each session are randomly selected by a person who is not present at the sessions. A "majority vote" procedure is carried out with the group to determine its consensus on the composition of the target picture. Upon the completion of this procedure, the sender-experimenter returns to the group and displays the target picture. Time is taken to discuss interesting individual experiences.

A pilot study using the above procedure and involving eight small groups has been carried out; it yielded a significant level of accuracy in picture retrieval ($P < .005$). Six sessions have also been run in a formal series (incomplete at the time of writing) in which the results were also significant ($P = .045$). Majority votes in this series involved groups ranging from 10 to 200 participants.

Summary of Induced Relaxation Studies

Altogether there have been 13 experimental studies of psi retrieval during induced relaxation. Ten of these studies gave significant overall levels of accuracy in target retrieval. This is a 77 percent success rate, compared to the expected chance rate of 5 percent. The combined significance of all 13 studies is associated with a probability of more than a billion to one. Quite clearly, induced relaxation procedures appear to enhance psi receptivity.

The finding by Stanford and Mayer (1974) that success in psi retrieval is correlated with degree of mental stillness fits especially nicely with Patanjali's internal concentration and with Mary Craig Sinclair's "blankness" of mind. Such internal cognitive noise reduction can only be achieved when somatic noise produced by physical tension is eliminated, and attention can be focused inward on internally-mediated mental processes. This also requires the attenuation of patterned perceptual input, which leads us to discussion of a parallel line of investigation, psi retrieval during conditions of relative sensory deprivation.

SENSORY DEPRIVATION

The reduction of patterned exteroceptive input is one of the defining characteristics of internal attention states. Psychophysiological investigations have confirmed that dreaming and meditation are associated with deafferentation. Patanjali's fifth stage, *Pratyahara,* is described by Taimni (1961) as imposing a "shutter between the sense-organs and the mind," restricting attention to internal memories and images. Several studies (Sanders and Reyher, 1969; Wickramasekera, 1969) have found significant increases in hypnotic susceptibility following sensory deprivation. Ernest Hilgard (1965) said of hypnosis, "The hypnotist has essentially a two-pronged strategy: that of sensory deprivation and that of developing a 'special' kind of human relationship." Heron (1961) found significantly greater changes in attitude toward psi phenomena for sensory deprivation subjects than for control subjects, after both groups listened to a record arguing for belief in various "psychic" phenomena. Peter Suedfeld (1969) summarized the research on susceptibility to external influence in sensory deprivation this way:

> Susceptibility to external influence, including both primary suggestibility and persuasibility, is clearly increased by [sensory deprivation]. The data indicate that this phenomenon originates with the lack of informational anchors in the SD situation: the subject is at loose ends, without guidelines for his behavior, . . . in a state of stimulus- and information-hunger . . . . This condition has the effect of maximizing the impact and the reward value of whatever information *is* made available to him (p. 166).

The first study of psi picture retrieval under conditions of sensory deprivation was reported by Honorton, Drucker, and Hermon (1973). Thirty volunteers each contributed a single 30-minute session in which they were confined in a sensory isolation cradle, supported and immobilized by straps. The cradle, suspended from a metal frame, carried the subject-receiver, moving in forward-backward, side-to-side, and rotating motions generated by the subject's involuntary body movements. The subject wore a light-proof blindfold and a headset to attenuate auditory and visual exteroceptive input. Following instructions to allow imagery to develop spontaneously, the subject was given "state report" instructions. The state report scale had been developed by Tart (1970), who found that it correlated significantly with objective measures of hypnotic susceptibility. In the adapted form used in this study, state reports designated the degree to which attention was directed internally. Prior research showed high state reports to be associated with increased EEG alpha activity (Honorton, Davidson, and Bindler, 1972) and significant psi performance in both guessing and free response tasks (Honorton, 1972; Honorton, Davidson, and Bindler, 1971; Parker, 1975). State reports were elicited from the subject every 5 minutes during the session. During the last 10 minutes of session, a sender located in another room attempted to influence the subject's spontaneous imagery with a randomly selected target picture. Subjects rank ordered pictures against their sensory deprivation imagery at the end of the session. Subjects with high state reports showed significant accuracy in target identification ($P = .025$), while those with low state reports obtained chance results. Subjects reporting strong shifts toward internalized attention, between the beginning of session and sending period, obtained an especially high level of target identification ($P = .011$). Using psi performance as a predictor of state, Honorton, Drucker, and Hermon found that subjects who were successful in psi retrieval showed a significantly larger shift in state than those who were unsuccessful in psi retrieval ($P < .05$).

Ganzfeld Stimulation

A homogeneous visual field ("ganzfeld") has been used to provide subjects with uniform visual input. Ganzfeld stimulation may be produced by placing halves of ping-pong balls over the subject's eyes and a uniform source of light in front of his face. The result is an experience of diffuse, unpatterned light and is characterized by reports of being immersed in a "sea of light," disorientation, and the occurrence of "blank out" periods in which there is a complete disappearance of visual experience, accompanied by an increase in EEG alpha activity (Avant, 1965). The "blank out" phenomenon is interpreted as indicating a functional similarity between continuous unpatterned visual input and no input at all (Cadwallander, 1958; Cohen 1957; Tepas, 1962). A similar phenomenon has been observed in studies of stabilized retinal imagery (Lehmann, Beeler, and Fender, 1967).

Ornstein (1971) has pointed out similarities between ganzfeld stimulation and concentrative meditation. The antecedent conditions are essentially the same; both ganzfeld stimulation and concentrative meditation provide constant, unpatterned input; both are associated with loss of contact with the external environment. Ganzfeld stimulation is associated with periods of "blank out," and concentrative meditation with periods of "void," both of which are accompanied by increases in EEG alpha activity.

Like other forms of sensory deprivation, ganzfeld stimulation is associated with increased attention to internal mentation. Bertini, Lewis, and Witkin (1964) exploited this association to develop an "experimental-hypnagogic" technique to facilitate the study of hypnagogic imagery. In addition to regulation of visual input, these investigators provided subjects with uniform auditory input via white noise delivered through headphones. Subjects were instructed to give continuous mentation reports of all on-going thoughts, images, and feelings during ganzfeld stimulation. Bertini, Lewis, and Witkin concluded that this procedure "facilitates the flow of ideation and imagery and is evocative of feeling." On the motivational level, they observed that "some subjects showed open preoccupation with the experimenter—what he is doing, what he is like as a person, . . . suggesting a 'budding' transference as an important source of feelings in the experimental situation."

From these observations, it would appear that ganzfeld stimulation, in the form used by Bertini, Lewis, and Witkin should fulfill the psi detection criteria described in the section entitled "Internal Attention States and Psi Detection Criteria." Specifically, this procedure satisfies the following conditions: (a) reduction of the sensory noise level through regulation of perceptual input, (b) deployment of attention toward internal mentation which could serve to "carry" psi impressions, (c) facilitation, through "stimulus hunger," of an affective link between the psi-receiver and a remote information source (sender-target), (d) recovery of target information through the receiver's continuous mentation report, and (e) confirmation of sender-receiver interaction through objective assessment of target-mentation correspondences.

The first study to utilize this procedure was reported by Honorton and Harper (1974). Thirty volunteer subject-receivers each participated in one 35-minute session in which their auditory-visual inputs were regulated via ganzfeld stimulation.

The sender was usually a member of the laboratory staff, though in some cases subjects brought along friends to serve in this role. Target material consisted of thematically-related, stereoscopic View-Master slide reels, selected on a random basis from a large number of such reels. At a randomly determined sending period during the session, the sender viewed the contents of the target reel, attempting to influence the receiver's ongoing mentation report with the general theme and specific contents of the reel. An experimenter located in a room between sender and receiver monitored the receiver's mentation report via intercom. Following a review of the receiver's mentation, after 35 minutes of ganzfeld stimulation, the receiver was shown four different View-Master reels, one of which had been viewed by the sender. Both experimenter and subject were blind as to which reel was the target. The subject then rank ordered the reels in relation to degree of correspondence with his mentation report. The correct target reels were identified with a significant degree of accuracy ($P = .017$), and the qualitative correspondences between targets and receiver-mentation reports were often striking. For example, when the target was "Birds of the World," the receiver reported: ". . . . I sense a large hawk's head in front of me . . . The sense of sleek feathers. Now it turns its head and flies away . . . ."

Terry and Honorton (1976) reported two replication studies using identical procedures. In the first experiment, 12 undergraduate students in an experimental parapsychology course given by Honorton completed 27 sessions, with a significant level of target retrieval ($P = .003$). Again, impressive correspondences were obtained between remote target material and receiver-mentation reports. When the target was "Rare Coins," the receiver reported: ". . . circles . . . Their sizes are not the same . . . some are really large, and others are very tiny—no larger than a penny . . . all these different sized circles . . . . Now I see colors . . . two in particular—gold and silver seem to stand out more than all the others . . . ." In the second experiment, six self-selected sender-receiver teams completed ten sessions each. Four of the six teams produced a level of accuracy in target retrieval which was at least double that expected by chance, and the overall results were highly significant ($P = .00059$).

A statistically significant independent replication and extension of these findings was reported by Braud, Wood, and Braud (1975). An especially noteworthy feature of this study was the inclusion of a control group of subjects who underwent the same procedures without ganzfeld stimulation. Twenty undergraduate students served as psi-receivers for one session each. Half of the receivers gave continuous mentation reports during 35 minutes of ganzfeld stimulation, while the other half gave mentation reports without ganzfeld stimulation. During the last 5 minutes of session, all subjects attempted to gain psi impressions of a target picture being viewed by a sender in another room. The sender was always one of the experimenters. The ganzfeld group produced a highly significant rate of target retrieval ($P = .001$), while the control group produced chance results. The level of psi retrieval for the ganzfeld group was significantly superior to that of the control group ($P < .025$). Questionnaire data indicated that the two groups did not differ significantly on factors such as belief in ESP, mood, expectancy, etc., which might otherwise have confounded the results. Shifts in body awareness were significantly greater for the ganzfeld group ($P < .02$). The ganzfeld group also showed greater shifts in self-rated state of consciousness than the control group, although the difference did not reach the .05 level of significance.

A different type of comparison was made by Terry, Tremmel, Kelly, Harper, and Barker (1976). They compared the information rate of psi retrieval in ganzfeld stimulation with mentation reports to psi guessing without ganzfeld stimulation. Thirty self-selected sender-receiver teams completed one session each. The teams were alternately assigned to ganzfeld-mentation and guessing groups. The ganzfeld-mentation group was run following the procedure described above. The guessing group was run under conditions similar to standard psi guessing experiments. Instructions to receivers in the guessing group were to guess which of the ten categories of content on a rating sheet were present in the target picture being viewed by the remote sender. This same format was used for the ganzfeld recievers, who were asked to code their ganzfeld mentation in relation to the presence of content in each of the ten binary categories. Target retrieval was significant for the ganzfeld group ($P = .018$) and at chance for the guessing group.

A comparison of psi ganzfeld retrieval and subliminal sensory ganzfeld retrieval was reported by Smith, Tremmel, and Honorton (1976). Twenty sender-receiver teams completed two sessions, one in each of two conditions. In one condition, the target picture was presented to the sender tachistoscopically for 1 millisecond. In the other condition, the sender was presented with the target picture supraliminally for 10 minutes. In both conditions, following target presentation, the sender (in addition to the receiver) went into ganzfeld stimulation and gave continuous mentation reports. Receivers were blind as to condition. Target material consisted of the binary-coded targets described above. At the end of 40 minutes of ganzfeld stimulation, both sender and receiver coded their mentation in relation to the presence or absence of content in each of the content categories. The receiver's score represented the rate of psi retrieval, and the sender's score represented the rate of subliminal visual retrieval. Overall psi results for both conditions combined were significant ($P = .015$). Psi retrieval was independently significant for the subliminal-sender condition ($P = .016$), and the rate of psi retrieval was comparable to the senders' subliminal sensory rate ($P = .015$). In other words, the receivers, who had no sensory contact with the target pictures, were nonetheless influenced by them to about the same degree as the senders, who *were* sensorially exposed to the target pictures for a brief duration.

Honorton (1976a) reported a short series of seven psi ganzfeld sessions bearing on the role of motivation and arousal in psi ganzfeld studies. In these sessions, psi retrieval was attempted in the presence of television film crews. The presence of TV cameras, lights, and the film crews generated a high level of excitement, especially on the part of the subject-receivers, who were "center stage." These sessions involved the same procedures as earlier Maimonides ganzfeld studies involving View-Master slides as targets and included the same precautions against sensory leakage. Six of the seven sessions resulted in correct identification of the target slides viewed by the sender ($P = .0013$). All but one of the subjects had participated in prior psi ganzfeld sessions, and they reported that their "TV ganzfeld" mentation was almost hallucinatory in quality. While this study did not assess motivational-arousal factors systematically, these findings are consistent with the "perceptual release" theory of dreams and hallucinations (West, 1962), according to which there is an optimal level of arousal necessary to maintain awareness in the absence of patterned exteroceptive input, and that the vividness of mentation in conditions of perceptual isolation is a function of the level of cortical arousal. This is contrary to the suggestion by W. G. Braud (1975), based primarily on his psi relaxation studies, that psi retrieval is associated with extremely low levels of arousal. Clearly, this is an area that requires further research, and the suggestion offered by this study is that the search for a psi-optimal level of arousal should carefully distinguish between cortical arousal and somatic arousal. The paradoxical combination of cortical arousal and somatic relaxation characterizes stage REM sleep which is the prototype of psi-conducive states.

Honorton (1976b) reported a ganzfeld pilot study in which 17 visiting scientists and journalists participated as psi receivers for one session each. In most cases, a member of the laboratory staff served as sender. Target material consisted of View-Master slide reels for some sessions and binary-coded pictures for others. A significant level of target retrieval was obtained ($P = .025$).

Palmer and Aued (1975) reported a study involving 40 volunteer subjects, mostly students. Each contributed a single 20-minute ganzfeld session. One of the experimenters served as sender and concentrated on a target picture for 3 minutes prior to the beginning of the session. However, "the agent rarely even saw the subjects and, when he did it was only briefly," "Think out loud" instructions, identical to those used in the Maimonides studies, were given to the subjects. The results were nonsignificant ($P = .55$).

Parker (1975) reported a psi ganzfeld study with 30 student subjects, each of whom completed a single session with continuous mentation reports. The experimenter served also as sender. State reports (Honorton et al., 1973) were elicited from the subjects at 10-minute intervals. At the end of the session, subjects were asked to make a brief record of their ganzfeld imagery. While no overt communication was allowed between experimenter-sender and subject, the judging procedure was supervised by the former, and the possibility of subtle sensory cues cannot be ruled out. Nonetheless, the overall results were statistically nonsignificant (P = .144). Contrary to prior studies using state reports, in this study subjects who gave high state reports produced significant psi-missing (P = .007).

Three psi ganzfeld studies were reported by Rogo (1976). In the first series, 28 volunteers contributed one session each as psi receivers. One of the experimenters served as sender. While visual ganzfeld techniques were used, there was no regulation of auditory input. Chance results were obtained (P = .50). In the second series, the most promising subject from the first completed ten sessions involving 7-15 minutes of ganzfeld stimulation. While qualitatively impressive target-mentation correspondences were observed, the overall results were not statistically significant (P = .055). Another short-duration ganzfeld series was run with 20 subjects. Again, the duration of ganzfeld stimulation was 7-15 minutes per session. The results were statistically nonsignificant (P = .30).

A comparison of psi retrieval in relation to varying auditory input in ganzfeld stimulation was reported by Habel (1976). Thirty sender-receiver teams completed three picture retrieval sessions each. Standard visual ganzfeld techniques were used throughout, but the nature of the auditory input was varied from session to session. One session involved standard white noise, another involved a highly structured and complex musical piece (Ravel's *Bolero*), and one session involved a simple drumbeat pattern. Target material consisted of View-Master slide reels, viewed by the sender located at a distance of $^1/_4$ mile from the receiver. While the overall results were nonsignificant (P = .83), Habel reported a post-hoc analysis based on the number of subjects run in the experiment per day. In the first half of the experiment, one to three subjects were run per day. During this period, the sessions involving white noise yielded a significant level of target retrieval (P = .046), while the sessions with musical and drumbeat patterns produced chance results. Conflicts over laboratory space, and the need to complete the experiment to meet a deadline, necessitated running between five and eight subjects per day during the second half of the experiment. Chance results were obtained during this period. Habel's impression that subjects run during this latter period were more negative toward the experiment than those run in the earlier, more relaxed period was confirmed by analysis of subjects' responses on the Nowlis Mood Scale, which showed significantly more negative affect during the second half of the experiment (P < .05).

Stanford and Neylon (1975) reported a clairvoyant psi ganzfeld study with 40 college-age volunteers. Each participated for a single 25-minute session, attempting to gain impressions of a target picture enclosed in an opaque wrapper, the content of which was unknown to anyone at the time of the session. Subjects were given an instructional set not to concentrate on the target picture, but to focus instead on their internal mentation. They were told that their "contact" with the picture would take place automatically because of their desire to succeed. Overall psi retrieval was nonsignificant ($P = .60$), but two important findings emerged from experimental predictions. Earlier, Honorton and Harper (1974) had noted informally that subjects in ganzfeld stimulation showed significant time distortion. Stanford and Neylon did not tell their subjects how long the session would last, and they elicited estimates of duration from the subjects. Those who were successful in psi retrieval underestimated the duration of session by 48 percent, whereas those who were unsuccessful in the psi task underestimated duration by 16 per cent. The difference between these two groups was significant ($P < .03$). Questionnaire data indicated a significant relationship between psi scores and percentage of autonomous mentation in session ($r = +.34$, $P < .04$). Body image changes also correlated significantly with psi performance ($P < .02$), confirming the finding obtained earlier by Braud, Wood, and Braud (1975).

Terry (1976) reported a study with 17 subject-receivers, each of whom completed two sessions as psi receivers, under conditions similar to those of Smith et al. (1976). Binary-coded targets were presented to senders tachistoscopically in one condition and supraliminally in the other. Overall psi retrieval was nonsignificant ($P = .61$), although there was a nonsignificant trend toward higher psi performance in the subliminal-sender condition.

Summary of Psi Ganzfeld Studies

Altogether there have been 16 experimental studies of psi retrieval during ganzfeld stimulation. Eight of these studies provided significant overall levels of accuracy in target retrieval. This represents a 50 percent success rate, compared to the expected chance rate of 5 percent. The combined significance of all 16 studies is associated with a probability of approximately 476 million to one. These findings provide compelling support for the hypothesis that psi receptivity is enhanced by relative perceptual isolation in the waking state. Perhaps a more accurate designation for these procedures is sensory relaxation.

The question arises as to whether there are consistent interstudy or interlaboratory differences which significantly discriminate between success and failure in the studies reviewed above. It does not appear that success or failure can be attributed to differences in type of target materials or specific instructions to subjects. While experimenter differences are probably as important as in other psi testing situations, the eight successful psi ganzfeld studies involved a total of nine different experimenters, compared to five different experimenters in the eight unsuccessful psi ganzfeld studies.

There appear to be three major candidates for interstudy variability: (a) laboratory differences, (b) duration of session, and (c) prior involvement of subjects in psi experiments. All of the successful studies originated in the two laboratories (Maimonides and Houston) which have specialized in studies of psi and internal states. Eight of the nine studies reported by these two laboratories provided overall significant levels of psi retrieval. The interaction of psi ganzfeld success with subject mood, reported by Habel (1976), may provide an important clue, and it seems clear that systematic work delineating set and setting variables in relation to psi success will be necessary in order to increase the interlaboratory reliability of these findings.

Investigators of sensory deprivation suggest that perceptual isolation effects are related to length of isolation in much the same way that drug effects are related to dosage (Cohen, 1957). This appears to be particularly true in the case of ganzfeld stimulation. The "blank out" phenomenon which indicates deafferentation has been found (Cohen, 1957) to occur after about 20 minutes of ganzfeld stimulation. For purposes of analysis, I have dichotomized the 16 psi ganzfeld studies on the basis of statistical significance, with length of ganzfeld isolation in each study as the dependent variable. The mean duration of ganzfeld stimulation in studies with overall significant ($P < .05$) psi retrieval was 37 minutes, compared with a mean of 22 minutes for the studies reporting overall nonsignificant psi retrieval. The successful studies were, therefore, on the average 15 minutes longer than the unsuccessful studies. This difference is statistically significant ($P = .005$), and although it may be confounded by laboratory differences, it suggests that further research on optimal session length may be productive.

The prior involvement of subjects in psi research is another variable requiring systematic investigation. Five of the successful psi ganzfeld studies involved subjects who, while not selected on the basis of prior performance, had participated in prior psi studies in the same laboratory. Two other successful studies involved subjects recruited from academic courses taught by one of the experimenters. Of the unsuccessful studies, only one involved subjects with prior laboratory psi experience.

CONCLUSIONS AND SPECULATION

Psi Enhancement through Internal State Procedures

This review has focused on more than 80 experimental studies involving procedures for inducing internal attention states to prepare subjects to receive information from their outer environment, or to influence specific aspects of that

TABLE 3. SIGNIFICANCE OF PSI PERFORMANCE IN FOUR PROCEDURES FOR INDUCING INTERNAL ATTENTION STATES.

Procedure	N Studies	N Signif. (P < .05)	Combined significance of all studies
Meditation	16	9	6×10^{-12}
Hypnosis	42	22	7.5×10^{-11}
Induced Relaxation	13	10	1.2×10^{-9}
Ganzfeld Stimulation	16	8	2.1×10^{-9}

environment, under conditions which preclude sensorimotor functioning. Table 3 shows the number of studies with each procedure, the overall significance of psi results, and the number of independently significant studies for each procedure.

The combined probability for all reported studies with each procedure is highly significant. The level of interstudy replicability for each procedure is also highly significant. These studies were contributed by a total of 26 different laboratories or teams of investigators, 17 of which obtained overall significant levels of psi functioning with internal state procedures.

These findings provide strong support for the following empirical generalization: *Psi functioning is enhanced (i.e., is more easily detected and recognized) when the receiver is in a state of sensory relaxation and is minimally influenced by ordinary perception and proprioception.*

Phenomenological, behavioral, and psychophysiological findings converge to suggest that psi-enhancing internal states share a number of common characteristics, the most firmly established of which are: (a) a sufficient level of cortical arousal to maintain conscious awareness; (b) muscular relaxation; (c) reduction of exteroceptive input from peripheral receptors; and (d) deployment of attention toward internal mentation processes. Other common factors may include right hemispheric modes of information processing (Braud, 1975) and an altered ("state specific") epistemology (LeShan, 1974).

Studies of subliminal perception indicate that retrieval of subliminal sensory influences is also enhanced by internal attention states and that such influences are often mediated through ongoing mentation processes (Dixon, 1971). Comparison of psi and subliminal input during internal attention states suggests that similar processes may be involved in the mediation of weak sensory and psi influences (Smith et al., 1976).

Filter Theory and Mind at Large

Surveying a variety of findings from sensory physiology, psychophysiological studies of meditation, and studies on the role of expectation in human perception, Robert Ornstein concluded, "Gathering information is certainly a major function of sensation, but sensory systems also act in just the opposite way. Our ordinary awareness of the world is selective and is restricted by the characteristics of sensory systems" (Naranjo and Ornstein, 1971).

Considering evidence that psi interactions may be occurring much more frequently than has hitherto been suspected, on an unconscious level (Kreitler and Kreitler, 1972; Stanford, 1974), and the evidence reviewed in this chapter that internal states involving attenuation of exteroceptive input enhance the detection and recognition of psi input, we have, I believe, the beginning of an empirical basis of support for the filter theory of Henri Bergson. According to this theory, the brain and nervous system function primarily as filters, protecting us from being overwhelmed by the "mass of largely useless and irrelevant knowledge, by shutting out most of what we should otherwise perceive and remember at any given moment, leaving only that very small and special selection that is likely to be practically useful" (Broad, 1953).

Aldous Huxley (1963) provided the following commentary on filter theory:

According to such a theory, each one of us is potentially Mind at Large. But insofar as we are animals, our business is at all costs to survive. To make biological survival possible, Mind at Large has to be funneled through the reducing valve of the brain and nervous system. . . . Certain persons, however, seem to be born with a kind of bypass that circumvents the reducing valve. In others temporary bypasses may be acquired either spontaneously or as a result of deliberate "spiritual excercises" (pp. 23–24).

REFERENCES

Altom, K., and Braud, W. G. Clairvoyant and telepathic impressions of musical targets. *Research in Parapsychology 1975*, pp. 171–174. Metuchen, N.J.: Scarecrow Press, 1976.

Anand, B. K., Chhina, G. S., and Singh, B. Some aspects of electroencephalographic studies in yogis. *Electroencephalography and Clinical Neurophysiology*, 1961, 13, 452–456.

Avant, L. Vision in the Ganzfeld. *Psychological Bulletin*, 1965, 64, 245–258.

Barker, P., Messer, E., and Drucker, S. A group majority vote procedure with receiver optimization. In J. D. Morris, W. G. Roll, and R. L. Morris (Eds.), *Research in Parapsychology 1975*, pp. 165–167. Metuchen, N. J.: Scarecrow Press, 1976.

Beloff, J., and Mandleberg, I. An attempted validation of the "Ryzl technique" for training ESP subjects. *Journal of the Society for Psychical Research*, 1966, 43, 229–249.

Bertini, M., Lewis, H., and Witkin, H. Some preliminary observations with an experimental procedure for the study of hypnagogic and related phenomena. *Archivo di Psicologia Neurologia e Psichiatria*, 1964, 6, 493–534.

Braud, L. W., and Braud, W. G. Further studies of relaxation as a psi-conducive state. *Journal of the American Society for Psychical Research*, 1974, 68, 229–245.

Braud, W. G. Psi-conducive states. *Journal of Communication*, 1975, 25, 142–152.

Braud, W. G., and Braud, L. W. Preliminary explorations of psi-conducive states: Progressive muscular relaxation. *Journal of the American Society for Psychical Research*, 1973, 67, 26–46.

Braud, W. G., Smith, G., Andrew, K., and Willis, S. Psychokinetic influences on random generators during evocation of "analytic" vs. "nonanalytic" modes of information processing. In J. D. Morris, W. G. Roll, and R. L. Morris (Eds.), *Research in Parapsychology 1975*, pp. 85–88. Metuchen, N. J.: Scarecrow Press, 1976.

Braud, W., and Thorsrud, M. Psi on the tip of the tongue: A pilot study of the influence of an "incubation period" upon free-response GESP performance. In J. D. Morris, W. G. Roll, and R. L. Morris (Eds.), *Research in Parapsychology 1975*, pp. 167–171. Metuchen, N. J.: Scarecrow Press, 1976.

Braud, W. G., Wood, R., and Braud, L. W. Free-response GESP performance during an experimental hypnagogic state induced by visual and acoustic ganzfeld techniques: A replication and extension. *Journal of the American Society for Psychical Research*, 1975, 69, 105–114.

Broad, C. D. *Religion, Philosophy, and Psychical Research*. New York: Harcourt, Brace, 1953.

Cadwallander, T. C. Cessation of visual experience under prolonged uniform visual stimulation. *American Psychologist*, 1958, 13, 410.

Casler, L. The improvement of clairvoyance scores by means of hypnotic suggestion. *Journal of Parapsychology*, 1962, 26, 77–87.

Casler, L. The effects of hypnosis on GESP. *Journal of Parapsychology*, 1964, 28, 126–134.

Casler, L. Self-generated hypnotic suggestions and clairvoyance. *International Journal of Parapsychology*, 1967, 9, 125–128.

Casler, L. Hypnotically induced interpersonal relationships and their influence on GESP. *Proceedings of the Parapsychological Association*, 1969, 6, 14–15.

Cohen, W. Spatial and textural characteristics of the Ganzfeld. *American Journal of Psychology*, 1957, 70, 403–410.

Dingwall, E. J. (Ed.). *Abnormal Hypnotic Phenomena*. London: Churchill, 1968. 4 vols.

Dixon, N. *Subliminal Perception: The Nature of a Controversy*. New York: McGraw-Hill, 1971.

Dukhan, H., and Rao, K. R. Meditation and ESP scoring. In W. G. Roll, R. L. Morris, and J. D. Morris (Eds.). *Research in Parapsychology 1972*, pp. 148–151. Metuchen, N. J.: Scarecrow Press, 1973.

Edmunds, S., and Jolliffe, D. A GESP experiment with four hypnotized subjects. *Journal of the Society for Psychical Research*, 1965, 43, 192–194.

Fahler, J. ESP card tests with and without hypnosis. *Journal of Parapsychology*, 1957, 21, 179–185.

Fahler, J., and Cadoret, R. J. ESP card tests of college students with and without hypnosis. *Journal of Parapsychology*, 1958, 22, 125–136.

Fahler, J., and Osis, K. Checking for awareness of hits in a precognition experiment with hypnotized subjects. *Journal of the American Society for Psychical Research*, 1966, 60, 340–346.

Gerber, R., and Schmeidler, G. R. An investigation of relaxation and of acceptance of the experimental situation as related to ESP scores in maternity patients. *Journal of Parapsychology*, 1957, 21, 47–57.

Glick, B. S., and Kogen, J. Clairvoyance in hypnotized subjects: Positive results. *Proceedings of the Parapsychological Association*, 1971, 8, 58–59.

Green, E., and Green, A. Regulating our mind-body processes. *Fields Within Fields*, 1973–74, 10, 16–24.

Grela, J. J. Effect on ESP scoring of hypnotically induced attitudes. *Journal of Parapsychology*, 1945, 9, 194–202.

Habel, M. Psi and varying auditory stimuli in the ganzfeld. In J. D. Morris, W. G. Roll, and W. L. Morris (Eds.), *Research in Parapsychology 1975*, pp. 181–184. Metuchen, N.J.: Scarecrow Press, 1976.

Haddox, V. A pilot study of a hypnotic method for training subjects in ESP. *Journal of Parapsychology*, 1966, **30**, 277-278.

Heron, W. Cognitive and physiological effects of perceptual isolation. In P. Solomon et al. (Eds.), *Sensory Deprivation*, pp. 6-33. Cambridge, Mass.: Harvard University Press, 1961.

Heywood, R. *ESP: A Personal Memoir*. New York: Dutton, 1964.

Hilgard, E. *Hypnotic Susceptibility*. New York: Harcourt, Brace, and World, 1965.

Honorton, C. Separation of high- and low-scoring ESP subjects through hypnotic preparation. *Journal of Parapsychology*, 1964, **28**, 251-257.

Honorton, C. A further separation of high- and low-scoring ESP subjects through hypnotic preparation. *Journal of Parapsychology*, 1966, **30**, 172-183.

Honorton, C. Significant factors in hypnotically-induced clairvoyant dreams. *Journal of the American Society for Psychical Research*, 1972, **66**, 86-102.

Honorton, C. Objective determination of information rate in psi tasks with pictorial stimuli. *Journal of the American Society for Psychical Research*, 1975, **69**, 353-359.

Honorton, C. Length of isolation and degree of arousal as probable factors influencing information retrieval in the ganzfeld. In J. D. Morris, W. G. Roll, and R. L. Morris (Eds.), *Research in Parapsychology 1975*, pp. 184-186. Metuchen, N.J.: 1976. (a)

Honorton, C. *Maimonides Division of Parapsychology and Psychophysics Annual Report: 1974-1975*. Brooklyn, N.Y.: Maimonides Medical Center, 1976. (b)

Honorton, C., Davidson, R., and Bindler, P. Feedback-augmented EEG alpha, shifts in subjective state, and ESP card-guessing performance. *Journal of the American Society for Psychical Research*, 1971, **65**, 308-323.

Honorton, C., Davidson, R., and Bindler, P. Shifts in subjective state associated with feedback-augmented EEG alpha. *Psychophysiology*, 1972, **9**, 269-270.

Honorton, C., Drucker, S., and Hermon, H. Shifts in subjective state and ESP under conditions of partial sensory deprivation. *Journal of the American Society for Psychical Research*, 1973, **67**, 191-197.

Honorton, C., and Harper, S. Psi-mediated imagery and ideation in an experimental procedure for regulating perceptual input. *Journal of the American Society for Psychical Research*, 1974, **68**, 156-168.

Honorton, C., and Krippner, S. Hypnosis and ESP performance: A review of the experimental literature. *Journal of the American Society for Psychical Research*, 1969, **63**, 214-252.

Honorton, C., and May, E. Volitional control in a psychokinetic task with auditory and visual feedback. In J. D. Morris, W. G. Roll, and R. L. Morris (Eds.), *Research in Parapsychology 1975*, pp. 90-91. Metuchen, N. J.: Scarecrow Press, 1976.

Honorton, C., and Stump, J. A preliminary study of hypnotically-induced clairvoyant dreams. *Journal of the American Society for Psychical Research*, 1969, **63**, 175-184.

Huxley, A. *The Doors of Perception* and *Heaven and Hell*. New York: Harper & Row, 1963.

Jacobson, E. *Progressive Relaxation*. Chicago: University of Chicago Press, 1929.

Keeling, K. Telepathic transmission in hypnotic dreams: An exploratory study. *Journal of Parapsychology*, 1971, **35**, 330-331.

Kreitler, H., and Kreitler, S. Does extrasensory perception affect psychological experiments? *Journal of Parapsychology*, 1972, **36**, 1-45.

Krippner, S. Experimentally-induced telepathic effects in hypnosis and nonhypnosis groups. *Journal of the American Society for Psychical Research*, 1968, **62**, 387-398.

Lehmann, D., Beeler, G., and Fender, D. EEG responses during the observation of stabilized retinal images. *Electroencephalography and Clinical Neurophysiology*, 1967, **22**, 136-142.

LeShan, L. *The Medium, the Mystic, and the Physicist.* New York: Viking Press, 1974.

Matas, F., and Pantas, L. A PK experiment comparing meditating versus nonmeditating subjects. *Proceedings of the Parapsychological Association,* 1971, **8,** 12–13.

McBain, W., Fox, W., Kimura, S., Nakanishi, M., and Tirado, J. Quasi-sensory communication: An investigation using semantic matching and accentuated affect. *Journal of Personality and Social Psychology,* 1970, **14,** 281–291.

Miller, S., and York, M. Perceptual defensiveness as a performance indicator on a free-response test of clairvoyance. In J. D. Morris, W. G. Roll, and R. L. Morris (Eds.). *Research in Parapsychology 1975,* pp. 162–164. Metuchen, N.J.: Scarecrow Press, 1976.

Mishra, R. *The Textbook of Yoga Psychology.* New York: Julian Press, 1967.

Moser, L. In E. J. Dingwall (Ed.), *Abnormal Hypnotic Phenomena.* London: Churchill, 1968. 4 vols.

Moss, T., Paulson, M., Chang, A., and Levitt, M. Hypnosis and ESP: A controlled experiment. *American Journal of Clinical Hypnosis,* 1970, **13,** 46–56.

Naranjo, C., and Ornstein, R. E. *On the Psychology of Meditation.* New York: Viking Press, 1971.

Nash, C. B., and Durkin, M. G. Terminal salience with multiple digit targets. *Journal of Parapsychology,* 1959, **23,** 49–53.

Orne, M. T. The nature of hypnosis: Artifact and essence. *Journal of Abnormal and Social Psychology,* 1959, **58,** 277–299.

Ornstein, R. E. The techniques of meditation and their implications for modern psychology. In C. Naranjo and R. E. Ornstein, *On the Psychology of Meditation.* New York: Viking Press, 1971.

Osis, K., and Bokert, E. ESP and changed states of consciousness induced by meditation. *Journal of the American Society for Psychical Research,* 1971, **65,** 17–65.

Palmer, J. Scoring in ESP tests as a function of belief in ESP. Part I. The sheep-goat effect. *Journal of the American Society for Psychical Research,* 1971, **65,** 373–408.

Palmer, J., and Aued, I. An ESP test with psychometric objects and the ganzfeld: Negative findings. In J. D. Morris, W. G. Roll, and R. L. Morris (Eds.). *Research in Parapsychology 1974,* pp. 50–53. Metuchen, N.J.: Scarecrow Press, 1975.

Palmer, J., and Lieberman, R. The influence of psychological set on ESP and out-of-body experiences. *Journal of the American Society for Psychical Research,* 1975, **69,** 193–214.

Parker, A. Some findings relevant to the change in state hypothesis. In J. D. Morris, W. G. Roll, and R. L. Morris (Eds.). *Research in Parapsychology 1974,* pp. 40–42. Metuchen, N.J.: Scarecrow Press, 1975.

Parker, A., and Beloff, J. Hypnotically-induced clairvoyant dreams: A partial replication and attempted confirmation. *Journal of the American Society for Psychical Research,* 1970, **64,** 432–442.

Prabhavananda, S., and Isherwood, C. *How to Know God: The Yoga Aphorisms of Patanjali,* New York: New American Library, 1953.

Pratt, J. G. A decade of research with a selected ESP subject: An overview and reappraisal of the work with Pavel Stepanek. *Proceedings of the American Society for Psychical Research,* 1973, **30.**

Rao, K. R. The differential response in three new situations. *Journal of Parapsychology,* 1964, **28,** 81–92.

Rechtschaffen, A. Sleep and dream states: An experimental design. In R. Cavanna (Ed.), *Psi Favorable States of Consciousness,* pp. 87–120. New York: Parapsychology Foundation, 1970.

Rhine, L. E. Psychological processes in ESP experiences. I. Waking experiences. *Journal of Parapsychology,* 1962, **26,** 88–111.

Rogo, D. S. An exploration of some parameters of psi in the ganzfeld. In J. D. Morris, W. G. Roll, and R. L. Morris (Eds.), *Research in Parapsychology 1975*, pp. 174-179. Metuchen, N. J.: Scarecrow Press, 1976.

Ryzl, M. Training the psi faculty by hypnosis. *Journal of the Society for Psychical Research*, 1962, **41**, 234-252.

Ryzl, M., and Ryzlova, J. A case of high-scoring ESP performance in the hypnotic state. *Journal of Parapsychology*, 1962, **26**, 153-171.

Sanders, R., and Reyher, J. Sensory deprivation and the enhancement of hypnotic susceptibility. *Journal of Abnormal Psychology*, 1969, **74**, 375-381.

Schmeidler, G. R. Rorschachs and ESP scores of patients suffering from cerebral concussion. *Journal of Parapsychology*, 1952, **16**, 80-89.

Schmeidler, G. R. High ESP scores after a swami's brief instruction in meditation and breathing. *Journal of the American Society for Psychical Research*, 1970, **64**, 100-103.

Schmeidler, G. R., and McConnell, R. A. *ESP and Personality Patterns*. New Haven: Yale University Press, 1958.

Schmidt, H., and Pantas, L. Psi tests with psychologically equivalent conditions and internally different machines. *Proceedings of the Parapsychological Association*, 1971, **8**, 49-51.

Sinclair, U. *Mental Radio*. Monrovia, Calif.: Sinclair, 1930.

Smith, M., Tremmel, L., and Honorton, C. A comparison of psi and weak sensory influences on ganzfeld mentation. In J. D. Morris, W. G. Roll, and R. L. Morris (Eds.), *Research in Parapsychology 1975*, pp. 191-194. Metuchen, N.J.: Scarecrow Press, 1976.

Stanford, R. G. EEG alpha activity and ESP performance: A replicative study. *Journal of the American Society for Psychical Research*, 1971, **65**, 144-154.

Stanford, R. G. An experimentally testable model for spontaneous psi events. I. Extrasensory events. *Journal of the American Society for Psychical Research*, 1974, **68**, 34-57.

Stanford, R. G., and Lovin, C. EEG alpha activity and ESP performance. *Journal of the American Society for Psychical Research*, 1970, **64**, 375-384.

Stanford. R. G., and Mayer, B. Relaxation as a psi-conducive state: A replication and exploration of parameters. *Journal of the American Society for Psychical Research*. 1974, **68**, 182-191.

Stanford, R. G., and Neylon, A. Experiential factors related to free-response clairvoyance performance in a sensory uniformity setting (ganzfeld). In J. D. Morris, W. G. Roll, and R. L. Morris (Eds.), *Research in Parapsychology 1974*, pp. 89-93. Metuchen, N.J.: Scarecrow Press, 1975.

Stanford, R. G., and Palmer, J. Meditation prior to the ESP task: An EEG study with an outstanding ESP subject. In W. G. Roll, R. L. Morris, and J. D. Morris (Eds.), *Research in Parapsychology 1972*, pp. 34-36. Metuchen, N.J.: Scarecrow Press, 1973.

Stanford, R. G., and Stevenson, I. EEG correlates of free-response GESP in an individual subject. *Journal of the American Society for Psychical Research*, 1972, **66**, 357-368.

Stephenson, C. Cambridge ESP-hypnosis experiments (1958-64). *Journal of the Society for Psychical Research*, 1965, **43**, 77-91.

Stevenson, I. *Telepathic Impressions*. Charlottesville: University Press of Virginia, 1970.

Suedfeld, P. Changes in intellectual performance and in susceptibility to influence. In J. Zubec (Ed.), *Sensory Deprivation: Fifteen Years of Research*, pp. 126-166. New York: Appleton Century Crofts, 1969.

Taimni, I. K. *The Science of Yoga*. Wheaton, Ill.: The Theosophical Publishing House, 1961.

Tart, C. Self-report scales of hypnotic depth. *International Journal of Clinical and Experimental Hypnosis*, 1970, **18**, 105-125.

Tepas, D. The electrophysiological correlates of vision in a uniform field. In M. Whitcomb (Ed.), *Visual Problems of the Armed Forces*, pp. 21–25. Washington: National Academy of Science, National Research Council, 1962.

Terry, J. Comparison of stimulus duration in sensory and psi conditions. In J. D. Morris, W. G. Roll, and R. L. Morris (Eds.), *Research in Parapsychology 1975*, pp. 179–181. Metuchen, N.J.: Scarecrow Press, 1976.

Terry J., and Honorton, C. Psi information retrieval in the ganzfeld: Two confirmatory studies. *Journal of the American Society for Psychical Research*, 1976, **70**, 207–217.

Terry, J., Tremmel, L., Kelly, M., Harper, S., and Barker, P. Psi information rate in guessing and receiver optimization. In J. D. Morris, W. G. Roll, and R. L. Morris (Eds.), *Research in Parapsychology 1975*, pp. 194–198. Metuchen, N.J.: 1976.

Van de Castle, R. L., and Davis, K. The relationship of suggestibility to ESP scoring level. *Journal of Parapsychology*, 1962, **26**, 270–271.

Vivekananda, Swami. *Raja Yoga*. New York: Ramakrishna-Vivekananda Center, 1955.

Wallace, R. K. Physiological effects of Transcendental Meditation. *Science*, 1970, **167**, 1751–1754.

Wallace, R., Benson, H., and Wilson, A. A wakeful hypometabolic physiologic state. *American Journal of Physiology*, 1971, **221**, 795–799.

West, L. J. A general theory of hallucinations and dreams. In L. J. West (Ed.), *Hallucinations*, pp. 275–291. New York: Grune and Stratton, 1962.

White, R. A. A comparison of old and new methods of response to targets in ESP experiments. *Journal of the American Society for Psychical Research*, 1964, **58**, 21–56.

Wickramasekera, I. The effects of sensory restriction on susceptibility to hypnosis: A hypothesis, some preliminary data, and theoretical speculation. *International Journal of Clinical and Experimental Hypnosis*, 1969, **17**, 217–224.

2

Sleep and Dreams

Robert L. Van de Castle

INTRODUCTION

Cicero, nearly 2,000 years ago, argued against the probability of prophetic dreams and whether it would ever be possible to discover any order or regularity in dreams. With regard to paranormal dreams, some hints as to their frequency and thematic content can be gained by examining surveys of psychic cases that include the incidence of dreams. Stevenson (1968) has estimated that "At least five thousand reasonably well-attested cases have been published in the English literature alone. Many other excellent cases have been published in French, German, Dutch, and other languages" (p. 116).

SPONTANEOUSLY OCCURRING PARANORMAL DREAMS

Documented Spontaneous Cases

A "documented" case is one which contains corroboration that a correspondence existed between a distant event and the person's report of a psychic experience. The largest survey of such cases was reported in the two volume work *Phantasms of the Living* (Gurney, Myers, and Podmore, 1886). Over 5,000 individuals were asked about possible psychic experiences. After sifting through letters, diaries, and interviews with witnesses, a total of 702 cases remained that the investigators felt contained some corroborative evidence for telepathy. Most of the cases concerned apparitions appearing to percipients while awake, but some paranormal events occurred while the percipient was sleeping.

The authors were well aware of the problems inherent in extracting any evidential value from dreams:

> The first objection to dreams, as evidence for transferred impressions of distant conditions or events, is this—that dreams being often somewhat dim and shapeless things, subsequent knowledge of the conditions or events may easily have the effect of giving body and definiteness to the recollection of a dream. . . .
>
> But there is a more general and sweeping objection. Millions of people are dreaming every night; and in dreams, if anywhere, the range of possibilities seems infinite; can any positive conclusion be drawn from such a chaos of meaningless and fragmentary impressions? Must not we admit the force of the obvious *a priori* argument, that among the countless multitudes of dreams, one here and there is likely to correspond in time with an actual occurrence resembling the one dreamed of. . . . Can the chances be at all estimated? . . .
>
> Before we can give weight to a dream-coincidence as pointing to anything beyond the operation of chance, we should inquire whether the event dreamed of is distinct, unexpected, and unusual. . . . amount of detail, and the number of connected events, are of immense importance, as each subsequently verified detail tells with ever-mounting strength against the hypothesis of accidental coincidence. Once more, dream content must be considered to some extent in relation to the dream-habits of the particular dreamer. Before estimating the value of the fact that a person has dreamt of the sudden death of a friend on the night when the death took place, we should have to ascertain that that person is not in the habit of dreaming of distressing or horrible events (Vol. 1, pp. 298–302).

A fairly typical example of the type of dream catalogued by these investigators is the following one where Mrs. Hilda West was the percipient and her father (or brother) was the agent:

> My father [Sir John Crowe, Consul-General for Norway] and brother were on a journey [to Norway] during the winter [of 1871–72]. I was expecting them home, without knowing the exact day of their return. . . . I had gone to bed at my usual time, about 11 p.m. Some time during the night I had a vivid dream, which made a great impression on me. I dreamt . . . I saw my father driving in a Spids sledge, followed in another by my brother. They had to pass a cross-road, on which another traveller was driving very fast, also in a sledge with one horse. Father seemed to drive on without observing the other fellow, who would without fail have driven over father if he had not made his horse rear, so that I saw my father drive under the hoofs of the horse. Every moment I expected the horse would fall down and crush him. I called out "Father! Father!" and woke in great fright. The next morning my father and brother returned. I said to him, "I am so glad to see you arrive quite safely as I had such a dreadful dream about you last night."

My brother said, "You could not have been in greater fright about him than I was," and then he related to me what had happened, which tallied exactly with my dream.

I have never had any other dream of this kind, nor do I remember ever to have had another dream of an accident happening to anyone in whom I was interested (Gurney et al., Vol. 1, p. 202).

Mrs. West's brother provided the investigators with a statement in which he verified the occurrence of the near-accident, adding that she had the dream "at the very time it happened, about 11:30 p.m."

In analyzing the 702 cases reported in *Phantasms,* it was found that 58 percent of the percipients were women, in 47 percent of the cases a blood relative was the agent, in 42 percent a friend or acquaintance, in 6 percent a husband or wife, and in 4 percent a stranger. Dreams were involved in 149 cases (21 percent) and 79 of these dreams (53 percent) represented or suggested the theme of death. The authors noted that "The passage from sleep to waking admits of many degrees; and a very interesting group of cases remain which cannot properly be classed as dreams, and yet which do not appertain to seasons of complete normal wakefulness" (Gurney et al., 1886, Vol. 1, p. 389). They called such experiences "borderland cases."

Dale (1946) examined the 110 "borderland" cases reported in *Phantasms* and divided them into three different groups. In 26 cases there was insufficient information for classification but for the remaining 84 cases she provided the following breakdown: in 25 percent of cases the percipient was just falling asleep, in 15 percent the percipient was just waking up, and in 60 percent the percipient was sound asleep and jolted awake by the impression that someone had entered the room or called their name. In all but six of the 50 "sound asleep" cases, the agent was dead or dying. Dale observed that when the percipient was falling asleep, he was more inclined to label his experiences as a "vision" and to describe the situation as if he were an on-the-scene observer, whereas percipients awakened from "deep" sleep without exception reported experiencing an exteriorized hallucination as if the agent were actually in the sleeper's bedroom.

Continuing in the tradition of *Phantasms*, E. M. Sidgwick published a paper in 1923 that was later incorporated into a one-volume abridgment of *Phantasms* published in 1962. Mrs. Sidgwick reviewed all the telepathic cases appearing in the then privately circulated *Journal* of the Society for Psychical Research (S.P.R.) from Volume 3 to 19 which had not been republished in the *Proceedings* of the S.P.R. or in the books by Podmore (1894) or Myers (1903). There were 54 cases excluded by the republication criterion. She also rejected any cases where the time interval between the presumed paranormal experience and the subsequent report of it exceeded 5 years or if she felt the evidence in the case was too weak. This left a total of 200 cases of which 30 were labeled as experimental or semiexperimental in nature. The percipient was reported to be dreaming in about one-third of the 170 remaining spontaneous cases.

Saltmarsh (1934) collated all the cases dealing with precognition since Volume 1 of the *Journal* and *Proceedings* of the S.P.R. These cases totaled to 349 of which 68 had occurred during mediumistic trance or while crystal-gazing. When vague, weak, and contemporaneous cases were excluded, a hard-core residue of 138 precognitive cases remained; 68 percent of these occurred during dreaming and 3 percent during "borderland" sleep. Death was the theme in 34 percent of the 138 cases.

In 1945 the American Society for Psychical Research (A.S.P.R.) sent a form letter to 203 subjects who had participated in a long-distance experiment and asked: Did the participant ever have (a) a dream or (b) a waking experience that corresponded to a distant event? Participants were also requested to supply an account of the incident. Of the 50 participants replying affirmatively to these questions, 52 percent acknowledged having had a dream corresponding to a distant event or one occurring later in time. Personal follow-up letters were sent to all respondents, but Dale (1946) reported that independent corroboration could only be obtained for eight cases, six of which involved female percipients. Only one of these cases involved a dream, and two occurred during "borderland" sleep.

In response to a popular article appearing in 1951, the A.S.P.R. received letters containing accounts of psychic experiences from 705 women and 244 men. Each letter was placed in one of five categories based upon interest and possibility of corroboration. Letters from the 89 people classified in category 1 were personally answered and further details and supporting documents requested (Dale, 1951). Of the 65 cases eventually considered as veridical, the agent-percipient relationship was either a close blood or marital tie in 28 cases. Nearly 50 percent of the themes concerned death. Dreams were involved in 41 percent of the cases, and 11 percent took place during "borderland" sleep.

The British S.P.R. received approximately 1,500 letters in response to a popular article published in 1957. An estimated average of 60 man-hours per case was required to follow through on correspondence and interviews. Eventually 300 cases were considered to be worthy of analysis (Green, 1960). The percipients consisted of 81 percent females while 64 percent of the agents were males. Death was the theme in 28 percent of the cases. The percipient was dreaming in 33 percent of the cases and in "borderland" sleep for 8 percent of the cases. Of the 103 cases involving precognition, 64 occurred during dreams and ten during "borderland" sleep.

Another popular article appearing in 1957 led to about 1,200 letters describing psychic experiences being mailed to the A.S.P.R. (Dale, White, and Murphy, 1962). Follow-up letters were sent to the most promising cases asking for confirmatory details. This article describes 17 corroborated events obtained from 16 individuals, 15 of whom were females. Of the 11 precognitive events, ten were based on dreams, and dreams were also involved in two of the other cases. Death was the theme for three of the 12 dreams.

Actuarial Studies of Spontaneous Precognitive Dreams

In 1927, J. W. Dunne published *An Experiment with Time.* This book stimulated a great deal of both popular and scientific interest in prophetic dreams. Besterman (1933) organized an experiment to examine Dunne's claim that precognitive dreams were as much to be expected as dreams of past events. In Besterman's first series, 20 members of the British S.P.R. were supplied with notebooks, carbon paper, and indelible pencils. They were instructed to write down their dreams upon awakening and mail off an original copy that same day. A carbon copy was retained by the dreamer, who was to notify Besterman if any correspondences to his recorded dreams occurred. Only two of the 265 dreams sent in during an 8-week interval had "moderate" value for suggesting precognition. Since Dunne complained that the middle-aged status of S.P.R. members may not have been optimal, Besterman utilized 22 Oxford students for his second series. Among the 148 dreams turned in, there were 12 "apparent" precognitions, including two "good" ones. Both of the two "good" dreams occurred to the same individual on the same night. For the third series, Dunne served as the subject. Only 17 dreams were forwarded during a 4-month interval of which he claimed five as revealing precognition. Besterman agreed that four of them offered "fair or moderate" precognitive material.

A few days after the kidnaping of the Lindbergh baby, the Harvard Psychological Clinic published a newspaper request for dreams that might bear upon the case (Murray and Wheeler, 1937). Other newspapers copied the request and over 1,300 dreams were received prior to the discovery of the baby's body. The mutilated body was discovered in a shallow grave, in some woods, several miles from the Lindbergh home in New Jersey. The man eventually convicted of the crime was Hauptmann, a German carpenter and ex-convict. The authors note that many of the dreams contained references to "foreigners" or "men with foreign accents." In about 5 percent of the dreams the baby was dead although the authors concluded that only seven dreams suggested the actual location of the body and the manner of its burial. One of these came from a Mrs. J. K.: "I thought I was standing or walking in a very muddy place *among many trees.* One spot looked as though it might be a *round, shallow grave.* Just then I heard a voice saying, 'the baby has been *murdered* and buried there'" (p. 310).

Also received were three dreams in which the writer stated that the dream occurred shortly before the kidnaping. In two of these dreams the Lindbergh baby was specifically identified, and both dreamers indicated they told other witnesses about the dream before the actual news was made public. The authors, however, made no efforts to verify the authenticity of these statements and were content to merely indicate that they "seem worthy of recording." The authors concluded:

> We have not the data for estimating the probabilities in a kidnaping case of this sort, but if one considers only the possible combination of listed items it appears that on the basis of pure chance one should expect a great many more dreams than were actually reported which combined the three crucial items . . . . The findings do not support the contention that distant events and dreams are causally related (p.313).

An attempt was made after the occurrence of two tragic events to discover whether any paranormal experiences may have been involved. Stevenson (1960, 1965) assembled 19 corroborated reports of percipients who apparently had extrasensory awareness that the *Titanic,* an "unsinkable" ship, had foundered. Of the ten precognitive cases, eight involved dreams. The other disaster was the Aberfan coal-tip slide that killed 144 persons, mostly school children, in a Welsh mining village in 1966. A week after the disaster, an appeal was made through a national newspaper for reports from people who might have had some fore-knowledge of it, and 76 letters were received. Of the 35 cases which seemed to stand up under examination, 25 were based upon dreams (Barker, 1967).

To act as a repository for possible precognitive dreams, the British Premonitions Bureau was set up in London, and Nelson (1970) arranged the Central Premonitions Registry at Box 482, Times Square Station, New York, N.Y. 10036.

In Holland, Tenhaeff (1968) has evaluated several hundred dreams from an engineer and noted that he seemed to develop the ability to have paranormal dreams about death events after his own father, to whom he was devoted, died. Bender (1966), in Germany, has collected over 1,300 dreams during a 10-year period from an actress and has estimated that approximately 10 percent of her dreams have been found to contain paranormal elements. Psychological attention has been directed toward exploring how her personality dynamics contribute to the particular precognitive dream symbols she employs.

Nondocumented Surveys of Spontaneous Cases

To evaluate the evidence for premonitions, E. M. Sidgwick (1888) examined 240 "good, bad, and indifferent" cases and reported that in about two-thirds of them, dreams had been the channel of expression. A few of her "good" cases were later utilized in Saltmarsh's precognition review (1934).

Flammarion, the French astronomer, made several published appeals in 1899 for accounts of psychic events associated with awareness of death at a distance. A total of 1,824 letters describing such experiences was received. Over 400 examples of the material he obtained appear in his book *The Unknown* (1900). Three chapters are devoted to dreams where he describes 49 cases involving "sight at a distance" when dreams or somnambulism were involved, 74 premonitory dreams, and 70 cases when the percipient was asleep.

The Boston S.P.R. mailed a questionnaire to 9,298 men and 718 women whose names appeared in *Who's Who in America* (Prince, 1931). A total of 430 persons from this distinguished group acknowledged a paranormal experience. Although only 7 percent of the persons polled were women, 12 percent of the cases were reported by women. Dreams accounted for 25 percent of the experiences with death being the theme in 45 percent and accidents in 20 percent.

As a result of public appeals, the Institute for Border Areas of Psychology and Mental Hygiene located at the University of Freiburg received over 1,000 letters describing psychic experiences. This material was analyzed by Sannwald in terms of statistical frequencies (1959) and motivational factors (1960). He reported that 70 percent of the percipients were females, and 61 percent of the agents were males. Death comprised 43 percent of the themes while incidents associated with love, marriage, and births only totaled 3 percent. Approximately 50 percent of the cases were based upon dreams, but if only precognition is considered, the figure rises to 60 percent.

The largest collection of nondocumented cases has been compiled by L. E. Rhine from letters sent to the Parapsychology Laboratory at Duke University. In one analysis based upon 3,290 cases of precognition, Rhine (1954) reported that 68 percent occurred in a dreaming state.

In an article describing paranormal dreams, Rhine (1962) indicated that her total case collection at that time numbered 7,119, and 65 percent of these consisted of dreams. Approximately 68 percent of the dreams could be classified as realistic, but a feeling of conviction was present in only 23 percent of such cases. This is surprising since 91 percent of the realistic dreams had specific enough details to warrant being labeled as a "complete idea" dream. A dream was considered as incomplete if no identity was established (all my relatives were there but I couldn't see who was in the coffin); if the identity was incorrect; or if the event were modified such as dreaming that a friend received a broken leg from a boating accident whereas in actuality it was a broken arm. In the incomplete unrealistic grouping, sometimes the dreamer inserted himself as the victim of a tragedy which befell another while in other cases the imagery was symbolic in nature. At the conclusion of her analyses, Rhine made the following observation:

> The pathway of ESP impressions from inception to consciousness . . . is not a sure and easy one. The impression may be deflected along the way with ease. It may be distorted, fragmented, or even quite blocked out of expression, and this may be occasioned not only by strong personal motivations, as one might expect, but also by weak and nameless cross-currents of association (p. 198).

Stevenson (1970) analyzed 125 precognitive dreams from "a miscellaneous collection" of uneven authenticity. He notes that 45 percent of these dreams were characterized as "vivid" or "realistic" by the percipients. Agents were close relatives in 31 percent of the cases and strangers in 9 percent. The percipient dreamed the future event would happen to himself in 49 percent of the cases. In 27 percent of the cases, percipients attempted to avert fulfillment of the precognized event. The precognitive dream occurred two or more times with little variation in 14 percent of the cases. Only 13 percent of the dreams were considered to contain symbols for the event.

An article by Stevenson (1963) refers to an unpublished survey of 372 ostensibly paranormal dreams made by J. F. Nicol from the publications of the A.S.P.R. Only four of the dreams were postcognitive in nature. Nicol (1968) made a brief reference to this survey and indicated that 66 percent of the dreams were precognitive.

On a questionnaire administered to nearly 2,500 eighth grade students in Northern India, 36 percent of the boys and 37 percent of the girls acknowledged some form of personal ESP experience (Prasad and Stevenson, 1968). Dreams were involved in contemporary experiences for 54 percent of the boys and 53 percent of the girls, and for 51 percent of the boys and 57 percent of the girls with precognitive experiences. Male agents, particularly brothers, were more frequent for both sexes, and the most frequent theme for both sexes was death (average 46 percent) when contemporary ESP was considered.

Brockhaus (1968) administered a questionnaire about paranormal beliefs to 182 university and 59 lycee students in the Ivory Coast region of West Africa. A belief in paranormal dreams was expressed by 57 percent of the students, and 33 percent answered that they had experienced prophetic dreams. Students who had been raised in urban settings professed a lower incidence of belief in parapsychological phenomena than those raised in the countryside.

Hanefeld (1968) gave a preliminary report based upon 1,000 German cases obtained from letters sent to a newspaper. He stated that 38 percent of the cases were based on dreams and that the dreamers felt their veridical dreams were more clear, more distinct, and easier to recall than their ordinary dreams.

A questionnaire containing 46 questions about ESP experiences was mailed to 700 residents of Charlottesville, Virginia, and to 300 local university students (Palmer and Dennis, 1975). Usable returns were obtained from 51 percent of the town and 89 percent of the student sample. One question was: "Have you ever had a rather clear and specific dream which matched in detail an event which occurred before, during, or after your dream, and which you did not know about or did not expect at the time of the dream?" Yes answers were given by 36 percent of the townspeople and 38 percent of the students. Since a more or less general psi factor emerged in the data analyses, respondents who had acknowledged paranormal dreams were much more likely to also acknowledge other forms of ESP experiences.

Commentary on Spontaneous Cases

Due to space limitations, it has not been possible to provide many illustrations of impressive paranormal dreams. Familiarity with such spontaneous material is strongly encouraged, however, for anyone wishing to appraise their evidential value or desiring to construct possible motivational models or theoretical hypotheses. For the reader interested in developing a firsthand appreciation for spontaneous dream material, the following books, each containing over 100 dream reports, should be consulted: *Phantasms of the Living* (Gurney et al., 1886), *The Unknown* (Flammarion, 1900), *Human Experiences* (Prince, 1931), *The Mystery of Dreams* (Stevens, 1949), and *Hidden Channels of the Mind* (Rhine, 1961).

What conclusions can be reached about paranormal dreams from the literature on spontaneous cases? It is difficult to establish any firm generalizations because most surveys of spontaneous cases don't report separate data analyses based only on the dream material and one doesn't know how much reliance to place upon the uncorroborated dream reports that have been mailed in by respondents to media requests.

Given these limitations, some recurrent threads of similarity can, however, be traced through the fabric of the collated studies carried out during the past 90 years. If various forms of ESP experiences are lumped together, all studies find that dreams are involved in somewhere between 33 percent and 68 percent of the cases. If only telepathic cases are considered, approximately 25 percent involve dreams; if only precognitive cases are considered, approximately 60 percent involve dreams. About 10 percent of cases occur while the percipient is in a "borderland" state of sleep.

Women outnumber men nearly two to one as percipients while men are the agents in approximately 60 percent of the cases. Close blood ties are involved in about 50 percent of the cases, and death looms as the most prominent theme, being present in close to 50 percent of the experiences, with accidents and injuries next in order of prominence.

Paranormal dreams are described as being unusually vivid and intense, and they have a peculiarly tenacious quality to them after the dreamer awakens. Although the scenario and characters are sometimes pictured in surprisingly accurate detail, the dreamer infrequently takes any assertive action to confirm or change the outcome portrayed in the dream. A fair number of paranormal dreams, however, have some psychological editing performed upon them so that various distortions or displacement of details occur or they may involve obscuring personal symbols. Due to this latter feature, many paranormal dreams may go unnoticed by an outside evaluator or even by the dreamer himself if he is not sufficiently attuned to the types of dream imagery he employs to represent certain emotionally pertinent ideas or interactions.

DREAMS IN THE THERAPEUTIC SETTING

Since considerable emotionality is stirred up by the painful probing activities associated with psychoanalysis and since dreams are utilized as a major mode of examination in that setting, it is not surprising that many parapsychologically oriented analysts have reported that the consultation room provides a fertile climate in which to observe the germination and development of psi-laden dreams.

A number of analysts have published clinical studies which trace out the genesis of presumptive paranormal dreams in the therapeutic situation (Ehrenwald, 1955; Eisenbud, 1970; Schwarz, 1965; Servadio, 1955; Ullman, 1959). An excellent collection of earlier studies by several analysts bearing upon this topic was compiled by Devereux (1953) in *Psychoanalysis and the Occult*. This book also contains six selections from Freud which bear upon possible relationships between psychoanalysis and telepathic or premonitory dreams. Among other comments, Freud remarked that the use of associations could help to ascertain whether doubtful phenomena were telepathic or not.

It is certainly not difficult to accept an instance of the following type described in Eisenbud (1970). One evening he had to phone his daughter in California to ask her to put off a planned visit home because he would be busy the coming week working with a patient. This woman had an unusual disorder and was to be housed in Eisenbud's home. That night one of his current patients had a dream in which she came to Eisenbud's office and found a child of about three there who looked as if she were Eisenbud's daughter. "You indicated to her somehow that you were busy. No words were exchanged. She knew she wasn't approved of, as if you had said, 'Go home, I have no time for you'" (p. 194).

In the case above, it is also not difficult to accept Eisenbud's hypothesis that his patient probably experienced this dream because she was identifying with his deeply disappointed daughter and felt jealous and threatened by the imminent arrival on the scene of a patient who would be a feminine competitor for the annalyst's attention.

Other incidents recounted in Eisenbud's *Psi and Psychoanalysis* (1970) are much less easy to follow. Several pages are generally required to trace the linkages forged by psi among events in the analyst's life, the stage of transference or countertransference currently existing in the therapy, and the patient's associations to the dream. At times, Eisenbud also finds it necessary to include events occurring in his wife's life, in other patients' lives, in friends' lives, etc., in order to diagram the psi-circuitry flowing between these various interpersonal poles.

Telepathic dreams are hypothesized to come forth most readily in the analytic setting whenever the patient feels neglected by the analyst or whenever an unresolved problem of the analyst is reactivated by the patient's effort to deal with that same issue. Therapists have been reluctant to publish accounts of psi dreams from their patients for several reasons. When such accounts are published, the author frequently receives very negative reactions from other professionals who do not accept a psi hypothesis. If the psychodynamic formulation sketched above is correct, publication of a psi dream is akin to an implicit admission that the therapist may have been guilty of ignoring a patient on some occasion. If the dream has been produced because the patient has zeroed in on some disowned problem of his, the therapist must be willing to make a public confession of that problem and to share all the intimate, embarrassing details that would be entailed by such a disclosure.

Some facets of clinical dreams seem to differ from those typically expected in spontaneous dreams. Themes of death, injury, or accidents are much less common. Family members are featured less prominently as agents, and it is the therapist who appears most frequently on front stage center, although often in disguised form. The events spotlighted from the analyst's life may involve such mundane matters as the floor plan in his new apartment (Ehrenwald, 1955) or the analyst's lack of sufficient silverware for expected dinner guests (Pederson-Krag, 1947).

DREAM PATTERNS AND ESP CARD-GUESSING SCORES

An unpublished dissertation by Miltiade Rhally from the Jung Institute in Zurich was reviewed by White (1965). Following each of 135 analytic sessions during a 2-year period, Rhally administered a clairvoyance test. The patient's task was to guess "down through" a deck of 50 standard ESP cards which had been randomized, sealed in an envelope, and placed on the analyst's desk by an assistant. Below-chance negative scores appeared during the 11 sessions when the patient reported a dream about the analyst or the analysis ($P = .04$), during the four sessions containing dreams of situations analogous to fellatio ($P = .0005$), and during the 19 sessions where a toilet was mentioned in a dream ($P = .003$). Above-chance positive scores were obtained following the 19 sessions when she reported dreams of attempting to escape from an existing situation ($P = .01$). These findings, in conjunction with the results of regularly administered psychological tests, enabled Rhally to formulate a dynamic motivational pattern that seemed to be reliably associated with ESP performance for this particular patient. Thus, rather than acting as a hindrance, the incorporation of a quantitative ESP procedure served as a useful additional analytic tool.

Van de Castle (1974) described a 5-year program of ESP testing carried out among the Cuna Indians of Panama. Each summer from 1968–1972, he administered group GESP tests to Cuna adolescents in a classroom setting. The ESP stimuli consisted of five colored drawings portraying objects familiar to

Cunas: a shark, jaguar, canoe, conch shell, and airplane. Van de Castle served as agent, and each of the 461 subjects completed 50 trials. Scores were checked and tabulated by an outside assistant. The overall scoring level was at a chance level for both sexes combined, but girls scored significantly higher than boys ($P < .01$).

Each student also wrote down his most recent dream. The 408 available dreams were scored by an outside assistant for the presence or absence of seven categories. These scoring categories received weights of 0, 1, or 2 points which allowed the total dream score to range from a theoretical minimum of 0 to a maximum of 10. For both girls and boys separately, there were significant differences ($P < .01$) in ESP scores in relation to the magnitude of the dream score.

Two separate scoring components seemed to be present in the dreams. Dreams that contained references to aggression, overt sexuality, and animals were associated with high ESP scores. The second component consisting of the presence of parental figures and relatives was also associated with high ESP scores. The first component was tentatively interpreted as a measure reflecting comfortableness with ego-alien impulses and the second as indicating acceptance of the traditional Cuna values of cooperation and helpfulness.

A few studies have also examined the relationship between dream recall and ESP scores. Johnson (1968) found a significant ($P = .01$) positive relationship between ratings of dream recall derived from a standardized "dream interview" and an ESP measure consisting of four clairvoyance and four precognition runs administered in a group setting to Swedish undergraduates. Honorton (1972) administered five precognition runs in a group setting to 28 members of an adult education class. Subjects who stated on a questionnaire that they remembered at least one dream a week scored significantly higher ($P < .01$) than those with less frequent recall. Haraldsson (1975) group administered to 223 Icelandic students 100 trials of a precognition test consisting of target digits from 0 through 9 and also had them complete a multiple-choice questionnaire dealing with dream recall and precognitive dream experiences. Groups differing in frequency of dream recall did not differ significantly in ESP scores, but there was a significant positive relationship ($P < .001$) between dream recall and the reported frequency of precognitive dreams.

ESP DREAMS IN THE LABORATORY

Probably the earliest published account of an experimental effort to paranormally influence a dream was reported by Weserman (1819). He was very impressed by "animal magnetism" and attempted to project his magnetic influence into the thoughts and dreams of friends at a distance. Weserman claimed five successful experiments, and Eisenbud (1970, p. 55) provides a brief account of one of them. Weserman's percipient was an elderly woman who was to see in a dream the funeral procession of Weserman's deceased friend C. When he went by the next day to investigate the outcome of his efforts, she immediately said that she had seen a funeral procession in her sleep and Weserman was the corpse. Weserman adroitly commented, "There was thus a slight error."

An Italian psychiatrist, Ermacora (1895), conducted a series of experiments with a 4-year-old girl, Angelina. The agent was a medium with a child trance control named Elvira. Angelina stayed with the medium, who was her cousin, while she visited Venice. Ermacora would come to her home at night, and while the medium was in trance, he would ask her control Elvira to transmit some suggested topic for Angelina to dream about. Ermacora then left the house. The next morning the medium would ask the child about her dreams, although at a later stage in the research, it was the medium's mother who carried out the questioning. One night, part of the message to be transmitted was that Angelina was to be a goatherder grazing goats on a hillside and that a lady would be carrying a parasol in her hand. The child was reported to have dreamed that she was in a high place, with a stick in her hand, among a lot of dogs with horns on their heads. Although a large number of dreams were reported that contain rather detailed incorporations of the topics selected by Ermacora, the experimental procedures were so lax on so many critical points that one cannot accept the findings with any degree of confidence. To Ermacora's credit, however, quite a few nights were noted where complete failure occurred.

A Viennese psychotherapist, Wilfred Daim (1953), used as targets a random pairing of a color and a geometrical symbol. Daim would concentrate on the stimulus early in the morning, when the percipient was presumably asleep. The percipient, who knew the pool of target material, wrote down his dreams before Daim asked for a more detailed report. Daim claimed that in 75 percent of the 30 trials attempted, the target material was directly reflected in the dream content. Percipients often reported a feeling of intrusion as when a three-cornered red fir tree suddenly appeared in an ongoing dream about music and soldiers. Since Daim was aware of the target when conducting his inquiry and also made the judgments as to whether incorporation had occurred, the study had obvious procedural shortcomings.

The Maimonides Research Program

The methodology and results associated with the various dream studies carried out during a decade of research at Maimonides Medical Center have been published in over 50 individual articles and have also been summarized in a technical monograph (Ullman and Krippner, 1970) and in a popular book (Ullman and Krippner, with Vaughan, 1973). A brief chronology of the major studies will be presented below.

Ullman undertook his initial effort to employ the objective EEG indicators for detecting the "dreaming" (REM) stage of sleep at the research quarters of the Parapsychology Foundation in 1960. Mrs. Eileen Garrett, a well-known sensitive, was the first percipient, and Ullman served as agent. During the two nights they worked as a team, there were some very good correspondences. A number of other percipients participated during this preliminary stage of research, and they also gave some encouraging results.

In 1962, a dream laboratory was established at the Maimonides Medical Center where Ullman was Chairman of the Psychiatry Department. With the help of Sol Feldstein, a graduate student, Ullman worked out the details of an experimental design that served as the protocol for all later studies. Krippner joined the laboratory in 1964 as the first formal studies were beginning.

The basic design was as follows: the percipient had EEG electrodes attached so that his sleep could be monitored while in bed in a soundproof room. After the percipient was going to sleep, an envelope containing a target picture, an art reproduction, was selected by a random number table and given to the agent. This envelope was not opened until the agent was locked into his room for the night. The agent's room in the first studies was 32 feet away, later it was 98 feet, and still later it was 14 miles away. A third person, the monitor, watched the EEG tracings all night long so that the percipient's REM periods could be detected.

As soon as a REM period began, the monitor signaled the agent to insure that he was awake and to alert the agent to renew his "transmitting" activities. After 10–20 minutes of REM activity, the monitor awakened the percipient via the intercom and requested that he describe his dreams in as much detail as possible. At the conclusion of the dream report, which was tape recorded, the monitor again signaled the agent so he could return to sleep if he desired. The same target picture was used for the entire night. The monitor continued to awaken the percipient for dream reports from each REM period, and the agent continued to concentrate on the target picture during each REM period after being signaled by the monitor.

The next morning, the percipient would generally be shown eight or 12 (depending on the study) art prints, one of which was a duplicate of the target picture the agent had attempted to transmit. The percipient then ranked the pictures and assigned a confidence rating from 1 to 100 for each picture in terms of how closely it matched the content or emotions of his dreams. The complete typescripts of the dreams were also sent to three outside judges along with the set of art prints for them to make independent rankings and confidence ratings. If eight pictures were included in the set, it was considered a "hit" if the target picture was assigned a rank of 1 through 4 and a "miss" if it was assigned a rank of 5 through 8. The number of "hits" vs. "misses" was statistically evaluated through the binomial expansion. The confidence ratings, ranging from a value of 1-100 points per picture, were evaluated by means of an analysis of variance (ANOVA) technique.

The design just described ruled out any sensory contact between the agent and percipient once the experiment was under way and also insured that the person conducting the dream inquiry had no knowledge about the identity of the target picture. Since the envelope containing the target picture was randomly selected from hundreds of potential choices in the files, it was extremely unlikely that it would consistently correspond with any stereotyped dream imagery that a percipient might possess. This design combined all the necessary procedural precautions so that any significant results it might yield could not be explained on the basis of a faulty methodology.

Several "major" studies were reported by the Maimonides group. In the first screening study, a male and female staff member served as alternate agents for 12 percipients, seven males and five females. Each percipient served for one night. Matching by three judges did not yield significant results with ANOVA but revealed that the male agent obtained significantly higher scores ($P < .05$) than the female agent. Percipients rankings were also significant ($P < .05$).

The second major study involved the successful male agent, Sol Feldstein, and the most successful of the percipients, William Erwin, a psychologist. A total of seven nights was completed before Erwin became ill. Significant differences for both ranks and ratings were obtained for the percipient's ($P < .05$) and the judges' evaluations ($P < .01$). These first two studies were described in a journal article (Ullman, Krippner, and Feldstein, 1966).

The third study was another screening one in which Feldstein alternated as agent with a female agent. Percipients were six men and six women who each slept one night in the laboratory. Significant results were not obtained for judges' or percipients' evaluations.

The most promising percipient from the second screening study, Robyn Posin, a psychologist, completed eight nights with Feldstein as agent, but neither her ratings nor that of the outside judges were significant. The second screening study and the Posin study are reported in a paper by Ullman (1969).

Another percipient from the second screening study, Theresa Grayeb, participated in the fifth major study (Krippner, 1969). A male research assistant served as agent for the eight nights when a target picture was being transmitted but, unknown to the percipient, there were eight nights when no target was involved. The percipient thought she was participating in a 16-night study. No significant differences between target and nontarget nights were found for either Grayeb's or the judges' ratings.

For the next major study, Erwin again was the percipient for an eight-night study with Feldstein acting as the agent (Ullman and Krippner, 1969). A novel twist was added to the role played by the agent. Each target had a "multisensory" kit associated with it so that the agent could immerse himself in the mood or theme of the target picture. For example, when the target was *Descent from the Cross,* the kit contained a crucifix, a small wooden cross, a picture of Jesus, some thumb tacks, and a red felt-tipped pen. The instructions in the kit read:

"Using these tacks, nail Christ to the cross; using this marker, color his body with blood." Excerpts from Erwin's dreams that night were:

> We were going to be sacrificed, or something, and there were political over-tones . . . what we would do is pretend we were the gods . . . in looking at the so-called king, chief, or whatever the native was . . . it would be almost like . . . looking at one of these totem-pole gods (Ullman et al., 1973, pp. 122–123).

The results of this study were statistically significant when evaluated by out-side judges $(P < .0001)$, and a "hit" was rated for each of the eight nights. Erwin had not evaluated the pictures.

I was the percipient for the next eight-night study (Ullman and Krippner, 1970). Peggy Kinder, a psychology student, was the agent the first two nights; Ullman was the agent the third night; and Barbara Lidsky, a social worker, was the agent the remaining nights. My rankings for the pictures yielded eight "hits" $(P = .004)$, and the ratings by an outside judge were also statistically significant $(P < .0004)$.

Another formal study involved four percipients who for half their eight nights had an agent concentrate on the same target for all four nights while on the other four nights the agent concentrated on a different target picture for each REM period (Honorton, Krippner, and Ullman, 1971). Three percipients ob-tained significantly higher scores in the different target condition, and the other percipient obtained significant results $(P < .0005)$ with no difference between conditions. An outside judge obtained significant results favoring the different target condition.

The agent was moved to the Foundation for Mind Research directed by Masters and Houston for the next formal study. Their laboratory is located 14 miles from Maimonides and contains facilities for providing the agent with a combined audio-visual experience. As he views a sequence of thematically related slides (e.g., Birth of a Baby) on an 8-foot screen, stereo loud-speakers play accom-panying mood music to provide a "sensory bombardment" arrangement (Kripp-ner, Honorton, Ullman, Masters, and Houston, 1971). Four nights were involved but two percipients participated each night. The eight percipients, of whom three were "sensitives," slept in the laboratory for one night. The judges' rank-ings gave eight "hits" and no "misses" in this series $(P = .004)$.

A variation of sensory bombardment was involved for a six-night study where the agents consisted of approximately 2,000 young people attending a rock con-cert of "The Grateful Dead" (Krippner, Honorton, and Ullman, 1973). While the rock group played, the audience viewed a target slide for 15 minutes and at-tempted to "send" the picture to Malcolm Bessent, a sensitive, who was located 45 miles away in the Maimonides Laboratory. As a control subject, Felicia Parise, whose existence was unknown to the audience, also attempted to dream about the target picture. She slept in her apartment and was awakened by a phone call every 90 minutes for a dream report. The judges' ratings for Bessent's dreams were statistically significant but those for Parise's were not.

Bessent was also the percipient for two major precognition series. In the first, an eight-night study, Bessent's task was to dream that night about a multisensory experience that he would participate in the following morning. After Bessent's dreams had been recorded and mailed off to a transcriber, someone not familiar with his dreams randomly determined the experience (Krippner, Ullman, and Honorton, 1971). When the target picture was "Hospital Corridor at St. Remy," for example, Bessent's experience consisted of listening to a recording of "Spellbound" while taking a pill and viewing paintings by mental patients. He was then dabbed with acetone and led through a darkened corridor of the laboratory. Evaluation by three judges produced statistically significant results ($P = .0002$).

The second precognitive series with Bessent involved 16 nights (Krippner, Honorton, and Ullman 1972). On eight nights, Bessent attempted to dream about a slide-and-sound sequence that he would be exposed to on the following night (future condition) and on that following night he would attempt to dream about the slide-and-sound sequence he had just finished viewing (past condition). When the transcripts of the 16 nights were ranked by the outside judges against each of the eight target sequences, they awarded seven "hits" and one "miss" for the precognitive nights, and their ratings were statistically significant ($P = .002$).

In addition to the formal series, there were also many "pilot" studies conducted to test out new ideas and subjects. The experimental precautions were just as careful as those exercised in the formal studies except that staff judges were frequently used for ratings rather than outside judges. These pilot studies can be placed in five broad groupings (Ullman et al., 1973, p. 277): telepathy sessions (72 "hits" and 21 "misses"); clairvoyance sessions (12 "hits" and 4 "misses"); precognition sessions (2 "hits" and 0 "misses"); non-REM sessions (3 "hits" and 2 "misses"); and napping sessions (22 "hits" and 10 "misses"). The results of the telepathy sessions were independently significant ($P < .0001$) as were the pooled results for the other types of pilot sessions ($P < .005$). There were also three sessions where the agent attempted to influence the directionality (horizontal vs. vertical) of the REMs rather than the dream content. Significant data were produced for each of these three sessions.

It was possible to examine the effectiveness of various interpersonal combinations in the pilot sessions. There were 11 sessions where a relative served as agent, and this combination produced nine "hits" and two "misses." Since most of the pilot sessions consisted of "one night stands," a large number of percipients was involved. If analyses are limited to just the first laboratory night, a total of 42 male and 38 female percipients were tested, and 14 males and 10 females served as agents (Ullman et al., 1973, p. 213). Males turned out to be significantly better percipients and had 76 percent "hits" regardless of whether a male or female served as agent while females obtained 67 percent "hits" with male agents but only 55 percent "hits" with female agents (Krippner, 1970).

The most recent dream project undertaken at Maimonides involves a comparison of extrasensory and presleep influences on dreams (Honorton, Ullman, and Krippner, 1975). Target stimuli were four brief films, two of them emotional and two neutral. On each of the first two ESP nights, an agent was shown a different film, and the percipient attempted to dream about the film. On the two presleep nights, the subject himself viewed the two remaining films before falling asleep. Forty agent-subject pairs, who were generally friends, were involved. Significant incorporation appeared on presleep nights, but neither the emotionally-arousing nor the emotionally-neutral film stimuli were incorporated on the ESP nights. Although individual percipients had content correspondences that were qualitatively and quantitatively similar to those obtained in the presleep condition, the degree of ESP influence was not consistent across subjects. Field independent subjects, as measured by the Rod and Frame Test and the Embedded Figures Test, obtained a significantly higher correspondence score in the ESP condition for the emotional films than for the neutral films ($P = .008$), but a similar difference was not found for these same subjects in the presleep condition.

Experimental Dream Studies By Other Investigators

Strauch (1970) served as agent and experimenter for 12 female percipients who each slept three nights in the laboratory at the Parapsychology Foundation. On the second and third nights, the agent attempted to transmit ESP target stimuli consisting of pictures. She reported that the judges' ratings did not achieve statistical significance but that "peripheral ESP phenomena seemed to occur outside the experimental design" (p. 49).

A pair of friends were the agent and percipient for a 17-night study at the Boston University School of Medicine (Globus, Knapp, Skinner, and Healy, 1968). The authors did not mention their sex. Target material consisted of 17 sets of four pictures. The experimenters recorded not only REM reports but also associations, hypnagogic fantasies, and non-REM reports. A group of judges did not obtain significant results in rating this collage of material, but unfortunately no separate analyses were made for just the REM reports. Judges were, however, found to be significantly more correct when they were most confident in their ratings, and one judge rated better than would be expected by chance.

Calvin Hall (1967) published a study in which six male percipients were involved. Hall acted as agent and attempted to pantomine the target activity as well as imagine it. Such activities as a boxing match, exploring a cave, or cutting one's finger were utilized, and a different one was employed for each REM period. Of the 121 reported dreams, Hall noticed a connection between the target material and dream content in 56. An undergraduate group of about 100 students rated 36 of these dreams by selecting which theme, out of four possibilities, best matched each dream. In 29 cases they were able to select the target theme to a significant degree. Since each percipient had contributed a large number of dreams while serving as a subject for an extended dream project, it was possible to compute how frequently the target theme had been dreamed of on control nights when the agent had made no effort to transmit any stimulus. These evaluations were also statistically significant. For example, I was one of the successful percipients (Osceola) and had dreamed about imagery peripherally relating to boxing in only four dreams out of the 97 on file, but I dreamed directly about this topic during the REM period when the agent was attempting to transmit it.

I was also the percipient for an eight-night attempted replication study of the Maimonides protocol at the University of Wyoming (Belvedere and Foulkes, 1971). Two local female undergraduates were utilized as agents on different nights. Neither my evaluations nor those of outside judges were significant. Although the design was very similar to that of the Maimonides protocol, there were some psychological differences which may have played a role in the outcomes being different. One involved the interpersonal climate existing in each of the two laboratories. At Maimonides, "the red carpet was rolled out" and everyone was extremely friendly, whereas at Wyoming, interactions with the staff were much more formal and detached. The following comments by Foulkes are pertinent concerning this issue:

> In retrospect, we may have erred too much on the side of "scientism" to the exclusion of creating conditions in which telepathy might reasonably (if it exists at all) be expected to flourish. It proved hard to escape the role of protector of scientific purity or guardian of the scientific morals. Were we sympathetic and encouraging observers, or scientific detectives out to prevent a crime from being committed before our very eyes? Sometimes it was difficult to be certain. Particularly revealing personally was a brief moment of intra-psychic panic when it seemed as though some telepathic influence might be "coming through"—how could it be? Where had I failed to prevent sensory leakage? Our subject (Van de Castle) clearly felt himself "on trial" before a not entirely sympathetic jury, and we also could not totally avoid the feeling that we too were on trial, with a favorable verdict for the subject raising doubts as to the scrupulosity of our judgment process.
>
> ... There is no place for sloppy dream research, whether on telepathy or anything else. But being rigorous is a different matter from insecurely flaunting one's rigor as we may have done in our first study (in Ullman et al., 1973, p. 236).

The moment of "intra-psychic panic" arose, I believe, when working with the same agent on the third and fourth nights, I obtained two direct "hits," i.e., when ranking the eight pictures I had correctly given the target pictures a ranking of 1. The picture sets also presented problems. I felt that they were not as differentiated as they could have been. After complaining about this feature part way through the study, all the remaining pictures were reassembled but it is questionable whether optimal heterogeneity was produced. On the sixth night the target picture was a close-up black and white photograph of a woman nursing a baby and on the seventh night the target picture was a close-up black and white photograph of a woman nursing a baby.

On the eighth night, I felt that I had had several dreams involving foreign places and on the basis of these dreams made a prediction about the type of target picture I expected. Here are some unpublished typescript excerpts from that prediction:

> My guess would be that it somehow deals with a foreign culture or people from a foreign culture. Now, by foreign culture it may be something like a hippy culture within America which would be sort of like a foreign culture . . . I think the clothing is going to be somewhat unusual . . . somewhat distinctive.

Ordinarily, such a specific prediction should have been useful in selecting out a single picture from the set that would more closely correspond to this description than would other pictures in the set. However, the eight pictures in the set were: two Indian women dressed in saris; a group of several dozen Chinese in long robes; a scene, apparently in Mexico, showing a kneeling peasant in coveralls and a man holding a parasol over a priest in a cassock; an Austrian postcard showing a seventeenth-century painting of cattle leaving an old adobe house with some peasants in front of it; some musicians playing for a couple sitting at an outdoor table in the French Quarter of New Orleans; two adolescent blacks standing in front of a spraying fire hydrant in what looks like a Harlem street scene; two young men, one with a black leather jacket and a suitcase, walking down some railroad tracks; and a photograph of The Milky Way or some galaxy.

Another aspect which was different was the interval between experimental nights. At Wyoming the entire series was completed within a 2-week period, whereas it took 44 weeks to complete the series at Maimonides since my visits were spaced 5 to 6 weeks apart.

The Wyoming staff also carried out a long-distance "sensory bombardment" study. The agent was Malcolm Bessent who viewed audiovisual material in New York City. The percipients, eight different females, each slept one night in the Wyoming laboratory. They had been selected by Bessent during an earlier Wyoming visit. No significant findings emerged when the dream transcripts were rated by three judges (Foulkes, Belvedere, Masters, Houston, Krippner, Honorton, and Ullman, 1972).

The only other published account that has bearing upon the Maimonides findings is one by me (Van de Castle, 1971b). This was not a laboratory study but involved morning recall of dreams. Approximately 70 members of a youth camp (aged 16+) served as percipients. The agent was a female staff member who attempted to transmit a colored magazine picture to all the campers. The following morning, the campers individually viewed a set of five magazine pictures and ranked them from 1 to 5 for correspondence to their remembered dreams. Ranks of 1 or 2 for the target picture were considered "hits," those of 4 or 5 as "misses." A different set of pictures was involved each night. More "hits" than "misses" were obtained on each of the four nights, and the overall total of 95 "hits" and 55 "misses" was significant ($P = .002$).

There have also been several unpublished or informal pilot attempts made by others to explore telepathic dreams. Rechtschaffen (1970) gives some examples of striking correspondences that he obtained when one subject (agent) was hypnotized and told to dream about a specific topic and the percipient attempted to dream about the agent's dream. He carried out one project involving six pairs of subjects that yielded 47 pairs of dreams. Two judges were not successful in matching the percipient's dreams to the topic suggested to the agent but he did find that "the results on dream-dream matching for all subjects combined were significant beyond the .001 level for one of the judges" (p. 91). The other judge had .01 probability for one subject and .07 for another subject.

Rechtschaffen noted that "When they were hits, they were quite good" (p. 92), and a refined technique was not needed to detect them. He went on to observe that "a hit does not reveal the degree of the hit. A simple matching procedure does not take into account the very unlikely probability of such a specific correspondence" (p. 92). Honorton (1975) has attempted to provide a solution to this problem through the use of a binary coding system where ten bits of information are coded as present or absent in a pictorial target and also in the percipient's response. With his system, if the response contains all ten features of the target, the associated P value would be .001.

In the book *Dream Telepathy*, reference is made to a telepathic dream study carried out at Centenary College in Louisiana (Ullman et al., 1973, p. 217). Some excerpts from dream reports are given that contain close correspondences to a target slide. I also gave a few brief examples of some correspondences between dreams and targets from some pilot work carried out by Liddon and me (Van de Castle, 1971a, p. 33).

An unpublished study was carried out by two male undergraduates at Virginia Wesleyan College in 1972. The study lasted for 20 nights, and the students alternated as agent and percipient for five nights at a time. After one of them had gone to sleep in his room, the other would wait for an hour and then begin to concentrate on a picture that had been randomly selected by another person. When his concentration wavered, the agent would begin to sketch the picture. After approximately 1 hour of "sending," the percipient was awakened by an observer unfamiliar with the target picture who recorded the dream reports. An outside judge rated the dreams, and a hit was recorded only if at least three exact physical correspondences had been incorporated in the dream. The judging standards were quite stringent, and a correspondence in terms of similar shape or function was not counted; the correspondence had to be an exact identity. One percipient was rated as showing four "hits" during his ten nights, and the other had five "hits" for his ten nights.

Commentary on the Experimental Studies

The work reviewed in the preceding section offers very encouraging evidence that telepathic incorporation of distant stimuli into dreams can be demonstrated under good experimental conditions. This does not mean, however, that one can confidently assume that positive results will be readily obtained by every investigator who attempts to duplicate the Maimonides protocol.

The important role played by the experimenter and the laboratory climate was suggested by the Wyoming study, as was the need to insure that the ESP stimuli are emotionally compelling and diversified. The findings by Globus et al. (1968) and Rechtschaffen (1970) bring out the marked differences to be found among judges; some seem to have a knack for recognizing similarities in themes, forms, functions, affects, etc., while others are more opaque in dealing with metaphors or cognitive idioms.

The characteristics of a good agent are not yet well delineated, but this individual must be sufficiently free from personal problems so that he or she will not be led into excessive personal preoccupations when viewing the target stimuli. There are parallels here to the therapeutic situation where the patient zeroes in on the therapist's unresolved conflicts. On several occasions when I was the percipient I described dream elements that dealt with family, sexual, or religious conflicts that the agents later acknowledged to me were in the forefront of their attention when they were supposed to be transmitting the target stimulus. It may be narcissistically gratifying for the percipient to subsequently find out that he was, in fact, telepathically "tuned-in" to the agent's private thinking, but the extraneous imagery produced by such nontarget ideation only acts to dilute the relevant target imagery and provides "red herrings" for the judges who have only the public set of pictures available for their ratings.

Successful percipients have generally been described by such adjectives as "open" or "frank." Several percipients have commented upon feeling threatened by the notion of being invaded or penetrated by the agent which weakens one's sense of ego-identity and intactness. There is also the "implicit demand" that every image and thought, no matter how embarrassing, must be verbalized when reporting on the dream because one can never be sure whether it might have some sort of connection to the target stimulus. In such a situation, the percipient obviously will be required to expose a great store of information concerning his private life and problems, and this can lead to various forms of inner resistance. It has been recognized that some percipients resonate more readily to certain classes of stimuli than to others because certain stimuli possess greater dynamic relevance for the percipient's unmet needs.

If we were to look for any consistencies that seem to hold for spontaneous, therapeutic, and experimental dreams they would have to reside in the area of motivation. There is every reason to assume that a paranormal dream does not arise within a vacuum nor that it is some random freak of nature. Such a dream should be considered as an end product of a complex motivational configuration that blends some intrapersonal need on the part of the "percipient" with some behavioral or emotional activity on the part of the "agent" that serves to satisfy or complement that need state. It is probably more accurate to consider this nexus of interpersonal patterning as being a psi gestalt that does not readily separate out into agent and percipient components. With precognitive dreams, it is obvious that this postulated "perceptual-affective" closure is not achieved within a chronological framework of temporal synchronicity. It seems rather that a sensitive psi scanning mechanism is utilized to select the dynamically most relevant event either currently available in fully materialized form or in the stages of nascent development already under way in the yet-to-be perceived, but tentatively formed, future.

Congruencies in psi functioning that parallel coping techniques employed in other tension-reducing situations can probably be found. Thus, when challenges to perceptual-affective closure arise, telepathic resolutions may be sought by individuals characteristically preferring immediate need-gratification strategies, while a precognitive paradigm may be more satisfying to someone accustomed to foregoing contemporaneous fulfillment in favor of long-term goal striving.

Having now reviewed the empirical evidence for paranormal dreams and advancing some brief speculations concerning their underlying motivational structure, it would be well to close with some remarks offered by Gardner Murphy in his introductory address to the first parapsychological symposium sponsored by the American Association for the Advancement of Science in 1970:

> In the half century in which I have tried to observe and evaluate the situation in parapsychology there has been a very notable increase in sophistication in the experimental procedures devised, and at the same time an increasing effort to develop a tentative yet systematic theoretical structure which may ultimately articulate with the moving contours of a general scientific theory concerned with living systems. . . . It will take much time and labor, but in both quantitative and qualitative terms the experimental analysis of dream telepathy is now a problem of such urgency that a mature science can no longer handle it either by ignoring it or by denying it. Fortunately, organized science has at last begun to recognize the need to look straight at the experimental data and their interpretation.

REFERENCES

Barker, J. C. Premonitions of the Aberfan disaster. *Journal of the Society for Psychical Research*, 1967, **44**, 169–181.

Belvedere, E., and Foulkes, D. Telepathy and dreams: A failure to replicate. *Perceptual and Motor Skills*, 1971, **33**, 783–789.

Bender, H. The Gotenhafen Case of correspondence between dreams and future events: A study of motivation. *International Journal of Neuropsychiatry*, 1966, **2**, 398–407.

Besterman, T. Report of an inquiry into precognitive dreams. *Proceedings of the Society for Psychical Research*, 1933, **41**, 186–204.

Brockhaus, E. Possibilities and limits for research in paranormal phenomena in West Africa. *Papers Presented for the Eleventh Annual Convention of the Parapsychological Association*. Freiburg, Germany: Institut für Grenzgebiete der Psychologie und Psychohygiene, 1968.

Daim, W. Studies in dream-telepathy. *Tomorrow*, 1953, **2**, 35–48.

Dale, L. A. Spontaneous experiences reported by a group of experimental subjects. *Journal of the American Society for Psychical Research*, 1946, **40**, 55–93.

Dale, L. A. A series of spontaneous cases in the tradition of *Phantasms of the Living*. *Journal of the American Society for Psychical Research*, 1951, **45**, 85–101.

Dale, L. A., White R., and Murphy, G. A selection of cases from a recent survey of spontaneous ESP phenomena. *Journal of the American Society for Psychical Research*, 1962, **56**, 3–47.

Devereux, G. (Ed.). *Psychoanalysis and the Occult*. New York: International Universities Press, 1953.

Dunne, J. W. *An Experiment with Time*. New York: Macmillan, 1927.

Ehrenwald, J. *New Dimensions of Deep Analysis*. New York: Grune and Stratton, 1955.

Eisenbud, J. *Psi and Psychoanalysis*. New York: Grune and Stratton, 1970.

Ermacora, G. B. Telepathic dreams experimentally induced. *Proceedings of the Society for Psychical Research*, 1895, **11**, 235–308.

Flammarion, C. *The Unknown*. New York: Harper, 1900.

Foulkes, D., Belvedere, E., Masters, R., Houston, J., Krippner, S., Honorton, C., and Ullman, M. Long-distance, "sensory bombardment" ESP in dreams: A failure to replicate. *Perceptual and Motor Skills*, 1972, **35**, 731–734.

Globus, G. G., Knapp, P. H., Skinner, J. C., and Healy, G. An appraisal of telepathic communication in dreams. *Psychophysiology*, 1968, **4**, 365.

Green, C. E. Report on enquiry into spontaneous cases. *Proceedings of the Society for Psychical Research*, 1960, **53**, 97–161.

Gurney, E., Myers, F. W. H., and Podmore, F. *Phantasms of the Living*. London: Trübner, 1886. 2 vols.

Hall, C. E. Experimente zur telepathischen Beeinflussung von Träumen. *Zeitschrift für Parapsychologie und Grenzgebiete der Psychologie*, 1967, **10**, 18–47.

Hanefeld, E. Content analysis of spontaneous cases. *Proceedings of the Parapsychological Association*, 1968, **5**, 7–8.

Haraldsson, E. Reported dream recall, precognitive dreams, and ESP. In J. D. Morris, W. G. Roll, and R. L. Morris (Eds.), *Research in Parapsychology 1974*, pp. 47–48. Metuchen, N. J.: Scarecrow Press, 1975.

Honorton, C. Reported frequency of dream recall and ESP. *Journal of the American Society for Psychical Research*, 1972, **66**, 369–374.

Honorton, C. Objective determination of information rate in psi tasks with pictorial stimuli. *Journal of the American Society for Psychical Research*, 1975, **69**, 353–359.

Honorton, C., Krippner, S., and Ullman, M. Telepathic transmission of art prints under two conditions. *Proceedings of the 80th Annual Convention of the American Psychological Association*, 1971, 319-320.

Honorton, C., Ullman, M., and Krippner, S. Comparison of extrasensory and presleep influences on dreams: A preliminary report. In J. D. Morris, W. G. Roll, and R. L. Morris (Eds.), *Research in Parapsychology 1974*, pp. 82-84. Metuchen, N. J.: Scarecrow Press, 1975.

Johnson, M. Relationship between dream recall and scoring direction. *Journal of Parapsychology*, 1968, **32**, 56-57.

Krippner, S. Investigations of extrasensory phenomena in dreams and other altered states of consciousness. *Journal of the American Society of Psychosomatic Dentistry and Medicine*, 1969, **16**, 7-14.

Krippner, S. Electrophysiological studies of ESP in dreams: Sex differences in seventy-four telepathy sessions. *Journal of the American Society for Psychical Research*, 1970, **64**, 277-285.

Krippner, S., Honorton, C., and Ullman, M. A second precognitive dream study with Malcolm Bessent. *Journal of the American Society for Psychical Research*, 1972, **66**, 269-279.

Krippner, S., Honorton, C., and Ullman, M. A long-distance ESP dream study with the "Grateful Dead." *Journal of the American Society of Psychosomatic Dentistry and Medicine*, 1973, **20**, 9-17.

Krippner, S., Honorton, C., Ullman, M., Masters, R., and Houston, J. A long-distance "sensory bombardment" study of ESP in dreams. *Journal of the American Society for Psychical Research*, 1971, **65**, 468-475.

Krippner, S., Ullman, M., and Honorton, C. A precognitive dream study with a single subject. *Journal of the American Society for Psychical Research*, 1971, **65**, 192-203.

Murphy, G. Introductory address: "Techniques and status of modern parapsychology." Presented at the First Symposium of the Parapsychological Association, 137th Annual Meeting of the American Association for the Advancement of Science, Chicago, 1970.

Murray, H. A., and Wheeler, D. R. A note on the possible clairvoyance of dreams. *Journal of Psychology*, 1937, **3**, 309-313.

Myers, F. W. H. *Human Personality and its Survival of Bodily Death*. New York: Longmans, Green, 1903.

Nelson, R. D. The Central Premonitions Registry. *Psychic*, 1970, **1**, 27-30.

Nicol, J. F. Discussion remarks. In R. Cavanna and M. Ullman (Eds.), *Psi and Altered States of Consciousness*, p. 147. New York: Parapsychology Foundation, 1968.

Palmer, J., and Dennis, M. A community mail survey of psychic experiences. In J. D. Morris, W. G. Roll, and R. L. Morris (Eds.), *Research in Parapsychology 1974*, pp. 130-133. Metuchen, N. J: Scarecrow Press, 1975.

Pederson-Krag, G. Telepathy and repression. *Psychoanalytic Quarterly*, 1947, **16**, 61-68.

Podmore, F. *Apparitions and Thought-Transference: an Examination of the Evidence for Telepathy*. New York: Putnam's, 1894.

Prasad, J., and Stevenson, I. A survey of spontaneous psychical experiences in school children of Uttar Pradesh, India. *International Journal of Parapsychology*, 1968, **10**, 241-261.

Prince, W. F. Human experiences. *Bulletin of the Boston Society for Psychic Research*, 1931, **14**, 5-328.

Rechtschaffen, A. Sleep and dream states: An experimental design. In R. Cavanna (Ed.), *Psi Favorable States of Consciousness*, pp. 87-120. New York: Parapsychology Foundation, 1970.

Rhine, L. E.   Frequency of types of experience in spontaneous precognition. *Journal of Parapsychology*, 1954, **18**, 93–123.

Rhine, L. E.   *Hidden Channels of the Mind*. New York: William Sloan Associates, 1961.

Rhine, L. E.   Psychological processes in ESP experiences. Part II. Dreams. *Journal of Parapsychology*, 1962, **26**, 172–199.

Saltmarsh, H. F.   Report on cases of apparent precognition. *Proceedings of the Society for Psychical Research*, 1934, **42**, 49–103.

Sannwald, G.   Statistische Untersuchungen an Spontanphänomenen. *Zeitschrift für Parapsychologie und Grenzgebiete der Psychologie*, 1959, **3**, 59–71.

Sannwald, G.   Zur Psychologie Paranormaler Spontanphänomene: Motivation, Thematik und Bezugspersonen "okkulter" Erlebnisse. *Zeitschrift für Parapsychologie und Grenzgebiete der Psychologie*, 1960, **3**, 149–183.

Schwarz, B. E.   *Psychic-Dynamics*. New York: Pageant Press, 1965.

Servadio, E.   A presumptively telepathic-precognitive dream during analysis. *International Journal of Psychoanalysis*, 1955, **36**, 27–30.

Sidgwick, E. M. (Mrs. H.)   On the evidence for premonitions. *Proceedings of the Society for Psychical Research*, 1888, **5**, 288–354.

Sidgwick, E. M. (Mrs. H.)   Phantasms of the Living. An examination of cases of telepathy between living persons . . . . *Proceedings of the Society for Psychical Research*, 1923, **33**, 23–429.

Stevens, W. O.   *The Mystery of dreams*. New York: Dodd, Mead, 1949.

Stevenson, I.   A review and analysis of paranormal experiences connected with the sinking of the *Titanic*. *Journal of the American Society for Psychical Research*, 1960, **54**, 153–171.

Stevenson, I.   A postcognitive dream illustrating some aspects of the pictographic process. *Journal of the American Society for Psychical Research*, 1963, **57**, 182–202.

Stevenson, I.   Seven more paranormal experiences associated with the sinking of the Titanic. *Journal of the American Society for Psychical Research*, 1965, **59**, 211–225.

Stevenson, I.   The substantiality of spontaneous cases. *Proceedings of the Parapsychological Association*, 1968, **5**, 91–128.

Stevenson, I.   Precognition of disasters. *Journal of the American Society for Psychical Research*, 1970, **64**, 187–210.

Strauch, I.   Dreams and psi in the laboratory. In R. Cavenna (Ed.), *Psi Favorable States of Consciousness*, pp. 46–54. New York: Parapsychology Foundation, 1970.

Tenhaeff, W. H. C.   Personality structure and psi research. *Papers presented for the Eleventh Annual Convention of the Parapsychological Association*. Freiburg, Germany: Institut für Grenzgebiete der Psychologie und Psychohygiene, 1968.

Ullman, M.   On the occurrence of telepathic dreams. *Journal of the American Society for Psychical Research*, 1959, **53**, 50–61.

Ullman, M.   Telepathy and dreams. *Experimental Medicine and Surgery*, 1969, **27**, 19–38.

Ullman, M., and Krippner, S.   A laboratory approach to the nocturnal dimension of paranormal experience: Report of a confirmatory study using the REM monitoring technique. *Biological Psychiatry*, 1969, **1**, 259–270.

Ullman, M, and Krippner, S.   Dream studies and telepathy. *Parapsychological Monographs No. 12*. New York: Parapsychology Foundation, 1970.

Ullman, M., Krippner, S., and Feldstein, S.   Experimentally-induced telepathic dreams: Two studies using EEG-REM monitoring technique. *International Journal of Neuropsychiatry*, 1966, **2**, 420–437.

Ullman, M., and Krippner, S., with Vaughan, A.   *Dream Telepathy*. New York: Macmillan, 1973.

Van de Castle, R. L. *The Psychology of Dreaming*. Morristown, N. J.: General Learning Press, 1971. (a)

Van de Castle, R. L. The study of GESP in a group setting by means of dreams. *Journal of Parapsychology*, 1971, **35**, 312. (b)

Van de Castle, R. L. An investigation of psi abilities among the Cuna Indians of Panama. In A. Angoff and D. Barth (Eds.), *Parapsychology and Anthropology*, pp. 80–97. New York: Parapsychology Foundation, 1974.

Weserman, H. M. Versuche willkürlicher Träumbilung. *Archiv, f.d. Tierischen Magnnetismus*, 1819, **6**, 135–142.

White, R. A. Review of a report on ESP testing in the analytic situation. *Journal of the American Society for Psychical Research*, 1965, **59**, 237–247.

3
Drug-Induced States of Consciousness

Charles T. Tart

PSI AND ALTERED STATES

One of the major problems in attempting to study and understand paranormal (psi) phenomena is simply that the phenomena don't work strongly or reliably. The average subject seldom shows any individually significant evidence of psi in laboratory experiments, and even gifted subjects, while occasionally able to demonstrate important amounts of psi in the laboratory, are still very erratic and unpredictable in their performance. Scientific knowledge of any phenomena generally advances by varying conditions that affect the phenomena and thus learning more about their nature. If you set up an experiment to test the effects of various variables, but the phenomena don't occur, you have mostly wasted your time. The tiny, unreliable amount of psi generally found in the laboratory makes this a typical happening. Thus a major interest of parapsychologists centers around what we can do to make the phenomena stronger and more reliable.

Because some of the most striking spontaneous cases take place when the percipient is in some unusual state of consciousness, such as dreaming, a reverie state, or a state of intense emotion, it is likely that unusual states of consciousness might be conditions in which paranormal phenomena occur more readily. Drug-induced states are of particular interest because it seems that we should be able to produce them readily by simply administering the requisite drugs.

Why should we expect more psi in altered states? Besides numerous anecdotal reports of apparently paranormal experiences in conjunction with drug use, my own survey of experiences of marijuana users (Tart, 1971) found that 31 percent of them sometimes thought they had telepathic experiences, 12 percent of them thought they had them fairly often, and 4 percent thought they usually occurred when they were intoxicated with marijuana. There have also been a few experimental attempts to study the effects of consciousness-changing drugs on paranormal phenomena (Cavanna and Servadio, 1964; Marti-Ibanez, 1965; Masters and Houston, 1966; Osis, 1961; Paul, 1966; Puharich, 1962; van Asperen de Boer, Barkema, and Kappers, 1966; Vasiliev, 1965; Whittlesey, 1960), which have recently been reviewed by Krippner and Davidson (1974). These studies were also encouraging although, in the light of the following discussion, they were methodologically very crude experiments. Because of this, I shall not review them here. Rather, I shall confine myself to an overview of the methodology needed for future studies of that class of consciousness-changing drugs generally known as psychedelics, such as marijuana or hashish, LSD, mescaline, psilocybin, and the like.

Given that we see a lot of potential for unusual states of consciousness favoring the operation of paranormal abilities, the obvious thing to do is to consult the factual knowledge and technology of whatever branch of science deals with altered states of consciousness and apply this information to our specific parapsychological problems. There are, for example, well over 1,000 experiments published in the scientific literature on the effects of powerful psychedelics like LSD and mescaline. Surely there must be an abundance of knowledge and techniques to draw upon.

Methodological Considerations

Unfortunately, most of the experiments are of very little value, as they simply did not take into account many of the methodological considerations discussed below. Although the situation is improving, many current experiments in this area are still methodologically flawed. If I were asked to summarize our knowledge of altered states of consciousness in general, I would characterize it as thousands of unrelated and often seemingly contradictory findings which do not fall into any kind of clear pattern at all. In many ways this is a prescientific area, in spite of having the appearance of scientific research.

To illustrate this, most of the published literature in this area will make an apparently scientific statement like the following: "Each subject, who had had considerable personal experience with LSD use on his or her own, was administered 1.25 micrograms per kilogram of body weight of pure LSD-25 orally. All interaction between staff and subjects was conducted under a standardized protocol, so that all subjects were treated essentially identically." The report then goes on to give the group averages on various kinds of performance tests and theorizes about the meaning of its findings in terms of various psychological variables.

This kind of description of procedures is usually considered highly rigorous (note the precise specification of drug dosage) and complete. I consider it highly incomplete and *dangerously misleading* in implying much more precision than exists.

Suppose there were five subjects in the experiment. We shall give their identities as Ann, Bob, Carl, Donna, and Ed. The reality of their reactions might be as follows.

Ann's previous experience with LSD had been entirely with black market substances, none of which actually contained more than a tiny amount of LSD, insufficient to significantly alter her state of consciousness. Her "experiences" that she wrongly attributes to LSD are almost all due to the excitement of doing an illegal, rebellious thing in the company of friends; i.e., she had many emotional highs, but no significant drug effects. In this experiment, as the drug began to take effect, a variety of new experiences began to happen which were so threatening to her that, half-knowingly, she mentally "applied the brakes," such that the LSD did not actually produce an altered state of consciousness in her.

Bob had actually taken potent doses of LSD a number of times in the past and experienced very warm, open contacts with his companions. His state of consciousness is altered by the LSD in the experiment, but the "standardized" interaction of the staff with him strikes him as so artificial, cold, and dehumanizing that he mentally isolates himself as much as possible from the experimental situation. Consequently he scores poorly on a variety of performance tasks. These results are interpreted as showing that LSD affects performance, but they reflect nothing more than Bob's lack of attention to the tasks.

Carl, while apparently well adjusted, actually has very intense unconscious fears which he keeps in check by his highly rigid personality structure. He has learned to cope with LSD in the past by only allowing certain kinds of experiences to happen and blocking others completely, so that the important dimensions of his personality are not destabilized. The rigid interaction pattern with the staff is a source of security to him, so he absorbs himself completely in following instructions precisely and generally trying to act as he believes good subjects should.

Donna has never worked through personal problems with her parents, stemming from their distant and formal relationship with her. Unconsciously she identifies the staff with her parents and in an adolescent style of rebellion deliberately gives bizarre and unusual reactions to various experimental tasks as a way of punishing laboratory staff and, indirectly, her parents, by messing up the results.

Ed has practiced a particular form of yoga meditation for many years before getting involved with LSD and, as a result, the effects of the LSD are organized into producing a very unusual state of consciousness that results primarily from his meditation practice rather than the LSD itself. Thus the state of Ed's consciousness is very different from that of almost all other LSD users, but his and all the other subjects' reactions are averaged together.

How good are data and conclusions which are drawn in ignorance of these kinds of factors? Unfortunately, I believe most of the published experimental literature on using drugs to induce altered states of consciousness is of this order. It can provide us with hints, but it is hardly a coherent, precise valid data base we can draw on to make paranormal phenomena happen reliably. Because of this, we cannot take the obvious route of drawing from the relevant literature. Instead, I shall briefly present my own systems approach to the nature of states of consciousness, described more fully elsewhere (Tart, 1975a; 1975b), for it has the virtue of providing an overall paradigm for understanding and using the many diverse bits of data about altered states. It is not limited to drug-induced states but covers states of consciousness in general.

THE NATURE OF ORDINARY CONSCIOUSNESS

A common, largely implicit working assumption is that our ordinary state of consciousness is somehow "natural" or given. A more accurate conceptualization is that our ordinary consciousness is a semiarbitrary *construction*. Because we are born as human beings, with a certain kind of body and nervous system operating in the environment of Earth, we begin life with potential access to an incredibly wide spectrum of human potentialities. These include abilities to learn language, arithmetic, to swim, to enter altered states of consciousness, etc. It also includes, for at least some people, the ability to exercise paranormal abilities. While there are undoubtedly genetic differences in the availability of various human potentialities for any given individual, we know little about these genetic limitations, and probably they are usually relatively minor compared with the limitations imposed by culture.

We are not born and raised in isolation, but as members of a particular culture. Any culture can be viewed as a group of people who, implicitly and explicitly, through their history, (a) have decided that certain human potentialities are good and so cultivate them; (b) have decided that other human potentialities are bad, and so try to block their development; and (c) are simply ignorant of a vast number of other human potentialities, and thus fail to develop them through disuse. Thus even in infancy there begins a diminution in the number of human potentialities available, as the parents begin the enculturation process. Many potentialities remain latent, and may be developed later in life, but those that form part of the infant's consciousness are clearly restricted. If you are born in an English-speaking culture, your potential to learn some non-English language steadily decreases, even though at birth you presumably could have learned Chinese just as easily as English.

As we grow into childhood, our peers and our formal schooling, as well as our parents, begin to shape our consciousness and our personality. While certain potentialities have now been developed to a high degree, our total range of potentialities is now less than it was. We no longer babble like infants, for example, using all the speech sounds found in all languages in the world, but we speak our own language well.

By the time we reached adolescence our peers are the primary influence on us, although in many ways we have internalized the values and life styles of our parents and they continue to affect us. Our latent sexuality now moves out of the realm of potentialities and into our consciousness. There is a possibility for profound changes in our ordinary consciousness at this time with the influx of these energies, as often occurs in adolescent conversion reactions. Because of the implicit selections of our culture up to this point though, the number of potentialities available for reshaping consciousness in a conversion reaction is quite limited.

Finally, we reach adulthood. Our peers continue to influence us, but our personality structure is largely fixed, with the influences of our parents and our earlier peers during childhood and adolescence internalized. We do not simply have a random collection of potentialities, but they have been organized along cognitive, bodily, and emotional lines to form a cohesive , functioning system.

Out of the vast selection of human potentialities available to us at birth, we have now settled on a relatively small number of potentialities which have been structured into a dynamic, functioning system. We are the beneficiaries of our culture selection in terms of our strengths. We are also the victims of it in terms of the narrowness of our lives and of the semiarbitrariness of the particular shaping that this selection of potentialities has undergone through our enculturation process. We function reasonably well within the consensus reality defined as important by our culture, but very poorly outside that consensus reality (Tart, 1974).

I emphasize that the state of our ordinary consciousness in adulthood is semiarbitrary, as we must all have minimum survival qualities in terms of the physical world; but since most of our life is now spent in the consensus reality of our social world, which reality varies enormously across cultures, this is very arbitrary.

The potential for paranormal functioning is largely residing among the latent potentials rather than among those consciously developed. Most of us cannot use any paranormal abilities at will. It is possible that not everyone is born with psi potential: We simply don't have any good evidence one way or the other on this. It is certainly the case that by the time we have reached adulthood, for some if not most people, the psi potential is no longer available even as a latent potential, much less a developed one: Given the forces that can be brought to bear within a particular culture, the psi potential is simply no longer reachable, or has extinguished through disuse, or has been so thoroughly blocked in terms of personality structure that for all practical purposes it is gone.

Another way of characterizing our ordinary state of consciousness is to see that the enculturation process builds a large number of semiarbitrary psychological structures, language structures, body skill structures, arithmetic structures, emotional reaction structures, etc. Most of the time these structures are latent, but some of them are activated by various psychological energies, particularly the energy constituted by paying attention, putting awareness into a particular structure. Until this moment while reading this paper, e.g., your "arithmetical skill structure" has been inactive, latent, but if I now ask you how much is two plus three, the answer "five" immediately pops into your head. Putting awareness in this area activates the appropriate structures produced by the enculturation process. The culture thus produces an ordinary state of consciousness which means certain structures are connected by certain preferred pathways for psychological energy and awareness to flow. Westerners think about cars and TV sets habitually, Australian aborigines think about the Dream Time, etc.

DISCRETE STATES OF CONSCIOUSNESS, NORMAL AND ALTERED

I have recently introduced (Tart, 1974; 1975a; 1975b), the terms of "discrete states of consciousness" (d-SoCs) and "discrete altered states of consciousness" (d-ASCs). A d-SoC for a given individual is a unique *configuration* or a system of psychological structures or subsystems, with probable, preferred ways of psychological energy/attention flowing between them. The structures or subsystems (related aggregates of structures) and energy flow pathways show some quantitative and minor qualitative variation in the way in which they process information, cope with the environment, or have experiences, but the subsystems, in their energetic pattern of interactions, comprise a *system*, an overall *pattern* having a recognizable feel or shape. The operations of the system components (structures and subsystems) interact on each other and stabilize each other's functioning such that the system, the d-SoC, maintains its overall patterning of function within a varying environment.

Psychologically one may say, "I'm perfectly awake but more relaxed than I was a moment ago," or "I am in my ordinary state of consciousness and paying less attention to the environment than I was," and the concept of remaining in our ordinary, awake *state* of consciousness is useful for understanding what is happening even though the specific content of our experience is different.

Some latent human potentialities are simply not connected into the pattern that constitutes our ordinary d-SoC. The psi potential would be one of these for most of us. Thus in our ordinary d-SoC we can try all the various mental tricks we know, but we have no immediate feel for the psi potential, we have no direct contact with it to make it work. Our maneuvering around in the experiential space of our ordinary d-SoC *may* set off unconscious processes which may or may not connect with our psi potential in desirable or undesirable ways, but that tends to be pretty much a matter of hit or miss. I can now rephrase as a question our earlier statement that we hope that in some altered state of consciousness we can use our psi potentials more directly: How can we rearrange the structure of our consciousness so as to have a more direct connection to this particular latent potential?

Recall that our ordinary d-SoC is a system, a pattern of relationships between various psychological structures and potentials. A d-ASC, given existing scientific knowledge, can be seen as different from our ordinary d-SoC in two ways. First, some potentialities available in the ordinary state may be temporarily inhibited, while some potentialities that were latent for the ordinary d-SoC may now be functioning or capable of being made to function. Second, the patterning, the connections, the system properties of the available potentials are different in the d-ASC, there is a qualitatively different gestalt to the d-ASC. To fully understand a d-ASC, we must grasp both the differences in potentialities available and the new pattern they are used in. To have access to a desired latent potential like the psi potential, then, we need to find (or deliberately create) a d-ASC where that potential is connected into the system pattern in an accessible way.

I deliberately stress the idea of a radical reorganization, a kind of quantum jump here in order to keep the concept of a d-SoC scientifically useful and to not simply mean any kind of change in the contents of consciousness. A d-ASC is quite clearly and importantly distinct from some other d-SoC. To illustrate this, you could dream about almost anything that you could experience in a waking state, there can be overlap in almost any particular content, yet the overall pattern of functioning in the dreaming state is quite different from that of our waking state, and people can readily distinguish the two d-SoCs.

STABILIZING A d-SoC

A d-SoC maintains its overall pattern despite variations in the particulars of its operation. The basic function of a d-SoC is to cope adaptively with some world or environment, so d-SoCs are tools for coping with various realities. Insofar as they are good tools, each should hold together and maintain its usefulness while performing its function. Given that a d-SoC is a pattern of dynamically changing relationships, then, we need stabilizing processes to hold the overall pattern of these relationships together.

There are four major ways in which a d-SoC is stabilized; I call them loading stabilization, negative feedback stabilization, positive feedback stabilization, and limiting stabilization.

Loading stabilization is a matter of keeping our thoughts and feelings occupied with experiences that fall within a prescribed range, thus keeping most or all of our attention and psychological energy in desired structures. In terms of stabilizing our "normal" d-SoC, this means keeping our minds busy with the approved aspects of consensus reality. As don Juan told Carlos Castaneda (Castaneda, 1971), the ordinary, repeated, day-to-day activities of people keep their energy so bound up within the known aspects of their social reality that they prevent them from becoming aware of nonordinary reality. Having to cope with physical reality, which varies within certain known patterns (ignoring the paranormal), is a major kind of loading stabilization. Similarly, sensing and operating our bodies also requires investing an immense amount of attention and energy in a familiar way and so further stabilizes our ordinary state.

Feedback stabilization is of two types, negative and positive. In both cases there are structures which sense the range in which other psychological structures are operating, and when the structures go outside these ranges a corrective process is initiated. Negative feedback stabilization involves damping or attenuating the erring process, sometimes through negative emotions, while positive feedback stabilization involves enhancing desired activity already going on in particular structures, often with the mechanism of positive feelings. Thus if we start to think about certain topics or have certain kinds of experiences we may become anxious and retreat from that area (negative feedback stabilization), while if we think of, say, a scheme for increasing agricultural productivity we feel is good, our internalized social value structures activate our reward system. So we are much more likely to think of increasing agricultural food production than of, say, ritual cannibalism, or of opening our minds to spirit influences.

Limiting stabilization refers to processes that do not allow other psychological structures and processes to go beyond certain limits. The action of tranquilizing drugs is a good example here: by not allowing emotions to exceed a certain intensity, the possibility of developing strong emotions which could destabilize our consciousness is limited.

A particular psychological action may constitute several kinds of stabilization simultaneously. If I fantasize intensely about past personal triumphs, for example, I am loading my consciousness by putting a lot of energy into this, thus decreasing the energy available for other processes. I am simultaneously calling up memory associations of feeling good, which I like, and this is positive feedback stabilization.

INDUCING A d-ASC

Given the above stabilization processes, which maintain the pattern of a d-SoC in spite of changes, how do we break that pattern down in order to restructure our selection and organization of human potentialities into a d-ASC?

The first basic induction operation is that of disrupting the stabilization of the baseline state of consciousness. We apply *disrupting forces*, attempting to directly disrupt stabilization processes, or we attempt disruption by pushing known psychological functions and subsystems beyond their normal limits of stable functioning. We might disrupt particular subsystems, for example, by overloading them with stimuli, depriving them of stimuli necessary for their operation, giving them anomalous stimuli which can't be processed in habitual ways, or by deliberately withdrawing attention or other psychological energy from them so that they cease to function.

At this point it is well to note that a d-SoC is *multiply* stabilized. In applying disruptive forces we may succeed in interrupting *some* stabilization processes, but those still functioning may be sufficient to hold the system in its normal pattern of operation. I may go out and remove a number of bolts from my automobile engine at random, but the engine may still function in a basically unchanged manner as other fasteners still hold it together, even though there is less of a margin of safety. The multiple stabilization of the ordinary d-SoC is particularly important in looking at the effects of drugs, for while a psychedelic drug may disrupt several stabilization processes, there may still be sufficient ones remaining so that no d-ASC is produced. Some people, for example, have taken very large doses of LSD and reported no psychological effects at all.

The second induction operation (these two operations are often carried out simultaneously) is to apply *patterning forces* or stimuli to the person. These are forces designed to call up particular latent potentials and to pattern the new structure, once the initial structure is disrupted, into the desired d-ASC.

If the disrupting operations are successful, we have a transitional phase, when the organization of the baseline d-SoC is broken down but the new organization of the d-ASC has not yet occurred. The patterning forces are of major importance now, although it may be necessary to continue applying disrupting forces to avoid a return to the baseline state from this period of transition. The transition phase may be very rapid and almost imperceptible in some subjects, especially those who are adept at attaining a particular d-ASC, but for those for whom it is more prolonged they may simply report "blanking out" or report unusual and unstable kinds of transitional phenomena that are seldom repeated.

If the patterning forces successfully shape the disorganized potentialities in the transition phase, a new system forms, the d-ASC. The d-ASC must have inherent stabilization factors in its organization and/or receive continuing stabilization support from the patterning forces.

Let us illustrate the induction process by taking a transition from one state of consciousness to another that we are all familiar with, falling asleep. We lie down in a dark, quiet room, which has the effect of taking away a multitude of environmental stimuli that tend to stimulate, load, and pattern our ordinary d-SoC. Lying down further allows the kinesthetic receptors in the body to adapt out, so that most of the stimuli from it disappear and no longer act as loading stabilization. We take a mental attitude of nothing being important: We all know what happens when we *try* to go to sleep! This attitude involves a deliberate withdrawal of attention energy from various structures and thus further destabilizes the functioning of the system. Tiredness, the physiological need to sleep, acts as a further disrupting force and as a patterning force. In cases of extreme fatigue, we may not even have to lie down to go to sleep; the fatigue is a sufficient disrupting and patterning force all by itself. If we are not at all tired, we may carry out the other operations without much success and not achieve the transition into sleep.

INDIVIDUAL DIFFERENCES

Lack of recognition of the vital importance of individual differences has led to a great deal of error and confusion in the scientific study of d-ASCs. This is especially important in looking at drug-induced d-ASCs, where individual differences in response to a given dosage of a known drug may be so enormous that quite different d-ASCs (or none at all) result in different subjects. Thinking that the same d-ASC has been reached because the same drug has been taken will result in enormous errors of interpretation.

Figure 1 shows a different way of presenting the concept of d-SoCs, namely through the process of mapping experience. For simplicity, here I make the assumption that a two-dimensional map would be sufficient to map the intensity or the quality of various experiences of a subject at different times. The dots represent two-dimensional coordinates of a subject's experience obtained at various times. In spite of some quantitative variation, the subject's experiences fall into three quite discrete clusters, and never into regions between them. These clusters in experiential space constitute d-SoCs. In terms of the transition from one to another, it is as if a person has to leap from one to the other and cannot stop and stabilize at any point in between these clusters.

For this particular example, I have labeled the vertical dimension of the map the ability to hallucinate, ranging from a high of seeing a mental projection with as much intensity as a sensory stimulus to a low of hardly being able to see it at all. I have labeled the horizontal dimension "rationality," in the sense of following the rules in a given logic. This can vary from following the rules perfectly to making many errors. We can then readily see how three d-SoCs, three clusterings of experience, fit here. In our ordinary state of consciousness, shown in the lower right-hand quadrant, our rationality is generally high to moderate, and, for most of us, our ability to image ranges from very little to somewhat moderate. Ordinary dreaming is shown in the upper left-hand quadrant. Here, by waking standards, we frequently have such bizarre things happen that our ability to fol-

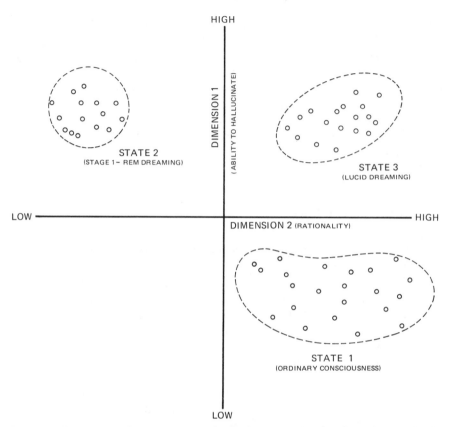

Figure 1. The concept of discrete states of consciousness as it arises from the experiential mapping of a single person's experiences over time.

low the rules of waking logic is quite poor. On the other hand, we perceive the dream world with an intensity that seems equal to that of ordinary sensory perceptions, so our ability to hallucinate ranges over a quite high range.

Lucid dreaming (van Eeden, 1913) is shown in the upper right quadrant. Here we have the experience of "waking up" within a dream. Since we still stay in a dream world and perceive it with extreme sensory intensity, the ability to hallucinate is quite high, but our reasoning seems quite good.

It is this kind of mapping of the qualities and intensities of experiences that is needed for really adequate descriptions of various d-SoCs.

This particular example also illustrates the inadequacy of two-dimensional mapping: Many ordinary dreams contain no logical errors at all, so the cluster for ordinary dreaming ought to extend much further to the right and overlap with the cluster for lucid dreaming, but this would confuse our example here. Yet on a three-dimensional or an N-dimensional map, what would appear to be

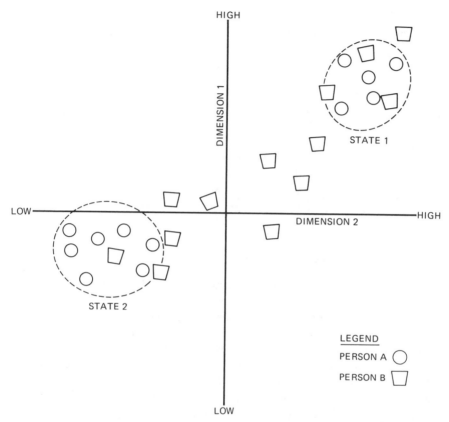

Figure 2. Experiential mapping over time of two peoples' experiences, showing the importance of considering individual differences in using the concept of discrete states of consciousness.

overlapping functioning in a lesser number of dimensions would seem to be quite different.

This kind of mapping will enable us to see the problems created by individual differences. Suppose we do this kind of experiential mapping for two different individuals. This is shown in Figure 2, where the experiences of Person A at various times are shown by the circles, and those of Person B at various times are shown by the cork-shaped symbols. Person A shows two discrete clusterings of experience, with no experiences in between. For Person A, the concept of two d-SoCs is a useful way of conceptualizing his experiences. Person B, however, reports experiences at various times to cover not only the two regions we characterized as two d-SoCs for Person A, but also experiences at values intermediate to these, in the "forbidden zone" of Person A. It would be highly misleading, in dealing with Person B, to say he was in *state* 2 when his experiences happened to fall in the lower left-hand quadrant or that he was in *state* 1 when his experiences fell in the upper right quadrant. For Person B, there seems to be only one d-SoC, whose range of functioning takes in what were two d-SoCs for Person A. It might be, for example, that state 1 is the ordinary d-SoC for Person A and by taking a certain drug he can move into state 2. Person B might be able to duplicate the experience simply by thinking about it for a moment, showing clear continuity with his ordinary state. Giving the same drug to Person B might produce a very different effect, or no effect at all.

As long as we recognize these individual differences, by adequately mapping the experiences of *each individual subject* and comparing them *before* combining results for different individuals, we do not have a problem. Unfortunately, almost all published studies have paid no real attention to possible individual differences and have simply assumed basic uniformity across subjects, thus giving us group results which might represent realities of no people at all.

USING DRUGS TO INDUCE d-ASCs

The basic thing we have to realize in using drugs to induce d-ASCs is that under no circumstances are we "simply" giving someone a certain drug. Nor can we even say that the "most important" thing we do is administer someone a certain drug. The unique individual who is our experimental subject starts from his ordinary state of consciousness which is an exceptionally complex, dynamic, stabilized system. He is in contact with many of our actions in conducting the experiment: In interpreting them, he brings his own understandings, values, and interpretations to the experiment, and he often alters these during the course of the experiment. We are a long way from the goal of being able to adequately specify all of these variables, and our understanding must remain crude until we do so. Let us consider some of these variables I found important during my investigations of marijuana intoxication (Tart, 1970a, 1971).

The obvious thing we do is administer the drug. Thus an important specification of conditions is the chemical nature of the drug, the exact quantity of the drug, and the method of administration. So we might say that we administered 350 milligrams of mescaline sulfate orally in several gelatin capsules. But while this looks like a precise statement, given our preference for physical variables, it is not sufficient. For example, people may vary considerably in their sensitivity to a given drug. A fixed quantity may be an overdose for one person, a subthreshold dose for a second. Swallowing some capsules might be easier for one person, for another it may maximize the possibility of nausea and its effects on his reactions. Further, many drug users are used to being able to control the amount of drug they take at any particular time, dividing the dose and taking more if they want more effect, but not taking more if they don't want a strong effect. If the control of quantity and method of administration is in the hands of the experimenter rather than under the subject's control, this may induce insecurity and other effects. Similarly, if the subject does not know the chemical nature of the drug he is getting (all too common in many studies), this may also induce anxiety.

The actual administration of the drug is accompanied by a host of nondrug, psychological forces impinging on the subject. I shall divide these into relatively long-term factors, things that have been with the subject for many years, into immediate subject factors operative primarily at the time of the experiment, and into particular situational or experimental factors.

The first major long-term factor is the cultural background of the subject. Has his culture given him positive or negative expectations about using drugs, and about this particular drug? Does the culture condone exploring d-ASCs, or has it declared them dangerous? Further, the person's particular personality structure within that cultural setting is important. Is this a neurotic person who will use the drug experience to express his or her problems? Is his personality adjustment fragile enough such that most energy will be devoted to fighting the drug reaction or keeping it within specified bounds? Are repressed elements of the personality liable to break through and cause conflict?

We must also consider physiological differences among individuals and their susceptibility to the particular drug, even though we do not have good data on this yet. Orientals, for example, tend to be more sensitive to alcohol for some physiological reactions than most Westerners. How to translate specific physiological differences into psychological outcomes is still generally unknown.

Finally, an important long-term factor is the subject's previously learned skills in reacting to drugs. Is this a "naive" subject who knows nothing about how to inhibit or intensify various drug effects? If so, much of his reactions will be of coping with novelty and stress, and the potentialities that are possible for a particular d-ASC may be buried under this reaction. Is this a person who, while not familiar with this specific drug, has generally learned to affect his drug reactions? If he is skilled in entering a d-ASC from this particular drug, might a much lower dosage be more optimal for operating in that d-ASC than the usual dose?

Then we come to a number of immediate subject factors. What is the subject's mood as he enters the experimental situation? Is he depressed, elated, anxious, curious, or what? Is the specific drug in its specific quantity and method of administration liable to amplify the incoming mood or replace it with something else? Which outcome do we want? What are the subject's expectations about what will happen with the drug? Does he expect to experience a lot of physical pain, does he think his psychological problems will be magically solved? And how do his expectations compare with his desires? That is, a subject may expect an unpleasant time and be willing to tolerate it, but he would really like to have a very pleasant experience.

Then there are important factors specific to the situation in which the drugs are taken, particularly if it is an experimental situation. What is the physical setting? The typical "scientific" or "medical" setting conveys a variety of messages to the subject about what is liable to happen and what is expected of him. A comfortable living room gives people a different psychological set than a sterile laboratory setting. Then, too, what are the social events that happened during the ingestion of the drug and the consequent reaction? Do assistants act in a friendly or cold way? If other subjects are taking the drug, might one of them have an especially bad reaction and communicate his anxiety to the other subjects, or vice versa? If this is an experimental situation, what are the formal instructions given to the subject, and what is his formal, conscious understanding of them and his reaction to them? Even more importantly, what are the implicit expectations, the biases of the experimenter that may be communicated to the subject? These problems of experimenter bias, or the demand characteristics of the situation (Orne, 1962), are vitally important, perhaps even more so than the formal experimental variables, and they warrant a more extended illustration.

In the late 50s and early 60s, there were a large number of studies on sensory deprivation. Putting a subject in a dark, soundproof room, with instructions to be still, so that bodily stimuli were taken away, and similar procedures produced a variety of unusual effects. At times they seemed to enter a d-ASC; often they experienced hallucinations, anxiety, alterations of thought processes, etc. These results were generally interpreted as showing that the brain needed a steady input from the environment in order to maintain its pattern of functioning. In terms of my systems theory approach, I would say they seem to show that without a good deal of loading stabilization from the environment, the d-SoC tends to break down. While I believe that this is generally true, it is now clear that the implicit biases in almost all of the experimental studies of sensory deprivation make it impossible to draw this conclusion from these studies. A striking demonstration of this was reported by Orne and Scheibe (1964).

Orne and Scheibe put subjects in an experimental situation which was not really sensory deprivation at all. For a couple of hours, individual subjects sat in a chair before a table in a well-lighted room in a hospital. The room had no windows, and was relatively blank and barren. It was not soundproof, as some noises from the corridor came in through the walls. The subject was required to sit there for 2 hours, but if he could not stand the full 2 hours, he could press a "panic button" on the wall which would bring the experimenter in to terminate the experiment. The situation is quite similar to one we experience frequently when, say, we have a long wait in a doctor's waiting room and there's nothing interesting to read and nobody to talk to. It is dull, but there is hardly any absolute lack of stimulation to the brain.

Subjects went through this procedure individually, but they were treated in two quite different ways. The subjects in the control group arrived at the hospital and were met by the experimenter, who was dressed casually and sloppily. He introduced himself as a graduate student who was doing a thesis project on people's reactions to sitting in a room for a couple of hours. The subject was put into the room and was told that the experimenter would come back in a couple of hours to interview him about how he reacted. The "panic button" was casually pointed out. Subjects in this group showed essentially no reaction, as reported in their later interviews, but boredom. Nobody pushed the panic button.

Subjects in the experimental group, although they received the same treatment of sitting in the dull room, were treated very differently when they first came in. The experimenter wore a suit and a white laboratory coat and introduced himself as Dr. So-and-So, a psychiatrist. He explained that the experiment they were participating in was one of "sensory deprivation." A long medical history was then taken, concentrating primarily on psychiatric symptoms. The subject was persuaded to sign a very long and complicated release form which released the experimenter, the hospital, and the granting agency from any untoward consequences resulting from this experimental procedure. In a corner of the interview room was a tray of hypodermic syringes, labeled "Emergency Tray." The experimenter did not say anything about this tray, although it was in plain sight, and if a subject happened to ask about it, he simply replied that it was of no consequence.

You can probably guess at the results. Some of the subjects in the experimental group pressed the panic button before their two hours were up. Many of them reported anxiety, altered thought processes, and unusual experiences. In brief, most of the experiences traditionally associated with sensory deprivation were produced, even though there was only a trivial degree of sensory deprivation involved. The expectations set up by the experimenter both explicitly (such as calling the experiment "sensory deprivation") and implicitly (everyone knows psychiatrists are interested in craziness) accounted for the results.

The unfortunate thing is that almost all studies of sensory deprivation have been carried out by psychiatrists or psychologists, typically in hospital situations, with medical release forms, and with the experimenters believing they are applying a very powerful psychological procedure to the subjects that might indeed disturb them. Thus we have no idea what proportion of the effects reported for sensory deprivation are actually due to a removal of loading stabilization and which are due to the implicit demands of the experimental situation.

Subjects are not completely passive recipients of the drug and nondrug forces acting on them. A subject may attempt to vary the nature of the forces impinging upon him, amplifying some and inhibiting others. But his attempts will be modified by his expectations and personality, and, of course, by his skill at being able to do these. Subjects may be able to overcome or modify some of the factors affecting them, but probably not all, and often not many at all.

It is also unfortunately true that almost all of the published scientific studies

TABLE 1. VALUES OF VARIABLES FOR MAXIMIZING PROBABILITY OF "GOOD" OR "BAD TRIP"

	Variables	Good Trip Likely	Bad Trip Likely
Drug	Quality	Pure, known.	Unknown drug or unknown degree of (harmful) adulterants.
	Quantity	Known accurately, adjusted to individual's desire.	Unknown, beyond individual's control.
Long-term factors	Culture	Acceptance, belief in benefits	Rejection, belief in detrimental effects.
	Personality	Stable, open, secure.	Unstable, rigid, neurotic, or psychotic.
	Physiology	Healthy.	Specific adverse vulnerability to drug.
	Learned drug skills	Wide experience gained under supportive conditions.	Little or no experience or preparation, unpleasant past experience.
Immediate user factors	Mood	Happy, calm, relaxed, or euphoric.	Depressed, overexcited, repressing significant emotions.
	Expectations	Pleasure, insight, known eventualities.	Danger, harm, manipulation, unknown eventualities.
	Desires	General pleasure, specific user-accepted goals.	Aimlessness, (repressed) desires to harm or degrade self for secondary gains
Experiment or situation	Physical setting	Pleasant and esthetically interesting by user's standards.	Cold, impersonal, "medical," "psychiatric," "hospital," "scientific."
	Social events	Friendly, non-manipulative interactions overall.	Depersonalization or manipulation of the user, hostility overall
	Formal instructions	Clear, understandable, creating trust and purpose.	Ambiguous, dishonest, creating mistrust.
	Implicit demands	Congruent with explicit communications, supportive.	Contradict explicit communications and/or reinforce other negative variables.

on the effects of drugs on consciousness have been carried out with the same kind of setting as the psychiatric studies on sensory deprivation. They were generally done by psychiatrists in medical settings with medical release forms and with the psychiatrists believing that they were doing something powerful and fairly dangerous to the subjects. This element of danger was justified because it was believed that we could learn important things about mental illness that might help in treatment. This was particularly true in the early days of drug research when psychedelic drugs were supposed to be "psychotomimetic." By and large, they were. The various nondrug factors resulted in a variety of unpleasant, psychotic reactions.

Table 1 summarizes extreme values that these many variables may take and the consequences. If many or most of the variables take certain values, a "good trip," a pleasant reaction, may take place that may result in a d-ASC in which a subject can do useful things, such as tapping latent potentialities like the psi potential. If many or most of the variables take the other values, however, a "bad trip" is likely, the subject's reaction will be one of mainly coping with anxiety or psychoticlike symptoms, performance detriments in a variety of areas are likely, and we should not expect to be able to get much useful work from him. Given the kind of data reported in most of the published studies, on both conditions and outcomes, it is clear that most conditions were in the "bad trip" direction in most investigations. Table 1 should serve as a useful reminder to experimenters about what to do and what not to do in future experiments.

THE DEPTH DIMENSION

Although it is important to realize that there is enormous variability in individual response to drugs, so that a dose under certain psychological conditions will induce a d-ASC in one person but will have little or no effect on another person, there nevertheless is a pattern of variation within d-ASC, once it is induced, that is commonly called the depth dimension, the intensity dimension, or various levels within a d-ASC. Knowing where a person is along this depth dimension is frequently important for an adequate specification of conditions and understanding of results. Saying that two people are both in their ordinary (presumably normal for our culture) d-SoC is a fine beginning, but further specification that one of them is very excited and the second is rather calm and sleepy adds to the precision of our description. This is still, of course, a very rough level of description.

In dealing with drug-induced d-ASCs, too many investigators, schooled in a pharmacological approach, have succumbed to the temptation of equating depth with dosage of the drug. Therefore, in this approach, a person who has taken 200 micrograms of LSD is basically twice as deep as a person who has taken 100 micrograms. For a variety of reasons (discussed in more detail elsewhere [Tart,

1975a]) dealing with the generally unknown values of the many psychological factors discussed above which control reactions to a drug, this equation is generally wrong. Of three people given the same dose of the same psychedelic drug, for example, one may experience some quantitative shift as to exactly where he is *within* the experiential space of his ordinary d-SoC, the second may move into the d-ASC but only reach a light depth in it, and the third may reach a profound depth in a d-ASC. Further, even when the same individual is given the identical dose at several different times, he may reach different depths of the d-ASC. Experienced marijuana users, for example, report that smoking the same amount of marijuana from the same batch at different times can result in quite different levels of intoxication (Tart, 1971). Thus knowing dosage may be useful, but it certainly cannot be considered a specification of depth.

The moral is that we do not assume that a d-ASC occurs simply because we have gone through the procedure (of giving a drug) for inducing it, nor does the intensity of the procedure (the dosage of the drug) necessarily tell us the depth reached. Rather we have to map the experiential space of the d-ASC, determine one or more appropriate depth dimensions, and then find a convenient way of assessing this depth at any time. Convenience is important here, especially if depth for a given d-ASC can vary unpredictably over short time periods. More precise indications for doing this are given elsewhere (Tart, 1972).

In my own investigations of hypnosis and marijuana intoxication, I have extensively investigated the process of allowing subjects to scale their own depth and report it by giving a number on a predefined scale. I have found the technique to be extremely useful, and the results have been reported in detail elsewhere (Tart, 1970b,.1971, 1972; Tart and Kvetensky, 1973).

To illustrate this, consider the case of experienced marijuana users. As a result of having been intoxicated and entered the d-ASC characteristic of marijuana intoxication many times, if they are exercising any self-observation at all they will have gotten a general idea of the various kinds of experiences expected and a feel for the ordering of these experiences along some kind of depth dimension. A typical report, for example, is that a person does not have to feel very intoxicated at all to experience some degree of sensory enhancement, but they have to feel very intoxicated to experience an obvious slowing down of time.

How reliable can such scaling be, especially from inexperienced observers? In my initial study of marijuana intoxication (Tart, 1971), I had subjects rate the minimum depth level necessary for experiencing a very wide variety of experiences. That study only allowed a kind of averaging across subjects to get a general feeling for the intensity level of various experiences. In order to see how consistent this kind of ranking of minimum levels for various effects was across subjects, Erma Kvetensky and I had a second, independent sample of experienced marijuana users rank eight of the more common phenomena as to minimal level of intoxication (Tart and Kvetensky, 1973). We took the (extrapolated) point at which 50 percent or more of the users indicated the minimal threshold of the various effects and then correlated the ranking of the earlier and later studies. We found a rank order correlation coefficient of .95, indicating a remarkable degree of agreement among experienced marijuana users on the relation of these phenomena to the depth dimension. When we compare each individual's rank ordering of these phenomena against the average standard found in the earlier study, the mean of these individual rank order correlation coefficients was .73, and almost half of the subjects had a correlation greater than .80 with the standard. Only 12 percent of the subjects showed correlations of less than .40 with the standard. Remember these are not trained observers dedicated to precise scientific observation; these are mainly students who are using marijuana for their own interest. Nevertheless an exceptionally high degree of consistency was shown. What might trained observers be able to do?

In general, I feel that at the present time self-report scales of the depth of a d-ASC, drug-induced or not, are probably the most useful measure we have of the depth dimension. Data on this are presented elsewhere (Tart, 1972). Charles Honorton has found that these kinds of self-reports also relate well to the degree of alpha rhythm and muscle tension that subjects show in learning to control their brain waves (Honorton, Davidson, and Bindler, 1971) and with how much ESP ability they show under various conditions (Honorton, 1972, 1974; Honorton, Drucker, and Hermon, 1973).

MAJOR PSYCHEDELIC DRUGS

In looking at the results produced by the powerful psychedelic drugs like LSD, mescaline, and psilocybin, the main thing we find is the extreme variability of results. It is clear that almost everyone who takes these more powerful psychedelics experiences important disruptions of his or her ordinary d-SoC, and we may say that the primary effect of the powerful psychedelics is to disrupt the stabilization processes of the ordinary state so that it breaks down. But, while there is enough commonality about the experiences produced by, say, marijuana intoxication (at least in our cultural setting), so that is is useful to speak of the "marijuana state" as a distinctive d-ASC, a state name that is useful when applied across subjects, the variability of the powerful psychedelics is so great that I interpret present evidence as showing that there is no particular d-ASC *necessarily* produced by the more powerful psychedelic drugs. To the contrary, we see a highly unstable condition in which one never gets more than rather transient formations of patterns that constitute d-ASCs. The potential d-ASCs seldom stabilize and persist for useful amounts of time. The colloquial phrase *tripping* is a very apropos description of this: One is continually going here and there, but never arriving and settling down anywhere.

While this is probably true for most of the experiences of powerful psychedelic drugs in our culture, it is not universally true. Carlos Castaneda's fascinating accounts (Castaneda, 1968, 1971, 1972, 1974) suggest that Castaneda's initial reaction to psychedelic drugs was this sort of tripping, but his mentor, don Juan, was not interested in this. Among other things, don Juan tried to train him to stabilize the effects of these drugs so that he could construct particular d-ASCs that were suited for particular kinds of tasks at various times. Thus with the addition of further psychological patterning forces to the primarily disruptive forces that psychedelic drugs constitute, it is possible that stable d-ASCs can be developed that will enable us to tap important human potentialities such as the psi potential. Discovering how to go about training a person to reach one or more stable d-ASCs with powerful psychedelic drugs is a major investigative task lying ahead of us.

PSYCHOLOGICAL AND PHYSIOLOGICAL EFFECTS

The reader may have noted that even though we are discussing drugs, I have not said a single thing about physiology, neurology, or neurochemistry. This is deliberate, for several reasons.

First, for the psychedelic drugs we know much about, the physiological knowledge that we have is of little value in explaining the psychological effects, and it is the psychological effects that are our primary interest here. If we ask what the major physiological effects of marijuana intoxication are, e.g., about all the evidence will allow us to say with any confidence is that there is a slight increase in heart rate and a reddening of the eyes due to dilation of their blood vessels and that neither is clinically significant. What such effects might have to do with various experiences or tapping the psi potential is not at all clear. While physiological investigations may some day tell us enough about psychological functioning to cast some light on the process, there is generally almost no relation between our knowledge of physiological and psychological reactions to drugs today and probably will not be for some time to come.

In terms of my systems approach to consciousness, drugs may indeed have specific effects on various neurological/physiological structures and subsystems, disrupting their operation, pushing them to extreme levels of functioning, or altering the interrelationships of various subsystems. That is, the drug may both disrupt and pattern on a physiological level, but this does not necessarily mean that it will induce a d-ASC, much less determine the specific form of it. Remember that any d-ASC is multiply stabilized, so a drug may disrupt several stabilization processes, yet the system of consciousness, the d-SoC, may still maintain its integrity.

A good example of this occurs again with marijuana intoxication. Most marijuana smokers have to *learn* how to achieve the d-ASC we call marijuana intoxication. Typically, the first few times most people smoke marijuana they feel nothing or only occasional, isolated effects like tingling, which do not affect their consciousness. The neophyte wonders why people make so much fuss about taking a drug that doesn't seem to do anything interesting. With the assistance of more experienced drug users, "a little help from my friends," who suggest that he focus his attention on certain kinds of happenings or attempt to have specified kinds of experiences, additional psychological factors begin to operate as patterning and disrupting forces, altering the flow of psychological energy among various structures. Eventually the neophyte learns to disrupt his ordinary state and pattern the d-ASC of marijuana intoxication. Often the transition takes place quite suddenly, and the neophyte finds that he is "stoned." The relatively invariant physiological effects of the drug have been there all the time, but they have not been combined with the right kind of psychological forces to bring about the d-ASC of marijuana intoxication.

LEARNING TO USE PSI WITHIN A d-ASC

A number of the earlier studies which attempted to use d-ASCs, whether drug-induced or not, to improve psi performance seemed to operate on an implicit, naive paradigm on the order of "This d-ASC is unusual, psi is unusual; therefore if we induce the d-ASC we should get psi." It does not seem to be that simple.

Inducing a d-ASC may indeed change the selection of human potentialities that go into consciousness to include one or more potentialities that involve psi, and/or the new pattern of structuring may allow access to that potential so that it can function. But we should not assume that that is all there is to it. We may now have to train the person to utilize that potential. Ways of training psi potential are, scientifically speaking, still largely unexplored, and this is not the place to deal with them, but I do want to point out the potential of immediate feedback training. There is some experimental evidence which indicates that giving a person immediate knowledge of results, which is presumably rewarding when a hit is made since the person is motivated to succeed, tends to eliminate the usual extinction of psi and produce learning in some subjects (Tart, 1976). This is a very elementary application of learning theory, and it would probably apply in various d-ASCs. Whatever the structure of the d-ASC is, the subject would try some kind of process that he hoped would activate his psi abilities, he would obtain immediate feedback on the degree to which it was effective, and he would be able to change or consolidate strategy, depending on whether he was unsuccessful or partially or completely successful.

OPERATIONAL DEFINITION, EXTERNAL AND INTERNAL

By now it should be clear that progress in this field will depend on our being able to describe accurately the particular experiential clusterings that we call d-SoCs and the operations necessary for inducing d-ASCs and functioning within them.

Given the scientific ethos of the last few decades, psychology was trapped in an *external* operationalism: describing the physical operations, how the experimenter and subject behaved, was a precise, highly repeatable kind of thing that was hoped would lead to scientific repeatability and control of psychological processes. Except in particular technical ways, this kind of focus on external behavior has not greatly advanced our psychological understanding and is on the wane as a dominant force. Particularly in dealing with d-ASCs, this kind of behaviorism or external operationalism is almost useless, for practically all phenomena of interest occur only in a person's experience. "Operationally defining" a hypnotic state as meaning that a person designated as a hypnotist has said the magic words or defining a marijuana state as existing because such and such a quantity of marijuana has been ingested are generally useless and misleading things to do. It results in our putting our data into categories that are highly inaccurate.

What we need is an *internal* operationalism. We need first to be able to specify the experiential/psychological characteristics of a subject's experience in detail. This requires a multidimensional specification. If we now find that our subject's experiences fall into several discrete, experiential clusters, then the concept of d-SoCs is useful in both describing and explaining his experience. We can then go on to specify the operations that must occur internally for a given d-ASC to develop. We may find, for instance, that if this subject *experiences* such and such a degree of physical relaxation, *experiences* deploying his attention on such and such a kind of image for some period, manages to avoid deploying attention on such and such a topic, etc., then the probability is very high that a certain kind of transition period will follow, and then his experiences will show the characteristics of a certain d-ASC. We may name that d-ASC whatever we wish. Then, given an experiential assessment that shows that the person is indeed in that d-ASC, we go on to devise certain ways of affecting him in that d-ASC that result in psi performance.

THE IDEAL EXPERIMENT

The parapsychologist is not going to be able merely to draw on well-developed techniques and knowledge in the area of d-ASCs and drug research, go into his laboratory, give a subject drug X, and see reliable psi functioning. Existing knowledge allows us to draw a general picture of the nature of d-ASCs, as I have sketched in the earlier part of this chapter, but the primary thing that this picture does is point out a variety of methodological problems in this area and give us some guidance for future research. Parapsychologists may either wait a decade or two until there is a well-developed science or, more profitably, begin carrying out studies which are basic contributions to our understanding of d-ASCs *per se,* as well as of parapsychological relevance. With this end in mind, I shall briefly sketch the outlines of the "ideal" experiment in this area, bringing together many of the methodological points made above. No investigator will do it exactly in this fashion, but it suggests things to keep in mind.

First, the investigator must answer satisfactorily such questions as why he thinks some particular d-ASC is likely to enhance psi functioning. Then, given what is known about that d-ASC, is it likely that the research he can put into it will pay off? This includes practical questions, such as whether a drug is legal or not; if it is legal, who will take the medical responsibility for the study; can proper investigational clearance for investigating the drug be obtained; can research funding in general be obtained? I raise these points because I suspect that, for the time being, the answer to some of them will be "No" for most parapsychologists. If it is, and yet the investigator wants to work in this area, I suggest that he investigate the ethical and legal considerations that would be involved in simply passing the word in a sympathetic population that people who are already under the influence of such and such drug drop by his laboratory at particular times and carry out some tasks. This would entail some ambiguities such as not really knowing the chemical nature of the drugs involved, their exact dosages, and the like; but since adequate psychological assessment of the actual configuration of subjects' consciousness is more important than these external, physical variables, this is not introducing as much ambiguity as one would suspect. I am not advising any investigator to break the law, but, given difficulties in carrying out investigations along orthodox lines in this area, plus the fact that untold millions of people are breaking the law anyway, it may still be possible to learn from the situation.

The second major consideration is to conceptualize your investigation, especially in its early stages, as a number of *individual case studies*. This means extensive work with individual subjects. What are the characteristics of his ordinary d-SoC? What d-ASC(s) can he enter, and what are the characteristics of each? Are they actually d-ASCs or simply different regions of the subject's ordinary d-SoC? Is a particular d-ASC consistent with itself across time, so as to warrant a state name? What can the subject and the experimenter do to further stabilize his d-ASC, to induce it readily, to bring the subject out of it readily? What is the personality structure of the subject? Are there psychological problems which are or might be exacerbated by the d-ASC, i.e., what are the risks involved in working with this subject in that d-ASC? Are the risks worth the potential gain? Might some d-ASCs be safe to use with this subject, but not others? Might new d-ASCs with desired characteristics be structured through appropriate work?

Third, given that you have a stable d-ASC for a given subject, how do you activate and refine psi potential in it? If free flowing imagery is a strong feature of the d-ASC, for example, might free-response GESP tests be more appropriate than repeated-guessing tests? Might emotionally significant targets be vital to activate the psi potential?

Fourth, assuming you have carried out the above procedure in several different subjects and tapped various psi potentials, then you can make comparisons across subjects. Is there enough similarity in various d-ASCs across subjects to warrant a common state name? If so, what does this say about the nature of the mind and/or of psi functioning? I do not think this state of the investigation warrants much discussion here, for there is so much to do in the earlier stages first.

Finally, but of as much importance as any of the preceding considerations, what is the experimental subject gaining from participation in these studies? Is he or she content with the abstract reward of helping to advance scientific knowledge, or perhaps the financial reward for participating in experiments? Is the relationship with the experimenter rewarding? Are there neurotic flaws, such as transference reactions, creating various games between the experimenter and the subject and so limiting experiences and results to certain "safe" territories? Might these neurotic interactions be reinforcing neurotic traits on the part of the subject or the experimenter's own neurotic traits? Can the experiment be carried out in such a way that the subjects will learn from it and grow from it as well as the experimenter? I think this last point is particularly important, as psychological and parapsychological research has often been dominated by an implicit "colonial" paradigm, where the "intelligent" and "wise" investigator uses subjects to find out things which will be useful to the investigator and his associates, but not to the subjects. This was resulted in a good deal of hidden resentment on the part of the subjects, which adds confusion and deliberate error to experimental results. I have tried to follow the practice of treating experimental subjects as coinvestigators, and I suspect that this style of investigation will have to become more prevalent if we are to eliminate some of the problems of experimenter bias.

REFERENCES

Castaneda, C. *The Teachings of Don Juan: A Yaqui Way of Knowledge.* Berkeley: University of California Press, 1968.

Castaneda, C. *A Separate Reality: Further Conversations with Don Juan.* New York: Simon and Schuster, 1971.

Castaneda, C. *Journey to Ixtlan: The Lessons of Don Juan.* New York: Simon and Schuster, 1972.

Castaneda, C. *Tales of Power.* New York: Simon and Schuster, 1974.

Cavanna, R., and Servadio, E. *ESP Experiences with LSD-25 and Psilocybin: A Methodological Approach.* Parapsychological Monographs No. 5. New York: Parapsychology Foundation, 1964.

Honorton, C. Significant factors in hypnotically-induced clairvoyant dreams. *Journal of the American Society for Psychical Research*, 1972, **66**, 86–102.

Honorton, C. State of awareness factors in psi activation. *Journal of the American Society for Psychical Research*, 1974, **68**, 246–256.

Honorton, C., Davidson, R., and Bindler, P. Feedback-augmented EEG alpha, shifts in subjective state, and ESP card-guessing performance. *Journal of the American Society for Psychical Research*, 1971, **65**, 308–323.

Honorton, C., Drucker, S. A., and Hermon, H. C. Shifts in subjective state and ESP under conditions of partial sensory deprivation: A preliminary study. *Journal of the American Society for Psychical Research*, 1973, **67**, 191–196.

Krippner, S., and Davidson, R. Paranormal events occurring during chemically-induced psychedelic experience and their implications for religion. *Journal of Altered States of Consciousness*, 1974, **1**, 175–184.

Marti-Ibanez, F. The gates to paradise. *MD Medical Newsmagazine*, June, 1965.

Masters, R. E. L., and Houston, J. *The Varieties of Psychedelic Experience*. New York: Holt, Rinehart and Winston, 1966.

Orne, M. T. On the social psychology of the psychological experiment, with particular reference to demand characteristics and their implications. *American Psychologist*, 1962, **17**, 776–783.

Orne, M. T., and Scheibe, K. The contribution of non-deprivation factors in production of sensory deprivation effects: The psychology of the "panic button." *Journal of Abnormal and Social Psychology*, 1964, **68**, 3–12.

Osis, K. A pharmacological approach to parapsychological experimentation. In *Proceedings of Two Conferences on Parapsychology and Pharmacology*, pp. 74–75. New York: Parapsychology Foundation, 1961.

Paul, M. Two cases of altered consciousness with amnesia apparently telepathically induced. *Psychedelic Review*, 1966, **3**, 4–8.

Puharich, A. *Beyond Telepathy*. Garden City, N. Y.: Doubleday, 1962.

Tart, C. T. Marijuana intoxication: Common experiences. *Nature*, 1970, **226**, 701–704. (a)

Tart, C. T. Self-report scales of hypnotic depth. *International Journal of Clinical and Experimental Hypnosis*, 1970, **18**, 105–125. (b)

Tart, C. T. *On Being Stoned: A Psychological Study of Marijuana Intoxication*. Palo Alto, Calif.: Science & Behavior Books, 1971.

Tart, C. T. Measuring the depth of an altered state of consciousness, with particular reference to self-report scales of hypnotic depth. In E. Fromm and R. E. Shor (Eds.), *Hypnosis: Research Developments and Perspectives*, pp. 445–447. Chicago: Aldine/Atherton, 1972.

Tart, C. T. On the nature of altered states of consciousness, with special reference to parapsychological phenomena. In W. G. Roll, R. L. Morris, and J. D. Morris (Eds.), *Research in Parapsychology 1973*, pp. 163–218. Metuchen, N. J.: Scarecrow Press, 1974.

Tart, C. T. *States of Consciousness*. New York: Dutton, 1975. (a)

Tart, C. T. *Discrete states of consciousness*. In P. Lee, R. E. Ornstein, D. Galin, A. J. Deikman, and C. T. Tart (Eds.), *Symposium on Consciousness*, pp. 89–175. New York: Viking Press, 1975. (b)

Tart, C. T. *Learning to Use Extrasensory Perception*. Chicago: University of Chicago Press, 1976.

Tart, C. T., and Kvetensky, E. Marijuana intoxication: Feasibility experiential scaling of depth. *Journal of Altered States of Consciousness*, 1973, **1**, 15–21.

van Asperen de Boer, S. R., Barkema, P. R., and Kappers, J. Is it possible to induce ESP with psilocybin? An exploratory investigation. *International Journal of Neuropsychiatry*, 1966, **2**, 447–473.

van Eeden, F. A study of dreams. *Proceedings of the Society for Psychical Research*, 1913, **26**, 431–461. Reprinted in C. T. Tart (Ed.),*Altered States of Consciousness*,pp. 145–158. New York: Wiley, 1969.

Vasiliev, L. L. *Mysterious Phenomena of the Human Psyche*. New Hyde Park, N. Y.: University Books, 1965.

Whittlesey, J. R. B. Some curious ESP results in terms of variance. *Journal of Parapsychology*, 1960, **24**, 220–222.

Part VI

PARAPSYCHOLOGY AND HEALING

1

Psi, Psychotherapy, and Psychoanalysis

Jan Ehrenwald

INTRODUCTION

Most modern schools of psychotherapy are wholly committed to the scientific model, and none more so than Freudian psychoanalysis. It is the scientific approach *par excellence*. As such, it faithfully reflects what has been the prevailing trend in modern clinical medicine up to our days. Psychoanalysis is essentially based on a cause-and-effect oriented medical model of treatment. Despite differences, the diverse approaches from Janet and Charcot to Freud, Adler, and Jung, have made a clean sweep of magic and demonology in their approach. The causes of mental disorder are sought within the individual, in his interpersonal relationships or in his society, not in malevolent spiritual agencies, in the decrees of the gods, in planetary constellations, or in mysterious astral influences.

FREUD AND THE OCCULT

Freudian psychoanalysis is perhaps the most consistent and the most uncompromising example of the scientific approach to psychotherapy. In Freud's topographical picture of personality, or in his metapsychological scheme of the human mind, there is no place for psi, for magic, animism, or the operation of external demoniacal agents. They are nothing but projections of repressed instinctual drives, personifications of internalized parental figures equipped with either protective, benign, or threatening, malevolent qualities. Neurosis is due to conflict between incompatible inner forces, and cure is contingent on the resolution of conflict. The analyst's task is to identify its sources, to lift it from the unconscious to the level of conscious awareness: He must make "the unconscious conscious." He must help the patient to finish unfinished psychological business within the transference—countertransference relationship through "working through" and reeducation.

It should be recalled at this point that Breuer and Freud developed their technique on the rebound from Liébeault's and Bernheim's use of hypnosis and hypnotic suggestion as their main therapeutic tool. Apparently Freud's early rejection of hypnosis was due to more than purely technical considerations. He felt uneasy over assuming the role of the hypnotist with his assumed omnipotence in relation to the hypnotized subject. Indeed, the analyst's detached, impersonal attitude in the psychoanalytic situation is the diametrical opposite of the therapist donning the mantle of the magician or medicine man and encouraging the patient's—as well as his own—regression "in the service of treatment."

Viewed in this light, the extreme rationalistic position of orthodox Freudian analysis can well be described as a reaction formation against the repudiated heritage of magic. Yet Freud's intransigent attitude against "oceanic feelings," against the mystical and the occult, is in striking contrast to his abiding fascination with it. He has dealt in a number of papers with the potential part played by telepathy in dreams and in the psychoanalytic situation.

One of Freud's first contributions to the subject of telepathy appeared in 1922. He confesses having hesitated for nearly 10 years with the publication of his observations "for fear of our scientific world picture being vitiated by them." The first case was of a lady of 43 of whom we learn only that she was undergoing treatment for neurosis. Her analysis discovered a strong fixation on her father which had prevented her finding happiness in her marriage. She had longed for children and hoped to reawaken her love for her husband by identifying him, as the father of her children, with her own father-image. When she learned there was no prospect of having children owing to her husband's illness, she became more deeply entangled in her neurosis. She was 27 when she turned to a "fortune-teller" in Paris, who, taking her for unmarried, "prophesied" that she would have two children at the age of 32. By the time her psychoanalysis began this prophesy had proved manifestly wrong: The patient had remained childless, and there was less hope than before of having children at the age of 43.

Yet her analysis showed, nevertheless, a surprising correspondence to reality with the fortune-teller's statement. The patient's mother was just 32 years of age when within the shortest possible interval she gave birth to two children, after almost resigning hope of having any at her age. It was clear that the patient, in her phantasy, took the place of her mother and that the fortune-teller, by his alleged prophecy relating to an intimate detail of her mother's past life, hit upon the daughter's most ardent secret desire. The wish to have children—one of the implications of her father complex—governed her unconscious life for years, and its frustration was one of the precipitating factors of her illness. Thus the fortune-teller's prophecy had proved wrong, it is true, but the striking fact remains that it disclosed precisely and in fully adequate manner a distinct unconscious idea existing in the patient's mind. Since there was no conceivable means of the fortune-teller understanding the significance to the daughter of either the reference to two children or to the age of 32, Freud had no option other than to attribute the incident to telepathy between the fortune-teller and his client.

Freud's second observation refers again to a fortune-teller's prophecy. This patient, a young man, fell ill at the time of his beloved sister's wedding. In this case analysis revealed strong fixation to his sister. This did not, however, prevent him from encouraging her marriage, in spite of the disapproval of their parents. Having undergone a first series of analytic treatments, the young man consulted an astrologer who "prophesied" her client's future by means of a horoscope starting from birth data. The young man gave her the birth data of his brother-in-law. The fortune-teller's forecast was gloomy. She prophesied that the young husband would die the next July or August from poisoning by crayfish or oysters.

Here, too, the prophecy proved entirely wrong. The brother-in-law did not die at the predicted time. Yet he had fallen ill during the past summer, before the patient had consulted the astrologer, and the cause of his illness was in fact poisoning from crayfish or oysters. Analysis made it clear that the patient had not, at that time, overcome his unconscious hatred of the rival who had married his sister. Hence his repressed wish that he might have died of the poisoning. According to Freud's conjecture he might have thought: "Such food-fads are likely to persist . . . Why should it not happen again"? As there was no possibility of the astrologer's knowing about this insignificant detail from the life history of the brother-in-law, Freud was compelled to suggest that here likewise this intelligence was due to some "supernormal" means of communication with the inquirer's unconscious. In this way only could the astrologer be supposed to have revealed to her client a certain item in his brother-in-law's biography related in a particular way to his own wishes and expectations.

The evidential value of these two observations is undoubtedly limited. Freud had to rely on secondhand information, and the possibility of misrecollection or misrepresentation on the part of his informants cannot be ruled out. Moreover, in both cases the incident dates back some considerable time prior to their recording, viz., 11 years in one, and several months in the other. Further, in both instances only one of the persons involved was accessible to direct inquiry, namely the patient, while his or her opposite number, the fortune-teller or astrologer, remains out of the picture. It may be that it was because of these shortcomings that Freud hesitated so long over their publication. On the other hand, he considered their evidence strong enough to justify his putting forward a working hypothesis. In both cases, he contends, it is emotionally colored mental content having an obvious relevance to repressed material which is reproduced in the minds of the percipients. In other words, the percipient is sensitive to such mental elements of an agent which are in a state of partial repression or which are apt to emerge from the unconscious to conscious awareness. To put it in terms of psychoanalysis: His sensitiveness refers to events in the stage of transition from primary to secondary processes.

In a further group of observations (Freud, 1933) the evidence was at least not impaired by the drawback of secondhand information. They occurred to Freud during the analytical situation, and it was he himself who seemed to be playing the role of the agent. Yet in these cases, too, Freud hesitated to acknowledge their genuineness without reservation. They are not impressive and, as so often happens in spontaneous phenomena, again open to the objection of chance coincidence. His first observation of this type goes back to 1919, when after the First World War Freud was greatly pleased by the visit of Dr. Forsyth, the noted London analyst, to his Vienna flat. Freud being engaged with a patient, Dr. Forsyth left his visiting card with the message that he would call again. While dealing with his next patient, Mr. P., Freud was still thinking of his distinguished guest—the first foreigner to visit him following the cessation of hostilities—when this patient unexpectedly produced the name *Herr von Vorsicht*. This is the German equivalent of Mr. Foresight, a name closely resembling that of Dr. Forsyth, and the patient mentioned it with reference to his own story. From the analytical point of view this reference fits in well with the patient's general attitude to the analyst. Freud interpreted it as an expression of his jealousy of the stranger to whom the analyst's attention had been diverted. Here again the point is that the patient could by no conceivable "normal" means have learned of the doctor's presence in Vienna and still less of his visit to Professor Freud.

Another observation of Freud's (1933) refers to the incidental reference by his patient during analysis to the word *nightmare*. This occurred precisely when Freud was concerned with the presence in Vienna of another distinguished visitor from London, Ernest Jones, whose book on the nightmare had aroused his keenest interest. Finally, in a third case, the name of Freud's friend, *Anton von Freund*, happened to intrude into the analytical conversation in the form of the patient's slip of the tongue, just when Freud was thinking of a visit he had paid to Anton von Freund's home.

Freud's interest in the occult is also borne out by his membership in both the British and American Societies for Psychical Research. In a letter to Hereward Carrington (Jones, 1957, Vol. 3, Chap. 14), he went so far as to say that if he had a chance to start his career all over again, he would dedicate himself to psychical research. But all these forays into the field of the occult notwithstanding, Freud never tried to integrate the available clinical and experimental observations with his own system of thought. Indeed, his attitude toward them remained ambivalent all along. In 1922, he expressed regret over having given the impression of supporting the reality of telepathy (Freud 1922):

> Have I given you the impression that I am secretly inclined to support the reality of telepathy in the occult sense? If so, I should very much regret such an impression; in reality, however, I was anxious to be strictly impartial. I have every reason to be so, for I have no opinion (p. 435).

It is interesting to note that Freud made these skeptical remarks some 3 years after his brilliant analysis of the Forsyth case.

In addition to some of the Freud articles reviewed here, an anthology edited by George Devereux (1953) contains early papers by N. Fodor, H. Deutsch, D. Burlingham, G. Pederson-Krag, E. Servadio, J. Eisenbud, and others. It also includes a spirited attack by Albert Ellis (1947) upon Eisenbud's and other psychoanalysts' contributions, as well as Eisenbud's masterly rebuttal to Ellis.

Hollós' (1933) contribution hews closely to the Freudian line. He focused on the emotional charge of telepathic communications and on their relevance to the transference-countertransference configuration. At times, he states, a patient's slip of the tongue may be made in direct response to telepathy from the therapist. The Devereux anthology also contains E. Servadio's (1935) pioneering paper, "Psychoanalysis and Telepathy," which emphasizes the importance of positive transference in the origin of telepathy. In a later paper (1955) he calls attention to the patient's ability to sense when the therapist turns his attention to a "rival." The resulting resentment may become a problem in his therapeutic management. The case is at the same time a graphic example of precognitive telepathy in the analytic situation. Among other contributions is Servadio's (1966) description of specific dovetailing patterns of interpersonal dynamics which are conducive to telepathy and his psychoanalytic study of trance mediumship (1937).

A paper by Hann-Kende (1953) likewise focuses attention on the dynamics of the transference-countertransference relationship. Pederson-Krag (1947) points to the part played by the therapist's anxiety and fear of exposure in the origin of telepathy. Helene Deutsch (1926) and Dorothy Burlingham (1935) published several observations of telepathy in adult and in mother-child relationships, as did Ehrenwald (1954) and Berthold Schwarz (1971). Schwarz described more than 1,000 examples of telepathy involving himself, his wife, and their two children.

In *New Dimensions of Deep Analysis* (1955), Ehrenwald applies the psychoanalytic method to both autopsychic and heteropsychic experiences. His argument is based on a number of telepathic dreams of patients in analysis and he shows that such dreams tend to occur in clusters at times when the therapist's interest in psi is heightened. He also calls attention to the minus-functions of the ego as important predisposing factors to psi, and stresses their similarity to the visual world of brain-injured patients, to their poor survival value, and to their acausal, metalogical quality.

Jule Eisenbud's pioneering contributions in his book *Psi and Psychoanalysis* (1970) range from the familiar type of telepathic dreams to telepathic "cross-dreaming" involving the therapist and several of his patients. He also presents his technique of "triangulation" to deal with such situations. This technique involves the therapist's and the patient's mental content viewed in conjunction with their surrounding external circumstances. Another new departure is Eisenbud's emphasis on the "psi-pathology" of everyday life. A number of precognitive dreams described by Eisenbud (1969, 1970) defy attempts at interpretation in terms of telepathic self-fulfillment as suggested earlier by Hitschmann (1924), Zulliger (1934), and others. The reading proposed by Eisenbud is that of day residues pertaining to the future. A challenging reinterpretation of the Oedipus conflict in precognitive terms is contained in Eisenbud's (1956) paper titled "Time and the Oedipus."

Eisenbud's *Psi and Psychoanalysis* is the first comprehensive presentation of the relevance of psi phenomena to analytic theory and practice. He considers the psi hypothesis as an important exploratory tool and stresses the advantages of its explicit use in therapeutic technique. In some cases only a telepathic interpretation can fill the gap in the dynamic understanding of the dream. The therapist, revealing to the patient the telepathic nature of his response, may then help to overcome an existing transference-countertransference difficulty that had been blocking progress. That the patient may occasionally catch the therapist "with his pants down," as Eisenbud put it, is another matter. It may reveal personal conflicts, anxieties, or other information embarrassing to him.

Another major contribution of Eisenbud's (1967) is his study of the psychic photography of Ted Serios, discussed elsewhere in this *Handbook*.

Marie L. Coleman's (1958) paper on a "paranormal triangle" closely follows Eisenbud's technique. The paper is concerned with telepathic incidents involving the patient, the therapist, and his supervisor. Another article (Nelson [formerly Coleman], 1964) focuses on ego-enhancing and revealing functions of precognitive dreams, with special reference to the dreamer's life style.

Nandor Fodor (1942) describes cases of telepathy *à trois*, involving himself and several of his patients. His book, *The Search for the Beloved* (1949) focuses on the need for closeness and intimacy sought by the patient on the telepathic level. In an early study of the poltergeist (1948), he suggests that the behavior of poltergeist children may in effect amount to an externalization of their repressed aggressive impulses.

Joost Meerloo (1964) considers telepathy an archaic function—a view shared by Fodor, Peerbolte (1964), and Freud himself. Telepathy, Meerloo holds, may play an important part in ecstasy and in panic reactions, as well as in other more pathological forms of mental contagion.

Montague Ullman (1949) emphasizes the personality traits of patients subject to repetitive telepathic experiences. They are of the withdrawn, shut-in, schizoid type. In these cases, telepathy may help to overcome their isolation and to restore lost contact with their fellow men. In later reports Ullman (1959, 1975) shows how striking correspondences of the patient's manifest dream with reality on the therapist's side may alert the latter to the possibility that telepathy had occurred. In a typical dream of this order, the appearance of an "unattached chromium soap dish" seems to be taken right out of Ullman's own experience in real life at the time of his patient's dream (1959). In another dream, the patient seemed to reflect Ullman's keen professional interest in a lecture about an "alcoholic cat" he had attended the night before the dream (1975).

Ullman considers dreams as metaphoric references to the patient's prevailing conflicts or personality problems surfacing at the time. The proper understanding of the metaphor may then reveal the meaningful nature of the telepathic element contained in the manifest dream content. According to Ullman (1975) spontaneous telepathy in crisis situations indicates "that in some way the mobilization of vital needs is implicated." He suggests that "dreaming is a state of heightened activation and that the vigilance function is oriented (in the human being at any rate) more to the detection of threats to the symbolic system linking the individual to his social milieu rather than to the detection of threats involving his state of bodily intactness."

The need for a sharper definition of the postulated telepathic correspondences between dream and reality led Ullman and his associates to their pioneering research project at the Maimonides Dream Laboratory (Ullman and Krippner, with Vaughan, 1973). It is discussed elsewhere in this Handbook.

More or less vague psychosomatic—or "telesomatic"—reactions of a telepathic nature were described by Eisenbud (1946), Ehrenwald (1948), Schwarz (1967), Stevenson (1970), and others. They are representative of a vast number of apparently telepathic incidents of the spontaneous type.

Ullman (1975) sums up some of the theoretical implications of his clinical and experimental dream studies in his emphasis on the REM state as one of openness to both autopsychic and heteropsychic experiences and that psi effects particularly are apt to occur when the sleeper's "significant relations are threatened, impaired, or destroyed." Thus psi may function "as an emerging communicative system in the interest of maintaining ties to the external world" which the individual, patient or nonpatient, has lost but tries to reestablish in a telepathic way.

Eisenbud (1970) assigns a much less specific yet biologically no less significant function of psi: "The goals psi serves are primarily not those of the individual at all, but of an ascending hierarchy of interrelated systems in which the individual is merely a messenger of sorts" (p. 337). Metaphorically speaking, he sees in psi the equivalent of the "vegetative nervous system of nature" at large.

Eisenbud is not usually given to mystical speculations, but such a formulation evokes distant echoes of Plotinus' ideas of a World-Soul and of the universe viewed as a large animal whose every part is indissolubly connected with every other part—if not of Jung's thesis of the Collective Unconscious and its miraculously endowed archetypes.

JUNG AND THE "SUPERNATURAL"

C. G. Jung's concern with the "supernatural" was of a deeply personal nature. It went back to his childhood years and was at the root of his interest in Spiritualism, astrology, and alchemy. His doctoral thesis (1957), first published in German in 1902, was devoted to the psychological study of a medium who happened to be a relative. It was sustained by a number of dramatic experiences which he recorded in his autobiography (1963).

In contrast to Freud, Jung's acceptance of telepathy, clairvoyance, and related "synchronistic" phenomena was wholly compatible with his overall system of thought. Indeed, it was Jung's mystical bent, his underlying "mythophilic" temper (Ehrenwald, 1968), colliding head on with Freud's rationalistic, causal - reductive, "mythophobic" orientation, which had led to the ultimate break between the two men. Nevertheless, Jung, too, failed to bring about a reconciliation in both theory and practice of the phenomena with his healing approach. On purely theoretical grounds, he agreed with Freud about the need to expand the range of the subject's consciousness: to "make the unconscious conscious." This expanded range of consciousness included the patient's confrontation with the collective unconscious and the archetypes. Such a confrontation, Jung stated, culminates in the individual's heroic struggle with the archetypes and in the release of potentially both malignant and beneficial forces of the collective unconscious. In some cases it involves the emergence of telepathy, clairvoyance, or precognition, or other numenous or synchronistic events. But in the last analysis he seemed to consider them as freakish intrusions from a mysterious external reality.

Numerous anecdotal accounts of this order can be found in his writings. One much quoted example is the sudden breaking, without apparent reason, of the blade of a large kitchen knife into four pieces (Jung, 1963). It happened in Jung's and his mother's presence a year or so after his father's death. Both were puzzled about the incident. Jung attributed it to the medium with whom he had been working at that time (1963). Some 30 years later, he described the incident to Dr. Rhine and sent him a photograph of the fragments. A similar incident involving the splitting of a heavy tabletop took place at about the same time. The story of Jung's "poltergeist" in Freud's bookcase happened during his visit to Freud in Vienna in 1909. In this case, too, Jung (1963) attributed the sudden explosive reports to his own mysterious PK activity.

Other incidents described in his autobiography (1963) and other writings are more relevant to his clinical practice. In one case he woke up from sleep with a dull pain in his head. He felt the presence of somebody who had opened the door and come into his room. The following day he received a telegram informing him that one of his patients had committed suicide by shooting himself in the head.   Another, more auspicious, incident is concerned with a Jewish patient, a young woman who had abjured her faith. "You have your neurosis because the fear of God has got into you," he told her. "That struck her like a bolt of lightening." The following night Jung himself had a dream in which he knelt before her and treated her "as if she were a goddess." And he adds: "I told this dream to her and in a week the neurosis had vanished" (p. 139). He notes that in this case he had applied no "method," but that the patient's response was indicative of a numenous, synchronistic event.

Another example of this order is the case of a young woman whose extreme rationalistic outlook made her inaccessible to psychological treatment. One day he sat opposite her with his back toward the window, listening to the flow of her rhetoric. The night before she had told him a dream about somebody who had given her a costly golden scarab as a present. At that very moment Jung heard something gently tapping on the window. It was a big insect trying to get into the dark room. He let it in, caught it, and it turned out to be a common rose chafer—a beetle closely resembling a golden scarab. He handed it to the patient: "Here is your golden scarab" (1955). "This experience," Jung notes, "punctured the desired hole in her rationalism and broke the ice of her intellectual resistance."

The case is a classical example of what Jung (1955) described as synchronicity, or an acausal connecting principle. It is based on a meaningful coincidence of events which are commonly described in parapsychological terms. Jung suggests that such meaningful coincidences may indeed hold the key to a successful therapeutic response. Unfortunately, the examples show that such incidents are plainly beyond the therapist's control. The best he can do is to be aware of their occurrence and to convey their deeper, numenous significance to the patient.

However, despite Jung's lifelong preoccupation with the matter, he stopped short of a definitive statement about the part played by the psi factor in his version of analytic psychotherapy. He saw himself as a healer, guided as much by scientific insight as by intuition and his personal myth. But the way he sought to reconcile the two opposing principles in his therapeutic practice has remained shrouded in mystery.

An attempt to conceptualize the problem can be found in the writings of Ehrenwald (1942, 1955) and more recently, Ullman (1975). In pursuance of Freud's remarks on the psychodynamics of telepathy and in concurrence with Hollós (1933), Servadio (1955), and Eisenbud (1970), Ehrenwald (1955) has tried to delineate the predisposing and conditioning factors of psi phenomena in the therapeutic situation. He noted that their origin is predicated on three well-defined criteria of telepathic correspondences: (a) uniqueness; (b) the presence of a number of distinctive features or "tracer elements"; and (c) the meaningful nature or "psychological significance" of the telepathic interpretation of a given case. He emphasized that, although the criterion of uniqueness carries the greatest evidential value, it is specific tracer elements, combined with the criterion of psychological significance, which tip the balance against mere coincidence and in favor of telepathy in both the treatment situation and everyday life. Using these criteria, Ehrenwald points to one more manifestation of the psi factor in therapy: the tendency to what he describes as the patient's doctrinal compliance—that is, the tendency to confirm with his dreams or other productions the therapist's pet scientific hypotheses, wishes, and expectations regarding the validity of his doctrine.

A third potential manifestation of psi in the treatment situation is closely related, but far more relevant in the present context. It is the patient's direct telepathic response to the doctor's emotionally charged therapeutic motivations. Unfortunately, such a response does not, however, carry the healer's voice-print or signature. It is not labeled with the criterion of uniqueness or specificity to pinpoint its telepathic origin.

The difficulty is compounded by the fact that, apart from the controversial instances of absent healing or "disembodied" placebos, it is virtually impossible to separate telepathy from suggestion, autosuggestion or other, more conventional, means of communication. The available evidence pointing to the part played by the psi factor in various forms of scientific psychotherapy is therefore largely circumstantial and at best unproven. In practice, it can be argued that the analyst should seek to integrate therapeutic interventions brought to bear on the ego and id level with those reaching the patient on the psi level. He should set his sights on practicing "three-level therapy" (Ehrenwald, 1955, p. 285).

However, the final integration of the psi level approach with scientific psychotherapy seems to be utopian at the present stage. The validation of the occurrence of psi phenomena is predicated on an essentially experimental and statistical inquiry: it has to be based on well-defined and, if possible, quantifiable criteria. Measured by the yardsticks of the scientific method, the use of the psi factor as a major ingredient of the healing touch is a persuasive, yet still unproven hypothesis. Still, there can be no doubt that the introduction of the psi factor is having a seminal influence upon the overall system of modern psychiatric thought.

REFERENCES

Burlingham, D. T. Child analysis and the mother. *Psychoanalytic Quarterly*, 1935, **4**, 69–92. (Also in G. Devereux (Ed.), *Psychoanalysis and the Occult*. New York: International Universities Press, 1953.)

Coleman, M. L. The paranormal triangle in analytical supervision. *Psychoanalysis and Psychoanalytic Review*, 1958, **45**, 73–84.

Deutsch, H. Occult processes occurring during psychoanalysis. *Imago*, 1926, **12**, 418–433. (Also in G. Devereux (Ed.), *Psychoanalysis and the Occult*. New York: International Universities Press, 1953.)

Devereux, G. (Ed.). *Psychoanalysis and the Occult*. New York: International Universities Press, 1953.

Ehrenwald, J. Telepathy in dreams. *British Journal of Medical Psychology*, 1942, **19**, 313–323.

Ehrenwald, J. *Telepathy and Medical Psychology*. New York: Norton, 1948.

Ehrenwald, J. Telepathy and the child-parent relationship. *Journal of the American Society for Psychical Research*, 1954, **48**, 43–55.

Ehrenwald, J. *New Dimensions of Deep Analysis*. New York: Grune and Stratton, 1955. (Reprinted by Arno Press, New York, 1975.)

Ehrenwald, J. Freud versus Jung: The mythophobic versus the mythophilic temper in psychotherapy. *Israeli Annals of Psychiatry*, 1968, **6**, 115–125.

Eisenbud, J. Telepathy and the problems of psychoanalysis. *Psychoanalytic Quarterly*, 1946, **15**, 32–87. (Also in G. Devereux (Ed.), *Psychoanalysis and the Occult*. New York: International Universities Press, 1953.)

Eisenbud, J. Time and the Oedipus. *Psychoanalytic Quarterly*, 1956, **25**, 363–384.

Eisenbud, J. *The World of Ted Serios*. New York: Morrow, 1967.

Eisenbud, J. Chronologically extraordinary psi correspondences in the psychoanalytic setting. *Psychoanalytic Review*, 1969, **56**, 9–27.

Eisenbud, J. *Psi and Psychoanalysis*. New York: Grune and Stratton, 1970.

Ellis, A. Telepathy and psychoanalysis: A critique of recent findings. *Psychiatric Quarterly*, 1947, **21**, 607–659.

Fodor, N. Telepathic dreams. *American Imago*, 1942, **3**, 61–87.

Fodor, N. The poltergeist psychoanalyzed. *Psychiatric Quarterly*, 1948, **22**, 195–203.

Fodor, N. *The Search for the Beloved*. New York: Hermitage Press, 1949.

Freud, S. Dreams and telepathy. *Imago*, 1922, **8**, 1–22. (Also in G. Devereux (Ed.), *Psychoanalysis and the Occult*. New York: International Universities Press, 1953.)

Freud, S. Dreams and the occult. In *New Introductory Lectures on Psychoanalysis*, Chap. 2. New York: Norton, 1933. (Also in G. Devereaux (Ed.), *Psychoanalysis and the Occult*. New York: International Universities Press, 1953.)

Hann-Kende, F. On the role of transference and countertransference in psychoanalysis. In G. Devereux (Ed.), *Psychoanalysis and the Occult*, Chap. 14. New York: International Universities Press, 1953.

Hitschmann, E. Telepathy and psychoanalysis. *International Journal of Psychoanalysis*, 1924, **5**, 423–438. (Also in G. Devereux (Ed.), *Psychoanalysis and the Occult*. New York: International Universities Press, 1953.)

Hollós, I. Psychopathologie alltaglicher telepathischer Erscheinungen. *Imago*, 1933, **19**, 529–546. (Summarized in G. Devereux (Ed.), *Psychoanalysis and the Occult*. New York: International Universities Press, 1953.)

Jones, E. *The Life and Work of Sigmund Freud*. New York: Basic Books, 1957. 3 vols.

Jung, C. G. On the psychology and pathology of so-called occult phenomena. In *Collected Works*. Vol. 1. New York: Pantheon, 1957. (Originally published in 1902.)

Jung, C. G. Synchronicity: An acausal connecting principle. In C. G. Jung and W. Pauli, *The Interpretation of Nature and the Psyche*. (Trans. by R. F. C. Hull.) Princeton: Princeton University Press, 1955.

Jung, C. G. *Memories, Dreams, Reflections*. (Recorded and edited by A. Jaffé; trans. by R. and C. Winston.) New York: Pantheon, 1963.

Meerloo, J. A. M. *Hidden Communion*. New York: Garrett/Helix, 1964.

Nelson, M. C. Paranormal patterns and the life style. *International Journal of Parapsychology,* 1964, **6,** 408–417.

Pederson-Krag, G. Telepathy and repression. *Psychoanalytic Quarterly,* 1947, **16,** 61–68. (Also in G. Devereux (Ed.), *Psychoanalysis and the Occult.* New York: International Universities Press, 1953.)

Peerbolte, M. L. Telepathy and psychoanalysis. *Psychics International,* 1964, **1,** 55–60.

Schwarz, B. E. Possible telesomatic reactions. *Journal of the Medical Society of New Jersey,* 1967, **64,** 600–603.

Schwarz, B. E. *Parent-Child Telepathy.* New York: Garrett/Helix, 1971.

Servadio, E. Psychoanalysis and telepathy. *Imago,* 1935, **21,** 489–497. (Also in G. Devereux (Ed.), *Psychoanalysis and the Occult.* New York: International Universities Press, 1953.)

Servadio, E. Processes of identification and conversion phenomena in a mediumistic clairvoyant. *International Journal of Psychoanalysis,* 1937, **18,** 89–90.

Servadio, E. A presumptively telepathic-precognitive dream during analysis. *International Journal of Psychoanalysis,* 1955, **36,** 27–30.

Servadio, E. The dynamics of so-called paranormal dreams. In G. E. von Grunebaum and R. Caillois (Eds.), *The Dream and Human Societies,* pp. 109-118. Berkeley and Los Angeles: University of California Press, 1966.

Stevenson, I. Telepathic impressions: A review and report of thirty-five new cases. *Proceedings of the American Society for Psychical Research,* 1970, **29,** 1–198.

Ullman, M. The nature of psi processes. *Journal of Parapsychology,* 1949, **13,** 59–62.

Ullman, M. On the occurrence of telepathic dreams. *Journal of the American Society for Psychical Research,* 1959, **53,** 50–61.

Ullman, M. Parapsychology and psychiatry. In A. M. Freedman, H. I. Kaplan, and B. J. Saddock (Eds.), *Comprehensive Textbook of Psychiatry,* 2nd ed., Vol. 2, pp. 2552–2561. Baltimore: Williams and Wilkins, 1975.

Ullman, M., and Krippner, S., with Vaughan, A. *Dream Telepathy.* New York: Macmillan, 1973.

Zulliger, H. Prophetic dreams. *International Journal of Psychoanalysis,* 1934, **15,** 191–208. (Also in G. Devereux (Ed.), *Psychoanalysis and the Occult.* New York: International Universities Press, 1953.)

2

Parapsychology and the Healing Arts

Jan Ehrenwald

INTRODUCTION

Parapsychology is concerned with that aspect of unorthodox healing which is attributed to the operation of a psi factor: with "psychic" healing. In turn, unorthodox healing covers a wide variety of remedial actions which do not conform to recognized principles of the scientific method or to procedures approved by the consensus of medical practitioners in a given culture. It is a relative term. What is deemed to be unorthodox in one society may well be considered wholly orthodox in another.

By the same token, some modern schools of psychotherapy that do not conform to the current medical or psychoanalytic model could likewise be described as yet other variations of an esoteric approach to treatment. On the opposite end of the scale is healing magic as it is practiced in preliterate societies, past and present. It is flanked by various forms of religious or spiritual healing, with or without a demonstrable psi factor involved in the process.

We shall see that the foremost differences between healing practices are not necessarily those of substance. Rather, they lie in the philosophies, preconceived ideas, and religious beliefs held by the respective practitioners. The primitive magician's faith in his omnipotence, in the possibility of thought and action at a distance, serves as a rationale for an elaborate system of thought and for a variety of rites, spells, incantations, and placebos used in his daily practice.

The ministrations of the faith healer are predicated on religious beliefs he may hold with equal fervor. They are based on religious observances, ritual prayers, sacraments, and other mysteries offered by the officiating priest. Yet despite the emphasis on spiritual aspects, faith healing is often combined with a variety of magic procedures. They range from the laying on of hands to sprinkling of holy water, the use of relics, sacred images, prayer mills, or rosary beads. It is invariably associated with suggestion and autosuggestion, while the part played by miracles—or by the psi factor—remains largely a matter of conjecture.

R. H. Thouless (1955), the noted Cambridge psychologist and parapsychologist, specifically distinguishes ritual healing from prayer healing. To this he adds a separate category of spirit healing in which healing powers are attributed to the spirits of the dead, made to appear in Spiritualistic séances or voodoo ceremonies. The list can be further extended to include such esoteric agencies as Mesmer's animal magnetism, Reichenbach's Od, Reich's orgone energy, or the bioplasmic or bioenergetic emanations proposed by modern Russian parapsychologists. More naive practitioners pin their hope on the operation of assorted vibrations, electromagnetic waves, radiations, or ethereal fluids transmitted from the healer to the healee.

Unfortunately, none of these theoretical assumptions have been borne out by the available scientific evidence. Indeed, one may ask whether insisting on such evidence is really called for where matters of faith, of religious dogma, or of cherished, emotionally charged beliefs are concerned. The answer is that if and when such an inquiry is apt to interfere with the therapist's and the patient's healing encounter, or with the mental set existing in the two, it should proceed with utmost tact and delicacy. But a dispassionate discussion of data is another matter. It is an established principle of both the physical and the behavioral sciences that the observer cannot help but affect and interfere with the delicate balance of events he is about to observe. Yet this very fact is in itself a valid subject for further scientific inquiry.

Stripped, at least for the present purpose, of its esoteric, supernatural, or ideological implications, unorthodox healing is a concatenation of magico-mythical, spiritual, and religious hopes and expectations, aided by suggestion or autosuggestion, so-called placebo effects, and a hypothetical psi factor involved in the interaction between the healer, the healee, and the group in which they are immersed.

Thus the classification of the varieties of unorthodox healing has to be guided by making allowance for the part played by (a) the healer, (b) the healee, and (c) their social environment. It is in the light of these considerations that a few representative examples of unorthodox healing will be discussed in the pages that follow.

HEALING MAGIC

The first sketches for the broad historic canvas of the healing arts can be found in the cave paintings of Altamira or Lascaux. The nomadic hunter made an image of his prey and hoped that in so doing he would gain mastery over it. The making of images, the naming of names, the manipulation of symbols, was in effect a magic procedure. As time went by, the maker of images, the knower of names, and the manipulator of symbols extended his magic powers from the control of wild animals to wresting rain from the clouds, raising tempests, soothing of ocean waves, to killing enemies by means of magic effigies, to fertility rites and curing of the sick.

His early prototype was the general practitioner of magic: he was Tribal Chief, Rainmaker, Witchdoctor, Soothsayer, and Priestly Healer rolled into one. We do not know whether or not a psi factor was involved in his ministrations. But the claims made by his latter-day descendants, the medieval sorcerer, the Hassidic *tzadik*, the Siberian shaman, the North American medicine man, show a striking structural resemblance with the modalities of what in contemporary terms can be described as the psi syndrome (Ehrenwald, 1972). He can read his clients' thoughts (telepathy); his soul can travel to and explore distant places (clairvoyance); he can effect changes in his physical environment (psychokinesis); he can presage the future (precognition); and he can heal the sick: psychic healing.

Healing magic has its roots in man's early belief in the arcane power of symbols, gestures, images, and words. To increase the power of the spoken words, they have to be repeated over and over again: They are strung together in spells, chants, and incantations. They may be reinforced by the acting out of their expected consequences in dramatic ritual and ecstatic dance, sometimes to the point of final exhaustion. Malinowski (1948), describing the behavior of the Trobriand Island medicine man in action, notes that "if a spectator were suddenly transported to some part of Melanesia and could observe the sorcerer at work . . . he might think that he had either to do with a lunatic or else he would guess that here was a man acting under the sway of uncontrolled anger." And he adds, "to the natives, knowledge of magic means knowledge of a spell, and in an analysis of any act of witchcraft it will always be found that the ritual centers around the utterance of the spell" (p. 74). Yet invariably both the spell and the medicine man's imitative behavior is imbedded in an expression of highly charged emotion.

There are more specific similarities of this picture with stress-induced or emotionally charged acting out and compulsive or perseverative actions seen under modern conditions. The infant, unable to make his environment comply with his wishes, throws a temper tantrum, kicks and flays with his limbs. He subscribes to the principle of what psychoanalysts term the omnipotence of movements. The rainmaker's or the Sufi dervish's frantic dancing and whirling is predicted on the same belief. The difference is that they no longer try to force the hands or the helpful ministrations of a benevolent parent figure, but the intervention of a supernatural agency or divinity. Their chanting and singing get louder and louder in intensity. They reiterate their plea over and over again; they shout as though they were talking to the hard of hearing and perseverate like patients suffering from a mental or neurological disorder.

The records of prayers and incantations addressed to ancient Egyptian, Assyrian, or Babylonian deities show a distinctly compulsive tendency.

> Sickness of the head, of the teeth of the heart,
> heartache,
> sickness of the eye, fever, poison,
> evil spirit, evil Demon, evil Ghost, evil Devil, evil God,
> evil Fiend
> Hag-demon, Ghoul, Robber sprite
> phantom of night, Night wrath, handmaiden of the phantom,
> Evil pestilence, noisome fever, baneful sickness,
> Pain, sorcery or any evil,
> Headache, shivering, etc.
> Unto the man, the son of his god come not nigh,
> Get thee hence!
>
> (C. J. S. Thompson, 1946)

Woe to him who fails to include in this compulsive recital any particular organ, part of the body, or type of affliction which is in need of protection or relief from suffering. The spell, the incantation, must make security double sure and should leave no loophole for the evil spirit to take hold and cause havoc in the patient's body or mind.

Thus the main features of the primitive medicine man's professional repertoire are: appropriate verbal, psychomotor, or motor acting out; compulsive perseveration; an itemizing of a complete laundry list of anatomical locations and bodily afflictions; and, if need be, a comprehensive roster of guardian spirits or protective deities called in on the case.

Commemorative tablets, records of successful cures, and votive offerings that have come down to us from ancient times and diverse cultures of classical antiquity testify to their belief in the efficacy of healing magic, with or without the intervention of a priestly healer. But contrary to popular belief fostered by the witch doctor, the thaumaturge, or the officiating priest, the records show that his therapeutic impact was invariably based on the combination of three interlacing and mutually reinforcing factors: (a) his own faith in the efficacy of his ministrations; (b) the patient's corresponding trust in the healer and his hope to be cured; and (c) the patient's friends and relations as participant observers, sharing both the anguish and hopes of their stricken fellow tribesman who occupy the center of the stage (Ehrenwald, 1966; Frank, 1961).

Here, again, the structural similarity of the ancient tribal scenario with interpersonal configurations favoring the emergence of psi phenomena is unmistakable. The medicine man and his client stand for the agent and percipient, respectively, in a modern ESP type of experiment. Their fellow tribesmen—the chorus of ancient Greek tragedy or the congregation in a revival meeting of our time—represent public opinion, the culture or subculture in which the principal protagonists are imbedded. Under favorable conditions, they are the Schmeidlerian "sheep," who help toward a favorable outcome—or the doubting Thomases, the Schmeidlerian "goats," who may cast a pall on the procedure and jeopardize success.

FAITH HEALING

The picture of the faith healer ministering to the sick in a biblical or medieval church setting could have been superimposed by a later artist on the wall paintings of ancient paleolithic or neolithic times. Here, too, essentially the same tripartite interpersonal configuration is readily descernible. Yet religion introduces a new factor into the therapeutic equation. The patient, the healer, and their devout following are all there. But to the religious believer God Himself takes a hand in bringing about the cure. The healer, the Christian Science practitioner, or the officiating priest disclaims magic omnipotence and serves merely as a mediator with the divinity. To be on the safe side, healing miracles are resorted to in order to buttress the faith of the devotee. Conversely, it is a basic proposition of the religious healer that it is the patient's unconditional faith which is one of the indispensible prerequisites of the cure.

Jesus, curing the woman with the hemorrhage, assured her: "Daughter, thy faith hath made thee whole," and he admonished the father of the epileptic boy to have the same faith in his ministrations lest the patient would fail to respond. At the same time, all four Gospels describe "the multitudes" or the "whole city" that congregates around and is getting in on the act of the unfolding drama of healing.

In turn, the subsequent dissemination of the news served to reinforce the curative effects of the happy tidings. Weatherhead (1954) points to the part played by the "atmosphere" surrounding incidents of this order. But here, again, the therapeutic triad involving the healer, the patient, and his group is clearly in evidence.

The healing miracles attributed to such shrines as Lourdes, St. Ann de Beaupres, the Madonna of Guadeloupe, or Mariazell are variations on the same theme.

They usually dispense with the mediation of a priestly healer, and it is the time-honored reputation of the shrine itself which takes his place. It serves as a catalyst or, to use a term applied in modern group therapy, as a facilitator of the therapeutic process. The milling crowd of the worshippers and other seekers of cure, the solemn services, the torch parades, the singing of hymns, the clouds of incense wafting through the candle-lit church provide powerful reinforcements of the patient's expectations to find relief for his suffering. It is further promoted by their gradual build-up in the course of what is usually a long or costly pilgrimage to a shrine.

It may be no coincidence that neither Lourdes, Mariazell, nor, for that matter, the Mental Hygiene Outpatients' Department of the Mayo Clinic in Rochester seem to hold the same attraction for the sick of the local population as for those who had to travel there from faraway places.

A significant feature of unorthodox healing, and particularly of faith healing, is its sovereign disregard of the cleavage between organic and functional pathology. For obvious reasons, the untutored practitioner is unaware of such neat nosological distinctions. But, like the Lord himself, even the sophisticated religious healer of our time is usually unconcerned about them. To the one who has the kind of faith that can move mountains, the removal of warts, of a malignancy, or of an anxiety neurosis is all in a day's work, and one affliction does not seem to constitute a greater challenge than the other.

Indeed, both the religious and medical authorities in Lourdes place chief emphasis on cures effected in organic conditions, and they are quite ready to attribute improvements in psychosomatic or neurotic conditions to mere suggestion or autosuggestion.

The *Bureau des Constatations* of Lourdes, set up under the auspices of the Catholic Clergy and a medical committee, focuses specific attention on physical symptoms and their removal as indications of what they hold may legitimately be described as a miraculous cure. They base such claims on four principal criteria:

1. Certification of the patient's condition before and after the visit.
2. The finding of organic or incurable illness.
3. Immediate recovery and disappearance of the existing pathology.
4. Persistence of cure after the visit.

It is claims of this order which are then acknowledged and designated as miracles by the Church. However, West (1957), who has investigated the records of the Lourdes healings in great detail, found only 11 cases coming close to meeting these criteria. He reaches the conclusion that the available evidence fails to meet the standards which would satisfy modern diagnostic and clinical criteria of fact finding.

Such a verdict does not, however, rule out the possibility that a psi factor was involved in whatever improvement occurred in the wake of the pilgrimage to Lourdes.

SPIRITUAL HEALING ON THE AMERICAN SCENE

Similar considerations apply to the claims of Christian Science practitioners, of Edgar Cayce, the Sleeping Prophet of Virginia Beach, and of other twentieth-century religious or spiritual healers in this country.

Mary Baker Eddy's (1934) *Science and Health with a Key to the Scriptures* was first published in Boston in 1875. It touched off a spectacularly successful spiritual movement at a time when extreme scientific materialism existed side by side with such antimaterialistic doctrines as Spiritualism, theosophy, and anthroposophy, both in this country and in Europe. Seen in historic perspective, it was one of the latest offshoots of the ancient magico-religious approach that followed in the footsteps of medieval astrological and alchemistic medicine and of Mesmer's theories of animal magnetism. Yet there is at least one way in which Christian Science marked a new departure. As a new religion, it dispensed with all the outer paraphernalia of magic, of the trappings of the Spiritualistic séance room, and confined itself to a direct appeal to the faith and suggestibility of the healer and the healee. It was, in effect, one of the first methodical attempts to the management of disease by purely psychological—or spiritual—means.

The rationale of the Christian Science approach is another matter. It emphasizes the illusionary nature of all flesh—and of all disease that the flesh is heir to. Indeed, sickness, disease, and death are merely due to the false testimony of "natural sense" which shuts off the "true sense of the Spirit." Therefore the struggle for the recovery of invalids goes on between "mortal minds and immortal Mind," and so forth.

Christian Science healing is predicated on such supposedly self-evident truths. It is done by a dedicated and properly trained Christian practitioner who offers the patient love, support, and intercessionary prayers. In addition, Mary Baker Eddy notes that "science can heal the sick who are absent from their healers," since space is no obstacle to "mind."

Here, again, our therapeutic triad of a hopeful healer, a trusting patient, and a devoted group of followers is unmistakeable. And here, again, we are offered a wealth of anecdotal accounts and testimonials of effected cures. They include a variety of both organic and functional conditions, yet adduce virtually no adequately documented medical data or controls to substantiate the claims.

Edgar Cayce, the Sleeping Prophet of Virginia Beach, is another healer whose exploits are essentially based on religious belief, shared with patients and the group. The Association for Research and Enlightment, which had assembled a devoted congregation around him and is now carrying on Cayce's spiritual legacy, does not adhere to any particular institutionalized religious denomination but is nevertheless inspired by a profound faith in Edgar Cayce's mission.

Cayce's exploits were chiefly based on his clairvoyant diagnosis of illness. They were usually arrived at in a trance state during which he gave his celebrated "readings." The readings pointed to the nature and location of the disease, and his advice combined simple homespun remedies with sound, commonsense recommendations to the patient and his family. Here, too, a special feature was absent healing and intercessionary prayer for the patient's recovery.

We learn that of 14,000 of Cayce's readings recorded over the years, some 9,000 were specifically devoted to matters of health (Carter and McGarey, 1972). As in the records of Lourdes or of Christian Science, the evidence presented in the voluminous Cayce literature is largely based on testimonials, letters of thanks, and glowing anecdotal accounts of cures effected by the healer. The case of Florence E., age 29, is a typical example. She is descibed as suffering from incurable scleroderma, with "inroads of a tubercle" in Florence's body (p. 22). Cayce's reading suggested: "Sponge off with saturated solution of bicarbonate of soda, then apply hot castor oil packs," etc.

On receiving this message from Cayce, the patient's parents and aunt were elated. "I knew Cayce would know!" the aunt exulted. It should be noted that several members of Florence's family had already been helped by Cayce. So was Florence herself on an earlier occasion. Dr. W. A. McGarey, a physician who reported on her case, claims that despite subsequent minor relapses, Florence has ultimately fully recovered from her disease. Yet there are no precise clinical data to support the original diagnosis of scleroderma, and there is no attempt to rule out the possibility of spontaneous remission. Still, what reaches even the skeptical reader is the account of an apparently marked improvement of a severe dermatological condition which followed in the wake of Edgar Cayce's clairvoyant consultation and his attempt at long-distance therapy.

In a large number of similar cases the clairvoyant impressions gained by Cayce and the apparent accuracy of some of his diagnostic statements may have played an important part in his impact upon his clients. Yet here, again, it is difficult to substantiate the extent to which a genuine psi factor had been involved in the total situation.

Among the more recent religious healers who have gained a wide following in this country, Ambrose and Olga Worrall (1965) should be mentioned at this point. Their work has been sponsored by a number of medical men, and one of their books has been introduced by Dr. Robert Laidlaw, the noted psychiatrist. The Worralls attended to their patients at the New Life Clinic at the Mount Washington Methodist Church, or in more informal casual settings. An important feature of their interventions was absent healing. It consists of Mr. or Mrs.

Worrall, or both, "holding" the patient in healing prayer at an appointed time, previously announced to the patient.

The patients and the illnesses treated are described in brief impressionistic vignettes (pp. 144–147): "A man who had suffered an injury to his eyes" and had virtually lost all vision; an elderly heart patient, the father of a physician; a man suffering from an obscure ulcer which was clairvoyantly diagnosed by Mrs. Worrall as a congested gall bladder, who was subsequently told he had cancer of the pancreas. In this latter case, Mrs. Worrall disagreed with the experts, and her initial clairvoyant impression was borne out by the subsequent surgical operation. In a case of lymphosarcomatosis Mrs. Worrall was "guided" to lay hands on the patient's abdomen. Subsequent X-ray examination reportedly showed no more evidence of a tumor, and the patient was "completely well."

Another case was the noted mystic, author, and philosopher, Gerald Heard, who had been suffering from an unspecified disease. Mrs. Worrall "held" him in her healing prayers when an apparition claiming to be Heard's grandmother appeared to her. After properly identifying herself, she asked Mrs. Worrall to convey a reassuring message to her grandson. Years later, Mr. Heard informed Mrs. Worrall that he was indeed very much improved in health in the wake of the "psychic incidents" described in her report.

It is needless to say that accounts of clairvoyant or healing exploits of this order cannot claim to be of any evidential value. Indeed, the Worralls (1965) themselves readily acknowledge that their clinic "was a pattern not only of success but also of failure" (p. 144). But they add that even in failure, "some help was given, some peace of mind, some acceptance of the universe of love" (p. 147). There can be no doubt that the wide circle of their followers, their enthusiastic fan mail, and the endorsement by numerous patients and ex-patients tend to bear out at least that aspect of their claims.

The same is true for Edgar Jackson, Kathryn Kuhlman, Agnes Sanford, and a large number of psychic healers of more local fame, to say nothing of the radio preachers and television personalities who have built their reputations on the press and electronic media. In effect, they rely chiefly on the third, the public relations, ingredient of our therapeutic triad.

One of the recent serious contributions to unorthodox healing on the American scene is Lawrence LeShan's book, *The Medium, the Mystic, and the Physicist* (1973). It is based on the theory that the "healing encounter" takes place outside the catagories of time and space, in what LeShan describes as nonsensory or clairvoyant, as opposed to ordinary or sensory reality. In order to prepare himself for such a venture, he enters an altered state of consciousness in which "positive biological or psychological changes in the healee's body may or may not occur." LeShan illustrates his results with six condensed case histories (pp. 121–128): a woman of 75 suffering from arthritis; a woman of 36 suffering from recurrent cold sores; another woman with a "loose knee joint"; a young lady with psoriasis; a boy with a broken back; and a sixth patient, a women of 65, with multiple myeloma—a malignant bone disease.

LeShan gives a graphic account of his own mental set during the healing sessions. He tries to conceptualize and to include the healer and the healee in one "functional entity." This is what he describes as Healing I. The attending state of transcendental meditation may then be conducive to positive biological change or to a process of organic self-repair in the patient. In some cases he combines such a procedure with traditional techniques of laying on of hands. On some occasions, intercessional types of distant healing, with or without the assistance of a group of student healers, were attempted.

As in virtually all unorthodox healers reviewed so far, LeShan's therapeutic successes were usually confirmed by his patients, and his theoretical assumptions won the support of a growing number of followers. To that extent they have indeed provided what can be described as their existential validation. His "healing encounter" with the patient, like the Hippocratic *Kairos* described by the psychoanalyst Harold Kelman (1960), has indeed proved an authentic and often deeply moving emotion experience. Yet LeShan does not—at least not in the present series—try to adduce documentary evidence to substantiate his claims. Nor does he produce convincing data to rule out the part played by suggestion or autosuggestion in a given case. Yet it can well be argued that only in the absence of such more conventional therapeutic factors can a legitimate claim of "purely" psychic healing be made.

THE EUROPEAN SCENE

Turning to more recent trends in unorthodox healing on the other side of the Atlantic, we can see striking similarities with the American scene. They can be found in both Catholic and Protestant countries, as well as in East European Jewish communities. Thus they are by no means confined to any particular religious denomination and seem to reflect still surviving archetypal residues of ancient Mediterranean, Eastern, and Far Eastern traditions.

Modern examples of unorthodox healing in England duplicate in many ways the claims of Christian Science practitioners; of Edgar Cayce, the Worralls (1965), Kathryn Kuhlman (1962), and many others in this country. A foremost exponent is Harry Edwards (1971) who flourished in England during and after World War I. Edwards was an unsuccessful politician and businessman turned Spiritualist who has treated thousands, if not tens of thousands, of patients in his long career. He would fall into trances in which he engaged in direct or absent healing, aided by what he described as "spirit doctors" or his spirit controls. The patients were supposed to "see" and "feel" his presence at their bedside, often many miles away. Working along these lines, Edwards has claimed the impressive improvement rate of 80 to 90 percent.

The English psychiatrist, Dr. Louis Rose (1968), has published a detailed account of his attempts to study and evaluate whatever case material from Edwards' files or personal communications he could lay hands on. He conducted several interviews with Edwards and attended a mass rally of some 1,800 people at Kingsway Hall without, however, having a real opportunity to examine any patient.

Rose's own survey of almost 100 cases showed: (a) 58 cases with incomplete records and unconfirmed claims; (b) 22 cases with records "so much at variance with the claims that it was considered impossible to continue with the investigation further"; (c) two cases in which the healer may have contributed to the amelioration of the organic condition; (d) one case in which demonstrable organic disability was relieved or cured after the intervention by the healer; (e) three cases improved but relapsed; (f) four cases in which a satisfactory degree of improvement in the organic state had occurred; (g) five cases in which improvement, when lasting, was received concurrently with orthodox medical treatment; and (h) one case examined before and after the treatment which continued to deteriorate.

In one case of purportedly "miraculous" return of vision the ophthalmologist wrote to Rose: "There is no miracle . . . patient was a case of spontaneous dislocation of lens which was cataractous" (p. 151).

Rose quotes a 1920 report of the British Medical Association stating that a BMA committee found no evidence in Harry Edwards' cases which could not be paralleled by similar cures effected by psychotherapy or spontaneous remission.

In a project sponsored by the Freiburg Institute for Borderline Areas of Psychology and Mental Hygiene, the German psychologist, Inge Strauch (1963), has made an extensive study of the mental healer Dr. Kurt Trampler—a holder of a doctorate in political science. Her collaborators in the project were members of the staff of the Medical Polyclinic of the University of Freiburg.

Trampler attributes his healing exploits to the operation of a "spiritual-energetic" principle. He tries to "switch his consciousness in the firm faith that he will find a way to the higher interrelationships of life," yet he insists that he is merely a catalyst in the healing process (p. 139). He works by "attuning" himself to the patient and by feeling his complaints in his own body. He can then localize the cause of the existing illness by some clairvoyant means. Trampler, too, practices "remote treatment"; or else he sees from 5-70 patients in groups. He also gives his patients sheets of aluminum foil which he has first "charged" with his hands. The sheets have to be applied to the ailing parts of the body.

The main purpose of Strauch's project was to determine the sociological make-up, the expectations, and the attitudes of a sample of 650 patients treated by Trampler. Patients were also given psychological interviews, tests, and thorough medical examinations before and after the treatment. The diseases included a wide spectrum of organic and functional pathology. During a follow-up period of up to 14 months, a subjective improvement rate of 61 percent was observed, with only 11 percent showing objective improvements as well. The author also notes that the severity of the conditions themselves did not materially affect the apparent improvement rate. She noted, furthermore, that the confrontation with Trampler was not the only factor in subjective improvements. It was largely determined by the patient's predispositions, especially his positive attitudes toward mental healing which were in turn inversely proportional to the patient's educational level and critical faculty.

It is interesting to compare the improvement rate reported in Strauch's study with the current rough estimates of 70 to 80 percent improvements obtained in conventional psychotherapy. This superior showing is in marked contrast to the generally enthusiastic response of Trampler's patients to his ministrations, reflected in the 650 testimonial letters of gratitude filed in the Freiburg Institute. Even 50 percent of those patients whose condition had objectively worsened during the period of treatment nevertheless declared that they had felt considerably better—at least temporarily.

It appears, therefore, that in an informal popularity poll Strauch's sample might well outscore the improvement rate obtained in traditional medical treatment. Indeed, there is reason to believe that the study of comparable selected samples of trusting, unsophisticated patient populations would show much the same results.

This is also borne out by the impression gained from reports of unorthodox healing in Italy. Servadio's (1963) studies of faith healing in the Lucanian countryside showed that the thaumaturgist's success depended more on his simple-minded clients' attitudes toward him than on his presumed faculties as a magician. Racanelli's book, *The Gift of Healing* (1953), points in the same direction. So does Colinon's study, *Les Guérisseurs* (1957), on the healers in France.

Reports of primitive healing from Asia, Africa, or Australia are difficult to measure by Western standards. They appear to be the more promising the less such standards are being applied to them. Recent claims of "psychic" surgery in the Philippines and Brazil (Puharich, 1974; Sherman, 1967; Valentine, 1973) are poorly documented. Such a seasoned observer as the American surgeon William Nolen (1974) described them as frankly fraudulent.

WHAT ARE THE FACTS?

I hinted that unorthodox healing is a relative term. One man's orthodox healing may be another man's superstition. One patient's savior and benefactor may be the American Medical Association's charlatan. The merits and demerits of the diverse approaches can only be validated within their respective frames of reference and in the light of their particular philosophy, belief system, and idiosyncratic method of validation. But while scientific medicine—and the laboratory experimenter—can rely on rigorous, quantifiable criteria to evaluate his evidence, such an expedient is rarely available to—or even sought by—the unorthodox healer. Of necessity, unorthodox healing usually remains outside the scientific orbit. Faith healing, diverse cultist, or spiritual practices are sealed off from science by a magic circle, as it were.

Nevertheless, there are four tentative conclusions which can be drawn from our condensed survey of the claims and more or less critical anecdotal accounts in the literature: (a) In spite of differences in the rationale adopted and the technique used by the individual practitioners, their approach is invariably geared to one or more of the ingredients of the therapeutic triad outlined on an earlier page. (b) Therapeutic success is usually contingent on the proper blend of hopes and expectations held by the healer, the healee, and the culture in which they are immersed. (c) Other things being equal, both functional, psychosomatic, and organic conditions tend to respond to the healer's ministrations. (d) Despite claims to the contrary, the response in organic cases (as well as functional conditions) is usually limited by the severity of the illness.

This point touches upon the controversial question of improvements or cures effected by faith healers in malignant conditions. It is a question closely linked with the problem of spontaneous remission in general. Spontaneous remission has been described as a cure or improvement in the absence of discernible external factors. The surgeons Everson and Cole (1966) have reviewed some 700 pertinent publications that have appeared since 1900 and found 176 such spontaneous remissions. Similar observations have since been reported in growing frequency (Booth, 1973). Such statistics have to be viewed against the background of tens, if not hundreds of thousands of sufferers from malignant tumors who have sought help from unorthodox healers during the past six or seven decades. It stands to reason that in such a huge population the random occurrence of seemingly freakish spontaneous remissions should be virtually inevitable. They may occur without any "discernible external factors." Yet if they do occur during or after the time the patient had been under the care of an unorthodox healer, the remission will readily be attributed to his ministration—in preference to the proverbially long but depersonalized arm of coincidence. Indeed, one single case of this order will suffice to establish the healer's reputation; it will serve to substantiate his claims, help to enhance his self-confidence as a thaumaturg, and to draw the multitudes to his public appearances.

PSYCHOTHERAPY AND THREE MODELS OF HEALING

What do these diametrically opposed claims and counterclaims add up to? They show once more that faith healers and miracle workers of various denominations tend to operate in a closed, self-sealing system of beliefs and practices, and that their exploits are well-nigh impossible to calibrate against the standards of clinical medicine. The closest approximation to the faith healer's rationale is the psychosomatic or psychotherapeutic model which can be invoked to account for most purported effects of "mind-over-matter," from hypnosis to Yoga practices; from Schultz's (1950) autogenic training to Transcendental Meditation, or Miller's "primitive learning" and the growing number of experiments with biofeedback.

In any case, these are the models which are usually invoked to account for most therapeutic results credited to unorthodox healers. We have seen that they range from the removal of warts to the improvement of a duodenal ulcer, of heart conditions, or of rheumatoid arthritis. They may culminate in the instant cure of a hysteric paralysis or other conversion symptoms. In all these cases, it is assumed that the leverage of words, gestures, or other symbolic communications is responsible for the effected cures. This is particularly true for manifestations of conversion hysteria, based as they are on what Charcot and Janet described as the "power of ideas." This is why it is functional disorders of this type which respond most readily to analytic psychotherapy, hypnosis, or other interventions trying to reach the unconscious through verbal or other symbolic means.

Psychosomatic disorders which are usually attributed to the slow, grinding effect of stress or emotional conflict respond less readily to such an approach. They are therefore the favorite proving grounds for the unorthodox healer, and it is in this group that he tends to obtain the best improvement rates.

Viewed within the psychosomatic frame of reference, such improvements can indeed best be understood in terms of autonomic reactions elicited by a psychoanalytic interpretation; by catharsis; by Franz Alexander's "corrective emotional experience"; by biofeedback training; by the effects of TM or of Schultz's autogenic training. What I described as the existential shift (Ehrenwald, 1971)—a global shift of inner attitudes and behavioral responses—is perhaps the common denominator of these many and varied interventions and responses. The existential shift embraces the whole range of the patient's inner experiences and behavioral repertoire. Even the healing powers of the Royal Touch, or the laying on of hands, can be attributed to the patient's emotional reaction to the symboblic meaning of a soothing gesture made by a benevolent parent figure. In a similar vein, his response to TM may well be due to its stilling effect on the electric activity of his restless brain.

But here, as in all forms of psychotherapy, both the psychoanalytic and the psychosomatic model usually ignore the potential part played by the psi factor in the process. The unorthodox healers' results, real or imaginary, are relegated to the closed circle of primitive magic, and attempts at their scientific verification are brushed aside as "intrinsically improbable," or at least impractical in the present climate of medical opinion, hospital policy, and malpractice legislation in this country. By contrast, the Filipino healers, Kathryn Kuhlman, Oral Roberts—to say nothing of God himself—have no malpractice problems.

Yet the burden of proof still remains with the parapsychologist or the worker in parapsychological medicine. This is, in effect, the challenge which such ambitious research projects as those of biologist Bernard Grad (1967) in Canada, or Sister Justa Smith (1968) and G. Watkins and A. Watkins (1971) in the United States are trying to meet. Their experiments seek to bridge the gap between the later-day magic of psi phenomena and animal or test tube models of experimental medicine in which the part played by suggestion, auto-suggestion, or doctrinal compliance is virtually eliminated and replaced by a testable ESP or PK hypothesis.

Although there still is a far cry from laboratory tests with enzyme solutions in a test tube or with mice handled by a purported healer, extrapolation from the laboratory to the medical model is a promising step towards the ultimate reconciliation of the magical, the psychosomatic, and psychodynamic models of healing.

REFERENCES

Booth, G. Psychobiological aspects of "spontaneous" regression of cancer. *Journal of the American Academy of Psychoanalysis*, 1973, 1, 303-317.

Carter, M. E., and McGarey, W. A. *Edgar Cayce on Healing.* New York: Paperback Library, 1972.

Colinon, M. *Les Guérisseurs.* Paris: Grasset, 1957.

Eddy, M. B. *Science and Health with a Key to the Scriptures.* Boston: The Trustees of the Will of Mary Baker Glover Eddy, 1934.

Edwards, H. *The Healing Intelligence.* New York: Taplinger, 1971.

Ehrenwald, J. *Psychotherapy: Myth and Method.* New York: Grune and Stratton, 1966.

Ehrenwald, J. Psi phenomena and the existential shift. *Journal of the American Society for Psychical Research*, 1971, 65, 162-172.

Ehrenwald, J. A neurophysiological model of psi phenomena. *Journal of Nervous and Mental Disease*, 1972, 159, 227-233.

Ehrenwald, J. *History of Psychotherapy: From Healing Magic to Encounter.* New York: Jason Aronson, 1976.

Everson, T. C., and Cole, W. H. *Spontaneous Regression in Cancer.* Philadelphia: Saunders, 1966.

Frank, J. D. *Persuasion and Healing.* Baltimore: Johns Hopkins Press, 1961.

Grad, B. The "laying on of hands": Implications for psychotherapy, gentling, and the placebo effect. *Journal of the American Society for Psychical Research*, 1967, 61, 286-305.

Kelman, H. *Kairos* and the therapeutic process. *Journal of Existential Psychiatry*, 1960, 1, 233-269.

Kuhlman, K. *I Believe in Miracles.* Englewood Cliffs, N.J.: Prentice-Hall, 1962.

LeShan, L. *The Medium, the Mystic, and the Physicist.* New York: Viking Press, 1973.

Malinowski, B. *Magic, Science and Religion.* Garden City, N.Y.: Anchor/Doubleday, 1948.

Nolen, W. A. *Healing: A Doctor in Search of a Miracle.* New York: Random House, 1974.

Puharich, A. Psychic research and the healing process. In E. D. Mitchell et al., *Psychic Exploration*, pp. 333-347. New York: Putnam's, 1974.

Racanelli, F. *Die Gabe des Heilens.* Berlin: Otto Wilhelm Barth, 1953.

Rose, L. *Faith Healing.* London: Gollancz, 1968.

Schultz, I. H. *Das Autogene Training.* Stuttgart: Thieme Verlag, 1950.

Servadio, E. *Unconscious and Paranormal Factors in Healing and Recovery.* (The Fifteenth Frederic W. H. Myers Memorial Lecture.) London: Society for Psychical Research, 1963.

Sherman, H. *"Wonder" Healers of the Philippines.* London: Psychic Press, 1967.

Smith, J. Paranormal effects on enzyme activity. *Proceedings of the Parapsychological Association,* 1968, **5,** 15–16.

Strauch, I. Medical aspects of "mental" healing. *International Journal of Parapsychology,* 1963, **5,** 135–165.

Thompson, C. J. S. *Magic and Healing.* London: Rider, 1946.

Thouless, R. H. Experiments in spiritual healing. *Newsletter of the Parapsychology Foundation,* 1955, **2,** No. 2.

Valentine, T. *Psychic Surgery.* Chicago: Regnery, 1973.

Watkins, G. K., and Watkins, A. M. Possible PK influence on the resuscitation of anesthetized mice. *Journal of Parapsychology,* 1971, **35,** 257–272.

Weatherhead, L. D. *Psychology, Religion and Healing.* (Rev. ed.) New York: Abingdon Press, 1954.

West, D. J. *Eleven Lourdes Miracles.* London: Duckworth, 1957.

Worrall, A. A., and Worrall, O. N. *The Gift of Healing.* New York: Harper & Row, 1965.

3

Psychopathology and Psi Phenomena

Montague Ullman

INTRODUCTION

In trying to relate psi events to psychopathology we face the uncomfortable fact that in neither instance are we dealing with clear-cut entities about which there is basic consensus. In the case of psi phenomena, for example, despite the fact that there is more general scientific agreement now concerning their existence than ever before, there is no agreement even among parapsychologists as to how they fit into the scheme of things.

Two broad theoretical approaches to psi start out with diametrically opposite assumptions. In one, there is an attempt to fit psi into an existing model of the universe. In the other, there is the conviction that we have to move beyond our present picture of the world to a radically revised one rooted in the reality of psi and the implications that follow from that reality. Advocates of the former view are hopeful that psi can be successfully incorporated into our present scientific outlook. Others are convinced that nothing short of a radical revamping of science itself is necessary. The controversy surfaces in concrete ways around questions of experimental design. Will object- and event-oriented positivist approaches be more fruitful than subjectivity-oriented psychological approaches? What characterizes the current scene is, perhaps, not so much the appearance of these issues but rather the sense of urgency concerning their resolution.

The contemporary scene with regard to a specialized area such as psychopathology is no less riddled with controversey. Although there is general consensus about the existence of psychopathology, there is little or no agreement as to what it is or which conceptual approach to its understanding will ultimately prove the most valid. Thus we have a variety of psychoanalytic theories focusing on developmental impediments and interpersonal tensions, communication theories concerned with the caliber of family interaction, and genetic and biochemical theories investigating the role of inborn and metabolic factors, particularly in the major psychoses. Perhaps the only unifying statement that can be made is that the specific content of the psychopathology will depend on the life experience of the individual. The various dynamic theories, despite their differences, all seek to provide a conceptual framework within which to understand the evolution and manifestations of psychopathology in the discrete individual.

Viewing the theories of psychopathology in historical perspective reveals a concern with ever-expanding fields of influence impinging on the individual, a fact which may have some converging relevance to developments in the theoretical approaches to psi phenomena. Prior to the elaboration of unconscious determinants of behavior, various neurological and constitutional theories were put forth to account for the occurrence of both the major psychoses and the various psychoneuroses. Psychiatric illnesses were looked upon as stigmata representing genetically and constitutionally determined degenerative processes in the nervous system. This view placed the individual in the role of helpless victim of an inexorable organic process.

As the concept of unconscious influences came to be dynamically elaborated— first through the work of Janet and then, more effectively, through Freud and his followers—a change occurred in the way the individual and his problems were conceptualized. No longer was he seen as victimized by forces totally beyond his control. He was now the victim of forces that were beyond his control only as long as they remained not understood. This dialectic, in the form of the struggle between the unknown·and the known, ushered in the modern era of dynamic psychiatry. The word *dynamic* refers to the elaboration of strategies (mechanisms) enabling the individual to cope with his needs as these are biologically, psychologically, and socially elaborated from birth on. Here, too, we see theoretical constructs moving perceptibly in the direction of a concern with a broader and broader field of interaction. If the appearance of the "Unconscious" on the scene freed the individual from the tyranny of a defective nervous system, then the interpersonal schools of psychoanalysis freed him from the tyranny of his own instincts. Communication theorists in turn, by elaborating the nature of the informational field generated in a family setting, helped liberate the individual from an exclusive concern with his own psychological structure by casting that structure in the context of a larger whole.

Holistic views extending outward and linking the individual more specifically to the entire social scene have been elaborated in different ways by Burrow (1927), Angyal (1941), Fromm (1941), and Laing and Cooper (1964). In each instance their contribution had a further freeing effect by noting more accurately and truthfully the context in which psychopathology arises. Each of these revisions has influenced our understanding of precisely what it is that is unconscious. There has been movement away from a particulate "Unconscious" (made up of specific and specifiable contents such as the Freudian concept of unconscious infantile wishes) to a "system" view in which whatever is not congruent with the dominant system organization controlling conscious awareness lies outside of awareness. Elaborated at the level of family dynamics by Jackson (1957) and others, at the level of personality by Angyal (1941), and at the social level by Laing and Esterson (1964) and Fromm (1963, 1973), the "Unconscious" becomes the domain of the potential rather than the hiding place of the instincts. The limitations imposed by earlier reductionistic approaches have been partially dissolved in recent years by both the evolution of techniques that more actively assault the presenting façades (encounter, Gestalt therapy) and by the growing interest in, and exploration of, altered states of consciousness for their capacity to reveal sources of untapped potential. We appear to be returning to a concept of the "Unconscious" that recalls some of the subliminal and supraliminal notions of Myers (1903).

In sum, theoretical approaches to psychopathology appear to be moving away from a positivistic stance toward a humanistic one. Instinct, mechanism, and energy transfer yield to purpose, meaning, and value in the context of field disturbances. The concept of the "Unconscious" becomes modified in the direction of a greater concern with social anarchy than biological anarchy and more to a state of creative unrest than tabooed yearnings.

It is precisely this more open, inventive, expanded view of the unconscious side of our lives that is setting the stage for a renewed exploration of the possible role played by psi events in the evolution of psychiatric disorder. Although historically the twin themes of psi and psychopathology have had closely related roots, they went through a period where separate developments took place as each sought to establish its own legitimacy. The beginnings of a new coming together are discernible. Let us briefly trace this development.

PSI AND PSYCHIATRY

At the time of the founding of the (British) Society for Psychical Research in 1882, there was a lively interest in hypnosis centering not only on its use as an instrument for investigating the unconscious and latent aspects of human personality but also in its relationship to paranormal perception. Early investigators like T. Weir Mitchell (1922), W. F. Prince (1915-1916), and Pierre Janet (1886) were intrigued by the possibility of psi linkages to altered states of consciousness. They investigated this connection not only in hypnosis (Janet, 1886), but also in the cases of hysteria (Mitchell, 1922), multiple personality (Mitchell, 1921;

Prince, 1915–1916), and paranoia (Prince, 1927). Myers' classic two-volume study, *Human Personality* (1903), not only outlined the evidence for survival but also provided a comprehensive survey of what was known at the time of the relationship between disordered internal states, including hysteria and insanity, and man's supraliminal (the term used to connote psi ability) capacities.

This early linkage of psi and psychiatry, forged as it was by the combined interests of some of the key investigators, soon loosened, giving way to two divergent developments representing two different kinds of historical necessities. The thrust of the psychoanalytic movement, led by Freud and his initial circle, was aimed at establishing, on the basis of observations, theory, and clinical practice, the nature, range, and significance of the unconscious determinants of personality and psychopathology. This goal required constant vigilance so as to preserve the scientific image of the newly emerging science of psychoanalysis. This is best illustrated by the kind of watch-dog attitude assumed by Ernest Jones (1957) with regard to Freud's show of interest in the "occult" and the constraints he succeeded in placing on this interest.

In the late 1920s, and in a somewhat analogous fashion, J. B. Rhine approached the monumental task of achieving scientific credibility for what was, at the time, a very odd and heterogeneous assortment of anomalous observations and beginning experimental endeavors. By his emphasis on the use of controlled laboratory methods, he too sought to achieve scientific respectability for the new science of parapsychology, a term he introduced. Parapsychology's concern with its own self-image, at least in the early stages, also had the effect of diluting its earlier ties to psychiatry. The Rhine school tended to eschew an active interest in and involvement with the dynamic contexts in which psi effects occurred. Its emphasis was by and large on rigorous quantitative assessment and the use of objective measures of evaluation.

The net result was that scientific parapsychology developed in a laboratory setting while clinical parapsychology was kept alive by the interest and writings of a handful of psychiatrists. These are reviewed from the point of view of dynamic and therapeutic considerations elsewhere in this volume. What now follows is a summary of the implications of this work for psychopathology. Since there is no sharp line between psychodynamics and psychopathology, some overlap will be inevitable.

PSI AND PSYCHOPATHOLOGY

Most of the writers on the subject of psi and psychiatry, being analysts, have stressed the dynamics of psi events as they arise in a clinical context. Only a few have gone further to theorize about the role psi may play in the evolution and symptomatology of the major psychoses.

Ehrenwald (1948) was the first in the modern era to undertake a serious assessment of the significance of the telepathy hypothesis for an understanding of paranoia and the schizophrenic psychoses. Favoring the view of psi as an archaic, regressive, or primitive faculty, he considers the occurrence of telepathy or heteropsychic input, as he refers to it, as evidence of some impairment of a filtering mechanism designed to ward off such influence. Heteropsychic stimuli operating in adult life pose a potential threat to one's sense of intactness and definition as a discrete entity. He notes as a possible exception the existence of a "psychic" character type as one who is able to accommodate in a positive and self-gratifying way to the existence of such a defective barrier and the consequent increased role of heteropsychic influences. Although sharing characterologic features in common with hysterical personalities, such types differ in the degree to which they are susceptible to heteropsychic influences and the organized manner in which these influences gain expression.

Central to Ehrenwald's conception of the way telepathy operates—or rather, the factors that account for its occurrence—is the notion of a minus-function. In the face of a functional or organic deficit that limits the range of the individual's interaction with the world about him, telepathic awareness emerges on the scene as a compensatory mechanism. Such functional deficits can exist either as discrete handicaps or as more global alterations in consciousness itself. They may be transient or lasting. Dreaming, hypnosis, and trance are examples of transient, reversible minus-functions, whereas psychosis, considered as an altered state, would be an enduring one.

Secondly, Ehrenwald emphasizes the significant role heteropsychic influences play in the early mother-child relationship in helping the child arrive at an intuitive orientation to the needs and expectations of the adults about him. Considering this early symbiotic matrix as the cradle of ESP, Ehrenwald (1971) sees subsequent psi manifestations as potentially regressive in character.

What Ehrenwald suggests in effect, in regard to both paranoia and the schizophrenic psychoses in general, is that, in addition to the characteristic sensitivity of these patients to hostility in others, there is also the ability to tap into the psyche of others telepathically. This sensitivity to heteropsychic stimuli often exposes deeply repressed sadistic-aggressive components of the personality of the source (agent) but may at times pick up scattered, more differentiated and specific thoughts and references at the level of the preconscious.

Telepathic sensitivity, according to Ehrenwald, plays its most significant role at the onset of a psychotic process and during the later, more deteriorated phases of the disorder. In the early stage of illness, telepathically perceived content may appear in the emerging delusional material, in which case the delusion cannot be completely understood on the basis of projection. At a more advanced stage, Ehrenwald interprets the picture of deterioration as resulting from the disorganizing effect of the intrusive flooding by both autopsychic and heteropsychic stimuli.

Applying these ideas more specifically, Ehrenwald suggests that catatonic nega-tivism can be understood in part as the effort to ward off uncanny experiences. Catatonic stupor occurs when the individual is chaotically overwhelmed by het-eropsychic input. The command automatisms sometimes seen in these patients can be looked upon as the consequence of heteropsychic influences on motor behavior. Ideas of grandeur, states of ecstasy, and ideas of mystic union may be viewed as a response to the enrichment of the personality from heteropsychic sources.

Ehrenwald's views were subject to certain criticisms at the time they appeared, by West (1948) because of the lack of supporting experimental evidence, by Eisenbud (1949) because of the lack of empirical evidence, and by Ullman (1948) because of the emphasis placed on paranormal factors. Nevertheless, offered at the time they were, Ehrenwald's theories were courageous beginnings. In the light of his conviction of the reality of the telepathy hypothesis, he gave some credence to the patient's own reading of his situation. He regarded the emergence of telepathy under these circumstances not as the primary cause of the illness, but as a compensatory effect secondary to a basic minus-function in the form of the intrinsic lack of rapport suffered by these patients.

Elsewhere in this volume (Chapter 3, Part VIII) Ehrenwald develops his ideas on the relationship of psi phenomena to hysteria. Drawing upon similar dissocia-tive tendencies in mediumship and conversion hysteria, he interprets psi effects as the mirror-image of the patterns of sensorimotor disturbances seen in conver-sion hysterics.

In another volume Ehrenwald (1955) has explored the possible role of telepathy in family patterns of neurotic interaction as well as in the tendency of marital partners to be involved often in complementary neuroses. He suggests that psi factors may play a role in the shaping of the pathological structure in the case of the former, and the choice of marital partner in the case of the latter.

The significance of Ehrenwald's work lies in the fact that, in going beyond Myers' early inferences concerning the relationship of telepathy to a variety of dissociated states (mediumship, hypnosis, multiple personality, hysteria, insanity) and re-viewing the problem in the light of current psychiatric concepts, he has made a strong case for including psi effects as a factor in the development of psychopathological disturbances. He has pointed to some of the ways in which our notions of psychosis may have to be revised. He has gone even further by suggesting a developmental model to account for the origin, appearance, and function of psi phenomena (Ehrenwald, 1971). He has taken Mahler's (1968) description of the early symbiotic period as the root source of psi and from that starting point has traced the role played by psi in the origins of paranoid hostility. He views such hostility as the outcome of a struggle against an imposed passivity and compliance. Either way out of this early symbiotic relationship, through autistic withdrawal or through passive surrender, results in heightened psi sensi-tivity. This sensitivity is used both to further the engulfing trend of the parent and to defend against it. What later emerges in the form of a paranoid delusion is the regressively distorted counterpart of this early, symbiotic model of communication. He regards the resurgence of psi in the analytic context as due to those features of the situation which tend to revive the early mother-child relationship.

There appears to be a number of ways in which conditions favoring the occurrence of psi bear a certain resemblance to the subjective states that accompany a psychotic process. In both circumstances altered states of consciousness play a prominent role. In the case of psi phenomena such states are known to exert a facilitating influence. In the evolution of a psychotic state feelings of unreality and depersonalization are often prominent. At a later point in the process the dissociated state becomes more globally organized, resulting in delusional systems, catatonic states, etc. The gross symptomatology that accompanies the movement into an organized psychotic state often takes the form of outright claims to mind reading ability or complaints of being victimized by the mind reading abilities of others.

Most of the striking anecdotal reports of psi occurrences are of the "crisis" variety, involving unexpected accidents, tragedy, and loss. An analogous kind of sense of desperation possesses the person sensing the imminence of a psychotic break with reality. He experiences himself as being in the grips of a process carrying him further and further away from all human supports and from a reality which, if not friendly, was at least familiar.

Ullman (1949, 1952), in his clinical observations, noted that patients who function close enough to a psychotic break to be aware of its possible imminence do manifest psi ability in the therapeutic context more frequently and more consistently than do other patients. It is as if, having for so long used language in the service of maintaining distance from others, they reach a point of no return in their efforts to maintain meaningful communicative bonds with others, including the therapist. This appears to be the circumstance under which telepathic faculties are mobilized. Conditioned by the expectations of hostility, the content of such telepathic forays into the private domain of the therapist is often embarrassingly revealing. Telepathic "needling" of this kind occurs at moments in the analysis when the patient feels the therapist, for reasons of his own, has become diverted, disinterested, and has shifted his concern away from him. At this stage the patient is neither consciously aware of his unusual ability nor of the way in which he is strategically employing it. That he is aware of it at some level is suggested by the fact that once an overt psychotic process takes over, much of the initially prevailing symptomatology is focused around the conviction that he can either read the thoughts of others or that others can read his thoughts and thus influence him.

Formal testing at this stage does not reveal any unusual ability and when psi effects do appear, they do so with less frequency and consistency than formerly and not within the context of the struggle to maintain a sense of relatedness.

They now seem to operate in the service of justifying the maintenance of the psychotic state. Bits and pieces of unconsciously hostile and rejecting thoughts are picked up and used destructively, often unerringly reaching their mark.

Ullman (1966, 1973b) links psi effects to the vigilance needs of the organism. Their occurrence with regard to any particular level of psychopathological organization would then have to be understood in terms of how time and space are structured in relation to different levels of pathological development and how the vigilance needs that characterize the resulting clinical syndromes are carried out in time and space. Does the psychopath, for example, who is inordinately concerned with maneuvering in the present, have to safeguard this way of operating by a kind of precognitive sensitivity to any impending events that may enhance the field of his self-seeking operations or that may interfere with his self-centered activities?

This question can also be raised with regard to the differential susceptibility to psi effects in the two major psychoses (Ullman, 1973a). All of the clinical reports linking psi to psychosis refer to schizophrenic processes, the possible exception being the incorporation of psi content into the rapid thought flow of the manic. Are these effects absent in the depressive psychoses? Ullman suggests that perhaps the answer lies in further exploration of how each of these categories of patients structure time.

The schizophrenic, sensing his vulnerability to unpredictable threats and assaults upon his isolation, relies on magical thinking to maneuver present reality. His weakened concern with real time and real events is augmented by a paranormal sensing of the sources of possible future danger. In the case of the manic-depressive, real time is also subject to alterations, and it is either retarded or accelerated, depending on which phase of the illness he is experiencing. Time is retarded in the depressive phase and accelerated in the manic phase. In the depressive phase the past overshadows the present and the future. In the manic phase the present overshadows both the past and the future. Ullman suggests the possibility that precognition would be more characteristic of schizophrenia (although for purposes of avoidance rather than manipulation as in the case of the psychopath), telepathy or clairvoyance of the manic state, and retrocognition of the depressive psychosis.

Similar questions have been raised with regard to characterological structuring of space and the possible relevance this might have to the occurrence of other psi effects, such as psychokinesis, in persons functioning at different levels of pathological organization (Ullman, 1973a).

Altered states of consciousness in general are characterized by unique time-space relations so that here too we have another point of convergence between psi and changes in the internal subjective milieu. Under the conditions of an altered state of consciousness, three transformations occur, all of which may have a bearing on the appearance of psi effects during such states. Alterations in space-time structuring expands the range of information available both temporally and spatially. The information once received is processed differently (in comparison with the processing of normal waking perceptions). The information is organized closer to the level of impression and feeling than for clarity of the cognitive content. The final transformation has to involve a motivational shift to a greater concern with internal processes and their effect on the arousal level of the organism. Dreaming is prototypic of this kind of transformation. The imagery that appears in dreams is processed in terms of its alerting potential (Ullman, 1973b). Psi messages have more of an alerting character than a clearly informational one.

Ullman's views on the relationship of the dreaming state to vigilance and to psi have been criticized by Eisenbud (1973), who feels there is insufficient evidence that dissociated states favor psi and that when psi does occur, its erratic nature makes it unlikely that it could serve any reliable vigilance function. Ullman, in response, called attention to the fact that in altered states of consciousness all stimuli, psi included, serve vigilance needs indirectly by mediating the level of arousal.

In a recent review of parapsychology and psychopathology Alberti (1974) reexamines the long held belief in the close relationship of psi to dissociated states such as are seen in hypnosis, hysteria, and psychosis. In addition to the early workers who strongly adhered to this point of view, for example, Myers (1903) and Janet (1886), he notes its restatement in contemporary terms by Moser (1935), Bender (1935), Ehrenwald (1948), and others. Alberti admits the association between certain hysterical features such as the tendency to dissociative states and the occurrence of various automatisms and psi phenomena, but he questions the nature of the correlation. He points to the fact, for example, that in reported cases of multiple personality genuine psi effects are the exception rather than the rule. He prefers to interpret the relationship as a contingent one rather than a causal one. He feels that proneness to dissociative states and guessing ability (ESP) are two distinct entities. When they are found together it is because the existence of dissociative states facilitates the emergence at a behavioral level of whatever it is that is responsible for a guessing performance indicative of ESP.

In further support of this point of view Alberti cites the experimental studies of Schmeidler (1960), Eysenck (1967), and Kanthamani and Rao (1972) correlating good ESP performance with extraversion and good social adaptation. He considers it unlikely, in view of results of this kind, that hysterics *per se* have any kind of intrinsic psi ability.

It seems somewhat risky to make comparative judgments of ESP performance without taking the context more into consideration. Extraverts and "expansives" may very well do better in a laboratory context where the atmosphere of a game prevails, whereas in a clinical or real life context the very existence of a dissociated state at either a functional or psychopathological level may contribute to the sense of urgency and "crisis" atmosphere that brings psi functioning close to being a necessity. Alberti himself comes to a somewhat similar formulation when he points out that discrepancies in the experimental results in laboratory testing of neurotics and psychotics can be explained on the basis that the existence of a psychopathological process will influence the way in which perceptual data are processed and cognitive data organized.

Complex mechanisms are involved, subfunctions of which may interact in ways that give different results on different occasions. Disturbances in these mechanisms consequent to mental illness will affect one or another aspect of ESP performance. This, Alberti believes, can account for some of the variations in the secondary aspects of ESP scores such as decline effects, the way results correlate with the expectations of the experimenters, etc. He suggests that the time is ripe for a more elaborate study of the pathology of ESP.

Working with the view of psychosis as a chronically altered state of consciousness, Rogo (1974b) has raised a number of issues with regard to the relationship of psi to the psychotic process. Basing his ideas on some of the early case reports of "obsession" and multiple personality, he suggests that not only do psi factors emerge initially in the early symptomatology, but that genuine psi ability is often seen to emerge after the cure of the disorder. He cites evidence in support of this from the autobiographies of recovered schizophrenics. He goes so far as to suggest that some cases of multiple personality can best be understood as a form of incipient mediumship.

A largely unexplored area having implications for our understanding of the interplay between psychopathology and bodily change has to do with the type of case where psi communications seem to take the form of transient somatic manifestations. Eisenbud (1970) describes several cases of what seemed to be psychosomatic symptoms initiated as psi-conditioned responses. Other observers, notably Schwarz (1967) and Stevenson (1970), suggest that the effect is more frequent than is generally suspected. Based on his studies of telepathic impressions, Stevenson feels it is reasonable to assume that somatic symptomatology ranging from obscure physical symptoms to identifiable psychosomatic syndromes may come about as physical analogies of a telepathic message. Schwarz coined the term *telesomatic* reactions for responses of this nature and reported on a number of illustrative cases drawn from his own practice as well as self-observation. He points out that, since reactions of this kind evolve unconsciously, they are apt to go unnoticed unless the telepathy hypothesis is kept in mind. He cites the work on the plethysmographic registration of ESP effects as suggestive of the possible mechanism responsible for physiological changes and somatic symptomatology.

Two types of reported experience are worth noting in their possible bearing on the problem of remotely induced bodily changes. One is a well-documented report of the extraordinary circumstances attending the unexpected simultaneous deaths of 32-year-old schizophrenic twins (Wilson and Reece, 1964) who were under observation at the time on different wards of a psychiatric hospital.

They died at approximately the same time and for causes that could not be determined at autopsy. In the analysis of the various factors that might have accounted for the simultaneity of death the authors included a "psychic" determinant.

Another kind of remotely induced organismic change is reported by Paul (1966) in her description of how two of her patients reacted during a period of time when she was under the influence of an hallucinogenic mushroom taken for experimental purposes. In each instance the patient went through a period of upset and disturbance followed by an amnesia of several hours duration correlating with the time the therapist herself was experiencing an altered state of consciousness. Temporary psychotic-like symptoms appeared to have been remotely induced, followed by a near total memory loss. Here again the question arises: if incidents of this kind do occur, how often do they go, if not unnoticed, then unrecognized as telepathically induced?

Another point of convergence between psi and psychopathology lies in the still largely unexplored area of the interpersonal milieu in which poltergeist phenomena are alleged to occur. Almost all modern writers on the subject such as Owen (1964), Roll (1972), and Rogo (1974a) have followed Fodor's (1959) lead in viewing the phenomena themselves as externally displaced paranormal manifestations of repressed aggression. Although preadolescent and adolescent youngsters are generally implicated as the key agents in connection with poltergeist phenomena, this is not necessarily always the case. In some instances an adult seems to be the focus of the disturbances. In line with prevailing trends, psychological interest in these problems has also shifted from an almost exclusive focus on the individual whose presence seems essential for the appearance of the phenomena to a broader concern with family dynamics and the way in which interpersonal crises generated in the family relate to the phenomena that occur.

Rogo emphasizes the importance of a psychotherapeutic approach to the members of the family as the surest approach to ameliorating the manifestations. Roll's elaborate investigation of poltergeist phenomena has led him to believe that the most consistent personality features of the implicated agent take the form of a combination of pent-up hostility with either strong repressive trends or a very low verbal ability. The implicated agent may be analogous to the identified patient in family therapy and like the latter may not be the source of the disturbance but rather, the victim. Considerably more work would have to be done along these lines, however, before any of these conjectures can be defined convincingly.

EXPERIMENTAL STUDIES

When we turn to the experimental studies that have been done to gauge the influence of psychiatric disorder on psi performance, we come upon an array of unrelated findings that fail to shed significant light on any intrinsic relationships between these two variables.

In what he considered an exploratory study using a STM (screen touch matching) procedure, Shulman (1938) tested 141 patients in a mental hospital. Most of them were diagnosed as having one or another form of psychosis. Positive scores were obtained with only one group, the manic-depressive depressed patients and surprisingly enough, these scores were significantly different from the negatively scoring involutional melancholia group. The author accounts for the difference in terms of the possible greater degree of negativism said to be present in the involutional melancholia group. Since the weight of current opinion is inclined to regard the involutionals as part of a continuum of depressive disorders, the results could be retrospectively interpreted as indicating that one group of depressives did better than another. As noted by Shulman, the attentional difficulties in working with actively psychotic patients are considerable and undoubtedly play a role in influencing the scoring level. Where the anxiety level is high, as it often is in involutionals, attentional difficulties would be expected. In this study the overall results for all patients were significant.

In another exploratory study (Urban and Kock, 1949), 216 psychiatric outpatients were tested for ESP. Although overall significance was achieved, the conditions under which the testing was carried out were far from optimal according to modern standards. Comparisons were made before and after shock therapy or various kinds of narco-analysis. Significant, but in some cases temporary, increase in scoring was noted during and upon completion of the treatment.

In a study conducted in 1938, but reported on in 1951 (Bates and Newton), ESP tests were carried out with 50 state hospital patients representing nine different diagnostic categories (six of which were psychotic disorders). Subjects were asked to get as many (high-aim condition) or as few (low-aim condition) "hits" as possible. While no significant differences in scoring ability were found for the various diagnostic groups, the overall results were highly significant, as was the difference in scoring rate in high- and low-aim conditions. Subjects classified as cooperative scored more successfully than those classified as apathetic or as irritable. In contrast with Shulman's results, both the manic-depressive depressed and the involutional melancholia patients scored significantly. The only group that did not succeed in getting results in the desired direction were the patients diagnosed as paranoid dementia praecox, who scored positively in both high- and low-aim conditions. Alberti (1974) notes that the difference in scoring level between high- and low-aim conditions was smallest in the three schizophrenic categories and in the organics. He suggests that since these are the patients in whom selective attention is apt to be most impaired, this factor may account for the fact that they were less successful in steering their ESP in the desired direction than were the patients in the five other diagnostic categories.

A series of tests by West (1952) was designed to see whether hostile and suspicious attitudes in psychotic patients would be conducive to negative scoring. No clear evidence of an ESP effect was found. As might be expected in patients of this kind, defects of attention, difficulty in maintaining contact, and stereotypy of behavior make for difficulty both in administering routine card-calling tests and in evaluating the results.

Humphrey (1954), working with psychotic patients in a London hospital, failed to confirm Urban and Köck's (1949) findings of increased scoring after electroshock therapy. She did, however, note positive scoring in all the schizophrenics tested.

Zorab (1957) tested a small sample of psychiatric patients (schizophrenic, manic-depressives, and a mixed group) using a standard card guessing technique and found no evidence of ESP in any of the groups.

Nash (1966), testing normal subjects for correlations between ESP and ten scales of the Minnesota Multiphasic Personality Inventory (MMPI) pertaining to schizophrenia, depression, and other psychopathological potential, found the correlations generally negative with regard to neurotic and psychotic tendencies.

These studies highlight some of the problems involved in carrying out experimental work with seriously disturbed patients suffering from the various psychoses. Aside from the practical problems in securing the patients' cooperation in carrying out a preset plan, there is also the limiting effects of attentional problems, distractibility, autistic response, etc. In addition there are nosological difficulties. Diverse classificatory systems are employed. Differences of opinion concerning diagnostic criteria exist. Diagnostic impressions vary not only with the observer but also with the context in which the observations are made. With regard to each diagnostic category, there are differing degrees of severity and differing symptomatology linked both to intrinsic processes and the setting in which the patient finds himself. Most of the reports described above did not go into detail concerning diagnostic criteria, context, or process.

The other problem that emerges in working with a too global categorization of patients is the likelihood, as indeed happened, that conflicting results, the product of the many unidentified variables, are apt to occur. In only a few instances were specific enough hypotheses set down for the experiment, such as testing high-aim versus low-aim (Bates and Newton, 1951) or the effect of paranoid ideation (West, 1952). The only specific hypothesis concerning the relationship of psi and psychosis to be tested was the one offered by Ehrenwald, dealing with heteropsychic influences on incipient schizophrenia and the role these played in the various manifestations of this illness. It is dubious whether West's study (1952) adequately put this hypothesis to the test. It is in situations like this that context and motivation play a significant role, and results obtained in a formal ESP card-guessing type of experiment cannot be automatically carried over as an indicator of what may or may not happen in the natural course of a psychotic process. Procedures have yet to be devised that would test the limits of psi abilities in a patient experiencing a particular kind of psychotic process under conditions where psi would play a meaningful role in terms of the motivation of the patient.

Beginnings have been made along these lines in designing tasks that are apt to mobilize psi functioning at an unconscious level in relation to genuinely felt needs. In this connection the line of research proposed by Stanford (1974) is of some relevance. He has evolved an experimentally testable model to account for spontaneous psi events based on evidence suggesting that psi operates unconsciously as a nonintentional but need-relevant response. His model, which he refers to as the psi-mediated instrumental response (PMIR) model, proposes that the organism uses psi nonintentionally to scan its environment for need-relevant objects or events or for information significantly related to such events. Once having obtained the information, the organism tends to act in ways which are instrumental in satisfying its need in relation to the particular object or event apprehended. This model links an unconscious psi-based scanning mechanism to the operation of unconscious needs. A model of this kind seems to fit precisely the dynamics connected with the appearance of psi in the clinical context. By inference it suggests the role psi might play in the evolution of a psychopathological structure since psi appears to be as readily deployable in the service of sick as well as healthy needs.

PROSPECTUS

Conceptual ferment is intrinsic to the nature of scientific inquiry. When the ferment rises to the point of challenging existing paradigms, resistance is encountered and change proceeds unevenly. Here and there specific disciplines send out exploratory pseudopods into the future. Humanistic psychology dabbles in the transpersonal. At a philosophical level the debate goes on concerning the shortcomings of a positivistically-oriented science. Theoretical physicists, having grown restive with the search for the elusive elementary particle, are seeking a more satisfactory view of the nature of physical reality. The consciousness of man has even been implicated as a factor influencing physical events at a distance (Wigner, 1970). While there is some evidence of movement and change in the conceptual underpinnings of psychopathology, the structure remains basically unaltered and therefore unaccommodating to psi effects. Where will the leverage come from to change this?

I would suggest that it will come from the same two sources that, in the last century, contributed to the rise of modern psychopathology. I refer to the science of physics and the budding science of psychical research. Newtonian-based physics profoundly influenced the approach to all scientific questions in the nineteenth century, and psychopathology was no exception. The mechanics, energy relations, and economic aspects of Freud's system bear witness to this influence. What is not generally appreciated are the contributions to psychiatry that came in the wake of the investigations of early psychical researchers into the claims of spiritism. This resulted in widespread interest in such phenomena as automatisms, multiple personalities, dissociated states in general, and what Myers (1903) referred to as the manifestations of our "supraliminal" self. Other examples of this psychiatric yield are given by Ellenberger (1970) in his scholarly treatise on the origins of the unconscious. In this connection he considers the appearance of Flournoy's *From India to the Planet Mars* in 1900 as one of the two books published that year that subsequently became classics in dynamic psychiatry. The other was Freud's *The Interpretation of Dreams*. Flournoy wrote his book after a lengthy study of a medium in Geneva who produced a variety of communications from purported discarnate entities both from the planet Earth as well as from Mars. Flournoy succeeded in tracing the sources of these messages to forgotten memories (for which he coined the term cryptomnesia). These memories in combination with the remarkable capacity of the unconscious for imaging and dramatic display and under the motivating influence of wish fulfillment provided the psychological underpinnings for what seemed to emerge as separate entities in the form of the medium's controls.

In the modern era the world of Newtonian physics has been transformed into the world of relativistic physics and the appreciation of this change, as Ehrenwald emphasizes in his writings, is necessary if the behavioral sciences are to accommodate the data of parapsychology. Some movement is occurring in psychiatry, but slowly. Thus far it has resulted in some shift away from a conceptual system based on the issues arising from the tension between safety and pleasure to a conceptual system more concerned with meanings, goals, and purposes. Psychiatry has become more holistic, field-oriented, relational, and interactional and is just beginning to send out transpersonal pseudopods. Helping in this process, hopefully, will be the conceptual fallout from the world of relativity physics, along with the newer behavioral technologies now available. From the former may come a greater awareness of, and sensitivity to, the way which our assumed spatial and temporal ordering of reality limits and impairs subject-object unity. It may also provide us with a deeper understanding of the role our notions of space and time play in structuring psychopathological processes.

The availability of the new technologies will inevitably move us further along in the process of conceptual review. The descriptive term *dissociation* can now be explored operationally in a number of ways. As an altered state of consciousness it can be dealt with along a physiological continuum of arousal; studied as a specific means of information processing; explored as a tension between right and left hemisphere function; or manipulated vegetatively through biofeedback techniques. Many of those exploring these new techniques approach their work without an antipsi bias so that the chances are greater than ever for a fruitful collaboration between behavioral scientist and parapsychologist in the interest of a deeper understanding of the psychological ills that befall us.

Psi is an effect in an interpersonal field and as such it presumably is incorporated into the ongoing dynamics of the members of that field. As psychiatry takes more cognizance of their occurrence, psi effects will move from an eccentric, anomalous position to whatever its rightful place may ultimately prove to be.

REFERENCES

Alberti, G. Psychopathology and parapsychology: Some possible contacts. In A. Angoff and B. Shapin (Eds.), *Parapsychology and the Sciences*, pp. 225-233. New York: Parapsychology Foundation, 1974.

Angyal, A. *Foundations for a Science of Personality*. New York: The Commonwealth Fund, 1941.

Bates, K. E., and Newton, M. An experimental study of ESP capacity in mental patients. *Journal of Parapsychology*, 1951, **15**, 271-277.

Bender, H. Mediumistische psychosen. In *Aufsatze zur Parapsychologie*. Munich: E. Reinhardt, 1935.

Burrow, T. *The Social Basis of Consciousness*. New York: Harcourt Brace, 1927.

Ehrenwald, J. *Telepathy and Medical Psychology*. New York: W. W. Norton, 1948.

Ehrenwald, J. *New Dimensions of Deep Analysis*. New York: Grune and Stratton, 1955.

Ehrenwald, J. Mother-child symbiosis: Cradle of ESP. *Psychoanalytic Review*, 1971, **58**(3), 455-466.

Eisenbud, J. Psychiatric contributions to parapsychology: A review. *Journal of Parapsychology*, 1949, **13**, 247-262.

Eisenbud, J. *Psi and Psychoanalysis*. New York: Grune and Stratton, 1970.

Eisenbud, J. In M. Ullman, and S. Krippner, with A. Vaughan. *Dream Telepathy*, pp. 253-258. New York: Macmillan, 1973.

Ellenberger, H. F. *The Discovery of the Unconscious*. New York: Basic Books, 1970.

Eysenck, H. J. Personality and extrasensory perception. *Journal of the Society for Psychical Research*, 1967, **44**, 55-71.

Flournoy, T. *From India to the Planet Mars*. New York: Harper, 1900.

Fodor, N. *On the Trail of the Poltergeist*. London: Arco, 1959.

Fromm, E. *Escape from Freedom*. New York: Rinehart, 1941.

Fromm, E. *Zen Buddhism and Psychoanalysis*. New York: Grove Press, 1963.

Fromm, E. *The Crisis of Psychoanalysis*. Middlesex, England: Penguin, 1973.

Humphrey, B. M. ESP tests with mental patients before and after electroshock treatment. *Journal of the Society for Psychical Research*, 1954, **37**, 259-266.

Jackson, D. D. The question of family homeostasis. *Psychiatric Quarterly*, 1957, **31**, Supplement, 79-90.

Janet, P. Deuxième note sur le sommeil provoqué à distance et la suggestion mentale pendant l'état somnambulique. *Revue Philosophique de la France et de L'Etranger*, 1886, **21**, 212-223.

Jones, E. *The Life and Work of Sigmund Freud*. New York: Basic Books, 1957, Vol. 3.

Kanthamani, B. K., and Rao, K. R. Personality characteristics of ESP subjects: III. Extraversion and ESP. *Journal of Parapsychology*, 1972, **36**, 198-212.

Laing, R. D., and Cooper, D. G. *Reason and Violence*. London: Tavistock Publications, 1964.

Laing, R. D., and Esterson, A. *Sanity, Madness and the Family*. London: Tavistock Publications, 1964.

Mahler, M. *Human Symbiosis and the Vicissitudes of Individuation*. New York: University Press International, 1968.

Mitchell, T. W. The Doris Fischer case of multiple personality. *Proceedings of the Society for Psychical Research*, 1921, **31**, 30–74.

Mitchell, T. W. *Medical Psychology and Psychical Research*. New York: Dutton, 1922.

Moser, F. *Der Okkultismus, Täuschungen und Tatsachen*. Munich: E. Reinhart, 1935.

Myers, F. W. H. *Human Personality and its Survival of Bodily Death*. London: Longmans, Green, 1903. 2 vols.

Nash, C. B. Relation between ESP scoring level and the Minnesota Multiphasic Personality Inventory. *Journal of the American Society for Psychical Research*, 1966, **60**, 56–62.

Owen, A. R. G. *Can We Explain the Poltergeist?* New York: Garrett, 1964.

Paul, M. A.   Two cases of altered consciousness with amnesia apparently telepathically induced. *Psychedelic Review*, 1966, **3**, 4–8.

Prince, W. F. The Doris case of multiple personality. *Proceedings of the American Society for Psychical Research*, 1915, **9**, 1–700; 1916, **10**, 701–1419.

Prince, W. F.   The cure of two cases of paranoia (through experimental appeal to purported obsessing spirits). *Bulletin of the Boston Society for Psychic Research*, 1927, **6**, 36–72. (Reprinted in *The Psychoanalytic Review*, 1969, **56**, 56–86.)

Rogo, D. S. Psychotherapy and the poltergeist. *Journal of the Society for Psychical Research*, 1974, **47**, 433–446. (a)

Rogo, D. S. Psi in the clinical framework of abnormal psychology. In A. Angoff and B. Shapin (Eds.), *Parapsychology and the Sciences*, pp. 52–65. New York: Parapsychology Foundation, 1974. (b)

Roll, W. G. *The Poltergeist*. New York: Nelson Doubleday, 1972.

Schmeidler, G. R. ESP in relation to Rorschach test evaluation. *Parapsychological Monographs No. 2*. New York: Parapsychology Foundation, 1960.

Schwarz, B. E. Possible telesomatic reactions. *Journal of the Medical Society of New Jersey*, 1967, **64**, 600–603.

Shulman, R. A study of card-guessing in psychotic subjects. *Journal of Parapsychology*, 1938, **2**, 95–106.

Stanford, R. G. An experimentally testable model for spontaneous psi events. I. Extrasensory events. *Journal of the American Society for Psychical Research*, 1974, **68**, 34–57.

Stevenson, I. Telepathic impressions: A review and report of thirty-five new cases. *Proceedings of the American Society for Psychical Research*, 1970, **29**, 1–198.

Ullman, M.   Review of *Telepathy and Medical Psychology*, by J. Ehrenwald. *Journal of the American Society for Psychical Research*, 1948, **42**, 72–77.

Ullman, M. On the nature of psi processes. *Journal of Parapsychology*, 1949, **13**, 59–62.

Ullman, M. On the nature of resistance to psi phenomena. *Journal of the American Society for Psychical Research*, 1952, **46**, 11–13.

Ullman, M. A nocturnal approach to psi. *Proceedings of the Parapsychological Association*, 1966, **3**, 35–62.

Ullman, M. Psi and psychiatry: The need for restructuring basic concepts. In W. G. Roll, R. L. Morris, and J. D. Morris (Eds.), *Research in Parapsychology 1972*, pp. 110–113. Metuchen, N.J.: Scarecrow Press, 1973. (a)

Ullman, M. A theory of vigilance and dreaming. In V. Zikmind (Ed.), *The Oculomotor System and Brain Function*, pp. 455–465. London: Butterworths, 1973. (b)

Urban, H., and Köck, F. Reported in: ESP tests with the mentally ill. *Parapsychology Bulletin*, 1949, No. 14, 1–2.

West, D. J. Review of *Telepathy and Medical Psychology*, by J. Ehrenwald. *Journal of the Society for Psychical Research*, 1948, **34**, 211–215.

West, D. J. ESP tests with psychotics. *Journal of the Society for Psychical Research*, 1952, **36**, 619–623.

Wigner, E. P. Physics and the explanation of life. *Foundations of Physics*, 1970, **1**, 35–45.

Wilson, I. C., and Reece, J. C. Simultaneous death in schizophrenic twins. *Archives of General Psychiatry*, 1964, **11**, 377–384.

Zorab, G. ESP experiments with psychotics. *Journal of the Society for Psychical Research*, 1957, 39, 162–164.

Part VII

SURVIVAL OF BODILY DEATH

1

Discarnate Survival

Alan Gauld

INTRODUCTION

Any attempt to survey the evidence for human survival of bodily death faces a dilemma. There are on the one hand some writers who regard as "evidence for survival" a wide assortment of alleged phenomena, some of which are "evidence for survival" only in the sense that they can be given an interpretation in terms of the survival hypothesis. Thus in 1946 a prominent British Spiritualist listed 34 classes of "proofs of survival" falling into ten categories (Collins, 1946, pp. 43–44), and at least one further class of phenomena, the so-called Raudive voices (Raudive, 1971), has come into prominence since that date. On the other hand, there are a number of writers who upon a priori grounds hold or hint that no empirical findings whatsoever could possibly constitute acceptable evidence for a person's having survived the dissolution of his body (e.g., Flew, 1972; Geach, 1969; Penelhum, 1970; with these cf. H. H. Price, 1959). It is claimed that the notion of personal identity is logically and inextricably tied to that of bodily continuity. If one follows the former writers, the task of surveying the "evidence for survival" becomes unduly extensive; if the latter, there is nothing to survey.

The present chapter will attempt to evade the above dilemma by adopting the following restrictions:

1. Only those cases will be counted as "evidence for survival" in which there is an apparent recrudescence of the personality of a person who has suffered bodily

death. The term *personality* is here used in the pragmatic or everyday sense in which someone's "personality," i.e., his characteristic attitudes and emotions, the style of his interactions with other people, his manners and mannerisms, his physical and intellectual skills, the sorts of knowledge he has, and especially his characteristic memory-knowledge, is largely independent of his physical appearance and can indeed be obliterated or radically changed while his body remains outwardly the same. Thus, cases in which there is simply an apparent post-mortem recrudescence of someone's voice or figure but no indications of recrude-scent "personality" will not count *per se* as "evidence for survival," and *a fortiori* cases just of allegedly inexplicable physical happenings will not do so either. Likewise, cases, such as the fascinating "Patience Worth" case (Litvag, 1972; Prince, 1927a), in which a distinctive personality manifests, but does not relate itself to any person known to have lived, will be excluded.

2. If "evidence for survival" is defined in the above way, then without doubt we have evidence for survival. The "problem of survival" is the question of how the cases which constitute this evidence are to be explained. It has been cus-tomary to set against each other two rival explanations, viz., the "survivalist" hypothesis, which proposes that the deceased persons whose personalities have apparently manifested after bodily death have survived undiminished in all essen-tials and are in some way or another operative in producing the phenomena con-cerned, and the "super-ESP" hypothesis, which attributes the phenomena to vast extrasensory powers possessed by persons still alive. Now the survivalist hypoth-esis, stated in this all-or-nothing fashion, has important shortcomings. In the first place, it runs full-tilt upon the conceptual problem, mentioned above, of whether or not a "person" could meaningfully be said to survive the dissolution of his body. In the second place, it makes no allowance for the possibility, em-phasized by Broad (1925, pp. 535–551; 1962, pp. 414–430) and easy to reconcile with much of the evidence, that something may survive which is less than a "person," something which is perhaps the bearer just of fragmentary "disposi-tions" which can only be actualized in the presence and through the agency of living persons. Accordingly this article will discuss principally what may be called the "continuity" hypothesis, that is, the view that the evidence for survival is to be explained in terms of the persistence of a *something*, whether mental or physical, whether or not a center of experiences or describable as a "person," a something which was once a part or aspect of a living human being and which, after the dissolution of that human being's body, somehow acts as a catalyst in the production of the very curious phenomena concerned. If this hypothesis be stigmatized as vague to the point of elusiveness, it may be replied that its rivals (e.g., the super-ESP hypothesis, the theory of demonic possession) only appear more definite so long as they are not closely scrutinized and that in any case we cannot in the present state of our information hope to do more than indicate possible frameworks within which more detailed theories may in the remote

future be developed. The strong version of the continuity hypothesis, the version which postulates the survival of a sentient agent who is in some sense the same person as a once living human being, will be referred to as the "survivalist" hypothesis. The term *incorporeal personal agency*, which implies that what survives must be wholly bodiless and must be a true "agent," will not be used.

3. Cases of ostensible reincarnation will not be considered (see Dr. Stevenson's chapter on Reincarnation).

The above restrictions will somewhat reduce the scope and complexity of the materials with which we are confronted. None the less these materials are still copious—some of the individual cases which will be touched upon were originally written up at a length greater than that of this article—and all that can be provided below is a brief classified guide to selected literature, together with a few amplifications and comments. Lengthier accounts which may usefully be consulted include Myers (1903), Holt (1915), Hyslop (1919), Z. Richmond (1938), K. Richmond (1939), Baird (1943, 1948), Murphy (1945), Hart (1959), W. H. Salter (1961), Ducasse (1961), Beard (1966), and Jacobson (1973). The following are the topics which will be treated:

1. Mediumship: general remarks.
2. Evidence for the continuity hypothesis from the phenomena of mediumship.
3. Apparitions and out-of-body experiences as bearing upon the continuity hypothesis.
4. Empirical considerations telling against the continuity hypothesis.
5. Concluding remarks.

MEDIUMSHIP: GENERAL REMARKS

The terminology generally used in discussions of mediumship has obvious shortcomings, but space does not permit any attempt to rectify them here. A "medium" may be defined as a person through whose agency or through whose organism there are received communications ostensibly from deceased human beings or other discarnate or remote entities. It is customary to divide the forms of mediumship into two broad categories, "mental" and "physical." In mental mediumship the communications are transmitted to persons other than the medium by the medium's own voice, hand, etc. In physical mediumship they are transmitted by ostensibly paranormal physical happenings in the medium's vicinity.

Mental and physical mediumship may each be further subdivided. Let us begin with mental mediumship. In what is commonly called "clairvoyant" mediumship (the term *clairvoyant* is here being used in an older and broader sense than that now current), the medium (who may be in a state of partial dissociation) "sees" or "hears" deceased friends and relatives of persons present and relays purported messages from them. Generally speaking, the experiences concerned seem not to have the distinctness of ordinary perception but are rather a seeing or hearing "in the mind's eye" or ear. Sometimes, however, the figures seen or voices heard may attain an hallucinatory vividness; the medium's experience then resembles that of the percipient of an apparition. Clairvoyant mediumship is extensively practiced within the Spiritualist movement, and a demonstration of it forms the centerpiece of most Spiritualist church services.

Other forms of mental mediumship involve so-called motor automatisms—speech, writing, gestures, sometimes even painting, drawing, or piano-playing, which are outside the conscious control of the automatist. They may assume the form of communications from the departed, and long literary or didactic works have not infrequently been thus "transmitted." Such automatisms may appear spontaneously, or as the result of suggestion or mental disorder, or may be deliberately cultivated by persons not otherwise abnormal. Ouija and planchette boards, tables so balanced as to tip easily, and other conjointly operated devices seem to facilitate the development of motor automatisms by relieving the automatist of a feeling of complete responsibility for the movements which occur.

The state of mind of an automatist during the production of such automatisms may be anything from normal alert wakefulness to a profound trance which is followed by complete amnesia for events occurring during that trance. Sometimes there is a feeling simply of being "overshadowed" by an external personality, and then the behavior executed is not "automatic," but seemingly directed and influenced from without. There are obvious affinities here with the "clairvoyant" mediumship just described. A sustained "overshadowing" of this kind can amount to an "obsession" by an alien personality (see Hyslop, 1919, Chap. 14; Prince, 1927b; 1929). In the case of mediums who pass into a trance, the ordinary personality may after a short interval seem to be completely replaced by that of a deceased person or other discarnate being. The new personality may in some instances attain almost complete control of the medium's organism. We then have what is ostensibly a transient "possession" of the organism by a second personality. Occasional instances of what purport to be longer term "possessions" by deceased persons are on record (see, e.g., Kerner, 1834; Myers, 1903, Vol. 1, pp. 360–368; Stevens, 1887).

It is by no means uncommon for the same medium to exhibit more than one of the "phases of mediumship" just described.

A little must now be said concerning what may be called the "dramatic form" in which mediumistic communications ostensibly from the deceased are commonly cast. It has become customary to divide the communicating personalities into "controls" and "communicators." "Controls" are ostensibly deceased persons who directly control the medium's hand or vocal apparatus and communicate *in propria persona*. "Communicators" are deceased persons with whom controls purport to be in touch and from whom they relay messages or of whom they give descriptions. The controls not infrequently speak as if they had themselves only a somewhat fluctuating awareness of the communicators for whom they purport to act as intermediaries. It is as if the controls are clairvoyant mediums once removed. The term *communicator* is also used generically to cover both controls and communicators.

There has been a good deal of controversy over the psychological status of controls. Some observers have been struck by the resemblances between many mediumistic controls and the secondary personalities of hysterical patients afflicted with "multiple personality" (see, e.g., Troubridge, 1922, pp. 348-359). Many controls are somewhat oppressively childish, as have been the secondary personalities which have emerged in certain cases of multiple personality. Few have given any very convincing evidence of identity with persons formerly incarnate; and attempts to explore the relationship between mediums and their controls by means of psychological tests have been largely inconclusive (Carington, 1934a, 1934b, 1935, 1937; Carrington, 1933; Thouless, 1937). More generally, it has been proposed that the whole drama of communication, with its controls and communicators, and the interplay between them, and its scientific-sounding accounts of the processes of control and transmission, can be shown on careful analysis to be even in the most favorable instances (i.e., those in which the purported communicators are most successful in giving correct information about their earthly careers) a construct of some ordinarily hidden level of the medium's mind. Thus in her classic studies of Mrs. Piper's mediumship, E. M. Sidgwick (1900, 1915) noted that Mrs. Piper's own personality showed through the personalities of the controls and communicators in divers ways. They displayed an ignorance of science, philosophy, and literature which had not characterized them in life, but which did characterize Mrs. Piper; they exhibited common associations and turns of phrase; they were unexpectedly interested in trivialities. Maintenance of the drama was everything and to that end controls would cover up mistakes in an absurd and evasive manner—including controls who in life had been persons of the utmost probity. The most convincing communicators and controls would unhesitatingly endorse the credentials of the least convincing, so that all stood or fell together. It must, however, be stated that other investigators with every claim to competence have found themselves able to accept certain mediumistic controls at face value and to write off the mistakes, confusions, and limitations as imposed by the conditions of communication and by the acquired organization of the medium's nervous system. This view was taken of, for example, the Piper controls by Myers (1903) and Hodgson (1898), and of Mrs. Leonard's controls by C. D. Thomas (1928).

The psychological problems of the status of mediumistic controls is fascinating and complex, but it cannot be taken further here. There is no satisfactory general study of the psychology of mediumship. A good deal of relevant material, however, can be found in Podmore (1902), Myers (1903), Flournoy (1911), Mitchell (1922), Lawton (1933), and Broad (1962), and cf. Murphy (1949, 1953), and Berg (1951). Among studies of particular mediums see, in addition to the references given in the preceding paragraph, Prince (1926), Broad (1955), Flournoy (1963), and Progoff (1964). The psychology of the mental medium has to be considered in the light of apparently quite similar phenomena observed in other societies than our own, and in other times. The historical and anthropological material may conveniently be approached through Lang (1894), Dingwall (1930), Oesterreich (1930), Barnouw (1942), Elliott (1955), Wavell, Butt, and Epton (1966), Beattie and Middleton (1969), Eliade (1970), and Dodds (1971).

It should be noted that the question of whether or not the claims of certain mediumistic controls and communicators to independence from their mediums are to be taken at face value cannot be simply equated with the question of whether or not the continuity hypothesis is true. Some writers, for instance E. M. Sidgwick, whose psychological analysis of the Piper controls was referred to above, have combined the view that controls and communicators and their interplay are all aspects of a drama evolved from the medium's subconscious, with the view that none the less behind that drama, and somehow directing its course or injecting material into it, are the deceased persons who figure in the drama as controls and communicators.

Among mental mediums who have been subjected to intensive investigations under the auspices of the British or American Societies for Psychical Research, the following may be particularly noted:

1. Mrs. L. E. Piper (1857–1950) of Boston, Massachusetts. Mrs. Piper's career as a medium began in 1884 after a visit to a healing medium at which she passed into a trance and wrote down a strikingly "evidential" message for one of the persons present. At first she used mainly to speak in trance, her principal control being a *soi-disant* French doctor of doubtful authenticity who called himself "Phinuit." In 1885 she attracted the attention of William James, then professor of psychology at Harvard, who undertook a sustained investigation of her mediumship. James arranged for her to visit England for study by the (British) Society for Psychical Research (Myers, Lodge, Leaf, and James, 1890), and shortly afterwards Richard Hodgson, a leading member of that Society, went to Boston to assume charge of the investigations (Hodgson, 1892). In 1892 there appeared as Mrs. Piper's principal control George Pellew (G.P.) a young man of literary and philosophical tastes who was known to Hodgson and had recently been killed in an accident. The G.P. control was extremely realistic, conversed freely and naturally with Pellew's own friends, and displayed an intimate knowledge of the living Pellew's own concerns (Hodgson, 1898). At the same period writing began to displace speaking in Mrs. Piper's trance. Between 1897 and 1905 a group of controls, claiming identity with certain notable persons, began to communicate under the pseudonyms "Imperator," "Rector," "Doctor," "Prudens," etc., and the communications assumed a more didactic tone. In 1905 Hodgson died and shortly thereafter appeared as one of Mrs. Piper's controls (James,

1909). Mrs. Piper's trance mediumship continued until 1911, and her automatic writing for some years afterwards. Her biography was written by her daughter (Piper, 1929). The longest general account of her mediumship is that in Holt (1915), with which cf. Sage (1903), Hyslop (1905), and W. H. Salter (1950). E. M. Sidgwick's studies (1900, 1915) of the psychology of her trance have already been mentioned above.   Among investigations of her mediumship the following may be noted in addition to the papers already cited: Newbold (1898), Hyslop (1901), Lodge (1909), Sidgwick, Verrall, and Piddington, (1910), and H. Verrall (1910).

2. Mrs. Rosalie Thompson (1868-?), an extremely versatile British medium whose mediumship began in 1897 with the production of divers physical phenomena. These, however, soon disappeared, and she became a clairvoyant and trance medium. Most of her trance communications were by voice (her chief control was ostensibly a deceased daughter, Nelly), but she also wrote automatically both in trance and in a waking state. The principal accounts of her mediumship are the following: Lodge (1902), Myers (1902), van Eeden (1902), Wilson and Piddington (1902), Hodgson (1902), M. Verrall (1902), Piddington (1904), and cf. Podmore (1910, pp. 184-198).

3. "Mrs. Willett" (Mrs. Winifred Coombe-Tennant, 1874-1956), a British "society" lady who had none the less strong social and political views of a radical kind and distinguished herself both in local and international politics. She was the wife of F. W. H. Myers' brother-in-law. She began automatic writing in 1908, after the death of a daughter, and in 1909 the deceased Myers and his friend, Edmund Gurney, ostensibly suggested to her that instead of writing automatically she should try to apprehend ideas and images which they would insinuate into her mind, and she should then record them by writing or speaking. This method she adopted. The principal investigators of her mediumship were first Sir Oliver Lodge (1911), and then G. W. Balfour (1935). Many of her sittings were occupied with discussions between Balfour and the ostensibly communicating Myers and Gurney about various philosophical and psychological issues, but together with certain automatists associated with the S. P. R., and especially Mrs. Verrall, she also played a part in various "cross correspondences" (see below) and was the medium for certain "literary puzzles" allegedly designed by two deceased classical scholars, A. W. Verrall and S. H. Butcher (see below). She was also the principal medium in the "Palm Sunday" case (J. Balfour, 1960), a series of messages ostensibly from Mary Catherine Lyttelton to the Conservative statesman Arthur Balfour, whose early love she had been. In these communications, matters not known to any person present were unmistakably referred to.

4. Mrs. Gladys Osborne Leonard (1882-1968), a British trance medium. Her principal control, "Feda," claimed to be one of Mrs. Leonard's ancestors, an Indian girl who had died in childbirth about the year 1800. The communications were generally spoken, although Mrs. Leonard occasionally wrote auto-

matically. A curious feature of her mediumship was an "independent voice," apparently not issuing from Mrs. Leonard's lips, which occasionally intervened to correct Feda's attempts to convey some message. Mrs. Leonard was investigated extensively by members of the British and American Societies for Psychical Research between 1916, when she became famous with the publication of some communications ostensibly from Sir Oliver Lodge's son Raymond (Lodge, 1916, 1918), and the beginning of the Second World War. Some of the "proxy sittings" in which she cooperated are discussed below. Other important investigations or discussions of her mediumship are: Radclyffe-Hall and Troubridge (1919), Troubridge (1922), H. Salter (1921, 1926, 1930), Allison (1929), C. D. Thomas (1928), and K. Richmond (1936). She has written an autobiography (Leonard, 1931). A brief general account of her mediumship is W. H. Salter 1950. For a popular but useful account see Smith (1964).

   5. Mrs. Eileen J. Garrett (1893–1970), a trance and clairvoyant medium born in Ireland, was trained as a medium in England and lived a good deal of her life in the United States. She became well known after the publication (H. Price, 1931) of some remarkable communications ostensibly from Lt. H. Irwin, commander of the ill-fated airship, the R101. Mrs. Garrett took a keen interest in the scientific investigation of mediumship and expressed doubts concerning the independence from her of her own "controls" (Angoff, 1974). She was the subject of a number of laboratory investigations (Birge and Rhine, 1942; Carington, 1934a, 1935; Carrington, 1933; Evans and Osborn, 1952; Goldney and Soal, 1938). In 1951 she established the Parapsychology Foundation in New York, which under her Presidency devoted itself to the furtherance of scientific parapsychology. She wrote several autobiographies (Garrett, 1939, 1968).

   Historically, physical mediumship, which is now uncommon, preceded mental mediumship. In the years following the inception in 1848 of the modern Spiritualist movement, many of the ostensible communications received from the departed were by means of raps or telekinetic phenomena not unlike those said to take place in poltergeist cases. There soon followed reports of partial or complete "materializations" and of communications by means of the "direct voice." Most of the attempts at scientific investigation of physical mediumship have concerned themselves primarily with the genuineness or otherwise of the alleged phenomena and only secondarily with the evidence for survival of which those phenomena are the apparent vehicles. On physical mediumship in general, see Amadou (1957). For the historical background Podmore (1902) is essential reading, and cf. Gauld (1968, Chaps. 1, 3, 4, 5, 9, and 10).

EVIDENCE FOR THE CONTINUITY HYPOTHESIS FROM PHENOMENA OF MEDIUMSHIP

Perhaps the most remarkable fact about the evidence for survival from the phenomena of mental mediumship is its quantity. The material on this topic published in the *Proceedings* of the S.P.R. alone would, if added together, yield a dozen or two bulky volumes. It might of course be remarked that in this field quality is of much greater importance than quantity. Not a few writers— especially, one suspects, those not well acquainted with the original case reports —seem to think that many mental mediums practice gross imposture on their clients, who "may have to arrange a sitting in advance," leaving their names and addresses. "This enables the medium . . . to assemble facts about the sitter's background . . . Further information is gleaned from the sitter's reactions to generalized but interrogatory remarks and by the interpretation of responses to feelers. Opportunities may meanwhile present themselves for the medium or her assistants to add to their dossiers on clients by examination of coat pockets and purses . . . . Investigators may even be sent to the client's home town to gather information" (Hansel, 1966, p. 223). When mediums' successes are not set down to fraud, they are attributed by these writers to "fishing" for information, to accumulated knowledge about the sorts of deceased relatives and friends a given type of person would be likely to have, to lucky hits among the clichés and generalities, and to possession of an unusually retentive memory for names, faces, and personal details.

Most of these suggestions are simply inapplicable to mediums who have been studied as extensively and as carefully as the five listed above. It was, for instance, a common practice of persons in charge of the investigations of these mediums to bring the sitters from as far afield as possible, to introduce sitters anonymously or pseudonymously, to pay particular attention to first sittings, and so on. (For some recent investigations in which extensive precautions were taken, but positive results none the less obtained, see Haraldsson and Stevenson, 1974.) Both Mrs. Piper and Mrs. Leonard were for a while watched by private detectives to make sure that they did not employ agents. So far as I am aware, an accusation of deliberate fraud was only once made against any of the mediums named above (by Richard Hodgson against Mrs. Thompson, see Hodgson, 1902, and cf. Podmore, 1910, pp. 157-158). It is, however, possible that some mediums may possess "flypaper" memories, especially when in a state of dissociation or trance. A striking example is given by Goldney (1939). The need to guard against this possibility was, however, early recognized (see, e.g., the "Huldah" episode, James, 1909, pp. 20-26), and it is not easy to see how a "sticky" memory could assist a medium to reveal intimate details of the personal concerns of anonymous sitters whom she is meeting for the first time. It is also quite true that even the best mediums (or their controls) to a greater or lesser degree "fill in" with clichés and generalities, the sitters' polite replies to which may open up further lines of plausible guessing. On this tendency in Mrs. Piper's mediumship see E. M. Sidgwick (1900, 1915) and cf. Parsons (1949). Attempts have been made to deal with this problem by devising statistical methods of assessment of mediumistic material (see, e.g., Greville, 1949; Pratt, 1969; Pratt and Birge, 1948; Saltmarsh and Soal, 1930; Scott, 1972; Stevenson, 1968b).

There are, however, many examples of mediumistic communications ostensibly from the deceased in which the correct information given is so specific and sometimes so detailed that the choice seems to lie straightforwardly between fraud and the exercise of some imperfectly understood paranormal faculty. The following case (Hodgson, 1892) may serve as an instance. This case is chosen not because it is particularly good, but because it is short—it took place before verbatim or near-verbatim recording of Mrs. Piper's sittings had been instituted as a matter of course:

Boston, *June 26th,* 1890

During the winter of 1885–6, I had my first sitting with Mrs. Piper. She was then on Pinckney-street, in this city. Immediately on becoming entranced, her control, Dr. Phinuit, said there were many spirit friends present. Among them he said was an old man, whom he described, but only in a general way. Then he said, "He is your father, and he calls you Judson." Attention was also called to the fact that he had a peculiar bare spot on his head, and Mrs. Piper put her hand on the corresponding place on her own head.

Now for the facts that gave these two apparently simple points whatever significance they possess. My father had died during the preceding summer, aged ninety years and six months. He had never lived in Boston, and Mrs. Piper, I am quite sure, had never seen him nor been in any way interested in him. He wasn't at all bald, but when quite young had been burned; so that there was a bare spot on the right side of the top of his head, perhaps an inch wide and three inches long, running from the forehead back towards the crown. This he covered by combing his hair over it. This was the spot that Mrs. Piper indicated. Now as to the name by which he addressed me: I was given the middle name, Judson, at the request of a half-sister, my father's daughter, who died soon after I was born. Out of tenderness for her memory (as I always supposed) father always used, when I was a boy, to call me Judson, though all the rest of the family called me by my first name, Minot. In his later life father also got to calling me by my first name. No one, therefore, had called me by my second name for many years. I was therefore naturally struck and surprised by suddenly having one who claimed to be my father giving me once more my old boyhood name. I was not consciously thinking of either of these things; and I am convinced that Mrs. Piper couldn't have known anything about them.

During this same sitting Mrs. Piper's control also said, "Here is somebody who says his name is John. He was your brother. No, not your own brother; your half-brother." Then, pressing her hand on the base of her brain, she moaned as she swayed to and fro. Then she continued, "He says it was so hard to die away off there all alone! How he did want to see mother!" She went on to explain that he died from a fall, striking the back of his head. Her whole account of this was realistic in the extreme. My half-brother John, the son of my mother—for both father and mother had been twice married—died several years previous to this sitting. While building a mill in Michigan he fell, striking the back of his head on a piece of timber. He was far from all friends;

and was a most tender lover of his mother. I was not thinking of him until told that he was present.

Many other things occurred during the sitting. But I mention only these, because, though simple, they are clear-cut and striking, and because I see no way by which Mrs. Piper could ever have known them.

M. J. SAVAGE

P.S.—I have had other sittings with Mrs. Piper. Most of the things told were, however, too personal for publication. Nearly all are inexplicable on any theory that does not go at least as far as telepathy (pp. 100–101).

The most economical explanation of Mrs. Piper's successes here is, as Mr. Savage indicates, telepathy from the sitter—provided, of course, that one accepts the evidence for telepathy. The theory of telepathy from persons present loses, however, some of its economy as against the continuity hypothesis in cases such as the Marble case (Lodge, 1909, pp. 255–279) or the Vandy case (Broad, 1962, Chap. 15; Gay, 1957) in which ostensibly the same communicator gave correct information about himself through different mediums and sometimes to different sitters. Thus in the Vandy case two pseudonymous sitters and three notetakers sat in various combinations and permutations with three mediums. The themes dwelt upon by the Edgar Vandy communicator were for the most part, though not always, ones which could have come from the mind of some person present; yet there is a consistency of theme which appears to transcend variations in sitters and mediums.

It is by no means difficult to find cases in which the correct information given was, so far as could be ascertained, not known to any person present. Sir Oliver Lodge (Myers et al., 1890, pp. 649–650) lists 41 such episodes which occurred in a series of sittings with Mrs. Piper (but cf. Podmore, 1910, pp. 306–307); Hyslop (1901, pp. 131–133) lists several instances with the same medium, and cf. Hodgson (1892, pp. 15–27). M. Verrall (1902, pp. 176–183) lists nine instances in sittings with Mrs. Thompson (cf. Podmore, 1910, pp. 310–311). A good many experiments with Mrs. Leonard were aimed at obtaining evidence of this kind (see below on "proxy" sittings, and cf. Radclyffe-Hall and Troubridge, 1919, pp. 487–546). In some of these cases the correct information given was, apparently, not merely not known to any person present, but not known *in toto* to *any* living person. See for instance the case of "Mrs. A.'s" sittings with Mrs. Thompson (M. Verrall, 1902, pp. 179–183; summarized in Z. Richmond, 1938, pp. 92–98). Under these circumstances the theory of telepathy from the sitters has to be enlarged into the super-ESP hypothesis: the view that the medium can telepathically locate distant persons with relevant pieces of information, disinter them from their unconscious minds (for, generally speaking, there is no reason to suppose that these persons were consciously thinking of the matters in question) and collate them appropriately; or can by clairvoyance apprehend the various states of affairs, documents, etc., to which the information given refers or from which it might have been gleaned.

The term *proxy sitting* is more or less self-explanatory. A sitter takes a sitting on behalf of an absent third party of whose concerns he knows little, in the hope of obtaining appropriate communications from some deceased person known to that third party but not to him. Prior to the sitting the proxy sitter may privately appeal to the desired communicator; at the sitting he may hand the medium some relic of the deceased person as a "token object," or may furnish her with that person's name. Unfortunately, nearly all such cases are too long to be satis- factorily summarized. As an example, however, we may consider some leading points from a case in which the Rev. C. Drayton Thomas was the sitter.

Mr. Thomas was asked by Professor E. R. Dodds to obtain a communication from a certain Frederic William Macaulay on behalf of the latter's daughter, Mrs. Lewis, who was married to a scientist friend of Professor Dodds. For this purpose Thomas had five sittings with Mrs. Leonard. Some distinctive references were made to Macaulay's work as an hydraulic engineer. The following extracts (C. D. Thomas, 1930) refer to more personal matters (Mrs. Lewis' annotations are in brackets).

> FEDA: There is also a John and a Harry, both with him. And Race . . . Rice . . . Riss . . . it might be Reece but sounds like Riss, and Francis. These are all names of people who were connected with him or linked up with him in the past, connected with happy times. I get a feeling of an active and busy home in which he was rather happy.
>
> [This is a very curious passage . . . Probably the happiest time of my father's life was in the four or five years before the war, when we, his five children, were all at school, and the home was packed with our friends during the holi- days. John, Harry and Francis could be three of these . . . But the most inter- esting passage is "It might be Reece but it sounds like Riss." . . . My elder brother was at school at Shrewsbury and there conceived a kind of hero- worship for one of the "Tweaks" (sixth form boys) whose name was Rees. He wrote home about him several times and always drew attention to the fact that the name was spelt "Rees" and not "Reece." In the holidays my sister and I used to tease him by singing "Not Reece but Riss" until my father stopped us . . .]
>
> FEDA: I get a funny word now . . . would he be interested in . . . baths of some kind? Ah, he says I have got the right word, baths. He spells it BATHS. His daughter will understand, he says. It is not something quite ordinary, but feels something special.
>
> [This is, to me, the most interesting thing that has yet emerged. Baths were always a matter of joke in our family—my father being very emphatic that water must not be wasted by our having too big baths or by leaving taps drip- ping. It is difficult to explain how intimate a detail this seems . . . The men- tion of baths here also seems to me an indication of my father's quaint humour, a characteristic which has hitherto been missing . . .]

FEDA: ... Godfrey; will you ask the daughter if she remembers someone called Godfrey. That name is a great link with old times.

[My father's most trusted clerk, one who specially helped in the hydraulic research, was called William Godfrey. He was with my father for years and I remember him from almost my earliest childhood ...]

FEDA: What is that? ... Peggy ... Peggy ... Puggy ... he is giving me a little name like Puggy or Peggy. Sounds like a special name, a little special nickname, and I think it is something his daughter would know ... [My father sometimes called me "pug-nose" or "Puggy".] (pp. 265-269.)

Over the five sittings, 124 items of information were given, of which 51 were classified as right, 12 as good, 32 as fair, 2 as poor, 22 as doubtful, and 5 as wrong. Thomas is inclined to set aside the hypothesis of telepathy from the living, though absent, Mrs. Lewis on the grounds that three items of information given were outside her knowledge. Dodds regards these incidents as too vague to be conclusive, but none the less remarks: "It appears to me that the hypotheses of fraud, rational inference from disclosed facts, telepathy from the actual sitter, and coincidence cannot either singly or in combination account for the results obtained" (C. D. Thomas, 1939, p. 294).

Other important accounts of proxy sittings are given by N. Walker (1927, 1935), C. D. Thomas (1933, 1935), Allison (1934), and J. F. Thomas (1937).

The theory of telepathy from the sitter and its inevitable extension, the super-ESP hypothesis, face perhaps their most formidable difficulties, at least with regard simply to the making of correct factual statements, in connection with certain cases of what have come to be called "drop in" communicators. Drop in communicators are communicators unknown, so far as can be discovered, to either medium or sitters. It is obvious that cases of verified communications from drop in communicators rule out the theory of telepathy from the sitters. If, further, the correct information communicated could not have been acquired telepathically or clairvoyantly from any single source but must rather have been assembled from a diversity of sources, even the super-ESP theory becomes somewhat stretched. For the problem must be faced of how the medium is able to single out, from the immense mass of material which *ex hypothesi* is clairvoyantly or telepathically available to her, just those items of information which will assist in the production of this particular drop in communicator (see Gauld, 1971, pp. 273-277).

Cases, or series of cases, of verified drop in communicators crop up from time to time in the annals of Spiritualism, but in many instances the possibility that the medium could have acquired the information by ordinary means has not been adequately considered (see the criticisms of this sort of evidence by Prince, 1933). The problems here are very similar to those which arise in the assessment of cases of ostensible reincarnation. There are, however, a number of cases on record which seem relatively free from such objections (e.g., Hill, 1934, pp. 97-102; Myers, 1903, Vol. 2, pp. 471-477; Stevenson, 1970b, 1973; Tyrrell, 1939;

Zorab, 1940), and recently two sets of cases, each centering on a different medium, have been and are continuing to be subjected to detailed study (Gauld, 1971; Haraldsson and Stevenson, 1975a, 1975b). In the cases which I have studied, the communications were spelled out by a ouija board operated by several persons, although it was quite clear that one particular person was the principal "medium" in their production. Communications from some 38 drop in communicators were scattered among a great deal of personal, didactic, and historical material. Of these, 10 were classified as wholly or partly verified (an 11th has subsequently been added), 15 (now 14) as unverified, and 13 as too vague to be susceptible of verification. A strong argument against deliberate fraud is that several of the most interesting cases were left unverified until I disinterred them from the records some 20 years afterwards. I will summarize one of the more curious cases (Gauld, 1971). At five sittings between 1950 and 1952 a drop in communicator calling himself "Harry Stockbridge" (pseudonym) spelled out the following items of personal information (verifications given in brackets):

> Second Loot attached Northumberland Fusiliers. Died Fourteen July, Sixteen.
> [A second lieutenant in the Northumberland Fusiliers, named Harry Stockbridge, was killed on July 14, 1916. This date is incorrectly given in the War Office official lists.]
> Tyneside Scottish. [Stockbridge was originally in a Tyneside Irish battalion of the Northumberland Fusiliers, but at the time of his death had been transferred to a Tyneside Scottish battalion, a fact which does not seem to have found its way into print.]
> Tall, dark, thin. Special features large brown eyes. [Verified by relatives and by a photograph, but not, so far as could be discovered, mentioned in any printed source.]
> I hung out in Leicester. [True.]
> Asked what were his likes and dislikes: Problems any. Pepys reading. Water colouring. [He studied mathematics and physics at University. His University career is referred to in print, but not his subject of study. Relatives could not answer for sure on the latter points.]
> Asked if he knew a "Powis Street" about which a sitter had dreamed: I knew it well. [It later transpired that there was a street of this name not far from his birthplace.] (pp. 322–327.)

Of the verified items, two have not, so far as can be ascertained, found their way into print. One printed source (a local newspaper obituary) contained all the remaining items, except that Stockbridge's rank was erroneously given as lieutenant instead, of second lieutenant. It is possible that there was at the time of the communications a surviving relative who possessed all the information concerned, but conversations with relatives suggested that their memories of him were too dim for this to have been likely. The powers of super-ESP which the medium would have required would in that case have been almost unthinkable.

Detailed inquiries into the life histories of the medium and sitters revealed no points at which their paths would have crossed Stockbridge's.

The "evidence for survival" which this article has so far considered has been evidence which taken at face value would suggest the survival of some of the memory-dispositions of a deceased person. A person's memory-dispositions are highly characteristic of him—the chance of finding two adult human beings with identical memory-dispositions must be enormously smaller than that of finding two people with identical fingerprints—and such evidence, if sufficiently detailed, is perhaps the most impressive single kind obtainable. However, the arguments brought to bear on this sort of evidence by proponents of the super-ESP hypothesis have led upholders of the continuity hypothesis to seek evidence of the post-mortem recrudescence of other aspects of personality. Evidence for such recrudescence—for the apparent recrudescence through mediums of, e.g., the characteristic mannerisms, turns of phrase, purposes, skills, and what may be called "personality organization" of deceased persons—has been found in very considerable quantities; but unfortunately this evidence is very often a great deal harder to connect beyond cavil with a certain formerly living person than is the evidence for persisting memory-dispositions. Furthermore, though this evidence may impress, and justifiably impress, the friends of the deceased person, these friends not infrequently find it almost impossible to convey its full force to outsiders.

There have, for example, been cases, not numerous, but not especially scarce either, in which a medium has reproduced, with startling exactness, the mannerisms, turns of phrase, habitual attitudes, even humor, of some deceased person not known to her in life. Mrs. Piper's mediumship provided a number of examples (especially in the case of her "G.P." control, referred to above), and so did that of Mrs. Leonard, e.g., the "A.V.B." communicator (Radclyffe-Hall and Troubridge, 1919) and the "John" and "Etta" communicators (C. D. Thomas, 1928). A recent series of automatic scripts in which the attitudes and manner of the ostensible communicator ("Mrs. Willett") are vividly conveyed is printed in Cummins (1965). There have even been cases, very difficult to assess, in which the handwriting of the communicator has been closely approximated (see, e.g., Flournoy, 1963, pp. 431–438; Myers, 1903, Vol. 2, pp. 231–234; Piddington, 1904, pp. 235–243). To account for the post-mortem recrudescence of such characteristics on the super-ESP hypothesis, it is necessary to invest the medium not only with sufficient powers of extrasensory perception to acquire paranormal information about the manners, mannerisms, attitudes, etc., of formerly living persons, but also with the imaginative intelligence necessary to assemble these findings into coherent representations of those deceased persons and the dramatic powers to carry the personations through.

Related problems arise over those relatively infrequent cases in which a deceased person ostensibly communicating through a medium exhibits some characteristic skill which that person possessed in life, but which is not, so far as can be ascertained, ordinarily possessed by the medium. The most obvious examples here are certain cases of xenoglossy—cases in which a communicator or control has spoken, written, or understood a language of which he was in life the master, but of which the medium is believed upon good grounds to be ignorant (see Lodge, Verrall, Feilding, Johnson, and Richet, 1905; Richet, 1905). A collection of cases of ostensible xenoglossy is given by Bozzano (1932), but the quality is to say the least uneven; Stevenson (1974) reviews the literature and discusses a single, though not especially impressive, case in unprecedented detail. There are occasional brief instances—too brief, perhaps, to be accorded much weight—in the records of Mrs. Piper's mediumship (see, e.g., Hodgson, 1892, p. 131; 1898, pp. 416–418, 480–482; Newbold, 1898, pp. 45–48; Sidgwick et al., 1910, pp. 51–62), and on one occasion a communicator through Mrs. Thompson, ostensibly a Dutchman, responded appropriately to phrases addressed to him in Dutch (van Eeden, 1902). A most remarkable case of apparent xenoglossy is that of the automatist "Rosemary," studied by Wood (1935, 1955) and by Hulme and Wood (1937). Rosemary's control, "Nona," claimed to have lived in ancient Egypt and communicated over a period of some years a very large number of apparently correct phrases and short sentences in the ancient Egyptian language. At the end of a close analysis of the case, Ducasse (1961) wrote, "The xenoglossy ... does provide strong evidence that the capacity once possessed by some person to converse extensively, purposefully, intelligently, and intelligibly in the Egyptian language of three thousand years ago, or anyway in a language closely related to it, has survived by many centuries the death of that person's body" (p. 256).

Fluent spoken conversation between a control and a sitter in a language unknown to the medium is very unusual. Most of the alleged cases have taken place through "direct voice" mediums, the best known of whom have been Mrs. Etta Wriedt (Moore, 1913) and George Valiantine (Bradley, 1924, 1925; Hope, 1932; Whymant, 1931). In neither case do we have adequate recordings or stenographic records, and Valiantine was detected in imposture of the grossest kind (Bradley, 1931; H. Salter, 1932).

Along with cases of apparent xenoglossy should perhaps be considered a small but curious collection of cases in which a child has ostensibly been controlled by a deceased person and written or spoken appropriate messages in language more advanced than that of which the child was ordinarily master (see, e.g., the cases referred to by Aksakow, 1898, Vol. 2, pp. 406–419; Myers, 1903, Vol. 2, pp. 171–172; Richet, 1923, pp. 220–227, and a case mentioned below on p. 619).

If these cases of the apparent post-mortem recrudescence of linguistic skills once possessed by a certain person are not to be dismissed as fraudulent (and some, at least, of them are in line to be so dismissed), they would appear to stretch the super-ESP hypothesis quite severely. For on this hypothesis it has to be supposed that the medium can telepathically obtain knowledge of the equivalents in her own language of words and phrases in a foreign language, and vice versa, and that in some cases she can do so with sufficient rapidity to permit natural conversation, which also involves her overcoming the physical difficulties of the novel pronunciations required.

A comment often made on the evidence for survival is that the personalities which manifest and claim, or are assumed to possess, identity with once living human beings generally appear static; they show little sign of developing, of forming and executing plans of their own, or otherwise of possessing any real independence or initiative. If this comment is justified, the continuity hypothesis can only be held in a form which postulates that what survives death is less than a person; and of course it might be suggested that the super-ESP hypothesis would be strengthened insofar as it becomes the more plausible to write off communicators as simply aspects or phases of a medium's personality. It is therefore of some theoretical interest to look at cases in which communicators have *prima facie* seemed to plan and act autonomously. It should be noted that such cases are *per se* only "evidence for survival" if the plans concerned are ones which can be considered characteristic of the alleged communicators.

A small collection of such cases will be found in Z. Richmond (1938). One of the more striking of these cases is in outline as follows (Myers, 1903):

In January, 1885, Mrs. A. von Wiesler (sister-in-law of Alexander Aksakow, a well-known Russian psychical researcher who reported the case), and her daughter Sophie, began to experiment with a planchette. They soon began to receive urgent and forceful communications from "Schura," the deceased daughter of somewhat distant acquaintances. Schura had adopted revolutionary political views and had, at the age of 17, committed suicide following the death of a like-minded cousin, Michael, while escaping from prison. She demanded that Sophie bring to a sitting Michael's brother, Nikolaus, who was, according to Schura, in danger of compromising himself politically. Sophie hesitated for reasons of social propriety. Schura's demands became more vehement at successive sittings, until on February 26, 1885, she wrote, "It is too late . . . expect his arrest." The von Wieslers then contacted Nikolaus' parents, who were, however, quite satisfied in respect of Nikolaus' conduct. Two years later Nikolaus was arrested and exiled because of political assemblies which he had attended in January and February, 1885. "The notes which Mrs. von Wiesler had made were read again and again by the families both of 'Schura' and of Nikolaus. 'Schura's' identity in all these manifestations was recognized as incontestably demonstrated, in the first place, by the main fact in relation to Nikolaus, by other intimate particulars, and also by the totality of the features which characterized her personality" (Vol. 2, p. 181).

An advocate of the super-ESP hypothesis would have to argue here that, having obtained by ESP a good deal of information about the affairs and characteristic concerns and purposes of two persons of whom they had only the sketchiest knowledge, Mrs. von Wiesler and her daughter then externalized this information in the form of the rather striking drama spelled out by the planchette.

By far the most celebrated cases in which there seems to be evidence of active planning on the part of the deceased are certain instances of "cross correspondences." A cross correspondence occurs when what is written or spoken by or through one medium or automatist corresponds or correlates to an extent that cannot be normally explained with what is written or spoken by or through another, and independent, medium or automatist. When "the cross correspondences" dignified by the definite article are referred to in the literature of parapsychology, what is meant is the extensive and interlinked series of cross correspondences which appeared between 1901 and 1930 in the automatic writings of a group of automatists associated with the British S.P.R. The originators and designers of these cross correspondences were, purportedly, F. W. H. Myers, Edmund Gurney, and Henry Sidgwick, the recently deceased early leaders of the S.P.R. All three of these men, but particularly Myers, had been classical scholars. Two of the automatists principally involved, Mrs. M. de G. Verrall, wife of Professor A. W. Verrall, the well-known classical scholar, and her daughter Helen (Mrs. W. H. Salter), both of whom had known Myers and Sidgwick, were also classical scholars, and their scripts were often loaded with classical phrases and allusions. Other automatists of the group included Mrs. Willett (Mrs. Coombe-Tennant), mentioned above, and Mrs. Holland (Mrs. Fleming, the sister of Rudyard Kipling). The work of unraveling the cross correspondences was principally undertaken by J. G. Piddington, Alice Johnson, and G. W. Balfour.

The cross correspondence materials, though of great psychological and parapsychological interest, are exceedingly voluminous and have not all been made public. In his valuable book on the subject, Saltmarsh (1938) lists 52 papers on or related to the cross correspondences from the *Proceedings* of the S.P.R., and many of these are very lengthy; see, e.g., M. Verrall (1906), Piddington (1908), A. Johnson (1908, 1910, 1911, 1914), Sidgwick et al. (1910), and Lodge (1911).

Saltmarsh (1938) distinguishes among "simple," "complex," and "ideal" cross correspondences. Simple cross correspondences "are those where in the scripts of two or more automatists there occurs the same word or phrase, or else two phrases so similar as to be clearly interconnected" (p. 41). An obvious explanation of simple cross correspondences would be that one automatist gains extrasensory knowledge of what the other is writing and writes something similar herself. Complex cross correspondences "are cases where the topic or topics are not directly mentioned, but referred to in an indirect and allusive way" (p. 42). An ideal complex cross correspondence would be one in which two independent automatists each wrote apparently unconnected meaningless messages. "Now, if a third automatist were to produce a script which, while meaningless taken by itself acts as a clue to the other two, so that the whole set could be brought together into one whole, and then show a single purpose and meaning, we should have good evidence that they all originated from a single source" (p. 34). Under these circumstances it might be argued that the second automatist could not have obtained the necessary information by paranormally cognizing what the first had written, and likewise with the third automatist and the writings of the first and second. For in this ideal case (to which perhaps no actual case has more than approximated) there is nothing in the words written, nor in the automatist's mind at the time of writing, to indicate what must be written to complete the cross correspondence.

An incomplete outline of a not excessively complex "complex" cross correspondence may perhaps most simply be presented in tabular form. It is the case generally called the "Hope, Star and Browning Case" (A. Johnson, 1914, pp. 28–49). It began on January 16, 1907, when Piddington asked Myers$_p$ (Mrs. Piper's Myers control) if he would indicate when a cross correspondence was being attempted by, for instance, drawing a circle with a triangle inside. This theme was apparently taken up and developed in the (quite independent) automatic writings of Mrs. and Miss Verrall (see pp. 596–597):

Here the drawings and the Browning references which appeared in the scripts of Mrs. and Miss Verrall are represented by Myers$_p$ on March 13, as having a common origin, viz. in effect his own associations to Piddington's suggestion of January 16. Saltmarsh (1938) says of this case: "[It] seems to fulfil the requirements for an ideal cross correspondence pretty nearly. We have a complex set of references made allusively and by implication in the scripts of two automatists, so that, taken by themselves, they are quite meaningless. In the third, Mrs. Piper's, the words are given outright and thus disclose the clue by means of which the whole puzzle is made clear" (p. 71). On the face of it there is at work here a purposive intelligence other than those of the various automatists. Whether it is the intelligence of the deceased Myers is an altogether larger question. One might construct an alternative explanation as follows: Mrs. Verrall, and to a lesser extent Mrs. Piper and Miss Verrall, were aware of the possibility of concordant automatisms and of the survivalist interpretation of them; each was also by this time aware of the identity of the other automatists whose scripts could be involved. Suppose that Mrs. Verrall, the central figure, was by ESP continually but unconsciously monitoring the activities and productions of the other automatists. Then she could have become at some level aware of Piddington's suggestion to Myers$_p$ on January 16. Her scripts of January 23 and January 28, with their "star" allusions, Browning quotations, and circle and triangle drawings, represent her own unconscious elaboration of Piddington's theme. It might next be supposed that the other automatists paranormally

Date	Mrs. Piper	Mrs. Verrall	Miss Verrall
Jan 16, 1907	Piddington suggests to Myers p triangle in circle sign for cross-correspondence.		
Jan 23, 1907		Writes: an anagram would be better. Tell him that—rats, star, tars and so on . . . [Myers in life was a devotee of the anagram].	
Jan 28, 1907		Writes: Aster [Greek = star] Teras [Greek = wonder]. The world's wonder. And all a wonder and a wild desire. The very wings of her. A WINGED DESIRE. Upopteros eros [Greek = winged love]. Then there is Blake. And mocked my loss of liberty. But it is all the same thing—the winged desire. Eros potheinos [Greek = love, the much-desired] the hope that leaves the earth for the sky— Abt Vogler—for earth too hard that found itself or lost itself—in the sky. That is what I want. On earth the broken sounds. Threads. In the sky, the perfect arc. The C major of this life. But your recollection is at fault. [Much of this consists of quotations from Robert Browning. The word "hope" has been substituted for "passion"]. There followed drawings of a triangle inside a circle and of a triangle inside a semicircle.	

Feb 3, 1907		Drew a monogram, a star and a crescent and wrote: A monogram, the crescent moon, remember that, and the star.
Feb 11, 1907	Myers$_p$ writes: Did she [Mrs. Verrall] receive the word evangelical [later corrected to Evelyn Hope, the title of a poem by Browning]? I referred also to Browning again. I referred to Hope and Browning . . . I also said star.	
Feb 17, 1907		Drew a star. Wrote: That was the sign she will understand when she sees it . . . No arts avail . . . and a star above it all rats everywhere in Hamelin town [reference to Browning's poem on the Pied Piper of Hamelin].
Mar 6, 1907	Myers$_p$ tells Piddington he has given Mrs. Verrall a circle and a triangle, but doubts that the latter appeared.	
Mar 13, 1907	Myers$_p$ reports that he drew a circle and a triangle for Mrs. Verrall and then said "But it suggested a poem to my mind, hence BHS" [i.e. Browning, Hope, Star].	
Apr 8, 1907	Myers$_p$ draws a circle and adds he drew a star and also a crescent.	

cognized the drawings and references to "star" and recognized the not very obscure Browning quotations. They then incorporated these themes in their own writings and threw the ball to and fro for a few weeks. At the end of this time Mrs. Piper brought the whole to an artistic conclusion by having her Myers control claim responsibility for the correspondences. Mrs. Piper was, however, a lady of slight education, and it might be that she could not herself have produced the literary references which her own scripts contained or have recognized such references in the scripts of others. In that case one might assign a more active role to Mrs. Verrall, or rather to her unconscious mind or subliminal self, and suppose that she somehow infiltrated her own literary fantasies, and the dramatic framework within which they were elaborated, into the depths of the other automatists' minds, whence they emerged in the forms set down above.

This is essentially the position taken by Podmore (1910, pp. 225-276), in his acute early critique of the cross correspondence cases, with which compare Pigou (1909), Maxwell (1912), and E. M. Sidgwick (1913). Podmore states: "From one point of view the experiments may be claimed to have been completely successful. The masterly collation and analysis of the three sets of scripts [i.e. Mrs. Verrall's, Mrs. Piper's, and Mrs. Holland's] (including also a few automatic writings by Miss Verrall) undertaken by Mr. Piddington reveal coincidences of thought and expression too numerous and too detailed to be accounted for by chance" (pp. 237-238). But beyond this Podmore is not prepared to go. He can "see no evidence whatever to justify the assumption, even provisionally, of a directing intelligence other than those of the automatists concerned" (p. 276). His principal reasons for adopting this view appear to be these: (a) Myers was the purported instigator of these cross correspondences; and yet the "Myers" who controlled Mrs. Piper and played an important part in the dénouement of some of the cases, was never able unequivocally to state the principle of the cross correspondences. (b) There is in at least one case, the "Sevens" case (A. Johnson, 1910, pp. 222-258), evidence that Mrs. Verrall was in some sense "behind" a highly complex and allusive cross correspondence. Between April and July, 1908, the scripts of a number of automatists, including Mrs. Verrall, were filled with allusions to the number *Seven*. Several of these allusions were also clearly references to passages in Dante's *Purgatorio*. It transpired that J. G. Piddington, one of the principal investigators of the cross correspondences, had all his life had an obsession with the number seven, and had deposited with the S.P.R. a sealed message to that effect which was to serve as a "posthumous test." There was, however, no reference to Dante in his letter. Mrs. Verrall, however, had lately been reading Dante. Podmore's view (1910) of the matter is as follows: "Mr. Piddington had for years been repeating *Seven* for all the world—that is, all the world within the range of his telepathic influence— to hear. His is a voice crying in the wilderness, however, until it happens that Mrs. Verrall reads the *Divine Comedy*, and the idea of *Seven*, already latent in her mind, is reinforced by a series of Dante images. Mrs. Verrall then . . . swells the stream of telepathic influence, and the effects, in the five remaining automatists, rise to the surface of the dream consciousness" (p. 273).

It is impossible here to discuss further the cross correspondences and the many problems they raise. On the "Plan" alleged to lie behind the whole series of writings produced by the S.P.R. automatists see H. Salter (1951) and W. H. Salter (1961). Two concluding comments may be made—firstly, that very few of those who have seriously investigated the cross correspondences are prepared to ascribe them to fraud or wholly to chance; and secondly, that Podmore's theory about Mrs. Verrall cannot give us the whole story, for the cross correspondences continued for some years after her death.

Closely related to the cross correspondences are the remarkable cases generally known as the "literary puzzles," with which should be compared certain communications through Mrs. Piper (Sidgwick et al., 1910, and cf. Podmore, 1910, pp. 255-276). The medium concerned in the literary puzzles was Mrs. Willett, and the ostensible communicators were two lately deceased classical scholars, A. W. Verrall and S. H. Butcher. Verrall had some, but not a close, connection with the S.P.R. automatists through his wife. It is important to note that Mrs. Willett, though well-read in general literature, was in no sense a classical scholar. The cases concerned are the "Statius" case and the "Ear of Dionysius" case (G. W. Balfour, 1914, 1918). Both are much too long to include an adequate summary. In barest outline, the "Ear of Dionysius" case involved mention of or allusions to the following topics in various Willett scripts (mostly during 1914):

The Ear of Dionysius. (A cave which Dionysius the Elder, tyrant of Syracuse 405-367 B.C., had utilized to listen to possibly seditious conversations among prisoners. This cave opens from certain stone quarries in Sicily. It had been referred to once in a Willett script of 1910, and Mrs. Verrall had asked Professor Verrall about it.)

The stone quarries of Syracuse.

Enna (in Sicily).

The heel of Italy.

Ulysses and Polyphemus (the one-eyed giant who imprisoned Ulysses in his cave).

Acis and Galatea (Acis, a shepherd, loved the nymph Galatea, and was murdered by the jealous Polyphemus).

Jealousy.

Music. A Zither.

Aristotle's *Poetics*.

Satire.

A script of August, 1915, contained the following, S. H. Butcher being the ostensible communicator (G. W. Balfour, 1918, pp. 220-221):

The Aural instruction was I think understood *Aural* appertaining to the Ear . . .

And now he asks HAS the *Satire* satire been identified . . .
the man clung to the fleece of a Ram and so passed out surely that is plain
[i.e. Ulysses leaving Polyphemus' cave] . . .
well conjoin that with Cythera and the Ear-man . . .
There is a Satire
write Cyclopean . . .
Philox He laboured in the stone quarries and drew upon the earlier writer
for material for his Satire Jealousy
The story is quite clear to me and I think it should be identified a musical
instrument comes in something like a mandoline thrumming . . .
He wrote in those stone quarries belonging to the Tyrant . . .

This script links together the cryptic references listed above. Philoxenus of
Cythera (435–380 B.C) is a far from well-known Greek poet (none of the investigators knew anything about him) who was at one time under the protection of
Dionysius the Elder of Syracuse. He was the author of a satirical dithyrambic
poem, entitled either *Cyclops* or *Galatea*, which, according to one story, had its
origin in the following way. Philoxenus seduced Dionysius' mistress, Galatea,
and was in consequence imprisoned in the stone quarries by the jealous tyrant.
After his release Philoxenus wrote the satire in question to revenge himself on
Dionysius. He represented himself as Ulysses, and Dionysius, who was blind in
one eye, as Polyphemus. Dithyrambic poetry was usually recited to the
accompaniment of a zither. Aristotle's *Poetics* (II, 4) mentions Philoxenus'
Cyclops.
The classical and literary knowledge displayed by the communicators in constructing this puzzle was considerable (only a most incomplete idea of it is
conveyed above). Such knowledge was possessed by the communicators but was
certainly not possessed by Mrs. Willett. The story of Philoxenus' imprisonment
was not to be found in the requisite detail in any of a number of standard reference books. It was given in a work which Mrs. Verrall discovered among Dr.
Verrall's books, a work which he had used in the preparation of certain lectures.
Butcher had translated Aristotle's *Poetics*. Mrs. Verrall stated that the name of
Philoxenus meant nothing to her and that she was entirely ignorant of the story.
Thus the supposition that Mrs. Willett obtained the classical information by
telepathy with Mrs. Verrall lacks evidential support.
In both the Statius and the Ear of Dionysius scripts, but especially the former,
there were many touches which those well qualified to judge regarded as highly
characteristic of Verrall and of Butcher, the latter of whom was not known to
Mrs. Willett.

APPARITIONS AND OUT-OF-BODY EXPERIENCES AS BEARING UPON THE CONTINUITY HYPOTHESIS

Prior to the start of the modern Spiritualist movement in 1848, it was in Western
Europe unusual, though not unknown, for an ostensible return *d'outre-tombe* to

take a mediumistic form. Far commoner were stories of *revenants*, apparitions of deceased persons. Such stories attracted a good deal of attention in the sixteenth century and were the subject of theological dispute between Protestant and Catholic writers (see, e.g., Lavater, 1572, and Leloyer's criticisms of him, 1605, pp. 556-679). In the seventeenth century attempts were made to counteract a growing religious skepticism by a systematic collection of contemporary ghost stories. More generally, one may say that apparitions are a perennial feature of human experience. They have been reported from all times and in all societies of which we have detailed records. The most commonly proferred explanation of them has perhaps been that we each possess, intermingled with our physical organism, a duplicate or subtle body of some exceedingly tenuous matter (see Mead, 1919), a body which may be or become the vehicle of our mental attributes and which may survive the dissolution of our fleshly bodies.

This view of apparitions has been rejected by the great majority of modern parapsychologists, who regard them as hallucinations, as having no external reality. The principal grounds for this assertion are the following (see Tyrrell, 1953, pp. 53-60): Although apparitions very often look and behave like ordinary human beings (the transparent or grotesque apparitions of legend, though known, are not common), they tend to vanish suddenly, leaving no trace behind; to perform physically impossible feats such as passing through doors or walls; and to move instantaneously from one place to another. Some apparitions have symbolic appurtenances or companions, or behave in an obviously symbolic manner. For example, L. E. Rhine (1961) cites a case in which the apparition of a person just deceased was accompanied by the figure of Christ and another in which the apparition floated away as if to a Heaven in the sky. There have even been cases in which apparitions have been seen, e.g., to open locked doors which upon examination proved to be still locked (Bennett, 1939, case 62). The opening of the doors was part of a whole hallucinatory episode. Against these considerations may be set firstly a small number of "ghost" photographs, exceedingly difficult to interpret, and secondly the very great theoretical difficulties raised by cases in which apparitions have been simultaneously perceived by more than one person (on these difficulties see, e.g., Broad, 1962, Chap. 9; Hart, 1956, pp. 201-215; Gurney, Myers, and Podmore, 1886, Vol. 2, pp. 277-316; Tyrrell, 1953, pp. 109-115). The balance of evidence undoubtedly favors the hallucination view, but one can hardly adhere to it without some reservation.

Even if one accepts that apparitions are hallucinatory, many problems remain. For among the somewhat numerous cases of which the firsthand records have been published by the British and American Societies for Psychical Research there are a substantial number in which the hallucinations—if hallucinations they were—may be described as "veridical." By this is meant that the hallucinations concerned corresponded, in ways for which no ordinary explanation is forthcoming, either with some external event or with the experiences of another percipient or percipients. Useful collections of such cases are found in Gurney et al.

(1886), Myers (1903, Vol. 1, Chap. 6), Podmore (1894, 1909), E. M. Sidgwick (1923), Prince (1928), W. H. Salter (1938), Bennett (1939), Dale (1951), Tyrrell (1953), MacKenzie (1971), Green and McCreery (1975). Among "veridical" cases the following kinds may be particularly noted:

1. *Collectively Perceived Apparitions.* In such cases two or more persons simultaneously see what is *prima facie* the same phantasmal figure in the same place. It sometimes happens that a person who is seemingly in a position to see an apparition which another person can see does not see it. Hart (1956, p. 204) states that of 46 cases in the literature in which second percipients were in a position to see an apparition, 26 were cases of collective percipiency. A review of the evidence for collective percipiency is given by Hart and Hart (1933). Cases of classes 2, 3, and 4 below may in addition be cases of collective percipiency.

2. *"Crisis" Apparitions.* Crisis apparitions (see especially Gurney et al., 1886; E. M. Sidgwick, 1923) are by far the most numerous cases of veridical apparitions. In such cases the percipient sees the apparition of some distant person (usually but not always a friend or relative) at or about the time when that person undergoes some unexpected crisis in his affairs (frequently death). The convention is that for an apparition to qualify as a "crisis" apparition, it must be seen within 12 hours before or after the crisis.

A most intensive effort was made by a group of early S.P.R. members to disprove what might be called the "chance-coincidence" view of crisis apparitions. According to this view, hallucinations as of seeing some person known to one are fairly common—common enough for a moderate number of them to coincide with the deaths of the persons concerned. When there is such a coincidence, the percipient will feel free to talk about his experience; otherwise he will remain silent, fearing to be thought abnormal. This argument was countered with the results of a number of "Censuses of Hallucinations" (Gurney et al., 1886, Vol. 2, Chap. 3; Sidgwick, Sidgwick, and Johnson, 1894). These censuses attempted to establish what might be called the "basic hallucination rate" in the population at large and then, by various statistical arguments, to show that the coincidences between "crisis" hallucinations and the deaths of the persons seen could not be ascribed to chance. In an analysis of the results of the largest of these censuses, a British one in which 17,000 persons were questioned, it was claimed that, when every allowance had been made for possibly contaminating factors, the number of death coincidences exceeded the chance prediction by a factor of 440. The methods and statistics used in these old censuses would not today be thought adequate, but this figure is so large that it is very difficult to dispose of. However, a later, but far less extensive survey conducted by more modern methods (West, 1948b) unearthed no satisfactory crisis cases. A further large survey seems called for.

Among those who accept that the death-coincidence cases cannot be explained away as due to chance, the theory of crisis apparitions propounded by Gurney

(Gurney et al., 1886) on the basis of a large collection of firsthand cases has, with one modification or another, found widespread acceptance. The essence of this theory is as follows: Crisis apparitions are, for reasons such as those indicated above, to be regarded as hallucinations. But there remains the problem, which cannot be dismissed by specious hypotheses about chance coincidence, of the correspondences between these hallucinations and the deaths or difficulties of the persons they represent. These correspondences, according to Gurney, may be explained on the theory that the percipients learn of the deaths, which are very often those of persons well known or closely related to them, through extrasensory perception. Extrasensory perception operates at unconscious or subliminal levels of the personality, which then dramatize the information received and transmit it to consciousness in the form of an hallucinatory quasi-perception. Gurney supports this proposal by two considerations (both of which receive ample support from his own and later collections of cases; see, e.g., L. E. Rhine, 1961). Firstly, cases of apparent spontaneous ESP can be arranged in a series beginning with those in which the percipient's experience is without sensory content (he simply "knows" that something is amiss; see, e.g., Stevenson, 1970a) and extending through innumerable gradations to cases, e.g., of ESP in dreams or on the border between sleep and waking, experiences between which and crisis apparitions no sharp line can be drawn. Secondly, the details of the figures seen very often correspond not to the actual situation and appearance of the dying person, but to the percipient's memory of that person, and the figures may even have symbolical accompaniments, e.g., a hearse, the figure of Christ, which harmonize with the percipient's ideas. However, difficulties arise for this theory in the case of apparitions which are collectively perceived (see above), and these difficulties have led some writers to follow Myers (Gurney et al., 1886, Vol. 2, pp. 277-316; Myers, 1903, Vol. 1, Chap. 6) in postulating some kind of actual "excursus" by the person whom the apparition represents.

3. *Haunting Apparitions.* In cases of haunting apparitions the same, or apparently the same, figure is seen in the same locality on a series of different occasions by the same or different percipients. Such cases may, but usually do not, also fall under the next heading. A useful collection of cases from the publications of the S.P.R. is given by Collins (1948). A classic early case history is reported by Morton (1892); see also Collins (1948). For some interesting experiments in which a series of mediums or sensitives were independently taken to the same "haunted" house, see Moss and Schmeidler (1968).

4. *Apparitions of Deceased Persons.* Such apparitions may be classed as "veridical" if either (a) the percipient did not know and had no reason to suspect that the person in question had died, (b) the apparition was of some deceased person not known to the percipient but subsequently recognized by him from a photograph or detailed description, or better still picked out by him from a series of photographs or descriptions, or (c) the apparition conveyed some information

once known to the deceased person concerned, but previously unknown to the percipient. Of especial interest here is information the conveying of which seems calculated to fulfill some desire characteristic of the deceased. Classic early papers on post-mortem apparitions are E. M. Sidgwick (1885), Myers (1889, 1890, 1892), and Podmore (1889).

The evidence for veridical apparitions is, of course, almost entirely anecdotal. How acceptable is evidence of this kind? Some writers (see especially West, 1948a) seem prepared to dismiss almost all of it, along with much of the evidence for spontaneous cases in general. Their principal grounds for skepticism are (a) that in only a few cases did the percipients at once write down a detailed account of their experiences, (b) that consequently there is every scope for errors of memory, which will naturally tend to exaggerate the veridical features of a case, (c) that there is both experimental and anecdotal evidence that memory of dramatic events or narratives is subject not just to errors of omission, but to quite considerable distortions and to the importation of fictitious material, and (d) that there is also experimental evidence that people may misperceive or fail to note important details of events taking place before their eyes. The principal counterarguments (see especially Stevenson, 1968c, pp. 99–115) are (a) that we do have such accounts in a modest number of cases (for an early list of such cases see Myers, 1903, Vol. 1, p. 642) and (b) that there is no evidence that experients in spontaneous cases have a *general* tendency toward retrospective exaggeration. On the contrary—Stevenson cites a number of instances in which responsible witnesses have rewritten their accounts many years after the event without substantial changes or exaggerations, and Hart (1956, pp. 169–172), surveying a large number of apparition stories, finds no sign of an inverse correlation between the evidential standing of reports and their dramatic qualities. There has come to light evidence that the case of retrospective exaggeration most commonly cited—the "Hornby" case—may not have been an example of exaggeration after all (Gauld, 1965, pp. 61–62). (c) and (d) The kinds of errors and distortions of memory found, e.g., by Bartlett (1932), generally tend toward making the accounts or events concerned less dramatic and more conventional. Furthermore, there is experimental evidence that persons who are under pressure to be accurate are less prone to distortions of memory than were the subjects in Bartlett's experiments (Gauld and Stephenson, 1967).

If we are prepared to discount the objections which have been offered against anecdotal evidence, the question arises: To what extent do cases of veridical apparitions constitute evidence for survival? It is, of course, obvious that only cases of veridical apparitions of deceased persons, cases of class 4 above, can yield such evidence, although these cases may in addition be cases of haunting or of collective percipiency. There are also in the literature one or two very extraordinary cases in which a large number of persons have individually or collectively seen the phantasm of a deceased person in or around the locality where that person once lived (see Ducasse, 1961, pp. 21–23, 154–156), but such cases do not *per se* constitute evidence for survival as that has been defined for the purpose of this article, for we stipulated that the mere post-mortem recrudescence of someone's external characteristics is not evidence for the survival of his personality.

Among cases of class 4, it is cases of class 4(c) which principally concern us. Cases of class 4(a), ones which are labeled "veridical" simply because the percipient learns, or guesses, from the apparition that the person whom the apparition represents has died, are not uncommon, but for the reasons just mentioned do not qualify as "evidence for survival" unless they also fall under class 4(c). Cases of class 4(b), ones in which the percipient sees a figure not known to him and subsequently recognizes it from a photograph or description as resembling a person who once frequented the spot, are rather uncommon. Some examples were collected by Bennett (1939, cases 5, 8, 18, 23, 25, 29, 31, 36; and cf. Lambert, 1966, and Tyrrell, 1953, case 45). But in none of these cases is there much to suggest the recrudescence of a personality as distinct from the recrudescence of someone's external characteristics or of some past scene.

Cases of class 4(c), ones in which the apparition conveys information once known to the deceased person concerned, especially information which tends to the fulfillment of some desire characteristic of the deceased, are likewise somewhat rare, though instances will be found in most of the collections of cases listed above. Popular legend often ascribes continuing purpose and recollection of the past to the traditional haunting ghost. But only rather rarely is it possible to "identify" the apparition, even tentatively, with a particular deceased person. Thus the question of continuing purpose and continuing memory can in general not even be raised. Furthermore, the majority of recurrent localized apparitions seem *prima facie* quite aimless. Occasional examples can, however, be found both of recurrent and of nonrecurrent apparitions which seem to fulfill the requirements for class 4(c). Several of those commonly cited, however, seem to have involved dreams rather than waking hallucinations. In the Chaffin Will case ("Case of the Will of Mr. James L. Chaffin," 1927; Z. Richmond, 1938, pp. 28-32) and the Conley case (Myers, 1903, Vol. 2, pp. 37-40), the deceased fathers of the percipients concerned appeared to them in dreams and revealed the location of objects (a will; a sum of money) whose whereabouts seem to have been unknown to any living person. (The last 13 Cantos of Dante's *Paradiso* are said to have been recovered through a similar incident.) In fact, it is hardly possible to draw any hard and fast line between veridical dreams and veridical apparitions, and in some cases, e.g., the Wünscher case (a nonrecurrent case of class 4[c]), an experience which began as a dream was continued as a waking hallucination (Myers, 1903, Vol. 1, pp. 433-435).

A nonrecurrent case of class 4(c) which may have been either an hallucination or a dream, and in which there is manifested both a continuing purpose and knowledge which the percipient did not previously possess, is the following (Myers, 1903) reported by Miss Lucy Dodson:

September 14th, 1891

On June 5th, 1887, a Sunday evening, between eleven and twelve at night, being awake, my name was called three times. I answered twice, thinking it was my uncle, "Come in, Uncle George, I am awake," but the third time I recognized the voice as that of my mother, who had been dead sixteen years. I said "Mamma!" She then came round a screen near my bedside with two children in her arms, and placed them in my arms and put the bedclothes over them and said, "Lucy, promise me to take care of them, for their mother is just dead." I said "Yes, mamma." She repeated, *"Promise* me to take care of them." I replied, "Yes, I promise you," and I added, "Oh, mamma, stay and speak to me, I am so wretched." She replied "Not yet, my child," then she seemed to go round the screen again, and I remained, feeling the children to be still in my arms, and fell asleep. When I awoke there was nothing. Tuesday morning, June 7th, I received the news of my sister-in-law's death. She had given birth to a child three weeks before, which I did not know till after her death . . . (Vol. 2, pp. 32–33).

Miss Dodson's statement is accompanied by various documents confirming the background circumstances of the case. Though at the time of the apparition she was in a state of anxiety about certain family matters, she was not specially thinking about her brother, whom she had not seen for 6 years. The case is, however, like most others in class 4(c), quite easy to interpret in terms of the super-ESP hypothesis. One need only suppose that Miss Dodson obtained by ESP the information about the interrelated birth and death, and somehow externalized this information as a phantasm of her deceased mother, symbolically with the two (living) children in her arms.

A special class of post-mortem apparitions which might be regarded as veridical is that of "take-away" apparitions, i.e., the not uncommon cases in which a dying person sees the apparition of a deceased individual known to him, which "calls him away" verbally, or by look or gesture. In some cases the figure has been seen by others present (see Prince, 1928, pp. 144–150). Osis (1961, 1975; cf. Barrett, 1926) reports that "take-away" apparitions are predominant among the hallucinations commonly experienced by dying persons. Osis (1975) believes that "the data give support to the hypothesis of survival after death." The hallucinations concerned are not, he says, the products of "brain sickness," for "people with these medical factors saw fewer apparitions which wanted to take them away. People who were clear-brained saw more such figures." They do not appear to be wish-fulfillments, for they are as likely to appear to percipients who believe that they will recover as to those who know that they are dying. They are not much affected by the percipients' religious hopes and expectations, for they take similar forms in different cultures. It might be argued that these facts are compatible with the view that the percipients in these cases precognize their own deaths and dramatize this knowledge in the form of an appropriate hallucination, just as they might have done if they had become paranormally aware of the death of a close friend or relative. However, on this view we might expect "take-away" apparitions to be frequent, as are crisis apparitions, when the imminent death is sudden and unexpected.

It will by now be apparent that I do not regard cases of veridical post-mortem apparitions as constituting very strong evidence in favor of the continuity hypothesis. Indeed, with only a very few exceptions, such as the unique and hence debatable Claughton case (Collins, 1948, pp. 187–212; Maitland, 1953; Myers, 1895, pp. 547–559), the experiences concerned are too brief to have the kind of evidential complexity which can stretch the super-ESP hypothesis. However, if other evidence for the continuity hypothesis—especially the evidence from mediumistic phenomena—is accepted as convincing, then it may well be that cases of veridical apparitions can easily and naturally be brought within its scope.

There is one class of phenomena which has been thought to link up with cases of apparitions in such a way as to support the continuity hypothesis of post-mortem apparitions, namely, the phenomena termed "out-of-body experiences" (OBEs) or "ecsomatic experiences." Green (1968) defines an ecsomatic experience as "one in which the objects of perception are apparently organized in such a way that the observer seems to himself to be observing them from a point of view which is not coincident with his physical body" (p. 17). Such experiences are by no means uncommon, but as yet no "Census of OBEs" has been carried out to give a proper idea of their frequency in our culture. Such an endeavor, perhaps combined with a more modern "Census of Hallucinations," would probably obtain a rich harvest of cases. A British press and radio appeal for cases in 1966 obtained some 400 replies (Green, 1968). Of "single" cases (i.e., cases which represented the experient's only OBE), 32.7 percent occurred when the subject was anesthetized or otherwise unconscious, and 12 percent were initiated during sleep. In 73 percent of cases the subject was lying down, but in a small number of instances he was engaged in physical activity, which generally continued more or less unimpaired during the OBE. Some 25 percent of cases were preceded by some form of short-term or long-term psychological stress. Other collections of spontaneous OB cases, mostly taken from printed sources, are to be found in Crookall (1961, 1964) and Muldoon and Carrington (1929, 1951). The experience of the percipient in these cases is usually that of seeing his own body and its immediate surroundings from a vantage point somewhere above it, but sometimes the percipient may appear to himself to travel a considerable distance from his body, and (rather rarely) to meet deceased persons, other "astral travelers," etc., or to reach the borders of the next world (usually visualized in some appropriate and symbolic form). Experiences of these more exciting kinds are commoner in accounts written by persons who claim to have developed techniques of having OBEs at will (Fox, 1962; Lancelin, 1913; Monroe, 1971; Muldoon and Carrington, 1929) than in the records of spontaneous OBEs. Such persons also commonly find themselves possessed of a second body, connected to their physical body by a tenuous "cord." (The idea that the "subtle body" is connected to the rather less than subtle one by such a "cord" is mentioned as early as Plutarch's *De Sera Numinis Vindicta*.) In contrast, 80 percent of Green's subjects (whose OBEs were almost always involuntary) reported that they found themselves a "disembodied consciousness," while only 3.5 percent mentioned the "cord."

It is impossible to pursue here a discussion of OBEs (on OBEs in general, see Durville, 1929; Eastman, 1962; Green, 1967; Heywood, 1968; B. Walker, 1974; Whiteman, 1961; for anthropological material, see Eliade, 1970). It is only with a rather small subclass of these cases that we are immediately concerned. Whatever the psychological interest of OBEs, and whatever their effects on the religious and philosophical beliefs of the experients, we should have no grounds for regarding them as anything other than somewhat bizarre hallucinations were it not for the fact that in a few apparently well-authenticated cases the percipient in an OBE has acquired by a quasi-visual process correct information about some matter of fact information which he could not have obtained through the sense organs of his physical body. (For experimental work relating to this question, see, e.g., Palmer and Lieberman, 1975; Palmer and Vassar, 1974; Tart, 1968.) Furthermore, in a very scanty number of these cases, the phantasm of the experient has been observed at the locality which he seemed to himself to have visited during his OBE. Small collections of cases of these two kinds, mostly taken from the publications of the S.P.R., are to be found in, e.g., Broad (1962, pp. 167–178), R. C. Johnson (1953, pp. 220–229), and Tyrrell (1953, pp. 149–154). A number of Green's cases fall into the former category.

Hart (1956), who cites various cases of conscious apparitions of the living, developed an ingenious argument. Analysis of the reported characteristics of apparitions of the dying and the dead and those of conscious "projectors" shows that the two categories of apparition belong, as it were, to the same population. They do not differ significantly in "externals." Since the apparitions of conscious projectors "have been shown (at least tentatively) to be of the same basic nature as apparitions of the dying and the dead," the experiences of the projectionists "may be regarded, provisionally, as conveying something of the nature of the experiences undergone at and (to a limited extent) after death" (p. 177).

This argument would, if valid, support not just the continuity hypothesis, but the continuity hypothesis in its strong or "survivalist" form. It has, however, to overcome at least the following objections: (a) Hart's argument seems to presuppose that when the apparition of a projectionist is observed at a spot which he seems to himself to be visiting, there is some sense in which the projectionist himself, having quitted his physical body, is present there *in propria persona* (cf. Myers, 1903, Vol. 1, pp. 264–265). It is, however, possible to interpret such cases in terms of reciprocal ESP between the projectionist and those who see his phantasm. The projectionist, so the story goes, acquires by ESP information about events transpiring in some distant locality and constructs therefrom a more or less accurate hallucination representing that scene. Persons at that scene acquire by ESP information as to the percipient's hallucination and embody this information in a phantasmal representation of him. Now if this be an admissible interpretation of these projection cases, Hart's transition from cases of "ESP projection" to cases of veridical apparitions of the dead loses much of its plausibility. For if the apparition of the projectionist is simply the mode in which the percipient dramatizes and makes manifest his paranormally acquired information about the projectionist's current hallucination, why should we not suppose that the percipients of post-mortem apparitions are simply dramatizing into hallucinatory form information, gleaned, e.g., by telepathy with the living, about the characteristics of some deceased person who once frequented the locality? (b) There are on record cases of "veridical" apparitions of living persons in which the person whose phantasm was seen had no abnormal experience, no experience as of traveling to a distant scene. For example, certain "arrival" cases—cases in which the phantasm of a living person has been seen at a certain spot a few minutes prior to his actual arrival at that spot—seem to fulfill these requirements (see Gurney et al., 1886, Vol. 2, pp. 96-100; Myers, 1903, Vol. 1, 255-257, 272-274). This strongly suggests that at least some apparitions do not constitute or contain centers of consciousness. Hence we can neither assume nor of course deny that veridical crisis or post-mortem apparitions do so.

EMPIRICAL CONSIDERATIONS TELLING AGAINST THE CONTINUITY HYPOTHESIS

The empirical considerations commonly advanced against the continuity hypothesis (see especially Dodds, 1934; Flew, 1953; Podmore, 1902, 1910) may conveniently be set forth under three headings:

1. Evidence suggesting that mediumistic controls and communicators are, despite the correct information which they sometimes deploy and the verisimilitude which they sometimes attain, only phases or aspects of the medium's own personality.

2. Evidence ostensibly telling against the continuity hypothesis in its strong, or "survivalist," form.

3. Evidence ostensibly telling against the continuity hypothesis in any form whatsoever.

1. This issue was touched upon earlier, and it was pointed out that though the evidence that mediumistic communicators are, generally at least, not independent persons is very strong, this does not altogether rule out the continuity hypothesis. It remains possible that the drama of ongoing communication with the dead, which the medium builds up from the dramatic resources of her subliminal self, is somehow influenced or even partly directed by entities or factors which enjoy

some kind of continuity with the organism or personality of a now deceased human being.

2. The arguments most commonly advanced against the strong or survivalist form of the continuity hypothesis are of two kinds. The first is put thus by Professor E. R. Dodds in a celebrated paper (1934):

> Now if the dead are really endowed with powers so varied and so remarkable . . . is it not matter for surprise that they refrained for so long from exercising their powers and making their existence known? During two and a half millennia of which we have fairly full written records—say from 650 B.C. to A.D. 1850—they failed so far as I know to produce satisfactory experimental evidence of their identity. Why? . . . Nor was there any lack of the necessary machinery or the necessary interest on the side of the living: the evidence collected in Oesterreich's book on Possession shows that the mediumistic trance is a fairly constant phenomenon in all ages and among all peoples; and curiosity about the state of the dead has left its mark on the literature alike of Greece and Rome, of the Middle Ages, and of the Renaissance. But there is something more singular still. The two groups of pre-nineteenth century mediums about whom we have most information, the κάτοχοι [those held down or overpowered, and hence, derivatively, possessed] of the late Graeco-Roman period and the witches of the sixteenth and seventeenth centuries, while performing a number of the feats performed by modern mediums, perversely attributed them in the one case to the agency of non-human gods or demons, in the other to the agency of the devil. Once again, why? (pp. 152–153).

Dodds perhaps exaggerates somewhat. In many non-European cultures ostensible communication with ancestral spirits by methods very much like those of modern mediums has without doubt been practiced for many centuries. Of course there is no "evidence for survival" here, but that could be because no one in these societies would think such evidence necessary. Even in our own culture it is possible to find occasional pre-1850 instances of ostensible possession by deceased persons (see, e.g., Kerner, 1834), and the κάτοχοι were sometimes ostensibly so possessed (Dodds, 1971, pp. 236–237). Stories of *revenants* have always been widespread. It would, however, not be unfair to say that even in the period since 1850 the initiative for ostensible mediumistic communication with the dead has in a large majority of cases come from the living. Yet if people survive death with their memories and affections more or less intact, surely many of them would wish to convey messages of comfort and reassurance to surviving relatives. Why are there not more "drop in" cases? If cases of verified drop in communicators with messages for living relatives were more numerous than they are, the survivalist position would surely be stronger; and if there were numerous drop in cases in which the same communicator delivered his message, or parts of his message, through different mediums, the survivalist position would surely be very greatly strengthened.

The second common line of argument against the survivalist hypothesis is based upon the triviality and banality of so many mediumistic communications, including ones ostensibly from persons who in life were noted for their literary and intellectual gifts. Furthermore, communicators who manifest through different mediums may well give accounts of the afterlife which differ in important details, e.g., as to whether reincarnation is the rule. However, this argument loses a good deal of its force if it be accepted that communicators do not literally control the medium's organism but may be aspects or facets of her own personality somehow shaped and (somewhat imperfectly) directed by the deceased persons whose names and superficial identities they assume. The banality is the medium's. The very occasional rising above banality—as when an ostensibly communicating Edmund Gurney showed a knowledge of philosophical terms greatly exceeding Mrs. Willett's (G. W. Balfour, 1935), and the ostensibly communicating Verrall and Butcher showed a knowledge of classical literature greatly exceeding hers—may represent the influence of the communicators.

3. The evidence which ostensibly tells against the continuity hypothesis in any form may be subdivided into (a) evidence that the "dispositions," memory and other, which are supposed to survive death depend entirely upon, and are indeed constituted by, certain aspects of brain functioning and thus cannot survive the dissolution of the physical organism, (b) evidence that ESP of something like the magnitude required by the super-ESP hypothesis can take place, and (c) evidence that such ESP is actually put to use by mediums in constructing their dramatic impersonations. The conjoint effect of (b) and (c) is of course simply to render the continuity hypothesis superfluous.

(a) This problem cannot be tackled in detail here. It seems to me, however, that although physiologists have acquired a great deal of information about the effect of brain lesions, brain stimulation, drugs, neurochemicals, and senile decay upon memory dispositions and other dispositions, they have not yet shown that these dispositions *are* states of the brain substance. To prove this, they would need to show not, e.g., that such-and-such a substance when absorbed into such-and-such an area of the brain disturbs or fortifies memory dispositions, but precisely how one can pass from an account of complex chemical processes within or between brain cells to an account of particular acts of conceptual memory, such as recollecting a person or incident from one's schooldays or what one was thinking about yesterday after dinner. This has not yet been achieved or even adumbrated, and there appear to me (Gauld, 1966) to be reasons of principle why it can never be achieved within a mechanistic framework of thought. So long as it has not been achieved, the continuity hypothesis has room in which to operate.

(b) The findings most commonly cited in this connection are those of Osty (1923) with certain French sensitives who might, without too much injustice, be described as fortune-tellers. These sensitives generally, though not invariably, were given and held some object which had been worn or carried by the person about whom the sitter desired information. The "psychometric objects" seemed in some way to link the sensitive to the absent person. In many cases cited by Osty, a sensitive gave detailed and correct information about the life history, characteristics, and future of the person with whom she was thus seemingly put in contact. The information given sometimes included points not known to any person present. In scope and accuracy the performances of some of Osty's sensitives, which may be compared with the performance of Mrs. Zierold, Pagenstecher's (1922; see also Prince, 1921) subject, rivaled those of fairly successful mediums, and yet they were given without any suggestion of communications from the dead or of help from the spirits. Thus we have here, it is claimed, evidence for what is truly "super-ESP."

It may be added that mediums, and their guides, frequently talk very much like fortune-tellers. They give information about the present concerns and future prospects of their sitters quite as often as they pass on messages from ostensible relatives and friends. There is no hard-and-fast line between the medium and the fortune-teller. It could accordingly be said that since we know from the work of Osty and others that fortune-tellers possess and utilize super-ESP in their performances, and since mediums cannot be sharply distinguished from fortune-tellers, we may reasonably ascribe even the more striking mediumistic communications to the medium's own super-ESP operating in conjunction with her religious presuppositions and dramatic tendencies.

Three *caveats* must be entered at this point. The first is that Osty's experimental methods and consequently his claims as to the paranormal powers of his sensitives are vulnerable to a number of quite serious criticisms (see, e.g., Schiller, 1924). The second is that there are indications that at least some of his sensitives held Spiritualist beliefs which Osty (1923, pp. 127n, 133) wished to extrude from the experimental situation. The third is that Osty seemed at any rate prepared to consider the possibility that just as sensitives obtain information about living persons by in some way "linking up" with them so they may obtain information about deceased persons by establishing a link with them in the same way as with living ones.

(c) What evidence is there that ESP (or super-ESP) is actually utilized by mental mediums in constructing their dramatic representations of deceased persons? Cases in which the material produced by a medium has apparently been shaped by the thoughts of the sitter are by no means uncommon. Dodds (1934) cites a number of examples:

> ... when Newbold was sitting for automatic writing with Mrs. Piper, an irrelevant (and rare) name, which he had erroneously associated with the supposed communicator, was reproduced as a spirit utterance in Mrs. Piper's script. Again, when the experimenter (Hodgson) thinks about Sir Walter Scott, an obviously fictitious "Sir Walter Scott" communicates next day at

the Piper sitting; when he thinks about D. D. Home, a similarly spurious "Home" presents himself next day. . . . Mrs. Salter heard one evening in conversation an anecdote about a man who wore several pairs of trousers simultaneously; next day at a Leonard sitting the control purporting to be Professor Verrall remarked to Mrs. Salter, "It isn't given to many men to wear two pairs of trousers. Well, I did once, I think you'll remember." Mrs. Salter did not remember (pp. 158–159).

An instance in which a medium apparently picked up the thoughts of the sitter is the "John Ferguson" case, recorded by S. G. Soal (1925, pp. 523-548). During a series of sittings with the London direct-voice medium, Mrs. Blanche Cooper, Soal received communications from a "John Ferguson," who gave various details about himself, all of which ultimately turned out to be false. Soal discovered that if, prior to a sitting, he invented definite hypotheses about John Ferguson and about persons and places supposedly connected with him, those hypotheses would often receive unambiguous confirmation at the sitting concerned. Eventually Mrs. Cooper's controls realized what had been going on, and one of them (ostensibly Soal's deceased brother) said that "His mind was a blank. He caught at any thoughts flying around—he'd have believed he was Jonah if you had told him so."

There is on record at least one case in which a medium apparently utilized in the construction of a communicator paranormal powers so far in excess of mere telepathy with a person present at the sitting that they might well be held to involve super-ESP. This case is again one recorded by Soal (1925, pp. 560-593; 1926) at his sittings with Mrs. Cooper, the case of Gordon Davis. At a sitting on January 4, 1922, Soal's deceased brother, Frank, said: "Sam, I've brought someone who knows you," Then a very clear and strong voice, which seemed "quite familiar" to Soal, began to speak and shortly gave the name "Gordon Davis" from "Roch" (Rochford). Gordon Davis was an old school acquaintance whom Soal believed to have been killed in World War I. Gordon Davis continued to speak. He did not state that he had been killed but said "My poor wife is my only worry now—and kiddie." He went on to refer correctly and unmistakably to persons, places, and events from their schooldays and to a chance later meeting. The communicator used forms of expression characteristic of the real Gordon Davis. Then "Nada," one of Mrs. Cooper's regular controls, took over and said, "Two E's . . . it has to do with the address of his wife." At two subsequent sittings, on January 9 and 30, 1922, Nada relayed further messages from Gordon Davis. These described in considerable detail certain supposed external features of Gordon Davis' house and also made some exceedingly specific references to pictures, ornaments, and furniture it was said to contain. In 1925 Soal learned that Gordon Davis was still alive and went to visit him. A great deal of the information given about his house, its contents, and the arrangement of its contents turned out to be correct. However, Davis and his "wife and kiddie" had not moved into the house until almost a year *after* the relevant sitting. The house was situated in "Eastern Esplanade" ("two E's"), Southend-on-Sea. Gordon Davis' diary showed that at the time of Soal's sittings of January 4 and 9, 1922, he had been busy seeing clients (he was a house agent). He had visited the house in Eastern Esplanade for the first time on January 6, 1922.

Nearly, though not quite, all the information which "Gordon Davis" gave at the first sitting was known to Soal, and, if one is prepared to accept the occurrence of telepathy, one might argue that Soal's recollections of Gordon Davis were stirred into life by an accidental similarity of tone and were then picked up and dramatized by the medium. The information given by Nada was less personal and in scope and content not at all unlike the information sometimes given by Osty's sensitives (1923, pp. 86–87) about persons with whom they had psychometric links. It resembles the Osty material also in referring to the future. It could have been obtained neither by telepathy from the sitter nor wholly by telepathy with the Gordon Davis of 1922. Precognitive telepathy·or clairvoyance relating to the distant Gordon Davis must seemingly have been involved and "super-ESP" does not seem too strong a term to apply to it.

The following line of argument can now be advanced. The cases cited by Dodds and the "John Ferguson" case prove that a medium can incorporate into a "communicating personality" material obtained through extrasensory contact with persons other than the ostensible communicator. The Gordon Davis case shows that a medium can build up a representation of a distant person by means of super-ESP somehow focused on that person, i.e., on the ostensible communicator. Hence it is plausible to assume that such super-ESP, focussed on spatially or temporally distant living persons or person-related events, can be utilized by a medium in building up a characterization of a deceased person, i.e., of someone *not* among those on whom the super-ESP was focused. The occurrence at mediumistic séances of information unknown to sitters, of verified drop in communicators, of correct statements made to proxy sitters, and so on, may then in principle be understood without resort to the continuity hypothesis.

This line of argument, however, like almost all lines of argument in the field of psychical research, is not without its weak points. To start with, the instances of alleged "telepathy with the sitters" cited by Dodds have been divorced from their backgrounds. Questions that need to be asked, and cannot be answered, are: how many times did a sitter think before a sitting of a famous person, or of an odd name, or of an amusing anecdote, and *not* find these things referred to at the next sitting; and how many times were famous persons, or odd names or odd happenings, mentioned at sittings without being antecedently thought of by sitters? The "John Ferguson" case, too, is by no means straightforward to interpret, as Soal himself remarks. Soal was an automatist of some note, and it is not in all instances obvious why his mind should be supposed to have influenced Mrs. Cooper's rather than the other way around.

With regard to the Gordon Davis case, the following remarks may be made:

(a) The standard Spiritualist explanation of such cases is an "impersonating spirit." However, this explanation is ruled out of court insofar as the case for believing in discarnate entities itself rests upon the dismissal of cases like the Gordon Davis case.

(b) Dodds (1934) says that the Gordon Davis communicator "wasn't Gordon Davis unless you are prepared to assume that he could simultaneously interview a client at Southend and converse with Soal in London through the lips of Mrs. Cooper. Personally I find this assumption more staggering than any which is involved in the telepathic hypothesis . . . " (p. 162). I do not wish to disagree with Dodds here. But perhaps it should be pointed out that Myers (1903) expressed the view, shared by some other writers, that there may be "an involuntary detachment of some element of the spirit, probably with no knowledge thereof at the main center of consciousness" (Vol. 2, p. 75). Myers supported his suggestion by citing cases in which the "double" of a living person has been seen.

(c) The case of Gordon Davis does not provide a complete parallel to the more striking cases of veridical mediumistic communications from the dead. For in these cases the information transmitted must, on the super-ESP hypothesis, have been assembled from sources other than the ostensible communicator. It is, of course, essential to the case against the continuity hypothesis that there should be satisfactory evidence that mediums can build up their "communicators" by ESP which is focused on sources other than the communicators themselves, for otherwise veridical communications from deceased persons would imply the post-mortem survival of those persons. Such evidence would be provided if several persons, not present at a sitting, were to agree upon a fictitious communicator, and each impress upon the medium's rendering of that communicator a supposed fact not known to the other members of the group.

(d) The Gordon Davis case, like the performance of Osty's sensitives, falls short of the best mediumistic performances in respects which will be touched on shortly.

For other examples of ostensible communications from living persons, see Myers (1893, pp. 52–61), Flournoy (1911, pp. 267–296), and H. Salter (1921, pp. 133–143).

CONCLUDING REMARKS

The continuity hypothesis and the super-ESP theory appear to have reached a position of virtual stalemate. Each can produce some sort of explanation of the other's most cherished data. The trouble is that the continuity hypothesis can give us no details of what it is that is supposed to survive, so that we do not know quite what to do to determine whether it is there or not. Likewise, the super-ESP theory is silent as to the laws and characteristics of ESP, so that we have no means of saying for certain whether or not it has been at work (see Gauld, 1961). To progress further with the problem of how the "evidence for survival" is to be explained, we must either find data which will enable us to make the rival hypotheses more definite, or else think of a way of testing them in the teeth of their inadequacies. Two kinds of proposals have commonly been made under the first heading and one under the second. They are:

1. (a) Perhaps it might be possible to detect by objective means the "subtle bodies" of projectionists and also of deceased persons.

1. (b) If ESP could be shown to possess some characteristic feature or to have definite limits, then we could in principle say whether ESP was or could have been at work in the production of any given piece of "evidence for survival."

2. We might try to find out before someone's death how much a "sensitive" can find out about him by ESP and compare this with the amount of information he is able to "communicate" after his death. If the latter exceeds the former, the continuity hypothesis would *prima facie* be vindicated, for the sources of information about a given person which might be accessible to ESP can at any rate hardly be more numerous after his death than before it.

Some brief comments will now be made on each of these possibilities:

1. (a) This possibility is one which few parapsychologists are prepared to take very seriously, and data bearing upon it are scanty and doubtful. Claims by various earlier writers to have instrumentally registered or detected the subtle bodies of deceased persons or to have detected a loss of weight at the moment of death are critically discussed, and for the most part rejected, by Carrington (1939). Still, we should not too lightly set aside the subtle body hypothesis, which is, after all, taken seriously by so acute a thinker as Broad (1962, pp. 415–428). This hypothesis must of course, be considered in relation to recent work on OBEs. A research project is currently being carried out under the auspices of the A.S.P.R. in an endeavor to determine whether or not something really leaves the body of an "ESP projectionist." Some interesting preliminary results have been reported (Osis, 1974; and cf. Palmer, Osis, Morris, and Tart, 1974). If experiments such as these yield clear-cut positive findings, certain survival-related lines of inquiry might be suggested; for instance, could a projectionist control a medium, and what light would such control, if achieved, throw upon ostensible control by deceased persons? Would the deceased persons be able to cooperate in experiments in the same way as the projectionists? Such proposals, however, remain at present in the realm of fantasy.

1. (b) This is the most frequently made suggestion for resolving the conflict between the two theories. Indeed, Osis (1966) has already carried out some heroic but inconclusive experiments in pursuit of it (cf. Dean, 1966). I cannot persuade myself, however, either that a characteristic of ESP is likely to be discovered which will differentiate the occurrence of ESP from the occurrence of any other high-grade cognitive activity or that we shall ever be able to lay down

any definite limits on the type and range of factual information which ESP may bring. With regard to the former possibility, L. E. Rhine (1966) remarks that "while the indications are clear that personality factors are involved in the expression of ESP just as they are in any other delicate mental process, still no special state or trait has been found to be specifically characteristic of ESP alone" (p. 127). With regard to the latter possibility she says, "All of this shows that the potential range of material accessible to ESP is as wide—but no wider than—the personal interests of the individual through whom it is expressed. But aside from these personal limitations, the ability appears to theoretically of unlimited scope" (p. 136).

The idea that it might be possible to assign limits to the factual information accessible to ESP seems to spring from a widespread covert assumption that ESP (in the form of clairvoyance) must be *something like* ordinary sense-perception, or (in the form of telepathy) *something like* the transmission of information along a communications channel. Both of these models are grossly implausible. The first has been devastatingly criticized by Broad (1953, pp. 29–45). The second is open to closely similar objections which are impossible to go into here, though it may be remarked that in any case the evidence for "pure" telepathy is so slender that J. B. Rhine (1974) has recently abandoned the concept altogether.

In short, ESP yields what is, in terms of empiricist views of how we acquire factual information, "anomalous knowledge" (see Carpenter, 1971, p. 33). Or rather—since the perceptual analogy implied in the term "ESP" is so misleading— ESP *is* "anomalous knowing." It consists in what might, following Jung (1972, pp. 43–44), be described as an *a priori* knowledge of matters of fact. As such, it belongs among conceptual phenomena rather than among sensory and perceptual ones. Perhaps the basic form of ESP experience is that of simply "knowing" something to be the case; the knowledge is cast in the form of sensory imagery, hallucinations, automatisms, etc., only when it does not succeed in reaching consciousness directly (see L. E. Rhine, 1961, pp. 63–68; Stevenson, 1970a). However strange this idea may appear, it has at any rate the advantage of cutting through various parapsychological Gordian knots. If we regard ESP as *a priori* knowledge of matters of fact rather than as a kind of surrogate sense-perception, we are no longer in danger of being forced to say that precognition requires us to postulate future causes of present percepts. For it is not a feature of epistemic concepts in general that the "object" of knowledge has to be among the causes of it. Again, controversy over whether one of the "forms of ESP"—precognition, retrocognition, telepathy, and clairvoyance—is fundamental in the sense that the others may be reduced to it loses most of its point. For this controversy devolves to questions about what sorts of "objects" anomalous knowledge may have; the issue is no longer that of whether, e.g., extrasensory knowledge of distant objects is acquired by a different (quasi-sensory) *process* than extrasensory knowledge of other people's thoughts. *Ex hypothesi* there are no such processes of knowledge acquisition; one simply *knows*.

Anomalous knowledge is, characteristically, personal knowledge. It is knowledge of facts of personal concern to oneself, or of facts of personal concern to one's friends and relations, and hence to oneself. Perhaps a "sensitive" is someone who, to a greater extent than most of us, makes other people's concerns her concerns and deploys her paranormal powers more widely than most of us are able to. Anomalous knowledge seems also to be knowledge which, as it were, moves along personal lines; a sensitive who has once "locked on" to the concerns of a particular person will stay with that person's concerns for a while, producing more and more information about them.

If ESP is thus looked upon as "anomalous knowing," there seems no reason why there should be any past, present, or future state of affairs, or any interlinked set of states of affairs (such as a person's life history), which a sensitive could conceive, of which she could not in principle have "anomalous knowledge." It would at any rate be extraordinarily difficult to argue that because no sensitive has heretofore exhibited anomalous knowledge of such-and-such a kind or extent, no sensitive *can* exhibit anomalous knowledge of that kind or extent. Again, we could no longer argue, for instance, that because in the case of a verified drop in communicator the relevant information could only have been gathered by the extrasensory collection of different currently existing items from different distant sources, the super-ESP hypothesis has been intolerably stretched. Anomalous knowledge could as well "lock on" to the life history, character, and characteristic goals and purposes of a deceased person as to living persons and present objects and events—or, for that matter—to future ones. (With regard to a verified drop in communicator, the problem would of course remain as to why, in the absence of a friend or relative, or of a psychometric object, the anomalous knowing was directed upon the life history and characteristics of that person.) What, if any, of the "evidence for survival"—or, indeed, what possible "evidence for survival"—would under these circumstances remain undigested by the super-ESP hypothesis? The following putative classes of evidence suggest themselves (they are classes of evidence which, arguably, would also remain on the quasi-perceptual view of ESP if that were tenable).

(i) Cases in which a communicator unmistakably refers to matters beyond the conceptual grasp of the medium or percipient, but within that of the communicator. For one can only "know" that which one has the conceptual equipment to know; hence, *ex hypothesi*, "anomalous" knowledge if limited in scope by the sensitive's own conceptual capacities. Unfortunately, it is in practice very difficult to decide for certain just what the limitations of someone's conceptual capacities may be. However, there are one or two cases in which it seems as though communicators may have touched on matters transcending the medium's conceptual capacities. The "Ear of Dionysius" case may perhaps be thought an example. In certain other communications received through Mrs. Willett (G. W. Balfour, 1935) philosphical terms were used which appeared quite beyond the medium's interest or comprehension. Indeed, it seemed sometimes as though the medium's rather circumscribed conceptual capacities were being skillfully manipulated so as to convey to more sophisticated persons ideas which she herself was incapable of grasping. Material of this kind is of the greatest interest and importance, and every attempt should be made to obtain more of it. It shades into material of the next class:

(ii) Cases in which the communicator has exhibited a skill, intellectual or otherwise, possessed in life by that communicator, but not possessed by the medium or percipient. The most obvious examples here are cases of apparent xenoglossy (see above). Such cases require the most careful critical scrutiny, and not many of them would be likely to pass it. However, in principle they strongly support the continuity theory. For the examples which we have of unambiguous "anomalous knowledge" are examples of *knowing that* so and so is the case. Possession of a skill, *knowing how to do* something, is not to be equated with knowing that such-and-such is the case. Knowing French, let us say, does not consist in knowing facts like the fact that in French *chien* means *dog*, and the fact that in French the interrogative may be formed by inversion of subject and verb if the subject is a pronoun other than *je*. It consists in being able to speak coherent and grammatical French, to read French books, etc. Even if one could obtain anomalous knowledge of innumerable facts like the fact that *chien* means *dog*, this would not *per se* even begin to give one the capacity to converse in French.

Similar points could be made about other kinds of skills, and also concerning those cases in which, allegedly, a communication of adult fluency or intellectual level has been received through a child medium. Ideally, of course, the recrudescence of a skill once possessed by the communicator should be accompanied by other evidence of identity. A case frequently quoted is one given by J. B. Rhine (1953, pp. 312–313) in which a boy of four wrote several sheets of old-fashioned square shorthand containing an evidential message to his mother from his recently deceased father who had learned to write shorthand in the old-fashioned way. This case unfortunately appears to lack contemporary documentation, but at least it serves to illustrate possibilities.

It is perhaps worth noting that if anomalous knowledge is indeed "knowledge that" rather than "knowledge how," we are precluded from explaining cases of fluent xenoglossy, child mediumship, etc., in terms of the medium having anomalous knowledge focused on the discarnate xenoglot communicator; we would have to suppose that the communicator was in some way capable of directly controlling the medium's neuromuscular apparatus.

(iii) Cases in which, on the super-ESP hypothesis, a medium would have to be credited not just with anomalous knowledge of amazing complexity and extent, but in addition with dramatic gifts and imaginative intelligence of a degree equally extraordinary. There is more, one might say, to creating a convincing representation of a deceased person than merely accumulating anomalous knowledge about his life, his home, his possessions, his relatives, his appearance, his mannerisms, his aims in life, his ailments, and so forth (here one might list all the sorts of details commonly supplied by Osty's sensitives), and then infiltrating this accumulated knowledge into a personation of him. There is also the way in which that accumulated knowledge is so to speak deployed. Consider these comments by W. F. Prince on some sittings which he and his adopted daughter had with Mrs. Soule:

> ... it was the peculiar selective character of the details purporting to come from my wife and relating to her last weeks on earth which most impressed me when I realized it . . . in the alleged communication there is no hint of the features of the case which to us stood out so prominently, and in fact she never knew what her malady really was, she never realized that there was an open wound, and she expected, up to her last five minutes, to get better and return to her home. On the contrary, what we do find is a multitude of true little details, her back being rubbed, her head rubbed in a particular way, the trouble with her foot and knee, continuing sensations of hunger, the sensitiveness of her head when her hair was washed or combed, feeling that she would be all right again, trouble with her back towards the last, yet not being permitted to lie on her side, the chicken broth which Theodosia brought her, the trouble her "store" teeth were to her, a sensation of fulness in the chest and of bad pain in the abdomen, pain stopping all at once (from opiate), comforting visions of her relatives, sense of rebellion associated with death, etc. It came to me as I scanned this list that it was these details and others like them that loomed large in my wife's sick mind . . . I, Theodosia, or both of us, knew all the above details, but some of them were but wan and fading images in our minds, luridly overshadowed by the memories I have mentioned and others (in Allison, 1929, pp. 202–203).

Thus the trance intelligence, whatever it may have been, deployed the information available to it concerning Mrs. Prince's last few weeks with an understanding of her situation and point of view more intimate and more sensitive than that of close relatives who were actually present. In other cases, too, the communicator has "come through" with extraordinary vivacity as an intelligent agent having a distinctive, characteristic, and consistent point of view, distinctive purposes pursued in a characteristic manner, and so on. Mrs. Piper's "George Pellew" control, for example, recognized and conversed with some 30 of the living Pellew's friends (pseudonymously introduced). He addressed each in the appropriate manner and tone, recollected incidents appropriate to their past relationships, and so forth (Hodgson, 1898, pp. 295–334). It was as if the sitters were seen through Pellew's spectacles. Some 10 or 12 years ago I spent a good deal of time studying the papers and diaries of F. W. H. Myers and Henry Sidgwick, thus learning a good many intimate details about their lives, characters, friends, families, and domestic arrangements. Yet I could no more deploy this accumulated knowledge to develop impersonations of them which would have passed muster before their close friends than I could fly. The gap between accumulating such knowledge and deploying it in the construction of a realistic communicator is enormous.

2. The principal suggestions made here have been the "cipher" and "combination lock" tests of survival proposed by Thouless (1948, 1960) and by Stevenson (1968a). The idea behind the cipher test (the combination lock test is similar in principle, though administratively easier) is that those interested in the problem of survival should encipher a passage of prose by the use of a "key word" which he does not write down but makes every possible effort to engrave upon his memory. While the researcher is still alive other interested persons are requested to sit with the mediums or sensitives and attempt to obtain the key word by ESP focused upon him. These attempts constitute a "control" experiment by which it is established whether or not the key word is accessible to the medium's ESP. If the key word proves to be inaccessible, and if it is then communicated after the researcher's death, we would appear to have a successful "test of survival" for which the super-ESP explanation is inadequate. In the light of what has just been said about the difficulty of assigning any absolute limits to ESP, it is obvious that the mediums used in the ante-mortem trial should also be used in the post-mortem ones. And even then it would be necessary to guard against the possibility that the "powers" of one or more of them had developed in the interval.

An obvious difficulty here is that in the ante-mortem trials the mediums or sensitives as a class might be expected to be reluctant to produce evidence which could be used against the continuity hypothesis. This problem might be dealt with in various ways; for example, by finding one of the rare mediums who, like the late Mrs. Eileen Garrett, was not committed to the survival hypothesis, by arranging proxy sittings in which the sitter did not know whether the person to be contacted was living or dead, by offering large rewards, or by disguising the experiment in one way or another.

More complicated forms of control might be devised. For example, a group of persons might encipher passages and memorize key words, and it would be decided by some random process (whose results would be stored in coded form until required) that such-and-such members of the group should endeavor to transmit their code-words after death and that such-and-such should endeavor to keep them back. Thus both "experimental" and "control" groups would be discarnate, and the mundane sources upon which ESP could be directed to crack the cipher would be the same for the members of each group. Or, one person might select a code word and another person agree to try to translate that word after the deaths of both into a language unknown to the former. It would then be "transmitted" in the foreign language and would require retranslation before the cipher could be broken. We would then have an instance of ostensible post-mortem collaboration between more than one communicator, which Murphy (1957, p. 132) regards as the strongest possible form of evidence for survival. It must be said, however, that work on these lines, like work on the survival problem in general, would require the cooperation of a number of dedicated and able persons, convinced of the importance of the question, and with modest funds at their disposal. At the end of the last century and during the earlier decades of this a few such persons were to be found. Now their number is small indeed.

REFERENCES

Aksakow, A. *Animismus und Spiritismus*. Leipzig: Oswald Mutze, 1898. 2 vols.

Allison, L. W. *Leonard and Soule Experiments*. Boston: Boston Society for Psychic Research, 1929.

Allison, L. W. Proxy sittings with Mrs. Leonard. *Proceedings of the Society for Psychical Research*, 1934, **42**, 104–146.

Amadou, R. *Les grands médiums*. Paris: Editions Denoël, 1957.

Angoff, A. *Eileen Garrett and the World Beyond the Senses*. New York: Morrow, 1974.

Baird, A. T. *One Hundred Cases for Survival After Death*. London: T. Werner Laurie, 1943.

Baird, A. T. *Case Book for Survival*. London: Psychic Press, n.d. [1948].

Balfour, G. W. Some recent scripts affording evidence of personal survival. *Proceedings of the Society for Psychical Research*, 1914, **27**, 221–243.

Balfour, G. W. The ear of Dionysius: Further scripts affording evidence of personal survival. *Proceedings of the Society for Psychical Research*, 1918, **29**, 197–243.

Balfour, G. W. A study of the psychological aspects of Mrs. Willett's mediumship. *Proceedings of the Society for Psychical Research*, 1935, **43**, 43–318.

Balfour, J. The "Palm Sunday" case: New light on an old love story. *Proceedings of the Society for Psychical Research*, 1960, **52**, 79–267.

Barnouw, V. Siberian shamanism and Western spiritualism. *Journal of the American Society for Psychical Research*, 1942, **36**, 140–168.

Barrett, W. F. *Death-Bed Visions*. London: Methuen, 1926.

Bartlett, F. C. *Remembering*. Cambridge: Cambridge University Press, 1932.

Beard, P. *Survival of Death: For and Against*. London: Hodder and Stoughton, 1966.

Beattie, J., and Middleton, J. *Spirit Mediumship and Society in Africa*. London: Routledge and Kegan Paul, 1969.

Bennett, E. *Apparitions and Haunted Houses*. London: Faber and Faber. 1939.

Berg, D. A. The *modus operandi* of trance communication: A comparison of theories. *Journal of the American Society for Psychical Research*, 1951, **45**, 17–36.

Birge, W. R., and Rhine, J. B. Unusual types of persons tested for ESP. I. A professional medium. *Journal of Parapsychology*, 1942, **6**, 85–94.

Bozzano, E. *Polyglot Mediumship*. London: Rider, 1932.

Bradley, H. D. *Towards the Stars*. London: T. Werner Laurie, 1924.

Bradley, H. D. *The Wisdom of the Gods*. London: T. Werner Laurie, 1925.

Bradley, H. D. *And After* . . . . London: T. Werner Laurie, 1931.

Broad, C. D. *The Mind and its Place in Nature*. London: Routledge and Kegan Paul, 1925.

Broad, C. D. *Religion, Philosophy and Psychical Research*. London: Routledge and Kegan Paul, 1953.

Broad, C. D. The phenomenology of Mrs. Leonard's mediumship. *Journal of the American Society for Psychical Research*, 1955, **49**, 47-63.

Broad, C. D. *Lectures on Psychical Research*. London: Routledge and Kegan Paul, 1962.

Carington, W. W. The quantitative study of trance personalities. Part I. *Proceedings of the Society for Psychical Research*, 1934, **42**, 173-240. (a)

Carington, W. W. Review of H. Carrington's *An Instrumental Test of the Independence of a Spirit Control*. *Proceedings of the Society for Psychical Research*, 1934, **42**, 241-249. (b)

Carington, W. W. The quantitative study of trance personalities. Part II. *Proceedings of the Society for Psychical Research*, 1935, **43**, 319-361.

Carington, W. W. The quantitative study of trance personalities. Part III. *Proceedings of the Society for Psychical Research*, 1937, **44**, 189-222.

Carpenter, J. C. Why psi, or parapsychology and the reification of anomaly. *Proceedings of the Parapsychological Association*, 1971, **8**, 29-34.

Carrington, H. *An Instrumental Test of the Independence of a Spirit Control*. New York: Americal Psychical Institute, n.d. [1933].

Carrington, H. *Laboratory Investigations into Psychic Phenomena*. London: Rider, n.d. [1939].

Case of the Will of Mr. James L. Chaffin. *Proceedings of the Society for Psychical Research*, 1927, **36**, 517-524.

Collins, B. A. *Death is Not the End*. (3rd ed. rev.) London: Psychic Press, 1946.

Collins, B. A. *The Cheltenham Ghost*. London: Psychic Press, 1948.

Crookall, R. *The Study and Practice of Astral Projection*. London: Aquarian Press, 1961.

Crookall, R. *The Technique of Astral Projection*. London: Aquarian Press, 1964.

Cummins, G. *Swan on a Black Sea*. London: Routledge and Kegan Paul, 1965.

Dale, L. A. A series of spontaneous cases in the tradition of *Phantasms of the Living*. *Journal of the American Society for Psychical Research*, 1951, **45**, 85-101.

Dean, E. D. Survival research and its ESP alternatives. *Journal of the American Society for Psychical Research*, 1966, **60**, 244-247.

Dingwall, E. *Ghosts and Spirits in the Ancient World*. London: Kegan Paul, 1930.

Dodds, E. R. Why I do not believe in survival. *Proceedings of the Society for Psychical Research*, 1934, **42**, 147-178.

Dodds, E. R. Supernormal phenomena in classical antiquity. *Proceedings of the Society for Psychical Research*, 1971, **55**, 189-237.

Ducasse, C. J. *A Critical Examination of the Belief in a Life after Death*. Springfield, Ill.: Charles C Thomas, 1961.

Durville, H. *Le fantome des vivants*. (7th ed.) Paris: Bibliothèque Eudiaque, 1929.

Eastman, M. Out-of-the-body experiences. *Proceedings of the Society for Psychical Research*, 1962, **53**, 287-309.

Eliade, M. *Shamanism: Archaic Techniques of Ecstasy*. (Trans. by W. Trask.) (2nd ed. rev.) London: Routledge and Kegan Paul, 1970.

Elliott, A. J. A. *Chinese Spirit-Medium Cults in Singapore*. London: London School of Economics, 1955.

Evans, C. C., and Osborn, E. An experiment in the electroencephalography of mediumistic trance. *Journal of the Society for Psychical Research*, 1952, **36**, 578-596.

Flew, A. G. N. *A New Approach to Psychical Research*. London: Watts, 1953.

Flew, A. G. N. Is there a case for disembodied survival? *Journal of the American Society for Psychical Research*, 1972, **66**, 129-144.

Flournoy, T. *Esprits et Médiums*. Geneva: Librairie Kündig, 1911.

Flournoy, T. *From India to the Planet Mars*. (Trans. by D. B. Vermilye.) (New ed.) Secaucus, N.J.: University Books, 1963.

Fox, O. Astral Projection: *A Record of Out-of-the-Body Experiences*. Secaucus, N.J.: University Books, 1962.

Garrett, E. J. *My Life as a Search for the Meaning of Mediumship*. London: Rider, 1939.

Garrett, E. J. *Many Voices: The Autobiography of a Medium*. New York: Putnam, 1968.

Gauld, A. The "super-ESP" hypothesis. *Proceedings of the Society for Psychical Research*, 1961, **53**, 226–246.

Gauld, A. Mr. Hall and the S.P.R. *Journal of the Society for Psychical Research*, 1965, **43**, 53–62.

Gauld, A. Could a machine perceive? *British Journal for the Philosophy of Science*, 1966, **17**, 44–58.

Gauld, A. *The Founders of Psychical Research*. New York: Schocken, 1968.

Gauld, A. A series of "drop in" communicators. *Proceedings of the Society for Psychical Research*, 1971, **55**, 273–340.

Gauld, A., and Stephenson, G. M. Some experiments relating to Bartlett's theory of remembering. *British Journal of Psychology*, 1967, **58**, 39–49.

Gay, K. (Ed.). The case of Edgar Vandy. *Journal of the Society for Psychical Research*, 1957, **39**, 1–64.

Geach, P. *God and the Soul*. London: Routledge and Kegan Paul, 1969.

Goldney, K. M. A case of purported spirit-communication. *Proceedings of the Society for Psychical Research*, 1939, **45**, 210–216.

Goldney, K. M., and Soal, S. G. Report on a series of sittings with Mrs. Eileen Garrett. *Proceedings of the Society for Psychical Research*, 1938, **45**, 43–87.

Green, C. E. Ecsomatic experiences and related phenomena. *Journal of the Society for Psychical Research*, 1967, **44**, 111–131.

Green, C. E. *Out-of-the-Body Experiences*. Oxford, England: Institute of Psychophysical Research, 1968.

Green, C. E. and McCreery, C. *Apparitions*. London: Hamish Hamilton, 1975.

Greville, T. N. E. On the number of sets required for testing the significance of verbal material. *Journal of Parapsychology*, 1949, **13**, 137–138.

Gurney, E., Myers, F. W. H., and Podmore, F. *Phantasms of the Living*. London: Trübner, 1886. 2 vols.

Hansel, C. E. M. *ESP: A Scientific Evaluation*. New York: Scribner's, 1966.

Haraldsson, E., and Stevenson, I. An experiment with the Icelandic medium Hafsteinn Björnsson. *Journal of the American Society for Psychical Research*, 1974, **68**, 192–202.

Haraldsson, E., and Stevenson, I. A communicator of the "drop in" type: The case of Runolfur Runolfsson. *Journal of the American Society for Psychical Research*, 1975, **69**, 33–59. (a)

Haraldsson, E., and Stevenson, I. A communicator of the "drop in" type in Iceland: The case of Gudni Magnusson. *Journal of the American Society for Psychical Research*, 1975, **69**, 245–261. (b)

Hart, H. Six theories about apparitions. *Proceedings of the Society for Psychical Research*, 1956, **50**, 153–239.

Hart, H. *The Enigma of Survival*. Springfield, Ill.: Charles C Thomas, 1959.

Hart, H., and Hart, E. B. Visions and apparitions collectively and reciprocally perceived. *Proceedings of the Society for Psychical Research*, 1933, **41**, 205–249.

Heywood, R. Attitudes to death in the light of dreams and other out-of-the-body experience. In A. Toynbee (Ed.), *Man's Concern with Death*, pp. 185–218. New York: McGraw-Hill, 1968.

Hill, J. A. *Experiences with Mediums*. London: Rider, 1934.

Hodgson, R. A record of observations of certain phenomena of trance. *Proceedings of the Society for Psychical Research*, 1892, **8**, 1-167.

Hodgson, R. A further record of observations of certain phenomena of trance. *Proceedings of the Society for Psychical Research*, 1898, **13**, 284-582.

Hodgson, R. Report on six sittings with Mrs. Thompson. *Proceedings of the Society for Psychical Research*, 1902, **17**, 138-161.

Holt, H. *On the Cosmic Relations*. London: Williams and Norgate, 1915. 2 vols.

Hope, C. Report on some sittings with Valiantine and Phoenix in 1927. *Proceedings of the Society for Psychical Research*, 1932, **40**, 411-417.

Hulme, A. J. H., and Wood, F. H. *Ancient Egypt Speaks*. London: Rider, 1937.

Hyslop, J. H. A further record of observations of certain trance phenomena. *Proceedings of the Society for Psychical Research*, 1901, **16**, 1-649.

Hyslop, J. H. *Science and a Future Life*. Boston: Turner, 1905.

Hyslop, J. H. *Contact with the Other World*. New York: Century, 1919.

Jacobson, N. *Life without Death*? New York: Delacorte Press, 1973.

James, W. Report on Mrs. Piper's Hodgson control. *Proceedings of the Society for Psychical Research*, 1909, **23**, 2-121.

Johnson, A. On the automatic writing of Mrs. Holland. *Proceedings of the Society for Psychical Research*, 1908, **21**, 166-391.

Johnson, A. Second report on Mrs. Holland's script. *Proceedings of the Society for Psychical Research*, 1910, **24**, 201-263.

Johnson, A. Third report on Mrs. Holland's script. *Proceedings of the Society for Psychical Research*, 1911, **25**, 218-303.

Johnson, A. A reconstruction of some "concordant automatisms." *Proceedings of the Society for Psychical Research*, 1914, **27**, 1-156.

Johnson, R. C. *The Imprisoned Splendour*. London: Hodder and Stoughton, 1953.

Jung, C. G. *Synchronicity*. London: Routledge and Kegan Paul, 1972.

Kerner, J. *Geschichten Besessener Neuerer Zeit*. Karlsruhe: G. Braun, 1834.

Lambert, G. W. An apparition of a child: The case of Johnnie M. *Journal of the Society for Psychical Research*, 1966, **43**, 428-431.

Lancelin, C. *Méthode de dedoublement personnel*. Paris: Durville, n.d. [1913].

Lang, A. *Cock Lane and Common Sense*. London: Longmans, Green, 1894.

Lavater, L. *Of Ghostes and Spirites Walking by Nyght*. London: R. Watkyns, 1572.

Lawton, G. *The Drama of Life after Death*. London: Constable, 1933.

Leloyer, P. *Discours, et histoires des spectres*. Paris: Nicolas Buon, 1605.

Leonard, G. O. *My Life in Two Worlds*. London: Cassell, 1931.

Litvag, I. *Singer in the Shadows*. New York: Macmillan, 1972.

Lodge, O. Introduction to the reports of sittings with Mrs. Thompson. *Proceedings of the Society for Psychical Research*, 1902, **17**, 61-66.

Lodge, O. Report on some trance communications received chiefly through Mrs. Piper. *Proceedings of the Society for Psychical Research*, 1909, **23**, 127-285.

Lodge, O. Evidence of classical scholarship and of cross-correspondence in some new automatic writings. *Proceedings of the Society for Psychical Research*, 1911, **25**, 113-175.

Lodge, O. *Raymond, or Life and Death*. London: Methuen, 1916.

Lodge, O. Recent evidence about prevision and survival. *Proceedings of the Society for Psychical Research*, 1918, **29**, 111-169.

Lodge, O., Verrall, M. de G. (Mrs. A. W. Verrall), Feilding, E., Johnson, A., and Richet, C. A discussion of Professor Richet's case of automatic writing in a language unknown to the writer. *Proceedings of the Society for Psychical Research*, 1905, **19**, 195-266.

MacKenzie, A. *Apparitions and Ghosts*. London: Arthur Barker, 1971.

Maitland, R. W. *The Snettisham Ghost*. London: Psychic Press, n.d. [1953].

Maxwell, J. Correspondances croisées et la méthode expérimentale. *Proceedings of the Society for Psychical Research*, 1912, **26**, 57–144.

Mead, G. R. S. *The Doctrine of the Subtle Body in Western Tradition*. London: Watkins, 1919.

Mitchell, T. W. *Medical Psychology and Psychical Research*. New York: Dutton, 1922.

Monroe, R. A. *Journeys Out of the Body*. Garden City, N.Y.: Doubleday, 1971.

Moore, W. U. *The Voices*. London: Watts, 1913.

Morton, R. C. (Despard, R.). Record of a haunted house. *Proceedings of the Society for Psychical Research*, 1892, **8**, 311–332.

Moss, T., and Schmeidler, G. R. Quantitative investigation of a "haunted house" with sensitives and a control group. *Journal of the American Society for Psychical Research*, 1968, **62**, 399–410.

Muldoon, S., and Carrington, H. *The Projection of the Astral Body*. London: Rider, 1929.

Muldoon, S., and Carrington, H. *The Phenomena of Astral Projection*. London: Rider, 1951.

Murphy, G. *Three Papers on the Survival Problem*. New York: American Society for Psychical Research, 1945.

Murphy, G. Psychical research and personality. *Proceedings of the Society for Psychical Research*, 1949, **49**, 1–15.

Murphy, G. Psychology and psychical research. *Proceedings of the Society for Psychical Research*, 1953, **50**, 26–49.

Murphy, G. Triumphs and defeats in the study of mediumship. *Journal of the American Society for Psychical Research*, 1957, **51**, 125–135.

Myers, F. W. H. On recognised apparitions occurring more than a year after death. *Proceedings of the Society for Psychical Research*, 1889, **6**, 13–65.

Myers, F. W. H. A defence of phantasms of the dead. *Proceedings of the Society for Psychical Research*, 1890, **6**, 314–357.

Myers, F. W. H. On indications of continued terrene knowledge on the part of phantasms of the dead. *Proceedings of the Society for Psychical Research*, 1892, **8**, 170–252.

Myers, F. W. H. The subliminal consciousness. VII. Motor automatism. *Proceedings of the Society for Psychical Research*, 1893, **9**, 26–128.

Myers, F. W. H. The subliminal self. IX. The relation of supernormal phenomena to time. *Proceedings of the Society for Psychical Research*, 1895, **11**, 408–593.

Myers, F. W. H. On the trance phenomena of Mrs. Thompson. *Proceedings of the Society for Psychical Research*, 1902, **17**, 67–74.

Myers, F. W. H. *Human Personality and its Survival of Bodily Death*. London: Longmans, Green, 1903. 2 vols.

Myers, F. W. H., Lodge, O., Leaf, W., and James, W. A record of observations of certain phenomena of trance. *Proceedings of the Society for Psychical Research*, 1890, **6**, 436–695.

Newbold, W. R. A further record of observations of certain phenomena of trance. *Proceedings of the Society for Psychical Research*, 1898, **14**, 6–49.

Oesterreich, T. K. *Possession: Demoniacal and Other*. New York: R. R. Smith, 1930.

Osis, K. *Deathbed Observations by Physicians and Nurses*. New York: Parapsychology Foundation, 1961.

Osis, K. Linkage experiments with mediums. *Journal of the American Society for Psychical Research*, 1966, **60**, 91–124.

Osis, K. Out-of-the-body research at the ASPR. *ASPR Newsletter*, 1974, No. 22, 1–3.

Osis, K. What did the dying see? *ASPR Newsletter*, 1975, No. 24, 1–3.

Osty, E. *Supernormal Faculties in Man*. (Trans. by S. de Brath.) London: Methuen, 1923.

Pagenstecher, G. Past events seership: A study in psychometry. *Proceedings of the American Society for Psychical Research*, 1922, **16**, 1–136.

Palmer, J., and Lieberman, R. The influence of psychological set on ESP and out-of-body experiences. *Journal of the American Society for Psychical Research*, 1975, **69**, 193–213.

Palmer, J., Osis, K., Morris, R. L., and Tart, C. T. Symposium: Research on out-of-the-body experiences. Where do we go from here? In W. G. Roll, R. L. Morris, and J. D. Morris (Eds), *Research in Parapsychology* 1973, pp. 107–120. Metuchen, N.J.: Scarecrow Press, 1974.

Palmer, J., and Vassar, C. ESP and out-of-the-body experiences: An exploratory study. *Journal of the American Society for Psychical Research*, 1974, **68**, 257–280.

Parsons, D. On the need for caution in assessing mediumistic material. *Proceedings of the Society for Psychical Research*, 1949, **48**, 344–352.

Penelhum, T. *Survival and Disembodied Existence*. London: Routledge and Kegan Paul, 1970.

Piddington, J. G. On the types of phenomena displayed in Mrs. Thompson's trance. *Proceedings of the Society for Psychical Research*, 1904, **18**, 104–307.

Piddington, J. G. A series of concordant automatisms. *Proceedings of the Society for Psychical Research*, 1908, **22**, 19–416.

Pigou, A. C. Psychical research and survival after bodily death. *Proceedings of the Society for Psychical Research*, 1909, **23**, 286–303.

Piper, A. L. *The Life and Work of Mrs. Piper*. London: Kegan Paul, 1929.

Podmore, F. Phantasms of the dead from another point of view. *Proceedings of the Society for Psychical Research*, 1889, **6**, 229–313.

Podmore, F. *Apparitions and Thought-Transference*. London: Walter Scott, 1894.

Podmore, F. *Modern Spiritualism: A History and a Criticism*. London: Methuen, 1902. 2 vols.

Podmore, F. *Telepathic Hallucinations: The New View of Ghosts*. London: Milner, n.d. [1909].

Podmore, F. *The Newer Spiritualism*. London: Fisher Unwin, 1910.

Pratt, J. G. On the evaluation of verbal material in parapsychology. (*Parapsychological Monographs No. 10.*) New York: Parapsychology Foundation, 1969.

Pratt, J. G., and Birge, W. R. Appraising verbal test material in parapsychology. *Journal of Parapsychology*, 1948, **12**, 236–256.

Price, H. The R101 disaster (case record): Mediumship of Mrs. Garrett. *Journal of the American Society for Psychical Research*, 1931, **25**, 268–279.

Price, H. H. Disbelief in the problem of survival. *Light*, 1959, **79**, 39–50.

Prince, W. F. Psychometric experiments with Señora Maria Reyes de Z. *Proceedings of the American Society for Psychical Research*, 1921, **15**, 189–314.

Prince, W. F. *The Psychic in the House*. Boston: Boston Society for Psychic Research, 1926.

Prince, W. F. *The Case of Patience Worth*. Boston: Boston Society for Psychic Research, 1927. (a)

Prince W. F. The cure of two cases of paranoia. *Bulletin of the Boston Society for Psychic Research*, 1927, **6**, 36–72. (b)

Prince, W. F. *Noted Witnesses for Psychic Occurrences*. Boston: Boston Society for Psychic Research, 1928.

Prince, W. F. Review of "A case of apparent obsession," by G. Burns. *Proceedings of the Society for Psychical Research*, 1929, **38**, 388–398.

Prince, W. F. A certain type of psychical research. *Bulletin of the Boston Society for Psychic Research*, 1933, **21**, 1–36.

Progoff, I. *The Image of an Oracle*. New York: Garrett/Helix, 1964.

Radclyffe-Hall, M., and Troubridge, U. On a series of sittings with Mrs. Osborne Leonard. *Proceedings of the Society for Psychical Research*, 1919, **30**, 339–554.

Raudive, K. *Breakthrough*. New York: Taplinger, 1971.

Rhine, J. B. *New World of the Mind*. New York: Sloane, 1953.

Rhine, J. B. Telepathy and other untestable hypotheses. *Journal of Parapsychology*, 1974, **38**, 137–153.

Rhine, L. E. *Hidden Channels of the Mind*. New York: Sloane, 1961.

Rhine, L. E. The range of ESP: Limited or unlimited? *Journal of the American Society for Psychical Research*, 1966, **60**, 125–136.

Richet, C. Xénoglossie: L'écriture automatique en langues étrangères. *Proceedings of the Society for Psychical Research*, 1905, **19**, 162–194.

Richet, C. *Thirty Years of Psychical Research*. (Trans. by S. de Brath.) New York: Macmillan, 1923.

Richmond, K. Preliminary studies of the recorded Leonard material. *Proceedings of the Society for Psychical Research*, 1936, **44**, 17–52.

Richmond, K. *Evidence of Identity*. London: Bell, 1939.

Richmond, Z. *Evidence of Purpose*. London: Bell, 1938.

Sage, M. *Mrs. Piper and the Society for Psychical Research*. (Trans. by N. Robertson.) London: Brimley Johnson, 1903.

Salter, H. de G. (Mrs. W. H. Salter). A further report on sittings with Mrs. Leonard. *Proceedings of the Society for Psychical Research*, 1921, **32**, 1–143.

Salter, H. de G. (Mrs. W. H. Salter). A report on some recent sittings with Mrs. Leonard. *Proceedings of the Society for Psychical Research*, 1926, **36**, 187–332.

Salter, H. de G. (Mrs. W. H. Salter). Some incidents occurring at sittings with Mrs. Leonard which may throw some light on their *modus operandi*. *Proceedings of the Society for Psychical Research*, 1930, **39**, 306–332.

Salter, H. de G. (Mrs. W. H. Salter). The history of George Valiantine. *Proceedings of the Society for Psychical Research*, 1932, **40**, 363–410.

Salter, H. de G. (Mrs. W. H. Salter). Some observations on the scripts of the S.P.R. group of automatists. *Journal of the American Society for Psychical Research*, 1951, **45**, 47–54.

Salter, W. H. *Ghosts and Apparitions*. London: Bell, 1938.

Salter, W. H. *Trance Mediumship: An Introductory Study of Mrs. Piper and Mrs. Leonard*. London: Society for Psychical Research, 1950.

Salter, W. H. *Zoar, or the Evidence of Psychical Research Concerning Survival*. London: Sidgwick and Jackson, 1961.

Saltmarsh, H. F. Report on the investigation of some sittings with Mrs. Warren Elliott. *Proceedings of the Society for Psychical Research*, 1930, **39**, 47–184.

Saltmarsh, H. F. *Evidence of Personal Survival from Cross Correspondences*. London: Bell, 1938.

Saltmarsh, H. F., and Soal, S. G. A method of investigating the supernormal content of mediumistic communications. *Proceedings of the Society for Psychical Research*, 1930, **39**, 266–271.

Schiller, F. C. S. Review of *Supernormal Faculties in Man* by E. Osty. *Proceedings of the Society for Psychical Research*, 1924, **34**, 333–335.

Scott, C. On the evaluation of verbal material in parapsychology: A discussion of Dr. Pratt's monograph. *Journal of the Society for Psychical Research*, 1972, **46**, 79–90.

Sidgwick, E. M. (Mrs. H. Sidgwick). Notes on the evidence, collected by the Society, for phantasms of the dead. *Proceedings of the Society for Psychical Research*, 1885, **3**, 69–150.

Sidgwick, E. M. (Mrs. H. Sidgwick). Discussion of the trance phenomena of Mrs. Piper. *Proceedings of the Society for Psychical Research*, 1900, **15**, 16–38.

Sidgwick, E. M. (Mrs. H. Sidgwick). A reply to Dr. Joseph Maxwell's paper on "cross correspondences" and the experimental method. *Proceedings of the Society for Psychical Research*, 1913, **26**, 375–400.

Sidgwick, E. M. (Mrs. H. Sidgwick). A contribution to the study of the psychology of Mrs. Piper's trance phenomena. *Proceedings of the Society for Psychical Research*, 1915, **28**, 1–657.

Sidgwick, E. M. (Mrs. H. Sidgwick). Phantasms of the living. . . . *Proceedings of the Society for Psychical Research*, 1923, **33**, 23–429.

Sidgwick, H., Sidgwick, E. M. (Mrs. H. Sidgwick), and Johnson, A. Report on the Census of Hallucinations. *Proceedings of the Society for Psychical Research*, 1894, **10**, 25–422.

Sidgwick, E. M. (Mrs. H. Sidgwick), Verrall, M. de G. (Mrs. A. W. Verrall), and Piddington, J. G. Further experiments with Mrs. Piper in 1908. *Proceedings of the Society for Psychical Research*, 1910, **24**, 31–200.

Smith, S. *The Mediumship of Mrs. Leonard.* New Hyde Park, N.Y.: University Books, 1964.

Soal, S. G. A report on some communications received through Mrs. Blanche Cooper. *Proceedings of the Society for Psychical Research*, 1925, **35**, 471–594.

Soal, S. G. A reply to Mr. H. Dennis Bradley. *Journal of the Society for Psychical Research*, 1926, **33**, 38–50.

Stevens, E. W. *The Watseka Wonder*. Chicago: Religio-Philosophical Publishing House, 1887.

Stevenson, I. The combination lock test for survival. *Journal of the American Society for Psychical Research*, 1968, **62**, 246–254. (a)

Stevenson, I. The analysis of a mediumistic session by a new method. *Journal of the American Society for Psychical Research*, 1968, **62**, 334–355. (b)

Stevenson I. The substantiality of spontaneous cases. *Proceedings of the Parapsychological Association*, 1968, **5**, 91–128. (c)

Stevenson, I. Telepathic impressions: A review and report of thirty-five new cases. *Proceedings of the American Society for Psychical Research*, 1970, **29**, 1–198. (a)

Stevenson, I. A communicator unknown to medium and sitters. *Journal of the American Society for Psychical Research*, 1970, **64**, 53–65. (b)

Stevenson, I. A communicator of the "drop in" type in France: The case of Robert Marie. *Journal of the American Society for Psychical Research*, 1973, **67**, 47–76.

Stevenson, I. Xenoglossy: A review and report of a case. *Proceedings of the American Society for Psychical Research*, 1974, **31**, 1–268.

Tart, C. T. A psychophysiological study of out-of-the-body experiences in a selected subject. *Journal of the American Society for Psychical Research*, 1968, **62**, 3–27.

Thomas, C. D. The *modus operandi* of trance-communication according to descriptions received through Mrs. Osborne Leonard. *Proceedings of the Society for Psychical Research*, 1928, **38**, 49–100.

Thomas, C. D. A consideration of a series of proxy sittings. *Proceedings of the Society for Psychical Research*, 1933, **41**, 139–185.

Thomas, C. D. A proxy case extending over eleven sittings with Mrs. Osborne Leonard. *Proceedings of the Society for Psychical Research*, 1935, **43**, 439–519.

Thomas, C. D. A proxy experiment of significant success. *Proceedings of the Society for Psychical Research*, 1939, **45**, 257–306.

Thomas J. F. *Beyond Normal Cognition*. Boston: Boston Society for Psychic Research, 1937.

Thouless, R. H. Review of Mr. Whately Carington's work on trance personalities. *Proceedings of the Society for Psychical Research*, 1937, **44**, 223–275.

Thouless, R. H. A test of survival. *Proceedings of the Society for Psychical Research*, 1948, **48**, 253–263.

Thouless, R. H. The empirical evidence for survival. *Journal of the American Society for Psychical Research*, 1960, **54**, 23-32.

Troubridge, U. The *modus operandi* in so-called mediumistic trance. *Proceedings of the Society for Psychical Research*, 1922, **32**, 344-378.

Tyrrell, G. N. M. A communicator introduced in automatic script. *Journal of the Society or Psychical Research*, 1939, **31**, 91-95.

Tyrrell, G. N. M. *Apparitions*. (2nd ed. rev.) London: Duckworth 1953.

Van Eeden, F. Account of sittings with Mrs. Thompson. *Proceedings of the Society for Psychical Research*, 1902, **17**, 75-115.

Verrall, H. de G. (Mrs. W. H. Salter). Report on the Junot sittings with Mrs. Piper. *Proceedings of the Society for Psychical Research*, 1910, **24**, 351-664.

Verrall, M. de G. (Mrs. A. W. Verrall). Notes on the trance phenomena of Mrs. Thompson. *Proceedings of the Society for Psychical Research*, 1902, **17**, 164-244.

Verrall, M. de G. (Mrs. A. W. Verrall). On a series of automatic writings. *Proceedings of the Society for Psychical Research*, 1906, **20**, 1-432.

Walker, B. *Beyond the Body*. London: Routledge and Kegan Paul, 1974.

Walker, N. *The Bridge*. London: Cassell, 1927.

Walker, N. *Through a Stranger's Hands*. London: Hutchinson, 1935.

Wavell, S., Butt, A., and Epton, N. *Trances.* New York: Dutton, 1966.

West, D. J. The investigation of spontaneous cases. *Proceedings of the Society for Psychical Research*, 1948, **48**, 264-300. (a)

West, D. J. A mass-observation questionnaire on hallucinations. *Journal of the Society for Psychical Research*, 1948, **34**, 187-196. (b)

Whiteman, J. H. M. *The Mystical Life*. London: Faber and Faber, 1961.

Whymant, N. *Psychic Adventures in New York*. London: Morley and Mitchell, 1931.

Wilson, J. O., and Piddington, J. G. A record of two sittings with Mrs. Thompson. *Proceedings of the Society for Psychical Research*, 1902, **17**, 116-137.

Wood, F. H. *After Thirty Centuries*. London: Rider, 1935.

Wood, F. H. *This Egyptian Miracle*. London: Watkins, 1955.

Zorab, G. A case for survival. *Journal of the Society for Psychical Research*, 1940, **31**, 142-152.

2

Reincarnation: Field Studies and Theoretical Issues

Ian Stevenson

INTRODUCTION

The word *reincarnation* refers to the concept that human beings (and perhaps subhuman animals) consist of two separable components, a physical body and a psychical entity or soul. At the death of the physical body the soul persists and, after a variable interval, becomes associated with a new physical body. As will be seen later, this is merely a short working definition which does not take account of the varying ideas held by different peoples about the nature and details of reincarnation. Although this chapter will be mainly concerned with describing and analyzing the evidence for reincarnation, the evaluation of such evidence requires some understanding of the diverse beliefs held about it throughout the world. This makes appropriate a summary account of some of these beliefs.

The Extent of the Belief in Reincarnation

Many different peoples have believed in reincarnation, and many believe in it today. Among Westerners the belief is most commonly associated with the Hindus and Buddhists of Southeast Asia, but this is probably due to the availability in the West of writings about Hindus and Buddhists and by them, and of translations of the scriptures which expound their beliefs. Western readers are usually less familiar with the fact that many other peoples of the world have also believed in reincarnation and do so at present. The scope of this chapter precludes a survey of all the peoples of past times who have believed in reincarnation. (Interested readers may consult Head and Cranston [1967] as a valuable introduction to the vast literature of this topic.) Students of this subject, however, need to understand how widespread have been the reports of the belief in reincarnation published by authors writing even within the present century. The belief has been reported among such groups as the following: some Islamic sects of western Asia such as the Alevis (Stevenson, 1970) and Druses (Stevenson, 1974a); numerous natives in North America, especially of the northwest areas, including Alaska (de Laguna, 1972; Slobodin, 1970; Stevenson, 1966, 1974a); many tribes of East and West Africa (Besterman, 1968; Deschamps, 1970; Noon, 1942; Parrinder, 1954, 1956; Thomas, 1968; Uchendu, 1964; Zahan, 1965); the Trobriand Islanders of the South Pacific (Malinowski, 1916); the northern tribes of Central Australia (Spencer and Gillen, 1904); and the Ainu of northern Japan (Munro, 1963). The foregoing list is not intended to be exhaustive, but should suffice to show that even in modern times many peoples outside Southeast Asia have believed in reincarnation and still do. The belief is in fact so widespread outside the culture of Europe and its derivatives in the Americas as to suggest the idea that all peoples not influenced by European ideas hold it. This, however, would be incorrect. Recent inquiries have shown that the Alevis of Anatolia do not believe in reincarnation (Bayer, 1970–71), although they may once have done so, as other Alevis of south central Turkey still do. Similarly, the Ismailis, an Islamic sect of the Shiite branch, no longer believe in reincarnation (Makarem, 1972, 1973) although their ancestors once did. And Van de Castle (1973) found no evidence of the belief in reincarnation among the Cunas of Panama.

Many Europeans and Americans (of South and North America), apart from the native groups mentioned above, also believe in reincarnation. A Gallup poll taken in 1968 in eight countries of western Europe showed that an average of 18 percent of persons in these countries believed in reincarnation. A similar poll carried out in the United States and Canada showed that 20 percent of the Americans and 26 percent of the Canadians questioned believed in reincarnation (Gallup International, 1969).

A consideration of the occurrence of a belief in reincarnation in widely separated cultures raises the question: How does (or did) the belief arise in these different cultures? In some instances we know or can surmise that the belief spread by normal means of communication. For example, there has been some communication between India and western Asia since protohistoric times and it is not improbable that the belief in reincarnation in India had some influence on its occurrence in western Asia. (There are also, however, important differences in the particular ideas about reincarnation found in Southeast Asia and in western Asia.) But such normal communication could not possibly account for the occurrence of the belief in reincarnation in northwestern Canada and West Africa, both of which have been effectively isolated (at least with regard to cultural influences) from Southeast Asia since man began to develop different cultures thousands of years ago. We are therefore on quite safe ground in supposing that the belief in reincarnation arose independently in different places and at different times.

It is possible to reach the idea of reincarnation through philosophical argument. The quickest route by this method is to assume the existence of a soul and its immortality and then to ask whether a soul that has no terminus to its existence can have had a beginning. Schopenhauer used this argument when he wrote: "Whoever believes that man's birth is his beginning must also believe that his death is his end" (Schopenhauer, 1908, Vol. 2, p. 558; my translation). And from the concept of the prenatal existence of the soul it is a short step to the idea that the soul had incarnated in other physical bodies before the birth of its present one.

Although other philosophers besides Schopenhauer have believed in reincarnation on purely rational grounds (McTaggart, 1915; Plato, 1910), it is unlikely that the belief arose in such a complicated way among groups of food gatherers and primitive cultivators. It seems more probable that they came to it through the examination of experiences that fell within their purview. These would be described by persons who claimed that they could actually remember having lived before. Such persons would presumably communicate their experiences at least within their own village and often, perhaps, to groups outside it. To the extent that observation in modern times has been possible, persons having such experiences have been found in every culture where the belief in reincarnation is strong and also in some where it is not.

We know, however, that some peoples in the past believed in reincarnation without our having received from them accounts of anything like the experiences of apparent memories and evidence that can be found today. In India, for example, the belief in reincarnation can be traced as far back as the later Vedas; but although early scriptures and myths of India contain scattered allusions to persons having memories of previous lives, we do not have any account of a fully developed case, such as this chapter will be mainly concerned with, until the eighteenth century A.D. Similarly, we know that some of the ancient Greeks believed in reincarnation, and Greek philosophers such as Plato (1910) argued the merits of the concept in detail, but without citing supportive case material of which, as in ancient India, there exist some fragmentary accounts. E. R. Dodds (1971) explained this by supposing that, if there had been any acceptable case material in ancient Greece, philosophers like Plato would have considered it irrelevant and almost undignified to descend from the heights of rational argument to the lower levels of empirical inquiry. A third example derives from the history of the Cathars, a heretical sect which flourished in southern France during the twelfth and thirteenth centuries (Madaule, 1961; Nelli, 1972). Rein-carnation formed an important tenet of their creed, but from them also we have received almost nothing comparable to modern case material. The explanation of this instance may lie in the systematic destruction by the Inquisition of the writings of the Cathars, with the result that most of what we know about them today derives not from their own documents, but from those of their persecu-tors and exterminators.

Notwithstanding the above examples from earlier times, it seems likely that empirical evidence from personal experiences has either established the belief in reincarnation or strengthened it where it already existed. Such evidence has probably contributed more than other factors to sustaining the belief, especially in the face of strongly held opposing systems such as those of Christians, ortho-dox (Sunni) Moslems, and most present-day scientists. A later section of this chapter will return to the topic of the relationship between the belief in rein-carnation and the occurrence of cases, but it may be helpful to say here that the relationship is almost certainly circular: The cases sustain the belief, al-though they are not necessary for it, and the belief fosters the cases by creating an ambiance favorable to their development and reporting.

The Types of Evidence Suggesting Reincarnation

Of the several different types of evidence adduced in support of a belief in reincarnation the weakest by far consists of statements made by one person, usually a sensitive, medium, or yogi, concerning the supposed previous life or lives of another person. In no department of parapsychology, if it may be called such, is the volume of utterance so disproportionately large in compari-son with the weakness of presented evidence. In nearly all instances of this type the statements of the person claiming to "read" another person's previous lives consist of completely unverifiable assertions about the previous life al-legedly perceived. Some persons have exploited claims to "read" other persons' past lives in sordid commercialism with regard to which one does not know whether to deplore more the cupidity of the profiteers or the gullibility of the deceived. The simple and not too expensive device of having several such "sensitives" make statements about the same person seems rarely to be adopted, although it would quickly unmask the pretensions of most of the practitioners in this field. This topic cannot be dismissed, however, without acknowledging that very rarely several sensitives have made the same (or very similar) state-ments about a presumed previous life of one person and that also very rarely mediums have made statements concerning the previous life of a person that were concordant with spontaneous memories the person himself had had. In these instances the most we can say by way of interpretation, assuming no normal leak of information, is that they provide evidence of extrasensory perception on the part of the medium or sensitive making the statements. They are not necessarily evidence of reincarnation, although harmonious with that interpretation.

On a slightly higher level of evidential merit are experiments with hypnosis and regression to presumed previous lives. But here again, interest and enthusiasm on the part of the general public has far outrun respectable data. The nature of the hypnotic state, and even its existence as an authentically different form of consciousness, have been much debated for more than a century. It can be agreed, however, that suggestions accepted by a subject may induce in him a condition in which he is more suggestible than usual, and that in this latter state he may be induced to experience images that, like the content of many dreams, ordinarily remain unconscious. Recall of childhood memories sometimes becomes greatly increased, with the recovery of surprising details previously forgotten but verified as correct (Reiff and Scheerer, 1959). Given this fact, it is possible to suppose that subjects could also easily be "taken further back" until they would remember real previous lives. But several difficulties interpose themselves before such a simple explanation. As already mentioned, the subject under hypnosis is in a condition of increased suggestibility, and he usually feels a strong inclination to conform to the wishes of the hypnotist. Therefore, when the hypnotist instructs the subject to "go back to a previous life," he will attempt to do so to the best of his ability; it matters little how explicit the instructions are because the subject responds almost as obediently to implied suggestions as to specific ones. Secondly, the hypnotic state (which was compared above to dreaming sleep) facilitates the mobilization of memories of all kinds that ordinarily remain dormant. These may include forgotten memories of books read, films seen, or radio and television programs heard. Some of these latent memories may furnish the materials for the construction of plausible, and even impressive, "previous lives" that are nevertheless completely imaginary. In some instances the "previous lives" may contain a mixture of fact and fiction as historical novels do. But even when they do include verifiable information the task of the investigator has only begun, because he must then show that the subject could not possibly have acquired the correct information by normal means of communication. This is formidably difficult and not made easier by the fact that in a number of instances the content of a hypnotically induced "previous life" has been traced to a book or other normal source of information to which the subject had been exposed. The subject is usually completely unaware of such exposure, a fact that leads to calling such instances "cryptomnesia" instead of examples of fraud. But this possibility also increases the difficulty in interpreting hypnotically induced "previous lives" and makes the need for caution particularly great. The fact that some of the "previous personalities" emerging during experiments with hypnosis show an impressive range of apparently appropriate emotions and much consistency over months or years has no bearing on the provenance of the details included in the "previous personalities" and merely shows, as dreams do, the dramatizing powers of levels of the mind that ordinarily remain unconscious.

When all the above has been admitted, however, there still remains a small number of cases of hypnotic regression in which something valuable has emerged. Two cases of responsive xenoglossy were developed during experiments with hypnosis (Stevenson, 1974b, 1976). And in the case of Bridey Murphy (Bernstein, 1956) the hypnotized subject mentioned recondite details about life in Ireland of which it seems extremely unlikely that she could have had normal knowledge (Ducasse, 1960). This case has not been improved upon in the many books since written for the general public that have reported experiments with hypnotic regression. Most of these contain absurd anachronisms and other solecisms. Nevertheless, the few substantial results from the use of hypnosis in such experiments justify a more extensive exploration of the technique with better controls. The possibility of developing additional authentic cases of responsive xenoglossy would alone warrant this effort. (These, however, may be better interpreted as evidence of discarnate survival than of reincarnation.) But as of now, by far the best evidence of reincarnation comes from the spontaneous cases of claimed memories of previous lives.

SPONTANEOUS CASES OF THE REINCARNATION TYPE

Kinds of Spontaneous Cases of the Reincarnation Type

Memories of apparent previous lives may occur to persons under a variety of conditions. They have been reported in the form of vivid (and recurring) dreams, during intoxication with certain drugs such as lysergic acid diethylamide (LSD), and during meditation. When the apparent memories occur during adulthood the same question arises as with experiments using hypnosis: Could the subject have acquired the content of his apparent memories—whether verifiable or not—from some source to which he had been normally exposed? The difficulties of answering this question in the majority of adult subjects, not with certainty, but just with reasonable probability, have made cases which begin when the subjects are young children seem much more promising. With them, one can in most instances achieve satisfactory assurance concerning whether the apparent memories could have come from normally acquired information. This is simply because the parents of a child of 2 or 3 (the age at which most children with spontaneous memories of previous lives begin to talk about them) usually know who has been in contact with the child, and they can give this information to an investigator. The possibility of greater control over normal sources of information has been responsible for the fact that most scientific investigations bearing on the evidence of reincarnation have started with cases having young children as subjects. This being so, most of the remainder of this chapter will be devoted to data derived from the investigation of such cases.

Features of Typical Cases of the Reincarnation Type

As already mentioned, the typical case of this type starts when a child between the ages of 2 and 4, but occasionally older, begins to narrate details of a previous life that he claims to have lived before his birth. The child often begins talking about this previous life as soon as he gains any ability to speak, and sometimes before his capacity for verbal expression matches his need to communicate so that he mispronounces words that are later better understood or uses gestures to supplement what he cannot yet say clearly with words. The subjects of these cases vary greatly both in the quantity of their utterances and in the richness of the memories of the previous lives talked about. Some children make only three or four different statements about a previous life, but others may be credited with 60 or 70 separate items pertaining to different details in the life remembered. It is conjecturable that in all cases the subject remembers more than he tells because his telling depends very much both on his own related emotions that lead him to confide in others about his memories, or to conceal them, and on the willingness of other persons to listen to him. (Even in Asia busy parents often do not make suitable audiences for the talk of small children.) In most cases the volume and clarity of the child's statements increase until at the age of between 5 and 6 he usually starts to forget the memories; or, if he does not forget them, he begins to talk about them less. Spontaneous remarks about the previous life have usually ceased by the time the child has reached the age of 8 and often before.

Unexpected behavior of various kinds nearly always accompanies the statements the child makes about the previous life he claims to remember, or occurs contemporaneously with them. This behavior is unusual for a child of the subject's family, but concordant with what he says concerning the previous life, and in most instances it is found to correspond with what other informants say concerning the behavior of the deceased person about whom the subject has been talking, if such a person is traced. (It has become conventional to refer to this person as the "previous personality" of the case; this phrase can be used without commitment to any interpretation of the case, and also without regard to whether a particular person has in fact been identified as corresponding to the subject's statements.) This unusual behavior may take the form of phobias, such as for guns or bladed weapons, or of philias, such as special interests and appetites for particular foods, motor vehicles, books, and other objects, as well as attachments to certain persons. The child often also shows "adult" attitudes and behaves with gravity, wisdom, and sometimes patronizing condescension toward other children. The latter conduct apparently derives, in instances with unusually vivid memories, from the conviction on the part of the subject that he is still an adult, not a child. Very often the child asks, or even clamors, to be taken to the place where he says he lived before, and shows marked concern over the people "he" left there. The unusual behavior on the part of the subject that relates to the previous life usually diminishes at about the time he stops talking about the previous life, but residues of it may persist for many years and long after the child has forgotten the imaged memories he once had of the previous life.

Nearly always, upon the insistence of the child or to satisfy their own curiosity, his parents take him to the place where he says he lived, and they try to find the family he is talking about. In most Asian cases this is not too difficult because the child usually gives enough details concerning proper names so that a corresponding person can be found without much effort. In some cases this person may already be known if the child refers to a previous life as a deceased member of his own family. In other instances, the subject gives so little detail that no one corresponding to his statements can be traced.

In many cases the subject has some birthmark or congenital deformity that corresponds in location and appearance to a wound (usually fatal) on the body of the related previous personality. The child may point to the birthmark as the place where "he" (in the previous life) was (for example) stabbed or shot. Or the birthmark may be noticed at the subject's birth and judged by his parents to indicate the identity of the "incoming" personality before the child himself has made any statements about a previous life. This occurs frequently in cases among the Tlingits of Alaska (Stevenson 1966, 1974a). In some cases the subject suffers from an internal disease that corresponds with one from which the related previous personality suffered but of which other members of his family have been free.

In addition to the features of typical cases mentioned above, several others occur in some cases, particularly in those of certain regions. In some cultures a person before he dies makes a prediction about his next incarnation. This may take the form of selecting the parents he has chosen for his next incarnation, indicating a certain mark on his body the appearance of which on his next body will identify him, or expressing some wish about the conditions and circumstances he will experience in that next life, such as not having flat feet or a stutter. In a small number of cases expressed wishes of these kinds appear to have been fulfilled according to the evidence of the case as later developed. Their chief present significance undoubtedly lies, however, in the fact that the expression of such wishes nearly always alerts other people, such as the intended next parents, concerning the possibility that this person will reincarnate in a particular family. And expectations thus aroused can influence the parents in their observation and reporting of the indicated child's statements and behavior; furthermore, the parents and other adults may encourage such statements and behavior in the child in a manner that does not occur when they have no acquaintance whatever with the person of whom the child is speaking. Thus cases with the feature of a pre-mortem prediction have the strength that a particular development was foretold, but also the weakness that self-fulfillment may have entered into the realization of the prediction.

The expression "announcing dreams" has been coined to indicate dreams experienced during a pregnancy, usually by the expectant mother but some-times by a relative or friend, in which a deceased personality indicates to the dreamer his intention to reincarnate as the baby of the pregnant woman. In a dream of this type the "communicator" may seem to state his intention verbally and explicitly or may indicate it only symbolically, as when the deceased person-ality (in the dream) appears at the front door of the dreamer's house with his suitcase as if he were arriving for a long visit. In a few instances the dreamer does not recognize the deceased person who seems to be coming to announce his rebirth. More often, however, he is recognized, and in these cases, as with the pre-mortem predictions mentioned above, the stage may be arranged for the parents to influence statements and behavior of their child that correspond to what is known or inferable about the identified deceased person.

The cases occur in all social strata of the cultures in which they are found, from the richest to the poorest. Not infrequently the two families concerned belong to widely different social classes, the subject being born in a poor family and remembering a previous life in a wealthy one, or vice versa. In the majority of cases, however, the subject remembers a previous life in his own culture and in a place within 15 miles of that where his family lives. However, numerous cases have occurred in which the two families concerned are much more widely separated. There is also an appreciable number of "international" cases in which the subject remembers a previous life as a person of another country (and culture); for reasons not well understood "international" cases tend to be weak in verifiable details or totally lacking in them.

The interval between death and presumed rebirth varies considerably. For Turkish (Alevi) cases the average interval is 9 months, for Sri Lanka (Sinhalese) cases it is 21 months, for Indian cases it is 45 months, and for Tlingit cases it is 48 months. The reasons for these differences are not yet understood.

The period of childhood when the memories are strongest is often fraught with conflict for the subject and his family. Any such turbulence usually passes away, however, as the child grows older and forgets, or stops talking about, the memories of the previous life. With rare exceptions the subjects of these cases develop normally during the years after the age of 10. (For further remarks on the later development of the subjects, see Stevenson, 1974a, 1975.)

Report of a Typical Case

To familiarize the reader with details of an actual case, I will now describe one in summary form. I have selected one in which the subject did not recall a great many details of the previous life he remembered, but for that reason its presentation can be briefer than is possible for reports of cases that are richer in detail. Reports of such cases can be studied elsewhere (Stevenson, 1974a, 1975, 1977, 1978). In other respects the case to be presented is rather typical, at least of cases in Lebanon, and it illustrates some of the strengths and weaknesses of these cases.

Pseudonyms will be used for the persons concerned in this case. And instead of giving the real names of the communities where the persons involved in the case lived, other communities of comparable size and in the same general area of Lebanon will be named. All the persons concerned were members of the Druse religion (Makarem, 1974; Stevenson, 1974a, 1978).

Summary of the Case and Its Investigation. The subject of the case is Kemal Andawar who was born on May 17, 1966. His parents were Fuad Andawar and his wife, Samiha. They lived in the small village of El Kalaa which lies in the mountains about 15 miles east of Beirut. Fuad Andawar was a collector and seller of pine cones (from which pine oil is derived) and a person of exceedingly modest means. Kemal was the sixth child and second son of the family.

When Kemal was only about 2 years of age someone mentioned a certain Dr. Arif Eldary in his presence. On hearing this name Kemal shouted "Arif is my brother." This appears to have been his first statement about a previous life. As he became older, and particularly when he was about 3 years old, he began to say that he was Abu Naef, meaning the father of a son called Naef, that his family name was Eldary, and that he was from Hammana, a larger village about 5 miles from El Kalaa. Kemal gradually told his family further details about the life he was remembering. He gave the names of the wife, Edma Eldary, he said he had, and those of two other sons besides Naef. These, he said, were called Abbas and Ramez. He also mentioned the name of a sister, Afafe, and another brother, Adnan.

He said he used to travel and lived outside of Lebanon. He remarked rather often that he was "boostaji." (This word has been romanized to approximate the sound of what Kemal said when pronounced by a speaker of English.) The word *boostaji* meant nothing to the members of Kemal's family, but as he mentioned the word at times in relation to what he had done (as occupation) in the previous life, they tried to think of some professional activity denoted by a word with a similar sound. They were not, however, successful in this.

Kemal asserted that in the previous life he had been wealthy, and he complained of the poverty of his family. He said the house he had had in Hammana was better than theirs and had a tile roof. (The Andawars' house had only a flat cement roof.)

Kemal also gave a rather circumstantial account of how he had died in the previous life. He said that he had been on a visit to Lebanon from the place abroad (which he did *not* name) where he was living. He had gone to the Cedars (an important resort in Lebanon) with his wife and had been killed in an automobile accident. The car, he said, had struck a wall of concrete blocks. He had opened the door of the car and had been struck by one of the blocks that fell down from the damaged wall.

Kemal made some other statements about the previous life he was remembering. It was learned later that not all of these were accurate, but the names of people and places he gave were sufficiently numerous and specific so that there was no doubt about the person to whom he was referring. This was Faruq Eldary, who had been the oldest of four brothers of a family living at Hammana. They had one sister. Faruq Eldary had been a businessman who had lived much of his life in Portuguese Guinea, where he had had the post of honorary consul. He traveled considerably and returned to Lebanon from time to time. He had died in an automobile accident during a visit to Lebanon on August 19, 1965.

On one occasion Kemal's father took him to Hammana mainly to verify some of the details of Kemal's statements. They went to the house of Faruq Eldary (without entering it) and then, passing it, to that of Faruq's brother, Adnan Eldary, who happened to be at home. When Fuad Andawar explained to Adnan Eldary that his son had been claiming to remember the life of his brother Faruq, Adnan Eldary responded coolly with an acknowledgment that such things "might happen." He did not encourage further conversation, and so Kemal and his father left quickly and never returned. (Fuad Andawar gave somewhat inconsistent statements about Kemal's age at the time of this visit; he said he was between 3 and 4 years old, but also that it took place in September, 1971, by which date Kemal was almost 5½ years old.) No member of Faruq Eldary's family subsequently visited Kemal until I asked them to do so during my investigation of the case.

I first learned about the case during a visit to Lebanon early in March, 1972, and began its investigation almost immediately. (Mr. Issam Abul-Hisn assisted me as interpreter and also obtained some additional information about the case independently.) The principal informants for Kemal's side of the case were his parents. Kemal himself, at that time not quite 6 years old, was still talking about the previous life and could answer some questions about it, so we obtained a statement from him. We visited Kemal and his family again in November, 1972, and once more in October, 1973. During the last visit to El Kalaa we also interviewed a neighbor and distant relative of the family. This person was Jamil Andawar, an elderly man living just across the street from Kemal's family. Kemal had often visited him and talked with him about his memories of the previous life. He added an independent corroboration of some of the statements about the previous life that Kemal's parents had credited to him.

For the family of Faruq Eldary the main informants were his younger brother, Dr. Arif Eldary, and a more distant relative, Tariq Eldary, who had driven the

car involved in the accident in which Faruq Eldary died. A nephew (Samir
Eldary) and another relative and former close associate of Faruq Eldary (Mahmoud Eldary) were also interviewed and furnished some relevant information.
They agreed (in October, 1973) to go to Kemal's home in El Kalaa with the
thought that he might be able to recognize them as from the life of Faruq Eldary.
So they accompanied me and Mr. Abul-Hisn to Kemal's home at El Kalaa. In
fact he did not recognize either of the visitors. Both of these men, however, had
changed considerably in physical appearance since the death of Faruq Eldary.
His nephew, Samir Eldary, had grown from a boy of 14 to a young man of 22.
And Mahmoud Eldary had grown a moustache and developed more grey hair
than he had had when Faruq Eldary had died.

Geographical Facts and Prior Acquaintance Between the Families Concerned. As
already mentioned, El Kalaa and Hammana are about 5 miles apart. In Druse villages as close together as they are, the inhabitants of one village are likely to
know those of another, at least by name. In this case the two families concerned
had some acquaintance. The Eldary family was a prosperous and prominent one
of the area. Dr. Arif Eldary was a well-known physician of Beirut. One of his
brothers, Adnan Eldary, was even better known since he was the local Member
of Parliament. He used to come to El Kalaa to solicit votes around election time
and so was a rather familiar person in the village. Faruq Eldary, the oldest
brother of the family, was not so well known as his two younger brothers, perhaps because he spent much of his life abroad. However, he returned to Lebanon
about once a year. The Andawars had some acquaintance with him. Kemal's
mother said that she had met him "several times." Kemal's father also said that
they had known Faruq Eldary but had not known the names of his wife or of his
sons other than Naef. They would know Naef's name because Faruq Eldary, like
most Arab men, became known by the name of his oldest son and was familiarly
called, according to the custom, Abu Naef. The two families thus knew each
other casually, but they had no close social relations. In view of the large gap
between their social and economic situations, no closer connection could be expected. Kemal's parents had attended the funeral of Faruq Eldary and his
mother thought that she was then pregnant with Kemal. (Attendance at funerals
among the Druses of Lebanon does not necessarily indicate an intimate relationship with the deceased or his family; it is customary for many casual acquaintances and even strangers to attend the funeral of a member of a prominent
family such as that of the Eldarys.) Despite having attended Faruq Eldary's
funeral, Kemal's parents had not learned the details of how he had died, and
when Kemal began talking about these they had to verify them from other
persons.

The Accuracy of Kemal's Statements about the Previous Life. According to
the information given by his parents and their neighbor, Jamil Andawar, Kemal

had made a total of 28 statements about the previous life he claimed to remember. Of these 17 were correct, 10 were not, and one was doubtful. (This tabulation includes seven statements Kemal made to me in 1972, but none that he made in 1973 when his memories seemed to be fading. For all the other 21 statements one or more of the adult informants attributed the statement to Kemal.) All of his statements about proper names of people and places were correct. Kemal's doubtful statement concerned a rifle which he said he had had in the previous life. When questioned about this item, Dr. Arif Eldary conceded that his brother had had a hunting gun, but was evasive about the rifle. Since nearly every family in Lebanon has a rifle, and since none admit to having one because private ownership of such weapons is illegal, readers may judge for themselves whether Kemal was correct on this item or not.

Kemal was wrong in several details related to the automobile accident in which Faruq Eldary died. Most of the information obtained about this accident was furnished by Tariq Eldary, who was the driver of the vehicle, and he may have been inclined to gloss over some details, although there is no reason to challenge the main features of his account. The accident had occurred, as Kemal had stated, after a visit to the Cedars, when the car had run into a wall of concrete blocks. Furthermore, a few of the concrete blocks had been loosened by the impact. However, Tariq Eldary denied that any of these had fallen on Faruq Eldary. After the car struck the wall he (Tariq Eldary) got out to inspect the damage and then observed that Faruq Eldary was sitting motionless in the front seat beside that of the driver. Their wives were in the back seat, and one of them (Tariq's wife) was also unconscious, evidently stunned at the moment of the crash. Faruq and Tariq's wife were sent to the hospital in the nearest town, Tripoli. Faruq Eldary died on the way to the hospital or soon after reaching it. Tariq Eldary thought Faruq had not been wounded at the time of the accident and attributed his death to heart disease. However, if the impact was sufficiently great so that another passenger (Tariq's wife) was concussed, it was probably strong enough to have fatally injured Faruq Eldary also. Be that as it may, Kemal was wrong in saying that Faruq had died from being hit on the head by a falling concrete block even though some such blocks had fallen from the wall at the time of the accident.

Kemal's Behavior Apparently Related to the Previous Life. During the period when Kemal was talking most actively about the previous life he also showed behavior that was unusual in his family and at the same time harmonious with that of the life he was claiming to remember. I have already mentioned his invidious comparisons between the house he claimed to remember from the previous life and that of his family. Toward its members Kemal adopted a tone of superiority they did not find altogether agreeable. He showed an unusual preoccupation with cleanliness and would not, for example, use any eating utensil, such as a drinking glass, that another person had used. (Faruq Eldary's brother, Dr. Arif Eldarv, said that Faruq had been unusually, almost obsessively, concerned about cleanliness and "could not tolerate dirtiness.") Kemal had some phobia of automobiles when he was young. He also commented on changes in his physical appearance of which he seemed to be aware. He said for example, "I am a man," and at times he asked to shave. He would say: "I was big, but now I am small." He was much concerned about Faruq Eldary's oldest son, Naef. He kept saying "I want to see Naef." And when he saw a car coming into El Kalaa he would say: "This is Naef coming."

Kemal's mother remarked that when he talked about the previous life he "became nervous and cried." No reason for his anguish was obvious, although it may have derived from Kemal's unhappiness over what he saw to be a drastic change in his situation as compared to what he remembered of the previous life. This brings us naturally to the next topic.

The meaning of the word *boostaji* has not been definitely found, but a plausible conjecture was offered by Tariq Eldary based on the fact that Faruq Eldary, who had lived for many years in Portuguese Guinea, could speak Portuguese. He suggested that Kemal had perhaps been trying to say that in the previous life he had had a "bom estado" (good position) and that his imperfect pronunciation had led his hearers to think that he was saying "boostaji" or something like it. (The Portuguese phrase *boa estaçao*, which also means "good position," provides an even better match with what Kemal seemed to be saying.) This suggestion also made sense of the hauteur Kemal showed toward his family and his complaints about their poverty. He could have been trying to communicate to them his perplexity over the fact that he had, as he saw the matter, changed not only in size, but in socioeconomic position, and that from once having had a "good position" he now found himself living among poor people. This sense of a marked change in circumstances might account also for the difference in mood noted by informants for Kemal and Faruq Eldary. Kemal invariably had a serious, almost somber demeanor. This fact was remarked upon by members of his family, and it contrasted with a statement that Dr. Arif Eldary made about his brother's mood. He said that Faruq Eldary had been invariably good-humored, cordial, and smiling.

The Attitudes of the Other Persons Concerned in the Case. Kemal's family, being Druses, believed in reincarnation. But his father was afraid that the Eldary family might conjecture that he was trying to exploit the case for his own or Kemal's profit. And so he and his wife tried to influence Kemal not to talk about the previous life he was remembering. Otherwise, Kemal's parents showed a kindly tolerance of his remarks, and they did not seem to mind greatly his snobbish pretensions of belonging to a better family. Children at the school Kemal attended, however, added to his inhibitions by teasing him about his memories. They jokingly said: "You are from Hammana. What are you doing here?"

Although members of the Eldary family knew about the case from the time of Kemal's visit with his father to the home of Adnan Eldary, none of them came to visit him spontaneously or otherwise took any notice of him and his claim to be one of their family reborn. When I suggested to Dr. Arif Eldary that he might visit Kemal at El Kalaa, he was quite uninterested and excused himself by saying that if Kemal seemed to recognize him the result would be meaningless since he was quite well known in the area. This was perfectly true, but members of the families of related previous personalities in these cases have often gone to visit the subjects for reasons other than the expectation that they would be recognized.

Kemal's Later Development. At the time of my last interview with Kemal in October, 1973, he was still talking some about the previous life. However, his memories had partly faded, and he was getting details of the previous life mixed up. His father said that he still talked about Naef and still showed an extraordinary concern about cleanliness. Otherwise he was developing normally and was progressing well in school. He was in the second class of the primary school at El Kalaa.

Comments. The main weakness of this case lies in the fact that the two families concerned had some prior acquaintance, although it is certain that they were not close friends. It is best to assume, however, that few if any of Kemal's statements about the previous life were of matters completely unknown (or unknowable) to his parents. In this respect the case is much weaker than some other Lebanese cases such as those of Imad Elawar (Stevenson, 1974a) and Suleyman Andary (Stevenson, 1973c). On the other hand, the different circumstances of the two families concerned give the case one of its main strengths. Kemal gained nothing from claiming to be a member of a well-known family, and the claim alienated him somewhat from his own family. They had made no effort to exploit the case in seeking publicity or in any other way, and they had tried to discourage Kemal from talking about the previous life. His expressions of superiority to them would alone have justified this, but his parents were, in addition, afraid of unjust charges on the part of the Eldarys who might have thought them guilty of exploiting Kemal's claims. And as for the Eldarys themselves, Kemal certainly gained nothing from them by his claims to be one of them. They either rebuffed or ignored him, and none of them had taken the trouble to visit him until the case was investigated.

Brief History of the Investigation of Cases of the Reincarnation Type

As already mentioned, some ancient writings of India and Greece contain allusions to persons who claimed to remember that they had lived before. Almost nothing, however, that corresponds to the typical fully developed modern case of this type was reported earlier than the late nineteenth century. Between then and 1940 sporadic reports of such cases began to appear, sometimes in single reports, sometimes in small groups of reports (Gupta, Sharma, and Mathur, 1936; Hall, 1898; Hearn, 1897; Osborn, 1974; Sahay, 1927; Sunderlal, 1924). In 1924 Delanne published a remarkable compilation of reports of cases which he had garnered from previously printed sources and his own correspondents. Although his collection reproduced some newspaper reports characterized by journalistic brevity and inattention to detail, it also included a small number of cases that had evidently received rather careful observation and documentation.

By 1960 it was possible to show that the quality of at least some reports of cases suggestive of reincarnation justified a systematic investigation of any additional cases that could be located (Stevenson, 1960). No one then seems to have realized how numerous such cases are in many different parts of the world. In the following year (1961) I began field investigations in India and Ceylon (now Sri Lanka) and gradually extended them to many other parts of the world. The first results of these endeavors were published in 1966 (Stevenson, 1966, 1974a) with further articles and books following in subsequent years (Stevenson, 1970, 1975, 1977, 1978; Stevenson and Story, 1970; Story and Stevenson, 1967).

Most of the case reports published between the 1890s and 1960 were included in books written for the general public or from the point of view of Spiritualists. They thus fell outside the literature and the growing tradition of psychical research which developed into modern parapsychology. It should be noted, however, that three reports of Indian cases published in the 1920s, two by Sahay (1927) and one by Sunderlal (1924), included the important feature of a written record made before any attempt at verifying the subject's statements was begun. The advances in the investigation of these cases since 1960 include, first, the more systematic collection of data from a large number of cases; second, the more careful recording of data obtained from firsthand informants; third, the analysis of each case with regard to interpretations alternative to reincarnation; and fourth, the increased attention given to observations of the physical and behavioral resemblances between subjects and related previous personalities of the cases. Some of these topics will next be considered in more detail.

The Distribution of Cases of the Reincarnation Type

As already mentioned, cases of the reincarnation type are reported (and found) much more frequently in those areas of the world where the belief in reincarnation is held by the majority of the population. Yet cases have also been reported and investigated in cultures having a majority of persons uninformed about reincarnation, uninterested in it, or actually opposed to the belief in it. In recent years more cases have been found in such groups, which include the Christians of

Lebanon and Sri Lanka, the Sunni Moslems of India, and the Christians of Europe, the United States, and Canada. It cannot be said as yet whether this has resulted from a softening of former opposition to the idea of reincarnation (and the related fear of seeming to endorse it by presenting a case), to better methods of finding cases, or to a combination of these and other factors.

The incidence of reported cases of the reincarnation type provides a quite inadequate guide to the real incidence of cases of this type. The figures for reported cases undoubtedly reflect the interest and effectiveness in reporting cases on the part of the public media of communication, such as newspapers, and the number and diligence of investigators seeking information about them. These factors almost certainly account for the fact that many more cases have been reported in northern India than in southern India. There are grounds for thinking that the cases occur just as frequently in southern India as in northern India, but they have not been publicized so much or searched for so thoroughly in southern India.

At one time it seemed possible that many more cases occurred in the West than were reported, but that they were suppressed by the parents of child subjects or by the subjects themselves. A certain number of cases have been exposed to this fate, and some have escaped it when someone, often the subject himself when older, informed me about the case. However, the increasing interest (among Westerners) in the topic of reincarnation in the 1960s and early 1970s, including some publicity given to its scientific investigation, has not brought to notice any great hoard of previously hidden cases. It therefore seems likely that the real incidence of cases in Europe and the United States is less than that in those parts of Asia (and northwestern North America) where the incidence of reported cases is high and where it may be expected that the real incidence of cases is also high.

Present methods of case-finding are haphazard and therefore far from satisfactory. But they are particularly deficient with regard to improving our understanding of the real incidence of the cases. This will require systematic surveys made with proper sampling methods in a variety of cultures. Considering the inadequacy of the methods of case finding and the paucity of persons actively engaged in locating and studying cases, it is perhaps surprising that the University of Virginia's collection of cases now numbers nearly 1,600. It should be emphasized, however, that these 1,600 cases are of uneven quality with regard to the richness of detail they have, the thoroughness of the investigations they have received, and the judgments of authenticity based on such investigations. About two-fifths of the cases have received extensive investigation by myself. Another (approximately) two-fifths have been investigated less thoroughly—either by myself or by one of my assistants who has worked as an interpreter with me in the study of other cases. One-fifth of the cases I have accepted into the series on the basis of published reports that seemed to justify credence or because I obtained reports about them from persons in whom I had confidence even though they were not working directly with me. All of the 1,600 cases have been provisionally accepted as authentic so that they have been included in a computerized analysis of the data of the entire collection to which I shall refer later. At least several hundred other cases have been notified to me, but set aside as insufficiently authentic and not meriting inclusion in the group to be studied further. Some of these latter cases could be dismissed on initial examination, others only after they had been given some investigation.

Probably more cases of the type than have come to my attention have occurred and are still occurring in many parts of the world. At the same time readers should not conclude from the rather large number of cases known about or conjectured, especially in Asia, that many persons remember previous lives. Cases of this type are rather rare even in Southeast Asia where, in comparison to the incidence of cases in the West, they occur relatively frequently. Thus in India it is unusual to find more than one case in a family or more than one in a village although some families do have several cases. It is more common to find two or several cases in the same family among the Druses of Lebanon and the natives of northwest North America.

Methods of Investigation

The methods of investigation used for these cases, described in more detail elsewhere (Stevenson, 1974a, 1975), derive from those developed by the early investigators of spontaneous cases in psychical research (Gurney, Myers, and Podmore, 1886; Myers, 1903). With due acknowledgment of the greatness of these pioneers I have made some efforts to improve upon their methods and also to modify them as required for the special features and circumstances of cases of the reincarnation type.

As with other types of spontaneous cases in parapsychology, the investigator of cases of the reincarnation type can rarely study the case while its main events are still unfolding. In the investigations of recent years it has been possible to reach more cases during this stage, but even when this happens the investigator in most instances has still the task of reconstructing as well as he can events that took place before he came on the scene. For this, reliance is placed mainly on interviews with firsthand informants, preferably several or more of them, and preferably also including a second interview (or more) with at least the main informants. Cross-questioning is used within the time available and the informants' tolerance for it, care being taken not to allow the investigation to be confused with legal proceedings. For most cases the principal informants on the side of the subject are his parents; his older siblings may also furnish valuable information.

When the subject of the case is still talking freely about the previous life he claims to remember, every effort is made to write down (or tape record) whatever he can say to the interviewers. Since the two families concerned have usually met by the time an investigator arrives, the subject's statements at that time have no value with regard to judgments about what he said *before* the two families met; but they have other values, not the least of which is the evidence they provide that the case was not simply invented by his parents, as critics have occasionally suggested. When the child himself makes statements corresponding to what his parents say he made earlier, then a minimal explanation of the case as one worked up dishonestly would have to include the subject as an apt pupil or co-conspirator with his parents.

Observations and notes concerning the behavior of the subject and other informants are also made. It not infrequently happens that the investigators can learn of some recent episode of the subject's unusual behavior of which I gave examples earlier. And sometimes the investigators themselves can observe such behavior directly. They also assess the apparent reliability of the informants with regard to accuracy of perception and memory for the events they are describing, their motives to tell the truth or to deceive, and any indications of less conscious influences that may lead them unintentionally to slant the evidence in one direction or another.

If informants additional to members of the subject's immediate family are available, and qualified by having firsthand knowledge of the case, their assistance is eagerly sought. Such persons are often uncles, aunts, grandparents, or neighbors. Their information may corroborate or supplement that of the subject and his parents, and it may help to evaluate the reliability of the principal informants. Every effort is also made to corroborate the oral testimony by whatever written documents are at hand or obtainable. These include birth certificates or horoscopes, diaries, notebooks, and school records.

After the investigation has been carried as far as it can be with the subject and his family, at least in its initial stages, the entire procedure of interviewing firsthand informants is repeated with the family of the deceased person about whom the child has been talking. If no such person has been identified and if the subject has given an apparently sufficient number of verifiable details, the investigators themselves try to find a person corresponding to the child's statements. It has happened, however, that in nearly every case in which the child has given sufficient details to permit verification its family has taken it to the previous family before an investigator reached the scene. It has been possible in fewer than 15 cases for the investigator to be the first person to trace the concerned previous family. For examples of these rare, but extremely valuable cases, see Stevenson (1974a, 1975, 1977).

Great importance is given to independent verification of the child's statements, the mere assertion by the child's parents that he was correct in a certain item being regarded as quite insufficient confirmation that he was. At the same time, when the two families have already met, care has to be taken that the family of the deceased person concerned does not compliantly, even if unintentionally, furnish false information that erroneously indicates the subject to have been more accurate than he really was. The investigators try to see buildings and objects mentioned by the child and to meet themselves any persons named by him who are still living. In this way they check on the accuracy or incorrectness, as the case may be, of many of the statements the child has made.

The data derived from field investigations are analyzed both with regard to individual cases and with regard to characteristics that recur in many cases. These types of analysis will next be considered separately.

Analyses of the Data of Individual Cases

The material derived from interviews and whatever written documents have become available are analyzed for consistencies and discrepancies among the statements of different informants and among those of one informant at different times. The information thus derived, together with any other evidence bearing on the reliability of the informants, is then taken into account in a consideration of various alternative interpretations of the case. The most important of these are the following.

Fraud. Dishonestly contrived cases have occurred, and at least some of them have been exposed. These have betrayed themselves by radical departures from the features of a typical case. It would be difficult to simulate a case with a young child as the subject. Small children are not easy to coach for the assumption of roles that do not seem natural to them. In a typical case the subject even up to the age of about 5 would still be talking about the previous life he remembered, and he could therefore be questioned about it. Also, in a typical case the child has made at least some remarks to informants other than his parents, such as uncles, aunts, and neighbors. Suspicion would be aroused by any case that depended on the unsupported statements of the subject's parents, although in some cases that seem from all other indices to be authentic, the child has made only a few statements about a previous life and these only to his parents. We have other clues to fraud besides the ones mentioned above, but it does not seem necessary to describe these here.

Apart from the practical difficulties of perpetrating a fraud, few motives exist for anyone to try, at least in Asia. Although in the West books may be written and fortunes made on fictitious and insubstantial cases, such opportunities do not exist in Asia, at any rate for the villagers among whom the majority of genuine cases occur. A few fraudulent cases in Asia have, however, been traced to unscrupulous journalists and "investigators."

Paramnesia. As already mentioned, the two families concerned in these cases have nearly always met before an investigator reaches the scene and begins to make written records of what has happened up to that time. Under these circumstances the families concerned may mingle their memories of what the child said with what they learn or remember about the identified previous personality, and they may then attribute to the child more knowledge about the previous personality than he really had before the two families met. In an extreme development of this kind the informants could elaborate a rather detailed case on the basis of a few statements made by the child. This could, at least in theory, happen without the people concerned being aware of what they are doing and without any intention to deceive.

The hypothesis of paramnesia may apply to a small number of cases, especially those in which the child has given out only a few details about the previous life he claims to remember, or is said to remember. But it seems an unlikely explanation for the many cases that are rich in apparently remembered details. Moreover, in at least some of the latter cases, that is, those richer in details, the informants are educated and thoughtful persons who have given their statements to investigators within a few weeks or months of the main events of the case. To account for such cases on the basis of faulty memory is to attribute to these informants deficiencies of observation and remembering for which there is no other evidence. Finally, the hypothesis of paramnesia cannot apply at all to those cases (unfortunately still very few) in which someone made a written record of what the child said about the previous life *before* any attempt at verification was made.

Cryptomnesia. In the hypothesis of paramnesia the child is credited with knowing more about the previous personality than he did; in cryptomnesia his knowledge about the previous personality is not in question, but he is thought to have come by it normally. In a small number of mediumistic cases, a medium has communicated information which she had acquired normally, perhaps through reading, although she had completely forgotten her exposure to the material which emerged in the communications. There is no question here of dishonesty, only that of a simple forgetfulness of what one had read or otherwise seen or heard. In some instances the medium may not even have been aware, at the time, of her exposure to the material later communicated, so that even the process of perception was unconscious.

Although cryptomnesia has been adduced as an explanation for at least some cases of the reincarnation type, no case has been identified yet as a proven example of cryptomnesia. Despite this weakness of the hypothesis—that it lacks examples from empirical studies—it remains an important possibility in certain cases. And it deserves special consideration when the two families concerned in a case have known each other before the case developed. In such instances members of one or the other family may well pass on to the subject more information about the deceased personality he later talks about than he or they afterwards recall. On the other hand, cryptomnesia does not seem a likely explanation for those quite numerous cases in which the two families concerned live in villages or towns separated by 50 or more miles and in which the persons on the two sides of the case assert, with good grounds for believing them, that they never had any acquaintance with each other prior to the development of the case. The very early age—2 or 3 years—at which most subjects begin to speak about the previous lives makes it unlikely that anyone could have had contact with such a child sufficient to communicate the information it seems to remember without the contact being known and remembered by its parents.

Extrasensory Perception and Personation. As explained above, certain cases may be explained by supposing normal channels of communication to the subject of information about the related previous personality. But this interpretation cannot reasonably apply to cases in which the two families concerned live in widely separated communities, in which the child begins to talk about a previous life at a very early age and with abundant detail, and in which the investigators reach the case when memories of events are still reasonably fresh. This has led to the proposal that the subjects are really gifted with extrasensory perception and that, using their paranormal powers, they obtain knowledge about a deceased person with whom they then identify themselves. The main sources for the information paranormally obtained by the subject are presumably the surviving relatives and friends of the deceased person. The previous personality thus constructed is viewed as a pathological secondary personality cast into a reincarnationist form under the influence of the culture surrounding him in which memories of a previous life are acceptable and expected. The hypothesis requires attribution of some degree of paramnesia to the subject himself, though not necessarily to other informants. He, however, comes to believe that information obtained contemporaneously derives from memories and so he falsely sets it in the past instead of in the present of his experiences. Chari (1962a, 1962b) and Murphy (1973) have persuasively argued the merits of this interpretation which they (with variations) favor. It is essential to include in this hypothesis the unusual behavior shown by the subject that corresponds to behavior reported for the related previous personality; a hypothesis of paranormal cognition alone will not suffice.

The hypothesis accounts quite well for the greater frequency of reported cases in cultures favoring the belief in reincarnation; it also accords with the fact that in the majority of cases the families concerned (those of the subject and the related previous personality) live in the same general geographical area. This would make easier paranormal communication to the subject through so-called psychometric objects that had been associated in some way with the deceased person or his family. The hypothesis does not, however, adequately account for the exceptions to the above general principles; that is, for cases that crop up in families and cultures unsympathetic or even hostile to the belief in reincarnation and those, alluded to above, with wide geographical separations between the families concerned. The most serious objection to it comes from the fact that, with rare exceptions, the subjects of these cases show no trace of paranormal powers apart from the memories of the previous lives they claim to remember If the accurate details in their statements derive from the use of paranormal cognition of an "ordinary" kind, it is surprising, to say the least, that it manifests so powerfully with regard to one particular person and no other, and for a few years of childhood and not thereafter. This argument seems to me strong, but it is not compelling since it has been found that some persons show paranormal abilities in only one particular task or situation (Pratt, 1973).

There are also difficulties for the hypothesis of extrasensory perception and personation in the subject's accurate knowledge of the condition of buildings and objects during the lifetime of the related previous personality and his (usual) ignorance of changes occurring to them after the previous personality's death. Nor is it clear how a theory of "ordinary" paranormal cognition could by itself account for the unusual behavior that almost invariably accompanies the subject's statements about the previous life he remembers. This behavior, as mentioned earlier, often extends over 5 years and sometimes many more. It may include attitudes and sometimes strong emotions and skills which it is not easy to conceive as being transmitted by "ordinary" extrasensory perception.

Other Hypotheses.   Several other hypotheses have been put forward to account for these cases. Each may apply to some of the cases, without being applicable to all of them.

Retrocognition is a variant of the hypothesis of extrasensory perception, and as such is liable to the same criticisms. Why, for example, should a child show strong retrocognitive ability in relation to only one particular deceased person and no other?

"Inherited memory" may apply to certain cases in which it is possible for the subject to be a lineal descendant of the previous personality, whether or not such genetic linkage is known to exist. Even in such cases, however, the hypothesis of "inherited memory" would be proposing transmission through genetic linkages of detailed imaged memories, something that is not envisaged in present-day theories of inheritance, although it is not for that reason impossible.   The hypothesis of "inherited memory" could not apply to the majority of cases of the reincarnation type in which the subject is born just a few years after the death of the previous personality in a family totally unrelated to the other one concerned. Thus the subject could not possibly be descended from the previous personality or have inherited any qualities from him.

"Possession" of the subject, whether temporary or permanent, by a discarnate personality has been put forward as an explanation for cases of the reincarnation type since at least as far back as the eighteenth century when Swedenborg (1906, p. 155) espoused it. Its gravest weakness is its failure to account for the cessation of the unusual statements and behavior expressed by the subject as he becomes older. As mentioned above, most subjects gradually cease talking spontaneously about the previous lives between the ages of 5 and 8, and their associated unusual behavior also diminishes, if sometime later. This process is much more often gradual than abrupt, and it is difficult to understand why "possessing spirits" would all (or mostly) withdraw themselves in such a fashion and when the subjects were of about the same age.

Reincarnation. In reincarnation research, as in other branches of parapsychology, one reaches paranormal interpretations, and especially those including survival as a part of them, only after trying to eliminate interpretations along normal lines or those that take account of processes for which we already have independent evidence. This means that reincarnation should only be considered the best interpretation of any case after the alternative interpretations mentioned above have been considered and found unsatisfactory, or at least less satisfactory than reincarnation in accounting for all the facts of the case. A later section of this chapter will attempt to summarize the present status of the evidence for reincarnation, but first I will consider the value of the analysis of large numbers of cases.

Analyses for Recurrent Characteristics in Numbers of Cases

Investigators in the early years of psychical research found it helpful to study the recurrent characteristics or patterns discoverable in large numbers of spontaneous cases considered together (Gurney et al., 1886; Sidgwick, Sidgwick, Johnson, Myers, Myers, and Podmore, 1894). The method was further developed by Green (1960); Hart (1956); Rhine (1953, 1954); and Sannwald (1959a, 1959b). In recent years the development of computers has made possible the handling and analysis of large amounts of data from many cases with less effort and time than was hitherto needed. In the application of this method to the data of cases of the reincarnation type two kinds of uniformities have emerged.

Characteristics Recurring in Cases from All Cultures Studied. Certain features have recurred, with some exceptions, in the cases of all cultures so far investigated. Examples of such features are: the usual age (2 to 4 years) when the subjects first start speaking about the previous lives; the usual age (5 to 8 years) when they stop talking about the previous lives; the high frequency of violent death in the related previous personalities (Stevenson, 1974a, 1974c, 1978); and the prominence of events connected with the death of the previous personality, or just preceding it, among the subjects' memories. These and other recurrent features found in cases of many different parts of the world appear to have two significances.

First, since at least some of the cultures in which these features have been found are effectively isolated from each other with regard to possibilities for mutual influence, and have been so for centuries, the occurrence of similar features in their cases is an indication of the authenticity of the cases. These "universal" features could not be explained as resulting from local cultural influences. They suggest instead some widespread human experience. This conclusion would not by itself tell anything about paranormal interpretations. Obviously other features of human experience have recurred in many (or perhaps all) different cultures which men have developed. The making of myths is certainly one of these, and the widespread occurrence of reincarnation cases could be an example of this mythopoeic tendency.

Second, the understanding of features that can be expected in a case of this type assists in the delineation of a "standard" case in comparison with which new cases can be evaluated. This may aid in such different matters as the earlier detection of fraudulent cases and reassurance to parents of a young subject of a case who are worried about whether he will later develop normally. The concept of a "standard" case is naturally modified from culture to culture by taking account not only of the "universal" features, but also of those that are culture-bound.

Culture-Bound Recurrent Features of the Cases. At least some of the features described as found in all cultures where cases of this type have been investigated vary to some extent from culture to culture. For example, although a high incidence of violent death has been found for the previous personalities in the cases of all cultures so far studied, the actual percentage of violent deaths ranges from a low of 38 percent in Sri Lanka cases to a high of slightly more than 78 percent in the Druse cases of Lebanon and Syria (Stevenson, 1974c, p. 409). Other features of the cases vary so much from one culture to another that we may properly speak of them as culture-bound. An impressive example of such a culture-bound factor in the patterns of the cases is the markedly variable incidence of those in which the subject claims to remember a previous life as a person of the opposite sex. No case of this type has been found among approximately 220 cases of the Alevis of south central Turkey and the Druses of Lebanon and Syria. Nor has any case of the "sex change" type been found in 85 cases occurring among the Tlingits of southeastern Alaska. (De Laguna [1972, p. 779] mentioned cases of the "sex change" type reported to her by two informants of the Yakutat Tlingits farther north.) At the other extreme, Slobodin (1970) has reported an incidence of 50 percent "sex change" cases in 44 cases that he studied among the Kutchin of northwestern Canada. In the University of Virginia collection of cases those of Burma and Thailand (consisting together of about 250 cases) have an incidence of approximately 20 percent of the "sex change" type. In all other cultures (not previously mentioned in this paragraph) the incidence of "sex change" cases is about 5 percent.

"Announcing dreams" and birthmarks also show a marked variation from one culture to another. Although these two features occur to some extent in the cases of all cultures so far studied, they have both been found much more abundantly in the cases among the Burmese, the natives of northwestern North America, and the Alevis of south central Turkey.

The connections between the subject and the family of the previous personality also vary significantly from one culture to another. For example, among the Tlingits of southeastern Alaska the subject and previous personality were related on the side of the subject's mother in 70 percent of the cases. Among the neighboring Eskimos (in a much smaller group of cases) subject and previous personality were related on the mother's side in only 27 percent of the cases. The incidence of such connections between the two families concerned in other cultures is extremely low, and although exact figures are not yet available for these, the incidence can be estimated as probably not higher than 2 percent among cases of Southeast Asia. For further information about apparently culture-bound variations in the characteristics of the cases, see Stevenson (1966, 1970, 1973a, 1974c.)

An interesting and probably important concordance occurs between the patterns in the cases of a particular culture and the beliefs held about them in that culture. For example, inquiries among the peoples where no cases of the "sex change" type occur almost always elicit the statement that "sex change" is "impossible." Beliefs concerning this and other features of the cases seem often to be held inflexibly and applied as standards assumed to be true for cases all over the world when the person making such an assertion has obviously had no experience of cases outside his own culture and perhaps of few within it. In interpreting the connections between beliefs and the patterns of the cases one naturally thinks that the local beliefs favor the development of cases congenial to the culture; the development of cases that seem discordant could be discouraged and even suppressed by scolding a subject whose memories seemed to depart from the norm acceptable in a particular culture, that is, the characteristics of that culture's typical case. We should remember, however, that an agreement between beliefs and patterns in the cases is not incompatible with reincarnation, and is indeed what we should expect if reincarnation occurs. It is altogether possible that the belief held by a person before he dies may influence what actually happens to him after he dies and if and when he reincarnates. Such an idea has been taught in Buddhism for centuries (Evans-Wentz, 1957).

THE PRESENT STATE OF THE EVIDENCE FOR REINCARNATION

Although systematic investigations of cases of the reincarnation type have been undertaken for less than 16 years, a considerable body of data has already been collected. Some parapsychologists have been surprised at the quantity of data that has been recorded and published so far, and most appear to agree that the results justify further investigations in this area.

Parapsychologists vary much more in their opinions concerning the interpretation as evidence for the survival of bodily death of the data so far obtained from these cases. Before 1960 few parapsychologists would have been willing to consider reincarnation as a serious interpretation for cases of this type, if they were aware of any. Today probably most parapsychologists would agree that reincarnation is at least entitled to inclusion in any list of possible interpretations of the cases, but not many would believe it the most probable interpretation.

All the cases (and all their reports) have deficiencies, as have most cases and reports of other types of spontaneous paranormal phenomena. The perfect case can be conceived (Stevenson, 1973b), but probably met only in fantasy and not in field work. We cannot reasonably expect to find any single case that will provide conclusive proof of reincarnation, nor is such proof a likely result from the study of all the cases considered together. Instead we may look for an accumulation of evidence, first from a larger number of cases, and second from an improvement in their average quality. The quality of the cases should improve as more scientifically trained persons of the countries where they occur begin to investigate them and reach them at early stages of their development more often than has been possible up to now. Some hopes may be expressed also for the results from the further investigation of cases having birthmarks and deformities. Cases with these features obviously require more than extrasensory perception for their interpretation. If it is argued, as some persons have done, that in such cases the account of a previous life has been made up to account for the birthmark or deformity, the latter themselves still have to be explained. If reincarnation seems a better interpretation of such cases, this suggests that some psychic "force" can influence human fetuses *in utero*, sometimes rather drastically.

OTHER THEORETICAL ISSUES RELATED TO REINCARNATION

Most of the hypotheses and theories with regard to reincarnation may be considered within two main categories: those concerned with alternative interpretations of the empirically derived evidence of reincarnation and those concerned with the processes of reincarnation, if it occurs. Because systematic research in this area is new, emphasis has been given to developing and analyzing evidence that indicates reincarnation as at least a reasonable hypothesis justifying further investigation. Previous sections of this chapter have already considered this category of theoretical issues.

With regard to theories of process, the field of reincarnation research is even less far advanced than other branches of parapsychology. We may, however, briefly consider such theories of process as have been developed, first by the peoples among whom the cases occur most frequently, and second by investigators working in the scientific tradition.

The peoples of regions where cases frequently occur often have some beliefs about the processes of reincarnation. Indeed, in some such areas, such as those of Southeast Asia where Hinduism and Buddhism predominate, there exist a number of scriptures alluding to concepts about reincarnation. What we may call local concepts of reincarnation vary considerably from one culture to another. For example, Hinduism decrees no fixed interval between death and presumed subsequent rebirth. But the Druses of Lebanon and neighboring countries believe that reincarnation occurs instantly at death, the released soul entering immediately into the body of a newly born baby (Stevenson, 1974a, 1978). The Jains of India have a somewhat similar belief but hold that the new connection between the recently deceased soul and its new physical body occurs at the moment of the conception of that body (Stevenson, 1975). Beliefs of this kind—and there are many of them—tend to be held dogmatically, and they can hardly be dignified with the name *theory* since they are promulgated as doctrines and not presented as testable hypotheses. Moreover, to the extent that they are confirmed by observation of cases occurring in the same area, this result may derive from a self-fulfilling prophecy as suggested in an earlier section of this chapter.

The few ventures in theorizing that Western scientists interested in this subject have made push our ideas only a little way ahead of the reasonably established facts. One example is the "law" mentioned above which suggests that what a person believes will happen to him after death will in fact happen to him. (But this idea, as already mentioned, has come to us from Buddhism.) Another tentative generalization derives from the observation mentioned earlier that the family of the subject usually lives within about 15 miles of the previous personality's family. Many exceptions have occurred to this general observation, but it has suggested another provisional "law" according to which, other things being equal, persons tend to be reborn near where they die. The tendency just mentioned and some other often observed features of the cases offer the hope of an eventual understanding of the factors which, if reincarnation occurs, influence a deceased person so that he is reborn in one particular family rather than in another of all those in which he might be reborn.

Some thought has been given, on the assumption that reincarnation occurs, to what it is that reincarnates. But here also concepts do little more than loosely connect observations. The subjects of the cases show three qualities corresponding to similar ones in the related previous personalities: imaged memories, behavioral traits, and physical characteristics, the last two occurring in some cases only. It may be supposed then that, if reincarnation occurs, some intermediate "body" comprised of nonmaterial "substances" acts as a carrier (during the interval between death and rebirth) between the previous personality and the new physical body in which its memories and other qualities will later manifest. Broad (1958) called this intermediate "something" a "psi-component," thus properly emphasizing its paranormal characteristics.

If, as now seems possible, the evidence for reincarnation increases and improves in the years ahead, more advanced theories related to it will be developed and tested. Already some predictions about the occurrence of birthmarks under certain conditions have been found accurate, and it seems likely that more and bolder predictions will be offered in the future. It is not difficult even to imagine in the future a whole demography of reincarnation that would attempt to study characteristics of groups of people from the point of view of the hypothesis of reincarnation.

Although research on cases of the reincarnation type developed to some extent away from traditional topics of inquiry in parapsychology (but not from traditional *methods*), nevertheless some links can already be discerned between the data of cases of the reincarnation type and those elicited in other branches of parapsychology. For example, "announcing dreams" purport to be communications from discarnate personalities. As such they relate closely to other types of apparent discarnate communications such as those conveyed through mediums, in some paranormal dreams not concerned with reincarnation, and in apparitional experiences. Another example of a connection with other areas of parapsychology occurs in the frequent claims by subjects of reincarnation cases in parts of Southeast Asia, especially Burma, Thailand, and Vietnam, that they remember events happening to them after death in the preceding lives and before their presumed rebirths. Such a subject may report having seen "his" previous physical body being buried or cremated and may also claim to remember having been in some kind of "intermediate body" during the "intermission" period between death and rebirth. Experiences of this kind have important affinities with those of living persons who, usually after some serious accident or during a near fatal illness, seem to leave their physical bodies and later remember that while "out-of-the-body" they seemed to see their physical bodies, lying inert, as from a different position in physical space. Persons having this latter type of experience recover and afterwards narrate what they remember to other persons; the mentioned subjects of reincarnation cases having somewhat similar experiences of being "out-of-the-body" say that they did not recover, but died, were reborn, and preserved memories of these experiences in their new lives.

In conclusion, something may be said about the potential contribution of the investigation of cases of the reincarnation type to branches of knowledge outside parapsychology. The other types of evidence bearing on the question of the survival of human personality after death do not impinge except peripherally on orthodox theories of child development and human personality. This is because the persons having the experiences from which such evidence derives, mediums for example, are (usually) adults and merely acting as temporary conduits or registrars of communications from ostensibly discarnate persons. In this process their own personalities, which are already in adult form anyway, become only transiently altered by the communications which they transmit. On the other hand, the subjects of the best reincarnation cases are young children whose personalities are not fully formed, and they often manifest unusual behavior during several years or more. Such children show a mixture of behavior that might be expected of children in their families and behavior that seems quite surprising. The unexpected behavior, however, may make sense if reincarnation is taken seriously as an explanation of it. Furthermore, there are many other children who, although they have no imaged memories of previous lives, nevertheless manifest strange, unexpected behavior that cannot be adequately accounted for either by heredity or by early environmental influences, but which might derive from patterns of conduct learned in previous lives. For example, in our efforts to understand children who are confused about gender identity it may be helpful to add reincarnation to the presently considered interpretations of this disorder. This suggestion receives support from some of the cases of the "sex change" type mentioned above; some subjects of such cases show behavior characteristic of a person of the opposite sex (Stevenson, 1973d, 1974a, 1975).

The study of cases of the reincarnation type thus holds out prospects for enriching our understanding of child development and, beyond that, of biology and medicine. If this occurs, an understanding of reincarnation will not replace present knowledge of heredity and environmental influences, but will supplement it. The greatest contribution from its investigation, however, will certainly derive from whatever additional evidence it adds to that already obtained, or to be obtained by other researches in the future, bearing on the important question of the fate of human personality after physical death. Future investigations of the evidence of reincarnation may confirm the prediction made many years ago by the English philosopher McTaggart (1915) who wrote: "If we succeed in proving immortality, it will be by means of considerations which would also prove pre-existence" (p. 113).

REFERENCES

Bayer, R. Personal communications, 1970–71.

Bernstein, M. *The Search for Bridey Murphy*. Garden City, N.Y.: Doubleday, 1956.

Besterman, T. Belief in rebirth among the natives of Africa (including Madagascar). In T. Besterman, *Collected Papers on the Paranormal*, pp. 22–59. New York: Garrett Publications, 1968.

Broad, C. D. *Personal Identity and Survival*. (The Thirteenth Frederic W. H. Myers Memorial Lecture.) London: The Society for Psychical Research, 1958.

Chari, C. T. K. Paranormal cognition, survival and reincarnation. *Journal of the American Society for Psychical Research*, 1962, 56, 158–183. (a)

Chari, C. T. K. Paramnesia and reincarnation. *Proceedings of the Society for Psychical Research*, 1962, 53, 264–286. (b)

De Laguna, F. Under Mount St. Elias: The history and culture of the Yakutat Tlingit. *Smithsonian Contributions to Anthropology*, 1972, 7, 776–781.

Delanne, G. *Documents pour servir à l'étude de la réincarnation*. Paris: Editions de la B. P. S., 1924.

Deschamps, H. *Les religions de l'Afrique noire.* Paris: Presses Universitaires de France, 1970.

Dodds, E. R. Personal communication, 1971.

Ducasse, C. J. How the case of *The Search for Bridey Murphy* stands today. *Journal of the American Society for Psychical Research,* 1960, **54,** 3–22.

Evans-Wentz, W. Y. (Ed.) *The Tibetan Book of the Dead.* (3rd ed.) London: Oxford University Press, 1957.

Gallup International. Report of polls concerning the belief in reincarnation in West Europe, Canada, and the United States. 1969.

Green, C. Analysis of spontaneous cases. *Proceedings of the Society for Psychical Research,* 1960, **53,** 97–161.

Gupta, L. D., Sharma, N. R., and Mathur, T. C. *An Inquiry into the Case of Shanti Devi.* Delhi: International Aryan League, 1936.

Gurney, E., Myers, F. W. H., and Podmore, F. *Phantasms of the Living.* London: Trübner, 1886, 2 vols.

Hall, H. F. *The Soul of a People.* London: Macmillan, 1898.

Hart, H. (and collaborators). Six theories about apparitions. *Proceedings of the Society for Psychical Research,* 1956, **50,** 153–239.

Head, J., and Cranston, J. L. *Reincarnation in World Thought.* New York: Julian Press, 1967.

Hearn, L. *Gleanings in Buddha-Fields.* Boston: Houghton Mifflin, 1897.

Madaule, J. *Le drame albigeois et le destin français.* Paris: Bernard Grasset, 1961.

Makarem, S. *The Doctrine of the Ismailis.* Beirut: The Arab Institute of Research and Publishing, 1972.

Makarem, S. Personal communication, 1973.

Makarem, S. *The Druze Faith.* Delmar, N.Y.: Caravan Books, 1974.

Malinowski, B. Baloma: The spirits of the dead in the Trobriand Islands. *Journal of the Royal Anthropological Institute of Great Britain and Ireland,* 1916, **46,** 353–430.

McTaggart, J. M. E. *Human Immortality and Pre-Existence.* London: Edward Arnold, 1915.

Munro, N. G. *Ainu: Creed and Cult.* New York: Columbia University Press, 1963.

Murphy, G. A Caringtonian approach to Ian Stevenson's *Twenty Cases Suggestive of Reincarnation. Journal of the American Society for Psychical Research,* 1973, **67,** 117–129.

Myers, F. W. H. *Human Personality and Its Survival of Bodily Death.* London: Longmans, Green, 1903. 2 vols.

Nelli, R. *Les cathares.* Paris: Grasset, 1972.

Noon, J. A. A preliminary examination of death concepts of the Ibo. *American Anthropologist,* 1942, **44,** 638–654.

Osborn, A. *The Superphysical.* (Rev. ed.) London: Frederick Muller, 1974. (First published in 1937.)

Parrinder, E. G. *African Traditional Religion.* Westport, Conn.: Greenwood Press, 1954.

Parrinder, E. G. Varieties of belief in reincarnation. *Hibbert Journal,* 1956, **55,** 260–267.

Plato. *The Meno.* (Trans. by F. Sydenham.) London: J. M. Dent, 1910.

Pratt, J. G. A decade of research with a selected ESP subject: An overview and reappraisal of the work with Pavel Stepanek. *Proceedings of the American Society for Psychical Research,* 1973, **30,** 1–78.

Reiff, R., and Scheerer, M. *Memory and Hypnotic Age Regression.* New York: International Universities Press, 1959.

Rhine, L. E. Subjective forms of spontaneous psi experiences. *Journal of Parapsychology,* 1953, **17,** 77–114.

Rhine, L. E. Frequency of types of experience in spontaneous precognition. *Journal of Parapsychology,* 1954, **18,** 93–123.

Sahay, K. K. N. *Reincarnation: Verified Cases of Rebirth after Death.* Bareilly: N. L. Gupta, 1927 (ca).

Sannwald, G. Statistische Untersuchungen an Spontanphänomenen. *Zeitschrift für Parapsychologie und Grenzgebiete der Psychologie,* 1959, **3**, 59–71. (a)

Sannwald, G. Zur Psychologie paranormaler Spontanphänomene: Motivation, Thematik und Bezugspersonen "okkulter" Erlebnisse. *Zeitschrift für Parapsychologie und Grenzgebiete der Psychologie,* 1959, **3**, 149–183. (b)

Schopenhauer, A. *Die Welt als Wille und Vorstellung.* Leipzig: F. U. Brockhaus, 1908. 2 vcls.

Sidgwick, H., Sidgwick, E. M., Johnson, A., Myers, F. W. H., Myers, A. T., and Podmore, F. Report on the census of hallucinations. *Proceedings of the Society for Psychical Research,* 1894, **10**, 25–422.

Slobodin, R. Kutchin concepts of reincarnation. *Western Canadian Journal of Anthropology,* 1970, **2**, 67–79.

Spencer, B., and Gillen, F. J. *The Northern Tribes of Central Australia.* London: Macmillan, 1904.

Stevenson, I. The evidence for survival from claimed memories of former incarnations. *Journal of the American Society for Psychical Research,* 1960, **54**, 51–71, 95–117.

Stevenson, I. Cultural patterns in cases suggestive of reincarnation among the Tlingit Indians of Southeastern Alaska. *Journal of the American Society for Psychical Research,* 1966, **60**, 229–243.

Stevenson, I. Characteristics of cases of the reincarnation type in Turkey and their comparison with cases in two other cultures. *International Journal of Comparative Sociology,* 1970, **11**, 1–17.

Stevenson, I. Characteristics of cases of the reincarnation type in Ceylon. *Contributions to Asian Studies,* 1973, **3**, 26–39. (a)

Stevenson, I. The "perfect" reincarnation case. In W. G. Roll, R. L. Morris, and J. D. Morris (Eds.), *Research in Parapsychology 1972,* pp. 185–187. Metuchen, N. J.: Scarecrow Press, 1973. (b)

Stevenson, I. Some new cases suggestive of reincarnation. III. The case of Suleyman Andary. *Journal of the American Society for Psychical Research,* 1973, **67**, 244–266. (c)

Stevenson, I. Some new cases suggestive of reincarnation. IV. The case of Ampan Petcherat. *Journal of the American Society for Psychical Research,* 1973, **67**, 361–380. (d)

Stevenson, I. *Twenty Cases Suggestive of Reincarnation.* (2nd rev. ed.) Charlottesville: University Press of Virginia, 1974. (First published in 1966.) (a)

Stevenson, I. Xenoglossy: A review and report of a case. *Proceedings of the American Society for Psychical Research,* 1974, **31**, 1–268. Also Charlottesville: University Press of Virginia, 1974. (b)

Stevenson, I. Some questions related to cases of the reincarnation type. *Journal of the American Society for Psychical Research,* 1974, **68**, 395–416. (c)

Stevenson, I. *Cases of the Reincarnation Type. Vol. 1. Ten Cases in India.* Charlottesville: University Press of Virginia, 1975.

Stevenson, I. A preliminary report on a new case of responsive xenoglossy: The case of Gretchen. *Journal of the American Society for Psychical Research,* 1976, **70**, 65–77.

Stevenson, I. *Cases of the Reincarnation Type. Vol. 2. Ten Cases in Sri Lanka.* Charlottesville: University Press of Virginia, 1977.

Stevenson, I. *Cases of the Reincarnation Type. Vol. 3. Fifteen Cases in Thailand, Lebanon, and Turkey.* Charlottesville: University Press of Virginia, 1978.

Stevenson, I., and Story, F. A case of the reincarnation type in Ceylon: The case of Disna Samarasinghe. *Journal of Asian and African Studies,* 1970, **5**, 241–255.

Story, F., and Stevenson, I.   A case of the reincarnation type in Ceylon: The case of Warnasiri Adikari. *Journal of the American Society for Psychical Research,* 1967, **61,** 130–145.

Sunderlal, R. B. S.   Cas apparents de réminiscences de vies antérieures. *Revue Métapsychique,* 1924, No. 4, juillet-août, 302–307.

Swedenborg, E.   *Heaven and its Wonders and Hell.*   Boston: New-Church Union, 1906. (First published in Latin, London, 1758.)

Thomas, L. V.   *Cinq essais sur la mort africaine.*   Dakar: Université de Dakar, 1968.

Uchendu, V. C.   The status implications of Igbo religious beliefs.   *The Nigerian Field,* 1964, **29,** 27–37.

Van de Castle, R. L.   Personal communication, 1973.

Zahan, D. (Ed.)   *Réincarnation et vie mystique en Afrique noire.*   Paris: Presses Universitaires de France, 1965.

Part VIII

PARAPSYCHOLOGY AND OTHER FIELDS

1

Parapsychology and Anthropology

Robert L. Van de Castle

PARAPSYCHOLOGICAL EVENTS FROM AN ANTHROPOLOGICAL PERSPECTIVE

Some Representative Views

There are probably as many viewpoints held toward parapsychology by anthropologists as there are individual anthropologists. Since cultural anthropologists have been exposed to such an array of different customs and belief systems, one would expect humbleness on their part with regard to declaring what the *correct* customs and the *true* belief systems should be. The kind of tolerance that one might hope from anthropologists is nicely brought out by Goldschmidt in his foreword to Castaneda's *The Teachings of Don Juan* (1969):

> Anthropology has taught us that the world is differently defined in different places. It is not only that people have different customs; it is not only that people believe in different gods and expect different post-mortem fates. It is, rather, that the worlds of different people have different shapes. The very metaphysical presuppositions differ: space does not conform to Euclidean geometry, time does not form a continuous unidirectional flow, causation does not conform to Aristotelian logic, man is not differentiated from non-man or life from death, as in our world (p. 9).

In some ethnographic accounts, however, a very paternalistic view is expressed. In describing the Mossi of West Africa, Mangin (1959) cautioned his European colleagues "Not to laugh at their ideas, no matter how childish they may seem to us. To laugh at them is the surest way of hurting their feelings and of making them hopelessly secretive. In any case, is not sincere belief worthy of some respect, even if this respect is mixed with a certain amount of pity?" (p. 124). Although their language is not so condescending, Middleton and Winter (1963) indicate that African viewpoints toward witchcraft and sorcery must be "termed magical from the point of view of the anthropologist because there are no grounds in terms of Western science for believing them able to accomplish the ends claimed for them" (p. 3).

As is true for most scientists, anthropologists are generally unfamiliar with the scientific literature of parapsychology and are therefore unlikely to conceptually consider the possible implications of the research findings from parapsychology for their own field. There have, however, been some notable exceptions. John Swanton, a past president of the American Anthropological Association, wrote a letter in 1952 to the Fellows of this association after he had retired from the Smithsonian Institution. Swanton had read widely in the parapsychological literature and urged his colleagues to familiarize themselves with the laboratory results of ESP studies because of their relevance for the field of anthropology. In his letter, Swanton stated: "A significant revolution which concerns us all is taking place quietly but surely in a related branch of science and it is not being met in an honest, truly scientific manner."

C. W. Weiant read a paper on parapsychology and its relationship to anthropology at a meeting of the American Anthropological Association in 1959. His paper (1960) noted the scientific recognition that parapsychology was receiving and reviewed some ethnographic accounts of possible psi events. Weiant remarked:

> I feel very strongly that every anthropologist, whether believer or unbeliever, should acquaint himself with the techniques of parapsychological research and make use of these, as well as any other means at his disposal, to establish what is real and what is illusion in the so-called paranormal. If it should turn out that the believers are right, there will certainly be exciting implications for anthropology (p. 8).

Anthropological Explanations for Possible Psi Events

In our own culture, we have many terms to designate individuals who claim various sorts of paranormal abilities; among them are: medium, sensitive, psychic, paragnost, and clairvoyant. Among the terms found in the anthropological literature to designate such individuals are: sorcerer, shaman, witch, diviner, seer, and wizard. The terms *witch doctor* and *medicine man* are more often used by nonanthropologists to refer to any member of a "primitive" culture who is engaged in the practice of magic or healing. The term *magical practitioner* will be used in this paper to refer to all individuals who might utilize paranormal powers in their cultural roles.

The personality of magical practitioners has interested anthropologists, and several case histories have been published (Casagrande, 1964; Handelman, 1967; Sachs, 1947). Since these magical practitioners make claims about possessing powers which the anthropologist "knows" are impossible to demonstrate, some anthropologists have concluded that the practitioner must obviously be delusional and suffering from schizophrenia or some other form of mental disorder (Devereaux, 1961; Kroeber, 1952; Silverman, 1967). A review of this issue by I. M. Lewis (1971) reveals that such a prejudiced view is not held by most modern anthropologists. A succinct summary of the situation has been provided by Handelman (1968): "Stated bluntly, data do not yet exist for properly evaluating the personality development and personality dynamics of shamans" (p. 354).

A strong case has been made by E. Fuller Torrey (1973) that magical practitioners are equally as effective in dealing with their fellow tribesmen as are American or European psychiatrists in dealing with their fellow citizens. Torrey slashes through our ethnocentric bias when he says: "If a person believes a mental disorder is caused by hormonal imbalance or a missing gene, then his therapy is automatically thought to be scientific, whereas if his theory of causation involves evil spirits, then his therapy must be magical" (p. 11). At another point Torrey observes: "The techniques used by Western psychiatrists are, with few exceptions, on exactly the same scientific plane as the techniques used by witch doctors. If one is magic then so is the other. If one is pre-scientific, then so is the other" (p. 9). After providing detailed accounts of the techniques used by healers in a wide variety of cultures, Torrey derives the common denominators underlying the therapeutic interactions between such practitioners and their patients. Among these factors are patient expectations of getting well, certain personality qualities of the therapist, and the sharing of a world-view that makes it possible for the practitioner to meaningfully name or identify the source of the patient's problems. This latter quality is called "The principle of Rumpelstiltskin" because it illustrates the magic of being able to come up with the right word which indicates to the patient that the practitioner understands, that the patient will not suffer alone with his sickness, and an optimistic prognosis is therefore possible.

I am not aware of any anthropological studies dealing with the physical appearance or physiological functioning of magical practitioners. Physical anthropologists are accustomed to making precise determinations of skeletal structure, muscular development, and genetic contributions to behavior and would therefore be in an excellent position to make a contribution to our understanding of the biological makeup of magical practitioners. A psychophysiological study involving European mediums was initiated by Assailly (1963). He inquired about 207 items of behavior, including physical disorders, during his interviews with a group of female mediums. Assailly reported these mediums characteristically complained of premenstrual abdominal swelling, a tendency toward bruising easily (ecchymosis), looseness of the ligaments, special sensitivity of the epigastric region, and excess hairiness.

Anthropologists have shown keen interest in attempting to understand the functional role played by magic in maintaining social institutions. Witchcraft is generally viewed as a projection of hostility, anxiety, or jealousy. Kluckhohn (1967) reported a correlation between the amount of fear and talk about witches and the general state of tension among the Navajo. Accusations of witchcraft are generally leveled by the deprived members of a culture against those who seem wealthier or more successful. Among the Nupe in Africa, economic dominance is maintained by the women, and only women are accused of being witches (Nadel, 1952). In another African society, where sex partners are relatively limited, witches are accused of engaging in relationships with a secret sex partner; or they are considered to lust after meat and milk in another African society, where the inheritance rules severely limit the possibility of a villager acquiring cattle (Wilson, 1951).

The qualities possessed by supernatural figures have also come in for considerable anthropological analysis. Margaret Mead (1937) observed that in societies where cooperation is characteristic, the supernatural system is conceived of as having its own pattern of rules, which man may propitiate in an orderly way; in societies where competition is characteristic, supernatural figures are perceived as being antagonistic, and there is a lack of trust or submission to any higher power. Many anthropologists have been strongly influenced by a psychoanalytic model which emphasizes the importance of early childhood practices in shaping later adult behavior. One cross-cultural study concluded that if children received indulgent treatment and a lack of pain from the nurturing agent during the first 18 months of life, adult members of that society would consider supernatural beings to be mainly benevolent (Lambert, Triandis, and Wolf, 1959).

From an anthropological perspective, magical and religious practices have evolved and continue because they provide a culturally acceptable explanation for misfortunes and offer remedies to alleviate the resultant anxiety. If one were willing to consider that genuine parapsychological phenomena are produced in such emotional settings, even if only on rare occasions, it could account for the persistence of such practices on another basis. A well-known axiom of learning theory is that conditioning established by aperiodic reinforcement is remarkably resistant to extinction. Just as pigeons will continue to peck for inordinate periods of time if they are given an occasional reinforcement of a tiny food pellet, perhaps members of primitive societies continue to engage in various magical and religious practices because they occasionally manage to produce genuine parapsychological phenomena as a consequence. This is but one example of how the conceptual framework of anthropology might be modified or enriched if the admissibility of parapsychological phenomena were to be more widely accepted.

ETHNOGRAPHIC ANECDOTES INVOLVING POSSIBLE PARANORMAL OCCURRENCES

Several anthropological theorists have been impressed by the frequent reports of apparent paranormal occurrences from observers in the field. In one of his last published papers, Robert Lowie (1956) commented:

> The accounts of occult experiences by otherwise intelligent and trustworthy reporters cannot simply be brushed aside. They ring true, whatever may be the interpretations of visions and auditions. As my best Crow interpreter phrased it, "When you listen to the old men telling about their mysterious experiences you've just *got* to believe them" (p. 16).

Somewhat similar sentiments were expressed by Ralph Linton in a letter written in 1942 to Weiant (Weiant, 1960):

> I have been struck, myself, in my experience with primitive groups, with the surprising uniformity of their stories about what we would call psychic phenomena. Beliefs regarding these phenomena coming from groups which could have had no possible contact, are, nevertheless, so much alike that they suggest either an amazing limitation on the human imagination, or the presence of a common basis of observed fact (p. 2).

Mircea Eliade (1966) declared:

> We now touch upon a problem of the greatest importance . . . that is, the question of the *reality* of the extrasensory capacities and paranormal powers ascribed to the shamans and medicine-men. Although research into this question is still at its beginning, a fairly large number of ethnographic documents has already put the authenticity of such phenomena beyond doubt (p. 87).

Unfortunately, there is a paucity of systematic reviews of ethnographic material dealing with observations of apparent paranormal phenomena. Outside of some brief articles (Humphrey, 1944; Pobers, 1956), the most detailed ethnographic reviews available in English are those by Lang (1900) and de Vesme (1931). Both of these are very dated. Three chapters in Oesterreich (1966) describe possession and trances among primitive groups, and the author discusses their possible parapsychological relevance. A review article has appeared in Dutch (Fischer, 1940), and de Martino (1946, 1973) and Bozzano (1974) have published fairly lengthy reviews in Italian of ethnographic accounts suggesting a possible psi factor at work. Books containing some interesting descriptions of psychic events in Australia (Elkins, 1944), in Africa (H. Trilles, 1914; R. G. Trilles, 1932), in Jamaica (Williams, 1934), and in Haiti (Huxley, 1969) are available. Zorab (1957) also lists several ethnographic citations.

Anecdotes Involving Possible ESP

To give the reader some feeling for the types of reports which may be found in ethnographic accounts, some representative examples will be presented. Weiant (1960) described the following experience which took place in Puerto Rico:

> With two friends I sat one night on the porch of a woman medium and listened with astonishment as this lady described in detail my home in Peekskill, N.Y., including references to the location of trees and shrubbery, the colors of blossoms, the arrangement of furniture and pictures, an enumeration of the members of my family and their approximate ages, and even the correct diagnosis of an ailment from which my mother-in-law was then suffering. She referred also to intimate details of my personal life. The circumstances were such that only clairvoyance could account for her knowledge (p. 7).

R. G. Trilles (1932) tells of an instance in which an African native provided an accurate description of Trilles' home in Paris and gave details of the final illness and death of his father which was confirmed several weeks later. A West African diviner offered a specific description of Geoffrey Gorer's (1935) home and companions in Dakar 1,000 miles away that proved to be very accurate. Predictions about Hallowell's (1942) father and the welfare of other members of his party was made by a Saulteux diviner that were subsequently confirmed when later information was obtained about them. While working with the Negas in India, Hutton (1921) noted that inquiries were made of him on three occasions as to whether certain relatives located in a regiment in France were dead, and in each case confirmation of the death of that person approximating the time of the inquiry was received several months later. Matthews (1886) reported that young girls who were members of a cult in the Bahamas would go into trances at the same time even though they were widely separated geographically and no scheduled events were related to the times of entering trances. These girls were also said to be able to reliably describe distant events when in a trance state.

Many anecdotes pertaining to the psychic ability of diviners in South Africa have been reported. Callaway (1884) wrote that a diviner had correctly informed him that he was concerned about a pregnant black goat and accurately predicted that she would deliver a white and grey kid by the time he returned home. The May 4, 1906, edition of *The Two Worlds* published in Manchester reprinted a story appearing in *The Natal Mercury* describing how Governor Shepstone of the English colony of Natal convened all of the *Izangoma* or diviners in 1891 to explain the new Code of Native Law which had reference to them. He told them that the government forbade *Ukbala* (consultation with a diviner) but that the rule would be waived if any of them would submit to an experiment and demonstrate the genuineness of their faculty. A series of tests was given them such as identifying the nature and location of hidden objects. Two of the diviners were so successful at the task that the Governor awarded them a certificate and gave them permission to continue their former practices.

A psychiatrist at Cape Town University, Laubscher (1938), made an effort to experimentally test the claims of Solomon Baba, a Tembu diviner. Unwitnessed by anyone, Laubscher buried a small purse wrapped in brown paper in the ground, covered it with a flat brown stone, and then placed a grey stone on top of the brown one. He immediately set off in an automobile and traveled 35 miles an hour to the home of the diviner who lived 60 miles away. When in a séance dance shortly after Laubscher's arrival, Solomon Baba described the purse, the wrapping paper, and the stones in minute detail. On another occasion Solomon Baba was also amazingly accurate in describing the appearance of some missing cattle from a distant region and correctly predicted the exact date of Laubscher's return to England even though the specified date was several months beyond the official date for which passage had already been booked.

Some recent examples of successful divination by South African *sangomas* have been provided by Adrian Boshier (1974). Boshier's background bears some resemblance to that of Castaneda (1969) in that Boshier has lived among African tribes for several years, has been officially adopted by some of them, and has begun an apprenticeship with a native sangoma teacher. In conversation, Boshier told me that he personally knows several hundred sangomas throughout South Africa. A good description of the "call to practice" and the training undergone by a sangoma is provided in his article.

Boshier indicates that sangomas must give empirical demonstrations of their divining ability before they can become officially accepted. In one test that he arranged, he hid the skin of a gemsbok underneath the canvas sail on the back of his Land Rover. Boshier's assistant, Miss Costello, stayed with the sangoma in Boshier's office while this concealment was taking place. Entering a trance state, the sangoma informed him of the approximate location where he had hidden the object, indicated that it came from an animal, had more than one color, and was raised up off the ground. Upon leaving Boshier's office, she was able to find the hidden skin within a matter of minutes.

Boshier also provides several other examples of successful divination by sangomas. On one occasion Boshier had spent about a week examining ancient copper mines. One day when he and a companion were about to enter a mine, a leopard bolted out of the tunnel past them. While visiting a sangoma on his way back to Johannesburg, she "threw her bones" and announced that the bones did not appear to be working properly because all she could see was Boshier being underneath the ground and that made no sense to her. When Boshier told her he had been spending considerable time exploring underground mines, the sangoma warned him to be careful about such trips because she also saw a leopard located right next to him in the underground place.

Anecdotes Involving Possible Psychokinesis

One area in which psychokinesis may play a role is psychic healing. David St. Clair (1971) attended a number of spiritualist meetings and healing ceremonies in Brazil and describes many instances of what sound like remarkable cures of physical disorders. In one session with a healer known as Palmério, St. Clair witnessed a young boy about 8 years old shuffling up to the healer on badly deformed feet that turned in at such an angle that he was almost walking on his ankles. Palmério prayed over the boy, violently shook the feet, and then kissed each foot gently. The boy got up from the examination table, took a few timid steps, and then walked away almost flat-footed. According to St. Clair, the boy's feet appeared to be normal after this "treatment." A female patient with a greenish-brown bruise on her breast had the discoloration disappear within a few moments after Palmério passed his hands over the breast. St. Clair's book contains photos of Arigó, a famous native "psychic surgeon," inserting knives under the eyelids of patients. Spiritistic healing has become so popular in Brazil that practitioners are said to be accepted in most of the nation's hospitals with a status comparable to that generally accorded physicians.

Many accounts of apparently remarkable cures (and hoaxes) have also been associated with "psychic surgeons" in the Philippine Islands (Valentine, 1973). Eliade (1966), in discussing "psychic surgery" carried out by shamans, wrote:

> Bogoras even witnesses an "operation"of this kind. A boy of 14 lay naked on the ground and his mother, a celebrated shamaness, opens his abdomen, the blood and gaping flesh were visible; the shamaness thrust her hand deep into the wound. During all the time the shamaness felt as though she were on fire, and constantly drank water. A few moments later the wound had closed, and Bogoras could detect no trace of it. Another shaman, after drumming for a long time to "heat" his body and his knife to a point at which, he said, the cut would not be felt, opened his own abdomen. Such feats are frequent through North Asia and they are connected with the "mastery over fire," for the same shamans who gash their bodies are able to swallow burning coals and to touch white hot iron (pp. 256–257).

In a book by Gaddis (1967), a summary table lists published sources which have described successful instances of "mastery over fire," most of which refer to examples of fire-walking. Kenn (1949), for example, claims that only nine individuals were burned out of the 576 participating in a walk over a 15-foot fire pit at the University of Hawaii. Experimental studies of fire-walks have been reported by Brown (1938) and Price (1936).

A frequent explanation offered for fire-walking is that the individual is in a trance state, but we still know very little about what constitutes a trance state. Imperviousness to external stimuli was shown in an EEG study of four yogis by Anand, Chhina, and Singh (1961). These investigators found that the yogis' control of attention during an alpha phase was so intense that they could not cause "alpha blocking" by stimulating them with flashing lights, sounding gongs, vibrations, or the touch of a hot glass test tube. Pain reduction has often been associated with hypnotic trance, and Hilgard (1973) has advanced a "neodissociative interpretation" to account for such findings.

Auto-suggestion is the explanation typically given to account for "miraculous" faith cures. Such "cures" are considered to take place only in the case of hysterical or other functional disorders. It is difficult to extend this hypothesis, however, to the healing of animals. In a joint research project conducted by members of the Medical School of the University of Manitoba and the Medical School of McGill University, it was found that the surgically-induced wounds of 100 mice healed significantly faster when held between the hands of a healer for two 15-minute periods a day than when a similar number of mice were held between the hands of nonhealers or when a third group of wounded mice remained unhandled (Grad, Cadoret, and Paul, 1961).

The full range of psychosomatic effects is poorly understood in modern medicine. Ever since Cannon's (1942) classic article on Voodoo-death, there has been speculation as to the probable causative mechanisms. Cannon attempted to account for this class of sudden deaths in the absence of any organic disease by attributing them to fear. Other explanations involving feelings of helplessness and hopelessness as important contributing dynamics have been reviewed by Halifax-Grof (1974). The "resignation" types of interpretations would suggest that victims die because of parasympathetic involvement rather than the sympathico-adrenal stimulation posited by Cannon. Hex death studies generally lack adequate descriptions of the events leading up to and surrounding the hex death as well as the necessary longitudinal physiological data. The dissertation by G. A. Lewis (1972) provides a good example of the type of information which should be included in such studies.

Some reports describe events involving inanimate external objects and would not be covered under the usual psychosomatic explanations. Jacolliet (1901) claimed that an Indian fakir at Benares was able to move, through mental energy, an extremely heavy bronze vase full of water in any direction that Jacolliet indicated and was even able to levitate it 7 or 8 inches above the ground. The types of sleight-of-hand tricks and conjuring effects that one must be on guard for in such situations are nicely documented in Chari's (1960) investigations in India.

An area of psychokinesis that has received considerable publicity in parapsychological circles is that of thoughtography. The most detailed study of this type is the one documented by Eisenbud (1967). His book contains many photographs of "mental images" from Ted Serios that Eisenbud indicates were recorded on film in such a manner that trickery was not a plausible explanation. Earlier successful results had also been reported by the Japanese investigator Fukarai (1931). In some of the work with Serios, Eisenbud described a class of photographs which he called "blackies." These are Polaroid photographs in which the entire picture is black even though the lens had been open and other pictures on the same roll of film were normally developed.

A friend of mine was an apprentice of Rolling Thunder, a Shoshone medicine man who lived in Nevada. This friend showed me a "blackie" Polaroid picture and described the circumstances under which it occurred. He said that on one occasion, a visitor to Rolling Thunder's home wished to take a Polaroid picture of him but Rolling Thunder did not wish the person to do so. Rolling Thunder told the individual to take as many pictures as he wished but that none of them would turn out properly because Rolling Thunder would mentally cause the camera to malfunction. After three successive "blackies" were obtained, Rolling Thunder began to feel sorry for the chagrined visitor. Rolling Thunder asked a couple of young women to stand next to him and smilingly told the photographer that a successful picture could now be obtained because he was in a better mood and would not jam the camera mentally. A perfectly normal picture of Rolling Thunder and the young women emerged after that point.

St. Clair (1971) describes an instance when he went to interview a Brazilian healer called Edu. As St. Clair, an experienced journalist, got his tape recorder into position for the interview, Edu indicated he would prefer that the tape recorder not be used. St. Clair protested and presented his arguments as to why it was necessary to have the healer's exact words on tape. Finally the healer shut his eyes for a few moments, looked intensely at the machine, and told St. Clair to turn it on. As soon as he did, the reels began to turn but the tape "came gushing out of the box like plastic spaghetti. I slammed at the stop button but it did no good. Soon his desk was a pile of forever-ruined tape" (p. 185).

EMPIRICAL INVESTIGATIONS OF PSI IN "PRIMITIVE" CULTURES

The preceding section on anecdotal accounts provides a strong suggestive case that parapsychological phenomena may occur with considerable frequency among members of "primitive" societies. Many counterhypotheses can be offered to explain apparent paranormal occurrences: inaccurate initial observations, exaggerations arising from faulty recall, sleight-of-hand trickery, hallucinations produced by altered states of consciousness, auto-suggestion, and collusion, to mention some of the more obvious alternative explanations. Such criticisms are less relevant when controlled experimentation is carried out. A few empirical studies involving members of "primitive" groups have been undertaken which do offer some support for the validity of the psi hypothesis.

Empirical Studies by Other Investigators

The first published study utilizing the traditional ESP cards with a native population was reported by Foster (1943). A group of 50 Indian children, ranging in age from 6 to 20 years, were individually tested at a school in Manitoba by a teacher whom Foster had trained. Each pupil completed 125 trials. They obtained more "hits" than would be expected on a chance basis, and the overall results were statistically significant.

The traditional ESP cards were also used in an unpublished study by a native school headmaster to test a group of nine male New Guinea natives about 21 years old and a group of six native teachers (Pope, 1953). Although the number of hits was above chance expectation, the results were not statistically significant. A drawing task was also attempted with this group. The target picture was a concealed photograph of an American-style living room, and seven of the nine drawings showed "more or less boxy-like looking likenesses of the exterior of a native house." The drawing results were not interpreted as evidence for ESP but rather as reflecting a rigid response to the task.

Another unpublished study was reported to me in a letter dated June 20, 1960, from Harmon Bro. He reported that some members of a parapsychology course that he taught at Northland College in Wisconsin had carried out an experiment comparing the scoring of school children on a local Indian Reservation with school children in a small town nearby. No significant differences were found between the two groups as a whole, although individuals among the children differed and in a few cases achieved "notable results" on clairvoyant runs.

The most extensive individual ESP testing program has been carried out by Ronald and Lyndon Rose in Australia. Their first research effort (Rose and Rose, 1951) was carried out at the settlement of Woodenbong where the natives were half-castes not engaged in tribal living. Ronald Rose served as the agent and looked at the ESP cards one at a time while his wife recorded the subject's verbal calls. The 23 subjects tested produced a highly significant number of hits above chance expectation for the 296 runs they completed ($CR = 6.57$). Their best subject was a 75-year-old diabetic woman who was frequently tested while trying to keep a lively 2-year-old grandson under control. She completed 68 runs and obtained an extremely significant above-chance number of hits ($CR = 9.03$).

During that same expedition, the Roses also tested their subjects with six-sided plastic dice containing different colors on each side. Twelve of these dice were placed in a shaker, and the subject attempted to influence a particular colored face to turn upward when they were thrown onto a blanket-covered table. The overall number of hits was not significant. The Roses pointed out that the average aborigine did not acknowledge any confidence at this task since he felt only the "clever men" were able to display psychokinetic phenomena.

Two groups in Central Australia, one de-tribalized and another that was almost tribal, were tested during the next expedition (R. Rose, 1952). The nearly tribal natives obtained a significant deviation above chance (CR = 2.96) in an ESP test, while the de-tribalized natives scored at chance level. The scores of two "clever men" were not significant. Dice supplied from the Duke Parapsychology Laboratory were utilized in a PK test, but the results again proved to be insignificant for both groups of subjects.

Four years later, the Roses returned to Woodenbong and retested the same natives (R. Rose, 1955). Of the 12 subjects tested on this occasion, all but one had been previously tested. Individually significant scores were obtained by several of the subjects. Lizzie Williams, the highest scoring subject during the first expedition, was again the highest scoring subject. Although she had been bedridden for the last 4 years, she obtained highly significant results for the 32 ESP runs that she completed (CR = 6.72). The PK results using the Duke dice were again insignificant.

The data obtained from all the testing expeditions were summarized in a book by Ronald Rose (1956). The approximately 50 aboriginal subjects tested in Australia had obtained a total of 545 hits above chance expectation for the 665 runs they completed (CR = 10.57). A total of 3,504 PK runs had been carried out, but the overall results were at the chance level. Although no details are provided, Rose indicates that the 279 runs resulting from two series of ESP tests carried out with Maori subjects from New Zealand produced significant above-chance scoring (CR = 9.25). Similar testing was also carried out in Samoa, but Rose reported that the above-chance scores were not significant for the 200 runs completed there. The Samoan natives had been given a PK test, but nonsignificant results were also obtained on that task. Rose suggested that the poor showing of the Samoan subjects may have been tied in to the repressive efforts by missionaries ever since their arrival in 1830 to stamp out any native beliefs in paranormal phenomena.

Jeffrey Mason has informed me through personal correspondence that he has carried out a series of ESP card tests with 396 subjects in Liberia that yielded nonsignificant results.

Empirical Investigations by the Author

I carried out an extensive group ESP testing program with Cuna Indian students between 1968 and 1974. These adolescents were attending Oller Junior High School on Nargana, one of the San Blas Islands, located off the eastern coast of Panama. Approximately 20 to 30 students were tested at a time in a classroom setting and each student completed 50 GESP trials. Instead of the regular ESP cards, a special deck of 75 cards containing colored pictures of five objects familiar to Cunas was developed. Each card displayed one of the following objects: a jaguar in a jungle setting, an underwater view of a shark, a conch shell on sand, a large canoe with a sail, and a propeller airplane in the sky.

I served as agent for the five testing series carried out between 1968 and 1972. In 1974, my wife, Doris, and I served as alternate agents within the same classroom testing session. A detailed description of the testing and scoring procedures has been published elsewhere (Van de Castle, 1974).

A total of 461 students were tested between 1968 and 1972. The 96 girls completed 362 runs (1 run = 25 trials) and obtained 67 hits above chance expectation. The 365 boys completed 1,258 runs and obtained 73 hits below chance expectation. Since some subjects had been tested in more than 1 year, a comparison based only upon scores obtained during the first testing session by each subject was made. The mean score obtained by the girls was 10.94 (chance = 10.00), while the boys had a mean score of 9.90. This difference in scoring is statistically significant ($P < .01$).

For those girls tested on more than one occasion, their scores declined significantly from their first year's testing session to subsequent testing sessions ($P < .01$), although they tended to maintain their relative scoring rank from the first year's testing session to the testing sessions in subsequent years ($r = +.30$, $P < .05$). The boys showed patterns of scoring similar to those of the girls, but their results were not significant.

The results of the 1968–72 testing series suggested that the girls were better performers at an ESP task than the boys. However, since I was the exclusive agent during this series, it is possible that the male agent–female percipient combination may have been an important dynamic factor. This possibility was explored during the 1974 testing series by utilizing agents of each sex with the same percipients in nine classrooms. In the classroom, I served as agent for the first run while my wife served as agent for the second run; in the second classroom, my wife served as agent for the first run while I served as agent for the second run. This counterbalanced order was continued for the remainder of the classrooms.

The 70 girls obtained a mean score of 10.17, while the 163 boys obtained a mean score of 10.16. The percipients' mean score was 5.18 with my wife as agent and 5.15 with me as agent. When the results were analyzed in terms of agent-percipient relationships, an interesting pattern emerged. The mean score for the girls when my wife was agent was 5.33; when I served as agent it was 4.84. This pattern was reversed for the boys; their mean score was 4.85 with my wife as agent and 5.31 when I served as agent. Although the mean scores were nearly identical when analyzed separately for the sex of the percipients and for the sex of the agents, the interactional effect between the sex of the percipient and the sex of the agent was significant. Percipients scored more successfully with an agent of the same sex. It was also noted that the girls scored significantly $(P < .03)$ higher on their first run than they did on their second run.

Some preliminary testing of the role of the agent's cultural identity was also attempted in 1974. After the regular testing series had been completed, two classrooms were informally retested using Cuna students as agents. Very high scores were obtained but since the testing conditions were not adequately supervised, I am hesitant to accept them at the same level of confidence as the formal work. This variable should definitely be studied in future work.

The agent's mood is also an important variable. During the 1969 and 1970 series, I made notes concerning my psychological state while serving as agent. These were recorded for each classroom session before any knowledge of the testing results for that classroom was available. Subsequent analyses indicated that percipients obtained low ESP scores whenever I had recorded comments suggesting I was exerting great will power to totally fuse with the target stimuli. High ESP scores resulted whenever I noted that I had been distracted, generally by some continuing noise, and my concentration had been less intense. The difference in scoring level between these two mental states was significant $(P < .001)$.

The personality of the percipient was also found to be a major factor in scoring success. This variable was investigated through an objective, quantitative analysis of dream content. The students each wrote their most recent dream on a special form with standardized instructions in Spanish. Mac Chapin, an anthropologist who has lived among the Cuna for several years, translated these reports. A research assistant, unfamiliar with the ESP scores, rated each dream for the presence or absence of seven categories, such as animal figures. This dream rating system is described elsewhere (Van de Castle, 1974).

High ESP scores, regardless of the sex of the percipient, were associated with the frequency with which two components of dream content were represented. The first component, possibly associated with reduced repression, consisted of the presence of long dreams, animal characters, direct sexuality, and aggressive interactions. The second component, possibly associated with cooperativeness, consisted of the presence of parental figures and relatives. Students with higher frequencies of these categories in their dreams obtained significantly higher $(P < .001)$ ESP scores than students with minimal representations of these categories.

Testing for psychokinesis was carried out during 1968 and 1969. Dice were employed, and the subject's task involved attempting to influence 12 dice to land on alternate sides of a wooden testing platform after they were mechanically released by the experimenter. A total of 108 subjects, mostly women and children, were individually tested, but no significant results were obtained. Subjects had great difficulty in comprehending this task and participated in a listless way because they had heard through the island "grapevine" that they would receive a gift if they sat near the American's unusual "box." Other factors probably contributing to the unsuitability of this PK testing arrangement are discussed in an earlier article (Van de Castle, 1970).

PSYCHIC OR INTUITIVE ARCHEOLOGY

"Psychic" or "intuitive" archeology involves the use of a "sensitive" to obtain information concerning where to locate a suitable dig site and also to offer hypotheses concerning the personal or cultural history of individuals responsible for producing artifacts found at archeological sites. Three papers bearing on this topic were presented at the 1974 meetings of The American Anthropological Association in Mexico City.

Goodman (1974) reported that a sensitive in Oregon had given information, while in a trance state, which enabled Goodman to locate a site near Flagstaff, Arizona which produced a large number of artifacts dating back earlier than 25,000 B.C. This sensitive predicted what types of artifacts would be found at various depths and what the nature of the geological strata would be to a statistically significant degree.

A previously unpublished manuscript was discovered by Wolkowski (1974) which describes extensive experiments carried out in 1937–1941 with the Polish sensitive, Ossowiecki. When this sensitive was handed an object from a museum collection, he was able to provide a detailed description concerning its origin and historical period. Examination of the veridicality of these psychic impressions is now being conducted.

The past president of the Canadian Archeological Association, J. N. Emerson, has reported (1974) that if he uses a sensitive called George when visiting Iroquois sites, George is able to "assess the age of the site, describe the people, their dress, their dwellings, economy and general behaviour" (p. 2). Emerson has estimated that George is "80% accurate." In a recent publication Emerson (1976) describes George's predictions while working in Egypt and Iran, and an instance is reported where he ordered a randomly arranged series of potsherds into correct chronological sequence when requested to do so by an archeologist from the University of Teheran. Emerson has proposed that a "psychic team composed of several sensitives could offer an important source of hypothesis-generating information to archeologists."

SOME SUGGESTIONS FOR FUTURE RESEARCH

Drug Studies

As can be seen by examining other chapters in this volume, considerable evidence has been garnered to support the hypothesis that enhanced ESP scoring levels are associated with altered states of consciousness. Since drugs are frequently used to induce altered states, it is to be expected that some authors have proposed that ESP ability is increased by hallucinogenic drugs (e.g., Blewett, 1963).

Masters and Houston (1966) recount several impressive examples of apparent ESP that were informally observed in their research on psychedelic drugs, which led them to carry out some systematic explorations. When they used ESP cards with subjects taking LSD in their laboratory, most of them initially found the task very trivial and uninteresting, and their scores at the beginning of the testing sessions were at a chance level. As boredom increased and their resentment at this waste of psychedelic time intensified, their scores dropped to significant below-chance levels for the final runs. Four friends of Houston, however, obtained impressively high scores (280 hits where chance expectation predicted 140) for their first seven runs, but their scores on the last three runs dropped to the chance level. For the next testing situation, Houston utilized pictures in envelopes as the ESP stimuli. She reported that "out of 62 subjects tested, 48 approximated the guide's image two or more times out of ten. Five subjects approximated the guide's image seven and eight times out of ten" (Masters and Houston, 1966, pp. 119-120). As examples of "approximation," Houston indicates that this term would be applied if the LSD subject reported "a snake with an arched head swimming in tossed seas" when the scene described in the envelope was "a Viking ship tossed in a storm." She also mentions that sometimes the guide would come up with an "accidental image" such as a forest fire which the subject would accurately pick up instead of the written target image of a skiing scene, but that these correspondences were charged as errors to the subject.

When describing his mescaline experiences, Langdon-Davies (1961) claimed to have demonstrated traveling clairvoyance and stated that he obtained 13 hits during an ESP run of 25 trials. Several anecdotes describing possible psi events among American Indians belonging to the peyote cult are mentioned by La Barre (1959).

Banisteriopsis caapi, also known as ayahuasca, or yage, is a vine used in South America to produce a hallucinogenic drink (Dobkin de Rios, 1972). McGovern (1927) provides some details about the telepathic abilities of the Indians in an Amazon village after ingesting ayahuasca: "Two or three men described in great detail what was going on in *malokas* hundreds of miles away, many of which they had never visited, and the inhabitants of which they had never seen, but which seemed to tally exactly with what I knew of the places and peoples concerned" (p. 263). McGovern, who was an assistant curator for the Field Museum of Natural History, also reported that a local medicine man correctly described the details about the sudden death of a chief who lived a great distance away.

An account of a Brazilian colonel named Morales with ayahuasca is given by Wilkins (1948). After drinking this liquid, Morales became conscious of the death of his sister located 2,900 miles away that was subsequently confirmed a month later by letter. A recent anecdote has been reported by Kensinger (1973):

> Several informants who have never been to or seen pictures of Pucallpa . . . have described their visits under the influence of ayahuasca to the town with sufficient detail for me to be able to recognize specific shops and sights. On the day following one ayahuasca party six of nine men informed me of seeing the death of my *chai*, "my mother's father." This occurred two days before I was informed by radio of his death" (p. 12).

Field Studies

Studies carried out in our own culture have indicated that the belief systems and attitudes held toward ESP are an important source of ESP scoring variations (Palmer, 1971, 1972). Belief in ESP among non-Western groups often remains high even when they have been exposed to university level training (Brockhaus, 1968). Studies should be carried out where the ESP scores of tribal members holding traditional versus "modern" views towards the paranormal are examined. Stevenson (1968) has compared cross-cultural beliefs on reincarnation with the incidence of reported reincarnation cases among such cultures, and similar studies concerning beliefs about other possible paranormal events and their frequency of occurrence are needed.

Bourguignon (1972) examined the data available on 488 non-Western societies and found some institutionalized form of dissociation present in 89 percent of these societies. If altered states of consciousness are associated with paranormal functioning, careful efforts should be made to document the possible psi events which might appear during the trance states induced by drinking, dancing, inhaling smoke from resinous plants, or drumming (Neher, 1962). The full range of Western technology including movie and tape recording as well as sensitive recording devices should be employed. Testing arrangements should be adapted to measure the particular talents claimed by a magical practitioner. For example, an investigator might request a practitioner noted for his PK powers to alternately speed up or slow down the time required for the sand to pass from one glass container to another on a "three-minute" egg timer. Statistical comparisons could be made between the trials when a faster versus a slower time was willed by the practitioner or healer. Other testing procedures which would yield quantitative data could readily be developed by any enterprising investigator. I hope that the material reviewed in this paper will challenge field workers to examine for themselves whether or not the numerous ethnographic accounts of paranormal events could originate from a verifiable factual basis.

REFERENCES

Anand, B. K., Chhina, G. S., and Singh, B. Some aspects of electroencephalographic studies in yogis. *Electroencephalography and Clinical Neurophysiology*, 1961, **13**, 452–456.

Assailly, A. Psychophysiological correlates of mediumistic faculties. *International Journal of Parapsychology*, 1963, **5**, 357–373.

Blewett, D. Psychedelic drugs in parapsychological research. *International Journal of Parapsychology*, 1963, **5**, 43–70.

Boshier, A. K. African apprenticeship. In A. Angoff and D. Barth (Eds.), *Parapsychology and Anthropology*, pp. 273–284. New York: Parapsychology Foundation, 1974.

Bourguignon, E. Dreams and altered states of consciousness in anthropological research. In F. L. Hsu (Ed.), *Psychological Anthropology*, pp. 403–434. Cambridge, Mass.: Schenkman, 1972.

Bozzano, E. *Popoli Primitivi e Manifestazioni Supernormali*. Milano: Armenia Editore, 1974.

Brockhaus, E. Possibilities and limits of parapsychological field research in West Africa. *Proceedings of the Parapsychological Association*, 1968, **5**, 9–10.

Brown, S. I. *Three Experimental Fire-Walks*. University of London: Council for Psychical Investigation. *Bulletin IV*, 1938.

Callaway, H. *The Religious System of the Amazulu*. London: The Folk-Lore Society, 1884.

Cannon, W. B. Voodoo death. *American Anthropologist*, 1942, **44**, 169–181.

Casagrande, J. (Ed.). *In the Company of Man*. New York: Harper Torchbooks, 1964.

Castaneda, C. *The Teachings of Don Juan*. New York: Ballantine, 1969.

Chari, C. T. K. Parapsychological studies and literature in India. *International Journal of Parapsychology*, 1960, **2**, 24–36.

de Martino, E. Magismo sciamanistico e fenomenologia paranormale. *Metapsichica*, 1946, **1**, 164–174.

de Martino, E. *Il Mondo Magico*. Torino: Universale Scientifica Boringhieri 98/99, 1973.

Devereux, G. Shamans as neurotics. *American Anthropologist*, 1961, **63**, 1088–1090.

de Vesme, C. *A History of Experimental Spiritualism*. Vol. 1. *Primitive Man*. (Trans. by S. de Brath.) London: Rider, 1931.

Dobkin de Rios, M. *Visionary Vine*. San Francisco: Chandler, 1972.

Eisenbud, J. *The World of Ted Serios*. New York: William Morrow, 1967.

Eliade, M. *Shamanism: Archaic Techniques of Ecstasy*. (Trans. by W. R. Trask.) Princeton: Princeton University Press, 1966.

Elkins, A. *Aboriginal Men of High Degree*. Sydney, Australia: Australasion, 1944.

Emerson, J. N. Intuitive archeology: A developing approach. Paper presented at a meeting of the American Anthropological Association, Mexico City, 1974.

Emerson, J. N. Intuitive archeology: Egypt and Iran. *A.R.E. Journal*, 1976, **11**, 55–63.

Fischer, H. T. Ethnologie en parapsychologie. *Tijdschrift voor Parapsychologie*, 1940, **12**, 1–15.

Foster, A. A. ESP tests with American Indian children. *Journal of Parapsychology*, 1943, **7**, 94–103.

Fukurai, T. *Clairvoyance and Thoughtography*. London: Rider, 1931.

Gaddis, V. H. *Mysterious Fires and Lights*. New York: David McKay, 1967.

Goodman, J. D. Psychic archeology: Methodology and empirical evidence from Flagstaff, Arizona. Paper presented at a meeting of the American Anthropological Association, Mexico City, 1974.

Gorer, G. *African Dances: A Book About West African Negroes*. New York: Knopf, 1935.

Grad, B., Cadoret, R. J., and Paul, G. I. The influence of an unorthodox method of treatment on wound healing in mice. *International Journal of Parapsychology*, 1961, **3**, 5–24.

Halifax-Grof, J. Hex death. In A. Angoff and D. Barth (Eds.), *Parapsychology and Anthropology*, pp. 59–73. New York: Parapsychology Foundation, 1974.

Hallowell, A. *The Role of Conjuring in Saulteux Society*. Philadelphia: University of Pennsylvania Press, 1942.

Handelman, D. The development of a Washo shaman. *Ethnology*, 1967, **6**, 444–464.

Handelman, D. Shamanizing on an empty stomach. *American Anthropologist*, 1968, **70**, 353–356.

Hilgard, E. R. A neodissociative interpretation of pain reduction in hypnosis. *Psychological Review*, 1973, **80**, 396–411.

Humphrey, B. M. Paranormal occurrences among preliterate peoples. *Journal of Parapsychology*, 1944, **8**, 214–229.

Hutton, J. *The Sema Negas*. London: Macmillan, 1921.

Huxley, F. *The Invisibles: Voodoo Gods in Haiti*. New York: McGraw-Hill, 1969.

Jacolliet, L. *Occult Science in India*. New York: Metaphysical Publishing Co., 1901.

Kenn, C. W. *Firewalking from the Inside*. Los Angeles: Franklin Thomas, 1949.

Kensinger, K. *Banisteriopsis* usage among the Peruvian Cashinahua. In M. Harner (Ed.), *Hallucinogens and Shamanism*, pp. 9–14. New York: Oxford University Press, 1973.

Kluckhohn, C. *Navaho Witchcraft*. Boston: Beacon Press, 1967.

Kroeber, A. L. Psychosis or social sanction. In A. L. Kroeber (Ed.), *The Nature of Culture*, pp. 310–319. Chicago: University of Chicago Press, 1952.

La Barre, W. *The Peyote Cult*. New York: Schocken Books, 1959.

Lambert, W. W., Triandis, L. M., and Wolf, M. Some correlates of beliefs in the malevolence and benevolence of supernatural beings: A cross-cultural study. *Journal of Abnormal and Social Psychology*, 1959, **58**, 162–169.

Lang, A. *The Making of Religion*. (2nd ed.) London: Longmans, Green, 1900.

Langdon-Davies, J. *On the Nature of Man*. New York: New American Library, 1961.

Laubscher, B. *Sex Customs and Psychopathology: A Study of South African Pagan Natives*. New York: McBride, 1938.

Lewis, G. A. *The Recognition of Sickness and Its Causes: A Medical-Anthropological Study of the Einu, West Sepik District, New Guinea*. Unpublished doctoral dissertation, London University, 1972.

Lewis, I. M. *Ecstatic Religion: An Anthropological Study of Spirit Possession and Shamanism*. London: Pelican Anthropology Library, 1971.

Lowie, R. Supernormal experiences. *Tomorrow*, 1956, **4**, 9–16.

Mangin, E. *The Mossi*. (Trans. by A. Brunel and E. Skinner.) New Haven: Human Relations Area Files, 1959.

Masters, R., and Houston, J. *The Varieties of Psychedelic Experience*. New York: Delta, 1966.

Matthews, F. B. An account of an outbreak of religious hallucination in the Bahamas, West Indies, with a brief sketch of some phenomena connected therewith. *Journal of the Society for Psychical Research*, 1886, **2**, 485–488.

McGovern, W. M. *Jungle Paths and Inca Ruins*. New York: Grosset and Dunlap, 1927.

Mead, M. (Ed.). *Cooperation and Competition Among Primitive Peoples*. New York: McGraw-Hill, 1937.

Middleton, J. F., and Winter, E. H. (Eds.). *Witchcraft and Sorcery in East Africa*. London: Routledge and Kegan Paul, 1963.

Nadel, S. F. Witchcraft in four African societies: An essay in comparison. *American Anthropologist*, 1952, **54**, 18–29.

Neher, A. A physiological explanation of unusual behavior in ceremonies involving drums. *Human Biology*, 1962, **34**, 151–160.

Oesterreich, T. K. *Possession: Demoniacal and Other, Among Primitive Races, in Antiquity, the Middle Ages, and Modern Times*. (Trans. by D. Ibberson.) New Hyde Park, N. Y.: University Books, 1966.

Palmer, J. Scoring in ESP tests as a function of belief in ESP. Part I. The sheep-goat effect. *Journal of the American Society for Psychical Research*, 1971, **65**, 373–408.

Palmer, J. Scoring in ESP tests as a function of belief in ESP. Part II. Beyond the sheep-goat effect. *Journal of the American Society for Psychical Research*, 1972, **66**, 1–26.

Pobers, M. Psychical phenomena among primitive peoples. In G. Wolstenshome and E. Millar (Eds.), *Ciba Foundation Symposium on Extrasensory Perception*, pp. 102–110. Boston: Little, Brown, 1956.

Pope, D. H. ESP tests with primitive people. *Parapsychology Bulletin*, 1953, **30**, 1–3.

Price, H. *A Report on Two Experimental Fire-Walks*. University of London: Council for Psychical Investigation. *Bulletin II*, 1936.

Rose, L., and Rose, R. Psi experiments with Australian aborigines. *Journal of Parapsychology*, 1951, **15**, 122–131.

Rose, R. Experiments in ESP and PK with aboriginal subjects. *Journal of Parapsychology*, 1952, **16**, 219–220.

Rose, R. A second report on psi experiments with Australian aborigines. *Journal of Parapsychology*, 1955, **19**, 92–98.

Rose, R. *Living Magic: The Realities Underlying the Psychical Practices and Beliefs of Australian Aborigines*. Chicago: Rand McNally, 1956.

Sachs, W. *Black Hamlet*. Boston: Little, Brown, 1947.

Silverman, J. Shamans and acute schizophrenia. *American Anthropologist*, 1967, **69**, 21–31.

St. Clair, D. *Drum and Candle*. Garden City, N. Y.: Doubleday, 1971.

Stevenson, I. Characteristics of cases of the reincarnation type in Turkey. *Proceedings of the Parapsychological Association*, 1968, **5**, 10–12.

Torrey, E. F. *The Mind Game: Witchdoctors and Psychiatrists*. New York: Bantam Books, 1973.

Trilles, H. *Fleurs noires et ames blanches*. Lille: 1914.

Trilles, R. G. *Les pygmées de la forêt equatorials*. Paris: 1932.

Valentine, T. *Psychic Surgery*. Chicago: Henry Regnery, 1973.

Van de Castle, R. L. Psi abilities in primitive groups. *Proceedings of the Parapsychological Association*, 1970, **7**, 97–122.

Van de Castle, R. L. An investigation of psi abilities among the Cuna Indians of Panama. In A. Angoff and D. Barth (Eds.), *Parapsychology and Anthropology*, pp. 80–97. New York: Parapsychology Foundation, 1974.

Weiant, C. W. Parapsychology and anthropology. *Manas*, 1960, **13**, 1–8.

Wilkins, H. T. *Devil Trees and Plants of Africa, Asia and South America*. Girard, Kansas: Haldeman-Julius, 1948.

Williams, J. *Psychic Phenomena of Jamaica*. New York: Dial Press, 1934.

Wilson, M. Witch beliefs and social structure. *American Journal of Sociology*, 1951, **56**, 307–313.

Wolkowski, Z. Archeological model-testing: Parapsychological experiments with Stefan Ossowiecki (1937–1941). Paper presented at a meeting of the American Anthropological Association, Mexico City, 1974.

Zorab, G. *Bibliography of Parapsychology*. New York: Parapsychology Foundation, 1957.

2

Parapsychology, Biology, and ANPSI

Robert L. Morris

INTRODUCTION

Parapsychology's findings have implications for biology at two levels. (1) Information appears to flow between organism and environment through some means other than those we presently understand. Thus our present understanding of information flow in biological systems may be badly flawed, since that understanding is founded upon research that could have involved more forms of information flow than were conceptualized by the investigators. The specificity of their conclusions can thus be questioned. An example of this within animal communication is the controversy over how many paths of information flow are involved in the apparent communication of honey locations in bee dances (e.g., Gould, Henery, and MacLeod, 1970; Von Frisch, 1967; Wenner and Johnson, 1967).

(2) If in fact such new modes of information flow (i.e. psi) exist, they must have some sort of explanation. Given the present limitations of our data, all attempted explanations at this time are speculative. Nevertheless, the eventual explanation of psi, whatever it may be, may come to have far deeper implications for our understanding of biological systems and of the nature of life than the direct implication of psi itself.

If we are to integrate parapsychology and biology, we should use concepts common to both. Parapsychology is defined in the glossary of 1975 issues of the *Journal of Parapsychology* as "the branch of science that deals with psi communication, i.e., behavioral or personal exchanges with the environment which are extrasensorimotor—not dependent on the senses and muscles." The core concept here is communication, a concept common throughout the biological sciences.

MacKay (1972) outlines five uses of the concept of "communication" between A and B: (a) a correlation between events at A and B; (b) a causal interaction between A and B; (c) transmission of information between A and B regardless of the presence of a sender or recipient; (d) an action by organism A upon organism B; and (e) a transaction between organisms A and B. MacKay feels the concept of communication has been overworked and should at least be restricted to categories (d) and (e), i.e., information flow between organisms. Within these categories, he further suggests that communication be applied only to cases in which each organism is aware of the other and information exchange is intended by the source organism. Some specialists in human communication prefer an even narrower definition. Worth and Gross (1974) define communication as "a social process, within a context, in which signs are produced and transmitted, perceived, and treated as messages from which meanings can be inferred." Gross (1975) has specifically taken parapsychology to task for not employing a comparably specific definition of its subject matter.

The concept of communication in the harder sciences does take on more general forms, however. Stent (1972), for instance, lists three general categories of cellular communication: genetic, metabolic, and nervous. All involve descriptions of continuous physiological information flow. Perhaps the most generalizable notion of communication was that of Shannon (1948), who represented communication systems in basic terms. An information source, not necessarily organic, places a message in a transmitter; the transmitter sends an encoded signal through a channel to a receiver, which then decodes the signal, allowing the original message to reach its destination (also not necessarily organic). Shannon also provided the notion of noise sources, which may act on the channel to distort the signal and reduce the effectiveness of the system. This basic model can readily be applied to many information flow systems in biology, although some of the specific mathematical models derived from it cannot be so generally applied, as MacKay (e.g., 1972) and others have pointed out. To apply even Shannon's basic concepts to ongoing physiological processes involves applying them simultaneously at several different levels of organization, such that transient biochemical events are regarded as interactive communication events within interactive cellular communication events, and so on up through interorganism communication events and interpopulation communication events.

To see where the phenomena of parapsychology fit in, let us return to MacKay's five usages of the term *communication*. Certainly the phenomena of spontaneous cases fit within (a), a correlation between events at A and B, with A being an organism and B being some aspect of the environment. In spontaneous cases, some aspect of the environment thematically matches or corresponds to some aspect within an organism, generally its reported experience, or intent, or observable behavior. Such correspondences have led us to infer communication between organism and environment.

Opinion has varied as to whether or not we are entitled to infer (b), a causal interaction between A and B. Some authors, e.g., Jung and Pauli (1955) and Koestler (1972), feel that psi is best construed as involving an "acausal connecting principle." Whether or not this is the case, or whether such a phrase is even linguistically tenable, is beyond the scope of the present paper.

In our controlled experimental studies, we tend to assume (c), transmission of information between A and B, and our experimental designs are very compatible with Shannon's basic model. In ESP studies, an experimenter creates a message in the environment and then monitors the isolated organism to see if the message can be detected. The experimenter, applying some randomizing technique to a target pool, serves as a message source. The selected target plus any agent involved serve as transmitters. The signal and channel at present are not specifiable. The percipient or subject serves as receiver, and the experimenter (or a second experimenter) serves as the message destination, once the behavior of the receiver is interpreted. In PK studies the same model applies. An experimenter creates a message of intention for the subject, who serves as transmitter, and an experimenter then monitors a target aspect of the environment which serves as receiver. The message destination once again is also an experimenter, who interprets the behavior of the receiver in order to extract the message. As with other complex biological systems, one could also insert multiple communication systems within the basic ESP and PK models outlined above, especially with regard to information processing within the organisms (including researchers) involved. It should be noted, of course, that in spontaneous cases the message source generally serves also as transmitter and the message destination as receiver.

With regard to (d) and (e), some studies and spontaneous cases do involve two organisms, each of which is aware that the other intends to communicate. On such occasions we can use the term communication in its most restricted senses. Psi communication as a whole could not be considered under (d) and (e), since pure clairvoyance and PK influences upon nonliving material have both been experimentally demonstrated (e.g., Schmidt, 1969; 1970a).

A few additional problems arise in interfacing psi with models of biological communications systems. Since we are unable to identify a specific channel, we have uncertainty as to the true transmitters and receivers and, therefore, the true path(s) of information flow. A second problem is that the moment of transmission is unclear. Given the uncertainties over the nature of the transmitter, information may become available at the moment it comes into existence,

or at the moment its final determinant comes into existence, or, in some probabilistic sense, information may become available *during the development* of its
determinants.   If one takes precognition seriously, an organism could conceivably acquire relevant information at any moment throughout its postfertil-
ization existence, and all hope of modeling biological communication systems
with any precision is lost.   A third problem is that the precise content of the
message is hard to specify in many cases, thus rendering any study of an encoded
and decoded signal very difficult. This is true in any study of complex behavior.
Also, any model involving PK must come to grips effectively with the concept of
goal-directedness and intention, a surprisingly complex and controversial issue.
From the above consideration it follows that any model involving specific stimuli for ESP and particular responses for the subject organism in PK will have
great difficulties.   Finally, just because our research assumes transmission of
information between A and B does not guarantee in itself that such is the case.

Although these difficulties exist, we must pursue our specific attempts to
interface psi with biology. Psi may act to cooperate with, or compete with, or
supplant our known biological communication systems. Before we explore these
speculative possibilities further, we must examine our data base in more detail.

IDENTIFIABLE CHANNELS OF INFORMATION FLOW

Before we discuss the evidence for psi interactions in biological systems, let us
summarize some findings about the range of nonpsi interactions that are possible
between organism and environment.

The Range of Animal Senses

Plants and animals, including humans, can apparently detect the presence of a
wide variety of weak physical stimuli. Presman (1970) summarizes evidence for
biological responsiveness to electromagnetic radiation ranging from the super-
high radio frequencies down to frequencies so low that they essentially represent
static electric and magnetic fields. Barnothy (1964) summarizes evidence for
responsiveness to strong and weak magnetic fields and to changes in field
strength. McNulty, Pease, and Bond (1975) indicate that when charged particles
such as pions and muons pass through the eyeball, they produce particle-induced
visual sensations (PIVS) in humans through Cerenkov radiation and other
mechanisms.   Many animals show great sensitivity to minute temperature
changes in their environments, such as rattlesnakes (e.g. Bullock and Cowles,
1952) and moths (Callahan, 1964). Some animals also have specialized sensors
for detecting pressure changes, e.g., the lateral lines of fish, which detect pressure changes in the surrounding water. By comparing the times of pressure
changes registered on each of its sides, the fish can localize the source of the

responsible disturbance (Dijgraaf, 1963). Most, if not all, animals, including humans, have the capacity to respond to small vibration movements in their environment, especially if the vibrations are conducted through solid material directly to some part of the body surface (e.g., Geldard, 1940). Although many animals seem responsive to changes in surrounding electrical or magnetic fields, a few have remarkable specialized adaptations. The knife-fish, *Gymnarchus niloticus*, detects the presence of objects near it by generating an electric field around its own body and detecting distortions in the way the electric lines of force enter the head region (Lissman, 1958, 1963). All organisms seem to respond to light; some have specialized adaptations to enable them to detect specific properties of light. Bees, for instance, detect the polarization of light through the arrangement of tiny tubules in the bottom of the eye which contain light-sensitive chemicals (Goldsmith, 1962; Goldsmith and Philpott, 1957). There is now some evidence that birds can respond to subtle changes in the angle of inclination of geomagnetic lines of force at the earth's surface, using changes in the angle for navigation and homing (Talkington, cited in Dröscher, 1969). In addition to the above, there are a great many sensors for various chemicals, generally receptors responsive to specific kinds of molecules, even in extremely low concentrations. For instance, some cells in the antennae of honey bees react only to carbon dioxide (Lacher, 1964).

Additional Aspects of Animal Senses

We know where the sensors for light, sound, taste, and so on are located on our own bodies; such sensors are often located in other places in other species. Many eyeless species, for instance, have light-sensitive cells over various surface areas of the body (e.g., Millott, 1957). Certain fish, such as minnows, appear to have olfactory detectors on the surface of parts of their skin (Whitear, 1965). It has often been suggested that humans can detect light through skin receptors. Although impressive demonstrations have been claimed (e.g., Ostrander and Schroeder, 1970), such demonstrations are easy to produce fraudulently (Christopher, 1975), and solid evidence for such abilities has yet to emerge.

Additionally, many of the senses described above are extremely sensitive, such as smell in dogs, vision in birds, hearing in bats and cetaceans, and so on. Even humans under the right conditions show great sensory acuity. In a completely darkened room, the human eye can apparently respond to as little as 5 quanta of light (Hecht, Schlaer, and Pirenne, 1941). Although the usual range of human hearing extends only up to 16–20 kilocycles, humans can respond to frequencies up to 200 kilocycles if the transmitter is in direct contact with the skull (Timm, 1950). At frequencies above 20 kilocycles there is no pitch discrimination with all frequencies sounding like a very high tone.

The above all represent examples of unusual sensitivities in animal sensation. These sensors are integrated with central processing and response systems in such a way as to amplify the usefulness of the information provided. Some can be quite complex. Kilian (1964) noted that horses, dogs, and some other species would respond strongly to vibrations from the subtle ground tremors that often precede earthquakes but would not react to comparable tremors that were not followed by earthquakes. Either the animals were extracting very specific information about differences in the two kinds of tremors, or else, as Kilian suggests, they were making use of additional geophysical cues associated with earthquakes such as storms in the earth's magnetic field or very high barometric pressure. The work of Sauer and Sauer (1960) with caged birds in a planetarium indicates that some birds navigate at night through the use of specific star patterns and that their capacity to do so is not a learned response.

Methodological Implications

There appear to be many potential pathways or channels of information flow available. There are differences from species to species, and the full range of any organism's capabilities are very difficult to specify.

Some of the findings described above are well established; others do not yet have as firm a data base from a variety of investigators as one might desire. Some researchers have failed to obtain the results of other researchers. To compare one communication study with another, testing conditions must be as similar as possible. Given the diversity of communication channels available, it is necessary to ensure that access to channels other than those being studied is adequately controlled and similar among the studies compared. It is also necessary to equate the organism's deployment of attention toward the information channel under study. This is especially true in humans; the effects of selective attention deployment in communication in general and psi in particular are well known and, in the latter case, are covered elsewhere in this volume. Deployment of attention is generally regulated by reducing competing input and by orienting the subject toward the specific target.

These problems reduce the likelihood that we presently have an accurate picture of the full range of the sensory capabilities of any organism. Nevertheless, we cannot say that the sensory capacity of any organism is in fact limitless. We can demonstrate sensory failure under certain specific conditions; if sufficient shielding and/or distance is involved, we can also demonstrate physically that no signal of a particular kind is available from the target.

In testing for psi, we must be aware of the full range of signals put out by the target and any other source containing information about the target. Living tissue, for instance, seems capable of producing weak magnetic fields (e.g. Cohen, 1975), as well as electrostatic fields and electromagnetic radiation at various frequencies (e.g., Presman, 1970). Such signals are generally weak and decay rapidly with distance. Often they are marked by stronger background noise and vary with small changes in the tissue, making them difficult to measure with precision. These fields may vary not only with the gross behavior of the organism; they may also vary with changes in the mental activity of the organism. Brenner, Williamson, and Kaufman (1975), for instance, found that visual stimulation could produce variations in the magnetic field of the human brain.

The above uncertainties must be understood before we can begin to assess the evidence for any truly new communication system (i.e., psi). The evidence for psi in humans is presented abundantly elsewhere in this volume. Let us now consider the evidence for psi in infrahuman species (animal psi, or anpsi, and plants).

PSI IN ANIMALS

Evidence from Spontaneous Cases

The most imprecise form of evidence for psi in animals is derived from analyses by researchers of large collections of reported spontaneous cases. The evidential value of each such report is limited for several reasons, among them: (a) distortion in the reporter's original perceptions, interpretations, memories, or final verbalization of the original experiences involved; (b) one can never re-create the original circumstances exactly, to examine all of the factors that may have been involved; (c) it is impossible to assess with any precision the likelihood that a given complex coincidence would have occurred by chance; (d) biases on the part of the investigator; (e) deliberate deception by reporter or investigator.

Additional difficulties occur when we try to draw inferences from large collections of such cases. A sampling bias is created by the fact that certain individuals or kinds of people may be more inclined to turn in cases, thus weighting any overall description of the cases in favor of those cases most likely to occur to such people. Also, the frequent lack of details about crucial factors makes conceptual comparison difficult. Drawing inferences from spontaneous cases often involves, in part, demonstrating the presence of relationships among variables common to many cases. This requires mathematical evaluation, which in turn requires some basis of comparison, either chance or a control group of some sort. Such a comparison is extremely difficult to make in analyzing spontaneous cases, once again due to the lack of detailed information about the relevant variables. Nevertheless, surveys of spontaneous cases can provide guidance for the conductance of more precise studies.

The most rigorous survey of anecdotes involving psi in animals was probably that of Rhine and Feather (1962), which was based on the extensive Duke collection of case reports. They described five categories of behavior suggesting psi: (a) behavior which suggests a reaction to impending danger to the animal itself or its master; (b) behavior which suggests a reaction to the death of the master at a distance; (c) behavior which suggests anticipation of the master's return; (d) homing behavior; and (e) psi-trailing. The strongest cases of the first three kinds generally involved a mammalian pet and a human with which it had been in close contact for considerable time. Included were examples of dogs refusing to enter vehicles that later crashed, horses shying from faulty bridges, dogs howling excessively at the same time as a distant owner was in trouble or dying, pets who became extremely excited just before the owner arrived home suddenly and unexpectedly following a long absence, and so on.

Category (d), homing, has been the subject of considerable research since Rhine and Feather wrote their article. The ability to return home after removal to a considerable distance regardless of direction has been well documented in many mammals and birds, plus in a variety of other organisms including some molluscs (e.g., Thorpe, 1963). Although we now have a fair understanding of how animals navigate, i.e., maintain direction, there has been less certainty about how they select the correct direction to begin with. Also, Rhine (1951) noted certain similarities between human psi performance and studies of mouse homing by Neuhaus (1948, 1950) and by Krüger and Vogelberg (1951): elusiveness of results; better results with fewer trials per day; absence of the ability in some animals; a rarity of high scorers; occasional significant negative results analogous to psi-missing; and a tendency for initial high scoring to be followed by a drop to chance scoring. Such similarities, plus the lack of a demonstrable mechanism for initial direction selection, led Rhine and Pratt (e.g., Pratt, 1953) to hypothesize that psi was involved in homing. Pratt and several coworkers attempted to develop an experimental design with pigeons that would provide a true assessment of the role of psi in homing (Pratt, 1956). The actual research failed to provide such an assessment, although they did develop a research plan refined to overcome the methodological difficulties (Pratt, 1966) but did not test it. At present there is therefore no experimental evidence directly suggesting that psi is involved in homing. In view of recent advances (e.g., Matthews, 1968) in testing various hypotheses about the use by birds of geomagnetic and celestial cues, it is likely that psi is not involved in the homing behavior of those species that perform it consistently. However, as was noted above, some species that have shown homing behavior experimentally have not necessarily done so with great consistency. Thus the potential involvement (if any) of psi in each species should be considered quite separately and may yet be tenable as a contributing factor.

Category (e), psi-trailing, involves cases in which an animal left behind trails its owner to a totally new location, or "home," which the animal has never visited previously. Rhine and Feather used four criteria in appraising psi-trailing cases: a reliable source of information for all the relevant aspects of the case; a specific characteristic by which the animal can be recognized, such as an unusual scar or a nametag; overall consistency and believability of the general details of the case; and adequate supporting data, such as corroborating testimony from several witnesses, availability of the pet for inspection, and so on. Rhine and Feather found 25 cases that met these criteria and involved over 30 miles of travel. Represented were ten dogs, twelve cats, and three birds. Some of the cases involved distances of several hundred miles. Explanation of such cases in terms of sensory acuity or "chance" is problematic, but there has yet been no attempt to verify psi-trailing experimentally.

Two other surveys of psi in animals are of interest. Bayless (1970) emphasizes cases relating to the survival question, such as the responses of animals in supposed "haunted houses," during mediumistic sittings, and so on. Gaddis and Gaddis (1970) describe many cases of unusual animal behavior, including apparently very intelligent animals, psi-trailing, and animals apparently reacting to distant events.

Such spontaneous cases are occasionally very impressive but lack persuasiveness for the reasons outlined earlier. Many cases involve pets with close bonds to humans, suggesting that psi in animals should be looked for especially in human-animal communication situations. Given that anecdotes are only registered when a human becomes aware of sufficient details, however, this finding is not surprising and may not portend a meaningful trend.

Evidence from Field Investigations

Field investigations are investigations of apparent spontaneous psi that recurs in the presence of an investigator, thus eliminating some but not all of the difficulties cited earlier with respect to spontaneous cases.

The only sizable body of data in this category for animals concerns so-called clever animals, generally dogs, horses, or pigs, that supposedly can do mathematics and communicate verbally through the use of a coded response system. Numbers are generally indicated by pawing, vocalizing, or tapping an appropriate number of times; letters of the alphabet are selected by consecutively touching lettered blocks in a tray. Generally such animals respond to simple questions from a trainer or from someone else in the presence of a trainer. Three hypotheses have been offered to explain such animals: genuine intelligence, subtle sensory cues from the environment, and psi. Genuine intelligence has been effectively ruled out by the general failure of such animals to succeed when no one present knows the correct answer, as well as by the findings of comparative psychologists regarding the limits of animal intelligence. Subtle sensory cues from the environment have been shown to be applicable in most cases. The classical example is that of Clever Hans (e.g., Pfungst, 1965), a horse who was being cued by subtle changes in the posture of whoever knew the correct answer. Whenever Hans began pawing the ground or moving his nose along the alphabet blocks, all humans present bent forward slightly to get a better look. When Hans reached the correct number of paws or the correct alphabet block, the person who knew the correct answer would lean back slightly, unintentionally, thus providing the cue. Pfungst also demonstrated this phenomenon in the laboratory using two humans. Rhine and Rhine (1929a, 1929b) conducted several investigations with Lady, a "mind-reading" horse. During their earlier investigations they found no specific cue that the horse was using, but someone present always had to know the correct answer. In later investigations, they found the horse using obvious body cues.

Some reports of such clever animals are more difficult to dismiss. Rolf, an Airedale terrier, would supposedly upon occasion paw or tap the answers to mathematics problems before the answers had been calculated, although in general someone present had to know the correct answer (Mackenzie, 1919). Bechterev (1949) described the work of the animal trainer Durov, who seemed able by mental concentration to direct certain of his dogs to perform specific tasks such as fetching sheet music from a piano, and so on. Screening the trainer's face from the dog reduced but did not eliminate the results. Vasiliev (1963) has expressed reservations about possible sensory cues and target selection, noting that when the trainer-sender was placed in a screened chamber, he was successful only when he could watch the dog through an opening. White (1964b) surveyed the field studies of clever dogs and added five new cases she had investigated personally. Of the five, only one seemed promising: Cookie, an 11-year-old female cocker spaniel, who could respond consistently when her trainer was in a separate dark room shielded from the dog by a thick curtain and with a loud masking noise in the background. White also noted that field research with dogs presents just as many psychological difficulties as does research with humans.

The best study of a clever animal to date is probably that of Chris the Wonder Dog, by Wood and Cadoret (1958). A preliminary investigation by Erickson (1969) of Chris indicated that he was responding to standard body language cues. At Cadoret's suggestion Chris was later taught by his owner, Wood, to call down through a deck of standard ESP cards by pawing once for circle, twice for square, and so on. Chris was then trained to respond to ESP cards enclosed in opaque envelopes. For each run, Wood's wife placed a closed deck of cards in the envelopes, shuffled them, and left the room. Wood later entered the room, cut the deck, and took it in to Chris. Chris made a number of pawings to each envelope in turn; the number was recorded by Wood. After the run each envelope would be opened and its contents noted independently. Chris scored well above chance ($P < .0001$) during a preset series of 500 trials, doing 10 to 20 trials per day. When Cadoret was brought back to observe the procedure, Chris produced a significant negative duration under a variety of conditions. Wood and Cadoret suggested that this psi-missing effect may be analogous to that in humans asked to perform under conditions of high stress (e.g., Rhine, 1952).

Pratt (1966), who also worked briefly with Chris, has suggested (1969) that Chris may have been responding to unconscious muscle cues from Wood, who would then have been functioning as the true psi subject. This possibility, plus the inconsistency in Chris's results, renders the research with Chris rather weak as evidence for psi in animals.

Chris's case is the best of its kind. The others are somewhat impressive collectively, but individually suffer from uncertainty as to whether or not sensory cues and experimenter bias were adequately eliminated.

In summary, neither spontaneous cases nor field investigations have provided strong support for the notion of psi in infrahuman species. We turn next to laboratory experiments.

Evidence from Laboratory Experiments

When done well, experimental studies under controlled laboratory conditions greatly reduce the sources of error cited earlier. By exercising control over the experimental variables, we can obtain a more detailed description of the relevant conditions and what actually took place, as well as describe the results in much more mathematically precise ways. Unfortunately the product of a study, its published report, often lacks details necessary for outside evaluation. Also, certain journals seem to have biases against publishing parapsychology studies that produce positive results (e.g. Honorton, Ramsey, and Cabibbo, 1975), and a leading parapsychology journal recently publicly declared a policy against publishing in detail research that does not contain positive results (Rhine, 1975). The resultant selective screening of publicly inspectable data makes the reviewer's task most difficult, and the potentially widespread existence of such policies should be borne in mind by those who read this chapter.

The Animal as Psi Source. Several studies have tested for animal psi using psychokinesis procedures. In general, such procedures involved placing the animal in a somewhat unpleasant environment, e.g., too cold, subject to periodic weak shocks, and so on. The pleasantness of the environment was periodically determined by decisions made by a random number generator (RNG) of the sort used in human PK research (e.g., Schmidt, 1970a). The hypothesis is that the animal, like the human, does not need to understand the mechanics of the environment in order to influence it; all that is necessary is that the animal be able to represent to itself the world as it would like it to be, e.g., "know what it wants," formulate an intention, etc., for the PK process to work. Success is defined in terms of the degree of bias in the favorable direction of the recorded output of the RNG during the time that its decisions affect the welfare of the animal, as opposed to the degree of bias on other comparable occasions.

The results of such studies are mixed. Schmidt (1970b) found that an RNG-controlled heat lamp stayed on significantly more often when his pet cat had access to the area under the lamp. He also found that cockroaches on a grid were shocked significantly more times by an RNG-controlled circuit than would be expected by chance, the apparent equivalent of psi-missing. Watkins (1971) found that lizards (*Anolis sagrei*) in a cool environment showed different tendencies to receive heat from an RNG-controlled heat lamp, depending upon ambient barometric pressure and humidity. These results are consistent with the differing heat needs of the lizards in these differing environments. Because of the complex and in part unanticipated nature of his findings, Watkins (1972) feels that this paradigm should be repeated and with stronger results before his findings be taken seriously. Schmidt (1974a) has recently obtained positive results with tanks of brine shrimp exposed to brief RNG-controlled electric shocks, e.g., the shrimp received fewer shocks than would be expected by chance. He has not been able to repeat the finding (Schmidt, 1974b).

Unfortunately, all of the above studies may be interpreted as human psi, since the experimenter wants the study to succeed and may just as easily as the animal be influencing the RNG. Schmidt's results with the cockroaches may be interpreted in this way. He dislikes cockroaches and was aware of when the cockroaches were shocked, because cockroaches often flip on their backs when shocked, and he had to be present to turn them right side up each time. Thus he may have produced the negative results himself. At any rate, these studies cannot in themselves be taken yet as evidence that animals can show PK.

The Animal as Psi Receiver for Emotional Information. A few preliminary studies have attempted to create emotionally salient events in the environment and measure the animal's somatic responses. Using a precognition paradigm, Morris (1967) found evidence that rats in an open field showed more tendency to freeze and not explore if they were about to die 10 minutes later than if they were not. This finding was true only for rats that were unfamiliar with the open field. Whether or not the rats were to die was determined by a second experimenter, blind to the open field score, through use of a table of random numbers. The scorer of the rat's open field responses likewise was blind as to the rat's fate. All rats used in this study had participated in perception studies by another researcher and were originally scheduled to die sooner. Schmidt (1970c) failed to find any differences in open field performance between those about to die and those who would remain alive, using a procedure similar to that of Morris. Craig (1973) found that rats about to die within 24 hours were more active than those who lived on. Craig's results may have differed from Morris' because of the different time intervals between testing and death. A rat that is very close to a predator in nature tends to freeze, and this was the response Morris anticipated before his study. A rat that is a considerable distance from a predator but which is at some level aware of its existence might well be motivated to take evasive action rather than freeze. Nevertheless, the discrepancies among these three studies do exist and prevent us from drawing any conclusions.

Morris (1967) also found that goldfish about to be picked up in a net and held aloft briefly were significantly more active, as rated by a blind observer, than goldfish that were not to be picked up. Which of three goldfish in the same tank was to be picked up was determined, immediately after their observation for a minute by an experimenter, by the experimenter's throw of two dice off a banking board. Thus the effect could have been due to experimenter PK. A later study (Morris, 1972) failed to obtain results when a concealed list of random numbers selected by someone not involved with the study was used to determine which fish was to be held aloft.

The studies in this section thus present no overall evidence for psi in animals, although in fairness it should be noted that they were all pilot studies in the process of methodological refinement. These procedures are of especial interest because they are directly related to the emotional involvement theme that emerged from the spontaneous case surveys.

The Animal as Psi Receiver for Choice-Related Information. The main research strategy for most anpsi research has been to present the animal with a specific set of behavioral options, or choices, only one of which leads either to reward or to avoidance of punishment. The animal is generally pretrained to expect each option to lead equally often to the reward or punishment. Without such pretraining, and even occasionally in spite of it, animals will develop biases and sequential patterns of response which may override any psi-mediated choice. The investigator has his choice of either modifying the conditions to reduce the likelihood of patterned behavior, or of taking such patterns into consideration by the method of data analysis.

Osis and Foster (1953) studied kittens running for food in a T-maze. Which of the two arms contained concealed food was determined randomly by an experimenter not otherwise involved. Olfactory cues were minimized by fans blowing air toward each foodcup, and the cups themselves were not visible to the kitten at the head of the maze, where it made its choices. The kittens in general scored positively under good conditions such as affectionate handling, yet tended to go to the wrong arm of the maze when distracted or handled poorly; the difference between the two conditions was statistically significant. Occasionally the animals developed fixed response patterns, e.g., entering the same arm time after time or alternating sides. Those trials in which the animals broke such a fixed pattern produced the strongest positive results.

Bestall (1962) used male mice in a two-choice maze. Each mouse made one choice. After all the mice in a given session made their choices, one side for each mouse was randomly designated as correct by an experimenter using the day's weather report and a list of random numbers. Correct choosers were given access to a female mouse 6 hours after having run the maze; incorrect choosers were killed 6 hours after having run the maze. Bestall obtained weak but significant positive results, with some evidence of cyclic variations in scoring from day to day.

Craig and Treurniet (1974) used a T-maze in a similar precognition paradigm with death as punishment for an incorrect choice. Overall results were chance, but those rats which chose the correct side took longer to make a choice. This finding was present in two consecutive studies. In a later study along similar lines (Treurniet and Craig, 1975), a suggestive relationship was found between success and phase of the moon.

Rhine (1971) worked with a trainer-dog team to see if they could locate dummy underwater mines buried 4 inches in the sand in shallow water at one of five possible predesignated locations. The dog was led by the trainer along a guide line above the water which indicated each of the five locations. The dog responded by sitting near the mine location. The mine box had been buried earlier by another experimenter and raked clean, while the trainer and dog were out of sight. The results were very strong but admit of three alternatives: (a) olfactory cues, since odors have been known to cling to such locations for quite some period of time; (b) tactile-vibrational cues, since the sand above the box may pack more densely when stepped upon than the sand at other places; and (c) the dog may have responded to unconscious cues from its trainer, who might know the correct location either through sensory cues or through psi.

Schouten (1972) placed thirsty mice in a box and trained them to press either of two levers to obtain access to water. Following this, the animals were tested for psi: only one of the levers led to water, as determined by an RNG that selected the correct lever at the beginning of each trial. The correct lever and the lever pressed by the animal were automatically recorded. Schouten found that his animals scored significantly above chance on those trials in which they were not showing patterned behavior in their selection of levers, but scored at chance overall. There was suggestive evidence that having another animal aware in advance which lever led to water helped the subject animal to choose that lever. In follow-up studies using thematically similar procedures, these results have not been confirmed (Schouten, 1973). Using a very similar procedure with thirsty rats, Terry and Harris (1975) found overall below chance results but significant positive results when the animals were not showing stereotyped behavior.

Parker (1974) used gerbils in a similar situation: They had two levers to depress, one of which would give access to a sunflower seed. A preprogrammed punch tape determined which lever would lead to food for each trial. The overall results were significantly positive and were strongest when the animals were not showing stereotyped behavior. Broughton and Millar (1975) obtained only chance results when they repeated this study in the same laboratory with the same equipment and some of the same animals.

Duval and Montredon (1968a) used mice in a shock-avoidance procedure. The animals were run in a small cage divided in half by a low wall which the animal could easily cross. Once every minute the animal's position was recorded automatically. A fraction of a second afterwards, and RNG selected one side to receive shock. If the animal was recorded as being on that side it received a mild shock through the floor for 5 seconds. The side selected and whether or not shock was administered was also recorded automatically. The overall results were positive but insignificant, i.e., the mice tended to avoid the shock. Often the mice showed stereotyped behavior, e.g., did not move from one trial to the next or moved only in response to shock. When these trials were dropped from the data, the results were significantly positive. In a follow-up work by the same team (Duval and Montredon, 1968b), significantly positive results also were obtained only during nonstereotyped behavior.

This shock avoidance paradigm has been examined extensively in the United States. One set of studies must now be dismissed because the senior researcher acknowledged fraud (see Rhine, 1974, for details). However, other research teams have attempted to repeat the Duval-Montredon studies, with procedural modifications. Levin (1975) describes four series of studies using a running wheel apparatus and one series using a box-shaped cage modeled after Duval and Montredon, all with gerbils as subjects. The wheel apparatus was a standard activity wheel with its inside running surface divided into halves by two low barriers 180 degrees apart. As the animal ran in the wheel it passed over the barriers easily, thus placing itself in each half of the running surface about half of the time. These halves of the wheel serve as the analogs of the two sides of the box in the Duval-Montredon studies. In these studies the animal's position was constantly monitored electronically. Nonrandom behavior was thus given a more precise definition: refusing to cross a barrier from one trial to the next, and crossing only immediately after receiving shock. At intervals of 10 seconds an RNG selected one of the two sides as target. If the animal was there it immediately received a very brief shock. All results were recorded and analyzed by computer. A preliminary series with shock level set low (100 milliamps for $1/8$ or $1/4$ second) gave chance results. A follow-up series varied shock intensity (but not duration) from 100–800 milliamps for $1/2$ second. Significant overall results were obtained only for 300 milliamps, and all other results were chance. A confirmatory series at 300 milliamps produced chance results. The final series, at 100 milliamps for $1/2$ second, produced overall significant positive results, but the RNG during the trials itself showed a significant side bias; this prevents firm interpretation of the results. In the series using a box apparatus instead of an activity wheel, the design was the same as Duval-Montredon, except that activity was monitored constantly and random behavior was defined as with the wheel; 1-minute intertrial intervals were used, with shock of 10 milliamps lasting for 5 seconds. Three subseries were run, none of which gave significant results overall or for random behavior trials by themselves.

Terry (1976) reports the results of four series he conducted with the box apparatus used by Levin, immediately following Levin's work. The procedure was similar to Levin's, except that a 20-second intertrial interval was used. Of the four series done, all were at chance save one, which produced overall significant positive results as well as significant positive results on random behavior trials alone. Terry considered several possible differences in procedure between his work and the earlier work that had been invalidated. He suggested that differences in housing may have been partly responsible, although there is no specific evidence in favor of this hypothesis.

Eysenck (1975) used rats of the Roman High Avoidance strain in a shuttle box divided in half by a low barrier, similar to the Duval-Montredon apparatus. A prearranged random order on a tape paper reader was used to designate which side would receive 0.1 milliamps of shock for 3 seconds. If the animal was on that side it was shocked; if not, no shock was administered. Random behavior trials were defined as by Levin and Terry. The results were independently statistically significant in the negative direction for both random and nonrandom behavior trials. A second series was run using the same procedure but with a shock level of 0.2 milliamps. This series produced chance results. Eysenck hypothesized that the difference in the two series may be due to the attractiveness of weak stimulation, even a mildly aversive one, for animals in a boring testing situation. In Series 1 the shock was weak enough that its stimulation value was not cancelled out by its painfulness, and the animals sought it out; in Series 2 the shock may have been too strong. Another way to regard the data is as one more example of initially significant findings that are not repeated in a follow-up study.

There are three major problems with the data on anpsi using choice behavior. First, the data are weak and unstable. Experimenters who obtain results the first time do not continue to do so in later studies. Duval and Montredon's own research may be an exception. Second, the definition of a random behavior trial has differed from study to study depending on the apparatus used and whether or not the animal's behavior was monitored continuously. The normal behavior of the animals in each apparatus should be studied in detail, to allow an empirically derived definition of random behavior. Also, selection of specific trials from the data for analysis places an additional burden on the experimental logic, to ensure that some artifact is not being introduced. Third, for those studies using an RNG instead of a prearranged set of random numbers, there is the possibility that a human, the experimenter, was producing the results rather than the animal, by influencing the RNG to generate a target in correspondence with the animal's behavior. The frequent initial successful study followed by unsuccessful ones in reminiscent of the PK decline effect discussed elsewhere in this volume and suggests some sort of experimenter interaction with the results.

Summary. The experimental evidence for psi in animals is encouraging but still weak. The research using animals as a source of psi information is inconsistent

and at best explainable in terms of human psi. The studies using animals as receivers for emotionally-related information were all brief pilot studies and need
methodological refinement before their results can be interpreted. The studies
using animals as receivers for choice-related information produce weak and inconsistent results which are occasionally strengthened if one selects only those
trials in which the animal seems to be making a true choice. It is also of interest
that none of the researchers reported evidence of improvement of performance
from beginning to end of the run, despite the fact that the animals were given
partial feedback. Also of interest, if repeated, are the suggestions that such
factors as stimulus strength and general treatment of the animal may affect performance. Consistent negative scoring would also be of interest were it to occur
consistently under certain specifiable conditions similar to those that induce
negative scoring in humans. Osis and Foster's cats are strongly reminiscent of
Honorton's similar findings with humans, e.g., those treated well scored above
chance while those treated poorly scored below chance (Honorton, Ramsey, and
Cabibbo, 1975). At present, unfortunately, our data on animals are not strong
enough to warrant specific speculation. Nor can we yet discuss meaningfully the
relationship between psi performance and level of central nervous system
development.

It should be noted that the data from studies involving attempts by humans to
influence animals have not been described in this chapter. Such studies may or
may not be construable as evidence for psi animals; most of us would not attribute psi ability to dice just because we seem able to influence them.

PSI IN PLANTS

Are the data any better for plants? Backster (1968) hypothesized that all
living cells are capable of "primary perception," a yet-undefined form of direct
biological communication. To test this hypothesis, he monitored the electrical
resistance on the surface of one leaf on each of three philodendrons to see if
they would respond at the moment of death of distant brine shrimp. The
shrimp were housed in a dump dish which would dump the shrimp into boiling
water during one of six possible dumping times. An RNG determined which of
the six times the animals were to be killed. The plants were monitored throughout all six time periods. The procedure was totally automated, and the experimenter left the premises during the actual running of the experiment. The
plant's responses were recorded on a strip chart recorder, which also recorded
the beginning of each of the six periods, each of which lasted for 35 seconds.
The charts were later analyzed by three blind judges according to standard psychogalvanic reflex measuring techniques. Tracings which showed excessive activity, no activity at all, or evidence of artifact, were eliminated by a blind judge.
Of those remaining (13 out of 21), there was a significantly greater amount of
activity on the dump trials than on the nondump trials. During seven control

runs done later, the mechanical dump was made but contained no brine shrimp; there was no differential response on dump vs. nondump trials.

There are no independent replications of this experiment available in the literature, and three investigation teams have failed to replicate. Johnson (1972) was unable to obtain any evidence of plant responsiveness to brine shrimp death when the plants were placed inside a controlled environment. He hypothesizes that minor temperature and humidity fluctuations associated with the dumping of the the shrimp itself were responsible for Backster's results. Unfortunately this critisism is hard to assess since Backster gives no details about changes in the ambient temperature in the room where the plants were housed; nor does he describe his control runs in sufficient detail to let us know how comparable they were to the experimental conditions. Finally, he does not evaluate the control runs with respect to the experimental runs mathematically.

Kmetz (1977) attempted to repeat the Backster procedure in all details except for the dumping method. Kmetz used six dumping vials containing shrimp and six containing plain water. The vials were dumped into the water once every 5 minutes, in alternating order. Kmetz claims no results. This may be because his controls were adequate and there is no effect to be found, or because he used too long an intertrial interval, or because by failing to arrange experimental and control trials randomly he inadvertently ran into a compensating natural periodicity of the plant's behavior. Kmetz also failed to find evidence that one cell culture's activity was modified by feeding a distant cell culture, a finding Backster had earlier claimed but not described in detail.

Perhaps the most intensive attempt to repeat Backster's work was that of Horowitz, Lewis, and Gasteiger (1975). Data were presented from five experimental sessions, each involving recordings from four philodendrons during a 15-minute period containing three brine shrimp killings and two control dumpings, randomly arranged. The data were scored from a polygraph recording by comparing the maximum peak-to-peak voltage deflections just after brine shrimp and water dumps, and comparing these with the voltage deflection during the immediately preceding control periods. No significant results were obtained. The report does not state whether or not the results were scored by blind judges.

The results of this report are additionally uncertain because the authors claim eight sessions were done, of which three have been dismissed due to unspecified equipment failure; yet a table of the results presents figures drawn from sessions 6, 7, 8, 10, and 12. Apparently the results given are from less than half the data.

The basic failure of these studies nevertheless casts doubt upon Backster's findings, especially since all three employed better controls than he did. Unfortunately, none of them was a replication in the usual sense. There were differences in general environment, arrangement of stimulus vs. control periods, methods of electrophysiological recording, data reduction, and statistical analysis.

As with the animal research, an additional problem is that we may be dealing with an experimenter effect, psi-mediated or otherwise. Although the experimenters made every effort to avoid physical involvement with the experiment while it was running, we still cannot rule out the possibility that, assuming the results of these studies are valid, the plants in Backster's study were activated by his own intent or that the natural activities of plants in the other three studies were suppressed by the intent of the experimenters involved.

BIOLOGICAL ASPECTS OF PSI INFORMATION PROCESSING IN HUMANS

Psi apparently becomes manifest only rarely. Either the message rarely arrives at the receiver, or the receiver generally has trouble decoding it, or both. If receiver decoding is in part involved, then we are dealing with biological processing in the organism. At present two research strategies have been used to gather more information on this point: examining the psychophysiological correlates of psi performance, and using psychophysiological responses themselves as measures of psi.

Psychophysiological Correlates of Psi Performance

Several researchers have done correlational studies in which they have measured some aspect of psi performance, e.g., card-guessing or free verbal response ability, while monitoring various physiological parameters.

Most frequently examined has been the occipitally recorded EEG, especially with regard to choice studies using a clairvoyance paradigm. The Research Committee of the American Society for Psychical Research (1959), Morris and Cohen (1969), and Wallwork (1952) found no relationship between alpha abundance and proportion of correct choices on standard ESP cards, nor did they find any overall evidence for the presence of psi in their tests, using unselected subjects. Honorton and Carbone (1971) and Stanford and Lovin (1970) found a significant negative relationship between alpha abundance and proportion of correct choices on standard ESP cards, using unselected subjects. Cadoret (1964), Honorton (1969), Honorton, Davidson, and Bindler (1971), and Morris, Roll, Klein, and Wheeler (1972) all found significant positive relationships between alpha abundance and proportion of correct choices on standard ESP cards. The first two studies and the fourth used subjects preselected for card-guessing ability; the third used subjects preselected for alpha abundance.

Morris et al. (1972) also found a positive relationship between alpha abundance and proportion of correct guesses on a task which involved choosing the sex of concealed yearbook photos. This study employed only one subject. Lalsingh Harribance, who had previously shown very strong positive psi on the tasks at hand. During the EEG study, his overall scoring rates were extremely strong. On very high-scoring runs he showed alpha abundance before and during the actual time of guessing itself. On the chance runs he showed alpha abundance just before making his choices, but during the choosing period itself his alpha abundance dropped. This study at present is the only EEG study involving very strong psi performance by the subject. Since only one subject was used, the results may not be generalizable.

Some results are more complex. Lewis and Schmeidler (1971) found a significant positive relationship between proportion of correct choices and alpha abundance when their subjects were not aware that they were participating in an ESP test, and a significant negative relationship on those runs in which the subjects were aware that they were participating in an ESP test. Stanford (1971) and Stanford and Stanford (1969) found no significant relationship between alpha abundance and overall ESP score but did find that high ESP scores were associated with an increase in the frequency of the alpha rhythm from just before ESP symbol guessing to the guessing period itself. Other studies have not reported alpha frequency shift data. Stanford interpreted such an increase in frequency as representing a possible "coping" response in which the subject is mobilizing himself for what he construes to be a difficult task, yet at the same time he maintains a general state of relaxed awareness. Stanford's procedures in these studies were described to the subjects as being precognition procedures rather than clairvoyance, even though in fact the random numbers that would determine the targets had themselves already been selected. Most people intrinsically regard precognition as a more difficult task than clairvoyance.

Only three EEG studies involving free-response procedures have been published. Stanford and Stevenson (1973), testing Stanford, found his alpha abundance not related to his ability to describe a concealed line drawing. However, they did find that alpha frequency during a preliminary mind-clearing period was negatively related to ESP success and also found that an increase in alpha frequency from the mind-clearing period to the following period of image formation about the target drawing was associated with psi success. The two findings are not independent, of course. Rao and Feola (1973) found that a single subject familiar with biofeedback and meditation was more successful at describing concealed magazine pictures when he was asked to produce high alpha than when he was asked to produce low alpha. Stanford and Palmer (1975) found that above-chance scorers on a free verbal response task involving concealed photographs showed significantly more alpha abundance than below-chance scorers, during both a preliminary period of listening to soothing music and during the imagery period.

As a whole, the EEG results are confusing and contradictory. Part of the problem is that the procedures and methods of data analysis varied widely from study to study. The most consistent finding was that alpha abundance tended to be positively associated with high ESP scores, especially for subjects preselected for expertise at the production of one or both. The studies which found no relationship between ESP and EEG also did not find overall positive evidence for ESP. The most difficult to explain are the studies that found a significant negative relationship between alpha abundance and ESP.

Very little work has been done with other psychophysiological measurements. Tenny (1962) failed to find any relationship between galvanic skin response activity (GSR) or vasomotor activity as measured by plethysmograph, and ESP choice success, although he did obtain significantly positive ESP results. Woodruff and Dale (1952) found a positive but not quite significant relationship between GSR activity and ESP card-guessing success, in two consecutive studies. Otani (1955) found significantly more hits on ESP cards during large skin resistance changes as measured by basal skin response (BSR). This result was obtained only under a subject condition of indifference toward the results and with eyes open. Braud and Braud (1974) found that subjects who heard taped relaxation-inducing instructions scored above chance in a free response GESP test, whereas those who heard a tension-inducing tape scored at chance. A related finding was that, over all subjects, positive scoring was significantly associated with less frontalis muscle activity (measured by electromyograph or EMG) during the target impression period, and with a decrease in frontalis activity from beginning to end of the session. The Brauds hypothesized that a physiologically-definable "relaxation state" was very conducive to psi in the receiving organism. In addition to reduced muscle activity, they suggested: lowered frequency and increased amplitude of EEG; lower heart rate, blood pressure, and vasomotor activity; increased basal skin resistance; lower oxygen consumption; and reduced blood lactate level. This overall schema is also compatible with the results of White's (1964a) finding that people purported to show strong free response ESP ability consistently described themselves as entering a period of relaxation and mind-clearing at the onset.

Too little work has been done to evaluate the accuracy or generality of the Brauds' "relaxation syndrome." Certainly the negative correlations between alpha abundance and psi performance in two studies, plus the findings of Stanford that an increased alpha frequency is correlated with psi on certain psi tasks, are at odds with the Brauds' ideas. Woodruff and Dale's and Otani's results with GSR and BSR are also contrary to the implications of this syndrome. However, the Brauds did not state that relaxation was the only condition for strong psi performance. Perhaps there are complex interactive relationships among state-trait subject variables, the nature of the psi task, and the optimum physiological processing of psi information.

Psychophysiological Responses as Measures of Psi Performance

There is evidence that physiological variables are correlated in a variety of ways with psi performance and are therefore in some way involved. Manifestations of psi are often complex, confused, and probably misprocessed within the organism at some level. Perhaps therefore we should look directly at changes in psychophsiological aspects themselves as indicators of the presence of a psi message. By so doing, we may be able to look crudely at the psi information during relatively early stages of its processing within the organism. Although the data will lack the richness of experience, they may be more consistent and may additionally eventually tell us a great deal about the processing elements themselves.

Targ and Puthoff (1974) flashed a strobe in the eyes of a sender and observed the response of the receiver's occipital EEG. One agent-receiver pair was selected for more extensive work, on the basis of preliminary success plus the monochromatic EEG spectrum of the receiver. During strobe periods, the average power and peak power of the receiver's alpha rhythms significantly decreased, indicating partial alpha blockage to remote visual information. At the same time, the subject was unable to guess with any accuracy above chance which periods were strobe periods and which were control.

Tart (1963) found that subjects in a soundproof room showed a faster and more complex EEG pattern plus more active GSR and plethysmograph responses when a distant agent was receiving strong shocks than during control times. At the same time, receivers showed no behavioral evidence of responsiveness to these distant events, in terms of frequency of key presses made during shock vs. control times. Kelly and Lenz (1976) employed a similar procedure with a receiver selected for monochromatic EEG, but without an agent. The receiver relaxed, eyes closed, and simply tried to visualize the target area and whether or not the strobe was on. No attempt was made to guess when the strobe was on or off. Using a variety of preliminary procedures, they obtained suggestive evidence that the EEG responded differentially to stimulus vs. control conditions and that the nature of the response may be dependent upon such parameters as intertrial interval, body position, and so on. Duane and Behrendt (1965) found some suggestion that increasing alpha abundance in one twin led to increased alpha in a remote identical twin, but the overall results were not significant. The Research Committee of the A.S.P.R. (1959) found no significant EEG changes in receivers during times in which agents were being emotionally stimulated.

Lloyd (1973) employed an averaged cortical evoked potential as a measure of responsiveness to the sudden onset of a distant stimulus. An agent was instructed to send a visual image each time a light flashed. During a run, 60 such flashes were entered on the EEG record in such a way that the EEG output before, during, and after the flash onset could be averaged to see if a coherent signal emerged in response to the onset of the remote stimulus. By visual inspection, such a cortical response seemed to be present. Lack of a control condition prevented statistical analysis, however. Millar (1976) repeated this procedure using control periods and found no evidence for psi. An important variable in such studies is the recording site from which the EEG is taken. The best recording sites are well known for various kinds of ordinary sensory stimulation. For psi information, we have no a priori reason to assume one site more important than another. To make evoked potential studies work for psi messages, exploration of a variety of potential sites would seem to be mandatory before the effectiveness of evoked potentials as psi responses can be assessed.

Another EEG measure that could be used as an indicator of psi processing is the contingent negative variation (CNV), a negative shift in cortical potential recorded by surface electrodes from the frontal portion of the brain. Also called the expectancy wave, it is generally regarded as a sign that the organism is imminently expecting some specific form of stimulation to which it must respond. Levin and Kennedy (1975) employed a reaction-time procedure to see whether or not the presence of a CNV could serve as evidence for anticipation of a yet-to-be determined event. Subjects were told to press a key when a green light appeared but not when a red light appeared. Which light appeared was determined by an RNG immediately before the light came on. In a preliminary study, subjects' CNV's showed significantly more evidence of expectancy just before the RNG selected green, the color to which the subject was to respond, than before red. A confirmatory study produced chance results, however. This procedure is very important, nevertheless, because the CNV represents a time-locked, precise event in central nervous system information processing.

Several other studies have employed psychophysiological measures other than the EEG. Tart's GSR and plethysmograph results have already been mentioned. Dean (1965), using a dream telepathy paradigm, found that active sending on the part of an agent significantly influenced the abundance of rapid eye movements during dream periods, even on occasions in which the subject's dream descriptions were unrelated to the target.

Beloff, Cowles, and Bate (1970) found no evidence that subjects' galvanic skin responses (GSR) were affected by mildly emotionally interesting messages sent by a remote agent, nor did Barron and Mordkoff (1968), Dean (1969), or Sanjar (1969). Rice (1966) found strong GSR deflections in receivers when the agents were exposed to startling stimuli, e.g., sudden immersion of feet in cold water, or hearing a blank cartridge fired. Hettinger (1952) claims that a group of preselected sensitives showed increased GSR activity when agents several miles away were stimulated or made to exercise, but does not provide sufficient details.

Figar (1959) measured peripheral vasomotor activity with a plethysmograph and found some indication that a receiver's vasomotor activity increased when a remote agent performed mental arithmetic. Unfortunately, no real attempt was made to analyze the data blind, nor was any precise statistical evaluation carried out. Esser, Etter, and Chamberlain (1967) found some indication that receivers' vasomotor activity increased when agents attended to sentences or names of emotional importance to the receivers, as opposed to control sentences, but the authors did not attempt any statistical analysis. Dean (e.g., Dean, 1962, 1969; Dean and Nash, 1967) found additional evidence that receivers' vasomotor activity increased when agents attended to names of emotional importance either to the agent or receiver. Sanjar (1969) found no relationship between receiver's vasomotor activity as measured by plethysmograph and agent arousal by loud noises or by being put through a psychiatric interview.

These studies are of considerable potential importance and should be pursued in more detail. Of especial interest is the fact that physiological responses were often correlated with the onset of the target event, whereas the cognitively processed verbal report or behavioral output of the subject was not. Perhaps such indices do give us a more direct access to less processed (and therefore less distorted) psi messages.

SUMMARY

There is not much that can be said in summarizing this material, other than that a few scattered promising beginnings have been made in developing the methodology for relating psi functioning to our present knowledge of biological communication. There is some evidence that psi communication is not restricted to humans. Before more specific speculation on the evolution of psi and its ecological significance can be seriously considered, we need much more data on more species. We also need to find functional relationships between anpsi strength and other relevant variables such as level of arousal, need strength, and so on to feel comfortable that we are not just dealing with experimenter psi effects.

Our knowledge of psi information processing in humans is little better off. There is fairly strong evidence, however, that psi expression does interact with detectable physiological events, some of which may serve as more direct indications of psi than our cognitively elaborated responses.

In conclusion, we must greatly expand our data base before we can truly assess the extent to which psi communication interacts with our presently known biological communication channels, either at a cellular or population level or somewhere in between.

REFERENCES

American Society for Psychical Research, Research Committee. Report of the Research Committee for 1958. *Journal of the American Society for Psychical Research*, 1959, 53, 69–71.

Backster, C. Evidence of a primary perception in plant life. *International Journal of Parapsychology*, 1968, 10, 329–348.

Barnothy, M. F. (Ed.). *Biological Effects of Magnetic Fields*. New York: Plenum Press, 1964. Vols. 1 and 2.

Barron, F., and Mordkoff, A. M. An attempt to relate creativity to possible extrasensory empathy as measured by physiological arousal in identical twins. *Journal of the American Society for Psychical Research*, 1968, 62, 73–79.

Bayless, R. *Animal Ghosts*. New York: University Books, 1970.

Bechterev, V. M. "Direct influence" of a person upon the behavior of animals. *Journal of Parapsychology*, 1949, 13, 166–176.

Beloff, J., Cowles, M., and Bate, D. Autonomic reactions to emotive stimuli under sensory and extrasensory conditions of presentation. *Journal of the American Society for Psychical Research*, 1970, 64, 313–319.

Bestall, C. M. An experiment in precognition in the laboratory mouse. *Journal of Parapsychology*, 1962, 26, 269.

Braud, L. W., and Braud, W. G. Further studies of relaxation as a psi-conducive state. *Journal of the American Society for Psychical Research*, 1974, 68, 229–245.

Brenner, D., Williamson, S. J., and Kaufman, L. Visually evoked magnetic fields of the human brain. *Science*, 1975, 190, 480–482.

Broughton, R., and Millar, B. An attempted confirmation of the rodent ESP findings with positive reinforcement. In J. D. Morris, W. G. Roll, and R. L. Morris (Eds.), *Research in Parapsychology 1974*, pp. 73–75. Metuchen, N.J.: Scarecrow Press, 1975.

Bullock, T. H., and Cowles, R. B. Physiology of an infrared receptor: The facial pit of vipers. *Science*, 1952, 115, 541–543.

Cadoret, R. J. An exploratory experiment: Continuous EEG recording during clairvoyant card tests. *Journal of Parapsychology*, 1964, 28, 226.

Callahan, P. S. Insects tuned in to infrared rays. *New Scientist*, 1964, 23, 137–138.

Christopher, M. *Mediums, Mystics and the Occult*. New York: Crowell, 1975.

Cohen, D. Magnetic fields of the human body. *Physics Today*, Aug. 1975, 34–43.

Craig, J. G. The effect of contingency on precognition in the rat. In W. G. Roll, R. L. Morris, and J. D. Morris (Eds.), *Research in Parapsychology 1972*, pp. 154–156. Metuchen, N.J.: Scarecrow Press, 1973.

Craig, J. G., and Treurniet, W. Precognition in rats as a function of shock and death. In W. G. Roll, R. L. Morris, and J. D. Morris (Eds.), *Research in Parapsychology 1973*, pp. 75–78. Metuchen, N.J.: Scarecrow Press, 1974.

Dean, E. D. The plethysmograph as an indicator of ESP. *Journal of the Society for Psychical Research*, 1962, 41, 351–353.

Dean, E. D. *Proceedings of the Parapsychological Association*, 1965, 2, 22–23.

Dean, E. D. Long-distance plethysmograph telepathy with agent under water. *Proceedings of the Parapsychological Association*, 1969, 6, 41–42.

Dean, E. D., and Nash, C. B. Coincident plethysmograph results under controlled conditions. *Journal of the Society for Psychical Research*, 1967, 44, 1–13.

Dijgraaf, S. The functioning and significance of the lateral-line organs. *Biological Review*, 1963, 38, 51–105.

Dröscher, V. *The Magic of the Senses*. New York: Dutton, 1969.

Duane, T., and Behrendt, T. Extrasensory electroencephalographic induction between identical twins. *Science*, 1965, 150, 367.

Duval, P., and Montredon, E. ESP experiments with mice. *Journal of Parapsychology*, 1968, 32, 153–166. (a)

Duval, P., and Montredon, E. Further psi experiments with mice. *Journal of Parapsychology*, 1968, 32, 260. (b)

Esser, A., Etter, T. L., and Chamberlain, W. B. Preliminary report: Physiological concomitants of "communication" between isolated subjects. *International Journal of Parapsychology*, 1967, 9, 53–56.

Erickson, R. Personal communication, 1969.

Eysenck, H. J. Precognition in rats. *Journal of Parapsychology*, 1975, 39, 222–227.

Figar, S. The application of plethysmography to the objective study of so-called extrasensory perception. *Journal of the Society for Psychical Research*, 1959, 38, 162–171.

Gaddis, V., and Gaddis, M. *The Strange World of Animals and Pets.* New York: Cowles, 1970.

Geldard, F. A. The perception of mechanical vibration. IV. Is there a separate "vibratory sense"? *Journal of Genetic Psychology,* 1940, **22**, 291–308.

Goldsmith, T. H. Fine structure of the retinulae in the compound eye of the honeybee. *Journal of Cell Biology,* 1962, **14**, 489–494.

Goldsmith, T. H., and Philpott, D. E. The microstructure of the compound eyes of insects. *Journal of Biophysical and Biochemical Cytology,* 1957, **3**, 429–438.

Gould, J. E., Henerey, M., and MacLeod, M. C. Communication of direction by the honeybee. *Science,* 1970, **169**, 544–554.

Gross, L. Yes, but is it really communication? *Journal of Communication,* 1975, **25**, 191–194.

Hecht, S., Shlaer, S., and Pirenne, M. H. Energy at the threshold of vision. *Science,* 1941, **93**, 585–587.

Hettinger, J. *Telepathy and Spiritualism.* London: Rider, 1952.

Honorton, C. Relationship between EEG alpha activity and ESP card-guessing performance. *Journal of the American Society for Psychical Research,* 1969, **63**, 365–374.

Honorton, C., and Carbone, M. A preliminary study of feedback-augmented EEG alpha activity and ESP card-guessing performance. *Journal of the American Society for Psychical Research,* 1971, **65**, 66–74.

Honorton, C., Davidson, R., and Bindler, P. Feedback-augmented EEG alpha, shifts in subjective state, and ESP card-guessing performance. *Journal of the American Society for Psychical Research,* 1971, **65**, 308–323.

Honorton, C., Ramsey, M., and Cabibbo, C. Experimenter effects in extrasensory perception. *Journal of the American Society for Psychical Research,* 1975, **69**, 135–149.

Horowitz, K. A., Lewis, D. C., and Gasteiger, E. L. Plant "primary perception": Electrophysiological unresponsiveness to brine shrimp killing. *Science,* 1975, **189**, 478–480.

Johnson, R. V. Letter to the editor. *Journal of Parapsychology,* 1972, **36**, 71–72.

Jung, C. G., and Pauli, W. *The Interpretation of Nature and the Psyche.* New York: Pantheon, 1955.

Kelly, E. F., and Lenz, J. EEG changes correlated with a remote stroboscopic stimulus: A preliminary study. In J. D. Morris, W. G. Roll, and R. L. Morris (Eds.), *Research in Parapsychology 1975,* pp. 58–63. Metuchen, N.J.: Scarecrow Press, 1976.

Kilian, E. Wie verhalten sich Tiere bei Erdbeben? *Naturwissenschaftliche Rundschau,* 1964, **17**, 135–139.

Kmetz, J. A study of primary perception in plant and animal life. *Journal of the American Society for Psychical Research,* 1977, **71**, 157–169.

Koestler, A. *The Roots of Coincidence.* New York: Random House, 1972.

Krüger, F., and Vogelberg, L. Versuche uber die Richtungsorientierung bei wissen Mausen und Ratten. *Zeitschrift für Tierpsychologie,* 1951, **8**, 293–322.

Lacher, V. Elektrophysiologische Untersuchungen an enizelnen Rezeptoren für Geruch, Kohlendioxyd, Luftfeuchtigkeit und Temperatur auf den Antennen der Arbeitsbiene und der Drohne. *Zeitschrift für Vergleichende Physiologie,* 1964, **48**, 587–623.

Levin, J. Unpublished manuscript, 1975.

Levin, J., and Kennedy, J. The relationship of slow cortical potentials to psi information in man. *Journal of Parapsychology,* 1975, **39**, 25–26.

Lewis, L., and Schmeidler, G. R. Alpha relations with non-intentional and purposeful ESP after feedback. *Journal of the American Society for Psychical Research,* 1971, **65**, 455–467.

Lissman, H. W. On the function and evolution of electric organs in fish. *Journal of Experimental Biology*, 1958, **35**, 156–191.

Lissman, H. W. Electric location by fishes. *Scientific American*, 1963, **208**, 50–59.

Lloyd, D. H. Objective events in the brain correlating with psychic phenomena. *New Horizons*, 1973, **1**, 69–75.

MacKay, D. Formal analysis of communicative processes. In R. A. Hinde (Ed.), *Non-verbal Communication*, pp. 3–25. Cambridge: Cambridge University Press, 1972.

Mackenzie, W. Rolf of Mannheim: A great psychological problem. (With notes by J. H. Hyslop.) *Proceedings of the American Society for Psychical Research*, 1919, **13**, 205–284.

Matthews, G. V. T. *Bird Navigation*. (2nd ed.) Cambridge: Cambridge University Press, 1968.

McNulty, P. J., Pease, V. P., and Bond, V. P. Visual sensations induced by Cerenkov radiation. *Science*, 1975, **189**, 453–454.

Millar, B. An attempted validation of the "Lloyd effect." In J. D. Morris, W. G. Roll, and R. L. Morris (Eds.), *Research in Parapsychology 1975*, pp. 25–27. Metuchen, N.J.: Scarecrow Press, 1976.

Millott, N. Photoreception in eyeless animals. *Endeavour*, 1957, **16**, 19–28.

Morris, R. L. Some new techniques in animal psi research. *Journal of Parapsychology*, 1967, **31**, 316–317.

Morris, R. L. Unpublished manuscript, 1972.

Morris, R. L., and Cohen, D. A preliminary experiment on the relationship among ESP, alpha rhythm and calling patterns. *Proceedings of the Parapsychological Association*, 1969, **6**, 22–23.

Morris, R. L., Roll, W. G., Klein, J., and Wheeler, G. EEG patterns and ESP results in forced-choice experiments with Lalsingh Harribance. *Journal of the American Society for Psychical Research*, 1972, **66**, 253–268.

Neuhaus, W. Untersuchungen uber die Richtungsorientierung bei Mausen. *Zeitschrift für Tierpsychologie*, 1948, **6**, 236–261.

Neuhaus, W. Versuche uber die Richtungsorientierung mit normalen und blinden Mausen. *Zeitschrift für Tierpsychologie*, 1950, **7**, 380–402.

Osis, K., and Foster, E. B. A test of ESP in cats. *Journal of Parapsychology*, 1953, **17**, 168–186.

Ostrander, S., and Schroeder, L. *Psychic Discoveries Behind the Iron Curtain*. Englewood Cliffs, N.J.: Prentice-Hall, 1970.

Otani, S. Relations of mental set and change of skin resistance to ESP score. *Journal of Parapsychology*, 1955, **19**, 164–170.

Parker, A. ESP in gerbils using positive reinforcement. *Journal of Parapsychology*, 1974, **38**, 301–311.

Pfungst, O. *Clever Hans*. (Ed. by R. Rosenthal.) New York: Holt, Rinehart and Winston, 1965. (1st American ed., trans. by C. L. Rahn. New York: Henry Holt, 1911.)

Pratt, J. G. The homing problem in pigeons. *Journal of Parapsychology*, 1953, **17**, 34–60.

Pratt, J. G. Testing for an ESP factor in pigeon homing: Requirements, attempts, and difficulties. In G. E. W. Wolstenholme and E. Millar (Eds.), *Extrasensory Perception: A CIBA Symposium*, pp. 165–186. Boston: Little, Brown, 1956.

Pratt, J. G. *Parapsychology: An Insider's View of ESP*. New York: Dutton, 1966.

Pratt, J. G. Personal communication, 1969.

Presman, A. S. *Electromagnetic Fields and Life*. (Trans. from Russian by F. L. Sinclair, ed. by F. A. Brown.) New York: Plenum Press, 1970.

Rao, K. R., and Feola, J. Alpha rhythm and ESP in a free response situation. In W. G. Roll, R. L. Morris, and J. D. Morris (Eds.), *Research in Parapsychology 1972*, pp. 141–144. Metuchen, N.J.: Scarecrow Press, 1973.

Reich, H. Cited by V. Dröscher, *The Magic of the Senses*, p. 268. New York: Dutton, 1969.

Rhine, J. B. The present outlook on the question of psi in animals. *Journal of Parapsychology*, 1951, 15, 230–251.

Rhine, J. B. The problem of psi-missing. *Journal of Parapsychology*, 1952, 16, 90–129.

Rhine, J. B. Location of hidden objects by a man-dog team. *Journal of Parapsychology*, 1971, 35, 18–33.

Rhine, J. B. Comments: A new case of experimenter unreliability. *Journal of Parapsychology*, 1974, 38, 215–225.

Rhine, J. B. Comments: Publication policy regarding nonsignificant results. *Journal of Parapsychology*, 1975, 39, 135–142.

Rhine, J. B., and Feather, S. R. The study of cases of "psi-trailing" in animals. *Journal of Parapsychology*, 1962, 26, 1–22.

Rhine, J. B., and Rhine, L. E. An investigation of a "mind-reading" horse. *Journal of Abnormal and Social Psychology*, 1929, 23, 449–466. (a)

Rhine, J. B., and Rhine, L. E. Second report on Lady, the "mind-reading" horse. *Journal of Abnormal and Social Psychology*, 1929, 24, 287–292. (b)

Rice, G. Emotional closeness, communication of affect, and ESP. *Proceedings of the Parapsychological Association*, 1966, 3, 25.

Sanjar, M. A study of coincident autonomic activity in closely related persons. *Journal of the American Society for Psychical Research*, 1969, 63, 88–94.

Sauer, F., and Sauer, E. Zugvögel als Navigatoren. *Naturwissenschaftliche Rundschau*, 1960, 13, 88–95.

Schmidt, H. Clairvoyance tests with a machine. *Journal of Parapsychology*, 1969, 33, 300–306.

Schmidt, H. A PK test with electronic equipment. *Journal of Parapsychology*, 1970, 34, 175–181. (a)

Schmidt, H. PK experiments with animals as subjects. *Journal of Parapsychology*, 1970, 34, 255–261. (b)

Schmidt, H. Personal communication, 1970. (c)

Schmidt, H. Animal PK tests with and without time displacement. Unpublished manuscript, 1974. (a)

Schmidt, H. Personal communication, 1974. (b)

Schouten, S. Psi in mice: Positive reinforcement. *Journal of Parapsychology*, 1972, 36, 261–282.

Schouten, S. Psi in mice: Role of target, spatial position of target and response preferences. Unpublished manuscript, 1973.

Shannon, C. E. Mathematical theory of communication. *Bell System Technical Journal*, 1948, 30, 50–64.

Stanford, R. G. EEG alpha activity and ESP performance: A replicative study. *Journal of the American Society for Psychical Research*, 1971, 65, 144–154.

Stanford, R. G., and Lovin, C. EEG alpha activity and ESP performance. *Journal of the American Society for Psychical Research*, 1970, 64, 375–384.

Stanford, R. G., and Palmer, J. Free-response ESP performance and occipital alpha rhythms. *Journal of the American Society for Psychical Research*, 1975, 69, 235–244.

Stanford, R. G., and Stanford, B. E. Shifts in EEG alpha rhythm as related to calling patterns and ESP run-score variance. *Journal of Parapsychology*, 1969, 33, 39–47.

Stanford, R. G., and Stevenson, I. EEG correlates of free-response GESP in an individual subject. *Journal of the American Society for Psychical Research*, 1973, 66, 357–368.

Stent, G. Cellular communications. In *Scientific American* (Ed.), *Communication*, pp. 17–28. San Francisco: W. H. Freeman, 1972.

Talkington, L. Magnetic-force theory on migration supported. *Medical Tribune*, 1965. Cited by V. Dröscher, *The Magic of the Senses*, p. 268. New York: Dutton, 1969.

Targ, R., and Puthoff, H. Information transmission under conditions of sensory shielding. *Nature*, 1974, **252**, 602–607.

Tart, C. T. Possible physiological correlates of psi cognition. *International Journal of Parapsychology*, 1963, **5**, 375–386.

Tenny, K. Physiological responses during an ESP test. *Journal of Parapsychology*, 1962, **24**, 272.

Terry, J. C. Continuation of the rodent precognition experiments. In J. D. Morris, W. G. Roll, and R. L. Morris (Eds.), *Research in Parapsychology 1975*, pp. 11–14. Metuchen, N.J.: Scarecrow Press, 1976.

Terry, J. C., and Harris, S. A. Precognition in water-deprived rats. In J. D. Morris, W. G. Roll, and R. L. Morris (Eds.), *Research in Parapsychology 1974*, p. 81. Metuchen, N.J.: Scarecrow Press, 1975.

Thorpe, W. H. *Learning and Instinct in Animals*. Cambridge: Harvard University Press, 1963.

Timm, C. Horempfindungen im Ultraschallgebiet. *Experientia,* 1950, **6**, 357–358.

Treurniet, W. C., and Craig, J. G. Precognition as a function of environmental enrichment and time of the lunar month. In J. D. Morris, W. G. Roll, and R. L. Morris (Eds.), *Research in Parapsychology 1974*, pp. 100–102. Metuchen, N.J.: Scarecrow Press, 1975.

Vasiliev, L. L. *Experiments in Mental Suggestion*. Church Crookham, Hampshire, England: Institute for the Study of Mental Images, 1963.

Von Frisch, K. Honey bees: Do they use the information as to direction and distance provided by their dances? *Science*, 1967, **158**, 1072–1075.

Wallwork, S. C. ESP experiments with simultaneous electroencephalographic recordings. *Journal of the Society for Psychical Research*, 1952, **36**, 697–701.

Watkins, G. K. Possible PK in the lizard *Anolis sagrei*. *Proceedings of the Parapsychological Association*, 1971, **8**, 23–25.

Watkins, G. K. Personal communication, 1972.

Wenner, A. M., and Johnson, D. L. Honey bees: Do they use the direction and distance information provided by their dancers? *Science*, 1967, **158**, 1076–1077.

White, R. A. A comparison of old and new methods of response to targets in ESP experiments. *Journal of the American Society for Psychical Research*, 1964, **58**, 21–56. (a)

White, R. A. The investigation of behavior suggestive of ESP in dogs. *Journal of the American Society for Psychical Research*, 1964, **58**, 250–279. (b)

Whitear, M. Presumed sensory cells in fish epidermis. *Nature*, 1965, **208**, 703–704.

Wood, G. H., and Cadoret, R. J. Tests of clairvoyance in a man-dog relationship. *Journal of Parapsychology*, 1958, **22**, 29–39.

Woodruff, J. L., and Dale, L. A. ESP function and psychogalvanic response. *Journal of the American Society for Psychical Research*, 1952, **46**, 62–65.

Worth, S., and Gross, L. Symbolic strategies. *Journal of Communication*, 1974, **24**, 27–39.

3

Psi Phenomena and Brain Research

Jan Ehrenwald

INTRODUCTION

Psi phenomena are inextricably tied together with human personality and with living beings in general. They are part of life itself. Psi does not occur "out there" like thunder and lightning, Brownian movement, or atomic radiation. Psi events impinge on an organism or emanate from it. They share the characteristic sensory-motor dichotomy and decline or position effects with ordinary sensory-motor skills. Psychoanalysts have found that they obey the identical psychodynamic laws as those governing unconscious mental processes, including those of subliminal perceptions. Thus the assumption that psi phenomena are closely correlated with brain functions is close at hand.

Yet such a proposition is by no means conclusive, and the hypothesis of a mandatory cerebral localization of psi has to be reviewed in a broader, and indeed all-encompassing, context of natural events.

Nearly a century ago, F. W. H. Myers was wondering whether telepathy stretched back to the amoeba or was reaching out to the angels. On raising this question, he may well have had the issue of animal psi in mind. But some of the recent findings of lingering effects in PK experiments or in poltergeist disturbances suggest that inanimate matter may not necessarily present an impenetrable barrier to psi events. So do the still controversial claims of alleged psychometry in which a gifted psychic or "paragnost" is supposed to be capable of responding to non-physical traces left by its owner on an inanimate object. This borderline aspect of psi is beyond the scope of the present inquiry. It will be confined to reviewing (a) relevant findings of animal psi in relation to brain function; (b) physiological variables; and (c) pertinent clinical neuropsychiatric observations in humans.

ANIMAL PSI

The need for this approach derives from the fact that such surgical interventions as excision or ablation techniques are precluded in human subjects. The available data on animal psi have been reviewed by Randall (1974) and Morris (1970) (see also Morris' chapter in this *Handbook*). The available observations range from unicellular organisms to moth larvae, wood-lice, cockroaches, goldfish, lizards and snakes, to rodents and higher mammals, including cats and dogs. In all these cases, it is largely the animals' behavioral or physiological responses that lend themselves to observations, while animals as primary sources of ESP or PK have not come as yet into the purview of methodical inquiry.

Smith's (1968) test-tube experiments with enzymes may be viewed as stepping stones toward psi in unicellular organisms. PK effects in paramecia described by Richmond (1952) belong in this category. So do Randall's (1971) PK experiments with wood-lice. Of a somewhat higher order are the Watkins' (1971) experiments with resuscitation of anesthetized mice and Grad's (1965) experiments with wound repair in mice handled by a healer. The prime targets in these cases are animal tissues, but they may have been under the control of the animal's vegetative nervous system at the same time.

More relevant in the present context are the experiments with mice, rats, and other rodents in which the animals were trained to select a lever in order to obtain food. In other series, they were exposed to randomly delivered electrical stimulation, but were able to avoid shocks when a precognized threat prompted them to jump over a barrier in their cage (Duval and Montredon, 1968). Craig (1975) and Craig and Treurniet (1974) studied the motor activity of rats in an open field situation in response to their presumed ability to precognize the threat of imminent death. Their behavior, as compared with a control group, suggested the operation of a psi factor in excess of chance expectation.

In early experiments with cats, Osis (1952) and Osis and Foster (1953) showed that a human agent could "will" cats to turn right or left in a maze and that hunger tended to mobilize their psi abilities. Schouten (1972) carried out psi experiments with mice in which psi-determined behavior was reinforced by rewards instead of electric shocks. The mice were trained to serve as "agents" or "percipients" respectively. Some scored high under telepathic, some under clairvoyant conditions.

An experimental procedure involving psi responses of a higher order was concerned with a cat who responded with measurably calm behavior when it was "visited" by its owner in an out-of-body state (Morris, 1974). Morris and his associates also noted that hamsters and gerbils were unresponsive to similar use of OB experiments.

The extensive literature of psi trailing in cats and dogs, though likewise suggestive of psi, is still amenable to rival sensory, in lieu of *extra*sensory, interpretations. So is the homing behavior of salmon, pigeons, cats, and dogs. More persuasive are the older observations on dogs, reported by Bechterev (1949) and the more recent findings by White (1964). Wood and Cadoret (1958) tested clairvoyance in a man-dog relationship by adapting the ESP card-calling technique to a dog called Chris. They found evidence of ESP in the presence of the owner.

These few representative samples of animal psi should suffice in the present context. They indicate that despite the many gaps in the available evidence, the occurrence of psi from the lowliest unicellular organisms to higher vertebrates, and especially rodents, cats, and dogs, can be taken for granted. It also appears that the observable psi responses tend to increase in complexity as we move from organisms with primitive neural structures to organisms with more highly differentiated central nervous systems. It should be noted at this point, however, that psi phenomena must not be lumped together in one single undifferentiated set of organismic functions—afferent or efferent, GESP, PK, and precognitive—as the case may be. Generically they may amount to the same thing, ranging over the whole spectrum of organic nature from plants to man. But we must realize that PK responses of paramecia differ from those of a cockroach, a hamster, or a dog, much in the same way as an apple and an appleseed differ from a full-grown specimen of an apple tree. By and large, evidence of psi-determined behavior in lower animals indicates that it may occur under the auspices of what McLean described as the archaic reptilian brain. In turn, the growing incidence of psi phenomena associated with the evolutionary increase of cortical structures would point to the part played by so-called uncommitted brain regions (Penfield, 1975) in the origin of psi functions of a higher order. Yet it is needless to say that the data of animal psi do not permit a fixed cerebral localization in any specialized brain region. Further insight into the problem has to be sought by turning our attention to additional neurophysiological and clinical observations in humans.

PHYSIOLOGICAL VARIABLES

It has always been suspected that a vast number of psi incidents, spontaneous and experimental, are taking place below the threshhold of conscious awareness. They are subliminal, preconscious, or unconscious and can only be gleaned from monitoring such variables as blood pressure, pulse rate, electromyogram, EEG, and other indices.

A typical example is Dean's (1962) plethysmographic experiments in which an emotionally charged stimulus word sent by an agent elicited measurable changes in the blood supply in the finger of a percipient. In a comparable series, Tart's

(1963) telepathic percipients produced subliminal physiological changes in response to mild electrical stimuli delivered to an agent.

Johnson (1974) of the University of Utrecht has studied subliminality in a modification of Pötzl's tachistoscopic dream experiments. He flashed "threatening" pictures and measured the degree to which the subject's defensiveness against the microtrauma affected his performance in ESP tasks. The results bore out the hypothesis that a "good" defensive posture was conducive to psi-missing.

Observations of this order appear to confirm that certain elementary forms of ESP tend to bypass conscious awareness. They are not tied to processing in higher cortical centers and point to subcortical, midbrain, or limbic regions as their substrate. Experimental psychologists described sensory perceptions of this order as subceptions. Eysenck (1961), Burt (1968), Beloff (1974), and others have specifically pointed to their relationship to perceptual defenses, while Dixon (1971) and Beloff emphasized the close relationship of both psi phenomena and subliminal perception to the reticular formation and the brainstem. Eysenck (1967) has noted, furthermore, that a high state of arousal of the cortex mediated by the ascending reticular formation is antagonistic to psi.

The EEG is particularly suited to telepathic experiments of this kind. Duane and Behrendt (1965) succeeded in inducing electroencephalographic changes in identical twins, bypassing conscious perception. Their observations have not been replicated by others. Earlier attempts by Ehrenwald, Kahn, and Ullman along the same lines were abandoned owing to inadequacies of the available instrumentation. In their article in *Nature*, Targ and Puthoff (1974) found that systematic alteration of ongoing electric activity can be elicited by a remote photic stimulus.

Needless to say that the exact determination of the sources of the EEG activity of the brain is still problematical. By and large, the occipital lobes have been identified as the sources of origin of alpha rhythm in certain altered states of consciousness. EEG data concerning lateralization of visually evoked potentials have been described by neurophysiologists, but no conclusive parapsychological findings have as yet been reported.

A striking series of EEG experiments has been reported by Lloyd (1973). His work has been sponsored by the New Horizons Research Foundation in Toronto. The Lloyd series is aimed at duplicating, by telepathic induction, the "average evoked EEG response" elicited by an actual auditory stimulus. It is claimed that the results indicate a direct brain response to a telepathic message, although Lloyd leaves open the question whether PK may have directly affected the monitoring equipment. We are told that T. H. Lloyd is a pseudonym, but the Editor of *New Horizons* testifies to the good faith and scientific qualifications of the author. Attempts at replicating the "Lloyd effect" elsewhere were unsuccessful.

The vast literature dealing with the relationship of ESP and alpha activity, and its reinforcement by diverse biofeedback methods, is described in other sections of this *Handbook*.

The Brauds (1975) have focused attention on the right versus the left hemisphere, and their relevance to facilitating psi functions. Their hypothesis that inducing mental states favoring right hemispheric dominance would be psi productive was not borne out. But the expected induction of left hemispheric dominance did lead to significant psi-missing.

Andrew (1975) applied the same procedure in reference to "active" psi, that is, psychokinesis. In this series, the right hemisphere group scored significantly above chance, and the left group showed an extrachance tendency to psi-missing. Results of assessing the activity of the two hemispheres during bilateral EEG recordings are not yet available. Whitten (1974) studied the EEG record of a gifted subject, Matthew Manning, while attempting to perform specified psychokinetic tasks. In this case, a distinct wave pattern, described as the ramp function, made its appearance.

The investigations of Broughton (1976), of the University of Edinburgh, focusing on brain hemisphere specialization, were based on the same rationale. Using an ingenious experimental paradigm to separate the two hemispheres in an ESP test, he found that improved performance could be elicited when the right hemisphere responses were encouraged while at the same time loading an additional conceptual task on the left hemisphere. He concludes that the right hemisphere of the brain is better at a receptive type of ESP.

We shall see that more light on the presumed lateralization of psi phenomena can be shed by clinical observations.

NEUROPSYCHIATRIC OBSERVATIONS

In human subjects we have to rely on the occurrence of organic pathology as a substitute for surgical removal or excision techniques used in animal experiments. The frequently cited instance of the dying serving as telepathic percipients or agents can be taken as the closest approximation to states of clinical "decerebration" or organic "minus function" (Ehrenwald, 1948) in which higher cortical functions are in abeyance. Similar considerations apply to the death defying feats of some out-of-body subjects (Ehrenwald, 1974). Telepathy in sleep, dreams, and the REM state (Ullman and Krippner, with Vaughan, 1973) points in the same direction. So do the countless reports of telepathy in trance conditions, in absent-mindedness, and in diverse altered states of consciousness.

The case of Ilga K., published by von Neureiter (1935), illustrates another facet of the problem. Ilga was a mentally defective girl of 9 with a severe reading disability. The samples of her handwriting, her general demeanor, and her photograph suggest the diagnosis of mental deficiency. Yet von Neureiter reported that the child could "read" any text if and when her mother, seated in another room, was reading the same text silently to herself. Ilga's case has been subject to some controversy. Yet the crucial point is that in this instance it was her mother's powerful motivation to compensate for her offspring's specific short-coming that was responsible for Ilga's telepathic ability. Another point to bear in mind is that her "minus function" consisted of a specific deficit on a higher cognitive level. It was of the nature of an alexia—that is, a cortical deficiency as described by Déjérine, Pötzl and others—and was not due to a peripheral sensory impairment. A similar picture was described by Drake (1938) in a mentally de-fective boy, little Bo, and, more recently, by Recordon, Stratton, and Peters (1968), in England. The latter case is known as that of the Cambridge Boy. Both Little Bo and the Cambridge Boy suffered from congenital spastic paralysis and were telepathically responsive to their mothers only.

The Los Angeles school psychologist Eloise Shields (1976) has investigated the psi abilities of 25 mongoloid, 25 brain-damaged, and 25 undifferentiated mentally defective children, age 5-21. They yielded an astronomical score of $P = .00000057$ against chance under telepathic conditions. Their performance scores under clairvoyant conditions were only slightly above chance.

Another significant experimental contribution is Schmeidler's (1952) series of ESP tests of 18 hospitalized patients suffering from cerebral concussion. The clinical picture in such cases is too ill-defined to permit any neurological diagno-sis beyond the conjecture that it amounts to a combination of a diffuse organic brain syndrome with some degree of psychological overlay. Using a control group of 11 hospitalized fracture patients without cerebral injury, Schmeidler found a significantly higher scoring pattern ($P = .002$) in the concussion group.

In such cases it can be argued that the postulated organic brain damage served as one of the predisposing or conditioning factors for the emergence of psi phenomena. Yet it should also be noted that lumping together forced-choice ESP responses of the card-calling type with ESP responses focusing on major targets of higher complexity, and trying to correlate the two with a supposedly all-encompassing functional deficit, "minus function," or assorted altered states of consciousness, is apt to miss the point. We shall presently see that to bring a semblance of order into the conflicting findings that have accrued on the inter-face between psi phenomena and neuropathology, we will have to think up a new twist to the conventional question of how a given function is supposed to be related to a specific brain region.

The new twist proposed here is to rephrase—or turn around—the usual question about the hypothetical cerebral localization of psi phenomena. Instead of won-dering what neural structures or brain region is responsible for their operation *some* of the time, we have to ask: What is it that *prevents* the organism from being flooded by the influx of both sensory and extrasensory stimuli *all* of the time? By the same token, we have to ask: What is it that puts the brake on the organism's motor or psychomotor organization, that stops it from reacting (or over-reacting) to external stimulation, that stops it from exhausting its store of psychomotor energy in the process—and from spending itself in a paroxysm of undirected and indiscriminate acting out like a Roman candle? Bypassing the question in regard to lower animals with less differentiated central nervous systems, the answer is that it is the neural structures in more highly developed species that are taking over the postulated protective, screening, or filtering functions.

Such a thesis goes back to Bergson's (1914) filter theory based on the principle of eliminating from consciousness external impressions that have no survival advantage or no relevance to the organisms's "attention to life." Bergson proposed that the brain, especially the brain cortex, is playing this role. He pointed out, furthermore, that, for the same reasons, telepathy and clairvoyance are subject to much the same process of screening or selective inattention. Bergson could not foresee that some 60 years later the discovery by Magoun and his associates of the reticular activating system (RAS) in the brainstem would provide some neurophysiological support for such a thesis.

We know today that the ascending and descending reticular tracks are concerned with facilitating or inhibiting the flow of sensory stimuli from both inside and outside the organism to and from higher centers. They are responsible for regulating arousal, vigilance, sleep, wakefulness, and fluctuations in the REM state. It may well be argued that, by the same token, it is the inhibitory function of the reticular formation which constitutes the first line of the organism's defense against the influx of such biologically indifferent or undesirable perceptual stimuli as ESP, or against the haphazard activation and "popping off" of such potentially wasteful motor impulses as PK. The concept of perceptual defenses and subliminal perceptions point in the same direction. According to McLean, Papez, and others, a secondary, limbic-midbrain system is likewise concerned with regulatory functions of this order. Dixon (1971) and Beloff (1974) suggested that the limbic system is particularly instrumental in the processing of subliminal stimuli. Pribram (1973) and Luria (1973) have noted, furthermore, that the frontal and temporal cortex play an important part in the mobilization of the volitional impulses and in the selective filtering of "afference" or input from outside.

It should be noted, however, that these considerations pay attention to the forced-choice micropsychological card-calling type of incidents only. As far as they go, they suggest that the fitful, capricious incidence of correct hits in a test series is due to the random occurrence of minor flaws in the screening or inhibitory function of the reticular formation and higher centers. This results in the intrusion of a few equally capricious bursts or clusters of psi incidents into a subject's scoring pattern. If this is true, psi responses of this order can be described as essentially *flaw*-determined: They are due to flaws in the operation of the subject's perceptual defenses, in the screening function of the Bergsonian filter or of what Freud described as *Reizschutz*, protecting the ego from being flooded by stimuli from the id. They can be contrasted with essentially *need*-determined responses of the spontaneous type involving ESP perceptions of a higher degree of complexity.

It goes without saying, however, that the filter theory cannot account for the

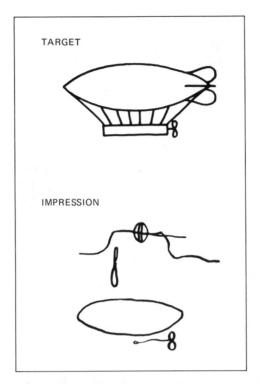

Figure 1. *Top:* An airship, drawn by the agent.
Bottom: Telepathic impression. Note the correct rendering of an oval shape. The propeller motif appears twice. The scribble above the oval is unexplained.

From: *Mind to Mind*, by René Warcollier.

occasional breakthrough of an emotionally-charged, psychologically and biologically relevant class of psi phenomena. The drawing tests by Warcollier (1948) in Paris or by Mr. and Mrs. Upton Sinclair in this country (1962) are convenient illustrations of this point. So are Carington's (1940) experiments on the paranormal cognition of drawings or the Maimonides dream experiments using telepathic targets exposed in the REM state (Ullman and Krippner, with Vaughan, 1973).

Figure 1 illustrates one of Warcollier's tests in which the subject was asked to draw his telepathic impression of an airship sketched by the agent. It shows an oval shape, barely recognizable as the superstructure of a dirigible, and two impressions of the propeller, one placed at the wrong spot, the other correctly under the oval shape. The match between target and telepathic impression is admittedly imperfect, and its poor quality may conceivably be challenged by the skeptic.

The fact is that most of the Warcollier and Sinclair drawings show considerable distortion and disorganization of the material. The percipient tends to pick out

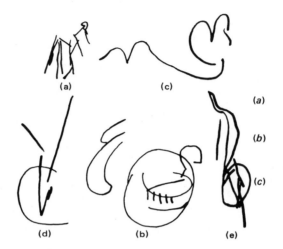

Figure 2. Drawings of the Vienna patient:
(a) A French window
(b) a face, *en face*
(c) the window latch
(d) a ship
(e) a tree drawn upside down, with (a) the root, (b) the trunk, (c) the crown.

From: Ehrenwald, 1930.

parts of the target picture and to miss the whole. He does not grasp its gestalt quality. He has a tendency to displace diverse elements in their relation to the original design. It is true that some samples of the Warcollier, the Sinclair, and the Ullman-Krippner series are of far better quality. Some of Uri Geller's telepathic responses in the recent Targ-Puthoff (1974) series came close to scoring a bull's eye right on the target. But we shall see that such exceptional feats are much less revealing about the nature of the telepathic process than the "near misses" which may be dismissed as unconvincing.

The significance of the "poor" samples becomes readily apparent when we turn our attention to drawings obtained under conditions seemingly worlds apart from experiments with healthy subjects under telepathic conditions. Figure 2 is a sample of drawings made by a 29-year-old patient of mine in the Neuropsychiatric Department of the University of Vienna in 1928 (Ehrenwald, 1930). He was admitted with a lesion in the parieto-occipital area of the left side of his brain due to a self-inflicted penetrating gunshot wound. Though the patient showed no evidence of psychosis, he was severely disoriented in space and time. His speech showed evidence of amnestic aphasia; his writing was agraphic. He was unable to perform the simplest calculations: He was suffering from acalculia. Above all, his drawings showed complete disorganization and distortion of his perceptual world: He presented the picture of optic agnosia as described in the neurological literature. Although his vision was by no means impaired, he was unable to make sense of his visual perceptions.

The similarity of such cases with telepathic drawings produced by normal experimental subjects is unmistakable. The fact is that on showing the two respective series to a lecture audience of graduate students in psychology, they mistook the drawings of the brain-injured patient for just another example of rather unconvincing ESP experiments. It is also interesting to note that agnosia patients, in addition to the impairment of their drawing ability, also tend to confuse the meaning of a given object or picture. They can perceive its parts but do not grasp it as a whole. My Vienna patient described the picture of a vase with flowers as a beer mug. One of Luria's (1973) cases, when shown the line drawings of a pair of spectacles said: "There is a circle . . . another circle . . . a stick . . . a crossbar . . . Why, it must be a bicycle" (p. 116).

Telepathic or clairvoyant percipients frequently have the same difficulty in giving a correct verbal description of the target. If their drawing is of higher quality than the productions of a brain-injured patient, it is due to the fact that they do not have the added handicap of impaired higher motor skills.

ESP, AGNOSIA, AND LATERALIZATION

What, then, do we learn from the striking similarity between productions of a normal percipient and the brain-injured patient? It suggests that the telepathic subject, like the patient suffering from optic agnosia, uses his *right*, rather than the dominant *left*, hemisphere for the central processing and organization of his impressions. The brain-injured patient has to fall back on the groping attempts of the "other side" of his brain to make up for the existing deficit on the left side. In turn, the telepathic percipient's productions carry all the hallmarks of the same difficulty in the organization and comprehension of his target material. That is, his responses likewise point to the part played in their origin by the right hemisphere. It is an interesting footnote to history that Myers (1885), close to a century ago, observed much the same difficulties in the communications of some subjects engaged in automatic writing. He compared their efforts with the clinical picture of aphasia or agraphia and suggested that in such cases the right hemisphere tries to take over. This he took as an indication that the right hemisphere may be specially attuned to receiving telepathic messages. We have seen that more recently the Brauds (1975), Andrew (1975), and Broughton (1975) have arrived at much the same conclusion.

An active, compensatory role of the right hemisphere has indeed been suggested by Sperry (1964), Bogen (1969), Gazzaniga (1967), Ornstein (1972), and others. They describe the left hemisphere as the logician, the specialist in linear, analytic thinking, while the much maligned right hemisphere is in effect the artist, the poet, the Listener with the Third Ear, presiding over the intuitive, nonanalytic mode of consciousness. If this is true, the distortion and disorganization of spatio-temporal relations in both telepathic percipients, and patients suffering from lesions in the left hemisphere, is readily understood. It is due to the absence of the traditional signposts of time (and space) in the repertoire of the right hemisphere. The fact is that the attending spatio-temporal and causal anomalies are characteristic features of the psi syndrome (Ehrenwald, 1972).

WHAT DOES IT ALL ADD UP TO?

What, then, do these amalgamated data about the neural correlates of the forced-choice or flaw-determined and the free-choice or need-determined psi phenomena add up to? They suggest that, by and large, the emergence of psi is based, (a) on bypassing the screening function of the reticular formation and the limbic midbrain system, and (b) on the central processing of incoming stimuli or outgoing messages in the right hemisphere. It goes without saying, however, that in any given case—under crisis conditions, in the psychoanalytic situation, and even in card-calling or drawing tests—we are likely to deal with a blend of both need- and flaw-determined factors. Without clear-cut tracer elements or a combination of a multiplicity of distinctive features, the occurrence of psi is difficult to ascertain. On the other hand, in the absence of emotionally-charged attitudes and motivations, e.g., in the experimenter-subject, or agent-percipient relationship, psi phenomena are unlikely to make their appearance. They need the proper motivation of Schmeidlerian "sheep."

Thus the presumed cerebral localization of psi phenomena is predicated on the concerted action of both cortical and subcortical brain regions. In the case of telepathy, such a cooperation involves brain regions pertaining to both agent and percipient. In other "agentless" modalities of psi, the presumed "interaction" is predicated on a percipient reaching out for, or being attuned to, stimuli derived from such inanimate objects as ESP cards or dice thrown from a cup. Indeed, the reach of the mind may extend to the outermost sectors of what elsewhere (Ehrenwald, 1972) I described as the symbiotic gradient: "To ships and shoes and sealing wax, and cabbages and kings."

Thus, despite the vast array of experimental and clinical observations reviewed here, the ultimate *modus operandi* of extrasensory perception or motor action in the absence of neural conduction is still shrouded in mystery. The intriguing suggestion made by Cyril Burt (1968) and others that the brain may be directly affected by PK, and that telepathy may be due to the direct clairvoyant perception of a brain state, provides only part of the answer. So does Eccles' (1970) observation that the firing of a group of a few brain cells, motor or sensory, or even of one "critically poised neuron" serving as a detector of remote spatio-temporal configurations, can be triggered off by a field of extraneous influences as well as by "willed action" (p. 127). It will be noted that once we are ready to adopt such a hypothesis, the role of Maxwell's Demon or of Koestler's Ghost in the Machine would be played by clairvoyance and psychokinesis "pure and simple." Moncrieff (1951) has indeed gone so far as to consider ordinary sensory perception itself as a clairvoyant process.

It is needless to say, however, that even such imaginative flights of fancy fall far short of solving the enigma of the cerebral localization of psi. We may conjecture that it is the right rather than the left side of the brain where the processing of incoming psi messages or the activation of outgoing PK impulses is taking place. But we are at a loss to tell how, in the last analysis, even "normal" sensory stimuli, originating from the outside world, are turned into conscious awareness. We don't know how a certain wavelength is perceived as *red*, or how an electric stimulation of the occipital cortex causes a hallucinatory experience. Nor do we know how volition or an "ordinary" motor impulse, originating somewhere in the frontal lobes, is converted into action. The last step in an extrasensory impression, or the first step in a volitional act or PK is no less—but neither more— mysterious. All we know is that both processes take place inside the skull. The difference between the two lies merely in the fact that in one case the gap in our understanding seems small and inconspicuous. At best, it is still baffling a few metaphysicians or theologians, while it is far more conspicuous, and indeed looms woefully large, in the other.

The fact is that both physicists and behavioral scientists have failed so far to fill the gaps remaining in our understanding of the cleavage between the mental and the physical—or to account for what Freud once called "the mysterious leap from body to mind." Yet both the physical and mental sciences have nevertheless been eminently successful in coping with the practical tasks encountered in their respective specialties. They have formulated theoretical models, devised testable hypotheses, and developed technologies and strategies of human betterment, of psychotherapy or drug treatment, even though they have not as yet come up with answers to some ultimately irreducible epistemological problems.

I submit that the parapsychologist engaged in his particular field of research should be extended the same privilege, without being pressed for ultimate answers to questions which have so far eluded those working in purportedly more solidly established fields of inquiry.

REFERENCES

Andrew, K. Psychokinetic influences on an electromechanical random number generator during evocation of "left-hemispheric" vs. "right-hemispheric" functioning. In J. D. Morris, W. G. Roll, and R. L. Morris (Eds.), *Research in Parapsychology 1974*, pp. 58–61. Metuchen, N.J.: Scarecrow Press, 1975.

Bechterev, V. M. "Direct influence" of a person upon the behavior of animals. *Journal of Parapsychology*, 1949, 13, 166–176.

Beloff, J. ESP: The search for a physiological index. *Journal of the Society for Psychical Research*, 1974, 47, 403–420.

Bergson, H. Presidential address to the Society for Psychical Research (1913). *Proceedings of the Society for Psychical Research*, 1914, **27**, 157–175.

Bogen, E. The other side of the brain. (Pts. I, II, and III.) *Bulletin of the Los Angeles Neurological Societies*, July, 1969.

Braud, W. G., and Braud, L. W. The psi-conducive syndrome: Free response GESP performance following evocation of "left-hemispheric" vs. "right-hemispheric" functioning. In J. D. Morris, W. G. Roll, and R. L. Morris (Eds.), *Research in Parapsychology 1974*, pp. 17–20. Metuchen, N.J.: Scarecrow Press, 1975.

Broughton, R. S. Brain hemisphere specialization and its possible effects on ESP performance. In J. D. Morris, W. G. Roll, and R. L. Morris (Eds.), *Research in Parapsychology 1975*, pp. 98–102. Metuchen, N.J.: Scarecrow Press, 1976.

Burt, C. *Psychology and Psychical Research*. (The Seventeenth Frederic W. H. Myers Memorial Lecture.) London: Society for Psychical Research, 1968.

Carington, W. W. Experiments on the paranormal cognition of drawings. *Journal of Parapsychology*, 1940, **4**, 1–134.

Craig, J. G. The effect of the experimenter on precognition in the rat. In J. D. Morris, W. G. Roll, and R. L. Morris (Eds.), *Research in Parapsychology 1974*, pp. 97–102. Metuchen, N.J.: Scarecrow Press, 1975.

Craig, J. G., and Treurniet, W. C. Precognition in rats as a function of shock and death. In W. G. Roll, R. L. Morris, and J. D. Morris (Eds.), *Research in Parapsychology 1973*, pp. 75–78. Metuchen, N.J.: Scarecrow Press, 1974.

Dean, D. The plethysmograph as an indicator of ESP. *Journal of the Society for Psychical Research*, 1962, **41**, 351–353.

Dixon, N. F. *Subliminal Perception: The Nature of a Controversy*. New York: McGraw-Hill, 1971.

Drake, R. M. An unusual case of extrasensory perception. *Journal of Parapsychology*, 1938, **2**, 184–198.

Duane, T., and Behrendt, R. Extrasensory electroencephalographic induction between identical twins. *Science*, 1965, **150**, 367.

Duval, P., and Montredon, E. ESP experiments with mice. *Journal of Parapsychology*, 1968, **32**, 153–166.

Eccles, J. C. *Facing Reality*. New York: Springer Verlag, 1970.

Ehrenwald, J. Disturbance of temporal and spatial orientation of drawing and calculation in a brain-injured patient. (Title trans.) *Zeitschrift für die Gesamte Neurologie und Psychiatrie*, 1930, **132**, 518–569.

Ehrenwald, J. *Telepathy and Medical Psychology*. New York: Norton, 1948.

Ehrenwald, J. A neurophysiological model of psi phenomena. *Journal of Nervous and Mental Disease*, 1972, **154**, 406–418.

Ehrenwald, J. Out-of-the-body experiences and the denial of death. *Journal of Nervous and Mental Disease*, 1974, **159**, 227–233.

Eysenck, H. J. *Handbook of Abnormal Psychology*. New York: Basic Books, 1961.

Eysenck, H. J. Personality and extrasensory perception. *Journal of the Society for Psychical Research*, 1967, **44**, 55–71.

Gazzaniga, M. S. The split brain in man. *Scientific American*, 1967, **508**, 24–29.

Grad, B. Some biological effects of the "laying on of hands": A review of experiments with animals and plants. *Journal of the American Society for Psychical Research*, 1965, **59**, 95–129.

Johnson, M. ESP and subliminality. In W. G. Roll, R. L. Morris, and J. D. Morris (Eds.), *Research in Parapsychology 1973*, pp. 22–24. Metuchen, N.J.: Scarecrow Press, 1974.

Lloyd, D. H. Objective events in the brain correlating with psychic phenomena. *New Horizons*, 1973, **1**, 69–75.

Luria, A. R. *The Working Brain*. New York: Basic Books, 1973.

Moncrieff, M. M. *The Clairvoyant Theory of Perception.* London: Faber and Faber, 1951.

Morris, R. L. Psi and animal behavior: A survey. *Journal of the American Society for Psychical Research,* 1970, **64**, 242-260.

Morris, R. L. The use of detectors for out-of-body experiences. In W. G. Roll, R. L. Morris, and J. D. Morris (Eds.), *Research in Parapsychology 1973,* pp. 114-116. Metuchen, N.J.: Scarecrow Press, 1974.

Myers, F. W. H. Automatic writing. *Proceedings of the Society for Psychical Research,* 1885, **3**, 1-63.

Neureiter, F. von. *Wissen um fremdes Wissen auf unbekanntem Wege erworben.* Gotha: Klotz, 1935.

Ornstein, R. E. *The Psychology of Consciousness.* New York: Viking Press, 1972.

Osis, K. A test of the occurrence of a psi effect between man and the cat. *Journal of Parapsychology,* 1952, **16**, 233-256.

Osis, K., and Foster, E. B. A test of ESP in cats. *Journal of Parapsychology,* 1953, **17**, 168-186.

Penfield, W. *The Mystery of the Mind.* Princeton: Princeton University Press, 1975.

Pribram, K. *Psychology of the Frontal Lobes.* New York: Academic Press, 1973.

Randall, J. L. Experiments to detect a psi effect with small animals. *Journal of the Society for Psychical Research,* 1971, **46**, 31-39.

Randall, J. L. Biological aspects of psi. In J. Beloff (Ed.), *New Directions in Parapsychology,* pp. 77-94. London: Elek Science, 1974.

Recordon, E. G., Stratton, F. J. M., and Peters, R. A. Some trials in a case of alleged telepathy. *Journal of the Society for Psychical Research,* 1968, **44**, 390-399.

Richmond, N. Two series of PK tests on paramecia. *Journal of the Society for Psychical Research,* 1952, **36**, 577-588.

Schmeidler, G. R. Rorschachs and ESP scores of patients suffering from cerebral concussion. *Journal of Parapsychology,* 1952, **16**, 80-89.

Schouten, S. A. Psi in mice: Positive reinforcement. *Journal of Parapsychology,* 1972, **36**, 261-282.

Shields, E. Severely mentally retarded children's psi ability. In J. D. Morris, W. G. Roll, and R. L. Morris (Eds.), *Research in Parapsychology 1975,* pp. 135-139. Metuchen, N.J.: Scarecrow Press, 1976.

Sinclair, U. *Mental Radio.* (Rev. 2nd printing.) Springfield, Ill.: Charles C Thomas, 1962.

Smith, J. Paranormal effects on enzyme activity. *Proceedings of the Parapsychological Association,* 1968, **5**, 15-16.

Sperry, R. W. The great cerebral commisure. *Scientific American,* January, 1964, 42-52.

Targ, R., and Puthoff, H. Information transmission under conditions of sensory shielding. *Nature,* October 18, 1974, 602-607.

Tart, C. T. Physiological correlates of psi cognition. *International Journal of Parapsychology,* 1963, **5**, 375-386.

Ullman, M., and Krippner, S., with Vaughan, A. *Dream Telepathy.* New York: Macmillan, 1973.

Warcollier, R. *Mind to Mind.* New York: Creative Age Press, 1948.

Watkins, G. K., and Watkins, A. M. Possible PK influence on the resuscitation of anesthetized mice. *Journal of Parapsychology,* 1971, **35**, 257-272.

White, R. A. The investigation of behavior suggestive of ESP in dogs. *Journal of the American Society for Psychical Research,* 1964, **58**, 250-279.

Whitten, J. Ramp functions in EEG power spectra during actual or attempted paranormal events. *New Horizons,* 1974, **1**, 174-183.

Wood, G. H., and Cadoret, R. J. Tests of clairvoyance in a man-dog relationship. *Journal of Parapsychology,* 1958, **22**, 29-39.

4

Parapsychology and Physics

J. H. M. Whiteman

INTRODUCTION

It is being increasingly recognized by parapsychologists that "the need for new basic insights is a paramount one and that acceptance of the findings of parapsychology by other scientists will not occur until a theory is available that 'makes sense' of psi phenomena" (Pratt, 1974, p. 134; see also Margenau, 1966, p. 215; Price, 1949, p. 20). Since all the exact sciences are based on physics, it is natural to seek a theory which is an extension or modification of physics. Whatever theory is proposed, the two research fields must in any case be consonant; hence the study of the relationship between them comes to be also of paramount importance.

An assumption commonly made is that physics is a system of established knowledge, on the interpretation of which all physicists of repute agree. That this is not the case will be seen below. It will be necessary, therefore, to study the conceptual foundations of contemporary physics with great penetration, so far as they bear on the interpretation of psi phenomena.

The research literature dealing with parapsychological evidence in relation to concepts or techniques of modern physics is vast; but, to date, little cognizance has been taken of the character of the mathematical languages of physics or the methods of philosophical analysis which throw light on its epistemology. In consequence a very varied spectrum of disconnected views and opinions is presented. Obviously a stand must be taken in favor of what we consider to be true insights, not as pressing any private opinion, but merely to bring rational order into a subject of exceptional difficulty.

THE COLLAPSE OF THE CLASSICAL ONTOLOGY

In a general way all scientists realize that the theory of relativity and the quantum theory have brought about a revolution in scientific ideas and orientation to the world. Nevertheless, the great majority continue to think about the world in very much the same way as before. It is remarkable how young graduates in physics, and many older physicists, can use formulas and techniques with hardly any realization of the acute conceptual difficulties raised by them. They continue to think in terms of nineteenth-century picturings, grafting the quantum formulas onto a classical foundation, and accustoming themselves not to be deterred when paradoxes appear.

There can be no doubt, however, in what respects the classical ontology has proved mistaken, both by its rational inadequacy as a conceptual system and by its practical inadequacy to give the correct experimental results. The deficiencies have been studied in detail and are widely agreed upon by philosophers of science in the field of modern physics (von Weizsäcker, 1971a, 1971b; Weyl, 1949; Whiteman, 1967; 1973, pp. 348-353). There seems to be a "systematic unity of physics which is as yet dimly seen" (von Weizsäcker, 1971b, p. 230). The main revisions of the classical ontology found to be necessary are thus closely related, but for convenience may be grouped under the following four heads:

1. *Measurement and Theories.* All measurement presupposes a theory (Popper, 1957, p. 189). A theory is a "conceptual system" which stands or falls as a whole but may be adjusted to fit new situations. Some conceptual systems (local Euclidean geometry, for example) may be "natural and necessary" (Poincaré, 1905, p. 152), while others are built on hypotheses which are to a varying extent ad hoc. But all, being conceptual, must be implemented approximately in experimental observations by "operational definitions" (Whiteman, 1967, Chaps. 8-13).

Thus, Special Relativity may be said to have arisen because the absolute time and common space-map for observers in relative motion, presupposed by the Galilean transformation $\bar{t} = t,\ \bar{x} = x - vt,$ imply the "classical" velocity-addition theorem (simple addition of velocities as, for example, when a man walks with velocity u along a train with velocity v); and this, applied to light, conflicts with experiment. Moreover, implementation of a "geometry" for cosmical measurement by a class of observers cannot begin with already measured differences in the velocity of light for them. Proceeding logically, then, we find that cosmical measurement must begin with a "geometry" in which, as it turns out, there is no absolute time and no common space-map for the various observers (Robertson, 1956).

The conclusion which is important here is that the rational structure of space and time and of physical laws expressible in those terms cannot be comprised in a material world but belongs to a realm of *universal reason* (or general logic for all possible observers and points of view). As will be seen below, quantum theory fully supports this conclusion.

2. *Mind-Matter Dualism.* It follows that, according to modern physics, Descartes' distinction between *res cogitans* and *res extensa* is oversimplified and misleading. The distinction which lies behind the common-sense opposition of matter to mind is between particular observations (by the senses, thought, feeling, etc., of the individual) and the potentiality for continuing existences in the universal reason. But four dualities are apt to be confused. One is the duality of the potential (or general) and the actual (or particular); another is of the universal and the individual; a third is of the conscious and unconscious; and the fourth is of the subjectively (or inwardly) directed and the objectively (or outwardly) directed.

Kant's "Copernican revolution" of the 1780s was to place all actual impressions of objectivity in the perceiving subject. "Space is a pure intuition" (Kant, 1933, bk. 39). But modern science cannot agree that "what objects may be in themselves . . . remains completely unknown to us" (Kant, 1933, bk. 59). At least one can say that objects are characterized by a potentiality to be known from various points of view, the various possible appearances being logically related by what are called in mathematics *transformation groups.* Thus the appearances of a cube to different observers are related by the possibility of translations and rotations combinable with each other in a logically consistent way. This structure of reason constitutes Euclidean geometry, not any inherent properties of "dead matter," and physical objects are specific structures in the general structure of space and time.

3. *Wholeness in Actualization.* Classical mechanics was founded on the concept of point-particles subject to equations of motion. The motion depends on a force-field, and this was supposed to be determined by the positions of the particles. The vicious circle can be overcome, in principle if not in practice, when the particles are finite in number and their initial motions are given, and when the unoperational character of a point-particle is ignored. This whole situation being unrealistic, mechanics must deal with continuous distributions; but the problems remain insoluble unless "boundary conditions" are arbitrarily chosen, either with all positions and velocities on the boundary given at one time (causal view) or with initial and final positions given (teleological view). The field-equation, which replaces the equations of motion, must then be solved as a whole, out of time, as it were.

Including the whole universe, supposed to be in infinite Euclidean space, does not relieve the conceptual and practical difficulties in the way of a realistic solution. In particular, paradoxes such as that of Olbera (Bondi, 1960, pp. 21–23) may arise. These facts were generally overlooked in the classical ontology.

In quantum theory the fields are required to be "potentiality" ones, in universal reason and subject to group transformation laws. Quantum absorptions and emissions cannot be theoretically predicted or experimentally controlled other than statistically. The fields thus determine only a distribution of possibilities for quantum exchange, and one such possible event is actualized, unpredictably, according to the whole circumstances on the occasion in question.

4. *Causality.* All these considerations combine to show that causality proceeds by three stages: from conveniently chosen boundary conditions for "objects" which are continuing potentialities in a mathematical "group-field"; through the developing potentiality-field which is characterized by a wave-function ψ; to a particular actuality in physical experience. There are no localized causal chains (except in a selective and incomplete sense depending on human interest), and no equation of motion or trajectories for "particles" in the classical sense.

It is clear, therefore, that the impersonal system of physics leaves a certain freedom from determinacy both "at the top," in the domain of universal reason and teleology, and "at the bottom," when particular actualizations arise from the wholeness of the circumstances. Thus above and below the level of scientific laws, which are essentially field-equations, there is a "cut-off" in normal scientific thinking. The "laws of universal causation" appealed to by opponents of parapsychology and behaviorists (W. R. Hammond, quoted in Burt, 1967, p. 112) do not exist in the form supposed.

PHYSICISTS AND THE MEANING OF PHYSICS

Jauch (1971) has remarked that "physicists very often do not know what they are actually doing, and equally often, what they do is different from what they say they are doing" (p. 23). D'Espagnat (1971a, 1971b), also, has drawn attention to the danger that when a man has understood a bit of nontrivial mathematics applied to physics he is so happy with himself that he may forget to try to make clear in his mind what conceptual ideas are underlying the whole thing.

The "conceptual ideas" which are thus clouded over may be of two kinds, mathematical and epistemological. Their clarity and validity need to be exposed by that kind of insight and analysis properly called *phenomenological* (Husserl, 1958a, 1958b; Whiteman, 1967). Unfortunately, by a disastrous misunderstanding, physicists and most of the Anglo-Saxon philosophical world have come to use this word for "looking to details of appearance," instead of "penetrating behind appearances" to the structure of ideas which gives them meaning and substance. Thus insight tends to be pushed aside in favor of theories which merely impose new formal devices on a background of classical conceptions. A glance at a few of the confusions resulting will be helpful for what follows.

In the theory of wave-packets it is well known that admissible solutions of the wave-equation require the combination of sinusoidal components which are *not* admissible (being not integrable-square). These sinusoidal components appear in the formalism because a standard technique for solving the field equations of physics is by first obtaining "separable solutions." Such solutions do not necessarily have any physical significance. For instance, if one interprets the sinusoidal components of a wave-packet as waves with average phase velocity u, and the group velocity (for the packet as a whole) is v, we find $uv = c^2$, where c is the velocity of light. Hence, since $v < c, u > c$. This means that the component "waves" do not exist in any possible physical frame of reference (since the transformation logically required breaks down). This conclusion is confirmed by the fact that in the case of a stationary wave-packet the calculated phase velocity would be infinite. But all that the mathematics shows is that the coefficient of x in the exponent vanishes; there is no identification of points in a traveling wave which could give meaning to the term *phase-velocity*.

Landé (1971, p. 222) uses the result $u > c$ as an argument, among others equally unsound, in an attempt to show the fallaciousness of what he calls "wave-particle duality." Dobbs (1967, p. 244) takes up the concept of "virtual particles," i.e., sinusoidal components of a field, which are represented with velocities greater than c, with the result that the formula for their momental mass yields an imaginary result. These components must of course be allowed for in the mathematics; but the arguments above show that they have no physical existence.

The fact that a formalism "works" in physics is no argument for the truth of the model according to which it is framed. Indeed, it is sometimes remarked that correct formulas are usually derived first by entirely wrong methods. One striking example of this is the formula for the "convection coefficient" when light travels through a moving medium such as water. This was first derived by Fresnel from the theory of an elastic ether. Another example is the formula for the fine-structure energy-levels of the Hydrogen spectrum, first derived by Sommerfeld from the entirely erroneous assumption that the electron travels in a spiraling relativistic orbit around the nucleus. The validity of a model can in fact be assessed only in the context of an entire world-view and physical theory grounded in phenomenological insights.

A common way of proceeding in physical research is to introduce a modified or extended formalism, altering or piling up postulates without much regard for mathematical consistency or the possibility of operational implementation. An example of this is the theory of the "collision" of quantal system and apparatus when a measurement is made—a theory adhered to by von Neumann (1955) and by Wigner (1971, pp. 6, 14) but held by others to "have no meaning" (Bohm,

1971, pp. 443, 440; also d'Espagnat, 1971c, p. 88; Ludwig, 1971; von Wiezsäcker, quoted in Whiteman, 1971, p. 71n; Zeh, 1971, p. 265). Such a theory may be described as an operationally unimplementable formalism (OUF, for short).

It will be important for what follows to note that in all operationally validated physical theories the measurements which are predicted or confirmed are obtained by very remarkable *infinite processes*. Thus integration, as in finding the length of a curve, involves what may seem at first sight the absurd idea of an infinite sum of vanishingly small parts. In contour integration we deliberately construct a function which diverges to infinity at certain points, in order to obtain the finite result. In the "momentum representation" of quantum theory, a state with a discrete spectrum is represented by *delta functions*. This means that one substitutes in integrals a succession of functions tending to infinity at one point and zero everywhere else and takes the limit toward which all the results tend in the process. Other than by such means, a representation does not exist. Every theory involving integral transforms embodies this feature.

Quantum Field Theory is sometimes criticized because of the divergences that may appear. According to what has just been said, there cannot be objection to the divergences as such. It is only a question of whether the most phenomenologically correct way of dealing with divergences by a modification of concepts has been found.

THEORY-BUILDING AND ANALYSIS

A few further general remarks are needed here on the kinds of theory which have been proposed for the purpose of reconciling parapsychology and physics. (For a discussion of particular theories, reference may be made to Professor Chari's article in this Handbook.)

The theories in question may be grouped in certain categories. Mention has already been made of theories which involve operationally unimplementable formalisms (OUF theories). A distinction can be made between these and ones which pile up applications of formulas which are individually implementable in a certain way but are not applied as a consistent mathematical theory requires. A simple example of this, in physics, is Landé's (1971) application of the formula $p = h/\lambda$, which is relativistically derived, to the nonrelativistic case, where p changes on transformation but not λ, so that a contradiction results. We can perhaps describe such theories as PUF theories (piling up formulas).

Thirdly, there are many theories which in one way or another presuppose the classical ontology. These may be called COD theories (classical ontology oriented). They usually combine classical and nonclassical models and formulas and so overlap with the PUF theories.

To be carefully distinguished from all these theories are ones in which a logically consistent language, mathematical or otherwise, is offered, along with the exhibiting of an unambiguous manner of application, to physical measurement at the level of physical observation, and to phenomenological insights at the level of meaning, so that the "language" is seen, on the one hand, to describe what is actually being done and experienced, and on the other hand, to provide a satisfying rational explanation. Special Relativity is such a theory. The chief question to be inquired into below is whether physics and parapsychology can be exhibited conjointly, in their foundations at least, as a theory of this kind rather than as one of the other kinds.

THE TELEOLOGICAL DERIVATION OF PHYSICAL LAWS

In considering what kind of theory should be looked for as an explanation of parapsychological phenomena, consonant with physics, we must take further account of the fact that the mere fitting of formalisms to phenomena tells us nothing about the validity or nonvalidity of the models or interpretations assumed. Some writers have supposed that a higher validity cannot indeed be attached to one model or interpretation over others, except on the ground of convenience, fertility, or aesthetic appeal. "All theories," Popper (1956, p. 366) asserts, "are, and remain, hypotheses—conjectures." And in the view of Kuhn (1962): "Nothing that has been or will be said makes [the development of science] a process of evolution toward anything" such as a "goal of truth" in any absolute sense (pp. 169f). Applied to psychology, this would mean that there is no such thing as a true insight, knowable as such, in distinction from error.

The authors of such views, however, have overlooked a vitally important fact concerning physics, namely, that the quantitative mathematical form of almost all the fundamental laws of physics can be derived, by phenomenological insight, from certain qualitative teleological requirements considered together with the possibilities for measurement of the phenomena in question. If our insight is deep and clear enough, we can thus distinguish between those laws that are, and always will be, correct in a certain way, and those which are in various ways faulty.

In illustration, and for later purposes, it will be helpful to survey very briefly the derivation of the laws of mechanics, Newtonian, relativistic, or quantal, by this means.

That measurement must begin with a local implementing of Euclidean geometry is shown elsewhere (Whiteman, 1967, Chap. 6). The necessity, established by Group Theory, of special relativity as a local geometry of space and time has already been mentioned.

Taking local approximations, with absolute time and for the present assuming determinacy, let us consider the rectilinear motion of a particle in a force field.

The beginning of dynamics is with the qualitative teleological demand that, given any initial velocity, the subsequent motion must be decided (otherwise nature would be random and chaotic) in some universal way, i.e., by a law meaningful and yielding the same result for all observers. We may propose laws relating the measurement of the force to the first, second, or higher order rates of change of distance covered by the particle. It is easy to see, however, that if the law involved explicitly the first order rate of change (velocity) it would not give the same result for all observers. If the law involved third or higher order rates of change, it would not give a unique result. Hence we arrive at the necessity for Newton's second law of motion, that the force is proportional to the second order rate of change, i.e., acceleration. The first law then covers the special case when the force is zero, and the third law arises chiefly because, given the qualitative condition for a reaction, the quantity must be determined uniquely from the quantity of the action.

The law of gravitation can be derived by the general theory of relativity, using tensor analysis, because there is only one tensor involving second order rates of change which is usable. It is then found that, locally, the gravitational field is conservative (i.e., has a potential). Rigid or elastic bodies count as "boundary conditions," the forces concerned being dealt with as "forces of constraint."

On such basis the whole of Newtonian mechanics stands logically (Pars, 1965) and results, if the forces have a potential, in the Hamiltonian formulation of dynamics with coordinates and conjugate momenta p. Since the argument from the teleological demand for determinate motion is a general one, we may expect the same broad logical structure to appear in the formulation of electrodynamics (as it does, both classically and relativistically) and in quantum mechanics, with a reinterpretation of concepts in every case.

A complete derivation of quantum mechanics by such means is not yet possible, but a few initial indications may be helpfully advanced here, because of their intimate bearing on parapsychological phenomena, as will appear in later sections.

As we have seen, structures of a conceptual system, such as straight lines and points, can be implemented in actuality only by successive approximation. To permit such approximation, or *average* agreement with the theory, the Hamiltonian formalism of mechanics must be reinterpreted in terms of average values for x and p instead of conceptually precise measures. The symbols should thus stand for "operations" which result in a spread of expectations because they operate on a continuous mathematical "field" or "state vector." As is well known, a Fourier transformation between a function $\psi(x, t)$ and an equivalent functional form $\phi(p, H)$, with a further functional relation between H and the other variables, provides just the necessary formulation, so that Hamilton's equations hold for expectation values. It requires a universal constant h; and, supposing a certain value for this is allocated, the "uncertainty relations" (commutators) and all other quantum formulas follow logically.

The quantum concepts turn out to be very different from the classical ones. Hence the relationship between the visible world of classical dynamics and the invisible "quantum world" is one of the correspondence only—but a *creative* correspondence, insofar as the quantum world of "fields" is the immediate cause of the actualized phenomena in the visible world.

The term *correspondence* has both the formal mathematical meaning of homomorphism (Jauch, 1971, p. 48; Piron, 1971, p. 276) and a psychological, hierarchical, or mystical meaning (Swedenborg, 1958; Whiteman, 1961). Here, as will be more clearly seen later, are the beginnings of a synthesis between psychology and physics.

THE EPISTEMOLOGICAL PROBLEMS OF QUANTUM THEORY AND THE "LANGUAGE" OF QUANTUM FIELD THEORY

We now have to see how far it is possible to gain insight into the status of the wave-function and thus into physical causation in general by consideration of experimental evidence in quantum physics. We shall find that in many ways a clue is also provided as to the manner of psychological causation. The problems have been discussed at great length in numerous research publications. Hence little more than a general view can be presented here.

Two kinds of physical occurrence are in question, broadly describable as "interference" and "collision," respectively. In the former there is a splitting and coming together of fields, so to speak, and in the latter there is a coming together and splitting. Paradoxes result when one attempts to carry over the classical concepts of "particle," "particle trajectory," "particle ensemble," "energy flow," "causal chain," and so on, regardless of the fact that, according to the previous discussion, these classical concepts must necessarily be reinterpreted.

A few of the paradoxes seem trivial, resulting simply from the joint application of quantum and classical formulas, or application of quantum formulas in a mathematically inconsistent way. The remaining difficulties can be considered under four heads:

1. The inseparability of localized particles or wave-packets in the free field (d'Espagnat, 1971b, 1971c; Whiteman, 1967, pp. 312*f*, 1971, p. 74). This is deduced from interference and diffraction experiments when the field is so weak that single scintillations or quantum absorptions are observed. The ψ-field is introduced to explain statistically the transference of quanta to the bound "systems" acting as detectors. We conclude that the quanta transferred can be counted, but they cannot be located otherwise than (if at all) in the field as a whole.

2. The inseparability of "systems" from the whole set-up; i.e., particular physical measures cannot be attributed to an existing "system" which collides with or confronts the measuring apparatus (d'Espagnat, 1971b, 1971c; Jauch,

1971, p. 29; Whiteman, 1971, p. 71*n*, pp. 75, 81–82). The measures in question appear only on the occasion of measurement.

3. The "collapse" of the wave-function on measurement. If the ψ-field is located in physical space, then, when a quantum is absorbed at a point, the field must collapse into it, implying velocities far greater than the velocity of light. This is in accord with other arguments indicating that ψ is an "as if" structure (d'Espagnat, 1971b, p. 90) or a "control mechanism" for absorptions (Whiteman, 1973, p. 352).

There seems to be a growing feeling that there is in fact no "collapse" because of the existence of a conceptual "boundary" between the sphere of macroscopic physical objects and the sphere of quantum concepts, consciousness, and life (Wigner, 1971, p. 17). So the concepts and picturings of the one sphere are simply not applicable to the other.

4. The correlation of "systems" not in normal physical communication with each other. Thus in the Compton Effect, when gamma rays "collide" with electrons (or an electron field), a quantum of the former (photon) may be absorbed at one angle of deflection afterwards, unpredictably, and synchronously an electron may be absorbed at another angle of deflection. The angles are correlated by conservation of momentum; but neither angle was settled until the first absorption took place, and this was after the two "systems" had separated. It may seem, therefore, as if the "information" concerning the photon's angle of deflection must have been communicated paranormally to the electron so that the latter's momentum could be properly correlated (Costa de Beauregard, 1975).

This argument clearly presupposes a picture of located "systems" in two separate fields. In line with what has been said above, however, we need to think in terms of "as if" ψ-fields, conjoint, and causally operating over physical space as a whole. What we then have is a "conceptual" or "transcendental" connection between the two observed absorptions, ensuring that these are correlated as regards momentum, without the need for any wave or other recognized form of physical communication between them.

The interesting result of this analysis is that physics itself seems to compel us to admit the possibility of what might be called "classically acausal" correlations, such as are considered in Jung's (1972) theory of synchronicity, Such correlations might be better described as the result of causation from a higher level, by correspondence, such as we have already found reason to admit on other grounds.

Almost without exception, the paradoxes of quantum theory have been discussed in the "language" of elementary quantum mechanics. This can be described as the adaptation of classical Hamiltonian theory by the substitution of approximate measures for exact ones, the formulation being "discrete," i.e., for a finite number of variables. Actualities, however, such as appearances of an existing straight line, are always presented as the outcome of an infinity of possibilities within a conceptually precise framework, seen "focally" or sensed "peripherally" (Husserl, 1931). It seems to follow, therefore, that the *continuous* formulation of Hamiltonian theory (as required for the motion of an elastic membrane) is the one that must be adopted; and this gives us Quantum Field Theory.

Some paradoxes arise simply because the language of elementary quantum mechanics (EQM) is not adequate to the experimental situation. For example, in EQM, the wave equation has to be formulated in such a way that if there are two or more particles they are separately identifiable and localizable; hence in many situations a rather fantastic correction has to be made (by the "exclusion principle," or "exchange forces") to allow for the fact that the "particles" are not in fact distinguishable. Again, in EQM, a sinusoidal wave and a wave-packet alike have necessarily only one quantum; but the former is usually interpreted as meaning that any number of quanta can be absorbed from it, in proportion to its intensity at the point.

The greatest inadequacies of EQM appear, however, in interaction theory, which can be made to give right results only by adding trial terms, supposing that an unquantized field is quantized, and making use of many other ad-hoc and often unconsistent devices (Schiff, 1955, Chap. X).

It is not widely realized that Quantum Field Theory (QFT) overcomes all these faults and astonishingly represents the experimental situation in a fitting language, some portions of which can be teleologically derived as in the last section. Early anomalies in the theory have been overcome, and although in many developments the mathematics is cruelly abstruse, basically the "language" is simple and deeply impressive as an account of natural law for physics on the small scale.

A fully covariant relativistic formulation is possible, with a 4-vector operator giving rates of change, derived from a 4^2-tensor. The field is compounded of two parts, the first of which, being now analogous to the electromagnetic field, is measurable, and therefore must be of operators, quantized. The other part, or "occupation vector," which merely gives the number of quanta for each component, is obviously unlocalizable. Thus the combined concept of "state vector" becomes closely in accord with actual experience.

The field in general is broken up into "orthonormal components" with multipliers a_k. If we then make the transition to "approximative" Hamiltonian theory by imposing a quantum rule (or uncertainty principle), we find that the field can contain only a discrete number of quanta of the energy-momentum vector, and that the operators a_k and its conjugate complex respectively destroy and create one quantum in the field. Every "particle" also has its "antiparticle."

In interaction between two fields, a scalar term must be added to the Hamiltonians of the two fields (if the Hamiltonian form is to be preserved); and for the

Compton Effect, for example, tensor analysis limits this term logically to $j\mu A\mu$, i.e., the scalar product of the current density (in the electron field) and the vector potential (in the photon field). The experimental results are then accounted for in detail.

It seems therefore that any attempt to unite parapsychology and physics should adhere, substantially at least, to the language of quantum field theory, in terms of "as if" fields at a level of creative potentiality.

THE UNION OF PSYCHOLOGY AND PHYSICS

Wigner (1964) has remarked that "there are many signs . . . that a more profound understanding" of observation and cognition "is a not too distant future step." He continues: "At any rate it should be the next decisive breakthrough toward a more integrated understanding of the world, after which we shall not have to treat physical phenomena and phenomena of the mind in such a way that we forget about the tools used for the consideration of one when thinking about the problems of the other" (p. xvi).

That this "higher integration" could not be achieved at that time Wigner (1964) imputed to the fact that "psychology is not yet ready for providing concepts and idealisations of such precision as is expected in mathematics or even physics" (p. xvi).

It happens, however, that the "number systems" in Eastern mystical philosophy, especially the Upanishads (with some confirmation by Western psychology and direct mystical testimonies), provide a basis of "precision," in such close correspondence with formulations of quantum theory that there is an obvious invitation to exhibit the two as aspects of an "integrated understanding of the world." In such a presentation the most basic field equations of quantum physics can be teleologically "derived," and various possibilities for further working out and testing can be proposed. It will be found also that parapsychological phenomena obtain explanation in full consistency with the physical ones.

It is the purpose of this section to give a general introduction to the holistic analysis of the total evidence, physical and psychological. Some of the mathematics must be outlined in order to exhibit the precision of the "language." For further details in regard to the axiomatic development, reference may be made to the original presentation, also given in outline only (Whiteman, 1975a).

1. In the physical part of the derivation it is simplest to begin with a postulate that everything actualized at the physical level can be accounted for on the basis of three spacelike variables x, y, z, and three timelike variables T, t, τ, with 15 "rotational directions" obtained by taking these two at a time. In this way a six-dimensional tensor calculus of antisymmetric tensors of rank 2 is constituted, with 15 independent components of each tensor; and the physical significance of scalar products obliges us to admit also a 16th component which is a scalar. For

the present we pass over the derivation of the original postulate from prior analyses.

For reasons to be given presently, two of the timelike variables are not subject to different points of view (i.e., transformation); these are also not concerned with the "field" level of causation. As a result, the 16 possible measures group themselves into two 4-vectors (transforming as in special relativity), a 4^2-tensor, and two scalars. Tensor analysis tells us that in an antisymmetric system of rank 2 tensors, the only products which can have physical significance are a cross-product, $P \times Q$, a vector product, $P \vee Q$, and a scalar product, $P . Q$. These happen to be produced all together in what is called the *sedenion algebra*, in which the various measures are attached to directional operators and added together, thus:

$$P = P^{12} \sigma_{12} + P^{13} \sigma_{13} + \ldots + P^{05} \sigma_{05} + P^{16}$$

where the symbols σ_{ab} obey rather elaborate multiplication rules.

(The σ-symbols should be understood as simply giving the row and column numbers [first and second suffixes respectively] of the corresponding component in the tensor when set out in a square array. The multiplication rules are then merely what is required to give all possible products, as above [see Appendix A]).

It now follows from tensor analysis that the only possible form of linear wave-equation (resulting in second order equations of motion as required) is $(\nabla + k) P = 0$, where ∇ is the gradient operator:

$$\sigma_{15} \frac{\partial}{\partial x} + \sigma_{25} \frac{\partial}{\partial y} + \sigma_{35} \frac{\partial}{\partial z} + \sigma_{45} \frac{\partial}{i \partial t},$$

k is a constant for the field in question, and P is the general 15-component vector ("complete field vector") constructed as above. If we conveniently label the components as follows:

$$P = (E_x \sigma_{14} + E_y \sigma_{24} + E_z \sigma_{34}) + i(H_x \sigma_{23} + H_y \sigma_{31} + H_z \sigma_{12}) +$$
$$(J_x \sigma_{15} + J_y \sigma_{25} + J_z \sigma_{35} + i\rho \sigma_{45})/k$$

putting the other five components zero, the result is found to be Maxwell's equations for the electromagnetic field, along with the continuity condition for the current vector J. If, on the other hand, we insert matrix forms for the symbols σ_{ab} and "factorize" P as $\psi i \chi j$, the equation for ψ is Dirac's linear wave-equation for the fermion field.

Some quantum problems, such as obtaining the formula for the fine-structure of the Hydrogen spectrum, can be solved more directly by working with the "complete" wave-equation as above instead of the spinor form in ψ. "Spin" enters the formalism because of the mathematical need for both "substitution" and "component-mixing" operators and turns out to be of the magnitude required experimentally. The Klein-Gordon equation for scalar mesons, with spin zero (Messiah, 1962, pp. 885–886), in the absence of an electromagnetic field, and its corrected form in the presence of an electromagnetic field, can be obtained by a familiar process (Messiah, 1962, pp. 890, 919). But this process should presumably be applied to the complete wave-equation. Clearly there is scope for further research here.

2. We must now consider the nature of the three spacelike and three timelike variables from what might be called the *psycho-mystical* angle and in reference to our previous analysis of causality, with a view to deriving the postulate from which we began.

For want of a better means of description, one can say that there are six *creative potencies* in all existence. Three are associated with change, being analogous to mass, motion, and force, respectively. Or again, they are analogous to (a) the actualization at the third stage of causation, (b) the changing due to the field equations, and (c) the intention which sets up boundary conditions. Corresponding to these we may expect three timelike operations, with associated "variables," (a) an "actualizing time" τ (which, as we shall see, involves the passage of the variable to infinity), (b) a "logical" or "field" time t for changes in the field, and (c) a cosmical or "planning" time T, to be explained in due course. Only the second of these, t, would be subject to different points of view.

Three more potencies are needed to provide the cognitive character of everything that exists. They may be described as categories of "timeless" ideas or concepts. There will be (a) a knowability of intention or purpose, (b) a knowability of change and difference, or intelligible relation, and (c) a knowability of substance, or sensory and fulfilling character. These may be thought of as analogous to the good, the true, and the beautiful, or to their opposites. In mystical correspondence, "height and depth," "breadth" (to right or left), and "near and far," represent qualities of fulfillment, intelligence, and harmony of intention or mood ("psychical distance"), respectively. But when different points of view are compounded by "rotations" so as to make the continuous actuality of a "world," the correspondences would inevitably be clouded over.

With regard to the "actualizing time" τ, the rotational transformation:

$$\begin{cases} \bar{x} = x \cosh \phi + \tau \sinh \phi \\ \bar{\tau} = x \sinh \phi + \tau \cosh \phi \end{cases}$$

yields $\bar{x} = x + x_o$ if $\tau \to \infty$, $\phi \to 0$, $\tau\phi \to x_o$. By this means, therefore, translations (space and time shifts) are formalized in the same way as rotations, and not anomalously as in the Euclidean and Poincaré groups.

The Euclidean group of transformations for space is a limited case of the Poincaré group for space-time; and the latter, we can now see, is a limited case of what might be called the "world-forming" or WF-group. The formalism implies that a "world" is created, so to speak, as follows:

Everything knowable is, in essence, a 16-fold structure of concepts, associated with an identifiable "source of consciousness" (in itself unlocated). The σ_{5a} "rotations," together with actualizing time, project the concepts as if onto a point in space and time (so that $\overline{x} = x_0$, instead of $x = 0$, etc.). Then all the rotations, conjointly, provide for an infinity of possible points of view, in absolute logical consistency with each other. This makes the "projections" *objective*. For there is nothing more real, definite, and substantial than what is compelled to be so by an absolute and precise logic, valid for all people. A "world" is projected because in all consciousness there is a *focus* and *periphery* ranging over a field or sphere of potentialities.

In such a way, physics may be considered to have solved the philosophical problem of perception, which arises from the paradoxical fact that objects are both privately conceptual and publicly objective.

3. We pass now to the further conclusion that the conceptual structure of every physical objectivity has an aspect in respect of which it is potentially present in the consciousness of the observing subject, and not in fact projected. Indeed, the whole "external" world must be so "present," being conceptual in essence. And not only the external world, but every other possible "world" must be present in a universal unconscious or potential conscious (cf. Price, 1953, pp. 12–15).

Among such compresent "worlds" there must be *thought-image* worlds in which the boundary conditions can be worked out, and an *ideal-purposive* world from which the unitive intelligence necessary to devise the planning of boundary conditions can proceed. At each level where 16-fold cycles project a "world," the possibility of consciousness requires also, as we shall see, the corresponding manifestation of 16-fold cycles of psychological action, finally expressing themselves correspondentially in bodily action at the physical level.

Each of the necessary spheres of ("subjective") psychological action and corresponding ("objective") nonphysical spatio-temporal perception must have its proper time t, and a correlation of time-instants in the various spheres is clearly needed to synchronize causal events in "inner" spheres with correlated ones in "outer" spheres. Hence we deduce the need for a cosmical or "planning" time T, relative to which the proper time in any sphere may suffer a time-shift, according to the changing correlations.

Thus in memory or retrocognition, we may suppose that a certain past event, at cosmical time T_0, has a potentiality (established in an individual's thought-image sphere by its actual occurrence—otherwise its actual occurrence would not be causal) and that an actualization of this is synchronized with a later physical event at time $T_1 > T_0$. The synchronization would be directed by purpose, desire, or need. The theory of actual memory-traces localized in the individual brain, it is hardly necessary to remark, is quite contrary to the epistemology of modern physics and also is subject to many other objections (Burt, 1967, pp. 109–116; Seeds and Vatter, 1971).

In tensor analysis applied to space and time, the field of events is analogous to the field of fixed positions on a space-map, and transformations merely present this field to different points of view. Consider now a change in boundary conditions in a certain region and at a certain time, made by "planning" (which can be likened to muscular action due to a "force of intention" at some cosmical time T). In such region and at such time new events are introduced, a new "map" is drawn, and the tensor laws therefore no longer apply. Hence the field equations and conservation laws implicit in them can no longer be derived. This fact establishes the necessary occurrence of *psychoenergetic systems* associated with the appearance of energy, momentum, etc., not balanced out by other quantities as required by the usual conservation laws. The effect of this would be as if energy, etc., were supplied from a higher causal level.

4. To complete the union of psychology and physics one needs to exhibit 16 psychological categories in every phase of consciousness, coordinated in a cycle which exactly corresponds to the "objective" cycle or set of 16 σ-operators by means of which a "world" is projected. A discussion of the voluminous psycho-mystical evidence in this connection would go far beyond the scope of this introduction; but the fact that remarkable correspondences do exist may perhaps be shown convincingly enough with the help of some tabulations and a few supporting references.

A fourfold cycle of creative functions or conditions, as described by Poincaré (Hadamard, 1945), is abundantly testified in mystical writings (Whiteman, 1961, pp. 179–181, 232–238, 242–243). Remarkable agreement is also shown with the "variables" 1–4 distinguished by Moriarty and Murphy (1967, pp. 207–208) for the rating of "creativity." The following table, associating the primordial spatio-temporal correspondences with number-suffixes, will enable us to connect the 16 σ-operators with the four chief "directions of spirit," each subdivided into four. Its justification is in the extraordinary agreement which results between the spatio-temporal significances and the psychological ones.

purpose $(x, 1)$ impulsion $(T, 0)$	means $(y, 2)$ change $(t, 5)$	fulfillment $(z, 3)$ ground $(\tau, 4)$

The six potencies exhibited here, when combined two at a time, characterize 15 of the stages in the "psychological" cycle, in agreement with the psycho-mystical evidence. The sixteenth, as we shall see, is an outermost identification or "talking to oneself."

The following tabulations show the correspondences in the case of the first and third "directions of spirit," called, in the Upanishads, *prāṇa* (forward spirit) and *apāna* (downward spirit), respectively, and elsewhere frequently likened to the sun rising in the east and setting in the west. It is to be noted that each "quarter" proceeds through impulsion, change, and ground to a function or aim linking with the next "quarter."

	σ-suffixes	potencies	combination	psychological term
Prāṇa "forward"	10	xT	impulsion of purposive ideas	enthusiasm
	15	xt	flow of purposive ideas	inspiration
	14	$x\tau$	grounding of purposive ideas	illumination
	23	yz	looking to adaptive means and fulfillment	circumspection
Apāna "downward"	40	$T\tau$	impulsion to ground	extroversion
	45	$t\tau$	movement to ground	application
	16	–	–	identification
	50	Tt	impulsion to change	checking, reaction

The reader may verify that the four stages in the second, or "reciprocal" and "adaptive," direction (*vyāna*) are suitably described by the terms: response, precising, perfect grounding, and purpose to fulfill.

The stages in the fourth direction (*samāna*, consummating spirit), as implied by this symbolism, are of special interest and importance. It is this direction or "quarter" with which the ancient mystical systems always associated "release" and "rebirth." The four stages in it will be seen to correspond to stages distinguished by White (1964, pp. 28–44) in the inducing of "altered states of consciousness." Relaxation is the preliminary checking of attachments or fixations and the imposing of general conditions of release instead. Then the four stages can be more easily isolated and sustained: the "demand"; the "waiting"; the release; and the breakthrough. When the stages are purely and strongly realized, they "lift" us to a more released state of "illumination," and the cycle begins again at the "higher" level.

REMARKS ON SCIENTIFIC METHOD IN PARAPSYCHOLOGY

One cannot relate physics to telepathy, clairvoyance, precognition, or other specific paranormal phenomena, unless one has a clear means of distinguishing these one from another. Recently it seems to have become widely agreed that such distinguishing is not possible, at least if the hypothetico-deductive method for science is adopted and only if evidence of a certain experimental type, physically recorded, is admitted (Rhine, 1974; Thouless, 1963, pp. 38, 141; West, 1962, p. 141). Thus Rhine (1974) declares that "a common circumstance is involved [in certain more or less major issues in parapsychology] : all the problems to be considered are without exception logically untestable by an experiment that could give an unambiguous result" (p. 138).

Here the assumptions are obvious: The "issues" are hypotheses, certain results of which are to be tested by physical experiment.

In the last decade or two the subject of scientific method and explanation has become unsettled and controversial. Valuable new insights have been gained, but their working-out has come in for much criticism (Hempel, 1965; Kuhn, 1962). "It is clear that 'science' and 'truth' and other similar expressions are not straightforward but highly ambiguous. . . . Contemporary methodology shows how diverse are the methods, and the value of their results, in various disciplines. . . . Reality, and hence the thought which tries to take it in, are obviously of enormous complexity (Bochenski, 1965, p. 126).

Many important advances in physics (special and general relativity, Planck's constant, wave and matrix mechanics) have been partly if not primarily inspired by epistemological considerations. This suggests that in most cases where a hypothetico-deductive method might seem to have been used, the hypotheses were in some barely conscious but nevertheless compelling way guided by phenomenological insight. And it is evident that later, when the "paradigm" (Kuhn, 1962) is being "tidied up," there is an impulsion to replace that method as far as possible by a derivation from direct phenomenological analysis. For hypotheses imposed blindly do no more than "save the appearances," and often result in paradoxes. In short, acceptable scientific hypotheses require comprehensive insight, not a mere anchoring in facts (Popper, 1956, p. 379; Weyl, 1949, p. 153).

For almost a century parapsychology has been at the "natural history" stage of science. The hypothetico-deductive stage was never reached because a physical paradigm was fairly obviously inadequate, while a psychological one could be achieved only by insights into the *psychological* evidence.

In this light let us consider the other common assumption of parapsychologists, mentioned above, that the evidence considered is to be provided by physical experiment. It is usual, indeed, to accept testimony by a sensitive as to his or her nonphysical experience, provided it is "veridical" (i.e., the facts reported correspond with physical ones). Presumably the chief argument for this proviso is that only in such a way can the "facts" be verified or confuted by another person. But if this argument were justified, it would seem, from what has just been said, that scientific explanation in psychology or parapsychology is impossible.

The self-defeating nature of the policy represented by the assumptions in question is seen particularly clearly in the fact that it prevents any possible distinction between a veridical dream and a veridical "out of the body experience." In physics it would prevent a distinction between the interpretation of the Lorentz transformation by Lorentz himself (in accord with the classical ontology) and the interpretation by Poincaré and Einstein.

Thus the positivistic concept of verification is "beset with serious difficulties"

(Bochenski, 1965, p. 55).   According to each field of inquiry a different kind of verification is reasonable.   In the case of nonphysical observation, a reasonable concept would seem to require agreement in respect of relevant particulars by another sensitive in similar circumstances (certainly not by all and sundry, in all particulars, and under any physical or nonphysical circumstances), always on the understanding that the testifiers have the same degree of honesty and powers of accurate description as are required in the physical sciences (Tart, 1972; Whiteman, 1975a).

But verification must also be within the framework of a conceptual system. As in confirming special relativity, or the real existence of other people than ourselves, it depends on the coherence of transcending insights rather than on following out specific rules for testing (Findley, 1966, pp. 185-186).

A similar interpretation must then apply to the concept of "repeatability" in parapsychological investigation (McCreery, 1967, Chap. 7; Murphy, 1971; Ransom, 1971, pp. 291-293; Tyrrell, 1953, pp. 163-164), a "repeat" being scientifically of interest only so far as it is a verification.

PHYSICS AND PARANORMAL "MENTAL PHENOMENA"

By the *paranormal* may be understood either (a) occurrences which are inexplicable in terms of the classical ontology, or (b) nonphysical experience other than "normal" thinking, memory, imagination, and dream (Burt, 1968, p. 7). In this and the following two sections we will be concerned with showing how the world-view and methodology to which modern physics has led us make the occurrences (a) explicable and (b) open up possibilities of scientific research into the nonphysical experience.

The first essential in this new world-view is, perhaps, the recognition that "objects" are potentialities for observation from various points of view and are thus *conceptual* and *intersubjective*.   Another essential is that there can be such "objects" not only at the level of physical potentiality but also at various thought-image levels and at ideal-purposive levels where they might be better called dispositions.   Thirdly, all these levels are linked by correspondences, so that the entire system of potentialities actualizable at the physical or any other level amounts to a Common Unconscious; and this, by a natural kind of fixation, is thought of as "within" the bodily organism which brings it to consciousness.

Conclusions of this kind have in fact been repeatedly advanced, independently of physics, on the basis of evidence concerning apparitions, multiple personality, mediumship of various kinds, or mystical experience.   Compare, for example, Myers' (1903) theory of a "comprehensive consciousness . . . which for the most part remains potential only" (Vol. 1, p. 12), Bergson's (1914) potentially unlimited ψ, McDougall's (1920, 1939) theory of a "systematic psychic field" and personality as a "graded hierarchy," Smuts's (1926) "holism" and "pull of the future," Tyrrell's theory of "grades of significance" (n.d., *ca.* 1930), Johnson's (1953) account of a "psychic ether," Ducasse's (1956) theory of dynamic "etheric objects," and Burt's (1968, pp. 49-50) theory of passive and active "psychic fields."

Veridical nonphysical experience (ESP) may thus be reasonably understood as the actualization of physical and nonphysical potentialities conjointly (Tyrrell, 1953, pp. 101-102) in the percipient's thought-image sphere *merged* with the physical sphere (Whiteman, 1961), the region of thought-image actualization being also subject to space-shifts or time-shifts according to correspondence and direction from the ideal-purposive level. It is important to realize that nothing is spatially "transmitted" because there are *two* spaces, in variable correlation, and if there are various minds concerned, they "work together" or "merge" (Sidgwick, 1923, pp. 419-423).

A few further remarks are needed on precognition. The reader may easily check that there is now neither an *epistemological* nor a *causal* difficulty (Broad, 1967, pp. 188-194; Dobbs, 1965, p. 252), since nothing prevents a provisional plan being worked out and the events logically involved in it being actualized at the thought-image level. The difficulty over "free will" remains. This arises from the fact that a "plan" drastically limits happenings possibly a great interval of time ahead and involving numerous human beings, some not yet born; and voluminous evidence testifies to such limitation (see, for example, Tyrrell, 1947, pp. 73-90, 179). Two questions then arise: By what means can the actions of human beings be so constrained? And if they are so constrained, how is there scope for "free will"?

This is not the place to consider these problems in detail. Reference may be made, however, to the distinction possible between subjective tendencies which are *cooperative* with the unitary wisdom at the Ideal-Purposive level and others which may be called *antioperative*. The latter may be presumed to be imaginary or erroneous in character, so that they are cut off from the possibility of making a "real" contribution to the universal plan. The "organic processes" behind the antioperative tendencies will be subject to both plan and field-equations (cf. Tyrrell, 1947, p. 95). But as far as the conscious subject is concerned, besides his freedom to cooperate with the plan there would appear to remain freedoms which are of a "private" or "small-bias" kind, corresponding to the openness "below" with which the physical theory of fields cannot deal.

PHYSICS AND SEPARATIVE EXPERIENCE ("OUT OF THE BODY")

In recent years the epithet "out of the body" has been applied to a great variety of ill-defined experience-types, understood as "altered" subjective states imposed on a basis of "objectively defined [physical] reality" (Palmer and Vassar, 1974, p. 259). The reported nonphysical spatial perceptions have even been dismissed as "theory" because they cannot be "proved" to be of the one "real" physical space (Eastman, 1962, pp. 289, 292). To forestall as far as possible such presuppositions of the classical ontology we shall speak here of "separative experience" (SE) or "separation" (Poynton, 1975; Whiteman, 1961, Part II). The "separation" is of life in a *perceived* nonphysical space from fixation on the physical space.

According to the above analysis, any "objective" 16-fold cycle requires a corresponding "psychological" 16-fold cycle, by which it comes to cognition. But such a cycle would be meaningless unless there were a potentiality for the various psychological states of the cycle to become conscious to particular individuals. We may infer, therefore, that at every level (including thought-image and ideal-purposive ones) there must be the possibility for a conscious human life, as complete as physical life, and with similar actualizations of bodily organisms or vehicles corresponding to the psychological functions expressed but otherwise having a character appropriate to the level in question (e.g., ideoplastic at thought-image levels).

Putting aside, therefore, all presuppositions of the classical ontology, we may define SE, in conformity with the evidence, as the "objective" (or intelligently responsive) perceiving by some individual, of a nonphysical "world" (or space-time) where such individual also "objectively" perceives his cognitive organism to be integrally situated.

SE must be carefully distinguished from experience of nonphysical phenomena "as from the physical body," even if the phenomena duplicate physical phenomena from another viewpoint (this would be the simple "space-shift" called "clairvoyance").

The qualification "objective" has been inserted in the definition in order to rule out dream and ensure that the "psychological" cycle is cognitively linked with the "objective" (nonphysical) one in the way which an appropriate scientific methodology would require. Here, particularly, dependence on positivistic verification by physical tests would be "self-defeating," and tests of "objectivity" must be centered on the details of reports which have been accepted as authentic. If appropriate tests of authenticity and objectivity are approved, this subject becomes open to far-reaching research, illuminating the structure of personality, the interrelationship of the various states and "worlds," mediumship, and survival. (For an introduction to this line of thought, see Balfour, 1935; Heywood, 1968, pp. 190–218; Tart, 1972, on "state-specific sciences"; Whiteman, 1965, 1975b).

PHYSICS AND PARANORMAL "PHYSICAL PHENOMENA"

The experimental and spontaneous phenomena (chiefly PK) which come under this head are considered in Part IV of this Handbook. Only a few matters of general principle, arising from previous discussions, call for attention here.

If we distinguish the level of field-equations, or normal physics, from the "planning" and "actualizing" levels, it seems clear, as has already been noted, that consideration of conservation laws (for energy, etc.) is irrelevant. Anything paranormal will be initiated from "above" or "below." There seem to be therefore two principal questions or fields of research:

1. How is an ideoplastic determination at the thought-image level translated into new or changed boundary conditions? This would seem to involve the creation of "sources," "sinks," and "bound systems," and possible "channeling" of fields with or without located materials such as ectoplasm. The process might occur by some direct kind of correspondence and could perhaps be likened to muscular action following a specific intention and visualized means.

2. How are specific quantum-exchanges initiated? If these occurred purely "by chance," it is clear that an experiment could be arranged so that any "plan" could be unpredictably disrupted. One may infer, therefore, that specific quantum-exchanges must be controllable by intention from a higher level (as confirmed by Schmidt, 1969, 1971, 1973). But normally one would expect "small-bias" deviations of which the plan need take no account.

That both topics 1 and 2 are concerned in the functions of the brain appears from researchers (Burt, 1968, p. 47; Eccles, 1953, p. 277) which indicate that single-quantum exchanges may be significantly involved at the synaptic junctions. The brain would then both fulfill and limit the intentional consciousness proceeding from higher levels into the physical one.

A bold attempt to reduce what may be going on in the brain to a deterministic "hidden-variable theory," assuming von Neumann's Projection Postulate, has been made by Walker (1975). Since the hidden variables are unlocalizable (Bell, 1964; 1971, pp. 178–180) in the brain or outside, and are not accessible to physical measurement, they are taken to correspond to paranormal faculties of consciousness. It remains to be seen whether there is something in this hidden-variable theory that goes beyond what Bell (1971) describes as an "ad-hoc scheme" such as can be made "to account for any experimental results whatever" (p. 175).

CONCLUSIONS

Alike in parapsychological researches today and in criticisms of these, presupposition of the classical ontology is frequent and obvious. This confuses the issues and raises insoluble pseudo-problems. Modern physics has reached the stage where the clear outlines of a new world-view and methodology are visible, and these provide an "integral understanding" of the world and its psychological and mystical background. With the wider acceptance of such world-view and methodology, new fields of research may be expected to open out, and parapsychology may be considered to have become an established science.

Opposition arises, however, not only from ignorance of modern physics, but also, and primarily it seems, from adherence to the simple one-level locational view of "reality" which nature offers, as it were, for ordinary practical purposes and for minds not yet capable of deeper insights. If it is impossible for us to think of a communion of minds transcending spatial separation, it is likely that we shall find it impossible to believe in telepathy or any other paranormal phenomenon, whatever the evidence or arguments.

If therefore the lessons of modern physics in this respect are to be thoroughly learned, practical aspects would seem to need as much attention as theoretical ones. It needs to be acknowledged that there is the possibility for everyone to cultivate powers of insight, transcending "simple location" (Whitehead, 1926, pp. 72-74, 82) in various well-recognized ways. To this conclusion, also, modern physics may be held to have pointed the way.

APPENDIX A

Note on the Field Tensor and Sedenian Algebra

The field tensor P may look more familiar when the components are set out in a square array:

$$\begin{pmatrix} 0 & iH_z & -iH_y & E_x & J_x & 0 \\ -iH_z & 0 & iH_x & E_y & J_y & 0 \\ iH_y & -iH_x & 0 & E_z & J_z & 0 \\ -E_x & -E_y & -E_z & 0 & i\rho & 0 \\ -J_x & -J_y & -J_z & -i\rho & 0 & 0 \\ 0 & 0 & 0 & 0 & 0 & 0 \end{pmatrix}$$

By taking the terms in the diagonal quarters "imaginary," and the others real, all equations of motion and effects of "rotation" become real. The multiplication rules for the σ-symbols are as follows:

$$\sigma_{ab}\,\sigma_{ab} = 1, \sigma_{ab} = -\,\sigma_{ba} \quad (a,b \text{ different})$$
$$\sigma_{ab}\,\sigma_{ac} = i\sigma_{bc} \quad\quad\quad (a,b,c \text{ different})$$
$$\sigma_{ab}\,\sigma_{cd} = \sigma_{ef} \quad\quad\quad (abcdef \text{ an even permutation of } 123450)$$

These can be obtained by multiplying two tensors each represented by a single term (σ_{ab}, σ_{cd}), calculating the sum of the three tensor products, $P \times Q + P \vee Q + P.Q$, and ensuring that the "quarters" are real or imaginary as required. The customary methods of dealing with the Dirac equation, using products of γ-matrices, with a few represented by σ-symbols (e.g., Messiah, 1962, pp. 893–905), appear very clumsy and confused. Eddington's (1946) E-numbers are related by $E_{ab} = i\sigma_{ab}$, but here again the theory runs into some confusion.

REFERENCES

Balfour, G. W. A study of the psychological aspects of Mrs. Willett's mediumship, and of the statements of the communicators concerning process. *Proceedings of the Society for Psychical Research*, 1935, 43, 43–318.

Bell, J. S.   On the Einstein–Podolsky–Rosen paradox. *Physics*, 1964, **1**, 195–200.

Bell, J. S.   Introduction to the hidden-variable question. *Proceedings of the International School of Physics "Enrico Fermi," Course IL*, pp. 171–181. New York: Academic Press, 1971.

Bergson, H.   Presidential Address. *Proceedings of the Society for Psychical Research*, 1914, **27**, 157–175.

Bochenski, J. M.   *The Methods of Contemporary Thought*. Boston: Reidel, 1965.

Bohm, D.   Quantum theory as an indication of a new order in physics. *Proceedings of the International School of Physics "Enrico Fermi," Course IL*, pp. 412–469. New York: Academic Press, 1971.

Bondi, H.   *Cosmology*. (2nd ed.) Cambridge: Cambridge University Press, 1960.

Broad, C. D.   The notion of "precognition." In J. R. Smythies (Ed.), *Science and ESP*, pp. 165–169. New York: Humanities Press, 1967.

Burt, C.   Psychology and parapsychology. In J. R. Smythies (Ed.), *Science and ESP*, pp. 61–141. New York: Humanities Press, 1967.

Burt, C.   *Psychology and Psychical Research*. London: Society for Psychical Research, 1968.

Costa de Beauregard, O.   Quantum paradoxes and Aristotle's twofold information concept. In L. Oteri (Ed.), *Quantum Physics and Parapsychology*, pp. 91–102. New York: Parapsychology Foundation, 1975.

d'Espagnat, B.   *Conceptual Foundations of Quantum Mechanics*. Menlo Park, California: W. A. Benjamin, 1971. (a)

d'Espagnat, B.   Letter to the participants. *Proceedings of the International School of Physics "Enrico Fermi," Course IL*, pp. xiii–xiv. New York: Academic Press, 1971. (b)

d'Espagnat, B.   Mesure et non séparabilité. *Proceedings of the International School of Physics "Enrico Fermi," Course IL*, pp. 84–96. New York: Academic Press, 1971. (c)

Dobbs, H. A. C.   Time and ESP. *Proceedings of the Society for Psychical Research*, 1965, **54**, 249–361.

Dobbs, H. A. C.   The feasibility of a physical theory of ESP. In J. R. Smythies (Ed.), *Science and ESP*, pp. 225–254. New York: Humanities Press, 1967.

Ducasse, C. J.   Letter dated 23 March 1954. Pp. 220–221 in H. Hart, Six theories about apparitions. *Proceedings of the Society for Psychical Research*, 1956, **50**, 153–239.

Eastman, M.   Out-of-the-body experiences. *Proceedings of the Society for Psychical Research*, 1962, **53**, 287–309.

Eccles, J. C.   *The Neurophysiological Basis of Mind*. Oxford: Oxford University Press, 1953.

Eddington, A. S.   *Fundamental Theory*. Cambridge: Cambridge University Press, 1946.

Findlay, J. N.   *The Discipline of the Cave*. London: Allen and Unwin, 1966.

Hadamard, J.   *The Psychology of Invention in the Mathematical Field*. Princeton: Princeton University Press, 1945.

Hempel, C. G.   *Aspects of Scientific Explanation*. New York: Free Press, 1965.

Heywood, R.   Attitudes to death in the light of dreams and other out-of-the-body experience. In A. Toynbee and others, *Man's Concern with Death*, pp. 185–218. New York: McGraw-Hill, 1968.

Husserl, E.   *Ideas: General Introduction to Pure Phenomenology*. (Trans. by W. R. Boyce Gibson.) London: Allen and Unwin, 1931.

Husserl, E.   *Ideen zu einer reinen Phänomenologie, II*. The Hague: Nijhoff, 1958. (a)

Husserl, E.   *Die Idee der Phänomenologie*. The Hague: Nijhoff, 1958. (b)

Jauch, J. M.   Foundation of quantum mechanics. *Proceedings of the International School of Physics "Enrico Fermi," Course IL*, pp. 20–55. New York: Academic Press, 1971.

Johnson, R. C.   *The Imprisoned Splendour*. London: Hodder and Stoughton, 1953.

Jung, C. G. *Synchronicity, An A-Causal Connecting Principle*. London: Routledge and Kegan Paul, 1972.

Kant, I. *Critique of Pure Reason*. (Trans. by N. Kemp–Smith.) London: Macmillan, 1933.

Kuhn, T. S. *The Structure of Scientific Revolutions*. Chicago: University of Chicago Press, 1962.

Landé, A. The decline and fall of quantum dualism. *Philosophy of Science*, 1971, **38**, 221–223.

Ludwig, G. The measuring process and an axiomatic foundation of quantum mechanics. *Proceedings of the International School of Physics "Enrico Fermi," Course IL*, pp. 287–315. New York: Academic Press, 1971.

Margenau, H. ESP in the framework of modern science. *Journal of the American Society for Psychical Research*, 1966, **60**, 214–228.

McCreery, C. *Science, Philosophy and ESP*. London: Faber and Faber, 1967.

McDougall, W. Presidential Address. *Proceedings of the Society for Psychical Research*, 1920, **31**, 105–123.

McDougall, W. *The Group Mind*. Cambridge: Cambridge University Press, 1939.

Messiah, A. *Quantum Mechanics, Volume II*. New York: Wiley, 1962.

Moriarty, A. E., and Murphy, G. Some thoughts about prerequisite conditions or states in creativity and paranormal experience. *Journal of the American Society for Psychical Research*, 1967, **61**, 203–218.

Murphy, G. The problem of repeatability in psychical research. *Journal of the American Society for Psychical Research*, 1971, **65**, 3–16.

Myers, F. W. H. *Human Personality and its Survival of Bodily Death*. London: Longmans, Green, 1903. 2 vols.

Palmer, J., and Vassar, C. ESP and out-of-the-body experiences: An exploratory study. *Journal of the American Society for Psychical Research*, 1974, **68**, 257–280.

Pars, L. A. *A Treatise on Analytical Dynamics*. London: Heinemann, 1965.

Piron, C. Observables in general quantum theory. *Proceedings of the International School of Physics "Enrico Fermi," Course IL*, pp. 274–286. New York: Academic Press, 1971.

Poincaré, H. *Science and Hypothesis*. London: Walter Scott Publishing Co., 1905.

Popper, K. R. Three views concerning human knowledge. In H. D. Lewis (Ed.), *Contemporary British Philosophy*, 355–388. London: Allen and Unwin, 1956.

Popper, K. R. Philosophy of science: A personal report. In C. A. Mace (Ed.), *British Philosophy in the Mid-Century*, 155–191. London: Allen and Unwin, 1957.

Poynton, J. C. Results of an out-of-the-body survey. In J. C. Poynton (Ed.), *Parapsychology in South Africa*, pp. 109–123. Johannesburg: South African Society for Psychical Research, 1975.

Pratt, J. G. Some notes for the future Einstein for parapsychology. *Journal of the American Society for Psychical Research*, 1974, **68**, 133–155.

Price, H. H. Mind over mind and mind over matter. *Enquiry*, 1949, **2**, 20–27.

Price, H. H. Survival and the idea of "another world." *Proceedings of the Society for Psychical Research*, 1953, **50**, 1–25.

Ransom, C. Recent criticisms of parapsychology: A review. *Journal of the American Society for Psychical Research*, 1971, **65**, 289–307.

Rhine, J. B. Telepathy and other untestable hypotheses. *Journal of Parapsychology*, 1974, **38**, 137–153.

Robertson, H. P. Cosmological theory. In A. Mercier and M. Kervaire (Eds.), *Jubilee of Relativity Theory, Proceedings*, pp. 128–145. Basel: Birkhäuser, 1956.

Schiff, L. I. *Quantum Mechanics*. New York: McGraw-Hill, 1955.

Schmidt, H. Quantum processes predicted. *New Scientist*, October 16, 1969, 114–115.

Schmidt, H. Mental influence on random events. *New Scientist*, June 24, 1971, 757–758.

Schmidt, H. PK tests with a high-speed random number generator. *Journal of Parapsychology*, 1973, **37**, 105–118.

Seeds, N. W., and Vatter, A. E. Synaptogenesis in reaggregating brain cell culture. *Proceedings of the National Academy of Sciences*, 1971, **68**, 3219–3222.

Sidgwick, E. M. (Mrs. H.). Phantasms of the living. . . . *Proceedings of the Society for Psychical Research*, 1923, **33**, 23–429.

Smuts, J. C. *Holism and Evolution*. London: Macmillan, 1926.

Swedenborg, E. *Heaven and its Wonders and Hell*. (Trans. by J. C. Ager, revised by D. H. Harley.) London: The Swedenborg Society, 1958.

Tart, C. States of consciousness and state-specific sciences. *Science*, 1972, **176**, 1203–1210.

Thouless, R. H. *Experimental Psychical Research*. Harmondsworth, England: Penguin Books, 1963.

Tyrrell, G. N. M. *Grades of Significance*. London: Rider, n.d. (ca. 1930).

Tyrrell, G. N. M. *The Personality of Man*. Harmondsworth, England: Penguin Books, 1947.

Tyrrell, G. N. M. *Apparitions*. London: Duckworth, 1953.

von Neumann, J. *Mathematical Foundations of Quantum Mechanics*. Princeton: Princeton University Press, 1955.

von Weizsäcker, C. F. The Copenhagen interpretation. In T. Bastin (Ed.), *Quantum Theory and Beyond*, pp. 25–31. Cambridge: Cambridge University Press, 1971. (a)

von Weizsäcker, C. F. The unity of physics. In T. Bastin (Ed.), *Quantum Theory and Beyond*, pp. 229–262. Cambridge: Cambridge University Press, 1971. (b)

Walker, E. H. Foundations of paraphysical and parapsychological phenomena. In L. Oteri (Ed.), *Quantum Physics and Parapsychology*, pp. 1–44. New York: Parapsychology Foundation, 1975.

West, D. J. *Psychical Research Today*. London: Duckworth, 1962.

Weyl, H. *Philosophy of Mathematics and Natural Science*. Princeton: Princeton University Press, 1949.

White, R. A. A comparison of old and new methods of response to targets in ESP experiments. *Journal of the American Society for Psychical Research*, 1964, **58**, 21–56.

Whitehead, A. N. *Science and the Modern World*. Cambridge: Cambridge University Press, 1926.

Whiteman, J. H. M. *The Mystical Life*. London: Faber and Faber, 1961.

Whiteman, J. H. M. Evidence of survival from "other-world" experiences. *Journal of the American Society for Psychical Research*, 1965, **59**, 160–166.

Whiteman, J. H. M. *Philosophy of Space and Time*. London: Allen and Unwin, 1967.

Whiteman, J. H. M. The phenomenology of observation and explanation in quantum theory. In T. Bastin (Ed.), *Quantum Theory and Beyond*, pp. 71–84. Cambridge: Cambridge University Press, 1971.

Whiteman, J. H. M. Quantum theory and parapsychology. *Journal of the American Society for Psychical Research*, 1973, **67**, 341–360.

Whiteman, J. H. M. Parapsychology as an analytico-deductive science. In L. Oteri (Ed.), *Quantum Physics and Parapsychology*, pp. 181–197. New York: Parapsychology Foundation, 1975.

Whiteman, J. H. M. The scientific evaluation of out-of-the-body experience. In J. C. Poynton (Ed.), *Parapsychology in South Africa*, pp. 95–108. Johannesburg: South African Society for Psychical Research, 1975. (b)

Wigner, E. P. The role of invariance principles in natural philosophy. In E. P. Wigner (Ed.), *Proceedings of the International School of Physics "Enrico Fermi," Course XXIX*, pp. ix–xvi. New York: Academic Press, 1964.

Wigner, E. P. The subject of our discussions. In B. d'Espagnat (Ed.), *Proceedings of the International School of Physics "Enrico Fermi," Course IL*, pp. 1-19. New York: Academic Press, 1971.

Zeh, H. D. On the irreversibility of time and observation in quantum theory. In B. d'Espagnat (Ed.), *Proceedings of the International School of Physics "Enrico Fermi," Course IL*, pp. 263-273. New York: Academic Press, 1971.

5

Parapsychology and Philosophy

John Beloff

INTRODUCTION

While there may be some argument as to how exactly one should construe the word *paranormal*, there would, I think, be general agreement that parapsychology is the empirical study of supposedly paranormal phenomena. No such agreement can be expected with regard to the definition of philosophy. For it is in the nature of philosophy to query all our concepts including, of course, that of philosophy itself. In discussing the relationship between parapsychology and philosophy it is necessary, therefore, to begin by making clear what, essentially, one understands by philosophy. We may compare two opposing schools of thought on this issue that have been influential in recent times. According to one view, that associated with the so-called ordinary language school, none of the findings of empirical science could have any bearing on the questions which are of concern to the philosopher. Philosophy may best be regarded, from this angle, as a form of mental hygiene whose object is to prevent people from falling into, or to rescue them from, the snares that come from the misuse of language. In special peril are those other philosophers who still cling to the belief that philosophy is concerned with certain general truths about the world or those scientists who step outside their own particular discipline to expatiate on the nature of reality. In short, philosophy is there to stop people from talking nonsense. It is for the philosopher to point out when the scientist is violating the common usage of some key word or offending against some rule of logic. Since the parapsychologist is peculiarly prone to talk nonsense he stands in special need of the services of the philosopher. But that is the extent of the relationship between science and philosophy.

A more traditional and more widely accepted view of philosophy is one that sees its primary role as that of providing a particular world-view or, if that seems too grand an objective, at least of providing answers to certain recurrent questions of a very general and far-reaching kind. It recognizes that much of philosophical activity is of an analytical and critical kind but that this should be subordinate to its synthetic and constructive aims. Philosophical problems are typically those that arise when there is a conflict between different ways of looking at the same set of facts and when there is no agreed basis for deciding which way is correct. This is why the classic problems of philosophy are so resistant to solution, although the unrelenting attempts to solve them have kept philosophy from withering away. On this view of philosophy, its relationship with the sciences is of a more intimate nature. The advances in scientific knowledge very often set the scene in which the philosophical issues have to be debated. One has only to think of the way in which the classic problem of free will and determinism has been fueled by the relentless encroachment of science into areas previously the preserve of moral and humanistic modes of thought.

It follows that, for those who take the first view, who see philosophy as concerned primarily with the proper use of language, the parapsychological evidence is either an irrelevancy or else a case requiring a conceptual disinfectant (Flew, 1953; French, 1975). On the second view, on the contrary, parapsychology, just because it contradicts so much that is part of both conventional science and common sense, is, or should be, of the utmost philosophical relevance. And yet it must be granted that the great debates that occupied the center of the European philosophical stage in its post-Cartesian phase proceeded with scant regard for the paranormal. Insofar as paranormal contingencies entered into the arguments at all it was in an hypothetical sense. With the bifurcation of European thought in the seventeenth century into the daylight world of reason which was the abode of the philosopher and scientist and the twilight world of archaic magical and occult beliefs, this was, no doubt, inevitable. Individual philosophers might turn aside to peer into this twilight world (Broad, 1950), but in none of the major systems of European philosophy do we find any clear recognition of the paranormal powers of mind. This contrasts sharply with the philosophical systems of India, rooted as they are in mysticism rather than in science. Only to the extent that the paranormal is represented in the supernaturalist or miraculous aspects of Christian religion and theology, which formed a permanent intellectual background against which European philosophy came to maturity, did it make any claim upon the attention of philosophers.

It was out of the conflict of science and religion that modern parapsychology emerged toward the end of the nineteenth century. At that time the progress of science seemed, to the layman at least, to point irrevocably toward a mechanistic world-view and a materialist view of mind. One way of resisting this conclusion was that taken by the Idealist philosophers. But, since their attempt to turn materialism on its head and show that reality was at bottom mindlike was wholly metaphysical in character, there was little need for them to invoke the existence of the paranormal in support of their position. A different way, however, was taken by Henry Sidgwick and those that followed him into the Society for Psychical Research and this was to use the methods and approach of the natural sciences in order to demonstrate the existence of nonphysical entities or principles and so challenge scientific materialism on its own ground (Broad, 1938). If parapsychology has so far failed to fulfill Sidgwick's aim of making paranormal phenomena entirely reputable, it has at least insured that they have remained problematical and cannot be ignored. This is the crucial service which parapsychology has performed for present-day philosophy of mind and philosophy of science (Mundle, 1967). But its achievement has resided preeminently in the patient accumulation of factual evidence and relevant case material, not as yet in any obvious theoretical advances. That parapsychology has not made more impact on science must be put down to the fact that the evidence so far, even the so-called experimental evidence, exists in the form of isolated case-studies. There is still no repeatable experiment on the basis of which any competent investigator can verify a given phenomenon for himself. In these circumstances the scientific community has preferred to stand aloof rather than commit itself on findings which, even if authentic, it could see no way to make intelligible.

The philosophical world likewise remained largely indifferent. Philosophers of the logical empiricist and allied schools, Russell, Carnap, Popper, etc., who looked to science as the exemplification of well-founded knowledge, had little to say on the question of the paranormal, but neither did those who, from the neo-Idealist standpoint, dwelt on the limitations of the scientific outlook, e.g., Whitehead or Polanyi. Parapsychology fared no better with the philosophers of the Existentialist schools that flourished on the Continent, who took their point of departure, not from science, but from actual experience in the real world. As for the ordinary language philosophers who followed in the wake of the later Wittgenstein and dominated Oxford during the ascendancy of Ryle and Austin, we have already alluded to their negative attitude. If one compares, say, the profound effect which the Freudian doctrines had on modern philosophy of mind with the relative lack of influence of parapsychology, even though the evidential basis of the former was in some respects much more open to question than that of the latter, it would, I think, be safe to say that the course of Western philosophy in the twentieth century would not have been appreciably different had there been no such thing as parapsychology. Those philosophers who did take an interest in the field and whose thinking was decisively affected in consequence were few and far between· and, whatever their claims to distinction might be, I doubt if any of them could be regarded as of central importance to modern philosophical thought. Some of the names that spring to mind in this connection are those of James, Bergson, Broad, Price, and Ducasse. Of these, Broad was, in my opinion, the most important (Broad, 1935, 1949; Ducasse, 1959).

But, if the actual interchange between parapsychology and philosophy has so far been slight and peripheral, this was not, I would suggest, due to any intrinsic reasons, but rather to the low level of credibility under which parapsychology labored. If parapsychology were, once and for all, to solve its authentication problem and become accepted generally as an incontestable body of knowledge, its impact on philosophy would, I surmise, soon become very pronounced and it, in turn, would stand to gain from the enhanced interest of the philosophers. In the remainder of this chapter I will endeavor, within the brief space at my disposal, to substantiate this conjecture by considering certain specific philosophical issues and seeing how they might be affected by taking more account of the parapsychological evidence. It is important from the outset, however, to appreciate how any set of contingent facts, be they normal or paranormal, relate to philosophical arguments. It should be obvious, in the first place, that they can never rebut such arguments if only because it is never the facts that are at issue but rather the construction that is to be put on them. If it were the facts that were decisive, we should know that it was a scientific hypothesis that we were dealing with, not a philosophical issue. The only way that a philosophical argument can be rebutted is by showing that it is internally inconsistent, that it leads eventually to a contradiction. What the empirical evidence can hope to do is to change the intellectual climate in which the controversy takes place and, in so doing, deprive a particular argument of its force and rationale. Assuming that the argument in question is coherent, it will still be tenable, no matter what the evidence may reveal, but, in the light of it, it may well come to seem pointless and will gradually lose its adherents. In what follows, I shall discuss four particular philosophical problems to illustrate my thesis.

THE MATERIALIST THEORY OF MIND

Cooper (1976) is perfectly correct in pointing out that the existence of ESP is not incompatible with a materialist theory of mind, not even if, for the sake of argument, we concede to the parapsychologist that ESP could never be explained in physical terms. This is not, however, as he seems to imply, due to some special resilience in the theory but follows from the very point w' have just considered, namely, that no contingent truth can ever be logically incompatible with any purely philosophical thesis. Yet even Cooper who, though open-minded about ESP, makes no secret of his commitment to materialism, acknowledges that "the general picture of the universe that the sort of person attracted to materialism had favoured has no room for ESP." But this is no mere historical accident.

There would be little point, purely in the interests of parsimony, to insist upon the identity of mind and brain if, behind this maneuver, there had not been a growing expectation that the entire range of mental capacities and processes would eventually yield to an explanation in terms of brain physiology. To the extent that the parapsychological findings cast doubt upon this prospect, they can hardly do otherwise than weaken the force and rationale of the materialist theory of mind.

It is intriguing that, in the same volume as Cooper argues his case, Lewis (1976) contends, *per contra,* that the materialist theory of mind is so inherently implausible that it is quite unnecessary to invoke psychic phenomena in order to demolish it. "If materialsim is false," he declares, "it must be shown to be so as a general account of behaviour and consciousness. If we fail to do this we cannot turn as a last resort to psychical research." Undoubtedly Lewis has a point here. Philosophers have argued forcibly on various grounds that the mind-brain identity theory, in any of its several versions that have been canvassed, is logically incoherent. To take one example, it has been pointed out that there are a great many things that can be said about our ordinary everyday mental processes that would make no sense at all if said about their corresponding brain processes. A thought, for instance, can always be said to be *about* something, but an electrical impulse in the neural circuits of the brain can scarcely be said to be *about* anything, it just *is.* Hence to equate mental events with brain events is to violate Leibniz' law of identity according to which whatever may be said about the one side of the equation must be applicable to the other side. Realization of this difficulty had led some materialists to shift from an identity theory to an "eliminative" theory according to which all talk about mental entities, processes, etc., can, in the last resort, be dispensed with as just so much outmoded theory on a par with talk about demons (Rorty, 1970). This solution of the mind-body problem, however, faces precisely the same objections that have led most philosophers to reject behaviorism, for not only is it contradicted by experience, but it allows no possibility of distinguishing between a person and a hypothetical insentient automaton that behaved just like a person. Any particular set of beliefs or theories, whether concerned with demons or with anything else, is always in principle dispensable. But what of the act of belief itself? We are surely in precisely the same position as Descartes found himself when he discovered that he could doubt anything except that he was doubting.

But, whether or not the materialist theory of mind can or cannot be formulated in a logically coherent way, the fact is that, outside the ranks of the professional philosophers, it has never been this aspect of materialism that has been influential. To the scientist and to the layman alike, what counts is the much vaguer idea that, whether we call mind a function of the brain or an epiphenomenon of brain processes, our mental life is wholly dependent upon the workings of the brain and has no autonomy of its own. It is materialism in this sense, i.e., as the denial of interactionist dualism, that has colored the outlook of modern man, not the misspent ingenuity of philosophers seeking to make materialsm proof against the criticisms of their fellow philosophers. And it is materialism in this sense that is undermined by the findings of the parapsychologists. For if it is true that people can acquire information about the world other than through any of the known sensory channels, or physically affect the world other than through any of the known effectors, then we are confronted with properties of mind which cannot plausibly be incorporated into a physiology of the brain (Price, 1949).

TELEOLOGY VERSUS MECHANISM

There is a whole cluster of problems in contemporary philosophy of mind that revolve around the question of explaining human actions. According to one school of thought, represented by miscellaneous materialists, determinists, and behaviorists, human behavior is no different from anything else in nature in being subject to the same categories of explanation as figure in any of the natural sciences. According to the opposing school of thought, which includes both the ordinary language philosophers as well as assorted teleologists and libertarians, actions can never be explained mechanistically in terms of causes for the simple reason that an action can be defined only in terms of its ends, as represented by the agent's intentions, and can therefore never be reduced to any sequence of movements which the agent may or may not execute in the performance of the action. Without an aim or intention no set of movements could ever amount to an action; conversely, granted the aim or intention there is always an indefinite range of such movements that would exemplify the action in question.

Within the teleological camp, however, there is a division of opinion as to whether this analysis implies that human behavior is free in some ultimate sense that would contradict physical determinism or whether the two positions are ultimately compatible and represent no more than two different ways of looking at one and the same set of facts, two different levels of explanation. The libertarians who believe in free will as a metaphysical reality, not just as a subjective experience, argue that actions are free in this absolute or contra-causal sense. The compatibilists or "soft determinists," on the other hand, argue that, while actions only become meaningful when interpreted in a teleological sense, this does not preclude the possibility that all the purely physical events involved conform to the deterministic assumptions of science. I shall now suggest that considerations deriving from parapsychology may be relevant to the issue between compatibilists and libertarians.

Consider PK. One feature which stands out from almost any instance of PK that one could cite from the literature is the following: A certain end is achieved without the subject ever being aware as to exactly how it was achieved. Furthermore, even if the subject did know how it was achieved, he would be in no better position to succeed with the task than if he did not know. The task might involve trying to bias the output of an electronic random number generator or it might be the healing of certain scars in the tissues of a living organism; what alone seems to be relevant is the setting up of an intention to attain a given target. Given the end in view, it seems to make not the slightest difference whether the physical conditions, which govern the means whereby that end is to be realized, are varied, without so much as informing the subject, from one run to the next. This aspect of PK has always been familiar to parapsychologists but, surprisingly, few before Schmidt (1974) have had the insight to realize its implications. Hitherto, the preferred way of conceptualizing the PK situation was to suppose that PK was invariably accompanied by clairvoyance. The PK was responsible for the actual physical effects, but the clairvoyance gave the subject the feedback, albeit at an unconscious level, necessary to apply the appropriate pushes and pulls as required. The analogy with ordinary sensorimotor tasks scarcely needs stressing. However, the weakness of such a conceptualization is not only that is is extraordinarily cumbersome but it implies a degree of efficiency of clairvoyance for which we simply have no independent evidence from the experiments designed specifically to test for clairvoyance. For, unless we suppose that the subject's clairvoyance is exceedingly accurate, and can function moreover at the microscopic level, it would be useless in guiding the energy exchanges involved in the PK. An enormous simplification is achieved, therefore, if we drop this paramechanical model altogether and agree to regard PK as an *inherently* teleological process; in other words, as a process in nature in which the means are *literally* governed by the ends.

If this teleological model of PK were to be accepted, it would throw a flood of light on our understanding of the ordinary purposeful actions that characterize human behavior. Thus, when we raise our arm, we know no more about the specific nerve fibers that have to be activated than Schmidt's subjects know about the construction of his random number generator. In normal action, it is always open to the physical determinist to argue that what actually causes the relevant nerve cells to fire is not anything mental, i.e., the intention in the mind of the agent, but rather his specific brain state of which the intention is but a subjective reflection. In the case of a paranormal action, on the other hand, this option is cut off since, *ex hypothesi*, every physical link between the subject's brain and the target system is presumed to have been excluded. If the recent advances in PK research were to become more widely known and accepted and began to figure in the deliberations of philosophers, it would seem more reasonable to drop the supposition of a cryptic physiological determinism in the case of normal action and to treat alike the normal and paranormal case as not merely teleological in character (about which there is no dispute), but as radically teleological in nature.

PERSONAL IDENTITY

The large literature on the philosophical problem of personal identity abounds in arguments that rely on hypothetical or imaginary instances, on the use of the "what if *per impossibile*" clause. What if I were suddenly to lose all my personal memories? What if, overnight, I developed a brand new personality? What if you and I were to swap bodies? What if I were suddenly to vanish and then rematerialize elsewhere? What if I were to witness my own funeral? (Flew, 1956; French, 1975). What if I were to persist in a disembodied form? (Penelhum, 1970) What if in a previous incarnation I was someone else, or if in a future incarnation I shall be someone else?

The point of all such questions is the same, namely, to test what weight our rather vague notion of a self will carry. With each new supposition we introduce one further breach in the continuity which we normally take for granted when assigning personal identity. Whether this continuity consists in the psychological connectedness associated with our personal memories or our abiding traits and dispositions or whether it is a physical continuity associated with the body, once the continuity is broken, if only by means of such a thought-experiment, we can no longer avoid asking ourselves whether it would be the same self that would exist on either side of this divide. The temptation to say "yes" is strong, and yet there are serious misgivings as to whether, by stretching the concept of the self beyond all the bounds of sense, our imagination may not have betrayed us and landed us in a looking-glass world of pure nonsense (Williams, 1968).

On the one hand, nothing would appear to be simpler than to imagine oneself engaged in time-travel, meeting the illustrious figures of history or visiting the Earth at some future period. Yet a moment's reflection is enough to show that this fantasy of the past or future contains one fatal anachronism that at one stroke destroys its logical coherence, namely, our own presence in that imaginary situation. We might arguably acquire direct knowledge of a past or future, but we cannot for logical reasons intervene in it. Is the same true of those examples in which some essential identity is supposed to persist through every conceivable empirical change of circumstances? If it is, the logical fallacy has still to be pointed out. Meanwhile philosophers remain undecided. Some find such questions meaningful (Lewis, 1969; Chap. 11); others dismiss them as nonsensical.

For the reasons we have already given, the parapsychological evidence cannot solve the problem of personal identity or any other such philosophical problem. What it can do is to inject a note of urgency into the controversy which no number of purely hypothetical examples could ever do. Of special interest in this connection is the problem of reincarnation which, thanks to the researches of Stevenson (1974, 1975), has acquired an evidential status such as it could not have had as a mere article of religious faith or occult belief. Since survival, in this case, is of an embodied kind, it avoids the arguments about individuation that have clung to the case of disembodied survival (Penelhum, 1970). At the same time there is, *ex hypothesi,* no physical continuity between the existing and the previous personality. The identification depends in the first place on a psychological continuity, the claimed memories of the past life, the correspondences in the personality of the two individuals, or, in some cases, certain bodily signs such as birthmarks, etc. None of this compels us to postulate a numerical identity; given an unlimited set of paranormal hypotheses to play with plus the long arm of coincidence there will always be other possible ways of interpreting the facts, assuming the facts are as alleged in the first place. But, at some unspecifiable point, it becomes the simplest interpretation of the facts (Ducasse, 1961, Part V). And, once we adopt it, once we have made the move from a "reincarnationist type case" to "a case of reincarnation," then there is no logical reason, even where there is no memory of any past life, why the hypothesis of such a previous existence should be discarded as meaningless. The problem of personal identity would persist but the debate would continue in a changed intellectual climate.

PRECOGNITION

My final example takes us beyond the philosophy of mind and raises questions of a fundamental cosmological nature. If the phenomenon of precognition were more common and more widely credited, it would be hard to see how we could preserve what I shall call the common-sense view of time. Indeed, it is precisely because the phenomenon threatens to overturn so much that seems indispensable in our ideas of time, causation, and so on, that philosophers, including some who are generally sympathetic to parapsychology, have questioned whether precognition, if taken literally to mean foreknowledge, is not an inherently incoherent idea like the kindred idea of time-travel which we have already discussed (Broad, 1967). Even some parapsychologists in the teeth of the empirical evidence have preferred to resort to certain expedients, at no matter what cost in deviousness and general implausibility, rather than acknowledge as meaningful a literal awareness of future events (Roll, 1961). Now, if it should turn out that the concept of precognition is, indeed, self-contradictory, then, of course, no amount of empirical evidence can save it; like time-travel, it would be a flawed concept, and we would be forced to look for alternative conceptualizations of the facts. I believe, however, that if we examine closely the arguments that have been put forward so far purporting to show that precognition is a logical impossibility, we shall find that none of them are valid. In that case the only question that remains is not whether precognition could occur but whether it ever does occur. And, if it does occur, then the common-sense view of time must be at fault.

I have space only to consider some of the more salient philosophical objections that have been voiced against the acceptance of precognition. A simple but persistent objection may be put as follows: How could I become aware of an event which, by definition, does not yet exist to be the object of my awareness or otherwise influence events in the present? This objection, however, begs the question, which is precisely whether, in some sense, the future *does* exist. Common sense holds that the future is open and unreal, that, of this instant, there exists only the potentiality that certain events may come about. But this is an assumption, and it has to be weighed against the alternative assumption on which a "realist" view of the future, as I would call it, is based. According to the realist view, the "now-point" of time is as relative to the observer's viewpoint as the "here" of space and is in no sense an objective feature of the space-time continuum in which what we are pleased to call "past, present, and future" events exist timelessly as a single four-dimensional or multidimensional block universe. This realist view, which the theory of relativity did much to promote, is defended on grounds that have nothing to do with precognition (Smart, 1963, Chap. 7).

A somewhat subtler and tougher objection runs as follows: Precognition implies backward causation since the event precognized is here assumed to be the cause of the subject precognizing it. But, if we allow backward causation we are implying that something we can do now could alter something which has already occurred in the past, and this is manifestly absurd (Gale, 1965). Just how absurd it is is sometimes brought home by pointing out that this would allow for the possibility that I could prevent myself from ever having been born. Yet, despite the number of eminent philosophers who have been swayed by this backward causation argument, it is, as Brier (1974) has painstakingly shown, based on a confusion. Certainly we cannot alter the past, what has been has been, but, if we are satisfied that an event at time t_0 would not have occurred *but for* an event at subsequent time t_1, we have all we need to postulate backward causation. After all, the future can no more be altered than the past, what will be will be, but, unless we are total fatalists, we would all accept that what we do now can have a bearing on what will happen and, similarly, there is no logical reason why what has happened should not depend on what we do now.

Of course this does not mean that backward causation is just as likely to occur as forward causation. Indeed, with certain marginal exceptions in the domain of quantum theory, it may be doubted whether we know of any instance in nature of backward causation other, that is, than the special case of precognition which is here in question. That is why we regard precognition as paranormal. But it is enough, for our present purposes, that, logically, precognition could occur. It may be pointed out here, parenthetically, that the existence of backward causation does nothing to support either determinism or fatalism. It may well be a free action of mine at time $_1$ that caused someone to precognize it at time t_0 (Brier, 1976).

Perhaps the one logical difficulty that does still cling to the concept of precognition is the intervention paradox. Traditionally, prophecy was always treated more as a form of warning than as a direct statement about the future. Consequently, if the precognition is unwelcome, and I am not a fatalist, I am likely to take steps to prevent its fulfillment. But here lies the rub. If nothing that I do makes any difference, then I have no option but to accept fatalism. If, on the other hand, I am successful and the disaster is averted, then the precognition was, at best, inaccurate. But, in that case, what was it that was precognized? For, had the ostensible precognition been entirely mistaken, how could it have helped me to avoid what otherwise would have been the consequences? Here the straightforward realist view of time does not seem able to provide a satisfactory answer. To say simply that the precognition was only partially veridical fails to do justice to the fact that, had it not been for my energetic intervention, the precognition might have been wholly veridical. Perhaps what we need is something more like a branching universe full of potential futures. Then which one becomes actual, which pathway the universe takes at any given juncture, is made to depend on whether a particular intervention does or does not take place. But this is a complex issue, and I cannot pursue it further here. I trust, however, enough has already been said to support my contention, as against Flew (1959, 1967), that the acceptance of precognition disturbs the philosophical *status quo.*

REFERENCES

Brier, B. *Precognition and the Philosophy of Science: An Essay on Backward Causation.* New York: Humanities Press, 1974.

Brier, B. The metaphysics of precognition. In S. Thakur (Ed.), *Philosophy and Psychical Research*, pp. 46–58. London: Allen & Unwin, 1976.

Broad, C. D. Normal cognition, clairvoyance and telepathy. *Proceedings of the Society for Psychical Research*, 1935, **43**, 387–438. (Reprinted in Broad, 1969, see below.)

Broad, C. D. Henry Sidgwick and psychical research. *Proceedings of the Society for Psychical Research*, 1938, **45**, 131–161. (Reprinted in Broad, 1969, see below.)

Broad, C. D. The relevance of psychical research to philosophy. *Philosophy*, 1949, **24** 291–309. (Reprinted in Broad, 1969, see below.)

Broad, C. D. Immanuel Kant and psychical research. *Proceedings of the Society for Psychical Research*, 1950, **49**, 79–104. (Reprinted in Broad, 1969, see below.)

Broad, C. D. The notion of precognition. In J. R. Smythies (Ed.), *Science and ESP*, pp. 165–196. New York: Humanities Press, 1967.

Broad, C. D. *Religion, Philosophy and Psychical Research.* New York: Humanities Press, 1969.

Cooper, D. E. ESP and the materialist theory of mind. In S. Thakur (Ed.), *Philosophy and Psychical Research*, pp. 59–80. London: Allen & Unwin, 1976.

Ducasse, C. J. Broad on the relevance of psychical research to philosophy. In P. A. Schilpp (Ed.), *The Philosophy of C. D. Broad*, pp. 375–410. New York: Tudor, 1959.

Ducasse, C. J. *A Critical Examination of the Belief in a Life After Death.* Springfield, Ill.: Charles C Thomas, 1961.

Flew, A. *A New Approach to Psychical Research.* London: Watts, 1953.

Flew, A. Can a man witness his own funeral? *Hibbert Journal*, 1956, **54**, 242–252. (Reprinted in A. Flew, *The Presumption of Atheism.* London: Elek/Pemberton, 1976.)

Flew, A. Broad and supernormal precognition. In P. A. Schilpp (Ed.), *The Philosophy of C. D. Broad*, pp. 411–436. New York: Tudor, 1959.

Flew, A. Precognition, philosophical implications of. In *Encyclopedia of Philosophy*. (P. Edwards, Ed. in Chief.) New York: Macmillan and the Free Press, 1967.

French, P. A. Can a man imagine witnessing his own funeral? In P. A. French (Ed.), *Philosophers in Wonderland*, pp. 318–329. Saint Paul, Minn.: Llewellyn, 1975.

Gale, R. M. Why a cause cannot be later than its effect. *Review of Metaphysics*, 1965, **19**, 209–234.

Lewis, H. D. *The Elusive Mind*. London: Allen & Unwin, 1969.

Lewis, H. D. Religion and the paranormal. In S. Thakur (Ed.), *Philosophy and Psychical Research*, pp. 142–156. London: Allen & Unwin, 1976. Pp. 142–156.

Mundle, C. W. K. ESP phenomena, philosophical implications of. In *Encyclopedia of Philosophy*. (P. Edwards, Ed. in Chief.) New York: Macmillan and the Free Press, 1967.

Penelhum, T. *Survival and Disembodied Existence*. New York: Humanities Press, 1970.

Price, H. H. Psychical research and human personality. *Hibbert Journal*, 1949, 47, 105–130. (Reprinted in J. R. Smythies (Ed.), *Science and ESP*. New York: Humanities Press, 1967.)

Roll, W. G. The problem of precognition. *Journal of the Society for Psychical Research*, 1961, **41**, 115–128. See also comments on Roll's paper (*loc. cit.*, 173–183) and his reply (*loc. cit.*, 1963, 42, 6–16).

Rorty, R. Mind-body identity, privacy and categories. In C. V. Borst (Ed.), *The Mind/Brain Identity Theory*, pp. 187–213. London: Macmillan, 1970.

Schmidt, H. Comparison of PK action on two different random number generators. *Journal of Parapsychology*, 1974, 38, 37–55.

Smart, J. J. C. *Philosophy and Scientific Realism*. London: Routledge and Kegan Paul, 1963.

Stevenson, I. *Twenty Cases Suggestive of Reincarnation*. (2nd rev. ed.) Charlottesville: University Press of Virginia, 1974.

Stevenson, I. *Cases of the Reincarnation Type. Volume I. Ten Cases in India*. Charlottesville: University Press of Virginia, 1975.

Williams, B. Imagination and the self. In P. F. Strawson (Ed.), *Studies in Thought and Action*, pp. 192–213. London: Oxford University Press, 1968.

6

Parapsychology and Religion

Walter Houston Clark

INTRODUCTION

I have defined religion as "the inner experience of the individual when he senses a Beyond, especially as evidenced by the effect of this experience on his behavior when he actively attempts to harmonize his life with the Beyond." In connection with the definition I have tried to hint at some of the difficulties encountered when even two people try to agree on just what religion is (Clark, 1958, Chap 2). I will have in mind this definition when in this chapter I make some observations relative to the relationship of religion to parapsychology. Yet when the term *religion* is mentioned, the average person, scholar or otherwise, will think of attendance at church, theology, or some other structurally expressed aspect of the religious impulse. But equally important, if not more so, are the nonrational factors that, whatever their ultimate metaphysical origin, come to consciousness mediated by the profound and mysterious activities of an individual's unconscious.

Thus William James stated that "the mother sea and fountain-head of all religions lie in the mystical experiences of the individual. . . . All theologies and all ecclesiasticisms are secondary growths superimposed" (Allen, 1967, p. 425). While the rational mind interacts with and guides the nonrational, as I have pointed out elsewhere (Clark, Malony, Daane, and Tippett, 1973, pp. 8-11), it is the nonrational that supplies the energies and the metaphysical essences which the reason tries to govern and out of which it tries to make sense. Even though reason can never hope to track down and explain the ghostly origins of what might be called "life forces," there appear to be reasons to believe, as I will explain below, that whether expressed as paranormal phenomema or as religious experience, the ultimate source is the same.

HOW CAN THE PARANORMAL AND RELIGION BE LINKED?

In the source I have already cited (Clark et al., 1973, Chaps. 2, 7) I have discussed my reasons for emphasizing the importance of ecstatic experiences of many kinds in the origins of the religious life and, in particular, the importance of the mystical consciousness as religion in its most characteristic and essential form. Without mysticism I do not believe we would have religion as we know it, nor would the great religious faiths have demonstrated the durability that has characterized their many centuries of existence. It is true that all have demonstrated periods of greater and of lesser creativity punctuated with episodes of cruelty and error hardly to be attributed to the truly mystical temperament, but the saving grace of fresh infusions of energy and intuition from the mystics perennially have saved religions and the cultures in which they have been embedded from ultimate obscurity. For the purpose of this chapter, therefore, I am identifying religion with mysticism.

In linking mysticism with the paranormal I am greatly indebted to the writings of Lawrence LeShan, particularly his *Toward a General Theory of the Paranormal* (1969) and *The Medium, the Mystic, and the Physicist* (1974). In these two works he uses the criteria set up by Bertrand Russell as the identifying characteristics of the mystic's consciousness and attitudes. They are: (a) There is a better way of gaining information than through the senses. (b) There is unity of all things. (c) There is no reality to time. (d) All evil is mere appearance (LeShan, 1969, p. 15).

LeShan then goes on to demonstrate that these basic attitudes also characterize the consciousness of the psychic or "the clairvoyant reality," as he calls it. Much of the evidential material on which he relies is based on statements by the eminent psychic, the late Eileen Garrett. For example, he points out that her statement in trance that a man on a journey is at once his goal and the road he is following recalls Emerson's poem *Brahma* (LeShan, 1969, p. 32).

> They reckon ill who leave me out,
>   When me they fly, I am the wings.
> I am the doubter and the doubt.
>   I am the hymn the Brahmin sings

Though not so immediately germane to the subject of our chapter, an even more striking observation by LeShan is that modern quantum physicists, though approaching their tasks from a wholly different direction, also exhibit similarities with both the psychics and the mystics. The similarities between physicists and mystics he strikingly demonstrates in an appendix to *The Medium, the Mystic, and the Physicist*. In this he mixes statements on the nature of reality by both physicists and mystics. It is almost impossible for even an expert in either field, unless he recognizes a particular statement, to determine with certainty whether the statement comes from a mystic or a physicist. This will help to illuminate the high opinion of mysticism held by Albert Einstein, who declared it to be "the sower of all true science" and "the center of true religiousness," while those who are strangers to it are "as good as dead" (Frank, 1948, p. 340). We will have occasion to return to the evidence of the physicists later in the chapter.

However, it must be said that not all religious people will accept the relationship between religion and the paranormal. Particularly at times when specific churches or a wider religious movement have been threatened by an upsurge of interest in parapsychology, there have been warnings against the seeking of contacts with departed and disembodied spirits, and of clairvoyant roads to higher understanding. Points often made are that clear evidence for the existence of an afterlife removes the need for religious faith and that the Bible prohibits mediumistic activities. But even some of those favorably disposed toward mysticism, like W. T. Stace (1960, pp. 45–55), distinguish between mysticism and paranormal events often confused with it. Furthermore, it is alleged that spirits communicating from "the other side," who might be supposed to be spending their time drinking at the fountains of truth, do not often reflect this advantage when they are summoned by the living to speak to them. But whatever we may think of such arguments, in my opinion it is a fact that the paranormal, certainly to the discursive intelligence, should be and is to be distinguished from the mystical. But that there is some deep-seated, even remarkable, similarity between the mystical and the clairvoyant consciousness is a truth that LeShan has obliged us to ponder. His carefully documented monograph almost by itself is sufficient reason for us to declare a relationship at a very deep level between these two strange expressions of human consciousness.

However, there is some experimental work that suggests support for LeShan's thesis. Though the idea involves considerable controversy, it has been alleged that the psychedelic drugs will often release experiences of a mystical religious nature. In an encyclopedia article (Clark, 1974) I have reviewed the situation with respect to religious cults which have used psychoactive drugs and herbs both today and through the ages to stimulate what cannot be denied as religious experiences. In addition, I have attended and ingested peyote in a dignified and impressive American Indian ceremony, which both objectively and subjectively was more deeply religious than any church ritual I have known and with results that were unmistakably mystical.

Furthermore, the most scientifically designed and best controlled experiment ever carried out in the area of religious experience had as its aim the testing of whether or not psilocybin, the chief active principle of a Mexican mushroom long used in all night cultic ceremonies by Mexican Indian shamans, will trigger mystical experiences. This was a Harvard doctoral experiment by Walter N. Pahnke, M.D. (Pahnke and Richards, 1973) in which ten theological student volunteers were given psilocybin before being sent to a Good Friday service. Evidence was overwhelming that they had experienced mystical experience to a far deeper extent than ten controls given a placebo. I have followed up and confirmed these results (Clark 1969, Chap. 6; 1973, Chap. 1).

Also I discovered that the same questionnaire that revealed reports of mystical experiences showed that a clear majority reported both out-of-body (OB) experiences and extrasensory perception (ESP). Of these, 28 percent reported OBEs that were "beyond anything ever experienced or imagined" while 22 percent reported ESP experiences of a like intensity. All of those who reported the paranormal experiences also reported elements of profound mystical experiences to some degree. Thus, the same triggers that released mystical experiences often released paranormal experiences as well. They both seemed to issue from the same deep levels of the personalities involved.

These results then would seem to give some experimental support to LeShan's speculative contention that there is a close affinity between parapsychology and religion. Therefore, the presumption will be accepted for the rest of this chapter that there is both strong theoretical as well as experimental support for a deep and significant relationship between religion and the paranormal.

However, many of those who have never had access to sophisticated theses such as those of LeShan, will tend to see a gulf between the humdrum though respectable religious lives that most of them live and the experiences that parapsychology studies. It is perfectly possible, at least in the world of ordinary consciousness, to separate paranormal from religious occurrences. I have referred above to the fact that W. T. Stace does so in his discussion of mysticism, even though he does acknowledge a kind of "family relationship" between mystical and paranormal events. It is when one considers the nature of the paranormal more carefully than does the average observer that one senses the deep-lying kinship of which LeShan speaks.

But there is another much more ordinary and common phenomenon that points in the same direction. This is that after being surprised by an experience with the paranormal, many people will report subjectively, perhaps without being able to give a good reason for their feelings, that the experience was in fact religious.

PARAPSYCHOLOGY AND THE BIBLE

The sacred writings of various religious traditions report paranormal happenings. When these occur in the more historical sections of such writings, we can suspect such passages of carrying veridical echoes of what were the original facts. In very general and over-simplified terms it might be said that the truer to life the bulk of such narratives appear to be, the greater the likelihood that paranormal events recounted may be true.

Also, the more that similar events have been observed and verified in our own times, the greater the presumption of truth in the narrative, and vice versa. For example, since there is no verified modern parallel occurrence to the story of the prophet Elijah's defeat of the priests of Baal when, in response to prayer, fire from heaven was sent which not only consumed the sacrificial bullocks drenched with water but also "licked up the water that was in the trench" (I Kings, 18: 17–40), even the more open-minded scientific intelligences will probably bracket such wonders until they can be shown to be attestable.

The prophets, visionaries, or seers, looked on as specially selected by Jehovah to lead and direct His people, were identified in the Jewish Bible or Christian Old Testament as the descendants of Jacob, or Israel, himself a visionary, as attested by the precognitive dream of "Jacob's Ladder" (Gen. 28: 10-17) and the night-long wrestling with God in the form of a man (Gen. 32: 24–30). In these stories the reader will become conscious of a pervasive note of awe, quite characteristic of any human surprised by his first encounter with the paranormal. This awe is also associated with many mystical experiences, with their suggestion of a descent into madness, described as the *mysterium tremendum*, or the mystery that makes one tremble, described by Rudolf Otto in *The Idea of the Holy* (1958). In these cases the sense of wonder is tinged with a religious intimation of overwhelming significance. Some of these same characteristics are found mingled in Moses' experience before the burning bush (Ex. 3: 1-6). During an experiment in which I ingested psilocybin, I looked at a flower which resulted in an experience that subjectively persuaded me was identical with that described as occurring to Moses when he saw the bush that burned and "was not consumed."

In this same narrative God speaks to Moses "out of the midst of the bush" and directs him to return to his people and deliver them out of the hand of Pharaoh. When Moses asks God his name so that he may tell who has sent him, God says "I AM THAT I AM! · · · Thus shalt thou say unto the children of Israel, 'I AM hath sent me unto you'" (Ex. 3: 14). The reader of the Hebrew Bible or Old Testament will notice that the Hebrew God always speaks in accents of dynamic authority and vigor, the source of which seems to come from a dimension far deeper than that commonplace consciousness out of which we transact most of our thought exchanges and business with one another. This existential characterization of himself given by God in the foregoing passage gives us a clue to the roots of this authority in that it suggests the radical truths of Eternity, the sense that time is an illusion that LeShan says is shared by the psychic, the mystic, and the quantum physicist.

In the Gospel of John (8: 58) Jesus reflects these passages from Exodus when he says "Before Abraham was, I am." This statement, which makes nonsense of ordinary time sense, shows Jesus to have participated in the mystical consciousness. To this kind of consciousness the ordinary man feels utterly strange. He has been brought up in the faith that "time is money!" That there might be a way of living which at one thrust sweeps away past, present, and future confuses and threatens him. Certainly intimations like this which could transform his "gentle Jesus" into a kind of freak with authority over both the future and the past, and the God, whom he always thought was on his side, into a Stranger whose awesome majesty derives partly from his dwelling place in Eternity, help to explain why the ordinary church-goer prefers his theology comforting, intellectualized, and bland. It also explains why even the average believers in the paranormal prefer this knowledge trivialized through wish fulfillment and an excessive gullibility.

The early stories of the Hebrew Patriarchs being partly mythological, it is hard to distinguish with precision their paranormal and mystical components except through the feeling tone for the numinous engendered by the exalted rhetoric so much better rendered by older translations like the King James Bible. Some sections of the Bible subsequent to Genesis and Exodus, being closer to history, tend to be more explicit and dependable. Such are the narratives found in the two Books of Samuel (See Moore, 1913, Chap. 10) in which historical reliability is suggested by the refusal of the sources to paint national heroes like Kings Saul and David as more than human. Here we find the story of the clairaudial calling of the child Samuel with the precognitive announcement of the Lord, "Behold, I will do a thing in Israel at which both the ears of everyone that heareth it will tingle" (I Sam. 3: 11).

We also have the story of how the young man Saul sought for the lost asses of his father and through the paranormal wisdom of the seer Samuel found himself the newly anointed King (I Sam. 9-10). Later on (Chap. 28) we have the story of this same King Saul, fearful and confused, breaking his own laws against witches by repairing at night to the witch at Endor, a medium who through a "familiar spirit," or control as we would call such today, calls up the apparition of the now dead Samuel, who predicts the defeat and death of the king. Such predictions could have been related after the fact, as is certainly the case in the Book of Daniel (Moore, 1913, Chap. 19), but it seems clear that the scribe believed in such happenings.

Another persistent paranormal theme throughout the Bible is that of healing. The dramatic story of the healing of the leper Naaman by Elisha through bathing in the waters of the Jordan river is a case in point (II Kings, 5). However, the most notable healer of Biblical times was Jesus of Nazareth. Unless one's attitude toward the Bible is that everything written therein should be accepted on faith without further scrutiny, or to the contrary, rejected as a series of fairy tales and nonsense, one is obligated to inquire how, in particular, the recorded paranormal events of the Bible could have occurred. I have already hinted at the indications that Jesus partook both of the clairvoyant and mystical attitudes toward reality. Elsewhere in this volume the reader will find chapters which give evidence that such healing takes place today and which discuss models of reality which help to explain such phenomena. J. C. Pearce (1971) produces evidence of these radically new ways of conceiving reality, into which the healing powers of Jesus are fitted by way of illustration.

LeShan (1974, pp. 99-167) not only gives illustrative evidence of psychic healing, but postulates two salient types of healing: one that occurs when the healer is in touch with clairvoyant reality, when the body repairs itself with much greater speed than is ordinarily the case, and an even more rapid, almost instantaneous, healing that occurs when the healer is in what LeShan calls "transpsychic" reality. Both are aided by a basic religious intention, but particularly the transpsychic healing, which only develops from a deeply moving mystical experience.

The healing "miracles" of Jesus seem to have been of the latter type, some of which occurred through actual touch, such as the woman with an issue of blood who was healed by touching his garment (Luke 8: 43-48), and some at a distance, as with the healing of the servant of the centurion (Luke 7: 2-10). We know that Christian bodies have sponsored healing clinics and have promoted the idea of psychic or "faith" healing both in words and sometimes by action; witness the well-known Roman Catholic healing shrine at Lourdes and the Christian Science church. Both have well-attested cures to their credit. Weatherhead (1951, Sec. 3) has given a constructively critical account of these and other healing movements with their well-documented successes.

THE SPIRITUALIST MOVEMENT

The foregoing discussion will serve as an important though inadequate explanation of the Spiritualist movement. It is important in that it has pointed to the essential and most durable of the forces and motives that have produced Spiritualism, inadequate in that such a brief discussion could hardly do justice to any considerable religious movement. For, such motives as wish-fulfillment, particularly through the promise of reunion with deceased loved-ones and a desire for personal survival, an interest in wonders, a desire for notoriety on the part of some leaders, ego-involvement, the need for fellowship, and a mixture of similar urges that are familiar to students of any religious movement are all important sources of the interest in Spiritualist churches.

The philosophical and spiritual ground in which nineteenth-century Spiritualism grew in America was dominated largely by the thinking of Emanuel Swedenborg, the eighteenth-century Swedish scientist and mystic, whose writings about his visions were stirring the spiritual waters of the early nineteenth century in America (Judah, 1967; Nelson, 1969). The seed which started Spiritualism growing as a self-conscious movement was the "spirit rappings" heard, and possibly produced, by the daughters of John Fox during 1848 in Hydesville, N.Y. Controversy arose about the genuineness of these phenomena in subsequent years, but at the time publicity given to the rappings led to the rapid rise of interest in the subject of the paranormal, some of which was scientific in nature, some mere curiosity, and some religious.

The latter led to the formations of many Spiritualist churches both in America and in England. Many cases of fraud were exposed, however, which hurt both the scientific and the religious interest in the paranormal. This led to the formation of societies as safeguards for the integrity of those who saw sound values in both of these movements. One of the most conservative of these, the National Spiritualist Association of Churches of the United States of America, was founded in 1893 and now has its headquarters in Milwaukee, Wisconsin. Since 1893 there have been schisms and the founding of new bodies. At this time the most visible expression of the movement is the Spiritual Frontiers Fellowship of Evanston, Illinois, not a church but with membership open to members of any religious organization or none at all.

This brief historical note has been given simply by way of emphasizing the fact that numbers of people do in fact see the paranormal as an important if not the chief building block in their personal religious faith.

SURVIVAL

The last section on the Spiritualist movement leads naturally to the subject of survival since this belief plays so large a part in the maintenance of Spiritualism. Swedenborg, through what he alleged were conversations with spirits and angels, gave detailed accounts of life after death, while Andrew Jackson Davis, a prolific writer influential with Spiritualists during the last century, wrote a book on life in what was called the "Summer-land" (1873), the presumed habitation of spirits after death, which contained rather detailed accounts of such matters as geography, language, and social intercourse there. Obviously such accounts are, at best, highly subjective.

Many people believe that there are traces in the universe of those who have died in such a form as occasionally to become visible and audible to those who are alive. Many well-attested cases can be found in the classic *Human Personality and its Survival of Bodily Death* by the English scholar Frederic W. H. Myers (1903, especially in Chap. 7). Even more careful and conservative is the American psychologist Gardner Murphy, who provides cases and a discussion of problems in *The Challenge of Psychical Research* (1961). (See also the chapter on survival in this volume by Alan Gauld.)

A special case of the idea of survival is to be found in the theories and beliefs surrounding reincarnation, to be distinguished from discarnate survival. Reincarnation is a very ancient concept. Among the Greeks it is found in Pythagoras and in Plato's *The Republic* and *Phaedrus* as well as among Eastern religions (Howe, 1974). Since it has been considered a heresy by most Christian churches from early times and is generally absent from the Jewish faith except among Kabbalists, it has never been quite respectable in the West. However, the modern interest in Eastern religion has given the idea a new impetus.

Since few people, if any, remember their presumed past incarnations with any distinctness, reincarnation makes a difficult field for research. Nevertheless, there have been a few careful and thorough investigators in the area, of which one is Ian Stevenson (1974). (See also the chapter on Reincarnation by Dr. Stevenson in this volume).

Obviously, the concept of reincarnation ethically and religiously performs much the same function as the idea of Heaven and Hell. These two differing concepts of the afterlife satisfy the average man's sense of justice. If a man spends his life in having a good time with no concern for right and justice and with no sensitivity to the suffering his behavior inflicts on his neighbor, those who have to endure the suffering will not be happy with the idea of a continuation of such inequity in a future life. Thoughts of Heaven and Hell will tend to warm the hearts of the earthly sufferers, and at the same time they warn those who aim to make life a succession of good times.

There are many believing in Heaven and Hell who look on these places not in the literal sense but simply as a myth that connotes much more than the bare idea can say, yet serving similar purposes. The same might be said for reincarnation, and its supporters will point out that subtle gradations in merit may more easily be taken care of in the case of reincarnation unless the idea of Purgatory is also accepted as a preparation for Heaven. Believers in Spiritualism are much more apt to take these concepts literally, and those who prefer the reincarnational model are quick to point out that no one could stand a life in Heaven as conventionally depicted for more than few days without being bored to death. Hell would not necessarily be preferable, but from almost any point of view reincarnation would seem to make more sense.

I have deliberately made my argument crass for purposes of clarity and have neglected the soaring or profound subtleties that cluster around these two approaches to immortality at their best. For they too can stir our perceptions to awareness of that undiscovered country that lies within us yet is as unknown as the heart of Africa. Once again it is only the mystic, the psychic, or perhaps the physicist who catches glimpses of his inner self when, like a carousel, the world of consciousness rolls round to disclose a universe wholly different from that to which most of us are accustomed.

Those who wish to arbitrate for themselves between these two models for a future life can do two things. First, examine the scientific evidence carefully gathered by such as Myers and Stevenson. Second, read the evidence of the seers and the mystics, like Swedenborg in his *Heaven and Hell* (see Van Dusen, 1974) or even Andrew Jackson Davis in his accounts of the Summer-land. It is necessary to add the insights of the mystics, who are forced to be the poets of the religious life if they are to speak about it at all, or the scientists who, like Einstein, possess the hearts of poets. Then, taking everything into consideration, such persons will come to the conclusion as to which view of the Beyond is that which is preferable for them. It is in this way that the study of parapsychology may be a practical step toward a religious decision.

NEGATIVE ASPECTS

There are many critical things that can be said of the paranormal approach to religion, despite the fact that the more sensitive psychics and researchers are often men and women of rare religious power and insight, like Swedenborg or F. W. H. Myers. But there are many church people and Spiritualists whose interest in the paranormal seems to distract them from the true spiritual and mystical goals of religion. Sometimes this is betrayed by a too explicit interest in what Heaven is like, along with a credulous recital of inconsequentialities gleaned from the control of a real or supposed medium. Such things help to explain the warnings often heard from Hindus that too much emphasis on the phenomena of the paranormal—or *siddhis*, otherwise accepted as a quite normal feature of Indian life— is a distraction in the pursuit of the deeply spiritual life. Swedenborg probably made a similar point when he said that miracles have a coercive effect on belief and destroy the free will in spiritual matters (Van Dusen, 1974, p. 140).

A final rather puzzling paranormal phenomenon linked to religion is that of possession. Taking its cue from Biblical and ancient times, the theory of possession has it that there are "evil spirits," sometimes representing malevolent human beings frustrated at the time of their deaths who remain trapped on the earth plane and who gain their satisfactions by haunting houses or entering the bodies of living beings and so "possessing" them. This was the theory of madness at the time of Jesus, who was able to "throw out" these spirits or devils. It is hard to demonstrate scientifically the existence of possessing "demons," though they constitute an interesting explanation of what disturbs some of the mentally ill, as in the history of the possession of the nuns at the Ursuline convent in Loudun, retold by Huxley (1952).

Taking his cue from Swedenborg, Van Dusen (1972) took the hallucinations of psychotic patients at their face value and entered into conversations with these discarnate entities in a nonthreatening way. He reported that he was able to help the patient, at the same time that he himself learned much about the unconscious. This does not mean that the concept of possession is thereby proved, but simply that perhaps there is a little more to it by way of usefulness than might be thought.

SUMMARY

In this chapter I have defined religion as the inner experience of the individual when he senses a Beyond. This suggests the need for a strongly nonrational, mystical element in religion, which in turn may be linked to the paranormal. There are many accounts of paranormal events in the Bible, particularly stories of healing and survival, which need checking against similar events that have been demonstrated today. Many persons intuitively associate the paranormal with religion, which helps to explain the Spiritualist movement. Evidences for survival also are important supports for Spiritualism, confirming as they do both the *human desire* for reunion with deceased loved ones and for personal survival.

Since psychics, physicists, and mystics seem to share the nonrational conviction that matter is a unity made up of a collection of forces and that time is but an illusion, it is important that the scientific study of the paranormal proceed with the help of the intuitive faculty of the mystic, the poet of the religious life.

REFERENCES

Allen, G. W. *William James*. New York: Viking, 1967.

Clark, W. H. *The Psychology of Religion*. New York: Macmillan, 1958.

Clark, W. H. *Chemical Ecstasy: Psychedelic Drugs and Religion*. New York: Sheed and Ward, 1969.

Clark, W. H. Pharmacological cults. *Encyclopaedia Britannica*, 1974.

Clark, W. H., Malony, H. N., Daane, J., and Tippett, A. R. *Religious Experience: Its Nature and Function in the Human Psyche*. Springfield, Ill.: Charles C Thomas, 1973.

Davis, A. J. *Death and the After Life*. 4th ed. New York: A. J. Davis, 1873.

Frank, P. *Einstein: His Life and Times*. New York: Knopf, 1948.

Howe, Q., Jr. *Reincarnation for the Christian*. New York: Harper & Row, 1974.

Huxley, A. *The Devils of Loudun*. New York: Harper & Row, 1952.

Judah, J. S. *The History and Philosophy of the Metaphysical Movements*. Philadelphia: Westminster Press, 1967.

LeShan, L. Toward a general theory of the paranormal. *Parapsychological Monographs No. 9*. New York: Parapsychology Foundation, 1969.

LeShan, L. *The Medium, the Mystic, and the Physicist*. New York: Viking Press, 1974.

Moore, G. F. *The Literature of the Old Testament*. New York: Henry Holt, 1913.

Murphy, G. *Challenge of Psychical Research: A Primer of Parapsychology*. New York: Harper & Row, 1961.

Myers, F. W. H. *Human Personality and its Survival of Bodily Death*. London: Longmans, Green, 1903. 2 vols.

Nelson, G. K. *Spiritualism and Society*. New York: Schocken Books, 1969.

Otto, R. *The Idea of the Holy*. (Trans. by J. W. Harvey.) New York: Oxford University Press, 1958.

Pahnke, W. N. and Richards, W. A. Religion and mind expanding drugs. In J. J. Heaney (Ed.), *Psyche and Spirit*, pp. 109–118. New York: Paulist Press, 1973.

Pearce, J. C. *The Crack in the Cosmic Egg: Challenging Constructs of Mind and Reality*. New York: Julian Press, 1971.

Stace, W. T., *Mysticism and Philosophy*. Philadelphia: Lippincott, 1960.

Stevenson, I. *Twenty Cases Suggestive of Reincarnation*. (2nd rev. ed.) Charlottesville: University Press of Virginia, 1974.

Van Dusen, W. *The Natural Depth in Man*. New York: Harper & Row, 1972.

Van Dusen, W. *The Presence of Other Worlds: The Findings of Emanuel Swedenborg*. New York: Harper & Row, 1974.

Weatherhead, L. D. *Psychology, Religion, and Healing*. New York: Abingdon-Cokesbury, 1951.

7

Parapsychology and Literature

Joseph M. Backus

INTRODUCTION

While there has been little application of parapsychology to the study of literature, or of the findings of literary study to the interests of parapsychology, the two disciplines have long been seen to move within the same circle—that ring which Robert Frost identifies in his couplet "The Secret Sits" (1942), at whose center the Secret sits "and knows." That the poet now and then catches sight of spirits, demons, and gods and "knows that a purposiveness out-reaching human ends is the life-giving secret for man" is noted by Jung (1933, p. 163), while Rhine (1947) observes that conditions favorable to psi occurrence are similar to those required for the "most delicately original and creative work in the arts" (p. 141). Some striking parallels have been drawn between poetic vision and psychedelic experience (Durr, 1970), and the pervasiveness of psi in literature has frequently been remarked; indeed, there is something "ghostly" in all great art, says Lafcadio Hearn (1965, pp. 91-92). Henry James has shown how the "unreal and the phantasmagoric are attached at a hundred points to daily existence" (Edel, 1970, pp. xiii-xiv). Traditionally the poet, or inspired writer, has been thought to possess special powers of perception, and writers of such varying temperaments as Blake, Balzac, and Bulwer-Lytton have been credited with doing much to reawaken the general consciousness of the unreal and phantasmagoric that characterized the Romantic Movement and began the development of modern parapsychology.

Nor were literary persons unmindful of its beginnings. Writers as different as Tennyson and Mark Twain became early members of the Society for Psychical Research (S.P.R.). So well known in literary circles had the S.P.R.'s activities become by 1887, when Oscar Wilde published his jesting story "The Canterville Ghost," that recurring blood stains on the floor cause one of his characters to write a "long letter to Messrs. Myers and Podmore on the subject of the Permanence of Sanguineous Stains When Connected With Crime," and 5 years later R. L. Stevenson wrote an earnest letter to Myers on his own "two con- sciousnesses" (Myers, 1893, pp. 9–11). While the poet Bryant joined a deputa- tion from Harvard to investigate the famous medium D. D. Home (Wilson, 1971, p. 466), other séances were attended by other literary notables as both patron and visitant; and to those attended by the living Victor Hugo came personifica- tions of The Novel, Drama, and Criticism (Ebon, 1971, p. 49). Other deliberate forays into the further reaches of the mind include the experiments with drugs of Coleridge and DeQuincy, as well as a study of "cultivated motor automatism" by Gertrude Stein, a pupil of William James, which she published in the *Harvard Psychological Review*.

Much psychical interest among men of letters has taken the form of book- length treatises, such as those by Scott (1830), Maeterlinck (1914), Romains (1924), Doyle (1930), Yeats (1918, 1927), Garland (1936), White (1937, 1940), and Huxley (1954, 1956). Shorter works include essays touching upon the psy- chical aspects of poetry by Emerson (1903) and Colin Wilson (1971) and one by Kenneth Burke (1970) on the creativity of verbal automatism. And certain small literary magazines, often the vanguard of scholarly concerns, now assume a metaphysical vocabulary and point of view to discuss "raising the levels of awareness/consciousness through sounds and rhythms," or the "psychic land- scape that is the universe of the poem" (Lamansky, 1974, pp. 3, 32).

PERTINENT SCHOLARSHIP: AN INDICATION

Since the parapsychologist and the literary scholar have in common the analysis of psychic responses to life by persons of exceptional sensitivity, and since both are committed to understanding man in relation to his surroundings, much literary scholarship deals with matters of at least tangential interest to parapsy- chology. These include the presence in literature of the mythic, the religious, the metaphysical, and especially the supernatural as treated by Scarborough (1917), Railo (1927), and Penzoldt (1952). More closely focused are studies of the literary influences of Spiritualism by Porter (1958), which is largely bio- graphical, and Kerr (1972), which discusses Spiritualism in the lives and works of Howells, Twain, and Henry James, among others. Roellinger (1949, p. 405) finds James' ghosts to be conceived "to a surprising extent" in terms of cases reported to the S.P.R.; and Banta (1972) goes further, to discuss James' explorations of the human consciousness. Another book on a single author argues for acceptance of the supernatural as a form of reality in the work of Defoe and notes in passing that scientific study by societies for psychical research has again made it permissible to discuss supernatural phenomena in scholarly circles (Baine, 1968, p. 73); but, while most of the works just cited are from university presses, academicians have by no means been won over. In his study of the occult sciences in the Renaissance, Wayne Shumaker (1972), a professor of literature at the University of California at Berkeley, has sought to dam the rising tide of interest in the occult with towering wagonloads of scholarly learning and right reason. And a recent article in *PMLA*, long an unassailable bastion of literary scholarship, means to show that Whitman's poetic intention was not to seek, after all, a condition of elevated consciousness but rather the cathartic method of psychological therapy superseded by Freud's "talking cure": "For Whitman, writing a poem may have had a function similar to talking to an analyst" (Black, 1973, p. 100).

Conversely, persons interested in parapsychology have sometimes turned to literature, on both professional and popular levels. The S.P.R. *Journal* has included, for example, an article suggesting that the witches in *Macbeth* could prophesy kingship by telepathically sensing Macbeth's ambitions, and comparing Shakespeare's keen insight to that of scientific psychology (Ehrenwald, 1941). An article in the *International Journal of Parapsychology*, on the other hand, calls Shakespeare England's first true psychic researcher, so completely did he understand, and accept, the psychic beliefs of his day (Yellen, 1970). In certain literary texts has appeared such parapsychological commentary as a brief discussion of reincarnation by Murphy (1963) appended to Jack London's novel *The Star Rover*, and clinical headnotes by Kline (1965) in *Favorite Stories of Hypnotism*. Containing noteworthy material from literary authors are texts on cosmic consciousness (Bucke, 1901), on various psi experiences (Prince, 1963), and on reincarnation (Head and Cranston, 1967). Literary authors make up about half the persons discussed by Ebon (1971) as having experienced psi phenomena, and a recent study of altered states of consciousness (Bro, 1970) draws repeatedly from Melville's *Moby Dick*. Since its establishment in 1969, the magazine *Psychic* has included a number of articles related to literature, two of which are of particular bibliographic interest (McCormick, 1972, 1973); and a bibliographical survey of modern occultism (Galbreath, 1972) includes literary references passim.

PURPOSE

In spite of much reciprocal interest between parapsychology and literature, however, their practical relationship is yet to be generalized and applied. The present chapter is therefore largely exploratory, concerning itself with a few specific kinds of psi experiences as they recur among certain literary works in the hope that such discussion will eventually lead to the formulation of a parapsychological approach to literature. Such an approach should be of value to both fields. The application of parapsychological knowledge to literature should certainly deepen the literary scholar's understanding of his subject; and the identification and interpretation of literary occurrences of psi phenomena should prove useful to the parapsychologist, not only as topological documentation *per se* (Lansing, 1970, p. 291), but also as documentation of the most perceptive and—within the limits of language—the most articulate kind. Even when the visionary poet is influenced by outside sources, as was Yeats, for example, following Swedenborg and Blake, or when the poet's perception is willfully embellished for artistic purposes, there must first be struck some vibrant inner chord; and any writer thus struck is likely to have seen further and told more than most readers have yet realized. If such is the case, and if a parapsychological approach to literature can be made to establish the reality of what the inspired writer has observed, then the much traveled circle around the Secret should be narrowed in good measure.

But where and how to begin?

Appropriate for parapsychological analysis are all those aspects of literature listed by Wellek and Warren in their still basic *Theory of Literature* (1956, p. 81) as admitting a psychological approach: (a) the author as individual or type, (b) the creative process, (c) the "psychological types and laws" present within literary works, and (d) the effect of literature on the reader; and while the present study is concerned chiefly with matters relating to their third category, limitations must still be set.

As a general means of interpreting literature, Wellek and Warren (1956, p. 157) find naturalistic psychology to be inadequate because much great art violates its standards by working "with improbable situations, with fantastic motifs." Of similar mind is Jung (1933, p. 157), who divides the informing experiences of literature into two kinds, as exemplified by the two parts of Goethe's *Faust*: those that never rend the curtain veiling the cosmos and those that rend "from top to bottom the curtain upon which is painted the picture of an ordered world." Into this latter division can be put those works where apparent disorder is the norm: ancient and retold myths, legends, and folk tales with their magical flights and metamorphoses; medieval and modern allegory; works by writers sometimes termed mystics; such works of high magic as those that center in Merlin, Prospero, and Faust himself; and certain works by writers of highest imagination, like Coleridge, who, often with rhythm, rhyme, and brilliant image, weave the spell to suspend disbelief. Here too can go literary outgrowths of short-lived artistic movements that have sought deliberately to rend the painted curtain (Art Nouveau, Surrealism) and the stream-of-consciousness writing of Joyce, Woolf, and Faulkner; as well as the Gothic novel, the ghost story, the weird tale, fantasy writing, and science fiction. Closely related are those works that depart the everyday world through some realistic form of transport, often a shipwreck in unknown seas or passage through some familiar point: a rabbit hole leading to Wonderland, an Arizona bus station on the road to Ixtlan. Often the bridge between real and unreal is some knowledgeable guide—be it don Juan Matus or the shade of Virgil—and the reader himself usually makes the crossing in the company of some conventional hero.

But, once identified, most literature of this kind seems less appropriate for discussion here than that which can be put into a third category, between Jung's two: that is, literature intended to mirror life as most readers know it and yet, like life, abounding with seemingly incidental instances of the improbable and fantastic. Most of the works considered here were written originally in English during the 100 and more years that parapsychology was developing; and while psi occurrences are to be expected in works of Romanticism, they also appear with telling frequency among those later writers who, like O'Neill, are "primarily concerned, not with the relationship between man and man, but with the relationship between man and God, between man and his own soul, between his conscious and unconscious needs and desires, [and for whom] realism and naturalism are clearly insufficient" (Törnqvist, 1969, p. 43).

PSYCHOMETRY: "SOMETHING HERE WHICH CRIES OUT IN MY EAR"

Perhaps the easiest way into the psychic landscape of literature is through psychometry, since psychometrical "readings" begin with actual, tangible objects that apparently call into play the full range of ESP capabilities: telepathy, clairvoyance, precognition, and retrocognition. According to most accounts, these impressions can register through any or all of the five physical senses, sometimes as fully realized scenes that include general moods as well as the thoughts and especially the feelings of particular people. By most accounts, impressions can relate to the past, present, or future of the owners of objects; but they also occur when no second human mind is apparently involved. The ability to psychometrize is usually thought peculiar to the psychic "sensitive," but something like psychometrical sensitivity, especially in reference to past events, also directs poetic vision. "There are worlds upon worlds, right here in front of us," says the Yaqui medicine man don Juan in *Journey to Ixtlan* (1972). Such ancient "magic" touches the arts through image-making, say Wellek and Warren (1956, p. 205), and fundamental to magic, they continue, "is the belief in the power of things."

Significantly enough, both the term and early explorations of psychometry have been called less scientific than "poetic" (Karagulla, 1967, p. 215; Roll, 1967, p. 221), the term having been introduced in 1842 by the discoverer of this ability, J. R. Buchanan, an American physiologist, to signify a measuring of the "soul" of things. It was a minor poet, the Reverend John Pierpont, in a sesquicentennial address at Yale College, who hailed psychometry as the dawn of a new civilization. And literature itself is full of its manifestations: portraits and personal memorabilia with stories to tell if they could but speak, as they sometimes do, precious jewels with curses attached and talismans with curative powers, secret places guarded by spirit, and places projecting translatable messages, as in Poe's "The Coliseum" (1845):

> We are not impotent—we pallid stones.
> Not all our power is gone—not all our fame—
> Not all the magic of our high renown—
> Not all the wonder that encircles us—
> Not all the mysteries that in us lie—
> Not all the memories that hang upon
> And cling around about us as a garment,
> Clothing us in a robe of more than glory.

"Psychometry" was a "newly coined word . . . called into active service in those days," wrote the American novelist John Townsend Trowbridge (Prince, 1963, p. 176) when remembering the 1850s. But the soul of things asserted itself before its naming, as in early versions of Poe's poem; in the "shadows and delusions" to which "Reason's self shall bow the knee" in Philip Freneau's "The Indian Burying Ground" (1788); and in Bryant's vision of the ancient mound-builders of "The Prairies" (1834). Nor is its appearance limited to works of nineteenth-century Romanticism. In Frank Waters' novel *The Man Who Killed the Deer* (1941), when a mare shies around a boulder marked with signs of the "Old Ones"—a circle enclosing a dot, the imprint of a hand, an animal with long legs and neck—her rider feels, as does the mare, the "lingering vibrations of the life that had never died but only lost its nonessential bodily form." And Robert Bly (1972, p. 6) makes the arresting observation that Pablo Neruda in his poetry "follows some arc of association which corresponds to the inner life of the objects; so that anyone sensitive to the inner life of objects can ride with him."

This kind of sensitivity is glimpsed in the life of such a visionary author as Yeats, who got impressions from flowers and leaves (1918, p. 49) and from a cardboard symbol (1927, p. 230). And when the psychically tormented Strindberg put his coat around the shoulders of a friend, thus sending the friend into convulsions, it was Strindberg's opinion that they were caused by emanations of his own "electric fluid" (Wilson, 1971, p. 97)—an incident that recalls Henry James' story "The Romance of Certain Old Clothes" (1868), where the vengeful spirit of the deceased owner of a rich and beloved wardrobe rises up from the trunk in which it is stored to strike dead a covetous sister. Certain other writers have acknowledged psychometry's influence on their work. In her autobiographical *Far Memory*, Joan Grant (1956) discusses her psychometrical experiences at length and attributes to an object from ancient Egypt her initial inspiration for the novel *Winged Pharaoh* (1937). And the poet and critic Allen Tate (1972, p. 229) tells of a psychometrist he happened to meet who held one of his antique shirt studs in her hand for "a silent minute," then described their original owner. "As I write these words the *frisson* of that moment returns," he says; and, brief and secondhand as it was, this seemingly immediate contact with another time and place caused Tate to write his only novel, *The Fathers* (1938). Even Browning showed respect for a similar demonstration while exhibiting a passionate impatience for certain other psychics. Again the psychometrist was a casual acquaintance, who is reported to have said, in Italian, after weighing one of Browning's cuff links in his hand: "There is something here which cries out in my ear, 'Murder, murder!'" "And truly," said Browning later, "those very studs were taken from the dead body of a great-uncle of mine, who was violently killed on his estate in St. Kitts, nearly eighty years ago" (Porter, 1958, p. 53; Prince, 1963, p. 132).

A trifling anecdote perhaps, but one that invites some searching questions, especially when appended by Browning's notion that he had given the truth away by his facial expressions!—a provocatively feeble gesture to Reason. Since he had been clearly sympathetic to the psychometrist, why did he remain so vindictively hostile to the lionized medium Home, for example, who became a model for the central figure of his scoffing 1,525-line dramatic monologue, "Mr. Sludge, 'the Medium'" (1864)? In addition to evident personal antagonism, could Browning as poet have considered himself something of a medium and one who produced a worthy product rather than merely exploiting process? This kind of comparison is made by his fawningly defensive Mr. Sludge, who, caught out in a lie, likens the professional spiritual medium to the revered author:

> He's Lowell—it's a world (you smile applause),
> Of his own invention—wondrous Longfellow,
> Surprising Hawthorne! Sludge does more than they,
> And acts the books they write: the more his praise!

If Browning can be considered a literary medium, did his mediumship, like that of some spiritual mediums, sometimes begin with psychometry? Is, for example, the title of his two-volume poem *The Ring and the Book* (1868, 1869) intended to carry some of psychometry's *frisson*? At the beginning he says the story of its murder came from an old book, partly written by hand, and possibly giving him more than he means to acknowledge:

> A book in shape but, really, pure crude fact
> Secreted from man's life when hearts beat hard,
> And brains, high-blooded, ticked two centuries since.
> Give it me back! The thing's restorative
> I' the touch and sight.

And could an influence on Browning's acceptance of psychometry have been another acquaintance of his in Italy, the "surprising Hawthorne" himself? At the beginning of *The Scarlet Letter* (1850), a historical romance of Hawthorne's own that predates Browning's by 18 years, Hawthorne indicates that he too drew literary inspiration from an emotionally charged object. "Certainly, there was some deep meaning in it, most worthy of interpretation," he says upon bringing to light a worn and faded red cloth "A" long after its cruel purpose had been served—a meaning "which, as it were, streamed forth from the mystic symbol, subtly communicating itself to my sensibilities, but evading the analysis of my mind." In *The Ring and the Book*, Browning quickly makes clear the symbolic meaning of the objects coupled in his title, which he doubtless intends as a distillation of the work's encompassing theme: the artist's power to transform "pure crude fact" (the book) into a vitalized and wholly humanized work of art (the ring). But even though the ring is most importantly an abstraction, he treats it too as an object more than inanimate: "Do you see this Ring? . . . found alive / Spark-like, 'mid unearthed slope-side figtree-roots / That roof old tombs at Chiusi." Thus he suggests a sense of the soul of things in both objects, streaming forth from one to inspire this particular work, from the other as artistic creativity itself.

Struck by the painted halo of light around a Byzantine figure of Christ, Karagulla (1967, p. 49) wonders if ancient artists could perceive human energy fields, and the same sort of question can be asked about psychometry. Was this ability once a natural property of the seer/poet? Did it help the blind Homer to repeople the dusty plains of Troy? Did he know that objects held close to the breasts of heroes carry more impressions—"Secreted from man's life when hearts beat hard"—than can actually be inscribed upon them? Does then the materially unrealistic shield he makes for Achilles simply follow an artistic convention, like statues, friezes, and pictographic symbols—all recognizably inadequate ways of investing the inwardly sensed with outward form? While disclaiming to be "psychic," Doyle (1930, pp. 50–51) writes of a "curious effect, almost a darkening of the landscape with a marked sense of heaviness, when I am on an old battlefield," which was especially strong at the scenes of Hastings and Culloden: "two fights where great causes were finally destroyed and where extreme bitterness may well have filled the hearts of the conquered." So too at Troy, and at the battles described in vigorous detail by Shakespeare, Tolstoy, Stephen Crane, and countless other writers dedicated not to war but peace.

But this is not to suggest that such writers had physically to visit old battlefields before they could write, or had to have at hand some battle-scarred object. To write *The Red Badge of Courage* (1895) without firsthand knowledge of the Civil War and without firsthand experience as a soldier, Crane is known to have studied records, maps, and pictures and to have interviewed veterans—all of which may have given him more than surface information, like Browning's old book, and like the photographs used by certain psychometrists to get accurate retrocognitive impressions, or like the living relatives or friends that certain mediums "psychometrize" to begin supposed contact with the dead. Still more suggestive is the apparent fact that psychic sensitives sometimes receive impressions without needing to touch the object psychometrized; for the same should hold true of literary mediums, the greatest of whom would seem to transcend a dependence on physical proximity altogether by unconsciously projecting consciousness to distant places, or by tapping what Yeats called the great memory (1918, pp. 50–51) or Jung, later, the collective unconscious. But unlike accomplished psychics, projecting authors would be impelled by specific literary needs, as Shakespeare may have been when wanting to dramatize certain ideas by drawing from Italian court life and other areas beyond his actual experience— an ability repeatedly challenged by detractors who would assign his work to a more materially sophisticated author.   "I'll put a girdle round about the earth / In forty minutes," says Puck in *A Midsummer Night's Dream*, speaking perhaps as Shakespeare's genius; for such swift-winged movements, such vaulting concepts crisscross like shooting stars the bright and boundless skies of literature.

PROJECTIONS: "PERFECT SPEED, MY SON, IS BEING THERE"

You will touch heaven the moment you touch perfect speed, the knowing Old Chiang tells the protagonist of *Jonathan Livingston Seagull* (1970). Perfect speed, he says, cannot be measured by miles per hour: "Perfect speed, my son, is being there." Like the Puck-like Lob at the end of Barrie's *Dear Brutus* (1917), Chiang then vanishes and reappears 50 feet away, vanishes and appears again "in the same millisecond" at Jonathan's shoulder. You can go to any place and to any time you want, he says, if you know that your true nature lives everywhere at once across space and time. Such a sense of ready movement and universality would seem to represent an extension of that which comes through psychometry, as in the case of so apparently capable a psychometrist as Mrs. William Denton, for example, holding an unidentified bit of mastodon's tooth and feeling herself a "perfect monster," unwieldy and heavy; or, with a fragment of aerolite at hand, seeming to travel with "great velocity and tremendous force" to reach some distant world—"for world it is, with plains and seas" (Denton and Denton, 1866, pp. 55, 77–78).

In literature, perfect and near-to-perfect speed is the speed of gods and godmothers, of witches, and of great Satan himself as seen by Milton, or by Meredith in "Lucifer in Starlight" (1883):

> And now upon his western wing he leaned,
> Now his huge bulk o'er Afric's sands careened,
> Now the black planet shadowed Arctic snows.

In more realistic works it becomes still more imperfect, sometimes taking the form of a kind of "traveling clairvoyance," as in Frank Norris' novel *The Octopus* (1901), where the "mystic" Vanamee searches for his dead Angéle by sending his mind out "across the enchanted sea of the Supernatural," or in Thomas Tryon's *The Other* (1971), where the young protagonist empathizes with a dragonfly until he goes soaring with it, "compound eyes taking in, grasping, everything...." Or, more often, superhuman speed occurs as a more usual kind of out-of-the-body experience (OBE), which can add considerable dimension to literature when it is recognized as a phenomenon that parapsychology has classified and studied as a "potentially psi-facilitating state of consciousness," as well as for its implications in regard to survival after death (Palmer and Vassar, 1974, p. 257).

Such experiences occur, for example, in two works about young American "primitives": Eudora Welty's short story "Livvie" (1943) and *Black Elk Speaks* (1932), a factual autobiography transcribed by the poet John G. Neihardt. As in many reported cases, both OBEs occur at times of crisis. Livvie, an unschooled black girl married to a much older, dying man, is carried away by the nostalgic chinaberry-like odor of a lipstick to look down from a cloud above a chinaberry tree and see her old home with her mother and father happily occupied in the yard. Still wearing the magical lipstick, she meets and falls for a young field hand, her brief psychic experience thus poignantly, and economically, marking the turning point from girl- to womanhood, at the same time anticipating the more earthly transport that is to follow. Black Elk's OBE occurs during an illness when he is 9. Carried by a cloud to his "Six Grandfathers," he beholds the "great vision" of his life: "Grandson, all over the universe you have seen. Now you shall go back with power ..." to mend the sacred "hoop" of his people. When he returns to his body, he learns that he has been lying like dead for 12 days—a long and powerful experience; but the circular way of the Sioux is irreparably broken, his inability to fulfill his vision becomes the tragic theme of his life, and a later OBE is pathetically like Livvie's. While traveling with a wild west show in Paris and ill again, he looks down on the passing countryside of France, the ocean, the Missouri River, the Black Hills, at last on his parents' tepee and his parents.

A knowledge of this phenomenon also lends substance to Kipling's *Kim* (1901), which might otherwise seem to end in little more than a cloud of whimsy. Throughout this novel Kipling surrounds his river-seeking Tibetan holy man with a strong enough aura of senility that his lamaistic views should amuse rather than offend the pious Victorian reader. So when, after nearly drowning, the lama tells Kim that "the wise Soul loosed itself from the silly Body and went free," the reader may pay as little attention as does his worldly disciple. But the lama goes on anyway, to close the book with an account of how he has looked down on "all Hind, from Ceylon in the sea to the Hills, and my own Painted

Rocks at Suchzen"—a perspective strangely like that of Jung (1963, pp. 289–290) during an illness more than 40 years later: "Far below my feet lay Ceylon, and in the distance ahead of me the subcontinent of India. . . . I could also see the snow-covered Himalayas. . . ." Both travelers record a beguiling sense of freedom and a strong unwillingness to return to earth. As in many reported cases, the lama returns to satisfy an unfulfilled commitment, to guide his "chela" to the Way; and by making this sacrifice he finds his river.

In naturalistic literature, OBEs can occur when naturalism grows too grim to bear, even in the physically-minded Hemingway's novel *A Farewell to Arms* (1929), where, however, the experience is but an autobiographical detail, quickly forgotten. In Hardy's *Tess of the d'Ubervilles* (1891), it does more, adding a significant winsomeness to this novel's beleaguered heroine when she says she can send herself hundreds of miles away from her body, which she then doesn't seem to want at all. And in London's *The Star Rover* (1915), astral projection accounts for the title and links its two main purposes: to expose the inhuman treatment of prison inmates and to show that man's spirit is the only reality that endures. The confessed-murderer/narrator of this hard-hitting, heavy-handed novel learns to preserve his sanity and his life by "killing his body," methodically eliminating its parts from his consciousness until he is off and away, projecting for most of the book into his past lives.

A novel owing much to *The Star Rover*, which it even mentions by name, is James Jones' *From Here to Eternity* (1951), whose protagonist escapes from tortuous confinement just as London's does, but only once, for an experience very briefly described and easily overlooked among the 861 pages of this long seamy story of World War II. The book might therefore seem to end without any evidential indication of survival, the talented but perversely prideful young protagonist evoking repeated abuse until he gets himself fatally shot; but book and title can be seen to carry a message similar to London's if the two works are compared in the light of some acquaintance with the nature of OBEs. And yet the reader can search the factual accounts of OBEs in vain for a symbolically (and naturalistically) truer simile for what is sometimes called the life line: "There was a kind of cord that looked like it was made out of jism connecting the two of him and he knew . . . that if that cord ever got broken he was dead. . . ." When he's shot, Jones refers again to this key concept: "The cord . . . that looked like it was made of come kept stretching and stretching . . . ." Until, "as if in a way he was seeing double, he realized that it wasnt [sic] really going to end after all, that it would never end."

Identification of this kind of experience among unlikely but fairly simple works gives one pause to wonder whether it occurs among those that are more complex. Is, for example, Hamlet's refusal to kill the king at prayer, when "fit and season'd for his passage," based more on practical considerations than on a penchant for inaction? When the king later tells the audience that he had not been able to project his thoughts to heaven, is Shakespeare justifying Hamlet's deliberation while revealing not only the king's guilt but also that Hamlet has missed exactly the opportunity he sought, thus emphasizing the psychic complexity of the problem confronting him? And at the end of "The Death of Ivan Ilyich" (1886), does Tolstory mean for the dying protagonist to leave his body after literally seeing the light? The curious repetition of events at the end of this work, one sequence viewed from Ilyich's prostrate body, the other viewpoint more detached, suggests a parting of consciousness that gives this long dark story a final, positive turn, at the same time deepening its moral. Freed from a lifelong preoccupation with the pettily materialistic only an hour before his departure, Ilyich realizes, like Jones' protagonist when he seems to be seeing double, that there is no death: "Death is ended. . . . It is no more." A naturalistic/psychological interpretation might see these statements as the last of Ilyich's self-delusions: death is ended because he dies; while a super-naturalistic/parapsychological one might see them as the beginning of self-realization—the tragedy being that it comes so late.

Considered together, the OBEs presented here help to explicate the following "mystical" poem, especially when it is remembered that most OBEs under normal conditions are reported as taking place at night, during sleep. The poem appears as "Introduction" to Blake's *Songs of Experience* (1794), where its rejoinder, "Earth's Answer," does much to clarify its meaning as a call to the earthbound to break free from darkness and seek the light by means of a return to spirit—a state of consciousness more readily open to the poet. It is symbolized here, apparently, by the imagery of out-of-the-body travel, which Blake himself is said to have experienced and which seems to inform his illustration for his hand-lettered version of this poem, surrounded as it is by a deep-blue starry sky where floats a naked, haloed human figure on a golden couchlike cloud, the head turned from looking down as if to heed the "Holy Word" (reproduced in Keynes, 1967, plate 30). As a whole, the poem represents in heady essence the office of the poet/seer:

> Hear the voice of the Bard!
> Who Present, Past, & Future sees
> Whose ears have heard,
> The Holy Word,
> That walk'd among the ancient trees.
>
> Calling the lapsed Soul
> And weeping in the evening dew:
> That might control
> The starry pole:
> And fallen fallen light renew!
>
> O Earth O Earth return!
> Arise from out the dewy grass:

Night is worn,
And the morn
Rises from the slumberous mass.

Turn away no more:
Why wilt thou turn away
The starry floor
The watry shore
Is giv'n thee till the break of day.

In her *Archetypal Patterns in Poetry*, Maud Bodkin (1934, pp. 317–318), agrees with A. E. Housman that the "music and magic" of this poem should not be destroyed by translation into any supposed argument in logical form. Instead, she analyzes her own subjective response to certain of its words, concluding at last that it contains the archetype of rebirth but completely missing its controlling image—which, once recognized as an OBE, reveals not only the idea so laboriously arrived at but also a thoroughly logical argument, in both literary and philosophical senses, its music and magic still intact. She also confesses that meaning began to come to her only after learning the poem "by heart," as if, like other of its commentators, and like countless other readers fascinated by the "ghostly" in literature, she had been possessed of an intuitive but thickly veiled awareness of the truth of its experience.

NEUTRAL SUBSTITUENT ENERGETICS: "IF A ROSE MIGHT SOMEHOW BE A THROAT"

The fair frequency with which OBEs occur in literature may be related to the fact that flying in a figurative sense has long been one of literature's characteristics. In ancient times, says Bly, the poet flew from one world to another, "riding on dragons" as the Chinese put it. Bly sees a recent return to the old "poetic leap," which he defines as a "leap from the conscious to the unconscious and back again" (1972, p. 3) by means of a process of association; and "the considerable distance between the associations, the distance the spark has to leap, gives the lines their bottomless feeling, their space, and the speed of the association increases the excitement of the poetry" (p. 6). Among such lines is one of his own from "Sleepers Joining Hands" (p. 88): "the outer eight-inch of the brain giving off smoke, like mist boiling off hailclouds." Certainly the many wide and rapid leaps back and forth between conscious and unconscious among associations here—from brain waves to smoke to mist to boiling to hailclouds, and back to seething brain when the full vault of the simile strikes the reader's own consciousness—speed this line along with the "flashing lights of flying saucers" that Bly finds characteristic of poetic leaping in general (p. 48).

And certainly this kind of contemporary brilliance makes certain older poetry pale to gaslight as far as leaping goes: When reading the monologues of Browning, for example, the reader usually need follow only the shorter, psychological jumps between the turns of a speaker's mind in reaction to an implied concurrent series of events. But still boldly luminous are the great unencumbered movements of Blake; and poetic leaps of varying intensity have occurred all along as a means of firing the reader's imagination. Even the most cohesive prose demands that the writer make an enormous leap, from living experience or conception to written symbols, and that the reader exercise an almost psychometrical sense if he is to follow from one life-invested word to another. A more conscious convention is the leap contrived by omission of transition, as between stanzas in the ballad, between scenes in fiction and drama, between lines in mid-twentieth-century verse. And, as Bly's discussion suggests, most frequent and variable are the leaps between the juxtaposed sensory images of metaphor—that greatest of all things for poets, says Aristotle, who saw a beginning of ultimate truth in what comes to us through the senses.

For any metaphor to achieve its intended effect, the reader of course must recognize the grounds upon which its parts (the "brain" and "hailclouds" of the line quoted above) are being compared, by consciously following the associational arc that has connected them. Sometimes the poet makes this jump very easy by disclosing his basis for comparison, sometimes even placing it as a kind of stepping stone between the parts, as Wordsworth does in the first line of untitled poem of 1807, "I wandered lonely as a cloud." Clearly, both poet and cloud have in common the quality of being lone. But even in this comparatively simple poem a much wider leap is required before its full meaning is understood. Its second line extends the metaphor by further describing the cloud—"That floats on high o'er vales and hills"—thus adding a note of yearning: the poet seems to wish he were like the cloud in this respect, too, floating evenly above the ups and downs of mundane existence as a harmonious and perhaps (like Blake's bard) an all-comprehending part of the whole. In the next lines he begins to find such identification when he comes upon a "host" of daffodils, golden in color and stretching out as a "never-ending line" of dancers: a bright, entrancing symbol of universal harmony upon which he "gazed—and gazed" until he himself, evidently, became a part of the scene. Now, "In vacant or in pensive mood, / They flash upon that inward eye" to renew a sustaining sense of union, his search for which is the fullest meaning of the introductory metaphor. And this kind of search may be called the most basic motivation for all metaphor, as well as for other leaps and flights in literature.

A more complex but more clearly unifying metaphor occurs in Sidney Lanier's "The Symphony" (1875), where it involves synaesthesia, or the rendering of one kind of sensation in terms of another, which Wellek and Warren (1956, p. 83) see as surviving from an "earlier comparatively undifferentiated sensorium" and expressing a "metaphysical-aesthetic attitude towards life." Indeed, parts of Lanier's poem can be read as particularizations of the effects of LSD described by one subject as a "symphony of variations" with "dimension and color and other things all ... mixed up ... [as] part of the whole pulsating ebb and flow" (Cohen, 1966, p. 141). Lanier's symphony begins with the "song-flow" of violins, which speak for "heart" as opposed to "head"; then presently:

> A velvet flute-note fell down pleasantly
> Upon the bosom of that harmony,
> And sailed and sailed incessantly,
> As if a petal from a wild-rose blown
> Had fluttered down upon that pool of tone
> And boatwise dropped o' the convex side
> And floated down the glassy tide
> And clarified and glorified
> The solemn spaces where the shadows bide.
> From the warm concave of that fluted note
> Somewhat, half song, half odor, forth did float,
> As if a rose might somehow be a throat:
> . . .
>
>   "Sweet friends,
>   Man's love ascends
> To finer and diviner ends
> Than man's mere thought e'er comprehends. . . ."

Thus mute Nature is translated by the flute and the flute by the poet; and to reproduce the flute-note for the printed page, Lanier adds to the sound effects of poetry such synaesthetic turns of metaphor as to blend four of the reader's five senses into a dizzying sense of oneness, which also supports the poem's main theme. "Music is Love in search of a word," it concludes fortissimo, for the driving force of both symphony and heart is the realization of harmonious union.

In a cynical little tale called "Julien" (1881) even Zola, dark father of literary naturalism, works toward the same end, but unconsciously and in lower key: Within a single paragraph he likens the sound of a flute to the trilling of a nightingale and to the charming voice of an old eighteenth-century marquise, its notes flying out with a rustling of wings as if from the darkness, "so closely did it blend with the hush of the night." Here again, as in all metaphor, superficially unrelated elements are fired together, as it were, to yield one common essence of reality. And Frank Norris, avowed follower of Zola, similarly violates naturalistic principle in *The Octopus* (1901) when describing Vanamee's feeling for Angéle: "the mingling of their lives was to be the Perfect Life, the intended, ordained union of the soul of man with the soul of woman, indissoluble, harmonious as music, beautiful beyond all thought, a foretaste of Heaven, a hostage of immortality." While Angéle dies before all this can be realized, Vanamee is able to achieve a transcendental sense of union with her through a gradual extension of consciousness, one of the few human triumphs of the book. And variations on the theme of super-naturalistic union through the medium of love are of course frequent in literature, ranging from the short-lived sexual transports of D. H. Lawrence (Wilson, 1971, pp. 491–492) to the infinitely expansive embrace of Whitman, who means to set flowing through all humanity one unifying warmth of spirit.

If a realization of transcendent unity, or "perfect speed," is the ultimate goal of out-of-the-body projection with its unifying perspective, of poetic flying or leaping, and of love, these are but a few expressions of the impulse toward such unity. The theme of cosmic union often takes the shape of direct assertion, as demonstrated by Durr (1970), juxtaposing statements from poets and LSD subjects. "All is in all . . . All is actually each," says Aldous Huxley (in Durr, p. 142), speaking for the latter group about a sense of "infinite Oneness"; and Emerson similarly, at the end of his poem "Each and All" (1839): "I yielded myself to the perfect whole." Thus do poets, more primitive and yet more civilized than their contemporaries, as T. S. Eliot has remarked (Wellek and Warren, 1956, p. 84), articulate man's primordial striving–if LSD has glanced the truth and not falsified or distorted. Less consciously may writers register the impulse toward union in the literary phenomenon of pathetic fallacy with its echo of cosmic sympathies, in the summing up of affairs at the ends of old novels, in the mandalic repetitions of poetry and poetic prose, and in the prevailing Aristotelian structural pattern of beginning, middle, and end. And if these manifestations of totality and fullness can be seen as microcosmic reflections of macrocosmic truth, it is reflected most significantly in the creative process itself. The poetic imagination, says Coleridge (1906), is that faculty which "dissolves, diffuses, dissipates, in order to recreate: or where this process is rendered impossible . . . it struggles to idealize and to unify. It is essentially *vital*, even as all objects (*as* objects) are essentially fixed and dead." The parenthetical phrase is worthy of note, for the unifying imagination of the poet can no more be satisfied with the traditional distinction between animate and inanimate, or between mind and matter, than can that of the parapsychologist.

The facts of parapsychology "not only do not require one to be a dualist–they do not *allow* one to be," says Rhine (1947, p. 179), after considering as a possible common denominator between mind and matter some "underlying order of neutral substituent energetics–a sort of nonpsychical and nonphysical substrate that is convertible into either mental or material manifestations." If the possibility of some single, and thus unifying, substrate can be accepted as a premise common to both parapsychology and literature, it should provide a likely basis for making further relationships between these two fields; and because this substrate, like Coleridge's imagination, must be essentially vital and, if vital, then synthetic or creative, such further study should do much to rid the world of darkness and demons. In the name of enlightenment, paradoxically, much applied psychology and much literary criticism derived from it now tend to limit rather than to extend perception by identifying those things extendedly perceived as illusions or delusions deriving from some common human failing, so that even the greatest of literary artists can be called a "victim and perpetrator of deception," as was long ago lamented by Jung (1933, p. 160). This critical sentiment can be readily leveled at any soaring work of "uplift" no matter how responsive an inner chord it strikes; and it can so intimidate or blind the contemporary writer that he seeks the Secret in not the bright sky but the depths of the abyss, to conjure forth the widely welcomed and destructive furies of *Rosemary's Baby*, *The Other*, or *The Exorcist*. Thus is ever drawn near the Gothic night—when the artist by nature must create, and a movement toward the light may be the most basic, if beclouded, urge of mankind.

REFERENCES

(Excluded from this list are references to literary works, most of which are available in numerous editions.)

Baine, R. M. *Daniel Defoe and the Supernatural*. Athens: University of Georgia Press, 1968.

Banta, M. *Henry James and the Occult: The Great Extension*. Bloomington: Indiana University Press, 1972.

Black, S. A. Radical utterances from the soul's abysms: Toward a new sense of Whitman. *PMLA: Publications of the Modern Language Association of America*, 1973, 88, 100–111.

Bly, R. Looking for dragon smoke. *The Seventies*, 1972 (Spring), whole issue.

Bodkin, M. *Archetypal Patterns in Poetry: Psychological Studies of Imagination*. London: Oxford University Press, 1934.

Bro, H. H. *High Play: Turning on Without Drugs*. New York: Coward–McCann, 1970.

Bucke, R. M. *Cosmic Consciousness: A Study in the Evolution of the Human Mind*. Philadelphia: Innes, 1901.

Burke, K. No word is an island: Some thoughts on the "creativity" of verbal automatism. In A. Angoff and B. Shapin (Eds.), *Psi Factors in Creativity*, pp. 184–197. New York: Parapsychology Foundation, 1970.

Cohen, S. *The Beyond Within: The LSD Story*. New York: Atheneum, 1966.

Coleridge, S. T. On the imagination, of esemplastic power. *Biographia Literaria*. London: Dent, 1906. Chapter XIII. (First published in 1817.)

Denton, W., and Denton, E. M. F. *The Soul of Things; or, Psychometric Researches and Discoveries*. (3rd ed. rev.) Boston: Walker, Wise, 1866.

Doyle, A. C. *The Edge of the Unknown*. New York: Putnam, 1930.

Durr, R. A. *Poetic Vision and the Psychedelic Experience*. Syracuse: Syracuse University Press, 1970.

Ebon, M. *They Knew the Unknown*. New York: World, 1971.

Edel, L. (Ed.) *Henry James: Stories of the Supernatural*. New York: Taplinger, 1970.

Ehrenwald, J. Telepathy in *Macbeth*? *Journal of the Society for Psychical Research*, 1941, 32, 99–102.

Emerson, R. W. The poet. In *The Complete Works of Ralph Waldo Emerson*, Vol. III, pp. 1–42. Boston: Houghton Mifflin, 1903. (Published in *Essays: Second Series*, 1844.)

Galbreath, R. The history of modern occultism: A bibliographical survey. In R. Galbreath (Ed.), *The Occult: Studies and Evaluations*, pp. 98–126. Bowling Green, Ohio: Bowling Green University Popular Press, 1972.

Garland, H. *Forty Years of Psychic Research: A Plain Narrative of Fact*.   New York: Macmillian, 1936.

Grant, J. *Far Memory*. New York: Harper & Row, 1956.

Head, J., and Cranston, S.L. *Reincarnation in World Thought*. New York: Julian Press, 1967.

Hearn, L. The value of the supernatural in fiction. In *Interpretations of Literature*, Vol. II, pp. 90–103. Port Washington, N.Y.: Kennikat Press, 1965. (First published in 1915.)

Huxley, A. *The Doors of Perception*. New York: Harper & Row, 1954.

Huxley, A. *Heaven and Hell*. New York: Harper & Row, 1956.

Jung, C. G. Psychology and literature. *In Modern Man in Search of a Soul*, pp. 152–172. (Trans. by W. S. Dell and C. F. Baynes.) New York: Harcourt, Brace and World, 1933.

Jung, C. G. *Memories, Dreams, Reflections*. (Recorded and ed. by A. Jaffé. Trans. by R. and C. Winston.) New York: Pantheon Books, 1963.

Karagulla, S. *Breakthrough to Creativity: Your Higher Sense Perception*. Santa Monica: DeVorss, 1967.

Kerr, H. *Mediums, and Spirit-Rappers, and Roaring Radicals: Spiritualism in American Literature, 1850–1900*. Urbana: University of Illinois Press, 1972.

Keynes, G. (Ed.) [William Blake's] *Songs of Innocence and of Experience*. London: Hart-Davis, 1967.

Kline, M. V. Introduction and headnotes. In D. Ward (Ed.), *Favorite Stories of Hypnotism*. New York: Dodd, Mead, 1965.

Lamansky, R. From the mountain. *Tantalus*, 1974 (Summer), pp. 3, 32.

Lansing, G. Psychic elements of poetic creativity. In A. Angoff (Ed.), *The Psychic Force: Essays in Modern Psychical Research from the International Journal of Parapsychology*, pp. 288–299. New York: Putnam, 1970.

McCormick, J. Psychic phenomena in literature. *Psychic*, 1972, 3(4), 40–44.

McCormick, J. Ghosts in literature. *Psychic*, 1973, 4(3), 44–48.

Maeterlinck, M. *The Unknown Guest*. (Trans. by A. T. de Mattos.) New York: Dodd, Mead, 1914.

Murphy, G. Jack London on transmigration. In J. London, *The Star Rover*, pp. 317–321. New York: Macmillan, 1963.

Myers, F. W. H. The subliminal consciousness. *Proceedings of the Society for Psychical Research*, 1893, 9, 3–128.

Palmer, J., and Vassar, C. ESP and out-of-the-body experiences: An exploratory study. *Journal of the American Society for Psychical Research*, 1974, 68, 257–280.

Penzoldt, P. *The Supernatural in Fiction*. London: Peter Nevill, 1952.

Porter, K. H. *Through a Glass Darkly: Spiritualism in the Browning Circle*. Lawrence: University of Kansas Press, 1958.

Prince, W. F. *Noted Witnesses for Psychic Occurrences*. Secaucus, N.J.: University Books, 1963. (First published in 1928.)

Railo, E. *The Haunted Castle: A Study of the Elements of English Romanticism*. London: George Routledge, 1927.

Rhine, J. B. *The Reach of the Mind*. New York: William Sloane, 1947.

Roellinger, F. X. Psychical research and "The Turn of the Screw." *American Literature*, 1949, 20, 401–412.

Roll, W. G. Pagenstecher's contribution to parapsychology. *Journal of the American Society for Psychical Research*, 1967, 61, 219–240.

Romains, J. *Eyeless Sight: A Study of Extra-Retinal Vision and the Paroptic Sense*. (Trans. by C. K. Ogden.) New York: Putnam, 1924.

Scarborough, D. *The Supernatural in Modern English Fiction*. New York: Putnam, 1917.

Scott, W. *Letters on Demonology and Witchcraft*. London: Murray, 1830.

Shumaker, W. *The Occult Sciences in the Renaissance: A Study in Intellectual Patterns*. Berkeley: University of California Press, 1972.

Tate, A. A lost traveller's dream. *Michigan Quarterly Review*, 1972, **11**, 225–236.

Törnqvist, E. *A Drama of Souls: Studies in O'Neill's Super-Naturalistic Technique*. New Haven: Yale University Press, 1969.

Wellek, R., and Warren, A. *Theory of Literature*. (3rd ed. rev.) New York: Harcourt, Brace and World, 1956.

White, S. E. *The Betty Book: Excursions Into the World of Other-Consciousness*. New York: Dutton, 1937.

White, S. E. *The Unobstructed Universe*. New York: Dutton, 1940.

Wilson. C. The poet as occultist. In *The Occult: A History*. New York: Random House, 1971.

Yeats, W. B. *Per Amica Silentia Lunae*. London: Macmillan, 1918.

Yeats, W. B. *Autobiographies*. New York: Macmillan, 1927. (New ed. with added materials.)

Yellen, S. The psychic world of William Shakespeare. In A. Angoff (Ed.), *The Psychic Force: Essays in Modern Psychical Research from the International Journal of Parapsychology*, pp. 267–288. New York: Putnam, 1970.

Part IX

PARAPSYCHOLOGICAL MODELS AND THEORIES

1

Some Generalized Theories and Models of Psi: A Critical Evaluation

C. T. K. Chari*

INTRODUCTION

Any discussion of generalized theories and models of psi must, in our present state of scientific knowledge, be very tentative. There has been so far no sustained consideration of the available theories with a view to ascertaining their scientific status. The only attempts to present some of the theories are those of Hans Bender (1966) and K. R. Rao (1966). They make no pretense of grouping the theories systematically or of formulating criteria for their assessment.

SCIENTIFIC THEORIES, MODELS, AND PARADIGMS VIS-À-VIS PARAPSYCHOLOGY

Contrary to some popular impressions, there is not much agreement in contemporary philosophy of science about the criteria for theories and models in any wide range of scientific speculation covering the physical, biological, psychological, and social sciences. On the well-known Hempel-Oppenheim "deductive-nomological" view, an event E (the *explanandum*) is said to be explained in

*I wish to thank Dr. P. J. Collipp, Nassau Medical Center, East Meadow, New York, for sending me an offprint of his article in the *Medical Times* and for offering some clarifications. I am grateful to Professor J. H. M. Whiteman for making available to me a predraft of the chapter which he has contributed to this *Handbook*. I acknowledge support and encouragement from the Parapsychology Foundation, New York City.

terms of covering laws, say $L_1, \ldots, L_n$, and other events, say $E_1, \ldots, E_n$. E is said to follow *logically* from the "laws" and the "states." Some authorities hold that a model is a suitable interpretation of a theory. A model in theoretical physics, for instance, may be a description in terms of physical states. If the physical theory is, say T, and t_1, t_2, are physical states in the theoretical language, then T and t_1 may together imply t_2, or, in the nomenclature of symbolic logic, $[T \cdot t_1 \supset t_2]$. Theories are usually regarded as having a greater generality than hypotheses.

The deductive-nomological view gives no secure guidance if more than one set of axioms, postulates, and deducible theorems can be set up. In Hempel's "inductive-probabilistic" framework, the role of a "covering law" is taken over by a probabilistic hypothesis. Unfortunately, we have an *embarras de choix* in constructing axiomatic systems of probability, especially in social sciences like economics involving considerations about "subjective" as well as "objective" probability.

The presumed symmetry of explanation and prediction in the deductive models becomes equivocal and controversial the moment we leave the idealized plane of mathematical physics. In medical pathology, a disease syndrome may have a kind of predictive value, but not necessarily an explanatory status. In the historical disciplines, we may have explanation, but without prediction (Gardiner, 1967; von Mises, 1958). Many social models are not so much mappings of an object-system on a postulated system as conceptualized sets of relations permitting at least some qualitative conclusions to be drawn about the relevant social group (McKinney and Tiryakian, 1970). The global features of the model may be more important than any logistic function, maxima, minima, and so forth.

Contemporary anthologies on political and social science (e.g., Apter and Andrain, 1972) point out that, if theories are explicit and generalized statements containing variables, and models are ways of expounding theories either by abstract symbolism or by descriptive and typological schemes, then social explanation must, at least implicitly, look beyond all these to a paradigm. Roughly speaking, a paradigm is a set of principles of orientation on which theories and models are based. Paradigms are polyvalent and elude precise characterization in a formal language. As Friedrichs (1970) remarks, apart from being the usual prime examples providing frames of reference, paradigms in the social and political sciences have typically linguistic rather than physical bases. They are pluralistic by being linguistic, and controversial by being irremediably pluralistic. In the political domain, we hear about the structural-functional, systems-analytical, rationalistic, and differential personality paradigms; in the social sciences, we hear about the normative, the structural, and the behavioral paradigms. For the normative paradigm, the "participant-observation" which furnishes the "facts" is never "value-free," but is always "value-laden." Whorfian hypotheses, Peter Finch's "quasi-causality" applied to social institutions, Parsonian systems-theories, various "models of man" using nonlinear analysis, path coefficients, path regression, etc., all illustrate selective ranges of social theory (Blalock, 1971; McKinney and Tiryakian, 1970). Even in the psychological sciences there is no unique and privileged way of forming constructs because there is no unique paradigm. If the stimulus is S, the response is R, and the organism is O, our "construct validity" may be in the language of $R = f(s)$, or $O = f(s)$, or even $R = f(O)$ (Neel, 1971).

Any full-dress explanation in parapsychology seems to need the whole gamut of the social, psychological, biological, and physical sciences (J. B. Rhine, 1971; Rhine and Pratt, 1957). Biological needs, personality characteristics (Schmeidler and McConnell, 1958), social attitudes and variables, and typologies can no more be excluded in an explanatory parapsychology than an obscure information-processing cutting right across the barriers of physical space-time and transcending the limits prescribed by orthodox biology and neurophysiology (Rhine and Pratt, 1957). It should be borne in mind that ESP and PK are never directly established by a single observation, or even by a series of observations. They have to be qualitatively or probabilistically established, at varying levels of significance, by the exclusion of some known stimuli, cues, variables, agencies, forces, and motives.

In spite of its avowedly rigorous experimental techniques, parapsychology reminds us of the situation in a complex social science where statistical reasoning alone is never sufficient to test theories, where the correlation language is too weak and the causal language too strong to suit even attempted middle-range explanations. The correlation language is rich but ambiguous. Whereas the relation of "if-then" (*modus ponens*) in a theory or hypothesis can be explicitly defined as transitive (i.e., if p, then q; if q, then y; therefore, if p, then y), rather strong requirements are needed to confer transitivity on empirically elicited statistical correlations between variables. If Durkheim's "pure individual case" has disappeared from much recent social research, the degree of falsifiability or testability of social theories often remains a formal or *a priori* characteristic of possible outcomes of distributions or probability considerations. Despite pious expectations in the social sciences, we are caught in the web between some generalizing (nomothetic) and singularizing (idiographic) speculation without hopes of immediate resolutions of conflicts.

To bring into focus the immensely difficult transition from methodology to interpretation in parapsychology, let us consider whether a "reinforced" or "diametrical" effect, with the subject scoring simultaneously on the cards immediately preceding and following the presented target (Tyrrell's "sandwich effect," 1946), occurred in the celebrated Soal-Goldney experiments (Soal and Bateman, 1954). For a tentative answer, we may have to resort to a second-order inference about, say, a sophisticated model (see Greville, 1954) involving quadratic or cubic equations and various extrapolatory assumptions about the continuous or sporadic character of the psi operation.

The crucial steps in parapsychological speculation consist in advancing from methodological (i.e., systematic but nonexplanatory) hypotheses to partial extrapolatory theories, and thence to a fundamental psi theory. The last step encounters an unprecedented difficulty. It is not like the genetic explanation of, say monozygotic and dizygotic twin correlations. The genetic information theory of orthodox biology suffices for twin correlations; it can, at least in principle, partition the genetic and environmental components of variance. The situation is very different in parapsychology. With all the psychological trait variables we can muster, with the whole fabric of biology, and with all the known laws of physics, we cannot produce a theory of psi which is both comprehensive and credible. The field is strewn with dead and dying hypotheses and desperate expedients.

The gap between methodology and theory in parapsychology may be illustrated by a glance at a variety of suggestions advanced in the past and in the present. H. H. Price's (1940) "collective unconscious," which is supposed to be a continuum for telepathic interaction, is a metaphysical construct which prescribes no methodological or explanatory links with the space-time of physics and with biopsychological variables. It affords only a philosophical climate favorable to psi. Whately Carington's (1972) "K-ideas" serving to link, in proportion to their associative strength, the agent and the percipient in an ostensible telepathic situation, is a quasi-descriptive hypothesis of no great generality (traditional associationism is outmoded even if some counterparts of it are not); it cannot be used for a methodological analysis of a wide range of ESP situations and so is not generally testable. The "shin" hypothesis of R. H. Thouless and B. P. Wiesner (1948) and the "psi-level" theory of Jan Ehrenwald (1955) presuppose a generalized perceptual-motor model. The "psi-gamma" and "psi-kappa" of the first theory and the "empathy" and "enkinesis" of the second theory are the transfigured counterparts of the afferent and efferent circuits of normal psychology. No *raison d'être* is offered for the theoretical extensions by analogy, and no inkling of the extended modes of operation in space and time. Ehrenwald, however, has the merit of seeking methodological links for his theory in psychoanalytic therapy and in depth-psychological observations.

Many recent proposals for psi models are tentative and exploratory. The "psi-mediated instrumental response" (PMIR) model sketched by Rex Stanford (1974) is methodological. It is assumed that PMIR can occur not only without conscious effort, but without even prior perception or awareness of the need-relevant condition. The research on dream-telepathy at Maimonides Medical Center (Ullman and Krippner, with Vaughan, 1973) is also largely descriptive and methodological. It is obvious that none of these quasi-explanatory models will work without a fundamental theory of psi-information processing in organisms. No such theory has been proposed by the model makers. The informational models built on the foundations of current information theories fail as comprehensive explanations of psi. The Osis-Bokert (1971) and the LeShan (1974) models speculate on relevancy, defense filtering, reorientation, etc., and bypass the whole problem of ESP information transmission over space and time. This omission is quite unwarranted if we really set out from significant informational models of human beings in which types of information processing are categorized and explicit relationships are spelled out between the amounts of information required and the adequacy of behavior. There is even a question today whether information theory should be confined to the stricter, narrower, and more mathematical contexts rather than being stretched to cover wider fields using informational concepts in some undefined way (Rosie, 1973).

It may be instructive to turn to another range of parapsychological problems. Any sufficiently generalized PK hypothesis must produce first principles capable of accounting not only for the physical forces acting paranormally on tumbling dice in obedience to conscious or unconscious volitions, but also for the rumored potent influence exercised by Uri Geller and Vinogradova on electrical and magnetic fields, by Nina Kulagina on floating hydrometers and Crookes' radiometers, and by Jurgenson on magnetic tape, as well as for some puzzling results of the "laying on of hands," for the alleged paranormal effects on fungus cultures (see L. E. Rhine, 1970), for the claimed phenomena of thoughtography (see Dr. Jule Eisenbud's chapter in this *Handbook*), and for massive psi healing running contrary to medical precepts. In 1969 P. J. Collipp described the presumed effects of collective prayer exercised on a group of randomly selected leukemic children compared with a control group, drug therapy being administered to both groups on more or less the same lines. Collipp (1973) is unimpressed by the criticism of the hemotologist Rosner that the control group was not matched carefully for the type of leukemia involved and the kind of drug therapy administered, and he remains convinced that the smallness of the sample was the chief handicap. Even more miraculous, if unsubstantiated, "cures" have been claimed by the enthusiastic disciples of the South Indian saint, Sri Sathya Sai Baba (Murphet, 1971).

We have no comprehensive theory accounting for all the reported physical, physiological, and therapeutic effects of psi. With some phenomena, e.g., the "laying on of hands," we have just reached the methodological and experimental stage. It is by no means certain that theories of the transmutation of gravitational, thermal, and other known forms of energy into psychokinesis do not flout established negentropic limits. Some proposed "autogravitation" hypotheses throw no light whatever on the static electrical effects claimed for Geller and Vinogradova. Theories of "biogravitation" seem to be cast in a holistic framework (the anomalous effect shows not in the individual living cells, but in the organism as a whole) and remain obscure for even the limited purposes of experimental testing and replication.

ON THE FALSIFICATION AND VERIFICATION OF THEORIES
IN SCIENCE AND IN PARAPSYCHOLOGY

It seems unwise, in parapsychological theory-building, to rely on any particular view of justifying scientific theories and models. A wise eclecticism, aware of the pitfalls of most of these methods, seems prudent. Inductivism, which is committed to the patient accumulation of facts, is no all-embracing ideal of scientific explanation but must be regarded rather as the codification of a popular myth about science. Alleged facts, especially in parapsychology, may permit mutually incompatible methodological and exploratory hypotheses. The blanket principle of "simplicity," exalted as the ideal of explanation, has proved illusory in the history of science (Harré, 1972; Theobald, 1968). The late Cyril Burt used to say that *Natura est simplex* cannot be a dictum of the psychological and social sciences. The ecological, contextual, historical, and cross-cultural fallacies are peculiar to the social sciences and have no counterpart in the physical sciences. Whether parapsychological research, especially in its excursions into anthropology, has freed itself from these fallacies is an open question, especially in view of the admission by such experts as Hook (1969) that even the most generalized semantic differential and other multicultural probes leave the separation of the culture-specific and the culture-invariant (pancultural) variables at the mercy of individual judgment which, in spite of professional training, is liable to err. The problems of equivalence in cross-cultural surveys, of translation, of using compound and coordinate bilinguals in investigations, of sorting out ethnic languages, are baffling. Irvine (1969) has gone so far as to question whether "intelligence" can be used as a construct of wide cross-cultural validity.

Operationism has become the fetish of some professional groups. To reduce every scientific concept to a finite set of operations, in accordance with the precepts of Bridgman, is to trivialize theory-building (Harré, 1972; Theobald, 1968). Theory in any large and fruitful sense, particularly in a domain like parapsychology, cannot be regarded as an ancillary to experimentation and prediction. Karl Popper's hypothetico-deductive version of inductivism, namely, falsification by instances, has no unimpeachable status (Harré, 1972; Theobald, 1968). Jarvie (1972) argues that the "logic of the situation" in the social sciences is normative as well as deductive.

According to both dogmatic and methodological falsificationism, scientific testing is a two-cornered fight between theory and experiment, its most important outcome being refutation. Lakatos (1970) has tried to refine the canons of rejection and acceptance. According to his sophisticated falsificationism, a scientific theory T_2 is falsified if and only if another theory T_1 is proposed which fulfills the three following conditions: (a) T_1 has an excess of empirical content over T_2; (b) T_1 explains the apparent previous success of T_2; and (c) some of the excess content of T_1 is corroborated. Applied to complex parapsychological research, even this version of falsificationism becomes dubious. Has the "survival hypothesis," in any of its formulations, an excess of content over the counterhypothesis of "ESP in the life-setting"? Can there be any decisive way of confirming the excess content? Needless to say, neither ESP nor survival is, as yet, a widely accepted hypothesis.

THE PLACE OF LOGICAL ANALYSIS IN PARAPSYCHOLOGICAL SPECULATION

Brier (1974), as a philosopher of science, has found it necessary to show that a psi phenomenon like precognition is not the outrageous claim it appears to be if "backward causation" in time is not logically incoherent or impossible. The gap between logical analysis and psi theories built on statistical evidence has already been underlined. It is not yet clear what type of logic psi theory needs. Will an analysis based on a Boolean logic, a distributive law, and an implicative "if-then" relationship do? Against the massive irreversibility of everyday biology and psychology, more than a logical demonstration of the bare possibility of "backward causation" is needed. *Suppose* backward causation in time were admitted; could there be a *two-way* circular process between a precognition and the future event, with a possible positive or negative feedback?

IS THERE A CONTEMPORARY RETREAT OF PHILOSOPHERS OF SCIENCE?

Our notions of explanation may well have to undergo some far-reaching and unprecedented changes before successful theory-building can come about in parapsychology. According to T. S. Kuhn's (1962) view, scientific revolutions are crises, tradition-shattering experiences, leading to major paradigm shifts. If he is right, the very concept of "truth" could be in the throes of a paradigm change. Popper and Kuhn both emphasize the interdependence of theory and fact, the insufficiency of a purely observational basis for science, the ethos of a scientific tradition, and Polanyi's fiduciary element. But whereas Popper's "criticism" can be a debate over fundamentals and can extend to the over-arching paradigm itself, for Kuhn scientific criticism is context-dependent; it operates *within* a paradigm since all rules, procedures, and methods, adopted by countless individual scientific workers, derive ultimately from the prevailing paradigm.

Does Feyerabend (1970), in advocating his "anarchistic theory of knowledge," sum up the contemporary retreat of philosophers of science? He says: "We find, then, that there is not a single rule, however plausible, and however firmly grounded in epistemology, that is not violated at some time or other."

DOES PARAPSYCHOLOGY AWAIT A REVOLUTION IN SCIENTIFIC PARADIGMS?

Does parapsychology await a major shift in scientific paradigms in Kuhn's sense? But Kuhn's view is not without its ambiguities and difficulties. Is Kuhn's "progress through scientific revolutions," which is not intraparadigmatic, cumulative or noncumulative? Is the illusion of cumulative progress generated by the mere rewriting of the history of science in the light of the new paradigm? Lakatos (1970) suggests that we should examine research programs, not paradigms, and he makes out a case for scientific progress by defending the notion of relative falsifiability. Stuewer (1970) pleads for a closer relationship between the philosophy of science and the history of science. Even so, what are we to make of the competing paradigms of the social sciences? Must they all be superseded by some new paradigm before a revolution can come about? Watson (1967) dubs psychology a "prescriptive science" because it lacks the clear paradigms of the more advanced sciences like physics. Krantz (1970, 1972) finds some indications that "operant" and "nonoperant" schools of psychology exist in mutual isolation.

One of Kuhn's major contentions may perhaps be stated in a less radical form than the one which he prefers. Our criteria for accepting very general theories of the universe are not understood or formulated; they may be very different from those tests (of falsifiability, etc.) which suffice for limited theories (Chari, 1975). The crying need in parapsychology may be for a meta-theory prescribing the criteria, the lines, and the limits for theories about psi phenomena and the universe. A meta-theory of this range is admittedly a stupendous task for which few parapsychologists or even teams of parapsychologists are equipped. The view that the whole material universe is just one convenient hypothesis, an "As-If" (*Als-Ob*), an approach unfolded in varying forms and with varying intents by G. N. M. Tyrrell (n.d., *ca* 1930; 1946), Hornell Hart (1965), and, more recently, by Charles McCreery (1973) and Lawrence LeShan (1974), may give a salutary jolt to smug and self-satisfied scientists, but this view cannot rank either as a major shift in paradigms or as a promising meta-theoretical framework for psi theories.

The following brief survey of some recently propounded generalized theories of psi may serve to show that parapsychology must have many more rallying points at a strictly exploratory level before it can mature into a truly explanatory discipline.

ELECTROMAGNETIC THEORIES OF PSI

Cazzamalli and others speculated on extrasensorial information being carried by some form of electromagnetic wave-propagation. The familiar objection that the signal-strength should then fall off according to an "inverse law" as the square of the distance increases is not enough to dispel the speculation. But the carefully designed experiments of Vasiliev (1963) rule out electromagnetic waves over a wide range in the ESP situation.

The electromagnetic theory can be harnessed to the postulates of current information theory. Complex relations hold among signal transmission, the mean transmitting power, sources of noise, the bandwidth of the channel, and the time required for transmission. Soviet workers like Lebedev and Levitin, by formulating the problem of "information transmission" in an electromagnetic field with both "wide-band" and "narrow-band" channels, have obtained the formulas of standard communication theory. It is, therefore, rather surprising to be told by a Soviet researcher, I. M. Kogan (in Rejdák, 1970), that with a suitably devised formula we can posit a hypothetical wave yielding a "telepathemic bit" (i.e., a binary psi unit) of information of specified duration at a specified temperature. Kogan admits that telepathy at longer distances does not fit very well into his theory.

Sophisticated modern variants of the electromagnetic theory of psi are much harder to refute than the commonplace garden variety. Wheeler and Feynman propounded an "absorber" theory of electromagnetic radiation and found that they had to introduce both "advanced" (future) and "retarded" (past) potentials. The two are inextricably mingled in the model. Suppose the "future absorbers" are not all cancelled out (as is usually assumed to be the case); then room can apparently be found for precognition. Feinberg and Good have invoked the hypothesis. Theoretical and experimental objections to the hypothesis have to be debated. Hoyle and Narlikar have demonstrated that a generalized model of an expanding universe incorporating the Wheeler-Feynman "absorber" theory does not allow the noncancellation of the "future absorbers." Full "retarded" and not "advanced" solutions are consistent with the model. Partridge and Pegg have found, in recent experiments, that absorption along the future cone in an expanding universe is better than one part in 10^8.

Ruderfer (see Chari, 1974a, 1974b) has amended the electromagnetic theory of psi by postulating neutrino and tachyon interactions with electromagnetic waves. The neutrino is a practically massless particle traveling with nearly the velocity of light. Pauli postulated its existence but wagered that it could not be detected. It was subsequently tracked by using the most delicate bubble chambers. Two kinds of neutrinos are known to exist. What are the implications for psi? While there are certainly many more neutrinos than atoms in the universe, there does not seem to be a sufficiently wide scope for high-energy neutrino interactions which could be used to support psi information transmission. Interactions may occur in certain nuclei, but not in others. While a neutrino theory of ESP cannot be positively falsified or verified at present, we must entertain many misgivings about it (Chari, 1974b).

The tachyon (so christened by Feinberg) is a hypothetical particle speeding with a velocity greater than that of light. The velocity of light, in the usual formulations of relativity theory, fixes an upper boundary for the transmission of all electromagnetic signals. Suppose, however, "ESP information" is carried by tachyons which interact with light particles (luxons) and slower-than-light material particles (tardyons); then could a "signal" in one frame of reference "arrive" *before* it is "sent" in another frame of reference? A tachyon hypothesis of ESP has been espoused by the Leningrad physicist Shiskin (in Rejdák, 1970) as well as by Ruderfer (see Chari, 1974b). Several issues about tachyons (assuming they exist) have not as yet been settled to the satisfaction of all physicists. Agreed formulations of the hypothesis in the "particle" and "wave" (field) forms have also not been reached. Some authorities question whether certain "preferred frames of reference" for tachyons violating the usual before-after categories are consistent with relativity (Chari, 1975). The proposed quantum restrictions ("cut-offs") are often quite arbitrary. The major question of information transmission by tachyons is wholly *sub judice* (Chari, 1972). Supposed methodological formulas for the "attenuation of ESP over increasing distances" make a poor start in speculation when the problem of precognition (transmission over *time*) is left largely unscratched. Brier's (1974) logical demonstration of the possibility of "backward causation" in time (even admitting that it is valid) is insufficient for any detailed theory of the *modus operandi* of precognition.

BIOELECTRIC, BIOENERGETIC, AND BIOPLASMIC THEORIES OF PSI

In grappling with ESP and PK problems, some enthusiasts have sought theoretical aid from the bioelectric fields postulated by Northrop, Burr, and their colleagues. These conjectural fields are supposed to influence the pattern and development of organisms. A majority of biologists would admit the coexistence of certain electrical and physiological phenomena without assenting to the deep-lying connections conjectured by Burr (see Chari, 1970). The Soviet researcher Inyushin (in Rejdák, 1970) envisages a "bioplasmic interaction" between a telepathic agent and percipient. The "bioplasm" is picturesquely described as a "fourth state of matter" which can be photographed, e.g., in a Kirlian field. The usual information-theoretic formulas would seem to ensure temporal irreversibility for most cases of what is called in theoretical physics Maxwellian or non-Maxwellian collision plasma. A "bioplasm" or "psychoplasm" with totally unknown properties cannot claim to be a rightful link between physics and psi phenomena.

GENERALIZED QUANTUM-MECHANICAL, RELATIVISTIC, AND COSMOLOGICAL THEORIES OF PSI

Quantum mechanics, especially the mathematical version of it made familiar by von Neumann (in Hooker, 1973), who extracted the essential features of the

Heisenberg and Schrödinger theories, seems to raise three far-reaching issues of possible relevance to parapsychology: (a) Consistent with the postulates of quantum mechanics, it seems possible for the constituents of a composite system to be in an indefinite state even when the system exists in a definite state. (b) The behavior of a quantum-mechanical system, so long as it is not interacting with an observer, is controlled by Schrödinger's equation. But during measurement by an observer, the system seems to undergo a sudden and nondeterminate transition which is not controlled by Schrödinger's equation. Helmut Schmidt (1975) has used a quantum set-up to demonstrate both ESP and PK. Can the "interaction with the observer" somehow explain the anomalies of physics as well as those of psi phenomena? (c) Von Neumann noted that the quantum-mechanical interaction of the observer with the observed greatly complicates the traditional theories of mind-body dualism. Von Weizäcker (1974) declared that we may have to consider the claims of Indian Vedanta sympathetically. He says that quantum physics makes the distinction between "in the body" and "out of the body" quite arbitrary and reduces so-called separate objects to the lack of knowledge of the coherent phases of reality.

A quantum-mechanical clue to the psi riddle has been sought along different lines. Ninian Marshall (1960) has attempted to account for the highly selective and well-nigh incredible ranges in which ESP information operates by postulating an "eidopoic influence" which is detectable only in highly organized material systems like the neural matter of organisms. The eidopoic influence can make what is virtually a "faint noise" available as a "signal" regardless of spatio-temporal distance. Wigner has dwelt on the contradiction of supposing that an eidopoic or other holistic influence is compatible with present-day quantum mechanics when there is no conceivable way of deducing it from the postulates of quantum mechanics.

Bohm, Bub, and others have introduced various "hidden variables" into the equations of quantum mechanics in order to make the paradoxical transition in measurement by an observer, the notorious "collapse of the wave packet," continuous and determinate. Von Neumann, Jauch, Piron, Gudder, and Misra (in Hooker, 1973) have all disputed whether "hidden variables" can be validly and consistently introduced into the postulates of quantum mechanics. From the critiques offered by Bell and Wigner (in Hooker, 1973), it would appear that "hidden variable" theories either (a) are not deterministic, but have quantum mechanics as a kind of "limit," or else (b) are deterministic, but are not able to reproduce quantum mechanics completely.

Walker (1974) has taken the bold step of introducing into quantum mechanics consciousness (or subconsciousness) as a "hidden variable." He attempts to explain ESP by demanding an intersubjective agreement in consciousness which brings about the "collapse of the wave packet," and he suggests that PK may be an accompanying divergent effect in the relevant energetic system. The theory makes the paradoxical claim that ESP does not mean that information is transmitted from the agent to the subject, but rather that in the very selection of the

ESP targets, however random, an agreed "collapse of the wave packet" has been engineered. Walker does not confront (any more than Marshall does) the problem of possible ESP in organisms lacking a central nervous system or even recognizable neural matter. It can be shown that even the simplest nontrivial "hidden variable" theory in quantum mechanics involves a set of unique nonlinear differential equations (Tutsch, 1973)—the Schrodinger equation in its usual forms is linear —and that all criteria for the observability of nonlinear systems are cryptical as well as global (Kou, Elliott, and Tarn, 1973).

Everett, Graham, and de Witt solve, or perhaps dissolve, the problem of the "collapse of the wave packet" by saying that *no* reduction of the wave packet occurs at any stage. There is a cosmos which breaks up into innumerable observers and observed systems. All of these are seen as equally real. In the multiparallel universe, various states can be endlessly superposed on one another. Good exploits this possibility by arguing that in ESP we may be dealing with various superpositions of the observer and the observed systems (see Chari, 1972). This theory makes the questionable supposition that the observer himself is "splitting" without being aware of the fact. The "branch" of the universe ostensibly available to him evolves stochastically and with quantum jumps. Some critics suspect that the whole theory provides only fodder for science fiction addicts. And for some parapsychologists too?

Dobbs (1965) and Shishkin (in Rejdák, 1970) abandon nonrelativistic quantum mechanics and welcome the relativistic generalization of it in quantum field theory. They try to account for precognition by invoking a Feynman model in which a particle like the positron moves backward in time. Dobbs gives a double twist to an already overweighted theory by speculating on a second virtual dimension of time in which probabilities, interpreted as Popper's objective dispositions or "propensities," can be copresent. Certain anomalous particles called "psitrons" register the probabilities in the second time-dimension and contribute to the EEG alpha rhythms of the brain. A below-the-threshold awareness of objective probabilities may emerge as a pre-image of a future event.

It may be questioned whether the wave function of quantum mechanics can signify the objective weights to be attached to the different possible states of an elementary particle like the electron and also whether time-reversals in a microtime can contribute decisively to the asymmetry of before-after during measurement in quantum mechanics when the observer makes, say, an "ESP hit." Can the hypothesized psitrons have anything at all to do the EEG alpha rhythms, whether these are interpreted as coupled oscillators with components which can be separated by a microcomputer and Fourier's method of transformation, or else treated as summated postsynaptic potentials largely under the control of recurrent inhibiting thalamic networks? Aleksandrova (1972) thinks that the measures of background activity (amplitude and index) may correlate with a level of nonspecific activity. According to her, the evoked potentials may correspond with changes in the stimulation of the reticular formation. The assumptions about the brain made in the professed psi theories are often gratuitous.

Pearson (Chari, 1970) invokes Dirac's negative energy states which are merely the mathematical counterpart of the Feynman positron. Pearson builds up a speculative hypothesis in which the energy densities of brain chemicals are supposed to be high enough to permit some anomalous manifestations (telepathy, clairvoyance, and precognition) of the "non-zero properites" of the "perfect vacuum." The fate of the theory is precarious.

In relativity theory, time intervals are not absolutely fixed; they are relative to the speed of the moving system. Attempts have been made to relate the clock paradox of the "asymmetrical aging of twins" in relativity to the precognition problem. But the "time-dilation effects"—e.g., in two-meson experiments and in finer analyses of the Mössbauer effect—are much too small to account for precognition in the typical laboratory setting.

Cosmological theories of ESP fare no better than the nonrelativistic quantum-mechanical theories and the relativistic quantum field theories. Kooy's world, with space and time *both* curved in cosmological reaches, leaves precognition in a terrestrial setting wholly unexplained (Chari, 1970). This may apply equally well to some recent fanciful constructs of Good, e. g., tachyons carrying "messages" in a curved universe. It has been shown by Albrow that, with complete symmetry of space, time, and electrical charge in an oscillating model of the universe, there would be no worthwhile observable consequences. Novel sub-spaces in a nearly closed universe, collapsed black holes, multiply-connected space-time with "worm-holes," matter-antimatter collisions (with or without the initial "big bang" of an expanding universe) are certainly curiosities for theoretical physics because they imply a partial or total abeyance of the known laws of nature, but they do not seem to be relevant to ESP occurring under ordinary conditions.

Gregory and Kohsen speculated on microevents occurring in quantal dimensions without time, and, by a kind of analogy, on macroevents having form and energy but no historical time. Unfortunately their elaborate theory of the "O-structure" relies dogmatically on a particular cosmological model, Eddington's "uranoid," and on a unified field theory in physics, the status of which is highly debatable.

MULTIDIMENSIONAL THEORIES OF PSI

Hornell Hart (1965) postulated the material universe as a cross-section of a five-dimensional manifold. Every observer is supposed to operate in a four-dimensional space-time by moving along a time-line, reading his past, but sometimes looking ahead noninferentially into the future. Intersection of four-dimensional structures will be in the five-space. J. R. Smythies would prefer to keep his physical dimensions and his psychic dimensions (3 of the former and $3n$ of the latter for n observers) apart. ESP and PK are unorthodox cognitive and energetic exchanges between the physical and the psychic spaces.

The term *dimension* in these theories is not sophisticated enough to establish

fruitful connections with mathematical topology, relativity, and quantum mechanics (Chari, 1958). Unorthodox exchanges in multidimensional space may
well disrupt the physical continuity of ordinary space, and they may even prevent
the extinction of an ordinary candle in our familiar 3-space. No cogent definition
of causality in the many-space universe has been offered.

J. W. Dunne postulated a multidimensional time and C. D. Broad a two-
dimensional time in an effort to solve the puzzle of precognition. A topological
generalization of these theories seems to be possible (Chari, 1957), but no coherent interpretation of the amended theory can be provided without the most
sweeping changes in all our usual conceptions of the passage of events. H. F.
Saltmarsh's (1934) conception of an extended "specious present" takes care of
the extensive aspect of time, but neglects utterly its passage aspect. Reductions
of temporal passage to nontemporal relations between suitably chosen terms are
overdone, at least in the case of psi. Either the precognized event or the precognition itself acquires a flagrantly indeterminate location in our one-way time
(Chari, 1970).

GENERALIZED PSI FIELD THEORIES

Generalized psi field theories such as those of G. D. Wassermann, Gardner Murphy,
Cyril Burt, W. G. Roll, and Campbell Garnett have been surveyed elsewhere
(Chari, 1970). Their status as theoretical rather than as methodological devices
is open to serious doubt. Wassermann's (1956) proliferation of field into bound-
matter P-fields, morphogenetic M-fields, behavioral and learning B-fields, with
psi fields as variants of B-fields, is purely ad hoc. He ignores the almost intract-
able difficulties which arise in relativistic quantum mechanics from the interaction
of fields, especially if we insist on a rigorous and consistent treatment of Hilbert
space. The difficulties have led Dirac, Bohm, and other authorities to speculate
on more general, if more obscure, spaces without reaching consensus. Quantum
Hilbert space is linear and admits of the endless superposition of states. The
classical Hamilton-Jacobi equation on which Wassermann seems to rely is nonlinear and admits of no superposition. Regarded as explanatory devices, Was-
serman's hypothesized fields are gratuitous. They have no analytic or predictive
value in psi research.

Cyril Burt's (1961) "informational fields" which elucidate clairvoyant or precognitive ESP could not have been deduced from any of the current versions of
information theory. Campbell Garnett's (1965) "neutral medium" for precognition, carrying patterns of future material and mental events, bears a most
dubious analogy to the *Urmaterie* of Heisenberg's nonlinear field theory. By
avoiding the mind-matter dichotomy, it seems to force a trichotomy on us.

Gardner Murphy's (1945) "interpersonal fields" are a cautious extrapolation
of Kurt Lewin's topology. Their diagnostic uses could certainly be explored
further. Theoretical issues are more controversial. An elaborate survey of

social and psychological fields by H. Mey (1965) would seem to suggest that these fields have not yet superseded causal and other modes of scientific explanation, contrary claims notwithstanding. And so long as there is no unambiguous mathematical or other method of constructing the "common space," the plural and particular "personal spaces" cannot be regarded as annulled or cancelled (Chari, 1970).

W. G. Roll's (1966) psi field theory may have some limited methodological uses, e.g., in discussing poltergeist phenomena. As a theoretical construct, however, it exhibits a hybrid character. By Roll's own admission, it partakes of some of the characteristics of Wassermann's P-fields and some of the characteristics of Murphy's interpersonal fields. One suspects that the weaknesses of both these constructs may be present. Technical criticism can also be offered of Roll's proposal to replace precognitive ESP by PK and nonprecognitive ESP, both acting in alliance with the psi field (Chari, 1970).

SYNCHRONICITY, CHANCE, AND PROBABILITY

Jung regarded synchronicity as a meaningful linkage of facts transcending the space-time-cause universe. Followers of Jung would interpret psi occurrences as "perfect coincidences." Hardy, Harvie, and Koestler (1973) hazard that a "coincidence-generating" acausal factor may operate in biological evolution and produce meaningful convergences, clusters, emergence of the new, and possibly psi occurrences. Whiteman regards synchronicity as a teleological causality operating from a higher to a lower level of a hierarchical universe.

Without going all the way with these writers or their critics, it must be pointed out that quantum mechanics calls for some drastic overhaul of the classical theory of probability developed in an axiomatic "label space" with its product spaces and product measures. In quantum logic, a new notion of "compatible random variables" precludes a joint distribution function for "incompatible variables." The distributive law of Boolean logic, which underlies so much of mathematical physics, computer technology, and the algebra of various proposed neural networks, ceases to hold sway in quantum lattice theory. Strongly non-Boolean logics may have a role to play in parapsychological theories and models.

SURVIVALISTIC AND REINCARNATIONISTIC THEORIES

Philosophers like Broad, Price, and Ducasse, in speculating on the implications of parapsychological survival data, have relied on some form of mind-body dualism theory. The logic of quantum mechanics raises some very deep and unexpected questions about the adequacy of any of these dualisms. Mind-body dualisms, at least in the forms hitherto favored, are not the necessary scaffolding of survival speculation.

A prerequisite of *any* theory of survival is an explicit and unequivocal answer to the twin questions: *What* survives death? And *how*? Parapsychology has traveled a long way away from experiments with "interatomic life quantities" and "four-dimensional astral bodies." Neither consciousness nor memory can decide exclusively the status of any θ-component of human personality which survives death. It should be clearly realized that survival is a much more fundamental issue than reincarnation. The latter *presupposes* the former, but the former does not *entail* the latter. Suppose two alleged "successive lives" of the "same ego" are separated in space and time (Stevenson, 1973, 1974); then we have to provide some clear notions of the "intermediate state" before reincarnation can rank even as a tentative methodological hypothesis for analyzing the data.

The problem of providing a methodological model of survival is greatly complicated by the urgent necessity, if we take the survival data seriously, of equipping the surviving θ-component with fairly extensive ESP and PK capacities. How, otherwise, can we even conceive of "discarnate communicators" finding purposefully, though temporarily, an anchorage in mediums and sensitives? And how, without ESP and PK on a spectacular scale, can the reincarnating ego select, however unconsciously, the place, time, and manner of its reentry into human societies, sometimes taking care to reproduce artificial marks made *after* death on its former body? Reincarnation, if it occurs on anything like a major scale, is a thinly disguised Lamarckism. The hypothesis demands that the habits, the memories, and even the scars on bodies, which were acquired by individuals in historically earlier times, are transmitted to later generations by their "surviving egos" being reborn in large numbers. There seems no way, either in modern molecular biology or in quantum-mechanical versions of it, of allowing reincarnating egos to influence genetic information systems directly. The presence of what is called a nonholonomic constraint in a quantum-mechanical system would transform the template replication of the average genetics manual into the far profounder *reliable* molecular code enforcing the one-directional flow of genetic information from the DNA of one generation to the DNA of another generation, or else from the DNA of the individual to the protein, via the DNA and the RNA, of the somatic cells. The reported rare instances of RNA-induced DNA synthesis (Temm, 1972) do not rob Crick's "central dogma of molecular biology" of its commanding position. Mediumistic possession, if it is a paranormal fact, would pose formidable problems for science, and yet no *ignoratio elenchi* for modern biology if the genetic information system is not directly involved, but only secondary informational systems organized in the central nervous system and related structures.

The persistence of memories is a major issue for all forms of the survival hypothesis, but for the reincarnationist doctrine it is something of a crux. Why do some persons, but not others, even in favorably situated Asian areas, recall their earlier lives? Why, even in the comparatively few cases that are reported, do the memories tend to fade away? An ordinary interference theory of memory (Stevenson, 1973) is worse than useless. Melton attacked the dichotomy of long-term memory and short-term memory and argued for a unitary memory following the general principles of interference. Evidence has recently been accumulating against the unitary view (Baddeley, 1972). Long-term memory has to be discussed in terms of search, signal theory, and retrieval of information. Few serious students can be satisfied with the pretended ethical justifications of the total autopsychic amnesia for former lives from which a majority of us must be suffering if reincarnation takes place on anything like a global scale.

H. H. Price (1972, Chap. 5) has sketched an ingenious theory of surviving clusters of "body images" having extension of a sort, but no "whereness" in any obvious sense in relation to sensory particulars. He ignores all tidy geometries and claims that his theory is a useful compromise between extreme "disembodied" and extreme "embodied" views. He finds, however, that he has to save the "surviving egos" from a dire solipsistic fate by supplying telepathic linkages between the several private "image worlds." One does not hear about any reincarnationist applications of this hypothesis. Are such applications feasible at all if the image worlds and physical worlds are incommensurable? The problem that haunts the Hart-Smythies multidimensional universes rears its head again. The complete lack of anything remotely like an explanatory theory of ESP and PK threatens to halt the most intrepid survivalist and make the whole speculation a gamble, and perhaps almost anybody's guess (Chari, 1974a). *Mors janua vitae* provides scientific workers with no reliable signposts indicating whether or not travelers return from the Great Bourne.

REFERENCES *

Aleksandrova, N. I. The correlation between background alpha activity and the characteristics of the components of evoked potentials. In V. D. Nebylitsyn and J. A. Gray (Eds.), *Biological Bases of Individual Behavior*, pp. 86–110. New York: Academic Press, 1972.

Apter, D. E., and Andrain, C. F. (Eds.). *Contemporary Analytical Theory*. Englewood Cliffs, N.J.: Prentice-Hall, 1972.

Baddeley, A. P. Human memory. In P. C. Dodwell (Ed.), *New Horizons of Psychology*, pp. 36–61. Harmondsworth, England: Penguin Books, 1972.

Bender, H. (Ed.). *Parapsychologie, Entwicklung, Ergebnisse Probleme*. Darmstad: Wissenschaftliche Buchgesselschaft, 1966.

Blalock, H. M. (Ed.). *Causal Models in the Social Sciences*. New York: Macmillan, 1971.

Brier, B. *Precognition and the Philosophy of Science*. New York: Humanities Press, 1974.

Burt, C. The structure of mind. *British Journal of Statistical Psychology*, 1961, 14, 145–170.

Carington, W. *Telepathy: An Outline of its Facts, Theory, and Implications*. New York: Gordon Press, 1972.

*A number of authors and sources discussed in this paper are not cited in the list of references for reasons of economy of space. Some of them will be found in Chari (1972, 1974a, 1974b, 1975).

Chari, C. T. K. A note on multi-dimensional time. *British Journal for the Philosophy of Science*, 1957, **8**, 155-158.

Chari, C. T. K. On the "space" and "time" of hallucinations. *British Journal for the Philosophy of Science*, 1958, **8**, 302-306.

Chari, C. T. K. An evaluation of some field-theoretical approaches to psi. *Psychocosmos*, 1970, **1**, 1-19.

Chari, C. T. K. Precognition, probability, and quantum mechanics. *Journal of the American Society for Psychical Research*, 1972, **66**, 193-207.

Chari, C. T. K. The challenge of psi: New horizons of scientific research. *Journal of Parapsychology*, 1974, **38**, 1-15. (a)

Chari, C. T. K. Letter. *Journal of Parapsychology*, 1974, **38**, 418-420. (b)

Chari, C. T. K. Parapsychology, quantum logic and information theory. In L. Oteri (Ed.), *Quantum Physics and Parapsychology*, pp. 76-90. New York: Parapsychology Foundation, 1975.

Collipp, P. J. The efficacy of prayer: A triple-blind study. *Medical Times*, 1969, **97**, 201-204.

Collipp, P. J. Personal communication, 1973.

Dobbs, H. A. C. Time and ESP. *Proceedings of the Society for Psychical Research*, 1965, **54**, 249-361.

Ehrenwald, J. *New Dimensions of Deep Analysis*. New York: Grune and Stratton, 1955.

Feyerabend, P. K. Against method: Outline of an anarchistic theory of knowledge. In M. Radner and S. Winokur (Eds.), *Analyses of Theories and Methods of Physics and Psychology*, pp. 17-130. Minneapolis: University of Minnesota Press, 1970.

Friedrichs, R. W. *The Sociology of Sociology*. New York: The Free Press, 1970.

Gardiner, P. *Theories of History*. London: Allen & Unwin, 1967.

Garnett, A. C. Matter, mind, and precognition. *Journal of Parapsychology*, 1965, **29**, 19-26.

Greville, T. N. E. A reappraisal of the mathematical evaluation of the reinforcement effect. *Journal of Parapsychology*, 1954, **18**, 178-183.

Hardy, A., Harvie, R., and Koestler, A. *The Challenge of Chance*. London: Hutchison, 1973.

Harré, R. *The Philosophy of Science*. London: Oxford University Press, 1972.

Hart, H. Toward a new philosophical basis for parapsychological phenomena. *Parapsychology Monographs No. 6*. New York: Parapsychology Foundation, 1965.

Hook, S. (Ed.). *Language and Philosophy: A Symposium*. New York: New York University Press, 1969.

Hooker, C. A. (Ed.). *Contemporary Research into the Foundations and Philosophy of Quantum Theory*. Boston: Reidel, 1973.

Irvine, S. H. Analysis of African abilities and attainments: Constructs across cultures. *Psychological Bulletin*, 1969, **71**, 20-32.

Jarvie, I. C. *Concepts and Society*. London: Routledge and Kegan Paul, 1972.

Kou, S. R., Elliott, D. L., and Tarn, T. J. Observability of non-linear systems. *Information and Control*, 1973, **22**, 89-99.

Krantz, D. L. *Schools of Psychology: A Symposium*. New York: Appleton-Century-Crofts, 1970.

Krantz, D. L. Schools and systems: The mutual isolation of operant and non-operant psychology as a case study. *Journal of the History of the Behavioral Sciences*, 1972, **8**, 86-102.

Kuhn, T. S. *The Structure of Scientific Revolutions*. Chicago: University of Chicago Press, 1962.

Lakatos, I. Falsification and the methodology of scientific research programs. In I. Lakatos and A. Musgrave (Eds.), *Criticism and the Growth of Knowledge*, pp. 91-195. New York: Cambridge University Press, 1970.

LeShan, L. *The Medium, the Mystic, and the Physicist*. New York: Viking Press, 1974.

Marshall, N. ESP and memory: A physical theory. *British Journal for the Philosophy of Science*, 1960, **10**, 265–286.

McCreery, C. *Psychical Phenomena and the Physical World*. London: Hamish Hamilton, 1973.

McKinney, J. C., and Tiryakian, E. (Eds.). *Theoretical Sociology: Perspectives and Development*. New York: Appleton-Century-Crofts, 1970.

Mey, H. *Studien zur Anwendung des Feldbegriff in den Sozial-Wissenschaften*. Munich: C. R. Piper, 1965.

Murphet, H. *Sai Baba, Man of Miracles*. London: Frederick Muller, 1971.

Murphy, G. Field theory and survival. *Journal of the American Society for Psychical Research*, 1945, **39**, 181–209.

Neel, A. *Theories of Psychology: A Handbook*. London: University of London Press, 1971.

Osis, K., and Bokert, E. ESP and changed states of consciousness induced by meditation. *Journal of the American Society for Psychical Research*, 1971, **65**, 17–65.

Price, H. H. Some philosophical questions about telepathy and clairvoyance. *Philosophy*, 1940, **15**, 363–385.

Price, H. H. *Essays in the Philosophy of Religion*. New York: Oxford University Press, 1972.

Rao, K. R. *Experimental Parapsychology: A Review and Interpretation*. Springfield, Ill.: Charles C Thomas, 1966.

Rejdák, A. (Ed.). *Telepatie a Jasnovidnost*. Prague: Svoboda, 1970.

Rhine, J. B. (Ed.). *Progress in Parapsychology*. Durham, N.C.: Parapsychology Press, 1971.

Rhine, J. B., and Pratt, J. G. *Parapsychology: Frontier Science of the Mind*. Springfield, Ill.: Charles C Thomas, 1957.

Rhine, L. E. *Mind Over Matter*. New York: Macmillan, 1970.

Roll, W. G. The psi field. *Proceedings of the Parapsychological Association* (1957–1964), 1966, **1**, 32–65.

Rosie, A. M. *Information and Communication Theory*. New York: Van Nostrand Reinhold, 1973.

Saltmarsh, H. F. Report on cases of apparent precognition. *Proceedings of the Society for · Psychical Research*, 1934, **42**, 49–103.

Schmeidler, G. R., and McConnell, R. A. *ESP and Personality Patterns*. New Haven: Yale University Press, 1958.

Schmidt, H. Toward a mathematical theory of psi. *Journal of the American Society for Psychical Research*, 1975, **69**, 301–319.

Soal, S. G., and Bateman, F. *Modern Experiments in Telepathy*. New Haven: Yale University Press, 1954.

Stanford, R. G. An experimentally testable model for spontaneous psi events. I. Extrasensory events. *Journal of the American Society for Psychical Research*, 1974, **68**, 34–57; II. Psychokinetic events. *Ibid*, 321–356.

Stevenson, I. Carington's psychon theory as applied to cases of the reincarnation type: A reply to Gardner Murphy. *Journal of the American Society for Psychical Research*, 1973, **67**, 130–146.

Stevenson, I. Some questions related to cases of the reincarnation type. *Journal of the American Society for Psychical Research*, 1974, **68**, 395–416.

Stuewer, R. H. (Ed.). *Historical and Philosophical Perspectives of Science*. Minneapolis: University of Minnesota Press, 1970.

Temm, H. M. RNA-directed-DNA synthesis. *Scientific American*, 1972, **226**, 25–33.

Theobald, D. W. *An Introduction to the Philosophy of Science*. London: Methuen, 1968.

Thouless, R. H., and Wiesner, B. P. The psi process in normal and "paranormal" psychology. *Journal of Parapsychology*, 1948, **12**, 192–212.

Tutsch, J. H. Mathematics of the measurement problem in quantum mechanics. *Journal of Mathematical Physics*, 1973, **12**, 1711–1718.

Tyrrell, G. N. M. *Grades of Significance*. London: Rider, n.d. (*ca.* 1930.)

Tyrrell, G. N. M. *The Personality of Man*. Harmondsworth, England: Penguin Books, 1946.

Ullman, M., and Krippner, S., with Vaughan, A. *Dream Telepathy*. New York: Macmillan, 1973.

Vasiliev, L. L. *Experiments in Mental Suggestion*. Church Crookham, Hampshire, England: Institute for the Study of Mental Images, 1963.

Von Mises, L. *Theory and History*. London: Jonathan Cape, 1958.

Von Weizäcker, C. F. Who is the knower in physics? In T. M. P. Mahadevan (Ed.), *Spiritual Perspectives*, pp. 147–161. New Delhi: Arnold-Heinemann, 1974.

Walker, E. H. Consciousness and quantum theory. In E. D. Mitchell and others, *Psychic Exploration: A Challenge for Science*, pp. 544–568. New York: Putnam's, 1974.

Wassermann, G. D. An outline of a field theory of organismic form and behavior. In G. D. Wolstenholme and E. Millar (Eds.), *Ciba Foundation Symposium on Extrasensory Perception*, pp. 53–72. Boston: Little, Brown, 1956.

Watson, R. I. Psychology: A prescriptive science. *American Psychologist*, 1967, **22**, 435–443.

2

Conceptual Frameworks of Contemporary Psi Research

Rex G. Stanford

INTRODUCTION

The functions of theory and theory-building in any scientific area are manifold. Some of these functions may be described as follows:

Explanation. A theory is capable of providing an explanation of the facts, findings, or functional relationships (laws) of a certain area of research. It does so by providing a framework within which such observations can be deduced from more general statements (Hempel and Oppenheim, 1953). Thus these observations are said to be subsumed by the theory.

Prediction of possible new discoveries. No theory is of any value which allows only the deduction of already known observations. In the first place, it is comparatively easy to produce a set of ad-hoc assumptions from which can be deduced the established findings of a given area of inquiry. Indeed, it should be possible to come up with a considerable set of such "theories" if there is no other requirement for theory building. But the problem is then how to decide between competing theories. (At this point the theory would generally be regarded as best which meets the above requirement through the use of the simplest or least numerous set of assumptions—the "Law of Parsimony" or Ockham's Razor—but this consideration is not central to our present concerns.) The way to decide between competing theories which adequately explain a given set of data is to make further deductions from the theories—deductions which predict heretofore undiscovered observations—and to conduct experimentation to aid in allowing a decision. Of course here it will be impossible to decide between two theories which give rise to predictions of the same "new" finding, so the trick is to see whether alternative theories lead to unique predictions and to pursue research to thereby confirm one theory and to disconfirm the other. In this way theory building leads to new research and possible new discovery. Indeed, were only one theory available, so long as it predicted possible new discoveries, it could play this function. To this point, then, it can be said that a good theory subsumes the known in a given area of inquiry and leads to predictions of new empirical knowledge.

Extralogical heuristic value of theories. A theory may encourage research for the purely logical reason just discussed and for certain other reasons which may be regarded as extralogical (though that is not to say they are illogical or unjustified). A good theory or model, and indeed any conceptual framework for scientific research, has the capacity to inspire research because of what might be termed the *affective value of theories*. Because a theory serves to organize the findings of research economically, it can have positive esthetic value which encourages new, incisive experimentation. The creation of a theory suggests that some degree of "closure" (in the Gestalt sense) may be about to occur and that heretofore relatively disparate findings can now be seen as parts of a meaningful whole. It at least suggests that this may happen pending the outcomes of further studies. On the other hand, because theories by definition explain certain empirical generalizations by subsuming them under higher-level generalizations, it is always possible that these most basic assumptions within a given theory will produce differing affective reactions in different scientists. Some persons will wish to use a different set of assumptions to subsume the same data. The choice will, of course, be based upon the feeling that one set of assumptions, rather than another, more clearly, more completely, or more elegantly accomplishes the job at hand. But the choice of sets of assumptions will often depend upon strong feelings or intuitions that some given approach works better or is more adequate. Whatever the reason, this, too, leads to further investigation. It should be noted that these extralogical heuristic functions of theory-building are possible only when a given theory has implications which go beyond current data.

Making explicit and clarifying assumptions. Sometimes research is carried out under implicit assumptions, assumptions which are often either taken for granted or may even be unrecognized. Ironically, it is just such assumptions which have a formative influence on the directions of research. If the assumptions are inadequate or incorrect, the result can be a serious and often long-term retardation of research. Elsewhere I have argued that parapsychology's progress has been retarded by its having "few if any *explicit* hypothetical constructs and . . . too many implicit and often unrecognized conceptual biases" (Stanford, 1974c, p. 137). The building of theories and models encourages the making explicit of the assumptions behind one's research and the clarification of these assumptions.

Encourages awareness of accomplishments and failures. Since theories are constructed in the light of and ultimately are intended to subsume current knowledge in a given area, theory-building and theory-based research help throw into clearer perspective exactly what is known and understood in a given scientific area and what is not. This function of theory is particularly relevant to young and relatively undeveloped sciences like parapsychology. Careful stock-taking in any scientific area can be a great boon. It allows building upon what is firmly established, provides encouragement toward strengthening of inadequately evidenced findings, and a stark realization of what areas remain untouched and thus must be pursued.

THEORY BUILDING IN PARAPSYCHOLOGY

The above remarks are intended to apply to any and all efforts at building conceptual frameworks for scientific research. What I have loosely termed theory building ranges over a wide span of activity from the highly formalized theories of physics to the (often) verbal conceptualizations in some of the social sciences. It also covers both general theories and much more delineated concepts aimed at explaining narrow ranges of facts. Many of the values of building conceptual frameworks to guide research nonetheless remain much the same in all the sciences and at all levels of conceptualization within a given science.

Bearing in mind these functions of theories, this paper will show both that parapsychology is now engaged in developing conceptual frameworks for its research and that this activity is exerting a major, important influence on the directions of research today.

To understand what is really happening in these respects, several questions can be asked: What concepts are guiding psi research at present? From what do these concepts derive? What kinds of research are they inspiring? Is the research actually leading to knowledge? Are useful new concepts being suggested by this concept-oriented work? How is any new knowledge in turn influencing the concepts of the field? Have any findings developed which have forced the reexamination or abandonment of earlier concepts? Are these developments leading toward real theory building, i.e., are there developing certain central concepts about psi function which have the capacity both to subsume prior observations and to suggest new ones? In what if any areas have parapsychologists failed to advance knowledge and conceptualization? Finally, granted that parapsychology is undergoing conceptual development and is engaging in concept-oriented research to an unprecedented degree, does it still retain certain implicit, unquestioned, untested, and perhaps unrecognized assumptions which should be subjected to examination?

The specific objective of this paper is to develop the evidence bearing on these questions and to suggest some answers for them.

SOME CONCEPTS CURRENTLY GUIDING PSI RESEARCH

It would be impossible to discuss all the concepts which are currently guiding parapsychological research. Whenever anyone tests a hypothesis, some concept is guiding that research. A careful examination of recent published research and integrative articles makes our task easier, however, for it suggests that the great bulk of published studies are being guided by certain central concepts which can be roughly divided into two models, each of which seems largely designed to integrate research in a particular major area of current concern.

One major area of research is the attempt to develop what Honorton (1975) has termed *receiver optimizing procedures*, that is, the search for experimental procedures which will optimize the function of the organism for the purpose of deliberate ESP performance of the perceptual-cognitive sort (e.g., attempts to perceive concealed pictures). Research in this area seems to be guided by the concept of a *psi-conducive syndrome* (the specific term is that of W. G. Braud, 1975; but also Honorton, 1974). The other major problem area to be considered is that of experiments intended to discover how psi functions in naturalistic contexts in which a person does not deliberately attempt to utilize psi capacities and may never become aware of them as such even when they function. The research in this area seems to be guided by concepts which have been described in Stanford's (1974a, 1974b) *psi-mediated instrumental response* (PMIR) model.

These two models are being highlighted in this review because they reflect the conceptualization behind a considerable bulk of contemporary psi research and because both models have to some extent already demonstrated their usefulness in subsuming earlier findings and in generating new ones. Further, both models seem to have considerable power, which means that they potentially have the capacity for organizing findings of diverse kinds. Both models have their precursors and have borrowed from earlier conceptualization. It must be emphasized, however, that these are not the only carefully articulated conceptual frameworks which guide psi research. They have been singled out only because each shares the characteristics mentioned above.

The reader may wonder why no "physical" models or theories of psi are to be discussed here. The reason is in essence simple: A "physical" theory of psi phenomena must either explain and/or predict functional relationships governing the occurrence of psi phenomena, *and these functional relationships must be statements involving physically measurable quantities*. This means quantities specifiable in the units physicists use in their equations. The unhappy truth is that no such functional relationship has ever been demonstrated, and none seems at present about to be demonstrated. Had such a physical functional relationship been demonstrated, much if not all of the controversy surrounding psi phenomena would likely have vanished in "the twinkling of an eye," or perhaps with the passage of a "psion." One implication of such a discovery would be that it would then be possible to specify under what condition(s) a specific form of psi interaction would and would not occur, and, ideally, it would indicate the specific (mathematical) form of the function relating the magnitude of the psi effect to the physical parameter(s) in question. Such a discovery would constitute the first real breakthrough in parapsychological research. Unfortunately, it does not seem close at hand. As more theoretical physicists become interested in psi phenomena, however, there is always the hope that the probability of such a discovery is increasing. Finally, it is conceivable that the testing of a "physical" theory of psi phenomena will have to wait upon either the development of better procedures for optimizing subject performance or upon better methods of measuring psi effects, or perhaps both.

A number of attempts have been made in the past to develop physicalistic models of psi function, but the problem discussed above still exists—deductions from such models have never been confirmed. Therefore no attempt to review these models will be made here.

Some readers may at this point wonder whether the observations with Kirlian photography might not have provided a useful basis for conceiving of psi phenomena within an energetic framework. There has been much popular writing about Kirlian photography, often coupled with wholly irresponsible claims that it has revealed the basis of the "psychic energy" which is supposed to underlie psi phenomena. Recent studies by Burton, Joines, and Stevens (1975), Montandon (1977), and Tiller and Boyers (described in Dobervich, 1974) cast very serious doubts on such claims. They indicate some very commonplace causes for the effects which appear in Kirlian photography.

Later in this paper I will suggest one possible reason why parapsychology has made no real progress in developing a basic framework for the *underlying* function of psi phenomena. One obvious reason which can be quickly mentioned here is that psi phenomena (as they are defined by parapsychologists) are almost certainly not mediated by known forms of energy and certainly do not seem to fit any model of energy transmission across space.

Given this currently unpromising state of affairs, let us turn to a consideration of the psychobiological models which are guiding many of the studies of psi phenomena.

THE PSI-CONDUCIVE SYNDROME

Since other chapters in this volume will discuss psi-conducive states in considerable detail, the remarks here will be confined to a description of the concepts which seem to be developing from and guiding such research, and some comment on and evaluation of these.

On the basis of extensive research on so-called altered states of consciousness (dreams, hypnosis, sensory isolation, etc.) and ESP performance (see chapters by

Honorton and by Van de Castle in this volume), Charles Honorton (1974) has developed a provisional framework regarding the circumstances which lead to receiver optimization for ESP performance. Extrasensory communication, according to Honorton's model, is facilitated by (a) a reduction in awareness of external stimuli, (b) a reduction in awareness of somatic stimuli, (c) a redirection of attention onto internal processes (mental processes such as imagery, feelings, impulses, etc.), and (d) elimination of internally generated distractions and noise. The first three points are supported by considerable experimental evidence, as Honorton noted in his review cited above, but the final point, as he also noted, has received little attention in laboratory studies. Reports of numerous psychics, however, concerning what they feel they must do in order to use ESP accurately provide nonexperimental support for the importance of using techniques to eliminate or reduce internally generated distractions and noise (for a review of some of the evidence on this point, see White, 1964).

Often psychics accomplish the elimination or reduction of internally generated distractions or noise by intense focusing of attention on some internal image or experience and then discarding that image or experience once the mind has become free of other activity. Then it is a matter of waiting for psi-mediated impressions to emerge into consciousness (White, 1964).

This technique bears a striking resemblance to that of yogic meditation as described by Patanjali (Prabhavananda and Isherwood, 1953) in which the stilling of the modifications of the mind is achieved by intense, and ultimately steady, focusing of the mind upon some object of concentration. Then when other modifications have ceased and awareness of only the object of concentration is achieved, the yogi lets go of even the "impressions" created by the object of his concentration. The Sanskrit word which describes this total process is *samyama*, and Patanjali finds in it the basis for the development of many psychic powers. Patanjali's many centuries-old speculations have begun to take on a new credibility because of the recent laboratory work on altered internal states and ESP. However, as noted earlier, there has been little laboratory work, if any, which has a direct bearing on the assertion that "stilling the modifications of the mind" (to use Patanjali's phrase) or "elimination of internally generated distractions and noise" (to use Honorton's) facilitates ESP performance. The reason is that there has been no real effort to study the effects of concentration exercises (as various psychics have used them) upon ESP communication. No doubt such studies will be forthcoming in the near future. The increased credibility of Patanjali's assertions about *samyama* and ESP derives from the close logical linkage of his assertions and what is already known of ESP receiver optimizing procedures.

What already seems fairly well demonstrated is the facilitation of ESP through nonmeditative techniques for reducing awareness of external and somatic stimuli and redirecting attention onto internal processes (e.g., sensory uniformity and isolation, and relaxation exercises). It seems not only rational, but scientifically demonstrated as well, that yogic meditation achieves exactly the same goals. Deeply meditating yogis seem behaviorally oblivious to external stimulation (Das and Gastaut, 1957). There have been several experimental demonstrations that external stimuli which would produce blocking of alpha rhythms in nonmeditating persons do not do so, or do not do so to nearly the same extent, in persons practicing one or another form of yogic meditation (Anand, Chhina, and Singh, 1961; Bagchi and Wenger, 1957; Banquet, 1973; Kasamatsu, Okuma, Takenaka, Koga, Ikeda, and Sugiyama, 1957). (Note that the blocking of alpha rhythms in response to sensory stimulation is an indication that this stimulation has caused cortical arousal in an individual and that his attention has at least momentarily responded to the stimulation.) Two studies have also shown that yogic meditation can result in a dramatic lowering of muscle tension (EMG) (Banquet, 1973; Das and Gastaut, 1957) and thus of somatic noise.

Therefore, what parapsychologists have accomplished in their subjects in the laboratory through externally imposed conditions and techniques—sensory uniformity or isolation to reduce attentiveness to external stimulation and progressive relaxation exercises to reduce muscle tension and thus somatic noise— can.be accomplished by the yogi through meditation in which he develops a strong, continuous focus of attention on some object. It should not be surprising, therefore, if meditationlike concentration exercises might prove to be a boon in the parapsychology laboratory, and, indeed, Dukhan and Rao (1973) have shown that ESP performance can be improved if the subject takes the test just after completing meditation. However, more research is needed, especially work which attempts to use meditationlike concentrative techniques to still the mind as a preparation for receiving ESP information in a free-response task. We in fact already have one such study (Stanford and Stevenson, 1972), and it suggests that when such a technique is successful in stilling the mind, ESP success is greater. However, in that study only one subject participated, and the success of the exercise in calming the mind was inferred from EEG measures rather than from introspective reports.

It is of interest that while parapsychologists have not studied ESP in yogis engaged in concentrative meditation, which accomplishes functional deafferentation (reduction of the effects of sensory stimulation) and reduction of somatic noise, they have studied another self-produced state of functional deafferentation and low somatic noise and have shown it to be a stronghold of ESP—the nocturnal (REM state) dream. REM state dreams are associated with very low responsivity to external stimulation and with a dramatic drop-off in EMG-measured muscular tension (see Foulkes, 1966). Indeed, this parallel may be more profound than it would seem at first examination: In two studies of deep, ecstatic states induced by yogic forms of meditation (Banquet, 1973; Das and

Gastaut, 1957) those experiencing these states (a) either behaviorally or electro-encephalographically (or both) acted essentially oblivious to sensory stimulation, (b) showed EEG patterns indicating high arousal (frequencies beyond the alpha range), and (c) produced dramatically reduced EMG records. In addition to producing functional deafferentation and reduced EMG traces, nocturnal dreams are associated with an EEG pattern reflecting high cortical arousal. All this is not to imply that these deep meditative states are functionally or exactly equivalent to REM dreaming, but it is to suggest that there are intriguing parallels and that they may share certain neurological features or functions.

It thus looks as though concentrative techniques of meditation may hold promise for ESP work because they seem to have potential for stilling the mind (reduction of internally generated noise), reducing awareness of external stimulation, and reducing somatically generated noise (muscular activity). It is suggested that in studying the effects of such exercises upon whether or not subjects become less aware of sensory stimulation, we should not rely on subjective reports alone for they are subject to several potentially contaminating factors. Rather, we should couple such reports with studies of whether or to what degree the alpha rhythms are blocked in response to such stimulation (as in the studies with yogis discussed earlier). In this connection it might also prove useful to study cortical event-related potentials (ERPs, sometimes also called evoked potentials). (For ERP literature reviews, see Donchin and Lindsley, 1969; McCallum and Knott, 1973; Regan, 1972.) There is mounting evidence that attentional factors can modify the effects of specific sensory events upon the electrical activity of the cortex as reflected in ERPs.

Exactly how attentional factors influence the effects of sensory stimuli upon the cortex is not fully understood, but there is considerable evidence that focusing the attention upon a particular object can cause peripheral gating (by means of centrifugal neural impulses) of incoming sensory information with inhibitory influences being exerted as early as the first sensory synapse and probably higher along the sensory tracts (see, e.g., Buño, Velluti, Handler, and García-Austt, 1966; Hagbarth and Kerr, 1954; Hernández-Peón, Guzmán-Flores, Alcáraz, and Fernández-Guardiola, 1957; Hernández-Peón, Scherrer, and Jouvet, 1956; Kerr and Hagbarth, 1955).

Finally, as concerns the Honorton model of receiver optimization, this model suggests an important relationship between the deployment of attention and the utilization of psi-mediated cues. This is that the psi percipient must not be entirely passive if he is to succeed. The model states that for there to be ESP success, a redirection of attention to internal processes must occur. This is not merely because one is thereby helped to ignore external stimulation. Rather, if psi-mediated cues are to be utilized they must be the objects of the subject's attention. According to the model the subject should be mentally calm and quiet, but he should also be inwardly attentive, ready to notice and be fully aware of psi-mediated cues which come into consciousness. He must be calmly *attentive*. This is an important point, so we will return to it while discussing the contributions of William G. Braud to the concept of psi-conducive states and the psi-conducive syndrome in particular.

Braud (1975) has developed the concept of the psi-conducive syndrome. This model indicates seven major characteristics of a "state" that Braud believes may be optimally psi-conducive. Because this state can be achieved through the coexistence of these seven "symptoms" in an individual, the state is termed a "syndrome"—a syndrome always being composed of a number of symptoms which, taken together, are indicative of some particular condition. Braud makes it clear, however, that any one of the seven features taken alone or any combination of them should facilitate ESP performance. It is not necessary for all of them to be present in order for a psi-conducive state to occur. ESP performance should, however, be optimal when these seven "conditions" or "symptoms" are all present.

Here in condensed form are the seven features of the psi-conducive syndrome as it is conceived by Braud:

1. physical relaxation
2. reduced "physical" arousal or activation (conceived to include autonomic, electroencephalographic, and basal metabolic rate measures of arousal or activation)
3. reduction in sensory input and processing (either by reduction of actual inputs or through the use of concentration exercises discussed earlier)
4. increased awareness of internal processes, feelings, and images (including dreams and fantasy)
5. "receptive mode/right hemispheric functioning" as opposed to "action mode/left hemispheric functioning"
6. an altered view of the nature of the world (especially one in which the unity and interrelatedness of "things" is emphasized; the concept of time is changed and the usual sense of time is no longer real to one; it is felt to be possible to know things more directly than we usually consider possible; and many of our usual evaluations of events in the world are changed—basically what LeShan (1969) has called the experience of "clairvoyant reality")
7. psi (or what might be accomplished through psi) must be (at least) momentarily important.

Points 1, 3, and 4 of this model, as they are discussed by Braud (1975), seem to cover essentially the points of Honorton's (1975) model. Examination of points 2, 5, 6, and 7 is therefore in order.

Points 5, 6, and 7 conceivably bring some extremely important additions to the assumptions in Honorton's model, but Braud's point 2 is problematic. In my opinion it is too diffusely or vaguely stated and is, in many respects, probably erroneous.

Braud (1975) states in support of this point that "ample evidence already exists in the literature that a state of lowered arousal is conducive to good psi performance" (p. 144). This statement needs qualification. A key point in the altered states—ESP literature is that dreams are often a stronghold of ESP. As it happens, the state in which dreaming normally occurs, ascending Stage 1 sleep or Stage REM, is characterized by features which in most respects contradict Braud's generalization. During Stage REM, heart rate often accelerates slightly (on the average); it becomes much more variable; breathing, if it changes in mean rate, is apt to accelerate somewhat, and it certainly becomes more irregular; and the EEG pattern is typically an aroused, desynchronized one (Foulkes, 1966). In many respects dreaming sleep is a highly aroused state.

There may be some truth to Braud's second proposition, but, as it is stated, it has overgenerality and seems to be inadequately conceptualized. Why, for example, should low arousal (of any of the three types mentioned by Braud) facilitate ESP performance? Braud does not discuss this issue, but it is an important one if the matter is to be seen in proper perspective. It seems reasonable that subjects must be *at least* aroused enough when they confront psi-mediated internal cues that they can be aware of them, notice them, and report them (or simply recall them later). If low arousal (of whatever kind) aids ESP performance, it is difficult to conceive of its doing so for any other reasons than that to some degree it results in lowered somatic and internally generated noise and that it may be indicative of the passive mode of experiencing which Braud mentions elsewhere in his model. In short, the point seems redundant with his other points. Further, the proposition is too general, and there is no specification of limitation on how low arousal has to go before it is no longer psi-conducive.

The importance of qualifying any emphasis on low arousal as being psi-conducive is evident in considering the experimental literature. Abundance of alpha rhythms (a sign of reduced cortical arousal) has not been shown to correlate reliably (across experiments) with ESP performance, either on a between- or within-subjects basis (reviewed by Stanford, 1976). There has, however, been one reliable relationship reported between alpha rhythms and ESP performance (Stanford, 1971; Stanford and Lovin, 1970; Stanford and Stevenson, 1972). This is that if a person is asked to relax or meditate prior to an ESP test, the resultant slowed alpha rhythms (characteristic of increased mental quietude and passivity) must, if the subject is to succeed at the ESP task, accelerate (shift upward in frequency) when he actually enters ESP testing and is attempting to utilize psi-mediated cues. Additionally, in two of the three studies cited (Stanford and Lovin, 1970; Stanford and Stevenson, 1972), the frequency of alpha rhythms during relaxation or meditation prior to the ESP task was negatively related to ESP performance. Taken together these two findings suggest that a period of mental quieting prior to an ESP task can be helpful, but that this lowered arousal must be followed by a period of somewhat increased arousal if the subject is to utilize psi-mediated cues successfully. There would appear to be an optimal level of arousal for successful ESP performance, a level at which the subject might be characterized as quietly or calmly attentive to internal cues.

As to whether autonomic, EEG, and metabolic "arousal" are related to cognitive-perceptual ESP performance in the manner Braud suggests, much more research would be required for a definitive answer. It is conceivable that in this way, too, Braud's proposition 2 may be overgeneral. However, it is clear that he regards it as a hypothesis rather than as established fact.

Braud's proposition 5 regarding "receptive mode/right hemispheric" versus "action mode/left hemispheric" function is possibly a very important addition to our conception of psi-conducive states. However, this proposition, like proposition 2, may involve more than at first seems obvious. Let us, therefore, consider first the matter of receptive mode versus action mode.

Psychics or "sensitives" from time immemorial, it would seem, have stressed that they cannot *make* ESP happen, but that they must adopt an attitude such that they can *let* it happen. The feeling is that any attempt to try to force ESP to happen is likely to end only in frustration. Although no poll has been taken on parapsychologists' impressions regarding this matter, one gains the impression that we would pretty much agree (in a tentative way) with this statement. LeShan (1969) formalized this idea as a part of his model some years ago. He said explicitly that "the harder a sensitive *tries* [LeShan's emphasis] to produce paranormal information, the less veridical evidence will be demonstrated" (p. 92). Unfortunately, definitive research experimentally comparing the attitudes of "letting it happen" and "making it happen" during an ESP test is still lacking. We do have some experimental evidence that this rule holds for PK, and that has been reviewed in the chapter on experimental PK in this volume.

Perhaps the inclusion of this idea in Braud's model will encourage some work on this problem, and the strong "clinical impressions" that the model is correct in this regard may provide added incentive. It should prove easy to experimentally manipulate subjects' approach (active or receptive) to the task, so that, too, should facilitate research.

Great caution will have to be used in carrying out such a manipulation so that it does not inadvertently change expectancy of success. In my opinion, confounding effects of this type would be less likely in clairvoyance studies than in GESP work. Subjects seem more likely to believe that passivity is a better approach in a telepathy or GESP task than in a clairvoyance one. In the former case the idea is that since someone is "sending," it is possible to "sit back, relax, and respond" to his or her active influence. Since no one is "sending" in clairvoyance tasks, subjects are apt to feel (probably quite irrationally) that they have to play an active role in gathering information about the target material. They may, for example, try to mentally "see through" the container concealing the target or to mentally "get inside" the wrapper and see what is there. The use of an independent-groups design to study this problem would probably have great advantages over a same-subjects design, and subject expectancies about the probability of success of the approach they work with should probably be manipulated by the experimenter in the direction of optimism and be held constant across conditions. (This would help eliminate individual differences in expectancy of success within a given condition, and this would be desirable, for if such expectancies relate to success, error variance in the study would be reduced.)

The assertion that right- versus left-hemispheric functioning facilitates ESP performance deserves special comment. This is an intriguing idea, and one that seems a likely candidate to attract much experimental interest. The fact that so many good ESP subjects seem to have strong artistic inclinations or seem unusually creative suggests that Braud's hypothesis may be correct. It is likely that many of the features of musical performance and appreciation and artistic creation may be associated to an appreciable extent with right-hemispheric function (see., e.g., Ornstein, 1972, for a review). And while there is evidence that individuals who by certain criteria are rather creative do well on ESP tasks (Honorton, 1967), there is also evidence that the use of rational, analytic thought processes (left-hemispheric functions) interferes with ESP performance (reviewed in Stanford, 1975a). Thus, both on the face of it and on the basis of indirect evidence the hypothesis of hemispheric lateralization of function being related to ESP performance deserves serious experimental study. Research on this topic is already under way in Braud's laboratory at the University of Houston (Andrew, 1975; Braud and Braud, 1975).

The hypothesis that right-hemispheric function is more hospitable to ESP performance than is left-hemispheric function should be carefully studied to assess its generality. Research on such a hypothesis should not be confined to one type of ESP task or one type of target material. For example, if such research were to involve the use of pictorial ESP targets, this might artificially bias the results in favor of a confirmation of the ESP-hemispheric lateralization hypothesis even if ESP success were not invariably favored by right-hemispheric function. For, as W. G. Braud (1975) notes in describing right-hemispheric function, the right hemisphere is associated with imagery and spatial, concrete thought processes. It is precisely that kind of thinking which would seem to be required by and would be emphasized by an ESP task with pictorial targets. Other forms of ESP tasks, involving other kinds of target material (e.g., linguistic targets or abstract concepts like mathematical operations used as targets), or other response modes (e.g., motor automatisms) might not show a similar relationship to hemispheric function (assuming such a relationship could be demonstrated at all). In short, it would be important to conduct studies to explore possible boundary conditions for the relationship suggested by this hypothesis.

It would be overly simplistic to imagine that the left hemisphere could not possibly play a positive role in ESP performance, at least under certain conditions. I vividly recall one experience I had as a subject in a study of nocturnal dreams and GESP which Robert L. Van de Castle and I conducted. On one particular night I had an experience which was very clearly related to the target picture, and this experience occurred largely during a period when I was drifting off to sleep. During that time I clearly heard a voice speak a clause or a sentence. I distinctly felt this "message" bore a meaningful relation to the target, so I aroused myself and reported it to the sleep monitor for tape recording. As it happened, what I heard in this speech provided the best clues of the entire night as to the nature of the target picture. These clues were much more reliable, in this case, than were my visual images. Thus I cannot but feel some sense of injustice to the left hemisphere, which is very much concerned with the perception and production of speech (in right-handed persons like myself), when I hear persons say that ESP is the exclusive province of the right hemisphere. (Braud has not said this, but there are some persons who have.) Furthermore, any number of skilled psychics have reported ESP experiences which come to them in the form of words, and a considerable number of spontaneous cases involve this feature (Rhine, 1956).

It would be surprising if both hemispheres were not intimately involved in most ESP success. The best psychics will tell you that using psi ability is not all impulse, images, guts, and gusto, but that there is some skillful disciplining of the mind involved, and the deliberate "focused attending" (Honorton, 1974) which is required to notice and consciously utilize psi cues is regarded as a left-hemispheric function. A reasonable hypothesis is that successful cognitive-perceptual ESP used intentionally, as in an experiment, depends not upon whether one hemisphere is active (e.g., the right) and the other idling (e.g., the left), but upon what each hemisphere is doing. Each must be doing the proper thing. What is the proper thing would only unfold during the course of research and would likely depend on the specific ESP task.

One can even think of some supposedly right-hemispheric functions which, it would seem reasonable, might interfere with free-response ESP on pictorial targets. Experimenters have often noticed that subjects seem to get a partial perception of the form of the target stimulus, but because of apparent premature perceptual closure come to perceive or interpret their image in the wrong way, so that they have roughly a "hit" on form, but not on "meaning." There are some indications that the right hemisphere manages "holistic" thought, the tendency, among other things, to create a Gestalt, a whole (image, object, etc.) in perception. On the other hand (or hemisphere!), the left hemisphere might have helped out here by saying, "Now wait, let this happen spontaneously, for that is what is required for psi function, let the image form itself, don't immediately leap to interpret it!" In short, again, a balanced relationship of right- and left-hemispheric function would seem useful.

W. G. Braud's (1975) discussion of the possible importance to ESP performance of an altered view of the nature of the world is strongly influenced by LeShan's (1969) intriguing model involving the concept of "clairvoyant reality." (See enumeration of Braud's seven points earlier.) It is difficult to comment incisively on this model or this particular point in Braud's conceptualization of psi-conducive states because neither LeShan nor Braud makes it particularly clear what it is about this kind of "altered view" which is supposed to allow facilitation of psi performance and why it should do so. Nonetheless, the general idea put forth by LeShan and echoed by Braud has a strong appeal and in a rather general way seems to fit in with a number of findings regarding psi function (e.g., the sheep-goat effect, the finding that some ways of inducing altered states are associated with improved ESP performance, etc.). It is also compatible with a widespread and venerable tradition that various mystics and others of exalted religious sentiment have often been associated with strange feats or manifestations which we would nowadays construe as possible psi events. The practice of yogic disciplines, for example, which are supposed to bring a change in one's way of experiencing the world, is thought to cause the unfoldment of psi capacities as the practice progresses (Prabhavananda and Isherwood, 1953). This particular point is not, incidentally, independent of Braud's point regarding right- versus left-hemispheric function since the mystical perspective emphasized in LeShan's thesis (adopted by Braud) would clearly seem to involve an abandonment, in many respects, of strong dependence upon left-hemispheric modes of thought (analytic, rational, etc.) as the basis of personal epistemology. This emphasizes once more the importance of eventually transforming the rather inexplicit assertion involved in this proposition into one or more specific hypotheses indicative of why and how such a changed world view should facilitate ESP performance (and should do so in a way not covered by other assertions of the model).

This should not be construed as an attack upon the idea that we must investigate the effects upon psi performance of those aspects of changed experiencing summarized under the term *clairvoyant reality*. Rather, it is a suggestion that we start with this concept, but that we should attempt to refine it into more specific, testable hypotheses to guide research. This proposal, I feel, concurs with the viewpoints of both LeShan and Braud on this matter.

As a starting (but hopefully not a stopping) point I would suggest that there are two aspects of the features of points 5 and 6 of Braud's model which may be of special importance.

Being in certain "altered states" and functioning in the "receptive mode" may have importance for ESP function not so much because of the positive aspects of those states as in what they eliminate during ESP testing. The first thing which may be eliminated is wrong effort. Note that the word *effort* has the qualifier "wrong" before it. Elsewhere I have elaborated on the concept of wrong effort as it applies to PK or combined ESP-PK events (Stanford, 1974b). White (1964) has done an excellent job of summarizing some of the techniques used by certain outstanding subjects to achieve their ESP performance. A reading of this valuable paper should convince the reader that good ESP performance is not derived from noneffort, but from elimination of certain types of effort—specifically the conscious effort to try to force psychic things (e.g., impressions or images or views "through" containers of target objects) to happen—combined with effective effort of other kinds (e.g., to concentrate on some inner mental image which is then dissolved and then is followed by the discipline of quietly but attentively waiting for (possibly) psi-mediated impressions to emerge). Let us interpret "receptive mode" in this fashion. It is likely that certain altered states facilitate this mode by helping one to experience the world in a way in which psi events happen naturally and easily (under the right circumstances—as, for example, after using the right ritual [see Stanford, 1974b] such that they are not so improbable or "difficult" that one has to "make" them happen). Indeed, ideally it might be good if one feels that the responsibility for errors or failure is outside one's hands, for this, too, helps one avoid frantic, anxious efforts to "make something happen" (Stanford, 1974b). An altered state may thus aid ESP performance by helping one feel less ego-involved in an ESP task. Two studies specifically suggest that the proper attitude toward the ESP task is not one of ego-involvement but task-involvement (Eilbert and Schmeidler, 1950; Stanford, 1965). It is also of interest that the stated belief that one can personally do well in an ESP test (an attitude likely to be associated with strong ego-involvement) has failed to correlate consistently with level of performance, whereas the belief that ESP is possible in the test at hand has been a much better predictor (for a review see Palmer, 1971). If an altered state can help one to view ESP as something one can help prepare for but cannot *make* happen (and thus cannot be responsible for failure at), it may boost ESP performance. Why? Because one's energies are not wasted in useless efforts to make things happen which may in fact block one's ability to "let it happen" and to be aware of psi-mediated cues. This is at least a possible interpretation of the data cited. But more study of this possibility is needed.

Second, part of the usefulness of altered states for ESP performance may lie in the fact that such states alter and weaken sequential, rational, and contextual constraints on associative (thought) processes, and thus psi-mediated cues may more easily emerge into consciousness. Dreams, for instance, often regarded by parapsychologists as a stronghold for ESP, show a dramatic breakdown of the usual rational, sequential, and contextual constraints encountered in waking mentation. Thus they may provide more opportunity for the emergence of psi information into the ongoing mentation. These possibilities are speculative and require experimental study.

Before leaving this topic, however, I must express some misgivings about whether all of the features associated with LeShan's "clairvoyant reality" are really necessary or even important to the expression of full-blown cognitive-perceptual ESP. I find no reason to believe that most or even many psychics are experiencing anything resembling the unitive or mystical experience when they are effectively manifesting ESP. Indeed, a full-blown mystical experience would seem an unlikely place for an ESP experience. Mystical experiences could conceivably help to remove some of the blocks to ESP experience, but this would likely be an after-effect of the mystical episode. The egocentric dispositions of some good psychics whom I have met suggest that they have seldom if ever experienced the ego-dissolving impact of a real mystical experience. Nonetheless, such persons often seem intellectually to adhere to a mystical or perhaps occult perspective, and one suspects that this helps them to evaluate and understand their psi experiences in what seems to them a meaningful context. Nor is there good evidence that most psychics genuinely evaluate "things of the world" in a different or more psychologically detached way than do most persons. Certainly they cannot be compared in this respect with most mystics.

The final ingredient of Braud's psi-conducive syndrome is that psi must somehow be momentarily important to a person in order for it to occur. What he is suggesting is exactly what I have suggested in the model for psi-mediated instrumental response (PMIR), to be discussed next below. Psi, spontaneous or otherwise, seems most often to function directly in the service of one's needs. When one is consciously trying to use ESP, as in the standard laboratory test, the chief sources of motivation may be a need to succeed for the pleasure of success *per se* and in order to enhance one's self-image and gain the favor of the experimenter and/or some other person(s) important to oneself. Much research is needed on this topic of need-strength and psi, both to experimentally confirm a relation between need strength and psi and to determine the possible form of the relationship. Work is under way on this in our laboratory at St. John's University in connection with the PMIR model. Braud's assumption of regarding motivation and psi has received striking anecdotal support at the Division of Parapsychology and Psychophysics of the Maimonides Medical Center. This laboratory is frequently visited by TV or film crews who wish to photograph ESP testing during a procedure (often the ganzfeld) designed to produce a psi-conducive state. When this occurs, it is exceedingly rare for the subject who "stars" to perform other than as a "star subject"—very fine performance is the rule. (The above is anecdotal based upon personal communication with Charles Honorton of the Maimonides laboratory.) There is an abundance of other anecdotal and spontaneous case material which could be adduced to support the idea that motivation is important to ESP performance. This motivational assumption is an important addition to the model of psi-conducive states. Here is a variable which may not merely reduce or eliminate sources of blockage, noise, inhibition, or constraint which may interfere with ESP success; it may actually determine the strength of the basic disposition toward a psi event. Later we will return to the topic of motivation.

In concluding this discussion of models for psi-conducive states some general observations are in order. Honorton's model is a rather conceptually refined and carefully articulated schema for understanding psi-conducive states. It has this characteristic because it is based upon careful consideration of large amounts of research already completed on the receiver optimization problem. Braud's model, though incorporating the salient features of Honorton's, is actually less of a formal, conceptual model. Rather, it is a bold and imaginative specification of certain conditions upon which future experimentation could likely, with profit, focus. So what it lacks in conceptual refinement and clarity it perhaps more than makes up in its capacity to guide research toward some important new understandings of psi-conducive states. The refinement of the concepts will undoubtedly come as the research progresses. Braud and his wife, Lendell, have already produced some excellent experimental studies built along the lines of their emergent conceptualization of psi-conducive states (Braud and Braud, 1973, 1974), and their work is already receiving experimental confirmation in other laboratories (e.g., Stanford and Mayer, 1974).

THE PMIR MODEL FOR EXTRASENSORY EVENTS

The conceptualization of psi function discussed to this point has centered on circumstances which increase the probability that the influence of psi information upon an individual will take the form of images, ideas, feelings, or intuitions which will provide conscious cues as to the nature of the object or event apprehended by psi. Although the models discussed above have value in aiding our understanding of extrasensory function in certain spontaneous contexts (e.g., during REM periods or during hypnagogic states), their focus seems to be one, as Honorton (1975) has put it, of "receiver optimization." Research on "receiver optimization" takes the form of studying ESP subjects who are aware they are involved in ESP testing and who wish to do as well as possible in developing images, ideas, etc., related to some target circumstance. Thus the focus of such research, while it has value for understanding certain classes of spontaneous events, is really on *intentional* extrasensory function of a perceptual-cognitive nature. (I prefer the term *intentional* to *conscious* since the latter term is extraordinarily vague and often seems to carry somewhat evaluative connotations.) The conceptualization of Honorton and Braud therefore emphasizes what has really been the thrust of experimental parapsychological research from its inception, the production in the laboratory of both quantitatively and qualitatively impressive evidence of the intentional use of extrasensory function.

Another, and by no means antithetical, approach to parapsychology is possible. This is to ask how laboratory research can directly enlighten our understanding of spontaneous psi events, events which by definition are nonintentional in character.

It is becoming increasingly obvious that not all spontaneous extrasensory events take forms which resemble perceptions or cognitions. Nonetheless, ESP in just that form has been the focus of traditional laboratory research. I have proposed (Stanford, 1974a) that the traditional types of spontaneous cases reported in the parapsychological literature represent a biased, misrepresentative sample of the spontaneous psi events which actually occur—a sample that all too strongly focuses on perceptual-cognitive cases. Earlier C. D. Broad (1969) convincingly made essentially the same point. Extrasensory influences on the organism may occur in ways or in circumstances in which they are seldom if ever recognized as such or even catch our attention. Even when they are recognized, they may not be reported because they are not regarded as having produced "strong evidence" of their being genuine psi. Even when persons who experience psi phenomena report them, further selective factors enter the picture when a parapsychologist goes over the cases and publishes only those regarded as "evidential" or dramatic. For these reasons traditional collections of spontaneous psi events feature perceptual-cognitive cases. Such cases are likely to be recognized as psi by those experiencing them and often seem convincing by their very nature. But even the largest collections of such cases do not provide any indications as to whether or to what degree more subtle and less easily recognizable psi influences may exist in daily life. There are odd and seemingly meaningful happenings in everyday life which are usually shrugged off as coincidences but which may sometimes be produced by subtle, nonintentional psi function.

In spite of the laboratory evidence that psi is a general human ability, few of us recognize in our own lives any of the kinds of ESP cases to be found in traditional case collections. This suggests that what is seen in these case collections is analogous to the tip of an iceberg. There may be many more instances of psi function in our everyday life experience than are betrayed by an examination of such case collections. To carry the analogy a bit further, the proposed mass of nonintentional psi cases which goes largely unrecognized may take forms which differ considerably from the more visible psi cases, just as the true shape of an iceberg is not betrayed by that part above the waterline.

In an earlier paper I gave several examples of spontaneous events which may represent the subtle psi functions proposed in the PMIR model (Stanford, 1974a). This is not the place for an exposition of such cases. Suffice it to say that they consist of the odd coincidences of everyday life which seem to have meaning and importance for persons involved in them. They range from "just happening" to do something or to be somewhere at the "right time" such that the outcome has unanticipated and logically unforeseen positive consequences for oneself, to making a mistake or forgetting to do something with the outcome having similar consequences. The proposal is that such "fortuitous coincidences" may be psi mediated. The model shortly to be detailed will, then, propose a considerable broadening of our concepts of spontaneous psi-mediated events.

It is necessary to conduct experimental research in order to arrive at any realistic understanding of such supposed spontaneous psi events. The reasons are twofold: (a) we ordinarily want to know the probability of the event(s) we are studying if chance alone were operating; and (b) we must experimentally manipulate the variables believed to influence spontaneous psi events if we are to draw definite conclusions about the variables which control such events.

The reader will naturally wish to know whether it is meaningful to try to make inferences about spontaneous psi on the basis of laboratory experiments. How can "experimental psi" ever be "spontaneous psi"? The answer lies in a rather radically different psi study than we are accustomed to expect from parapsychology laboratories. These new studies are aimed at producing experimentally induced spontaneous psi events. This involves placing persons in settings which "invite" spontaneous (nonintentional) ESP and/or PK, without those persons being told to attempt to use psi and without their realizing that psi is being studied. The crux of the matter is that in all such studies there is an element of nonintentional psi, and it is precisely this nonintentionality which gives such studies special potential for discovering how psi functions in life situations (in which it is always nonintentional). The specific forms that such studies take will become clearer with the discussion of the experimentally testable assumptions of the PMIR model.

The italicized propositions which follow are the assumptions of the PMIR model. This model is intended to subsume laboratory findings which may have a bearing on nonintentional (and therefore spontaneous) psi function and to lead beyond those findings. It is an attempt, within a psychobiological framework, to provide some very tentative explanations of psi function, both in the laboratory and outside it, and to generate a set of experimentally evaluable assumptions which may lead to new discoveries.

In the presence of a particular need the organism uses psi (ESP), as well as sensory means, to scan its environment for objects and events relevant to that need and for information crucially related to such objects or events.

This proposition accepts the common assumption of parapsychologists that psi events are strongly influenced by the motivations or needs of the person involved, but it goes beyond that to propose that we use extrasensory potential in a very active way. The organism is assumed to actively scan its environment for information relevant to its needs. Perhaps the most important experimentally testable implication of this "scanning" assumption is that the organism will, through extrasensory mediation, respond to need-relevant objects and events even though it has no sensory knowledge even of the existence of those objects or events. A considerable number of successful studies exist in which this requirement would seem to have been met (Carpenter, 1971; Johnson, 1973; Schmidt, 1975; Stanford and Associates, 1976; Stanford and Stio, 1976; Stanford and Thompson, 1974; Stanford, Zenhausern, Taylor, and Dwyer, 1975; plus an unpublished study of Stanford, similar to Carpenter, 1971, mentioned in Stanford, 1974a). In two of these studies, a combination of extrasensory scanning and PK was seemingly involved (Schmidt, 1975; Stanford et al., 1975).

When extrasensory information is thus obtained about need-relevant objects or events (or information crucially related thereto), a disposition toward psi-mediated instrumental response (PMIR) arises.

That is, the organism then tends to act in ways which are instrumental in satisfying its needs in relation to the need-relevant object or event. Any study which demonstrates the occurrence of PMIR provides support for this proposition.

Each of the studies cited as supporting the first proposition also lends support to this one, since PMIR occurred in them. The third proposition spells out specific ramifications of the second proposition.

Preparation for or production of PMIR often involves such changes as motivational or emotional arousal, attention-focusing responses, and other preparation for response.

This indicates that there are other evidences of nonintentional psi function than just the overt instrumental response involved in PMIR. These might be present even if something should block the occurrence of the actual instrumental response. One might look for various indications of arousal such as cortical, muscular, and even behavioral indices.

A study by Tart (1963) showed physiological evidence of emotional arousal to an extrasensory target. Work by Dean (1962) and by Dean and Nash (1967) showed a similar effect involving cardiovascular arousal measured by the plethysmograph. At the behavioral level Morris (1967) found that a goldfish which was shortly to be suspended in a net out of water exhibited more swimming activity than did control goldfish which would not be picked up.

Some indirect evidence for this proposition comes from Carpenter (1971). His sample of male college-age believers in ESP scored better on standard ESP cards which, unknown to them, had inserted along with them pictures of humans engaging in sexual intercourse than they did on standard cards not thus loaded. This suggests that there was some form of emotional arousal to the hidden stimulus which influenced their response to the standard cards. Johnson (1971) and Johnson and Nordbeck (1972) reported analogous findings.

That a certain amount of arousal may be useful to the organism in integrating and responding to incoming extrasensory information is suggested by a series of EEG-ESP studies (Stanford, 1971; Stanford and Lovin, 1970; Stanford and Stevenson, 1972).

All else being equal, the strength of the disposition toward PMIR is directly and positively related to: (a) the importance or strength of the need(s) in question; (b) the degree of need-relevance of the need-relevant object or event; and (c) the closeness in time of the potential encounter with the need-relevant object or event.

Subproposition (a) regarding need-strength or need-importance refers to how strong a given need is and how central (important) it is in the hierarchy of needs found in a given organism. The subproposition regarding need-relevance refers to what psychologists would term the incentive value of the so-called goal object or event (that which the organism is disposed toward encountering through PMIR). The importance of incentives in nonpsi settings has been reviewed by Klinger (1971, 1975). The third subproposition proposes that there exists a psi analogue to the fact that as an organism approaches a goal-object or goal-event the effects of that incentive (whatever they may be) upon the behaviors and physiological state of the organism typically intensify. We work harder as we get close to an exam, and we become more anxious as the time approaches for us to go to the dentist. We would expect that if a response mediated by psi is capable of producing an encounter with a desired goal event, that response will be more likely to occur if it would result in an immediate reward than if it were to result in a delayed reward. Similarly, we should expect effects related to this proposition to be evident in the case of the forms of arousal mentioned in the third proposition of the PMIR model.

The subproposition involving need-strength or need-importance has had abundant support since the beginnings of parapsychology from anecedotal and spontaneous case materials, but such evidence, even if it is widely regarded as strongly suggestive, cannot be taken as conclusive. What is needed is direct experimental evidence. The sheep-goat finding has often been interpreted as reflecting differential application of psi in the service of the subject's need to confirm his own beliefs (for a review see Palmer, 1971), but this is something less than an experimental demonstration of the role of motivation in psi-mediated behavior. In our laboratory at St. John's University we recently completed a study in which a direct attempt to manipulate need-strength did produce a significant effect in the anticipated direction upon the tendency of subjects to produce PMIR (Stanford and Associates, 1976).

The proposed relationship of need strength and measured disposition toward PMIR may very well reverse at high levels of need strength, especially when the response required is complex (Yerkes-Dodson Law derived in nonpsi situations).

An organism can be "overdriven," resulting in deficiencies of behavioral response. It is another question whether such a high level of need strength could be realistically or ethically accomplished in the laboratory.

The subproposition regarding degree of need-relevance of the need-relevant object or event has not received direct experimental study, though results of studies like those of Carpenter (1971) might be considered to provide some indirect support. Direct study of this proposition is needed. It will be of special interest to learn whether there may be high levels of incentive value which reverse the proposed relationship of incentive value and disposition toward PMIR. The issues in this connection are potentially complex, so no further effort will be made here to analyze them. What is needed is some careful parametric research.

The subproposition regarding closeness in time of the potential encounter with the need-relevant object or event appears to have support from studies of spontaneous cases. Work on spontaneous cases of possible precognition (premonition) has produced the pattern suggested by the subproposition in question (Barker, 1967; Stevenson, 1970). Reported psi cognitions of future events are much more frequent close to the event in time than earlier. It must be borne in mind, however, that the consistent effect noted with spontaneous cases could conceivably be partially or even wholly an artifact. If one "precognizes" an event, and if that occurs a considerable time before the confirming event, the precognitive experience is less likely to be remembered.

One interesting bit of experimental data with goldfish as subjects supports the closeness-in-time subproposition. Morris (1967) did a study of "precognition" in goldfish. He and a coexperimenter observed the amount of swimming activity in three goldfish; immediately thereafter one goldfish was randomly selected to be picked up out of the water and held for a short period in a net. The supposition was that the goldfish which was later to be picked up would be more active shortly beforehand. They studied swimming behavior during time intervals at two temporal distances from the traumatic event in question. Only the one providing measurement closer to this event reliably produced more swimming in the goldfish to be picked up. Replication of this work with attention to the question of reliability of measurement and reduction of the possibility of experimenter psi is needed. The study does seem very relevant to the subproposition being discussed, and it might even be termed a PMIR study since what was merely "swimming behavior" in this case might have been "escape behavior" in a free situation and thus would have involved a psi-mediated instrumental response.

PMIR can (but need not always) occur: (a) without a conscious effort to use psi; (b) without a conscious effort to fulfill the need subserved by PMIR; (c) without prior sensory knowledge even of the existence of the need-relevant circumstance; (d) without the development of conscious perceptions (e.g., mental images) or ideas concerning the need-relevant circumstance; and (e) without awareness that anything extraordinary is happening.

This means that PMIR can occur under any one of the conditions specified in (a)-(e) and that it can occur when any number of these conditions are combined.

The conceptually most important test of this proposition is derived from any experiment in which the conditions of all five subpropositions are met. If PMIR can occur under those conditions, it could have very important implications for understanding human behavior outside the laboratory. Three studies have provided support for the proposal that PMIR can occur when the conditions of all five subpropositions have been met (Stanford and Associates, 1976; Stanford and Stio, 1976; Stanford and Thompson, 1974).

Ten studies (some including a number of substudies) have provided support for proposition (a), that psi can occur without a conscious effort to use psi (Johnson, 1973; Kreitler and Kreitler, 1972, 1973; Lewis and Schmeidler, 1971; Schmidt, 1975; Stanford 1970; Stanford and Associates, 1976; Stanford and Stio, 1976; Stanford and Thompson, 1974; Stanford et al., 1975). Three studies have supported proposition (b), that PMIR can occur without a conscious effort to fulfill the need subserved by PMIR (Stanford and Associates, 1976; Stanford and Stio, 1976; Stanford and Thompson, 1974). Proposition (c) which states that PMIR can occur without prior sensory knowledge even of the existence of the need-relevant circumstance appears to obtain support from all the studies cited above as supporting proposition (a) and, in addition, from a study by Carpenter (1971) and a similar, unpublished study of my own. Subpropositions (d) and (e) receive at least indirect support from most and probably all of the studies cited so far in this section.

PMIR occurs in part through psi-mediated facilitation or triggering of otherwise ready or available responses (including actual behaviors, thoughts, memories, or feelings).

PMIR tends to be accomplished in the most economical way possible.

The two propositions are closely linked. They propose that PMIR functions as simply and economically as possible through psi interactions with conditions or processes already existing in the organism.

While PMIR is conceived to occur through psi-mediated facilitation or triggering of responses in the organism's normal repertoire, PMIR can, if the necessity arises, be accomplished through psi-mediated inhibition or blocking of responses which necessarily have to be blocked in order for PMIR to occur. This is not a contradiction, however. This response-blocking or inhibition is conceived to occur via psi-mediated facilitation of responses which compete with (or, ultimately replace) those responses which would have to be eliminated or slowed in order for PMIR to occur. Under the assumptions of this model, response inhibition (slowing) or blocking may be more or less efficient (as compared with response facilitation for PMIR), depending upon whether the response which must be facilitated to produce inhibition or blocking is relatively weak or strong (under comparable nonpsi circumstances) as compared with the response which must be blocked or inhibited. A recent study (Stanford and Stio, 1976) compared the strength of the disposition toward PMIR when simple response facilitation was required as contrasted with when PMIR demanded response inhibition involving facilitation of a relatively weak competing response. The measured disposition toward successful PMIR was reliably greater in the former condition, confirming the assumption (expressed in the first of the two PMIR assumptions immediately above) of associative mediation of response in PMIR. The associative-mediation hypothesis of the PMIR model earlier received confirmation in a study of word association as a vehicle for ESP (Stanford, 1973). That study showed that well-established associative responses make particularly good vehicles for ESP provided they are not so prepotent in the test situation that they cause excessive "false-alarms." One of the great values of the associative-mediation hypothesis of the PMIR model is that it allows some quite specific predictions about how easy PMIR will be to accomplish in a given situation and thus about the probability of its occurrence in that situation.

Consideration of the two PMIR assumptions under discussion will reveal some interesting possibilities in this model:

Influence upon timing. Sometimes in life situations we unexpectedly encounter a favorable event or avoid an unfavorable one simply by "happening" to be at the right place at the right time. In principle this could simply involve a slowing down or speeding up of our arrival at a particular place, and the PMIR model suggests that this process may occur through psi mediation. Specifically, it might occur through the interposition, in an action sequence, of ready behaviors which are simply released or triggered through psi guidance; by a similar suppression of particular actions (through psi-facilitation of one or more competing responses); by affecting the general rate of performance of an action sequence (through the mechanisms suggested above); or by influencing directly the time of initiation of a preplanned action sequence (through mechanisms discussed above). I have in my files a number of cases of possible PMIR which seemingly depended upon some such influence upon timing. Most importantly, three experimental studies have now demonstrated the occurrence of PMIR when its occurrence depended upon the timing of the production of a certain response (Stanford and Associates, 1976; Stanford and Stio, 1976; Stanford and Thompson, 1974).

Forgetting or remembering. One possible expression of PMIR might be forgetting or remembering something in a situation in which this forgetting or remembering has logically unpredictable favorable consequences. Elsewhere I have reported a spontaneous case possibly involving a forgetting mechanism (Stanford, 1974a, Case 1). One experimental study has provided evidence of psi-mediated forgetting (or at least of psi-mediated inhibition of some aspect of whatever is involved in memory) (Stanford, 1970). A study of word-association as a vehicle for ESP provided some evidence supportive of the concept that learned responses (memories) can be triggered by psi (Stanford, 1973).

Mistakes. Possibly through PMIR, mistakes sometimes occur which work to an unexpected advantage. I have several cases on file which illustrate this idea (see, e.g., Stanford, 1974a, p. 48). The concept of a mistake as a mediating vehicle for PMIR seems highly plausible when one considers the concept of psi-mediated facilitation of competing responses.

Associations. Sometimes a thought comes into one's mind which leads to the initiation of action which has unexpectedly favorable consequences. A hypothetical example would be thinking of a friend, and this causing one to call him, thus learning from him some unanticipated news of special interest. This might happen without one's having any "hunch" or intuition that one's friend had anything of special interest to say. Such a mechanism is simply a variety of the remembering mechanism discussed above which is not concerned with specific memories of past events but with potentiating into consciousness particular ideas. The word-association ESP study cited earlier (Stanford, 1973) provided evidence that psi can prime both particular responses and particular meanings (ideas).

Psi-mediated cognitions and/or "perceptions." As in typical spontaneous case reports, PMIR can be mediated by psi-produced ideas and/or apparent perceptions of need-relevant circumstances. Such modes for PMIR have been overemphasized historically. This has led to a somewhat misleading term, *extrasensory perception,* being used to designate the entirety of extrasensory function. Even as applied to many "cognitive-perceptual" ESP cases the term *perception* may be a misnomer. Many veridical psi-mediated "images" and "impressions" are really based upon psi-selection and psi-elicited recall of specific memories from out of the sensitive's sensory past which will represent to his or her consciousness the essential nature of the event being cognized or "perceived" by psi (Honorton and Harper, 1974; Roll 1966; Tyrrell, 1946). The idea that in "perceptual-cognitive" ESP, psi influence potentiates memories—including, often, some remote, improbable ones—may account for the common observation that after a good ESP "reading" a psychic may not be able to recall some of the most salient, accurate points in the "reading."

The strong sense of conviction often associated with cognitive-"perceptual" ESP cases likely derives not from the intrinsic nature of such events but from the circumstance that the ideas, feelings, images, etc., psi-mediated into awareness in such instances are so unusual or inappropriate in the life-context in which they appear that the person experiencing them is inclined to impute to them an unusual or psychic origin (Stanford, 1967).

The proposition that PMIR tends to be accomplished in the most economical way possible suggests, among other things, that a full-blown, conscious, psi-mediated cognition or "perception" (in the waking state) of the need-relevant object or event is unlikely when PMIR can be accomplished in some simpler, less demanding, and less potentially disruptive way.

There may nonetheless be certain circumstances in which a psi-mediated cognition or "perception" of a need-relevant event would be necessary to the occurrence of PMIR. Suppose that through the extrasensory scanning mechanism posited earlier, one encountered information regarding a tragic event to occur in one's own life or in the life of someone very near to oneself. What might constitute an *instrumental response* (PMIR) in this case? If one could come to know about or "perceive" the event before it happened or before physically encountering it, it might be possible to avoid some of its associated unpleasantness or disruptiveness. One might be able to become psychologically adjusted to the event or be better prepared for the encounter with it. The extrasensory foreknowledge could provide a kind of immunizing inoculation which would likely reduce the stress of the event when it was actually encountered and might enable one to better adapt to it. This may account for the fact that many cognitive or "perceptual" expressions of ESP refer to tragic events.

The possible expressions of PMIR discussed above are not intended to be either exhaustive or entirely exclusive categories one from another.

The PMIR model, as can be seen, provides a basis for remarkably subtle, yet powerful, psi function in the service of one's needs. If such a model is to be realistic it must also include assumptions which limit the possibility for the occurrence of PMIR. Otherwise, life would be one delightful "goal event" after another, and PMIR would allow us to avoid many of the normally unforeseen misfortunes which we encounter.

Certain factors limit the possibility for or the effectiveness of PMIR. Many such factors are situational. Others are psychological and include behavioral rigidity, inhibition, stereotypy, response chaining, and strong preoccupations blocking the expression of PMIR.

One effect of certain situational factors, as noted above, is to force the disposition toward PMIR to take the difficult cognitive-"perceptual" form (difficult at least for the waking state), if it is to have any chance of being effective. Much internal work seems to be required in that instance. It is easy to imagine that certain kinds of situational factors would entirely defeat the possibility of effective PMIR.

The term *behavioral rigidity* refers to preplanning a block of one's time such that it becomes a rigid schedule or regimen from which little or no deviation is permitted. *Behavioral inhibition* refers to an either long- or short-term tendency toward the imposition of tight rational or stylistic constraints upon behavior such that one must be quite sure of what one is doing or how one is doing it before taking any action, particularly if the action is unusual, unexpected, or deviant in terms of one's usual style of action. A person who exhibits high behavioral inhibition seldom acts on impulse. He requires strong justification for all that he does and must feel sure his action is appropriate to what he knows of or how he typically responds to the circumstances at hand. *Behavioral stereotypy* refers to a tendency to repeat a specific action, or a specific action sequence, in exactly the same way it has been done before. *Response chaining* occurs when a given act tends strongly and automatically to follow another particular act. Response chaining does not always derive from rational planning or scheduling. *Strong preoccupations* is self-explanatory. All the above factors put predetermined constraints on behavior. Numerous experimental studies confirm that factors such as these do inhibit the expression of ESP (for a review of these studies see Stanford, 1975).

Of all the possible mechanisms for PMIR, it seems likely that the influence upon timing and the mechanisms of forgetting and mistake-production would more likely be effective in the face of such behavioral constraints than would the other mechanisms. Of these three, the influence upon timing would perhaps be the most robust and thus might sometimes allow PMIR influence even in the face of strong behavioral constraints. Because it therefore has considerable conceptual and practical importance, it has been the focus of recent experimentation (Stanford and Associates, 1976; Stanford and Stio, 1976; Stanford and Thompson, 1974).

If young adults, adolescents, and perhaps, especially, children, can be assumed to be relatively more free as compared with older adults of the behavioral constraints discussed above, it may be that the formative influence of PMIR on their lives is proportionately greater than for adults. However, this would be a relative consideration, and it is not at all to suggest that PMIR is absent from adult life. Its role might simply be diminished. In any event, particular adults who retain more flexible cognitive styles and life styles might be more amenable to PMIR influence. There have been no studies of the role of age or life style on nonintentional psi or PMIR.

Certain factors dispose toward systematic misuse of PMIR, i.e., use of PMIR in ways which would normally be regarded as against the organism's own best interests. Factors disposing toward this misuse of PMIR are considered to include neuroticism, a negative self-concept, and direct motivational conflicts such as guilt or an approach-avoidance conflict. In the case of guilt or an approach-avoidance conflict, whether PMIR is used to approach or to avoid the goal (need-relevant object or event) should depend upon the same factors which govern behavior in ordinary approach-avoidance situations.

This proposition suggests conditions under which PMIR may be misused. There have been no direct experimental tests of this proposition. Direct tests are definitely needed even though results from studies of intentional ESP performance and personality variables seem to reflect at least in a general way, the pattern suggested in this proposition (see Stanford, 1974a). In the case of nonintentional ESP (PMIR) there is evidence (Stanford and Thompson, 1974) that persons who do well or poorly tend to do the same on an intentional ESP task. This encourages the supposition that personality-ESP results involving intentional ESP may generalize to nonintentional ESP.

As concerns the subproposition about guilt and motivational conflicts and PMIR, work with quasi-nonintentional ESP tasks by Carpenter (1971), Johnson (1971), and Johnson and Nordbeck (1972) with emotionally-loaded targets provides suggestive support. Subjects tended to psi-miss in attempting to match targets when, unknown to them, the targets had associated with them what might be construed as a negative emotional loading. Carpenter (1971) found that high-anxious junior high school subjects tended to psi-miss when trying to match targets associated with an erotic loading, even though they did not know that any targets had special loadings.

Stanford and Associates (1976) attempted an indirect test of the subproposition relating self-concept and PMIR. We attempted to influence what might be termed "momentary self-concept" by providing one group with strongly positive reinforcement for their performance on an experimental task (prior to the PMIR task) and another group with no feedback about their ostensible performance on the task. No attempt was made to actually create a negative self-concept in subjects. Therefore the test of the proposition above was an indirect one. Experimental results, though in the direction anticipated, fell far short of statistical significance. We did find that our male college-age subjects, when given the positive reinforcement by a female experimenter, performed significantly well and that a comparable group of male subjects given the positive reinforcement by a college-age male tended to perform poorly on the PMIR task. This suggests that a morale factor was at work. Further work is certainly needed to learn whether a boost in morale (a sense of personal efficacy, capability, or well-being) may increase the probability that persons can use PMIR constructively.

One of the subpropositions under discussion asserts that subjects using PMIR in an approach-avoidance situation will manifest behavior typical of nonpsi approach-avoidance situations. In ordinary approach-avoidance situations the organism makes approach responses until it gains a certain perceived proximity to the goal and then it becomes more and more inhibited as it further approaches the goal, and, upon closer approach, may start to retreat from the goal. Too close an approach causes the organism to reach a point at which the aversive aspects of the situation exceed the positive aspects. This would suggest, for example, that a person who has inner conflicts about having real success in his area of work might constructively use PMIR to allow himself some minor accomplishments, but would use it to defeat himself when undertaking projects which might lead to major success. No experimental study of this subproposition has been undertaken.

Extending the PMIR Model

Repeated casual observations and consideration of certain kinds of cases to be found in traditional spontaneous case collections suggest a generalization of the concept of "need" (in the PMIR model) to one of "response disposition."

The organism uses psi to scan its environment and when it thus encounters information about objects or events regarding which it has (in nonpsi circumstances) a definite response disposition (whether that disposition represents a tissue need, a learned need, a conditioned response, or some combination of these), it will tend to respond in a manner appropriate to the nature of that disposition and in a degree positively and directly related to its magnitude (as it is found in nonpsi situations). The psi-apprehended likelihood of actually encountering that object or event will also positively and directly determine the strength of that disposition, as will the closeness in time of the encounter with it. Objects or events similar to one regarding which the organism has developed a response disposition will be responded to, through psi mediation, to the degree that they resemble the original object or event; the principles of stimulus generalization will apply.

The inclusion of these statements in the model give it considerable explanatory power above and beyond its originally published form (Stanford, 1974a). The model would now seem capable of explaining such frequently noted observations as that an employee feels inexplicably nervous before an unexpected visit from an executive in his company; that one sometimes thinks about another person just before unexpectedly receiving some news about that person or a call from him or her; and it would seem to expand the scope of the model to explain a still larger range of the events often simply labeled "synchronistic." Whether the model proposes a correct explanation of such events must, of course, wait upon considerable experimentation. Some earlier experimental work would seem to provide support for this extension of the model (Dean, 1962; Dean and Nash, 1967; Morris, 1967; Tart, 1963). Much further work is clearly needed, both for testing the subpropositions in this extension of the model and in refining them.

Methodological Ramifications of the PMIR Model

Research on the PMIR model involves an attempt to model the way psi may function in life situations. The basic experimental paradigm usually involves a single opportunity for an individual nonintentionally to produce a psi-mediated response instrumental in serving his or her own needs. In such work whether or not the subject makes a particular kind of response at a particular time determines whether he will encounter a favorable or less favorable circumstance in the next (or a later) part of the experiment. The subject does not know that the study involves psi in any way and of course knows nothing sensorially of the response-reward (or punishment) contingencies. This paradigm models the likely function of psi outside the laboratory in which an individual usually has a chance, through psi mediation, to make a response which will either direct him toward a favorable event or away from an unfavorable one, or perhaps both. If appropriate PMIR occurs, the results are favorable; if not, they are less favorable. The outcomes are definite and clear-cut, and behavior has irrevocable consequences. Outside the laboratory there is often only a single opportunity to produce PMIR with respect to a given goal event or at least only one opportunity for PMIR to take a given form. Repeated "trials" of the same kind do not exist. The emphasis in experimental PMIR studies is thus on a single PMIR trial for each subject, and the outcome of that single trial is irrevocable. Many subjects are tested in a given experimental condition so that the effects upon the disposition toward PMIR in that condition can be examined.

Many variations of this paradigm are possible. The most basic requirement is that the experimental situation provide an opportunity for the use of psi in the service of the subject's needs, but that it do so without his awareness that psi is being studied and without his awareness that there is any connection between his behavior (during the PMIR task) and the experience(s) he will later encounter. Specific examples of this method are to be found in recent studies (Stanford and Associates, 1976; Stanford and Stio, 1976; Stanford and Thompson, 1974).

In such work it is often possible to design the study such that even though each subject has only one trial he can be assigned an interval-scale score measuring his disposition toward adaptive PMIR, and parametric statistics can be performed on the data of the experiment (see, e.g., Stanford and Thompson, 1974). In other applications only ordinal or nominal data may be possible or perhaps desirable.

General Comments on the PMIR Model

The PMIR model considerably broadens our conception of psi events. (This is all the more true if one considers the applications of the model in the area of psychokinesis, a topic to be considered in another chapter in this volume.) It does so by questioning, on rational, empirical, and experimental grounds, the common assumption that ESP's basic function is to produce cognitive or perception-like experiences and that other manifestations of extrasensory influence represent degraded, inhibited, suppressed, or partially blocked expressions of information that was somehow struggling for expression in the "true" form. The PMIR model instead proposes specific means by which psi can produce very subtle but powerful behavioral effects in the service of one's needs or in accord with one's nonpsi dispositions and can do so without being highly disruptive or causing the individual to feel that anything unusual is happening. Thus many of the most common functions of psi may go unnoticed, unrecognized, and thus unrecorded in spontaneous case collections. As has been shown, experimental studies are absolutely necessary in order to effectively study the broader nature of psi function.

The model takes very seriously the possible involvement of psi factors in life experience even among persons who have never claimed anything resembling a "cognitive-perceptual" ESP experience. It suggests that at least some of the seemingly meaningful events in life which are usually dismissed as "sheer coincidence" may be psi-mediated and actively produced by the organism in accord with its individual needs, dispositions, and typical modes of adaptation.

SOME CONCLUDING THOUGHTS

Earlier the reader was promised some thoughts on whether parapsychology retains certain implicit, unquestioned, untested, and perhaps unrecognized assumptions and some suggestions as to why this science has made no real progress in developing a basic framework for the underlying function of psi phenomena. I make no claim to having the answers in this area, but I do feel that the issue of unquestioned assumptions and our lack of progress on basic questions may be closely related.

A basic unquestioned assumption amounting essentially to a prejudice which pervades parapsychology is that psi interactions are specifically and exclusively associated with "living systems." At this point and even without the aid of precognitive clairaudience I fancy I can hear many readers saying, "What?! Have you really gone off the deep end? Do you really mean to suggest that anyone should entertain the idea that dead matter has consciousness, cognitive, conation, and all the other qualities of living systems which seem to be involved in psi?" My answer is that if this is your reaction it simply illustrates how strongly conditioned you—and most of us—are toward adopting a biopsychological view of psi phenomena. Let us step back a bit and examine the bases of that understandable prejudice.

It derives in large part from the historical background of parapsychological research, a background steeped in the dualism of spiritistic and spiritualistic orientations, in many years of sticky and none too enlightening entanglement in "survival" research, and in decades of research conducted exclusively from the perspective of the psychologist and the biologist. The result has been an implicit, unquestioned dualistic perspective on psi phenomena—either a mental-physical dualism or a living systems versus dead matter dualism or a combination of both. Psi phenomena are unquestioningly called "mental phenomena" and are attributed either to the unique attributes of a nonphysical "mind" or are considered somehow the emergent product of biological development.

We must at last raise the question of whether psi interactions are really specifically and exclusively associated with "living systems." If we as parapsychologists (and look at the biases implicit in that word!) do not stand back and question our fundamental, implicit assumptions, who will? Will it ever be possible to break out of the present cul-de-sac without doing this?

Now it is possible to reconsider what we confront if we drop the assumption that psi interactions are the exclusive province of "living systems." It is not necessary to try to impute to nonorganic systems all the supposed properties of living systems which seem to us to be associated with psi interactions. Rather, it is possible to reassess what is meant by psi events, to try to abstract from their appearances the basic nature of the interactions, and to ask whether analogous interactions may occur outside the biological realm. Admittedly this is vague, but there is no space here to discuss the matter further. In any event my own further thoughts on the matter are in their embryonic stages.

In conclusion it will only be possible to ask whether so far we may not have vastly misconceived the nature of psi events due to the vicissitudes of our history as a science. Might it not be that we have in psi phenomena hints of certain basic interaction potentialities present even in nonliving systems, but that we have never looked for them because we have been blinded by a biopsychological perspective on psi? Should this view prove correct—and I make no claims that it is—the study of psi events would have made a major contribution to physics, and, finally, physics would probably cast new light upon the origins and development of living systems.

These are bold proposals, but I suspect that our slow development in parapsychology has derived in part from too little bold thinking and, in part, from unbridled, untestable ponderings in the realm of dualistic metaphysics. Perhaps we can cure both ills with a single pill.

We shall have to do something, for our findings even within a biopsychological paradigm are beginning to make that paradigm, at least in its present form, look patently absurd. And lest the reader feel that I do not recognize this as a case of the pot calling the kettle black (given that the PMIR model is a solidly psychobiological one), I must confess that it is the nature of the ESP and PK events with which that model confronts us which forces the conclusion that to make sense of psi events even at the biopsychological level, progress at more basic levels is absolutely essential. The biopsychologistic paradigm, while it works reasonably well in promoting an understanding of specific behavioral features related to psi events, bogs us down in incredible complexities as soon as we attempt to apply it to anything even so basic as the possibility of influencing the fall of dice in a PK study. Ironically, in the final analysis it is the remarkable goal-orienting capacity of psi (ESP and PK) events, a feature stressed in the PMIR model, which may deliver the death-dealing blow to any biopsychological psi paradigm which has been so far devised. In the chapter in this volume on PK events I also discuss this topic, for it is precisely this which is at once the most embarrassing, exciting, and potentially important finding of psi research. It must certainly become a major focus of future conceptualization in this field.

REFERENCES

Anand, B. K., Chhina, G. S., and Singh, B. Some aspects of electroencephalographic studies in yogis. *Electroencephalography and Clinical Neurophysiology*, 1961, **13**, 452–456.

Andrew, K. Psychokinetic influences on an electromechanical random number generator during evocation of "left-hemispheric" vs. "right hemispheric" functioning. In J. D. Morris, W. G. Roll, and R. L. Morris (Eds.), *Research in Parapsychology 1974*, pp. 58–61. Metuchen, N.J.: Scarecrow Press, 1975.

Bagchi, F. K., and Wenger, M. A. Electrophysiological correlates of some yogi exercises. *Electroencephalography and Clinical Neurophysiology*, 1957, Suppl. 7, 132–148.

Banquet, J. P. Spectral analysis of EEG in meditation. *Electroencephalography and Clinical Neurophysiology*, 1973, **35**, 143–151.

Barker, J. C. Premonitions of the Aberfan disaster. *Journal of the Society for Psychical Research*, 1967, **44**, 169–180.

Braud, L. W., and Braud, W. G. Further studies of relaxation as a psi-conducive state. *Journal of the American Society for Psychical Research*, 1974, **68**, 229–245.

Braud, W. G. Psi-conducive states. *Journal of Communication*, 1975, **25**, 142–152.

Braud, W. G., and Braud, L. W. Preliminary explorations of psi-conducive states: Progressive muscular relaxation. *Journal of the American Society for Psychical Research*, 1973, **67**, 26–46.

Braud, W. G., and Braud, L. W. The psi-conducive syndrome: Free response GESP performance following evocation of "left-hemispheric" vs. "right-hemispheric" functioning. In J. D. Morris, W. G. Roll, and R. L. Morris (Eds.), *Research in Parapsychology 1974*, pp. 17–20. Metuchen, N. J.: Scarecrow Press, 1975.

Broad, C. D. *Religion, Philosophy and Psychical Research*. New York: Humanities Press, 1969.

Buño, W. (Jr.), Velluti, R., Handler, P., and Garćia-Austt, E. Neural control of the cochlear input in the wakeful free guinea pig. *Physiology and Behavior*, 1966, **1**, 23–35.

Burton, L., Joines, W., ans Stevens, B. Kirlian photography and its relevance to parapsychological research. In J. D. Morris, W. G. Roll, and R. L. Morris (Eds.), *Research in Parapsychology 1974*, pp. 107–112. Metuchen, N.J.: Scarecrow Press, 1975.

Carpenter, J. C. The differential effect and hidden target differences consisting of erotic and neutral stimuli. *Journal of the American Society for Psychical Research*, 1971, **65**, 204–214.

Das, N. N., and Gastaut, H. Variations de l'activité électrique du cerveau, du coeur et des muscles squelettiques au cours de la méditation et de l'extase yogique. *Electroencephalography and Clinical Neurophysiology*, 1957, Suppl. 6, 211–220.

Dean, E. D. The plethysmograph as an indicator of ESP. *Journal of the Society for Psychical Research*, 1962, **41**, 351–353.

Dean, E. D., and Nash, C. B. Coincident plethysmograph results under controlled conditions. *Journal of the Society for Psychical Research*, 1967, **44**, 1–14.

Dobervich, C. Kirlian photography revealed? *Psychic*, 1974, **6** (1), 34–39.

Donchin, E., and Lindsley, D. B. (Eds.), *Average Evoked Potentials*. Washington, D.C.: NASA, SP-191, 1969.

Dukhan, H., and Rao, K. R. Meditation and ESP scoring. In W. G. Roll, R. L. Morris, and J. D. Morris (Eds.), *Research in Parapsychology 1972*, pp. 148-151. Metuchen, N.J.: Scarecrow Press, 1973.

Eilbert, L., and Schmeidler, G. R. A study of certain psychological factors in relation to ESP performance. *Journal of Parapsychology*, 1950, **14**, 53-74.

Foulkes, D. *The Psychology of Sleep*. New York: Scribner's, 1966.

Hagbarth, K. E., and Kerr, D. I. B. Central influences on spinal afferent conduction. *Journal of Neurophysiology*, 1954, **17**, 295-307.

Hempel, C. G., and Oppenheim, P. The logic of explanation. In H. Feigl and M. Brodbeck (Eds.), *Readings in the Philosophy of Science*, pp. 319-352. New York: Appleton-Century-Crofts, 1953.

Hernández-Péon, R., Guzmán-Flores, C., Alcáraz, M., and Fernández-Guardiola, A. Sensory transmission in visual pathway during "attention" in unanaesthetized cats. *Acta Neurologica Latino Americana*, 1957, **3**, 1-8.

Hernández-Péon, R., Scherrer, H., and Jouvet, M. Modification of electric activity in cochlear nucleus during attention in unanaesthetized cats. *Science*, 1956, **123**, 331-332.

Honorton, C. Creativity and precognition scoring level. *Journal of Parapsychology*, 1967, **31**, 29-42.

Honorton, C. Psi-conducive states of awareness. In E. D. Mitchell et al., *Psychic Exploration*, pp. 616-638. New York: Putnam's, 1974.

Honorton, C. Receiver optimization and information rate in ESP. Paper presented at the Annual Meeting of the American Association for the Advancement of Science, New York, N.Y., January 26-31, 1975.

Honorton, C., and Harper, S. Psi-mediated imagery and ideation in an experimental procedure for regulating perceptual input. *Journal of the American Society for Psychical Research*, 1974, **68**, 156-168.

Johnson, M. An attempt to affect scoring behavior in a group test of precognition by means of manipulation of motivation and by the use of individually assigned emotionally loaded targets. *Research Letter* of the Parapsychological Division of the Psychological Laboratory, University of Utrecht, December, 1971; Utrecht, The Netherlands.

Johnson, M. A new technique of testing ESP in a real-life, high-motivational context. *Journal of Parapsychology*, 1973, **37**, 210-217.

Johnson, M., and Nordbeck, B. Variation in the scoring behavior of a "psychic" subject. *Journal of Parapsychology*, 1972, **36**, 122-132.

Kasamatsu, A., Okuma, T., Takenaka, S., Koga, E., Ikeda, K., and Sugiyama, H. The EEG of "Zen" and "Yoga" practitioners. *Electroencephalography and Clinical Neurophysiology*, 1957, Suppl. 9, 51-52.

Kerr, D. I. B., and Hagbarth, K. E. An investigation of olfactory centrifugal fiber system. *Journal of Neurophysiology*, 1955, **18**, 363-374.

Klinger, E. *Structure and Functions of Fantasy*. New York: Wiley-Interscience, 1971.

Klinger, E. Consequences of commitment to and disengagement from incentives. *Psychological Review*, 1975, **82**, 1-25.

Kreitler, H., and Kreitler, S. Does extrasensory perception affect psychological experiments? *Journal of Parapsychology*, 1972, **36**, 1-45.

Kreitler, H., and Kreitler, S. Subliminal perception and extrasensory perception. *Journal of Parapsychology*, 1973, **37**, 163-188.

LeShan, L. Toward a general theory of the paranormal. *Parapsychological Monographs No. 9.* New York: Parapsychology Foundation, 1969.

Lewis, L., and Schmeidler, G. R. Alpha relations with non-intentional and purposeful ESP after feedback. *Journal of the American Society for Psychical Research*, 1971, **65**, 455-467.

McCallum, C. W., and Knott, J. (Eds.). The contingent negative variation. *Proceedings of the Vancouver Symposium*. Amsterdam: Elsevier, 1973.

Montandon, H. E. Psychophysiological aspects of the Kirlian phenomenon: A confirmatory study. *Journal of the American Society for Psychical Research*, 1977, **71**, 45–49.

Morris, R. L. Some new techniques in animal psi research. *Journal of Parapsychology*, 1967, **31**, 316–317.

Ornstein, R. E. *The Psychology of Consciousness*. San Francisco: Freeman, 1972.

Palmer, J. Scoring in ESP tests as a function of belief in ESP. Part I. The sheep-goat effect. *Journal of the American Society for Psychical Research*, 1971, **65**, 373–408.

Prabhavananda, S., and Isherwood, C. *How to Know God: The Yoga Aphorisms of Patanjali*. Hollywood: Vedanta Press, 1953.

Regan, D. *Evoked Potentials in Psychology, Sensory Physiology, and Clinical Medicine*. New York: Wiley-Interscience, 1972.

Rhine, L. E. Hallucinatory psi experiences: An introductory survey. *Journal of Parapsychology*, 1956, **20**, 233–256.

Roll, W. G. ESP and memory. *International Journal of Neuropsychiatry*, 1966, **2**, 505–521.

Schmidt, H. Observation of subconscious PK effects with and without time displacement. In J. D. Morris, W. G. Roll, and R. L. Morris (Eds.), *Research in Parapsychology 1974*, pp. 116–121. Metuchen, N.J.: Scarecrow Press, 1975.

Stanford, R. G. A further study of high- versus low-scoring sheep. *Journal of Parapsychology*, 1965, **29**, 141–158.

Stanford, R. G. Response bias and the correctness of ESP test responses. *Journal of Parapsychology*, 1967, **31**, 280–289.

Stanford, R. G. Extrasensory effects upon "memory." *Journal of the American Society for Psychical Research*, 1970, **64**, 161–186.

Stanford, R. G. EEG alpha activity and ESP performance: A replicative study. *Journal of the American Society for Psychical Research*, 1971, **65**, 144–154.

Stanford, R. G. Extrasensory effects upon associative processes in a directed free-response task. *Journal of the American Society for Psychical Research*, 1973, **67**, 147–190.

Stanford, R. G. An experimentally testable model for spontaneous psi events. I. Extrasensory events. *Journal of the American Society for Psychical Research*, 1974, **68**, 34–57. (a)

Stanford, R. G. An experimentally testable model for spontaneous psi events. II. Psychokinetic events. *Journal of the American Society for Psychical Research*, 1974, **68**, 321–356. (b)

Stanford, R. G. Concept and psi. In W. G. Roll, R. L. Morris, and J. D. Morris (Eds.), *Research in Parapsychology 1973*, pp. 137–162. Metuchen, N.J.: Scarecrow Press, 1974. (c)

Stanford, R. G. Response factors in extrasensory performance. *Journal of Communication*, 1975, **25**, 153–161.

Stanford, R. G., and Associates. A study of motivational arousal and self-concept in psi-mediated instrumental response. *Journal of the American Society for Psychical Research*, 1976, **70**, 167–178.

Stanford, R. G., and Thompson, G. Unconscious psi-mediated instrumental response and mediated instrumental response. *Journal of the American Society for Psychical Research*, 1976, **70**, 167–178.

Stanford, R. G., and Lovin, C. EEG alpha activity and ESP performance. *Journal of the American Society for Psychical Research*, 1970, **64**, 375–384.

Stanford, R., and Mayer, B. Relaxation as a psi-conducive state: A replication and exploration of parameters. *Journal of the American Society for Psychical Research*, 1974, **68**, 182–191.

Stanford, R. G., and Stevenson, I. EEG correlates of free-response GESP in an individual subject. *Journal of the American Society for Psychical Research*, 1972, **66**, 357–368.

Stanford, R. G., and Stio, A. A study of associative mediation in psi-mediated instrumental response. *Journal of the American Society for Psychical Research*, 1976, **70**, 55–64.

Stanford, R. G., and Thompson, G. Unconscious psi-mediated instrumental response and its relation to conscious ESP performance. In W. G. Roll, R. L. Morris, and J. D. Morris (Eds.), *Research in Parapsychology 1973*, pp. 99–103. Metuchen, N.J.: Scarecrow Press, 1974.

Stanford, R. G., Zenhausern, R., Taylor, A., and Dwyer, M. Psychokinesis as psi-mediated instrumental response. *Journal of the American Society for Psychical Research*, 1975, **69**, 127–133.

Stevenson, I. Precognition of disasters. *Journal of the American Society for Psychical Research*, 1970, **64**, 187–210.

Tart, C. T. Possible physiological correlates of psi cognition. *International Journal of Parapsychology*, 1963, **5**, 375–386.

Tyrrell, G. N. M. The "modus operandi" of paranormal cognition. *Proceedings of the Society for Psychical Research*, 1946, **48**, 65–120.

White, R. A. A comparison of old and new methods of reponse to targets in ESP experiments. *Journal of the American Society for Psychical Research*, 1964, **58**, 21–56.

3

Science and Reality*

Arthur Koestler

Some of my friends and well-wishers professed to be shocked because my last book, *The Roots of Coincidence*, is concerned with parapsychology—i.e., telepathy and the even more puzzling phenomena of psychokinesis, short-term precognition, and apparently meaningful coincidences. I would like to take this opportunity to mention briefly some of the reasons which may prompt a rational person—which I believe myself to be—with a strong scientific bent, to get involved in these unorthodox branches of research.

The evidence for ESP can be divided into two broad categories—on the one hand experiments in the laboratory and on the other hand what one might call out-of-the-blue phenomena which occur spontaneously, such as veridical dreams, clocks which stop at the moment of a person's death, and other meaningful coincidences. Such events do not constitute scientific evidence, although a great many people have experienced them; however strong their emotional impact, rationality prompts us to attribute them to chance.

But the evidence produced in the laboratories cannot be thus dismissed. Any single event—like the stopping of the clock—however improbable, can be ascribed to chance because the laws of probability do not apply to single events, only to large numbers of events on a statistical scale. But probability statistics is precisely the method in modern ESP laboratory research, based on the same type of

*"Science and Reality" from THE HEEL OF ACHILLES: Essays 1968-1973, by Arthur Koestler. Copyright © 1974 by Arthur Koestler. Reprinted by permission of Random House, Inc.

calculation as that employed by physicists, geneticists, market-researchers, and insurance companies. And the *same* logic which compels us to dismiss the stopping of the clock as a chance event also compels us to *exclude* the possibility of chance if a telepathic subject persistently, in thousands of consecutive card-guessing or dice-throwing experiments, scores a persistently higher number of hits than the probability calculus permits—because here the odds against chance are on an astronomical scale.

It was a strictly orthodox, statistical approach, applied to an unorthodox subject, which gradually wore down academic resistance—and incredulity—in the course of the 45 years since J. B. Rhine established the first Laboratory for Parapsychology at Duke University, North Carolina. Since then, a great number of similar laboratories have been established all over the world—including Soviet Russia and other Communist countries—in which scientists work under the same rigorously controlled test-conditions as researchers in other fields, using sophisticated computers and electronic apparatus to eliminate as far as possible human error in evaluating the results. And the results show that ESP—extrasensory perception—is a fact, whether we like it or not. In 1969 the American Association for the Advancement of Science approved the application of the Parapsychological Association to become an affiliate of that august body. That decision conferred on parapsychology the ultimate seal of respectability.

Nevertheless, even open-minded people feel a strong intellectual discomfort or even revulsion when confronted with phenomena which seem to contradict what they believe to be the immutable laws of physics. The answer is that the laws of physics are by no means immutable, but in constant flux; and that since the advent of Planck, Einstein, and Heisenberg, modern quantum physics has discarded all our classical, common-sense notions of time, space, matter, and causality. Thus both physics and parapsychology point to aspects or levels of reality beyond the reach of contemporary science—a coded message written in invisible ink between the lines of a banal letter. Though we can only decipher tantalizingly small fragments of the message, the knowledge that it is there is exciting and comforting at the same time.

4

Mind and Body:
A Contribution to a
Theory of
Parapsychological
Phenomena

Benjamin B. Wolman

INTRODUCTION

One of the main issues of scientific research in parapsychology concerns the nature of parapsychological phenomena. Are they mind or body? Do they belong to physics or psychology? Are telepathic messages transmitted by physical carriers such as electromagnetic waves or by some inconceivable, nonspatial, psychological processes? Rhine and Pratt (1957) maintain that parapsychical phenomena "are distinguishable from the other phenomena of psychology merely by the fact that they can be *shown* to be nonphysical in character" (p. 10). Furthermore, "the evidence is now conclusive enough in parapsychology to leave no doubt that, so far as present concepts go, we are dealing with nonphysical principles and processes." However, Rhine and Pratt admit that this distinction "is only relatively thorough-going" (p. 11). Apparently, the evidence is not conclusive.

Some researchers in parapsychology believe in the physical nature of parapsychological phenomena; e.g., the Soviet scientist, Vasiliev (1963) conducted experiments in transmission of mental images. In the first series of experiments, the subjects were put in a closed metal room, and in the second series of experiments, the metal barrier was substituted by a wooden one which did not prevent electromagnetic waves. No significant differences were discovered between the two sets of experiments, and the theory of electromagnetic nature of telepathy was not proven. However, these negative results did not prevent further experimentation nor did they exclude physicalistic interpretations. Apparently, there is no conclusive evidence for either psychological or physical explanations.

The theoretical controversy concerning the nature of parapsychological phenomena cannot be resolved within the framework of parapsychology. It seems that parapsychological phenomena are but a fraction of a wide range of borderline processes, such as the entire field of the unconscious, dreams, hypnotism, psychosomatic and somatopsychic symptoms, and they must be examined in such a broad perspective. A review of all the relevant knowledge may offer the much needed framework for a parapsychological theory building. The present chapter intends to be a contribution to this complex task.

THE MIND-BODY DICHOTOMY

As early as 3000 B.C., that is, about 5,000 years ago, when an Egyptian Pharaoh died, several slaves were killed and buried in his grave in Gerzeh to provide service for him in the hereafter. The great pyramid of Gizeh, the grave of the Pharaoh Khufer, was built by 100,000 slaves who labored for almost 20 years in order to provide adequate care for the Pharaoh's soul after his bodily death.

The mind-body dichotomy is probably as old as humanity. Were men immortal, they wouldn't have to face the mind-body problem. Their mortality makes them aware of the fact that as long as they live, they act, but when they die, all actions stop. Small wonder they assumed the existence of a nonbodily force that activates the body; and when it leaves the body, all actions come to an end.

The ancient Israelites called this nonbodily force *neshama* (soul) which is a derivative of *neshima* (breath). God created man out of corporeal "dust" but blew the *neshama* into Adam's nostrils. The same nonbodily driving force was called by ancient Romans *anima*, or soul. The soul made bodies move. Without soul, men were like inanimate objects. No one would dare kick a live enemy, but one could do it to a dead enemy whose soul had left him.

The belief in immortality of the soul is more plausible than the lack of such a belief. Sun and moon, oceans and rivers, mountains and valleys are for ever. Bodies die, but souls last forever. The immortality of the soul was a generally accepted belief, and it was not easy to doubt it. Dualism is a common-sense, widely accepted philosophy, irrespective of one's belief in the immortality of the soul.

The soma-psyche problem, as presented in dualistic way, has no solution. The psyche is not material, while the body is material, perishable, born to die. There is no bridge, no connection, no common elements between the soul and the body.

Dualism became the fundamental philosophy in the Aristotelian system; dualism is a dogma in the monotheistic religions, elaborated in the writings of Maimonides and Thomas Aquinas. Dualism is often publicly denounced but always present as an unsurmountable obstacle.

All efforts to solve this problem outside religion, either by empirical studies or by philosophical speculations, have led nowhere. Descartes accepted two systems and invented an arbitrarily set connection system between them. But the perplexing fact of communication between mind and body could be neither denied nor explained away. Alcohol changes human moods; moods alter respiration and blood circulation. These facts have been known for a very long time, but it is not easy to find adequate interpretation.

The occasionalists, such as Guelinx, assumed that mind and matter "run on parallel never-intersecting tracks. The good God has so arranged things that the activities of mind and matter correspond exactly to one another, and keep in such perfect step that each seems to influence the other without actually doing so. In the same way . . . the makers of a cinematograph film arrange that the voices and action should correspond and synchronize through the whole length of the film" (Jeans, 1958, p. 26).

A somewhat similar solution was suggested by the Gestalt school of psychology. Their principle of isomorphism means that the order of psychological experiences is "a true representation of a corresponding order in the processes upon which experience depends." This corresponding order is the "functional order in the sequence of correlated brain processes" (Köhler, 1947, p. 62).

The main stream of psychology and psychiatry has been guided by a monistic-materialistic philosophy. Hippocrates and Galen in ancient times, and in modern times Pinel, Esquirol, Pavlov, and Kraepelin strongly emphasized the organic factors in behavior. The division of mental disorders into organic and functional excluded mentalism. Functional disorders were believed to be the disorders whose organicity was not yet proven. In lack of anatomical and histological abnormalities, the disorders were believed to be caused by a general dysfunction of the nervous system.

REDUCTIONISM

Whoever tries to develop a comprehensive theory of parapsychological phenomena must be reminded of the fate of Galileo Galilei and Copernicus. Even today, hundreds of years later, common sense militates against the idea that the earth is round and it does, indeed, rotate. Everybody's daily experience flies in face of scientific theories, for whenever one goes for a walk he finds the earth to be flat and not moving at all, Galileo and Copernicus notwithstanding.

Even more difficult is to accept Einstein's relativity theory. Taken literally, Einstein's theory should make one throw away his wristwatch, for time is merely a fourth dimension. One must not dare to sit on a chair for chairs ceased to be the old, traditional, solid wood or metal and turned into an everchanging aggregate of rapidly moving units of energy.

Apparently, parapsychology adds additional headaches. Our daily observations are clearly dualistic, and they either deal with mind or matter, and the dualism of soul and body is deeply entrenched in the Judeo–Christian tradition. Everyone *knows* for sure that human bodies decay eventually, and some people believe that the souls will live forever in the Hereafter. Descartes drew a sharp line between the *res cogitans* and *res extensa*. I. P. Pavlov (1928) maintained that the study of conditioned reflexes had always to do with "necessarily spatial" facts, while the status of psychology which deals with "subjective states" is "completely hopeless" (p. 219).

Some scientists and philosophers hoped to build bridges between the "spatial" neurophysiology and the nonspatial psychology if they could reduce psychology to neurophysiology.

One must distinguish between the *theoretical* and the *methodological* reductionism. The first intends to reduce the theoretical body of the to-be-reduced science to terms of the reducing science which is believed to encompass the data of the to-be-reduced science, e.g., some philosophers of science believe that biology could be reduced to chemistry.

The methodological reductionism advocates the application of research methods of one science to another, such as, e.g., the application of statistical methods developed in agriculture to economics or the application of physicalistic methods of measurement and other quantitative techniques to the study of human behavior.

One may distinguish three types of theoretical reductionism. Theoretical reductionism in the realm of psychology is a belief that

1. The subject matter of psychology can presently be presented in terms of the subject matter of another science, for example, neurophysiology—which is *radical reductionism*,
2. future research may discover that such a reduction is feasible—*hoped-for reductionism*,
3. the scientific propositions and theories derived from empirical studies in psychology could and should be presented as logical consequences of scientific propositions of other sciences—*logical reductionism*.

The subject matter of psychology—human personality—is reduced to biochemical and neurological processes.

Not all psychologists share the belief that such a reduction is possible, and they oppose *radical reductionism*. They feel that presently radical reductionism is an untenable hypothesis, yet they share the belief that such a reduction may become possible in the future. This belief, the *hoped-for reductionism*, is widely accepted in psychology.

The third alternative, the *logical reductionism*, tries to reduce the formal logical propositions derived from empirical studies and conceptualization of psychological theory to scientific propositions of other sciences.

Radical reductionism insists that events described by the "science to-be-reduced" are mere appearances or illusions. Actually, these events are more truthfully explained in terms of the other, "reducing" science. The facts as described by the "science-to-be-reduced" are believed to be unreal and have to be replaced by scientific data described by the "reducing" science. The reducing science must "take over" the science to be reduced.

The history of philosophy and science offers several instances of such developments. The pre-Socratic philosophers introduced the concept of four elements in an effort to reduce the universe of the sensorily perceived variety of phenomena to the four elements of the "true" world. Plato believed the material world was to be seen as a mere reflection of the world of ideas. So it was in Hegel's philosophical system. Galileo's theory of falling bodies was "reduced" by Newton's theory of gravitation and mechanics. In our times, metabolic processes are being reduced to chemistry.

Although the efforts to solve the psyche-soma dichotomy can develop in either direction by reducing body to mind or mind to body, the latter has been more common. Karl Vogt in *Vorlesungen über den Menschen* (1863) defended the idea that consciousness should be regarded as one of the many brain functions. Vogt asserted that human thought is related to the brain as gall is to the liver. Similar ideas were expressed by H. Nikescgitt: "No thought without phosphorus." Moleschott, in his *Kreislauf des Lebens* (1857), made an effort to reestablish the unity of the universe instead of the "hopeless" division of the world into material and spiritual which, he believed, was a division between the real and the imaginary. Also, Herbart advocated radical reductionism and presented mental life as a function of material units (Wolman, 1968).

The difference between psychology and physiology, as Watson (1919, p. 20) saw it, was that physiology studied separate physiological functions whereas psychology dealt with the functions of the organism as a whole. "The findings of psychology become the functional correlates of structure and lend themselves to explanation in physico-chemical terms" (Watson, 1913). Bechterev (1913, pp. 45ff) believed that consciousness *is* a state of physical energy related to central inhibition and resistance in cortical processes. Hebb (1949) wrote about "the kind of activity *throughout the cerebrum* which we call consciousness" (p. 219). He also believed that "interest or motivation" can be "provisionally translated into the stability and persistence of the phase sequence" in nerve cells (p. 223).

Some psychologists vigorously rejected any sort of theoretical reductionism. According to Skinner (1953), "modern science has attempted to put forth an ordered and integrated conception of nature.... The picture which emerges is almost always dualistic. The scientist humbly admits that he is describing only half of the universe, and he defers to another world—a world of mind or consciousness—for which another mode of inquiry is assumed to be required" (p. 276). According to Skinner (1950), there is no valid reason to reduce psychological data to physiology, physics, or chemistry. Also, Kurt Lewin (1951) saw no advantage in reducing psychology to physiology and objected to the Gestaltists' isomorphic theory of mind and body.

Most psychological theorists have neither accepted nor rejected reductionism, but professed a hoped-for-reductionism. For instance, C. L. Hull (1943) maintained that there is no adequate neuropsychology to which psychology could be reduced at the present time. Also, Freud (1949) believed that "the future may teach us how to exercise a direct influence, by means of particular chemical substances, upon the amount of energy and their distribution in the apparatus of mind" (p. 79).

Another way out was suggested by logical reductionism. According to Nagel (1953),

> The objective of the reduction is to show that the laws or general principles of the secondary science are simply logical consequences of the assumptions of the primary science (the reducing science). However, if these laws contain expressions that do not occur in the assumptions of the primary science, a logical derivation is clearly impossible. Accordingly, a necessary condition for the derivation is the explicit formulation of suitable relations between such expressions in the secondary science and the expressions occurring in the premises of the primary discipline (p. 541).

However, logical reductionism does not prove that mental and somatic processes are the same nor that they are different. Experts in brain science find little help in logical reductionism and, as Sherrington (1941) put it, "mind and brain, for all I can tell, remain refractory apart" (p. 212).

THE CONCEPT OF IDENTITY

Apparently, the problem of mind and body cannot be resolved within the framework of reductionism. One should, perhaps, embark on the road of logical analysis. Are mind and body two different things, or could they be perceived as one and the same thing?

In order to tackle this question, one must start with clarification of the terms *the same*, *identical*, and so on. Let us start with the mathematical sign "equals."
Consider the equation

$$a + b = 0 \tag{1}$$

This equation does not imply identity. The sign "a" and the sign "b" have the same numerical value, one of them positive, the other negative.

The sign symbol "zero" is not necessarily identical with the composite sign "$a + b$." The equation merely represents a mathematical operation, but not an identity relationship. Translated into simple English, it reads as follows:

a added to b *equals* 0, but they are a and b, and they are *not* a zero.

Philosophy of science is full of concepts uncritically borrowed from mathematics. Such a state of affairs was perhaps justified in times of Spinoza or Kant when philosophers believed in the alleged superiority and self-evidence of mathematical propositions. However, the development of newer mathematical systems, such as, e.g., Riemann's and Lobatchevski's geometry, Boyle's system, matrix algebra, topology, etc., have challenged the axiomatic nature of the mathematical systems and have made mathematics into a systematic aggregate of symbolic signs and operations, sort of a language or game (Wolman, 1960, p. 528).

This change in the role of mathematics permits a far-reaching revision of several concepts. Consider the equation:

$$a = a \tag{2}$$

This equation seems to be self-evident, but this alleged self-evidence could be questioned.

For instance, in traditional algebra:

$$a + b = b + a \tag{3}$$

but in matrix algebra:

$$\{a + b\} \neq \{b + a\} \tag{4}$$

In topological mathematics the equation $a + b = b + a$ may become meaningless, for the relative position of the elements in regard to each other is the relevant issue in topology.

Furthermore, consider the chemical equation:

$$C + C + O = C_2 O \tag{5}$$

Is $C_2 O$ identical with $C + C + O$?

The empirical evidence militates against such an assumption, for the *quality* of $C_2 O$ is different from two unbound C's and an O. Thus the above equation:

$$C + C + O = C_2 O$$

does not represent identity but merely describes a complex process by which C and C and O can *become* $C_2 O$. Moreover, this description is far from being accurate, which may undermine one's belief in the applicability of simple mathematical signs toward description of complex phenomena. One is tempted to remark at this point that the irrational mathematical sign "i" presented in the equation:

$$i = \sqrt{-1} \tag{6}$$

has played a constructive role in the history of electricity.

The development of thermodynamics should have aroused serious doubts concerning the possibility of anything ever being identical with anything else, including itself. In thermodynamics heat *changes* into kinetic energy; does this mean that heat *is* kinetic energy? Is fuel identical with energy? Is water identical with vapor and ice?

Empirically speaking, ice $\neq$ water $\neq$ vapor. Are they, therefore, the same? Or are they not?

Heraclitus said that no one can bathe twice in *the same* river. It seems, however, obvious that no one could ever remain the same person. A person "P" in time unit "t_1" and environment "e_1" is not exactly the same as the "same" person a while later in time unit "t_2" and in an environment "e_2." Thus

$$P_{t_1 e_1} \neq P_{t_2 e_2} \tag{7}$$

K. Lewin (1951), H. S. Sullivan (1947), B. B. Wolman (1960), and many others have pointed to the *field-theoretical* nature of human personality. Prognosis of mental or physical diseases can be, at best, a statistical approximation. In order to predict an individual case, a clinician must possess a complete knowledge of *all* relevant factors affecting his patient, and the prediction, if any, must be field-theoretical. "The same" patient reacts differently to "the same" disease in a different environment and under a different type of treatment.

CONTINUITY IN CHANGE

Apparently no one is nor can ever be identical with oneself, and the term *identical* should be put in the vocabulary of archaic terms together with witchcraft, phlogiston, ether, and so on. The fact that heat may *turn* into motion, electric current into light, and an egg into a chicken does not mean that in any of these cases the antecedent is identical with the subsequent one. Complex processes of change take place in each of the three above-mentioned instances, and each process of change is different.

But change does not imply discontinuity. A fertilized egg becomes a zygote, and the zygote becomes an embryo, fetus, neonate, infant, toddler, little child, adolescent, college student, and eventually, e.g., a famous pediatrician. Is the pediatrician "the same" as or "identical" with the nursery child he or she was

40 or 50 years ago? *The answer is "Yes" in the sense of continuity, but "No" in the sense of identity.*

It is an undeniable fact that, under certain conditions, certain bodies change, merge, split, grow, shrink, move, stop, fall apart, and so on. The Montana Indians used to squeeze the skulls of their newborn infants to make them look prettier by the standards of the prevailing fashion. Contemporary women starve themselves to meet the standards set by the Garment Center's fashion designers. When a woman has lost 20 pounds, is she still the same woman or not? When a child has grown up, when an attic has been added to a house, when a man has shaved his beard: are these all still the same?

Obviously, there are degrees of change. When a pot of water is put on a stove, the temperature of the water changes. When the water reaches a boiling point, further changes take place. Logically speaking, as long as at least one element A_1 persists in A_2, we speak of *continuity*.

There are a great many types and degrees of change and, as mentioned before, there is no reason to prescribe to them one path and one pattern. The fact of continuity in change is evident in many, if not all, phenomena and events in the universe. As observed by Greek philosophers and by the Hebrew Ecclesiastes, rivers evaporate and turn into clouds, and clouds give rain and fill rivers with water. Lava erupts and turns into fertile soil, and some fertile soil is eroded or covered by dunes. Species develop and perish, and new worlds develop out of old ones.

This continuous change is expressed in a universal theory, the theory of *monistic transitionism*. Monistic transitionism (a) takes into account the diversity and variability of nature, (b) unites this empirical diversity into an over-all continuous *unity*, and (c) introduces the general idea of continuous changeability of things. Transitionism does not assume uniformity of the universe; it assumes only its continuity.

Monistic transitionism is neither reductionism of any type nor an emergence theory. It simply states that, empirically speaking, heat is not motion; heat and motion are measured by different units and have different impact on things. They act differently; they are different.

Yet heat and motion can be, under certain conditions, transformed into one another. Thus transitionism at the empirical level states that although things are different, some things have many similarities, and certain things can be transformed into other things.

Obviously, certain phenomena, although empirically different, can be partially reduced to each other. This rule does not apply to all phenomena, for unity does not mean uniformity. Certain sciences can be reduced in a radical sense, while other sciences only in the sense of logical reductionism, that is, interpreted in terms of the laws of other sciences. Perhaps chemistry will be formally reduced to quantum mechanics. Certain areas are, however, not reducible. But even those areas that are not reducible can be presented in a continuum of changes. The issue is not an issue of faith, but of empirical evidence and logical inference.

TRANSITIONISM

M. Scriven (1962, p. 104) wrote that parapsychology provides us with a factual basis on which there is yet to be built a theory. He was wrong, for not all empirical data of parapsychology are adequately proven, and there have been several efforts to order the available data to a theoretical system. The present paper endeavors to introduce a set of theoretical constructs.

The underlying hypothesis is that of *monistic transitionism* (Wolman, 1965). Specifically, transitionism aims at the development of a set of theoretical constructs applicable to living organisms. These theoretical constructs would permit us to present mental phenomena as a continuum of all other organic processes. Organic processes, called O, under certain conditions, called k_1, are transformed ($\Rightarrow$) into mental processes, called M. Thus, the formula,

$$O_{k1} \Rightarrow M \text{ (which means } O_{k1} \text{ is transformed into } M) \tag{8}$$

A reverse process of transformation of mental processes (M) into organic ones (O) is also feasible under the condition k_2. Thus,

$$M_{k2} \Rightarrow O \text{ (which means } M_{k2} \text{ is transformed into } O) \tag{9}$$

Transitionism is a general theory which views the universe as a system of continuous transitions from one form into another. It is a theory of unity and continuity. Transitionism encompasses Einstein's principle of transformation of energy into matter; then it presents the evolution of matter in three recognizable phases: (a) The inanimate or inorganic matter at a certain point of evolution undergoes changes and becomes (b) organic, as described in experimental studies of Oparin (1957). Then, at a certain phase in evolution, matter turns into (c) psychological processes (which can also be called behavioral). Transitionism links all three phases into one process of change and continuity. This process is also reversible: for, as the inorganic matter may become organic matter and the organic matter may become psychological, the psychological elements can turn organic and organic elements may turn inorganic. For example, under the impact of alcohol, human feelings can change; under the impact of human feelings, bodily chemistry may change. Nature crosses this bridge from mind to body and from body to mind every day in a series of psychosomatic and somatopsychic phenomena. Extrasensory perception and psychokinesis are but particular cases of the universal process of transition.

The principles of *monistic transitionism* can be summarized as follows:

1. The change does not disrupt continuity of the universe.
2. The unity of the universe remains always the same in a continuous process of change.
3. Einstein's formula $E = mc^2$ is a particular case of the more general principle of a continuous transition.
4. Biological evolution is a particular case of the universal process of change which may go in any direction, from energy to matter, from mind to body, from past to future, and vice versa.
5. Mind and body are two levels of transition, the mind being merely a higher level of evolution.
6. Higher evolutionary levels incorporate the lower ones but not vice versa. Thus, both theoretical and methodological reductionism must be limited to clearly reducible issues.
7. Causal thinking is, in a sense, anthropomorphic, for it ascribes human features to the universe. However, causality, as a biological phenomenon, applies to human behavior and partly to all life processes.
8. Parapsychological phenomena are the area where mind and body transform into each other. These phenomena do not occur everywhere; they are determined by complex factors just as other psychosomatic and somatopsychic processes.

TRANSITIONISM IN NEUROPHYSIOLOGY

Soviet experiments in interoceptive conditioning (Ayrapetyants, 1952; Bykov, 1957) prove that the viscera are closer to the unconscious than to the conscious. The inner organs can be conditioned without the subject being aware of it. For example, in an experiment performed by Balakshina in denervated kidneys with a destroyed hypophysis, the physiological processes in the kidneys could be interpreted in terms of physics. In experiments on pain reception, where speech signals were used, the role of the cerebral cortex was established. Stimulation of exteroceptors has usually been accompanied by a "subjectively perceived sensation." In Russian psychology, this term denotes mental processes. Stimulation of interoceptors was either not perceived subjectively at all or, at least, not accompanied by any definite, localized perception. Soviet research contributed to the differentiation of what might be called "levels" in the transition from organic to mental. Interoceptive conditioning in man was proven to be unconscious.

Russian psychologists emphasize that mental processes are not reducible to physiological processes but represent a new, unique, higher level of development.

In a paper published in 1956 in the journal *Voprosy Psikhologii*, S. L. Rubinstein (1957, a reprint of original paper) expressed this trend of thought:

> The discovery of the biochemical nature of physiological phenomena has not resulted in the disappearance of those as specific phenomena. . . . However far-reaching the discoveries of biochemical regularities controlling the formation of cortical connections, reflexes will not cease to be reflexes. . . . Since psychic phenomena obey the physiological laws of higher nervous activity they appear as the effect of the operation of physiological laws; similarly, those physiological and biological phenomena which obey the laws of chemistry appear as effects of the operation of chemical laws. But physiological processes represent a new, unique form of manifestation of chemical laws, and it is precisely the discovery of these new specific forms of manifestation that is covered by the laws of physiology. In the same way, the physiological laws of neurodynamics find in psychic phenomena a *new unique form of manifestation which is expressed in the laws of psychology*. In other words, psychic phenomena remain psychic phenomena, even though they appear as a form of manifestation of physiological laws; just as physiological phenomena remain physiological, though as an outcome of biochemical investigation they also appear as a form of manifestation of the laws of chemistry. Such, in general, is the interrelationship of the laws governing the lower and higher forms of movement of matter, the relationship between "lower" and "higher" regions of scientific investigation. The fact that the more general laws governing the lower regions spread to the more specialized regions does not exclude the necessity of discovering the specific laws of these higher regions (pp. 268–269).

The neuropsychologist John Eccles, in *The Neurophysiological Basis of Mind* (1953) introduced the hypothesis of the mode of operation of "Will" on the cerebral cortex (quoted from Koestler, 1972, p. 72):

> A great part of the skilled activity evolving from the cerebral cortex is stereotyped and automatic, and may be likened to the control of breathing by respiratory centres. But it is contended that it is possible voluntarily to assume control of such actions. . . .
>
> An important neurophysiological problem arises as soon as we attempt to consider in detail the events that would occur in the cerebral cortex when, by the exercise of "will," there is some change in response to a given situation. . . .
>
> Eccles proposed a theory of how a minute "will-influence," affecting "a single neuron" in the cortex, would trigger off very considerable changes in brain activity. The trigger-action can affect neurons which are "critically poised" in unstable equilibrium, just below the threshold of discharging a nerve impulse. In view of the fact that there are some four thousand neurons packed together per square millimetre (approximately 1/700 square inch) of the cerebral cortex, and that each neuron has several hundred synaptic

connections with other neurons, we have here a network of such density and complexity that in the active cerebral cortex within twenty milli-seconds, the pattern of discharge of even hundreds of thousands of neurons would be modified as a result of an "influence" that initially caused the discharge of merely one neuron. This fact supports the hypothesis that the "will" modifies the spatio-temporal fields of influence that become affected through this unique detector function of the active cerebral cortex.

So far, Eccles has been discussing the action of individual minds on their own brains. In the concluding sections of his book, Eccles included ESP and PK into the theory. He accepted the experiments of Rhine, Thouless, Soal, and others as evidence for a generalized "two-way traffic" between mind and matter, and for a direct traffic between mind and mind. Eccles believes that ESP and PK are weak and irregular manifestations of the "same" principle which allows an individual's mental volition to influence his own material brain, and the material brain to give rise to conscious experiences (quoted from Koestler, 1972, pp. 73–74).

According to the astronomer Firsoff (1967) human mind is "a universal entity or interaction of the same order as electricity or gravitation." And, therefore, "there must exist a modulus of transformation, analogous to Einstein's famous equation $E = mc^2$, whereby 'mind stuff' could be equated with other entities of the physical world" (p. 102).

DREAMS

Monistic transitionism endeavors to explain several areas hitherto unexplainable. Some of these areas border on parapsychology, and some are traditionally included in parapsychology proper. Dreaming, hypnosis, and empathy belong to the first category, while telepathy and other extrasensory phenomena as well as psychokinesis belong to the latter. The intention of this paper is to prove that all these phenomena could and should be grouped together under the heading of body-mind and mind-body transition.

For millennia people saw in dreaming something that transcended common occurrences. In the waking state people were aware of (they experienced) walking, talking, eating, etc., only when their body was actively pursuing these functions. In dreams, however, people could experience bodily functions without actually performing them. The "mind" acted, while the "body" rested, and the physically nonexisting activities were vividly performed in the dreamer's mind. Small wonder that these phenomena were viewed as supernatural, and, as such, possibly caused by visitations of ghosts, spirits, and gods. Joseph's dreams in Egypt were believed to be inspired by the Lord.

Freud's interpretations of dreams hinged on the concept of the unconscious. The concept of the unconscious links in a peculiar manner the mental and physical aspects of human life. On one hand, Freud's theory of dreams sounds thoroughly psychogenic, and the terms *wish, dream work, manifest dream content*, etc., are clearly nonorganic. However, all this takes place in the "province" or "layer" of the unconscious, and repression, cathexis, and so on imply physical forces. Apparently, Freud was much influenced by Herbart's materialistic push-and-pull psychology (Wolman, 1968).

Moreover, while Freud's physicalistic model of "mental state" (the topographic theory) was criticized by several contemporary psychologists and psychoanalysts, the "structural" concept of the id is the link between somatic and mental processes. The id is the seat of "instinctual cathexes seeking discharge"; the id is a "cauldron of seething excitement." The id contains whatever originates in the body and is transformed into mental processes. The id, Freud (1964) wrote, stands "in direct contact with somatic processes, and takes over from them instinctual needs and gives them mental expression" (p. 104).

Freud's theoretical "hoped-for reductionism" has found considerable support in recent dream research. Several dream researchers have discovered a connection between physiology and the psychological aspects of dreams. Auditory stimuli in dreams occur frequently in association with the muscle activity of the middle ear. Frightening dreams and nightmares are associated with acceleration of heartbeat and respiration. The neuron firing in the visual part of the cortex and the pyramidal system is the same in REM sleep and during the waking state, but it is lower during non-REM sleep. However, during the REM sleep the flexor and extensor reflexes are inhibited, but there is an increase in oxygen consumption, blood flow, and brain temperature (Webb, 1973).

On several occasions patients' dreams gave me the opportunity to diagnose their physical ailments of which they themselves were unaware. In some instances, the physicians misdiagnosed their diseases and, in some cases, erroneously interpreted disease as a psychological overreaction or psychosomatic disorder.

Several years ago a patient of mine, Dr. J., complained of stomach trouble. Since all physical examinations were negative, he maintained that his symptoms were psychosomatic.

> I disagreed with his self-diagnostic statements. I believe that physical disease can strike everyone, and neurotics are not immune to TB, pneumonia, and typhoid fever. I have always been opposed to the throwing of all physical symptoms into the wastebasket of psychosomatics. In all the years of my practice, whenever a patient complained of pain or ailment, I always demanded a thorough medical examination. Accordingly I asked Dr. J. to consult his physician. He chided me. "I knew," he said sarcastically, "that you would send me for a physical. That's your old-fashioned philosophy; body comes first."

However, upon my insistence he went to see his family physician. Next he reported triumphantly: "My doctor could not find anything wrong with me. It's all in my mind. It's psychosomatic, positive."

...A week passed, and Dr. J. reported a strange dream. In his dream his brother, with whom he had strongly identified, was hit in the kidneys by a bomb and was dying. At this point I became absolutely convinced that Dr. J. had cancer of the kidneys or some other serious kidney disease.

I decided to act immediately. I did not communicate my suspicions to Dr. J., but I put to him an ultimatum: either he immediately go for a GI series or I would refuse to see him any longer. I sent him to a top internist. The examination discovered cancer of the kidneys. He was hospitalized immediately and, unfortunately, never came back (Wolman, 1972, pp. 249–250).

Apparently, the sad experiences of Dr. J.'s kidneys were not communicated to his consciousness. They remained unconscious—and the unconscious voice of the dream called for help. His disease was somato-psychic, and the damage caused to the kidneys was *transformed* into the symbolism of a dream.

HYPNOSIS

Hypnotism belongs to the broad category of borderline mind-body transitions together with parapsychological phenomena. Hypnosis is reported to reduce even the pains of childbirth. Hypnotic suggestions can be effective "in producing physiological effects such as alterations in gastric secretions, inhibition of gastric hunger contractions, inhibition or augmentation of allergic responses, reduction of warts, and production of skin changes which resemble warts or dermographism" (Barber, 1973). However, similar results have been obtained also by nonhypnotic suggestions.

Patients under hypnosis receive clues from the hypnotist even if he does not express them and often when he himself is unaware of what he is communicating. Some therapists report a frequent release of sexual and/or aggressive fantasies and often overt actions in their patients under hypnosis. Other therapists rarely if ever witness these fantasies. Apparently, some therapists unconsciously communicate and elicit these feelings in the hypnotized patients (Wolberg, 1967).

EMPATHY

Dreams and hypnosis certainly are unconscious phenomena, but empathy cannot be viewed as an entirely unconscious nor as a purely mental process. Empathy has been defined in Wolman's (1973) *Dictionary of Behavioral Science* as the ability to perceive the mood and feelings of another person and the understanding of the feelings, sufferings, and situation of another person without these feelings being communicated by words.

Moreover, empathy encompasses communication across large distances: thus it borders on and often transgresses the borders of ESP. The ability to perceive communication not expressed in words is a prerequisite of a successful patient-therapist relationship in practically every type of psychotherapy, but this is a one-to-one proximity relationship.

Sullivan (1947) interpreted empathy in organismic terms. Sullivan's theory invites comparison with Cannon's homeostatic system: *Tension* and *relief* follow each other, especially since tension and relief are interpreted by Sullivan in purely physiological terms, as a contraction and relaxation of muscles. This physiological process is later modified by social influences. The child soon learns that on certain occasions the immediate relaxation of muscles meets with parental disapproval. Parental disapproval causes a feeling of discomfort. This *empathized discomfort* stems not from the organism but from *interpersonal relationships*. This discomfort is so strong that it destroys the original comfort of relaxation. For example, as soon as there is any tension in bladder or bowels, the proper muscles act immediately to bring relief. However, this automatic relaxation may invite parental hostility, which produces in the child a feeling of "empathized discomfort." This feeling will bring the child to learn "to suffer increasing tension in the bladder and rectum and to resist the automatic relaxation of the sphincter muscles concerned in retaining the urine and feces. Failures in this are often accompanied by empathized discomfort, and success is often the occasion of empathized comfort which is added to the satisfaction from relief of tension" (Sullivan, 1947, p. 44).

TRANSITIONISM IN PARAPSYCHOLOGY

Apparently, parapsychological phenomena belong to the "transitionalistic" area of change and continuity together with hypnosis, dreams, empathy, unconscious, cathexis, and a host of other psychosomatic and somato-psychic phenomena. They are the infant and "the same" infant who grew up and became an adult; they are the seed and the tree; the mind and the body. They do not stand alone; modern physics has accepted the dual nature of light, and Firsoff's (1967) theory of *neutrino* offers an important *sequitur* to Einstein's theory of transformation of energy into matter. According to Firsoff (quoted from Koestler, 1972).

> The universe as seen by a neutrino eye would wear a very unfamiliar look. Our earth and other planets simply would not be there, or might at best appear as thin patches of mist. The sun and other stars may be dimly visible, in as much as they emit some neutrinos. . . . A neutrino brain might suspect our existence from certain secondary effects, but would find it very difficult to prove, as we would elude the neutrino instruments at his disposal.
>
> Our universe is no truer than that of the neutrinos—they exist, but they

exist in a different kind of space, governed by different laws. . . . In our space no material body can exceed the velocity of light, because at this velocity its mass and so inertia becomes infinite. The neutrino, however, is subject neither to gravitational nor to electro-magnetic fields, so that it need not be bound by this speed limit and may have its own, different time. It might be able to travel faster than light, which would make it relativistically recede in our time scale.

From our earlier analysis of mental entities, it appears that they have no definite locus in so-called "physical," or better, gravi-electromagnetic, space, in which respect they resemble a neutrino or, for that matter, a fast electron. This already suggests a special kind of mental space governed by different laws, which is further corroborated by the parapsychological experiments made at Duke University and elsewhere. . . . It seems . . . that this kind of perception involves a mental interaction, which is subject to laws of its own, defining a different type of space-time (pp. 63–64).

Parapsychology may exercise a beneficial influence on the studies of human life, whether they are conducted from the organic, biochemical, and neuro-physiological side or from the psychological angle. Parapsychology challenges the traditional concepts of time, causation, and individualistic isolation so well entrenched in both the organismic and psychogenic theories. Viewed from the historical perspective, parapsychology introduces new ideas, keeping pace with theoretical physics and contemporary philosophy of science (Wolman, 1973).

The concept of positive and negative time, introduced by R. P. Feynman in 1949, revolutionized theoretical physics. Strangely enough, the hypnotic regression in age has evoked much less interest, although it may serve as an empirical proof of moving back and forth in time analogous to moving back and forth in space. Several parapsychological phenomena could be similarly interpreted.

One of the problems in any psychological research, including parapsychology, stems from the notion that every human being is a separate and discrete entity. Psychiatrists and clinical psychologists often try to make prognostic judgments, ignoring the fact that no one lives in a vacuum, and the fate of every individual is greatly influenced by environmental factors. This applies also to parapsychology. Everything that happens in this area is influenced by the subjects involved, the experimenter or the observer, and a host of other factors. Moreover, the traditional causal relationship can be applicable to isolated systems and thus preserved in certain psychological situations, but it may not be applied when human behavior is viewed in a broad context of the universe. Certainly the transfer of thoughts and images across large spaces could not be interpreted in a narrow, one-to-one relationship. Broadly speaking, "any local agitation shakes the whole universe. The distant effects are minute, but they are there . . . There is no possibility of a detached, self-contained evidence" (Whitehead, 1934, p. 181).

The fact that not all parapsychological experiments yield significant data adds additional proof to the variability of nature. Not all oaks are the same size, and not all human organisms have the same chemistry. Apparently, some individuals are closer to the transitional processes than others. There are far-reaching organic and psychological differences between individuals, e.g., the IQ correlation between two randomly chosen individuals is zero. Some human organisms vehemently react against penicillin which produces miracles for others. There is, therefore, no reason to assume that all people are equally able to respond to telepathy, hypnotism, and, for that matter, to any other stimulus.

Both empathy and telepathy are instances of *transfer* of psychological elements such as emotional states, perceptions, thoughts and so on, but such a transfer is facilitated by the particular somatopsychic or psychosomatic nature of the individuals concerned. Future research in parapsychology must, therefore, focus on a most thorough study of the "paranormal" individuals, the "sensitives."

In summary, are parapsychological phenomena mind or body? They are either or both. They exemplify the facts of nature, the continuity in change. And as such, parapsychology opens new vistas in science, joining psychoanalysis, hypnotism, psychosomatic medicine, and theoretical physics.

REFERENCES

Ayrapetyants, E. S. *Higher Nervous Function and the Receptors of Internal Organs*. Moscow: U.S.S.R. Academy of Science, 1952.

Barber, T. X. Experimental hypnosis. In B. B. Wolman (Ed.), *Handbook of General Psychology*, pp. 942–963. Englewood Cliffs, N.J.: Prentice-Hall, 1973.

Bechterev, V. M. *Objective Psychologie-Reflexologie*. Leipzig: Teubner, 1913.

Bykov, W. H. *The Cerebral Cortex and the Internal Organs*. New York: Chemical Publishing, 1957.

Eccles, J. C. *The Neurophysiological Basis of Mind*. Oxford: Clarendon Press, 1953.

Feynman, R. P. *Quantum Electrodynamics*. New York: Benjamin, 1961.

Firsoff, V. A. *Life, Mind and Galaxies*. Edinburgh and London: Oliver & Boyd, 1967.

Freud, S. *Outline of Psychoanalysis*. New York: Norton, 1949.

Freud, S. *New Introductory Lectures on Psychoanalysis*. Vol. 22, *Standard Edition*. London: Hogarth Press, 1964.

Hebb, D. O. *The Organization of Behavior*. New York: Wiley, 1949.

Hull, C. L. The problem of intervening variables in molar behavior theory. *Psychological Review*, 1943, 50, 273–291.

Jeans, J. *The Mysterious Universe*. New York: Dutton, 1958.

Koestler, A. *The Roots of Coincidence*. New York: Random House, 1972.

Köhler, W. *Gestalt Psychology*. New York: Liveright, 1947.

Lewin, K. *Field Theory in Social Science*. New York: Harper, 1951.

Nagel, E. *The Structure of Science*. New York: Harcourt, Brace, 1953.

Oparin, A. I. *The Origins of Life on Earth*. New York: Academic Press, 1957.

Pavlov, I. P. *Lectures on Conditioned Reflexes*. New York: Liveright, 1928.

Rhine, J. B., and Pratt, J. G. *Parapsychology: Frontier Science of the Mind*. Springfield, Ill.: Charles C Thomas, 1957.

Rubinstein, S. L. Questions of psychological theory. In B. Simon (Ed.), *Psychology in the Soviet Union*, pp. 264–278. Stanford, Cal.: Stanford University Press, 1957.

Scriven, M. The frontiers of psychology: Psychoanalysis and parapsychology. In R. G. Colodny (Ed.), *Frontiers of Science and Philosophy*, pp. 79–129. Pittsburgh: University of Pittsburgh Press, 1962.

Sherrington, C. S. *Man on his Nature*. New York: Macmillan, 1941.

Skinner, B. F. Are theories of learning necessary? *Psychological Review*. 1950, 57, 193–216.

Skinner, B. F. *Science and Human Behavior*. New York: Macmillan, 1953.

Sullivan, H. S. *Conceptions of Modern Psychiatry*. Washington, D.C.: White Foundation, 1947.

Vasiliev, L. L. *Experiments in Mental Suggestion*. Church Crookham, England: Institute for the Study of Mental Images, 1963.

Watson, J. B. Psychology as the behaviorist sees it. *Psychological Review*, 1913, 20, 158–177.

Watson, J. B. *Psychology from the Standpoint of a Behaviorist*. Philadelphia: Lippincott, 1919.

Webb, W. B. Sleep and dreams. In B. B. Wolman (Ed.). *Handbook of General Psychology*, pp. 734–748. Englewood Cliffs, N.J.: Prentice-Hall, 1973.

Whitehead, A. N. *Nature and Life*. Cambridge: Cambridge University Press, 1934.

Wolberg, L. *The Technique of Psychotherapy*. New York: Grune and Stratton, 1967.

Wolman, B. B. *Contemporary Theories and Systems in Psychology*. New York: Harper & Row, 1960.

Wolman, B. B. Principles of monistic transitionism. In B. B. Wolman and E. Nagel (Eds.), *Scientific Psychology: Principles and Approaches*, pp. 563–585. New York: Basic Books, 1965.

Wolman, B. B. Johann Friedrich Herbart. In B. B. Wolman (Ed.), *Historical Roots of Contemporary Psychology*, pp. 29–46. New York: Harper & Row, 1968.

Wolman, B. B. (Ed.). *Success and Failure in Psychoanalysis and Psychotherapy*. New York: Macmillan, 1972.

Wolman, B. B. Concerning psychology and the philosophy of science. In B. B. Wolman (Ed.), *Handbook of General Psychology*, pp. 22–48. Englewood Cliffs, N.J.: Prentice-Hall-1973.

Wolman, B. B. *Dictionary of Behavioral Science*. New York: Van Nostrand Reinhold, 1973.

Part X

SOVIET RESEARCH IN PARAPSYCHOLOGY

1

Soviet Research in Parapsychology

J. G. Pratt

INTRODUCTION

The task of summarizing research developments in parapsychology in the Soviet Union differs in two main respects from the assignments accepted by other contributors to this volume. On the one hand, only a few scientific reports on research in parapsychology have been published in the USSR, and a survey limited to them would be quite brief. But on the other hand, there has sprung up in Russia during the past 15 years an unusually large popular literature on parapsychology—most of it describing Soviet research that has not yet been presented in the scientific literature. This material has been recognized as a golden opportunity by enterprising journalistic writers in the West. Working without the background to use scientific judgment or the need to impose restraints, they have exploited the situation by sensationalizing and exaggerating the information. The result has been a widespread impression in the West that there has been a tremendous development in parapsychology in the USSR—one that has outstripped progress in those areas of the world where work in the field has been pursued for a much longer time. I see my responsibility, therefore, as extending not only to the Soviet research that has been presented in the scientific literature but also to developments that are not so well defined, for the purpose of bringing them into proper scientific perspective. When we move beyond the solid ground of formal research reports we will inevitably have to be somewhat speculative regarding the research as well as tentative in our judgments concerning the future of parapsychology in the USSR.

The next three sections describe research developments on which adequately reported scientific information is available. In the first two instances the investigations were published by the Soviet scientists (V. M. Bechterev and L. L. Vasiliev) who were principally involved in the work. The third section deals with a special subject, Nina Kulagina, and the principal Russian investigator in this instance, G. A. Sergeyev, has not yet published a full account of his work. He has, however, discussed his findings with several Western scientists, and some of them have been able to make their own observations of Kulagina and have jointly prepared a survey of all the observations available on this subject from both Soviet and non-Soviet sources (Keil, Herbert, Ullman, and Pratt, 1976).

The fourth section will consider Soviet work in parapsychology as it is reflected in a bibliography on this subject and related areas by two Russians who have been active in promoting educational activities, scientific meetings, and private exchanges on an international scale.

The fifth section of the chapter will examine and undertake an evaluation of an official statement of the Soviet position on parapsychology as formulated by four leading spokesmen for the psychologists. Finally, some effort will be made to interpret the research developments and related activities as regards the likely future course of parapsychology in the Soviet Union.

THE WORK AND INFLUENCE OF V. M. BECHTEREV

The modern history of parapsychological research in the USSR (the period with which this chapter will deal) can be traced to the World War I period and to the interest and efforts of V. M. Bechterev, founder and director of the Institute for Brain Research in Petrograd (now Leningrad). Just before the war Bechterev was approached by a trainer of circus animals, V. L. Durov, with the request to join in an investigation of an apparent ability of his dogs to carry out silent commands. Tests conducted at that time in Bechterev's apartment convinced him that the claim merited further study, and after the end of the war a series of tests were conducted by Bechterev and his colleagues during several visits to Moscow.

In the typical test conducted with Durov's fox terrier, Pikki, the experimenter would decide upon what complex task he wished the dog to perform. Then he would take the dog's head between his two hands, stare into the animal's eyes, and concentrate upon the series of actions required to carry out the task. For example, one task was "to jump upon one of the chairs at the wall behind Durov, then to climb on the little round table beside it, and, stretching himself, scratch the big portrait hanging on the wall above the table" (Bechterev, 1949, p. 168). This task as well as many others of similar degrees of complexity were carried out, usually with complete success, but with occasional partial or complete failures that often provided clues bearing upon the *modus operandi* of the dog's behavior.

The research was advanced through stages of testing and excluding conceivable sensory explanations of the dog's behavior. To limit possible sources of unconscious sensory cues, only the experimenter knew the task to be performed. On one occasion Durov, while looking into the eyes of the dog and concentrating upon a serious task that the animal was to perform, deliberately changed his facial expression to that of laughter. At other times the eyes of the experimenter were blindfolded to conceal any possible cues from movements of the eyes while giving the suggestion. Again, the dog's trainer was entirely excluded from contact with the dog immediately before and during the testing period. An assistant who did not know the task held the head of the animal between his hands while the experimenter merely looked into the dog's eyes and concentrated upon what task was to be performed. In other tests the experimenter was concealed from the animal behind screens of different material (wood, metal, paraffin). Finally, the person who knew the task concentrated upon it while he was in another room completely out of the dog's sight. Complex tasks were successfully performed under all of these conditions, though sometimes only after initial failures.

Three reports on these animal studies were published during 1920 in the *Proceedings* of the Institute for Brain Research (Bechterev, 1920; Flecksor, 1920; Ivanov-Smolensky, 1920). An abbreviated English translation of Bechterev's paper was published three decades later (Bechterev, 1949). These investigations led Bechterev to conclude that animals, especially dogs trained to obey, may be directly influenced by mental suggestion in the absence of any overt sign by which they could be guided.

Between 1920 and his death in 1927, Bechterev was active in organizing and promoting investigations into mental suggestion and related problems as a part of the research program of the Institute for Brain Research. A description of these developments is provided by Vasiliev (1963). A Commission for the Study of Mental Suggestion attached to the Brain Institute was formed in 1922 with multidisciplinary membership, and papers covering some of its work on telepathy and related problems were presented at the Second All Russian Congress of Psychoneurology held in Petrograd in January 1924. The Congress went on record as recognizing the importance of further research on mental suggestion and recommending participation of Russian scientists in the work of the International Committee for Psychical Research that had been organized in 1921. At the initiative of the Soviet Minister of Education a Russian committee affiliated with the international body was formed, with Bechterev as one of its members.

The original commission had ceased to function after 2 years, and the work of carrying out the resolution of the All Russian Congress was assigned to the Society for Neurology, Reflexology, Hypnotism, and Biophysics which functioned within the Institute for Brain Research. Individual members of the Society at first carried out investigations on their own initiative, and at a meeting held in

1926 L. L. Vasiliev reported on some of his own research in a paper with the title: "The Biophysical Foundations of Direct Thought Transmission," a theoretical discussion that was subsequently published in popular form in *Science News* (No. 7, 1926).

The Board of the Society instructed a group of its members to attempt to confirm and extend the work of Vasiliev, and this interest led to the formation in 1926 of the Experimental Commission on Hypnotism and Psychophysics under the chairmanship of Bechterev and numbering among its members two physicists, two physiologists, three psychiatrists, and others. Until Bechterev's death in 1927 this Commission carried out an intensive program of research, study, and reporting at a total of 16 meetings on the progress of investigations in a number of areas.

The activities outlined above surely testify to the seriousness of the interest in parapsychology among Soviet scientists, especially in the Institute for Brain Research during Bechterev's presence and leadership. However, the strength of this interest was yet to be ascertained through the answer to the question: Would the research in parapsychology endure beyond the leader's death?

THE RESEARCH AND INFLUENCE OF L. L. VASILIEV

In this section we will be dealing chiefly with information drawn from a Soviet publication with which the Western scientist can feel comfortable as to form if not substance. This is a book published in September 1962 by Leningrad State University and brought out in an English translation the following year with the title: *Experiments in Mental Suggestion* (Vasiliev, 1963). We learn from the front matter of the English edition that the book was published "on instruction from the Editorial Council of the University of Leningrad" and that the "English translation [was] authorized and revised by Professor Vasiliev."

The author was Chairman of the Department of Physiology in the University of Leningrad, having advanced to that position during the years since 1921 when he joined the staff of the Institute for Brain Research in Petrograd as a "beginner in physiology." The account in the previous section covering the Institute's activities in parapsychology during the Bechterev period is based upon the Preface of Vasiliev's book.

The book is further characterized in the front matter in the following words:

> In this book are presented in outline the results of investigations which the author has pursued in conjunction with his collaborators in the field of so-called mental or wordless suggestion. The author has studied questions connected with mental suggestion of acts of movement, visual images and sensations, sleeping and waking. Original experiments, both with and without hypnosis, are described, and there is an account of the so-called electromagnetic theory of mental suggestion and of the present position of the question of the

energetic nature of these phenomena.   The book is intended for biologists, physiologists, psychologists, doctors, physicists and specialists in other disciplines.

The Preface also traces developments in parapsychology in the Institute after the death of Bechterev. In 1928 Vasiliev, in connection with a scientific mission to Germany and France, visited parapsychological centers in Paris and Berlin and established personal contacts that were continued through correspondence and were, he says, of great help to his later studies on mental suggestion.

In 1932 the Institute for Brain Research, then under the leadership of Professor V. P. Ossipov, "received an assignment to commence an experimental study of telepathy with the aim of determining as far as possible its physical basis" (Vasiliev, 1963, p. 4). A research team was formed under the leadership of Vasiliev, and work along the lines indicated in the above quotation was continued on a sustained basis until 1938, a period of 5½ years.

Their first efforts were directed toward confirming the claims of the Italian physicist Cazzamalli that he had discovered brain waves approximately 1 centimeter in length which, theoretically, could be the physical basis of telepathy. Soviet scientists failed to confirm this claim.

They then directed their efforts toward first finding evidence of telepathy and subsequently testing whether the process depended upon electromagnetic radiations. These experiments, which we will examine more closely shortly, were interrupted (as Vasiliev says in his book and as he later repeated personally to me) by World War II and the economic and political upheaval it caused for the following decade.

In 1956 Vasiliev began a correspondence with R. Warcollier and later with R. L. Kherumian, both members of the Paris Institut Métapsychique. Gradually, under the more favorable conditions of the Khrushchev period, steps were taken toward resuming active work in parapsychology. In 1959 Vasiliev published a book for the general reader on unsolved problems in psychology in which he included a chapter on telepathy (Vasiliev, 1965). That same year he received from Kherumian two popular articles that claimed to describe a highly successful ESP experiment carried out in the USA between a laboratory on land and a subject working in the submarine *Nautilus* while under way and submerged at sea. This story was later shown to be a hoax of fiction masquerading as science, but it was apparently taken quite seriously in Russia. From the political point of view the authorities, it appears, were reluctant to ignore parapsychology if there was any likelihood that the American military establishment was conducting successful experiments in ESP.

While Vasiliev was quick to seize the advantage provided by this story of a *Nautilus* experiment, he did not give the chief weight to the possible military importance of ESP research. Rather, he saw the use of the submarine and the great thickness of sea water as a condition that provided screening against electromagnetic radiation, and this was the feature of his own research during the 30s that he regarded as its principal contribution. He therefore moved with dispatch to publish that work to establish the Soviet right to priority of discovery. Simultaneously, he obtained the official approval of the University of Leningrad to establish a special laboratory within the Physiological Institute of the Biology Faculty for research on telepathic phenomena. Beyond briefly tracing the historical developments leading to the founding of the laboratory, the book (1963) reports the experimental work from the 20s and 30s, with the most important results coming from the latter period. The investigations fell into three logical groups from the point of view of experimental approach and basic method, and the findings from each kind of test are presented separately in the book and will be described similarly here.

One type of investigation, muscular movement in response to silent commands given to a subject in hypnosis, took as its starting point some French work reported at the end of the last century (Joire, 1897). The Russian experiments appeared to be clearly successful in achieving responses to such commands as "raise your right arm"; "show your tongue"; "scratch your left cheek and the bridge of your nose." Such tests, first conducted in 1926 and then discontinued, were resumed in 1937, but the investigators found that initial success in a receptive subject diminished as the work continued. It appeared that the subject became "trained" through repeated tests and thus began to act on his own in anticipation of what the experimenter might expect him to do. The method was changed, therefore, to one in which silent suggestions were given that the subject, while standing in the hypnotic state, would sway forward or backward. An objective record of body movement was obtained by having the subject stand on a special platform that recorded shifts in weight. Summarizing the efforts along these lines, Vasiliev says that he regards the results as sufficient to support the claims of Joire, but the experimental conditions were not adequate to meet the requirements for rigorous evidence in support of the telepathic hypothesis.

The second general method is discussed under the heading of "mental suggestion of visual images and sensations." Like the former approach, this one was also used in the earlier period of work under Bechterev as well as during the 30s. The first efforts were along the lines of what we have come to designate as free-response tests: A sender would select some target object, and the subject would attempt to draw or describe it without having been given any clue as to what had been chosen for the trial. Out of a total of 269 such trials performed during the 20s, in approximate figures 14 percent were accurately received to an unmistakable degree, 34 percent seemed partially or symbolically correct, and 52 percent were judged to be failures. As with non-Russian experiments along the same lines done prior to or during that period, there was no effort to use random procedures in the selection of the targets, and the results were not evaluated objectively by such procedures as have now become routine. Vasiliev therefore once more expressed appreciation for the Soviet results from the point of view of their exploratory value in providing clues to the nature of the telepathic process, but not as evidence for ESP good enough to satisfy the strongly skeptical.

A smaller number of tests of this kind were also conducted during the 30s. The primary emphasis, however, in testing for the transmission of mental images was placed upon having volunteer subjects, working individually, guess on each trial whether a sender was looking at a white or black ball or disk. Target selection in these tests was random, and the results lent themselves to simple statistical evaluation by appropriate methods. In one such experiment conducted by Vasiliev, 22 subjects were used in a total of 26 sessions, each involving 80 trials. The total of 2,080 trials completed showed a margin of success that was only 5.6 percent above the fifty-fifty level expected, but this success rate is nevertheless statistically highly significant. When this method was adapted in a later test by having the subject inside a closed metal room for half the trials and in the same room with a wooden cover substituted for the metal one to eliminate the screening against electromagnetic waves during the other trials, the experiment failed as a test of the radiation hypothesis because no significant evidence of telepathy was obtained under either condition.

The third method, this one modeled on earlier French work by P. Janet and M. Gibert (1886), involved initiating and terminating hypnotic sleep by means of silent suggestions made at randomly-chosen times. This approach was found not to suffer from the disadvantages of the other two methods, and work along this line was developed to an advanced stage with a level of safeguarding and a degree of success that the investigators considered conclusive regarding their main objective. This was to find out whether a kind of electromagnetic radiation formed the basis of telepathic transmission. To their great surprise they found that this hypothesis was not supported. As with other lines of work, however, these "sleep" and "wake up" experiments were only gradually improved in methodology over the period they were conducted.

During 1933–1934 a total of 260 trials were performed at putting a susceptible subject into hypnosis or waking him up by silent suggestion. Vasiliev reports that success was achieved approximately 90 percent of the time. An objective method was used for registering when sleep began and when it ended—the subject was given the task of pressing continuously upon a bulb of air which had a tube connected with a marker resting on moving paper, and the subject unconsciously interrupted the pressing while in the sleep state. However, during this stage there were no control trials, and the matter of success or failure depended upon the judgment of the investigators.

By 1935–1936 the technique had been improved as regards both the use of a control condition and the use of improved screening, this also with a control condition of no screening, with the subject not knowing which condition was being used. These tests involved having the subject relax in readiness to fall asleep while the hypnotist in another room followed written instructions to silently suggest the onset of sleep or to avoid doing so. Highly significant statistical differences were found indicating quicker onset of sleep when the hypnotist was suggesting it than when he was not.

From the point of view of testing the radiation hypothesis, tests of this kind were carried out when the subject was inside a screening chamber of sheet iron in one room and the hypnotist was inside a screening lead chamber in another room. The procedure required that the hypnotist close himself inside the lead chamber with the lid down before he opened and read his instructions. If they called for a screened trial, he left the chamber closed while suggesting sleep; if unscreened, he lifted the lid and stuck his head through the opening while suggesting. A control condition with instructions not to suggest also involved having the head exposed while the hypnotist kept his mind blank or thought of things not connected with the experiment. There was no significant difference between the screened and unscreened trials with suggestion of sleep, but both of them showed a significant shortening of the time for the onset of sleep as compared with the trials with no suggestion.

The effectiveness of mental suggestion at a distance in bringing on sleep or waking the subject was tested in 12 series, most of them conducted in 1934, with the standards of safeguarding and evaluation applied in other research at that time plus the additional safeguarding against sensory cues. The distances varied from 25 meters to 1,700 kilometers, and success, achieved in every trial in from 1 to 6 minutes, was unrelated to the distance used.

Vasiliev (1963) recognized clearly in his discussions of previous non-Russian research in parapsychology that far more evidence had been presented for the reality of ESP than the Soviet work reported in his book represented. He appears, therefore, to have regarded the matter of independently proving telepathy as being of less importance than making some contribution toward a better understanding of its nature. He concluded that their research showed that the electromagnetic radiation hypothesis did not apply, which was contrary to what the Russian scientists expected their research to show.

In summary, we may reasonably say that this Soviet research in parapsychology does not have a place of major importance in the large body of experimental findings in the field, but it does have, quite independently of its geographical and historical setting, its own value as an independent scientific study. The major value, however, is the light it throws upon the basic similarity of approach to parapsychological problems in Russia and in the West in spite of different cultures and political systems, provided the comparison is made appropriately in terms of the same period and stage of development of parapsychology (that is, when Russian research of the 20s and 30s is compared with Western work of the same time).

Vasiliev lived to direct the laboratory he had founded for only 6 years, some of the time handicapped by poor health, and he died early in 1966. If he and his staff completed any new research during that time, we do not have any record of it. Apparently the laboratory did not issue the proceedings for which Vasiliev told me in 1963 they were gathering material. It is no small credit to him to be able to note here the fact that he discovered the psychic abilities of Nina S. Kulagina, a subject who is best known for her exceptional PK (psychokinesis) abilities. The research subsequently done with Kulagina is the topic for discussion in the next section.

INVESTIGATIONS OF NINA KULAGINA

The Soviet research conducted with this subject (movement of objects and other directly observable PK effects) has not been fully reported in the Russian scientific literature. However, the special circumstances that apply in this case appear to justify including this research here as meeting our criterion of acceptable Soviet scientific work in parapsychology.

In 1968 G. A. Sergeyev, a neurophysiologist and electroencephalographer in Leningrad, presented a film on Kulagina before an international parapsychological meeting in Moscow. He said he had investigated this subject's claims and had obtained compelling evidence of the genuineness of her PK abilities. The Western parapsychologists who were present thought that the effects shown in the film, mostly the movement of small objects in the presence of the subject without the use of any apparent physical means, clearly deserved further scientific study.

Over the next few years two of the foreign participants in that meeting (H. H. J. Keil of the University of Tasmania and the present writer) visited Leningrad, between us, a total of five times to discuss this work with Sergeyev and to seek opportunities to observe Kulagina moving objects. On three of these visits (only one time when we were there together) we were successful in meeting Kulagina and seeing her move objects that we provided for the purpose. On one visit Keil went with J. Fahler, a clinical psychologist in Helsinki.

Two other parapsychologists from the West, B. Herbert of the Paraphysical Laboratory in England and M. Ullman of the Maimonides Medical Center in Brooklyn, had similar opportunities to observe successful PK demonstrations by Kulagina on other, separate occasions. Herbert was accompanied on his visit by a colleague, M. Cassirer.

In addition, a Czech psychologist, Z. Rejdak (1970), has published an account of his observations of Kulagina's performance made in 1968 under favorable conditions. Also, the engineer husband of Kulagina, V. V. Kulagin, prepared a paper describing many of the phenomena observed over a period of at least 2 years. This paper was translated into English and published (Kulagin, 1971).

Add to these sources of information the fact that the *Journal of Paraphysics* published in 1969 and 1970 the results of an intensive study and analysis of two Russian films in which Kulagina can be seen demonstrating her ability and the further fact that none of the observers of Kulagina have found any direct reason to suspect fraud in any of her effects. Taking the whole situation on the investigation of this case into account, four of us who had visited Leningrad and observed Kulagina moving our own objects decided to pull together in one publication (Keil et al., 1976) all the information available on this case from scientific sources, including what has been learned through personal exchanges with Soviet investigators.

Before the decision to publish a survey paper was reached, an international, interdisciplinary team of scientists that was officially sponsored by the American and West German governments requested the permission of the appropriate Soviet authorities to make an independent investigation of Kulagina. This request was disapproved by the Soviet authorities on the ground that "parapsychology is not studied in the Soviet Union." The prospects therefore did not appear to be encouraging for gathering further evidence under more formal experimental conditions. After some later successful private meetings with Kulagina in which there were growing signs of disapproval of such efforts by the Soviet authorities, we decided that there was much to be gained and nothing to be lost by bringing together all the evidence already available.

The evidence for Kulagina's moving of objects by PK and other observations bearing upon the nature of her performance are too extensive to be summarized here in detail. I will, instead, first give a brief description of the subject's general behavior during a session and of the principal physiological changes that have been recorded while she is demonstrating her PK ability. Then I will describe in detail an event observed by two visiting parapsychologists that provides unusually strong evidence of movement of an object for which we are unable to find any ordinary physical explanation and which, even considered in isolation, is very strong evidence for the PK interpretation.

In a typical session, Kulagina sits in a straight chair before a table. At first she appears to be relaxed, though she may become nervous if she has come outside her own environment to meet strangers in an unfamiliar location. She takes some time to prepare herself mentally and emotionally for the effort to demonstrate her ability, which may be as short as a fraction of a minute or as long as an hour or more. As part of her preparation, she sometimes breathes deeply several times. Then she holds one or both hands near (approximately 10-20 centimeters) some small object that has been placed on the table before her. Usually, the object is one chosen by an observer and may be any object that he happened to have on his person. Sometimes two or more objects are placed on the table at the same time, and under informal conditions Kulagina may touch one of them briefly in order to separate it from the others or to put it in a position that she finds more comfortable for her effort to make it move.

It is by no means the case, however, that the subject always touches an object before she moves it. In many observations on record the experimenter has placed the objects on the table and immediately covered them with an inverted plexiglass cube, and Kulagina has moved some of the objects under the cube without touching the cover.

The objects that are moved vary widely as to material, shape, and weight. They are organic or inorganic, magnetic or nonmagnetic. Long objects, such as a cigarette, are moved more easily when they are standing on end. Such objects show a remarkable characteristic of remaining vertical over a considerable distance even when moving over a textured cloth surface. The experimenters were not able to duplicate this effect when they tried to move a cigarette with a pin in the bottom end by means of a magnet held under the table. The cigarette could be moved, but it always toppled over.

The reported weights of objects that were moved range from a fraction of a gram to 50 grams. Kulagina caused one pan of a scale that was in balance (with each pan holding weights of 30 grams) to be lowered, and she continued to cause that pan to stay down when an additional 10 grams were added to the higher pan.

The movement of an object may come almost immediately after Kulagina shows by her behavior that she is beginning her effort to make it move. At other times movement is delayed for some seconds or up to a minute. If movement does not occur after such an interval of time Kulagina usually admits failure and stops the trial, during which she may have been under great physical strain from the effort to succeed.

When an object moves, it generally advances approximately in the direction of the subject, traveling usually in short steps interrupted by longer pauses. There is sometimes a slow rotation of the object that occurs during the forward movement. Wide variations have been observed in the pattern of movement, and occasionally an object, once it starts, travels at a slow, steady speed until it reaches the edge of the surface on which it is resting, which may be the edge of the table at a distance of 10–20 centimeters.

Sergeyev and other Soviet scientists report that Kulagina has achieved vertical levitation of an object, and visiting parapsychologists have been given copies of a photograph showing a small sphere, probably a ping-pong ball, apparently suspended in the air between her two hands.

Very striking physiological changes have been observed and recorded in the subject while she was giving a successful demonstration of her object-moving ability. Electrodes attached to the occipital region of the skull recorded brain waves that are much stronger than usual, the amplitude estimated to be 50 times as great as those recorded when the subject was normally relaxed. Electrodes attached to other regions of the skull showed no change during PK.

Sergeyev invented a sensitive device (the principle on which it works still kept secret) by which he was able to register some effect up to a distance of 3 meters from Kulagina when she was moving objects. This electrode probe required no direct physical contact with the subject, and the effect that was being detected was registered on a polygraph along with the EEG recordings.

The rate of heartbeat increases to as much as 150–240 beats per minute. Loss of body weight during a 2-hour session was reported to be as high as 2,000 grams. The figures cited more frequently are within the range of 700–1000 grams of weight loss after sessions of 30 minutes to 1 hour. Commonly, the subject becomes fatigued, and she is sometimes extremely exhausted after a session. At other times, such as when she is working in her own environment under informal and pleasant social conditions in the company of persons with whom she feels on good terms, there is little or no evidence of undue strain and no noticeable fatigue.

Physical changes other than the movement of objects have also been observed. Unexposed photographic film wrapped in lightproof paper was found, when later developed, to have become fogged when Kulagina caused an object to move along the length of the covering envelope. The fogged area appeared to be the part of the film directly under the path taken by the moving object, and the fogging was heavier where the object was momentarily stationary during the pauses between movements. Control tests with the same object made by moving it normally in imitation of the Kulagina effect produced no changes in the film. Kulagina also causes, in some persons, a reddening of the skin at a point on the body which she lightly touches with her hand, and this effect may be unbearably painful and the reddening may last for hours while gradually fading away.

I will now describe the single event that, even considered alone, seems to provide strong evidence for PK.

The observers were Keil and Fahler (1975; see also Keil et al., 1976). They witnessed and recorded on film a number of successful demonstrations by Kulagina. The advance preparations for the event that is of particular concern here were made without the knowledge of the subject. The first time she saw the test device was when it was brought out by the observers and placed on the table at the beginning of the session, and it was not at any time during the testing period removed from the table nor out of sight of the observers.

The device was a 10-centimeter plexiglass cube with one open side, with one end of a very weak coil spring glued to the inside center point of one of the side walls. The other end of the spring was glued to a ping-pong ball, and the length of the spring was such that, when the cube was placed with the point of attachment at the top and the ball hanging straight down, the weight stretched the spring only far enough to hold the lowest point of the ball approximately 1 centimeter above the inner bottom surface of the cube. This is clearly shown in the film when the ball is at rest: The reflected image of the ball, visible in the plexiglass surface below it, is approximately 2 centimeters lower than the ball itself.

Kulagina did not at any time reach inside the cube and touch the ball or spring. The film shows, however, that she touched the outside of the cube and changed its position on the table so that its open side was toward her. At this point there is a momentary break in the filming. When we next see the cube, the subject is holding her hands on each side of the cube and making her usual effort to produce movement, and the ball is already on the floor of the cube, obviously pulled down by a force strong enough to extend the length of the spring further than is normal for the weight of the ball. Then the ball moves upward slightly, but not as far as it hangs when at rest, and it is immediately captured again by the downward force and returned to the floor of the cube.

This "tug of war" is repeated several times until, after a few seconds, the force extending the spring prevails over its upward pull, and the ball remains steadily in contact with the floor. Almost immediately, it begins to slide horizontally across the cube toward the corner that is on the subject's right side, staying in contact with the plexiglass surface as it does so.

When the ball, stretching the spring further as it goes, reaches the front edge of the cube, Kulagina appears to relax and cease her effort, and the ball is jerked upward in the direction of the point of attachment of the spring at the top of the cube.

Let us consider the difficulties that this event interposes in the way of any efforts to find a normal explanation. If a magician had prepared his trick cube in advance and had taken it away so that the viewers were unable to examine it, we would have no right to suppose that anything more than a magical trick had been performed. He would have needed a very fine thread glued to the ball and threaded through a small hole in the bottom of the cube or a small countersunk staple in order to pull the ball vertically downward. It is difficult to imagine how he could have kept the ball constantly in contact with the floor while making it travel to the front edge of the cube by pulling a second string.

Let us concede that these effects might be possible with painstaking advance preparations. But they could be detected by examination of the cube afterward. In Kulagina's case, she had no opportunity to make the preparations, and the cube belonged to the experimenters and was brought away by them afterward.

We do not need to consider the possibility of switching a trick cube for the genuine one at the start of the session and then switching again at the end, because neither the subject nor anyone associated with her knew that this device would be presented and therefore no one could have prepared a trick duplicate.

We have tested whether a strong magnet—one capable of lifting 3.5–4 pounds— would attract the lower end of the spring and thus pull the ball down to the floor of the cube. We found that the magnet had no effect even when it was held directly against the outside bottom surface of the cube. If a magnet had been used during the test session, it would have had to be held under the table top, farther from the spring. Even if a stronger magnet could move the ball, it would have to be so large that it is scarcely conceivable that it could have been introduced and manipulated without its presence being observed by the experimenters and detectable in the film. The hesitating movements near the beginning of the event seem particularly difficult to fit into the magnet hypothesis. Either the magnet would be strong enough to hold the ball down (assuming that it could pull it down in the first place), or it could not immediately recapture the spring once it had broken free of the pull of the magnet.

These are the reasons why we say that there is no conceivable normal explanation for the movements that occurred during this event. Can any reader succeed where we have failed? If not, then PK remains as the only available explanation.

There are precedents in the parapsychological literature for what Kulagina is able to do, but one must go back at least 60 years to find them. More important is the question: Will there be successors without another such intolerable interruption? Fortunately, the answer already appears to be in the affirmative, and the survey article (Keil et al., 1976) describes the first stages of research with several other subjects who have successfully demonstrated directly observable PK effects. In this area, at least, the Soviet research in parapsychology may have played an essential part in reopening investigations in the West in a long-neglected area of parapsychology.

A BIBLIOGRAPHY OF SOVIET PUBLICATIONS ON PARAPSYCHOLOGY

An unofficial listing of publications bearing upon this area was compiled by E. K. Naumov and L. V. Vilenskaya in mimeographic form. Since this was in the Russian language, it may have been intended primarily for use within the USSR. Almost immediately, however, copies reached the West, where the document was translated and issued as a U.S. Government Publication. This English edition is the publication discussed here and listed at the end of the chapter (Naumov and Vilenskaya, 1972).

The compilers state that their survey covers publications in the field since 1900, and it seems reasonable to assume that the listing of scientific publications would have been made as complete as possible. This document therefore provides a reasonable basis for judging the progress made in parapsychology in the USSR in comparison with the work done in other countries.

The first section is titled "Parapsychology," and it is divided into scientific publications (63 items) and popular scientific literature (209 items). In contrast, a survey of the world-wide scientific literature of parapsychology, one restricted largely to publications during the period 1940–1966, lists 1,251 items (Rao, 1966). Since this survey is international in scope, it naturally contains some Soviet publications; but it clearly shows that the number of scientific publications on parapsychology in the USSR is small in relation to those found in other parts of the world.

Furthermore, closer examination of the titles of the 63 scientific USSR publications suggests that many of them are not directly concerned with problems of parapsychology as the field is usually defined. A few examples will illustrate the basis of this opionion: item 15, "Dynamic Systems in Physics and Biology"; item 27, "Physico-Chemical Modulation of Information and Thinking Processes. Communication 1. The Thermodynamics of the Information Process"; item 40, "Investigation of Conditioned-Reflex Modifications of the Electroencephalogram in Man to a Nonspecific Stimulus."

If we similarly judge from the titles, the section on popular literature is more consistently concerned with parapsychology. The length of this list shows clearly that there is a strong public interest in this general topic. The period covered by the popular publications (almost exclusively 1960–1971) was one during which governmental regulation of the press in the USSR was less strict. Taking advantage of their opportunity, Soviet editors responded in the manner characteristic of that profession around the world: They published what their readers wanted to read.

During this period the USSR editors also frequently presented popular forum-type, debate-style discussions reflecting a range of opinions on parapsychology, pro and con. The bibliography lists ten such public discussions, most of them giving the views of eminent USSR scientists and scholars.

Other sections of the bibliography cover literature in areas that are characterized as related to parapsychology. These sections include articles on dowsing (called "the biophysical effect"), Kirlian photography, capacities of the brain, dermo-optic sensitivity, electric and magnetic fields of living organisms, yoga, hypnosis and autohypnosis, and effects of the sun on the organism. In the West, most of these topics would not be considered to merit inclusion in a bibliography on parapsychology unless particular studies had specific parapsychological aspects.

The impression one gets from the document as a whole is that the Russian compilers of this list know what is included in parapsychology in the West but that they were impelled for undefined reasons to blur the boundaries of the field and include many areas that are not included under definitions accepted in other countries.

We shall have occasion later to allude further to this Russian bibliography and to inferences that may be made from it.

THE ATTITUDE OF USSR PSYCHOLOGISTS TOWARD SOVIET RESEARCH IN PARAPSYCHOLOGY: AN "OFFICIAL" POSITION PAPER

An article published in a scholarly journal linked with the Soviet Academy of Pedagogical Sciences was written by four leading psychologists (Zinchenko, Leont'yev, Lomov, and Luria, 1973) after the Society of Psychologists had devoted a session to the question of the status of parapsychology. Such "official" recognition as this publication represents is, in itself, compelling evidence that developments in parapsychology in the USSR have advanced so far that established science there can no longer ignore them. This publication has therefore been widely recognized in the West as an important scientific document that should provide clues regarding the direction that Soviet research in parapsychology will likely take in the future.

Opinions among parapsychologists in the West regarding how to interpret this document have varied widely. At one extreme have been the views that the article amounts to a formal, even if reluctant, acknowledgment of parapsychology as a legitimate area of scientific endeavor and that the time has come for it to be officially organized and pursued in the Soviet Union. At the other extreme are those (among whom I belong) who see this document as a reaction of Soviet psychologists to the fact that public and scientific interest in this field has become so strong that it can be tolerated only if further research is officially organized and regulated. The writers say that parapsychology is not a legitimate branch of science, though some of the phenomena investigated by parapsychologists are real—they do not say which ones. The legitimate problems should be investigated as special human abilities within the established branches of science to which they are relevant. As we attempt to evaluate this document, the important consideration must be to reach a judgment regarding which of these contrasting views is more likely the correct one.

Most of the article is taken up with describing what, in the views of the Soviet writers, the parapsychologists consider the field to include. The resulting outline is recognizable in its main divisions, but the subdivisions are strange both for some of the topics included as relevant research problems as well as for areas of research that are omitted. The result is a grossly inadequate representation of the range of research areas covered in parapsychology.

In the attention they give to the history and the current status of parapsychology in the West, the Soviet psychologists also show themselves to be poorly informed. Their article abounds in factual errors and distortions, including exaggerations of the number of parapsychology laboratories now actively working in the field and the number of scientific journals devoted to this area. Their figure on periodicals could be justified only if popular magazines at all levels of quality were added to the strictly professional journals. The article also is obscure on the amount of serious literature in that it fails to draw a clear distinction between the scientific reports and the popular literature.

My impression of the description given by the Soviet psychologists of the current status of parapsychology in the USSR is that it is, on the whole, quite accurate and fair. They represent the interest as that of persons who are devoting time to the field unofficially, most of them only during their leisure hours and without pay. They point out that there have been a few sections organized for special attention to parapsychology attached to institutions in different cities, most of these parent organizations being in areas of technical and applied science. They decry the interest and support that such efforts have received from scientists whose professional competence is in fields not closely related to psychology and therefore not qualifying them for working in parapsychology.

To insure that the views of the Soviet psychologists are correctly-represented, I will let them speak in their own words by quoting a few paragraphs from their concluding section, where they are making specific recommendations regarding what must no longer be allowed to occur and what positive steps should be taken. I have added the superscript numbers to refer to the numbered paragraphs commenting on different points following the quotation.

Analysis of the status of what is called parapsychology reveals that it is extremely cluttered with anti-scientific concepts and to a significant degree it has become a field of activity for alleged "specialists." Some of them have declared themselves as leaders and coworkers of organizations which have never existed in our country, for example, the "Institute of Technical Parapsychology." It is necessary to suppress the activity of unqualified and militant parapsychologists who take on themselves the spreading of propaganda, voluntarily and by no means unselfishly, by presenting numerous reports and lectures on parapsychology, including some also given before scientific audiences. These lectures are an unconscientious mixture of mythology and reality.[1] The non-critical attitude toward parapsychology on the part of some serious scientists can be explained only by a positivistic indifference in their attitude toward scientific theory and methodology. There are no legitimate bases for the existence of parapsychology as a special science since the only thing that unites parapsychologists is the mysteriousness and unsolvability of the phenomena they study.

Likewise appearing inadmissable to us is the practice of publishing in the pages of newspapers, journals, and popular publications sensational and scientifically unsubstantiated materials on parapsychology. In this instance, for some reason or other, the tradition, usually observed by scientists who respect themselves, is being destroyed: serious scientific achievements are first published in special scientific literature and only after that in popular literature.[2]

The need to regulate scientific research work in the field of study of those real phenomena which are described in parapsychology has certainly matured.[3] Taking into account that many investigations in the field of parapsychology are performed by physicists and engineers, it is expedient in the Institute of Biophysics of the Academy of Sciences USSR and in the Institute of Problems in the Transmission of Information of the Academy to discuss the direction and scientific level of the study of the biophysical effect [dowsing] and electromagnetic fields generated by living organisms as a possible means of biological communication, as well as a series of other phenomena. Attention to these phenomena on the part of biophysics and the theory of communication will help in their demystification.

Psychological institutes of the Academy of Psychological Sciences within the Soviet Academy and other psychological institutes should also examine the possibility of rigorous scientific research into these phenomena. Apparently it would be advisable to organize in the structure of one of the psychological institutes a laboratory for the study of people actually possessing unusual abilities (which are by no means always necessarily paranormal). The results of such investigations, after a careful check, naturally should be published in scientific literature (and only then in popular literature).

It seems to us that the attention of serious scientific organizations to phenomena described in parapsychology will aid in revealing their true nature; it will close the door to charlatans profiting on the completely natural interest of the general public in many unfathomable secrets of human psychic phenomena; and it will disperse the myths about the existance of a "parapsychological movement" in the USSR.

1. Up to this point, this paragraph in the Soviet article seems to be directed explicitly against the parapsychological activities of E. K. Naumov, who has been the most active promoter and organizer of parapsychology in the Soviet Union and encourager of international cooperation. In one respect, the description does Naumov an injustice, since he did not claim to be the head of an "*Institute* of Technical Parapsychology," but rather of a "*Department* of Technical Parapsychology." The distinction between *institute* and *department* may be one of crucial importance in the Soviet scientific system, for the former connotes official approval and status whereas the latter may not. Perhaps the mistaken impression of the Soviet psychologists arose from the fact that some foreign friends of Naumov, in writing about his activities, mistakenly said that he was head of the Institute for Technical Parapsychology. The statement, "It is necessary to suppress the activity of unqualified and militant parapsychologists . . ." reads like an accusation calling for Naumov's arrest and punishment, and it is perhaps not merely coincidental that he was arrested a few months later and sentenced to a period in a labor camp (Regelson, 1974).

2. In this paragraph the Soviet writers correctly describe the predominance of material on parapsychology in the popular USSR press without prior (or even subsequent) publication in the scientific literature. Their parenthetical expression, "for some reason or other," ducks the issue of why this has been the situation and thus leaves the readers with the impression that this is a situation that has come about as a matter of choice on the part of the research workers in parapsychology. It seems more likely that the avenue of popular presentation of work in this field was taken by many of the scientists because this was the only one open to them. Officially approved laboratories led by scientists who were personally committed to research in parapsychology could include scientific reports on work in this field in their regular publications, and during the Khrushchev period, as shown by the example of Vasiliev, it was possible to get approval for the publication of parapsychological books. These instances, however, are

the exceptions that only prove the rule that the ordinary channels for scientific publication have been closed to research in parapsychology.

3. This sentence reflects the fact that there is no recognized research in the Soviet Union except what is officially approved and regulated. Unofficial work done by an individual as a part-time interest or "hobby" is tolerated so long as it does not attract too much attention. It was particularly annoying to the Soviet authorities to find that tourists from the West, especially from the USA, were really coming to the Soviet Union because of their interest in talking with Russian scientists about their work on parapsychology and to attend unofficial public meetings dealing with this area. Invariably, visitors who went there expecting to go into Soviet laboratories were denied that privilege, but often not until they had pressed their Russian hosts to make the effort to obtain permission, thereby further annoying the authorities. It has been said that Naumov's major (and unannounced) offense was that he persisted after repeated warning in keeping up correspondence with foreign parapsychologists and in promoting meetings with them in the USSR (Regelson, 1974).

CONCLUDING REMARKS

The developments in Soviet research in parapsychology since the second decade of the century occurred during the first 50 years within established academic situations and along carefully-regulated lines. While Vasiliev took aggressive and successful steps in the direction of accelerating this development of parapsychology, he was careful to do so while attempting to make the research acceptable in terms of orthodox Soviet science. He was removed from the scene by his illness and his death before the laboratory was established in a way to insure that his successor would continue along the same lines.

The initiation of the Brezhnev period marked a slow turning of the political system away from the liberalization that had marked the Khrushchev era, and this fact made it once more difficult for parapsychological research to be done openly in university and institute laboratories. It was in this "vacuum" of official opinion about the field that Naumov and other interested individuals began to work for the advancement of the field, particularly in spreading information about it among the general population. Among those active during the decade 1965-1975 were a few scientists who were outstanding in their own fields, and at least one of them (Sergeyev) did important research in parapsychology. It is entirely possible, I freely admit, that a few others did so as well and that I have not done them justice because of the language barrier. But undoubtedly the major success was along educational lines: the building up of public interest through fostering publications in the popular press.

This groundswell of public interest, particularly when it assumed the proportions of an international movement sustained by both correspondence and meetings between Soviet and foreign enthusiasts, was what eventually forced an official reaction. The remedy to be applied to the situation has been prescribed by the four Soviet psychologists in plain language. I see no reason to doubt that they were speaking with authority and without any need to conceal their intention. In my opinion, their pronouncements foretell a new era during which Soviet Science will permit and even support research on unusual human abilities so long as those problems to be researched offer some hope of solution in terms that can be reconciled with the principles of dialectical materialism.

REFERENCES

Bechterev, V. M. "Direct influence" of a person upon the behavior of animals. *Journal of Parapsychology*, 1949, **13**, 166–176. (Abridged translation of original article in *Problems in the Study and Training of Personality*, 1920, Petrograd, 2nd ed., pp. 230–265. The English article is translated from a German translation published in the *Zeitschrift für Psychotherapie* in 1924.)

Flecksor, P. Experiments in so-called mental suggestion on animals. In *Problems in the Study and Training of Personality*, 1920, Petrograd, 2nd ed.

Ivanov-Smolensky, A. G. Experiments in mental suggestion on animals. In *Problems in the Study and Training of Personality*, 1920, Petrograd, 2nd ed.

Janet, P., and Gibert, M. Sur quelques phénomènes de somnambulisme. *Revue Philosophique*, 1886, I and II.

Joire, P. De la suggestion mentale. *Annales des sciences psychiques*, 1897, No. 4, 193

Keil, H. H. J., and Fahler, J. A strong case for PK involving directly observable movements of objects recorded on cine film. In J. D. Morris, W. G. Roll, and R. L. Morris (Eds.), *Research in Parapsychology 1974*, pp. 66–69. Metuchen, N. J.: Scarecrow Press, 1975.

Keil, H. H. J., Herbert, B., Ullman, M., and Pratt, J. G. Directly observable voluntary PK effects: A survey and tentative interpretation of available findings from Nina Kulagina and other known related cases of recent date. *Proceedings of the Society for Psychical Research*, 1976, **56**, 197–235.

Kulagin, V. V. Nina S. Kulagina. *Journal of Paraphysics*, 1971, **5**, 54–62.

Naumov, E. K., and Vilenskaya, L. V. *Bibliographies on Parapsychology (Psychoenergetics) and Related Subjects*. Washington: Department of Commerce, 1972. (Originally published privately, Moscow, 1971.)

Rao, K. R. *Experimental Parapsychology: A Review and Interpretation*. Springfield, Ill.: Charles C Thomas, 1966.

Regelson, L. An appeal to Soviet and foreign public opinion. *Journal of the Society for Psychical Research*, 1974, **47**, 521–524.

Rejdak, Z. Die psychokinetischen Phänomene von Nina Kulagina. *Zeitschrift für Parapsychologie und Grenzgebiete der Psychologie*, 1970, **12**, 106–110.

Vasiliev, L. L. *Experiments in Mental Suggestion*. Church Crookham, England: Gally Hill Press, 1963. (Originally published in 1962 by Leningrad State University.) (An American edition of this book [paperback] with an Introduction by Anita Gregory was published in 1976 by E. P. Dutton, New York, under the title of *Experiments in Distant Influence*.)

Vasiliev, L. L. *Mysterious Phenomena of the Human Psyche*. New Hyde Park, N.Y.: University Books, 1965. (Originally published by the State Political Printing House, USSR, in 1959.)

Zinchenko, V. P., Leont'yev, A. N., Lomov, B. F., and Luria, A. R. Parapsychology: Fiction or reality? *Voprosy Filosofii* [*Questions of Philosophy*], 1973, No. 9, 128–136.

POSTSCRIPT

Just as the Handbook was going to press, an article by R. A. McConnell, "Parapsychology in the USSR," was published in the *Journal of Parapsychology*, 1975, **39**, 129–134. His article is concerned with only the current situation, and it is based upon an analysis of two Soviet documents (Regelson, 1974; Zinchenko et al., 1973) previously referred to in this chapter. In most respects I find that McConnell and I are in close general agreement regarding the situation for Soviet parapsychology at this time, but there may be one noteworthy difference in our interpretations. I see the recent developments as pointing to an official dismemberment of parapsychology so that the phenomena that are accepted as real and as being compatible with the Communist point of view are assigned appropriately to different scientific institutes for investigation. McConnell, on the other hand, considers that the reality of psi phenomena has now been officially recognized and the study of them will henceforth be conducted in government laboratories. Perhaps we would both agree that this apparent difference is more a matter of emphasis than of substance.

I conclude by quoting the final two paragraphs of McConnell's article:

> From the information given above it is a reasonable inference that for many years the scientific leaders of the USSR have knowingly allowed parapsychology to flourish at a popular level until they could make up their minds as to whether psi phenomena are real or imaginary. They have decided in favor of those phenomena, the study of which will now be undertaken within government laboratories. As a preliminary step, popular and indiscriminate investigation must be halted. Eduard Naumov's punishment will serve to warn his more scientific colleagues that they, too, must conform to government policy.

> After reading the two publications described above, if there were any doubt that the Soviet KGB has an active interest in the Russian psychic, Kulagina, that doubt would be dispelled by the stories of surveillance, harassment, and intervention that have been brought back in recent years by Western parapsychologists who visited or tried to visit her in Leningrad (pp. 133–134).

Part XI

SUGGESTED READINGS AND GLOSSARY OF TERMS

Suggested Readings in Parapsychology

Compiled by *Rhea A. White*

Preliminary Note: This list of in-print books on parapsychology was prepared at a time when many new books of presumed worth were in the process of being published and many old classics being made available once more, while in addition a sizable number of core books that have been available for several years were still in print. Limiting the number of titles on this list was therefore difficult. It is hoped that those selected will provide a basic understanding of what parapsychology is, of how parapsychological research is conducted, and of what the implications of psi phenomena are for the understanding of man's nature. Reference should be made to book reviews in the parapsychological journals for additional titles of worthwhile books as they are published.

GENERAL PSYCHICAL RESEARCH

Angoff, A., and Shapin, B. (Eds.). *Parapsychology and the Sciences.* New York: Parapsychology Foundation, 1974. 289p. $7.00.

Most of the papers in this conference proceedings offer a view of the impact of other scientific disciplines on parapsychology. The broad spectrum of subjects covered consists of abnormal psychology, psychopathology, psychoanalysis, psychology, subliminal perception, biology, meteorology, physics, genetics, and chemistry. The remaining papers discuss parapsychology as a science, approaches to the scientific investigation of psi, and the implications of psi for other sciences.

Beloff, J. (Ed.). *New Directions in Parapsychology.* Metuchen, N. J.: Scarecrow Press, 1975. 174p. $8.50. (First published in 1974).

This compilation contains seven hitherto unpublished "state of the art" papers by well-known parapsychologists on key areas in the field. The topics covered are instrumentation used in psi research, altered states and psi, personality and psi, biology and psi, high-scoring subjects, poltergeist research, and survival of bodily death. There is a postscript by Arthur Koestler. Beloff provides helpful commentaries and a glossary.

Broad, C. D. *Lectures on Psychical Research.* New York: Humanities Press, 1962. 450p. $16.50.

Surveying the whole field of psychical research, the first main section of the book contains three chapters on major quantitative experiments and the second deals with theoretical points arising from spontaneous psi phenomena. The final section discusses trance phenomena and the work of several gifted sensitives. The book concludes with an epilogue on human personality and survival of bodily death.

Heywood, R. *Beyond the Reach of Sense: An Inquiry into Extrasensory Perception.* New York: Dutton, 1974. 252p. $3.45 (paper). (First published in 1959.)

In this readable introduction to psychical research, the emphasis is on qualitative studies of psi phenomena and on survival research. In the first of two appendices representatives of other disciplines discuss "some explanations and hypotheses" for psi; in the second, the author assesses progress in the field during the 15 years since publication of the first edition of the book.

McConnell, R. A. *ESP Curriculum Guide.* New York: Simon and Schuster, 1971. 128p. $5.95; $1.95 (paper).

This guide was written for high school and college teachers to enable them to teach parapsychology "in an honest, accurate, and exciting way." The investigation of ESP and PK is presented within the wider framework of scientific method in general. In addition to a theoretical framework, practical information on conducting experiments, evaluating their results, and building apparatus is presented.

Mitchell, E. D., and others. Edited by J. White. *Psychic Exploration: A Challenge for Science.* New York: Putnam, 1974. 708p. $17.50.

This is a compendium of articles on various aspects of parapsychology by parapsychologists and members of related disciplines. The papers were written specifically for this volume; primarily they are surveys which, with their attendant bibliographies, are useful introductions to parapsychology. Several of the more speculative contributions, however, are both uninformed and misleading. It is suggested that readers of the book consult reviews of it by J. G. Pratt (*Journal of Parapsychology*, March, 1975) and John Beloff (*Journal* A.S.P.R., October, 1975).

Murphy, G. (with L. A. Dale). *Challenge of Psychical Research: A Primer of Parapsychology.* New York: Harper & Row, 1961. 297p. $6.50; $1.95 (paper).

This is a collection of basic source materials on spontaneous cases, quantitative psi investigations, and the survival question. Murphy introduces each section with a discussion of the evidence and an interpretation of its meaning. The aim of the book is not to survey the field, but to provide a "primer of working materials with which the reader may struggle."

Pratt, J. G. *ESP Research Today: A Study of Developments in Parapsychology since 1960.* Metuchen, N. J.: Scarecrow Press, 1973. 195p. $6.00.

Though intended for the general reader, this survey of recent work in parapsychology is written from the viewpoint of an active research worker in the field. There are two general chapters as well as seven which are devoted to specific topics: psi research in the Soviet Union and the author's own experiments there with the Russian psychokinetic medium,

Nina Kulagina; the high-scoring ESP subject, Pavel Stepanek; Van Vuurde's "ESP alarm clock"; psychic photography; poltergeists; reincarnation; and parapsychology as a science.

Randall, J. L. *Parapsychology and the Nature of Life*. New York: Harper & Row, 1975. 256p. $8.95.

The purpose of this book is to describe the place of parapsychology in the assessment of the nature of human personality and of life itself. The first part, "Mechanism triumphant," reviews the scientific findings which form the basis of the deterministic theory of life. The second and longest part, "Counter-attack," is a review of parapsychological evidence. The final part, "Towards a new synthesis," offers some speculations about the nature of reality which take into consideration the findings of parapsychology as well as those of the biological and physical sciences.

Schmeidler, G. R. (Ed.). *Parapsychology: Its Relation to Physics, Biology, Psychology, and Psychiatry*. Metuchen, N. J.: Scarecrow Press, 1976. 178p. $11.00.

The papers in this volume were originally delivered at a symposium held by the American Society for Psychical Research to "present authoritative accounts of research to a public whose sources of information about parapsychology often contain much that is unreliable." The 12 chapters are by practicing physicists, psychologists, and psychiatrists who have also had many years of experience in parapsychology. This book may serve both as a primer of facts about the paranormal and as a handbook of observations, hypotheses, and strategies of parapsychological research.

Shapin, B., and Coly, L. (Eds.). *Education in Parapsychology*. New York: Parapsychology Foundation, 1976. 313p. $12.50.

This Parapsychology Foundation conference proceedings is on a topic of considerable current importance: education in parapsychology. Included are general papers such as R. G. Stanford's "Preparing for a career in parapsychology," J. Beloff's "The study of the paranormal as an educative experience," and R. L. Morris' "The responsibilities of instructors in parapsychology." There are also papers devoted to specific subjects such as parapsychology in the liberal arts curriculum, in the teaching of philosophy, and in the secondary school curriculum. Some of the 16 chapters are aimed at students and some at instructors, but all are relevant to the concerns of anyone interested in parapsychological education.

Smythies, J. R. (Ed.). *Science and ESP*. New York: Humanities Press, 1967. 306p. $14.25.

The editor selected 13 papers which present the views of a number of scientists from different disciplines on the nature of psi phenomena. Some of the topics dealt with are psychology and parapsychology, attitudes toward psi, theories of psi, psychiatry and parapsychology, and anthropology and ESP. The theoretical contributions, in particular, are still relevant, and the survey articles provide useful insights into the nature of psi.

Tyrrell, G. N. M. *Science and Psychical Phenomena*. New York: Arno Press, 1975. 379p. $22.00 (First published in 1938.)

This is one of the best introductions to the full range of parapsychological phenomena. Tyrrell evaluates the evidence for psi provided by spontaneous experiences, describes the experimental findings (1882 to 1938), and discusses mediumship and survival. Special emphasis is given to theoretical aspects of trance phenomena, the prevailing attitudes toward psi phenomena, and the significance of the paranormal for our concepts of human personality and normal sense perception.

West, D. J. *Psychical Research Today*. New York: Hillary House, 1956. 144p. $3.25 (paper).

This is still one of the best critical introductions to basic parapsychology. West gives equal attention to quantitative research, mediumistic investigations, and studies of spontaneous phenomena, with emphasis on British work. A theoretical chapter concludes the book.

Wolstenholme, G. E. W., and Millar, E. C. P. (Eds.). *Extrasensory Perception: A Ciba Foundation Symposium*. New York: Citadel Press, 1966. 240p. $2.25 (paper.) (First published in 1956.)

The Ciba Foundation conferences are well-known to scientists everywhere. This book records the proceedings of one such conference which brought together 23 participants, including physicists, psychologists, psychiatrists, biologists, and parapsychologists. Fourteen papers and seven discussion periods are included. The major topics covered are criticisms, evaluations of the evidence for ESP, theoretical approaches, anpsi, medical parapsychology, and ESP in primitive and peasant societies.

EXPERIMENTAL PARAPSYCHOLOGY

Morris, J. D., Roll, W. G., and Morris, R. L. (Eds.). *Research in Parapsychology 1975*. Metuchen, N. J.: Scarecrow Press, 1976. $9.00.

This is an annual publication which until 1972 was known as the *Proceedings of the Parapsychological Association*. Each volume consists of abstracts of papers and full texts of the presidential and invited addresses given at the annual convention of the Association (the professional parapsychological organization), thus providing an ongoing summary of the developments and findings in the field. The volumes are well indexed.

Pratt, J. G. *A Decade of Research with a Selected ESP Subject: An Overview and Reappraisal of the Work with Pavel Stepanek*. (Proceedings of the A.S.P.R., Vol. 30.) New York: American Society for Psychical Research, 1973. 78p. $4.00.

The author presents a .step-by-step account of the many experiments carried out by himself and by other parapsychologists with the Czech high-scoring ESP subject, Pavel Stepanek. The investigations span a decade, the longest period over which any ESP subject has been able to maintain a significant scoring level. Pratt describes how Stepanek's ESP works, what he is like as a person, and the impact of the research on parapsychologists and on other scientists.

Rao, K. R. *Experimental Parapsychology: A Review and Interpretation*. Springfield, Ill.: Charles C Thomas, 1966. 255p. $9.50.

This book presents short, systematic reviews of all the psi experiments published from 1940 through 1965. A critical survey of several theories of psi and a discussion of "parapsychology and the nature of man" is also provided. There is a comprehensive bibliography of 1,251 items.

Rhine, J. B. (Ed.). *Progress in Parapsychology*. Durham, N. C.: Parapsychology Press, 1971. 315p. $7.00.

This is a collection of 20 papers presented at review meetings held at the Institute for Parapsychology, Foundation for Research on the Nature of Man, during 1968 and 1969. The reports were submitted from all over the world, and those "giving the most representative survey of the field" were selected for inclusion. The areas covered are "new approaches," "mind over matter," "factors in psi test performance," and "main lines of continuity," and "parapsychology in perspective." Also included is a tribute to William McDougall for his contributions to parapsychology.

Rhine, J. B., and others. *Extrasensory Perception After Sixty Years.* Boston: Branden Press, 1966. 483p. $5.95. (First published in 1940.)

Subtitled "a critical appraisal of the research in extrasensory perception," this classic work is a survey of "everything that is of importance to know in deciding whether ESP occurs, and what it is like if it does occur." The book covers the experimental literature from 1882 to 1939. Criticisms of ESP research and answers to them are stressed. It also functions as a handbook of experimental methods and a survey of problem areas. There is a bibliography of 361 items.

Rhine, J. B., and Pratt, J. G. *Parapsychology: Frontier Science of the Mind.* (Rev. ed.) Springfield, Ill.: Charles C Thomas, 1962. 224p. $6.00.

This volume was conceived as a textbook of experimental parapsychology. Part I reviews what has been learned about the nature of psi and its relation to other fields. Part II is on techniques for testing, including basic procedures, methods of statistical evaluation, and the psychology of successful psi testing. Each chapter has a bibliography and a list of additional readings.

Schmeidler, G. R. (Ed.). *Extrasensory Perception.* New York: Lieber-Atherton, 1969. 166p. $7.95; $2.95 (paper).

This anthology is in the "Atherton controversies" series of books reviewing "conflicting views of key controversial subjects" and aimed at college teachers. As the title indicates, only one aspect of psi is dealt with—extrasensory perception. Three papers are centrally concerned with criticisms of ESP, and the remaining six are research reports dealing with psychological factors influencing ESP. In her introduction the editor provides an informative overview of the evidence for ESP and what is known about its psychology. She also provides introductory and concluding remarks for each selection which help to place it in the context of ongoing research.

Schmeidler, G. R., and McConnell, R. A. *ESP and Personality Patterns.* Westport, Conn.: Greenwood Press, 1974. 136p. $9.00. (First published in 1958.)

This is a survey of experiments dealing with belief in ESP in relation to ESP scoring level— the "sheep-goat" effect. The initial chapters describe the senior author's own investigations on this effect and attempts by others to repeat her results. The last part of the book deals with personality correlates of ESP success, with chapters on the Rorschach test, experiments with cerebral concussion patients, and frustration in relation to ESP. The evidence for ESP is evaluated and suggestions made for further research.

Thouless, R. H. *From Anecdote to Experiment in Psychical Research.* London and Boston: Routledge and Kegan Paul, 1972. 198p. $10.00.

This introduction to experimental parapsychology is intended for readers familiar with other areas of scientific research. All the major approaches to the investigation of psi are presented and their methodological advantages and disadvantages delineated. The basics of what has been learned about the nature of psi from empirical research is discussed.

SPONTANEOUS PSI

Gurney, E., Myers, F. W. H., and Podmore, F. *Phantasms of the Living.* Gainesville, Fla.: Scholars' Facsimiles and Reprints, 1970. $47.50. 2 vols. (First published in 1886.)

This is one of the classics of psychical research, compiled by three of the foremost pioneers of the subject. It is a collection and survey of what was known about ESP in the late nineteenth century. The emphasis is on spontaneous phenomena as expressed in dreams and hallucinations, including collective and reciprocal cases, but some experiments are also described. Counterhypotheses and theories are considered in detail.

Heywood, R. *ESP: A Personal Memoir*. New York: Dutton, 1964. 224p. $3.45 (paper).

This is an autobiographical account of what it feels like to be, to use the author's term, an "experient" (sensitive). She provides numerous accounts of her experiences, which she classifies in two categories: "a passive awareness, usually fleeting . . . of apparent presences or of situations not perceptible *via* the senses; and an inner prompting to action or comment on behalf of other people, which seem either beyond my normal capacity, or absurd in the light of facts known to me at the time, but turn out to be relevant in the light of other facts learnt later on." The book is a courageous attempt to be objective about one's own subjectivity.

MacKenzie, A. *The Unexplained: Some Strange Cases of Psychical Research*. New York: Popular Library, 1970. 173p. $.75 (paper).

Most of the experiences described in this book were taken from the publications of the Society for Psychical Research. Emphasis is on cases involving apparitions and poltergeists. As a result of interviews and correspondence the author had with the persons concerned, he was able to add biographical and other new material of interest and value to some of the accounts. A brief history of the S.P.R. is given in an appendix.

Sidgwick, E. M. *Phantasms of the Living: Cases of Telepathy Printed in the Journal of the Society for Psychical Research during Thirty-five Years*. Bound with *Phantasms of the Living* (Gurney, Myers, and Podmore, 1886), abridged and edited by E. M. Sidgwick. New York: Arno Press, 1975. $56.00. Two vols. in one.

Two of Mrs. Sidgwick's earlier published papers on telepathy are reprinted in this double volume. The first paper contains experimental and semi-experimental reports and accounts of spontaneous experiences, including some interesting collective and reciprocal cases. The second paper is entitled "On hindrances and complications in telepathic communication." The remainder of the volume is devoted to her abridgment of the monumental *Phantasms of the Living* (see annotation on p. 908), which she nearly halved by omitting many cases while retaining most of the text. The contents of this reprint constitute what is undoubtedly the largest and most valuable collection of spontaneous cases ever published.

Stevenson, I. *Telepathic Impressions: A Review and Report of Thirty-five New Cases*. Charlottesville: University Press of Virginia, 1970. 198p. $6.75. (First published as a Proceedings of the A.S.P.R., Vol. 29, 1970.)

The author presents a survey and analysis of 160 published cases of telepathy which involved only "impressions" or "intuitions" about distant persons and lacked clear-cut imagery. He also describes 23 new cases of this type which he investigated personally, some of them indicating that pain and other physical symptoms may be telepathically communicated. The two final chapters discuss the processes of telepathic communication and the evidence for psi provided by cases of the impression type.

Tyrrell, G. N. M. *Apparitions*. New York: Macmillan, 1962. 192p. $.95 (paper). (First published in 1942.)

This is perhaps the most provocative study of apparitions ever published. The author presents a psychological approach to the production of veridical apparitions. In his view, the percipient receives a kernel of information telepathically, and then subconsciously stages the apparitional show as a means of becoming consciously aware of this information. He presents a number of key cases to illustrate his theory and speculates on the bearing that veridical apparitions of the deceased may have on the evidence for survival of bodily death.

PSYCHOKINESIS AND POLTERGEISTS

Eisenbud, J. *The World of Ted Serios*. New York: Paperback Library, 1969. 367p. $.95 (paper).

Subtitled "'Thoughtographic' studies of an extraordinary mind," this volume describes the author's extensive investigations of Ted Serios' ability to imprint mental images on photographic film by other than normal means. A number of Eisenbud's colleagues at the University of Denver collaborated in the experiments, which were carried out under a variety of conditions to explore the parameters of the phenomena. The style of the book is both scholarly and readable. There are 150 illustrations relating to Serios' work.

Owen, A. R. G. *Can We Explain the Poltergeist?* New York: Garrett/Helix, 1964. 436p. $8.50.

This book provides a thorough survey of poltergeist phenomena. There are four parts, covering spurious cases, genuine poltergeists (many case accounts and an entire chapter devoted to the Sauchie poltergeist), the powers and limitations of poltergeists (including forms of expression), and interpretations of poltergeist phenomena (biological, psycho-neurotic, and the relation of poltergeists to physical mediumship). A final chapter makes suggestions for future investigators.

Rhine, L. E. *Mind over Matter: Psychokinesis*. New York: Macmillan, 1970. 402p. $7.95; $1.95 (paper).

This book presents a detailed survey of the various types of evidence for psychokinesis, with emphasis on the pioneer experiments carried out at the Duke University Parapsychology Laboratory. There are chapters on confirmatory work carried out at other centers, physiological and psychological variables, spontaneous PK, possible practical applications (e.g., in unorthodox healing), and the theoretical implications of PK.

Roll, W. G. *The Poltergeist*. Metuchen, N. J.: Scarecrow Press, 1976. 208p. $7.50. (First published in 1972.)

In this book the author describes a number of cases he has investigated personally as well as others from the literature. There are important chapters on the psychology, psycho-pathology, and theory of the poltergeist. An appendix gives detailed guidelines for the investigation of poltergeist and haunting phenomena.

MEDIUMSHIP AND POST-MORTEM SURVIVAL

Ducasse, C. J. *A Critical Examination of the Belief in a Life After Death*. Springfield, Ill.: Charles C Thomas, 1961. 318p. $8.75.

This is one of the major works on the question of survival after death. After an exhaustive discussion of the problem from a philosophical, religious, and logical point of view, Ducasse reviews the empirical evidence afforded by parapsychology, concluding that on balance it points to survival "of the most significant capacities of the human mind, and of continuing exercise of these." He also considers the various forms which life after death could plausibly take should it be a reality.

Jacobson, N. O. *Life Without Death? On Parapsychology, Mysticism and the Question of Survival*. New York: Delacorte Press, 1974. 334p. $10.00.

The dual aim of the author is to provide a survey of all the major phenomena studied by parapsychology and to show how investigations in all these areas may shed light on the possibility of survival. Both pros and cons are presented. Finally, on the assumption that we do survive, he describes what life after death might be like.

Murphy, G. *Three Papers on the Survival Problem*. New York: American Society for Psychical Research, 1945. 90p. $3.00 (paper).

Under this title are reprinted three articles dealing with the survival question which were originally published in the A.S.P.R. *Journal* (Vol. 43, 1945). In the first, "An outline of survival evidence," the various types of evidence are defined and illustrative case material cited; in the second, "Difficulties confronting the survival hypothesis," the author discusses the obstacles in the way of obtaining final proof of survival and says that "if progress is to be made, it will be through squarely confronting the difficulties, not by seeking to escape them"; the third paper suggests new ways of formulating the survival question and indicates what would constitute the best evidence for survival.

Osis, K. *Deathbed Observations by Physicians and Nurses*. New York: Parapsychology Foundation, 1961. 113p. $1.75 (paper).

This is a study of experiences of terminal patients as described by 640 doctors and nurses who took part in a large-scale survey carried out by the author. The data, obtained by means of questionnaires, revealed that in 753 cases the patients experienced an elevated mood during their last hours. A total of 888 reported visions (hallucinations of a nonhuman nature), and 1,370 saw apparitions, mainly of deceased relatives and friends. Most of the data came from patients who were fully conscious and whose mentality was not disturbed by sedation. The results of the investigation are interpreted by the author as consistent with the survival hypothesis.

Salter, W. H. *Zoar; or, The Evidence of Psychical Research Concerning Survival*. New York: Arno Press, 1975. 238p. $13.00. (First published in 1961.)

This book presents a thorough sifting of the evidence for survival, and the author's main thrust is to show why a definite *yes* or *no* answer is not possible. All types of evidence are described and evaluated: apparitions and hauntings; poltergeists; the phenomena of ecstasy and inspiration; dissociative states; and mediumistic phenomena, including the cross correspondences. Previously unpublished evidence regarding the latter, with which Salter was intimately involved, is included.

Smith, S. *The Mediumship of Mrs. Leonard*. Secaucus, N. J.: University Books, 1964. 260p. $7.50.

This is a popular but well-documented account of the life and work of one of England's most gifted mediums, Gladys Osborn Leonard. There are chapters describing her controls, the role of the sitters, proxy sittings, book and newspaper tests, word-association tests, precognitive experiences, and direct-voice phenomena. The *modus operandi* of trance is also discussed.

Stevenson, I. *Twenty Cases Suggestive of Reincarnation*. (2nd rev. ed.) Charlottesville: University Press of Virginia, 1974. 396p. $15.00. (1st ed. published as a Proceedings of the A.S.P.R., Vol. 26, 1966.)

This is a revision of an important book describing a scientific approach to the age-old question of reincarnation. In addition to carefully researched case histories, Stevenson provides a thorough survey of the literature on reincarnation, including theories and criticisms. New material in this edition includes follow-up interviews with the subjects of 18 cases.

PSYCHOLOGY, PSYCHIATRY, AND PSI

Burt, C. *Psychology and Psychical Research*. London: Society for Psychical Research, 1968. 109p. £.50 (paper).

This expanded version of a lecture delivered by the author to the Society for Psychical Research is aimed at answering the need for a "comprehensive statement of the psychological problems involved in parapsychology." He deals with changing trends in psychology and neurology which make the existence of psi seem more likely, ways of rectifying the present lack of a scientific theory to account for parapsychological data, and the need for modifying the goals currently pursued by parapsychology in the light of data from other scientific disciplines.

Devereux, G. (Ed.). *Psychoanalysis and the Occult*. New York: International Universities Press, 1971. 448p. $15.00; $3.95 (paper). (First published in 1953.)

In addition to papers by the editor, there are contributions from 17 psychoanalysts, beginning with several by Freud. Devereux describes them as "*psychoanalytic* studies of so-called 'psi phenomena'" and views them "primarily as contributions to the theory and practice of clinical analysis." Two historical and methodological papers are included. Some of the contributions were translated into English for purposes of this book. There is a bibliography of 204 items.

Ehrenwald, J. *History of Psychotherapy: From Healing Magic to Encounter Groups*. New York: Jason Aronson, 1975. 589p. $20.00.

This is a greatly expanded version of Ehrenwald's earlier history of psychotherapy, *From Medicine Man to Freud* (1956). He points out that whereas his first history to the 1950s comprised some 400 pages, it took that many in this edition simply to cover developments since 1950! The book is an anthology of passages from representatives of the various psychotherapies. A chapter is devoted to parapsychology. He points out that all forms of psychotherapy may be examples of doctrinal compliance and that whatever theories of psychotherapy one may espouse, "man is the most important therapeutic agent for man."

Ehrenwald, J. *New Dimensions of Deep Analysis*. New York: Arno Press, 1975. 316p. $18.00. (First published in 1954.)

Part one is a review of cases of telepathy and precognition in the psychoanalytic setting, with emphasis on those occurring in dreams. Part two presents a theory of the functioning of psi, particularly in the family situation. The final section shows how the psi hypothesis can facilitate the aims of psychotherapy.

Ehrenwald, J. *Telepathy and Medical Psychology*. New York: Gordon Press, 1974. 212p. $24.95. (First published in 1948.)

Observing that psi phenomena are most likely to occur during deficit states of the organism such as sleep or trance, the author postulates that psi develops as a compensatory or, as he puts it, "minus function." He documents cases indicating that the psi hypothesis can shed light on psychiatric disorders, particularly schizophrenia. He concludes with a chapter on telepathy and human personality.

Eisenbud, J. *Psi and Psychoanalysis*. New York: Grune & Stratton, 1970. 359p. $12.95.

After providing numerous examples illustrating the occurrence of psi in the psychoanalytic situation, the author proposes that many of the data of analysis (symptoms, dreams, associations, etc.) are psi-conditioned and can be fully understood only by taking the psi hypothesis into consideration. He explores the theory of psi-conditioned behavior as it applies to the transference and countertransference situations, to other analytic situations, to ordinary life events, and to scientific world views. There is a bibliography of 332 items.

Van Over, R. (Ed.). *Psychology and Extrasensory Perception*. New York: New American Library, 1972. 416p. $1.95 (paper).

In his introduction to this collection of readings the editor provides an overview of the relation of parapsychology and psychology, pointing out that although they share a common need to explore scientifically "the conscious-unconscious mind" they have tended to go their separate ways. In three parts, the book contains 18 selections. The first part includes early writings on the relationship between parapsychology and psychology; the second offers papers concerned with a scientific approach to psi and psychology; and those in the final part deal with the implications of parapsychology for psychology.

PHILOSOPHY, RELIGION, AND PSI

Broad, C. D. *Religion, Philosophy and Psychical Research*. New York: Humanities Press, 1969. 308p. $7.50. (First published in 1953.)

This collection of previously published essays by Broad is in three sections. The first, and longest, is on psychical research. In it he deals with the relevance of psi phenomena to philosophy; J. W. Dunne's theory of serialism, which was offered as an explanation of precognition; clairvoyance, telepathy, and normal cognition; and the role in psychical research played by Kant, Swedenborg, and Henry Sidgwick. The second section, on religion, contains a discussion of the evidence for and against the survival hypothesis.

LeShan, L. *The Medium, the Mystic, and the Physicist: Toward a General Theory of the Paranormal*. New York: Viking, 1974. 279p. $8.95.

In the first half of this book the author presents a compelling case for his theory that the "reality" of mediums, mystics, and physicists is the same and that it differs from our commonsense, everyday conception of the world. Having propounded his theory, he decided to test it by devising a psychic training method which would be based on its postulates and which could be checked against everyday reality. He chose paranormal healing as the psi faculty he wanted to develop because of its potential usefulness as a cultural tool. The last half of the book describes his efforts, attended with some success, to train himself and then others to heal.

Wheatley, J. M. O., and Edge, H. L. (Eds.). *Philosophical Dimensions of Parapsychology*. Springfield, Ill.: Charles C Thomas, 1976. 483p. $24.50.

This collection of 27 papers by well-known parapsychologists and philosophers is arranged in five sections, each with an introduction by the editors. These sections cover psi and (a) philosophy, (b) cognition, (c) precognition, (d) survival, and (e) science. Some of the specific topics deal with knowledge, empiricism, and ESP; ESP and memory; survival, reincarnation, and the problem of personal identity; the reconciliation of psi and physics; and states of consciousness and state-specific sciences.

ALTERED STATES AND PSI

Cavanna, R., and Ullman, M. (Eds.). *Psi and Altered States of Consciousness*. New York: Parapsychology Foundation, 1968. 208p. $6.00.

The 17 papers in this conference proceedings relate psi to hypnosis, dreams, drugs, yoga, and altered states in general. There are historical surveys, review articles, theoretical contributions, and methodological contributions included. The orientation of the book is toward future research. Most of the papers are by parapsychologists, but some are by experts in other fields, primarily psychiatry and neurology.

McCreery, C. *Science, Philosophy and ESP*. London: Hamish Hamilton, 1969. 199p. £2.25.

This research-oriented book is in two parts. The first presents several well-known cases from the literature of psychical research, experimental and spontaneous. In Part Two, McCreery reviews the various types of evidence shedding light on the psychological conditions which are "necessary but not sufficient" to the demonstration of psi. Altered states of consciousness figure prominently in the discussion.

Myers, F. W. H. *Human Personality and its Survival of Bodily Death*. (Abridged and edited by S. Smith.) Secaucus, N. J.: University Books, 1961. 416p. $10.00 (First published in 1903, 2 vols.)

The original two-volume *Human Personality* is parapsychology's first classic. It is also a seminal work on altered states of consciousness, particularly those associated with hypnosis, automatism, and trance. While retaining much of the material on altered states, trance phenomena, and phantasms of the dead, the present abridgment has deleted some of the illustrative case histories presented in the lengthy appendices in the two-volume edition and incorporated the remainder in the text. (The original two-volume edition, long out of print, has been reprinted by Arno Press, $80.00.)

Ullman, M., and Krippner, S. (with A. Vaughan). *Dream Telepathy*. New York: Macmillan, 1973. 300p. $8.95; Baltimore: Penguin, $2.95 (paper).

This popular introduction to the investigation of ESP in dreams through the REM technique is useful to laymen and professionals alike. It also presents a history of earlier approaches to the study of dreams and psi. Spontaneous telepathic dreaming is reviewed in Part 1. The second and longest part presents a history of the experimental investigation of dreams and psi, with major emphasis on the pioneering experiments Ullman and Krippner carried out in the Dream Laboratory (now the Division of Parapsychology and Psychophysics) at Maimonides Medical Center in Brooklyn. The last part deals with the theoretical implications of dream telepathy.

HISTORICAL STUDIES

Gauld, A. *The Founders of Psychical Research*. New York: Schocken, 1968. 387p. $10.00.

After surveying the development of Spiritualism in the United States and its spread to England, the author, a British psychologist, gives detailed accounts of the life and work of three major pioneers in parapsychology who founded the Society for Psychical Research in 1882: Henry Sidgwick, F. W. H. Myers, and Edmund Gurney. The roles of a number of other leading scientists and scholars in establishing psychical research as a scientific endeavor are also described. There are chapters on apparitions, mental and physical mediumship, and Myers' theory of the subliminal self, with synopses of some of the S.P.R.'s major publications and the controversies they engendered.

Murphy, G., and Ballou, R. O. *William James on Psychical Research*. New York: Viking Press, 1969. 339p. $2.25 (paper). (First published in 1960.)

William James was a pioneer in parapsychology as well as psychology. He helped to form the American Society for Psychical Research and was president of the Society for Psychical Research. This volume brings together his numerous writings on various aspects of the field. It includes a number of general articles, as well as papers on clairvoyance, levitation, out-of-body experiences, survival, and the Boston medium, Leonora Piper, who was discovered by James himself. Murphy provides introductory and concluding essays which delineate James' role in parapsychology.

Podmore, F. *Mediums of the 19th Century.* Secaucus, N. J.: University Books, 1963. $20.00. 2 vols. (First published in 1902.)

Originally titled *Modern Spiritualism*, this work provides a thoroughgoing survey of the phenomena and the personalities associated with Spiritualism and psychical research during the nineteenth century. It includes sections on early spiritualistic phenomena, Spiritualism in America and England, and "problems of mediumship." Of the author the British parapsychologist Eric Dingwall wrote: "As a historian and critic of psychical research Podmore was the most outstanding figure of his generation."

Tietze, T. R. *Margery.* New York: Harper & Row, 1973. 201p. $6.95.

The period of the 1920s was an important one in the history of psychical research in America because it was during this time that many persons interested in parapsychological research turned away from the séance room to the laboratory as the only sure place to control experimental conditions. One of the most controversial figures on the scene during these years was Margery (Mrs. Crandon), the internationally known Boston medium who brought to a head the frustrations inherent in the study of physical mediumship because it was never possible to decide once and for all if any of her phenomena were genuine. Tietze provides a detailed and absorbing account of Margery, her mediumship, the men who investigated her, and the status of psychical research during that turbulent period in its history.

Van Over, R., and Oteri, L. (Eds.). *William McDougall, Explorer of the Mind: Studies in Psychical Research.* New York: Garrett/Helix, 1967. 319p. $8.50.

William McDougall was not only a pioneer of psychology but of parapsychology as well. This is a collection of 23 of his papers on psychical research and related subjects such as hypnotism, automatisms, hallucinations, and suggestion. There is a useful 30-page biographical introduction by J. W. Evans.

CRITICISMS

Angoff, A., and Shapin, B. (Eds.). *A Century of Psychical Research: The Continuing Doubts and Affirmations.* New York: Parapsychology Foundation, 1971. 212p. $6.00.

The papers in this conference proceedings were written with the purpose of assessing progress in parapsychology during the past hundred years, and nearly half are of a critical nature. Of particular relevance are "Parapsychology: The views of a critic," by Hansel; "Confusion about 'ESP' and skepticism about ESP," by Mundle; "Responsibility in parapsychology," by Dingwall; "Parapsychology: Doubts, difficulties, and possibilities," by Cutten; "A critical examination of the survival hypothesis," by Roll; and "Reasons for continuing doubt about the existence of psychic phenomena," by West. The remaining papers deal with a variety of subjects, chief among them mysticism, religion, and parapsychology.

Hansel, C. E. M. *ESP: A Scientific Evaluation.* New York: Scribner's, 1966. 263p. $10.00; $2.45 (paper).

The author attempts to show how the results of certain key parapsychological experiments and other investigations in the field could have been produced by fraudulent means. The emphasis is placed on the work of J. B. Rhine and S. G. Soal. The book has stimulated extensive critical reviews, for example, by Ian Stevenson (*Journal* A.S.P.R., July, 1967) and Charles Honorton (*Journal of Parapsychology*, March, 1967).

Murchison, C. A. (Ed.). *The Case For and Against Psychical Belief.* New York: Arno Press, 1975. 365p. $22.00. (First published in 1927.)

Most of the papers in this book were prepared for a symposium held at Clark University in 1926, although some had originally been published elsewhere. The contributions depict varying attitudes and opinions on the reality of psi phenomena. There are three parts for the three major attitudes held by the symposiasts: those who were convinced of the reality of psi, those who were "convinced of the rarity of genuine phenomena," and those who held that psi phenomena do not exist.

Prince. W. F. *The Enchanted Boundary.* New York: Arno Press, 1975. 348p. $20.00. (First published in 1930.)

This book presents the results of the first large-scale attempt to review and assess the criticisms of psychical research. The criticisms of 111 persons are reviewed in all, those in part one of the book being taken from published sources from 1820–1930, and those in part two being an analysis of responses to a query Prince put to prominent men and women regarding the existence of psi phenomena.

REFERENCE BOOKS

Pleasants, H. (Ed.). *Biographical Dictionary of Parapsychology with Directory and Glossary 1964-1966.* New York: Garrett/Helix, 1964. 371p. $9.00.

This volume is "the beginning of an attempt to collect the widely scattered information regarding all those who have been or are engaged . . . in parapsychology." A total of 467 persons are listed, including some primarily identified with other fields who nevertheless made significant contributions to psychical research. In addition to the biographical data, bibliographies are given in the case of persons who have published in parapsychology.

Cavendish, R. (Ed.). *Encyclopedia of the Unexplained.* New York: McGraw-Hill, 1974. 304p. $17.95.

This encyclopedia covers magic, occultism, and parapsychology. J. B. Rhine served as the consultant for the parapsychological entries and wrote several of them himself. Entries range from a paragraph to several pages in length. The longer articles are signed and include suggestions for further reading. Until a basic and authoritative encyclopedia of parapsychology comes along, this work will help fill the gap since the publication in 1933 of Fodor's *Encyclopaedia of Psychic Science.*

Naumov, E. K., and Vilenskaya, L. V. *Bibliographies on Parapsychology (Psychoenergetics) and Related Subjects.* Arlington, Va.: Joint Publications Research Service, 1972. 101p. $3.00 (paper).

This two-part bibliography was compiled by two Russians who wanted to put together a list of references on parapsychology stressing foreign as well as Russian work published over the preceding 70 years. The longest section is a list of Russian materials with English titles. The list of "foreign" materials consists mainly of English, French, Italian, and German titles. There is also a list of 20 landmark events in the history of Soviet parapsychology.

White, R. A. (Ed.). *Surveys in Parapsychology.* Metuchen, N. J.: Scarecrow Press, 1976. 484p. $17.50.

This is a collection of review articles originally published in parapsychological journals. There are 19 papers in five categories: Some basic areas of parapsychological study; Psi phenomena in specific subject populations; Insights into how psi operates; Theories of psi phenomena; and Criticisms of parapsychology. As an aid to students and researchers, the editor has provided up-dated bibliographies for each of the selections.

White, R. A., and Dale, L. A. *Parapsychology: Sources of Information*. Metuchen, N. J.: Scarecrow Press, 1973. 302p. $7.50.

The major portion of this book consists of an annotated bibliography of 282 books on parapsychology arranged by subject. Reading level ratings and book review citations are provided for each title. There are additional sections describing coverage of parapsychology in general and specialized encyclopedias, the major research organizations, periodicals, a chronology of important events in the scientific recognition of parapsychology, and a list of parapsychological theses accepted in partial fulfillment of graduate degrees. A glossary of terms and an index to illustrations are also included.

Glossary of Terms Found in the Literature of Psychical Research and Parapsychology

Compiled by *Laura A. Dale* and *Rhea A. White**

Preliminary Note: The purpose of this glossary is to provide definitions of most of the terms** a reader is likely to come across in ranging through the literature of parapsychology from its beginnings in the 1880s to the present. Thus we have included not only terms relevant to contemporary parapsychology, but also terms appearing in early works on Spiritualism and psychical research even though many of them are no longer much used and are now primarily of historical interest. It should be noted that terms involving certain alleged phenomena are merely defined as they are used in the literature, and no judgments are made as to the strength of the evidence for their reality.

Absent Healing. See *Healing, Absent.*
Absent Sitting. See *Proxy Sitting.*
Active-Agent Telepathy. See *Mental or Behavioral Influence of an Agent.*
Agent. In GESP tests, the person who looks at the target; in telepathy tests and in spontaneous ESP experiences, the person whose thoughts and feelings are apprehended. See also *Target Person.*
Anpsi. Psi in animals.

*We would like to express our gratitude to Drs. J. G. Pratt and Ian Stevenson, who read an earlier draft of this glossary and made many helpful suggestions for its improvement.

**We have not included a number of statistical terms which are discussed in the chapter by Drs. Burdick and Kelly in this volume. Definitions followed by an asterisk have been taken from various editions of the glossary appearing regularly in the *Journal of Parapsychology*, with the kind permission of the Editors.

Apparition. A visual appearance, usually manifesting only once or rarely, which suggests the presence of a deceased person or animal, or of a living person or animal not within the sensory range of the percipient. See also *Ghost*; *Hallucination.*

Apport. An object alleged to arrive by paranormal means in a closed space, indicating the supposed passage of matter through matter. See also *Teleportation.*

Arrival Case. A type of spontaneous case in which the percipient has a strong but inexplicable impression that he is about to meet a specific person, and that person arrives soon thereafter.

Association Theory of Telepathy. Theory proposed by Carington which holds that if two ideas are associated in one mind, this association may become effective in another mind which is presented with one of these ideas. See also *K-Idea*; *K-Object.*

Astral Body. Primarily a Theosophical term for the "double," or replica of the self, which is said to leave the physical body during an out-of-the-body experience, or at the moment of death.

Astral Projection. See *Out-of-the-Body Experience.*

Augury. See *Divination.*

Aura. A field of multi-colored luminous radiations said by some sensitives to surround living bodies.

Authentication. The verification of the facts associated with spontaneous psi experiences by independent statements from witnesses, newspaper or other written accounts, or other corroboratory material supporting the account of the percipient concerning his experience and the events to which it was apparently related. See also *Corroborator.*

Automatic Writing. Writing that is not under the conscious control of the writer. See also *Ouija Board*; *Planchette.*

Automatism. Any complex sensory or motor activity carried out by a person without his conscious direction and usually when in a dissociated state. See also *Motor Automatism; Sensory Automatism.*

Automatist. A person who practices or experiences automatism. The term is sometimes used as a synonym for sensitive or medium.

Autoscopy. The act of seeing one's "double," or one's body as if from a point outside the center of consciousness.

Average Score. The average number of hits per run, or the total score divided by the number of runs. See also *Score; Total Score.*

BT. See *Basic Technique.*

Backward Displacement. See under *Displacement.*

Basic Technique (BT). The clairvoyance technique in which each card is laid aside by the experimenter as it is called by the subject. The check-up is made at the end of the run.*

Bidirectionality of Psi. Term used by Rao to indicate that in the experimental situation psi may manifest itself in either a positive (above chance) direction or a negative (below chance) direction. See also *Differential Effect; Preferential Effect.*

Billet Reading. A test in which the sitter writes a question on a slip of paper and seals it in an envelope; the medium then answers the question and sometimes gives additional information relevant to the sitter, purportedly by paranormal means.

Bilocation. The experience of seeming to be in two different locations at the same time. See also *Out-of-the-Body Experience.*

Biocommunication. Term for telepathy in Soviet parapsychology.

Bioinformation. Term for extrasensory perception in Soviet parapsychology.

Biolocation. Term for clairvoyance in Soviet parapsychology.

Book Test. A test for survival occurring in mediumistic sittings in which an attempt is made to exclude telepathy between medium and sitter by having the communicator transmit a message referring to topics on specific pages of a book that the medium could not have seen normally. See also *Newspaper Test.*

CR. See *Critical Ratio.*

CR_d. See *Critical Ratio of the Difference.*

Call. The response made by the subject in guessing the target in an ESP test.

Card Guessing. A common method of testing for ESP in which the subject tries to guess the identity of cards arranged in random order and placed out of sensory range.

Case, Spontaneous. See *Spontaneous Psi Experience.*

Chair Test. A test for precognition, associated especially with the Dutch sensitive Gerard Croiset, in which a sensitive describes the appearance, characteristics, and events in the life of a person unknown to him who will later attend a public meeting and sit there in a randomly selected chair.

Chance. The complex of undefined causal factors irrelevant to the purpose at hand.* See also *Mean Chance Expectation.*

Change Effect. Term used by Thouless to indicate that a change of conditions in an experimental task is often associated with a temporary drop in scoring level.

Checker. The person who matches targets and responses in a psi experiment in order to determine the subject's score. See also *Experimenter.*

Checking Effect. See *Confidence Call.*

Chi-Square. A sum of quantities, each of which is a deviation squared divided by an expected value. Also a sum of the squares of CRs.*

Cipher Test for Survival. Test proposed by Thouless in which a person encodes a message in a cipher of his own devising, unbreakable by rational means, with the intention of communicating after his death the key to the decipherment of the message.

Clairvoyance. Extrasensory awareness of objects or objective events.*

Clairvoyance, Precognitive. In ESP tests, the prediction of a target order not yet in existence and which will never be known sensorially to any mind.

Clock Card Test. An ESP test devised by Fisk and Mitchell in which cards showing the position of one hand of a clock are used as targets.

Closed Deck. A target pack for use in an ESP test which contains an equal number of each type of symbol. See also *Open Deck.*

Cognition, Paranormal. See *Extrasensory Perception.*

Coincidence, Acausal. See *Synchronicity.*

Collective Hallucination. Hallucination experienced simultaneously by two or more persons who are together at the time. See also *Reciprocal Hallucination.*

Combination Lock Test for Survival. Test proposed by Stevenson in which a person sets a combination lock to a combination known only to himself with the intention of communicating after his death the numbers to which the lock must be set in order to open it.

Communicator. A personality purporting to be that of a deceased individual which communicates with the living, usually through a medium.

Confidence Call. A response that the subject feels relatively certain is correct, and so indicates before the data are checked.

Confirmatory Experiment. A formal, large-scale experimental attempt to verify a finding or hypothesis suggested by earlier exploratory work. See also *Pilot Experiment.*

Consistent Missing. The tendency of some subjects in ESP tests to respond with the same incorrect call to a certain target; e.g., consistently calling "star" when the target is a circle.

Control. In trance mediumship, the personality which habitually relays messages from the communicator to the sitter.

Control, Direct. Manipulation of and/or communication through a medium by a communicator without the mediation of a control.

Cooperator. A person who participates in a test for psychometry by submitting a token object, or other means of identification; the cooperator also participates in evaluating the results by scoring or annotating the records with regard to their applicability to him. See also *Psychometry.*

Corroborator. A witness in a spontaneous case who either observed the subject at the time of his experience, observed events connected with it, or received a report about it soon after it occurred, thus being in a position to confirm in whole or in part the subject's own account. See also *Authentication.*

Covariance Effect. Term used by Murphy and Taves to describe the finding that if ESP is evidenced in two tasks carried out concomitantly, high scores on one task tend to be accompanied by high scores on the other task and, conversely, low scores on one task tend to be accompanied by low scores on the other task. See also *Differential Effect; Dual Task.*

Crisis Apparition. An apparition seen at or about the time the supposed agent is undergoing some unexpected crisis, frequently death.

Critical Ratio (CR). A measure to determine whether or not the observed deviation is significantly greater than the expected random fluctuation about the average.*

Critical Ratio of the Difference (CR$_d$). The observed difference between the average scores of two samples of data divided by the standard deviation of the difference.*

Cross Correspondence. A series of independent communications through two or more mediums such that the complete message is not clear until the separate fragments are put together.

Cryptesthesia. Older term for ESP, coined by Richet.

Cryptomnesia. Unconscious memory of an event or experience forgotten by the conscious mind.

Crystal-Gazing. See *Scrying.*

Cumberlandism. See *Muscle-Reading.*

DT. See *Down Through.*

Deathbed Experience. Apparent awareness of the presence of deceased relatives or friends and/or an altered state of consciousness such as exaltation on the part of a dying person. See also *Peak in Darien Case.*

Decline Effect. The tendency for positive scoring in psi tests to decrease, within either a run, a session, or a longer period of testing. See also *Incline Effect.*

Déjà Vu. An illusion of memory in which one experiences a new event or scene as if it had been lived through before.

Deviation. The amount an observed number of hits or an average score varies (either above or below) from mean chance expectation of a run or series or other unit of trials.*

Diagnosis, Paranormal. The diagnosis of illness by means other than those recognized by medical science. See also *Healing, Unorthodox.*

Diametric Hypothesis. Theory that ESP comprehends the elements in a complex situation by a single act rather than by a step-by-step process.

Differential Effect. In experiments incorporating contrasting conditions, the tendency of subjects to score above chance in one condition and below chance in the other. See also *Bidirectionality of Psi; Preferential Effect.*

Direct Control. See *Control, Direct.*

Direct Voice. A phenomenon of mediumship in which a voice purportedly not produced by the medium's vocal cords is heard, usually (but not always) issuing from a trumpet which floats around the room.

Discarnate Entity. A disembodied being; i.e., a spirit.

Displacement. ESP responses to targets other than those for which the calls were intended.*

Backward Displacement: ESP responses to targets preceding the intended targets. Displacement to the targets one, two, three, etc., places preceding the intended targets are designated as (−1), (−2), (−3), etc.*

Forward Displacement: ESP responses to targets coming later than the intended targets. Displacement to the targets one, two, three, etc., places after the intended targets are designated as (+1), (+2), (+3), etc.*

Divination. The use of various practices such as tea leaf reading, palmistry, scrying, *I Ching,* Tarot cards, etc., to reveal hidden knowledge, diagnose illness, or foretell the future. See also *Scrying.*

Doctrinal Compliance. Term used by Ehrenwald to indicate the tendency of patients to produce dreams and other material which validate the therapist's special ideas and theories about psychotherapy; he concludes that unconscious telepathic leakage between patient and therapist plays a role in bringing this about. See also *Experimenter Effect; Telepathic Leakage.*

Double. A replica of oneself, appearing to be separate from the physical body. See also *Astral Body; Autoscopy; Out-of-the-Body Experience.*

Down Through (DT). A technique for testing clairvoyance in which the subject guesses the order, top to bottom, of a pack of cards before any are removed or matched with the calls. See also *Up Through.*

Dowser. A person who practices dowsing.

Dowsing. A form of motor automatism in which a divining rod (forked twig or other device) is used to locate underground water, oil, etc., or other concealed items by following the direction in which the rod turns in the user's hands. See also *Map Dowsing.*

Dream, Veridical. A dream presumptively paranormal in that it corresponds in some of its details to events beyond the dreamer's normal knowledge or sensory range.

Drop in Communicator. A communicator appearing spontaneously at a sitting and entirely unknown to the medium, sitters, or anyone else present.

Dual Aspect Target. See *Multiple Aspect Target.*

Dual Task. An ESP or PK task in which the results obtained under two conditions are contrasted.

ESP. See *Extrasensory Perception.*

ESP Cards. Cards, each bearing one of five symbols: circle, square, cross (plus), star, and waves (three parallel undulating lines). The standard deck is made up of 25 cards. See also *Closed Deck; Open Deck.*

ESP Projection. An out-of-the-body experience during which the individual is seen at a distant point and/or brings back a veridical description of what he observed at that point. See also *Out-of-the-Body Experience; Traveling Clairvoyance.*

Ectoplasm. A substance alleged to issue from the bodies of some physical mediums and out of which materializations are said to be formed.

Error Phenomenon. Term coined by Rao to indicate that a procedural error made by the experimenter or by the subject may be causally related to the occurrence of psi; the error is conceived of as either activating psi or occurring as a result of psi.

Expectation. See *Mean Chance Expectation.*

Experient. Term proposed by Dodds to be used instead of "percipient" to take into account the fact that psi may be mediated through modalities other than sensory ones. See also *Percipient; Subject.*

Experimenter. The person who conceives and designs an experiment and is thus most closely identified with its outcome. He may or may not also conduct the testing and act as randomizer or checker.

Experimenter Effect. Term used to refer to the finding that experimenters working under the same objective conditions and with subjects from the same population may get different or conflicting results which conform to their own expectations. See also *Doctrinal Compliance*.

Exploratory Experiment. See *Pilot Experiment*.

Extrasensory Perception (ESP). Knowledge of or response to an external event or influence not apprehended through known sensory channels.

Faith Healing. See *Diagnosis, Paranormal; Healing, Unorthodox*.

False Memory. See *Déjà Vu; Paramnesia*.

Fire-Immunity. The alleged ability to come into direct contact with fire or red-hot coals without being burned.

Focusing Effect. The general tendency for ESP success to be concentrated upon particular targets more than upon others; also, a form of target preference exhibited by the subject Pavel Stepanek, who consistently favored particular targets among a set of concealed objects which were apparently similar pieces of cardboard.

Forced-Choice Test. A test in which the subject is required to respond to a target which is one of a fixed number of items, as in a card-guessing test. See also *Free-Response Experiment*.

Foreknowledge. See *Precognition*.

Forward Displacement. See under *Displacement*.

Free-Response Test. A test in which the target range is unknown to the subject, thus permitting him to respond with any impressions that come to mind. See also *Forced-Choice Experiment*.

GESP. See *General Extrasensory Perception*.

General Extrasensory Perception (GESP). ESP which could be either telepathy or clairvoyance or both.*

Ghost. An apparition which is observed more or less regularly over a period of time in a specific house or locality and sometimes conveys veridical information about the former history of the locality. See also *Apparition; Haunting*.

Gift of Tongues. See *Glossolalia*.

Glossolalia. Speaking "in tongues," that is, in a fabricated or unknown language; it usually occurs in a religious context or is attributed to religious inspiration.

Goat. See *Sheep-Goat Effect*.

Greville Correction. A method developed by Greville for the statistical evaluation of data based upon two or more sets of responses to one set of targets. See also *Stacking Effect*.

Guess. The subject's response to the target in an ESP test.

Hallucination. An experience having the characteristics of a sense perception (visual, auditory, tactile, etc.) but without sensory stimulation; it is termed "veridical" if it corresponds to an event or circumstance unknown to the percipient.

Haunting. The more or less regular occurrence of ostensibly paranormal visual and/or auditory phenomena associated· with a particular locality and usually attributed to the activity or residual effect of a discarnate entity. See also *Ghost*.

Healing, Absent. Paranormal healing effected when the healer and healee are not within sensory range of each other.

Healing, Unorthodox. Healing effected by nonmedical means (such as prayer, the "laying on of hands," etc.) and inexplicable in terms of present-day medical knowledge. See also *Diagnosis, Paranormal; Psychic Surgery*.

High-Dice Test. A test for PK in which the subject tries to throw two dice so that they will fall with the two uppermost faces totaling eight or more. See also *Low-Dice Test*.

High-Scoring Subject. A person who consistently obtains extrachance results in psi experiments.

High Variance. Fluctuation of scores beyond mean chance variance.*

Hit. A correct response in a psi test.

Homing. Term applied to an ability of some animals to return to their original home when released from a distance. See also *Psi-Trailing.*

Hypnosis-at-a-Distance. The induction of hypnosis in an individual who is not within sensory range of the hypnotist.

IPA. See *Incorporeal Personal Agency.*

Incline Effect. The tendency for psi scoring to increase at the end of a run, session, or other experimental unit. See also *Terminal Salience.*

Incorporeal Personal Agency (IPA). Synonym for post-mortem survival.

Intervention. Term used by L. E. Rhine to indicate the possibility that a person having a spontaneous precognitive impression can avert or avoid the foreseen event, or some aspects of it.

K-Idea. Term coined by Carington to refer to an idea (other than that of the target) shared by agent and percipient and thought to facilitate telepathic transmission of the target by means of association. See also *Association Theory of Telepathy.*

K-Object. An object (often a photograph) associated with the agent and present with the percipient during an experiment to enhance the shared K-idea and thus facilitate telepathic transmission of the target by means of association. See also *Association Theory of Telepathy.*

Kirlian Photography. A type of high-voltage photography, developed in Russia by S. D. Kirlian, which reveals radiations or energy fields surrounding both organic material and inorganic substances.

Laying on of Hands. See *Healing, Unorthodox.*

Levitation. The raising of objects or bodies in the air by supposedly paranormal means.

Linkage Design. A design used in proxy sittings with mediums in which a chain of human links is interposed between the medium and the living source of information (usually the distant sitter) in order to make less likely the transfer of information from the latter to the medium by means of ESP; each participant in the experimental design is aware only of the link(s) adjacent to him in the chain. A similar design may be used in GESP experiments.

Low-Dice Test. A test for PK in which the subject tries to throw two dice so that they will fall with the two uppermost faces totaling six or less. See also *High-Dice Test.*

Low Variance. Fluctuation of scores below mean chance variation.*

Lucid Dream. A dream in which the dreamer is aware that he is dreaming.

Lucidity. An early term for clairvoyance, coined by Richet.

MCE. See *Mean Chance Expectation.*

MOBIA. See *Mental or Behavioral Influence of an Agent.*

Majority Vote Technique. An evaluative method in ESP testing in which the symbol called most often by a subject (or a group of subjects) for a given target is defined as the response to that target.

Map Dowsing. A form of dowsing in which the dowsing rod or other device indicates the location of water, oil, etc., on a map of the area rather than in the geographical area itself.

Materialization. A manifestation of physical mediumship in which living entities, or sometimes inanimate objects, become temporarily visible in apparently solid form by allegedly paranormal means. See also *Ectoplasm.*

Mean Chance Expectation. In an ESP or PK experiment, the average number of hits expected if only chance factors are involved.

Mean Variance (Theoretical). The expected variance of the theoretical mean score.*

Medium, Mental. A person who regularly receives communications purporting to come from the deceased and transmits them to the living. See also *Communicator; Control; Trance.*

Medium, Physical. A person who, usually sitting with a group of other persons, produces physical effects alleged to be paranormal and sometimes attributed to discarnate agency. See also *Apport, Ectoplasm; Levitation; Materialization.*

Mediumship, Polyglot. See *Xenoglossy.*

Mental Healing. See *Healing, Unorthodox.*

Mental or Behavioral Influence of an Agent (MOBIA). Term suggested by Stanford as a new term for "active-agent telepathy"; he proposes that the agent can play an active role in telepathy and that such "telepathy" is really a form of psychokinesis.

Mental Phenomena. Term usually associated with Spiritualism and referring to those phenomena of mediumship which involve purported communications from the deceased via the mind of the medium by means of sensory or motor automatism. See also *Medium, Mental.*

Metagnome. French term for a sensitive.

Metapsychics. An alternative designation for the subject matter of psychical research; the word derives from a French one coined by Richet.

Midas Touch in Reverse. Phrase coined by Taves and Dale to describe the tendency of scores in psi research in which experimenter and subject are aware of the ongoing results to be in line with the experimenter's objectives in the first stages of the work, and thereafter to drop to chance or below; the effect is attributed to both experimenter and subject.

Mind Reading. See *Telepathy.*

Minus Function. Observation by Ehrenwald that psi phenomena are likely to occur during sleep and other deficit states of the organism, thus leading him to postulate that psi is a compensatory extension of normal capacities.

Miss. An incorrect response in a psi test.

Motor Automatism. A complex motor act, such as automatic writing, carried out by a person without his conscious direction and usually when in a dissociated state. See also *Automatism; Sensory Automatism.*

Multiple Aspect Target. A target with two or more features, each of which may be guessed correctly or incorrectly by the subject; e.g., playing cards, which have three aspects: color, suit, and number.

Muscle-Reading. A form of "pseudo-telepathy" in which the subject is able, for example, to find a hidden object by means of physical contact with a person who knows of its whereabouts, due to subtle muscular cues the latter provides unconsciously; also known as Cumberlandism.

Newspaper Test. A test for survival occurring in mediumistic sittings in which an effort is made to exclude telepathy between medium and sitter by having the communicator transmit a message referring to topics on specific pages of a newspaper that the medium could not have seen normally; this test can yield evidence of precognition when reference is made to newspapers not yet published. See also *Book Test.*

Nonintentional Psi. Term used by Stanford to denote ESP responses to need-relevant material which one is not consciously trying to apprehend; the term is extended to encompass the nonintentional use of PK implicitly guided by extrasensory means. See also *Spontaneous Psi Experience.*

Null Hypothesis. The hypothesis tentatively held to be true when a statistical analysis of data is undertaken, and generally asserting that an experimental result represents only the effects of sampling from a single population of scores or from a particular specified population; if the statistical test of significance produces results very improbable (usually defined as two-tailed $P < .05$) under the assumption that the null hypothesis is true, then it is rejected and the findings are tentatively accepted as due to the causes specified in the experimental hypothesis. See also *Type I Error; Type II Error.*

OBE. See *Out-of-the-Body Experience.*

Object-Reading. See *Psychometry.*

Obsession, Spirit. Supposed partial invasion of the mind of a living person by a discarnate entity, usually for purposes of the latter's gratification. See also *Possession.*

Occultism. Term for various esoteric theories and practices for attaining hidden powers.

One-Tailed Test. A statistical test used to evaluate the results of experiments in which the direction of deviation (either above or below chance expectation) has been specified in advance. See also *Two-Tailed Test.*

Open Deck. A target pack for use in an ESP test in which the order of symbols is random and the number of each type of symbol is not fixed in advance. See also *Closed Deck.*

Optional Stopping Hypothesis. Raised as a counterhypothesis to the occurrence of experimental psi, it argues that extrachance deviations may be obtained in what is actually a chance series if testing is stopped at a favorable point.

Ouija Board. A board marked with letters and numbers, plus a smaller board with a pointer; the user places his finger tips on the latter and by means of involuntary muscular movements the pointer spells out a message. See also *Planchette.*

Out-of-the-Body Experience. An experience, either spontaneous or induced, in which one's center of consciousness seems to be in a spatial location separate from that of one's physical body. See also *Autoscopy; Bilocation; ESP Projection; Traveling Clairvoyance.*

P (Probability). The fraction of times in a great number of chance repetitions that the observed result is expected to be equaled or exceeded.*

p (probability). The number which the fraction of successes approaches in the limit with a sufficiently large succession of chance trials; e.g., in chance matchings with five targets, $p = 1/5$, or one success in five trials.*

PK. See *Psychokinesis.*

PK Placement Test. A test for psychokinesis in which the subject tries to influence falling objects to land in a designated area of the throwing surface.

PMIR. See *Psi-Mediated Instrumental Response.*

PQ. See *Psi Quotient.*

Paragnost. Dutch term for a sensitive.

Paramnesia. A distortion of recognition or memory; the term is often used synonymously with its best known form, déjà vu.

Paranormal. A synonym for psychic or parapsychological; beyond ("para") what should occur if only the known laws of cause and effect are operating.

Paraphysics. The study of the physics of psi phenomena.

Parapsychic. J. B. Rhine's term for a high-scoring subject in psi research.

Parapsychical. A synonym for paranormal, i.e., attributable to the operation of psi.

Parapsychology. The branch of psychology which deals with behavior which cannot now be explained or described in terms of known physical principles; modern term for psychical research.

Passage of Matter through Matter. See *Apport, Teleportation.*

Peak in Darien Case. Term introduced by Frances Cobbe to indicate a special type of deathbed experience in which a dying person seems to be aware of the presence of a deceased relative or friend of whose prior death he could not have been normally aware.

Pendulum. A device, such as a weight on the end of a thread, which can, when held over letters of the alphabet, move automatically and spell out or otherwise specify a message without conscious control of the person holding it. See also *Ouija Board; Planchette.*

Percipient. A subject in an ESP test, or a person who has a spontaneous ESP experience. See also *Experient; Subject.*

Persona Theory. Hypothesis proposed by Hart postulating that apparitions of the dead and mediumistic communicators are temporary re-creations of the personality-structures ("personas") of the deceased by the unconscious dramatizing powers of the percipient or the medium; however, they may (according to Hart) sometimes derive ingredients from actual discarnate personalities.

Phantasm. See *Apparition.*

Photography, Paranormal. See *Psychic Photography; Spirit Photography.*

Physical Phenomena. Term usually associated with Spiritualism and referring to those phenomena of mediumship which involve alleged paranormal physical effects. See also *Mediumship, Physical.*

Pilot Experiment. A preliminary or exploratory test carried out for purposes such as finding suitable subjects, determining workable experimental conditions, and/or developing tentative hypotheses for testing in later full-scale investigations. See also *Confirmatory Experiment.*

Placement Test. See *PK Placement Test.*

Planchette. A small board on rollers and supporting a pencil which spells out a message on a writing surface by means of involuntary muscular movements when the user places his finger tips on it. See also *Ouija Board.*

Poltergeist. Poltergeist phenomena involve the unexplained movement or breakage of objects, etc., and often seem to center around the presence of an adolescent; they differ from hauntings in that apparitions are rarely seen.

Poltergeist Medium. A person, often a teenager, who appears to be the focal point of a poltergeist outbreak; the poltergeist "agent."

Polyglot Mediumship. See *Xenoglossy.*

Position Effect. The tendency of hits in psi tests to be systematically distributed according to the position of the trial on the record sheet. See also *Decline Effect; Psi-Missing; Salience Ratio.*

Possession. A state in which a person's organism appears to be under the control of another agency or center of consciousness. See also *Obsession, Spirit.*

Postcognition. See *Retrocognition.*

Post-Mortem Communication. A communication allegedly from a deceased to a living person, usually through a medium.

Pratt-Birge Method. A method developed by Pratt and Birge in which the Greville correction is used in statistically evaluating the accuracy of free-response material, especially the content of mediumistic communications.

Precognition. Knowledge of a future event which could not have been predicted or inferred by normal means.

Precognitive Clairvoyance. See *Clairvoyance, Precognitive.*

Precognitive Telepathy. See *Telepathy, Precognitive.*

Prediction. See *Precognition.*

Preferential Effect. A subclass of the differential effect in which the contrasting condition associated with positive ESP or PK scoring is the one for which the subject had an expressed preference. See also *Bidirectionality of Psi; Differential Effect.*

Preferential Matching. A method of scoring responses to free material. A judge ranks the stimulus objects (usually in sets of four) with respect to their similarity to, or association with, each response; and/or he ranks the responses with respect to their similarity to, or association with, each stimulus object.*

Premonition. See *Precognition.*

Prevision. See *Precognition.*

Probability. See *P; p.*

Proxy Sitting. A sitting with a medium or sensitive at which the person desiring to receive communications is represented by someone else, a "proxy."

Psi. A general term to identify a person's extrasensorimotor communication with the environment. Psi includes ESP and PK.*

Psi Dexterity. Combination of manual manipulation and the exercise of psi such that apparatus or objects are affected in a way that cannot be entirely accounted for in terms of normal sensorimotor activity.

Psi Field Hypothesis. Theory proposed by Roll which postulates that events connected with physical objects produce changes in the "psi fields" surrounding the objects such that these fields may be apprehended by ESP.

Psi Gamma. Neutral term for extrasensory perception (ESP) proposed by Thouless and Wiesner.

Psi-Hitting. The use of psi so that the target at which the subject is aiming is hit significantly more often than would be expected by chance. See also *Psi-Missing.*

Psi Kappa. Neutral term for psychokinesis (PK) proposed by Thouless and Wiesner.

Psi-Mediated Instrumental Response (PMIR). Term proposed by Stanford to indicate an organism's nonintentional use of psi in everyday life in order to make responses which are instrumental in satisfying its needs.

Psi-Mediating Vehicle. Any symbol, image, or object which enables the percipient to bring information received by ESP into conscious awareness.

Psi-Missing. The use of psi so that the target at which the subject is aiming is missed significantly more often than would be expected by chance. See also *Psi-Hitting.*

Psi Quotient (PQ). A measure of psi efficiency in a given test performance. $PQ = 1000$ (CR^2/n) where n is the number of trials.*

Psi-Trailing. A form of anpsi in which a pet "trails" its owner to a distant location where it has never been before and under circumstances in which normal means of tracking (e.g., by scent) could not have been used. See also *Homing.*

Psychic Healing. See *Healing, Unorthodox.*

Psychic Pathology of Everyday Life. Term used by Eisenbud to indicate that slips, lapses of memory, seemingly accidental physical events, and other anomalous occurrences become meaningful when viewed as instances of psi-determined or psi-conditioned behavior.

Psychic Photography. The projection by allegedly paranormal means of mental images on film or photographic plates.

Psychic Surgery. A form of unorthodox healing in which it is alleged that portions of diseased tissues are removed without the use of instruments, and bleeding, infection, etc., are inhibited paranormally.

Psychical Research. The systematic study and investigation of phenomena which cannot be described or explained in terms of established physical principles; older term for parapsychology.

Psychoboly. Term coined by Tanagras to denote psychokinesis, especially when used for malevolent purposes, as in alleged "evil-eye" phenomena.

Psychoenergetics. Soviet term for parapsychology.

Psychokinesis (PK). The influence of mind on external objects or processes without the mediation of known physical energies or forces.

Psychometric Object. See *Token Object.*

Psychometrist. A person (sensitive) who practices psychometry.

Psychometry. Term coined by Buchanan which literally means "soul measurement"; refers to tests in which a sensitive holds an object and obtains impressions relating to its history and/or events in the lives of persons who have been in contact with it.

Psychon Theory of Mind. Theory of Carington in which the mind is viewed as consisting only of psychons (images and/or sensa) grouped by means of associative links; he applies the theory to survival, suggesting that what survives are the psychon systems resulting from earlier sensory stimuli together with others linked with them, especially through telepathic interaction with other minds (i.e., other psychon systems).

Psychotronics. Czech term for parapsychology, but including certain phenomena that are not now generally accepted as parapsychological.

Pure Clairvoyance Technique. A method of testing for clairvoyance in which a machine generates the targets and scores the responses but records only the *total* scores, thus ruling out telepathy as an explanation for extrachance results.

Pure Telepathy Technique. A method of testing for telepathy in which no objective record is ever made of the targets, thus ruling out clairvoyance or precognition as an explanation for extrachance results.

Pygmalion Hypothesis. Survival hypothesis proposed by Eisenbud which states that while seemingly surviving personalities may be living in certain restricted senses, they are not surviving portions of the deceased; they are re-creations by the living of certain aspects of the deceased. Once organized, such entities may have varying degrees of autonomy, but they continue to exist only for as long as their life is sustained by the living.

QD. See *Quarter Distribution.*

Qualitative Experiment. A test for psi using target material which does not have defined probabilities of appearance and therefore does not permit direct statistical evaluation of the results obtained.

Quantitative Experiment. A test for psi using target material which has prescribed probability values and therefore permits direct statistical evaluation of the results obtained.

Quarter Distribution (QD). The distribution of hits in the record page (or in a logical subdivision thereof . . .) as found in the four equal quarters formed by dividing the selected unit horizontally and vertically.*

RSPK. See *Recurrent Spontaneous Psychokinesis.*

Random Behavior Trial. Term used primarily in connection with anpsi experiments to indicate those trials on which the animal reacts, for no apparent reason, in a way contrary to its usual side habits or customary patterns. See also *Response Bias.*

Randomizer. The person who prepares the random order of the targets for a psi experiment.

Raudive Voice Phenomena. See *Voice Phenomena.*

Reading. The protocol or record of the statements made by a sensitive or medium during a sitting.

Rebirth. Term generally used as a synonym for reincarnation, but some Buddhists make a distinction between them, using rebirth to indicate the idea that from one life to another a continuity of personality occurs, but not an identity. See also *Reincarnation.*

Reciprocal Hallucination. An hallucination, elements of which are shared by two or more persons out of sensory range of one another. See also *Collective Hallucination.*

Recitative Xenoglossy. See *Xenoglossy.*

Recurrent Spontaneous Psychokinesis (RSPK). Spontaneous physical effects inexplicable in terms of known physical energies which occur repeatedly over a period of time, especially poltergeist disturbances.

Reincarnation. A form of survival in which the mind, or some aspect of it, is reborn in another body. See also *Rebirth; Survival.*

Reinforcement Effect. Tendency (e.g., found in Soal's experiments with Shackleton) for displacement hits to occur more frequently when the target card lies between two cards bearing the same symbol than when it lies between two cards bearing different symbols. See also *Displacement.*

Repeated Guessing Technique. See *Majority Vote Technique.*

Response Bias. Tendency to show specific behavior patterns, e.g., to call certain target symbols frequently and to avoid calling others.

Response Bias Hypothesis. Theory first developed by Stanford postulating that bias against a given response increases the likelihood that this response, when made, will be a hit. See also *Random Behavior Trial.*

Responsive Xenoglossy. See *Xenoglossy.*

Retrocognition. Knowledge of a past event which could not have been learned or inferred by normal means.

Reversal Effect. Term used to indicate the finding in replicative studies of results in the opposite direction from the original ones.

Run. A group of successive trials in psi testing which may be of any predetermined length, but usually consisting of 25 calls of an order of target cards in an ESP test or of 24 die throws in a PK test.

Run-Score Variance. The fluctuation of the scores of individual runs around the theoretical mean.*

SD. See *Standard Deviation.*

STM. See *Screened Touch Matching.*

Salience Ratio. A measure of the relation of the rate of success in the end segments of the run (or in the end trials of the segment) and that of the middle segments (or trials).* See also *Terminal Salience.*

Scatter Effect. Ehrenwald's term for the finding that psi responses are rarely in one-to-one agreement with the target, but may be displaced in time or space; the responses are likely to be scattered around the target rather than hitting the bull's eye.

Scatter Theory. Hypothesis proposed by Ehrenwald to account for the scatter effect by attributing it to the fact that psi phenomena are biologically incongruous.

Score. The number of hits made in any given unit of trials, usually a run.* See also *Average Score; Total Score.*

Screened Touch Matching (STM). An ESP card-testing technique in which the subject indicates in each trial (by pointing to one of five key positions) what he thinks the top card is in the inverted pack held by the experimenter behind a screen. The card is then laid opposite that position.*

Scrying. The use of a crystal ball or other bright reflecting surface upon which to project hallucinatory images; e.g., crystal-gazing. See also *Divination.*

Séance. See *Sitting.*

Second Sight. See *Clairvoyance.*

Secondary Effect. Term referring to significant psi scoring revealed by effects such as consistent missing, displacement, etc., rather than by direct hitting on the target.

Sender. See *Agent.*

Sensitive. A person who has frequent psi experiences and can at times induce them at will; similar to a medium, except that communications purporting to come from the deceased are usually not involved. See also *Medium, Mental.*

Sensory Automatism. Visual or auditory imagery, sometimes fully externalized, experienced by a person without his conscious direction and usually when in a dissociated state. See also *Automatism; Motor Automatism.*

Series. Several runs of experimental sessions that are grouped in accordance with the stated purpose and design of the experiment.*

Session. A unit of a psi experiment comprising all the trials, usually predetermined in number, carried out during one test occasion; an experiment may consist of one or more sessions. The term is also used as a synonym for "sitting" in mediumistic experiments.

Set. A subdivision of the record page serving as a scoring unit for a consecutive group of trials, usually for the same target.*

Sheep. See *Sheep-Goat Effect.*

Sheep-Goat Effect. Term first used by Schmeidler to indicate the relationship between acceptance of the possibility of ESP under the given experimental conditions and ESP scoring level, those accepting the possibility (sheep) tending to score above chance and those rejecting it (goats) at or below chance. See also *Supersheep.*

Significance. A numerical result is significant when it equals or surpasses some criterion of degree of chance improbability. The criterion commonly used in parapsychology today is a probability value of .02 (odds of 50 to 1 against chance) or less, or a deviation in either direction such that the CR is 2.33 or greater. Odds of 20 to 1 (probability of .05) are regarded as strongly suggestive.*

Singles Test. A PK technique in which the aim of a subject is to try to influence dice to fall with a specified face up.*

Sitter. A person who sits with a medium or sensitive.

Sitting. An interview with a medium or sensitive, often for the purpose of obtaining communications from the deceased.

Sitting, Absent. See *Proxy Sitting.*

Slate Writing. The supposedly paranormal appearance of written messages on slates in the presence of a medium.

Speaking in Tongues. See *Glossolalia.*

Spirit Photography. The projection of images, usually self-portraits, on film or photographic plates allegedly accomplished by the activity of deceased persons. See also *Psychic Photography.*

Spiritism. French term for Spiritualism.

Spritualism. A religion with doctrines and practices based on the belief that survival of death is a reality and that communication between the living and the deceased occurs, usually via mediumship.

Spontaneous Case. See *Spontaneous Psi Experience.*

Spontaneous Psi Experience. Any unanticipated experience of ESP or PK occurring in the course of daily living; such experiences are characterized by the lack of planning and control characterizing laboratory experiments in which, however, spontaneous psi may play an important part. See also *Nonintentional Psi.*

Stacking Effect. An effect resulting in spuriously high or low ESP scores which may occur when two or more subjects make calls for the same target order, and due to similarity of target preference on the part of the subjects. See also *Greville Correction.*

Stage Telepathy. "Pseudo-telepathy" (usually involving the use of prearranged codes, conjuring tricks, or muscle-reading) carried out by stage performers for the purposes of entertainment.

Standard Deviation (SD). Usually the theoretical root mean square of the deviations. It is obtained from the formula $\sqrt{npq}$ in which n is the number of single trials, p the probability of success per trial, and q the probability of failure.*

Subject. A person who is tested for psi; also, a person who has a spontaneous psi experience. See also *Experient; Percipient.*

Subject Variance. The fluctuation of a subject's total score from the theoretical mean of his series.*

Super-ESP Hypothesis. Theory postulating that psi in the living is adequate to account for any evidence for survival thus far adduced.

Supernormal. Older term for paranormal.

Supernormal Cognition. Synonym for extrasensory perception, coined by Osty.

Super-Sheep (Supersheep). Term introduced by Beloff and Bate to describe a subject in an ESP experiment who is sure that his score will be high because of his ESP ability. See also *Sheep-Goat Effect.*

Surgery, Psychic. See *Psychic Surgery.*

Survival. Continued conscious existence in disembodied form for at least a time after bodily death; differs from immortality in that eternal existence is not implied (although neither is it ruled out). See also *Reincarnation.*

Synchronicity. Term used by Jung to indicate the acausal but meaningful coincidence in time of events having the same or similar meaning, and related to archetypal forces; the simultaneous occurrence of a given subjective state and an external event which appears to be a meaningful parallel to that subjective state, or vice versa.

Table Tipping. A form of motor automatism in which several persons place their finger tips on a table top, causing it to move and rap out messages by means of a code.

Target. In ESP tests, the objective or mental event to which the subject is attempting to respond; in PK tests, the objective process or object which the subject tries to influence (such as the face or location of a die).*

Target Card. The card which the percipient is attempting to identify or otherwise indicate a knowledge of.*

Target Face. The face of the falling die which the subject tries to make turn up by PK.*

Target Pack. The pack of cards, the order of which the subject is attempting to identify.*

Target Person. The person about whom a sensitive is trying to get impressions (especially in object-reading tests) or the agent in a telepathy or GESP test.

Target Preference. The tendency in an ESP test for some subjects to call certain symbols more often than others. See also *Focusing Effect; Response Bias.*

Telekinesis. Older term for psychokinesis, still preferred in the USSR and Eastern Europe.

Telepathic Leakage. Defined by Ehrenwald as a form of telepathy between patient and therapist in which the emotionally charged interests which preoccupy the therapist are mirrored in the patient's productions. See also *Doctrinal Compliance.*

Telepathy. Extrasensory awareness of another person's mental content or state.

Telepathy, Precognitive. Extrasensory awareness of another person's future mental content or state.

Teleportation. A form of PK phenomena in which objects allegedly move over a distance and/or through other objects. See also *Apport.*

Telesthesia. Term coined by Myers to indicate perception at a distance. See *Clairvoyance.*

Terminal Salience. A higher rate of deviation on the end segments of the run (or in the end trials of the segment) than in the middle segments (or trials). See also *Salience Ratio.*

Test Administrator. The person who actually presents the experiment to the subjects and is their main contact with the experiment. See also *Experimenter.*

Theta. The first letter of the Greek word for death (*thanatos*), a term proposed by Roll to mean (as an adjective) "relating to the question of survival," as in "theta phenomena," and to denote (as a noun) inquiry into the possibility of survival, as in "research on theta."

Thought Transference. See *Telepathy.*

Thoughtography. See *Psychic Photography.*

Token Object. In psychometry, an object associated with the target person and held by the sensitive to provide a focal point for receiving impressions.

Token-Object Test. See *Psychometry.*

Total Score. The score resulting from pooling all scores in an experimental series. See also *Average Score; Score.*

Tracer Effect. Term coined by Ehrenwald to indicate the appearance in the manifest content of a dream, or other response, specific and distinctive features relating to a target event.

Trance. A dissociated state characterized by lack of voluntary movement in which various forms of automatism may be expressed; usually exhibited under hypnotic or mediumistic conditions. See also *Automatism.*

Trance Personality. See *Communicator; Control.*

Traveling Clairvoyance. A form of clairvoyance in which the subject (often in hypnotic trance) seems to "travel" to a distant location and describes scenes or events taking place there. See also *ESP Projection.*

Trial. In ESP tests, a single attempt to identify a target object; in PK tests, a single unit of effect to be measured in the evaluation of results.*

Two-Tailed Test. A statistical test used to evaluate the results of experiments in which the direction of deviation (either above or below chance expectation) has not been specified in advance. See also *One-Tailed Test.*

Type I (Alpha) Error. Rejection of the null hypothesis when it is in fact true. See also *Null Hypothesis.*

Type II (Beta) Error. Acceptance of the null hypothesis when it is in fact false. See also *Null Hypothesis.*

Unorthodox Healing. See *Healing, Unorthodox.*

Up Through. A technique for testing clairvoyance in which the subject guesses the order, bottom to top, of a pack of cards before any are removed or matched with the calls. See also *Down Through.*

Variance-Differential Effect. Significant difference between variances of run scores (or other units) in two experimental series designed to affect results differentially.* See also *Differential Effect.*

Variance, Theoretical. A measure of the dispersal of a group of scores about their theoretical mean.*

Veridical Dream. See *Dream, Veridical.*

Verification. See *Authentication.*

Voice Phenomena. Phenomena first reported by Jürgenson and popularized by Raudive in which voicelike sounds purporting to have originated from deceased persons are recorded on magnetic tape; these sounds are usually not heard at the time of recording, but only when the tape is played back.

Waiting Technique. Term used by Beloff to indicate a method of responding to ESP targets in which the subject deliberately waits for images to develop, as described by White.

Water Witching. See *Dowsing.*

Witness Effect. An effect resulting in a change in psi scoring level sometimes occurring when a stranger is brought into an experimental session in the role of an observer.

Xenoglossy. Term coined by Richet for the act of speaking in a recognized foreign language not normally learned by the subject; in recitative xenoglossy the subject merely utters, as from rote memory, fragments of the language, while in responsive xenoglossy he is able to converse more or less freely in it.

Zener Cards. See *ESP Cards.*

Name Index

937

Subject Index